Encyclopedia of Morals

MIDCENTURY
REFERENCE LIBRARY

DAGOBERT D. RUNES, Ph.D., *General Editor*

AVAILABLE

Beethoven Encyclopedia
Dictionary of American Grammar
 and Usage
Dictionary of the American Language
Dictionary of American Literature
Dictionary of American Maxims
Dictionary of American Proverbs
Dictionary of American Synonyms
Dictionary of Ancient History
Dictionary of Anthropology
Dictionary of Arts and Crafts
Dictionary of the Arts
Dictionary of Civics and Government
Dictionary of Dietetics
Dictionary of Early English
Dictionary of Etiquette
Dictionary of European History
Dictionary of Foreign Words
 and Phrases
Dictionary of Last Words
Dictionary of Latin Literature
Dictionary of Linguistics
Dictionary of Magic
Dictionary of Mysticism
Dictionary of Mythology
Dictionary of New Words
Dictionary of Pastoral Psychology
Dictionary of Philosophy

Dictionary of Psychoanalysis
Dictionary of Russian Literature
Dictionary of Science and Technology
Dictionary of Sociology
Dictionary of Spanish Literature
Dictionary of Word Origins
Dictionary of World Literature
Encyclopedia of Aberrations
Encyclopedia of the Arts
Encyclopedia of Atomic Energy
Encyclopedia of Criminology
Encyclopedia of Literature
Encyclopedia of Psychology
Encyclopedia of Religion
Encyclopedia of Substitutes and
 Synthetics
Encyclopedia of Vocational Guidance
Illustrated Technical Dictionary
Labor Dictionary
Liberal Arts Dictionary
Military and Naval Dictionary
New Dictionary of American History
New Dictionary of Psychology
Protestant Dictionary
Slavonic Encyclopedia
Theatre Dictionary
Tobacco Dictionary
Yoga Dictionary

FORTHCOMING

Buddhist Dictionary
Dictionary of American Folklore
Dictionary of the American Indian
Dictionary of American Men and Places
Dictionary of American Names
Dictionary of American Superstitions
Dictionary of Astronomy
Dictionary of Discoveries and Inventions
Dictionary of Earth Sciences
Dictionary of Explorations
Dictionary of French Literature
Dictionary of Geography

Dictionary of German Literature
Dictionary of Hebrew Literature
Dictionary of Law
Dictionary of Mechanics
Dictionary of Poetics
Dictionary of the Renaissance
Dictionary of Science
Dictionary of Social Science
Encyclopedia of Morals
Personnel Dictionary
Teachers' Dictionary
Writers' Dictionary

PHILOSOPHICAL LIBRARY, INC.
Publishers

15 E. 40th Street   New York 16, N. Y.

ENCYCLOPEDIA
OF MORALS

edited by

Vergilius Ferm

PHILOSOPHICAL LIBRARY
NEW YORK

Editor's Preface

This Encyclopedia has been planned on the theory that substantial articles rather than brief notations of widely scattered topics serve better to fulfill the purpose of reference information. To round out the service of such a work it has seemed best to be somewhat meticulous with the furnishing of cross-references so that the reader, if he chooses, may handily find the multitudinous ideas associated with morals as these have been treated, however much or little, in the contexts of the larger topics. Thus the topic contents are indexed.

Moral behavior and ethical ideas are as complex as human relationships. This being so, there is no presumption here to attempt to exhaust the subject in a one volume venture. However, many major ideas and their proponents are presented as well as a fairly generous slice of interesting examples of social behavior among societies quite unfamiliar to most readers.

There are, of course, two exhibitions of morals: the views of theorists who reflect upon such matters and have come up with their various theories and explanations; and there are the practical relationships which are lived out in interpersonal and communal living which are the result less of theory and more of practice and custom. In the former group one finds the philosophers who turn their attention to that branch of their profession known as ethics; in the latter one finds the sociologists and anthropologists who describe situations as they find them. In this book, the theories of philosophers naturally come into large and wide focus. At the same time, it has been felt that moral behavior apart from mere theory should have its representation if the volume is to serve its purpose. Among the latter group we have singled out the anthropologists since there is something fresh and revealing which such students present in their accounts of moral codes, which add up to a fuller understanding of morals.

I am indebted to many colleagues in my profession for help (through a wide correspondence) in selecting topics and finding the proper people to deal with them. In the field of anthropology I have had to turn outside my field and consult with those who are familiar with the work of such investigators. The anthropological field has a surprisingly large number of workers whose researches are far less well known even to the average professional reader. Chief among those who have guided me in the selection of topics and introduced me to scholars have been Professor Melville J. Herskovits and his colleagues in

Northwestern University's Department of Anthropology. I have followed Herskovits' suggestion of preference of selected expositions of the moral systems of two or three specific peoples over any attempt to present the dubious characterization of continental areas, such as African, South Asian, South American and North American Peoples. The diversity found among groups classified according to geography is so great as to make such general classifications inexact. The reader will find here samples of the moral behavior and codes of indigenous and non-historical peoples from remote corners of the globe.

In the religious area, some, but not all of the major religions are included, particularly those which do not divert their devotees to an over-emphasis upon the supernatural world as over against the day-to-day existence of the natural order. A religion emphasizing social escapism or quietism needs hardly to be considered in such a volume as this since the accentuation is here not upon religions as such.

The list of the names of the contributors is its own guarantee of authoritative reporting. The editor is grateful to each one for his and her painstaking work to make this volume possible. In some cases authorship has included two and even more articles as the signatures attest. Grateful acknowledgment is particularly directed to the Trustees of The College of Wooster and to Dr. Howard F. Lowry, President, for a third sabbatical year for research and writing making possible the sustained time to bring this and other work to undelayed completion.

It is hoped that this volume will prove useful to students and disciplined scholars in whatever manner they approach the subject of morals.

Vergilius Ferm

The College of Wooster

Contributors

HERBERT BALDUS, Ph.D.
Head of the Department of Ethnology of the State Museum of S. Paulo (Museu Paulista) and Professor of Ethnology of Escola de Sociologia e Politica de S. Paulo, Brazil

LEWIS W. BECK, Ph.D.
Professor of Philosophy and Associate Dean of the Graduate School, The University of Rochester

HERMAN A. BRAUTIGAM, Ph.D.
Director, Division of Philosophy and Religion, Colgate University

HOWARD H. BRINTON, Ph.D., Litt.D.
Director Emeritus and Lecturer, Pendle Hill Graduate School of Religious and Social Study

JAMES COLLINS, Ph.D.
Associate Professor of Philosophy, St. Louis University

FRANCIS J. CONNELL, C.SS.R., S.T.D., LL.D.
Professor of Moral Theology and Dean of the School of Sacred Theology, The Catholic University of America

CYCLONE COVEY, Ph.D.
Professor of History and Government, Amherst College

MERVIN M. DEEMS, Ph.D.
Dean, Bangor Theological Seminary and Chairman of the Department of Homiletics and Professor of Christian History

EDWARD P. DOZIER, Ph.D.
Assistant Professor of Anthropology, Northwestern University

JOSEPH DUNNER, Ph.D.
Chairman of the Political Science Department, Grinnell College

JOSÉ R. EROLA
Captain, Tribal Administrator (Interventor) in Territoria del Rif, 1950–1955 and now District Administrator of Aith Wariyaghir

MARTIN ESHLEMAN, Ph.D.
Chairman of the Department of Philosophy, Carleton College

VERGILIUS FERM, B.D., Ph.D.
Compton Professor and Head of the Department of Philosophy, The College
of Wooster

WILLIAM K. FRANKENA, Ph.D.
Chairman of the Department of Philosophy, The University of Michigan

LUCIUS GARVIN, Ph.D.
Chairman of the Department of Philosophy, The University of Maryland

WILLIAM H. GASS, Ph. D.
Assistant Professor of Philosophy, Purdue University

ALFRED BOULIGNY GLATHE, Ph.D.
Until recently, Assistant Professor of Philosophy, Stanford University; Now,
Research Analyst, Controller's Department, Bank of America Headquarters,
San Francisco, California

IRVING GOLDMAN, Ph.D.
Professor of Anthropology, Sarah Lawrence College

RUBIN GOTESKY, Ph.D.
Associate Professor of Philosophy, University of Georgia

DAVID M. HART, M.A.
Research Fellow in Spanish Morocco, Ford Foundation, 1952–1953

HELENE ISWOLSKY, B.A.
Instructor of Russian Language and Literature, Fordham Institute of Contemporary Russian Studies. Formerly, Visiting Instructor, Vassar College

WALTER KAUFMANN, Ph.D.
Associate Professor of Philosophy, Princeton University

GEORGE L. KLINE, Ph.D.
Assistant Professor of Philosophy, Columbia University

CLYDE KLUCKHOHN, M. A. (Oxon.), Ph.D., L.H.D.
Fellow, Centre for Advanced Study in the Behavioral Sciences (1954–1955);
Professor of Anthropology, Harvard University

CLIFFORD G. KOSSEL, S.J., S.T.L., Ph.D.
Associate Professor of Philosophy, Mount St. Michael's College, The School
of Philosophy and Science of Gonzaga University

JOHN M. KRUMM, B.D., Ph.D.
Professor of Religion and Chaplain, Columbia University

ARCHIBALD T. MacALLISTER, Ph.D.
Associate Professor of Italian, Princeton University

WILLIAM MADSEN, Ph.D.
Assistant Professor of Anthropology, The University of Texas

H. B. MAYO, M.A., D.Phil. (Oxon).
Professor of Political Science, University of Alberta

YI-PAO MEI, Ph.D., LL.D., L.H.D.
Professor of Oriental Studies, The State University of Iowa

PHILIP MERLAN, Ph.D., J.D.
Professor of German Literature and Civilization, Scripps College and Professor of Philosophy, Claremont Graduate School

LEONARD G. MILLER, Ph.D.
Assistant Professor of Philosophy, University of Washington

ROBERT F. MURPHY, Ph.D.
Assistant Professor of Anthropology, University of California

SWAMI NIKHILANANDA.
Monk of the Ramakrishna Order of India. Founder and Leader of the Ramakrishna-Vivekananda Center of New York

BERNARD PEACH, Ph.D.
Assistant Professor of Philosophy, Duke University

HORACE ABRAM RIGG, Jr., Ph.D.
Professor of the History of Religion and Chairman of the Department of Biblical Literature, Western Reserve University

NATHANIEL W. ROE, Ph.D.
Assistant Professor of Philosophy, Wellesley College

EDWARD A. RYAN, S.J., Docteur en Sciences Historiques (Louvain).
Professor of Church History, Woodstock College

GEORGE H. SABINE, Ph.D.
Professor Emeritus of Philosophy, Cornell University

HAROLD K. SCHNEIDER, Ph.D.
Instructor in the Department of Anthropology and Sociology, Lawrence College

ix

KERMIT SCHOONOVER, B.D., S.T.M., Ph.D.
Dean of the School of Oriental Studies, The American University at Cairo, Egypt

HAROLD M. SCHULWEIS, M.A., M.H.L.
Rabbi, Temple Beth Abraham, Oakland, California. Formerly, Lecturer in Philosophy, College of the City of New York

FREDERICK SONTAG, Ph.D.
Assistant Professor of Philosophy, Pomona College

ELMER SPRAGUE, D.Phil. (Oxon.)
Instructor in the Department of Philosophy, Brooklyn College

ROBERT H. SPRINGER, S.J., S.T.D.
Professor of Moral Theology, Woodstock College

RIA STAVRIDES, Ph.D.
Assistant Professor of Philosophy, Vassar College

JEROME STOLNITZ, Ph.D.
Assistant Professor of Philosophy, University of Rochester

IRACH J. S. TARAPOREWALA, Ph.D.
Director of Iranian Studies in the *Vaidika Samshodhana Mandala* (Vedic Research Institution), Poona, India

JACOB TAUBES, Ph.D.
Assistant Professor of Religion, Columbia University

FRANK A. TILLMAN, B.A.
Instructor in Philosophy, The College of Wooster

BERNARD WAND, Ph.D.
Assistant Professor of Philosophy, Carleton College

RICHARD A. WATERMAN, Ph.D.
Associate Professor of Anthropology and Head of the Laboratory of Comparative Musicology, Wayne University

Encyclopedia of Morals

A

abnegation: *see* Schopenhauer, Arthur.
abnormal and normal, the: *see* Freud,
Sigmund.
**Aboriginals of Yirkalla, N.E. Arnhem
Land, Australia,[1] the Moral Values
of**
The system of morals to be outlined
herein is that of the group of Australian Aboriginals inhabiting the area
around Yirkalla, just north of Cape
Arnhem at the most northeastern point
of Arnhem Land, where the Gulf of
Carpentaria opens into the Arafura
Sea. They have no distinctive name for
themselves as a group, but have been
dubbed Murngin by Warner[2] and Wulamba by Berndt.[3] I shall refer to that
section of the population with which I
am dealing as the people of Yirkalla.
This group has tended since the end of
the third decade of the century to cluster around the mission station at Yirkalla, and the area in the vicinity of the

station had, by 1953, become the established residential site of members of
many clans formerly distributed over
a territory extending as far as a hundred miles south and west of the point.
Actually, the Yirkalla population is a
floating one, since the traditional clan
territories are frequently visited and
only about half the group lives at
Yirkalla at any given time. Normally,
the Yirkalla population is in the neighborhood of 300.

Northeastern Arnhem Land is an
area with adequate food resources. Fish
abound in the coastal waters, and there
is much game. These Aboriginals,
therefore are in economic circumstances differing greatly from those of
the better-known groups of the barren
center of Australia; yet the getting and
eating of food forms a veritable cultural focus and, as we shall see, many
moral values cluster about food. In the
Yirkalla area the terrain is divided between swampy areas of monsoon jungle
and clean forests of eucalyptus, and a
few rock outcrops provide the land's
only elevations.

The Aboriginals are organized in
patrilineal clans or lineages, each possessing a distinctive dialect, territory,
set of totems, myth, and graphic art
style. Each member of the society is
related in one of seventy-three ways to

[1] The field research of which this paper is
one of the results extended from March 1952
to March 1953, and was supported by a grant
under the provisions of the Fulbright Act,
supplemented by a grant of the American
Philosophical Society. For information concerning the morality of Yirkalla women the
writer is indebted to his wife and co-worker,
Patricia Panyity Waterman.

[2] *Cf.* W. Lloyd Warner, *A Black Civilization*
(New York, 1937), p. 15.

[3] *Cf.* Ronald M. Berndt, *Djanggawul* (New
York, 1953), p. xix.

each other member and, conceptually at least, to everyone else in the entire world. Thus, a man may have "fathers," "brothers," and so on, in clans other than his own, and he is expected to act towards them in rather rigidly defined ways. At times, interpersonal relations based on the kinship categories run counter to the principle of clan loyalty, and it is evident that the clan system and the kinship system are, to a certain extent, independent variables. Cross-secting both of these systems is an almost completely independent one: that of the sub-sections, called by the Aboriginals, "skins." There are eight of these, each with a men's and a women's division. Membership in a skin is determined by a complex kind of matrilineal descent, whereby a child belongs not to his mother's skin, but to one determined by it. The one principle of social organization consistent with all three of these role-defining mechanisms, and one that serves to a great extent as the unifying principle in Yirkalla social organization, is that of the division of the world into moieties. Thus, half of one's own kinship affiliations are within one's own moiety; the other half, in the opposite. About half the clans belong to each moiety, as do four of the skins.

The moral code, so far as it refers to sexual practices, is intimately connected with the social organization. Having anything to do sexually with a woman who is a member of a man's own clan, or even of another clan in a man's own moiety is so grossly and outrageously immoral that it occurs only in the sacred myths. While cases of infringement of this "extended incest taboo" possibly occur, neither the writer nor his wife were able to collect a single instance of even a gossiping reference to an actual occurrence of this kind.[4] Avoidance, of a sort, is practised by a man toward his sisters, and especially toward those women classed as his mothers-in-law, but any open association between adult man and woman in which there is any evidence of affection is immoral. For example, the writer and his wife were considered immoral until they learned never to hold hands while walking along the beach.

Relations with women of the opposite moiety but of one of the "wrong" skins in that moiety are regarded as immoral. On the other hand, sexual advances or relationships with women of the "right" skin are not immoral at all, regardless of any difference in age that might be involved. Thus, it is not immoral for an elderly man to kidnap, for purposes of marriage, the small daughter of another man, pro-

---

4 In adhering to standard mission policy, the kind and capable missionary at Yirkalla nullified in advance most of the effects of any attempts he might make to connect Christian morality with Aboriginal morality by having the Aboriginals call him by the word for brother, and his wife by the word for sister. This not only left him self-convicted of moral depravity in the minds of the Aboriginals but, further, provided them with an intolerable situation in that there was no way at all for them to relate to his child. Fortunately, most of the Aboriginals simply considered this official stand regarding kinship terminology further evidence of the pre-logical mentality of the whites.

vided that the other man be of the opposite moiety and his daughter of the proper skin; it is simply an affront to the clan from which she is stolen. It might be punishable by death, but it is not immoral. Situations of a similar kind exist with respect to competition for wives between real or classificatory brothers. Normally, all men who call each other brothers call the women open to them by a term translatable as "wife," although a better translation would be "mother's brother's daughter." These women call each other "sister." There is considerable competition between "brothers" for these "wives," even for those who are married. As it happens, there is a highly-developed pattern of sexual jealousy at Yirkalla and almost half the camp brawls recorded during the period from, roughly, the middle of 1952 to the middle of 1953 were the direct results of sexual dealings between men and their "brothers'" wives. Nevertheless, there was not the slightest indication that such dealings were looked upon as immoral. Too much or too frequent sexual experience on the part of either man or woman is, however, immoral.

The main focus of the moral sense at Yirkalla centers around economic matters, rather than around sex. While it is not immoral to steal a wife, especially if she has not been promised to someone else, if one can get away with it, it is definitely contrary to ethical principles to fail to give substantial gifts to one's wife's father. In this case, we have an act of omission that can bring punishment from the father-in-law, and at the same time places the husband in the status of an immoral person of bad character. Since one's father-in-law is one's mother's brother, and since the tie between a man and his maternal uncle is ideally a very strong one, this kind of reneging is not likely to happen between real relatives. However, most "mother's brothers" are classificatory—maternal uncles in name only—and a man may very likely be tempted to default in his gift-giving to some very distant father-in-law. If punished, however, he may expect no sympathy, except from members of his immediate family who may, in effect, join him in his immorality.

The basis of the system of economic exchange at Yirkalla is a combination of gift-giving and simultaneous maneuvering to place others under obligation to one. The latter is a motivation quite well understood and as thoroughly accepted as is sharp bargaining in our own culture. Yet the Yirkalla moral sense serves to keep the gift-giving going even when no such advantage seems likely to accrue from it. In this gift-exchange society, the ordinary person is not particularly generous, as this term is interpreted in Western society, yet he behaves as if he were. If he does not, he is immoral. One who receives a prized gift may wish to retain it, but he cannot, for he will be surrounded by relatives who demand it. He surrenders it with as good grace as he can muster, unless it is the kind of gift of which he can immediately consume a part, whereupon the recipient finds himself almost at once in the same situation as the former owner.

3

Beyond the very basic tools—spear, spear-thrower, digging-stick—no secular item of material culture can be retained for very long. The writer on several occasions presented informants with lengths of gaudily printed trade cloth, of identifiable design, and kept a record of the line of succession of owners. In the space of a week, such an article might change hands fifteen times. First it would appear as a loincloth, then, perhaps, as a woman's wrap-around skirt, then it would be seen on a series of adults and would usually end up, mutilated and faded, as the garment of a succession of children.

The writer's storeroom, inviolate by mutual agreement, provided a theatre for certain acts of immorality that threw the moral principle behind Yirkalla gift-giving into sharp relief. Especially with regard to an economic good of highest value, such as tobacco, did the character of the motivation for constant gift-giving become apparent. The conflict between greediness for tobacco and the moral obligation to give it away was quickly resolved when the notion of the savings bank occurred, almost simultaneously, to a number of the people at Yirkalla. Informants, particularly those who were working intimately with the writer and his wife, began to accumulate surplusses of tobacco. There is no room in orthodox Yirkalla economics for the concept of surplus, and, indeed, any "surplus" tobacco taken home would be immediately consumed, even if it were so much that every adult in the camp had to make himself sick in the process.

Therefore, the custom grew up of presenting this tobacco to the writer, with the express stipulation that the return gift expected from the writer would be nothing else than the same tobacco. In other words, the tobacco was banked. Very soon the practice spread, and people who were comparative strangers began to appear with tins of treacle, bottles of hair oil, cakes of soap, small bags of flour—all acquired at the mission station, which was out of sight of the writer's camp—with the request (phrased in terms of reciprocal gifts) that I save the goods for the owners.

Two observations can be made in connection with this evanescent development. One indicates its superficiality as regards the totality of the Aboriginal economy: no "Aboriginal" goods were banked, only things acquired either from the mission or from the ethnographer. The other is that the constant gift-giving in this society springs from no deep-seated feelings of generosity, but rather from the moral necessity to give gifts. While the banking arrangement remained the secret of a few informants, it served its purpose. After the first few days, however, the secret became far too open, and quite soon the gift-giving system basic to the economy began to operate in a new way. A man would appear, declaring that his nephew had deposited tobacco and that he wanted it. This sort of thing obviously leads into a problem in ethics for the ethnographer: the problem of how and when to honor verbal checks in a non-literate society. As a temporary measure, the writer adopted the policy of requiring the de-

4

positor to appear in person to authorize all withdrawals. This proved extremely annoying to the informants, especially in the frequent cases when they had in fact given no such authorization but were, so to speak, caught red-handed in the immoral act of saving economic goods.[5] Finally, the novel institution of the bank became a matter of public knowledge and, thus, lost its immoral function. No one mourned when it was closed.

Observance of food taboos is strongly reinforced by the Yirkalla moral sense, since the supernatural sanctions involved in many cases descend on the family group rather than simply on the persons who break the taboos. This is not the place to list food taboos in detail, but some indication of their importance for this society may be afforded by the statement that these taboos affect the lives of all persons at Yirkalla. Even the male elders, for whom all ordinary taboos are lifted and who may even declare particular foods taboo to all but themselves, are forced on certain occasions to abstain from certain foods, while the lives of younger men and all women are hedged about with ceremonial proscriptions on types of food. While there is no effective taboo on the eating of one's own totemic animals in this area, there are many plants and animals that may not be eaten in various circum-

stances. Food taboos concerning pregnancy are particularly strong, and these are observed both by the expectant mother and by her husband. Some of these follow the principle of sympathetic magic. For example, the eating of any spiny sea-animal, such as the crab, will induce skin diseases in the yet-to-be-born child. Not all the taboos are so "logical": the eating of hot eggs by an expectant mother is believed to bring about abortion; the same thing results from the eating of certain wild fruits. The mother continues to observe these taboos after the birth of the child, relaxing most of them after the child begins to walk. The taboo against crocodile flesh and crocodile eggs, however, continues for the mother until well after the child has learned to talk, and that against emu and emu eggs until the child is old enough to be married. In this last case, we have a taboo effective at almost any given time for nearly all grown women except the old.

In a sense, the breaking of any of these taboos concerning pregnancy and children is an offence against the child's whole lineage, and this fact serves at least to reinforce the moral sanctions supporting the taboos. Gossip, and the fear of gossip, is in most cases an effective factor in buttressing the individual's own moral sense concerning food taboos; a woman, however, may be beaten by her husband for a lapse and, although wife-beating is generally immoral, in this particular case his act will meet with the approval of even her own kinsmen.

Another set of taboos concerns the

---

[5] Incidentally, there were occasions where fraudulent checks were cashed and even where informants were guilty of attempted overdrafts. These involved no immorality; an ethnographer is always fair game for his informants.

5

realm of the sacred. The ceremonial camp of the old men is off-limits for women and children, and younger men appear there only by invitation. A woman who approached one of these sacred spots would be warned away if her approach were detected before she came too close; she would be guilty of an immoral act either of curiosity or of carelessness. If she actually set foot on the hallowed ground she would have to be killed. Drawing a sacred design or singing a sacred song belonging to a clan not one's own is immoral unless one has obtained explicit permission from the owners to perform this act. To a lesser extent, the use of a dialect belonging to another clan falls in the same category, although this is actually closer to what we would term a breach of etiquette.

A double standard of morals prevails, in a way, at Yirkalla. Immoral acts for women include careless exposure of the genitals, and resting or being lazy during the daylight hours; these apply not at all to men. Women may, and are expected to, use obscene language fairly constantly, whereas a man who does this is immoral.

Moral standards enter in conflicting ways into the conceptual area of the blood feud. Vengeance is a moral necessity in specific instances; one must avenge the killing of a kinsman. Yet in general there is a sentiment that the continuing of feuds is bad. This of course parallels the attitudes about war in the Western world to some extent, but it is interesting to observe this ambivalence in the Yirkalla microcosm. Uniformly, male informants would declare, quite sincerely, that all the killing that went on among the Aboriginals of the area was a very bad thing for all concerned. Yet most had participated in retaliatory raids, or intended to whenever opportunity arose. In 1953 there were two militant pacifists in the Yirkalla area, both outstanding individuals. Djiring, son of Wonggo, the "Old Man" of the extremely powerful Djapo clan, was by general admission the best hunter and strongest man in the society. About 1939 he announced that there would be no more killing of men in the region, and by sheer personal power forced his kinsman, including his father, to refrain from entering into what at the time promised to be one of the bloodiest raids in the history of Yirkalla. Precisely what his position in Yirkalla society was at the time of his decision, the writer was unable to determine, but by 1953 Djiring had become symbolically, at least, a one-man police force and was accorded a form of respect amounting to reverence. Obviously, in acting out a kind of ideal behavior usually only verbalized, he was making a logical extension of one of the two sides of Yirkalla morality regarding war. Equally obviously, it was his own warlike reputation that made it possible for him to enforce his dictum. In 1953, the prestige of Djiring functioned with considerable success in holding down the number of feud-killings at Yirkalla.

Highly influenced by Djiring, one of whose sisters he married, was Naradjin. A good hunter, although not of the stature of Djiring, Naradjin was

6

in 1953 Djiring's equivalent in the opposite moiety. Naradjin differed from Djiring in two notable ways. While Djiring evidenced no hint of a desire to attain any measure of political power, being entirely motivated, apparently, by his sincere abhorrence of feuding, Naradjin, no less sincere in this respect, had a tendency to arrange meetings where the old men could discuss these matters, and where his own persuasiveness could gain prestige for him—where, in effect, his authority would be recognized. Thus, in a society without political institutions, Naradjin used his pacifism in a political manner. [6] In the second place, Naradjin was extremely co-operative with, and influenced by, the White Australian element, with which he had had more contact than anyone else of the Yirkalla population. Djiring, on the other hand, avoided contact with whites as much as possible; he pitched his camp a day's journey from the Yirkalla mission, whereas Naradjin lived on the mission grounds and functioned as interpreter for the missionary.

Both these leading men, at any rate, indicate a shift in the moral system regarding feuding at Yirkalla—a shift in emphasis from vengeance towards pacifism. The very fact that they were able to take and hold the stand they did both showed the potential effectiveness of the residual pacifism in Yirkalla morality and provided the neces-

sary nudge for its implementation in the actual behavior of the population in general. Djiring and Naradjin were not, in 1953, uniformly successful in banning the blood-feud, but since the weight of the Australian Native Affairs Administration was squarely behind them in this regard, it would seem that the entire system of feuds was on the wane, leaving a curious gap in Yirkalla culture, since no other institutionalized method of acting upon disputes between lineages had yet been devised.

A comparison of certain Yirkalla behavior patterns having moral connotations, with corresponding ones of our own society, will serve to point up some of the characteristics of the former. In Western culture the adoption of a mendicant role—whining and begging for gifts—is not, for upstanding members of the community, moral. At Yirkalla, on the contrary, this is precisely the approach prescribed for one who requests a gift, and is a matter of etiquette more likely to be observed by the socially important and "correct" persons than by others. In Western culture the recipient of a gift is normally supposed to express gratitude; at Yirkalla this would be regarded as somewhat insulting since it would be taken to indicate surprise on the part of the recipient that the giver had been willing and able to present the gift.

It may, perhaps, be unnecessary to mention that many of the most cherished rules of right behavior for European culture—rules actually very infrequently encountered in human culture—are absent at Yirkalla. Among these are universalistic notions of "kindness

6 This is not without interest for the theoretical study of the development of political systems, and will be discussed at length in another place.

to dumb animals" and "kindness to the handicapped." In specific instances persons at Yirkalla may, indeed, be kind to dumb animals or to the handicapped, but no moral value seems to be attached either to observance or to non-observance of these Western canons of behavior. The same is true of "fair-play" and "sportsmanship." There are no organized competitive sports at Yirkalla, and the rules for the conduct of the blood-feud—perhaps the closest approximation to a competitive sport to be found in the area—exalt stealth, treachery, and the harrassing of the underdog. Most of the attitudes associated with the concept of romantic love, and with "momism" are likewise not to be found at Yirkalla. It is, in fact, not at all surprising that Westerners, conscious of the elements of their own moral code and altogether ignorant of the nature of the strict morality of the Aboriginal, tended, at least in earlier days, to view the Aboriginal as a non-moral creature.

We have seen, however, that the Aboriginal at Yirkalla has an entirely consistent moral system, regulating much of his behavior and dealing with the most important aspects of his life: sex, economics, religion, and warfare. The moral system, however, controls his life no more completely than does the moral code of any other human society control the lives of its individual members. While Yirkalla society is, by and large, non-competitive, it is nevertheless intensely individualistic. There is not complete consensus of moral ideas there, in spite of the fact that the immeasurably greater degree of social homogeneity there than in, for example, the Western world would perhaps lead one to expect such consensus. Sex differences in moral attitudes have been alluded to above; these are more than matched by differences in interpretation of the moral code among members of either sex. While this paper has been concerned with those matters of right and wrong about which there was, in 1953, essential agreement among the people at Yirkalla, it should be understood that not only was there some difference of opinion about these matters in strictly Aboriginal times, but also in the contemporary situation the impact of various moral codes stemming from the Western world had tended further to accentuate these divergences.

Richard A. Waterman
Wayne University

8

phonsus and Catholic Moral Philosophy.

absolutism: *see* Cudworth, Ralph; Dewey, John; French Existentialism and Moral Philosophy; Khomiakov, Alexey; Major Ethical Viewpoints; Marxist Theory of Morals; Morals and Religion; Muslim Morals; Quakerism, Classical, The Morality of; Soloviev, Wladimir; Zuni Indians, Morals of.

absorption: *see* Schopenhauer, Arthur.

abstinence: *see* Aboriginals of Yirkalla; Hindu Ethics; Hobbes, Thomas; Jewish Ethics and Its Civilization; Minor Socratics; More, Henry; Puritan Morals.

Abū Bakr: *see* Muslim Morals.

Abu Sa'id: *see* Muslim Morals.

Academy, the: *see* Stoics, the.

acceptance: *see* Stoics, the.

accountability, moral: *see* Muslim Morals.

acculturation: *see* Mundurucu Indians, A Dual System of Ethics; Primitive Morals; Rio Grande Pueblo Indians.

accusations: *see* Hammurapi, Code of.

activity: *see* Aquinas, Thomas, Moral Views of; Hindu Ethics; Stoics, the.

Adam, the new: *see* Hegel, G. W. F.

Adam, the old: *see* Hegel, G. W. F.

Adamses, the: *see* Moral Philosophy in America.

adaptation: *see* Major Ethical Viewpoints.

Adeimantus: *see* Sophists, the.

Adler, Alfred: *see* Freud, Sigmund.

admiration: *see* More, Henry; Ross, Sir (William) David.

adoration: *see* Jewish Ethics and Its Civilization.

adultery: *see* Augustine and Morals; Aztec Morals; Hindu Ethics; Jewish Ethics and Its Civilization; Muslim Morals; Navaho Morals; Pakot, the Moral System of; Tapirape Morals, Some Aspects of; Zuni Indians, Morals of.

advice: *see* Aztec Morals.

aesthetic, the: *see* Green, T. H.; Scheler, Max.

aesthetic enjoyment: *see* Ross, Sir (William) David.

aesthetic experience: *see* Schopenhauer, Arthur.

aesthetic morality: *see* Cooper, Anthony Ashley.

aesthetic self-expression: *see* Soviet Morality, Current.

affections: *see* Balguy, John; emotions; feelings; More, Henry.

Africa: *see* Pakot, the Moral System of.

after-life: *see* Aztec Morals; hereafter; Hindu Ethics; immortality; Pakot, the Moral System of.

agape: *see* Schopenhauer, Arthur.

age-levels: *see* Psychology and Morals.

aggression: *see* Freud, Sigmund.

Ahura-Mazdā: *see* Zoroastrian Morals.

Aikin: *see* Reid, Thomas.

Aka-Marnyu: *see* Zoroastrian Morals.

Akiba, rabbi: *see* Jewish Ethics and Its Civilization.

Akselrod-Ortodoks, L. I.: *see* Soviet Morality, Current.

Albee, Ernest: *see* Cooper, Anthony Ashley.

Albertus Magnus: *see* Hegel, G. W. F.

alcoholism: *see* Psychology and Morals; Puritan Morals.

Alcott, Bronson: *see* Moral Philosophy in America.

9

al-Ghazali: *see* Muslim Morals.

al-Junaid: *see* Muslim Morals.

allegiance: *see* loyalty; Minor Socratics.

Allen, Ethan: *see* Moral Philosophy in America.

alms-giving: *see* Hindu Ethics; Muslim Morals.

Al-Muhasibi: *see* Muslim Morals.

altruism: *see* China, Moral Philosophies of; Dewey, John; Hume, David; Kant, I.; Utilitarianism.

ambiguity: *see* French Existentialism and Moral Philosophy;

ambition: *see* Machiavelli, Niccolo; Plato; Zuni Indians, Morals of.

Ameretat: *see* Zoroastrian Morals.

America, Moral Philosophy in: *see* Moral Philosophy in America.

American Puritanism: *see* Puritan Morals.

Ames, William: *see* Puritan Morals.

Amesha-Spentā: *see* Zoroastrian Morals.

Amnesia: *see* Forgetting; Freud, Sigmund.

Amraphel: *see* Hammurapi, Code of.

amulets: *see* Zuni Indians, Morals of.

amusements: *see* Quakerism, Classical, The Morality of; Stoics, the.

Analects of Confucius: *see* China, Moral Philosophies of.

analogy: *see* Clarke, Samuel; Kant, I.

analysis: *see* Hobbes, Thomas; Language and Ethics; Meta-ethics and Normative Ethics.

analytical philosophy: *see* Moral Philosophy in America.

anarchy: *see* Quakerism, Classical, the Morality of.

ancestor worship: *see* China, Moral Philosophies of; Zuni Indians.

ancient Mexican Morals: *see* Aztec Morals.

anger: *see* Butler, Joseph; Dante, Alighieri; Hindu Ethics; Machiavelli, Niccolo; Mundurucu Indians, A Dual System of Ethics; Muslim Morals; Navaho Morals; Rio Grande Pueblo Indians; Zuni Indians, Morals of.

Anglicanism: *see* Puritan Morals.

angst: *see* Freud, Sigmund.

anguish: *see* French Existentialism and Moral Philosophy.

animals: *see* Aboriginals of Yirkalla; cattle; Hindu Ethics; Quakerism, Classical, Morality of.

animism: *see* China, Moral Philosophies of; Muslim Morals.

Annikeris: *see* Minor Socratics.

anthropocentrism: *see* Sophists, the.

anthropology: *see* Primitive Morals; Rio Grande Pueblo Indians.

anti-hedonism: *see* Minor Socratics.

anti-individualism: *see* Soviet Morality, Current.

anti-materialism: *see* Freud, Sigmund.

antinomies of value: *see* Hartmann, Nicolai.

antinomy of ought value: *see* Hartmann, Nicolai.

Antiphon: *see* Sophists, the.

Antisthenes: *see* Minor Socratics.

anxiety: *see* angst; China, Moral Philosophies of; Jesuits, the, Moral Theology of; Rio Grande Pueblo Indians.

apathy: *see* Stoics, the.

apologetics: *see* Jewish Ethics and Its Civilization.

a posteriori truths: *see* Scheler, Max.

apparel: *see* Puritan Morals.

appetite(s): *see* Cooper, Anthony Ashley; Cudworth, Ralph; Hobbes, Thomas; More, Henry; Reid, Thomas; Spinoza.

approbation: *see* Reid, Thomas; Utilitarianism.

approval: *see* Balguy, John; Broad, C. D.; Freud, Sigmund; Major Ethical Viewpoints; Primitive Morals; Socrates.

a priori, the: *see* Broad, C. D.; Clarke, Samuel; Hartmann, Nicolai; Jewish Ethics and Its Civilization; Kant, I.

a priori truths: *see* Scheler, Max.

aptitude: *see* Cudworth, Ralph.

Aquaviva: *see* Jesuits, the, Moral Theology of.

Aquinas, Thomas, Moral Views of

Biography

Thomas Aquinas was born in the castle at Rocasecca, near Naples, in 1225. His father, Landulph, was Count of Aquin; his mother, Theodora, was Countess of Teceno and related to the imperial family. At the age of five Thomas became an oblate at the monastery of Montecassino where he studied till Frederick II closed the monastery temporarily in 1239. In Autumn of the same year he began studies at the University of Naples.

Attracted by the life of the Dominicans in the city he asked and was granted admission to the young mendicant order in 1244, contrary to the wishes and threats of his family. Waylaid by his brothers on his way to Paris, he was imprisoned in the ancestral castle until Autumn, 1245. Released at the insistence of the Pope, he made his way to Paris to begin advanced studies

under one of the most learned teachers of the time, the Dominican, Albert the Great. Albert recognized the genius of his pupil, and in 1248 brought Thomas with him when he was assigned to teach at the Dominican house of studies in Cologne. Here, probably in 1250, Thomas was ordained to the priesthood.

In 1252 he returned to Paris to prepare for the degree of Master in theology. As Baccalaureus he lectured for two years on the Bible and then for two years on the Sentences of Peter Lombard. In 1256 he received the degree, and held the Dominican chair of theology at the University until 1259. During this period he took a decisive part in the controversy between the secular and religious teachers at the University.

At the command of Alexander IV he went to Anagni to lecture at the school attached to the papal court, and then spent almost nine years teaching and preaching at Orvieto, Rome, and Viterbo. In the beginning of 1269 he returned to Paris where he taught until Easter of 1272. He was then sent to Naples to direct the Dominican provincial house of studies there. Summoned by Pope Gregory X to attend a General Council at Lyons, he fell ill on the journey and died in February, 1274, at the Cistercian monastery of Fossanuova, between Naples and Rome.

Considered by many the greatest philosopher and theologian of his age, he played a major role in clarifying and developing the position of traditional Christian thought in relation to

11

the rising tide of Greek philosophical wisdom. From the first teaching period until shortly before the end of his life he engaged in almost constant writing and controversy. Through his many writings, especially the great *Summa Theologiae,* he has had great influence on the subsequent development of philosophy and theology. He was recognized as a prudent guide, a kind and genial companion, and a man intent on God in study and prayer. His outstanding holiness was recognized officially when he was proclaimed a saint by Pope John XXII in 1323.

1. *The Moral Problem: Freedom and Finality*

For Thomas Aquinas a primary datum of moral knowledge is that man is a unique kind of being; he is different from, although related to, everything else in the visible universe. And this uniqueness is manifest in his actions. He does not simply fall like a rock; nor does he merely move like a dog, determined by instinct to the particular sensed object. Man chooses, selects, proposes ends and adapts varied means to their attainment. By virtue of intelligence and free will he is truly judge and master of his own acts.

With mastery, however, goes responsibility which is one of the premises of man's social life and law. But man is not only accountable to society. He also recognizes an accountability to himself, more precisely, to the judgment of his own reason. In spite of his freedom to choose, he finds this freedom, not removed, but urged on

or restrained by his own judgment asserting an *ought* or *ought not.*

What is the root of this apparent limitation of freedom? Basically it is man's recognition of his own uniqueness and of the actions fitting it. Just as he knows that a pen-knife should not be used as a chisel to hammer marble, he also sees that a man should not be used, nor use himself, like a pen-knife or a pig. There is a basic design in man which indicates a unique function or law of operation. This is what Aquinas calls nature, an internal structure making a thing the sort of thing it is, with pre-designed ends and a tendency to realize those ends in appropriate operations.

The moral problem enters exactly here. Non-intelligent beings move with sureness to the ends of their own nature; only extrinsic causes can interfere with their fulfillment. But man has both the glory and the misery of directing himself freely to the ends of his nature, or of destroying himself. His problem is to bring his freely chosen actions into accord with the finalities of his nature which he neither makes nor chooses. Only thus will he find the good he truly seeks; any other course is an attempt to be what he is not and leads only to frustration.

2. *Nature of Moral Science*

The function of moral science is to aid man in discovering his true end or ends and the means to fulfill them. The moral science of Aquinas is deeply rooted in metaphysics and theology. Not that morality is deduced a priori from these sciences; there are original moral data and the science must develop from these. But morality can be fully understood and finally justified only when seen as a manifestation of those energies which permeate the whole of reality and have their source and end in God.

This is clear from the fact that moral science is a guide of human action, and man neither exists nor acts in a vacuum. He is part of a universe of things and other men; he has necessary and observable relations to them. The universe is an ordered whole in which man has a proper place, and in and through which he must work out his salvation. Moral science is practical from the beginning. It may ask what are apparently speculative questions, but it asks them only in order to know what to do, not merely to know what is. Its aim is to set up norms for action.

Although moral science is normative, it must contain a large factual element. If a man does not know what, where and when he is, he can no more act properly than he could use a saw properly if he did not know what the thing is and carefully observe its condition. The facts may come from many sources. If we are assured that God has spoken to tell us what to do, this is a fact which must be faced for the Creator of nature understands nature and to bypass His direction would be disastrous. If observation and philosophical and scientific analysis show us something of the structure and laws of the universe and man, we cannot disregard these facts; reality is very hard on those who attempt to defy its order. Finally the historical and social disciplines not only help us to discover more about the intrinsic character of man, but also give us the facts about man's situation, the concrete circumstances in which every human action takes place and which, therefore, must be taken into account in the moral decision.

This concreteness of human actions points to another fact. Moral science, like all science, deals with the universal and necessary. But human actions are individual and contingent. Moral science, then, cannot be the whole of moral knowledge. There must be a knowledge which applies the universal norms properly to the varied and complex circumstances of a present contingent action. A painter must know how to apply the general rules of painting to this material in these conditions and with these instruments. For this he develops the habit of art. A similar part is played by the ruling moral virtue of the practical intellect, prudence, which is a developed insight enabling one to apply moral rules to contingent actions.

Finally, let us make no mistake about the power of moral science; it will not make a man good. It is a guide which can be freely accepted or rejected. Yet for those who seek honestly it is an important support and help to the natural tendency to good. Aquinas agrees with Aristotle: like archers, we are more likely to hit the target if we can see it.

3. The Ultimate End

We are aware that we act for purposes. Yet it is true of every agent that it acts for an end. This is as obvious as to say: if there is nothing to be done, there is nothing to do. But the ends of different things are in some way different according to the capacities of their natures. Finally, in a series of ends there is one ruling end in regard to which the others are mere means or partial ends. There must, then, be a terminal or ultimate end to give significance to the subordinate ends or means in the series. Except in relation to this ultimate the others are not sought, as a man does not seek medicine unless he wishes to be healthy.

Human activity, then, has an ultimate goal. On at least one aspect of this goal men do, and by nature must, agree. The goal is happiness which Aquinas defines as the good or sum of goods which brings appetite to rest because there is nothing left to desire or seek. In metaphysical terms, this means that man, like other things, seeks the full actualization of his potencies. The human good is the realization, the full perfection, of human nature.

But here agreement ends. Man has many appetites, and men, as a matter of fact, place their hope of happiness in many things. They seek life, health, pleasure, security, power, prestige, knowledge, virtue, love. These are all good, but since man is one they cannot be merely disparate; there is an order and hierarchy among them. Some are superior; some are subordinate; and one must be supreme, informing, governing, and elevating the others. What is this highest good? First, Aquinas agrees with Aristotle that the full

flowering of a nature is in its operation, so man's good must be in some activity appropriate to his nature. Since man's distinction and superiority lie in intelligence, his final perfection must be in some activity of intelligence, and other activities and ends must subserve this one.

Now intellect, as practical, guides the production of things and the performance of moral actions for the end. The one, then, tends to the perfection of the thing made and the other deals with the means. But the activity we are seeking must be essentially a perfection of the agent and be the end, not merely tend to it. There remains the contemplative activity of intellect. The value of this operation lies, first, in its complete spiritual immanence. It begins and ends in the subject and is a perfection, an expansion of its existence. Secondly, its superior value is in the range of its object. For it expands the being of the knower precisely by an assimilation of the being of other things. It goes out, as it were, only to bring in; it is a spiritual nourishment by which, as Aristotle noted, the soul can become all things. As it is a capacity for being, it is a hunger for truth which is the good of intellect, and for which the will, rational appetite, reaches out as man's highest good.

What object can satisfy this desire? Clearly only God who is Being and the source of all being as He is Good and the source of all good. Man's capacity for total being and his appetite for total good meet in the intellectual assimilation of this highest object. For this man seeks life, for it is his highest life; for this he seeks the goods of the body, that it may serve the soul; for this he seeks all those other goods of the soul, that it may be disposed for contemplation.

Yet man differs from other things not in the object he seeks, but in the manner in which he seeks and attains it. Everything in seeking its good is unknowingly seeking God, for there is no good that is not a derivation of His goodness. However, non-intelligent beings attain God only by a mute imitation of His being and causality in their own being and operation. Man alone consciously returns to God by an operation directly related to Him. And it is by the attainment of his own personal end and perfection that man at the same time fulfills his proper place in the universe. For it is through him, by serving him, that other things also finally return to their source. Thus the universe fulfills its purpose, the manifestation of the divine perfection by an ordered and operative unity of the many.

One question remains. How can we know God? Are we confined to the sort of knowledge of God to be attained in this life by the highest speculative sciences, metaphysics and theology? This would yield a good life much as Aristotle has described it—a mixture of contemplation and action, for we would have to engage in the personal and social activity necessary to secure the conditions for contemplation. Such a life has a high value, but aside from the discontinuity plus the chance reversals and death which can end it,

this kind of contemplative life would not exhaust man's desire. While scientific reason can know the existence of God, what it knows of His nature is little and only through analogy with His effects. But intellect seeks more—to grasp the First Cause in His own proper being. This, however, being a share in the uncreated Life, is beyond the active power of any created nature.

Yet God has told what He alone can and will accomplish. In the life after death we are destined to see Him, no longer through a glass, darkly, but face to face in intuitive vision. By His liberality a special gift of light will be given the intellect to strengthen it for this blinding vision. Even the body after its resurrection will share a redundance of this contemplative act of intellect and of the joy of the will unalterably exhausting its love in the possession of its complete good. The supernatural end of man is the true perfection of the whole man.

4. Good Will, Right Reason, and Conscience

Obviously we do not attain this ultimate term in one leap. But this life is already the beginning of the end, and we must make sure that we are going in the right direction. In short, man must find out what sort of actions are good and, therefore, lead to his final goal. Our discussion of the end has already told us much about the way. Since the end is the perfection of nature, actions are good in so far as they are suited to promote this perfection. Since the end is also the activ-

15

ity of intellect, which is the specific character of man, we have the principle of the hierarchy of goods man must pursue. Good moral life is nothing but the free direction of our actions to these ends. In the light of a new metaphysics of man, Aquinas takes up and develops the old Greek doctrine: the good life is life according to nature and reason.

The internal complexity of the human act and the external complexity of the human situation often make it difficult to discover the reasonable action. And we are very liable to error and inadequacy in our judgments. Does this mean that we cannot know that we are tending to our end? No, for moral goodness lies essentially in the quality of good will which need not be affected by these mistakes. But we must see just what will and good will are.

The will is the specific appetite of man which tends to the good of the whole man and each of his powers. It naturally and necessarily tends to man's ultimate end in its character as his perfect good. Since no good that is presented to it in this life is that total good, it freely embraces, tends to, particular goods as partial realizations or means to the perfect good. Note that any end short of the ultimate end has the character of a means relative to the ultimate goal, although it may itself be viewed as an end in regard to a given series of actions. Moreover, since the will chooses means only under the influence of its movement to the end, the embracing of means-and-end constitutes one moral act. Further, since

the will is the first mover, as efficient cause, in all human actions, the morality of the will carries over to the actions of the other powers which are moved by it and to the exterior actions which result from it. What matters, then is that the will embrace good ends-and-means.

But the will is not an autonomous source of morality. Being non-cognitive, a blind power, it cannot move until its natural tendency to good in general is channelled by a concrete, real good to be sought. It must be specified, as Aquinas says. Now as man's highest appetite, it is coordinate with his specifying power, the intellect; will is rational appetite. This means that the judgment of intellect proposes the concrete good to be sought and orders means to attain it, and it is this intellectual apprehension of the good which specifies and moves the will as its object and end.

But neither is reason an autonomous guide. It is naturally ruled by the objective reality and order of things in so far as it can discover them with the aid of the senses and its own intuitive, analytic, and reasoning powers. It must consider the proposed action, the particular circumstances, and its end to see that all are fitting to the proper order of man's tendencies and his relations to the rest of the universe. Reason is right reason and the proper norm of morality in so far as its practical conclusions are conformed to this order. If it concludes that, everything considered, this is an action fitting human nature and present circumstances, it pronounces the final moral

16

judgment which is called conscience: I ought to do this.

It is this end-and-means as determined by right reason that finally specifies the will's act as good, for then the act has all that a free human act should have—proper order to the ultimate end. If there is any known deficiency in this total object—either in the action itself, its circumstances, or its end—which makes it unsuitable to my nature, and, therefore, to my end, it is evil and the will embracing it is evil. We say any *known* deficiency, for only what is known is an object of the will.

Suppose, however, that there is some objective deficiency in the action which, owing either to lack of information or faulty reasoning, I have not seen. My conscience is erroneous; is my will good or evil in following it? This depends on whether or not the will itself is the cause of that error. We have said that the will moves all the other powers, and this includes even the intellect. Once having understood and embraced the human good in general, I can keep my reason on the track of this good and of the proper means. I can move it to observe and reason according to objective realities and principles—to make itself right. Yet in a given situation in which I have to act there may be matters beyond my present capacity or control which occasion an erroneous conclusion. If I have done my best to see the true moral situation, I must follow conscience and my will is good because the object as apprehended by reason is good.

But it can also happen that under the influence of appetites for particular goods not properly subordinated to my nature and end, I may prevent or neglect the movement of my reason according to the objective order. I rationalize this particular good, closing the mind's eye to the total good and the principles that should govern this situation. I still follow the last practical judgment which specifies my will act, but now I am the cause of the deficiency in the object. Hence my will is evil and the action evil.

We may conclude, then, that a good will is what finally makes an act morally good; that a good will is one firmly set to follow rational judgment and to render this judgment itself conformed to the objective order of natures and ends so far as possible. This places morality in the interior of the agent, but does not make the human agent an autonomous source of morality.

5. *Natural Moral Law*

The possibility of inculpable error and also the necessity of starting points for practical reasoning raises a problem. Could reason be totally wrong or doubtful from the beginning and thus render the whole of moral reasoning inculpably erroneous or doubtful? Aquinas maintains that in the practical order as in the speculative there are certain first principles which are *naturally* known. This does not mean that they are inborn in a Cartesian manner, although Thomas uses the term *innatus*. Rather the intellect itself is an innate power which, given the proper experience of concrete ob-

17

jects, by its nature sees without a reasoning process an absolute significance and necessity involved in the particular object.

In the speculative order the intellect recognizes being and its necessities in whatever is offered to it by the senses. In the practical order it immediately recognizes in being its aspect of good or desirability, and so grasps the principle that good is to be done and evil avoided. This is simply the first specification of the will by intellect proposing to it the good. But this most general principle is not all. With proper growth and the attainment of maturity every man naturally experiences certain fundamental tendencies of his own nature, and he recognizes that the objects of these are properly human goods.

In one sense these very tendencies are themselves natural law. Law is simply the practical judgment of a ruler imposed on subjects to direct their actions to the common good. Everything has tendencies to operations appropriate to its nature. In other things we call them laws of nature because they are in the nature and derived from the eternal reason of God, the eternal law, who makes natures adapted to their function in the universe. Since man's will and nature are free, these tendencies do not become guides of his action till he formulates them in his own practical judgment. For reason is the first principle in the guidance of human action; hence until these tendencies enter the sphere of reason they cannot specify the will act and are not moral prin-

ciples. Natural law is thus a participation in the eternal law, for both the natural appetitive tendencies and the natural power of reason to formulate them as guides of human action are from God.

Involving as they do a recognition of appetite, these first principles can be formulated only inadequately in conceptual terms. In a sense the head must here listen to the heart. But Aquinas manifests the levels of tendency which reason recognizes as good and to be followed. Like every being, man tends to be, that is, to exist and develop. This might be called the law of self-preservation by food, clothing, and shelter. Like all animals he tends to the good and preservation of the species. This may be formulated as the need and responsibility for family life. Finally, by virtue of what is proper to his nature, reason, man tends to live in society and to know the truth about himself, his destiny, the universe, and God. The last tendency is recognized as the highest if not the most fundamental.

Aquinas also includes in natural law other principles which are easily discovered as immediate conclusions without an involved process of reasoning. These are best expressed in the Decalogue which God has revealed because men can be so perverse in their habits and customs that even these may be obscured. They remain very general rules whose proper application may often escape even the best will. But the development of moral conscience by experience, especially in societal life, and by divine revelation and rational endeavor gradually brings man to a developed state of culture; progress lies not so much in the development of technological instruments as in man's growing awareness of the true requirements of his nature in its tendency to its end. Natural law, then forms the beginnings of right moral reasoning and a point to which one can return for justification. But it cannot constitute a nice set of rules to tell what to do on every occasion. Under the guidance of these norms and of experience man must still use his intelligence.

6. *The Passions, Virtues, and Grace*

Man is not a pure intellect, and it would be unreasonable for him to live as though he were. To know is his highest operation, but to know he must live and, therefore, there is a time to eat. But in judging and following the objective hierarchy of values, the forces that may bend a man from the right course are the strong appetites for particular goods which may obscure his vision of the total good. Especially difficult to control are the strong movements of sense appetites, which Aquinas calls passions, drawing us to sensible goods and pleasures.

These inclinations and their pleasures are not evil. They are designed in nature by God precisely to preserve it, and so are good. But when they dominate the judgment of reason and tendency of will, they are disordered and, therefore, introduce evil into the moral action. Neither reason nor will are necessitated by these passions, but they can hardly resist for long without the development of firm and stable tendencies of control. By the repeated exercise of acts under rational control we are able to instil new operative tendencies, called habits, into practical intellect, will, and the powers that come somewhat under their direction. If these are habits tending to human good, they are called virtues, otherwise vices.

Thomas arranges the acquired virtues under the traditional four cardinal virtues according to the chief areas of moral problems. The strong desires of sensible pleasure and fear of pain obviously need habitual control. Hence we need to develop the virtue of temperance to moderate by reason and will the tendency to pleasure, especially in the realm of touch involving food, drink, and sex. Likewise we require the virtue of courage to encounter the difficult and painful obstacles in the path of the reasonable pursuit of our end.

Aside from the sense appetites, there is a special difficulty in the will about our relations to other people and things. There is little danger that we will overlook our private interests, but it is sometimes quite difficult to see and accept that our own good requires us to attend to the reasonable good of others and, above all, to the common good through which we attain our own good. Hence we need to acquire the general and particular virtue of justice to incline our appetite to submit our private interests to the requirements of the common good and to constantly give to others the goods and services which are theirs.

The above virtues are in and rectify

19

the appetites themselves. But presupposing the rightness of our appetites, the practical intellect ordering the means to fulfill these right tendencies must develop the aptitude for properly deliberating, accurately diagnosing a situation, and finally grasping the reasonable mean in the matter of all the appetites. Good general moral principles and good appetites ("good intentions" in the popular sense) do not guarantee fully good or virtuous actions unless they are informed by reasonable order in each particular. This is the function of prudence, which is not mere caution, but the reasonable apprehension of the means to good ends in concrete situations.

If man were destined for a purely natural contemplation of God, these virtues would suffice to direct his moral life. Since he is destined by God for a supernatural contemplation and participation in the divine life, he requires supernatural means which, during his temporal existence, will begin and lead to that life. The root of this life is the free gift of God which in Christian theology is called grace. It may best be described as a sort of entitative habit in the manner of a quality of the soul which does not change its nature but augments and elevates the nature to a new life.

This gift is accompanied by operative habits, the theological virtues, which relate our operations properly to God as our supernatural end. Faith inclines the intellect to accept what God has revealed though we do not fully understand it. Hope inclines the will to seek and expect through grace supernatural union with God as our final happiness. Greatest of all is charity which inclines the will to love God in and for Himself above all things, even myself. Thus we are firmly attached to the highest personal and common good, God, and must from that very fact love all who have communion with us in that good, all men save those who are already finally excluded from the society of God.

7. Society and Liberty

One may by natural temperament be predisposed to certain virtues or vices, or one may acquire virtues by a divine gift. But the natural virtues which are needed to live an habitually good moral life and make the moral character are normally acquired by training and exercise. However, one man by himself alone is incapable of advancing far either in the general knowledge of moral aims necessary for a fully rational moral life or in the discipline of the appetites necessary to hold to the line of reason in guiding himself to the good life. The "noble savage" in the woods is more likely to be a slave of ignorance and passion. Hence Aquinas says with Aristotle that man is by nature a social and political animal; only through society can he find the capacity and liberty to realize his nature.

The minimal but most fundamental social unit is the family. Although entered freely, the monogamous and lifelong union of man and woman has its end and character set by nature. Its primary good is the child. From his parents the child receives not only the physical sustenance which he cannot get for himself, but the basic moral and intellectual training that enables him to enter the larger society as a free man. Yet the family is not exhausted in concentration on the child; by the communion in virtuous life it is a good of husband and wife as well as of the children. The love, fidelity, and devotion to the common interest are not only a living model for the young of the best social friendship but a development of the best selves of the parents.

Yet neither can one family provide all that man needs for the full flowering of his nature. Stretching out from the family in ethnic, economic, moral, and cultural lines, society grows towards that quantitative and qualitative sufficiency which Aquinas calls the perfect community. For this there is required a sufficient diversity of functional groups so that man's needs in all these lines may be more nearly satisfied. Most important is the need of society for political form involving authority to direct individuals and lesser societies for the common good of the whole people.

Political authority, rooted in man's social nature, and therefore in God, belongs to the whole people or to one who, as their vicar, is charged with the care of the common welfare. The chief instrument of political authority is law which is a reasonable directive of action for the common good and binds the consciences of the citizens by the virtue of justice. In part human law merely formulates the conclusions of natural law and thus besides fulfilling a need of social order holds up to the citizenry the ideal of rational life. But as properly human law it serves as a kind of societal prudence, adapting the general norms of natural law, determining its indeterminacies, according to the concrete conditions and maturity of the people. Even thus its authority derives from the eternal and natural law, for the latter indicates that man as a social being must seek reasonable means to organize social life to fit the nature of man and his situation.

The immediate objective of civil law is to establish social unity and peace by establishing an order of justice in which all the citizens and lesser societies may have security in their goods and be enabled to share in the fruits of social cooperation according to their contribution. This very order is the first common good, but it is ordained to a further end, the virtuous life of the citizens. Law immediately takes care of the external order and the external acts required for that order. But by its directive and coercive power it aims ultimately to lead the citizens to act from true interior virtue by habituation to these acts. Yet it cannot by itself effect this. Hence while the very establishment of law and order makes possible the liberty by which individuals and lesser communities can carry out their proper functions, it also stimulates and calls for their free cooperation in actually bringing about the virtuous life and communion in that life through the communication of their goods with one another. This is civic friendship, the final aim of the legislator.

The scope of political authority, then, is clearly limited by its end, the maintainance of a temporal order which makes possible the free and full development of men. It needs and leaves room for other societies, autonomous in caring for their own ends, moderated by the requirements of the larger society without which their own good could not be attained.

As man needed special aids from God to render his operations apt to attain his supernatural end, so he needs a special society to attain the means, a society in but not of the temporal order. This is the Church established by Christ and His Mystical Body. It is charged with providing the guidance and means by which the virtuous life will lead man to his ultimate end, the vision of God. Since this is the end of all men, and therefore the highest common good, the Church which cares for it has a dignity and value superior to that of political society. Hence, while Church and political society have distinct spheres, the latter, as subordinate in its end, must make sure that its own order is such that it gives adequate scope for the work of the Church.

In so far as it is an external organization the Church has its own law to govern the external order of its members. But the chief law of the Church is that interior grace and charity which frees men from the slavery of sin and gives them the liberty of the sons of God. From this love flows that friendship with God and men which effects, and is augmented by, the communication of the spiritual goods of faith, hope, and charity, and the communion in the sacramental life and worship. This is the earthly beginning of the eternal society of the saints with the Trinity in heaven.

True, grace reaches all men though they be not professing members of the true Church. But this grace comes through Christ and through the Church, His Body, by its Sacrifice and sacraments. Yet such grace will be fruitful for eternal life only to those who cooperate with it, to those who with genuine good will sincerely and humbly seek the Way, the Truth, and the Life.

Bibliography

A. G. Sertillanges, *La Philosophie Morale de Saint Thomas,* nouvelle edition (Paris, 1946; first edition, 1916).

M. Wittmann, *Die Ethik des hl. Thomas von Aquin* (Munich, 1933).

Etienne Gilson, *Moral Values and the Moral Life,* (St. Louis, 1931).

——, *Le Thomisme,* 5me ed. (Vrin, Paris, 1944).

O. Lottin, *Principes de Morale,* 2 vols. (Louvain, 1947).

V. J. Bourke, *Ethics* (New York, 1951).

Yves Simon, *Critique de la Connaissance Morale* (Desclee, Paris, 1934).

J. Maritain, *Natural Law and the Rights of Man* (New York, 1943).

——, *The Person and the Common Good* (New York, 1947).

Clifford G. Kossel, S.J.
Mount St. Michael's College
and Gonzaga University

Aquinas, Thomas: *see* Dante, Alighieri; Hegel, G. W. F.; Jesuits, the,

Moral Theology of; Jewish Ethics and Its Civilization; Liguori, St. Alphonsus and Catholic Moral Philosophy; Major Ethical Viewpoints.

Arabia: *see* Muslim Morals; Primitive Morals.

Arabs: *see* Muslim Morals; Riffian Morals.

Aristippus: *see* Major Ethical Viewpoints; Minor Socratics.

aristocracy: *see* Berdyaev, Nicolas; Hammurapi, Code of; Minor Socratics.

Aristotle

The most notorious fact concerning Aristotle's life is that he was for a considerable time the pupil of Plato. In the history of philosophy Aristotle is usually given credit for being the chief opponent of Platonism, although one indication that this opposition is not a simple matter is that Aristotle makes a reference several times to 'we Platonists.' His life began approximately forty-five years after Plato's birth in 384 B.C. in the little town of Stagira, and this historical proximity to Plato is probably the most famous of all overlappings between the lives of great philosophers. His father was a physician, from whom he might have inherited his interest in biology, and his mother's family belonged to Chalcis, where Aristotle took refuge from his enemies in his last days. At eighteen he entered Plato's academy at Athens, and he remained there until Plato's death nineteen years later. Paralleling Plato's experience, Aristotle accepted in 343–2 B.C. a position as teacher for Philip of Macedon's young son, Alexander, although Aristotle's experience was less ill-fated than that of Plato. In 335–4 he returned to Athens to found his own school, which became known as the Lyceum, and thence began the most fruitful period of his life. In 323 B.C. an absurd charge of impiety was brought against Aristotle, and, determined not to let Athens sin twice against philosophy, he left Athens for Chalcis where death overtook him in 322 B.C.

Whereas with Plato the entire set of his dialogues must be combed in order to piece together a complete ethical theory, there is a great temptation when dealing with the more systematic Aristotle to accept the *Nicomachean Ethics* as his definitive statement and to let it go at that. One difficulty in having only Aristotle's lecture notes instead of his finished works is that it increases the difficulty of determining Aristotle's exact view on any subject. We cannot be absolutely sure how he might have grouped his own thoughts on any issue if he had prepared his own words for publication. It is true that he tells us that ethics is an entirely separate inquiry from his physical and logical works, which would tend to reinforce the temptation to use the *Nicomachean Ethics* and the two minor ethical works as the sole expression of his ethical thought. However, this contention of the separateness of value questions from philosophy in general is crucial to his ethical doctrine and therefore cannot simply be taken for granted, if we are to understand critically Aristotle's ethics. This forces an examination of such statements of ethi-

23

cal import as can be found in his work as a whole, followed by a final interpretation of the *Nicomachean Ethics* within this general framework.

On first thought the logical writings would seem to be the least likely place to discover much of ethical significance. While this is true as far as explicit statements are concerned, a general understanding of Aristotle's logical doctrine yields certain points of ethical interest. Primarily what emerges in the logic is Aristotle's stress on formal proof, on exactly stated argument and on the ability to prove conclusions—an emphasis almost entirely missing in Plato. What also becomes quite clear is Aristotle's insistent stress on the primacy of the sensible individual and of the necessity of working with only the essential attributes of an object. Reason looks for abstract conclusions, but it can reach these only by generalizing from immediate experience, which is the method of procedure to be used in ethical inquiry. The natural movement of each object toward its appointed end is also an important concept to be carried over from the physical treatises, as is the attempt to understand the nature of each thing through a description of its causes and its characteristic pattern of motion in the process of generation and decay.

No concept is so characteristic of Aristotle as his habit of thinking in the inclusive-exclusive relationship of species. Each subject matter, then, is to be treated in a manner appropriate to it, and this means that ethics is a distinct kind of inquiry to be treated differ-ently from other philosophical problems. Knowledge, however, always proceeds scientifically to yield necessary conclusions. Whereas Plato feels that one of the central problems of ethics is to control the unlimited, Aristotle denies on physical grounds the actual existence of an unlimited. All knowledge comes from prior knowledge, just as all movement comes from prior motion. The soul, then, is not a self-moved mover as it was for Plato. Instead, the basic fact for Aristotle is that the soul is always set in motion by something external to itself, probably sensible things. (*De Anima,* 406 b 10)

Where Plato characterized the soul primarily by intellection, Aristotle tells us that the two characteristics which distinguish the soul from other things are movement and sensation. (*De Anima,* 403 b 25) Any substance is compounded of both matter and form. "Matter is potentiality, form actuality." (*De Anima,* 412 a 10) Now the soul is by nature inseparable from the body, since it is the body's form, which of course by nature ties the soul closely to sense objects. It is quite natural, then, that the soul should locate its ends in the objects which it finds about it and of a similarly compound nature, that is, other sense objects. Mind, however, has the ability to become all things in knowledge, due to its active powers of abstraction, a power which is central to man and which frees him from being bound completely to sense knowledge. In fact, knowledge always means an abstract and universal grasp of forms for Aristotle. Although the soul is closely linked with sensation, it

24

has the power to transcend it to produce abstract knowledge in the mind, a capacity of considerable importance ethically.

The *Metaphysics* is perhaps the most difficult book in all of Aristotle's writing to relate to his ethical doctrine. For instance, for Plato the Good is the first principle both of ethics and of ontology. On the other hand, while Aristotle mentions that the status of the good as a first principle is an important question, (*Metaphysica*, 1091 a 29–33) the location of his only complete study of the good is in the ethical writings, and then it is carried out primarily in nonmetaphysical terms. Here he denies that anything can be gained by giving Good an independent ontological status, (*Nic. Ethics*, 1096 b 2) principally on the grounds of ethical utility. However, his more serious argument stems from the logical categories. "Since 'good' has as many senses as 'being'," (*Nic. Ethics*, 1096 a 22) and since being is treated only according to the divisions of the categories, then good cannot be treated as a general concept but only as a group of particular concepts applying to particular uses. An ontological analysis of good requires that it be capable of generalized treatment, but its asserted diversity prevents this, and besides "however much there are Ideas and in particular Ideas of good, they are perhaps useless to a good life and to action." (*Ethica Eudomia*, 1217 b 24)

Ethics and politics, then, define good in such a way that it has little or no direct bearing upon ontology, and the question of the status of the Good in ontology is not of major concern to ethics or to politics. However, certain sections of the *Metaphysics* raise important questions concerning Aristotle's treatment of the Good. He has rejected the view that treats the Good as a first principle, saying that "as being is not one in all the categories that we have mentioned, so neither is good; nor is there one science either of being or of the good." (*Ethica Eudemia*, 1217 b 33) This is really the crux of Aristotle's argument against the Good as an ontological principle, and yet in the *Metaphysics* he announces that his purpose there is to consider being qua being, not in any particular sense but as being in general. (*Metaphysica*, 1003 a 20) Therefore, if he retracts his statement that being cannot be considered in general, and if, as he has said, good has as many senses as being, then the objection against treating good as a general principle also seems to be removed.

At one point Aristotle indicates that good probably must be treated as a cause and promises to speak about this elsewhere. (*Metaphysica*, 1078 b 6) This promise remains unfulfilled, and the Good, therefore, remains a secondary part of Aristotle's *Metaphysics*. At one point he makes the interesting suggestion that "to say that the first principle is good is probably correct," (*Metaphysica*, 1091 b 20) but again, in spite of this statement, the rest of the *Metaphysics* proceeds just as if good could be safely ignored in ontology.

When branches of exact science are listed in the *Metaphysics*, ethics is not included, which indicates Aristotle's view that such questions require a quite different approach and yield less precise knowledge. When we reach the famous argument for the existence of an unmoved mover, we find that he is not necessarily spoken of as being good and is not conceived to be the cause of the world, except in the non-involved sense of acting as a final cause for motion. One of the basic arguments involved in the proof of the unmoved mover is that actuality is better and more valuable than potentiality (*Metaphysica*, 1051 a 4) which is a principle that does carry over into ethics.

The *Nicomachean Ethics* opens with the primary statement of the goal oriented nature of human activity. "Every art and every inquiry, and similarly every action and pursuit, is thought to aim at some good." (*Nic. Ethics*, 1094 a 1) The sudden appearance of value concepts as primary may seem strange after so much of Aristotle's discussion has been carried out on a valuationally neutral plane. Yet this merely points to the fact that values enter as an important consideration primarily in the realm of human interaction, and here Aristotle seeks to find the chief good, that which is desired for its own sake. This must take place through a different mode of inquiry from the physical and metaphysical treatises, and we must be content to have it yield only a rough and probable conclusion, since this subject matter admits of only limited precision.

We all agree that happiness is always desirable in itself, but what we must discover is just what happiness is and how it is produced. "Happiness, then,

is something final and self-sufficient, and is the end of action." (*Nic. Ethics*, 1097 b 20) "Now if the function of man is an activity of soul which follows or implies a rational principle," (*Nic. Ethics*, 1098 a 7) then "human good turns out to be activity of soul in accordance with virtue." (*Nic. Ethics*, 1098 a 17) This makes our specific task quite clear: If we are to discover what happiness really is, since Aristotle cannot agree that it is pleasure, we must be able to define virtue and its relation to the activity of the soul.

First of all we discover that, although it does not constitute happiness, prosperity is needed as a pre-condition for the attainment of happiness. "It needs external goods as well; for it is impossible, or not easy, to do noble acts without the proper equipment." (*Nic. Ethics*, 1099 a 31) This immediately links happiness closely to material affairs and limits it primarily to people who can first acquire the necessary material means. This cannot, however, be a part-time or short-term affair, for "he is happy who is active in accordance with complete virtue and is sufficiently equipped with external goods, not for some chance period but throughout a complete life." (*Nic. Ethics*, 1101 a 15)

Turning to the central consideration of the nature of virtue, we find that all virtues naturally divide into two classes: "Some of the virtues are intellectual and others moral." (*Nic. Ethics*, 1103 a 5) After stating that "intellectual virtue in the main owes both its birth and its growth to teaching, while moral comes about as a result of habit,"

(*Nic. Ethics,* 1103 a 15) Aristotle leaves the intellectual virtues and begins to define the moral. Moral virtue requires inborn capacities, and then these natural character traits are made perfect by habit. We learn by imitation, becoming just "by doing just acts, temperate by doing temperate acts, brave by doing brave acts." (*Nic. Ethics,* 1103 b 1) Given good natural endowments, education becomes the other crucial factor in the perfecting of virtue. "It makes a very great difference, or rather *all* the difference" (*Nic. Ethics,* 1103 b 25) whether or not we have first rate training from childhood up. Moral virtues become states of character, but only after the natural qualities have been properly shaped.

Beginning with the assertion that "temperance and courage are destroyed by excess and defect, and preserved by the mean," (*Nic. Ethics,* 1104 a 25) we have the statement of the famous Aristotelian doctrine of the golden mean. Since virtue has to do with passions and actions, the intermediate is praised as a form of success, and virtue is, then, "a state of character concerned with choice, lying in a mean." (*Nic. Ethics,* 1107 a 1) What determines such a mean? It is not at all a fixed reference point, but rather merely a general principle for the man of practical reason to apply. However, "not every action nor every passion admits of a mean," (*Nic. Ethics,* 1107 a 10) which tells us that the theory of the mean cannot be stressed too strongly, since it applies only in areas which admit variance consistent with the maintenance of virtue. The principle of the mean, then, is misinterpreted if it is taken as an avenue of compromise with such things as ambition or greed which are never consonant with virtue.

Aristotle is one of the first to introduce the question of freedom, asserting that the voluntariness of the action must be determined before it can be called virtuous. To qualify as virtuous the action must flow from the nature of the individual, uncompelled by external circumstances. A virtuous action must be a genuine expression of the character of the person, or it does not really indicate the presence of strength of character in the individual. Ignorance, too, means that the action is not voluntary, and compulsion exists when the moving principle is outside the person, "the person compelled contributing nothing." (*Nic. Ethics,* 1110 b 15) "The voluntary would seem to be that of which the moving principle is in the agent himself, he being aware of the particular circumstances of the action." (*Nic. Ethics,* 1111 a 23)

"Choice, then, seems to be voluntary" (*Nic. Ethics,* 1111 b 7) and to relate to things that are in our power and can be done. We deliberate only about things which are capable of being changed, and "we deliberate not about ends but about means." (*Nic. Ethics,* 1112 b 12) Thus, choice is a highly limited function, confined to what we are able to effect, taking its goals as given to it and finding freedom only in the route by which these stated goals shall be achieved. Some of this we can learn, but, again, fundamentally natural endowment is crucial, since "one must be born with an eye, as it were, by which to judge rightly and choose what is truly good." (*Nic. Ethics,* 1114 b 7)

Following this the traditional virtues are defined and discussed, such as courage and temperance, but these are more particular illustrations of the general ethical position than additions to the fundamental view. When Aristotle turns to liberality, magnificence and pride, he comes as close to confining virtue exclusively to the aristocratic class as he does in his entire discussion. "The refined and well-bred man will be . . . a law unto himself," (*Nic. Ethics,* 1128 a 32) and, if this section were read in isolation, happiness would seem to be attainable only by a selected aristocracy. That there is such an overtone in Aristotle's ethical view is undeniable, but it is not as simple or as unrelieved as it appears at this point.

Returning to the doctrine of the mean as the goal of ethics, Aristotle is the first to recognize the vagueness inherent in the concept of always striving for the mean. If this lack of clarity is to be remedied, "it should be determined what is the right rule and what is the standard that fixes it." (*Nic. Ethics,* 1138 b 34) Similarly to the course of the discussion in Plato's *Republic,* Aristotle pauses here to discuss the nature of the soul and of knowledge, since unless this is discovered we cannot determine exactly what establishes the mean in conduct. Here the scientific or precise part of the soul is separated from the calculative or practical. Only the intellect which aims at the practical is capable of causing movement,

and its good state is "truth in agreement with right desire." (*Nic. Ethics,* 1139 a 30) The man of practical wisdom is able to deliberate well about what is good and expedient for himself and "good action itself is its end." (*Nic. Ethics* 1140 b 8) The contemplative intellect moves nothing and its good state is simply truth.

Then, in an almost unexpected shift of emphasis, Aristotle declares that "wisdom must plainly be the most finished of the forms of knowledge." (*Nic. Ethics,* 1141 a 17) Man is not to be thought of as the best thing in the world, so that while it is true that practical wisdom involves a rational principle and produces good actions, in the end the practical "is not supreme over philosophic wisdom." (*Nic. Ethics,* 1145 a 7) Thus, Aristotle begins to shift from the early emphasis on goods and action, to the rational principle necessarily involved in good action, and then finally to philosophical reason which by nature produces no action but still is the ultimate goal for the virtuous man. At first the moral virtues seem to occupy the center of the stage as the picture of the happy man *per se,* but gradually Aristotle moves on to an increasing stress upon the cultivation of intellectual virtues, which removes the discussion from what was previously a necessarily aristocratic level. Moral virtues are by nature exclusive, but intellectual virtues are less directly involved with non-sharable properties.

Returning toward the end of the *Nicomachean Ethics* to the original discussion of happiness, Aristotle insists that it must be an activity and not a passive disposition. But "if happiness is activity in accordance with virtue, it is reasonable that it should be in accordance with the highest virtue; and this will be that of the best thing in us." (*Nic. Ethics,* 1177 a 11) This activity, he asserts firmly, is contemplative, and it is best because it is of all activities the most self-sufficient. Although nothing arises from this apart from the contemplation, the philosopher needs the aid of no other man to contemplate truth. "The activity of reason, which is contemplative, seems both to be superior in serious worth and to aim at no end beyond itself, and to have its pleasure proper to itself." (*Nic. Ethics,* 1177 b 20) Reason is the authoritative and the better part of man, and it would be strange if he did not choose the life of his best self.

Even at this point we cannot ignore the fact that some external equipment is needed for such a life of contemplation, but the man of the contemplative life needs nothing near the amount of money, for instance, that the liberal man needs to exercise his virtue. Being thus more self-sufficient, the life of contemplation best fulfills the requirements of happiness, although the moral virtues of property and activity are nowhere rejected. However, it is true that the contemplative life is akin to the divine, and, being like the activity of God, the contemplative must surpass other lives in its blessedness and must be that which is most akin to the nature of happiness. Finally Aristotle states the outcome explicitly: "Hap-

piness extends, then, just so far as contemplation does and those to whom contemplation more fully belongs are more truly happy." (*Nic. Ethics,* 1178 b 30)

The final problem in the interpretation of Aristotle's ethical view is the reconciliation of this later stress on reason and contemplation with the earlier emphasis on action and its accompanying rejection of Plato's Good as not being helpful to the practical man. Aristotle has, of course, still left room for the moral virtues as the earlier level of virtue which must be present to some extent in the higher level of contemplation as the basis of its operation. The interesting result, however, is that in some sense it turns out that Aristotle's highest level of virtue is less directly concerned with action than Plato's philosopher-king. Aristotle seems to endorse contemplation as an end in itself, although never forgetting the moral virtues, whereas Plato does not allow his good man to remain at the contemplative level as his self-sufficient goal. In this respect, it is possible that Aristotle is more associated with the stress on the contemplative life in the middle ages than Plato.

Although Aristotle leaves the life of contemplative reason as his highest ethical goal, for an overall picture of his ethics one cannot ignore the natural transition to the *Politics* which appears at the end of the ethical discussion. Men are slow to change and often do not yield to rational argument. Few people actually live temperately, and the bad man, whose

29

desire is for pleasure, can only be corrected by pain like a beast of burden. Therefore, having once learned the principles of ethics, the man who really wants to make men better by his care must try to become capable of legislating, since public control is effected by law and, in turn, good control chiefly by good laws. In this transition we have a parallel to Plato's philosopher-king. "Must we not, then, next examine whence and how one can learn to legislate," (*Nic. Ethics*, 1180 b 29) and thus we are carried from the purely ethical into the political as the natural completion of the ethical goal.

Just as Plato's ethical principles apply alike to the state and to the individual, so it is equally impossible to give an adequate account of Aristotle's ethical views without placing them in their social context. While it is true that the emphasis which he has placed on the contemplative life would seem to remove ethics from an immediate and direct connection to society, this stress—while interesting and important —is not mentioned nearly as often as the famed Aristotelian principle that man is by nature a social animal. At the basis of his thinking Aristotle may actually approve the contemplative life as the most independent and the best, but such an emphasis has to be placed beside Aristotle's keen interest in man's social relations, if the Aristotelian ethics is to be seen as a whole.

Similarly to the fact that every individual action is said to aim at some good, so also is every community "established with a view to some good." (*Politica*, 1252 a 1) Furthermore, just as the moral virtues are the ground for the development of intellectual virtue, so is the supply of material needs the basis upon which society is first formed. The family is the natural unit of the state, since the family is conceived as the operating household held together by its interdependence for the supply of mutual needs. Nevertheless, the state is prior to the family as the whole is said to be prior to its parts, since the individual when isolated is not self-sufficient. Man in the undeveloped state can become the worst of the beasts; education perfects him to become the best of animals, but he is dependent upon the prior existence of the state for his education. Little or no good can be accomplished by the individual man without the education and the context provided for him by society. The achievement of the good life, then, cannot afford to overlook the establishment of a well-ordered social structure. "It is characteristic of man that he alone has any sense of good and evil," (*Politica*, 1253 a 15) but he can only develop this within the context provided by society and its established educational program.

The Aristotelian doctrine of the so-called 'natural slave' has been much abused, but it is undeniable that Aristotle sees society in a hierarchical order with some in inferior capacities as far as management of the state is concerned. All men do not have equal talents, and for this reason some will work in menial tasks as long as these functions have to be performed. More than this, however, the discussion of slavery is meant to point up the more general fact that some men place themselves in the position of being dominated by others, and this means that they are not free, since they have surrendered their ability to deliberate about their own affairs. Such people are like Plato's despot with a master passion enthroned in their soul.

Like Plato, Aristotle feels that the best is often unattainable, and the statesman must, therefore, not only know what is best in the abstract but also what is best "relatively to the circumstances." (*Politica,* 1288 b 27) Life requires adjustment, and the good man will keep both his ideal and the relative circumstances in mind in planning action. Similarly, we must consider "not only what form of government is best, but also what is possible and what is easily attainable by all." (*Politica,* 1288 b 37)

When one has finished reading, the primary impression which Aristotle leaves is of the balance between the active and the contemplative, just as his theory of knowledge tries to balance the importance of sensation with the value of abstract knowledge, the particular alongside the universal. To the extent that the practical reason is stressed, the moral virtues are emphasized and seem consistent both with the importance placed upon sensation and with the separation of ethics from the rest of philosophy as a different subject. On the other hand, when contemplative knowledge is claimed as the most important—and Aristotle does not assert that this is man's distinctive feature—then the intellectual virtues seem paramount and the mind's ability to know universals becomes the crucial point. Transcendence of the natural order is also involved here, and ethics becomes more closely related to metaphysics, since this emphasis on the contemplative makes men tend toward the divine and away from the animal. Either stress in Aristotle changes the perspective which we have of his ethical views, but the undeniable fact is that neither facet can ever be lost, since they are both equally present in his original statement.

Bibliography

E. Barker, *The Politics of Aristotle* (London, 1946).

J. Burnet, *Nicomachean Ethics,* Text and Commentary (London, 1900).

G. Grote, *Aristotle* (London, 1872).

W. Jaeger, *Aristotle: Fundamentals of the History of His Development* (London, 1948).

T. W. Organ, *An Index to Aristotle* (Princeton, 1949).

W. D. Ross, *Aristotle* (London, 1945).

J. D. Steward, *Commentary on the Nicomachean Ethics,* 2 vols. (Oxford, 1892).

A. E. Taylor, *Aristotle* (London, 1919).

Frederick Sontag
Pomona College

Aristotle: *see* Aquinas, Thomas, Moral Views of; China, Moral Philosophies of; Dante, Alighieri; Goethe, Johann Wolfgang von; Green, T. H.; Hegel, G. W. F.; Jesuits, the, Moral Theology of; Kant, I.; Major Ethical Viewpoints; More, Henry; Muslim Morals; Nietzsche, Friedrich; Prichard, H. A.; Sophists, the; Spinoza; Stoics, the.

Arminianism: *see* Moral Philosophy in America; Puritan Morals.

Arnhem Land: *see* Aboriginals of Yirkalla.

Arrian: *see* Stoics, the.

arrogance: *see* Dante, Alighieri; Navaho Morals.

art (the arts): *see* beauty; Schopenhauer, Arthur; Sophists, the.

artistic shaping of ideals: *see* Soviet Morality, Current.

Aryas, ancient: *see* Zoroastrian Morals.

asceticism: *see* Hindu Ethics; Jesuits, the, Moral Theology of; Jewish Ethics and Its Civilization; Khomiakov, Alexey; Minor Socratics; Muslim Morals; Nietzsche, Friedrich; Puritan Morals: Quakerism, Classical, The Morality of; Schopenhauer, Arthur; Soviet Morality, Current; Stoics, the; Utilitarianism.

Asha: *see* Zoroastrian Morals.

assassins: *see* Muslim Morals.

assent: *see* Stoics, the.

association of ideas: *see* Utilitarianism.

association psychology: *see* Utilitarianism.

associationism: *see* Scheler, Max.

Ātar: *see* Zoroastrian Morals.

atheism: *see* Spinoza.

atomism: *see* Cudworth, Ralph.

atonement: *see* Jewish Ethics and Its Civilization.

attitude: *see* Hindu Ethics; Major Ethical Viewpoints; Muslim Morals.

attitude and morals: *see* Christian Moral Philosophy.

attitude theory: *see* Language and Ethics.

attributes: *see* Spinoza.

attrition: *see* Jesuits, the, Moral Theology of.

Auerbach, E.: *see* Hammurapi, Code of.

Augustine and Morals

Son of Monnica, a Christian, and Patricius, a pagan, Augustine was born November 13, 354, at Tagaste, North Africa, where he received his early education. About the age of eleven he continued his studies at Madaura and some six years later moved on to Carthage where he studied and then taught rhetoric. The Carthaginian students proved unruly and Augustine transferred to Rome only to find that students there often would not pay their fees and drifted from teacher to teacher. After a few months he accepted a position as teacher of rhetoric offered by the city of Milan. Meantime there occurred an odyssey of soul. He had been signed with the cross at birth, though not baptized, but despite his Christian mother he had grown up with no concern for Christianity, his student days marked with roistering and dissolute living ("the thorns of lust grew rank over my head," *Conf.* ii. 3). Recalling an early escapade of pear-stealing he concluded that he had sinned not only for the fun of it but from pride. Then "to Carthage I came where a cauldron of unholy loves bubbled up all around me" (*Conf.* iii. 1). A reading of Cicero's *Hortensius* aroused within him a love of wisdom ("O Truth, Truth! how inwardly even then did the marrow of my soul pant after thee . . ." *Conf.* iii. 6). He joined the Manichæans who promised to lead him to all truth. From Manichæism he drifted into Skepticism and Neoplatonism, the latter influencing him profoundly. In Milan he and his faithful mother listened to the sermons of the great Ambrose and here Augustine's conversion took place in 386. He received baptism in the Easter season of 387. Having resigned his official position he and his friends set out on the long journey home. At Ostia, Monnica, her mission accomplished, died. Returning to Tagaste Augustine established there a monastic community of laymen but in 391 he was ordained a priest and four years later received appointment as Bishop of Hippo Regius, a position he filled with great distinction for thirty-five years. He died August 28, 430 as the Vandals approached the gates of his city. Hardly had Augustine attained inward peace in his soul-struggle before the Roman culture of the western European world broke and disintegrated from the assaults of invading tribes. On the last day of the year 406 many Vandals, Alani, and Suevi crossed the Rhine. Four years later Rome itself fell to Alaric and his Visigoths. Ten years before, Augustine's *Confessions* had described his struggle for peace of soul. Rome's fall called forth embarrassing criticism by the pagans of the powerless Christian God and caused the great theologian to contrast the two cities, the city of earth and the city of God, differentiated by the loves (of self, or of God) of their citizens. Just as the *Confessions* was a unique writing in the area of religious devotion, so the *City of God* gave a Christian philosophy of history to a dying culture.

In addition to the convulsion of society the Church of Augustine's day suffered from attacks by heretics and schismatics. Arianism persisted in Gaul, Montanism and Manichæism were rife in North Africa (and the latter in Rome). Puritanic Donatism laid claim to being genuine Christianity, a claim which the doughty Bishop of Hippo could not countenance. Latest of the heresies and perhaps the most subtle, Pelagianism advocated a greater freedom of the will in contrast to predestination. Augustine defended the Church by much preaching and voluminous writing. Scholars would be inclined to disagree about which were his most important writings but in any such collection the following works would probably find a place: *Soliloquies, Morals of the Catholic Church, On Christian Doctrine, Confessions, On the Trinity, On the Spirit and the Letter, City of God, Concerning Nature and Grace, Enchiridion, On Grace and Free Will,* the *Retractions.*

The supreme question of the classical age and so of Augustine's century was: What is man's chief good? How, asks Augustine, ought man to live? (*De Mor. Eccl. Cath.,* 3) Since man desires happiness (Cf. *De Beata Vita*) and this may be found only "where man's chief good is loved and possessed," there is only one way of attaining one's goal: the pursuit of God which brings to the soul both virtue and wisdom. "The perfection of all our good things and our perfect good is God" (*De Mor. Eccl. Cath.,* 8). But this is because through his governance God provides judgment and punishment for our sins, and a gracious and merciful salvation.

Thus, "following after God is the desire of happiness; to reach God is happiness itself. We follow after God by loving Him; we reach Him, not by becoming entirely what He is, but in nearness to Him, and in wonderful and immaterial contact with Him, and in being inwardly illuminated and occupied by His truth and holiness" (*Ibid.* 11). "As to virtue leading us to a happy life, I hold virtue to be nothing else than perfect love of God" (*Ibid,* 15). Such love of God involves love of neighbor, or brother, and proper love of self (*De Trin.* viii. 8; *De Civ. Dei,* xix. 14; *In Joan. Evang.* lxv. 1; lxxxiii. 3; xvii. 8) and exemplifies eternal law (*De Civ. Dei,* xix. 14). Thus, the highest aim of man in the classical age, the happy life, is grounded by Augustine in the Christian religion where to be turned toward God and to cling to Him is blessedness and peace, but to be turned away from God is sin and destruction (*De Trin.* xii. 11).

Man and Sin

Furthermore, God originally created man morally upright (*De Civ. Dei,* xiv. 11) but man fell, not through inherently evil nature, but because of an evil choice by his will (*Ibid.* xii. 7), a choice which the bad angels had made earlier (*Ibid.* xii. 6). In both cases such behavior vitiates their natures (*Enchir.* 48) and arises from pride, for the beginning of sin is pride (*Ecclesiasticus* x. 13; *De Civ. Dei,* xii. 6; xiv. 13). Augustine's conception of pride as the originator of sin is more comprehensive than, though allied to, the acts of violence, rage, and rebellion called hubris (ὕβρις) by the classical writers. To be sure the quality of defiance is much the same but with the Greeks it was man against implacable Fate, or the decrees of the gods; with Augustine the conception is of such an exaltation of self as to produce an inner aversion to God who is love. Even the gross fleshly sins are really vices of the soul (*De Civ. Dei,* xiv. 2). How then may one escape this pride which is the beginning of sin? Through humility which is found in the City of God and in its King, Jesus Christ (*Ibid.* xiv. 13). Obedience ("the mother and guardian of all the virtues in a reasonable creature") has been so fashioned by God that submission becomes advantageous, but selfish defiance produces destruction (*Ibid.* xiv. 12). This explains the origins of the two cities, their histories, present experiences, and eventual destinies. Thus *humilitas* stands over against *superbia*. If the latter is the beginning of sin, the former is the beginning of wisdom and of love. Through humility, and enabled by God's grace, we repudiate self and turn toward God. Only when we are humble are we in the mood to learn of Him who is meek and lowly in heart, and such a mood is required for the attempting of other virtues.

The Christian and Society

The inhabitants of the City of God keep on working out their salvation and seek to convert and change the world. They are socially minded (*De Civ. Dei,* xix, 5, 19), and are aware of all the distress and disturbances which family, civic, and national life entail.

34

How can the Stoics deny the ills of this life (*Ibid.* xix. 4)? Here the Christian ethic operates especially, trying to bring body and soul to that well-ordered peace of God which is eternal law (*Ibid.* xix. 13; Cf. also *De Ordine*), but the Christian also realizes that no city or state of this world can demonstrate ultimate justice (*De Civ. Dei,* xix. 24). He knows further that lasting peace will be experienced only in immortality (*Ibid.* xix. 27).

The Christian Virtues

Nevertheless, despite the low morality of the Romans already cited by Cicero and others (*De Civ. Dei,* ii. 21) the philosophers, especially the Platonists, contributed much that is valuable ("liberal instruction . . . some most excellent precepts of morality . . . some truths even in regard to the worship of the One God," *De Doc. Christ.,* ii. 40. 60) which ought to be incorporated to better use in the preaching of the Gospel. Virtues desired on their own account are still virtues but are apt to lead to pride (*De Civ. Dei,* xix. 25). Just as life needs a deeper reference than flesh so virtue needs to be related to God. Thus the Greek virtues of self-control, courage, justice, and wisdom are, for the Christian, four expressions of love: "temperance is love giving itself entirely to that which is loved; fortitude is love readily bearing all things for the sake of the loved object; justice is love serving only the loved object, and therefore ruling rightly; prudence is love distinguishing with sagacity between what hinders it and what helps it" (*De Mor. Eccl. Cath.,* 15). But the object of these four forms of love is God the greatest good (Cf. *De Nat. Boni,* 7).

The Morality of the Christian

Citizens of the City of God in this life keep his commandments, following either the contemplative or the active life, or a combination of both. But they are careful neither to withdraw from life as to shun their duty to serve their neighbors, nor to embroil themselves with worldly affairs as to neglect contemplation of God (*De Civ. Dei,* xix. 19). But, since man is a composite of body and soul, when we wish to benefit our neighbor we must show him by the Holy Scriptures how to fear God and then how to love him. This will lead our neighbor to the knowledge of truth (*De Mor. Eccl. Cath.,* 28). Furthermore, Augustine preaches the New Testament ethic of love for one's enemies: "In no way can thine enemy so hurt thee by his violence, as thou dost hurt thyself if thou love him not" (*Serm.* vi; Ben lvi). In his congregations were more poor people than rich. He has no desire for the poor to remain poor, but he warns them against pride of poverty, and the rich against having everything except God (*Serm.* xxxv; Ben. lxxxv). Augustine is under no illusion concerning the world. If times are hard and evils abound, it is men who make the times. So righteous must be the Christian that tribulation will prove to be merely an exercise *Serm.* xxi, Ben. lxxxi; Cf. *Serm.* xxx, Ben. lxxx). Unlike the Stoic the Christian may never escape his troubles by suicide (*De Civ. Dei,* i. 20).

Rather he endures evil things through patience which he possesses because he loves God (*De Pat.* 14). The Christian, of course, may not lie (*De Mend., Contra Mend.*), either to protect a refugee seeking shelter (for lying kills not the body but the soul, *De Mend,* 9) or even to preserve one's own chastity (for the body cannot really be despoiled if integrity of mind is kept, *Ibid.* 10). Altogether the way the Christian goes is a hard and narrow road but he has the Church, the Scriptures and Christ himself who is the way (*Enarr.* Ps. xci. 13) to help him.

The Monk and Labor

Augustine has high regard for the disciplined and scheduled life of the faithful monk (*Enarr.* Ps. c. 9). Furthermore, not only Christians in the world but those withdrawn from the world in monasteries should engage in manual labor (*De Opere Mon.*). A monk may still meditate while he works with his hands (*Ibid.* 20). Indeed, Augustine wishes he could exchange his "pastoral counseling" for the scheduled life of the monastery with its provision for definite hours of labor and study (*Ibid.* 37). Faithful performance of monastic duties will tend to offset the disastrous effects caused by hypocrites garbed as monks who jump about from place to place telling lies and selling relics of martyrs (*Ibid.* 36).

Marriage and Virginity

Augustine's position on marriage and virginity while based on Paul is also that of many of the Church Fathers,—a position adopted by the medieval and modern Roman Catholic Church. Augustine writes four essays on this general theme, *De Continentia, De Bono Conjugali, De Virginitate,* and *De Bono Viduitatis.* Marriage is good but continence is better. The "first natural bond of human society is man and wife" (*De Bono Conj.* 1) and marriage is a sacrament not broken even by separation. The bonds are of iron, bound tighter by the Bishop (*Enarr.* Ps. cxlix. 10). Marriage is a good given by God not for its own sake but for friendship and procreation (*De Bono Conj.* 9), so that the faithful may be kept from adultery and fornication (*De Bono Vid.* 21). However, married persons through faith may exemplify wedded chastity (*Serm.* xliii, Ben. xciii). Although second marriages are not wrong, chaste widowhood is preferable (*De Bono Vid.* 6). Continence, a virtue of the soul and the product of righteousness, restrains lusts, even those of emulation and strife (*De Con.* 1; 25; 17). Still, according to the Scriptures and, for that matter, according to reason, although marriage is no sin it is not as high a good as the gift of virginity (*De Virg.* 19). Virgins in a unique sense may follow the virgin road trod by the Lamb (*Ibid.* 29). They are, therefore, peculiarly subject to the sin of pride, since virginity may be thought of as pleasing oneself (*Enarr.* Ps. lxxvi. 11). Again Augustine pleads for humility, counseling virgins to come to Jesus, who is meek and lowly of heart (*De Virg.* 35). Just as these devoted Christians have adopted virginity, their conduct throughout ought to be as unsullied as their flesh. They not only abstain from gross sins (murders, thefts, drunkenness, etc.) but lighter sins (wandering eyes, unbecoming mien, unbridled tongue, etc.). This sort of conduct coupled with virginity would show forth an angelic life provided charity and humility are also displayed (*Ibid.* 54).

The Christian's Righteousness Relative

Meanwhile, the average Christian has a high moral standard to follow, as Augustine shows in recounting the Beatitudes and after each one adding "imitate him" (*De Virg.* 28). All may thus follow the Lamb, though the way is narrow (*Enarr.* Ps. lxix. 1). But the great pastor also knew how impossible the Christian ethic was, at least for many. The Manichæans need not point out those Christians who hold still to superstitious practices or who veil their gluttony and drunkenness with the name of religion (*De Mor. Eccl. Cath.* 75). The same people who today fill the churches will fill the theatres tomorrow. Life is a turbulent sea (a favorite metaphor with Augustine), but the faithful look to Christ and so triumph. Yet even the righteousness of the Christian is only relative, consisting "rather in the remission of sins than in the perfecting of virtues" (*De Civ. Dei,* xix. 27). Never can a man be good unaided! "The just man doth live by faith, which worketh by love; whereby men cleave to God, who worketh in man both to will and work according to good will" (*Enarr.*

Ps. lxxviii. 8). The pilgrims of the City of God always pray "Forgive us our debts as we forgive our debtors," a Scriptural reference which Augustine never wearied of quoting. It appears again and again in his many writings.

The Highest Ethic: Christian Love

What differentiates one society or group of people from another? If "a people is an assemblage of reasonable beings bound together by a common agreement as to the objects of their love," then what they love will also reveal their character. Augustine thus puts a moral or spiritual interpretation upon society and the political state. But society is composed of individuals who make choices. Just as the law of gravity operates in the physical world, the law of love works in the spiritual realm. So Augustine says, "My love is my weight" (*Conf.* xiii. 9), and so he can also say, "Love, and do what thou wilt" (*In Epis. Joan.* vii. 8). The origin of the two cities is a matter of their respective loves: "Accordingly two cities have been formed by two loves: the earthly by the love of self, even to the contempt of God; the heavenly by the love of God, even to the contempt of self" (*De Civ. Dei,* xiv. 28).

Church and State

According to the most enlightened Christian faith of this twentieth century Augustine's acquiesence to coercion of schismatics by the State was immoral. We have to take into consideration not only the point in history when Augustine lived but also the fact

37

that he came to his conclusion gradually and reluctantly. To him a schismatic was practically a heretic, or a lost soul. In his letter to Vincentius (*Epis.* xciii) he explains that originally he did not believe in coercion, since no one may force another's will. But examples of successful edicts by the State (one in his own town) in behalf of the Church have convinced him that kings of the earth by making good laws serve Christ. Not coercion but the objective or end result, is to be judged good or bad. If salvation, that is to say, the Apostolic doctrine in Christ's Church, is worth all it may cost then coercion presents two advantages. Through fear of suffering the one in error may renounce his prejudice, or he may be led to examine the truth of which he has been ignorant. And Augustine has seen this work in many cities which once were Donatist but which, through fear, had become Catholic. One can only say, as one must say, that this use of expediency in religion, this justifying the means for the end, was neither good religion nor high philosophy.

Note.—All references and quotations from Augustine's works as found in *A Select Library of the Nicene and Post-Nicene Fathers of the Christian Church,* edited by Philip Schaff, First Series, Vols. I–VIII (The Christian Literature Company, 1888).

Bibliography

P. Alfaric, *L'évolution intellectuelle de saint Augustin* (Paris, 1918).

M. C. D'Arcy, *A Monument to St. Augustine* (London, 1930).

R. H. Barrow, *Introduction to St. Augustine, The City of God* (London, 1950).

Roy W. Battenhouse, Editor, *A Companion to the Study of St. Augustine* (New York, 1955), esp. chap. xiv.

Vernon J. Bourke, *Augustine's Quest of Wisdom* (Milwaukee, 1944).

C. Boyer, *L'idée de vérité dans la philosophie de saint Augustin* (Paris, 1921).

C. N. Cochrane, *Christianity and Classical Culture* (Oxford, 1939).

J. N. Figgis, *The Political Aspects of St. Augustine's City of God* (London, 1921).

Etienne Gilson, *Introduction à l'étude de saint Augustin,* 3rd ed. (Paris, 1949).

Gustav Krüger, *Augustin: Der Mann und sein Werk* (1930).

Hugh Pope, *St. Augustine of Hippo* (London, 1937).

G. G. Willis, *Saint Augustine and the Donatist Controversy* (London, 1950).

Mervin M. Deems
Bangor Theological Seminary

Augustine, St.: *see* Jesuits, the, Moral Theology of; Puritan Morals; Scheler, Max; Spinoza.

austerity: *see* Hindu Ethics; Riffian Morals.

Australian Aboriginals: *see* Aboriginals of Yirkalla.

authenticity: *see* French Existentialism and Moral Philosophy.

authoritarianism: *see* Berdyaev, Nicolas; Cooper, Anthony Ashley; Khomiakov, Alexey; Soviet Morality, Current.

authority: *see* Aquinas, Thomas, Moral Views of; Balguy, John; China, Moral Philosophies of; Hindu Ethics; Kant, I; More, Henry; Muslim Morals; Primitive Morals; Rio Grande Pueblo Indians; Spinoza.

autonomy: *see* Aquinas, Thomas, Moral Views of; Jewish Ethics and Its Civilization; Kant, I.; Soviet Morality, Current.

autonomy, moral: *see* Scheler, Max.

avarice: *see* Dante, Alighieri; greed; Hindu Ethics; Muslim Morals.

Avenarius: *see* Soviet Morality, Current.

Averroës: *see* Schopenhauer, Arthur.

Averroism: *see* Dante, Alighieri.

aversion: *see* Hobbes, Thomas; Stoics, the.

Avesta: *see* Zoroastrian Morals.

axiological realism: *see* Hartmann, Nicolai.

axioms: *see* More, Henry.

Ayer, Alfred Jules

Alfred Jules Ayer was born in London, October 29, 1910. While still a young man and while a research student at Christ Church, Oxford, he wrote the brilliant and cryptic *Language, Truth and Logic,* 1936, which he announced as being derived from the thought of Bertrand Russell and L. Wittgenstein some of whose work was the logical outcome of the empiricism of Berkeley and Hume. The work of Ayer, who is now Grote Professor of Mind and Logic at University College, London is a part of the movement of scientific empiricism called logical positivism (a name which was later changed to logical empiricism) which was first given full expression by members of the Vienna Circle under the leadership of M. Schlick.

Ayer's ethical theory was first enunciated as a defence of the consistency of his general philosophical position, according to the main tenet of which a sentence is held to be literally meaningful if and only if the proposition it expresses is either analytic (its truth follows from the definition of its terms) or synthetic (verifiable in principle or in practice). The immediate consequence was that according to this principle all value statements were held to be meaningless on the grounds that they were neither empirical nor true by definition. The formulation of the verification principle was to undergo extensive technical modifications in the face of serious criticism. Yet, while the terminology in which it was originally framed was changed and the methods according to which a statement were verifiable in a weak or strong sense was drastically revised, though not altogether successfully, the central thesis of radical empiricism remained the same. While Ayer's emotive theory of ethics is not a necessary consequence of his philosophical position and may be examined independently, the theory was never anywhere extensively developed apart from considerations of his position. Thus it will be useful in understanding the theory of non-cognitive ethics to develop it in the way in which he presents it.

If the empiricist principle was to be maintained consistently, Ayer thought that he would have to provide an answer for the intuitionists who held, as did G. E. Moore, that statements of value and statements of fact are both synthetic but each requires different methods for its validation. Accordingly, statements of value do not predict the course of our sensations in just the same way in which empirical statements do, but rather they are unanalyzable and must be apprehended directly by our intuitive faculties. In order to maintain the principle of verification, Ayer agreed that ethical terms are not analyzable, but instead of assuming them to require a special method of verification, he maintained that if they were not factual in the usual sense they were simply pseudo-propositions which at best were expressions of feelings.

The actual working out of this position took the following form. Ayer believed there to be four kinds of statements relevant to ethics: 1) definitions of ethical terms, 2) descriptions of moral phenomena, 3) exhortations to moral virtue, and 4) ethical judgments themselves. Only one of these forms the subject-matter of ethical philosophy, namely, 1) the definition of ethical terms. The second [2)] belongs exclusively to sociology or psychology and 3) and 4) are held not to be meaningful propositions at all. Accordingly, ethical philosophy makes no moral pronouncements; a part of its business is to determine whether statements containing ethical terms are reducible to statements of empirical fact. Ayer rejects the naive subjectivist and utilitarian reduction of "x is good" to "x is pleasant" or "x is desired" on the ground that according to such views an individual would not be contradicting himself if he held that some pleasant things are not good or that some bad things are desired. The assumption here is that disagreement can take place only if formal contraction is possible. And since these locutions do violence to actual usage, with which the verification principle is in accord, such reductions must be ruled out as unsuccessful.

Ayer holds that normative statements to the effect that certain actions are right or wrong are statements about which we may never significantly disagree. The only conditions under which it is allowed that statements of the moral type are empirical propositions are when they are either assertions to the effect that a certain type of action is condoned or not condoned by the customs of a given society at a given time, in which case they are empirical propositions belonging to the science of sociology, or assertions about the state of a person's mind, in which case they belong to the field of psychology. Usually, however, when an individual says that a certain action is right or wrong he is not making an assertion about the mores of his culture nor is he asserting something of the state of his mind; rather, he is expressing a sentiment or feeling. To say, "You acted wrongly in stealing that money," is to say no more than what is asserted by, "You stole that money." And to say that stealing is wrong one does not assert a proposition at all, but rather one expresses a certain feeling of moral disapproval. It is for this reason that there can be no criterion for the validity of these kinds of statements and not, as Moore supposed, that their validity must be guaranteed by intuition. The method of intuition Ayer rejects out of hand because it does not permit us to decide between two conflicting intuitions. Disputes about moral judgments arise, according to Ayer, not because two different unanalyzable qualities are being apprehended, but because the disputes are really about the particular facts of the case in terms of which it is possible to have formal contradiction. In short the answer he supplied to the intuitionists in defense of his empiricist thesis was that ethical judgments are matters of feeling about which it is irrelevant to ask for their truth or falsity.

The force of Ayer's verification principle has been vitiated somewhat by his recent admission (contained in the second edition of *Language, Truth and Logic*) that the principle was never intended to be an empirical hypothesis, but it was entertained as a stipulative definition of meaning; however, the definition was not an arbitrary one for it was intended to be in accord with ordinary usage. The harshness of his analysis of value statements was lessened in two ways: 1) he admits that we may significantly disagree about statements of value without formal contradiction—a case in point would be a dispute concerning tastes in which case a person may attempt to persuade us to his view by drawing attention to the facts or by making use of suitable emotive expressions; 2) he admits that a survey of actual usage will reveal consensus on the fact that moralists do make statements of fact; but, Ayer maintains, no matter what we call these statements their use reveals that they have a significantly different function which distinguishes them from the function of statements about matters of fact; their function is exclusively emotive.

Ayer's contribution to ethical theory is a recommendation of a new way of speaking which will, if accepted, reveal the distinct office of moral discourse. He has indicated that at least one of its many functions is emotive. Ayer, himself, did not work out the full implications of this theory. It remained for others, notably C. L. Stevenson in *Ethics and Language,* to elaborate this aspect of ethical judgments and to present detailed analyses of certain specimens of moral agreements and disagreements.

Bibliography

A. J. Ayer, *Language, Truth and Logic* (1936).
——, Introduction to the second edition of *Language, Truth and Logic* (New York: 1946).
——, *Philosophical Essays* (London: 1954).

Frank A. Tillman
The College of Wooster

Ayer, A. J.: *see* Language and Ethics.
Aztec Morals

The ancient Aztecs of Mexico observed a rigid moral code designed to please their bloodthirsty gods. Man's primary moral obligation was to honor his gods and feed them with human blood and hearts. The Aztecs migrated to the Valley of Mexico in 1299 and established their capital at Tenochtitlan some twenty-five years later. To provide their gods with an ample supply of sacrificial victims the Aztecs waged wars that extended their empire from northern Vera Cruz to Guatemala. During the expansion of the Aztec Empire the province of Mexico-Tenochtitlan prospered and grew to a population of approximately one million by the time of the Spanish Conquest.

Bravery was the supreme virtue among the Aztecs. Warriors won honor and prestige by executing brave deeds in battle and by dying heroically for Aztec gods. Aztec warriors gave their lives in battle not only for personal honor but also because they believed that their gods needed human blood and hearts to sustain them. Without human food the gods would grow too weak to provide men with sun, rain, food, health and victory. The Aztec concept of the relationship between men and gods is eloquently expressed in an Aztec priest's oration to the god Tezcatlipoca asking for victory in battle (Sahagun 1938, 2:51–52):

"The god of the earth opens his mouth with hunger to swallow the blood of the many who will die in this battle . . . We want to give food and drink to the gods of the sky and to the gods of the underworld, providing them with a feast of the blood and flesh of the men who will die in this war . . . They (the nobles) want to die in war because truly it was for this that they were sent to this world so they could feed the sun and the earth with their flesh and blood."

To provide their gods with regular supplies of hot food the Aztecs continually waged religious wars and sacrificed their captives whose blood and hearts were offered to the gods. Aztec warriors who captured the sacrificial

victims achieved great prestige for their brave deeds.

The Aztec esteemed bravery in peaceful activities as well as in war. Death in childbirth was the female equivalent of death on the battlefield and the dead mother was deified for her brave act. Traveling merchants sought honor by courageously facing hardships such as hunger, thirst and fatigue and by risking their lives in journeying over dangerous paths. Some men proved their bravery by swallowing live snakes and frogs at religious ceremonies honoring the rain god called Tlaloc.

Humility before the gods constituted a virtue second only to bravery in the Aztec ethical system. A man who humbly begged the gods for help might be granted strength to shed the blood of his foes in battle, a position of military leadership, or earthly riches. The Aztec demonstrated his humility and respect for the gods by sweeping the temples, offering incense, sighing and crying before images of the gods during night vigils. He was obliged to participate in religious dances, songs, feasts, and processions. Parents admonished their children to be sad in the presence of the gods and constantly warned children that they might be killed by the gods for failure to show proper humility.

Honesty was an important virtue particularly in human relations with the gods. In time of personal misfortune the Aztec frequently called on a god for help and made a solemn vow to repay the deity with an offering. As a guarantee that he would keep his promise the Aztec ate a small amount of dirt in homage to the gods. Sahagun stated that the Aztecs always kept their promises to the gods. If a man wanted to make certain that someone was telling the truth he demanded that the doubted individual perform the rite of eating dirt after which he was firmly believed.

Tranquility and courtesy in daily relationships between relatives and neighbors were moral qualities highly valued by the Aztecs. Elders repeatedly urged young people to show respect for others, including their inferiors, and to be discreet at all times. Parents taught their children to convey the quality of tranquility by cultivating well modulated voices, stately bearing, and good manners.

Aztec children learned to honor their parents and follow their advice. Fathers advised their sons to be brave, humble, courteous, discreet, serious and honest. Mothers taught their daughters to be industrious in their housework, content with their lot, peaceful in their daily relationships with others, and faithful in marriage. A wife was expected to be loyal to her husband even if he failed to provide her with enough to eat or wanted to leave her.

Cowardice was perhaps the most contemptible quality in the Aztec moral code. The coward never achieved prestige, good fortune, or happiness. Tezcatlipoca, the god of night, tormented cowards by frightening them at night when he appeared as a phantom. The god manifested himself as a hopping skull, a shroud, a female dwarf, and as a headless-footless body. In these forms Tezcatlipoca often chased the coward until he fell ill or died from fright.

Haughtiness was a vice despised by the Aztecs. The haughty man deprecated his inferiors, failed to look up to his elders, and showed contempt for everybody. Men who acquired riches often became haughty and overbearing. Tezcatlipoca, the god who granted wealth, punished the haughty man by taking away his riches. Tezcatlipoca also inflicted poverty, sickness and misfortune on rich men who abused their slaves.

Quarrelsomeness was an uncondoned vice among the Aztecs. Children were admonished to refrain from spreading malicious gossip, using bad language, and ridiculing others. Vociferousness and tale bearing were qualities commonly attributed to quarrelsome women.

Dishonesty was deprecated in relations with the gods and in relations with human beings. The gods killed any man who broke a solemn vow. Theft constituted a civil crime punished by death. Lying and cheating were considered immoral acts but they were not usually punished.

Murder and adultery were crimes punished by death. Civil officials executed the criminal by crushing his head between two stones. A murderer or adulterer could escape punishment, however, by confessing his crime to a priest and swearing that he would never again commit the same crime. Tlazolteatl, the goddess of carnality had the power to produce lust and pro-

43

voke illicit love affairs including adultery. She also possessed power to cleanse men of carnal sins if they confessed to their priests and performed penance.

Drunkenness was a vice greatly disparaged by Aztec elders. The privilege of becoming intoxicated was supposed to be limited to old people but public orations on the evils of drink indicate that drunkenness was a widespread habit among old and young. One Aztec official asserted that drunkenness caused nearly all other vices including adultery, corruption of virgins, violation of relatives, robbery, defamation and quarreling. A youth caught drunk in public was beaten or bludgeoned to death.

Witchcraft was a sin that subjected the witch to the hatred of the entire community. Sahagun described Aztec witches as poor, friendless and morose individuals.

The Aztecs believed that good deeds were rewarded and evil deeds punished both on earth and in the afterworld. The gods granted worldly wealth, honor and happiness to virtuous individuals and punished immoral individuals with poverty, sickness and unhappiness. The manner of a man's death determined his destination in the afterworld.

Brave men who gave their lives in battle for the gods went to a glorious sky world after death. Women who died in childbirth and captives who died on the sacrificial stone also went to the sky world. Each day the spirits of the dead warriors accompanied Huitzilopochtli, the god of sun and war, on his journey to the center of the sky. Souls of the women who died in childbirth guided the sun from the center of the sky to the west. Four years after death the souls of men who went to the sky world were transformed into birds and permitted to return to earth to feed on the nectar of flowers. Souls of the dead women returned to earth in the form of terrifying phantoms who afflicted children with illness.

Men and women who offended the gods by failure to fulfill their religious obligations often were afflicted with fatal illnesses which destined them to an afterlife in the cold, dark underworld called Mictlan. Before reaching Mictlan the souls had to suffer for four years on a tortuous journey to the underworld.

A third afterworld was the earthly paradise called Tlalocan where the rain deities dwelled. Individuals chosen by the rain gods to go to Tlalocan were killed by drowning, lightning, and certain diseases caused by the rain gods. Sixteenth century Spanish chronicles do not say whether the individuals who went to Tlalocan were chosen on the basis of their earthly behavior.

The moral character of the individual was largely pre-determined by the gods before his birth. Persons born under lucky signs in the Aztec sacred calendar were destined by the gods to be brave and fortunate whereas persons born under bad signs were doomed to commit evil deeds and encounter misfortune. The individual born under a good sign could lose his luck by neglecting his ritual obli-

44

gations and a person born under a bad sign could improve his lot a little by performing penance for the evil he was destined to commit.

After the Spanish Conquest of Mexico the Aztecs in large part rejected Christian morals. Nahuatl Indian descendants of the Aztecs living in the southwestern corner of the Valley of Mexico today continue to reject a number of important Christian moral precepts.

In the village of San Francisco Tecospa, delegacion of Milpa Alta, where I carried out an ethnographic study sponsored by the Wenner-Gren Foundation for Anthropological Research the Nahuatl Indians have rejected the commandment that they should love the Christian God and they do not believe that God loves them. Tecospan Indians say that God is an enemy of mankind who wants to destroy the world and all its people. He is prevented from doing so only by the Virgin of Guadalupe who intervenes with him on behalf of the Mexicans who are her children. God cannot destroy mankind without her consent.

The Indians of Tecospa have rejected the Christian commandment that they should worship no other deities but God. Religion in the Valley of Mexico always has been and still is polytheistic. Today Catholic saints have replaced Aztec gods as village patrons. Tecospans worship the saints not merely as intermediaries with God but also as deities in their own right. The Indians still venerate Aztec rain dwarfs called "ahuatoton" meaning "water spirits."

Humility toward deities is a virtue in Tecospan ethics but meekness in dealing with an enemy is a sign of cowardice. The Christian virtues of righteousness and purity of heart are lacking in Tecospan ethics which emphasize proper behavior rather than good thoughts and beliefs. An individual may think what he likes so long as he acts according to the local code of ethics. Today, as in Aztec times, the Indian's primary moral duty is to fulfill his ritual obligations to the deities who grant him rain, crops and health.

Bibliography

Charles S. Braden, *Religious Aspects of the Conquest of Mexico* (Duke University Press, Durham, N. C., 1930).

Alfonso Caso, *The Religion of the Aztecs*. (Editorial Fray B. de Sahagun, Mexico, D. F., 1937).

William Madsen, *Christo-Paganism: A Study of Mexican Religious Syncretism*. Ph.D. thesis in University of California library (Berkeley, Calif.).

Fray Toribio Motolinía, *The Indians of New Spain*. Translated by Elizabeth Foster (The Cortes Society. Berkeley, Calif., 1950).

Bernardino de Sahagun, *Historia General de las Cosas de Nueva España*. 5 tomos. (Editorial Pedro Robredo, Mexico, D. F., 1938).

George Vaillant, *Aztecs of Mexico*. (Garden City, N.Y., 1944).

William Madsen
University of Texas

Azzariah, Eliezer: *see* Jewish Ethics and Its Civilization.

B

Babbitt, I.: *see* Major Ethical Viewpoints.

Babylonia, ancient: *see* Hammurapi, Code of.

Bacon, F.: *see* Moral Philosophy in America; Spinoza.

bad, the: *see* Aboriginals of Yirkalla; Augustine and Morals; Ayer, Alfred J.; beyond good and evil; Dewey, John; evil; French Existentialism and Moral Philosophy; Kant, I.; Liguori, St. Alphonsus and Catholic Moral Philosophy; Morals and Religion; Muslim Morals; Navaho Morals; Prichard, H. A.; Psychology and Morals; Puritan Morals; Riffian Morals; Rio Grande Pueblo Indians; Ross, Sir (William) David; sin; Socrates; Sophists, the; Spinoza; Tapirapé Morals, Some Aspects of.

Bahnsen, J.: *see* Schopenhauer, Arthur.

Bakunin: *see* Soviet Morality, Current.

balance: *see* Liguori, St. Alphonsus and Catholic Moral Philosophy; More, Henry; Pakot, the Moral system of; Rio Grande Pueblo Indians; Ross, Sir (William) David.

Balguy, John

John Balguy was born at Sheffield August 12, 1686. He was educated by his father before entering St. John's College, Cambridge in 1702. He received his bachelor's degree in 1706 and was ordained to the ministry in 1710 serving first at Lamesly and Tanfield in the county of Durham. In 1728 he was made a prebend of Salisbury by Bishop Hoadley, whose views he had supported in the "Bangorian Controversy" under the pen-name of Silvius. In 1729 he became vicar of Northallerton, York, and remained in this position until his death in 1748.

Balguy's moral philosophy represents a significant modification of the rationalistic system of Samuel Clarke. Though constructive in many respects, it is presented in large part within a polemical context, primarily against Hutcheson (*The Foundation of Moral Goodness Part I*, 1728; *Part II*, 1729) but also against Shaftesbury (*A Letter to a Deist concerning the Beauty and Excellency of Moral Virtue, and the support and improvement which it receives from the Christian Religion*, 1726). Against Shaftesbury Balguy argues that while love of virtue as such is the highest reach of morality, the rewards and punishments promised by the Christian religion are valuable, even necessary, sanctions of conduct. In *The Foundation of Goodness* Balguy improves his position considerably.

He does not make explicit what he

means by 'foundation,' but it is possible to infer from context several possible meanings, and to see why he states his problem as he does. He is, for example, willing to admit that the affections are important aids to reason and reflection in the performance of duty but he denies what he takes to be Hutcheson's view that they are the foundation of moral goodness:

[Hutcheson] does not consider this natural Affection or Instinct, merely as a Help or Incentive to Virtue, but as the true Ground or Foundation of it. He makes Virtue entirely to consist in it, or flow from it. (*Foundation*. Part I, p. 7.)

In language which still remains figurative he denies that affections and the moral sense can be the "only Pillars on which moral Goodness rests." He thus suggests that the foundation of virtue is 1) what it consists in, 2) what it flows from, 3) what it rests on. Balguy also considers that the problem of the foundation of virtue is not only to enquire into its "first original" but also into the reason for the universal approbation of virtue:

To enquire what it is that originally constitutes Virtue or Moral Goodness, and whence arises that universal approbation which it meets with from rational Beings are undoubtedly Speculations of very great Moment. (*Foundation*, Part I, p. 4.)

A search into foundations, then, is for the purpose of discovering why virtue is approved. In this respect the foundation of morality will be "the reason why" virtue is approved and Balguy's opening polemic against Hutcheson reveals why he holds that

the affections cannot be the foundation of morals; if they were, then no one would be likely to approve of virtuous actions. Balguy points out five consequences of the doctrine that virtue is founded upon, flows from, or consists in, the affections: Virtue would be arbitrary; a man without instincts could not perform any moral acts; animals would be virtuous; degree of virtue would be directly proportional to strength of affection. Hutcheson himself denied this last consequence, as Balguy points out, and thus his theory falls under a double difficulty: It not only enunciates a doctrine which does not agree with moral facts but is internally inconsistent. Finally, on Hutcheson's foundations morality is "dishonored":

Now if Virtue and the Approbation of Virtue, be merely instinctive, we must certainly think less highly and less honourably of it, than we should if we looked upon it as rational; for I suppose it will readily be allowed, that Reason is the nobler Principle: It is therefore to be wished that it may be found to have the first and chief place in the original Idea of Virtue. (*Foundation,* Part I, p. 19.)

Balguy argues in a similar way that the moral sense cannot be the foundation of morals, and although he finds a place for the affections, the moral sense, and even self-love, in the pursuit of virtue, he never admits that they are more than auxiliaries or accompaniments of it. In the end he concludes:

In short, I cannot have any other idea of moral Merit, than conforming, or endeavouring to conform, our Actions to the Reasons of Things. And this I am persuaded, is the real Foundation of all Goodness, whether human or divine. (*Foundation*, Part I, p. 55.)

Balguy reaffirms Clarke's answer to the question 'What are the foundations of morals?': "truth" and "the natures of things." But he represents a modification of Clarke in that he explicitly calls attention to the fact that the similarity between morality and logic or mathematics, so strongly emphasized by the rationalists, is analogical. The analogical character of the comparison in Clarke and Wollaston had more often than not been obscured by the extreme way in which it was drawn. Balguy on the other hand specifically recommends that the term 'contradiction' be replaced by the term 'counteraction' when it refers to the lack of agreement between the nature of a situation and an action. He admits that actions may be true or false in a figurative sense, but considers that it reduces confusion and ambiguity to refer to them as right or wrong (*Foundation*, Part I pp. 34–35). He also makes clear that what he intends by asserting an analogy between morality and mathematics is primarily that it is possible to have *as* certain knowledge in the one as in the other:

Can . . . such an Equality or Proportion be ascribed to . . . Moral Ideas as belongs to . . . Mathematical ones? Those Terms are used and applied to both Kinds, but not precisely in the same Sense. They belong originally to Idea of Quantity; and when they are used to denote Moral Fitness, their Signification is somewhat figura-

tive. But concerning the Meaning, or Propriety of Terms, I have no Dispute at present. However the Agreement between Moral Ideas may be denominated or distinguished, what I contend for is, that the Ideas themselves invariably bear such Relations to each other; which are no less certain, and oftentimes more immediately evident than the Equality or Proportion between the forementioned Angles and Figures. (*Foundation*, Part II, p. 6.)

In the second part of *The Foundation of Moral Goodness,* under the impetus of his questioner, Balguy had to deal explicitly with the relation between the foundations of morality and obligation.

In Part I of *The Foundation of Moral Goodness* he had distinguished obligation as "internal" and "external." External obligation is the compulsion laid upon one by a just authority. With this type of obligation he expresses no concern. On the other hand,

Internal obligation is a State of the Mind into which it is brought by the Perception of a plain Reason for acting, or forbearing to act, arising from the Nature, Circumstances, or Relations of Persons or Things. The Internal Reasons of Things are the Supreme Law, inducing the strongest Obligation, and affecting all intelligent Beings. (*Foundation*, Part I, p. 29.)

Of the fourteen objections or questions in *Part II* of *Foundation* which deal directly with obligation, four are central: the third, fourth, fifth, and sixth. The third and fourth in effect admit that the ideas of "bounty" and "gratitude" are moral ideas but deny that any obligation can be deduced

49

from them "if we suppose no senti- ment." Balguy denies the denial, but the closest he comes to exhibiting such a deduction here is in answer to the fourth objection where he provides an argument in incomplete, yet deductive, form:

If receiving of Benefits be a good Reason, as it certainly is, why the Receiver should be grateful, then it obliges him so to be. (*Foundation*, Part II, p. 8.)

These issues are pushed further in Articles V and VI where Balguy's questioner raises questions not only about the foundations of morals but also about knowledge of the relationship between knowledge, deduction and reason, on the one hand, and obligation, on the other:

Art. V. If you will affirm, that by comparing these Ideas in your Mind, you can perceive any such Moral Proposition necessarily included, viz., that a Man ought to be grateful; I ask, whether you see that necessary Consequence immediately upon comparing these Ideas, or mediately by the Help of some intermediate Reasoning or Proof. If you see such a Connection immediately, or, as it were, intuitively, I wonder everybody else cannot see it. If you have any intermediate Reasonings or Proofs, pray let us have them. (*Foundation*, Part II, pp. 9–10).

Art. VI. I know not well what you mean by this Expression, viz., that our Understandings are capable of Moral Perceptions. I believe every body agrees that in some sense they are; that is, that the Mind is capable of receiving or forming Moral Ideas: But it does not follow from hence, that obligation is deducible merely from

our Moral Ideas, without supposing any sentiment. (*Foundation,* pp. 11–12.)

In answer to the fifth article Balguy affirms first that the statement that a man ought to be grateful to his benefactors is one which is true self-evidently, even though he goes on to show in two enthymemes how obligation is deducible. He has no answer to the question why there should be disagreement over self-evident truths.

In answer to the sixth article, he does not attempt to uphold the self-evidence of his doctrine of obligation but instead attempts to justify further the deduction of obligation from fittingness (or reasonableness). In answer to article V he had argued that since bounty and gratitude are morally fitting, gratitude is reasonable; and that since it is reasonable it is obligatory. If we provide the missing premises, the arguments run as follows:

[1.] [Everything that is morally fitting is reasonable.]
2. Bounty and gratitude are morally fitting.
3. Therefore, Gratitude in return for bounty is reasonable.
[4.] [If any act is reasonable then it ought to be done.]
5. Gratitude in return for bounty is reasonable.
6. Therefore, Gratitude in return for bounty ought to be done.

His contribution to these arguments in his answer to Article VI consists primarily in his justification of [4.] which had been a suppressed premise in his discussion of Article V. He argues in support of [1.], which had also been suppressed in the discussion of V, by offering the exclusive alternatives of admitting actions to be reasonable for the doing of which a good reason can be given or admitting that no actions are reasonable. He assumes without argument that the answer is in favor of the first alternative and then offers a final exclusive alternation in support of his view of the deducibility of obligation:

How does it appear that we ought to do what is reasonable? As moral agents, we are either obliged to do this, or nothing. (*Foundation*, Part II, p. 13.)

His alternation then amounts to this: either we are obliged to act in accordance with reasonable grounds or we must disavow all significance to acting. It seems possible to suggest in the light of this that for Balguy the foundation of morality is not so much "the nature of things" as "the nature of active, rational, things" where the emphasis is upon activity no less than upon rationality.

An ambiguity that has run through Balguy's discussion, however, may seem to mar the significance of this important doctrine. He has not distinguished between the meaning of 'reasonable' as 'having good reasons (grounds)' and 'in accordance with the processes of reasoning (deduction),' and often shifts between them. But his further discussion of obligation indicates that he here intends 'reasonable' to mean 'having good reasons (grounds)' since he puts it forward in support of the view that there is no serious alternative to being obliged to do what there are good reasons to do.

[Obligation] supposes likewise some Perception in the Mind, since no agent can be obliged to or by anything while he is ignorant of it. What is it then, which as soon as perceived, produces that State of Mind which we call Obligation? It must be some Motive, some Inducement, some Reason that is fit to influence and incline the Will, and prevail with it to choose and act accordingly. (*Foundation*, Part II, pp. 13–14.)

With respect to sensible agents, Balguy admits that "Pleasure or natural Good" is such a motive (or end). But for moral agents there is a moral end rather than a natural one. This end is moral goodness which in *Part I* Balguy explained as acting in accordance with the natures of things. Here he distinguishes, within "good reasons" for acting, between internal and external, moral and natural, but unfortunately does not discuss the distinction:

. . . whatever Agent is said to be under an Obligation to the Performance of any Action, the true Meaning of such an Expression, as it appears to me, is, that he perceives some good Reason, either internal or external, moral or natural, for the Performance of it. (*Foundation*, Part II, pp. 15–16.)

In the light of this passage, then, in spite of Balguy's polemic against Hutcheson, there is a similarity between the two men. Hutcheson distinguished between obligation to an action in order to obtain happiness or avoid misery and obligation to an action the performance of which every spectator or the agent himself would approve if he considered all the relevant circumstances fully. (*Illustrations upon the Moral Sense.*) The first of these corresponds to Balguy's obligation based on an internal natural reason; the second corresponds to Balguy's obligation based on an internal moral reason, the chief difference in the latter case being between Hutcheson's criterion of "approval" and Balguy's criterion of "agreement with the nature of active, rational beings." Balguy would probably argue that Hutcheson's criterion is merely a limited version of his own.

Such an argument would be basically correct but leaves a more important matter to be considered. The chief difficulty with the doctrine that the foundation of morals is to be found in the nature of things is not that it is false or that it excludes certain situations or acts. Rather, it is so broad and vague that it supplies no more than a starting point for ethics. Balguy took some of the first steps beyond this rationalistic starting point in his attempt to explicate obligation in terms of "good Reasons." In so doing he also emphasized the central importance of the problem of obligation in any moral philosophy, after a period in which it had been neglected or submerged by others in the rationalistic tradition. The polemical aspects of Balguy's writing also served to usher in a new phase in British moral philosophy. Although criticism of Hobbes was still an important concern, reflections in ethics turned in a new direction as a result of the awareness of the issues between the rationalists and the empiricists which Balguy's polemic had made plain.

Bibliography

John Balguy, *Letter to a Deist concerning the Beauty and Excellency of Moral Virtue, and the support and improvement which it receives from the Christian Religion* (1726).

——, *The Foundation of Moral Goodness, Part I,* (1728).

——, *The Foundation of Moral Goodness, Part II,* (1729). [Part II was written in answer to forty objections to Part I. Rachel Kydd has suggested (*Reason and Conduct in Hume's Treatise*) that Hutcheson himself wrote the objections. But Balguy's son, Thomas, in his notice of his father's life in *Biographia Britannica,* Vol. I, p. 551, asserts that the objections were written by Lord Darcy.]

——, *Divine Rectitude: or, a Brief Inquiry concerning the Moral Perfections of the Deity, particularly in respect of Creation and Providence* (1730).

——, *A Second Letter to a Deist, concerning a late book, entitled "Christianity as old as the Creation,"* more particularly that chapter which relates to Dr. Clarke (1731).

——, *The Law of Truth, or the Obligations of Reason essential to all Religion* (1732). [These were collected and published in 1734 in London by J. Pemberton.]

——, *An Essay on Redemption* (1741).

——, *Sermons* (1746).

Hugh David Jones, "John Balguy," *Abhundlung zur Philosophie und ihrer Geshichte,* Heft 4, (1909).

Bernard Peach
Duke University

Balguy, John: *see* Clarke, Samuel; Cooper, Anthony Ashley; Price, Richard.

banishment: *see* Rio Grande Pueblo Indians.

Barclay, Robert: *see* Quakerism, Classical, the Morality of.

Bayes, Thomas: *see* Price, Richard.

Bayle: *see* Cooper, Anthony Ashley.

Baynes, Paul: *see* Puritan Morals.

Bazarov, V. A.: *see* Soviet Morality, Current.

beatitude: *see* Dante, Alighieri.

beatitudes, the: *see* Augustine and Morals.

beauty: *see* art (the arts); Cooper, Anthony Ashley; Cudworth, Ralph; Major Ethical Viewpoints; Plato; Puritan Morals; Stoics, the.

Beauvoir, Simone de: *see* French Existentialism and Moral Philosophy.

Beccaria: *see* Utilitarianism.

Bedouin: *see* Primitive Morals.

beer drinking: *see* Puritan Morals.

begging: *see* Aboriginals of Yirkalla; mendicant; Minor Socratics.

Bellamy, Joseph: *see* Moral Philosophy in America.

Bellers, John: *see* Quakerism, Classical, The Morality of.

Benavides: *see* Rio Grande Pueblo Indians.

beneficence: *see* Reid, Thomas; Ross, Sir (William) David.

benevolence: *see* Butler, Joseph; Clarke, Samuel; Cooper, Anthony Ashley; Cumberland, Richard; Hobbes, Thomas; Hume, David; Hutcheson, Francis; Moral Philosophy in America; Navaho Morals; Price, Richard; Reid, Thomas; Sidgwick, Henry; Utilitarianism.

Bentham, Jeremy: *see* Cumberland, Richard; Green, T. H.; Major Ethical Viewpoints; Marxist Theory of

Morals; Moral Philosophy in America; Schlick, Moritz; Utilitarianism.

Berbers, Moroccan: *see* Riffian Morals.

Berdyaev, Nicolas

The revival of Russian religious thought, which marked the end of the 19th century (see: A. Khomiakov, F. Dostoyevsky, W. Soloviev, Leo Tolstoy), was carried on and developed by Nicolas Berdyaev in the first half of the 20th century. In fact, as Berdyaev himself tells us (*Dream and Reality*), he was directly influenced and stimulated by Russian 19th century religious teachings. He owes many of his basic principles and even some of his terminology (as, for instance, in the definition of love and freedom) to the Christian philosophy of the East. However, Berdyaev must be considered not only as the most brilliant representative of Russian philosophic achievement, but also and essentially as a philosopher in his own right, independent of his predecessors at home, as well as of Western philosophies, of which too he had a thorough knowledge and understanding.

The son of a country-gentleman, whose estate was located in the province of Kiev, Nicolas Berdyaev (born in 1874) was brought up in early childhood and adolescence in the framework of traditional Russian nobility: landed gentry, military commanders and civil servants. Berdyaev's family, however, mingled this conventional set-up with what was at that time known as "Western enlightenment." This meant certain intellectual traits borrowed from European culture: a taste for Western philosophy, for Voltaire and the French Encyclopedists, as well as for Kant and Schopenhauer, whose writings gradually minimized, and even tended to replace Russian Orthodox education. According to Berdyaev's own testimony, (*Dream and Reality*), he received at home no true Christian formation, but was only taught the outward, conventional rituals of the Church. His mother, descendent of a French emigré family, (she was *née* Countess de Choiseul) initiated him in her own country's tradition. From his mother he learned to speak French fluently. He also became familiar with the Western religious background. Though through marriage, Berdyaev's mother became Russian-Orthodox, she retained something of her early Roman-Catholic training. His mother's origins, as well as her kindliness and understanding, account for Nicolas' own congenial and friendly attitude toward things European, which he blended throughout his life, with a deeply Russian national consciousness.

While studying in his teens at Kiev University, Berdyaev was attracted by the young radical intelligentsia to which most of his fellow-students belonged. This was the time, when (at the turn of the century) Russian radicalism, in its extreme socialist wing, was strongly influenced by the Marxist doctrine. He became an ardent Marxist and took part in revolutionary activities which led to his arrest. He was tried and exiled to Vologda, a town in the North of Russia, where many revolutionaries were banished at that time. During his stay in Vologda he had ample opportunity to meet the leaders of Russian Marxism and to become familiar with their ideology and methods. Both disappointed and repulsed him. The totalitarian element of Marxism, its complete absence of spirituality, i.e., of freedom, turned him against the very men, whose struggle he had so willingly shared, and whose punishment he had taken upon himself in a sincere spirit of self-sacrifice. He returned from Vologda a confirmed anti-Marxist. However, his early experience in the Marxist field proved extremely valuable in later years when he undertook the criticism of communism and all other totalitarian doctrines. He was thoroughly aware of their inner springs and not merely of their outward manifestations.

Having rejected Marxism—the social doctrine without God *par excellence,* Berdyaev still wanted social justice and strove above all toward the defense of the human person. This humanist ideal he now discovered in the teaching of Christianity. Even as a Marxist, he had been strongly drawn to Tolstoy. Now he not only reread Tolstoy but went beyond him, and fully accepted the Church and Divine Revelation (which Tolstoy did not adhere to). In Berdyaev's return to the Church, Khomiakov's teaching of Sobornost (commonalty), i.e., love binding all members together under the one and only authority, Jesus Christ, played a decisive role. So did Soloviev's ecumenic spirit. From Dostoyevsky, Berdyaev retained in particular the notion of the free-will, i.e., Christian freedom. As to his initial teacher, Tolstoy, Berdyaev continued to defend and to support most fervently Tolstoy's concern with the poor, with suffering mankind, and with all that should be done for them: bread and bodily comfort. But he did not believe that this was *all* man needed. Man also needed to assert his spiritual dignity and freedom. Like Soloviev, Berdyaev did not accept Tolstoy's doctrine of non-resistance to evil. On the contrary, he looked upon himself as a fighting champion of the good provided, of course, that the weapons used against evil were not evil themselves.

The subsequent development of Berdyaev's religious, social and ethical philosophy belongs to the most decisive period of the above-mentioned Russian spiritual revival. This period, from 1900 to 1917, brings us to the very threshold of the Russian revolution, and far beyond this historical landmark. During the first decade of the 20th century, other young men of his generation had followed the same evolution from atheist materialism to the spirit of Christ and His Church. Among these young men, who had abandoned Marxism, most noteworthy were Prof. Sergius Bulgakov (who later became a priest and famous theologian), the political writer, Peter Struve, and Prof. Semyon Frank, outstanding contributor, to the Russian-Orthodox renaissance.

Berdyaev's articles on behalf of Christian humanism and freedom were published in reviews and journals specially founded in order to defend this new platform. The "Religious-Philosophical Societies" of Saint Petersburg (today Leningrad) and Moscow were also active in Russia's religious revival. Even after the Communist coup d'état in 1917, Berdyaev could still continue for some time his writing and was permitted to lecture in Moscow. But in 1922, his activity in Russia was suddenly interrupted. Together with a number of prominent intellectuals, including S. Bulgakov, N. O. Lossky, S. Frank, P. Sorokine, and others, he was expelled from his native land. He stayed for a time in Germany, and later settled in France. There he spent more than twenty years, writing most of his major works, lecturing in Russian and French, and becoming one of the leading philosophers of his time. It can be truly said, that while remaining essentially a Russian religious thinker, Berdyaev can be considered as internationally famous. His works, translated in many languages, are held in high esteem not only by the Russian-Orthodox, but also by Catholics and Protestants. Though some of these works may appear controversial to members of his own Church, as well as to representatives of other denominations, all of them agree on a number of essential points: his fine and alert consciousness of man's spiritual value and immortal destiny have scarcely been surpassed by any of his contemporaries. His profound and brilliant criticism of totalitarian doctrines (Communist, Nazi, Fascist) are most illuminating to all those who want to fight these ideologies, which he branded as modern "idolatries." On the other hand, he denounced the sins of capitalism also, insofar as capitalism pursued its own materialistic aims, as long as industrialism enslaved man and stifled legitimate aspirations. Last but not least, Berdyaev denounced the false pretence, lack of true faith and pharisaism too often manifested by the established churches. This criticism set its sharpest pattern in a brief essay entitled *Of the Worth of Christianity and the Unworthiness of Christians.* This article, translated in French had a very great influence not only on the Russian-Orthodox, but also on French Catholic and Protestant social minded youth. He died in 1948.

The impact of Berdyaev's teaching was founded on the principle that Christian ethics must not only be applied to each man separately but to humanity *in its entire scope,* The commandment of love is *not* fulfilled if it does not embrace all men. To be a humanist in separate cases, to save one's soul alone, and not to be a humanist in society is what Berdyaev bitterly described as *"double-book-keeping."* Christianity teaches us that man is free, therefore all men are free. If one single man is enslaved, then all men are enslaved. To be free, society must first of all serve man, not make of man its instrument.

But *who* is this man whom Berdyaev places above society? He is the *person,* made in the image and semblance of God. He is a living link in the natural *and* supernatural world. To ignore man's spiritual essence, to submit him to man-made regulations, means to "objectivize" subjective values, to impose upon them the dead letter of "legalism." "The human person," writes Berdyaev, "is defined above all not by its relation to society and cosmos, not by its relation to the world which is enslaved by objectivization, but by its relation to God" (*Slavery and Freedom*).

This conception of man as a free child of God is generally described as Berdyaev's Personalism. But this personalism does not separate man from his fellows as individualism does. On the contrary it brings men together in Sobornost as presented in Russian-Orthodoxy (see Khomiakov). "A society of personalities is not either a monarchy, or a theocracy, or an aristocracy or a democracy, nor is it authoritarian society, nor a liberal society, nor a bourgeois society nor a socialist society: it is not fascism nor communism, nor even anarchism . . . There is only one, acceptable, non-servile meaning of the word Sobornost, and that is the interpretation of it as the interior concrete universalism of personality" (*Slavery and Freedom*).

The human person is then, according to Berdyaev, both *free* and *universal.* This means that the human person, in the Christian ethical conception, is both separate, independent, *and* all-embracing. Responsible for himself, man is responsible also for each of his brothers. "Moral consciousness," writes Berdyaev, "began with God's question: 'Cain, where is thy brother Abel?' It will end with another question on the part of God: 'Abel, where is thy brother Cain?' (*The Des-*

56

tiny of Man). Thus, Berdyaev sharply outlines an ethical system *both* personalist and participating in all-humanity, the Mystical body of Christ: "Paradise," he writes, "is possible for me if there is no everlasting hell for a single being that has ever lived. One cannot be saved singly, in isolation. Salvation can be only communal, universal deliverance from torments."

As Prof. N. Lossky writes: "Berdyaev is convinced that ways of redeeming evil and conquering hell can be found and believes in universal salvation. . . ." However, Berdyaev continuously points to 1) the failure of Christianity in our time; and 2) the full realization of the human person in Christ only at the end of times.

"The history of Christendom," he writes, "has been too often a crucifixion of Christ." (*An Essay on Eschatological Metaphysics*). As long as history prevails *in time,* we cannot attain the Kingdom of God. However, man's destiny is not in time, but in Eternity. This is why we should not be concerned with the "abstract norm of the good," a norm, which is "objectivized," and "does not care about man" (*The Destiny of Man*).

Berdyaev often pointed out that we do not sufficiently grasp the significance of spirit over matter. Not only is this underestimation of spiritual values manifest in materialist doctrines—but so-called Christians also operate with material values only.

Man's soul, wrote Dostoyevsky, is an arena, in which good and evil struggle. Berdyaev implemented this famous utterance by saying:

The human soul is an arena in which there takes place the interplay of freedom and necessity, the spiritual and the natural world (*Freedom and the Spirit*).

And he goes on to say:

Man is determined from within, from the inmost depths of his being, in so far as the spirit subdues in him the psychical and natural elements, and the soul is absorbed by the spirit, and the spirit enters into the soul. Freedom belongs only to those phenomena of the soul which can be called spiritual (*Ibid*).

Berdyaev's fundamental thesis then, as implemented in his many writings, is that the material, natural world is the world of necessity, but that there is another world, the world of *freedom,* which obeys no earthly laws, and ignores earthly phenomena in time. His message is crystal clear on these main points. His most remarkable achievement was to combine time and eternity, the human person and society, each man responsible for himself, and all men responsible for each other.

Bibliography

N. Berdyaev, *Dream and Reality* (Russian title: *Samopoznanye*). Translated into English (New York, 1951).

——, *The Destiny of Man*. Translated into English (New York, 1937).

——, *Slavery and Freedom*. Translated into English (New York, 1939).

——, *Essai de Metaphysique Eschatologique*. Translated into French (Paris, 1946).

——, *The Fate of Man in the Modern World*. Translated into English (Morehouse-Gorham, 1934).

——, *The Bourgeois Mind*. Collected Articles, including "Man and the Machine" and "The Worth of Christianity and the Unworthiness of Christians." Translated into English (New York, 1934).

——, *Freedom and the Spirit.* Translated into English (New York, 1935).

——, *The Russian Idea.* Translated into English (New York, 1948).

For Berdyaev's complete bibliography see: Matthew Spinka, *Nicholas Berdyaev* presenting some 30 titles of books and as many essays and articles by Berdyaev, many of them translated into English, French and German. (Philadelphia, 1950).

Matther Spinka, *Nicholas Berdyaev, Captive of Freedom* (1950, as above).

N. O. Lossky, *History of Russian Philosophy* (Int. University Press, 1951).

George Seaver, *Nicholas Berdyaev* (New York, 1950).

Helene Iswolsky
Fordham Institute of Contemporary Russian Studies

Berdyaev, Nicolas: *see* Dostoyevsky, Fyodor; Khomiakov, Alexey; Soviet Morality, Current.

Berkeley: *see* Ayer, Alfred J.: Cudworth, Ralph; Moral Philosophy in America.

Bernheim: *see* Freud, Sigmund.

bestiality: *see* Dante, Alighieri.

beyond good and evil: *see* Hindu Ethics; Nietzsche, Friedrich.

Bhagavad Gita: *see* Hindu Ethics.

Bible: *see* Hammurapi, Code of; Hindu Ethics; Jewish Ethics and Its Civilization; Moral Philosophy in America; New Testament; Old Testament; Primitive Morals; Puritan Morals; Scripture; Spinoza.

bibliolatry: *see* Jewish Ethics and Its Civilization.

bigotry: *see* Puritan Morals.

Bion: *see* Minor Socratics.

Birch, Elizabeth: *see* Cooper, Anthony Ashley.

birth control: *see* Soviet Morality, Current.

blame: *see* Cudworth, Ralph; Jesuits, the, Moral Theology of; Moore, George Edward; More, Henry; Price, Richard; Reid, Thomas; Rio Grande Pueblo Indians; Utilitarianism.

Blanshard, Brand: *see* Moral Philosophy in America.

blasphemy: *see* Dante, Alighieri; Jewish Ethics and Its Civilization; Liguori, St. Alphonsus and Catholic Moral Philosophy.

"blat": *see* Soviet Morality, Current.

blessedness: *see* Augustine and Morals; Spinoza.

bliss: *see* Hindu Ethics.

blood feud: *see* Aboriginals of Yirkalla.

blood revenge: *see* Muslim Morals.

boasting: *see* Mundurucu Indians, A Dual System of Ethics.

Bogdanov, A. A.: *see* Soviet Morality, Current.

Bolsheviks: *see* Marxist Theory of Morals; Soviet Morality, Current.

bondage: *see* Hindu Ethics.

boniform faculty: *see* More, Henry.

boredom: *see* Schopenhauer, Arthur.

Borgia, Caesar: *see* Machiavelli, Nicolo.

Bosanquet, B.: *see* Green, T. H.; Hammurapi, Code of.

bounty: *see* Balguy, John.

bourgeoisie: *see* Marxist Theory of Morals; Soviet Morality, Current.

Bowne, B. P.: *see* Moral Philosophy in America.

Bowring, John: *see* Utilitarianism.

Bradford, William: *see* Puritan Morals.

Bradley, F. H.: *see* Green, T. H.; Major Ethical Viewpoints.

Bradstreet, Ann: *see* Puritan Morals.

Bradstreet, Simon: *see* Puritan Morals.

Brahman: *see* Hindu Ethics.

brahmin: *see* Hindu Ethics.

bravery: *see* Aztec Morals; Riffian Morals.

Brazil: *see* Tapirapé Morals, Some Aspects of.

Breuer: *see* Freud, Sigmund.

Brewster, William: *see* Puritan Morals.

British School of Psychologists: *see* Psychology and Morals.

Broad, C. D.

C. D. Broad (1887–), Fellow of Trinity College, Cambridge, and Knightbridge Professor of Moral Philosophy in the University of Cambridge, has been for the past thirty years one of the most important and influential of contemporary philosophers. The breadth of his philosophic interests will be indicated by the titles of his best known books: *Scientific Thought* (1923), *The Mind and Its Place In Nature* (1925), and *Five Types of Ethical Theory* (1930). More recently a number of his papers have been collected and reprinted in *Ethics and the History of Philosophy* (1952), and *Religion, Philosophy and Psychical Research* (1953). His ethical views, to which this short article is confined, are contained in *Five Types of Ethical Theory,* in his two recent volumes, and in a number of papers appearing in professional journals.

Broad maintains that it is not the business of the moral philosopher to tell people what they ought to do, for he has no special information of this sort to offer. Rather, it is the philosopher's unique task to reflect on moral concepts and beliefs, to analyze and clarify them, to seek out the various relations between them, and to see what evidence, if any, there is for them. In short, his task is critical, not speculative or didactic.

Broad has devoted a good part of his time to a careful and detailed examination of the philosophical views of others. In *Five Types of Ethical Theory,* for instance, he marshals, dissects, and comments on the views of Spinoza, Butler, Hume, Kant and Sidgwick. He has also been much concerned with the problems raised by men like G. E. Moore and Sir David Ross, his contemporaries, and with the controversies stirred up by the protagonists of "naturalism," "non-naturalism" and "emotivism." Unfortunately, as valuable as Broad's analyses of theories and problems are, they do not lend themselves to a brief summary, for they are too many and too diverse. We can touch on them only insofar as they throw light on Broad's own views.

A summary of Broad's views will be misleading if it suggests that he has expounded, elaborated, and defended an ethical theory. He has not. On the contrary, as suggested above, he has

59

concerned himself mainly with the analysis and evaluation of the views of others. Sometimes he gives the impression that he can make a more valuable contribution to ethical theory by clarifying current issues than by arguing for yet another theory, and at other times he is clearly of the opinion that the complexity of the problems forestalls any definite choice between proposed solutions. But, for whatever reasons, he presents his own views very infrequently and then only briefly, and usually as a prologue or appendage to the main business at hand. For instance, in *Five Types of Ethical Theory*, the first two hundred and eighty pages are devoted to a searching examination of five important ethical theories while only the last five pages are given over to a statement of his own position. Despite this characteristic of his work, the several brief statements he does make and the tenor of thirty years writing reveal a general pattern. In *The Mind and Its Place in Nature* and *Five Types of Ethical Theory* he asserts very briefly a position which is stated less firmly but elaborated in greater detail in later papers. It will become obvious as we proceed that his views have been greatly influenced by the thought of men like Moore and Ross.

Broad starts by noting that there are two quite different classes of moral concept—that of "good" and related concepts like "valuable" and "desirable" and that of "right" and related concepts like "fitting," "duty," and "obligation." Consequently the task he sets himself is that of investigating

the nature of each of these sorts of concept and the relations between them. He says that good and right are characteristics (relations or properties), and thereby commits himself to the view that moral utterances are propositions, a view he affirms more vigorously in later writings when he rejects emotivism. Having said that good and right are characteristics he goes on, as Moore had, to consider whether they are "natural" or "non-natural." In an effort to clarify this distinction, he suggests that a "natural" characteristic is either a) one that we become aware of by inspecting our sense-data or introspecting our experiences, or b) one that is definable in terms of the sort of characteristic just mentioned together with the concepts of substance and cause. Using this criterion, he finds that right and good are non-natural characteristics, and supplements this finding by arguing that no naturalistic analysis of these concepts elaborated so far is at all plausible and that it is "very likely, though not absolutely certain that Ethical Naturalism is false. . . ." He thinks it is obvious that right and good are not pure relations and therefore that they are properties of some kind, but he is not as sure as Moore is that they are simple and unanalyzable. He is "almost certain" that "right" cannot be defined in terms of "good," hence suggesting that right may be a simple non-natural property, but he thinks it is possible that "x is good" means "x is such that it would be a fitting object of desire to any mind which had an adequate idea of its non-ethical characteristics," thus suggesting that good may be a relational property.

Since an *a priori* notion is, by definition, the notion of a characteristic that is not manifested in sensation or introspection, and since a non-natural characteristic, by definition, is not manifested in sensation or introspection, it follows that the concepts of non-natural characteristics like good and right are *a priori* concepts. He supposes, as a corollary to this conclusion, that non-natural properties are apprehended by some cognitive act. He also says that the apprehension of these properties is frequently accompanied by uniquely moral emotions like moral approval or disapproval, remorse and indignation, and suggests that we might not have become aware of the moral properties in the first instance if these moral emotions had not been roused in particular situations.

An act is never just right, it is right because it possesses some property that makes it right. For instance, an act is right if it is an act of showing gratitude to a benefactor, of keeping a promise, of telling the truth, or of avoiding the infliction of pain. Because an act cannot be right if it does not possess such a property and because it must be right or have a tendency to be right if it does possess such a property, these are said to be "right-making" or "right-inclining" properties. Similarly, a thing will not be good unless it is characterized by a "good-making" or "good-inclining" property like that of being pleasant. Since there is a necessary connection of the sort just described between right or good on the one hand and right- or good-making properties on the other, general moral statements such as "It is wrong to deliberately mislead others," "It is wrong to kill other people," and "Pleasure is good" are necessarily true. Since these statements are not analytic, there are synthetic *a priori* statements in ethics. The truth of judgments about particular situations, however, is not so evident. Since there is a multiplicity of both good- and right-making characteristics, it is frequently the case that a number of morally relevant factors are found in a given situation. For instance, an action might be right insofar as it involves returning a kindness to a benefactor but wrong insofar as it involves telling a lie. In situations of this sort it is necessary to weigh all the relevant right-making factors and come to a conclusion about the "net-fittingness" of an action to the situation. Because this can be difficult (there are no general rules for doing this), we are frequently far less certain about the judgment than we are about the various principles that apply to the situation in which it was made. There is yet another sort of error inherent in the making of judgments, the sort that arises when the judge is not aware of or cannot ascertain all the morally relevant matters of fact. If it turns out that the judgment was mistaken, then it was "materially wrong," but it may still be "formally right" provided that the error stemmed wholly from unavoidable ignorance or misinformation.

Broad concludes that the multiplicity of good- and right-making properties defeats both the attempt to systematize value judgments by explaining all values in terms of some one ultimate sort of value and the attempt to systematize moral judgments by justifying them all in terms of some one ultimate moral principle or rule. There are a number of self-evident, independent value statements and many self-evident independent moral principles. Consequently he rejects both the value theory and the moral theory of the Utilitarian. At the same time he emphasizes that he does not go to the other extreme, as he believes some Intuitionists do, to deny that the goodness or evil an act produces is irrelevant to the question of right and wrong. The characteristic of producing good, he insists, is one of many right-making characteristics.

It is hard to determine how much of this general theory Broad was prepared to accept at any given time and to what extent it represents his present views. As I mentioned at the outset, the main tenets were affirmed very briefly in some of his earlier writings and the implications of some of them were examined in greater detail in later writings. But in the very places where he does elaborate on them he seems least inclined to commit himself to them. For instance, in an article entitled "Moore's Ethical Doctrines" (contained in *The Philosophy of G. E. Moore,* ed. Paul A. Schlipp, New York, 1943), he weakens his earlier position by saying that it is not at all certain that "good" is the name of a property. He goes on to state as a conditional conclusion that if good is a property it

is a non-natural property and the idea of good is an *a priori* concept. According to the position he took in *Five Types of Ethical Theory,* he should be committed to these views but in this article he says simply that anyone who thinks good is a property will be so committed. Again, he had said earlier that there is a necessary connection between good and the good-making property and that there are, consequently, synthetic *a priori* statements, but here he says only that if the connection is a necessary one then there are synthetic *a priori* statements, and if there are synthetic *a priori* statements then the widely held doctrine that all *a priori* statements are analytic must be mistaken. But having pointed out that the doctrine that there is a necessary connection between good and good-making properties is not compatible with the doctrine that all *a priori* statements are analytic, he does not try to choose between them. In an article written several years later ("Moral sense Theories in Ethics," *Proceedings of the Aristotelian Society,* 45, 1944–45) he says he feels the strength of both of these apparently incompatible positions but is not sure enough of either to reject the other. In the view of statements like these it is difficult to say exactly how much of the original theory Broad is still prepared to accept.

In trying to determine what Broad's present views are there is another difficulty of a different but perhaps related sort. Some of his later articles reveal a more sympathetic attitude towards naturalism than the earlier ones do, thus suggesting that his views may have changed considerably. In "Moral sense Theories in Ethics," for instance, he says there are three sorts of moral theory worth discussing: Interjectionism or Emotivism, the Objective theory according to which right and good are non-naturalistic characteristics belonging to the act and apprehended by us (the view he was earlier disposed to accept), and a subjectivistic form of naturalism which I shall describe in a moment. He dismisses emotivism without discussion. The Objective theory states that right is a property we become aware of and this implies, according to Broad, that seeing that an act is right is analogous to seeing that an object is yellow; that is, when we see that an act is right we must be having a peculiar sensation or something like a sensation. Broad rejects the theory on the ground that this is not so, and goes on to defend a variety of subjectivism. According to subjectivism, he says, a moral judgment is a judgment concerned with some peculiar experience that human beings have when they realize that an act has a right-making property. This experience will be either some sort of sensation or some sort of emotion. Since he has already denied the first alternative, he is left with the second. After mentioning various right-making properties he concludes "In respect of each of these aspects of the act and its consequences I have a tendency to feel towards the act a certain kind of moral emotion of a certain degree of intensity. . . . It seems to me that I call the act "right" or "wrong" in accordance with my final moral-emo-

tional reaction to it, after viewing it under all these various aspects, and after trying to allow for any permanent or temporary emotional peculiarities in myself which may make my emotional reaction eccentric or unbalanced." Although this conclusion is stated in the first person it is difficult to determine whether it is Broad's own considered view, for he is not unequivocal and he discusses it nowhere else. But if it is, it marks a radical change from his earlier views. This interest in naturalism is also reflected in his recent sympathetic exposition of the moral views of the late Axel Hägerström.

The most probable conclusion is that Broad has always preferred to maintain the aloofness of the critic, and that despite tendencies to be attracted to one or another of the theories with which he has been most concerned, he has never given wholehearted allegiance to any. This would explain the brevity and infrequency of his firm statements, the tentative nature of others, and the differences between them. But insofar as there has been a dominant pattern in his thought it has been that sketched in the body of this article.

Leonard G. Miller
University of Washington

Broad, C. D.: *see* Moore, George Edward; Price, Richard.
brotherhood of man: *see* Freud, Sigmund; Hammurapi, Code of.
Brunner, Emile: *see* Major Ethical

Viewpoints; Moral Philosophy in America.

Buddha: *see* Hindu Ethics.

Buddhism: *see* China, Moral Philosophies of; Hindu Ethics.

Bukharin: *see* Soviet Morality, Current.

Bulgakov, Sergius: *see* Berdyaev, Nicolas; Soviet Morality, Current.

Bulwer, Edward: *see* Utilitarianism.

bundling: *see* Puritan Morals.

Burkitt, M. C.: *see* Primitive Morals.

Bury, J. B.: *see* Primitive Morals.

Butler, Joseph

Joseph Butler, the youngest son of a successful Presbyterian linen draper, was born in Wantage, Berkshire, in 1692. In the hope that he would enter the Presbyterian ministry, he was sent to the dissenting academy of Mr. Samuel Jones, located first at Gloucester and later at Tewkesbury. However, partially as a result of correspondence with Samuel Clarke, the greatest theologian of the time, he transferred his allegiance to the Church of England, and entered Oriel College, Oxford, in 1715, to prepare himself for the priesthood of that church. In due course he graduated, was ordained, and received an appointment as preacher at the Rolls Chapel in London, a position he held until 1726. In this year he published some of his sermons under the title *Fifteen Sermons Preached at The Rolls Chapel.* In 1736 he published his other important work, *The Analogy of Religion,* in which he defended theism against the currently ascendant doctrine of deism. In this same year he was appointed Clerk of the Closet by Queen Caroline, a position which

brought him to the attention of many of the leading figures of the time and which won for him the respect and friendship of the Queen. As a result of increasing recognition he was appointed Bishop of Bristol in 1738 and eventually Bishop of Durham in 1750. He died in 1752 after a lengthy illness.

Butler was friendly and charitable but quite retiring in nature. Perhaps the most dramatic incident in an otherwise rather uneventful life was his clash with John Wesley, a priest in the see of Bristol, over the latter's decision to break with the established church. Although he took no active part in social or political affairs, as a bishop he sat dutifully in the House of Lords. Horace Walpole was led to say of him, ". . . the Bishop of Durham had been wafted to that see in a cloud of metaphysics, and remained absorbed in it."

Despite his retiring nature, Butler was very much concerned with the general moral laxity and cynicism of the time. Addressing a fashionable congregation in the Rolls Chapel he defended the life of virtue against that of self-interest. He argued first that conscience makes a claim of its own and that this claim should be heeded, and secondly, that there is no conflict between the life dictated by conscience and that recommended by enlightened self-interest, and consequently no reason for the self-interested man to sneer at the life of virtue. His defense of these views led him to criticize and reject psychological egoism, the doctrine that all man's actions are motivated by a concern for his own welfare. Butler's present reputation rests upon his discussion of these matters and upon the analysis of human nature which emerges in this discussion. His views on these topics are developed in the *Fifteen Sermons,* especially Sermons One, Two, Three, Eleven, and Twelve, and in the *Dissertation Upon The Nature Of Virtue* which was appended to *The Analogy of Religion.*

Butler, like most men of the Eighteenth Century, believed that the universe was made by an intelligent and capable creator, that it was put together in a neat and orderly fashion, and that its patterns, connections, and relations can be discovered by man if he but subject it to a careful and intelligent scrutiny. Directing his attention to man specifically, he assumed that God had some particular way of life in mind for man and that He designed him accordingly. He believed that man can discover this way of life by investigating his own nature. He embarked, therefore, on a detailed analysis of human nature on the assumption that such an examination would reveal not only what human beings actually do, but also what they are designed to do and ought to do.

An examination of our own behavior and that of others will show, says Butler, not only that we are motivated by many things, but also that our motives are not a mere congeries of impulses and drives of co-equal status. Human nature is a synthetic whole in which the passions, appetites, affections and impulses are subject to the control of several higher principles, and all of these to that of one supreme

principle. Human nature can be viewed as a hierarchical structure containing three levels.

The basic and elemental motives, those occupying the first level, are the passions, appetites, impulses, feelings and affections, exemplified by such things as anger, hunger, sexual desire, envy and love. These various things, which I shall henceforth call "impulses," share the following characteristics. First, the object of an impulse is some specific thing, state or action. For instance, the object of anger is retaliation and the object of hunger is food. Secondly, on at least their first appearance impulses occur spontaneously, and not because of any intent that they should occur. Subsequently, certain of them may be aroused deliberately upon some occasions, but on the whole their occurrence will still be unpremeditated. Thirdly, having occurred, each operates blindly—urging, goading, or driving us to action without regard to the effect that action will have on the fulfilment of any other impulse or on the total welfare of the agent. So far as the structure of human nature is concerned, they occur and operate prior to any control which may be exercised over them later. Butler is not unaware of the differences between feelings, affections, appetites, passions and impulses, but he groups them together because they share the above characteristics, characteristics which are important for his argument.

Each impulse, in the attainment of its own specific goal, ministers incidentally to the interests of the agent or to the interests of others. For instance, when I satisfy my desire for supper I do more than satisfy my desire; I also do what I must do if I am to maintain my physical existence and I do this even though the thought of doing it is far from my mind. The fact that all impulses tend to further the welfare of the agent or the welfare of others, even though this is not their object, is an indication that we were designed both to help ourselves and to help others. A close examination of our behavior will reveal the two general motives this analysis suggests; a general concern for our own welfare, which Butler calls "self-love," and a general concern for the welfare of others, which he calls "benevolence." These two general motives or "rational principles" occupy the second level in the hierarchy of human nature. They differ from impulses in several respects. First, they are general principles. They are not concerned with some particular object or state in the way in which impulses like hunger and anger are; rather, they are concerned with the production or modification of a great number of these particular states and they are so concerned because their goal is the overall welfare of the agent or others. Secondly, as implied in the first point, these principles depend on the impulses in the sense that the gratifications, pleasures, or miseries they are concerned to produce or avoid are those associated with the pursuit and satisfaction of impulses. Happiness, he says, consists of the enjoyment of the objects of our several particular appetites, passions and affections. Take away these and self-love and benevolence will have absolutely nothing to employ themselves about. Thirdly, they are regarded not merely as psychological tendencies, capacities or dispositions, but as standards. This important distinction is reflected in his view that these principles not only do regulate the impulses, but that it is appropriate and proper that they should. They have authority over our impulsive nature. The difference between the first level and the second, between impulse and principle, is the difference between action flowing spontaneously from the impulse of the moment and action chosen deliberately in the light of possible alternatives and consequences.

Butler realizes that these two principles are not, as a matter of fact, co-equal in strength or influence, for our concern for our own welfare is developed more fully and exercised more frequently than our concern for others. But he does insist that we do have a concern for others and that we should develop it more fully. In saying this he is not asking us to inhibit our concern for ourselves, for there is nothing wrong with a strongly developed sense of self-interest provided that it does not stifle the benevolent side of our nature. Enlightened self-interest, however, will not do this, for it will give careful consideration to the personal satisfactions to be obtained from benevolence and to the disappointments frequently associated with narrow selfishness. Butler can recommend the full development of both enlightened self-interest and benevolence because he believes the behavior recommended by the former will agree almost completely with that recommended by the latter.

An examination of our own experience and that of others will reveal that we have a moral faculty, conscience, and that this faculty occupies by itself the third and highest level in the hierarchy of human nature. It is that faculty which pronounces moral judgment upon persons, acts and behavior, condemning some as evil, wrong, or unjust and approving of others as good, right or just. While it is a rational principle it is not patterned after the principles of self-love and benevolence; if it was, it would simply be the concern to act morally just as self-love is the concern to act prudently. When a person has to make a decision in some particular situation, self-love prompts him to look out for his own interests but does not tell him what these are or how he should decide. On the other hand, conscience proceeds, not by cautioning him to act morally, but by telling him what his duty is. Conscience is not a disposition to act in a certain way and it is not a standard; it is a faculty which makes specific decisions or pronouncements about specific situations.

In delivering such decisions or pronouncements, conscience does more than provide us with moral information for it enjoins us to act upon pain of violating our nature and of incurring the displeasure of God. If we would only heed it we would not go astray. In the Preface to the Sermons, Butler says ". . . the very constitution of our nature requires that we bring our whole conduct before this superior faculty, wait its determination, enforce upon ourselves its authority, and make it the business of our lives, as it is absolutely the whole business of a moral agent to conform ourselves to it." Conscience possesses this authority, he argues in Sermon Two, even though it can be and frequently is flouted. "Had it strength, as it has right; had it power, as it has manifest authority, it would absolutely govern the world."

Butler assumes that most men have a conscience, that conscience operates clearly and decisively in almost all situations, and that the judgments of one man will agree on the whole with those of another. He is not concerned with questions about moral conflict, indecision, and perplexity because he thinks these things are almost non-existent. Furthermore, just as benevolence and enlightened self-love do not conflict with one another, so conscience does not conflict with either of them nor they with it. He maintains that human beings and the world, including the hereafter, have been constructed in such a way that the intelligent exercising of any one of these principles will lead to the same behavior as the intelligent exercising of any other. Yet, he emphasizes that they are distinctly different principles and that conscience is invested with supreme authority.

Butler does not stress moral rules or principles, for given the sort of conscience he describes, these would be superfluous at best and possible sources of moral error at worst. He criticizes

67

utilitarianism specifically by reminding us of the deplorable things done by men who have deliberately tried to implement what they thought was best for their fellows. Persons who think that morality can be reduced to a concern for the happiness of mankind run a double risk, for, in the first place, ignorance of what is good for their fellows may lead to moral error, and in the second, overzealous adherence to the principle may result in unjust, violent or vicious behavior. Butler is willing to consider the hypothesis that God is a utilitarian, but he insists that conscience is the only reliable guide for men. Indeed, God has endowed us with a conscience for this very reason. For human beings, conscience is the source of morality.

In this summary of Butler's analysis of human nature I have already indicated the general nature of his attack on psychological egoism. According to Butler, human nature is an organic, systematic whole composed of a number of elements related to each other in definite ways. If any of these elements is ignored or distorted or if the relations between them are upset, then our nature has been violated. In asserting that all actions are motivated by self-love the psychological egoist denies the existence of benevolence and conscience and consequently the existence of the relations of authority between them and the impulses and between conscience and self-love. The egoist's description of human nature is far from being the realistic description is purports to be; it is, rather, a gross distortion.

In the following paragraphs I shall discuss some of the details of Butler's attack on psychological egoism. He believes that the doctrine of the egoist can be discounted frequently by reminding the person that he does have a conscience and that he does act benevolently. But he does not rest his case on such a simple reminder; he goes on to discuss some of the confusions which make psychological egoism seem plausible. He begins by pointing out, as I have indicated above, that the object of an impulse differs considerably from that of self-love; self-love deliberately aims at the happiness of the agent while an impulse does no such thing. The object of hunger is food, not the happiness of the agent. A person may eat deliberately because eating gives him pleasure, but hunger is not a desire to obtain this pleasure. It is what it is, a desire for food. In arguing that we are always motivated by a concern for our own welfare the egoist is mistaken, for he ignores our impulses or misconstrues their nature.

It may be thought that we are psychological egoists because we do only that which we desire or choose to do and because we obtain pleasure from the gratification of our desires. Butler admits both of these facts but denies that either of them provides evidence in favor of psychological egoism. With respect to the first, it is the case, of course, that the agent's desires are the agent's desires, but this is irrelevant to the question of egoism. The question to be answered is, "What is the object of the desire?" rather than "Who has the desire?" My desire to help my neighbor is my desire but this does not make me selfish. The second fact is also irrelevant. A person could obtain pleasure from the successful completion of his endeavor, whether it be selfish or benevolent. I am not selfish in virtue of the fact that helping my neighbor makes me happy; I am selfish only if I help him in order to obtain that personal pleasure. Even if the egoist could show that I obtain pleasure from everything I do, he would not have shown that I am always motivated by the desire to further my own interests. Perhaps the confusion centers about the use of the word "selfish." If the egoist is using the word, intentionally or unintentionally, to refer to the facts that our desires are our desires and that the pleasures arising from their gratification are our pleasures, then it follows, of course, that we always act "selfishly." However, Butler says, even if we accept this usage, we will still want to distinguish between action intended to further the welfare of others and action intended to further our own welfare, a distinction we usually make by using the terms "benevolent" and "selfish." This is the distinction Butler is defending and this is the distinction the psychological egoist is denying if his theory is one about human behavior and not one about the use of a word. The two facts discussed earlier in this paragraph do not provide evidence in support of egoism; reference to them only confuses the issue.

Having drawn our attention to various confusions, Butler proceeds by analyzing cases in which the inadequacy of the egoist's theory is obvious. The clearest example occurs at the beginning of Sermon Five where he destroys Hobbes' claim that "Pity is imagination or fiction of future calamity to ourselves, proceeding from the sense of another's calamity." Butler says that when I observe the misfortune of another I may be afraid a similar misfortune will or could happen to me, but he insists that such a feeling must be distinguished from pity itself. I may be both compassionate and afraid but these feelings must not be confused with each other. If the egoist is right ". . . fear and pity would be the same idea, and a fearful man and compassionate man the same character, which everyone immediately sees are totally different." It simply is not the case that the more sympathetic a man is the more fearful he is. Secondly, we are prone to admire a person who has acted compassionately, while we are not inclined to admire a person who has acted fearfully. Fear for ourselves and compassion are quite different, as is evidenced by the different ways in which we react to them. The same sort of considerations also make it clear that compassion cannot be equated with thankfulness that we have escaped the calamity which has befallen another. Thankfulness and fear frequently accompany pity but must not be confused with it; only the latter "carries us with calmness and thought" to the assistance of the one in distress.

At other times Butler proceeds, not by giving an analysis, but by offering counter arguments. In Sermon One he attacks Hobbes' claim that benevolence is "only the love of power, and delight in the exercise of it" by pointing out that the benevolent side of our nature makes itself heard in cases where there is no exercise of power. For instance, a man might desire to help his unfortunate neighbor even though he is unable to do so, and he might approve enthusiastically if a third person gives the assistance he is unable to give. In this case, love of power cannot account for the desire or the approval.

These are typical Butlerian arguments; no matter how the egoist tries to explain away benevolent action Butler will counter by calling our attention to cases which cannot be accounted for in terms of the egoist's theory. In presenting such cases he intends not merely to discredit some particular person or doctrine, but to make it clear to us that men, ourselves included, do recognize benevolent acts. After this detailed criticism it is hardly necessary to go on to labor the point that the existence and operation of conscience also upset the egoist's theory. In Sermon Eleven he sums up his case: "How much soever therefore is to be allowed to self-love, yet it cannot be allowed to be the whole of our inward constitution, because, you see, there are other parts or principles which come into it." Thus Butler concludes what has become the classic refutation of psychological egoism.

Bibliography

The Works of Joseph Butler, With an Introduction and Notes by J. H. Bernard (London, 1900), 2 vols.

C. D. Broad, *Five types of ethical theory* (London, 1930).

Thomas H. McPherson, "The development of Bishop Butler's Ethics," *Philosophy,* XXIII (1948), XXIV (1949).

Ernest C. Mossner, *Bishop Butler and the Age of Reason,* (New York, 1936).

William J. Norton, Jr., *Bishop Butler, Moralist and Divine* (New Brunswick, 1940).

D. Daiches Raphael, "Bishop Butler's View of Conscience," *Philosophy,* XXIV (1949).

Leonard G. Miller
University of Washington

Butler, J.: *see* Broad, C. D.; Clarke, Samuel; Cooper, Anthony Ashley; Cumberland, Richard; Hobbes, Thomas; Price, Richard; Prichard, H. A.

Byron: *see* Schopenhauer, Arthur.

C

calamity: *see* Puritan Morals.

calculus: *see* Minor Socratics.

calculus, hedonistic: *see* Utilitarianism.

Callicles: *see* Sophists, the.

calmness: *see* Hindu Ethics; serenity; tranquility.

Calvin, John: *see* Calvinism; Puritan Morals.

Calvinism: *see* Clarke, Samuel; Moral Philosophy in America; Puritan Morals; Soviet Morality, Current.

Cambridge ethics: *see* Sidgwick, Henry.

Cambridge moralists: *see* Broad, C. D.; Ross, Sir (William) David.

Cambridge Platonists: *see* More, Henry.

cannibalism: *see* Minor Socratics; Primitive Morals.

capital punishment: *see* Quakerism, Classical, The Morality of; Tolstoy, Leo.

capitalism: *see* Berdyaev, Nicolas; Marxist Theory of Morals; Quakerism, Classical, The Morality of; Soviet Morality, Current.

caprice: *see* Spinoza.

caprice, principle of: *see* Clarke, Samuel; Utilitarianism.

cardinal sins: *see* Jewish Ethics and Its Civilization; sin.

card playing: *see* Puritan Morals.

Carmagnola: *see* Machiavelli, Niccolo.

Carnap, Rudolf: *see* Language and Ethics; Schlick, Moritz.

Carritt, E. F.: *see* Clarke, Samuel; Price, Richard; Ross, Sir (William) David.

Cartwright, Thomas: *see* Puritan Morals.

caste: *see* Hindu Ethics.

categorical imperative: *see* Jewish Ethics and Its Civilization; Kant, I.; Major Ethical Viewpoints; Scheler, Max.

Catholic Moral Philosophy: *see* Liguori, St. Alphonsus and Catholic Moral Philosophy.

Catholicism: *see* Aquinas, Thomas, Moral Views of; Augustine and Morals; Aztec Morals; Berdyaev, Nicolas; Jesuits, the, Moral Theology of; Khomiakov, Alexey; Moral Philosophy in America; Rio Grande Pueblo Indians; Scheler, Max; Soloviev, Wladimir; Spinoza.

Cato: *see* Stoics, the.

cattle: *see* animals; Pakot, the Moral System of.

causal inference: *see* Hume, David.

causality: *see* Schopenhauer, Arthur; Stoics, the.

cause: *see* Hindu Ethics; Kant, I.; Soviet Morality, Current; Spinoza.

celibacy: *see* continence; Hindu Ethics.

censor: *see* Freud, Sigmund.

censure: *see* Primitive Morals; Rio Grande Pueblo Indians.

Cercidas: *see* Minor Socratics.

ceremony: *see* Jewish Ethics and Its

71

Civilization; Navaho Morals; Rio Grande Pueblo Indians; rites; Tapirapé Morals, Some Aspects of.

certainty: see Balguy, John; Jesuits, the, Moral Theology of; Liguori, St. Alphonsus and Catholic Moral Philosophy; Spinoza.

certitude: see Liguori, St. Alphonsus and Catholic Moral Philosophy.

chain reaction: see Hindu Ethics.

chance: see caprice.

change: see Dewey, John; Marxist Theory of Morals; Minor Socratics.

Channing, W. E.: see Moral Philosophy in America.

chaos: see Spinoza.

character: see Aristotle; Green, T. H.

Charcot: see Freud, Sigmund.

charity: see Aquinas, Thomas, Moral Views of; Dante, Alighieri; Dostoyevsky, Fyodor; Hindu Ethics; Jewish Ethics and Its Civilization.

chastity: see Augustine and Morals; Hindu Ethics; Jewish Ethics and Its Civilization; Liguori, St. Alphonsus and Catholic Moral Philosophy; Puritan Morals; Schopenhauer, Arthur.

cheating: see Aztec Morals; Puritan Morals; Zuni Indians, Morals of.

Cheka (Secret Police): see Soviet Morality, Current.

chief good, the: see Aristotle; Broad, C. D.; good; Hindu Ethics; summum bonum.

childhood: see Psychology and Morals.

children: see China, Moral Philosophies of; Hammurapi, Code of; Hindu Ethics; Puritan Morals; Soviet Morality, Current; Tapirapé Morals, Some Aspects of; young, the.

China, Moral Philosophies of

I
Early Moral Ideas in China

Prior to the Age of Philosophers in China, Chinese moral ideas and ideals are recorded and expounded in the Classics. This material is important in itself, and it is also important as the common intellectual heritage of all the philosophers, beginning with Confucius. The portion of this literature that has come down to us is known as the Five Classics, namely, the *Classic of Poetry,* the *Classic of History,* the *Classic of Changes,* the *Classic of Ceremonials,* and the *Spring and Autumn Annals.* The last item is an annual history kept by Confucius of his native State, while each of the other four is a collection or anthology representing layers of chronological strata of an accumulated literary tradition, the earliest of which are probably older than the Old Testament and comparable to the oldest portions of the Vedas of Hinduism.

The dawn of Chinese history ushered in the Three Dynasties, namely, Hsia (2205–1766 B.C.?), Shang (1766–1122 B.C.?), and Chou (1122–256 B.C.). In the very story of the succession of the Three Dynasties are rooted some of the earliest and strongest patterns of moral conviction among the Chinese people. The capable founding emperors of these dynasties have become personified symbols of virtue just as their degenerate descendants who brought about the downfall of their dynastic power, similar symbols of vice. History is shown to be going in cycles, and rulers are exhorted to be virtuous because the sure penalty for vice is self-destruction. These precepts are expounded from all angles in the Classics, and they have doubtlessly contributed towards the stability of society and benevolence in government in China.

These politico-moral convictions were further buttressed by a growing understanding about the gods and nature. By the time of the Shang dynasty there had already developed the worship of ancestor spirits, deities, as well as a God, the practice of which has been variously named animism, universism, and siniticism by Western scholars. Marriage and family relations had become institutionalized, and in connection with the religious and social functions, ceremonials had been codified and musical instruments constructed.

When the Chou replaced the Shang, they grafted their own "Heaven" concept to the Shang cult of worship of ancestors, heroes, gods and other deities. Since Heaven was the abode of the gods, the Heaven concept soon began to serve as a kind of collective deity. There also arose the notion of there being some one fundamental principle that gave sense to existence and it was generally called the *Tao*. The embryonic idea of the dual force of the *Yin* and the *Yang* is found in the *Classic of Changes*, while that of the Five Elements, in the *Classic of History*. Since the *Tao* is the norm of all existence, to follow the *Tao* is also the proper code of conduct. There is thus a unity of ethics and metaphysics.

Toward the last phase of the Chou dynasty, the pattern of feudalistic hierarchy, which was the distinctive character of the political and social organization of the era, was on the decline. After the imperial power had lost its potency, a kind of league of the feudal states was instituted among the states themselves, with stipulated covenants for maintaining peace and settling disputes. Even when armed conflicts became unavoidable, there were accepted gentlemen's codes regarding warfare, such as "A superior man does not inflict a wound on a wounded enemy, nor does he take one prisoner who is gray-haired." Eventually, however, force replaced all other considerations, and interstate relations sank to the level of the jungle, causing untold suffering and devastation to the people. The classical philosophers all lived in this period, and the question of the day was how order could be restored out of chaos, and how virtue could again be made the basis of conduct, individually, socially, and politically.

This long course of development of moral consciousness is accompanied by a corresponding rise in the value of man, the individual man. Like most peoples, in early antiquity the Chinese consisted of masters and slaves, aristocrats and plebeians. Often the slaves were captives of war. Of a still earlier day, there were even traces of human sacrifice, and a lord's servants and harem being interred together with his coffin. At the height of the feudalistic system, men working the land were not only slaves but slaves tied down to the land, i.e., the ownership of the slaves went together with the ownership of the land. Eventually slaves were pried loose from the land, and there is preserved a record of one deal by which five men were exchanged for one horse plus eleven skeins of silk.

The crumbling of the well-ordered hierarchical society late in the Chou dynasty promoted phenomenally the worth of the common man. As the rival princes competed for man-power in order to expand their armies and fill the granaries, the value of the common people enjoyed an unprecedented boom, whereas members of the nobility, on the other hand, became displaced and dispossessed in increasing numbers. There was generally a narrowing down of the gap between the aristocrat and the plebeian, together with an emergence of a significant middle class, among whom may be counted most of the philosophers.

II

Confucius (551–479 B.C.), the Humanist

Of all moral philosophers of China, Confucius is the most important. As a matter of fact, Confucius may be said to have laid down the pattern for the Chinese way of life and the Chinese way of thought. Even in his boyhood, Confucius was sober-minded, bent on learning, and particularly fond of history. Though he had to go to work early in life, he managed to have a period of study and travel. As Confucius grew in stature and reputation, young men of all stations of life came to him to seek instruction. He taught every one with equal enthusiasm, and declared, "In education there is no discrimination." Eventually he was said to have had three thousand pupils. Confucius was the first professional teacher in Chinese history, and his birthday is now observed as Teachers' Day in China. The popularization of education at the hands of Confucius brought about an intellectual revolution as radical as it was imperceptible. It resulted in extending the educational opportunities from the aristocrat to the commoner, and in transferring the cultural authority from the court to a class of private scholars that is sometimes spoken of as the intelligentsia.

And yet Confucius did not feel teaching was his primary mission in life. All educated men in China have wanted to be men of affairs as well as men of learning and wisdom. Theirs is a dual ideal of "sageness within and kingliness without," that of the philosopher-king. For a few years, Confucius did hold an appointment to public office. Records showed that he was a wise and successful administrator and that his rise on the official ladder was very rapid. But being unwilling to compromise his principles, he soon found it necessary, because of the waywardness of his Prince, to relinquish his post of Acting Premiership in his home state, and started travelling from one state to another in the hope of finding a ruler sincerely receptive to his politico-educational program.

At the end of a futile sojourn of some thirteen years, he finally returned home when he was nearly seventy. He resignedly devoted his remaining years to the instruction of his disciples and to the editing of the Chinese Classics. Notes and records of his instructions, conversations and travels were brought together and edited after his death, and these are preserved in the work known as the *Analects of Confucius.*

The key to the Confucian moral philosophy lies in the concept of *jen* which has been translated as love or magnanimity among several other suggested equivalents. Many of the recorded sayings of Confucius have to do with *jen.* His briefest and definitive remark about it was, "*Jen* is to love all men." One early amplification of the text says, "*Jen* is to love men joyously and from the innermost of one's heart," while another early commentary underlines the etymological significance of the character *jen* as "denoting that which is common in two men." *Jen* is the common denominator of humanity, as well as the distinctive mark of man from birds and beasts. It is both the innermost nature and the highest ideal of true manhood, the beginning and the end of life. *Jen* is therefore not only a moral virtue but also the metaphysical essence of man. According to Confucius, the man of *jen* has no anxieties and is free from evil, and it is only he who can love men or hate men. All virtues like reciprocity, loyalty, courage, trustworthiness, etc. may be regarded as expressions of *jen,* and *jen* is thus, like the Socratic Justice, the super-virtue of all virtues. *Jen* is the unifying principle of all conduct. A superior is said not to act contrary to *jen,* but holds himself true to it under all circumstances. And when necessary,

the man of *jen* would rather give up his life than permit the *jen* in him to be injured. Confucius must have had *jen* in its supreme form in mind, when he said, "Hearing the *Tao* in the morning, one dies content in the evening."

How, then, do we acquire this all-important *jen?* One arrives at *jen* not so much by way of intellect or emotion as by intuition. *Jen* is inborn in us all and our hearts know it. He whose intuition is more sensitive than others, has a better grasp of *jen* and attains it to a higher degree. Curiously, the equivalent for "paralysis" in Chinese medical language is literally "absence or lack of *jen.*" The extent of *jen* defines the size of the man, so to speak. Confucius said, "Is *jen* something remote? If I want *jen,* behold, *jen* has arrived." Again, "The attainment of *jen* depends upon oneself. What has it got to do with others?" *Jen* is something immediate, intimate, and intrinsic, and the seeker after *jen* should seek it in himself for it is something near at hand indeed.

The man of *jen* is called a Superior Man or a Sage, according to the degree of his attainment. One of the distinctive marks of the superior man over against the inferior man is that whereas the former is always composed and contented, the latter is constantly worried and full of distress. In describing his own moral development, Confucius said: "At fifteen I set my heart on learning; at thirty I was firmly established; at forty I had no more doubts; at fifty I knew the will of Heaven; at sixty I was ready to listen to it; at seventy I could follow my heart's desire without transgressing what was right." Confucius can truly be said to have achieved an ease and serenity in himself and attained a harmony and identity with what is fundamentally true and real in the universe. In him the educational, moral and religious values are perfectly blended, and the inner and outer worlds become one. If Confucius appeared to be reticent about the highest reaches of the life of the spirit, which has not infrequently given rise to the impression that he was a skeptic or agnostic on such matters, it was because he knew instinctively that such a state of the mind or soul was neither reducible to conceptual analysis, nor subject to systematic teaching. But his personal example has stood through the centuries in China like a beacon light to all seekers after the good life—good life in the highest sense. Worthily indeed has Confucius been revered by the Chinese as their Supreme Sage and Foremost Teacher!

Confucius understood only too well that although the *jen* is inborn in us all, it could not be more than the very few who would reach the final stage of the pilgrim's progress of the soul. For the guidance of the many, he discoursed repeatedly on the various virtues and proper relations of men in their several stations of life. And it should not be difficult to understand why the family was regarded as the natural cradle for the maturing and flowering of the *jen* feeling. Confucianists of a later age developed out of these ideas the code of the five social relations, and particularly of filial piety and ancestor worship. While *jen* takes on various expressions in these various relations, one controlling principle, the principle of reciprocity (*shu*), a derivative of *jen,* might be taken as "the one word that might serve as a principle of conduct for life: Do not do to others what you would not want others to do to you." Besides the small Confucian *Classic on Filial Piety,* there came to be written, also on the basis of Confucius' ideas, the *Great Learning* in which the eight-step plan from the cultivation of the individual to harmony in the world is outlined, and the *Doctrine of the Mean.* Confucius also made much of the rites of propriety and music. A moral act is to be prompted by the motive of *jen,* to be sure, but its highest value will not be fully attained unless it is performed in the right manner and with proper grace.

All in all, Confucianism insists upon grounding morality and value in man himself. No external standard, though it be from God, will be necessary or even acceptable. Self-conscious, self-critical, and self-realizing manhood is the center of all goodness and the origin of all virtues. Here is the first dawn of humanism, perhaps, in the world history of ethics.

III
Mo Tzu (470–391 B.C.?) the "Altruist"

Mo Tzu, or Mo Ti, was born a few years after Confucius had died and was a close contemporary of Socrates.

76

He was widely read and well-versed in the classics. Some even said he was at first a follower of Confucianism but became a renegade because of the elaborate Confucian ceremonials. Like Confucius he also travelled about trying to find a receptive prince to put his teachings in practice and the world in order. With universal love and condemnation of offensive wars as major items of his platform, however, his failure with the ambitious, greedy rulers was a foregone conclusion. He kept a school and recommended several of his pupils to public office. The book bearing his name, the *Mo Tzu,* contains records of his sayings and doings.

Rigorism is perhaps a proper characterization both of the man and of his teachings. He was the kind of person who practised what he preached. When examining his doctrine of "Condemnation of Offensive Wars," for instance, it should be borne in mind that more than once, upon being advised of a forthcoming predatory attack on a small state by a large state, he actually betook himself to the court of the offending party to prevent the perpetuation of the outrage. On one of these peace missions, it was said, he had to walk ten days and ten nights, and tear off pieces of cloth from his garment wherewith to wrap up his sore feet. An ancient critic said of Mo Tzu, "Despite all personal hardships, he held fast to his ideas—a man of distinction indeed!" Because of this spirit of selflessness of his life and because of his teachings of universal love and the will of Heaven, Mo Tzu has

sometimes been called the Chinese Jesus.

"Universal love and mutual profit" is the key idea of Moism. All the disorder of the day, in the last analysis, was patently due to selfishness and partiality. Such was the diagnosis; hence the prescription: "partiality should be replaced by universality." With genial satire and cutting logic it was demonstrated that when every one regards the states and cities of others as he regards his own, no one will attack the others' states or seize the others' cities. And the argument was applied all the way down to personal safety and welfare of the individual: The peace of the world and the happiness of man lie in the practice of mutual love.

Now universal love implies the abandoning of an emphasis upon such distinctions as high and low, near and far, essential elements in the traditional life of China. Naturally many objections were directed against the new doctrine—its impracticability, its neglect of the special claims of one's parents, etc. Mo Tzu demonstrated that, on the one hand, the principle of universal love is rooted in the concept of the will of Heaven, while, on the other, it serves a useful purpose. Convinced of the identification of the virtuous with the useful, *honestum* with *utile,* Mo Tzu spoke of "universal love and mutual profit" without embarrassment or apology. As a matter of fact, to Mo Tzu the Confucian idea of *jen,* as something derived from the direct intuitive sense, was quite unintelligible. For instance, he was greatly annoyed when a Confucianist announced, "We make music for music's sake." To Mo Tzu this was sheer nonsense, the same as telling people, "we build houses for houses' sake." What one ought to have said is that "a house is built so as to keep off the cold in winter and the heat in summer, and to separate the men from the women in accordance with the codes of propriety." His own doctrine of universal love was proposed because it would result in mutual benefit, and, eventually, order and harmony for all.

Mencius (372–289 B.C.?), the great exponent of Confucianism and the Second Sage of China, was perhaps the most forceful critic of Mo Tzu. Universal love contrasted to *jen* in action —call it graded love if you must—is not at all a higher level of moral sentiment, according to Mencius, but simply an artificial and arbitrary notion about human relationships. What could be more natural and, at the same time, more ideal than to let the well-spring of the human heart issue forth freely in its natural course and to its natural degree? To say that one loves the man on the street as much as one's own parents is untrue, and to say that one should do so violates every sense of rationality. Mencius even compared Mo Tzu to birds and beasts. He did so because to him the all-important *jen* in a person was the line of demarcation between man and animal, and Mo Tzu was so busy trying to "universalize" love that he completely neglected the true character of the *jen* that was in him.

IV

Yang Chu (420–340 B.C.?), the "Egoist"

When Mencius raised his voice in condemnation, he condemned Yang Chu and Mo Ti in the same breath, thus:

The words of Yang Chu and Mo Ti fill the empire. If you listen to people's discourses, you get the impression that they have adopted the view of the one or the other. Now Yang's principle is "Each one for himself," which does not acknowledge the claims of the sovereign. Mo's principle is "To love all indiscriminately," which does not acknowledge the peculiar affection due to a father. To acknowledge neither king nor father is to be in the state of a beast. If these principles are not stopped and the principles of Confucius set forth, their perverse doctrines will delude the people and stop up the path of *jen* (love) and *yi* (righteousness).

Yang Chu and Mo Ti, with the distinction of being denounced by the Second Sage of China in such strong language, have become widely known as the representative Chinese "egoist" and "altruist." Of the altruism of Mo Tzu we have seen something in the last section.

Yang Chu was evidently one of those wise-man recluses about whose life we know next to nothing. The seventh chapter of the *Lieh Tzu* bears the title, "Yang Chu," and within the space of a few pages is set down clearly and candidly a refreshingly unorthodox view of life and value. The author of the chapter was interested in such problems as those of name and reality, pleasure and pain, and untrammelled freedom. He might be said to be an exponent of nominalism, hedonism, and egotism. There is even a touch of fatalism about him. He might also be regarded as a precursor of Taoism, though not in the chronological sense, as he shared with Lao Tzu and Chuang Tzu a strong sense of naturalism. Yang Chu impresses one with about the same charm and limitations as Epicurus, whom he immediately preceded across the seas.

First of all, Yang Chu is deeply impressed by the brevity of life. Even if the usual three-score-and-ten should be stretched to a round hundred, what with one's helpless infancy and senile old age, sleep at night and idleness during the day, sickness and sorrow, bereavement and anxiety, a man's actual span of life is very brief. And of this remainder Yang Chu says, "I wonder if he can enjoy a single hour of contentment and serenity undarkened by the gloom of care." If the sand of life runs so quickly, the scythe of death mows every one down inevitably and without exception. Whatever difference there might be among men while they live, the intelligent and the stupid, the honorable and the humble, they are obliterated by death. "It is only in life that all things have variety; in death all is equality," says Yang Chu. The art of life eschews tampering with life on the one hand—both striving after longevity and committing suicide being equally condemnable—and worrying about and beyond death on the other. And it consists in making the most of life, in the sense of "following the desires of one's heart and refraining from contradicting the inclinations of nature." "The only way to treat life," continues Yang Chu, "is to let it have its own way, neither hindering it nor obstructing it." The good life is then a life of pleasure, but pleasure in accordance with nature, and therefore a life of contentment. If Epicurus said, "You cannot live pleasurably without living virtuously and justly," his Chinese predecessor Yang Chu seemed to have said, "You cannot live pleasurably without living naturally and contentedly."

It is in this same spirit that we should consider the "egotism" of Yang Chu. Since Mencius' day, Yang Chu has carried the onus as the teacher of the principle of "Each one for himself," and as the man "who would not give up a single hair for the benefit of the whole world." Actually Yang Chu's "egotism" is just another expression of his insistence on letting nature run its own course. This is what he says, "Among the men of old, even if one could benefit the whole world by destroying a single hair, he would not do it. Even if one could have the whole world for the benefit of oneself, he would not take it. When nobody would sacrifice a hair, when nobody would benefit the world, the world would become orderly." Yang Chu, like Epicurus, considered the pleasurable life the good life, but the pleasure that is good is far from being passion run wild. Every one for himself, yes; every one for himself at the expense of others, decidedly no.

79

V

Lao Tzu (575–485 B.C.?) and Chuang Tzu (369–286 B.C.?), the Naturalists

Lao Tzu is the most noted hermit philosopher in China and one of the best known in the world. Because of the man's preference for obscurity, few details are known about his life. Presumably he was a kind of historian-librarian of the Chou Court. He was an older contemporary of Confucius, and in fact there is the traditional story of a meeting between the two, in which Lao Tzu told young Confucius to relax. Evidently Lao Tzu never bothered to have pupils. In his old age, he rode beyond the Pass and disappeared in the west. As Lao Tzu stopped at the Pass, so the story goes, the keeper begged Lao Tzu to leave his teachings to him. The result is the "5000-word" classic, the *Tao Te Ching*. The little work is written in eighty-one chapters, mostly in verse. Because of the uncertainties surrounding the man and the work, many theories have been advanced regarding both. Probably there actually lived such a mystic thinker older than Confucius by a score of years, but the work, which might well have been inspired by him, and even embody some of his teachings, seems to be of a much later date.

The influence of Taoism in China is second only to that of Confucianism, and of Taoism the *Tao Te Ching* has come to be regarded as the symbol and the scripture. The main theme of the *Tao Te Ching* has to do with the nature and working of the *Tao*. It is an attempt to deal with the problem of reality, particularly that of the one and the many, by proposing a way of thinking that might be called naturalistic mysticism. The *Tao* is fundamentally nameless and unnamable. Therefore anything that we say about the *Tao* is said as a concession to the human intellect and has to be so understood. Thus the *Tao* is said to be absolute and immutable. It has no beginning and no end; it is antecedent to everything, essence of all substance, and regulator of all movement. And the fundamental character of the cosmic dynamic is return, reversal and renewal.

When applied to the sphere of moral conduct, the way of the *Tao* finds it necessary first of all to demolish the established, i.e., artificial, scale of values. The slogan is to "banish sageness, discard wisdom," "banish *jen* (love), discard *yi* (righteousness)," because as soon as you set up a man-made standard the people will begin to scheme and contend. The right way, instead, is the way of *wu-wei. Wu-wei* literally means non-doing. Just as non-being is considered by the Taoists as the highest reality, even higher than being, so is non-doing considered as the highest virtue. While the term sounds like doing nothing, it means doing nothing extraneous; non-doing means for the most part non-fussing, no ado. "Do nothing and yet there is nothing that is not done," says the *Tao Te Ching*. The plea is to give nature a chance.

When nature is permitted to run its own course, we shall soon come by, among other things, the realization of strength in weakness. It is said, "The most yielding of things has the run over the most unyielding." The reason for this lies in the fact that weakness rather than strength is a fundamental characteristic of the *Tao*—"Reversal is the movement of the *Tao;* weakness is the application of the *Tao*." By way of assisting us to this understanding, the *Tao Te Ching* calls our attention to water, the female, the child. Though apparently the most yielding and weak of all things in the world, yet nothing is superior to water when it comes to attacking what is unyielding and strong. Water symbolizes the *Tao* because, "The highest good is like water. Water benefits all things generously and is without strife. It dwells in the lowly places that men disdain. Thus it comes near the *Tao*." One citation will have to suffice for the significance of the female and the child: "He who knows the masculine but keeps to the feminine becomes the ravine of the world. Being the ravine of the world, in constant virtue he dwells, to the state of the babe he returns." Evidently the way of the feminine is superior to the way of the masculine, and the way of the babe symbolizing original innocence is the best of all.

Another result of the doctrine of *wu-wei* is the life of detachment, the highest virtue by the Taoist standard. Thus it is said in the *Tao Te Ching:* "To give life but not to own, to achieve but not to cherish, to lead but not to be master—this is the Mystic Virtue!" This is also pretty much the same doctrine that in India is known as *Karmayoga*.

Chuang Tzu was an outstanding philosopher, poet, and mystic. Unlike Confucius or Mo Tzu or Mencius, he led the life of a carefree recluse and not much was recorded about it. The book *Chuang Tzu* is a very intriguing work. Several of the chapters are literary masterpieces. Imageries, anecdotes, parables as well as allegory and parodox fill the pages and each bit is done with humor, charm and detachment. With Chuang Tzu, Taoism reached another stage of development. The main points in Chuang Tzu's teachings may be summarized as relativity, equality, and absolute freedom. The world for most people is one of relativity and unreality, a dream world. Here we operate through our senses and we make distinctions between right and wrong, good and bad, life and death. It is only in the *tao* that we find reality. In the *tao* all distinctions vanish, everything exists in and of itself, and there is complete spontaneity, hence absolute freedom. At this level it is no more the senses but an intuitive understanding that serves as our guide. Viewed from this level, all contradictions are resolved in a sea of identity and life and death become only alternate states of existence. Life is something that should be "let come as it comes and let go as it goes." And one who has attained such a vision is, in Taoist terminology, a true man, or a man of the *tao*.

VI

Hsün Tzu (306–218 B.C.?), the "Environmentalist."

Towards the end of the Classical Age in the history of Chinese philosophy, there flourished two men, Hsün Tzu and Han Fei Tzu, a teacher-student combination. Hsün Tzu claimed to be a Confucianist and Han Fei Tzu has come to be regarded as the undisguised spokesman for the "Legalists." Actually both were well acquainted with the teachings of the various schools of Confucianism, Taoism, Moism, and the Logicians, and there are traces of influences from these several sources in their teachings. In Hsün Tzu, in particular, we find an interweaving of all the important strands in ancient Chinese thought. His universality of interest, his matter-of-fact manner of approach, as well as the many penetrating observations about nature and man that we find scattered throughout his works, the *Hsün Tzu,* remind one irresistibly of Aristotle. In spite of his claim to Confucian orthodoxy, he had too much originality to be just another exponent of the "line." As a matter of fact, there are startling differences between his fundamental ideas and those of Mencius, representative of the other wing of Confucianism. In the end, the Chinese people accepted Mencius and rejected Hsün Tzu, and Confucianism has come to mean the orthodoxy of the Confucius-Mencius axis. All the more refreshing it should be for us to learn what Hsün Tzu had to say about the way of Heaven and man.

The Chinese idea of Heaven covers a very wide range. For the unquestioning multitude it is an anthropomorphic living God, for the more sophisticated intelligentsia it is a cosmic principle more or less moral in character, and for a handful of iconoclasts it is nature pure and simple. Hsün Tzu was an exceptionally tough-minded thinker among the Chinese. To him, "Heaven conducts itself with constant regularity." It does not prevail on account of the virtues of a sage-king; nor does it cease to prevail because of the wickedness of a tyrant. Heaven is no source of blessing; neither is it a proper object of worship. For man the part of wisdom is therefore to know his own place and fulfill his own duties. Heaven does not help him who helps himself; all the more, man should help himself. Instead of relying on Heaven, Hsün Tzu exhorts people to "employ," "domesticate," and "exploit" it, a unique Baconian touch in the history of Chinese thought.

If Heaven is not a moral force but an indifferent blind process, human nature is not good, but evil. "The nature of man is evil," says Hsün Tzu, "his goodness is acquired." On the point of human nature Hsün Tzu takes the diametrically opposite position to that of Mencius. Mencius says human nature is good. Hence the keynote in education is "extension," individual freedom is to be enjoyed by all, and whatever authority there is comes from within. Hsün Tzu says human nature is evil. Hence the keynote in education is "accumulation," social control is indispensable, and authority comes from without. To Hsün Tzu it is environment that makes the man, and it is obedience to the precepts of sage-kings that produces the goodness that is in man. Where the desired goodness is easily brought about, as in the case of scholars and ministers, apply decorum; where it is not, as in the case of the common people, let the laws be enforced. Though the standards are external and the efforts are strenuous, yet Hsün Tzu could see in every man on the street the possibility of a sage. What is needed is "straightening and bending," "grinding and whetting."

Thus Hsün Tzu might be regarded as the realistic wing of Confucianism, ethically the left wing because of its mechanistic tendencies while politically the right wing because of its authoritarian inclinations. Mencius, to the contrary, might be said to be the idealistic wing of Confucianism, ethically right and politically left.

VII
Han Fei Tzu (280?–233 B.C.), the "Legalist"

Han Fei Tzu is the representative spokesman of the Legalist School in ancient Chinese thought. By legalism is here meant a kind of Machiavellian view of government and politics as well as human nature. Many practising politicians, since time immemorial, may be regarded as precursors of the school, but most of them are too busy or too ashamed to preach what they practise. The *Han Fei Tzu* is a rare work for its frankness and honesty. Han Fei was a stutterer, but as a writer he was forceful and clear. Han Fei was a pupil of Hsün Tzu, as we have noted, and a famous schoolmate was Li Ssu. Li Ssu had already ingratiated himself into the favor of the King of Ch'in by the time Han Fei arrived at the Ch'in Court. Han Fei, though appreciated by the King of Ch'in, was put in prison and then to death through intrigue for which his schoolmate Li Ssu was more than suspect. Eventually Li Ssu was also condemned to die by being torn to pieces. Since those times, the Chinese have taken the lesson to heart: Those who preach the gospel of the sword die by the sword.

The teacher Hsün Tzu taught that human nature was evil; the pupil Han Fei learned his lesson by heart. But where Hsün Tzu still had room for decorum and environment and the virtuous examples of the sage-kings as factors for bringing about goodness, Han Fei could see the only effective disciplinary force in strict laws and severe punishment. Both emphasized the necessity for "straightening and bending," but the eventual goal for Hsün Tzu was the development of the individual towards sagehood, whereas for Han Fei it was submissiveness of so many obedient subjects of a powerful state. Here lies perhaps the dividing line between the Confucianist teacher and the legalist pupil. Here lies also the dividing line between Han Fei Tzu on the one hand and practically all the other Chinese thinkers on the other, for rarely indeed in Chinese thought has the state been placed above the individual.

Since Han Fei Tzu's doctrines are so unorthodox, he is entitled to a fuller hearing. The following passage is a good example of his view of human nature and education:

Now take a young fellow who is a bad character. His parents may get angry at him, but he never makes any change. The villagers may reprove him, but he is not moved. His teachers may admonish him, but he never reforms. The love of his parents, the effort of the villagers, and the wisdom of his teachers—all the three excellent disciplines are brought to bear upon him, and not even a hair on his shins is altered. It is only after the district-magistrate sends out his gendarmes and in the name of the law searches for wicked individuals, that the young man becomes afraid, and changes his ways and alters his deeds. So while the love of parents is not sufficient to discipline the children, the severe penalties of the district-magistrate are. This is because men become naturally spoiled by love but submissive to authority.

The nature of man, as far as Han Fei could see, shows not only a lack of native goodness but also a lack of native intelligence. He had no patience with those who insisted on the slogan of "Win the hearts of the people." To him "the intelligence of the people is not to be relied upon, just like the mind of a baby." And the people are too ignorant to appreciate the decrees of the rulers issued for their good. Therefore, "Assuredly, subtle and intricate theories are no business of the people."

Human conduct is a functional variable. It varies with the material conditions of the time and place. To uphold some such universal standard as love (*jen*) and righteousness (*yi*) is to be unrealistic and operate in a vacuum. Han Fei Tzu says:

Now people who dwell in the mountains and have to draw water from the gorges give water to each other as gifts at festivals; those who live in swamps and are troubled with too much water hire labor to open channels for it. Likewise, in the spring following a year of famine one is unable to feed one's younger brother, while in the autumn of a year of plenty, even casual visitors are offered food. Not that men neglect their blood relations and love passers-by, but that the material provisions on the respective occasions are so different. . . . Therefore circumstances go according to their time and the course of action is planned in accordance with the circumstances.

And it is in the *Han Fei Tzu* that we find the well-known parable of the farmer and the hare. One day while the farmer was tilling his land, a hare running at full speed hurled itself against the stump of a tree that stood in the field, broke its neck, and died. Thereafter the farmer left his plough and kept watch at the stump, thinking that he had discovered a much easier way of earning a living. The moral of the parable: history never repeats itself.

The above is a very simplified, probably an over-simplified, survey of the most important types of moral philosophies of China. They all happen to come out of the Classical period, but, then, all really great philosophies and religions in any culture seem to spring forth from its classical age. The introduction of Buddhism into China shortly after the beginning of the Christian era made a big difference to Chinese thought, but the effect was more on metaphysics and methodology than moral philosophy. During the last several decades, Chinese thought was struggling with problems growing out of China's contact with the West. Possibly a fresh pattern of moral philosophy might emerge as a result. But before the situation had an opportunity to work itself out to its natural conclusion, the Communist ideology was imposed upon the nation arbitrarily, replacing all other thought systems, Chinese or Western.

Bibliography

Fung Yu-Lan: *A Comparative Study of Life Ideals* (Shanghai, Commercial Press, 1924).
Herbert Finley Rudd, *Chinese Moral Sentiments Before Confucius* (University of Chicago [doctorate thesis], 1914).
K. J. Spalding, *Three Chinese Thinkers* (Mo Tzu, Chuang Tzu, Hsŭn Tzu) (Nanking, National Central Library, 1947).
Arthur Waley, *Three Ways of Thought in Ancient China,* (Chuang Tzu, Mencius, Han Fei Tzu) (London, Allen & Unwin, 1939).
On Confucius, *The Analects of Confucius,* W. E. Soothill tr. (London, Oxford University Press, 1910, 1945).
On Mo Tzu, *The Ethical & Political Works of Motse,* Y. P. Mei tr. (London, Arthur Probsthain, 1929).
On Yang Chu, *Yang Chu's Garden of Pleasure,* Anton Forke tr. (London, Murray, Wisdom of the East series, 1912).
On Lao Tzu, *The Way and Its Power,* Arthur Waley tr. (London, Allen & Unwin, 1934).
On Chuang Tzu, *Chuang Tzu,* Fung Yu-lan tr. (first seven chapters only), (Shanghai Commercial Press, 1933).
On Hsün Tzu, *The Works of Hsün Tzu,* H. H. Dubs tr. (London, Arthur Probsthain, 1928).
On Han Fei Tzu, *The Complete Works of Han Fei Tzu,* vol. I (vol. II has not been published), W. K. Liao tr. (London, Arthur Probsthain, 1939).

Yi-Pao Mei
State University of Iowa

Chinese Jesus, the: *see* China, Moral Philosophies of.

chivalry: *see* Muslim Morals.

choice: *see* Augustine and Morals; freedom; French Existentialism and Moral Philosophy; Kierkegaard, Soren; Major Ethical Viewpoints; More, Henry; Psychology and Morals; Soviet Morality, Current; Stoics, the; Zoroastrian Morals.

Chou dynasty: *see* China, Moral Philosophies of.

Christian ethics: *see* Augustine and Morals; Berdyaev, Nicolas; Christian Moral Philosophy; Dante, Alighieri; Kant, I.; Moral Philosophy in America; Quakerism, Classical, The Morality of; Schlick, Moritz; Soloviev, Wladimir; Soviet Morality, Current; Stoics, the. *See* also Christianity.

Christian existentialism: *see* French Existentialism and Moral Philosophy.

85

Christian Moral Philosophy

By Christian moral philosophy we mean that process of inquiry by which a Christian, precisely because he is a Christian, seeks to determine what he ought to do. Christian moral philosophy begins with the assumption that the answer to this question can only be discovered in that relationship with God made possible by the revelation of God's own character and purpose in nature and history and more particularly in that special history which is the history of the people of Israel, culminating in the person of Jesus Christ and carried on since His Resurrection and Ascension in the life of the Spirit-led community which is the Christian Church.

Christianity has its rootage and origin in the Hebrew religious and national tradition, and its moral philosophy was profoundly affected and at a number of points conclusively determined by the form and content of that tradition. One of its characteristic and influential elements was the life and thought of the prophets. The impact of the prophetic insights is felt everywhere in the Old Testament. The history of Israel was written largely by men who saw that history through eyes sharpened and focussed by the prophetic movement. The Law of Israel represented a codification of —and to some extent, a compromise with—the prophetic message. The prophet spoke out of a sense of the presence of God in the historical crises of his time. The priest ministered to men's eternal needs; the authors of the wisdom literature interpreted the meaning of the commonplace experiences of life. The prophet spoke out of the midst of a great national crisis in which he believed God had given him an authentic word to speak, the obedient response to which was the primary test of the nation's loyalty to God. The domestic and international situation in which the prophetic movement first achieved its importance (the early 8th Century, B.C.) was—perhaps unexpectedly—a highly favorable one, marked by relative security, luxury and stability.

The prophetic word was spoken not as a result of a political and economic analysis of a dangerous and deteriorating social and international situation but as a consequence of the over-powering conviction that God was about to inaugurate a new stage in His great purpose for men in history. The prophetic message was not a carefully reasoned system of social and political reform. It consisted rather in "the making known of God's will . . . to be performed in the concrete situation, and of threats and promises of divine activity." (Minear). The prophets spoke for a God who was "high and lifted up," holy and righteous and utterly self-sufficient and self-existent. There is no suggestion in the prophetic message that God's own reputation or prestige is involved in the moral failures of His people. "Are ye not as children of the Ethiopians unto me, O children of Israel?" (Amos ix, 7).

It is precisely such a transcendent God who in His mercy and righteousness has initiated with Israel an extraordinary covenant relationship, an agreement in which God promises His utter fidelity, and in response man promises obedience and trust. Israel is charged by the prophets with having forgotten this covenant, with failing to recall the meaning of her own history in which God made Himself known as a faithful God in such significant and powerful experiences as those of the Passover, the Red Sea, the years in the wilderness. This lack of remembrance is compounded with a degree of social injustice and of religious syncretism, all of which constitute a deep and thoroughgoing rebellion of Israel against her God, a rebellion which the prophets are convinced can lead only to national disaster. The prophets saw little hope that their message would be heeded and were quite unprepared to make any specific proposals in the realm of social or political action to remedy the evils which they delineated so clearly. They demanded repentance for the injustice and religious laxity which they saw all around them, but Jeremiah speaks for all of them when he asks Israel mockingly, "Can the Ethiopian change his skin or the leopard his spots? Then you will do good who are accustomed to do evil." Their task was to give meaning and moral significance to the impending national catastrophe and to see God's righteous purpose fulfilling itself even in the destruction of His people.

Even in the most pessimistic of the prophets, however, there was the recognition of the possibility that a tiny minority of the people might by obedi-ence and faith transcend the catastrophe and come to serve as the nucleus of a re-established national community. Even in his despair the prophet himself constituted some exception to the prevailing hardness of heart, and by his own obedient proclamation of the Word of God that came to him he proved that the link of God with His covenant people was not wholly destroyed. Isaiah promises explicitly that "a remnant shall be saved."

Through the prophetic movement, three great ideas passed into the Judaic-Christian tradition: (1) that religion and ethics are indissolubly united. God's relationship with man is predicated upon a contractual relationship, man's part of which is not only faithfulness to God but, equally crucially, justice toward his fellowmen. (2) That man's responsibilities toward his fellows are measured by God's own faithfulness and care for His people. The great acts of God by which Israel's deliverance from Egypt was accomplished are rehearsed as reminding the nation of its unbounded duty to care for the oppressed, the stranger, the victim of injustice. (3) That history is the scene of God's righteous judgments and that one of man's responsibilities is to discern the signs of the times and to perceive the meaning of his contemporary life. The deep involvement of Israel's God in the historical movements of the world is a powerful deterrent to any renunciation or withdrawal from the urgencies of this present life.

The earlier prophets were dramatically vindicated by the catastrophic series of wars with Assyria and Babylon, climaxing in the capture of Jerusalem by the Chaldeans in 586 B.C. In the period that followed, several developments took place which profoundly affected the later Judaism out of which Christianity sprang. One of these was a kind of "atomization" of ethical thought, accomplished by the teaching of the prophet Ezekiel, whereby attention was directed toward the individual and his standing before God rather than toward the nation and her achievements of social justice and religious purity. ("The soul that sinneth *it* shall die"— Ezekiel xviii, 4). Ezekiel's motivation was doubtless a pastoral one, a desire to lift the burden of despondency and hopelessness, which the Exile had induced, by assuring his hearers that each man will be judged on his own merits rather than by his association with an evil and unrighteous nation. The second development was a narrowing of the area of ethical concern, with less attention paid to social injustice—a reflection of the loss of social responsibility on the part of the refugee Jews—and a preoccupation with cultic behavior which might serve to maintain the people's sense of identity and continuity (e.g. the observance of the Sabbath and the avoidance of defilement by the use of "unclean" foods). The third development was a deepening sense of the evil character of man's present existence and a new anticipation in sharper and more precise form of the future time when God's righteousness would be vindicated and His will obeyed. This concentration on future vindication tended to put the emphasis on behavior that symbolized loyalty to God against all opposition and persecution (e.g. Daniel's quiet persistence in refusing to compromise his religious loyalty for the sake of royal favour). This deepening pessimism about the present time was reenforced by Israel's own history during the post-exilic period, marked by foreign invasion and threatening encroachments of Greek culture. More and more it appeared that only in some golden age in the future could Israel hope to serve God freely and to realize His purposes of righteousness and peace.

A wide variety of response to this religious and ethical situation characterized the Judaism of Jesus' time. The most conspicuous school of thought was that of the Pharisees, legitimate heirs of the prophet Ezekiel, whose concern was to promote the most careful and scrupulous observance of the Law, interpreted by the scholarship of an impressive tradition of commentators. Though marred often-times by an unfortunate degree of self-righteousness and by an anxiety about personal purity, there was a genuine zeal for doing God's will among the Pharisees which must have made them a natural audience to whom Jesus would want to speak. Another party of Jewish ethical and religious thought had felt the full impact of Greek influence. They were the Sadducees, and they were primarily found not unnaturally in the larger towns and cities where commercial and political currents flowed most consistently. The prophetic insistence upon God's righteousness was here transmuted into a more urbane calculation of what was reasonable and prudent in life. It was perhaps the wisdom of a book like Proverbs that was most congenial to the Sadducee with his common sense approach to life's problems. Widespread among Jesus' contemporaries were various forms of eschatological expectation, sustained by a considerable literature and by the spoken word of numerous itinerant preachers and teachers. (Cf. John the Baptist and his message that "the axe is laid at the root of the tree," Luke iii, 1–18) The eschatological expectations of Jesus' contemporaries are difficult to characterize in any general way, so greatly did they vary as one aspect or another of the literary tradition was interpreted or emphasized in a new way by some popular preacher. The central thought in most speculation, however, was that of an imminent Kingdom of Heaven, which would replace the present world order in some cataclysmic judgment and would substitute an era in which all wrongs would be rectified and the constancy and faithfulness of the righteous would be vindicated. This theme, of course, became a central feature in the teaching and preaching of Jesus himself. It was generally anticipated that the arrival of the Kingdom would be preceded by "signs of the end," calamities and woes both in society and in nature; and the inauguration of the Kingdom was expected to be accomplished through a judgment, which would reveal the wickedness of men and punish them appropriately while admitting the righteous to the joys and fulfillment of the Kingdom. It will be at once apparent that Jesus made use of many of these eschatological elements as the form and background for his own ethical and religious teachings.

The ministry of Jesus was associated historically with the mission of John the Baptist. The exact relationship between the two may be obscure, due to the efforts of the evangelists to exaggerate the extent to which the Baptist recognized his role as a precursor of Jesus. What seems beyond dispute is that Jesus consciously associated himself with much of the spirit and purpose of John's ministry, proceeding on the basis of its assumptions and emphases. Unlike some of the current eschatological expectations, John insisted that considerations of social justice were of primary importance in the preparation for the imminent arrival of the kingdom. The summary of his teachings as given in Luke lay primary emphasis not on the more familiar aspects of the Jewish Law, e.g. the observance of the Sabbath or ritual observances in connection with food and washing, but rather with questions of justice and charity. "He that hath two coats, let him impart to him that hath none; and he that hath meat, let him do likewise . . . Exact no more than that which is appointed you . . . Do violence to no man, neither accuse any falsely; and be content with your wages." (Luke iii, 10–14). The ethical emphasis is re-enforced by being set in contrast to the supposed privilege of belonging to the Jewish tradition. "God is able of these stones to raise up children unto Abraham . . . Every tree which bringeth not forth good fruit is hewn down and cast into the fire." (Luke iii 8–9). This insistence that the onrushing Kingdom would judge Israel sternly on the basis of the degree of justice and equity manifested in her national life is repeated again and again in some of the sayings of Jesus in an equally rigorous and searching way. (Cf. Luke xi, 42 or Luke xx, 46–47).

Like John, Jesus began his preaching with the warning that the final period of human history was about to be inaugurated and that the appropriate response was a realization of the moral ambiguity of one's life—both personal and as a member of the nation of Israel—and a hopeful trust in what God was about to do about it. "The time is fulfilled, and the Kingdom of God is at hand; repent ye, and believe the gospel." The ethical teachings of the New Testament are all to be understood against this background—the old order of existence is about to pass away forever, to be succeeded by the rule of God over all life. In view of the urgency of the situation, we must begin to live our lives on the new basis that God demands. In one of the collections of Jesus' ethical teachings, known as the Sermon on the Mount, the eschatological setting is unmistakable. The so-called Beatitudes with which the "sermon" begins are all cast in the future tense. "Blessed are the meek, for they *shall* inherit the earth." The reference is to the time of the Kingdom's advent. The "sermon" concludes with a description of two kinds of houses, one built upon the sand, the other firmly founded upon a rock. Only the woes and catastrophes which are about to come ("the rain descended and the floods came and the winds blew") will disclose the difference between the two foundations. The ethic of Jesus in the Sermon on the Mount is an ethic which looks for its fullest possibilities of realization and expression in the time of the Kingdom.

The eschatological setting of Jesus' ethics meant that they did not involve long-term calculations of effects and influences. It was not supposed that the kind of behaviour enjoined in the Sermon on the Mount, for example, would be the strategy which could overcome or check the power of evil in human life. There is no suggestion that allowing an aggressor to strike one on both cheeks will soften his heart and cause a deep reformation of his character with a rejection of aggressive violence in the future. Indeed the sort of ethical decisions described in the "sermon" are obviously highly artificial ones, involving only two persons who are thought of without reference to the sort of network of obligations and responsibilities in which the ordinary man is constantly involved. The injunction, for example, to give to everyone that asks and lend to anyone that desires to borrow could not be considered a binding rule for bank presidents to follow. The "sermon" ignores the responsibilities one

90

may have within the structure of the present world-order, assuming that the Kingdom of God is soon to replace the present world-order.

The main body of the Jesus ethical teachings are to be found in the Sermon on the Mount and consist for the most part in the enunciation of the thesis that fundamental to all ethical legislation of the Jewish tradition—referred to as the Law or the Torah—was the virtue of love. The reconstruction which Jesus undertakes of the things which were "said by them of old time" was based on the assumption that he was only recovering and bringing into prominence the original meaning of the whole Torah. Early in St. Matthew's formulation of the "sermon" there is the statement of the thesis: "I came not to destroy but to fulfill." Jesus accepts the general authority of the Torah. He is critical only of the distortions and misunderstandings of it that have resulted from misleading commentaries and interpretations. Since the Torah was the codification of what the prophets had taught under the inspiration and tutelage of the Spirit of God it was natural to the Gospel writers to assume that after the Spirit had descended upon Jesus in the baptism he was entirely qualified to distil the true meaning out of the words once again and to illuminate their real meaning. In the Gospel the authority of Jesus as an ethical teacher grows out of His Messianic character and qualification.

The word "love" as used by Jesus is a word of special quality and meaning. Its dimensions are to be found pri-marily in the character and mind of God Himself, and the Sermon on the Mount includes the injunction that we are to imitate the love of God in all human relationships. (cf. Luke vi, verses 35–36 and Matthew v, verse 45). Love as we see it in God is primarily an activity rather than an emotion, and Jesus' ethic, in consequence, is ineradicably activistic in its implications. It is expressed always in positive form—"give to him that asketh," "love your enemies," etc. It is never content with abstaining from evil but is always seeking ways of engaging in life situations with a constructive and positive purpose. Rooting the understanding of love in the being and purpose of God also emphasizes its self-giving quality. There is no hint that love is to be pursued as a policy of enlightened self-interest, since to describe it in this way would have no meaning with respect to God in His perfection and self-sufficiency. Love, as Jesus speaks of it, has the same quality among men that it has in the relationship between God and man—it is utterly self-forgetful and condescending, overlooking the lack of merit or quality in the recipient. ("He maketh his sun to rise on the evil and on the good, and sendeth rain on the just and on the unjust"). The love of the Sermon on the Mount does not recognize and respond to value in the object so much as it confers value and importance by its own outgoing and creative activity. The customary distinctions and gradations that are involved in any administration of justice are irrelevant insofar as the Sermon on the Mount is con-

91

cerned. No questions are raised as to the degree of need represented in the man who wants your coat or the justice of his law-suit which seeks to obtain it. The undiscriminating quality of love is everywhere in the "Sermon" underlined and emphasized.

Although this love is inevitably expressed in appropriate action, Jesus makes clear that it has to do also with inner feeling and motivation. His interpretation of the meaning of the Torah commandments penetrates to the area of inner attitude, and he brushes aside attempts to limit the application of love to specified activity and behaviour. A series of examples in the Sermon on the Mount makes this clear.

Murder, adultery, divorce, perjury, vindictive revenge, and generous helpfulness are all traced to inner attitudes (Matthew vi, verses 21–48). Not only murder but hateful anger, not only adultery but the lust which looks upon another person primarily as an object to satisfy personal desire, not only illegal abandonment of the wife but any evasion of the responsibility for life-long conjugal affection and care, not only the violation of a sworn oath but any dishonesty in intention, not only neglect of concern for friends and close associates but any lack of love even toward enemies—all these are set down as violations of the original commandment of God. The weight of the Jewish Torah is here made humanly unbearable. Most illuminating of all for Jesus' attitude toward the Torah is his condemnation of judging. "Judge not, that ye be not judged . . .

Why beholdest thou the mote that is in thy brother's eye, but considerest not the beam that is in thine own eye? . . . First cast out the beam out of thine own eye; and then shalt thou see clearly to cast out the mote out of thy brother's eye." Here the concern is not to condemn the act of discriminating judgment. Indeed the last portion of the quotation implies that the purpose of self-analysis is in order that a more exact and careful act of discriminating judgment may be made in the case of "the brother." What is condemned—symbolized by the beam in one's own eye—is the sort of self-righteousness and assumption of moral superiority and infallibility which makes any sort of loving discrimination in the judgment of others quite impossible. Jesus' condemnation is not of the activity of discriminating judgment—an obvious necessity in any administration of justice —but rather of the kind of censoriousness which is the peculiar temptation of the complacent and self-righteous. Love, for Jesus, is obviously an inner quality of heart and mind, a disposition of the whole person toward sympathetic concern and helpfulness for others. This disposition implies continuous responsibility for and involvement in all the areas of human need. It carries implications of positive, outreaching and creative activity. It is above all else a description of God's own nature, and as a word it is inseparably linked to the idea of the divine power and energy, creating and sustaining all things.

There is abundant evidence in the Gospels that Jesus often spoke on another level of ethical concern—the immediately relevant and practical. It is difficult on any other grounds to explain what appear to be glaring inconsistencies in his ethical injunctions or between his injunctions and some of his own decisions and activities. It is not easy to reconcile "bless them that curse you do good to them that hate you" with another verse that occurs within the Sermon on the Mount as reported in St. Matthew's Gospel, "Give not that which is holy unto dogs, neither cast ye your pearls before swine." Surely the undiscriminating love of the Sermon on the Mount would take no account of the character of those to whom the Gospel might be preached, and the fact that they might reject it scornfully would not qualify the obligation of continuous and loving concern. Even more perplexing to some has been the apparent contrast between the patient endurance of evil suggested in the injunction: "Resist not evil" and the use of coercion and force to drive the money changers from the Temple—an event recorded in all four gospels. Apparently even in the case of Jesus himself there is a recognition of the distinction between the absolute standard of the Kingdom of God and the prudential accommodation of that standard to the present evil world. In explaining the reason for the Mosaic permission of a bill of divorcement, Jesus uses the expression "because of the hardness of your hearts." (Matthew xix, 8). Although Jesus rejects this exception in enunciating the original purpose of God in marriage ("from the beginning it was not so"), he nevertheless recognizes here the conditioning and qualifying facts of human sin and of ingrained wickedness. One of the perennial questions of Christian moral philosophy is to determine under what circumstances we are in effect confronted with situations of "hardness of hearts" and what accommodations of the Kingdom ethic of love are appropriate in such circumstances. Jesus' own sayings of a prudential and accommodating sort make it clear that such questions are a central concern of any Christian moral philosophy.

Essentially the same insights into the nature of the ethical problem are represented in the thought of Saint Paul, although some aspects of the teachings of Jesus as recorded in the Gospels are here expanded upon or emphasized more sharply. Paul is preoccupied with the problem of the righteousness which God requires in man and the paradoxical relation of the Jewish Law to this righteousness —declaring it plainly and yet frustrating the realization of it. Jesus had expressed this insight into the ambiguous character of the Law and its involvement in pride and self-righteousness by his frequent and penetrating denunciations of the Pharisees. The parable of the Pharisee and the Publican with its concluding judgment that the latter "went down to his house justified rather than the other" despite the Pharisee's model behaviour in terms of the Torah requirements is perhaps the clearest example of this insight of Jesus. (Luke xviii, 9–14) Paul brings to bear on the problem the acute analytic powers of a mind that has been sharpened in the agony of self-accusation and guilt. In Romans vii, 7–24 Paul examines the intention and actual effect of the Law on man's ethical life, noting the following:

1. The Law confronts man with the realization of his sin. Without the Law man would not have known the extent and depth of his sinful condition.

2. The very knowledge of the prohibitions which the Law enacts stirs rebellious and self-centered man to a greater degree of lawlessness than ever before. The Law which was intended to forbid sin thus results actually in enhancing its power and reenforcing it.

3. The Law leads man to despair since it sets up the unresolvable tension between conscience and the self-assertive drives of the ego, between "the law in my mind" and "the law in my members." The consequence is that one conceives of righteousness and justice and finds himself hindered from achieving it by the subtle and insidious influences of the self in its aggressiveness and anxiety. The final cry is "Wretched man that I am! Who shall deliver me from the body of this death?"

In all this discussion, St. Paul means by "the Law" more than just the recorded words of the Torah; he means the whole approach to religion which the Pharisees represented, the way of moral struggle in the interests of self-justification. He sees that this kind of self-conscious striving is in the sharpest sort of contrast to the kind of heed-less self-forgetful love which is the essence of the Torah. He applies the same criticism, incidentally to the moral strivings of mankind in general, perceiving that the corruptions and frustrations of the Jewish religious and ethical are no less characteristic of the Gentile world. St. Paul grants the existence of a kind of natural law among the Gentiles (Romans i, 19–20) and says that this leaves the Gentile world "without excuse." But it is at once apparent that the natural law in the conscience is no more able than the revealed law of Moses to maintain man in the path of righteousness, and Paul's critical analysis of the Gentile world is no less condemnatory than his evaluation of Jewish ethical endeavor. It is of the Gentiles that he speaks when he writes: "Knowing the judgment of God, that they which commit such things are worthy of death, not only do the same but have pleasure in them that do them." (Romans i, 32).

Even more explicitly than in the Gospels, ethics in the Pauline are shown to be inextricably involved in religious attitudes and faith. The clear connection between the two is shown, for example, in the discussion of the Gentile world mentioned above. Paul passes from a discussion of inadequacies in theology to a discussion of ethical failure in the same verse: "And even as they did not like to retain God in their knowledge, God gave them over to a reprobate mind, to do those things which are not convenient." (Romans i, 28) Just as a "reprobate mind" and unrighteousness are closely connected so are "faith in Jesus

Christ" and the "righteousness of God" (cf. Romans iii, 22). Obviously sin, as Paul uses the term, refers not primarily to specific acts of misbehaviour but rather to a condition of man's whole being, alienated and separated from God, torn between a lingering yearning for righteousness and an untamable self-assertiveness, existing in a "body of death" from which there is no human way of deliverance.

In a number of passages, Paul associates this condition of man with the fleshly side of his nature (sarx). (Cf. Galatians v, 17: "The flesh lusteth against the Spirit, and the Spirit against the flesh; and these are contrary the one to the other so that ye cannot do the things that ye would.") One should beware of taking this passage and similar ones in Pauline literature as evidence of a thorough-going spirit-flesh dualism. An examination of the following verses, for example, in which Paul details for purposes of contrast the "works of the flesh" and the "fruit of the Spirit" makes it clear that the fleshly side of man's nature is understood in such a way as to include much more than would usually be described as gross and materialistic. Among the "works of the flesh" catalogued are, for example, idolatry, hatred, rivalry (variance), jealousy (emulations), and envy. The ordinary flesh-spirit dualism would not normally classify these kinds of behaviour as materialistic and fleshly. Paul's view seems to be that man's sin involves a disorientation of his whole being, a terrible confusion as to meaning and

purpose which often results in a desperate kind of physical and fleshly excess. Man in this state of existence is referred to as "fleshly" (sarkikos) in contrast to man in a new and right relationship to God who is termed "spiritual" (pneumatikos).

For Paul the crucial moment that must precede ethical reformation is the moment of "justification," i.e., of being accepted and given status by the mercy and creative love of God. This mercy and creative love do not, however, annul or cancel out God's justice and righteousness. Paul's phrase is "justified by his (Christ's) blood" (Romans v, 9) and his preaching centered, according to his own claim, on "Jesus Christ and him crucified" (I Cor. ii, 2) The same act of God which accepts man as an adopted son of the divine love also proclaims the eternal penalty against man's unrighteousness and exhibits the cost of the divine forgiveness. This assurance of acceptance by God, personally appropriated by a trusting and obedient opening of the heart and life to God which Paul calls "faith," results in the flooding into the self of God's own impulse of love and self-giving (Cf. Romans v, 5—"the love of God is shed abroad in our hearts"), and the consequence is that a man henceforth walks "not after the flesh but after the Spirit" (Romans viii, 1).

The Christian life is understood by Paul to be characterized by a large degree of freedom accompanied by a complete absence of anxiety or fear. A favorite word of Paul's, used to describe the Christian life, is "boldness." There will be ethical questions and

95

ethical decisions but fundamentally the Christian man is free from the sort of anxious and timorous calculations about ethics which Paul had known as a Jew. "Owe no man anything but to love one another, for he that loveth another hath fulfilled the Law" (Romans xiii, 8). What Paul could not accomplish in his divided state, preoccupied with his own status and fearful of God's displeasure, he now finds himself empowered to do and to be insofar as he trusts God for his love and mercy, and lives in the light of that confidence.

The only qualification that Paul would put on freedom is the qualification which love itself implies, the concern for the welfare of brother men. "Take heed lest this liberty of yours become a stumbling block to them that are weak." (I Cor. viii, 9). Paul expresses himself as ready to accept any discipline and to submit to the prejudices and tastes of anyone if by this means he can commend God's love in Christ to them (Cf. I Cor. ix, 19). On the other hand, he cannot allow the Church to compromise the essential freedom of discipleship by insisting upon any legalistic or ritualistic qualification for receiving what is essentially the free gift of God in Christ. The bitterly argued question of the place of circumcision in the Christian Church is the focus of this latter concern.

In the adaptation of these ethical insights to the wide variety of ethical questions which his many Christian friends referred to him for solution, Paul was deeply influenced by the eschatological thinking of the time.

There is some evidence that the sense of the near approach of the end of this age and of its characteristic responsibilities and institutions had induced in some Christians a kind of "idealistic anarchism" and a "radical indifference or hostility toward the rest of the social order" (Troeltsch). Paul's fervid exhortations to do one's political duty, to avoid fornication, to engage in one's daily work—all imply that among his hearers were those who under the emotional impact of a belief in the imminence of the triumphant return of Christ were casting aside all responsibilities and devoting themselves to ecstatic anticipation of the Parousia. Paul, on the other hand, like Jesus himself, recognized the importance of the present orders of society and the need for making such accommodations to them as might serve to help maintain justice and order. The famous passage on obedience to civil authority, for example, cites two reasons for the general injunction to conformity: "Wrath" and "conscience sake," and both of them suggest that it is a part of the responsibility of Christian love to maintain the structure of government by which good is rewarded and evil punished. To neglect this responsibility would mean a violation of Christian love and would therefore be risking divine wrath and would run counter to the impulses of the Christian conscience. It is inconceivable, of course, that Paul would have written this passage in a time when the civil authority was enforcing idol worship, for example. Here Paul is taking into account a specific situation in the Empire and a specific line of anarchistic thought within the Christian community. He was also perhaps reflecting his own experience with the Roman government which had provided protection against the rioting crowds that often threatened his work of preaching the Gospel.

Similarly in his treatment of marriage, he writes under the impression that the present order of society is not long to continue and that the fewer social responsibilities one takes on himself the better. Indeed Paul anticipates that the immediate future will be a time of troubles and tumults and says that the Christian will be wise to spare himself the anguish that family ties will add to days such as these. (I Cor. vii, 25–40). However, Paul is wise enough to recognize that this may present a problem of special urgency especially to a young couple who have been preparing for marriage, and he concludes that if the choice is to marry or "to burn" (i.e. with the sexual desire) it is obviously better to marry. (I Cor. vii, 9 b). On the other hand, Paul is clear (assuming that he is the author of the epistle to the Ephesians) that marriage is not only a lesser of two evils or an accommodation to baser physical necessities but presents unique opportunities for the expression of Christian love, and he goes so far as to compare the relation between husband and wife to the care and love which Christ showed for the Church (Ephesians v, 22–33).

Paul's teaching about economic life is similarly conservative in tone, accepting by and large the present struc-

ture of relationships and urging diligence and patience and Christian love in and through these relationships. As against a heedless lack of concern for the immediate economic future, Paul instructs his readers to stay at their daily work. He points out the obligation to maintain oneself and not rely upon the labour of others (I Thess. iv, 11–12) and also reminds his readers that by diligence in business one makes it possible to relieve the necessities of needy brethren (Ephesians iv, 28). Nothing is said to suggest the essential evil of the master-slave relationship. Instead Paul urges diligence and hardwork upon the slaves, reminding them that their work is a way of serving Christ and their thought must be of Him rather than of the worthiness of the human master. At the same time, the master is urged to regard his slave in the same spirit of brotherly concern, and is reminded that "neither is there respect of persons with Him (i.e. God)." (Ephesians vi, 5–9). This final verse reminds us of Paul's conviction that the distinctions and barriers of the present social order were already in principle transcended in Christian experience, not only in economic matters but in the relationship between the sexes and in the case of cultural and national differences as well. "There is neither Jew nor Greek, there is neither bond nor free, there is neither male nor female; for ye are all one in Christ Jesus." (Gal. iii, 28). That this fundamental insight was not more adequately translated into terms of social and political reconstruction was due, of course, to (1) the supposed shortness of the time and (2) to the relative insignificance and impotence of the Christian movement. Paul has tasted the joy and the freedom and the assurance of the Christian life and yearns for the day when the whole creation will be renewed and transformed as an appropriate environment for the kind of life that Christian love at its fullest would require. In the meantime, he has a sober sense of responsibility for the adjustment of the love impulse that has been released by Christ to the complex of human relationships in which man finds himself. In principle no man has any obligation except to love, but in experience he finds himself in a network of obligations through which love must be expressed. Paul himself shows the way in which one incisive Christian mind sought to discharge this obligation which Christian love itself lays upon him.

Bibliography

Emil Brunner, *The Divine Imperative* (London, 1937).

C. J. Cadoux, *The Early Church and the World*.

Martin Dibelius, *The Sermon on the Mount* (New York, 1940).

Alexander Miller, *The Renewal of Man*.

Paul Minear, *Eyes of Faith* (Philadelphia, 1946).

Reinhold Niebuhr, *An Interpretation of Christian Ethics* (New York, 1935).

A. Nygren, *Eros and Agape,* vol. I, translated by P. S. Watson (London, 1953).

Paul Ramsay, *Basic Christian Ethics*.

Holmes Rolston, *The Social Message of the Apostle Paul*.

R. Y. B. Scott, *The Relevance of the Prophets* (New York, 1944).

Ernst Troeltsch, *The Social Teaching of the Christian Churches,* vol. I (New York, 1931).

Amos Wilder, *Eschatology and Ethics in the Teaching of Jesus*.

Nils Ehrenström et. al. *Christian Faith and the Common Life* (An Oxford Conference Book).

John M. Krumm
Columbia University

Christian morality: *see* Nietzsche, Friedrich.

Christianity: *see* Aquinas, Thomas, Moral Views of; Augustine and Morals; Aztec Morals; Balguy, John; Berdyaev, Nicolas; Clarke, Samuel; Cudworth, Ralph; Freud, Sigmund; Hegel, G. W. F.; Jesuits, the Moral Theology of; Jewish Ethics and Its Civilization; Kant, I.; Khomiakov, Alexey; Moral Philosophy in America; Puritan Morals; Quakerism, Classical; Rio Grande Pueblo Indians; Soloviev, Wladimir; Spinoza.

Chrysippus: *see* Stoics, the.

Chuang Tzu: *see* China, Moral Philosophies of.

Chuang Tzu, **the:** *see* China, Moral Philosophies of.

church: *see* Aquinas, Thomas, Moral views of; Augustine and Morals; Khomiakov, Alexey; Moral Philosophy in America; Puritan Morals; Quakerism, Classical, The Morality of; Soviet Morality, Current. *See* also Christian Moral Philosophy.

church and state: *see* Augustine and Morals; Puritan Morals.

Cicero: *see* Augustine and Morals;

Dante, Alighieri; Primitive Morals; Stoics, the.

circumcision: *see* Jewish Ethics and Its Civilization; Pakot, the Moral System of; Primitive Morals.

city-state: *see* Puritan Morals.

civilization: *see* Jewish Ethics and Its Civilization.

civil law: *see* Aquinas, Thomas, Moral Views of.

claim: *see* Dewey, John; Ross, Sir (William) David.

clans: *see* Aboriginals of Yirkalla.

Clark, G.: *see* Primitive Morals.

Clarke, John: *see* Price, Richard; Wollaston, William.

Clarke, Samuel

Samuel Clarke was born October 11, 1675 in Norwich, England. He entered Caius College, Cambridge, in 1691, where his career was marked with distinction. Soon after taking his degree, he became chaplain to the Bishop of Norwich. He published in 1697 a translation of Rehault's *Physics,* a textbook based on Cartesian principles. His translation included notes and comments indicating weaknesses of the Cartesian system and the superiority of the Newtonian. Clarke is considered, therefore, one of the most influential persons in introducing the Newtonian physics into English universities. His next years were devoted primarily to ecclesiastical duties and his publications reflect this concern. He next became rector of Drayton and in 1704 was appointed to the Boyle lectureship. His subject was *Demonstration of the Being and Attributes of God.* His lectures being extremely well-received, he was reappointed the following year and chose as his subject *A Discourse Concerning the Unchangeable Obligations of Natural Religion, and the Truth and Certainty of the Christian Revelation.* The second series of lectures, along with some of his sermons, contain the body of his ethical writings. In 1706 he wrote a refutation of Dodwell on the immortality of the soul and was drawn into a controversy with Anthony Collins. In the same year he was appointed rector of St. Bennett's and also completed a translation of Newton's *Opticks.* Shortly afterward he became a chaplain to Queen Anne. In 1709 he received the rectory of St. James's Westminster. In the same year he took the degree of doctor of divinity defending two theses: 1) No article of the Christian faith, delivered in the Holy Scriptures, is disagreeable to right reason. 2) Without the liberty of human actions there can be no true religion. In 1712 he raised a controversy by publishing a treatise on *The Scripture Doctrine of the Trinity.* In 1715 and 1716 he engaged in written controversy with Leibniz on several issues dealing mainly with human freedom. In 1719 he became master of Wigston's Hospital, Leicester. In 1724 he published seventeen sermons and in 1727 refused the position of Master of the Mint which had become vacant when Newton died. In 1728 the *Philosophical Transactions* of the Royal Society published a discussion of velocity and force in natural bodies which he had debated with Bishop Hoadley. In 1729 he published the first twelve books of his translation, with notes and commentary, of the *Iliad*. The remaining books and ten volumes of sermons were published after his death May 17, 1729.

Clarke had a cheerful, even playful, disposition, sometimes being referred to as the "capering genius." He was considered, during his lifetime, and for some years afterward, to be the intellectual equal of Newton and Leibniz. But this did not dampen his animal spirits which enabled him to amuse himself and others with witticisms and antics such as swimming upon a table and leaping over tables and chairs.

Clarke is generally credited with giving ethical rationalism in England both a considerable impetus in development and a more rigid form than his predecessors. Being a great admirer of Newtonian physics and the methods of the *Principia* it is not surprising that he attempted to set forth his doctrine in the "mathematical manner" and that he laid great stress on the analogy between mathematics and ethics.

The manner of Clarke's procedure and the matter of his basic ethical views are both exhibited in the first proposition of *The Unchangeable Obligations of Natural Religion:*

The same necessary and eternal different relations that different things bear to one another; and the same consequent Fitness or Unfitness of the Application of different things or different Relations one to another, with regard to which, the Will of God always and necessarily does determine itself, to choose to act only what is agreeable to Justice, Equity, Goodness and Truth, in order to the Welfare of the whole Universe—ought likewise constantly to determine the wills of all subordinate rational Beings to govern all their actions by the same Rules, for the Good of the Public in their respective stations—That is, these eternal and necessary differences of things make it fit and reasonable for Creatures, so to act; they cause it to be their duty, or lay an obligation upon them . . . separate from the consideration of these Rules being the positive will or command of God; and also antecedent to any respect . . . of Advantage or Disadvantage . . .

Almost the whole of Clarke's ethical views are contained in his "proof" of this proposition. His insistence upon the *a priori* nature of ethical knowledge is exhibited early in this proof:

That there are differences of things, and different Respects or proportions, of some things toward others, is as evident and undeniable, as that one magnitude or number, is greater, equal to, or smaller than another. That from these different Relations of different things, there necessarily arises an agreement or disagreement of some things with others, or a fitness or unfitness of the application of different things or different relations one to another, is likewise as plain as that there is any such thing as Proportion or Disproportion in Geometry or Arithmetick . . .

These passages also indicate that for Clarke the basic moral concept is "fitness." Unfortunately the only explication of it he offers is in several examples:

(1) 'Tis a thing absolutely and necessarily fitter in itself that God should govern, (a) according to law than caprice; (b) for the universal good of creation than for universal misery.

(2) 'Tis undeniably more fit, absolutely and in itself, that all men should (a) endeavor to promote the universal good and welfare of all, than the universal destruction of all; (b) deal with one another according to the known rules of justice than to disappoint the expectations of their neighbors.

(3) 'Tis without dispute more fit and reasonable in itself to preserve the life of an innocent man in my power than to kill him.

These absolute fitnesses Clarke claims are so "plain and self-evident" that nothing but extreme stupidity or perverseness could account for anyone's doubt of them. Indeed, to doubt or deny them is on a level with doubting or denying that a rectangle has twice the area of a triangle of equal base and height.

In addition to the positive attempt in these examples to explicate the notion of fittingness (and, thereby, of moral rightness) Clarke is arguing against any arbitrary basis of morality, as for example, that right and wrong are created by the will of the Leviathan and as a result of an "arbitrary compact." He maintains that these eternal fitnesses are independent of the will of God, a denial of a Calvinistic doctrine and one that had appeared in certain parts of Locke's ethical views.

Clarke argues from an *a priori* understanding of fitness to the existence of obligation. God, in his omniscience, determines his will always according to the eternal reason of things, i.e., according to their eternal relations of fitness or unfitness. Therefore, his creatures, made in his image, are also obliged to act in accordance with their understanding of the eternal relations which hold between different things. For Clarke, then, reason is rationally intuitive and carries an inherent obligatory authority. Clarke draws an analogy with mathematical reasoning in terms of the similarity in the way we arrive at knowledge of the relations of things. He admits a disanalogy also, but does not permit it to carry any weight: In the operation of pure reason in mathematics, understanding the relations of things necessarily binds assent. But because of the possibility of the foreign influence of the passions it is possible to understand relations of fittingness and yet not be bound to act in accordance with that understanding. We really have no excuse for waywardness of this kind, however, since we are rational creatures and are free to follow reason. Clarke's emphasis, therefore, is much more upon the analogy than the disanalogy.

Although Clarke admits that sanctions of rewards and punishment are the most effective means of guaranteeing that persons will perform their obligations, this is secondary to the obligations of reason. The judgments men make of the actions of others, of themselves, and of injuries to themselves prove the absolute obligation of the law of reason. The ignorance of savages presents no obstacle to this doctrine. That they need instruction in right and wrong is no less evident than their need for instruction in mathematics, and argues just as little

101

that there are not eternal and necessary relations and circumstances of fittingness as that there are not necessary proportions between numbers.

When Clarke proceeds from the epistemological foundations of ethics to a statement of detailed duties, he does not unambiguously assert that particular duties are deduced from the fundamental principle that we are absolutely obliged to act in accordance with our understanding of fittingness. Some commentators say he merely enumerates the branches of duty, others say he deduces them. Clarke himself is not clear, although he seems to think he is carrying out a deduction. In any case, he holds that there are three main classes of duties: to God, ourselves, and others. Duties to God are the acts and sentiments of veneration, love and worship, to which we are bound by an understanding of God's nature. Such duties are too sublime to admit drawing significantly any analogy with mathematics. Duties to others are divided into Justice and Benevolence. Justice is epitomized in the principle that we should act towards others as we want them to act towards us. Here it is significant to draw an analogy with mathematics. Iniquity in action is like falsity or contradiction in demonstration: what makes the latter absurd makes the former unreasonable: "It would be impossible for men not to be as much ashamed of doing Iniquity, as they are of believing contradictions." Universal love or benevolence is the promotion of the welfare and happiness of all. It is obligatory on several grounds. For example, it is unquestionably fit that a single person should be happy and enjoy well-being. By a simple progression Clarke infers that therefore it is most fit and therefore most obligatory that all should be happy and enjoy well-being. God's actions are determined by the principle of benevolence; therefore ours should also be. Duties to ourselves are, e.g., self-preservation, temperance and contentment. These derive from the fact that we are not creators of our own being. Therefore we do not have the right to destroy that being either directly as in suicide or indirectly as in debauchery or any other form of self-abuse.

The eternity and immutability of the laws of reason and of moral obligation are absolute and therefore independent of even the will of God himself. Thus, although in one sense God is the creator of all things and the relations between them, these things and relations in so far as they are morally fitting are so in themselves, not because God creates them. God himself is guided by their fittingness and creates them because of it. This independence is complicated, however, by Clarke's admission that it would be unreasonable to expect men to give up things they desire in this life if there were no promise or hope of future reward. He attempts to retain the independence by arguing that since God is pure reason (i.e., acts in accordance with "the reason of things") there must be rewards and punishments in a future state.

Clarke's position in the development of ethical rationalism is a central one, often regarded as more important and influential than the quality of his thought justifies. The fact is that the earlier rationalism of men like Cumberland, Cudworth and More was made more explicit and rigid in Clarke's treatment. Martineau puts it well in saying that the earlier rationalism lost its "glow" in Clarke's hands. But just because he did formulate rationalism in a much more explicit and relatively more rigid way, his philosophy in many respects is a focal point from which divergent strains of rationalism and empiricism departed.

In the first place his writings enjoyed a widespread circulation and, on the whole, popularity and acceptance. He challenged Hobbes, he appealed to values that were strongly favored by the prejudices of his audience, he claimed to present the methods of the incomparable Newton in his ethical doctrines and made a wide appeal to the mathematical analogy. Both of these last factors appealed to the convictions of an educated audience; the first, because, as Pope later put it, most educated Englishmen felt that Newton was the manifestation of the divine dictum "Let there be light"; the second, because the hope of a "universal mathematics" had developed nearly into a conviction in the years from Descartes to Newton.

One line of ethical writers therefore took Clarke as their point of departure in a positive sense. Wollaston attempted to make more specific the mathematical analogy and to draw a more specific parallel between the values of mathematics, truth and falsity, and the ethical values, right and wrong. Balguy and Price attempted to introduce modifications into his rationalism that would retain its general form and yet avoid its difficulties. The influence of these men has extended to the present in the writings of Carritt, Ewing and Ross.

Another line of ethical writers took Clarke as their point of departure in a negative sense. It is not clear that Shaftesbury knew Clarke's writings or his views. Shaftesbury's *Inquiry* appeared in an unauthorized version in 1699, six years before Clarke's second Boyle lectures. But the authorized version of Shaftesbury's *Characteristicks* appeared in 1711 and though lacking in explicit references to Clarke, presents an opposing view. At any rate, there is no question that Hutcheson and Hume wrote in explicit rejection of the rationalism of Clarke, and another of Clarke's earliest critics was Joseph Butler. Hutcheson's references to Clarke are limited and unsystematic, but many of the polemical parts of Book III of Hume's *Treatise* read like a systematic refutation of Clarke.

It is undeniable that many doctrines in Clarke's system justify the criticism they received from the empiricists. The appeal to the notion of fittingness, a concept that is relative certainly to situations and often to human purposes, as an absolute concept, was one such point. Another was his assertion of a necessary connection between cognition and conduct or, putting it another way, his identification of practical and theoretical reason. Closely associated with this is his over-emphasis of the analogies between how we reach mathematical conclusions and how we reach ethical conclusions, to the neglect of the disanalogies. Thus the empiricist critics had good grounds for arguing that he confused rightness with obligatoriness, that he failed to take account of the difference between understanding the nature of a proposition and acting in accordance with that understanding, and for arguing that he claimed to find *a priori* knowledge of relationships where none could exist, namely, *a priori* knowledge that certain acts are right (fitting) and that right acts ought to be done. In general Clarke's attempt to deal with the problem of obligation is confused. Sometimes he seems to identify rightness and obligatoriness and sometimes he seems to indicate that they are different, if not distinct. Finally, there was his attempt to maintain both of two antithetical doctrines; one out of his concern to deny Hobbes, the other out of his concern to provide a place for religion in the foundations of morality. On the one hand he maintains that right and wrong, and therefore virtuous conduct, are absolutely independent of (arbitrary) will, whether God's, a will expressed in a compact, or a Leviathan's. On the other hand he maintains that it is reasonable to expect that virtuous conduct should have its reward, if not in this life then in another and infers the attribute of justice in the Deity at the expense of introducing self-interest where there should be only virtuous conduct in accordance with "the absolute reason of things."

But if Clarke's doctrines themselves are open to the criticism of the empiricists, or even the more moderate rationalists, it is nevertheless true that Clarke's was one of the earliest attempts to analyze the concept of rightness; that he had the strength that rationalism in ethics has always enjoyed, namely, the emphasis upon the impartiality and objectivity of ethical values. As a final judgment then we may say that he was much more significant in his failures than in his successes, and much more influential than the quality of his writing seems to justify on current reading. This is because the modifications and criticisms that his theories aroused have become so much a part of ethical theory since his time that his contributions as a focal point in a significant shift and development have become increasingly difficult to recognize and appreciate.

Bibliography

Samuel Clarke, *A Discourse Concerning the Being and Attributes of God, the Obligations of Natural Religion and the Truth and Certainty of the Christian Revelations, in opposition to Hobbes, Spinoza, the author of the Oracles of Reason, and other Deniers of Natural and Revealed Religion* (London, 1706).

——, *Correspondence with Leibniz* (London, 1717).

——, *Sermons,* (London, 1724 and 1730).

William Whewell, *Lectures on the History of Moral Philosophy in England,* (London, 1852), Lecture V.

John Hunt, *Religious Thought in England,* (London, 1870), Vol. II, 444–457, Vol. III, 20–29, 109–115.

R. Zimmerman, "Samuel Clarke's Leben und Lehre. Ein Betrag zur Geschichte des Rationalismus in England," *Denkshriften der kaiserlichen Akademic der Wissenschaften, Abhandlung der Philosophisch-Historisch Klasse,* Band 19 (Vienna, 1870), 249–336.

J. Martineau, *Types of Ethical Theory* (Oxford, 1889), Vol. II, 459–474.

R. M. Kydd, *Reason and Conduct in Hume's Treatise,* (Oxford, 1946), Chapters 1 and 2.

Bernard Peach
Duke University

Clarke, Samuel: *see* Balguy, John; Cudworth, Ralph; Cumberland, Richard; Reid, Thomas.

class basis of morality: *see* Marxist Theory of Morals.

class distinctions: *see* Quakerism, Classical, The Morality of.

class interest: *see* Marxist Theory of Morals.

class society: *see* Marxist Theory of Morals.

class struggle: *see* Marxist Theory of Morals; Soviet Morality, Current.

classes, economic: *see* Green, T. H.; Marxist Theory of Morals.

classical morality: *see* Nietzsche, Friedrich.

Classical Quakerism: *see* Quakerism, Classical, The Morality of.

classless society: *see* Marxist Theory of Morals.

cleanness: *see* Pakot, the Moral System of.

cleansing, ceremonial: *see* Pakot, the Moral System of.

Cleanthes: *see* Stoics, the.

clergy: *see* Puritan Morals.

clumsiness: *see* Navaho Morals.

Code of Hammurapi: *see* Hammurapi, Code of.

codes: *see* Jewish Ethics and Its Civilization; moral codes; Navaho Morals; Puritan Morals; Spinoza; Zuni Indians, Morals of.

codes, legal: *see* Hammurapi, Code of; Sophists, the; Soviet Morality, Current; Stoics, the.

coercion: *see* Augustine and Morals; Hobbes, Thomas; Puritan Morals; Rio Grande Pueblo Indians; Soviet Morality, Current.

cognition: *see* Knowledge; More, Henry.

cognitivist theories: *see* Major Ethical Viewpoints.

coherence: *see* Green, T. H.

Colerus, John: *see* Spinoza.

collectivism: *see* Marxist Theory of Morals; Mundurucu Indians, A Dual System of Ethics.

collectivity: *see* Zuni Indians, Morals of.

Collins, Anthony: *see* Clarke, Samuel.

comforts: *see* Hindu Ethics; Zuni Indians, Morals of.

command(s): *see* Cudworth, Ralph; Kant, I.

commandments: *see* Hindu Ethics; Jewish Ethics and Its Civilization; Spinoza; Zoroastrian Morals.

commandments, five: *see* Tolstoy, Leo.

commandments, twelve: *see* Soviet Morality, Current.

commitment: *see* Psychology and Morals.

common good: *see* Green, T. H.

common man: *see* China, Moral Philosophies of; Machiavelli, Niccolo.

common sense: *see* Moore, George Edward; Reid, Thomas; Utilitarianism.

Common Sense School, Scottish: *see* Price, Richard.

commonalty: *see* Khomiakov, Alexey.

commoners: *see* Hammurapi, Code of.

communion with the Divine: *see* Hindu Ethics.

communism: *see* Berdyaev, Nicolas; China, Moral Philosophies of; Marxist Theory of Morals; Soviet Morality, Current.

Communist Manifesto: *see* Marxist Theory of Morals.

community: *see* Aquinas, Thomas, Moral Views of; Moral Philosophy in America; Quakerism, Classical, The Morality of; Zuni Indians, Morals of.

community of wives: *see* Stoics, the.

compact theory: *see* Clarke, Samuel; Cooper, Anthony Ashley; Cudworth, Ralph; Sophists, the.

compassion: *see* Butler, Joseph; Hindu Ethics; Hobbes, Thomas; Reid, Thomas; Scheler, Max; Schopenhauer, Arthur; Tolstoy, Leo.

compensation: *see* Zuni Indians, Morals of.

competition: *see* Hindu Ethics; Marxist Theory of Morals; Mundurucu Indians, A Dual System of Ethics; Reid, Thomas; Zuni Indians, Morals of.

compromise: *see* Stoics, the; Zuni Indians, Morals of.

compulsion: *see* More, Henry.

Comte, Auguste: *see* Major Ethical Viewpoints.

conation: *see* will, the.

conceit: *see* Minor Socratics.

concentration: *see* Hindu Ethics.

concupiscence: *see* lust; More, Henry.

conduct: *see* Hindu Ethics; Hume, David; Meta-ethics and Normative Ethics; Moore, George Edward; Muslim Morals; Rio Grande Pueblo Indians.

confession: *see* Jesuits, the. Moral Theology of.

confessional, the: *see* Liguori, St. Alphonsus and Catholic Moral Philosophy.

confessors: *see* Jesuits, the, Moral Theology of.

configuration: *see* Mundurucu Indians, A Dual System of Ethics.

conflicts: *see* Cudworth, Ralph; Dewey, John; Hegel, G. W. F.; Hindu Ethics; Hobbes, Thomas; Major Ethical Viewpoints; Marxist Theory of Morals; Price, Richard; Prichard, H. A.; Psychology and Morals; Reid, Thomas; Sophists, the; Zuni Indians, Morals of.

conflicts of duties: *see* Ross, Sir (William) David.

conformity: *see* Hindu Ethics; Jewish Ethics and Its Civilization; Kant, I.; Pakot, the Moral System of; Rio Grande Pueblo Indians; Soviet Morality, Current; Stoics, the; Zuni Indians, Morals of.

Confucianism: *see* China, Moral Philosophies of.

Confucius: *see* China, Moral Philosophies of.

Congregationalism: *see* Puritan Morals.

congruity: *see* More, Henry.

connivance: *see* Soviet Morality, Current.

conscience: *see* Aquinas, Thomas, Moral Views of; Butler, Joseph; Christian Moral Philosophy; Cooper, Anthony Ashley; Freud, Sigmund; Green, T. H.; Hartmann, Nicolai; Hindu Ethics; Hume, David; Jesuits, the, Moral Theology of; Jewish Ethics and Its Civilization; Liguori, St. Alphonsus and Catholic Moral Philosophy; Primitive Morals; Psychology and Morals; Puritan Morals; Quakerism, Classical, The Morality of; Reid, Thomas; Rio Grande Pueblo Indians; Schlick, Moritz; Soviet Morality, Current; Tolstoy, Leo; Zoroastrian Morals.

consciousness, self: *see* Green, T. H.

consensus gentium: *see* Reid, Thomas.

consequences: *see* Kant, I.; Major Ethical Viewpoints.

consequential theory: *see* Ross, Sir (William) David.

consistency: *see* Cumberland, Richard; Hume, David; Jewish Ethics and Its Civilization; Stoics, the; Wollaston, William.

contemplation: *see* Aquinas, Thomas, Moral Views of; Aristotle; Hindu Ethics; meditation; Schopenhauer, Arthur; Sophists, the; Stoics, the.

contemptible, the: *see* Nietzsche, Friedrich.

contentment: *see* China, Moral Philosophies of; Clarke, Samuel; Cudworth, Ralph.

contextual reference: *see* Dewey, John.

continence: *see* Augustine and Morals; celibacy.

contingency: *see* Aquinas, Thomas, Moral Views of.

contraceptives: *see* Soviet Morality, Current.

contract: *see* Zoroastrian Morals.

contract theory: *see* Utilitarianism.

contradiction: *see* China, Moral Philosophies of; Clarke, Samuel; Kierkegaard, Soren; Wollaston, William.

contrition: *see* Jesuits, the, Moral Theology of.

control: *see* Hindu Ethics; More, Henry.

control, state: *see* Soviet Morality, Current.

convention: *see* custom; Goethe, Johann Wolfgang von; Sophists, the; Spinoza; tradition.

conversion: *see* Hegel, G. W. F.

Cook, J.: *see* Primitive Morals.

Cooper, Anthony Ashley, Third Earl of Shaftesbury

Shaftesbury was born in London, February 26, 1671. It is reported that the marriage from which he issued was arranged by John Locke, friend and adviser to his grandfather, the first earl of Shaftesbury. He grew up under the guardianship of his grandfather and the educational precepts of Locke, although Locke was not his actual tutor. He was taught by a Mrs. Elizabeth Birch in accordance with principles put forth in Locke's *Thoughts Concerning Education*. In 1686, after a brief and unpleasant period as a warden's boarder at Winchester, he traveled abroad where it is reported he much preferred conversation with the tutors of other young Englishmen to conversation with the young men themselves. He returned to England in 1689, and after a period of five years of quiet and study he was a successful candidate for the borough of Poole. By family and education he was a Whig; but he did not vote the party line, being always ready to support causes that appeared to promote individual liberty or the independence of parliament. He never was in strong health and in 1698 the aggravation of his asthma by the London smoke obliged him to retire from the political scene. He spent a year in Holland where he enjoyed unrestricted conversation on philosophy, politics, morals, and religion in the company of LeClerc, Bayle, and other members of a circle of which Locke had been a member several years before. It was during this period that Toland published, without Shaftesbury's authority, an imperfect edition of the *Enquiry Concerning Virtue or Merit*. In 1700 after his return to England he succeeded his father as third earl of Shaftesbury and was active in the general elections of 1700 and 1701. These were successful for the Whigs and William III offered Shaftesbury the position of secretary of state but his ill health made it impossible for him to accept. William's death and Shaftesbury's disfavor with Anne soon led him to leave England for Holland and after his return in 1704 his time was devoted almost entirely to literary pursuits. He married at the age of forty, apparently because of the concern of his friends about a successor to the title. When he took the project in mind he found almost immediately a woman with whom he fell in love. She was the daughter of a lord and possessor of a fortune so large that Shaftesbury was ready to marry her without dowry in order not to seem a fortune-seeker. But opposition from her father to a man in Shaftesbury's health stopped the match. He soon afterward married a Miss Jane Ewer, a woman "with little or no fortune, and not in the highest degree of quality either," but possessing the more important qualities of "a right education, simple innocence, modesty and the plain qualities of a good mother and a good nurse." (Letter to Molesworth, Letter XIII, referred to in Fowler's *Shaftesbury and Hutcheson*, p. 29.) These qualities stood her in good stead, for whatever degree of sentiment is characteristic of Shaftesbury's ethical theories he was no sentimentalist about marriage. Although he clearly held the woman in high respect he wrote to Molesworth that he feared he could not speak of marriage without offending the most part of "sober married people, and the ladies chiefly: for I should in reality think I did wonders, in extolling the happiness of my new state and the merit of my wife in particular, by saying that I verily thought myself as happy a man now as ever." (*Ibid.*) Their only child was born about a year later, bringing into prominence Lady Shaftesbury's qualities as a mother; and Shaftesbury's increasingly poor health, requiring warmer air, took them to Naples, where for something over a year that remained of his life his wife showed in the highest degree her qualities as a nurse. He died in February 1713.

The polemical parts of Shaftesbury's moral theory are directed primarily at two doctrines: those of Hobbes and those which base morality upon religion considered formalistically or as a matter of orthodoxy. The religious doctrines against which Shaftesbury argues are the ones that make, with various degrees of subtlety, virtuous conduct a matter of fear of consequences, either present or future; and the source of right and wrong the authority of God. In opposition Shaftesbury contends that the virtuous life is one that is found good, even beautiful, in the very living of it; and that anyone who believes in a God who is just and good implicitly accepts standards of justice and goodness independent of God's will. This rejection of egoism and authoritarianism assumes a more explicit and heavier task in his polemic against Hobbes: The whole picture of man in a "state of nature," the compact that brought society into existence, and the egoism and authoritarianism that hold it together is considered by Shaftesbury an impossible picture. In the first place, all known forms of human existence have been social in nature; anything like the state of nature described by Hobbes is not even to be found among animals or insects. The whole notion of a compact or agreement requires that circumstances of communication, understanding and agreement about goals, obtain; in short, the compact theory itself presupposes a modicum of social organization. And, finally, no society could endure if human nature is motivated by fear and selfish desire.

Shaftesbury has of course taken the easy way with Hobbes, much of the plausibility of his arguments against him being grounded in taking Hobbe's doctrines as history. Hobbes himself had suggested that this was not his intent and that his doctrine of the state of nature was to be understood as an elaborate contrary-to-fact conditional providing a logical analysis of the justification of the dominance of authority over the individual: a description of what it would be like if we had no organized and dominant civil authority. Despite this weakness of Shaftesbury's refutation of Hobbes, however, his emphasis on the social nature of man and his psychological and empirical-inductive approach to problems of morals are important factors in moral philosophy generally and provide important bases for the positive construction of Shaftesbury's theory in particular.

Closely associated with Shaftesbury's insistence upon the social nature of man is his concept of "system" and the phenomenon of sympathy. To "sympathize" is to "feel together and be united in one sense or feeling." This admits a broad enough application that Shaftesbury finds sympathy not only in the social affection of fellow-feeling but also in the parts of animal bodies, the fibres of plants and the order and unity of the heavenly bodies. But it is in man that sympathy and other social affections reach their highest level and provide the basis for a theory of morality.

The basic concept in Shaftesbury's moral theory is "good." This is a concept that applies most importantly to creatures with "affections," but he insists that no judgment concerning the good is significant that does not also take into account the system within which it belongs. The natural affections are "naturally" good, the unnatural ones correspondingly vicious. A natural affection is one that is harmonious within its system, i.e., neither "too much" nor "too little." Such "mere" goodness lies within the reach of every sensible creature and must be distinguished from moral goodness or virtue, which man alone can achieve: this consists of a new affection, achieved as a result of an awareness and understanding of the affections that constitute mere goodness. Virtue according to Shaftesbury in the *Enquiry,* is a "reflex" approbation, love, or appreciation of good affections. On the personal level virtue will be a harmony among the various passions and of these with reason. It will exemplify itself on the social level as an approval of affections that contribute to the good of the entire system. There are both "inner" and "outer" aspects of virtue, then, although he does not always distinguish between them. The one is an internal economy of affections, the other a social economy within which each virtuous individual is one who approves of and acts in accordance with the naturally good affections that lead to the good of the whole system.

Shaftesbury does not offer a hierarchy of virtues, but it is plain that benevolence is very important; important enough that Butler, was perhaps referring to Shaftesbury when he warned against theories that identify virtue with benevolence. But from Shaftesbury's listings of the "natural affections" and the "self-affections" both classes of which are involved in determining vice or virtue it is evident that he did not make the identification. Benevolence, however, may be understood as a "motivating affection" for Shaftesbury and provides a possible way of reading the significance of the title of the *Enquiry Concerning Virtue or Merit.* Merit is the process of acting for the good (harmony) of the system, virtue the harmony that results. This would mean that *acting* benevolently is meritorious and *being* benevolent is virtuous. But this is still not the whole of merit or virtue since acting for the harmony of the "personal system" is part of merit and the personal harmony achieved is a part of virtue and they would both belong in the class of the "self-affections." This problem led Hutcheson later to hold that a person can be the object of his own benevolence; but Shaftesbury does not go to this extreme.

Shaftesbury's theory is often described as a theory of sentiment; but reason plays an important part, both cognitive and conative: We must know what affections lead to an harmonious system, for example, before we can be virtuous since virtue consists of a reflex approval (affection) for these affections. This knowledge is furthermore considered by Shaftesbury to be a necessary condition of virtuous acting not only in the sense that without it we wouldn't know what we ought to do, but also in the sense that it provides a motive to the will. In addition, Shaftesbury appreciates the importance of considering evidence, weighing alternatives, and the other rational processes that go into the determining of an action. His position on the matter, though it remains vague, seems to be that reason and appetite are both necessary, but neither sufficient, for virtuous action, with appetite in some sense the more important.

In any case, the non-rational factors in his theory receive more emphasis, both from Shaftesbury himself and from most commentators. He insists, for example, upon the sensitivity of human nature to the peculiar beauty of a moral act or a moral character. We have a natural sense of good and evil, of the virtuous and the vicious. Here are at least the rudiments of the "moral sense" which was to be developed, though eventually in effect dismissed, by Francis Hutcheson. Emphasis upon the apparent immediacy of moral judgments, upon harmony and proportion, made it easy and natural for Shaftesbury to appeal to the "esthetic analogy" and his theory has sometimes been called an "esthetic" morality. Shaftesbury maintained that virtue is like beauty in many ways both in itself and in the way by which we become aware of it. Moral judgments are frequently compared to judgments of art objects; they are primarily, though not solely, a matter of having a proper ("refined," "gentlemanly") feeling when confronted with certain kinds of "objects." Judgments

of virtue and vice are like the awareness of beauty and ugliness. In some passages Shaftesbury goes beyond this to assert that virtue and vice are species of beauty and ugliness and even suggests in some passages that they are identical. A further element in the analogy is that just as taste in art can be developed so the appreciation of virtue can be developed. By the same reasoning, Shaftesbury admits that both kinds of appreciation could be corrupted although he denies that the moral sense can ever be completely eradicated. But in his discussion of the moral sense it appears that its development consists largely in the development of the cognitive aspects of moral judgments. Shaftesbury accordingly speaks of a natural sense of right and wrong, a moral sense and conscience, without attempting to distinguish them or the relative components of reason and sentiment involved in each.

The respects in which this sense is treated like conscience raises the problem of obligation. With his emphasis upon benevolence, general welfare, and altruistic affections it is surprising to find Shaftesbury doing two things: First, raising the question, 'Why should I be moral?' and, second, answering it by showing that it is to one's own greatest self-interest to do so. At least he answers the question 'What obligation is there to virtue?' by arguing, at great length and in great detail, that a balanced harmony of public affections and private affections and the eradication of the unnatural affections is the way to maxi-

111

mize "self-enjoyment" and to minimize "misery and ill."

There is fairly widespread agreement that Shaftesbury inaugurated a new era in English ethics. He was not the first to react and argue against Hobbes' egoism and authoritarianism in ethics, but in the phase of English ethical philosophy that grew out of answers to Hobbes he was the first writer who influenced others with an approach to ethics that concentrates on man's psychological nature and attempts to demonstrate the compatibility of self-regard and public-regard. (There is a complication here in that Cudworth, despite the rationalism of his *True Intellectual System of the Universe* and *Treatise on Eternal and Immutable Morality,* had worked out a moral psychology that was similar to that of Shaftesbury, Hutcheson, Butler and Hume; but most of it still remains unknown in the Cudworth manuscripts in the British Museum.) He also represents a beginning point of a conflict between rationalistic and empirical ethics that is still bearing fruit. Although Shaftesbury's polemic was against Hobbes he in turn became the object of polemic by John Balguy and Richard Price and thus, within the phase of ethical reflection that grew up out of a reaction against Hobbes, Shaftesbury constitutes a starting point for the opposition between empirical and rational systems of ethics in the British Moralist tradition, probably one of the richest veins in the history of ethical reflection. Whether or not his contribu-

tions qualify him to receive Ernest Albee's accolade "the greatest of English moralists" (*Philosophical Review,* vol. VI) certainly the influence of the man who contributed the basic starting point to the tradition that includes Butler, Hutcheson, Hume and Adam Smith and consequently runs to our own day must be regarded as a very significant influence. In addition, his influence upon both French and German writers was considerable, particularly upon LeClerc, Voltaire, and Diderot, Lessing, Mendelssohn, Herder, and extending even to Leibniz.

Finally, however, it must be recognized that he was much more a moralist and a suggester than a philosopher in any systematic sense. It would therefore be churlish to criticize him for failing to accomplish something he didn't even attempt to accomplish. There is one apparent inconsistency, however, which seems major enough to warrant attention, namely, his doctrine that the life of virtue is a life that is found good in the living of it and his concern to show that we are obliged to virtue because of the compatibility of personal and public affections. Looking at Shaftesbury with the advantage of the intervening years it is apparent that this need not be considered a contradiction in any logical sense, but a revelation of the complication of the facts and language of morality. If, that is, we remain within the system which Shaftesbury first proposes as the system where virtue is "its own reward," the question "What reason is there for my being virtuous?'

112

is inappropriate. It amounts to asking 'Why ought I to do what I ought to do?' Within Shaftesbury's explanation of *what* virtue is, the very description of an act's being virtuous carries with it, though implicitly, the ultimate reason for doing it. It is therefore inappropriate, *within* the system, to ask for a *further* reason for doing the act. But 'ought,' 'virtue,' 'reason' and most other key concepts in the language of morality function in various ways and at various levels. (This is one of the things Hutcheson learned from Shaftesbury, although whether the awareness or learning was explicit or implicit in either case raises fine points of interpretation, scholarship and history.) It is a function of an indefinitely large number of factors in human nature just how far such a series of requests for reasons will in fact be pushed. In effect what Shaftesbury does in answering the question 'What reason is there for pursuing virtue?' is simply to shift to a more inclusive framework within which the whole process of acting virtuously can in fact be questioned. Within this more inclusive framework it is appropriate to ask why anyone should be affected practically by the explanation of virtue which Shaftesbury has formulated. Butler, it may be noticed, in his famous "cool hour" passage was dealing with the same kind of problem. What is implicit in these cases, and important to learn from these writers, is that the moral context, broad, vague, ramified as it may be, is an *included* context that still permits challenge and demand for justification. To this recognition Shaftesbury's writings, whether he explicitly intended so or not, represent significant contributions.

Bibliography

Shaftesbury's published works:

Select Sermons of Benjamin Whichcote, ed. with preface by Shaftesbury (1698).

Characteristicks of Men, Manners, Opinions, Times, three volumes (1711). Includes:

Letter Concerning Enthusiasm

Sensus Communis; an essay on the Freedom of Wit and Humour

The Moralists, a Philosophical Rhapsody

Soliloquy, or Advice to an Author

An Enquiry Concerning Virtue or Merit

Miscellaneous Reflections on the preceding Treatises, and other Critical Subjects

Historical Draught or Tablature of the Judgment of Hercules

Letter Concerning Design

Several Letters, written by a Noble Lord to a Young Man at the University (1716).

Letters from the late Earl of Shaftesbury to R. Molesworth Esq. (1721).

The Original Letters of Locke, Sidney and Shaftesbury, ed. by T. Forster (1830).

The Life, Unpublished Letters and Philosophical Regimen of Anthony, Earl of Shaftesbury, ed. by B. Rand (London and New York, 1900).

Second Characters, or the Language of Forms, ed. by B. Rand (Cambridge, 1914).

Commentaries:

Thomas Fowler, *Shaftesbury and Hutcheson* (London, 1882).

James Martineau, *Types of Ethical Theory* (Oxford, 1889), pp. 487–513.

James Bonar, *Moral Sense* (New York and London, 1930), Ch. 1.

E. T. Mitchell, *A System of Ethics* (New York, 1950), Part II, Ch. 10.

R. L. Brett, *The Third Earl of Shaftesbury* (London,, Hutchinson's, 1951).

Bernard Peach, "Shaftesbury, the Mathematical Analogy and Conduct," *The Personalist*, forthcoming.

Bernard Peach
Duke University

Cooper, Anthony Ashley (Shaftesbury, Third Earl of): *see* Balguy, John; Clarke, Samuel; Cudworth, Ralph; Cumberland, Richard; Goethe, Johann Wolfgang von; Hutcheson, Francis; Major Ethical Viewpoints; More, Henry.

cooperation: *see* Marxist Theory of Morals; Mundurucu Indians, A Dual System of Ethics; Navaho Morals; Rio Grande Pueblo Indians; Spinoza.

corruption: *see* Soviet Morality, Current; Zuni Indians, Morals of.

corruption of human nature: *see* Christian Moral Philosophy.

cosmology: *see* Hindu Ethics; Pakot, the Moral System of.

cosmopolitanism: *see* Minor Socratics; Stoics, the.

Cotton, John: *see* Puritan Morals.

Council of Trent: *see* Jesuits, the, Moral Theology of.

counteraction: *see* Balguy, John.

courage: *see* Aquinas, Thomas, Morals of; Aristotle; Augustine and Morals; Aztec Morals; China, Moral Philosophies of; Minor Socratics; Muslim Morals; Navaho Morals; Plato; Riffian Morals; Stoics, the.

courtesy: *see* Aztec Morals; Hindu Ethics; Muslim Morals; Navaho Morals.

Cousin, Victor: *see* Moral Philosophy in America.

covenants: *see* Cudworth, Ralph; Puritan Morals.

covetousness: *see* Hindu Ethics; Muslim Morals; Zuni Indians, Morals of.

cowardice: *see* Aztec Morals.

Crates: *see* Minor Socratics.

creation: *see* Augustine and Morals; Clarke, Samuel; Jewish Ethics and Its Civilization; Primitive Morals; Spinoza.

creativity: *see* Soviet Morality, Current.

creeds: *see* Jewish Ethics and Its Civilization.

crimes: *see* Marxist Theory of Morals; Pakot, the Moral System of; Soviet Morality, Current; Zuni Indians, Morals of.

criminal, the: *see* Freud, Sigmund.

criteria: *see* Meta-ethics and Normative Ethics.

criticism, philosophical: *see* Morals and Religion.

Cromwell: *see* Puritan Morals.

cruelty: *see* Hindu Ethics; Major Ethical Viewpoints; Marxist Theory of Morals; Puritan Morals; Schopenhauer, Arthur; Stoics, the; Tapirapé Morals, Some Aspects of.

Cudworth, Ralph

Ralph Cudworth was born at Aller, Somersetshire, England, in 1617. He received his early education from his stepfather, Dr. Stoughton, entering Emmanuel College, Cambridge in 1632. He received his M.A. in 1639 and became a fellow. In 1641 he became rector of North Cadbury in Somersetshire. In 1642 he published *A Discourse Concerning the True Notion of the Lord's Supper* and a treatise entitled *The Union of Christ and the Church.* In 1644 he received his B.D. and became master of Clare Hall. In 1645 he was appointed professor of Hebrew. On March 31, 1647 he preached before the House of Commons. In 1654 he became master of Christ's College. During the Protectorate he was frequently, though confidentially, consulted about university and governmental appointments. In 1662 he became rector of Ashwell in Hertfordshire and in 1678 prebend of Gloucester. In 1678 he also published *The True Intellectual System of the Universe.* He died in 1688. His daughter, Damaris, later became Lady Masham, friend of John Locke at whose estate the great philosopher spent the last years of his life. *A Treatise on Eternal and Immutable Morality* was published in 1731, and in 1838 *A Treatise on Free Will.* Both of these are portions of the greater work suggested in various places in the *True Intellectual System* that Cudworth never carried through to completion. The remainder of his work remains in manuscript form in the British Museum where, until the recent excavations of J. A. Passmore (*Ralph Cudworth: An Interpretation,* Cambridge, 1951) its significance remained almost entirely unappreciated. This is particularly so with Cudworth's "psychology of morals," and on that subject most of my exposition is derived from Passmore's summary of the manuscripts.

It is impossible to separate Cudworth's theory of knowledge and metaphysics from his ethics. Indeed in his published works there are only metaphysical and epistemological prolegomena to ethics, and even in his manuscript remains there is little that could be called a system of ethics in any sense that would imply a system of specific rights and duties. This reflects his conviction that the best method of preparing a person to be moral is to prepare his mind to understand the foundations of morality, and these are metaphysical, epistemological, psychological and theological. The task of the moral philosopher is to describe the good life, not to draw up a set of rules.

Cudworth's metaphysic is basically a dualism combining Hobbesian atomism and Platonic realism. Cudworth admits, indeed insists on, atomism as a true description of the material universe. But he equally insists that it is incomplete, calling for an explanation of motion that can be provided only by something completely different from passive matter; therefore, active mind. There are of course many complications that can arise from such a metaphysical dualism, not the least of which is the epistemological dualism which also characterizes Cudworth's doctrine. The fields of sense and understanding are different from one another, yet sense is not wholly material and passive. There is some activity (cogitation) even in sensing; yet it is not knowledge. Knowledge is an activity of the immaterial soul involving judgments and relations. Many

115

relations are not derived from sense but are innate in the activity of the mind itself, e.g., cause, effect; means, end; similarity, dissimilarity; genus, species; whole, part. Some of them are of particular ethical significance, e.g., order, proportion, symmetry, aptitude, for in so far as these are components of moral judgments they cannot be explained as generalizations from sense observations. The mind itself "gives rise to them." Such relations, however, are not therefore fictitious entities. They are the basic components of true reality. Reality is relational and rational and, as such, reality must be regarded as the mind of God. The discovery of truth is a discovery of an aspect of universal mind, something eternal and immutable. On such metaphysical, epistemological and theological foundations Cudworth argues that moral relations and concepts of such relations are not arbitrary, but are eternally and immutably moral, by their very nature. No arbitrary power, whether a group of citizens compacting with one another, an absolute monarch, or God himself by an arbitrary act of will, can make moral what is in its nature immoral, or conversely, any more than such a power could alter the sum of the interior angles of a triangle, or make true what is false.

Still Cudworth cannot rule out altogether the ethical significance of commands of a superior. So he draws a distinction between things that are good in themselves, "by nature" or "materially" and those that are good "by accident" or "formally":

There are some things which the intellectual nature obligeth to *per se,* of itself, and directly, absolutely and perpetually, and these things are called naturally good or evil; other things there are which the same intellectual nature obligeth to by accident only, hypothetically, upon condition of some voluntary action either of our own or some other person's by means whereof those things which were in their own nature indifferent, falling under something that is absolutely good or evil and thereby acquiring a new relation to the intellectual nature, do for the time being become such things as ought to be done or omitted, being made such not by will but by nature.

Indifferent things commanded, considered materially in themselves remain still what they were before in their own nature, that is, indifferent . . . all the moral goodness, justice and virtue that is exercised in obeying positive commands, and doing such things as are positive only and to be done for no other cause but because they are commanded, or in respect to political order, consisteth not in the materiality of the actions themselves, but in that formality of yielding obedience to the commands of lawful authority in them . . . wherefore in positive commands the will of the commander does not create any new moral entity, but only diversely modifies and determines that general duty or obligation or natural justice to obey lawful authority and keep oaths and covenants.

These doctrines are the characteristic ones on the basis of which Cudworth is usually classified as a rationalist. But when we come to his concern for conduct, we find in his unpublished manuscripts a moral psychology that is quite different from the rigid rationalistic doctrines of, say, Samuel

Clarke, usually considered a "follower" of Cudworth.

Cudworth rejects the faculty psychology of "Reason, Will and Desire." They cannot be so sharply distinguished, a complication of all three entering into many acts. It is the whole man who understands, wills, and desires. Cudworth therefore asserts that mere reason is not sufficient to explain either the cognizance of moral qualities or relations or action following upon such cognizance:

As the first spring of vital action is not from the speculative understanding, so neither is dry and insipid ratiocination the only measure of good and evil. . . . It is not sapless speculative knowledge that is the proper rule or judge of good and evil, but vital touches, tastes and savours. . . . The first principle by which good and evil are distinguished is vital, not notional. (Passmore, *Ralph Cudworth*, p. 66.)

It is the person who judges, desires, and acts, not reason that knows, appetite that desires, and will that acts. This is an artificial division of the unity of the moral agent that creates more problems for moral philosophy than it solves.

On the other hand Cudworth does not uncritically overemphasize this unity of person. There are in fact divisive factors operating in conduct. What Cudworth does insist upon is that these conflicts are not conflicts between different faculties but between different ways of life. He calls them, in the Christian tradition, the way of the flesh and the way of the spirit; but no soul (person) is ever wholly encompassed in one or the other. They are in fact divisive factors operating in conduct. They are simply "higher" and "lower" manifestations of the complex elements that make up the whole person; and the reason that functions in the one case is "superior" to the reason that functions in the other. Both, however, are integrated with the emotional elements of the person. "Inferior Reason" is prudence. "Superior Reason" is love of moral excellence. The animal appetites are egoistic, the spiritual appetites are impartial, dominated by a passion for universality, free from self-love.

The problem of freedom, then, is not whether the will is free but whether the person is free to choose between the egoistic forces of the animal appetites and the spiritual forces of universal love. In attempting to deal with this problem Cudworth distinguishes three kinds of freedom, in connection with each of which he says things that are difficult to reconcile with what he says of the others. First, we have some power, he asserts, to promote the good life, that is, the life concerned with and devoted to the higher good of the life of spirit. Second, he asserts that the operation of this power is not a matter of sheer spontaneity. He emphatically rejects the "vulgar doctrine" that freedom is "indifferency to act or not to act." It is not "in accord with the phenomena" to hold that "the wickedest person might in a moment by his free will make himself as holy as a seraphim." The freedom we do have in this sense is a freedom to choose the good life as opposed to its opposite, because as

117

persons we are neither totally perfect nor totally imperfect. Freedom in this sense then is the capacity to prefer the spiritual to the animal life. Third, there is a freedom of not exercising this capacity. Recognition of this freedom is required because the second doctrine does not explain sin by attributing it to man's freedom. Sin is considered by Cudworth to be a failure to realize our greatest possibilities; and it is due to man because he has the freedom of not exercising his capacity to choose the spiritual life.

Cudworth's final problem is whether there is freedom, in the metaphysical sense, to make these choices. He proposes "an indifferent voluntaneity," "the voluntary non-exercise of free-will," in an effort to solve this problem, but recognizes that he is not successful. Although he must finally remain dissatisfied with his own discussion of freedom, he knows of none that is more satisfactory. And he does consider it at least satisfactory enough to provide a foundation for his views about what constitutes the good life and about the relation of religion to ethics.

The good life is the impartial life—loving good as good, universally. In it there is mutual compliance and promotion. It is a life of system and order. It is a life of beauty—a triumph of unity over diversity. It is a creative life—"the active exertion of love itself." Happiness is not the reward of goodness but is contained in the processes that make up the good life.

Religion is no set of propositions or ceremonies. It is not a way of achieving salvation by adopting severities. Religion is a combination of a certain state and a certain process: having a good mind and living a good life. Since it is not necessary to regard every act as either opposing or assisting the will of God there is no need to regard every act as either opposing or assisting our search for salvation. The general character of a life is the important thing, not necessarily every minute act. Yet Cudworth's doctrine of virtue is made up of the traditional Christian virtues. Of these he greatly emphasizes love, but also includes "mortification of lust," patience, contentment, resignation. His theory of freedom is an important basis for his insistence upon the importance of praise and blame and his consequent insistence that everyone must have an equal chance to follow the good life. Cudworth's emphasis upon goodness as the basic ethical concept rather than obligation leads him to reinterpret "obedience" as "participation in God's will." Such participation is a direct contact with the source of universal love—the release from all bondage to egoism.

Although it is difficult to evaluate the historical significance of Cudworth from the standpoint of his influence, it is quite clear that he influenced Locke, particularly in Locke's arguments for the existence of God and in the rationalistic doctrines of Book IV of the *Essay Concerning Human Understanding*. In ethics the famous but undeveloped doctrine of the mathematical demonstrability of morals is probably the most direct influence and there is similar internal evidence of influence in Locke's attack on the "indifferentist" doctrine of free-will, his definition of volition and other details of moral psychology. With the new awareness of the significance of the Cudworth manuscripts it now seems likely that there could have been a direct influence even upon Shaftesbury, often regarded as an enemy of rationalism and Platonism in its theological adaptations. The similarity between doctrines of Cudworth and Shaftesbury is undeniable: the humanism of their ethics, an intellectualism that is compatible with a recognition of the importance of the emotions, an appeal to the mathematical analogy, the regarding of virtue as really "something in itself" . . . not arbitrary or factitious," the emphasis upon system and order, and the view that selfishness is the basic vice. On external evidence there is also a good case for influence. Shaftesbury refers twice to Cudworth in his published writings, linking his name sympathetically with that of his predecessor. Cudworth's daughter lent books to Shaftesbury and the manuscripts could have been among them. So it is possible, even likely, that Shaftesbury knew the doctrines of the Cudworth manuscripts and therefore somewhat more likely that the similarities of doctrine are the result of fairly direct influences. On the other hand, a recognition of the moral psychology of the manuscripts indicates that the influence of Cudworth upon Samuel Clarke was not so great as has been previously supposed. The theory of motivation there is certainly not Clarke's and it appears from Clarke's references that many of his rationalistic doctrines derive from certain passages in Cumberland and Whichcote.

The references of Richard Price, to Cudworth, however, are frequent and explicit. Passmore in fact asserts that Price's epistemology and metaphysics are "simply appropriated from Cudworth." This may do Price an injustice, but certainly the influence was very strong. Price's ethical theory, on the other hand, Passmore finds, is much more like Clarke's than Cudworth's, although it is like the view tradition has ascribed to Cudworth in ignorance of his manuscript remains.

Cudworth's influence upon many minor British thinkers, and upon Berkeley and Leibniz, the French Encyclopedists and Janet is an investigation that remains to be undertaken, but one which would almost certainly lead to results that would be enhanced both in breadth and depth by a recognition of the significance of Cudworth's manuscripts.

Undoubtedly there are many difficulties in Cudworth's doctrines. He compromises his eternal and immutable morality by maintaining that certain indifferent acts can become moral by becoming the object of a command. And he cannot save the immutability by drawing a distinction between "moral by nature" and "moral by accident." He cannot hold the humanistic ethics of some of the manuscripts and sermons without compromising the theological and Christian basis which he also attempts to provide for his ethics. Indeed he is aware of the difficulty, although he does not recognize its strength, when he asserts that if he had to choose between Christianity and philosophy he would choose philosophy. The inadequacies of his doctrine of human freedom he himself recognized and admitted. He attempted to make goodness the central concept of his ethics and also retain the traditional Christian emphasis upon obligation and obedience. This creates a tension in the relation between goodness and obligation which leads him toward either a fragmentation of the unity of the self, with reason and passion opposing one another, or to an admission that obligation and goodness are not so closely connected as some of his doctrines would indicate. And there is a difficulty in his attributing the tremendous variety of impartial, non-egoistic engagements of individuals to a source in a unitary and single person even though that person is greater than human. Nevertheless it must be recognized that Cudworth strongly influenced the two main streams of ethical development of the eighteenth century: rationalism and sentimentalism. And in so far as those movements have extended an influence, the influence of Cudworth has also extended.

Bibliography

Ralph Cudworth, *A Sermon Preached Before the Honourable House of Commons* (Cambridge, 1647).
——, *A Sermon Preached to the Honourable Society of Lincolnes-Inne* (London, 1664).
——, *The True Intellectual System of the Universe, Wherein all the Reason and Philosophy of Atheism is Confuted, and Its Impossibility Demonstrated* (London, 1678).
——, *A Treatise Concerning Eternal and Immutable Morality* (London, 1731).
——, *A Treatise on Free Will* (London, 1838).
——, For a description on the Manuscript Works, see J. A. Passmore, *Ralph Cudworth: An Interpretation* (Cambridge, 1951).
Wm. Whewell, *Lectures on Moral Philosophy* (Cambridge, 1852), Lecture IV.
C. E. Lowry, *The Philosophy of Ralph Cudworth* (New York, 1884).
J. Martineau, *Types of Ethical Theory* (Oxford, 1889), Vol. II, pp. 427–458.
W. R. Scott, *An Introduction to Cudworth's Treatise Concerning Eternal and Immutable Morality* (London, 1891).
J. H. Muirhead, *The Platonic Tradition in Anglo-Saxon Philosophy* (London, 1931).
E. Cassirer, *The Platonic Renaissance in England* (Austin, Texas, 1953).
A. N. Prior, *Logic and the Basis of Ethics* (Oxford, 1949).
J. A. Passmore, "The Moral Philosophy of Cudworth," *Australasian Journal of Psychology and Philosophy*, Vol. 20.
——, *Ralph Cudworth: An Interpretation* (Cambridge, 1951).

Bernard Peach
Duke University

Cudworth, R.: *see* **Clarke, Samuel; Cooper, Anthony Ashley; More, Henry; Price, Richard.**

cult: *see* **Jewish Ethics and Its Civilization.**

cultural isolation: *see* **Riffian Morals.**

cultural pressures: *see* Rio Grande Pueblo Indians.

culture: *see* Aboriginals of Yirkalla; Ayer, Alfred J.; Marxist Theory of Morals; Morals and Religion; Pakot, the Moral System of; Primitive Morals; Psychology and Morals; Rio Grande Pueblo Indians; Zuni Indians, Morals of.

Cumberland, Richard

Richard Cumberland was born in London in 1632 and educated at St. Paul's school and at Magdalene College, Cambridge. He took the degree of B.A. in 1653 and in 1656 received the M.A. degree from both Cambridge and Oxford. He acquired a B.D. in 1663 and a D.D. in 1680. During the years immediately after graduation from Cambridge he studied medicine although he never practiced. His knowledge of biology, anatomy and medicine shows up frequently in the examples that appear in his main ethical writing. His main work in ethics, *The Laws of Nature* (full title in English translation from the original Latin: Philosophical Inquiry into the Laws of Nature, Wherein the Essence, the Principal Heads, the Order, the Publication, and the Obligation of these Laws are Deduced from the Nature of Things, Wherein also the Principles of Mr. Hobbes' Philosophy both in a State of Nature, and of Civil Society are Examined into and Refuted) was published in 1672 when Cumberland was forty years old. This was the same year Puffendorf's *De Jure Naturae et Gentium* appeared. Puffendorf's favorable attitude toward Cumberland's book aided its popularity on the Continent where it had several editions and was translated into French.

Cumberland's advancement in the Church was aided by men who had been his friends during his college days, although Cumberland was no favor-seeker. He was successively Chaplain to the lord keeper of London, rector at Brampton in Northamptonshire, preacher to Cambridge University, rector of Allhallows at Stamford and finally Bishop of Peterborough.

He retained a healthy vigor throughout his long life, remaining active physically well beyond his eightieth year. He learned the Coptic language at the age of eighty-three and discussed helpfully the Coptic translation of the New Testament with its translator, Dr. Wilkins. He died in 1718 in his eighty-seventh year sitting in a chair with a book in his hand.

He was a man of such serenity it is reported that he never displayed anger throughout his entire life.

He did not marry.

Cumberland's moral philosophy can be formulated and explained independently of his appeal to the laws of nature, but using his own framework in which the laws of nature are central is more appropriate to his own attitude and approach. His appeal to the concept of the laws of nature was due historically to the influence of the works of Grotius, Hobbes and others, who used the concept in enunciating their political and moral philosophies. He considered that his doctrine of the laws of nature, indeed, that his entire moral and political philosophy opposed that of Hobbes, but the opposition between them on the concept of natural laws is a matter of detail. They were agreed in regarding them as "eternal and immutable principles regulative of voluntary action." They disagreed, however, about the content of natural law and the means of making it effective.

Cumberland gives several versions of the one fundamental law of nature, to which all the various laws of nature (which he does not enumerate) can be reduced. These various statements reflect Cumberland's conviction that a law does not have to be stated in a special form to be a law. It sometimes appears as a statement of fact, sometimes as an explicit command or imperative, and sometimes in the "gerundive" form as an ascription of obligation: The version offered in Chapter I, section IV illustrates the factual and imperative aspects:

There is one fundamental law of nature: The greatest benevolence of every rational agent towards all constitutes the happiest state of all in general and of each in particular, as far as is in their power to procure it; and is necessarily requisite in order to attain the happiest state to which they can aspire; and therefore the common good of all is the supreme law.

If we combine the major emphases of the other versions of the one fundamental law of nature they summarize in this way: Benevolence, an active concern for the welfare of others, is the best means of achieving happiness and perfection in the social whole, as a whole, and in its individual members,

as individuals. Benevolence is commanded; everyone ought to be benevolent.

Much of Cumberland's book is devoted to "establishing" the law of nature in this protean significance and much of his moral philosophy can be understood from the various claims he makes in this regard. He explicitly states that the law can be established in either of two ways; but he attempts to do so in several others also.

Some ways of establishing the law of nature are epistemological. We may, for example, show how we come to know it. Cumberland maintains we may "start from effects and infer causes" or "start from causes and infer effects." Those who appeal to empirical moral similarities in various cultures and eras use the first method. Cumberland prefers the second because it indicates more conclusively the divine source of the law of nature: The general import of many arguments, by which Cumberland claims to illustrate this method, is that purpose is apparent throughout the natural realm, most natural events contributing to man's well-being. Such a teleological system must be the effect of a universal mind. Knowing that God is the cause of the laws of nature we thereby also know, in opposition to Hobbes, that no words or arbitrary signs are needed to "promulgate" them. That the laws of nature are laws "in the nature of things" is abundantly evident to all "rationals" in the good consequences which follow their obedience and bad consequences that follow their breach. It is perhaps unnecessary to remark that Cumberland is here following the first epistemological method rather than the second. His claim to certainty in his conclusions, therefore, represents a confusion in his methodology.

He also claims the law of nature can be established by showing that we can come to know it "analytically." He considers each word and phrase from the standpoint of whether we understand them by "internal sense" or "external sense." In short, he offers what would be called an empirical analysis of the law of nature.

He also argues that the law of nature can be established by showing that it is the foundation of morality. He does not clearly distinguish between this claim (which turns out to be that virtue is a form of benevolence) and the claim that the law of nature can be established by showing that it is the essence of rightness. What makes a right act right, he maintains, is that it contributes to the "greatest good of the universe of rational beings." This is of course one version of the natural law itself. The "foundations of morals" were as vaguely treated by Cumberland as by most of his successors.

He also claims to justify the natural law by a deductive argument: If there is a law of nature then particular moral laws must prohibit acts that contribute to the misery rather than to the happiness and perfection of the individual or group. He consequently argues that the law of nature is established because particular moral laws prohibit murder, theft, covetousness and ingratitude. The logical fallacy is no less glaring in the original than in this exposition of it.

There is a close correlation between this argument and another which claims to show that the law of nature is "necessary" and implies not only particular moral laws but also such general moral principles as equality. He claims that it is necessarily the case that benevolence is the best means to happiness, both individual and social and that this implies the necessity of the traditional virtues of industry, patience, moderation, gratitude, honesty and the like. It also implies the right to private property since social well-being is impossible without private property. It implies the moral equality of all men in a way that anticipates Kant's better-known version: "It is inconsistent to act after one manner in relation of oneself and after another manner in relation to others having the same nature."

In another group of arguments Cumberland claims that the law of nature can be established by showing we are obliged to it and that it is a "practical proposition." Cumberland's theory of obligation is legislative in nature and requires a law-giver to declare that actions conformable to his law are necessary for those to whom the law applies. The pains and pleasures consequent upon malevolence and benevolence are a declaration of God's position as law-giver. In addition there are the rewards and punishments in after-life, although Cumberland only mentions these and does not emphasize them, in general avoiding appeal to any tenets of revealed religion in his moral philosophy.

Finally, he asserts that the natural law can be established by showing that it is a "practical proposition." He means by this that the natural law provides, in Hume's later terms, an influencing motive of the will. But in his concern to establish the necessity of this characteristic he fails to distinguish between the right which the natural law has to influence the will and its actual power of influencing the will. There is a suggestion that the natural law will not in fact be practical unless a man in fact accepts as his goal the welfare of others. But Cumberland is more concerned to argue that the natural law has a necessary *de jure* practicality even though it may not have a *de facto* authority . He appeals to the mathematical analogy to support such *de jure* authority, his general argument being that there is as necessary a connection between benevolence as means and general welfare as end as there is between the methods of mathematics as means and valid conclusions as ends. He assumes uncritically that such an analogy necessarily provides a motivating influence to the will. This is an extreme rationalism that tends, by indirection, to raise doubts about the strength of his rationalistic basis for the principles of moral equality and consistency in action.

In "establishing" the natural law Cumberland contributes many suggestions to epistemological methods in ethics. He also makes suggestive contributions to the discussion of the foundations of ethics, offering views that are utilitarian, hedonistic, perfectionistic, and legislative all at once. He combines both an emphasis upon the rationality of morals and a recognition of the function of emotion, the latter often combined with physiological or biological factors that represent the result of empirical observation and experiment. He proposes the basic utilitarian principle that acts are right according as they contribute to the welfare of rational agents and considers society an organic unity within which personal well-being will necessarily derive from social well-being. He formulates an objective theory of morality within which 'right' means 'in accordance with reason.' His appeal to the principle of contradiction in supporting the role of reason in morality avoids any acceptance of innate ideas and is based upon an analogy between consistency in action and in mathematics: The choice of a lesser good in preference to a greater good is the same sort of inconsistency as the affirmation that the whole is equal to, or less than, a part. This is just the kind of practical inconsistency that egoism commits: "In practice it argues as great an imperfection [as in speculation to hold contrary judgments of like things] and is a direct contradiction, in cases perfectly alike, to have different judgments and different volitions, according as myself or another is involved." Practically consistent actions bring a pleasure that he describes as tranquillity or absence of conflicting desires. Morally significant pleasure then is a complex for Cumberland, necessarily connected with unimpeded and effective normal activities of mind and body, a knowledge that others around us are happy. It consists in a tranquil frame of mind, the feeling that we have acted consistently, and the consciousness that we have acted for the common welfare.

We find in Cumberland, then, though never with great clarity, and not always without some confusion, a great many important suggestions for ethics. He is in fact suggestive enough that one writer has said of him that "a careful study of the ethical system of Richard Cumberland in its relation to its predecessors and successors will show it to be one of the three or four most powerful influences in the history of British ethics." (F. C. Sharp, *Mind*, Vol. 21.) His influence was largely transmitted through the writings of Samuel Clarke and Shaftesbury. The first, emphasizing the rationalistic aspects of Cumberland's theory, in turn influenced a long line of rationalistic writers in ethics, extending with more or less directness down to the present, e.g., in W. D. Ross. The latter, emphasizing the empirical aspects of Cumberland's system, in turn influenced a long line of empirical ethical writers including Butler, Hutcheson, Hume, Adam Smith, Jeremy Bentham, John Stuart Mill, and hence extending to the present day in such writers as John Dewey and C. L. Stevenson.

F. C. Sharp claims that Cumberland was the first writer to declare explicitly that the essence of morality is the aim to bring about the greatest attainable good for those affected by the ac-

tion and to derive the corollary that the agent's self has no greater claims than any other self. He finds that many of Cumberland's views about the place of reason in ethics are original; not his doctrines of objectivity of moral distinctions, their independence of God or their "source" in reason; but in his interpretation of the practical application of the rules of logical consistency. Whether these are evaluations which exceed the evidence of history only a careful examination of history's record would reveal. In any case, it would seem clear that Cumberland is one of the most suggestive writers in the history of ethics.

Bibliography

Richard Cumberland, *De Legibus Naturae* (London, 1672). English translation by John Maxwell (London, 1727).

John Tyrell, *A Brief Disquisition of the Laws of Nature* (London, 1672).

Ernest Albee, *A History of English Utilitarianism* (London, 1901).

F. C. Sharp, "The Ethical System of Richard Cumberland and its Place in the History of British Ethics," *Mind*, Vol. 21.

Bernard Peach
Duke University

Cumberland, R.: *see* Clarke, Samuel; Cudworth, Ralph.

cupidity: *see* Dante, Alighieri.

cures: *see* Rio Grande Pueblo Indians.

curiosity: *see* Aboriginals of Yirkalla.

Current Soviet Morality: *see* Soviet Morality, Current.

curse: *see* Pakot, the Moral System of; Puritan Morals.

125

custom: *see* Aboriginals of Yirkalla; Ayer, Alfred J.; convention; Dewey, John; Major Ethical Viewpoints; Morals and Religion; Pakot, the Moral System of; Primitive Morals; Puritan Morals; Riffian Morals; Sophists, the; Tradition; tribal custom.

cycle: *see* Hindu Ethics; Spinoza.

cynicism, moral: *see* Marxist Theory of Morals.

Cynic schools, the: *see* Goethe, Johann Wolfgang von; Minor Socratics; Stoics, the.

Cyrenaics: *see* Goethe, Johann Wolfgang von; Minor Socratics.

Cyrus, the Elder: *see* Minor Socratics.

D

da-da-da: *see* Hindu Ethics.

dancing: *see* Puritan Morals; Rio Grande Pueblo Indians.

Dante Alighieri

Dante Alighieri (1265–1321) was born in the free city-state of Florence in central Italy of a family which belonged to the lesser nobility and to the Guelph or anti-Imperial faction. This party's definitive victory over the Ghibelline partisans of the Emperor, which almost coincided with Dante's birth, provided a setting of comparative calm for his youth and early manhood, thus permitting him to acquire a good education for his day and to pursue his natural artistic, poetic and intellectual bent with only a minimum of military interference. The outstanding event of this youthful period was his romantic, idealized attachment for a girl of his own age, Beatrice Portinari, whom he immortalized in his first work, the *New Life* (1292), and later in his masterpiece, the *Divine Comedy*. This ideal love, like those of the troubadours it resembles, did not prevent him from marrying and establishing a family, nor did his scholarly inclinations keep him from participating in the conduct of public affairs. His name appears with increasing frequency in government records after 1295, and in 1300 he was elected to the commune's highest office, that of prior. At that very moment the more than 30 years' peace was broken by a violent division within the Guelph party. Dante joined the moderate "White" faction. Pope Boniface VIII contrived to secure the victory of the "Blacks" in 1301 and in 1302, Dante, as a leader of the unsuccessful opposition, was condemned to death. Fortunately for himself and posterity he escaped; but he was forced to spend the rest of his life in exile at one or another of the small courts of Northern Italy. He died in the service of Guido Novello da Polenta, of Ravenna, in 1321. His major works are the *Banquet,* a series of philosophical poems with an encyclopedic commentary, begun in the first decade of the fourteenth century and abandoned at about one-quarter of its planned length; the *De Monarchia* in Latin, complete in three books, written probably before the middle of the second decade; and the *Divine Comedy,* completed just before his death.

Each of these works would be of interest in a detailed study of Dante's moral system, for each is concerned directly or indirectly with the philosophical education of mankind; yet it would have been far better for our clear understanding of his final views had only the *Comedy* survived. The vagueness of their chronology, which is still far from any precise solution, the extent and complexity of the works themselves, the mass of accumulated scholarship (and of scholarly ignorance) have combined to obscure the evolutionary relationship of the first two to the *Comedy* and the latter's unquestioned supremacy as a definitive statement of its author's position in all matters philosophical or theological.

Nowhere is this more true than in the all-important question of the role assigned by Dante to Philosophy and the relation he saw between it and Theology; for it is as true of the Florentine as it is of his master, St. Thomas Aquinas, that the first cannot be discussed without some reference to the second. Much is made of his unorthodox separation of the two, in accordance with his theory of the two ends of man, earthly happiness and eternal beatitude, and he can be quoted, quite faithfully, as assigning to Philosophy full charge of this life, leaving to Theology practically no sway this side of the grave. Such quotations, however, will be from the earlier works, especially the *De Monarchia,* and to use them indiscriminately as glosses for the *Comedy* is to deny the authority of the masterpiece to supersede all prior statements, and tends to nullify one of the poem's most urgent and repeated messages: the limitations of human wisdom and its dependence on divine guidance. Virgil's subservience to Beatrice, his powerlessness before the gates enclosing the sins of Injustice, the mad voyage of Ulysses, all underline the correction of an earlier position perilously close to Averroism.

Yet, subject to the above reservation, Dante did entrust to moral philosophy a major role in the education of the will he deemed essential for man to realize the potential of his Christian heritage. This he symbolized in *Purgatory* by having the four stars representing the cardinal virtues, Prudence, Justice, Temperance and Fortitude, shine during the day, the only time when conscious, rational progress might be made; while by night the pilgrim rested secure in the symbolic light of the theological virtues of Faith, Hope and Charity; his education during this time was imparted by visions. In this central book of the *Comedy,* and in the central cantos of the book and consequently of the whole poem, he expounds the Thomistic doctrines of responsibility and free will, of Love as the motivating force of good and of the various categories of evil.

All creatures feel love; in the lower orders this is instinctive and not subject to error, but in man it may err through having an evil object, or through excess or defect of vigor. Man may not desire his own harm nor, as creature, hate his Creator; if he seeks evil, it must be for another; that he rise through another's fall (Pride), that he fear being overshadowed by another (Envy), that he desire unreasonable vengeance for wrong or insult (Anger). Deficient pursuit of the Highest Good is Sloth or Acedia; excessive pursuit of worldly goods and pleasures leads to Avarice, Gluttony and Lust. These, in order of diminishing gravity, are the Capital Vices found in *Purgatory*. Obviously Malice and Heresy have no place here, for no one can be saved in whom these sins persist at the moment of death.

Dante had a particular interest in establishing individual responsibility; first, as justification for his elaborate system of rewards and punishments, and, second, to combat the Epicureanism which was rife among his contemporaries. The newly created soul (he says) moves instinctively toward anything pleasing to it, and that motion is Love, felt by all worldly creatures. Man alone among them, however, is endowed with intellect, which enables him to control his responses; his will is free to choose and the responsibility of his choice is therefore also his.

Rewards of the right choices are, of course, admission to the educative processes of Purgatory where the remaining tendencies toward evil are purged from the subconscious will by variously administered lessons in the corresponding virtues; and, when this has been completed, the vision of God which is Paradise. Punishment of the persistent habit of wrong choices is eternal consignment to Hell, the description of which constitutes the first book of the *Comedy*.

This first book, the well known *Inferno*, represents Dante's understanding of classical (pagan) moral philosophy, reconciled with those of the Christian sins which lend themselves to interpretation on the moral level. His purpose thus closely resembles that of St. Thomas, but to refer to his work as a versification of the *Summa* is inaccurate and unjust, for while he does generally follow the Aquinate, he does so with a full awareness of the older scholar's sources and of his divergences from them. It has been more accurately said that Dante is a faithful follower of St. Thomas's method and that he applies it with considerable skill to Aristotle, Cicero and St. Thomas himself. Indeed, in the predominantly moral *Inferno* he is much more inclined to prefer Aristotle, whom he honors there with the title of "Master of those who know."

His grouping of sins into the three major "dispositions" of Incontinence, Violence and Fraud, in that order of gravity, is a good example of his method and of his independence. His chief authorities, Aristotle, Cicero and St. Thomas, had been in general agreement as to Incontinence and its being least offensive; Dante reflects this in characteristic fashion by seeming to neglect this category in his theoretical discussion. Basing himself on Aristotle's three "moral states to be avoided," he translates the other two as Malice and Mad Bestiality, but makes no distinction between them since the corrupt text of his day made no clear distinction possible. Cicero, however, in his *De Officiis*, had adopted the terms Force and Fraud and had arranged them in that order. St. Thomas, in reviewing past theories, had ignored Cicero and, to achieve some purpose of his own, had assigned to Force or Violence the lowest position. Dante in turn ignores St. Thomas and satisfies his own conviction by following Cicero both as to terminology and scale of values; although he does not openly refer to the Roman, he provides a devious clue by condemning Fraud as "proper to Man." The complexity of the whole problem is again reflected characteristically by the occasional use of other terms and by the introduction of complicating elements.

Complications, indeed, appear at the very outskirts of Hell, where Dante locates those guilty of refusing to act in accordance with any moral principles, such as the angels who sided with neither God nor Lucifer. By some this is linked with Aristotle's *Ignavia;* it is at least possible that it represents Acedia of the Active Life. Immediately inside Hell, but not subject to punishment, are the victims of Original Sin: unbaptized children and virtuous heathens, among whom are found several famous Moslems.

The first of the standard vices encountered under Incontinence is Lust, most natural and hence most excusable of deviations. Here we meet the retributive principle of the counter-passion in its imitative form: for having allowed themselves to be carried away by passion, these souls are eternally carried along by a tempestuous wind. Next come the Gluttons, guilty of a natural but ignoble vice, and these lie prostrate in filth under a cold rain. After them we find an interesting example of the Aristotelian interpretation of vice as deviation from a virtuous mean; in this case, Avarice and Prodigality. These sinners push great weights half-way round a circle, in opposition in Hell as they were in life.

In the fourth and final sin of Incontinence, Anger, we meet a novelty, for not only are the two excesses represented by Sullenness and Violent Anger, but Dante himself illustrates the virtue of Just Anger or Righteous Indignation as he takes pleasure in seeing one of the damned set upon not only by the others but, in his blind rage, by himself.

Between this "disposition" and the second occurs the area of complications alluded to above. It begins with the first of the warnings against overconfidence in Philosophy or Reason as Virgil, its representative, is powerless to penetrate the citadel of Lower Hell without the aid of a Divine Messenger. Appropriately enough, the Christian sin of Despair is here suggested allegorically, though Dante carefully refrains from assigning it a place by name. No such scruples hide the next "intrusion" of Christian sin, for these damned are clearly identified as Arch-heretics. This is rationalized, however, by calling them "Epicurus and his followers," although only Christians are singled out. It is clear, too, that this was the heresy of unbelief in the immortality of the soul; schismatics will be found in the lowest major category. It can be argued that it represents, under its allegorical veil, another Christian sin, Acedia of the Contemplative Life; the location is suggestive, since it serves to introduce Lower Hell, as the opposite form of the vice can be said to have introduced Upper Hell.

Before proceeding to illustrate Violence, Dante has Virgil discourse on its several categories which are, in order of increasing seriousness, violence (1) against one's neighbor in his person or his goods (2) against oneself, likewise in person or goods, and (3) against God, Nature or Art. The second "disposition" is therefore so divided. It is worthy of note that from here on we find sins or vices defined with reference to external operations; so in the first subdivision of Violence we are shown tyrants, assassins and robbers-with-assault immersed in varying degree in a river of blood. In the middle division, lower and hence more serious, are the suicides, deprived eternally of their human form, and the wastrels pursued and torn by dogs. In the final and worst category of Violence the blasphemers against God (the sole example is pagan, Capaneus) lie motionless under a fiery snow, while the sodomites run eternally over the unnatural landscape.

Dante's method of showing an otherwise estimable and beloved character destroyed by a vice here finds one of its greatest expressions in the episode of Brunetto Latini. A person of essential nobility, philosopher and scholar, a man of letters who had grasped the value of the intellectual life, he is eternally lost through his unnatural vice. This great moral lesson is intensified if one looks back to the person used as an example of Violent Anger, Argenti, described as a completely unworthy, unsympathetic man, and compares his lighter punishment with that meted out with growing severity to the series of far worthier characters each of whom has nullified his accomplishments by his transgression of moral law.

Such a backward glance will reveal also the close connection Dante saw between that worst sin of Incontinence, whose violence constantly threatens injury to one's neighbor (which is contrary to the basic characteristic of Incontinence) and the "disposition" of Violence itself. The contrary is true of the transition from the second to the final category, Fraud; Dante literally separates these by an enormous gulf which indicates that he felt the latter to be not only worse but immeasurably so. The total deterioration of character implied by Fraud is symbolized in Geryon, the beast which carries Dante and Virgil down through the gulf; its body recalls the false attractiveness of sins of the appetite, its forepaws suggest the violence and force we have just left, while its human head and face ("That of a just man") represents the corruption of the intellect which Dante associated with Fraud.

There is no question that Dante arranged his *Hell* for the purpose of condemning Injustice under the guise of Fraud. This derives logically from what we know of his attitude toward its opposite; for him, Love of Justice is the crowning virtue. In fact, he follows the *Summa* in equating Charity with Justice, thus effecting a sort of union of the theological and philosophical systems. Following scattered statements made by his predecessors about the danger to society of several forms of Injustice, Dante divides Fraud into two chief types: the first breaks only the natural or social bond which should unite all men; the second breaks some special tie of loyalty or love, and this worst of all sins is Treachery.

In order to stress the social menace of Simple Fraud he organizes the arrangement of its various outer manifestations into a sort of community with ten compartments, called "Malebolge" or "Evil Pouches." But there is a further moral significance in this title: "pouches" suggests "pockets" or "purses," and almost every one of these sins is rooted in Cupidity. This is not to be confused with the Avarice of Incontinence, for where this is conservative, tenacious, Dante's Cupidity is aggressive; Greed, perhaps, as contrasted with Illiberality. Another contrast between the first "disposition" and this last is also stressed: whereas Incontinence destroys itself and Violence-Bestiality may be directed against another, Fraud-Malice invariably aims to destroy one's neighbor.

We thus meet first those who made use for their own gain of the sexual appetite of others—Panders and Seducers. Here we have a compounding of Lust, Fraud and Greed. Next come the Flatterers, who cater to the natural hunger for praise and are prodigal with it. The third "pouch" contains the Simonists who sold sacred things for love of money. The counterpassion is interesting here: as they inverted values in life, so they are here inverted and placed in holes or pockets. Then we see the Fortune Tellers who attempted to defeat Fortune for their gain. After them we see the Grafters, who misused public office for gain;

this is more serious than Simony, for it attacks the very government of Society, whereas Simony cannot destroy the true essence of the Church which should be spiritual. Hypocrisy, which follows, is a counterfeiting of virtue prompted by the sort of pride and arrogance we earlier saw linked with Anger. In the seventh "pouch" we find Theft by Stealth, as contrasted with Theft by Violence encountered in the second great division. It also suggests Usury, found in the same earlier division, in its attempt to defeat Art.

The most memorable incident in this rather gruesome parade of vice occurs in the eighth "pouch," where Dante meets Ulysses, as a "Fraudulent Counselor," who suffers for the many wiles he practiced himself and prepared for others. Yet what he narrates is his imaginary final voyage beyond the Pillars of Hercules, on till he sighted his goal, the mountain of Purgatory; then his presumption is punished by divine fury. This is the last of Dante's warnings of the inadequacy of human reason, at least in the *Inferno*. The next-to-the-last "pouch" is where we find the Schismatics, sowers of discord in church, state and family; it has been pointed out that their sin seems more akin to sedition than to heresy. The final "pouch" is essentially a sin against Truth: counterfeiting of metals, of persons, of coinage. In counting this vice lowest of all in Simple Fraud, Dante was following St. Thomas: ". . . it would be impossible for men to live together unless they believed one another."

The final category, Treachery, is

likewise subdivided. There are four such divisions, for betrayers of relatives, for traitors to country, betrayers of guests and, finally, of benefactors. Appropriately they are embedded in ice, to symbolize the absence of love and the hardness of heart associated with this vice. Dante himself is cold and cruel to the souls he encounters, and indulges in a cold humor. The final example is Lucifer, angelic intelligence and beauty reduced to bestial ugliness, rebellious pride converted to an impotent, servile instrument of Divine Justice.

It will be observed that there is no mention made by Dante of the gravest capital sins of Pride and Envy. As with Acedia, their presence can be deduced as the root of other manifestations, especially in the categories of Fraud. It must be remembered that Dante's is a philosophical, not a theological hell; the Capital Vices, so clearly present in *Purgatory*, have no overt place in Hell and even those treated under Incontinence are there, in all probability, because Dante thought them basic to both systems.

Bibliography

M. Baldini, *La costruzione morale dell'Inferno di Dante* (Città di Castello, 1914).
A. H. Gilbert, *Dante's Conception of Justice* (Durham, N.C., 1925).
E. Gilson, *Dante the Philosopher* (New York, 1949).
E. Moore, *Studies in Dante,* Second Series (Oxford, 1899).
B. Nardi, *Dante e la cultura medievale* (Bari, 1949).
——, *Nel mondo di Dante* (Roma, 1944).
——, *Saggi di filosofia dantesca* (Milano, 1930).
W. H. V. Reade, *The Moral System of Dante's Inferno* (Oxford, 1909).

Archibald T. MacAllister
Princeton University

Dante, A.: *see* Goethe, Johann Wolfgang von.
Darwin, Charles: *see* Freud, Sigmund; Major Ethical Viewpoints; Moral Philosophy in America.
Darwinism: *see* Soviet Morality, Current.
death: *see* Aztec Morals; China, Moral Philosophies of; Hobbes, Thomas; Schopenhauer, Arthur; Pakot, the Moral System of; Primitive Morals.
death impulse: *see* Freud, Sigmund.
debauchery: *see* Clarke, Samuel.
Deborin: *see* Soviet Morality, Current.
debts: *see* Jewish Ethics and Its Civilization.
Decalogue: *see* Aquinas, Thomas, Moral Views of.
deceit: *see* Freud, Sigmund; Hindu Ethics; Kant, I.; lying; Riffian Morals; Sophists, the.
decency: *see* Hindu Ethics; Puritan Morals.
decision: *see* Psychology and Morals; Schlick, Moritz.
decorum: *see* Navaho Morals; Puritan Morals.
deduction: *see* mathematics; Reid, Thomas; Spinoza.
definability: *see* Price, Richard.
degeneracy: *see* Plato.
degrees of goodness: *see* Stoics, the.
deism: *see* Butler, Joseph; Moral Philosophy in America.

delinquency: *see* Puritan Morals; Riffian Morals.

de Lugo, J.: *see* Jesuits, the, Moral Theology of.

demands: *see* Schlick, Moritz.

Dembski: *see* Soviet Morality, Current.

demeanor: *see* Puritan Morals.

de Medina, B.: *see* Jesuits, the, Moral Theology of.

demerit: *see* Reid, Thomas.

Demetrius: *see* Minor Socratics.

democracy: *see* Berdyaev, Nicolas; Dewey, John; Kant, I.; Marxist Theory of Morals; Moral Philosophy in America; Quakerism, Classical, The Morality of; Sophists, the; Soviet Morality, Current; Utilitarianism.

Democritus: *see* Sophists, the.

demon: *see* Hindu Ethics.

denial: *see* Schopenhauer, Arthur.

deontological ethics: *see* Hartmann, Nicolai.

deontologism: *see* Ross, Sir (William) David.

dependence: *see* Freud, Sigmund.

depravity: *see* Stoics, the.

depth psychology: *see* Psychology and Morals.

Descartes, R.: *see* Clarke, Samuel; Major Ethical Viewpoints; Moral Philosophy in America; More, Henry; Price, Richard; Spinoza.

descriptive ethics: *see* Major Ethical Viewpoints.

design: *see* Aquinas, Thomas, Moral Views of.

desirable: *see* Ayer, Alfred J.; Broad, C. D.; Psychology and Morals; Sophists, the.

desires: *see* Aquinas, Thomas, Moral Views of; Butler, Joseph; Cudworth, Ralph; Dewey, John; Freud, Sigmund; Hindu Ethics; Hobbes, Thomas; Kant, I.; Machiavelli, Niccolo; Major Ethical Viewpoints; Moral Philosophy in America; More, Henry; Plato; Prichard, H. A.; Rio Grande Pueblo Indians; Russell, Bertrand; Schlick, Moritz; Schopenhauer, Arthur; Socrates; Sophists the; Spinoza; Stoics, the; Wollaston, William.

despair: *see* Dante, Alighieri; French Existentialism and Moral Philosophy; Jewish Ethics and Its Civilization; Kierkegaard, Soren; Schlick, Moritz; Soloviev, Wladimir.

despised, the: *see* Freud, Sigmund.

destiny: *see* Aquinas, Thomas, Moral Views of; Berdyaev, Nicholas; Liguori, St. Alphonsus and Catholic Moral Philosophy.

detachment: *see* China, Moral Philosophies of; Hindu Ethics; Minor Socratics.

determination: *see* Hindu Ethics; Psychology and Morals.

determinism: *see* Dewey, John; Freud, Sigmund; historical determinism; Kant, I.; Marxist Theory of Morals; Russell, Bertrand; Soviet Morality, Current; Spinoza; Stoics, the.

Deussen, P.:*see* Schopenhauer, Arthur.

Deuteronomic law: *see* Jewish Ethics and Its Civilization.

devotion: *see* Aquinas, Thomas, Moral Views of.

Dewey, John

John Dewey was a moral philosopher of a new kind. Born at a time when the effects of modern science were just beginning to be felt and its implications to be more or less clearly rcalized, he developed his moral theory slowly and painfully out of existing experience. Unlike many philosophers before him and some after, he spoke to his generation. By suggesting new ideas, implementing them, he sought to make his generation critically aware of the revolutionary meaning of science and democracy for the present and the future. As he said of himself in a rejoinder to critics of his philosophy, his main objective in life was to seek a sensible integration of men's "scientific beliefs" with their beliefs about values. But he felt this objective not merely as his; it was the fundamental problem of modern man. If mankind failed to solve it, modern civilization was destroyed. Before he died, he realized that mankind had approached this critical moment with the development of the atomic bomb.

John Dewey was born in the quiet town of Burlington, Vermont, October 20, 1859, the same year that saw the publication of Charles Darwin's *Origin of the Species*. He went through the public schools to the state university where he graduated in 1879. In 1884, he received his Ph.D. in philosophy at Johns Hopkins University. Between his birth and his doctoral degree, tremendous events occurred: the Civil War came and went; Darwinism won an apparently lasting victory over theology and fundamentalism; Democracy, even though bitterly fought here and abroad, went from one triumph to another; science, too, was conquering new field after field of knowledge. Medicine and psychology were coming into their own. Education was being

placed on both a universal and scientific basis. The new philosophies of Pragmatism and Experimentalism were beginning their struggle to conquer the philosophical world.

Dewey was caught up and enveloped in the vortex of these events. Very soon after receiving his doctorate, he became one of the acknowledged leaders and interpreters of experimental philosophy. As he went from the Universities of Michigan, Minnesota, Chicago, to Columbia University, he published a continual stream of books and articles which analyzed and profoundly affected every phase of American life. His *Education and Democracy, School and Society,* and *Experience and Education* influenced the American educational system so profoundly that it was revolutionized. His psychological theories are just beginning to find application in fields like perception and experimental aesthetics. In logic, he wrote three important books: *How We Think* (1910), *Essays in Experimental Logic* (1916), and *Logic, the Theory of Inquiry* (1939), in which he sought to integrate logic with the actual procedure of valid investigation. In politics, he sought constantly to give an experimental meaning to the problems of a mass-production society. To vivify the sense in which democracy and scientific inquiry are socially interrelated, he wrote the *Public and its Problems* (1927), *Individualism, Old and New* (1930), and *Liberalism and Social Action* (1935). To establish the experimental nature of morality, he wrote *Ethics* (1938), in collaboration with his friend and colleague, James H. Tufts, and the *Theory of Valuation* (1939).

After Dewey retired emeritus from Columbia University, he stopped neither his creative writing nor his interest in public affairs. In the thirties, he attempted to create a Peoples' Party in opposition to the conservative and totalitarian parties. In 1937, he served on a committee to investigate Trotsky's role as a leader of opposition to the Stalin regime in the Soviet Union. He died of pneumonia June 1, 1952, at the age of ninety-two, just at the time when the social tide in America was beginning to turn strongly against all of the ideas for which he had fought so trenchantly and triumphantly during his lifetime.

Dewey and Some Basic Assumptions Concerning Ethical Development

To Dewey, as to many others, the social order is the matrix of ethical theory. There are no ethical schools or doctrines in societies which are both internally and externally harmonious, i.e., in societies which are so fortunately situated that custom is sufficient to solve all basic individual and group problems. However, a changing society, no matter how slowly, creates conflicts both as to ethical norms and consequences. Such conflicts inevitably require ethical clarification and formulation.

The method of solving such conflicts, of achieving ethical clarification and formulation, depends upon the theoretical and technical knowledge at the disposal of a given social order and the attitudes, desires, interests, hopes and expectations of men and groups at a given historical moment or period. As societies rise and fall, they accumulate a huge and conflicting tradition of moral rules and methods all of which are not necessarily acceptable to all groups or individuals living in those societies. Not only in the daily practice of life, but on the higher levels of theoretical analysis, will these rules and methods be opposed to each other as adequate or inadequate.

In general, the majority of men in any given society have taken one or all of three ethical approaches: (a) that what his group or society accepts as right is right; (b) that what derives from some high source—the Gods, Nature, Reason, etc., is right; and (c) that what derives from the way one feels, wants, enjoys, is right. Most men have combined all three methods according to need and circumstance without evaluating them. Moral philosophers in general, have supported either (b) or (c), rejecting (a) as insufficient rationally to support any set of moral principles.

Whatever the approach, the usual ground for its justification has been that it produces the best results for mankind, as a whole. Few philosophers or prophets have argued that evil and suffering are thereby avoided, but merely that less evil and suffering follow from pursuing one or another of the methods espoused.

To Dewey, these traditional methods were outmoded; they no longer sufficed even as rationalizations of the failure of men to solve their social problems. The defects of these methods were too obvious. Neither custom, eternal principles, nor passion has produced rational principles capable today of rationally ordering the lives of millions of humans. Today these methods hamper the objective investigation and solution of problems facing a society based on science. To Dewey, therefore, the only method adequate for this formidable task is scientific method. He pointed out that, wherever it has been applied, it has solved problems previously considered insoluble. The one area where this has not been done is in the social sphere.

The Nature of Scientific Method

Dewey's conception of the experimental method, despite more than half a century of exposition, has been consistently misunderstood by his opponents and even by some of his supporters. Dewey does not identify the experimental or scientific method with the specific procedures of any of the sciences—their specific devices of language, instruments, testing procedures. These, he believed, were the outcome of trying to solve the specific problems which this or that science faced. On the other hand, he did not mean to say that some of these procedures, devices, techniques might not be useful to some other science. Whether this is so or not can only be determined experimentally.

The experimental or scientific method was to Dewey a method of acting and using instrumentalities whether those of language or physical device in such a way that differences of opinion over anticipated consequences or outcomes in nature could be decisively tested and resolved satisfactorily. He meant by "satisfactory solution" one which could be used again and again in predicting with a high degree of success other similar and even different outcomes. The kinds of procedures to be used in any given science are not determinable in advance; they depend upon the nature of the outcomes sought, the conditions under which such outcomes are produced and the relation of human beings to these conditions and outcomes, anticipated and unanticipated, controlled or uncontrolled. Dewey again and again pointed out that the experimental methods of a science like psychology might be very different from those of a science like physics. He objected vigorously to the mechanical transfer of such techniques, based on the naive assumption that what was successful in solving problems in one science is necessarily useful or appropriate to another.

The Experimental Method in Ethics

In general, therefore, what Dewey wanted carried over to ethics is the general procedures of scientific method, those which are characteristic of all the sciences. Whatever else is carried over or used is to be done purely for purposes of testing, experimentation, to see whether they help solve problems. Certain rules, therefore, were established by Dewey as special conditions for the scientific analysis of ethical problems.

137

One rule was that ethical problems, conflicts, must be viewed as part of a given social matrix, as having meaning, significance only in terms of the kinds of difficulties which actually harass individuals and groups at that time. To separate ethical problems from the matrix in which they are born is to reduce them to the arbitrary, to make them, in principle, insoluble. Dewey pointed to the following consequences of the failure to abide by this rule:

(a) that the specific conditions which produce given moral problems are not taken into account, resulting in socially ineffectual proposals;

(b) That moral rules are often proposed which are simply tautological reformulations, not solutions, of the problem;

(c) That moral rules are taken to be unchanging and eternal: This assumption results in intensifying social conflict, since it assumes as fact what is not fact: (i) the non-existence of moral conflict, and (ii) that such conflict ought not to exist, since the right solutions are already known;

(d) That moral rules have no rational basis and can not be justified by any consideration of evidence: Obviously, if the conditions of moral conflict are not to be taken into account, then the conflict over moral rules becomes irrational and unjustifiable. Where are the grounds for the conflict? What relation have they to observable consequences or to the conditions which produced the social conflict?

Dewey pointed out that none of these consequences follow, if one takes moral conflicts as rising out of the conditions of social living. Studying them, one can discover the factors which have produced specific moral conflict, whether individual or social. One can discover (a) where the conflict lies (i) whether in the ends-in-view sought, i.e., the outcomes desired, (ii) in the ends-in-view not sought or desired, (iii) or in the suggested means which will prevent (i) and (ii); and (b) what obstacles—prejudices, institutions, groups, etc.—lie in the way of solution. Moreover, one can concern oneself with (c) finding ways of testing suggested means, and (d) anticipatorily analyzing the adequacy or inadequacy of the suggested means in relation to the ends-in-view sought; and (e) setting up controls derived from these anticipated outcomes for the purpose of evaluating the actual outcomes.

A second rule was to develop new techniques for the observation and control of suggested moral solutions or, as Dewey called them, moral hypotheses. Here Dewey emphasized the need for creative inventiveness and ingenuity. He did not blame ethics for the absence of serious effort to develop such new techniques: he blamed existing institutional obstacles and ideological prejudices. The difficulties to the development of a moral science are, he believed, factual not logical.

The Program for Ethical Inquiry

In the *Theory of Evaluation,* Dewey developed a large-scale hypothesis or program for ethical investigation. For living creatures, and for man, in particular, objects, events, happenings, are not merely scientific—facts, as such; they are also enjoyed or capable of being enjoyed, suffered or capable of causing suffering. As enjoyed or suffered, such objects, events, happenings are not different from any other sort of fact: they are simply facts. But as enjoyable, as desirable, as insufferable, or aversive, they are merely possible verifiers of judgments made about them. The judgments made about them as enjoyable, as desirable, are *value judgments,* and what makes them judgments, propositions, albeit of a special kind, is that they make predictions about the capacity or incapacity of given objects, events or actions to satisfy desires, needs, interests. These as-yet-not-experienced objects, these as-yet-not-enjoyed, not-suffered objects, serve as verifiers of the value-judgments.

Dewey objected strongly to calling the enjoyed or suffered objects values, as Perry and others did. These objects are not values, but only the conditions for the formation of values or value-judgments. Only when such enjoyed or suffered objects are evaluated, i.e., judged as enjoyable, desirable, i.e., as valuable, do they become values.

Expressed linguistically, statements about enjoyed objects, such as "I like this or enjoy this," are not *value-judgments* but *fact-judgments.* Such fact-judgments of course, are necessary for, without them, value judgments are impossible; but they are merely the necessary *not* the sufficient condition for value-judgments. Value-judgments such as "Enjoying this is worth-while," have as their basis past enjoyments expressed in statements like "I like this."

If value judgments then, are essentially predictions about the enjoyability of given objects, i.e., enjoyable objects, then they are inseparable from the conditions which verify them. Thus, said Dewey, two things are true with respect to them: (a) all value (moral) judgments are tentative, subject to and falsifiable by empirical tests and (b) if this is true, then all value (moral) judgments must be tested by the same methods essentially used to test the validity of any other kind of empirical judgment. The empirical nature of moral judgments, Dewey believed, is often obscured by language and their logical complexity over-simplified. Consequently the logical elements composing a moral judgment are rarely realized. Actually, every moral judgment, explicitly or implicitly, states (a) that a certain experience or situation is desired, and (b) that there are ways (these are usually not made explicit) of attaining the desired experience or situation. In addition, it may assert that (c) a given situation is not wanted, i.e., is bad; and (d) that such and such experiences constitute a test of the validity or truth of the moral judgment.

To Dewey, the mistakes of Subjectivism and of proponents of the Emotive Theory of Value rest in their failure to analyze the logical constituents of a moral judgment or any value judgment. The first mistake is to misunderstand the nature of *desire* or

139

interest. Dewey pointed out an important difference between impulse and desire. Desire is rooted in impulse, for impulse is the basis of desire; but impulse is not desire. All organisms have impulses, i.e., tendencies to act to fulfil needs. Impulse is rooted in the absence of something needed or to be avoided by the organism. It is transformed into desire only by the addition of knowledge. A desire, in other words, is a vital impulse fused with an idea. Desire comes into existence when the organism has *knowledge* of its needs, i.e., it knows what it needs; it has a goal, an end-in-view. However, there is more to desire than this. A desire is not yet fully a desire so long as it is merely limited to an end-in-view. So far it is merely a *wish,* something akin to a dream, lacking available or known means of being satisfied. Only when vital impulse is fused with an end-in-view *and* the means of attaining it, does it become desire.

It is desire which transforms fact-judgments like "I like this," into value-judgments or propositions; and such judgments as judgments are in no respect different from scientific judgments. Like scientific judgments, they are either true or false and subject to the test of experience. Ethical judgments simply report the fact that certain desires are approved or rather that certain ends-in-view when attained will satisfy given vital impulses. Thus organisms capable of desire have a body of ethical judgments, more or less complicated, well-developed, well-ordered, depending upon the total conditions of their existence. Human beings, for example, have a highly complex system of such judgments trained into them from childhood.

However, the existence of a large body of ethical judgments does not mean that either the judgments or the desires (interests) upon which the judgments are based are eternal. Human experience—the changing conditions of environment, including changes within man—may produce new situations making impossible the satisfaction of old established desires. Either new desires have come into existence which are in conflict with the old, or desires are not being fulfilled by the means which ethical judgments explicitly or implicitly assert will fulfil them. Whichever is the case, the result is ethical reflection, deliberation or re-evaluation. If new judgments follow from such reflections they are not, in any logical sense, different from the old. Like the old judgments, they are judgments *relating means to consequences*; they differ from the old only in that they are believed to be able to bring satisfaction.

At this point, we can state the difference Dewey saw between any ordinary experimental or scientific judgment and a moral judgment. Moral judgments do not differ as judgments; they differ only in asserting a relationship of means-to-consequences, of means-to-outcomes. Ordinary scientific judgments do not. That moral judgments assert such a relationship is the ground for holding them to be hypotheses, subject to controlled experimentation and observation.

Moreover, Dewey insisted that ethical judgments are more than evaluations of means; they are also re-appraisals of ends. Dewey pointed out that ethical judgments assert ends as consequences, but as asserted, they are not *actual* consequences; they are *consequences-in-view, goals, ends-in-view*. The *actual* consequences may either correspond with the consequences-in-view, the goal, or they may not. In other words, they may or may not verify it. Or they may include other consequences which are not foreseen or considered essential elements of the consequences-in-view. Such mis-judgment can lead to re-appraisals of the ends-in-view. In other words, approved desires may no longer be approved; and this means specifically that all or any one of the constituents of ethical judgment—the ends-in-view, the foreseen consequences or the means—may be reconsidered. While it is true that ethical judgments have not been consciously rejected or modified by the use of scientific criteria, Dewey believed that psychology, sociology and anthropology would show that the failure of ethical judgments to coincide with predicted outcomes is the cause for human beings changing their ethical values. And if these sciences can show that this is the case, they would justify his program for establishing ethical judgments.

The Scientific Construction of the Good, the Ideal

Among the tremendous complex of ethical judgments which control the life of man, there are some which have a higher place than others. These are often called "ideals." To Dewey, ideals are simply names for activities which help to integrate the total life of man. Sometimes, they are spoken of as separate and distinct goals, thus, as ideals; at other times, they are taken as integrated, as systematized, and then they are spoken of as an "ideal." Sometimes, they are taken to be that set of goals which is to be preferred over all others; and then they are spoken of as "The Ideal." In whatever sense they are referred to, they mean for Dewey that set of goals which presumptively lead to the integration of the total life of man. For example, Dewey defined a "utopian" ideal as that end-in-view or set of ends-in-view for which the means of attainment are completely lacking; and he defined the "wrong" ideal as simply one which reduces the total life of man to drudgery.

Ideals are simply another way, said Dewey, of designating or denoting the *Good*, but this is so if and only if the Good is taken to mean those consequences which promote a "given course of activities" leading to the satisfaction of vital impulses and actual needs. In this sense, a "scientific" ideal or "scientific" ideals, or the Good, can be set up to meet all the requirements of observation and testability.

To Dewey, of course, the setting up of such ideals can only be done if they are positively related to the social matrix in which men live; and of course, this also means that existing ideals, those established by tradition and human experience, must be taken into account. Existing ideals, after all, indicate what men at present believe must be created and what must be done in order that approved desires and interests can be satisfied. There would be no need for scientific ideals, if existing ideals could not or need not be subjected to criticism. However, for good and sufficient cause, there are always competing ideals in any advanced civilization expressing the fact of the failure of dominant ideals to attain predicted goals or to discover appropriate means. Competing ideals and the failure of such ideals to attain goals or to use the right means seem to Dewey to provide the basis for justifying the use of scientific methods in ethics. How else can sensible choices be made between competing ideals? How many false ideals—for lack of scientific testing—have been followed by men to the death? How tragic have been the social costs of following "utopian" ideals for lack of appropriate procedures for testing them?

Failure to seek or even want to establish such experimental tests, said Dewey, has caused men to transform their local, vague, contradictory, unrealizable ideals into eternal finalities to be rejected only at the peril of their souls. This finality is simply the unwarranted extension of the fact that ideals are accepted as final for the time being either because of social habit or because no serious objections have been raised against them. That ideals are not final is proven by the existence of what men call "evils":—

the lack of things considered good, the frustrations experienced, and the failure of human effort to attain desired goals. Evils are the clear evidence that given ideals are not justified or have not yet justified themselves.

To view ideals and evils scientifically—i.e., to consider them neither as finalities nor as inexpungible actualities—was for Dewey the only way of making possible the rational consideration and experimental solutions of all social and individual problems. Thus evils are to be taken as symptoms or conditions to be studied and investigated; ideals are to be viewed as integrally related to such symptoms or as hypotheses for their removal; and the existence of conflicting ideals is not to be taken as evidence of eternal and irrational incompatibilities, but as evidence of problems needing resolution.

Factors Involved in the Construction of the Good

If evils are problems or conditions and ideals are hypotheses, then Dewey believed no testable ideals can be developed without recourse to psychology, sociology, the sciences of man. These sciences reveal man's vital impulses, biological drives and needs; and from them can be derived the kind of personal desires and social interests which will best satisfy them. Further, Dewey believed that such ideals must be related to the means actually or probably available at the given time so that they can be acted upon. Lastly, the analysis of means must include consideration of existing institutions in terms of their capacity to develop habits that can control vital impulses destructive of approved personal desires and social interests. In short, such analysis involves considerations of the social means to develop *good* character and *right* conduct on a social scale.

Rights, Goods, Claims and Duties

In complex societies, there is always a conflict of rights and goods, even to the highest good, the Ideal, the Good. This is due to the fact that people make demands, claims, which by this very act become "rights" or "goods" for those at least who make them. But how do such claims become "rights" or "goods"? To Dewey, the answer is simple: when they are recognized and accepted by others. Failure to recognize them means that they have not yet attained the status of rights or goods. Recognition of claims, of course, may have narrower or wider peripheries. Thus some claims may be recognized as rights or goods only within a small group. Others may achieve legal recognition. Still others may attain international or human-wide recognition. The recognition of claims may be based upon different grounds; power, social position, sheer authority, rewards or punishments, or personal acceptance. Any or all of these factors may influence or determine the status of a claim as right or good, but in the long run, Dewey believed claims are recognized as rights and goods primarily through the benefits which their recognition confer directly and indirectly upon all involved. Thus, in the long run, what is established as right or good through custom or law indicates rightly or wrongly what men believe at that time and place benefits them all.

Serious disagreements about rights or goods, about the "rightness" of this right or the "goodness" of this good,— in short, about the rightness of any given custom or law, indicate that the claims for either made by the majority or by powerful groups within a society are not completely justified. While disagreements about rights and goods are not particularly serious where few people are involved, they are of serious moment to any established order when many are involved. Such disagreements often become the causes and occasions for wars, civil wars and revolutions.

No matter how serious may be the nature of such disagreements, they do not affect the status of law or custom in general. For Dewey, no matter what the society, disagreements about rights and goods are not so thorogoing as to involve all rights and goods. Examination of the most varied societies will show the prevalence or the recognition of certain rights and goods. Thus ethical theorists who attack law and order as such are merely theorizing; their theorizing has little or no relevance for the solution of moral disagreements in any existing society. Law and custom are essential to any society. However, Dewey is just as intolerant of the other point of view that, because law and custom, in general, can not be questioned, no specific law or custom can be questioned. Neither extreme subjectivism nor dogmatic intolerance is ethically useful to any society. That men do dispute over rights and goods and have done so in almost all societies shows the practical necessity for an objective methodology to settle satisfactorily such disputes as well as for tolerance in order to recognize that differences over moral matters are justifiable.

Whenever men make claims, demands, they expect compliance or obligation. Obligation is simply the logical counterpart of a claim. This is why every claim seems to be both a right and a duty. But neither one nor the other follows for anyone unless the claim is recognized. Thus by the very fact that men accept a claim, they impose upon themselves an obligation or a duty of a specific sort. It is at the moment of social acceptance that claims are transformed into moral facts expressed either in law or custom.

To Dewey the endless discussion as to which is first, right or good, seems futile. Right is no less primary than good; both are born from the same situation. Right is simply the good from the point of view of the demands or claims made by a society upon its members or by its members upon it so to act as to achieve the good of each and all. The good, then, is simply the appropriate consequences of right actions by persons in a society. Theoretically, what is good is the consequence of right action and right action the consequence of the good.

The theoretical coherence of right and good is the ground for rational criticism of either one or the other or both when viewed as means, as ideal or as expected consequences. Where consistency does not exist, it produces such distinctions as individual versus group or institutional rights and goods or institutional versus "ideal" rights and goods. Absence of theoretical coherence leads not only to these distinctions, but to efforts to re-evaluate goods and rights so as to eradicate them.

Moral Standards

Whatever may be the specific cause for the making of new claims, they invariably involve new ends-in-view, new means to socially approved ends-in-view, or both. When these claims are accepted into law or custom, they become standard for all concerned, even for those who do not accept them. Generally, it is believed that compliance with such standards produce happiness; non-compliance, unhappiness. Thus all individuals—parents, teachers, rulers, etc.,—and institutions concern themselves with developing habits which will make compliance with these standards automatic, since compliance means happiness and non-compliance, unhappiness. Thus happiness to Dewey can never be general; it must be specific. Either the individual is fulfilled or he is not. The specificity of happiness is the reason which led Dewey to believe that the failure of any moral standard to bring fulfilment to any person places that standard so far under a theoretical cloud.

Moreover, to Dewey, moral standards may be long-lived or short-lived. Their length of life depends upon their significance to the group, to society. If significant, they are transmitted from generation to generation frequently with unfortunate results. Their very significance often gives them a sacred authority which prohibits legitimate criticism. Thus they are often transformed from significant moral guides into obstacles stunting the moral life and inimical to the healthy growth of society.

Even when moral standards are vital, Dewey did not consider them to be rules specifically defining what is permissible or impermissible. He considered them to be generalized statements of probable consequences respecting approved or disapproved situations. Consequently he thought of them as serving as guides, schemas, methods for making intelligent choices in any given situation; they did not determine like rules what must be chosen or done. When standards are reduced to rules, they stultify moral intelligence and prevent the objective solution of moral problems.

Even though moral standards change or become obsolete, Dewey did not believe that this made them relative to personal feelings or beliefs. Their being changed or their obsolescence is caused by their failure to predict consequences, but this is not their fault. New conditions, actuality, are the causes of their insufficiency as moral guides.

The Development and Utility of the Moral Self

To Dewey, the formation of the good self, or of good selves, is the dominating purpose of all education, whether private or public, since the good self is by definition the *social* self, the self capable of living with others, of social co-operation, of maintaining the good society. Consequently the kind of good selves produced reflects both the common goods as well as the moral conflicts flaring within a society at a given period.

In most complex societies, the good self, according to Dewey, is described more or less in the following terms: (a) as possessing wisdom or prudence; (b) as desirous of lasting satisfactions embracing others as well as itself; (c) as aware of and sensitive to the just claims (rights and goods) of others; (d) as alert, through knowledge and experience, to new values and situations; (e) and as always ready, as a consequence, to reconsider all ideals in order to establish better ones.

Plainly this is Dewey's conception of the good self for a modern society constantly subject to the effect and shock of change. It is not the conception, in all respects, of others. It is Dewey's idealization of the sort of man he thinks a modern society requires. But whether acceptable to others or not, the formation of "good" selves is unquestionably a problem of social education, a problem of creating persons whose "impulsive tendencies" will be controlled by values which "contribute to the enrichment of the lives of all."

145

The important fact about the Deweyan good self is that it is neither *mere* means nor *mere* end. It is neither so self-active that it is moved to act completely from within nor so completely determined from without that it acts only upon external stimulation. To Dewey, the external stimulus is as important as the inner "motive," since neither is meaningful without the other. The effects of things, events, environment, upon the self are important for judging the rightness of any standard or the goodness of any good.

Consequently, Dewey rejected absolutistic ethical theories like Egoism or Altruism. The interests of the self and the interests of other selves can have no meaning apart from each other. The principle of the welfare of all—the so-called principle of Altruism—involves the principle of the welfare of the self—the so-called egoistic principle. The welfare of all selves logically involves by definition the welfare of the one self: otherwise there is no welfare of all. And any moral principle becomes self-contradictory if it applies to all without at the same time applying to the individual.

Growth: The Basis of Moral Responsibility and Freedom

If one were to seek for one word upon which the moral theory of Dewey rests, it would be found in the word "growth." The capacity of a society or an individual to "grow" is the basic criterion of either's capacity for goodness. Growth did not mean to Dewey merely change or increase in size. Change of course is always involved in growth but not necessarily increase in size. Two dimensions are particularly important to the concept of growth: (1) continuity of change, and (2) incorporation of what is worthwhile in past experience into the new habits, structures, and outlooks of the present. Growth, as distinct from death, is the continuous actualization of new possibilities arising in experience. The creation of such new possibilities, any one of which can be chosen, is the essence of freedom; the prevention or prohibition of such new possibilities the essence of unfreedom. Deliberation, intelligent consideration of new possibilities in the light of consequences, already experienced or anticipated, is the essence of responsibility; the rejection of intelligent consideration of new possibilities, irresponsibility.

Not merely every person but every society can be judged by these criteria. A closed society is one without responsibility or freedom, for it rejects growth; it struggles to exclude the new and different and punishes those who give them serious consideration. Except for some individuals, the closed society deprives its members of both responsibility and freedom, thus keeping most of its members morally immature and stunted.

Bibliography

John Dewey, *The Theory of Valuation*, International Encyclopedia of the Unity of Science, VII. N. 4. (Chicago, 1939).
——, *Human Nature and Conduct*, (New York, 1932).

——, *The Quest for Certainty,* (New York, 1929).

——, *Liberalism and Social Action,* (New York, 1935).

——, *Psychology* (New York, 1891).

John Dewey and James H. Tufts, *Ethics,* rev. ed. (New York, 1938).

Rubin Gotesky
University of Georgia

Dewey, John: *see* Cumberland, Richard; Major Ethical Viewpoints; Moral Philosophy in America; Psychology and Morals; Soviet Morality, Current.

dharma: *see* Hindu Ethics.

Dhu al-Nūn Misri: *see* Muslim Morals.

dialectic: *see* Hegel, G. W. F.; Kierkegaard, Soren; Marxist Theory of Morals; Plato.

diatribe: *see* Minor Socratics.

dictatorship of the proletariat: *see* Soviet Morality, Current.

Diderot: *see* Cooper, Anthony Ashley.

dietary laws: *see* Jewish Ethics and Its Civilization.

dignity: *see* Berdyaev, Nicolas; Hammurapi, Code of; Hegel, G. W. F.; Kant, I.; Khomiakov, Alexey; Puritan Morals; Soviet Morality, Current; Stoics, the; Utilitarianism.

diligence: *see* Quakerism, Classical, The Morality of.

Dio: *see* Minor Socratics.

Diogenes: *see* Minor Socratics; Stoics, the.

Diogenes Laertius: *see* Stoics, the.

disanalogy: *see* Clarke, Samuel.

disapproval: *see* Broad, C. D.; Major Ethical Viewpoints; Primitive Morals; Puritan Morals.

discipline: *see* China, Moral Philosophies of; Hindu Ethics; Major Ethical Viewpoints; Navaho Morals; self-discipline.

discretion: *see* Aztec Morals.

disease: *see* Rio Grande Pueblo Indians; Stoics, the.

disease, moral: *see* moral disease.

disequilibrium: *see* Rio Grande Pueblo Indians.

dishonesty: *see* Aztec Morals; More, Henry.

dishonor: *see* Sophists, the.

disinterested benevolence: *see* Moral Philosophy in America.

disinterested liking: *see* Schopenhauer, Arthur.

disinterestedness: *see* Hume, David.

disobedience: *see* Quakerism, Classical, The Morality of; Sophists, the.

disorder: *see* Hindu Ethics; Major Ethical Viewpoints; Puritan Morals.

dispositions: *see* Hindu Ethics; Schlick, Moritz; Stoics, the.

disrespect: *see* Zuni Indians, Morals of.

dissipation: *see* Puritan Morals.

distrust: *see* Mundurucu Indians, A Dual System of Ethics.

disunity: *see* Quakerism, Classical, The Morality of.

disvalues: *see* Major Ethical Viewpoints.

diversity: *see* Cudworth, Ralph.

divination: *see* Riffian Morals.

divine judgment: *see* Hammurapi, Code of.

divine law: *see* Marxist Theory of Morals; Muslim Morals.

divine love: *see* Puritan Morals.

divine positive law: *see* Liguori, St. Alphonsus and Catholic Moral Philosophy.

Divine spark: *see* Zoroastrian Morals.

Divine truth: *see* Jewish Ethics and Its Civilization.

divorce: *see* Liguori, St, Alphonsus and Catholic Moral Philosophy; Marxist Theory of Morals; Muslim Morals; Soviet Morality, Current; Tapirapé Morals, Some Aspects of; Zuni Indians, Morals of.

Dodwell: *see* Clarke, Samuel.

Donatism: *see* Augustine and Morals.

Dostoyevsky, Fyodor

Dostoyevsky's works belong to the highest level of Russian literature, and moreover belong to the treasury of world culture. This is due of course to Dostoyevsky's genius as a novelist, to be compared only with Tolstoy's. But just as in Tolstoy's case, Dostoyevsky's literary value is only *one* aspect of his extraordinary prestige. Like Tolstoy, Dostoyevsky is a religious thinker, a Christian moralist,—and to a far greater extent than his famous contemporary. Indeed, Dostoyevsky's own faith,—that of the Russian-Orthodox Church, was never basically doubted by him (as by Tolstoy), though also often put to severe trial. We must, moreover, keep in mind that Dostoyevsky not only presents the highest religious and ethical interpretation of man but, in his writings— especially in his four major novels and in some of his shorter fictional works— he analyzes and brings out with intense dramatic force all the elements of the human person's character, nature and destiny. This is why Dostoyevsky's novels and stories have been studied by psychologists, physicians, psycho-analysts and psychiatrists. To these "specialists" of the human mind and body we must add the sociologist and the political philosopher, who can also find sufficient food for meditation in Dostoyevsky's conception of man in society (as for instance in *The Possessed* and in certain chapters of *The Brothers Karamazov*). The careful student of his thought, is not necessarily satisfied with his novels and stories. We have, in addition to these, *The Diary of A Writer,* in which, at the end of his life, Dostoyevsky noted many of his ideas and reactions. We also have his letters, especially his correspondence with his brother.[1] Finally, we have his note-books and initial drafts, which offer us the blueprints to his novels.[2]

In spite of this abundance of firsthand material, or perhaps precisely because of it, Dostoyevsky's contribution to morals *per se* cannot be easily deduced. The problem has too often been confused, due to a variety of interpretations: the psychologist and the psychiatrist tend to ignore anything which in his writings reaches out to a higher, religious, supernatural sphere. The religious philosopher, Christian moralist and mystic (for Dostoyevsky appeals also to the mystic) are too often inclined to ignore Dostoyevsky's presentation of natural man. Maybe, only an expert theologian do the final summing up. This has been already attempted by Russian-Orthodox authors, like Berdyaev, Lossky, Frank, and others, as well as

---

1 Michael Dostoyevsky. This correspondence is published *in extenso*.

2 Published in separate volumes.

by Catholic scholars, like Romano Guardini and De Lubac.

After examining these various interpretations of Dostoyevsky's thoughts, we shall hold in mind a few essential propositions: First: Dostoyevsky is fundamentally a religious and Christian thinker—his psychology, sociology, personal and social ethics are centered in God. Second: Dostoyevsky's religious and ethical ideas (with the exception of those expressed in *The Diary of A Writer*) are not formulated as a doctrine, but presented as a living phenomenon, reflected in the behavior of human beings. These human beings, do not merely speak (though there are many dialogues and soliloquies in his novels). Even when the characters in the novels argue with others and analyze themselves, they are not content in doing so. They *test* themselves, or life tests them, or sometimes even death. Third: Each character in Dostoyevsky's fiction has his own special destiny, just as men have in true life; he is above all a human person, and as such obeys the natural law, or disobeys it; being endowed with a free will, man *chooses* between good and evil. Fourth: while man makes his choice, there is a struggle, a *tension*. Dostoyevsky very clearly stated that "the soul of man is a battle-field between God and the devil." This is why sin, and the devil himself (as in Ivan Karamazov's hallucinations, when he actually conversed with the devil) are pictured with a truly dramatic, often terrifying impact. It is not always apparent *who* finally wins. Actually his novels and stories end in disaster. Only in *The Brothers Karamazov,* in which sin and its consequences are no less tragically projected, there is the victory of good over evil, and the promise of resurrection. True, Dostoyevsky himself did not consider this novel as a final solution. He intended to write a second part, entitled *The Atheist,* in which the crucial problems discussed in his previous works, would receive another, perhaps decisive, analysis. Could he have added anything to that which he had already written? We doubt it. As the profound Russian literary critic and essayist, V. Rozanov, wrote: "Dostoyevsky said all he had to say in *The Brothers Karamazov.* He died soon after the completion of this novel. His last message can be very clearly deduced from the chapter of *The Brothers Karamazov* entitled "Conversations and exhortations of Father Zossima,"[3] and especially the ethical problem with which we are here concerned:

"The Eternal Judge [says Father Zossima, the old and wise monk] asks of you what you can comprehend and not what you cannot."

This is an allusion to the natural law to which man is bound. But Zossima goes on to say that natural law itself is informed by the supernatural:

"You will know that yourself hereafter, for you will behold all things truly then and will not dispute them. On earth indeed, we are as it were astray, and if it were not for the precious image of Christ

[3] *The Brothers Karamazov,* Book VI, The Russian Monk.

before us, we should be undone and altogether lost."

And so Dostoyevsky goes on to say, in the old monk's words:

"Much on earth is hidden from us, but to make up for that we have been given a precious mystic sense of our living bond with the other world. . . This is why the philosophers say that we cannot apprehend the reality of things on earth."

This is why, most commentators of Dostoyevsky's writings, even those who do not accept his faith, come to the conclusion that his entire *scale* of moral values is founded on the experience of God. Writes another outstanding Russian writer, poet and philosopher, Vyacheslav Ivanov analyzing Dostoyevsky's ethics:

Where atheism has been elevated to the practical norm of social existence, Dostoyevsky holds that this entails first of all a deterioration and corruption of the moral sense, and subsequently its complete extinction. For morality not founded on religion is not capable, in the long run, of maintaining even the independence, much less the absoluteness, of its own values."[4]

Concerning his scale of values, projected by Dostoyevsky, whether in the individual or social moral field, Romano Guardini tells us, that all of Dostoyevsky's world is filled with a religious atmosphere.[5] We shall go further, by stressing that this moral world of his is filled by a *Christological* content. Without Christology, Dostoyevsky's entire conception of

man and of the moral law guiding him would not make sense. In order to realize this more clearly, we must go back to his own spiritual development, beginning from his early years and ending with the last period of his life.

The son of a physician in charge of the medical care of an orphanage in Moscow, Fyodor Dostoyevsky (born 1821) was brought up in a family of limited means and drab environment. His father was strict and scarcely knew how to make himself loved by his children. But his mother was a gentle and kind woman; she died, however, when her sons, Fyodor and Michael were still quite young and thus were deprived of the tender care she gave them. It was from his mother that Fyodor learned the rudiments of the Russian-Orthodox faith: not only in his home but also in the churches and monasteries where she often took her children. Of this early religious education, he retained a lasting memory. As a young child, he was much impressed by the book of Job, which was read aloud in church, and by a prayer to Our Lady, which he recited often throughout his entire life. Forced by his father to study at the school of military engineers in Petersburg, Fyodor showed but little interest in a soldier's career. Graduating from school, he did not enter the army but turned to literature, which fascinated him. His father's violent death—the old physician was murdered by his serfs in a small country estate—caused a shock which seems to have had the most serious consequences. The shock was the greater because father and son had

---

[4] *Freedom and the Tragic Life, A study in Dostoyevsky.*

[5] *L'Univers Religieux de Dostoyevsky.*

been in sharp disagreement. Dostoyevsky's biographers often point out that this brutal murder of the father caused the son's terrible disease, from which he suffered all his life: epilepsy. The famous Sigmund Freud, creator of psychoanalysis, affirmed that Dostoyevsky was afflicted with a neurotic derangement, classified by him as the Oedipus (father's) complex.[6] We find no further proof of Freud's diagnosis, except in the fact that in Dostoyevsky's writings, especially in *The Brothers Karamazov*, and in the novel entitled *The Raw Youth*, the antagonism between father and son is vividly depicted. If he was stricken at that time with epilepsy in his youth, another far more serious experience must have rendered his condition even more acute and dangerous. Shortly after having published his first story, *Poor People*, which made him famous, Dostoyevsky became intimate with the most brilliant representatives of the Russian literary world. Most of them were radicals and atheists; they had formed in the 40's a secret political society, with which he was acquainted and whose meetings he attended. True, he did not share their extreme revolutionary views nor did he accept their atheist teachings. On the contrary, the *godless* society which these radicals wanted to create in Russia, inspired him with repulsion. He had the opportunity closely to study a social utopia from which Christ was absent. This is why he could later so

clearly expose this utopia and disclose the evil aims of its initiators in *The Possessed*. But meanwhile, Dostoyevsky became involved in the conspiracy without even clearly realizing its full meaning. He was arrested together with the other members of the secret society, imprisoned, submitted to severe questioning (during which he never betrayed his fellow-prisoners) and finally condemned to death. It was only after having been brought to the place of execution and faced a firing squad, that he and his associates were reprieved. The death sentence was commuted to four years of hard labor in Siberia. Dostoyevsky told of his imprisonment in his book: *The House of the Dead*. He was subjected to the regime of condemned criminals of common law, robbers and murderers. Instead of antagonizing him against these men, this tragic encounter with sin, taught him the full meaning of charity, forgiveness and also the possibility of expiation and salvation. But this supernatural enlightenment would perhaps have been impossible, were it not for an incident related to his first introduction to convict life. On his way to the Siberian prison, to which he was assigned, Dostoyevsky met a woman, Mrs. von Vizin, who devoted her life to the care and comfort of convicts. Mrs. von Vizin gave him a small volume: the Four Gospels. These Dostoyevsky read on his journey to prison and in prison, as well as after his liberation. The Gospels which of course he knew from his childhood, yet never fully grasped, now became to him a revelation. The

---

6 Freud wrote an essay presenting a psychoanalysis of Dostoyevsky out of the latter's biography and novels.

well-known French novelist André Gide says in his lectures on Dostoyevsky: "The great, external events of Dostoyevsky's life . . . are less important than one small fact [meaning his reception of the Gospels from Mrs. von Vizin]. All his subsequent written works are steeped in the Gospels."[7]

After his liberation from prison, Dostoyevsky wrote to Mrs. von Vizin; he explained to her how great was the impact of Christ's message in the most tragic period of his life, and also how close he had been to the rejection of the Gospels' truth:

"I shall tell you about myself that I am a child of the century of disbelief and doubt. . . . What terrible tortures I now suffer because of this thirst for faith which is all the stronger in my soul that the arguments against it are more numerous. And yet sometimes God gives me moments of complete serenity. In such moments I compose for myself a profession of faith, in which everything is clear and sacred. This profession of faith is simple: I believe that there is nothing more beautiful, more profound, more appealing, more reasonable, more courageous, more perfect than Christ."[8]

It seems that Dostoyevsky's entire experience after his liberation and up to his death, as well as the basic structure of his moral teaching, can be deduced from this letter. A detailed analysis of his major works, and his note-books and further correspondence implement and confirm his Chris-

tological approach. On the other hand, we have sufficient evidence that his way toward Christ was neither smooth nor secure nor untroubled unless, perhaps, at the very end. His shattered health, due to prison life, to say nothing of his experience of last-minute reprieve, precipitated and rendered more and more acute his epileptic condition. Moreover, his personal and emotional life, even after liberation, was far from happy. His first marriage with Maria Issayeva was disappointing, causing him pangs of jealousy, and accentuating his loneliness and sickliness. His liaison with Appolinarya Suslova, a cruel, heartless and wayward young woman, who betrayed and mocked him, was marked with more bitterness and jealous resentment. It was at that time, that he surrendered to his fatal vice: gambling. It was only after Maria's death and his second marriage with his devoted stenographer Anna Snitkina, that brought him relative peace of mind. Poverty, sickness, distress, due to his gambling passion, the intolerable demands imposed on him by his creditors and publishers, the death of his favorite child, and almost uninterrupted work—all these trials accompanied Dostoyevsky to his grave. And yet, during these years of exceptional trial and tribulation, he wrote his major novels, in which, step by step, he affirmed and reaffirmed his faith, his profound moral conviction, his unshaken trust in Christ, expressed in Zossima's exhortations. His death occurred in 1881.

---

7 André Gide, *Lectures on Dostoyevsky.*

8 Dostoyevsky's letter to Mrs. von Vizin, Feb., 20, 1854.

To read Dostoyevsky's works in their true light means also to take step by step the long pilgrimage leading to the moral law *par excellence*. Let us briefly recall the main landmarks of this trail, as they appear in his four great novels.[9] *Crime and Punishment* is the first step. Here we have, so to say, the premises of the problems raised in all the novels. Raskolnikov, the hero of *Crime and Punishment* believes himself to be a superman. As such, he thinks, he is permitted to do anything he chooses and is capable of doing everything. Raskolnikov commits a murder to test himself because he considers this murder justified: 1) because he is a superman; 2) because his victim, the old, greedy and rapacious pawn-broker does not deserve to live; 3) because the goods stolen from her after the murder will somehow help Raskolnikov to continue his studies, help his poor mother and sister, and finally offer him the means of becoming a benefactor of humanity; 4) because to perform such a deed will prove that he is absolutely free to *choose* between good and evil, without being obliged to suffer the consequences which ordinary men would have to face. As soon as the crime is committed, Raskolnikov discovers that he is not a superman, and that actually there are no superior or inferior beings in the ethi-

cal world; all have to obey the moral law. This realization first comes to him through his own miserable condition: physical and mental, bred by the terror of being found out or of giving himself away. But the final consciousness of good and evil is attained by Raskolnikov through Sonya, the prostitute, to whom all is forgiven because she loves, and who teaches others to ask forgiveness. Sonya reads the Gospels to Raskolnikov (how clearly this scene of *Crime and Punishment* is reminiscent of Dostoyevsky's own discovery of the Gospels in Siberia!). Raskolnikov confesses to Sonya his crime and explains his motives: "After all, Sonya, all I did was to kill some ignoble malevolent vermin." Sonya cries: "But yet the vermin was a human being . . . you turned away from God, and God has punished you, by giving you up to Satan." In a few simple, naive, but extraordinarily convincing words, Sonya persuades Raskolnikov to confess his crime publicly and to give himself up to justice. She offers him her devotion and pity; after he has confessed, been tried and condemned, she follows him to Siberia. "But now," writes Dostoyevsky, "a new history commences: a story of the gradual renewal of a man."

Analyzing the premises, posed by Dostoyevsky in *Crime and Punishment,* and developed in the three other novels, Nicolas Berdyaev writes that when man turns away from God, in order to become a superman for whom everything is allowed, his freedom *degenerates* into self-will. Raskolnikov "does not give the impression of a free

9 The religious and moral issues we here discuss were raised by Dostoyevsky in most of his other fictional works, as well as in his *Diary of a Writer*. Space does not allow us to examine them, but the main patterns all appear in the four novels.

man at all, but of a maniac," suffering from a "fixed idea." He wanted to test his freedom and his strength; the experiment fails. "I have murdered myself, not her" (the old pawn-broker), Raskolnikov cries in his confession; this, Berdyaev tells us is "the suicide of man by self-affirmation."

Raskolnikov is saved from spiritual death and is renewed through confession and contrition. Not all of the main characters of Dostoyevsky's novels attain this ethical and religious rebirth. In *The Idiot,* there is only one man who has attained true freedom, but he has never turned away from God. He is Myshkin, "the perfectly good man," as Dostoyevsky describes him in his letters to friends, when planning his second novel. Myshkin is Christlike; he is meek and humble of soul. This is why people jeer at him, and call him "idiot." And what about those who surround him?— Pride, lust, greed, jealousy, violence, —such are the fatal forces which drive all other characters, to whom Myshkin can only offer his kindness, his gentleness, pity and forgiveness. "Humility," writes Dostoyevsky, "is a terrible force." So is the force which is described in *The Idiot* as *love-pity,* which, as Myshkin cries out, "is greater than love." But indeed this is the kingdom, which is "not of this world." But can such meekness conquer evil immediately? *The Idiot,* as we have already pointed out, is a story which ends in disaster: murder, suicide, despair; and yet, the personality of Myshkin shines triumphant and the darkness grasps it not.

In *The Possessed* there is a reversed situation: the kingdom of God, together with natural law, are completely obliterated. Pride, lust, violence, are actually impersonated in all characters, except the very few who are their scape-goats. "The Possessed" is usually interpreted as Dostoyevsky's forceful and prophetic denunciation of atheist political and social doctrines. True, we can easily recognize in this novel the picture of the communist conspiracy: a secret society, resolved to employ every means, in order to seize power and build a "perfect" godless society. Actually, the problem of good and evil, of God and godlessness, is raised in *The Possessed,* not merely on the social and political level. This is a struggle in the soul of each of these characters: Stavrogin, the instigator of the secret society, is also a sinner, and even a criminal, in his individual life (see his "confession"). Kyrillov, one of the most fanatical members of the society, seeks to prove to himself, that he is equal to God, and can defy Him by ending his own life, whenever he chooses to do so. Verkhovensky, the leader of the group, is an abject character of all, and says of himself: "I am a scoundrel."

Now we have only to take one more step, in order to find Dostoyevsky's final answer to the moral problem raised in the preceding novels: the answer, as we have already said, is given in *The Brothers Karamazov.* These problems, or as Dostoyevsky called them himself, these "accursed questions," are presented with extraordinary force and spectacular impact,

154

in this, his last work. The three "brothers," and their father, the corrupt and greedy old man, and the illegitimate half-brother Smerdyakov, are each of them, not only vivid, admirably depicted personalities, they are each of them *symbols* of a religious and ethical equation. Old Karamazov: lust and immoralism on the bestial level. Dmitry Karamazov: primitive passion, violence, yet mingled with honesty and a direct intuition of the good. Ivan: rationalism, intellectual pride, the vain desire to "correct" the justice of God, to substitute the Gospels by dialectics. Smerdyakov: whose sick mind and criminal instincts seem to be the result of the Karamazovs' collective sins. Then finally, Alyesha Karamazov: who, thanks to his teacher, the monk Zossima, acquires the spiritual strength to wander through this family jungle, and emerges unscathed. Like *The Idiot,* Alyesha is the projection of the "kingdom of heaven," but unlike Myshkin he does not suffer disaster. He helps his brothers save themselves, he prevents them from "giving themselves up to Satan." It is a remarkable fact, that Alyesha, who symbolizes the *Christological solution,* speaks out less often than Sonya in *Crime and Punishment,* and Myshkin in *The Idiot.* His testimony is almost unspoken. At the end of the famous discourse with his brother Ivan (see book V, *Pro* and *Contra,*), in which the proud rationalist defies the young novice, "Alyesha looked at him in silence." For him it seems, the solution of the problem is so obvious, it needs no demonstration: where Christ

is, there too is the ethical rule, as taught Zossima. From Dostoyevsky's letter to Mrs. von Vizin in the 40's to *The Brothers Karamazov* in the 80's, there is one continuous way toward Christ,—not only as the Saviour of the world, but also as the original and only source of the world's moral law.

Bibliography

F. Dostoyevsky, *The Brothers Karamazov,* Translated by Constance Garnett. Modern Library (1929). *Crime and Punishment* (1928). *The Idiot* (1928). *The Possessed* (1931). *The Diary of a Writer,* Translated by Boris Brazol (New York, 1949). *Letters and Reminiscences,* Edited by Koteliansky & Middleton Murray (New York, 1923). *Letters to Family and Friends* (New York, 1917). *Note-books.* In Russian (Centrarkhiv, Moscow) Arkhiv Dostoyevskogo (1922–31–35).

A. G. Dostoyevskaya (Snitkina), *Dostoyevsky portrayed by his wife,* Translated by Koteliansky (London, 1926).

N. Berdyaev, *Dostoyevsky,* Translated (New York, 1934).

S. Freud, "Dostoyevsky and Parricide," Article in *Realist* (1929), v. I.

André Gide, *Dostoyevsky,* Translated (New York, 1949).

Romano Guardini, *L'Univers Religieux de Dostoyevsky,* Aux Editions du Seuil (1947).

H. De Lubac, S. J. *The Drama of Atheist Humanism,* Translated (New York, 1950).

Helene Iswolsky
Fordham Institute of Contemporary Russian Studies

Dostoyevsky, F.: *see* Berdyaev, Nicolas; Freud, Sigmund; Khomiakov, Alexey; Soloviev, Wladimir.

double moral standard: *see* Aboriginals of Yirkalla; Marxist Theory of Morals.

doubt: *see* China, Moral Philosophies of; Clarke, Samuel; Hindu Ethics; Jesuits, the, Moral Theology of; Liguori, St. Alphonsus and Catholic Moral Philosophy.

dreams: *see* Freud, Sigmund.

dress: *see* Puritan Morals.

drinking: *see* drunkenness; Hindu Ethics; Navaho Morals; Puritan Morals.

drives, original: *see* Freud, Sigmund; Hume, David; Impulses; Psychology and Morals.

Drŭj: *see* Zoroastrian Morals.

drunkenness: *see* Augustine and Morals; Aztec Morals; Psychology and Morals; Puritan Morals; Zuni Indians, Morals of.

dual system of ethics: *see* Mundurucu Indians, A Dual System of Ethics.

Dumont: *see* Utilitarianism.

Durkheim, E.: *see* Major Ethical Viewpoints.

duties: *see* Augustine and Morals; Balguy, John; Broad, C. D.; Butler, Joseph; Clarke, Samuel; Cudworth, Ralph; Dewey, John; dharma; Hindu Ethics; Hume, David; Jesuits, the, Moral Theology of; Jewish Ethics and Its Civilization; Kant, I.; Kierkegaard, Soren; Major Ethical Viewpoints; Marxist Theory of Morals; Moore, George Edward; Moral Philosophy in America; More, Henry; Muslim Morals; obligation; Price, Richard; Prichard, H. A.; Psychology and Morals; Puritan Morals; Reid, Thomas; Ross, Sir (William) David; Scheler, Max; Schlick, Moritz; Sophists, the; Soviet Morality, Current; Stoics, the.

Duvergier, de Hauranne, Jean: *see* Jesuits, the, Moral Theology of.

Dwight, Timothy: *see* Moral Philosophy in America.

Dymond, Jonathan: *see* Quakerism, Classical, The Morality of.

Dynamic School of British Psychologists: *see* Psychology and Morals.

E

eating: *see* food; Hindu Ethics.

Eckermann: *see* Goethe, Johann Wolfgang von.

economic determinism: *see* Marxist Theory of Morals.

economic needs: *see* Riffian Morals; Zuni Indians, Morals of.

economics and morality: *see* Aboriginals of Yirkalla; Marxist Theory of Morals; Soviet Morality, Current.

ecstasy: *see* Minor Socratics.

ecumenical movement: *see* Soloviev, Wladimir.

ecumenicity: *see* Quakerism, The Morality of.

education: *see* China, Moral Philosophies of; Dewey, John; Green, T. H.; Hindu Ethics; Primitive Morals; Sophists, the; Soviet Morality, Current.

Edwards, Jonathan: *see* Moral Philosophy in America; Puritan Morals.

egalitarianism: *see* Soviet Morality, Current.

ego, the: *see* Freud, Sigmund; Hindu Ethics; self.

ego assertion: *see* Hindu Ethics; Mundurucu Indians, A Dual System of Ethics.

egocentricity: *see* Morals and Religion; Psychology and Morals.

egoism: *see* China, Moral Philosophies of; Cooper, Anthony Ashley; Cudworth, Ralph; Cumberland, Richard; Dewey, John; Green, T. H.;

Hindu Ethics; Hume, David; Schlick, Moritz; Schopenhauer, Arthur; selfishness; Utilitarianism.

egoism, enlightened: *see* Moral Philosophy in America.

egoism, ethical: *see* Major Ethical Viewpoints; Sidgwick, Henry.

egoist: *see* psychological egoism.

egoistic hedonism: *see* Major Ethical Viewpoints.

elders: *see* Aztec Morals; Pakot, the Moral System of; Primitive Morals.

Eleatic school, the: *see* Minor Socratics; Sophists, the.

Eliot, John: *see* Puritan Morals.

emancipation: *see* Schopenhauer, Arthur.

Emerson, R. W.: *see* Moral Philosophy in America.

emotions: *see* Ayer, Alfred J.; Cudworth, Ralph; feelings; Hindu Ethics; Language and Ethics; Major Ethical Viewpoints; Reid, Thomas; Spinoza; Utilitarianism.

emotions and morals: *see* feelings; Hume, David; Utilitarianism.

emotive theory: *see* Ayer, Alfred J.; Major Ethical Viewpoints; Ross, Sir (William) David; Russell, Bertrand.

emotive theory of value: *see* Dewey, John.

emotivism: *see* Broad, C. D.; Freud, Sigmund; Moore, George Edward.

empathy: *see* Scheler, Max.

157

Empedocles: *see* Sophists, the.

empirical sciences: *see* Soviet Morality, Current.

empiricism: *see* Ayer, Alfred J.; Balguy, John; Clarke, Samuel; Cooper; Anthony Ashley; Cumberland, Richard; Dewey, John; Green, T. H.; Hume, David; Language and Ethics; Moral Philosophy in America; More, Henry; Russell, Bertrand; Spinoza; Utilitarianism.

emptiness: *see* French Existentialism and Moral Philosophy.

endeavor: *see* Hobbes, Thomas; Stoics, the.

Endecott, John: *see* Puritan Morals.

ends: *see* Aquinas, Thomas; Moral Views of; Dewey, John; Green, T. H.; Kant, I.; Liguori, St. Alphonsus and Catholic Moral Philosophy; Major Ethical Viewpoints; Reid, Thomas; Soviet Morality, Current; Stoics, the; teleology, ethical.

ends and means: *see* Aquinas, Thomas; Moral Views of; Jesuits, the, Moral Theology of; Kant, I.; Soviet Morality, Current.

endurance: *see* Muslim Morals.

enforcement of morality: *see* Puritan Morals.

Engels, Frederick: *see* Marxist Theory of Morals; Soviet Morality, Current.

English Puritanism: *see* Puritan Morals.

enhancement: *see* Morals and Religion.

enjoyment: *see* Dewey, John; Minor Socratics.

enlightened egoism: *see* Butler, Joseph; Moral Philosophy in America.

Enlightenment, the: *see* Jewish Ethics and Its Civilization; Kant, I.

environment: *see* China, Moral Philosophies of.

envy: *see* Butler, Joseph; Dante, Alighieri; Machiavelli, Niccolo; Muslim Morals; Spinoza; Zuni Indians, Morals of.

Epictetus: *see* Minor Socratics; Stoics, the.

Epicureanism: *see* Dante, Alighieri; Goethe, Johann Wolfgang von; Minor Socratics; Stoics, the.

Epicurus: *see* China, Moral Philosophies of; Dante, Alighieri; Major Ethical Viewpoints.

epigrams: *see* Jewish Ethics and Its Civilization.

Epimetheus: *see* Sophists, the.

epistemology: *see* Clarke, Samuel; Cudworth, Ralph; Green, T. H.; Kant, I.; Knowledge; Meta-ethics and Normative Ethics; More, Henry; Price, Richard; Prichard, H. A.; Reid, Thomas; Scheler, Max; Soviet Morality, Current; Stoics, the.

equalitarianism: *see* Quakerism, Classical, The Morality of.

equality: *see* China, Moral Philosophies of; Hammurapi, Code of; Quakerism, Classical, The Morality of.

equality of sexes: *see* Zoroastrian Morals.

equanimity: *see* Hindu Ethics; serenity.

equilibrium: *see* balance.

equi-probabilism: *see* Jesuits, the, Moral Theology of; Liguori, St. Alphonsus and Catholic Moral Philosophy.

equity: *see* Clarke, Samuel.

eros: *see* Schopenhauer, Arthur.

eros cult: *see* Soviet Morality, Current.

error: *see* falsity; Freud, Sigmund; Liguori, St. Alphonsus and Catholic Moral Philosophy; Puritan Morals; Reid, Thomas; Spinoza; Wollaston, William.

eschatology: *see* Hegel, G. W. F.; Jewish Ethics and Its Civilization.

eschatology and Jesus' ethics: *see* Christian Moral Philosophy.

Escobar, Antonio: *see* Jesuits, the Moral Theology of.

essences: *see* Hartmann, Nicolai.

Essenes: *see* Jewish Ethics and Its Civilization.

esteem: *see* Zuni Indians, Morals of.

eternal law: *see* Aquinas, Thomas, Moral Views of; Liguori, St. Alphonsus and Catholic Moral Philosophy.

ethical absolutism: *see* Major Ethical Viewpoints.

ethical egoism: *see* egoism, ethical.

ethical naturalism: *see* Moral Philosophy in America; naturalism; Ross, Sir (William) David.

ethical rationalism: *see* Major Ethical Viewpoints.

Ethical Viewpoints, Major: *see* Major Ethical Viewpoints.

ethics: *see* Hindu Ethics; Major Ethical Viewpoints; Meta-ethics and Normative Ethics; Moral Philosophy in America; Psychology and Morals.

ethics and language: *see* Ayer, Alfred J.; Language and Ethics; Meta-ethics and Normative Ethics; Moral Philosophy in America.

ethics and metaphysics: *see* Aristotle; Hindu Ethics.

ethics and morals: *see* Major Ethical Viewpoints.

ethics, philosophical: *see* Hartmann, Nicolai; Morals and Religion.

ethics, social: *see* social ethics.

ethics, traditional: *see* Moore, George Edward.

etiquette: *see* Aboriginals of Yirkalla.

Eucken, Rudolf: *see* Scheler, Max.

Eucleides: *see* Minor Socratics.

euthanasia: *see* Liguori, St. Alphonsus and Catholic Moral Philosophy; Marxist Theory of Morals.

evil: *see* Aquinas, Thomas, Moral Views of; Augustine and Morals; Aztec Morals; bad, the; Berdyaev Nicolas; Broad, C. D.; Butler, Joseph; China, Moral Philosophies of; Cudworth, Ralph; Dante, Alighieri; Dewey, John; Freud, Sigmund; good and bad; good and evil; Hammurapi, Code of; Hindu Ethics; Hobbes, Thomas; Jesuits, the Moral Theology of; Jewish Ethics and Its Civilization; Liguori, St. Alphonsus and Catholic Moral Philosophy; Machiavelli, Niccolo; Major Ethical Viewpoints; Moore, George Edward; More, Henry; Muslim Morals; Navaho Morals; Pakot, the Moral System of; Plato; Psychology and Morals; Quakerism, Classical, The Morality of; Reid, Thomas; Rio Grande Pueblo Indians; Ross, Sir (William) David; Scheler, Max; Schlick, Moritz; Schopenhauer, Arthur; Soloviev, Wladimir; Sophists, the; Soviet Morality, Current; Spinoza; Stoics, the; Tapirapé Morals, Some Aspects of; Tolstoy, Leo; vice; wickedness; Wollaston, William; Zoroastrian Morals.

evolution: *see* Major Ethical Viewpoints; Primitive Morals.

evolutionary ethics: *see* Moral Philosophy in America.

159

Ewing: *see* Clarke, Samuel; Price, Richard.

excess: *see* Hindu Ethics; Navaho Morals; Zuni Indians, Morals of.

excommunication: *see* Spinoza.

existence: *see* Spinoza.

existential ethics: *see* Soviet Morality, Current.

existentialism: *see* French existentialism; French Existentialism and Moral Philosophy; Kierkegaard, Soren; Moral Philosophy in America; Scheler, Max.

expediency: *see* Augustine and Morals; Kant, I.; Marxist Theory of Morals; Soviet Morality, Current; Utilitarianism.

experience: *see* Jewish Ethics and Its Civilization; Moral Philosophy in America.

experimentalism: *see* Dewey, John.

exploitation: *see* Marxist Theory of Morals.

extrinsic principles: *see* Liguori, St. Alphonsus and Catholic Moral Philosophy.

F

Fabritius, L.: *see* Spinoza.
failure: *see* Hindu Ethics.
Fairchild, J. H.: *see* Moral Philosophy in America.
fair-play: *see* Aboriginals of Yirkalla; Pakot, the Moral System of; Rio Grande Pueblo Indians.
faith: *see* Aquinas, Thomas, Moral Views of; Dante, Alighieri; Jewish Ethics and Its Civilization; Kant, I.; Khomiakov, Alexey; Moral Philosophy in America; Spinoza; Zoroastrian Morals.
faithfulness: *see* Hindu Ethics; Muslim Morals.
falsehood: *see* Hindu Ethics; Zoroastrian Morals.
falsity: *see* Ayer, Alfred J.; Clarke, Samuel; error; Hammurapi, Code of; lying; Reid, Thomas; Wollaston, William.
fame: *see* Hindu Ethics.
family: *see* Aquinas, Thomas, Moral Views of; China, Moral Philosophy of; Hindu Ethics; Marxist Theory of Morals; Riffian Morals; Rio Grande Pueblo Indians; Soviet Morality, Current; Tapirapé Morals, Some Aspects of.
family loyalty: *see* Hindu Ethics; Navaho Morals.
famine: *see* Rio Grande Pueblo Indians.
fanaticism: *see* Puritan Morals.

fasting: *see* Jewish Ethics and its Civilization; Muslim Morals.
fatalism: *see* China, Moral Philosophies of; Muslim Morals; Psychology and Morals.
fate: *see* Augustine and Morals; Aztec Morals; Freud, Sigmund; Stoics, the.
fatigue: *see* Aztec Morals.
Faust: *see* Goethe, Johann Wolfgang von.
favorite child, the: *see* Tapirapé Morals, Some Aspects of.
fear: *see* Augustine and Morals; Butler, Joseph; Cooper, Anthony Ashley; Freud, Sigmund; Hindu Ethics; Hobbes, Thomas; Kant, I.; Muslim Morals; Psychology and Morals; Puritan Morals; Quakerism, Classical, The Morality of; Spinoza; Tapirapé Morals, Some Aspects of; Utilitarianism.
fear of God: *see* Augustine and Morals.
fearlessness: *see* Hindu Ethics.
fecundity: *see* Utilitarianism.
feelings: *see* Ayer, Alfred J.; Balguy, John; Cooper, Anthony Ashley; emotions; Language and Ethics; Machiavelli, Niccolo; Price, Richard; Prichard, H. A.; Reid, Thomas; Schlick, Moritz; Utilitarianism.
Feigl: *see* Schlick, Moritz.
felicity: *see* Muslim Morals.

161

fetishes: *see* Zuni Indians, Morals of.

feudalism: *see* Hammurapi, Code of; Marxist Theory of Morals.

feuds: *see* Aboriginals of Yirkalla; Riffian Morals.

Fichte, J. G.: *see* Goethe, Johann Wolfgang von; Hegel, G. W. F.; Schopenhauer, Arthur.

fiddling: *see* Puritan Morals.

fidelity: *see* Aquinas, Thomas, Moral Views of; Ross, Sir (William) David.

fighting: *see* pugnacity; Puritan Morals; Riffian Morals.

fines, payment of: *see* Hammurapi, Code of; Pakot, The Moral System of; Puritan Morals; Rio Grande Pueblo Indians.

Finkelstein, L.: *see* Jewish Ethics and Its Civilization.

Finney, C. G.: *see* Moral Philosophy in America.

fire worshippers: *see* Zoroastrian Morals.

first principles: *see* Aquinas, Thomas, Moral Views of; Reid, Thomas.

Fiske, John: *see* Moral Philosophy in America.

Fite, W.: *see* Major Ethical Viewpoints.

fitness: *see* Kant, I.; Plato.

fitting(ness): *see* Balguy, John; Broad, C. D.; Clarke, Samuel.

Fitzroy, R.: *see* Primitive Morals.

Five Classics, The: *see* China, Moral Philosophies of.

flattery: *see* Dante, Alighieri; Machiavelli, Niccolo; Quakerism, Classical, The Morality of.

Flornoy, B.: *see* Primitive Morals.

folklore: *see* Puritan Morals.

food: *see* Aboriginals of Yirkalla; Aztec Morals; eating; Primitive Morals.

force: *see* China, Moral Philosophies of; Hobbes, Thomas.

forgetting: *see* amnesia; Freud, Sigmund; Psychology and Morals.

forgiveness: *see* Augustine and Morals; Christian Moral Philosophy; Dostoyevsky. Fyodor; Hindu Ethics; Quakerism, Classical, The Morality of.

formalism: *see* Jewish Ethics and Its Civilization; Wollaston, William.

formalism, ethical: *see* Hartmann, Nicolai.

formalistic ethics: *see* Kant; Moral Philosophy in America.

fornication: *see* Augustine and Morals.

fortitude: *see* Augustine and Morals; Dante, Alighieri; More, Henry.

fortune: *see* Aztec Morals.

foundation of morals: *see* Balguy, John; Cudworth, Ralph.

Fowler, E.: *see* More, Henry.

Fox, George: *see* Quakerism, Classical, The Morality of.

frame of reference: *see* Psychology and Morals.

Frank, Semyon: *see* Berdyaev, Nicolas.

Frankena, William K.: *see* More, Henry; Reid, Thomas.

Franklin, Benjamin: *see* Moral Philosophy in America.

fraud: *see* Dante, Alighieri; Hobbes, Thomas; Navaho Morals; Soviet Morality, Current.

Frazer, J. G.: *see* Primitive Morals.

free association: *see* Freud, Sigmund.

free love: *see* Soviet Morality, Current.

free thinkers: *see* Moral Philosophy in America.

free will: *see* Cudworth, Ralph; Dante,

Alighieri; Jewish Ethics and Its Civilization; More, Henry; Soviet Morality, Current; Utilitarianism.

freedom: *see* Aquinas, Thomas, Moral Views of; Aristotle; Berdyaev, Nicolas; Christian Moral Philosophy; Cudworth, Ralph; Dewey, John; Dostoyevsky, Fyodor; French Existentialism and Moral Philosophy; Hartmann, Nicolai; Hindu Ethics; Jesuits, the, Moral Theology of; Jewish Ethics and Its Civilization; Kant, I.; Khomiakov, Alexey; Liguori, St. Alphonsus and Catholic Moral Philosophy; Minor Socratics; Moore, George Edward; Moral Freedom and Responsibility; Moral Philosophy in America; More, Henry; Quakerism, Classical, The Morality of; Russell, Bertrand; Soviet Morality, Current; Stoics, the; Zoroastrian Morals.

freedom, human: *see* China, Moral Philosophies of; Cudworth, Ralph; Freud, Sigmund; Goethe, Johann Wolfgang von; Green, T. H.; Hegel, G. W. F.; Hindu Ethics; Hume, David; Price, Richard; Schopenhauer, Arthur; Spinoza; Utilitarianism.

freedom, moral: *see* Kant, I.; Soviet Morality, Current.

freedom of thought: *see* Spinoza.

French Encyclopedists: *see* Cudworth, Ralph.

French Existentialism and Moral Philosophy

There are moments in every man's life that are so bewildering that like Peer Gynt in Ibsen's play he would give everything he has for a signpost saying: "This is the way." Crucial situations strike at the heart of man and his many concerns, his innumerable plans, his multiple intentions seem to flee from him and leave him with but one: What is his way? Sometimes man turns to philosophy for help and indeed the great ethical doctrines of the past have tried to show ways for him to follow. Does the philosophy of Existence help?

All contemporary existential thinkers have at some time or other been asked to write an ethics. None of them has done so as yet and indeed it would seem that their very method of inquiry would exclude such a possibility. They are phenomenologists and as such have set themselves the task of describing man in the world rather than theorizing about him and it. They are concerned with what is and not like traditional metaphysics with what can be or like moral philosophers with what ought to be. Their ontology is a description of the structures of being, the being of man, the being of the world, and the being of things, stemming from a pre-reflective level of consciousness; a view of man and his world free of the customary ways, logical or empirical, idealistic or materialistic, of looking at them. In circumventing these usual ways of thinking, they have had to circumvent the usual ways of writing, and their unorthodox forms of expression are not the clear and precise language of strict philosophy. This is the reason they are sometimes accused of obscurity. Their descriptions of human existence and the world break the ordinary bounds of grammar and seem to require a freer

163

means of communication and a new structure of language. When they leave the ontological level, instead of writing philosophical treatises they choose an artistic medium in which to express their ideas.

This article is concerned with the French school of Existentialism of which the outstanding representatives are: Jean Paul Sartre, Simone de Beauvoir, Maurice Merleau-Ponty and Gabriel Marcel.

Jean Paul Sartre

Jean Paul Sartre was born in Paris in 1905, studied at the "Ecole Normale" and received from there a degree in philosophy. He taught philosophy in Havre, Laon and Paris. He traveled in Germany, Italy, Spain, England and Greece. During the second World War he served in Alsace and was taken prisoner in 1940 and released in 1941. After his discharge he played an active role in the "Résistance." He gave up teaching to devote his time to writing. He is a successful playwright and novelist in addition to being a philosopher.

At the end of his philosophical work *L'Être et le Néant,* Sartre states that it is not possible to draw ethical imperatives from his phenomenological ontology. However, he adds that his descriptions open up a new horizon within which to view questions concerning the conduct of life. He calls this "moral description" and promises to dedicate another of his works to it. Simone de Beauvoir in her *Ethics of Ambiguity* and Merleau-Ponty in his *Humanism et Terreur* in the mean-

time have already started on this enterprise. Gabriel Marcel's position is different since he is a Christian existentialist but he, too, in so far as he remains existential in the Kierkegaardian sense, rejects submission to dogma, both religious and ethical.

Since they, like all existential philosophers, take away the belief in dogma, the adherence to ethical principles and the hope of finding a universally valid standard of judgment, how do they throw light on the complexities of human conduct? Can they help poor Peer find his guidepost?

Since Sartre is regarded as the most profound as well as the most explicit of this group of existentialists, it is well to start with him. In *L'Être et le Néant* he rejects the two classical ways of looking at the question of the natural and social connection between man and his world which form the bases for either a relative or an absolute ethics. According to one of these views man is seen as the product of physiological, psychological and sociological influences, shaped by them and to be understood through them. He differs from all other natural phenomena in degree but not in kind. According to the other, he is said to have a freedom found no where else in nature. That is, in one, man is reduced to a thing in the world, in the other his consciousness is free to form the world. While the first view gives rise to naturalistic and relative standards of morality and the second to the "ought" as an absolute, both provide an objective justification for man's action. He is promised that if he plays the game

164

of life according to the rules he will win.

Sartre does not see eye to eye with either of these views. According to him, man's difference from things is not one of degree but precisely one of kind, and his description of freedom is such that man cannot be said to "have" it. A "thing," Sartre explains, obeys the laws of nature, enclosed within certain limits, a fullness of being, identical with itself. It is what it is. Sartre calls this region of being "l'Être-en-soi." Man, when he is identified with his body, seems to belong to it and this identification has given rise to the belief in "human nature" as something that can be known, that can be shaped and controlled by outside influences and which therefore can also be expected to act in accordance with generally accepted rules of behavior. But, says Sartre, in spite of this seeming, the self is never merely an "être-en-soi." It can do what no object can do, it can question its own being. It originates in a No. Only man knows he is not something and from this original negation stems his selfhood. "Things" are what they are without negation, they are "positivité." The self, on the other hand, has to be what it is, a "Néant," a not-being, a nothingness. Man is characterized by a lack of being, "he is what he is not and he is not what he is." Therefore there can no longer be any question of "human nature" nor the generalizations about man which this concept entails. Man is not a "thing" therefore there can be no relative ethics.

In Sartre's philosophy there can be no absolute ethics either since his concept of freedom differs fundamentally from the traditional ones on which such an ethics is based. His affirmation of man's freedom is neither the result of a logical demonstration nor of an hypothesis verified by empirical data but is, instead, the outcome of phenomenological analysis. While in traditional thought consciousness is considered the fruition of nature, for Sartre it breaks into the fabric of nature like a flaw. It is an emptiness, a nothingness, and this nothingness he calls freedom. No "thing" can be free but man's very being is his freedom. He cannot not be free; he is, in Sartre's words, "condemned to be free." In traditional concepts, freedom pertains to man's essence as one of its attributes or qualities, while for Sartre on the contrary, it is through his freedom that man creates his essence. He becomes what he is through his acts. According to Sartre and all existential philosophy, the mistaken premise of the different types of idealism and their absolute ethics is that they take the subject with its essence as their starting point instead of viewing "subjectivity" as that toward which we constantly struggle. As soon as the concept of essence as something given is abandoned and is looked at in Sartre's way as created through man's choice, general principles and absolute standards are meaningless. Sartre tells us how he thinks value arises. The tension created by the constant striving between the two types of being, the "en soi" and the "pour soi," which is human existence, gives birth to value.

165

Consciousness or "pour soi" experiences itself as lack, as not-being, and just as Nature abhors a vacuum this nothingness, this void, strives to fill itself and in so doing produces values.

Traditionally, the ultimate value, Sartre says, is God. God by definition as "causa sui" and "ens a se" would be the synthesis which this striving of the "pour soi" is constantly trying to achieve and never can since by its nature it has to say "No" to the en soi. In other words man tries to become God and can't but instead succeeds in putting what pertains to the structure of his being outside himself in much the same way as a primitive separates his soul from himself. Man objectifies his own striving and worships it under many different names. All lesser or derivative values come about in the same way as the ultimate one. Once the values are objectified and regarded as principles they conceal from man his true being which is freedom, and so instead of creating his own values he adheres to collective ones. Man is constantly tempted to do this because freedom means anguish and by following established values he escapes this anguish. The turning away from freedom of which the acceptance of ready made values is a prime example Sartre calls "bad faith." Although the term "bad faith" might lead one to think it is tinged with a moral sense it has nothing to do with morality. What it does have to do with is Sartre's conception of "authenticity." By creating one's own values one can lead an authentic life, by adopting the "objective" ones an inauthentic one, but neither is good nor bad. In Sartre's philosophy it is true the authentic way seems to be preferred, but this is not because it is conceived of as "good" but because in it man knows the truth of his being. In choosing his freedom he becomes the "homo creator" who creates his own being and his own world and is responsible for both. This freedom is nothing and everything. It is a curse as well as the source of all human greatness and, just as it has ceased to be an ideal and has become instead his very being, so is his "total responsibility" no longer a moral precept but the outcome of his being.

It is as if Sartrean man had abandoned the study of metaphysics in order to embody it and this metaphysical power bursts all ready made absolutes. In utter loneliness he makes his own choices and thereby chooses for all mankind. He is alone and yet indissolubly linked with all men. In Sartre's philosophy human existence begins in a "No" and arrives at a "Yes," the ultimate Yes to the truth and affirmation of its being.

Simone de Beauvoir

Simone de Beauvoir was born in Paris in 1909. She studied at the Sorbonne and holds the "licence de philosophie" from there. She taught in "lycées" in Marseilles, Rouen and Paris. In 1943 she gave up teaching to dedicate herself to writing. She is the author of many novels, essays and plays. In 1947 she spent four months in the United States on a lecture tour sponsored by the French Embassy. She has been a friend of Jean Paul Sartre's since the early twenties when they were both students at the Sorbonne. Much of her work has been written at the "Café des deux Magots" and the "Café de Flore" both of which are meeting places for artistic and philosophical spirits in present-day Paris.

Simone de Beauvoir accepts Sartre's view of man and draws from it moral implications. Her basic concern is with freedom as the being of man. How is it to be engaged in a specific situation and why? On Sartre's ontological premise is not one action as "good" or "bad" as another? Why seek at all since what I attain today will be surpassed tomorrow? Her struggle with these questions finds its philosophical expression in her book *The Ethics of Ambiguity*, whose very title reveals her stand on moral questions. Since existence is ambiguous, she suggests that we accept ambiguity instead of trying to flee from it. "It is in the knowledge of the genuine conditions of our life," she says, "that we must draw our strength to live and our reason for acting," and means that all reasons and justifications for man's actions are to be won from the structure of existence itself. And so, instead of being considered as "ideals" and "precepts" they have become possibilities of one's being and their formulation or expression is a "moral description." Man, says Simone de Beauvoir, is originally free, in the sense that he spontaneously casts himself into the world. His morality, or, in traditional terms, his "good" is the affirmation of his "freedom." Here the question arises, "Does it make sense to speak of affirming freedom when man cannot

not be free?" It does, since his freedom also permits denial. Man denies it by hiding his own structure from himself, veiling the truth of his being, living in untruth or inauthenticity.

Through her concept of existence, Simone de Beauvoir tries to show what it means to act freely in a specific situation. Existence moves between two extreme possibilities. In one of them the individual lives in the moment, in the immediate, in diversions and pastimes; his experience is not connected since by emphasis on the fleeting "now" he holds it only bit by bit at a time, his existence crumbles into nothing. In the other, the individual, far from living in pure immediacy and the moment, runs away from the immediate, thrusts himself into the future so far that his possibilities become unreal, mere phantoms out of reach. He is the "stargazer" of the ancients who, by looking too far cannot see what is near him; he empties his existence and misses his time. He sees innumerable possibilities and is able to seize none; yet to him it seems as if everything were possible. Such a man, although conscious of his freedom, engages it in mirages instead of realities. True existence lies between these poles and creates itself through its decisions and choices. It escapes immediacy because through its goals and intentions it stretches towards the future and also towards the past by ceaselessly returning to it to incorporate it into the whole of its intention. Thus freedom confirms itself in the unity of time, each act being one of its embodiments

167

and foreshadowing new possibilities for itself.

Simone de Beauvoir draws a vivid picture of those who by trying to negate their freedom restrain the free movement of existence. She calls them submen. "He," (the subman), "discovers around him only an insignificant and dull world. How could this naked world arouse within him any desire to feel, to understand, to live? The less he exists, the less is there reason for him to exist, since these reasons are created only by existing. . . He would like to forget himself, to be ignorant of himself, but the nothingness which is at the heart of man is also the consciousness that he has of himself . . . His negativity is revealed positively as anguish, desire, appeal . . . He is thereby led to take refuge in the ready made values of the serious world . . . He will take shelter behind a label . . . One day a monarchist, the next day an anarchist, he is more readily anti-semitic, anti-clerical or anti-republican . . . He realizes himself in the world as a blind uncontrolled force which anybody can get control of."

The subman lives in untruth, he takes flight from himself, while the authentic man accepts the ambiguity of his existence and adheres to his self. True morality in Beauvoir's view does not consist in following fixed principles or in respecting objective values. There are no ready made means by which to be justified and saved. True morality consists in being actively what we are by accident, the incarnation of freedom.

Maurice Merleau-Ponty

Maurice Merleau-Ponty also starts with Sartre's analysis of man but has, as his special work, developed a conception of the "conscience engagée" (Sartre's pour-soi engagé), believing that it solves difficulties he sees in Sartre's analysis of man's "being-in-the-world." He does this on two levels: the ontological and the historical. Both studies are based on the concept of the ambiguity of existence. His ontological inquiry into the problem has resulted in a phenomenology of perception ("Phenomenologie de la Perception"), which describes perception as a mode of being in which an engaged consciousness organizes the field of perception and presents us with our world. He has tried, in his inquiry into the problem of "being-in-the-world" from the historical perspective, to arrive at a philosophy of history, and has presented his ideas in a series of essays entitled *Humanism et Terreur*. While, from the basic concepts of the ambiguity of existence and "the conscience engagée," Simone de Beauvoir develops implications for the meaning and conduct of the individual and his relations to others, Merleau-Ponty relates them to historical action. What criteria are there for the statesman? What signposts does he have to show him the way to the "right" decisions? Just as for Simone de Beauvoir there are no objective standards for human conduct, so for Merleau-Ponty there are no criteria for the statesman's actions. It is how his deed turns out that matters, and its evaluation takes place later in the light of circumstances which the doer cannot possibly be aware of at the time he acts. "An historical situation cannot be treated," Merleau-Ponty says, "as if it were a problem in geometry, where, although there are unknowns, there are no indeterminates." It is precisely the indeterminates, according to him, which make history a terror. For, he says, while history remains "open," and "the truth" of a situation is truth for some only and arbitrariness for others, man is not able to be a spectator but has to be an actor. Plunged into an unfinished historical situation he has to act with no guarantee of the outcome. What sense does it make, then, to speak of conscience engagée? How is it to be engaged? Merleau-Ponty answers that the problem is not to be considered in the light of principles and ideologies but in the light of human relations. A society is worth exactly what the relations that make it up are worth. The tragedy of human relations lies in the fact that though men are subjects they "perceive" each other as objects and so use, exploit and mistrust one another.

It is here, Merleau-Ponty says, in the field of human relations, that, by involving itself in them, consciousness can be "engaged." And it is this, this involvement, that is the actions of men who see all men as subjects, that is historical freedom.

Otherwise, he says, quoting St. Paul, freedom is a cruel God who demands his hecatombs. To translate his own words, "Man's views and actions, relative as they are, are the absolute itself because there is nothing else, there is no destiny. By our acts and by our ideas we touch the absolute, or rather the relations between men are the absolute." Merleau-Ponty views history as a tragedy because its possibilities are many and the actuality is one, and because of the predicament in which man is of having to choose a possibility and act upon it as if it were already realized. As he says, "Whatever we do is a risk." But this ambiguity and contingency which he sees at the heart of history does not lead him to relativism. He definitely states, "What we have to say is not that in history all is relative, but rather that all is absolute." Man cannot help looking at the future any more than he can stop breathing. He shares with others a historical situation, argues about it and gives it meaning. The world, in the words of Merleau-Ponty, "is an open and unfinished system and the same contingency that threatens it with discord also gives it the possibility of getting out of it." Any historical situation is ambiguous but it need not therefore be absurd. All one has to remember is that it is made by the acts of men.

Gabriel Marcel

Gabriel Marcel was born in 1889 as the son of the minister of France to Stockholm. His father was a non-practicing Catholic; his mother, who died when Gabriel Marcel was four, was Jewish. Marcel himself became a Catholic in 1929. He lives in Paris, where he is a music critic and a successful playwright.

While Sartre, Beauvoir and Merleau-Ponty can be said to form a "school" of Existentialism, Gabriel Marcel stands by himself. He is an original existential thinker who, like Kierkegaard, wants neither system nor school and who takes philosophy to be a search or an investigation. It is interesting to know that he had not read Kierkegaard when he called his own philosophy "Philosophie de l'Existence." Although Marcel is a Christian existentialist, he says that his philosophy was not predicated on Christian thought but as he proceeded he found Christianity fitting in naturally with his metaphysics.

He describes modern man as a man of functions who identifies himself with them, and allotting to each function a certain amount of time, he runs on a schedule. The whole world is functionalized. In his essay "On the Ontological Mystery," Marcel describes the sadness that the impression of such a world produces. "It is sufficient to recall the dreary image of the retired official, or those urban Sundays when the passers-by look like people who have retired from life. In such a world, there is something mocking and sinister even in the tolerance awarded to the man who has retired from his work." But the sadness is also experienced by the man himself who has surrendered to his functions. He feels the lack of something which he cannot define but which shows itself in his experience as restlessness, uneasiness, "emptiness" and despair. He cannot cope with the many problems that occur in his life; he does not know where to turn for help, which is not surprising since in the eyes of Marcel such a

life has lost its reality, it has "emptied" itself, it has become nothing. According to Marcel, men in this state are never really "present," they are always "absent"; their physical presence does, of course, not overcome their "absence" as beings who can be "with" others in the genuine sense. That is why they vanish when there is need for them, a fact which they try to cover up with a lot of talk, and why the mark of their relationships with others is betrayal.

To escape this plight, man needs to recognize his sense of being. He can only do this as a result of his experience of the emptiness of existence, and it is this experienced need to fill the void that is the first step out of despair. When he takes this step his life can be authentic and despair is vanquished by hope. In speaking of hope, Marcel makes it clear that he speaks of it as a metaphysical concept and not a psychological one. Hope in his sense has nothing to do with fear and desire. It implies an assertion, not a doubt. It is, he says, "the assertion that there is at the heart of being, beyond all data, beyond all inventories and all calculations, a mysterious principle which is in connivance with me, which cannot but will that which I will, if what I will deserves to be willed and is, in fact, willed by the whole of my being." Through hope man makes his link with being, or absolute presence; through it he overcomes his alienation from himself and the world which means, in other words, he finds his salvation. He has become "faithful" to being, and therefore can be faithful to himself and to others. This faithfulness is not an ideal or principle, for Marcel, but rather it is an "active perpetuation of presence and the renewal of its benefits." Such a man can now be "present" to others, can be "with" them in the genuine sense; he is capable of love in its Christian meaning. In fact, a man's knowledge of himself should be based on the love shown him by others. "Fundamentally," Marcel says, "I set no other store by myself, except in so far that I know that I am loved by other people." And in *The Mystery of Being* he writes, "Love tends away from the functional world"; the more I am "present" to others, the more I can say "I am." Through love man becomes a subject in truth. Marcel's thought is essentially metaphysical and one cannot speak therefore of an ethics proper, although it is possible to infer moral implications from it. His conceptions of "faithfulness," "hope," "love" are metaphysical, not moral. They are descriptive of man's being and may be affirmed or denied through his freedom.

* * *

It is apparent that the philosophy of these French Existentialists will not furnish man with any ready made guideposts, any traditional ethical principles or moral precepts, but it may furnish him with something better; with examples of men who can look at their own being, face what they see and so assume a responsibility in a sphere which, maybe, is at once larger and more wonderful than that bounded by rules and dogma. It is a philosophy grounded in non-being and negation. While it looks at the tragic aspects of existence, despair, betrayal, death, it does so for the sake of affirmation, for on the other side of despair, they say, life begins.

Bibliography

Jean Paul Sartre, *L'Être et le Néant,* Bibliothèque des Idées, Libraire Gallimard (Paris, 1943). English translation by Hazel E. Barnes: *Being and Nothingness* (Philosophical Library, New York, 1956).
——, *Les Chemins de la Liberté,* Bibliothèque des Idées, Librairy Gallimard (Paris, 1945).
——, *No Exit and The Flies* (New York, 1947).
Gabriel Marcel, *The Philosophy of Existence* (New York, 1949).
——, *Du Refus à l'Invocation* (Paris, 1940).
——, *Journal Métaphysique* (Paris, Aubier, 1914).
Maurice Merleau-Ponty, *La Structure du Comportement* (Paris, Presses Universitaires de France, 1953).
——, *Sens et Non Sens* (Paris, éditions Nagel, 1948).
——, *Humanism et Terreur* (Paris, Gallimard, 1947).
Simone, de Beauvoir, *Ethics of Ambiguity* (New York, 1948).
——, *The Second Sex* (New York, 1953).
——, *L'invitée* (Paris, Gallimard, 1943).

Ria Stavrides
Vassar College

French Existentialism: *see* existentialism; Freud, Sigmund.

Freud, Sigmund
Freud was born in Freiberg (then Austria-Hungary, now Czechoslova-

kia) on May 6, 1856. Being a Jew, he tells us, he learned early to discount the judgment of the compact majority. He studied medicine, took his M.D. in Vienna in 1881, specialized in brain anatomy, and in 1885 was made a lecturer for neuro-pathology. He studied hysteria with Charcot in Paris, and a little later came very close to establishing the use of cocaine as a local anaesthetic. In 1886 he got married. Then he studied hypnosis with Bernheim in Nancy and, back in Vienna, hysteria together with Breuer. Out of these studies he gradually developed his own theories, and in 1900 he published his first major work which he continued to consider his greatest: *The Interpretation of Dreams*. 600 copies were printed, and it took eight years to sell them; but before Freud's death the book went through eight editions and was widely translated. More than any other single event, publication of this book marks the beginning of psychoanalysis which Freud created and for which he coined the name. (Nazi antiSemites, who belittled Freud's contribution, sometimes claimed that Breuer was the real founder—not knowing that Breuer too was a Jew.)

Before the first World War, Freud published several other fundamental works, including *The Psychopathology of Everyday Life*, his *Three Contributions to the Theory of Sex*, and *Totem and Tabu*. In 1911 and 1912 Alfred Adler and C. G. Jung seceded from Freud's school. During the War, Freud summed up his conclusions so far in a notable series of lectures, soon published and translated as *General Introduction to Psychoanalysis*—still by far the best introduction to the subject.

After the War Freud tried to systematize his theories, an attempt that led to some modifications and to the introduction of several new concepts, including the death impulse, the ego, the id, and the superego. These concepts represent afterthoughts; psychoanalysis does not stand or fall with them, and Freud's claim to fame might not have been greatly diminished had he stopped writing in 1920. Yet his attempt to systematize was by no means prompted by dogmatism: books like *Beyond the Pleasure Principle* and *The Ego and the Id* show a determination to examine the adequacy and sufficiency of the concepts previously employed and a willingness to effect even drastic revisions where necessary. Freud's lack of respect for those who broke with him was motivated by his conviction that their modifications of his theory were prompted less by evidence than by a false regard for public opinion and, in Jung's case, also by a penchant for the occult.

In his later works Freud applied his ideas to a critique of religion as a product of wishful thinking (*The Future of an Illusion*) and to general cultural criticism and philosophic anthropology (*Civilization and Its Discontents*). When the Nazis entered Vienna in 1938 he escaped to London where he went on working until the last, in spite of cancer. He died on September 23, 1939.

Freud's few explicit references to ethics in his later works and even his theory of conscience may well be less important for ethics than the implications of his earlier work. We shall therefore begin with a brief sketch of Freud's approach to human nature.

Psychoanalysis began as a therapeutic method when Freud abandoned hypnosis. Much has been made of his "determinism"; but the whole purpose of his therapy, if not of his life, was to restore their freedom to people who had become unable to do what they wanted to do, or to stop doing what they wanted to stop doing. Moreover, Freud abandoned hypnosis because it represents an encroachment on the patient's freedom and therefore does not lead to a permanent or complete cure: he did not want his patients to buy back their freedom at the price of permanent dependence on another human being. It is extremely doubtful whether Freud ever denied freedom in any sense in which it would be worth having.

The new method consisted first of all in question and answer, in the course of which Freud encountered frequent resistance and amnesia. The association of these two phenomena led to the conception of repression which, as Freud himself pointed out, had been aphoristically anticipated by Nietzsche in section 68 of *Beyond Good and Evil*: " 'I have done that,' says my memory. 'I could not have done that,' says my pride and remains inexorable. Finally, my memory yields."

When he was able to overcome the patient's resistance and amnesia, Freud found that the repressed materials were very frequently concerned with sexual experiences of early childhood. Few of his contentions met with more initial opposition than the claim that young children are vitally interested in sexual functions, and few are such commonplaces today. Much more controversial is Freud's conception of the Oedipus complex to which we shall return later.

To avoid prejudicing his results by leading questions, Freud came to replace the method of question and answer by recourse to free association and by the interpretation of dreams which he called "the royal road to the unconscious." The central claim here is this: although internal physiological stimuli or external stimuli, like a noise, a smell, or a change of temperature, may trigger dreams, and although day residues turn up in dreams, every dream represents a wish fulfillment, almost always in disguised form. In the face of frequent misrepresentations, Freud insisted repeatedly that the wish need not be sexual. He illustrated the *Interpretation of Dreams* with Schwindt's "The Dream of the Prisoner," which shows gremlins sawing through the iron bars across the window and the prisoner escaping; and Freud reports, for example, the dream of a child who, after being denied a second helping of strawberries, dreamt of having it after all. Generally, however, the overt dream must be distinguished from the latent content which is disguised by an elaborate symbolism. Although some symbols are held to be almost invariable, a dream can be interpreted only with some knowledge of the dreamer's personal background and associations. The symbolism as well as other disfigurations of the latent content are charged to a "censor."

Even if one admits that the analysis of dreams, and of our associations with various elements in a dream, is a royal road to the unconscious, one may well question some of Freud's assumptions; e.g., that every dream has one, and only one, latent meaning, and that the symbolism is to be explained in terms of self-deception.

The central purpose of Freud's therapeutic interpretation of dreams, however, and indeed of his entire treatment, should not be overlooked. It is well stated in the 27th lecture of Freud's *General Introduction to Psychoanalysis:* "By raising the unconscious into consciousness, we overcome the repressions, abolish the conditions for symptom formation, and change the pathogenetic conflict into a normal conflict which must somehow find a resolution." "We hold that whoever has successfully passed through an education for truthfulness toward himself, will thereby be protected permanently against the danger of immorality, even if his standard of morality should somehow differ from social conventions."

Although Freud says in the same context, "Where there is no repression to be overcome, nor any analogous psychical process, there our therapeutics has no business," he exerted himself to show that repressions and analogous psychical processes were by no means confined to neurotics. Not only do other men dream too, but there is what Freud called "the psychopathology of everyday life." Here the key term is *Fehleistung,* one of Freud's many felicitous coinages, inadequately rendered as "error" or "slip." The coinage "mischievement" seems preferable. The theory here is that forgetting and slips in speaking, writing, or doing things, though triggered by tiredness or distraction, actually vent suppressed or repressed thoughts or wishes. A man who forgets his wedding, to give an extreme example, presumably does not wish to get married; and when Portia says to Bassanio, "One half of me is yours, the other half yours—Mine own, I would say," she shows that she has been thinking, though she did not mean to say it, that her whole heart belongs to Bassanio.

This last example is Freud's own and merely one instance among scores of illustrations from, or applications to, literature and art. Freud liked to show that what seemed fantastic to his contemporaries had long been known by Spinoza, Schopenhauer, and Nietzsche, and utilized by Shakespeare, Goethe, Schiller, and Dostoevsky. He also tried to illuminate literary problems, as he did in his famous footnote on *Hamlet* which was subsequently expanded into a book by Ernest Jones.

Most important, however, world literature furnishes powerful evidence against the common objection that the truth of Freud's theories is limited to the Vienna socialites around 1900 or, at best, to our own civilization.

Sophocles' Jocasta soothes Oedipus, saying: "many men have in their dreams had intercourse with their mothers." Plato says, at the beginning of the ninth book of the *Republic:* "Of the unnecessary pleasures and desires some seem to me to be unlawful. They threaten to rise up in everybody; but suppressed by the laws and the better desires with the help of reason, they disappear completely in some people, or only a few weak ones remain, but in others they remain stronger and more numerous. . . . those that awake in sleep when the other soul sleeps . . . but the animalic and wild part, overfull of food and drink, leaps up, shakes off sleep, and goes forth to satisfy its cravings. In such a state, as you know, he dares do anything, free of all shame and insight. He does not even think that he should shrink from intercourse with his mother . . ." And Dostoevsky's Ivan Karamazov, whose brother has been accused of murdering his father for the sake of a woman whom both father and son desired, shouts at the court: "Who doesn't desire his father's death?"

Such evidence of course does not establish the universality of these desires: only certain types in these civilizations, widely separated in space and time, might be troubled by such wishes; or such desires might be encountered only in some types of cultures, not in others. Freud argued powerfully, but not conclusively, that all men, regardless or race, color, or creed, are brothers under the skin. Those who disagree with him cannot rest satisfied with allegedly self-evident dif-

ferences but must deal explicitly with the evidence adduced by Freud and others, notably including Otto Rank's *Das Inzest-Motiv in Dichtung und Sage.*

There remains Freud's later work in which the Oedipus complex becomes, if anything, more important. In his *New Introductory Lectures on Psychoanalysis* (Chapter 5), he characterizes "the boy's Oedipus complex, in which he desires his mother, and wants to get rid of his father as a rival . . . The threat of castration forces him to give up this attitude. Under the influence of the danger of losing his penis, he abandons his Oedipus complex; it is repressed and in the most normal cases entirely destroyed, while a severe super-ego is set up as its heir." The super-ego, which has been facetiously characterized as the part of the personality which is soluble in alcohol, is the psychoanalytic equivalent of the conscience. But the universality of the process here described, or even of the Oedipus complex, has never been established, nor have Freud's followers made systematic studies of orphans, semi-orphans, children brought up by only one parent or neither parent, etc.

A theory suggested to Freud by Darwin but long since abandoned by anthropologists, leads to Freud's least plausible thesis: "We cannot get away from the supposition that the guilt feeling of mankind is derived from the Oedipus complex and was acquired when the father was killed by the association of the brothers," he says in section VII of *Civilization and its Dis-*

175

contents; and the notion of the murder of the primal father by his sons plays an even more decisive role in Freud's last book, *Moses and Monotheism.*

In the same section of *Civilization and its Discontents* Freud suggests that besides the sex impulse there is another basic urge, aggression. As the individual develops, "aggression is introjected, made inwardly—really, sent back to where it came from, namely, turned against one's own ego. There it is taken over by a part of the ego which, as the super-ego, stands opposed to the rest of the ego; and in the form of 'conscience' it now vents that same aggression against the ego which the ego would have liked to vent on other individuals. The tension between the severe super-ego and the ego subjected to it we call the consciousness of guilt; it finds expression in the need for punishment." The wording depends on Freud's assumption that aggression is, in its original form, directed against the self as a death impulse.

Freud's theory of conscience is similar to Nietzsche's which is expounded in somewhat greater detail in the second essay of the *Genealogy of Morals.* Freud himself says: "Nietzsche, the other philosopher whose premonitions and insights often agree in the most amazing manner with the laborious results of psychoanalysis, I have long avoided for this very reason. After all, I was less concerned about any priority than about the preservation of my impartiality." (*Selbstdarstellung*). Since his remarks about conscience do not represent "laborious results" but bold speculations, it may have been unfortunate that Freud did not give more careful attention to rival naturalistic theories—and especially to Nietzsche's attempt to explain in terms of a single basic drive the phenomena which led Freud after World War I to modify his earlier psychological monism by postulating a death impulse.

A few more quotations from the same section may round out Freud's ideas about the genesis of conscience. "Evil is thus originally that for which one is threatened with loss of love; one must avoid it from fear of such loss." And a couple of pages later: "Fate is considered as a substitute for the parents; when one suffers misfortune this means that one is no longer loved by this highest power; and threatened by this loss of love, one submits again to the parent surrogate in the super-ego which one was ready to neglect as long as everything went well." Even though it takes misfortune to make us submit, Freud argues only a few pages later that, once the super-ego is developed, the feeling of guilt becomes chronic: "The denial of gratification does not help sufficiently, for the wish remains and cannot be hidden from the super-ego. In spite of the successful denial, therefore, a feeling of guilt will develop . . ." In the last chapter, finally Freud says "that the feeling of guilt . . . in its later phases is one and the same thing as fear [*Angst*] of the super-ego."

Freud's later theories, here outlined, certainly give no adequate picture of his importance for ethics. At best they require such sympathetic modification as, for example, David Riesman's suggestion in *The Lonely Crowd* that the super-ego account fits what Riesman calls the "inner-directed" person but not the "tradition-directed" or "other-directed" type.

Freud's significance for ethics can perhaps be summed up best in terms of a brief comparison first with Socrates and then with Jesus. With Socrates he shares first of all the motto, "know thyself!" Freud lent substance to this demand when he showed how ingeniously we deceive ourselves, hiding from consciousness what pains us or does not meet with our approval; and he suggested techniques for attaining self-knowledge. Freud has often been censured for overemphasizing the dark side of man, a charge against which he defended himself in the *General Introduction*, chapter IX: "We dwell on the evil side of man with greater emphasis only because other men deny it, which makes man's psychic life not better but incomprehensible." As a theory of human nature, psychoanalysis seems partial indeed: one might say that, unlike Kant, Freud furnished a "critique of *un*-reason." To be sure, he did not intend to deny man's reason: Robert Waelder recalls how Freud said to him, "To me the moral has always seemed self-evident"; and Theodor Reik recalls how Freud refused to accept Reik's pessimistic estimate of man's future. Even so Freud's explicit comments on the aspirations of the artist, the seeker after truth, and the religious genius are simplistic, and his philosophical anthropology does not

commend itself. But it should not be forgotten that his reason for focussing attention on the irrational was that he had come to the conclusion that we must face and understand it before we could become autonomous. His approach was initially therapeutic and has pedagogical value, even though it does not yield a complete theory of human nature.

The second parallel with Socrates may be found in the belief of both men that virtue is knowledge—knowledge not of transcendant verities or of God but of ourselves. At this point Freud, like Socrates, is an optimist: the man who knows himself will not only cease to be neurotic but—and this passage was quoted above—he "will thereby be protected permanently against the danger of immorality, even if his standard of morality should somehow differ from social conventions."

The third and last parallel with Socrates concerns the maieutic method, the art of midwifery: Freud too seeks to give the needed knowledge not by teaching, leave alone preaching, but by way of eliciting memories. He tries to bring to light knowledge that is present in the subject but cannot be "born" without help.

The parallels with Jesus can be stated summarily. There is first of all, to borrow a title from Stefan Zweig (the book contains a fine essay on Freud) "healing through the spirit." Freud's work is based on a radical anti-materialism which attacks physical symptoms via the psyche. Secondly, there is Freud's devotion to the despised and rejected, the outcasts of society. He had no liking for Jesus, Christianity, or the Jewish religion, and he argued that it was impossible to love one's neighbor as oneself, leave alone one's enemies. Plainly, he valued honesty above both sentiments. But many Jews and Christians might well join in the wish that more men might love their neighbors in Freud's fashion!

There remains yet the most important point of all. No man before Freud had given equal substance to one of the most striking sayings in the Gospels (found only in the fourth Gospel, and not even in the early manuscripts of that, but first related of a Stoic sage): "He that is without sin among you, let him first cast a stone." Nothing that Freud has done, and little that anyone else has done, is more relevant to ethics than his success in breaking down the wall between the normal and the abnormal, the respectable and the criminal, the good and the evil. Freud gave, as it were, a new answer to the Gospel query, "who is my neighbor?" The mentally troubled, depressed, hysterical, and insane are not possessed by the devil but essentially "as thyself." Freud made men seek to understand and help where previous ages despised and condemned.

After Freud moral judgments become altogether questionable: they appear symptomatic rather than cognitive and tell us more about the judges than about those who are judged. In this respect Freud differs radically from Socrates and Jesus, and in many ways he is certainly closer to the Stoics and to Spinoza. The conception of moral judgments as symptoms can be found in Nietzsche, but recent proponents of an emotivist theory of ethics probably owe more to Freud, and the French existentialists are equally indebted to both men.

Plato once defined justice as the health of the soul. Freud suggests that to have a healthy soul *is* to be ethical, the moral codes of mankind notwithstanding. In fact, the moral codes are symptoms of imperfect health and self-deception. Those who know themselves neither are wicked, according to Freud, nor call any man wicked: they are healthy and try to help the sick.

Bibliography

Works: In German there are two collected editions: *Gesammelte Schriften* (12 vols). and *Gesammelte Werke* (18 vols.). The first complete English edition, in new translations, is now in process of publication, but most of the important books and papers have long been available in English, though often in unreliable translations. This criticism applies also to *The Basic Writings of Sigmund Freud* which offers six of the most important works in one volume. See also Robert Waelder's introduction to *The Living Thoughts of Freud* (1941) and E. B. Holt, *The Freudian Wish* (1915); J. Jastrow, *The House that Freud Built* (1932); T. Reik, *From Thirty Years with Freud* (1940); Ernest Jones, *The Life and Work of Sigmund Freud* (1953 ff.).

Walter Kaufmann
Princeton University

Freud, Sigmund: *see* Dostoyevsky, Fyodor; Nietzsche, Friedrich; Psychology and Morals; Spinoza.

Friends, Society of: *see* Quakerism, Classical, The Morality of.

friendship: *see* Aquinas, Thomas, Moral Views of; Augustine and Morals; Hindu Ethics; Major Ethical Viewpoints.

frivolity: *see* Puritan Morals; Quakerism, Classical, The Morality of.

frugality: *see* Riffian Morals.

fruits of the Spirit: *see* Christian Moral Philosophy.

frustration: *see* Psychology and Morals.

Fuegians: *see* Primitive Morals.

functionalism: *see* Dewey, John; Moral Philosophy in America; Psychology and Morals.

functioning will: *see* Stoics, the.

fundamental needs: *see* Hume, David.

fury: *see* More, Henry.

G

gain: *see* Hindu Ethics; profit, mutual.
Galileo: *see* Hobbes, Thomas.
gambling: *see* Hindu Ethics; Navaho
  Morals.
games: *see* Puritan Morals.
games of chance: *see* Muslim Morals.
Gandhi: *see* Tolstoy, Leo.
Gathas, the: *see* Zoroastrian Morals.
Gay, John: *see* Utilitarianism.
general truths: *see* Ross, Sir (William)
  David; truth(s).
generosity: *see* Aboriginals of Yirkalla;
  Mundurucu Indians, A Dual System
  of Ethics; Muslim Morals; Navaho
  Morals; Reid, Thomas; Riffian Mor-
  als; Rio Grande Pueblo Indians;
  Tapirapé Morals, Some Aspects of.
Geneva: *see* Puritan Morals.
Genicot, E.: *see* Jesuits, the, Moral
  Theology of.
Gentillet: *see* Machiavelli, Niccolo.
gentleness: *see* Hindu Ethics; Puritan
  Morals.
Gheerbrant, G.: *see* Primitive Morals.
ghetto: *see* Jewish Ethics and Its Civi-
  lization; Spinoza.
gift-giving: *see* Aboriginals of Yirkalla.
Gillen, F. J.: *see* Primitive Morals.
glaucon: *see* Sophists, the.
gloom: *see* Jewish Ethics and Its Civi-
  lization.
glory: *see* Hobbes, Thomas.
gluttony: *see* Dante, Alighieri.
God: *see* Augustine and Morals;
Clarke, Samuel; Cudworth, Ralph;
Green, T H.; Hammurapi, Code of;
Hindu Ethics; Hutcheson, Francis;
Jewish Ethics and Its Civilization;
Kierkegaard, Soren; Major Ethical
Viewpoints; More, Henry; Pakot,
The Moral System of; Puritan Mor-
als; Reid, Thomas; Scheler, Max;
Spinoza; Stoics, the; Theology and
Ethics.
godliness: *see* Hindu Ethics; Puritan
  Morals.
God realization: *see* Hindu Ethics.
Gods: *see* Aztec Morals; Hindu Ethics;
  Primitive Morals; Sophists, the.
Goedel: *see* Schlick, Moritz.
Goethe, Johann Wolfgang von
  Goethe was born in Frankfurt a M.
(Germany) on August 28, 1749. He
studied law at the universities of Leipzig and Strassburg, practised law in
Frankfurt (1771–75), and in 1775 was
called to Weimar by the young duke
Karl August. Henceforth he spent
most of his life in Weimar where he
died on March 22, 1832. He invites
comparison with men of the Renaissance, Leonardo in particular, as a
"universal man." As a member of the
state government he took his official
duties seriously and devoted a good
deal of time to them; but he took an
even greater interest in the arts and
in several of the natural sciences;

he made an anatomical discovery, proposed an important botanical hypothesis, and developed an intricate theory of colors; he directed the theatre in Wiemar from 1791 to 1817 and had Mozart's works performed more often than those of anyone else; and he came to be widely recognized, some thirty or forty years before his death, as Germany's greatest poet. That estimate still stands.

Goethe never considered himself a philosopher, but he read some of Kant's works as they first appeared, and he personally knew Fichte, Schelling, Hegel, and Schopenhauer. He admired Spinoza, and was also influenced by Leibniz and Shaftesbury. At no time did he develop his thought systematically, and once he wrote: "Doing natural science we are pantheists; writing poetry, polytheists; and ethically, monotheists." (*Maxims and Reflections*). In the context of ethics he might be considered in at least three ways. *First,* one might concentrate on his explicit observations, distinguished by great range and wisdom and many happy formulations. It would be easy to compile a pertinent anthology from the 143 volumes of his works, diaries, and letters (*Sophienausgabe*) and the 5 volumes of his collected conversations (ed. Biedermann). Both Goethe's own *Maxims and Reflections* and his celebrated conversations with Eckermann are among the world's great books of wisdom. *Secondly,* one might concentrate on his works to determine the ethical implications of his major poems, plays, and novels. In such a study *Iphigenia* and *Elective Affinities*,

Faust and *Wilhelm Meister* would probably deserve special attention. *Finally,* it might be argued that Goethe's life has influenced the history of ethics far more than any of his works. In the following article an attempt will be made to combine all three approaches, at least to the extent of giving some idea of the merits of each.

The outstanding fact about Goethe is his development—not from mediocrity to excellence but from consummation to consummation of style upon style. *Goetz von Berlichingen* (1773) and *Werther* (1774) represent, and were immediately acclaimed as, the culmination of Storm and Stress. In Goethe's two great plays, *Iphigenia* (1787) and *Tasso* (1790), German classicism reached its perfection. Then, still before the end of the century, *Faust: A Fragment* and *Wilhelm Meister's Apprenticeship* gave a decisive impetus to romanticism, and *Meister* all but created a new genre, the novel that relates the education and character formation of the hero, the *Bildungsroman*. *Elective Affinities* (1809) is one of the outstanding German novels, and *Dichtung und Wahrheit* (3 parts 1811–14, last part 1833) is not only a strikingly original autobiography but created a new perspective for the study of an artist, or indeed of man in general: life and work must be studied together as an organic unity and in terms of development.

The evolution of Goethe is best reflected in his poetry. It is doubtful whether any other man has written so many so excellent poems; certainly no one else has left a comparable record of the development of a poetic sensibility over a period of approximately sixty years. Anacreontic lyrics, the magnificent defiance of Prometheus, hymns, earthy *Roman Elegies* (1795), biting *Venetian Epigrams* (1796), the epic *Hermann and Dorothea* and the wonderful ballads of 1798, the sonnets of 1815, and, at seventy, the epochmaking *West-Eastern Divan*—nothing in world literature compares with this. And in all these periods Goethe writes the most moving love poems, from *Willkommen und Abschied* in his twenties to the *Marienbader Elegie* in his seventies. These poems help to account for the fact that Goethe's loves have been, for decades, part of the curriculum in the German secondary schools: not to know Friedrike, Lotte, Lilli, and the rest was to be uneducated. The inference seems warranted that men so brought up would on the whole tend to favor a self-realizationist ethic and that at least some forms of intuitionism would strike them as evidently absurd. What is good is not, as it were, seen once and for all; as he develops, a man's moral ideas change, and wisdom is attained, if ever, only in old age; but the emphasis falls not on the eventual conclusion but on the development.

This question is central in Goethe's *Faust* which also reflects, better than any other single work, the poet's own development. Off and on Goethe worked on it for sixty years. His first magnificent attempt, the so-called *Urfaust,* was published only posthumously in 1888; Goethe himself published *Faust: A Fragment* in 1790, *Faust: The First Part of the Tragedy* in 1808, and completed Part Two shortly before he died, leaving it to be published after his death. Partly as a result of this, partly also owing to Goethe's conception of poetry and its relation to ideas, *Faust* is not only no allegory but does not embody or try to communicate any single philosophy of life. "They come and ask me what idea I sought to embody in my *Faust*. As if I knew . . . that myself! . . . Indeed, that would have been a fine thing, had I wanted to string such a rich, variegated . . . life . . . upon the meagre thread of a single . . . idea! It was altogether not my manner as a poet to strive for the embodiment of something abstract." *Faust* is more epigrammatic than any other great work of literature except the Bible, and it has enriched the German language with more "familiar quotations" than could be found in *Hamlet*. The one among these that has most often been taken for the central idea of the drama is "Who ever strives with all his power, We are allowed to save," sung by the angels, "floating through the higher atmosphere, carrying Faust's immortal part," in the last scene. But these two lines require some explanation.

Morally, Goethe did not condone Faust's every action merely because Faust kept "striving." But there was no place in Goethe's world picture for hell or damnation. In a conversation Goethe once spoke of writing a scene "where even the Devil finds grace and mercy before God" (Pniower, #973);

and while this scene was never written, the Lord's comment on Mephistopheles in the Prologue expresses the same attitude: "Of all the spirits that negate, The knavish jester gives me least to do. For man's activity can easily abate, He soon prefers uninterrupted rest; To give him this companion hence seems best, Who roils and must as Devil help create." More concisely, Mephistopheles characterizes himself in his first encounter with Faust as "Part of that force which would do evil evermore, and yet creates the good."

Goethe's attitude clearly invites comparison with Hegel's, but it has probably been best epitomized by Nietzsche when he calls Goethe (in *The Twilight of the Idols*) "the man of tolerance, not from weakness but from strength, because he knows how to use to his advantage, even that from which the average nature would perish. . . . Such a spirit who has *become free* stands amid the cosmos with a joyous and trusting fatalism, in the *faith* that only the particular is loathsome, and that all is redeemed and affirmed in the whole—*he does not negate any more*. Such a faith, however, is the highest of all possible faiths."

Goethe's attitude may also remind us of the words of Spinoza whom Goethe so admired: "to hate no one, to despise no one, to mock no one, to be angry with no one, and to envy no one." (*Ethics,* end of Part II) Only mockery was part of Goethe's genius— a mockery, however, that was free from hatred, anger, and envy: in the young Goethe it seems like the overflow of his exuberant high spirits; in the old Goethe, a rare Olympian malice which was probably closer to Einstein's impish playfulness than to Bertrand Russell's more tendentious variant. His attitude was affirmative without ever becoming entirely serene, leave alone saintly; and if there was any resentment in the man it was resentment of convention, not of individuals, though he came to use convention as a protective shield against individuals who might have upset his creative economy.

One might almost say that Faust is saved for two reasons. First, and most important, there is Goethe's general attitude which has been sketched here: he was not one to consign any man to hell; he lacked what we might call "the moralistic resentment"—the dissatisfaction with oneself which, instead of creatively enhancing the self, deceives itself about its own nature and damns others. Secondly, Goethe saves Faust to show his opposition to convention, moralism, and resentment. In this sense, the conclusion of *Faust* is more polemical than is usually recognized. The title of the penultimate scene, "Entombment," is plainly parodistic, and so are the portable "hell's jaws" which furnish a light-hearted contrast to Dante's awesome portal to the inferno. And while Dante, in what Goethe called his "gruesome greatness," sent Francesca da Rimini to hell, Goethe elevates even Faust into heaven. While a contemporary usage conditioned by liberal Protestantism would call Goethe's attitude "Christian," it is well to remember that Goethe himself considered it anti-

Christian. Having finished the last scene, he turned to writing Act IV with its malicious passages about the church; and in his letters, during the last year of his life, he calls the cross "the painful torture wood, the most disgusting thing under the sun [which] no reasonable human being should strive to exhume"; and he scorns Schlegel's conversion: "Friedrich Schlegel suffocated in the end of his rumination of ethical and religious absurdities . . . he fled into Catholicism." (June 9 and Oct. 20, 1831.)

Faust was early based on an alternative which, as Goethe later found, was by no means exclusive. It is the alternative on which the famous bet in the pact scene is based: "If ever I recline, calmed, on a bed of sloth, You may destroy me then and there. If ever flattering you should wile me That in myself I find delight, If with enjoyment you beguile me, Then break on me, eternal night. . . . If to the moment I should say: Abide, you are so fair— Put me in fetters on that day, I *wish* to perish then, I swear." Goethe later found that one could appreciate the present without being a Philistine, that could live in the moment without betraying one's striving, and that could find delight in oneself without becoming smug and slothful. Early in the last act, he has Lynkeus sing: "In all things I see The eternally bright, And as they please me, In myself I delight." And to Eckermann Goethe says (Nov. 3, 1823): "every moment is of infinite value, for it is the representative of a whole eternity"; and he urges: "ever hold fast to the present."

In fact, Goethe considered romanticism essentially "sick"; he thought that its typical dissatisfactions with the present and flight either into an imaginary past (often medieval) or the future or something remote and bizarre was motivated by the romantic's sense of his own inadequacy.

Thus Goethe came to distinguish two kinds of striving, that of the romantic and his own; and he made this point emphatically in the seventh and eighth books of *Wilhelm Meister's Apprenticeship,* after the early installments of the novel had been misunderstood and hailed by the German romantics. Three quotations will readily illustrate this: "Wherever you may be . . . work as best you can . . . and let the present be a cause of good cheer to you"; "Man cannot be happy until his unconditional striving limits itself"; and "Whoever wants to do or enjoy all and everything in its whole humanity . . . will only spend his time with an eternally dissatisfied striving." (7.8; 8.5; 8.7)

The two kinds of striving correspond to, and probably helped to inspire, Hegel's contrast between the "good" and the "bad infinite." Even more important, Hegel used his vast influence as a professor of philosophy at Berlin to impress on his students: "Whoever wants something great, says Goethe, must be able to limit himself." (*Philosophy of Right,* Addition to Par. 13) The whole *Philosophy of Right* is profoundly influenced by Goethe's example: it teaches that freedom must be sought within the limitations of a responsible role in the civic life of a community, and that the realm of the Absolute Spirit, i.e., art, religion, and philosophy, does not involve a rejection of civic life but only its fulfillment. The British Idealists were to teach much the same doctrine, under the dual influence of Hegel and Goethe himself.

No doubt, Goethe thought of embodying this idea in *Faust* when he decided to let Faust end up winning land from the sea. Here was some possibility of representing concretely the limitation of a previously unconditional striving. Any number of details suggest, however, that Goethe did not go through with this notion: in the end, Faust is still thoroughly dissatisfied with the here and now; he is ruthless with his neighbors and employs slave labor while dreaming of freedom in the future; and in the last scene he is not only physically blind but completely unaware of his immediate environment. Nothing whatever will come of all his efforts, and while he thinks drainage ditches are being dug, it is in fact his own grave.

While the dry antitheses of *Wilhelm Meister* lack the force required to balance *Faust,* there is at least one major work in which Goethe represents a beautiful image of ideal humanity: *Iphigenia.* Goethe's male heroes are generally not ideals; they are partial self-projections, magnified images of Goethe's own failings—or rather of qualities which, when separated from the whole personality, become failings. In this sense, Faust and Mephistopheles, Tasso, and Antonio, Egmont and Oranien are almost caricatures of

the poet—so many ways of dividing himself in half, with the result that both male leads are lesser men than Goethe himself. In the figure of Iphigenia, the poet himself is out of the picture (he appears as Orestes and Pylades); and while the conception of the heroine is partly inspired by Charlotte von Stein and, no doubt, by Goethe's early feelings for his own sister, Iphigenia is perhaps his most nearly ideal figure, and no account of Goethe's ethic would be complete without quoting Goethe's famous words in a dedication of the drama, penned in 1827: "Every failing that is human / Pure humanity atones." No *deus ex machina* is required, as in the Greek drama, nor any Christian God, nor yet the Promethean defiance of Sartre's Orestes. In Goethe's world the Promethean striving is tempered by "the eternal womanly." For him, the relation between man and woman—as brother and sister or, above all, as lovers—redeems life. It does not of itself furnish an adequate content for life, but neither is it to his mind the setting of inhumanity and tragedy. The end of *Faust I,* the culmination of Goethe's dramatic powers, is exceptional for him and deliberately balanced by the conclusion of Part Two. His outlook on life is essentially not tragic but confident, affirmative, and tolerant.

The ethics of Plato and Aristotle, the Cynics and the Cyrenaics, the Stoics and the Epicureans was largely inspired by the personality, the life, and certain observations, of Socrates. Goethe is one of the exceedingly few men whose personality has left a comparable impact in contemporary and subsequent reflection. He was not a philosopher and did not offer conceptual analyses like Socrates, not to speak of modern philosophers; but what he did offer is far rarer: his character became normative for others; so did some of the characters he created; and his tolerance as a man and a poet furnishes a prime example of an ethical attitude free of moralistic resentment.

Above all, his *Wilhelm Meister* and, even more, *Dichtung und Wahrheit,* established the development approach to the understanding of man and a new, organic conception of the relation of works of art to their maker, and deeds to the doer.

Bibliography

Works: There are innumerable editions in German of which the so-called *Sophienausgabe* in 143 volumes is the most complete. In addition, there are *Goethes Gespräche* (5 vols), ed. Biedermann. *Goethes Gespräche mit Eckermann* are available in many editions. In English there is no adequate edition, and many works are available only in poor translations—even *Faust* of which there are over fifty different English versions.

A. Bielschowsky, *Goethe,* 2 vols. (1895).

Pniower, *Goethe's Faust* (1899).

F. Gunhold, *Goethe* (1916).

B. Fairley, *A Study of Goethe* (1947).

L. Lewisohn, *Goethe* (2 vols., 1949).

A. Bergstraesser, *Goethe's Image of Man and Society* (1949).

W. Kaufmann, "Goethe and the History of Ideas" and "Goethe's Faith and Faust's Redemption" in *Journal of the History of Ideas* and *Monatshefte* (1949).

K. Viëtor, *Goethe: The Thinker* (1950).

Walter Kaufmann
Princeton University

Goethe, J.: *see* Freud, Sigmund; Nietzsche, Friedrich; Schopenhauer, Arthur; Zoroastrian Morals.

golden age: *see* Christian Moral Philosophy.

golden mean, the: *see* Aristotle.

Golden Rule: *see* China, Moral Philosophies of; Clarke, Samuel; Hindu Ethics; Hobbes, Thomas; Jewish Ethics and Its Civilization; Meta-ethics and Normative Ethics; More, Henry; Sidgwick, Henry.

Gonzalez, Tirso: *see* Jesuits, the, Moral Theology of.

good: *see* Augustine and Morals; Aquinas, Thomas, Moral Views of; Aztec Morals; Aristotle; Ayer, Alfred J.; Balguy, John; Berdyaev, Nicolas; Broad, C. D.; Butler, Joseph; China, Moral Philosophies of; Clarke, Samuel; Cooper, Anthony Ashley; Cudworth, Ralph; Dante, Alighieri; Dewey, John; French Existentialism and Moral Philosophy; Freud, Sigmund; Green, T. H.; Hartmann, Nicolai; Hindu Ethics; Hobbes, Thomas; Jesuits, the Moral Theology of; Kant, I.; Language and Ethics; Liguori, St. Alphonsus and Catholic Moral Philosophy; Machiavelli, Niccolo; Major Ethical Viewpoints; Marxist Theory of Morals; Meta-ethics and Normative Ethics; Minor Socratics; Moore, George Edward; Moral Philosophy in America; Morals and Religion; More, Henry;

Muslim Morals; Navaho Morals; Pakot, the Moral System of; Psychology and Morals; Prichard, H. A.; Puritan Morals; Quakerism, Classical, The Morality of; Reid, Thomas; Riffian Morals; Rio Grande Pueblo Indians; Ross, Sir (William) David; Russell, Bertrand; Scheler, Max; Schlick, Moritz; Sidgwick, Henry; Socrates; Soloviev, Wladimir; Sophists, the; Soviet Morality, Current; Spinoza; Summum bonum; Tapirapé Morals, Some Aspects of; Utilitarianism; virtue; Wollaston, William; Zoroastrian Morals.

good and bad: *see* Nietzsche, Friedrich.

good and evil: *see* Dostoyevsky, Fyodor; Hindu Ethics.

good and evil, beyond: *see* Hindu Ethics; Nietzsche, Friedrich.

good feeling: *see* Rio Grande Pueblo Indians.

good life, the: *see* Cudworth, Ralph; Hindu Ethics; Spinoza; Stoics, the; Zoroastrian Morals.

good self, the: *see* Dewey, John.

good, the supreme: *see* Plato; Summum bonum.

good will: *see* Aquinas, Thomas, Moral Views of. Hindu Ethics; Jewish Ethics and Its Civilization; Kant, I.

Gorgias: *see* Sophists, the.

Gorky, Maxim: *see* Soviet Morality, Current.

Gospels, the: *see* Christian Moral Philosophy; Dostoyevsky, Fyodor; Tolstoy, Leo.

gossip: *see* Aboriginals of Yirkalla; Hindu Ethics; Rio Grande Pueblo Indians.

government: *see* China, Moral Philosophies of; Hobbes, Thomas; Moral Philosophy in America; Puritan Morals; Soviet Morality, Current; Utilitarianism.

grace: *see* Aquinas, Thomas, Moral Views of; Augustine and Morals; Hindu Ethics; Jewish Ethics and Its Civilization.

graft: *see* Dante, Alighieri.

graphic art: *see* Aboriginals of Yirkalla.

gratification: *see* Butler, Joseph; Freud, Sigmund.

gratitude: *see* Aboriginals of Yirkalla; Balguy, John; Broad, C. D.; More, Henry; Price, Richard; Reid, Thomas; Ross, Sir (William) David.

Great Awakening: *see* Puritan Morals.

greed: *see* Aboriginals of Yirkalla; avarice; Dante, Alighieri; Hindu Ethics; Machiavelli, Niccolo.

Greek ethics: *see* Aristotle; Augustine and Morals; Hindu Ethics; Minor Socratics; Plato; Schlick, Moritz; Socrates; Sophists, the; Stoics, the.

Greek ethics and Islam: *see* Muslim Morals.

Green, Thomas Hill

Thomas Hill Green (1836–1882) was born in the village of Birken (Yorkshire) where his father was rector. He was educated at Rugby and at Balliol College, Oxford, where he was a pupil of Benjamin Jowett. Green became a Fellow of Balliol in 1860 and after 1870, when Jowett became Master, he had an important part in the internal management of the college. He was elected Whyte's Professor of Moral Philosophy in 1878. With the exception of a lengthy criticism of British empiricism in the standard edition of Hume's *Philosophical Works* (1874–

75), which he edited with T. H. Grose, Green's publications were mostly posthumous. The manuscript of the *Prolegomena to Ethics* (edited by A. C. Bradley, 1883) was nearly complete when he died. His *Works* (3 vols., 1888; 2nd edition, 1889–90) were edited from manuscripts and lecture notes by R. L. Nettleship.

Though Green's life was mainly devoted to his academic work, he was continuously interested in public education and in civic affairs. In 1864 he was investigator for a Royal Commission on secondary education for which he wrote a report, and in 1876 he was elected to the town council of Oxford. He took an active part in local politics as a Liberal, in behalf of the extension of the suffrage, publicly supported elementary education, the opening of the universities to middle-class students, and local option. Green's influence was considerable but it was chiefly exerted through his teaching and personal relations with his students; it is not adequately represented by his writings. His pupil R. L. Nettleship appraised his character and thought as follows: "The strongest elements in Green's nature seem to have been the sense of public duty and the sense of religious dependence, and in the creeds of modern liberalism and modern evangelicism he found a congenial language, which he had no difficulty in translating when he wished into German metaphysic" (Green's *Works*, Vol. III, p. xxix).

Green's philosophy was an important example of the so-called Neo-Hegelian idealism which dominated Anglo-American philosophical thought in the last quarter of the nineteenth century. The extent of Green's dependence on Hegel has been variously estimated; it seems clearly to have been less than that of his pupil Bernard Bosanquet or perhaps of F. H. Bradley. His theory of knowledge depended more directly on Kant's conception of the transcendental unity of apperception, and his ethics elaborated Kant's principle that "nothing is good without qualification except the good will." But as Nettleship suggests, any form of German philosophy may have been a "language" into which Green translated ideas still more deeply rooted in his thought. He was profoundly influenced by Aristotle's conception that personal good is achieved by participation, through citizenship, in values resident in civilization as a social product. Perhaps the most powerful factor in his ethics came from his deep sympathy with English Puritanism, its belief in the inherent worth of personality and its strong sense of civic obligation.

Green regarded ethics as part of a total philosophy based on a theory of knowledge which in turn supports an idealist metaphysics. The whole he conceived to be a coherent system logically implied by presumptions required to validate knowledge of reality and moral conduct. Only such a philosophy can demonstrate the real or essential nature of man, his relations to nature, to God, and to his fellows. The central principle of Green's theory of knowledge was the absolute difference which he held to exist between a series of data and the consciousness of them as a series. Experience depends upon a unity of consciousness that sensations can neither produce nor explain. Phenomena do not cause self-consciousness; rather, the fact of there being phenomena implies a pre-existing self-consciousness. The world as known must be conceived as a system of unalterable relations and such a system must be conceived as the work of thought. The principle of nature, Green inferred, is an eternal self-consciousness, in some sense comparable to intelligence as the principle of human experience, and this eternal consciousness becomes operative in man through the idea of a perfect life which is already actual in God. Since man as an animal organism thus becomes the agent of an eternally complete consciousness, his conduct is not determined by natural forces; he is a free and responsible cause and hence the subject of rights and obligations.

Green's critics even among idealists often found his terms vague or ambiguous, his transitions of thought too rapid, and his arguments at points confused. A critic who was not an idealist would of course reject the procedure of deriving metaphysics from theory of knowledge and might question the assumption that ethics depends either on a theory of knowledge or on metaphysics. Apart from the question of its validity, however, Green's philosophy, and idealism in general, performed an important critical function by its examination of the then current sensationalist empiricism. The association of ideas was not an adequate theory of mental structure, and egoistic individualism was not an adequate theory of ethics.

Green's ethics belonged to the self-realization type of theory: the perfect development of human capacity is the ultimate standard of good. As sensations when organized by thought are transformed into knowledge, so animal wants are transformed by moral reflection into conscious ends and motives, and these into will and character. These terms refer to stages or levels at which conduct has been made coherent rather than to faculties. This organization of inclinations or desires is at once personal, objective, and social. It is personal in the sense that it is guided by the conception of ends in which the self can find its true satisfaction and realize its capacities. It is objective in the sense that what is desired is not a feeling but an actual state of affairs to be brought into being. This is the ground for Green's rejection of hedonism; pleasure is not the object of desire but an incident in the satisfaction gained by accomplishing concrete purposes. The organization is social because the self is inherently social and can realize its capacities only in activities and goods shared with other persons. The will is free because, in the course of this threefold development, action becomes self-determined; its motives lie within the character or personality of the agent. Green's analysis of moral development, like the analysis of intellectual development in his theory of knowledge, depends upon the assumption, characteristic of Neo-Hegelian idealism, that logical consistency or coherence is sufficiently inclusive to provide a standard of both fact and value; it is a principle of objectivity for knowledge of what really is and also of what ought to be. His theory of value postulates that good in general means that which satisfies an interest; the greater good is that which satisfies a more permanent interest or a more inclusive context of interests. Moral self-reflection reveals a conception both of human capacities that are partly realized and of a development in which they might be further realized. Hence it enforces a personal responsibility for a more complete realization of one's own powers and a social responsibility for creating the conditions in which a more general realization of human capacities is possible. Beyond any present state of moral achievement there is the idea of a better state, and ultimately of a possible best state or perfection of human nature.

This analysis is regarded by Green as providing a general form or criterion of morals. In all actual cases, however, the form always has a content supplied by accepted rules of moral practice and existing institutions. These represent capacities that man has tried to realize, though only with partial success. The consciousness of having these capacities is "the parent of the institutions and usages, of the social judgments and aspirations, through which human life has been so far bettered; through which man has so far realized his capacities and

marked out the path that he must follow in their further realization" (*Prolegomena,* §180). The content of good or of duty varies from generation to generation; the formal ideal of a true good, consisting in a higher type of character and more adequate conditions for attaining it, is a regulative idea or principle of criticism which, by acting as a constant reminder that what has been achieved is not the best that might be, provides a driving force toward improvement. Thus conscience is at once conservative and progressive; it demands loyalty to goods already achieved and to a higher standard which can be conceived but is not yet accepted. Green believed that such a progress of morals can be perceived in history. There has been, first, an extension of the range of persons recognized as entitled to moral respect or admitted to being ends in themselves; as in the abolition of slavery and the acceptance of universal citizenship. In the second place there has been an enrichment of the ideal itself; as by the inclusion in it of higher intellectual and esthetic values beyond the satisfaction of material needs.

For Green as for Aristotle there was no more than a difference of emphasis between individual ethics and social or political philosophy. The most important element in his theory of human nature was his affirmation that the self is a social self. "Without society, no persons; this is as true as that without persons . . . there could be no such society as we know" (*Prolegomena,* §190). A personal good, indeed, requires the satisfaction of the agent's fundamental interests, but for a social being these include the interests of other persons. The good which he desires for himself must be a common or a shared good, and a shared good implies that others must be treated as ends in themselves in the same way that a man is an end to himself. A moral society, as Kant said, is a "kingdom of ends," a community of equals united by respect for each other and by loyalty to the ends of the society, in which each member has both moral and legal rights and duties. The fundamental right of every person is to have a part in the goods of civilization which society has created and to contribute to them. He has a personality by virtue of his membership, by claiming the rights and performing the duties that membership implies. At the political level, Green argued, this implies that freedom is not negative only, consisting in the absence of legal restraints, but includes opportunity, "a positive power or capacity of doing or enjoying something worth doing or enjoying." The state is morally obligated to use its legislative power to remove hindrances that stand in the way of self-realization and hence of the general good, by supporting education, by preventing discrimination, and by protecting the interests of classes whose economic position is weak.

Green's use of ethical terms was deficient in exact analysis and was not always consistent. It is questionable whether "self-realization" offers a better guide to the ethical criticism of legislation than Bentham's "greatest happiness principle," and to Sidgwick, who was Green's most important contemporary among English moralists, the term was not necessarily less egoistic in its implications than "pleasure." Green's use of the expression "common good" was vague if not actually ambiguous; it was a source of disagreement among successors who were in general agreement with him. His statement that the self is essentially "social" was profoundly suggestive, but it opened up, rather than solved, a wide range of questions about the psychological dependence of personality on the social *milieu* and about the ethical relationship between individual and social values. The importance of Green's ethics can perhaps be best expressed by saying that it represented a change in point of view: it put in question the individualism that had appeared axiomatic throughout so much of modern moral and social philosophy. In this respect it fostered a change already perceptible in J. S. Mill's restatement of utilitarianism. This change reflected a wide-spread shift in the climate of social opinion, away from *laissez faire* and toward the use of public authority to ameliorate conditions regarded as injurious to general welfare.

Bibliography

W. H. Fairbrother, *The Philosophy of Thomas Hill Green* (London, 1896).

W. D. Lamont, *Introduction to Green's Moral Philosophy* (London, 1934).

J. H. Muirhead, *The Service of the State: Four Lectures on the Political Teaching of T. H. Green* (London, 1908).

R. L. Nettleship, *Memoir of Thomas Hill Green*. In Green's *Works*, Vol. III; reprinted (London, 1906).

Henry Sidgwick, *Lectures on the Ethics of T. H. Green, H. Spencer, and J. Martineau* (London, 1902).

George H. Sabine
Cornell University

Green, T. H.: *see* Hammurapi, Code of; Major Ethical Viewpoints; Prichard, H. A.

Grotius: *see* Cumberland, Richard.

group behavior: *see* Primitive Morals; Rio Grande Pueblo Indians.

growth: *see* Dewey, John.

Guadalupe: *see* Aztec Morals.

guilt: *see* Major Ethical Viewpoints; Quakerism, Classical, The Morality of; Rio Grande Pueblo Indians; Schopenhauer, Arthur; Tolstoy, Leo.

guilt feeling: *see* Freud, Sigmund.

Gurrich: *see* Soviet Morality, Current.

Gury, J. P.: *see* Jesuits, the, Moral Theology of.

H

habit: *see* Aquinas, Thomas, Moral Views of; Aristotle; Dewey, John; Hume, David; Psychology and Morals; Puritan Morals; Reid, Thomas, Stoics, the; Utilitarianism.

Haddon, A. C.: *see* Primitive Morals.

Hadfield, J. A.: *see* Psychology and Morals.

Hägerström, Axel: *see* Broad, C. D.

hair: *see* Puritan Morals.

Halacha: *see* Jewish Ethics and Its Civilization.

half-truths: *see* Hindu Ethics.

Hamlet: *see* Freud, Sigmund.

Hammurabi: *see* Hammurapi, Code of.

Hammurapi, Code of

Hammurapi (this seems to have been the correct pronunciation, though today he is often called Hammurabi) was a king of ancient Babylonia, probably from 1728–1686 B.C. He may be the man referred to in Genesis 14 as "Amraphel, king of Shinar." His law code was discovered in the winter of 1901–2 in the course of excavations at Susa (the Shushan of Esther and Daniel) in Southern Persia, where an Elamite raider had taken the diorite stela about the 12th century B.C. The stela, topped by a bas-relief showing Hammurapi with the sun god Shamash, was found by French archeologists who took it to the Louvre.

The code is not the earliest code of laws known to us, but in its preservation and comprehensiveness it has no equal of comparable antiquity, save only the Mosaic legislation which is younger. Ever since the code was found, its relation to the Books of Moses in the Old Testament has excited the greatest interest; and it is this topic that shall be stressed here.

The legislation, which is framed by a poetic prologue and epilogue, deals with the following matters: accusations, witnesses, and judges; theft and robbery; a military feudal system; field, garden, and house; tradesmen and female wine sellers; articles left with another person for safekeeping; family relationships; injuries; ships; rents; and slaves. In this central portion there are no digressions, and the arrangement is far more systematic than in the comparable sections of the Old Testament. This, added to the many parallels in detail, led early scholars to underestimate the striking originality of the Mosaic legislation. Confronted with such an unusually significant and unexpected discovery, these scholars could scarcely have been expected to react differently; and the tremendous influence of the Code of Hammurapi on the Law of Moses cannot be doubted. The most fruitful perspective is that suggested by Elias Auerbach (*Wüste und Gelobtes Land,* vol. I, 154ff.):

"Now that we know that the political hegemony of Babylonia extended to Palestine too for a long time (precisely under Hammurapi and his successors), while the cultural hegemony actually lasted for centuries, parallels in the legal ordering of life cease to be surprising. The Code of Hammurapi once was the law of the land and had to . . . leave traces as deep as those which Roman law or the Code Napoléon left in the development of German law. What is therefore important for an understanding of the spiritual structure of Israel is less the parallels than the *differences.*"

The two central principles of the Code of Hammurapi are, first, *ius talionis* and, secondly, that the law is a respecter of persons. Both principles, of course, are anathema to most contemporary penologists, and a widespread attitude considers the first of them, retaliation, practically synonymous with the Law of Moses. The arguments of T. H. Green, Bernard Bosanquet, and other apologists for *ius talionis* not withstanding, both principles clearly have a common presupposition: they distinguish insufficiently between human beings and material objects. And the crucial difference between the Code of Hammurapi and the Law of Moses is that in the latter the unique worth of man as such is proclaimed and implicit—for the first time in human history.

The Code of Hammurapi recognizes three classes of people: an aristocracy, commoners, and slaves. Accordingly, it generally provides three kinds of punishment, depending, for example, on whether an injury has been inflicted on a member of the aristocracy, a commoner, or a slave. The slave is considered less as a human being than as a piece of property. So, however, are the sons and daughters even of a noble. And the way in which the principle of retaliation is applied suggests that the body of the noble himself too is considered as essentially a material object.

Here are a few illustrations, accompanied in each case by a contrast with the Law of Moses. The punishment of injuries depends on the social status of the injured person, and the man who has destroyed an eye or broken a bone of another man's slave is to pay one-half his value. In other words, he only has to compensate the owner for the damage done to his property. It is quite consistent with this outlook that for destroying an eye or breaking a bone of one's own slave there is no penalty whatever. This should be compared with Exodus 21.20 and 21.26ff. where the man who as much as breaks a tooth of his own slave must let him go free for his tooth. In the Law of Moses, the slave is first of all a human being and has to be treated as such.

According to the Code of Hammurapi, if a man either helps a fugitive slave "escape through the city gate" or harbors him in his house "and has not brought him forth at the summons of the police, that householder shall be put to death." (15ff.) Compare this with Deuteronomy 23.15f.: "Thou shalt not deliver unto his master the servant which is escaped from his master unto thee: He shall dwell with thee, even among you, in that place which he shall choose in one of thy gates, where it liketh him best: thou shalt not oppress him."

In the Law of Moses, being a slave is an accidental condition. This is further emphasized by constant reminders that the children of Israel have themselves been slaves in Egypt and should know how it feels to be a slave. On the Sabbath the slave too should rest, and every Sabbath thus becomes a celebration of the brotherhood and equality of men. The contrast in this respect between the Code of Hammurapi and the Law of Moses is most neatly illustrated by Hammurapi's last law (282): "If a male slave has said to his master, 'You are not my master,' his master shall prove him to be his slave and cut off his ear." In Exodus 21 we find a faint but, no doubt, deliberate echo of this law—an echo, however, that is designed to bring out the deep difference between the two legislations: "If thou buy an Hebrew servant, six years he shall serve: and in the seventh he shall go out free for nothing. . . . And if the servant shall plainly say . . . 'I will not go out free' . . . his master shall bore his ear through with an awl; and he shall serve him for ever."

As mentioned above, Hammurapi considers a man's children too as his property and not as human beings in their own right. If a man strikes the daughter of another man, "if that woman has died, they shall put his daughter to death." (210) A man's

daughter may thus be put to death merely by way of imposing a severe fine upon the father. The fine becomes less severe if the woman killed in the first instance was the daughter of a commoner (one-half mina of silver); and if she was a slave, the owner gets a little less still (one-third mina).

Similarly, if a man builds a house for another man, and he builds it badly and the house collapses—if it causes the death of the owner, the builder shall be put to death; but "if it has caused the death of a son of the owner of the house, they shall put the son of that builder to death." (229ff.) To such provisions there is no parallel in the Law of Moses which insists, with striking originality, that there is only one God and that all men alike are made in his image and thus altogether incommensurable with things or money.

The law of talion, to be sure, still appears in the Law of Moses too, but in an almost polemical manner: The Mosaic phrase, "an eye for an eye," might be said to conceal a revaluation of Hammurapi's values. Consider the three passages in which the phrase occurs, and the first two will make plain the new spirit, while the third brings out an interesting continuity.

The first occurrence of "life for life, eye for eye, tooth for tooth" is in Exodus 21 where it is immediately followed by the provision, already cited: "If he smite out his manservant's tooth, or his maidservant's tooth: he shall let him go free for his tooth's sake." This provision shows immediately what is amply borne out by the entire Law of Moses, namely that the prin-

197

ciple of retaliation was never applied mechanically and in accordance with the letter of the phrase. Rather the emphasis was on the spirit; to wit, that an injury is an injury, and that the law is no respecter of persons. Or, to put it positively, the words of the ancient law of talion are employed to promulgate the new principle of equality before the law.

This interpretation is corroborated by the second passage in the Bible in which the phrase occurs, in Leviticus 24, where the ancient formula is followed by this declaration: "Ye shall have one manner of law, as well for the stranger as for one of your own country: for I am the Lord your God."

The third passage, finally, in Deuteronomy 19, echoes and expands a similar law in the Code of Hammurapi: "If a false witness rise up against any man to testify against him falsely . . . the judges shall make diligent inquisition: and if they see that the witness . . . hath testified falsely against his brother; Then shall ye do unto him as he had thought to have done unto his brother: so shalt thou put the evil away from among you. And those which remain shall hear, and fear, and shall henceforth commit no more such evil among you. And thine eye shall not pity: life for life, eye for eye, tooth for tooth, hand for hand, foot for foot." In Hammurapi's substantially similar law there is no reference to the intention of the witness: the man who accuses another of murder and then cannot prove his charge is put to death. It is customary today to decry "an eye for an eye" as the epitome of legal bar-

barism; but to arrive at a judicious evaluation one will have to compare this last application with contemporary morality in the United States, for example, where a late Senator who advised one of his colleagues to accuse as many people as possible to increase his chances of making at least some his accusations stick is widely admired for his exemplary honesty and integrity.

It is widely but falsely assumed that the principle of talion was, as it were, left behind by Jesus' counsel to love one's enemies. In fact, the passage in which Jesus repudiates the ancient maxim, "an eye for an eye, and a tooth for a tooth" is the one in which he proceeds: "But I say unto you, That ye resist not evil: . . . And if any man will sue thee at the law, and take away thy coat, let him have the cloak also." Where he rejects talion, he rejects the courts altogether; but where he speaks of the divine judgment, he again and again returns to talion; e.g., to cite the Sermon on the Mount once more: "For with what judgment ye judge, ye shall be judged: and with what measure ye mete, it shall be measured to you again." (Matthew 5 and 7) Elsewhere the New Testament goes far beyond both Moses and Hammurapi by holding out *eternal* punishment for, to give only a single example, not accepting the teachings of Jesus' apostles.

It seems fair to say that talion in one form or another has become, increasingly since Hammurapi's time, inseparable from the Western sense of justice. Jesus' counsel to love one's enemies is on an entirely different plane: it is a maxim for personal relations, on a level with the Mosaic injunction, "If thou meet thine enemy's ox or his ass going astray, thou shalt surely bring it back to him again." (Exodus 23.4. Cf. also 5 and many similar passages in the Law and the Prophets and the later books of the Old Testament.) In personal relations Hammurapi did not advocate retaliation either; and in court Christian countries have not distinguished themselves from non-Christian countries by renouncing the principle of "life for life," let alone the underlying conception of talion. In this respect contemporary Western law is essentially continuous with the Code of Hammurapi, though modern penologists are moving away from retaliation and advocating a penal system based on the primacy of reform.

In conclusion it should be noted that perhaps the most striking parallel to the Law of Moses is to be found not in the legislation of Hammurapi but in the Prologue and Epilogue where Hammurapi declares that he is giving these laws "in order that the strong might not oppress the weak, and that justice might be dealt the orphan and the widow."

Text: Ancient Near Eastern Texts Relating to the Old Testament, ed. James B. Pritchard (2nd rev. ed. 1955), pp. 163–180, and *Altorientalische Texte und Bilder zum Alten Testamente,* ed. Hugo Gressmann with A. Ungnad and H. Ranke. (1909), pp. 140–171. See also "The Current Controversy over the Dating of the First Dynasty of Babylon in Term of Years B.C." in A. J. Toynbee, *A Study of History,* vol. X (1954), pp. 171–212, and Elias Auerbach, *Wüste und Gelobtes Land,* vol. I (1932).

Walter Kaufmann
Princeton University

Hampshire, S.: *see* Prichard, H. A.; Reid, Thomas.
Han Fei Tzu: *see* China, Moral Philosophies of.
Han Fei Tzu, the: *see* China, Moral Philosophies of.
happiness: *see* Aquinas, Thomas, Moral Views of; Aristotle; Augustine and Morals; Aztec Morals; Butler, Joseph; Clarke, Samuel; Cudworth, Ralph; Cumberland, Richard; Dante, Alighieri; Dewey, John; Green, T. H.; hedonism; Hindu Ethics; Kant, I.; Liguori, St. Alphonsus and Catholic Moral Philosophy; Major Ethical Viewpoints; Minor Socratics; Moral Philosophy in America; More, Henry; Muslim Morals; Navaho Morals; Plato; Pleasure; Price, Richard; Prichard, H. A.; Rio Grande Pueblo Indians; Ross, Sir (William) David; Schlick, Moritz; Sidgwick, Henry; Socrates; Sophists, the; Spinoza; Stoics, the; Utilitarianism; Wollaston, William; Zoroastrian Morals.
hardship: *see* Minor Socratics.
Hardy: *see* Schopenhauer, Arthur.
Hare: *see* Reid, Thomas.
harm: *see* Sophists, the.
harmony: *see* China, Moral Philosophies of; Cooper, Anthony Ashley; Hindu Ethics; Mundurucu Indians, A Dual System of Ethics; Plato; Quakerism, Classical, The Morality

of; Rio Grande Pueblo Indians; Sophists, the; Spinoza; Stoics, the; Zuni Indians, Morals of.

Harris, W. T.: *see* Moral Philosophy in America.

harsh words: *see* Muslim Morals.

harshness: *see* Zuni Indians, Morals of.

Hartmann, E. von: *see* Schopenhauer, Arthur.

Hartmann, Nicolai

Nicolai Hartmann, a leading intuitionist and realist in recent ethics and the author of what has been called "the most comprehensive systematic treatise on ethics ever published," was born in Riga in 1882. He was educated at St. Petersburg and Marburg, and he taught at the Universities of Cologne, Berlin, and Göttingen. He was one of the most prolific writers in recent philosophy, being the author of substantial treatises in epistemology, metaphysics, history of philosophy, philosophy of science, and aesthetics, as well as an ontology in several volumes. The chief influences on his work are those of Kant, Husserl, and Aristotle, and, in ethics, Nietzsche and Max Scheler. He died in Göttingen October 9, 1950.

Hartmann began his philosophical career as a neo-Kantian, but by the time his greatest works, including the *Ethics,* were written, he had broken with Kantianism and affiliated himself with the phenomenologists, the school of Husserl which rejected the Kantian theory of the *a priori* and argued for a direct *a priori* insight into the essences which give content and structure to experience.

Though Hartmann was in no sense a disciple of any other philosopher, and is outspoken in his criticism of many of the views of Scheler and other phenomenologists, both the strengths and weaknesses—each in exaggerated form—of the phenomenological method appear in Hartmann's *Ethics.* The greatest strengths of Hartmann's *Ethics* are an almost incredible subtlety of discrimination in complex phenomena of morality that had never before been analyzed so exhaustively, and an exemplary and unique ability in leaving the phenomena with which he dealt unforced into any alien theoretical mold. The weaknesses are likewise inherent in the method of phenomenology: an appeal to the moral sense for the settlement of theoretical disputes when the disputes themselves had been historically engendered by the ambiguities in the deliverances of such alleged intuitive faculties and by the lack of unanimity among consciences. Hence Hartmann's *Ethics* is likely to speak persuasively only to those already committed to general agreement with his axiological realism. With Hartmann, the reader does not make one or two concessions and then find himself dialectically committed to the rest of the theory, but he is called upon to consult his moral sense in almost every chapter, sometimes on every page. If the outcome is not what Hartmann says it is, the book has no further argument to make or persuasion to offer. But to one who is sympathetic to this way of philosophizing and whose moral sense is more often than not in agreement with Hartmann's, there is no other book that has such fineness of texture and delicacy of judgment. And any reader, whether in agreement with Hartmann or not, must acknowledge that there is no other book in moral philosophy that is as comprehensive and detailed as Hartmann's *Ethics*. For this reason there are lessons in it for defenders and critics of all ethical theories.

Hartmann starts with experiences of value of all kinds, but especially with conscience, which is the primal moral sense of value. The purpose of philosophical ethics is the Socratic midwifery of moral consciousness; in aim it is theoretical, but by bringing to light aspects or species of value obscured or neglected in the original moral consciousness, ethics can become a normative, transforming power in life.

Philosophical ethics is not an empirical study of conscience and conduct as natural or social. It is, however, empirical in the phenomenological sense of the word: it seeks to bring to clear and evident salience the essential contents and structures present in all phenomena of valuation, without prior theoretical decision as to what is genuine and what is spurious, what objective and what subjective. Its goal is to find, amid the variety of value experiences, the ideal phenomenon or phenomenological essence, which will illuminate, render intelligible, and provide a standard for the very kinds of valuational experiences which are its own starting point. The ideal phenomenon or essence is the object of a clear and evident insight (*Wertblick, Wesensschau*); it is not, in the Kantian sense, a transcendental condition of the experience that is itself never phenomenally given, but it is essential *content* of the experience, not oversimplified yet stripped of irrelevancies. Because it is always present and at least dimly adumbrated in all experiences of the relevant kind, every valuational experience has an *a priori* character. We do not learn by induction from experience what is of value; experience is only the occasion which brings the value, by a kind of Platonic *anamnesis*, before full consciousness. We do not "read into" experience the values; they are rather found there as essences of the objects, situations, experiences, and dispositions they characterize.

Hartmann distinguishes two fundamental types of value experience, which, while they interpenetrate, are logically and phenomenologically distinct. One consists of experiences relevant to answering the question, "What is valuable?" Such experiences are contemplative. The other consists of experiences proffering answers to the question, "What ought I to do?" They presuppose some answer to the former question, but Hartmann gives first place to the latter question, since our sense of obligation is more vivid and articulate than our contemplative vision of values outside the context of obligation to actualize them. But the first question is not neglected; the loving attention to details of values isolated from the context of obligation is a unique feature of Hartmann's philosophizing, and no other ethical writer has so celebrated the value-character of the contemplation of values, of taking up an inward attitude in the absence of obligation.

Hartmann's moral philosophy and theory of value may best be summarized under three headings: (a) Values in general, and the Ought, (b) Moral values proper, and (c) the Person.

(a) *Values and the Ought.* Values are essences, Platonic ideas. Like the structures of logic and mathematics, they have an ideal self-existence (*Ansichsein*), which is to say that they are not, as such, either actual or subjective. Unlike the structures of mathematics and logic, however, they are not formal and empty; they are, in Scheler's sense, material essences, each with its own qualitative uniqueness to be discerned by an *a priori* ethical insight instead of by philosophical dialectic. With the experience of value there is discerned, by an *ordre du coeur*, some intimation of its position, its height and depth and bearing upon other values.

It is not quite correct to say that values are, for Hartmann, Platonic ideas, for Platonic ideas are thought to be categories of existence and to apply to the actual world. In a consistently Platonic world, being and value must ultimately coincide, because the supreme principles of value are likewise categories of existence. But this feature of Platonism, according to Hartmann, diminishes the autonomy of ethics by equating value with being, either now or in eternity, and independently of man's activity. Hartmann condemns any metaphysical commitment which obscures or diminishes the absolute indispensability of

moral action, on which alone the realization of moral values and, so far as we know, the realization of all other values depends. Many metaphysical theories—not only mechanism but also finalism, Platonism, all varieties of monism, pantheism, and even theism—derogate from man's autonomous position as the agent solely responsible (so far as we know) for the actualization of value. The "rehabilitation of man," says Hartmann, is the "miracle of the ethical phenomenon," which shows that men are neither mere parts of a world-machine without value nor mere organs in an organic universe in which value and existence are brought together without his effort; this rehabilitation of man, therefore, requires a distinction between the being of values and that of Platonic ideas. Values do not inevitably manifest themselves in actual conduct. They directly determine existence *as it ought to be,* not existence itself.

Hartmann then distinguishes three meanings of the "ought." (i) The ideal ought-to-be (*Seinsollen*) is the formal condition of any value. To say "*x* is a value" is to say "*x* ought to be." The ought-to-be is the "formal cause" of value, and value (what it is that ought to be) is the "material cause" of the ought. The ideal ought-to-be sanctions reality when it exists, but in itself it is independent of whether reality corresponds to it or not. The ought-to-be-character does not disappear when it happens to qualify an actuality, and value does not relinquish its ought-to-be-character when actuality does not show its presence. (ii) The positive ought-to-be is a relational property of a value which ideally ought-to-be but is not realized in existence. There is no positive ought-to-be that is not also an ideal ought-to-be; but many a thing in the world is as it ought to be. Therefore many values are not qualified by the positive ought-to-be and are objects of axiological contemplation, not of practical striving. (iii) The ought-to-do (*Tunsollen*) has a wholly different foundation. The positive ought-to-be, when its realization becomes the goal of striving of an active and free agent, commands what the person ought to do. The conversion of the positive ought-to-be into a goal occurs by means of an imperative which fixes the ought-to-do. What a person ought to do depends upon the positive ought-to-be and upon his existential situation and power.

Hartmann gives an elaborate exposition of the interrelationships of the various values and their corresponding oughts and formulates a set of axiological laws of these relations. The most important of the conclusions of this study are as follows. (i) The realm of value is characterized by ineradicable antinomies between values. Incompatibilities arise because some opposing values cannot be fully realized in one world (e.g., brotherly love and "love of the remote"), or because the values themselves are antithetical (e.g., love and justice). Every choice of a value or fulfilment of an obligation is not merely a choice of value against an anti-value but also of one value over against another value, which may be of equal worth. The notion of a sys-

tematic ideal of values is, therefore, so far as we know illusory and chimerical. (ii) Values cannot be arranged in a single scale of worth. All scaling must be multi-dimensional. Two of the most important dimensions are those of height and strength. A higher value, in one of several ways, is dependent upon a lower value, but the lower value is the stronger. Over against the lower, the higher value possesses a unique *novum* which is its freedom, its being not wholly determined by its lower condition. The most stringent prohibitions are against infringing the lower but stronger values; the most demanding positive ideals are those directed to the realization of the highest but weakest values. Hartmann formulates the "law of inverse variation of strength and height," according to which the higher a value, the more praiseworthy its attainment and the less blameworthy its absence; the stronger a value, the more blameworthy its absence but the less praiseworthy its presence.

(b) *Moral values.* There are two fundamentally distinct species of values: those that characterize things and situations, and those that characterize persons as free agents and their acts and dispositions. While essentially distinct, they do in fact overlap. For instance, life is a good that must characterize a moral agent, but it is not restricted to moral beings; truthfulness on the other hand is a moral value, but it is also a social good.

Both types of value are involved in every moral action. The moral situation always involves the following elements: (i) a person as agent, as the "executor of values in the realm of existence"; (ii) a person as patient or recipient of an action by the agent directed to the realization of some non-moral good for him; (iii) a moral value attaching to the disposition of the agent. (The person as agent may be the same as the person as patient.)

The moral value is realized even when the end is not as a matter of fact achieved; therefore moral value is not an instrumental value, and Hartmann's ethics is not "teleological" in the usual sense of the word. But unless there is a quest for some non-moral good, moral value does not emerge, and Hartmann is not a "formalist" in the sense in which it is generally said that Kant was a formalist, denying the admissability of seeking non-moral values in morality. We cannot be good "for the sake of the good;" we always aim at something that would be a goods value for a person, ourselves or another; but the moral value "rides on the back" of our action and is not the goal of it. Scheler had insisted that moral values, therefore, cannot ever be the object of striving; Hartmann, on the other hand, rightly says merely that the value aimed at may be in fact the possession of a moral value, but it is never the *same* moral value as the one characterizing the act itself. In spite of his criticism of Scheler, however, Hartmann does not adequately account for the "attractive power" of moral values themselves; he recognizes that they have this power, but he does not seem to have a secure place in his system for this important fact, for he denies that moral values themselves have an ought-to-do-character.

The height of a moral value is related in no simple way to the height of the goods value intended, and Hartmann often seems to waver, in particular cases, between the ethics of "ideal utilitarianism," with its emphasis upon the determination of the "right" by the "good," and "deontological ethics" with its assertion of the priority of the right over the good in moral decision. Were there any simple relation between the heights of the conditioning and the conditioned value, Hartmann could avoid these conflicts; but he finds none, and leaves decisions to casuistry.

On the basis of the relation between the two species of value, Hartmann builds his theory of specific moral values. He discusses, with matchless acuteness, the Christian and Aristotelian virtues, the values of unique personality, Nietzsche's "love of the remote" and "radiant virtue," and others either fixed in our tradition or only inchoate in contemporary moral consciousness. But the most interesting part of his account of moral value is his unprecedented study of the "four fundamental moral values": the good, the noble, the rich in experience (*die Fülle*), and the pure.

These values, characterized by an ought-to-be of great height but of little strength, emerge as perduring values of personality when an agent "by nature" realizes a specific structure of value in the patterns of all his action. They are structural values and characterize personality as a whole. Yet they are antithetical to each other, and a unique ideal of human perfection cannot be formulated.

Goodness is the moral value characterizing the person who strives for the higher values; the good man converts values into ends; the good is "the teleology of the highest." The noble is the value of the pursuit of one value to the exclusion of others; the value pursued may be high or low, and Satan himself is noble, though not good. Richness of experience is the opposite of both; it is the value of personal many-sidedness, including much that is not good, and is radically opposed to the one-sidedness of the noble. Purity contrasts with richness and is like nobility in being founded on single-mindedness, but it is predicated upon obliviousness of the conflict and opposition inherent in the good and noble character; while the man of rich experience may look with disdain (or envy) upon the pure and innocent. Much of Hartmann's detailed study of individual virtues is concerned with the ramifications of this moral typology and the oppositions and affiliations of the basic moral types.

(c) *The Person.* Each type of value is applicable only to a definite order of carrier in the world. Some apply to things, some to living beings, and some to conscious beings or subjects. A subject that can discern values, cultivate attitudes towards them, and pursue them by voluntary action is a *person,* which is the highest level of existing organization that we know. Moral values are values characterizing persons in so far as they are free.

While a human person is the only mediator between the realm of ideal values and the order of nature, he is not automatically so. Values do not ingress into existence through the mere being of the person; and if they did so, the value of the person would be only that of a means to some non-moral end. Moral values characterize the person as free and responsible, not as inevitably actualizing values.

To be moral, therefore, presupposes to be free. Freedom means at least partial exemption from the laws of natural processes. Hartmann accepts Kant's "demonstration" of freedom in this sense ("negative freedom"), but he disentangles it from the simple bifurcation of natural and moral law which is the limit of Kant's theory. Hartmann generalizes Kant's solution and asserts that the necessary condition of freedom in this sense is an "added determinant" that can initiate new causal sequences, this added determinant being a higher stratum in the manifold stratification of the world. The added determinant is a condition of *moral* freedom, of course, only at that level where the added determinant is concerned with value.

Hartmann argues that Kant did not, however, secure the autonomy of the person, and, moreover, that his own generalization of Kant does not, taken alone, accomplish it. All that is secured by Kant and by Hartmann's extension, thus far, is the autonomy of the higher level (the moral law) over the lower (nature). For Kant, the person is determined either by the law of nature or by the law of morality; but in either case the person is determined, not free and autonomously responsible. Hartmann, as we have seen, rejects every metaphysical theory which in the least infringes on human responsibility, and here he discovers a new antinomy, "the antinomy of ought and value": If the person is determined by value, he is not free; and if not determined by values, the person is not moral; hence in neither case can moral value be realized.

Hartmann resolves this antinomy by denying that values "determine" the person even when natural law does not. Values are not themselves the "added determinant." They command, but they do not determine. If they did determine, values would themselves be ontological principles fully realized in the world without the intervention of a person *responsible* for their actualization; and such a world would be one lacking moral value proper. Evidence that they are not determinants is found in the classical argument that moral values are actual and therefore must be possible; hence freedom is possible. But Hartmann suspects this argument, since our moral sense of values might be delusive. Better evidence he finds in an original argument based upon the conflicts among values themselves, especially in the conflict between the strong universal values and the high values of individual personality (unique personal *ethos*). The realm of value does not issue unequivocal edicts to its executive officers in the world of existence. Its commands are contradictory, and the person who cannot adjudicate

these conflicts intellectually must decide them by fiat and *thereby* take responsibility and guilt. Conflicts of obligation cannot be solved, they must be decided. Decision is choice, coerced by neither values nor causes. Thus man is not only free "under law," as Kant held, but has freedom "above the law" itself, and his decisions are qualified by moral value, either positive or negative.

How man can be free in this way is admitted by Hartmann (as by Kant) to be an unsolvable problem. But the categorial stratification of the world, in which each level is characterised by a unique *novum* undetermined by its lower categorial conditions, gives Hartmann at least an analogical key to this mystery. But he confesses that he can push the door open only a little way. And Hartmann's *Ethics* ends with a chapter perhaps unique in the history of philosophy, a chapter on the apparent and real weaknesses of his own theory of freedom.

In this way he not only showed a caution and humility all too rare among moral philosophers, but also gave point to an idea governing all his work, to wit, that the objective, phenomenological study of values is only in its beginning stages, that we must not be impatient for theoretical results, and that—as he wrote and often said in his lectures—"We do not yet know what is good and bad."

Bibliography

Works by Hartmann. *Ethik* (Berlin, 1925, second edition, 1935, third edition, 1949; English translation by Stanton

Coit, 3 volumes, London, 1932); *Das Problem des geistigen Seins* (Berlin, 1932); *Neue Wege der Ontologie* (Stuttgart, 1943; English translation by Reinhard Kuhn, Chicago, 1953).

Works on Hartmann, Roger Hazelton, "On Hartmann's Doctrine of Values as Essences," *Philosophical Review*, XLVIII (1939), 621–32; H. Heimsoeth and R. Heiss, *Nicolai Hartmann, der Denker und sein Werk* (Göttingen, 1952; contains essays by Hartmann's students, a paper by Hartmann on "personality," a transcript of a seminar in ethics conducted by Hartmann, and a good bibliography); Sidney Hook, "A Critique of Ethical Realism," *International Journal of Ethics*, XL (1929), 179–92; O. C. Jensen, "Nicolai Hartmann's Theory of Virtue," *Ethics*, LII (1942), 463–79; E. J. Koehle, *Personality. A Study according to the Philosophies . . . of Scheler and Hartmann* (Newton, New Jersey, 1941); John E. Smith, "Hartmann's New Ontology," *Review of Metaphysics*, VII (1954), 583–601; Merle G. Walker, "Perry and Hartmann, Antithetical or Complementary?" *International Journal of Ethics*, XLIX (1939), 37–61.

Lewis White Beck
University of Rochester

Hasan al Basri: *see* Muslim Morals.
Hasidism: *see* Jewish Ethics and Its Civilization.
hate: *see* China, Moral Philosophies of; Goethe, Johann Wolfgang von; Hindu Ethics; Major Ethical Viewpoints; More, Henry; Spinoza.
hatred: *see* Muslim Morals; Quakerism, Classical, The Morality of.
haughtiness: *see* Aztec Morals.
Haŭrvatat: *see* Zoroastrian Morals.

Haven, Joseph: *see* Moral Philosophy in America.
healing: *see* Freud, Sigmund.
health: *see* Freud, Sigmund; Hindu Ethics; Jewish Ethics and Its Civilization; Navaho Morals; Puritan Morals; Rio Grande Pueblo Indians; Sophists, the; Stoics, the.
heaven, Chinese idea of: *see* China, Moral Philosophies of.
Hebrew moral philosophy: *see* Christian Moral Philosophy; Jewish Ethics and Its Civilization.
hedonism: *see* China, Moral Philosophies of; Cumberland, Richard; Green, T. H.; Hume, David; Major Ethical Viewpoints; Minor Socratics; Moore, George Edward; Muslim Morals; pleasure; Schlick, Moritz; Sidgwick, Henry; Utilitarianism.
hedonism, psychological: *see* Utilitarianism.
heedlessness: *see* Muslim Morals.
Hegel, Georg Wilhelm Friedrich

I

In his last attack on the Christian foundations of Western civilization Nietzsche ironically remarked "that philosophy has been corrupted by theologians' blood. The Protestant parson is a grandfather of German philosophy; Protestantism itself, its *peccatum originale*. Definition of Protestantism: the partial paralysis of Christianity—*and* of reason. One need merely say "Tübingen Seminary" to understand what German philosophy is at bottom: an *insidious* theology. The Swabians are the best liars in Germany: they lie innocently." (*The Antichrist* I, 10, in: *The Portable Nie-*

tzsche, [1954], p. 576.) In this attack Nietzsche directs his arrows against Hegel who is a son of the pietistic Swabia of the eighteenth century and was stamped for life by his theological education in the Tübingen Seminary. Nietzsche's critique reveals in spite of its violent tone remarkable insight into the crux of Hegel's philosophy, which is Christian by origin but post-Christian by consequence. Hegel's philosophy is Christian in its language, but post-Christian in its meaning.

The transition from the Christian to the post-Christian realm is usually tagged with the perjorative term "secularization." What is peculiar to Hegel's philosophy is that the theological original text itself is transferred into a new realm: the language of Christian faith is translated into the language of Christian reason. This transformation occurs, however, on the very premises that are contained in the theological language. No wonder that a merciless critic could describe this tension in Hegel's philosophy as a partial paralysis of Christianity and of reason.

Hegel's philosophy of man is essentially built on the premises of the Christian concept of man. It is fundamental for this concept of man that man can convert. In the Christian frame of reference conversion is originally not a magic ritual act but implies a total transformation of man: the old Adam can become a new Adam, an essentially different man. The stages of the dialectic which Hegel describes in various ways throughout his work are nothing but a series of conversions,

successive stages of the transformation of man on his way through history.

History begins, according to Hegel, in the first meeting between man and man. This general thesis needs some specification: Hegel argues (in the spirit of Hobbes) that history begins with the first struggle between man and man that results in their division between master and slave. In the nascent state of society man is not simply "man" but always and necessarily either master or slave.

With Aristotle, Hegel admits in man a radical division between master and slave. But note also the difference. For Aristotle the division of man into master and slave is the perennial human condition that will last forever: man is "born" either with a servile or a free nature. This condition of human life can never be modified or changed. Masters and slaves constitute two distinct species of man. "It is thus clear, that, as some are by nature free, so others are by nature slaves, and for these latter the condition of slavery is both beneficial and just." (Aristotle, *Politics,* Ch. V, 11, 1255a). These two species of man are irreducible to each other and eternally bound to their natural topos, to their natural place in an immutable cosmos.

For Hegel, however, the division of man into master and slave is only the start of history and this difference will be overcome and erased in the course of time. The characteristics of mastery or servitude are not given or innate to man. Man is not born a slave or master, he *becomes* slave or master in a historic action. The master is the one who is ready to go until the end in the struggle, ready to die if he is not recognized by others as master while the slave accepts out of fear of death the superiority of the master, submits voluntarily to him and recognizes the master as master without being recognized by him in the dignity of the human person. But there is no necessity, no innate factor that makes one human being a master and subjugates the other to become a slave. The division results from a free historic action and is in no way predetermined by "nature." Man can overcome his condition and transform his servile status. History is for Hegel nothing but a progressive negation of the state of servitude by the slave: a series of conversions to become a free and recognized man. The old Adam who lives in the state of servitude becomes a new Adam who lives in the state of freedom.

History (which contains the story of the interaction between warrior-masters and workmen-slaves) comes to an end at the moment when the master will cease to rule as a master and the slave will cease to work as a slave. History will be fulfilled at the moment when the "synthesis" of the master and the slave will be realized. This conception, according to which history is an interaction or a dialectic of mastery and servitude, enables us to understand the meaning of Hegel's division of the historic process into three major phases (which are however of quite different length). If history begins with the struggle after which a master dominates a slave, it follows that the first historical phase must be one where

the human existence is totally determined by the rule of the master. In the course of this phase, therefore, it is the spirit of mastery which will reveal its human possibilities. But if history is a dialectic between mastery and servitude it is necessary that servitude also should become manifest through historic action. Therefore the first phase must be followed by a second one in which human existence will be determined by the consciousness and action of the slave. Finally, if the end of history represents a synthesis of mastery and servitude (and the understanding of this synthesis) these two phases must be followed by a third phase during which human existence neutralizes the antagonism between man and man. At this stage there arises also the possibility of a scientific understanding of man, i.e., of an understanding that is not tainted by the antagonism between the ideology of the master and the ideology of the slave. Hegel considered the advent of Napoleon as a caesura in history in which a universal homogeneous society could be established. It is this moment in history that offers, according to Hegel, for the first time, the possibility of an interpretation of the human condition in a definite, in a scientific way.

In short, the dialectic of Hegel spells out in the language of philosophy the fundamental categories of Christian eschatology. History is possible only in a meaningful way where the events do not reoccur eternally and man walks around in circles, but where man, in successive or progressive stages of negation transforms given orders and structures and establishes the city of reason on earth.

II

In one sentence to his preface to the *Phenomenology of the Spirit* Hegel offers us a key to interpret his philosophy: "In my view . . . everything depends on grasping and expressing the ultimate proof not as Substance but as Subject as well" (*Phenomenology of Mind,* 2d ed.; [London], 1931, p. 80). This sentence is of cardinal importance for it contains Hegel's critique of classical ontology, the critique of the Philosophy of Plato and Aristotle, and may well serve as a guide to understand the anti-ontological ("transcendental") critical philosophy of Kant, Fichte and Hegel.

Philosophy has been divided by some historians into:

1). philosophy of substance: ontology
2). philosophy of subject: epistemology: critical philosophy

We can put the difference between ancient and modern philosophy into the rough scheme

1). philosophy of nature: realism: philosophy of substance: ontology: (Plato and Aristotle).
2). Philosophy of spirit: idealism: philosophy of subject: Philosophy of history: (Kant and Hegel).

Greek philosophy has developed its categories by unfolding the concept of nature. Its ontology is an explication of the realm of nature and its categorical frame is the logic of identity: if I ask what is the *nature* of man? What is the *nature* of the world? what is the *nature* of the gods? I am asking always for the identical a-a. The Greek philosophical inquiry "into the nature of the cosmos, into the nature of man, into the nature of the gods" presupposes an identical, "eternal" sameness. Note that an inquiry into the nature, i.e., into the always same and identical nature of x, y and z works with patterns developed in cosmology. Its origin is the inquiry into the nature of nature (*physis*). The Greek concept of nature rules still in the medieval Christian philosophy. Albertus Magnus and Thomas Aquinas add only a "supernatural" realm to the natural base. Philosophy and theology are construed in the Middle Ages like a two storey house.

Only from Kant and Hegel on can we date a philosophy of the spirit: philosophy of subject: epistemology: philosophy of history, and in Hegel's philosophy we reach the full opposition to the framework of classical ontology. Nature is no longer the matrix of things, but the universal category is a concept of spirit; man, the subject, is no longer explicated in terms of substance, of nature, but substance, nature, is interpreted in terms of spirit.

There is nothing sublime or Sundayish about Hegel's concept of the spirit. It is the concept which comprises the trinity of man; freedom, historicity, personhood. Hegel's analysis is philosophy of the *spirit* because it tries to interpret man in his freedom, i.e., man in his activity. His philosophy of the spirit is not a contemplative theory but a theory of action. Hegel's philosophy is a theory of action because it is an analysis of history.

In the concept of the spirit Hegel emphasizes the element of negativity, which was neglected in classical philosophy. In classical ontology the category of identity is fundamental for describing "being qua being." Ultimately every inquiry into the nature of x, y and z can only bring to the fore the identity of being with itself and must end up in an elaborate ontology identifying being and thought. In the light of the category of identity being remains always the same, eternally identical with itself. Against Aristotle's logic and ontology of identity, Hegel developed the historic category of negativity. Spirit is negativity. Due to the spirit a being can negate, contest or suppress, the identity with itself and become something other than itself. It no longer needs to represent an eternal idea in a static cosmos but it can break through the fixed barriers, the so-called natural limits, and become other than itself.

For Hegel freedom, action, and negativity are interdependent categories describing man in his historicity. At the end of the passage that states *in nuce* the content of his philosophy, Hegel returns to the theme of the relation between substance and subject and says: "that the truth is only realized in the form of system, that substance is essentially subject, is expressed in the idea which represents the Absolute is spirit—the grandest conception of all and one which is due to modern times and its religion" (*ibid.*) The Absolute is spirit, this again is a statement to oppose Greek ontology. Hegel does not seek the key for the interpretation of man in the cosmos, in the "eternal" nature but in the triad of freedom, action and negativity, i.e., in the historic, transformative action of man.

The Greek doctrine of man specifies for him an always identical topos, a natural place in the cosmos. Change and development are only secondary. The logos does not change or transform the given nature, but only "reveals" what is eternally given and predetermined. In the perspective of Hegel, however, man is essentially through his spirit engaged in a transformative action. The statement: "man is spirit" implies that man is a person, a free historic individual, beyond the cosmic or natural structure. Man can and should overcome his nature, he should convert, he should transform the world. By changing the world, man is also transforming himself. Man can become a new man. In the historic world man acts by way of conversion and transformation. When Hegel summarizes his philosophy in a sentence like: "substance is essentially subject" he is translating into the language of reason what has been considered central in the drama of eschatology: the conversion of the old Adam into the new Adam, and this is precisely the reason why Hegel uses in the summary of his philosophy the key word: Spirit. Spirit is for Hegel a modern term, opposing the pagan philosophy of substance, the pagan ontology of being, the Greek emphasis on the primacy of nature.

And still, Hegel, who stresses the Christian origins of the concept of spirit entitles the sixth chapter of his *Phenomenology* with the emphatic term "Spirit." This chapter, however, does not deal with the kingdom that is not of this world, but presents precisely the development of human history from the Greek city-state to the French revolution and the Empire of Napoleon. Hegel's concept of spirit is not transmundane but historic. The realm of the spirit is the arena of human history. The temporal realm itself which Christian religion has separated for centuries from the temporal realm.

Christian theologians would have, like Nietzsche, to accuse Hegel of transforming Providence into a cunning reason, of translating the stages of the history of salvation into the stages of world history and, to make the accusation full, of elevating world history to the high court of justice. Hegel, however, would argue that what his opponents would call "secularization" of the Christian drama of salvation does indeed mean the realization of the Christian spirit on earth, the fulfillment of the original meaning of redemption—fulfillment in an ambiguous way: by transforming the origin, by taking the subsequent evolution of Christian society into consideration. If there is a meaningful history of the Christian era as a history that unfolds the element of the messianic hope contained in the original message, then the incarnation of the spiritual into the secular realm is a warranted conclusion. Those who deny the transformation of the messianic drama into a drama of history must with Kierkegaard and Nietzsche deny the history of Christendom as Christian history and reduce the Christian experience to the ivory tower of man's individual soul.

Bibliography

I. Biographical Data of Georg Wilhelm Friedrich Hegel (1770–1831):

1784–	88	Gymnasium Stuttgart
1788–	93	Tübingen Seminary
1793–	96	Tutor at Berne, Switzerland
1797–1800		Tutor at Frankfurt
1800–1806		Professor at Jena
1807		Editor of a Journal at Bamberg
1808–1816		Rector of Gymnasium at Nuremberg
1816–1818		Professor at Heidelberg
1818–1831		Professor at Berlin

II. Writings by Hegel relevant to his social theory:
   a. *Early Theological Writings,* transl. by T. M. Knox (Chicago, 1948).
   b. Political Essays, in: *The Philosophy of Hegel,* edited by Carl J. Friedrich (New York, 1953).
   c. *Phenomenology of Mind,* transl. by J. B. Baillie, 2d ed. (London, 1931). Especially chapters 4, 5 and 6.
   d. *Philosophy of Right,* transl. by T. M. Knox (Oxford, 1942).
III. Writings about Hegel's social theory:
   a. Sidney Hook, *From Hegel to Marx,* 2d ed. (New York, 1954).
   b. Herbert Marcuse, *Reason and Revolution, Hegel and the Rise of Social Theory,* 2d ed. (New York, 1954).

Jacob Taubes
Columbia University

Hegel, G. W. F.; Hegelianism: *see* Goethe, Johann Wolfgang von; Green, T. H.; Kierkegaard, Soren;

Major Ethical Viewpoints; Marxist Theory of Morals; Moral Philosophy in America; Schopenhauer, Arthur; Soviet Morality, Current.

Hegesias: *see* Minor Socratics.

hell: *see* Dante, Alighieri; Goethe, Johann Wolfgang von.

Helvetius: *see* Utilitarianism.

Heptad, the Supreme: *see* Zoroastrian Morals.

Heracles: *see* Minor Socratics.

Herder: *see* Cooper, Anthony Ashley. Kant, I.

hereafter: *see* after-life; immortality; Rio Grande Pueblo Indians.

heredity: *see* Hindu Ethics.

heresy: *see* Dante, Alighieri; Spinoza.

Herford, R. T.: *see* Jewish Ethics and Its Civilization.

Herskovits, M. J.: *see* Pakot, the Moral System of.

heteronomy: *see* Jewish Ethics and Its Civilization.

hierarchy: *see* Butler, Joseph; Ross, Sir (William) David.

Hildreth, Richard: *see* Moral Philosophy in America.

Hillel: *see* Jewish Ethics and Its Civilization.

Hindu Ethics

Hindu philosophers have discussed ethics both from the subjective or personal and from the objective or social standpoint. Subjective ethics emphasizes personal discipline. Its purpose is the individual's purification of mind, leading to his attainment of the Highest Goal, which transcends and fulfils all relative values. Objective ethics deals with social welfare. It is based upon the Hindu conception of dharma or duty, determined by a man's position in society and his stage of life, and also upon certain universal duties common to all human beings. But social ethics, too, ultimately helps the individual to attain the Knowledge of the Self or God. Hindu ethics, however, stresses the personal value of actions. The reason for this emphasis will be discussed later.

The ethical theories of the Hindus are derived from certain metaphysical concepts laid down in the Upanishads, which contain the philosophy of the Vedas, and also from other subsidiary scriptures based upon the Vedic teachings. According to the general Upanishadic view, the value of an action is to be judged by the degree of personal sacrifice involved. An action is meritorious if it requires a voluntary denial of personal comforts and material advantages on the doer's part, though the action in itself may not be conducive to the immediate well-being of others. But the Upanishads do not deny the social value of action. A good action is thus extolled: "As the scent is wafted afar from a tree laden with flowers, so also is wafted afar the scent of a good deed." Self-Knowledge is denied to him "who has not first turned away from wickedness, who is not tranquil and subdued, and whose mind is not at peace." Among the various social duties are included "hospitality, courtesy, duties to the wife, children, and grandchildren." In one Upanishad a king says: "In my kingdom there is no thief, no miser, no drunkard, no man without an altar in his house, no ignorant person, no adulterer, much less an adulteress."

213

As already stated, Hindu ethics is primarily concerned with self-discipline leading to the liberation of the individual. Thus the Bhagavad Gītā says: "Let a man lift himself up by his own self; let him not depress himself; for he himself is his friend and he himself is his enemy. To him who has conquered himself by himself, his own self is a friend, but to him who has not conquered himself, his own self is hostile, like an external enemy." The chief self-disciplines are austerity and renunciation. Through the practice of austerity a man curbs his selfish impulses and also acquires superhuman and supernatural powers which exalt him far above the world of men, nay, even above the world of the gods. Through self-control and concentration he can penetrate into the mysteries of nature and acquire wisdom which is unattainable by any other means. But asceticism, in India, has sometimes been abused with the selfish aim of exciting wonder or securing personal profit, thus depriving it of its spiritual significance.

The sense-organs are ordinarily inclined to material pleasures. They should be controlled in order to create inner calmness without which profound spiritual truths cannot be perceived and the Highest Goal cannot be realized. The Upanishads make a sharp distinction between the ideal of pleasure and the ideal of the good. They are like light and darkness. "He who chooses the pleasant misses the end." "The fool chooses the pleasant out of greed and avarice."

But the practice of austerities does not mean the suppression or the torturing of the sense-organs. If the sense-organs are weakened then the spiritual goal cannot be achieved. The *Katha Upanishad* explains this through the illustration of a chariot. The body is compared to the chariot, the intellect or discriminative faculty to the driver, the mind to the reins, the senses to the horses, the sense-objects to the roads, and the embodied soul to the master of the chariot. The chariot can serve its purpose if it is well built, if the driver knows his way, and if the reins are strong, the horses firmly held in control, and the roads well chosen. The spiritual seeker should possess a healthy body and vigorous organs, unfaltering determination, and an undistracted mind. His discrimination should guide his senses to choose only those objects which are helpful to the realization of his spiritual ideal. If, on the other hand, the body, the mind, or any of his faculties is injured or suppressed, he cannot attain the goal, just as the rider cannot reach his destination if the chariot and its other accessories are not in good condition. Thus the two important elements emphasized in the practice of self-control are discrimination and will-power. The Bhagavad Gītā extols the man who is "temperate in his food and recreation, temperate in his exertion at work, temperate in sleep and waking."

Renunciation is the other discipline for self-perfection. This is the basis of the Hindu conception of duty pertaining to the stages of life and caste or position in society.

Each stage in life and position in

214

society has its appropriate duties and obligations, the right discharge of which requires self-control and renunciation. Through the four stages of life a man learns progressive renunciation and gradually becomes purified of all earthly attachment. During the first stage he is a celibate student, observing chastity of body and mind. Reverence and obedience mark his relationship with his teacher. At the end of this period, the student, while taking leave, is admonished by the teacher to speak the truth, do his duty, pursue the study of the scriptures, and to see that the line of his family is not broken. He is further asked not to neglect his health and possessions, to honour father, mother, and guests, to bestow alms in an appropriate manner, and in all doubtful cases to follow the judgement of approved authorities.

The life of the householder represents the second stage. It is required of him to establish a family, beget children, perform duties according to his position in society, and lead a life of self-control. The householder's life is the foundation of a healthy society.

At the approach of old age, husband and wife enter the third stage; they hand over the family duties to their children, retire into solitude for the contemplation of the deeper mysteries of life, and commune with God chiefly through meditation.

During the final stage, a man renounces the world and becomes a monk, though he can embrace the monastic life at any time if he feels intense dispassion for material things. Now he is a free soul cultivating the virtues of chastity, poverty, truthfulness, and non-injury. He gives an assurance of fearlessness to all living beings. A living demonstration of the reality of God, he no longer strives for ethical perfection; the moral virtues embellish all his actions. He devotes himself to the welfare of others without seeking any personal gain. Thus ethical disciplines prepare one for this, the consummation of human life.

From the caste system we learn about the social morality of the Hindus, that is to say, morality as represented in a code of external acts and requiring outward conformity. The caste-system is based on men's admitted inequalities, intellectual and spiritual, at the moment of birth. These are the result of actions performed in a previous birth, and each person, therefore, is himself responsible for his peculiar condition. In a future birth he will be born in a higher caste by cheerfully discharging the duties of his present position, and be degraded if he acts otherwise.

Each caste has its appropriate duties and obligations. The brāhmin is the priest and the spiritual guide, the kshatriya the protector of the country from external enemies and internal disorder, the vaiśya the guardian of wealth, and the śudra the performer of manual work. At first based on virtues and actions, caste later became hereditary. The higher caste must show gentleness and compassion to the lower. The four castes are the four principal parts of society; the welfare of one depends upon the welfare of the others. The original purpose of the caste-system was to eliminate ruthless competition from society and promote social harmony, though in later times power corrupted the members of the upper castes. Through the caste-system India demonstrated the superiority of knowledge over the power of the military, wealth, and organized labour.

Social morality is determined by a man's position in caste. There is no absolute moral standard equally applicable to all. Morality, called dharma in Hindu ethics, is the law of a man's inner growth and cannot be imposed from outside. It determines a man's reaction to the outer world. What is demanded of a brāhmin cannot apply to a merchant or a labourer. Each person must observe his respective dharma, however imperfect, and should not try to imitate the dharma of another, however perfect the latter may appear to be. Through the faithful performance of dharma a man's heart becomes pure and he thus becomes fit to contemplate profound spiritual truths. In the end he gives up all social duties and communes with God alone, in whom he finds the culmination of worldly values. But he cannot realize this exalted state without at first fulfilling his social obligations.

The purpose of social morality is to create an ideal society, offering its members facilities for developing their higher potentialities. Such a society gives its members an opportunity to cultivate personal morality for the purification of the mind, which in the end enables them to realize the Highest Goal.

The Highest Goal may be either acosmic or cosmic, according to the metaphysical theories with which it is related. According to non-dualistic philosophers, the Highest Goal is transcendental or acosmic. Based upon the oneness of existence, it transcends all moral imperatives, personal or social. A perfect non-dualist may no longer strive after moral excellence, but he can never perform an immoral act. But according to the dualists, the Highest Goal is cosmic, it is the realization of the Personal God. A dualist does not give up the moral virtues, but they acquire for him a new significance. As he has already completely suppressed his lower nature, passion, greed, or egotism can no longer disturb his mind. He retains his personality, but it has been completely purged of all selfish traits.

A few words may be said here to explain why social ethics has been given a secondary position by Hindu philosophers. First, society consists of individuals; if they are perfect, social welfare will follow as a matter of course. Second, in ancient Hindu society the general moral tone was very high. Everyone was expected to follow his dharma or duty, which included rendering help to his less fortunate fellow beings. The country was prosperous and men were generous and hospitable. Thus no great need was felt for organized charity, which, in European society, became prominent only in the wake of the Industrial Revolution. Third, a spiritually illumined person should serve others, either seeing in them the manifestation of his own Self or regarding them as the children of God. Such help was generally in the nature of spiritual teaching, which is, in a sense, the highest of all forms of service. Finally, all material values are transitory in this ever changing empirical world. The pairs of opposites—such as good and evil, pain and pleasure—constitute its very structure. The sum total of human happiness and suffering remains constant. The idea of progress—if it means the gradual elimination of evil and the increase of good, so that in the end only good will remain in a perfect world—is not accepted by Hindu philosophers. Suffering, like chronic rheumatism, only moves from one place to another but cannot be totally eradicated. Yet we must do good to others, because only in that way can we attain individual perfection. Hence moral laws have only an instrumental, and not an ultimate value.

Dualistic philosophers accept the world as real. The non-dualists deny its ultimate reality, but admit, during the state of ignorance, the empirical reality of the individual and the universe. As long as a man regards the body as real, he cannot deny the existence of his individual soul or of the universe. Thus non-dualism has propounded its own system of theology, ethics, and cosmology. An individual is endowed with volition, desire, conscience or consciousness of duty, emotion, etc., which must be trained in such a way as to lead him to the realization of Liberation. It is expected of the moral agent to follow the virtues and shun their opposites.

The will may be classified as impious and pious. The impious will leads to unrighteousness and produces evil. The pious will leads to righteousness and is conducive to the Highest Good. The purpose of ethics is to suppress unrighteousness and stimulate righteousness.

Unrighteousness may be physical, verbal, or mental. Physical unrighteousness manifests itself as cruelty, theft, and sexual perversion; verbal unrighteousness, as falsehood, rudeness, insinuation, and gossip; mental unrighteousness, as ill-will, covetousness, and irreverence.

Righteousness, also, is threefold: physical, verbal, and mental. Physical righteousness consists in charity, helping the distressed, and service to others; verbal righteousness, in gentle speech conducive to the welfare of others; and the righteousness of the mind, in kindness, detachment, and reverence. Righteousness and unrighteousness cover both personal and social duties. Broadly speaking, virtue is defined as what is conducive to the welfare of others, and vice as what causes them pain and misery.

Patanjali, the great Hindu psychologist and philosopher, enumerates the principal virtues as non-injury, truthfulness, abstention from theft, chastity, and non-attachment to material objects. Non-injury, the mother of all virtues, implies positive goodwill and kindness to all beings. It requires self-restraint, self-sacrifice, abstention from greed, the control of hate, and mental alertness, without which one may inadvertently commit an act of greediness, hatred, or cruelty. It also includes

217

gentleness or abstention from harsh words.

Truthfulness is opposed to falsehood. A person practising truthfulness must ascertain the facts by such valid proofs as direct perception, correct inference, and reliable testimony. In addition, he must faithfully describe the facts, without any intentional deceit or unnecessary verbiage. Half-truths and evasions are regarded as lies. But truthfulness, in order to be a virtue, must not hurt others. Its purpose is the welfare of others. When such a purpose is not served the wise remain silent. A Hindu injunction says: "Speak the truth, speak the pleasant, but never an unpleasant truth."

Abstention from theft implies that one must not unlawfully appropriate another's property or harbour greediness. What it really amounts to is indifference to the material advantages of life. The accumulation of material objects is generally tainted by cruelty or other blemishes. One certainly cannot hoard wealth without some sort of deceit or injury to others.

The practice of chastity, highly extolled by Hindu philosophers, includes abstention from lewdness in thought, speech, and action through any of the sense-organs.

The virtues here defined and enumerated are called by Patanjali universal virtues and admit of no exceptions arising from class, profession, place, or occasion. They are compulsory for spiritual seekers aiming at Self-realization, and they differ from the ordinary moral standards by which we treat differently men and animals, our fellow countrymen and foreigners, relatives and strangers.

According to Jainism, an offshoot of Hinduism, an action is immoral if it is impelled by the impious thought of the agent, and moral if there is pious thought behind it. Forgiveness is the highest virtue. The Jaina ethics aims more at self-culture than at social service, though in actual practice the Jainas of India are most forward in alleviating the misery not only of afflicted men, but also of dumb animals and insects.

Buddhist philosophers recognize sub-conscious morality and not merely conscious moral action. It is not manifest actions or words alone that are moral or immoral, but even the disposition of the mind. Thus unrighteousness begins to accumulate from the day when a man resolves that from a certain date he will earn his living by plundering and killing others, though this resolution may remain dormant for a long time. Likewise, a man begins to accumulate virtue from the day he makes a pious resolution, even though the conscious action may take place much later. Furthermore, Buddhists speak of institutional morality, according to which the founder of an institution is responsible for its good and evil effects upon others.

In contrast to Hindu ethics, which aims at personal Liberation, Greek ethics emphasizes the social virtues. Two of the characteristic Greek virtues are justice and friendship, the former stressing proper regard for the rights of others, and the latter being a social quality.

218

According to many critics, both Eastern and Western, absolute non-dualism, the outstanding philosophical system of India, which denies the ultimate reality of the phenomenal universe and the individual, has no scope for ethics. After all, it is argued, morality can function only in a world of multiplicity. This criticism is hardly valid. It will be appropriate to discuss here briefly the ethics of non-dualism.

The non-dualistic ethics is based upon the non-dualistic metaphysics, which affirms Ultimate Reality as one without a second or as the oneness of existence. Birthless, deathless, immutable, fearless, incorporeal, attributeless, nameless, and formless, this Reality is called Brahman or the Pure Spirit, which alone exists. In the absence of duality no moral laws can operate in the realm of Pure Spirit. Thus a person who has realized his identity with Brahman has transcended all ethical imperatives. Since such a person sees himself in all beings and all beings in himself, no unethical traits—such as falsehood, selfishness, secretiveness, greed, anger, or lust—are found in him.

But non-dualistic Vedānta does not altogether deny the reality of the material universe and individual souls. Under certain conditions they appear real, though neither the embodiment of the soul nor the materiality of the universe is final or original. How the infinite and the absolute Brahman becomes the finite soul and the relative universe will for ever remain an enigma to the limited human mind. According to Vedānta, there exists in Brahman an inscrutable power called māyā or nescience, which is responsible for the projection of the universe and living beings. When this cosmic ignorance is destroyed, these very individual souls and the physical universe are then seen in their true nature, that is to say, as Pure Spirit. Till that Unity of Existence is realized, the empirical reality of the world and the diverse beings are admitted. The world functions within the framework of time, space, and causation and is changeable. An embodied being is a victim of birth and death, pain and pleasure, good and evil, virtue and vice, and the other pairs of opposites which constitute its bondage. Ethical disciplines play an important part in the liberation of the soul. The non-dualistic ethics can be regarded from two standpoints: ascetic or positive. Let us consider first the ascetic aspect.

Under the influence of nescience or ignorance, there appears the individualized soul, who regards the world of diversity as real. He regards other individuals as entirely distinct from himself and develops love and hate for some of these individuals and remains indifferent toward the rest. Thus, as a consequence of ignorance, the individual soul first forgets his real, spiritual nature; second, holds the wrong belief that he is separate from others; and lastly comes to see a physical and social environment to which he reacts in diverse ways. Suffering, which is the result of ignorance, springs from the second of these consequences, namely, the wrong belief that he is separate from other beings. The notion of ego,

219

due to the individual's identification with the body and senses, through ignorance, brings the conflict between "I" and "you." Ego is the source of all evil. Selfishness is sin, as has been declared by all religions. Hence a man seeking Knowledge and Liberation should first of all renounce the ego, that is to say, give up all private and personal interests. Therefore the non-dualistic morality, in one of its phases, preaches the ascetic ideal of self-denial.

Now for the positive aspect of ethics: As stated before, ignorance hides from a man the real truth, which is his identity with Brahman or the Pure Spirit. Man is more than the finite or narrow self. He is really the Universal Soul. It is his duty to recognize his oneness with Brahman. But an intellectual recognition is not enough; his daily action must be influenced by it. Every man searching for the nature of his relationship with others can be told that all individuals are, in essence, the same as the Pure Spirit. Men are not fundamentally different from one another. Consequently it is the duty of all to avoid discrimination between one another and cultivate a feeling of kindliness and love for all.

For the non-dualist this love is not confined only to men, but extends to all living creatures. When a man is asked to love his neighbour, he should also be told that every living being is his neighbour. This all-embracing attitude is based upon the belief that all living beings have souls, though all souls may not have reached the same state of spiritual growth. The universal love taught by non-dualism pre-cludes not only all hatred, but also emphasizes the attitude of non-difference. It denies the anthropocentric view that man is the centre of creation and that he alone is endowed with a soul. Universal love is based upon the fundamental oneness of all living beings. The reason advanced for such love is the unreal nature of the commonly felt difference between one sentient object and another, which difference is the result of ignorance. Any expression of love that is not related to this oneness is but a reflection of true love; for whether one knows it or not, the unity of existence is the ultimate truth.

Ethical action, in some form or other, is incumbent upon all human beings who regard themselves as part of society and the phenomenal world. Through appropriate ethical disciplines, the brutish man becomes the decent man of society; the decent man, the ideal man; and the ideal man is transformed into God. This is illustrated by a story in one of the Upanishads. Once a god, a man, and a demon—the three offspring of the Creator—sought his advice for self-improvement. In reply, the Creator uttered thrice the letter *da*, which is the first letter of three Sanskrit words, meaning, respectively self-control, charity, and compassion. He asked the god to practise self-control, the man charity, and the demon compassion. There exist in human society three types of people: god-like men, ordinary men, and demoniacal men. The god-like man, in spite of his culture and refinement, often lacks self-control and may go to excess in certain matters like eating, drinking, or gambling. Hence he needs to practise self-control. The ordinary human being is greedy; he is always eager to grab what belongs to others. Therefore he should practise liberality. The demoniacal person is cruel and ruthless. It is his duty to practise the discipline of compassion. The Upanishad says that the Creator, even now, gives the same advice about the moral law to the different types of human beings through the voice of thunder, which makes the reverberating sound *da - da - da*.

It is the observance of moral laws that distinguishes men from beasts. Now the question arises whether a man, still living on the ethical plane, can transcend the strife and conflict of life and realize the peace and freedom which his higher nature demands. Is ethics an end in itself or does it lead to a higher state in which ethical laws are transcended? The Hindu philosophers and modern Western thinkers seem to hold divergent views on this matter.

Though Hindu ethics extols the personal value of action over the social value, yet it may be stated here that the Hindus can learn much from the West about the application of ethics to the welfare of society. Conditions have changed in India. The concept of dharma, which was the foundation of Hindu life, has somewhat lost its hold upon the people. The struggle for existence in a competitive society has become keen. The wealth is not evenly distributed. There exists in India a widespread misery due to

ignorance, poverty, ill health, and general backwardness of life, and here lies the importance of social ethics in India. Even in this new orientation, India must not forget the ultimate goal of ethics, namely, the liberation of man from the imperfection of the phenomenal world.

Moral life cannot be dissociated from struggle—an incessant struggle for perfection which does not seem possible of attainment on the moral plane. Ethics is concerned with life as it *ought* to be lived, with the ideal of conduct. A moral man constantly says to himself: "I ought to have done this, I ought not to have done that"; "I ought to be this, I ought not to be that." *Oughtness* is the very essence of morality and implies a habitual struggle for self-improvement. Thus moral life belongs to the plane of imperfection. No one can be *merely* moral and at the same time perfect. Where there is no imperfection there is no *ought;* where there is no *ought,* there is no morality. Where there is no self-contradiction there is no *ought.* The *ought* itself is a self-contradiction.

The struggle of the moral man against evil cannot be resolved by moral precepts: The sinner cannot be absolved from his sin by mere morality. The Bible speaks of the woman taken in adultery—brought before the judges, who condemned her by the moral laws of the time, but redeemed by the spiritual man, *der reine Tor,* who was the embodiment of guilelessness and innocence. How could the moral judges, still struggling against *sin,* wash away the sin of the guilty woman? Redemption comes from grace, which belongs to the realm of the Spirit.

Hindu philosophers have suggested means for resolving the conflict involved in moral action. Both optional action, which has a particular end in view and is performed by the agent who seeks that end, and obligatory action, which it is the duty of all to perform, must not violate moral laws. But all actions, optional or obligatory, produce a bondage for their doers. An action leaves in the mind a subtle impression, which under suitable conditions becomes the cause of another action. This second action, too, leaves an impression which becomes the cause of a third action. This chain reaction does not seem to stop anywhere, and man works under necessity or compulsion. He is compelled to act. This is called the binding effect of action. How can one be free from this bondage? The Bhagavad Gītā says that subtle impressions are formed when the doer is looking for the result and becomes attached to it. It is not action itself, but attachment, that creates bondage and suffering. The agent must relinquish all attachment to the fruit of action. He must remain unagitated in success or failure. Hinduism advocates renunciation *in* action, not renunciation *of* action. A duty must be done because it ought to be done; the hankering for the result is irrelevant. If anyone is benefited by the action, well and good; but that should not be the impelling motive of the doer. The Bhagavad Gītā says: "To work you have the right, but not to the fruit thereof. Do not seek the result; do not long for non-action." What happens if an action is performed in this way? Though the doer rejects the immediate and limited fruit, he is preparing himself for the supreme fruit of life, namely, the attainment of perfection. Through non-attached action the mind and heart become free of lust, greed, and anger and attain serenity, without which supramental spiritual truths cannot be realized. Thus we see ethics opening the door to a realm which lies beyond ethics.

Two kinds of perfection have been defined by Hindu philosophers: For the believer in God it means God-realization, and for the non-dualist, Self-realization. The devotee of God regards himself as God's instrument, subordinates his will to God's will, dedicates his work entirely to God, and preserves equanimity of mind in success and failure, gain and loss. Work done in this spirit of non-attachment purifies the mind and brings about communion with God.

The non-dualist regards his true Self as the witness of action, unconcerned with its fruit. He sees the difference between the Self and the non-Self. The Self is the Pure Spirit, always free and peaceful. The non-Self consisting of ego, mind, senses, and body, plans a work, uses suitable means to accomplish it, and experiences the result. It is the non-Self that cherishes desire and clamours for the result. But the real Self remains immutable, as one indifferent to the result. After long practice, the Self succeeds in detaching itself from identification with the non-Self and in realizing its true nature of Pure Existence, Knowledge, and Bliss. This Knowledge liberates it from bondage to the world. Illumined dualists and non-dualists are both utterly unselfish. Free from ego, they transcend the moral *ought*. While dwelling in the body, both the Knower of God and the Knower of the Self may perform action, but without the impelling sense of duty. They do not act under pressure, but out of love. Action flows spontaneously from the fullness of their hearts. The question of improving the world is meaningless to them. The dualist sees the world as God's world. God dwells in all beings. Through loving service to men he worships God alone. The non-dualist is always conscious of the unity of existence. There exists for him only one Soul, and that is the Universal Self. He loves his neighbours as himself because they are his own Self. And these neighbours include all living beings.

Work of lasting benefit to humanity has been done by blessed souls like Christ and Buddha, who were free from the moral struggle. The action done by many so-called social reformers is not wholly disinterested. Such action has no doubt helped men physically and intellectually, but could not produce the Highest Good. In activities involving social service or philanthropy, there lurks somewhere in the sub-conscious mind of the doer a desire for fame, power, or recognition. He is not altogether motiveless. Only an illumined person, whose ego has either been burnt in the fire of Self-Knowledge or totally transformed by the touch of God, is free from selfish motives.

An illumined person is no longer troubled by the idea of good and evil. After the realization of Truth he never makes a false step. His struggles are over. With the destruction of the cosmic ignorance which has conjured up the dream of duality, he is no longer haunted by the notion of good and evil. The Upanishad declares: "Evil does not overtake him, but he transcends evil. He becomes sinless, taintless, free from doubts, and a Knower of Truth." He does not strive after morality from fear of punishment or hope of reward, or for the attainment of any mundane goal. Moral virtues such as humility, self-control, and tranquillity become his natural attributes.

Bibliography

S. Dasgupta, *A History of Indian Philosophy* (Cambridge, 1932).
S. Radhakrishnan, *Indian Philosophy* (London, 1929).
M. Hiriyanna, *Outlines of Indian Philosophy* (New York, 1932).
P. Deussen, *The Philosophy of the Upanishads* (1906).
S. K. Maitra, *The Ethics of the Hindus* (Calcutta, 1925).
P. S. Sivaswamy Aiyer, *Evolution of Hindu Moral Ideals* (Calcutta, 1935).
S. Radhakrishnan, *The Principal Upanishads* (New York, 1953).
Swami Nikhilananda, *The Bhagavad Gita* (with notes based on Sankara), (New York, 1944).
Swami Nikhilananda, *The Upanishads*, Vols. I & II (New York, 1949 & 1952).

Swami Nikhilananda
Ramakrishna-Vivekananda Center, New York

Hinduism: *see* Minor Socratics; Schopenhauer, Arthur.

Hindus: *see* Zoroastrian Morals.

Hippias: *see* Sophists, the.

historical determinism: *see* Soviet Morality, Current.

history: *see* Hegel, G. W. F.; Marxist Theory of Morals; Spinoza.

Hitler, A.: *see* Marxist Theory of Morals.

Hoadley, Bishop: *see* Clarke, Samuel.

Hobbes, Thomas

Thomas Hobbes was born near Malmesbury in the year in which England, through her victory over the Spanish Armada, attained security against external foes. However, Hobbes lived to spend most of his life witnessing his country's internal dissension which did not finally end till 1688, nine years after his death. This experience of civil discord, with its constant threat to life and property, influenced the fundamental aim of his moral and political philosophy: to discover a way to establish and guarantee peace.

Deserted by his father early in life, Hobbes' education was taken over by his uncle who sent him to Oxford in 1603. On leaving Oxford in 1608 he joined the Cavendish household as a tutor. His relationship with that family afforded him the opportunity to visit continental Europe and to become acquainted with the new sciences of the day. In 1636 he met Galileo and was profoundly influenced by him. This influence, together with his discovery of geometry which had taken place some eight years earlier, is revealed in the method which Hobbes employs in his investigation into the nature of the world, man and the state.

With the approach of the civil war Hobbes withdrew voluntarily to Paris as he feared reprisals for his political doctrine which had been circulated in manuscript form.

Although his sympathy lay with the Royalists his position, in its disparagement of tradition and its anti-clerical bias, met with their disfavor; and with the establishment of peace by Cromwell Hobbes returned to England. However, his desertion of the Royalist cause was readily forgiven by Charles II at the Restoration and the remainder of his life was spent peacefully enough.

For Hobbes, ethics, as a branch of philosophy, must in its enquiry into the behavior of men employ the philosophic method. And that method, on Hobbes' view, is concerned generally with the knowledge of consequences and specifically in ethics with the knowledge of the consequences which follow from the passions of men. Philosophical and scientific knowledge are identical and the method which is employed in the investigation of, say, geometry or physics is no different, in its basic rules of procedure, than the one used to investigate politics or ethics.

But the Hobbesian method is not the method of the scientific procedure of today. It is a method of analysis and synthesis which is characterized by an extreme rationalism. In the investigation of any subject matter we may begin with the given and try to analyze or resolve this whole into the simplest, ultimate components or we may begin from ultimate components and synthesize or compound these so that they constitute a complex whole. In either case the process is one of reasoning or deduction.

When applied to ethics this method rules out certain considerations which had traditionally influenced ethical theorists. The history of the past is irrelevant. For it is merely a record of our previous experiences and, as such, involves no reasoning, no deduction of consequences from ultimate facts. Thus the appeal to tradition, custom and legal precedent has no significance for Hobbes. For these supposed guides to conduct are often haphazardly formed and have no solid basis. Indeed, they may often misguide us. Nor is prudence an authoritative guide. For prudence, depending on experience and imagination, is limited to the particular actions of particular men. Science, however, must be universal and yield conclusions which are applicable to all men.

With this method in mind Hobbes' first task—the task of analysis— is to isolate the ultimate components of human behavior. To do this it is necessary to abstract all the influences which, in their various ways, affect men and consider them as isolated units. Thus Hobbes is concerned with depicting not the observable behavior of day to day living in a normal society but the kind of human behavior one might expect to find where no such society exists. The concept of the individual as a solitary unit, completely free from all social influences and hence the "natural" man, functions in Hobbes' ethical theory very much as the concept of a rigid body functions in theoretical physics. In neither case do we come across any such entities in our experience but in both cases the concepts prove fruitful for the understanding of the particular subject.

This natural man will be affected in a definite way both by his external environment and his internal passions. His behavior will be analogous to that of a machine. For just as a machine is made up of parts which interact with each other, so too is man. And just as the movement of a machine is to be explained by reference to its contact with other bodies so too is human activity. Man is part of nature's causal nexus and his actions must be understood, whether as causes or effects, in the same way as physical events.

Movement in man is of two sorts: vital and animal. The former includes the significant biological functions and requires no help from the imagination to move body and limbs; the latter needs the aid of the imagination to move body and limbs. Of these two types vital motion is the more important. For any action which a man may voluntarily undertake will be directed towards the preservation of his biological well being.

The beginning of animal motion prior to its appearance in a specific action is termed endeavour. Endeavour may be towards an object, in which case it is desire, or it may be from an object, in which case it is aversion. Desires or aversions may be instinctive or

225

they may be aroused by experience. Since the desire for an object depends on its furthering a man's vital motion its appearance is pleasurable and, similarly, since aversion from an object hinders vital motion its appearance is painful. But this does not mean that the object of action is to seek pleasure and avoid pain. The object is to seek self-preservation of which pleasure or pain are merely indications of success or failure. Here Hobbes fails to note that some pains may be conducive to self-preservation; and that there are many pleasures which are destructive of it.

Prior to the performance or omission of any action a man will be influenced by a series of appetites or aversions. The last passion in this series is, for Hobbes, the will. And the will is invariably directed towards the action which seems most advantageous to its agent. But since deliberation is merely the succession of alternating passions to or from any given object Hobbes cannot distinguish purely spontaneous or instinctive acts from planned or deliberated ones. Nor can there be at this level any distinction, as Hobbes himself readily admits, between human and animal behavior.

The dominating passion for man is fear—a fear not only for his present security but for his future. This passion may be manifested as a desire either for gain or for glory. And there is no passion which cannot be reduced to it. Although pity may appear to be a disinterested concern for the ills of others it is ultimately due to the fear which we have of such ills happening to ourselves. That fear for oneself might be expected to dominate over compassion is at least an arguable position. But it is scarcely plausible to believe, with Hobbes, that the benevolent passions are fundamentally selfish. For as Bishop Butler, the most acute critic of Hobbes' social psychology, pointed out the distinction which we make between benevolence and malice would be meaningless if both were merely aspects of the same desire.

The natural man, then, is a creature of his passions. But in itself this characteristic need not lead to disastrous consequences. These arise because the objects which men pursue in their search for guaranteed security are limited in number and must be competed for. And even competition for these objects need not itself be disastrous if men were naturally unequal. The challenge to another man's possessions arises only because each man, as naturally equal in strength to his neighbor, has the hope of successfully purloining his possessions and the fear of losing his own. Thus ethics—the science which deals with the consequences of the natural passions of man—reasons: given this hypothetical situation as described, then there must follow a constant warfare amongst men in which each man appears as a wolf to every other man. Here the cardinal virtues will be force and fraud. But, it must be emphasized, it is only under such conditions that Hobbes considers these as virtues.

Finally, the natural man will consider the objects of his appetite good and the objects of his aversion evil.

Nothing is ever good or evil in itself; and no consideration of objects, taken by themselves, can yield any standard or universal rule of conduct. Thus where there is as yet no society each man's good is dependent entirely on his passions. Good and evil then are terms which are relative to the person who employs them. Moreover, since one man's desires will vary from time to time, and place to place, and equally since different men will vary in their desires, so too will an object's goodness. And the antagonism between men in their natural state will be paralleled by their contradictions concerning good and evil.

Out of this welter of conflict, however, there is one aim which all men would desire to achieve — security — and one end which they would all desire to avoid—death. And, reason, having drawn the consequences of the uncontrolled operation of the passions is also able to indicate the appropriate remedy. There is one basic rule which, if all men adopted, would bring about peace and lift man out of his condition of being a wolf and enable him to become more like a God: that each man should not do to another that which he would not have done to himself. The golden rule is formulated by Hobbes in this negative way to make explicit that it is mutual abstinence that is to be the guide to conduct, not mutual assistance.

But although the reason of each man may well discern this rule, as well as others, which must be followed if peace is to be attained, and although each man may even feel obliged to follow it, yet it cannot be expected that any man will ever actually abide by it without some guarantee of his own security. Consequently, it is necessary that a coercive power, having effective means of punishment at its disposal, be established to ensure its observance. The establishment of society is coincident with the establishment of this coercive power. And just as the war of all against all ceases, so too do the quarrels over the nature of good and evil. For decisions on moral matters now rest ultimately with the coercive, civil power. But this power is neither arbitrary nor irresponsible. It must guarantee the safety of the members of society and the security of the state.

Although man escapes the chaos of his natural condition in society no change takes place in the nature of his passions. The preservation of his vital motion still constitutes the driving force of his actions; society merely provides a convenient framework in which he may operate. And here again Hobbes is reacting against the traditional view of man as a social animal. It is not only that the Hobbesian man is not instinctively gregarious but that the values which he may realize as a member of society are no different than those which he might realize, if possible, in his natural condition. Society does not create new values; it merely guarantees the attainment of the natural ones.

It is easy to criticize Hobbes. His view of the ultimate selfishness of all our passions is indefensible. His reduction of the obligation to civil obedience to self-interest is, where plausible, ambiguous and, where clear, destructive of the very meaning of the term. But his importance cannot be overestimated. For there are at least three aspects of Hobbes' thought which will remain of permanent value. First: he has given us the most pungent picture of the then rising commercial class with its insistence on freedom from restraint and its dominant value of non-interference into the lives of other men. Second: he has shown us the wolf that lies behind every man once social restraint is removed and this aspect of human nature, to which sentimentalism has blinded most of us till quite recently, is always with us. Third: he has taught us the fundamental lesson that the only fruitful method of resolving the predicaments in which men may find themselves is through the use of their reason. It is not merely that knowledge is power but that knowledge is the only power. And once we abandon it we must also abandon hope.

Bibliography

Hobbes' chief writings in ethics are to be found in *The Elements of Law* (1640), *De Cive* (1647) and *Leviathan* (1651). The best fairly recent books on Hobbes are: A. E. Taylor, *Hobbes* (1909); J. Laird, *Hobbes* (1934); L. Strauss, *The Political Philosophy of Hobbes* (1936). Michael Oakeshott's introduction to the Blackwell edition of *Leviathan* is undoubtedly the most masterful summary of Hobbes' argument.

Bernard Wand
Carleton College, Ottawa

Hobbes, Thomas: *see* Balguy, John; Butler, Joseph; Clarke, Samuel; Cooper, Anthony Ashley; Cudworth, Ralph; Cumberland, Richard; Hegel, G. W. F.; Hume, David; More, Henry; Utilitarianism.

Hocking, W. E.: *see* Moral Philosophy in America.

holiness: *see* piety; Spinoza; Zoroastrian Morals.

Holy Immortals, the: *see* Zoroastrian Morals.

homo sapiens: *see* Primitive Morals.

homosexuality: *see* Soviet Morality, Current.

honesty: *see* Aztec Morals; Freud, Sigmund; Hume, David; Kant, I.; Price, Richard; Quakerism, Classical, The Morality of; Rio Grande Pueblo Indians.

honor: *see* Aztec Morals; Major Ethical Viewpoints; Reid, Thomas; Sophists, the; Zuni Indians, Morals of.

Hooton, E. A.: *see* Primitive Morals.

hope: *see* Aquinas, Thomas, Moral Views of; Dante, Alighieri; French Existentialism and Moral Philosophy; Spinoza.

Hopkins, E. W.: *see* Primitive Morals.

Hopkins, Samuel: *see* Moral Philosophy in America.

Horatio: *see* Minor Socratics.

hospitality: *see* Hindu Ethics; Mundurucu Indians, A Dual System of Ethics; Muslim Morals; Navaho Morals; Riffian Morals; Rio Grande Pueblo Indians.

Hsia dynasty: *see* China, Moral Philosophies of.

Hsün Tzu: *see* China, Moral Philosophies of.

Hsün Tzu, the: *see* China, Moral Philosophies of.

Hudde, Johann: *see* Spinoza.

Huguenots: *see* Puritan Morals.

Huitzilopochtli: *see* Aztec Morals.

human life: *see* Soviet Morality, Current.

human nature: *see* Aquinas, Thomas, Moral Views of; Berdyaev, Nicolas; Butler, Joseph; China, Moral Philosophies of; Freud, Sigmund; Hindu Ethics; Jesuits, the, Moral Theology of; Major Ethical Viewpoints; Marxist Theory of Morals; nature of man; Puritan Morals.

human nature, laws of: *see* Hume, David.

human positive law: *see* Liguori, St. Alphonsus and Catholic Moral Philosophy.

human sacrifice: *see* China, Moral Philosophies of.

humanism: *see* China, Moral Philosophies of; Cudworth, Ralph; Jewish Ethics and Its Civilization; Major Ethical Viewpoints; Morals and Religion; Sophists, the; Soviet Morality, Current.

humanism, Christian: *see* Berdyaev, Nicolas.

humanistic ethics: *see* Major Ethical Viewpoints.

humanitarianism: *see* Marxist Theory of Morals.

humanity: *see* Goethe, Johann Wolfgang von; Stoics, the.

Hume, David

Introduction

David Hume, rather belatedly recognized as a philosophic genius of the first rank, was born in Edinburgh on the 26th of April, 1711. His family were genteel, but the estate was meagre; and a career was necessary for his support. Discovering that his taste (and as he hoped his ability) ran toward letters rather than law or business (both of which, somewhat desultorily, he tried), Hume decided to "make a very rigid frugality supply my deficiency of fortune, to maintain unimpaired my independency, and to regard every object as contemptible, except the improvement of my talents in literature." Retreating to La Flèche in Anjou at the age of twenty three, he there produced in three years his masterpiece (and one of the great works of Western philosophy), *A Treatise of Human Nature.* This work, anonymously published in England, aroused little comment, and Hume, who as a man of letters had an obvious need for an audience, settled down to writings less ambitious (and less abstruse) than one which had aspired to "introduce the experimental method of reasoning into moral subjects."

By 1742, two volumes of *Essays on Moral and Political Subjects* appeared, and by 1751 Hume had reissued the substance, if not the intricately detailed reasonings, of the *Treatise* in two shorter works composed in his mature, occasionally over-elaborate style, namely, the *Enquiry Concerning the Human Understanding* and the *Enquiry Concerning the Principles of Morals.* Hume's request that these "may alone be regarded as containing [my] philosophical sentiments and principles" has been ignored, and the *Treatise,* as the chief source of his

229

views, is more vigorously studied today than ever before.

In Edinburgh, Hume's name early became associated with scepticism and heterodoxy; and in 1745 he vainly sought a professorship in the University of Edinburgh. In 1746 he was appointed secretary and judge-advocate to General St. Clair, and this situation resulted in some slight military (and later, some diplomatic) experience in France and Italy. By 1752, the only work of philosophic power comparable to that of the *Treatise* was in manuscript: this was the *Dialogues on Natural Religion*. Hume's philosophic writing was therefore largely concluded by the time he was forty.

In 1752 Hume published the *Political Discourses*, which dealt chiefly (and astutely) with economic theory. Translated into French, they brought him an enduring continental reputation. In the same year he secured appointment as librarian of the Advocates' Library in Edinburgh; and with source materials close at hand he began the composition of a *History of England*. A decade was devoted to this work, which although now all but obsolete brought Hume much of his literary fame, as well as his fortune, in its day. Indeed, at fifty Hume had achieved his avowed ambition of winning both acclaim and independence as a Scottish man of letters.

Hume deferred a longed-for retirement to his native Edinburgh until after a stay in Paris, from 1763 to 1769. This episode marked the climax of his career. His writings, philosophical and otherwise, were applauded, his presence was eagerly sought after, and he was accepted into the intellectual peerage composed of d'Alembert, Diderot, Holbach, Buffon, Turgot, and others. He left France with some regret but "determined to abandon the fine folks, before they abandon me." His final retirement in Edinburgh was agreeably spent in the company of friends and books, but he could not be tempted to enter, in print, any further into the political, moral, and religious disputes of the time. Hume made careful preparations for the posthumous publication of his *Dialogues,* a masterful work on a limited topic. They were published in 1779 by Hume's nephew, David, both Hume's printer, Strahan, and his friend, Adam Smith, having declined the honor.

On August 25th, 1776, Hume died with a calm that chagrined those (who like Boswell) had hoped for a death-bed recantation of his sceptical opinions regarding immortality and similar topics. In *My Own Life* (which is incomparably the best short sketch), Hume summarized his personal qualities as follows:

"I am, or rather was, (for that is the style I must now use in speaking of myself, which emboldens me the more to speak my sentiments)—I was, I say, a man of mild dispositions, of command of temper, of an open, social, and cheerful humour, capable of attachment, but little susceptible of enmity, and of great moderation in all my passions. Even my love of literary fame, my ruling passion, never soured my temper, notwithstanding my frequent disappointments. My company was not unacceptable to the young and careless as well as to the studious and literary; and as I took a particular pleasure in the company of modest women, I had no reason to be displeased with the reception I met with from them. . . . I cannot say there is no vanity in making this funeral oration of myself, but I hope it is not a misplaced one; and this is a matter of fact which is easily cleared and ascertained." .

Everything that is known of Hume today confirms this self-appraisal.

Hume's Theory of Morals

For Hume as for Spinoza, moral theory is an attempt to explain the moral behavior of human beings. Moral theory is not a science which *asserts* judgments of value in relation to human conduct. It is, rather, a science which shows how such judgments arise in the context of human society and how they are conditioned by the needs, drives, emotions, habits, and attitudes of people who, because they are born into an already existing social organization, become moral agents willy-nilly. The chief sources of Hume's ethical views are *Treatise*, Part III, and the *Enquiry Concerning the Principles of Morals*. The latter in comparison with the former appears almost as a slight work, an elegantly written but somewhat jejune combination of hedonistic ethics with utilitarianism, together with some trenchant critical remarks on other systems. In Part III of the *Treatise*, however, moral theory appears as part of a general philosophy of human nature and as having an intimate dependence upon the epistemological theories of Part I and upon the intricate psychology expounded in

Part II. While there is no intention to set the *Enquiry* aside, the present exposition will be drawn largely from the *Treatise*.

It is fairly clear that in the *Treatise of Human Nature* Hume intended, as Laird observes,[1] "to become the Newton of the Human Mind," that is, to account for all of its varied activities, including those praisings and blamings of human character and action which we regard as moral, as being results of a few general, simple laws operating under circumstances peculiar to the context at hand. The analogy is to the way in which the trajectories of material particles are predictable in terms of a few "simple" laws together with "initial conditions" upon the particular context under consideration. The grand scheme of the laws of human nature is developed in the *Treatise,* and Hume's contribution to moral theory cannot be fully appreciated without reference to it. To be sure, as the work progresses, it becomes evident that the laws of human emotion and ideation from which moral phenomena are to be derived are neither few in number nor particularly simple. But the Newtonian spirit of undertaking to explain only what is observed and to do this only in terms of what is observable prevails throughout.

Hume's moral theory has a negative part which chiefly depends upon his theory of knowledge and a positive part which depends upon, if indeed it is not merely a portion of, his psychology of the emotions. The negative part

[1] Laird, Hume's *Philosophy of Human Nature*, p. 20.

231

may be summarized in the thesis that no moral conclusion (such, e.g., as that I must repay my debts, or that kindness toward one's enemies is better than anger) ever follows by a logical process from premises which are logico-mathematical in content or from scientific premises such as deal, e.g., with the co-variation of measurable quantities or with predictions of probable effects from assumed causes. A rational being without feelings and sentiments would never recognize duty or moral worth although he could master the theory of equations or predict the position of the moon a hundred years hence. To the reply that such a being could not be termed *fully* rational, Hume's rejoinder is in effect that since, as a matter of plain logic, "it ought to be" does not follow from "it is," any more than "it is good" follows from "it is," *moral* rationality (or as some would put it, the possession of conscience) is a species distinct from the logical and the scientific. Arithmetic may tell us to what *in toto* our debts amount; alone, it can never, by its very nature, tell us that we ought to repay them. Causal reasoning may inform us that a bridge is about to collapse; alone, it cannot admonish us to warn a stranger of his peril in walking across it. Hume is not concerned to deny the *reality* of conscience, moral insight, and the sense of duty—he asserts their reality with vigor—but only that they proceed from purely intellectual operations properly so-called. To his exploration of the sources of moral ideas, in other words to the

positive part of his theory, we now turn.

Hume looks for the sources of conscience or a "sense of morals" in the quasi-instinctual drives, the feelings, sentiments, attitudes, and habits of individuals who must, by natural necessity interact with and preserve some form of social union with their neighbors. The primitive, or as Hume terms them, the "original" drives and response-patterns of human beings are materials out of which morality is to be fashioned; but nowhere, however, among these primitive drives can there be found the moral sense itself. This notion, namely that "*no action can be virtuous, or morally good, unless there be in human nature some motive to produce it, distinct from the sense of its morality*" (*Treatise*, Selby–Bigge edition, p. 479), is of the utmost importance for Hume's ethical naturalism, and it marks the sharpest break between his theory and a formalistic one such as Kant's. Hume's argument is simple: if an action (e.g., returning borrowed money) is praised because the agent's motive is virtuous (he performs out of a sense of obligation), it must be at least possible for the agent to have had another, distinct motive for returning the money. Otherwise, we arrive at the result (meaningless to Hume) that A returns the money because he senses that it is his duty to do so, i.e., he senses that feelings that one ought to return borrowed money are so constituted as to be sensed as being obligatory. For Hume, therefore, no duties are self-justifying; all actions which at any given time are regarded as morally necessary to perform (or abstain from) have come to be so from some prior time in which they were non-moral and performed for non-moral (i.e. "natural") reasons.

Hume most clearly exhibits the (largely hypothetical) evolution of the sense of morality in his account of justice, by which he means not only the rules governing property (real and personal) but also those providing for formal government and even the rudiments of international law. "Justice," to Hume, covered the greatest part of one's obligations to one's neighbors, both near and far. Rules of property are obviously unnecessary in relation to friends or other objects of a natural benevolence which (contra Hobbes) is real but severely limited. Respect for the property of persons outside the small circle of personal benevolence is dictated at first because it is (so Hume thinks) indispensable to the social organization relied upon by all for their mutual survival. It is a set of conventions, habits or usages naturally slipped into because of their social utility. Subsequently, observation of the conventions becomes a moral obligation and deviation subjects the agent to moral censure if not to formal penalties. It is upon the explanation of this transition that Hume brings to bear the most general principles of his theory of human nature. Some digression upon these may be helpful at this point.

Part I of the Treatise culminates in Hume's celebrated analysis of causal inference, or in his usual term, of "belief." To put the upshot in terms whose simplicity does Hume but small injustice, our belief, e.g., that we shall be burned if we touch a glowing poker has as an indispensable (if only partial) basis some regularity within our sensorial experience such as an experience of touching being followed by one of burning. When instead of being burned we believe that we inevitably shall be, this is because (in an ultimately inexplicable way) the "vivacity" of the actual, sensorial experience has "transfused" itself into what otherwise would have been a mere idea, converting it thereby into a belief, into a piece of "empirical knowledge." This disarmingly simple theory, which raised questions that even today are still the center of controversies over the foundations of empirical knowledge, must be borne in mind when dealing with Hume's moral theory, to which we now return.

As mentioned above, one of Hume's chief tasks is to explain how a conventional pattern of conduct, slipped into because of its convenience to the participants, acquires a *moral* character. In the case of property, it is obvious why A would object to B's stealing A's possessions. It is also obvious why A would be displeased if B were to steal from C, a friend of A. For in this case, A desires the pleasure of C and is defeated in this benevolent desire if C is distressed. What does require explanation is why A is displeased at the mere idea of B's stealing from D, a stranger to A, when (apart from this displeasure, which Hume denies is an "original" response) the fate of D is of no consequence to A. Hume's theory is analogous to his explanation of belief: through sympathy, a native capacity of most human beings, A finds himself in the position of D and of all other members of the social group whose interests would be similarly injured by an act of stealing. A's pallid, perhaps merely latent ideas of the interests of others are given a "transfusion" of vivacity from the vividness of his own ever-present interests, and A feels B's injury of D an injustice to all society, himself included. Through sympathetic identification of his own interests with those of his social group, A has become, paradoxically, a disinterested spectator and judge of the character and actions of others: the moral agent judges his neighbor's actions and intentions not in terms of their impact merely upon himself or his friends (the objects of his benevolence) but upon himself as representing the fundamental interests of the community. The judgment of good or evil is immediate, akin to the operation of a special sense (hence the term, "moral sense"). And a judgment of character or action is moral only if (a) it is directed toward some mental quality (or action proceeding therefrom) in a person and (b) only if the approbation or disapprobation which *is* the judgment proceeds from a disinterested observer. Otherwise, judgments of good and ill are merely personal, idiosyncratic, and have no claim to be heard before the "party of humanity."

Sympathy thus plays a role in Hume's moral theory analogous to that played in his theory of knowl-edge by belief. Belief, based upon our indubitably real but severely limited sensorial contact with reality, takes our minds cognitively out of themselves and offers a surrogate—which on the whole is pragmatically acceptable —for past, future, or otherwise sensorially inaccessible realities. Sympathy in the moral sphere enables us to feel and react appropriately to influences upon the weal or woe of others whose interests, although actually related to ours, would but for sympathy be ignored. It is actually to one's interest to promote honesty, as a matter of general social utility. But how can one be motivated toward a *general* observance of the rules of honesty if one reacts with disapprobation only of those who are dishonest in their dealings with himself or his friends? Justice, then, the sum total of those obligations, rights, privileges, and immunities which enable communal living to be carried on (with more or less success) by men whose native benevolence and altruism are severely limited, is made possible by the mechanism of sympathetically shared interests,—by one's taking an interest in the interests of another. (In the *Enquiry,* Hume unfortunately confused benevolence, defined in the *Treatise* as an appetite for the good of another person, with sympathy, which is not an emotion but a process into which emotions enter.) It is important to notice that although for Hume, conventions of justice would never have arisen if the pattern of conduct they represent had had no social utility, nevertheless, when conventions have become morally (i.e., disinterestedly) approved, their original basis in utlility may become forgotten. When this happens, moral sense degenerates into dogma. Honesty for the mere sake of honesty becomes the rule: let justice be done, though the heavens fall. Hume's theory is an enduringly valuable critique of this type of ethical dogmatism.

With the example of justice in mind, one would expect that perhaps every quality of human beings which is of social utility might have become disinterestedly admired and therefore have become a virtue. Hume's analysis finds this actually to be the case. Qualities such as meekness, beneficence, charity, generosity, and clemency, while non-conventional in origin, are called social virtues merely because it is universally recognized that they tend to the good of society. Our sympathetic appreciation of the benefits conferred to others by these qualities arouses our disinterested admiration; the qualities, therefore, become virtues and their owners virtuous. A third set of qualities usually regarded as virtuous is comprised by such as prudence, temperance, frugality, industry, and enterprise. These are disinterestedly admired because of their usefulness to their owners. (Hume, perhaps overoptimistically, posited that one can even admire disinterestedly the qualities of an enemy which are advantageous to *him!*) And fourth, as well as of least importance, are qualities such as wit and eloquence, which are merely agreeable to their owner. Because we can sympathetically (and hence disinterestedly) enjoy the pleasure which

the witty person derives from his own possession of wit, this quality must be ranked as a virtue, albeit of a minor kind. It is apparent that on Hume's theory there is no sharp line to be drawn between the sternly obligatory, such as honesty, and the merely praiseworthy, such as "moderation" or even "eloquence." Hume finds no problem here. Traditionally, the line is drawn between the voluntary and the involuntary: one can (by punishment) make a child honest, at least in his actions, but Hume finds no good reason why virtuous qualities must be wholly voluntary.

Hume's treatment of altruism is interestingly paralleled by his view of freedom of the will. Benevolence is not altruism; it is merely the capacity (very limited in most persons) for forming friendships within a small and largely non-competitive circle. Altruism in the sense of getting somehow outside the circle of one's own interests (usually, and rather meaninglessly called "selfish") is impossible. The true meaning of altruism for Hume is the incorporation of the interests of others into the pattern of one's own. As mentioned above, this is possible through sympathy, which enables us at least to *feel* praise or blame toward the actions or characters of others even if we are not sufficiently bestirred to take appropriate action. (We despise corrupt public officials oftener than we actively seek their removal from office.) Analogously, for Hume, there is no freedom in the sense of an escape of the will from its determining motives. Freedom in the sense of an absence of regular patterns of stimulus and response, of conditioning and habituation is for Hume (as for Hobbes) meaningless. The only intelligible form of freedom, and the only one which men seek actually for themselves or their social group, is the freedom of one's own will from interference by the will of others. When we act (with perfect predictability, it may be) from our own motives alone and not because of the wishes of others, we act freely and responsibly. This is the *meaning* of human freedom; whether and to what extent we are free in this sense is a question Hume leaves largely unexplored.

Hume's moral theory has been characterized by hostile critics as seeking (*inter alia*) to 'reduce all morality to that of the common man in his least inspired moments.' The criticism is irrelevant in the light of Hume's profession that "we must therefore glean up our experiments in this science [i.e., the "science of man"] from a cautious observation of human life, and take them as they appear in the common course of the world, by men's behavior in company, in affairs, and in their pleasures." (*Treatise,* Selby-Bigge edition, *Intro.,* p. xxiii.) Hume found the world to be one in which the main patterns of communal living were outgrowths of socially necessary give-and-take arrangements which became objects of admiration by disinterested third parties. In an age in which moral tautologies and other empty but high-sounding phrases (cf. Locke's dictum that where there is no property, there can be no injustice) still exerted an influence, were read as well as heard

from the pulpit, Hume directed attention back to the fundamental sources of morality, namely in behavior resulting from fundamental needs and drives modified by local environmental conditions. It is true that Hume is at a loss to "prove" that one ought to remain "just" even if an opportunity for profitable transgression is presented and if one's concern for oneself is no longer affected negatively by a knowledge of secret guilt. According to Hume's philosophy, however, there is no such ultimate proof in any case. For example, if morality depended upon maintaining a kind of internal consistency among one's volitions (as with Kant) one could always ask (with as much or as little meaning) for a "proof" that we *ought* to maintain this consistency. On Hume's general view, we infer "one yard" from "three feet" ultimately because we wish to keep our meanings consistent. In the causal realm, we infer dangerous heat from the glowing of a poker ultimately because in terms of its consequences for our future dealings with the poker, this inference seems preferable (in the light of other, past experiences) to its alternatives. And we are moral—if so we choose to be—when with the "party of humanity" we align ourselves steadily and cooly against the socially destructive forces of primitive egoism which survive in adult society. To be sure, the egoism itself can never be abolished; but if Hume is correct, it is still highly modifiable, and its modification so as to provide social peace compatibly with the enhancement of individual values is, if actual, the sub-

236

stance, just as it is, if reflected upon, the meaning of morality.

Bibliography

I. Chief Philosophical Works of Hume
A Treatise of Human Nature (1739).
An Enquiry Concerning Human Understanding (1748).
An Enquiry Concerning the Principles of Morals (1751).
Dialogues Concerning Natural Religion (1779).

II. Works on Hume
C. W. Hendel, *Studies in the Philosophy of David Hume* (Princeton, 1925).
C. D. Broad, *Five Types of Ethical Theory* (London, 1930) Chapter 4 is on Hume.
J. Laird, *Hume's Philosophy of Human Nature* (New York, 1931).
B. M. Laing, *David Hume* (London, 1932).
N. K. Smith, *Hume's Philosophy of Human Nature* (London, 1941).
Hume's Moral and Political Philosophy, edited with an Introduction by Henry D. Aiken (New York, 1948).
A. B. Glathe, *Hume's Theory of the Passions and of Morals* (Univ. of Calif. Press, 1950).

Alfred B. Glathe
Recently, Stanford University;
Now, San Francisco, California

Hume, David: *see* Ayer, Alfred J.; Broad, C. D.; Clarke, Samuel; Cooper, Anthony Ashley; Cumberland, Richard; Green, T. H.; Hutcheson, Francis; Meta-ethics and Normative Ethics; Moral Philosophy in America; Price, Richard; Primitive Morals; Reid, Thomas; Utilitarianism.

humility: *see* Aztec Morals; Augustine and Morals; Hindu Ethics; Machiavelli, Niccolo; Muslim Morals.

humor: *see* Navaho Morals; Tapirapé Morals, Some Aspects of.

hunger: *see* Aztec Morals; Butler, Joseph; Minor Socratics.

Husserl, Edmund: *see* Scheler, Max.

Hutcheson, Francis

Francis Hutcheson was born on the eighth of August, 1694, at Drumalrig in County Down, Ulster. He was the son and grandson of Presbyterian ministers. In 1711, he matriculated at the University of Glasgow. He completed both the arts and the theological courses there, finishing, probably, in 1717. He returned to Ulster, and in 1719 the Presbyterians licensed him as a probationer preacher. Shortly thereafter, he was invited to Dublin by the Presbyterian clergy to found an academy for Presbyterian youths, which he headed for the next ten years. In Dublin, he met admirers of the third Earl of Shaftesbury's philosophy; and through them, Shaftesbury came to be an influence on Hutcheson. While in Dublin, he published his first and most important philosophical works: the *Inquiry into the Original of our Ideas of Beauty and Virtue,* in 1725; and the *Essay on the Nature and Conduct of the Passions with Illustrations on the Moral Sense,* in 1728. Hutcheson was elected Professor of Moral Philosophy in the University of Glasgow in 1730, a post which he held until his death on the eighth of August, 1746.

As a professor at Glasgow, Hutcheson devoted himself to softening the theology and broadening the culture of the Presbyterian clergy and people. Some estimate of the magnitude of his task can be gained from the anecdote that the youthful Hutcheson outraged his father's congregation by preaching about a good and benevolent God, who would allow even heathens to enter Heaven, if they had followed the light of their own consciences. Not a word did the daft boy say about the good, old comfortable doctrines of election, reprobation, original sin, and faith. What is more, the mature Hutcheson was tried by the Presbytery of Glasgow for teaching, "in contravention to the Westminster Confession the following two false and dangerous doctrines, first that the standard of moral goodness was the promotion of the happiness of others; and second that we could have a knowledge of good and evil, without, and prior to a knowledge of God." But nothing came of what Hutcheson called the "whimsical buffoonery about his heresy." As a professor of moral philosophy, Hutcheson was a preacher of morals rather than a moral philosopher. The spirit of his teaching is reflected in his rebuking the young David Hume for lacking "a certain warmth in the cause of virtue, which all good men would relish, and which could not displease amidst abstract enquiries."

In moral philosophy, Hutcheson is a member of the moral sense school. The third Earl of Shaftesbury, Hume, and Adam Smith are other members of this school, which in the course of the history of philosophy loses itself in

Utilitarianism, to appear again in the moral philosophy of the third Earl Russell. Hutcheson was the philosophical correspondent of Hume, and a teacher of Adam Smith. Like a number of other Eighteenth Century British clergymen, Hutcheson turned to philosophy, and finally to philosophizing, to answer questions raised by his religion. Hutcheson wanted to know how virtue and vice are distinguished, and why it is that men strive to be virtuous. He answered these questions by showing how the moral sense works. The moral sense is the basis of Hutcheson's moral philosophy, and it retains its importance in each of his four works on morals. Thus, this article will be devoted to an account of the moral sense.

The starting point for Hutcheson's moral philosophy is virtue. When we characterize someone by using a virtue word (or a vice word) to describe his behavior, we are generalizing about the way he has acted in the past, and predicting the way he will behave in the future. Thus, virtues are ways of acting. The virtue for Hutcheson is benevolence; and in his early writing his interest in benevolence is overshadowed by his account of why it is a virtue. This is not surprising, for in his first essays his chief interest is in explaining and defending his account of the moral sense as our means of knowing that an action is virtuous. When he has established the existence of the moral sense, Hutcheson can go on to expound his view that benevolence is the summit of individual moral excellence and the virtue which makes human society possible. In his later writing Hutcheson regards it as established that the moral sense is a part of human nature, and that he is entitled to use it in his moral philosophy without detailed explanation or lengthy apology.

How, then, do we know that benevolence is a virtue? Hutcheson rejects two sorts of answers to this question. He rejects the answer that the list of human virtues has been drawn up by God, and thus that one's knowledge of virtues is a knowledge of God's list, gained by revelation. He also rejects the answer that virtues, spoken of as the fitting thing to do, are features of the world which one learns to pick out and identify, in the same way that one knows what stars, leaves, or cart wheels are. In contrast with the theological and the objectivist views, Hutcheson argues that we know that benevolence is a virtue because it pleases us by means of our moral sense.

In claiming that men have a moral sense, Hutcheson is extending Locke's epistemology to account for what it is we know when we know that someone's actions are virtuous. Locke taught that knowledge is ideas, and that the two sources of ideas are sensation and reflection. When we know that an action is virtuous, this knowledge must be an idea; and, for Hutcheson, this idea is a perception of pleasure.

Hutcheson's claim that men are equipped with a moral sense is much less startling than his words suggest. He is not claiming that men have extra noses for moral smells, or any other special organ. He is rather locating the source of moral knowledge. Since

moral ideas must follow our ideas of actions, they are properly, in Locke's scheme, ideas of reflection; and reflection is, for Locke, "the perception of the operations of our own mind within us, as it is employed about the ideas it has got." Since moral ideas are ideas of reflection, Hutcheson might have spoken of moral reflection rather than a moral sense. Locke, however, gives Hutcheson some license to speak as he does. For Locke says of reflection, "This source of ideas, every man has wholly in himself; and though it be not sense, as having nothing to do with external objects, yet it is very like it, and might properly enough be called internal sense." Leaving the question of names aside, how does the moral sense work?

The operation of the moral sense depends on knowledge. Before I can tell whether or not someone's action is virtuous, I must know whether or not it is benevolent. Is the action done for the welfare of someone other than the actor; or did the actor, at least, intend the welfare of someone else? When I find that the action was indeed benevolent, at least in intention, then it pleases me. I have found it to be virtuous. It may be objected that Hutcheson has simply defined benevolent actions as virtuous, and that whenever one discovers a benevolent action one knows that it is to be called virtuous. But this objection overlooks the power of Hutcheson's system to explain why benevolent actions are virtuous. They are so because they please. It is their pleasingness and not their benevolence which makes benevolent actions virtuous. Then, is any action that pleases us virtuous? Hutcheson's answer to this question is "No"; and the answer depends on the introduction of God to complete his account of the moral sense. Benevolent actions are the only actions that come under the purview of the moral sense, and God has determined man to be pleased by benevolent actions. For Hutcheson, our knowledge of virtue is not derived from custom, education, example, or study.

As well as being our means of discovering virtue, the moral sense is also our means of approving of it. Thus, Hutcheson is able to use the moral sense to explain not only how men come to know virtue, but why they are virtuous. Hutcheson takes it as a universal characteristic of human nature that men would rather approve than disapprove of themselves; and when they are virtuous, they can approve of themselves. What is more, our approval of the virtue of others is likewise an encouragement to them to continue to be virtuous.

It has been urged against Hutcheson that, if all men have a moral sense, they ought to find the same actions virtuous. Since they do not, we may suppose that men do not have a moral sense. Hutcheson's reply is that differences about the virtuousness of actions prove not that men lack a moral sense, but that some men are careless or mistaken in their assessment of the benevolence of actions. Thus, if a man is led to be pleased by an action, which he accordingly finds virtuous, through a faulty estimate of its benevolence, he should blame not his moral sense

for his being pleased, but his reason for its faulty assessment of the effects of the action. The efficiency of the moral sense depends on the accuracy of the knowledge it has to work on. It would appear to be implied by Hutcheson that everyone could finally agree on what actions are benevolent. In further support of his claim that all men have a moral sense, Hutcheson argues that all men do approve of benevolence, and cite it as an admirable quality of their actions, even though they may disagree about which actions are benevolent. But Hutcheson's most telling argument in favor of the moral sense is his pointing out that, if men were not disposed to be pleased by some actions and displeased by others, they would be indifferent to any action, and there would be no basis for distinguishing virtue and vice.

To conclude this brief sketch of Hutcheson's moral philosophy, two problems may be noticed. First, except for regarding being pleased as a perception, Hutcheson leaves the moral sense unanalysed. Today's supporters or opponents of Hutcheson's philosophy must carry this matter more deeply than he did. Second, the piety of some readers may not afford them the confidence which permits Hutcheson to declare that God has determined men to find benevolence pleasing, and thus virtuous. But rather than abandon moral sense philosophy on this account, it may be possible to strengthen its case by discovering more exactly the place of custom, education, example, and study in our discernment of virtue. Hutcheson discounted the importance of these factors in our moral judgments, because he supposed that to admit them weakened the case for the moral sense; but on more careful scrutiny, we may discover that a recognition of their place makes moral sense philosophy more plausible. Indeed, this is the line that Hume takes. What is more, a departure from Hutcheson's theological determinism would enable moral sense philosophy to account for the virtuousness of other qualities besides benevolence. At the same time it must be recognized that such a departure is also a departure from the view that at least one quality, benevolence, is absolutely virtuous. Whether or not such a conclusion is to be regretted is a matter for speculation. Hutcheson, however, would have thought his moral sense philosophy worth nothing if it was not both in accord with the facts of human nature and a means of promoting virtue; and it is doubtful that moral sense philosophy requires absolute virtues to meet these conditions. As for the conditions themselves, we can do no less than judge moral sense philosophy by the same severe standards Hutcheson employed.

Bibliography

Francis Hutcheson, *Inquiry into the Original of our Ideas of Beauty and Virtue* (London, 1725; 2nd Edition, 1726; 3rd, 1729; 4th, 1738 [with addendum]; 5th, 1753; Glasgow, 1772 [with corrections and additions in their proper places]). Most of the second part of this work, the *Inquiry Concerning the Original of our Ideas of Virtue or Moral Good,* is reprinted in *British Moralists,* L. A. Selby-Bigge, Ed. (Oxford, 1897).

Essay on the Nature and Conduct of the Passions, with Illustrations upon the Moral Sense (London and Dublin, 1728; and later ed.).

Short Introduction to Moral Philosophy (Glasgow, 1747; and later ed.).

System of Moral Philosophy, with Life by Leechman (Glasgow, 1755).

D. Daiches Raphael, *The Moral Sense* (Oxford, 1947).

William Robert Scott, *Francis Hutcheson* (Cambridge, 1900). The biographical facts in the above sketch are taken from Scott.

Elmer Sprague
Brooklyn College

Hutcheson, Francis: *see* Balguy, John; Clarke, Samuel; Cooper, Anthony Ashley; Major Ethical Viewpoints; Moral Philosophy in America; More, Henry; Price, Richard; Prichard, H. A.; Reid, Thomas; Utilitarianism; Wollaston, William.

Hutchinson, Ann: *see* Puritan Morals.

Huxley, J.: *see* Major Ethical Viewpoints.

Huyghens: *see* Spinoza.

Hvare: *see* Zoroastrian Morals.

hypnotism: *see* Freud, Sigmund.

hypocrisy: *see* Augustine and Morals; Dante, Alighieri; Jewish Ethics and Its Civilization; Muslim Morals; Soviet Morality, Current.

hysteria: *see* Freud, Sigmund.

I

Ibn al- 'Arabi: *see* Muslim Morals.

Ibn al-Farid: *see* Muslim Morals.

Ibn Maskawaihi: *see* Muslim Morals.

Ibn Paquda: *see* Jewish Ethics and Its Civilization.

id, the: *see* Freud, Sigmund.

ideal morals: *see* Morals and Religion.

ideal religion: *see* Morals and Religion.

ideal utilitarianism: *see* Hartmann, Nicolai; Major Ethical Viewpoints.

idealism: *see* French Existentialism and Moral Philosophy; Jewish Ethics and Its Civilization; Moral Philosophy in America.

idealism, metaphysical: *see* Green, T. H.; Major Ethical Viewpoints.

ideals: *see* Dewey, John; Hindu Ethics; Jewish Ethics and Its Civilization; Major Ethical Viewpoints; Marxist Theory of Morals; Plato; Psychology and Morals; Rio Grande Pueblo Indians.

idolatry: *see* Jewish Ethics and Its Civilization.

ignorance: *see* Aquinas, Thomas, Moral Views of; China, Moral Philosophies of; Clarke, Samuel; Hindu Ethics; More, Henry; Plato; Socrates; Sophists, the; Stoics, the; Zoroastrian Morals.

illiberality: *see* Dante, Alighieri.

illiteracy: *see* Aboriginals of Yirkalla.

illness: *see* Rio Grande Pueblo Indians.

illumination: *see* Hindu Ethics; Schopenhauer, Arthur.

illumination, inner: *see* Zoroastrian Morals.

illusion: *see* Freud, Sigmund; Minor Socratics; Schopenhauer, Arthur; Spinoza.

immediacy: *see* intuitionism.

immorality: *see* Aboriginals of Yirkalla; Freud, Sigmund; Hindu Ethics; Machiavelli, Niccolo; Morals and Religion; Pakot, the Moral System of; Psychology and Morals; Soviet Morality, Current.

immortality: *see* after-life; Augustine and Morals; Clarke, Samuel; hereafter; Schopenhauer, Arthur; Spinoza; Zoroastrian Morals.

immutability: *see* Cudworth, Ralph.

impartiality: *see* Cudworth, Ralph; Zuni Indians, Morals of.

imperative: *see* categorical imperative; Hindu Ethics; Kant, I.

imperfection: *see* Hindu Ethics; More, Henry.

impersonalism: *see* Soviet Morality, Current.

imprudence: *see* Kant, I.

impulse: *see* Butler, Joseph; Dewey, John; drives; Freud, Sigmund; Hin-

243

insatiability: *see* Schopenhauer, Arthur.

insight: *see* Minor Socratics; Scheler, Max.

instincts: *see* Balguy, John.

institutional morality: *see* Hindu Ethics.

instrumental value: *see* Hindu Ethics; Major Ethical Viewpoints.

instrumentalism: *see* Dewey, John; Language and Ethics; Major Ethical Viewpoints; Psychology and Morals.

integration, inner: *see* Major Ethical Viewpoints.

integrity: *see* Psychology and Morals; Quakerism, Classical, The Morality of.

intellect: *see* Liguori, St. Alphonsus and Catholic Moral Philosophy.

intellect, unicity of: *see* Schopenhauer, Arthur.

intelligence: *see* Aquinas, Thomas, Moral Views of.

intentions: *see* Aquinas, Thomas, Moral Views of; Hammurapi, Code of; Jewish Ethics and Its Civilization; Prichard, H. A.; Reid, Thomas; Ross, Sir (William) David; Stoics, the; Utilitarianism.

interest: *see* Dewey, John; Green, T. H.; Hindu Ethics; Kant, I.; Major Ethical Viewpoints; Prichard, H. A.; Ross, Sir (William) David; Sophists, the; Spinoza.

interest theory: *see* Major Ethical Viewpoints.

Interjectionism: *see* Broad, C. D.

internal sanctions: *see* Rio Grande Pueblo Indians.

intolerance: *see* Dewey, John; Rio Grande Pueblo Indians; Spinoza.

intrigue: *see* Riffian Morals.

intrinsic goodness: *see* Prichard, H. A.; Ross, Sir (William) David.

intrinsic principles: *see* Liguori, St. Alphonsus and Catholic Moral Philosophy.

intrinsic value: *see* Major Ethical Viewpoints; Moore, George Edward; Russell, Bertrand; Scheler, Max.

intuition: *see* Aquinas, Thomas, Moral Views of; China, Moral Philosophies of; Jewish Ethics and Its Civilization; Khomiakov, Alexey; Moral Philosophy in America; non-cognition; Reid, Thomas; Scheler, Max; Sidgwick, Henry; Spinoza.

intuition, rational: *see* Clarke, Samuel; Reid, Thomas; Schlick, Moritz; Spinoza.

intuitionism: *see* Ayer, Alfred J.; Broad, C. D.; Goethe, Johann Wolfgang von; Hartmann, Nicolai; Language and Ethics; Major Ethical Viewpoints; Meta-ethics and Normative Ethics; Moore, George Edward; Price, Richard; Prichard, H. A.; Quakerism, Classical, The Morality of; Ross, Sir (William) David; Utilitarianism; Zoroastrian Morals.

intuitionism, ethical: *see* intuitionism; Moral Philosophy in America.

intuitionism, philosophical: *see* intuitionism; Sidgwick, Henry.

intuitive induction: *see* Ross, Sir (William) David.

inward light: *see* Reid, Thomas.

inwardness: *see* Jewish Ethics and Its Civilization.

Iran, ancient: *see* Zoroastrian Morals.

irrational, the: *see* Freud, Sigmund; Sophists, the.

irresponsibility: *see* Dewey, John.

irreverence: *see* Hindu Ethics.

Islam: *see* Muslim Morals; Riffian Morals.

Isocrates: *see* Sophists, the.

isolation: *see* cultural isolation.

isolation method: *see* Moore, George Edward.

Israel, ancient: *see* Hammurapi, Code of; Jewish Ethics and Its Civilization.

ius talionis: *see* Hammurapi, Code of.

J

Jacobinism: *see* Soviet Morality, Current.

Jainism: *see* Hindu Ethics.

James, William: *see* Major Ethical Viewpoints; Moral Philosophy in America.

Janet: *see* Cudworth, Ralph.

Jansenism: *see* Jesuits, the, Moral Theology of; Liguori, St. Alphonsus and Catholic Moral Philosophy.

Jansenius, Cornelius: *see* Jesuits, the, Moral Theology of.

jealousy: *see* Navaho Morals; Spinoza; Zuni Indians, Morals of.

Jefferson, Thomas: *see* Moral Philosophy in America; Puritan Morals.

jen: *see* China, Moral Philosophies of.

Jesuits, the, Moral Theology of

St. Ignatius Loyola (1491–1556), the founder of the Society of Jesus, prescribed in the Constitutions of the Order (Part IV) that the theological studies of the members would have a pragmatic end, the welfare of souls and their eternal salvation. With this in view he enjoined that his followers should defend only the doctrines which the Roman Catholic Church lays down and approves and among the approved doctrines those which are surer and more commonly accepted, *securiorem et magis approbatam doctrinam.* As a theologian to be followed he recommended by name St. Thomas

Aquinas (1226–1274). St. Ignatius was also solicitous for unity of doctrine and endeavored by his recommendations to exclude divergences of opinion among his followers in preaching, teaching, and publications. By this he did not intend to exclude freedom of thought but only to limit it to the extent necessary for orthodoxy of doctrine and fraternal union of Jesuits among themselves.

Condition of Moral Theology at the time of St. Ignatius

St. Thomas, whom St. Ignatius chose as the guide of his sons, had in the 13th century developed in his *Summa Theologica (Prima Secundae* and *Secunda Secundae)* the first complete system of Christian moral theology on principles laid down by St. Augustine. The metaphysic at the base of St. Thomas' moral teaching was derived from the Christian faith and not from Aristotle whose influence was more on the form than on the thought content.

The decree of the Fourth Lateran Council (1215), imposing yearly confession on all the faithful who had attained the use of reason, led to the composition of books which sought to guide confessors by giving the solution to cases of conscience. The *Summa de casibus paenitentiae* of the Dominican

247

St. Raymund of Peñafort (1275), the *Summa astesana* (1317), the *Summa pisana* (1338) and the *Summa summarum* of Sylvester Prierias (1518) were the most important of these works which contained handy summaries of medieval casuistry for the use of confessors. When the Jesuits appeared on the scene, therefore, the reasoned development of Christian moral teaching in the writings of St. Thomas Aquinas and handbooks containing the fruits of centuries of casuistic endeavor were available. Members of the Society of Jesus were destined to follow this double lead.

Moral Theology of the early Jesuits

The leading theologians among the early Jesuits, e.g., F. Toledo (✝1596), G. Valencia (✝1603), G. Vásquez (✝1604) and F. Suarez (✝1617) in commenting on the *Summa Theologica* of St. Thomas developed a moral teaching based on theological principles. Others, e.g., L. Molina (✝1600), L. Lessius (✝1623), and J. de Lugo (✝1660) wrote systematic studies of parts of moral theology. The tradition of the medieval casuists was also continued in the *Summa casuum conscientiae* of F. Toledo (✝1596) and the *Aphorismi confessariorum* of Emmanuel Sa (✝1596).

One of the most significant developments in the field of morals in the Catholic Church of the 16th and 17th centuries was the gradual separation of moral theology from dogmatic theology. The reasons for this cleavage are obscure but the decree of the Council of Trent enjoining the confession of

each and every mortal sin along with the differentiating circumstances had something to do with it. This development has been criticised as unfortunate on the grounds that it tended to turn moral theology into a study of sins rather than of the virtues, to separate it unduly from its principal sources in Holy Scripture and to encumber it with much extraneous material derived from philosophy, law and pastoral practice. The *Opus morale in praecepta decalogi* (Madrid, 1613) of the Spanish Jesuit Thomas Sanchez was the first moral theology which abandoned the method of the virtues of the *Summa Theologica* of St. Thomas for the more negative schema of the Ten Commandments. This treatment became standard outside as well as in the Society of Jesus.

The Controversy on Probabilism

In the 17th century a struggle arose in the Church on the question of the use of probable opinions. A brief exposé of the theory of probabilism is here presented as a prelude to its history. Probabilism, like its counterparts probabiliorism and equiprobabilism, sets itself to answer the age-old question: must a doubtful law be obeyed? It has thus no application to the vast complex of duties which are certain and clear. But when a law only doubtfully commands an act, probabilism asks, is one obliged to observe the law, or may he decide in favor of his personal liberty? Thus it seeks to establish a sure rule of conduct in cases of doubt, a rule which is not destructive of the spirit of submission to law and is morally correct. For this reason probabilism has no right to speak out when a doubt of conscience concerns the validity of an act, some necessary end to be achieved at all cost, or a certain right to be protected. Such instances apart, probabilism teaches that a well-founded doubt exempts one from the moral obligation of the observance of a law. It says the same even when in a given instance there is greater evidence in support of the law than for the opinion favoring personal liberty. The moral justification for probabilism is not simply that the obligation is doubtful; therefore man is free in the matter of which there is doubt. Such an attitude is not worthy of the true Christian conscience. It is tantamount to saying, "I am probably obliged by the law, but I don't care; I will not observe it anyhow." Rather one must first use moral prudence to solve the doubt and arrive at certainty. Secondly, when a certain conscience cannot be achieved directly, recourse must be had to a so-called reflex principle to attain the requisite certitude. This is done by appealing to the principle: a doubtful law does not oblige. This truth in turn finds its justification in an implicit intention of the legislator. He may licitly be presumed not to intend his law to be binding where it only doubtfully applies. A contrary intent on his part would lead to anxiety of conscience on the part of his subjects, imposing heavy burden on them. Moreover it would be unjust to demand obedience to obligations which probably do not exist. For the lawmaker has a duty to make clear his legislative mind. The precision used in wording legislation in exact legal language is evidence of the intent to render the meaning of law clear and beyond doubt. Where reasonable doubt exists, then, as to the meaning or existence of the law, there is a valid presumption that the legislator does not will his law to be operative.

The principle: a doubtful law does not oblige, had long before the origin of the Jesuits been applied by theologians to solve doubts of conscience. Its use, however, had been haphazard. It had never been elaborated into a moral system or theory applicable to doubts in general. Furthermore it was not a Jesuit but a Dominican, B. de Medina (†1581), who fathered the system of probabilism. Others improved and further refined the doctrine. Outstanding among the Jesuit contributors was Suarez. In a short time probabilism came into peaceful possession and enjoyed widespread acceptance by theologians in general until the middle of the 17th century. It was in time espoused by Jesuit theologians, who stoutly defend it today against the supporters of the stricter moral systems. A bizarre episode in Jesuit history, however, was introduced by the election as General, through the influence of Pope Innocent XI, of Tirso Gonzalez, a Spaniard. Gonzalez, a theologian of note and one of the few Jesuits to oppose probabilism, endeavored strenuously to impose his views on his confreres.

In the meantime the opponents of Jesuit morality had found in Jean Duvergier de Hauranne, abbé of Saint-

Cyran, a leader, and in Cornelius Jansenius, bishop of Ypres, a theorician. These founders of Jansenism professed a desire to save the Catholic Church from what they considered the corrupt morals of the Jesuits by installing their nightmare creed which closed the gates of God's mercy to all but a select coterie. Saint-Cyran and Jansenius both died before their efforts constituted a real threat to the Jesuits. But their disciple, Blaise Pascal (1623–1662), delivered a devastating attack on the Jesuits in his *Lettres Provinciales*. These letters, which enjoyed a popular success rarely equalled in the history of literature, are for the most part devoted to the ridicule of the moral theology and ascetical training of the Jesuits. Although characterized by alterations and incomplete citations, they produced a reversal in public opinion because of their matchless style. It is certain that Pascal with very little knowledge of the subject matter holds up to ridicule very upright and worthy men, particularly Antonio Escobar (1589–1669).

In 1690 Pope Alexander VIII condemned the following expression of the Jansenistic moral system called tutiorism: "Non licet sequi opinionem vel inter probabiles probabilissimam" (It is illicit to follow even the most probable of probable opinions). On the other hand, the Holy See never frowned on probabilism properly understood and prudently applied. While Innocent XI did at one time insist that Jesuit professors should be free to teach probabiliorism if they chose, and while some misconceptions of the doctrine and abuses in practice were condemned by Alexander VII (1665–1666) and Innocent XI (1689), yet a proposition which would have condemned the theory itself was deliberately rejected by the same Innocent XI.

The disturbance created by the Jansenists was not allowed to die down until the suppression of the Society of Jesus by Clement XIV in 1773. Indeed one of the main reasons for that suppression seems to have been the accusation of debased morals founded on Jansenistic charges.

Subsequent Developments

Throughout the 18th century Jesuit moralists were engaged in combating the rationalism of the epoch. The traditional Christian teaching was maintained, and Johann Michael Sailer (†1832), who had been a member of the suppressed Society of Jesus, produced a moral theology founded on the principles of the faith and the explanation of the virtues which lead to Christian perfection.

The moral theologians of the restored Society have continued the traditional Jesuit teaching. Especially distinguished among them have been J. P. Gury (†1866), E. Génicot (†1900), A. Lehmkuhl (†1917), and H. Noldin (†1922). A. Vermeersch (†1936) has in recent years made another attempt to return to the virtues as the schema of moral theology. His initiative is being continued by others.

Characteristics of Jesuit Morality

A study of the Jesuit moral literature reveals three characteristic traits:

a sacramentarian approach, a sane optimism, and mildness in moral judgment.

1) Jesuit moralists are resolute sacramentarians and reject all efforts to reduce Christian life to a pure religion of the spirit. They have been ardent exponents of frequent confession. To facilitate the reception of the sacrament of penance they have defended the sufficiency of attrition for its reception. As contrasted with contrition, attrition is sorrow for sin for a lesser motive than the love of God, e.g., to detest sin because of its intrinsic turpitude or from fear of the pains of hell which sin merits. Jesuit theologians have, moreover, always looked on the reception of Holy Communion as an antidote to temptation and sin and not as a reward of virtue.

2) Jesuit moralists have defended a sane optimism against Jansenistic pessimism which claimed to represent the thought of St. Augustine. With St. Thomas they refuse to admit that man has been lessened *in suis naturalibus* by original sin. They contend that our nature, even though deprived of supernatural and preternatural gifts, is not properly evil in itself. They maintain with Molina that the liberty of fallen man is complete if not integral, since without it responsibility would be an empty word. Jesuit moralists conceive the creation of man as a mark of the overflowing love of God the Father for all men and not merely for some. They defend the real universality of the divine salvific will.

3) This sane optimism has led Jesuit moralists to incline after the example of the Good Shepherd to kindness in judgment rather than to severity. If some of their number have leaned too far in this direction, they have been called to order by the Fathers General of the Society: Aquaviva in 1597, Vitelleschi in 1617, and Piccolomini in 1650, as well as by the General Congregations of the order in 1652 and 1661.

Characteristic Theses

Certain theses of Jesuit moral teaching stand out as distinctive and characteristic. Among these are probabilism, already treated above, the Jesuit position on moral responsibility, and gravity of matter in unchastity. Other teachings, tyrannicide and "the end justifies the means," have been falsely imputed to them. Each of these doctrines must be briefly considered.

Jesuit theologians from the beginning have insisted that there can be no moral responsibility in the absence of actual advertence. This means that man does not acquire merit or blame before God for his moral acts, unless he is actually aware of the good or evil in these acts. In this they crossed swords with theologians of the Augustinian and Aristotelian traditions who held that interpretative advertence to the morality of the act suffices for responsibility. For them the fact that one could and should have been aware of the objective evil inherent in his action makes him culpable. But Jesuit morality has always taught that there can be no question of sin, if subjective advertence is not present at the moment the given act is placed. Expressed positively this teaching holds that genuine good faith exempts man from moral blame for the evil he has done, no matter how wicked the objective malice may be. For moral goodness and evil consist essentially in that the will embraces an object which is in accord with, or contrary to, God's law. If then man's intellect is not actually aware of the good or bad in what he is doing, it is psychologically impossible for him to will the good or the evil. The nature of man is such that he can only will that which is known to the intellect. *Nil volitum nisi praecognitum.*

This view of responsibility, now in undisputed possession of the field, was long in combat before it won the day. Previous centuries had witnessed almost exclusive preoccupation with the objective requisites for responsibility. Indeed it is only today, after the great strides made by modern psychology, that the subjective is reaching full recognition. This is not to say that the Jesuits were the authors of this interpretation of responsibility. It had always been taught, though imperfectly realized. And previous to the arrival of Jesuit scholars on the scene its theological elaboration had already been begun, notably by Dominicans. The Jesuits did, however, so champion it as to make of it a characteristic moral thesis of the order.

There was another controversial issue of the 16th century in which the Jesuits took a distinctive stand. It was the doctrinal dispute whether directly willed unchastity always involves an objectively grave violation of the moral law. Reputable authors denied this thesis. Some Jesuit writers sided with them, among whom was Sanchez (†1610) in his celebrated treatise *De matrimonio.* The majority of Jesuits, however, took a sterner view of the question. The sexual faculty exists in man not for his individual good, they reasoned, but for that of the human race. The use of sex, therefore, for the personal gratification of the individual exclusively is a substantial perversion of this essential relation of sex to the race. As such it is necessarily a serious infraction of the law of nature. Judging the former opinion of questionable merit and dangerous to Christian morals, Aquaviva, General of the Order (1581–1615), forbade his subjects to teach or hold it. Subsequent Generals confirmed this decision. Outside the Order, however, the opinion was still sustained by some theologians. In virtue of this extrinsic authority Jesuit confessors did not, indeed might not, deny sacramental absolution to a penitent convinced that he had sinned only venially by unchastity. Today with the progress of moral science no Catholic theologian holds light matter in directly willed impurity. Thus the majority view of earlier Jesuits and the vigorous action of the heads of the Order have been vindicated by theological science.

It is false to attribute a doctrine of tyrannicide to the Order. In the treatise *De rege et regis institutione* (Toledo, 1599), the Spanish Jesuit Juan Mariana permitted tyrannicide in certain extreme cases. But the Order never adopted his doctrine and explicitly reprobated it in 1614. Again the principle "the end justifies the means," while it is capable of a true interpretation in certain contexts, has never been taught by the Society of Jesus in its immoral sense. An unbiased examination of Jesuit writings affords complete proof of this.

Bibliography

Dictionnaire de Théologie Catholique, VIII, 1069–1092.

J. Brodrick, *The Economic Morals of the Jesuits* (London, 1934).

M. Bishop, *Pascal, the Life of Genius* (New York, 1936).

F. Tillmann, *Die Idee der Nachfolge Christi,* pp. 26–45 (Düsseldorf, 1949).

I. von Döllinger and H. Reusch, *Moralstreitigkeiten in der römisch-katholischen Kirche* (Nördlingen, 1889).

The Catholic Encyclopedia, XIV, 601–611.

Edward A. Ryan
Robert H. Springer
Woodstock College

Jesuits: *see* Marxist Theory of Morals; Puritan Morals.

Jesus of Nazareth: *see* Augustine and Morals; Christian Moral Philosophy; Dostoyevsky, Fyodor; Freud, Sigmund; Hammurapi, Code of; Hindu Ethics; Kant, I.; Liguori, St. Alphonsus and Catholic Moral Philosophy; Quakerism, Classical, The Morality of; Tolstoy, Leo; Zoroastrian Morals.

Jewish Ethics and its Civilization

I. *A Word of Caution*

It is the wont of liberal authors on the subject to characterize Jewish ethics as idealistic, universal, this worldly, optimistic, rational, anti-ascetic, humanistic.[1] Writers of the orthodox school depict the same subject matter quite differently. To them it appears nomian, other-worldly, particularist, largely concerned with ritual and obedience to Divine Will. With few exceptions,[2] Christian theologians find it abounding in ceremonialism, legalistic, parochial, formalistic.

Much of these conflicting presentations of Jewish ethics springs from the twin evils of polemics and apologetics. The polemicist seems forever in search of distinguishing differentia between systems of ethics and is thus tempted to caricature the characteristics by glossing over the nuances. The apologist, whether in reaction to outside attack or in defence of a particular sectarian position, nearly always ignores the non-supporting texts. In the instance of Jewish ethics, these extremes have led to convenient classifications which set up the battle of Law vs. Spirit, Nationalism vs. Universalism, Formalism vs. Inwardness, Materialism, vs. Idealism, Justice vs. Love. Corroborative evidence is carved from the huge and manifold tradition, some citations exaggeratedly pronounced, others chipped away to fall unnoticed by the side. To the uninitiated spectator, the end product appears either as

---

[1] See Samuel Schulman's popular essay "Jewish Ethics," reflecting the liberal reform approach to the subject: in *Popular Studies in Judaism.*

[2] Notable among these exceptions are G. F. Moore and R. T. Herford.

an unrelieved paragon of virtues or a monstrous anachronism. He is either amazed by its contemporaneity[3] or repelled by its primitive crudeness.

Even after closer scrutiny, the reader discovers that each contradictory school is capable of producing a most impressive array of scriptural and Talmudic quotations and utterances vindicating each position. These, however, are easy to produce. For one thing, neither the Bible nor the Talmud treats ethics as a disparate discipline. There is no apparent concern for system or consistency. Further facilitating the one-sidedness of either vantage point is the absence of a single, authoritative text which would reconcile the patent contradictions even within the same treatise. Yet another factor is the long and varied history which forms divergent backgrounds for the plethora of ethical expression in Judaism.[4] It is

not surprising that different levels of civilization and divergent social and economic situations should produce a diversity of ethical response. But that the response of one period or of one mood should be seized upon as "typical" or "dominant" is more disturbing.

We will consider it of value, then, to ignore those partisan, single-stranded characterizations of Jewish ethics which lay claim to represent the authentic tradition. We will note that there are two principal sources of ethical directive in Judaism: the maxims and epigrams aphoristically strewn throughout the entire body of the literature; and the ethics both implied and articulated in the codes of law and ritual practice. We will not hope to fashion a coherent, uniform and homogeneous ethics out of this civilizational complexity. The resulting picture may not be as sharp or distinct as a systematic treatise but we believe it to capture more candidly the gamut of pluralistic moods and manners through which the Jewish experience has evolved.

II. *The Humanistic Bias*

Most modern liberal ethicists attempt to demonstrate that Jewish ethics is optimistic, this-worldly and peculiarly congenial to a naturalistic approach.[5] This version of Jewish ethics is easily bolstered by such typically cheerful citations as follows:

---

[3] Illustrations of the Kantian formulation of Jewish ethics are conspicuous in the writings of Lazarus' *The Ethics of Judaism*, Kaufman Kohler's *Jewish Theology* ("The Ethics of Judaism and the Kingdom of God,") Emil Hirsch's "Ethics" in the Jewish Encyclopedia.

[4] Biblical ethics alone includes a period ranging from primitive times to the second century of the common era. Not all of this is of one coherent mood. It contains period ethics of priestly theocracy, with that of the Prophets, and Wisdom series. To this must be added the centuries of Talmudic era (ending about 500 C.E.), the philosophic efforts of the Middle ages, the mysticism of Kabbalah, the romance of Hasidism, the period of Enlightenment, Reform, and the contemporary religious and secular philosophies. For the sake of economy and because works on Jewish ethics usually restrict themselves to the major sources of Bible and Talmud, we have concentrated on these classic periods.

---

[5] See Van Meter Ames' review of Israel Mattuck's *Jewish Ethics* for such a version. The review may be found in *The Menorah Journal* (Spring–Summer 1955).

BIBLICAL:

(1) "Be fruitful and multiply and replenish the earth and subdue it." (Genesis 1:28.)

(2) "And God created man in His own image, in the image of God created He him." (Genesis 1:27.)

(3) "Ye shall therefore keep My statutes and My ordinances which, if a man do, he shall *live* by them." (Leviticus 18:5.)

RABBINIC:

(1) "Every man will be held accountable before God for all the permitted things he beheld in life and did not enjoy." (Jerusalem Talmud, Kiddushin, end.)

(2) "God's commandments are intended to enhance the value and enjoyment of life, but not to mar it and make it gloomy." (Yoma 85a.)

(3) "The spirit of God rests upon man neither in a state of gloom nor in a state of indolence, but solely in the joy of performing a duty." (Sabbath 30b.)

(4) "Rabbi Samuel declared: 'He that fasts is called a sinner' basing this on an interpretation of Numbers 6:11." (Taanit 11a.)

The liberal, humanistic strain is unmistakable. But it is partial. Let us cite a few illustrations of what has been omitted:

BIBLICAL:

(1) "Cursed is the ground for thy sake; in toil shalt thou eat of it all the days of thy life. Thorns also and thistles shall it bring forth to thee. . . . In the sweat of thy face shalt thou eat bread. . ." (Genesis 3:17–19.)

(2) ". . . for the imagination of man's heart is evil from his youth." (Genesis 8:21.)

RABBINIC:

(1) "Rabbi Jacob said: 'This world is like a vestibule before the world to come.' " (Ethics of the Fathers (Pirke Aboth) 4:21–22.) ". . . better is one hour of blissfulness in the world to come than the whole life of this world."

(2) "In order to be holy it is necessary to abstain even from things that are permitted." (Yebamoth 20a.)

(3) "This is the way of Torah: a morsel of bread with salt must thou eat, and water by measure must thou drink, thou must sleep upon the ground and live a life of anguish the while thou toilest in the Torah." (Pirke Aboth 6:4.)[6]

(4) For two-and-a-half years, debate between the two rabbinic Schools of Shammai and Hillel raged as to the merit of life. A vote was finally taken and it was decided that "it were better for man *not* to have been created than to be created, but now that he has been created let him investigate his past deeds or as

---

[6] Israel Mattuck's apology for this dictum seeks to soften its ascetic tone by asserting "This should probably be interpreted not absolutely but relatively." *Jewish Ethics,* p. 139.

others say, let him examine his future actions." (Erubin 13b.)[7]

(5) "Rabbi Eleazer declared: 'He that fasts is called holy'" interpreting Numbers 6:5 for his support. (Taanit 11a).

(6) "Rabbi Judah, the Prince, said: 'He who accepts the pleasures of this world is deprived of the pleasures of the world to come and vice versa.'" (Aboth d. Rabbi Nathan verse I, XXVIII, 43a.)

When confronted by such quotations and illustrations from rabbinic conduct and temperaments contrary to the humanistic mood, the liberal theoreticians invoke quantitative and/or qualitative criteria for determining their true significance. Typically, Lazarus explains, "But in all the controversies, the party of energetic action and joyous living is represented by the best names and outnumbers by far its antagonists."[8] Yet, aside from the notable ascetic traditions of Rechabites, Essenes and Nazirites, the Talmud includes prominent and compelling rabbinic personalities who not only advocated but practiced a quite severe asceticism. Such, for example, as Mar, son of Rabina, who sat in fast the entire year excepting a few festivals;[9] (Pesachim 68b); or Rabbi Judah, the compiler of the Mishnah who proudly practiced asceticism as evidence of his piety.[10]

Nor can the mystic saints in Jewish post-Talmudic life who advocated asceticism, or the writings of a number of eminent Jewish theologians and moralists be so readily dismissed. The 10th century Ibn Paquda includes "renunciation of luxuries and love of the world" as the ninth fundamental principle of the religious "duties of the hearts" in his influential work of the same name.[11] Moses Hayyim Luzzatto, the 18th century author of *The Path of the Upright* (*Messilat Yesharim*) demonstrates that "abstinence is the beginning of saintliness," that man should therefore "avoid contact with worldly affairs as much as possible."[12]

Better, then, to frankly state that the strain of Jewish ethics we emphasize is determined by the philosophy of the age and the selective discrimination of ourselves or of the ethicist we read. The manifest development of the latent sources of optimism in the Bible and Talmud is the creation of thinkers who have absorbed the values of the Enlightenment. The age of confidence in human progress which experienced the joy of this worldly life found little point in citing the Talmudic heeding that there be "no unrestrained laugh-

---

7 C. Montefiore, commenting on this pessimistic note, apologetically assures the reader that "the passage is clearly a record of some famous dialectical discussion, without any true bearing upon the arguer's *real* views about actual life." p. 539, *A Rabbinic Anthology* (London, 1938).

8 M. Lazarus *The Ethics of Judaism*, Vol. II, p. 120.

9 Berachoth, 30b, where Rabbi Jochanan, Rabbi Ashi and others assent to this mournful attitude.

10 Ketuboth 104a.

11 Bachya Ibn Paquda: *Duties of the Heart*, p. 17.

12 *Messilat Yesharim*, p. 122.

ter in this world." (Berachoth 13a.) Essays composed and sermons preached filter the wellsprings of the Bible and Talmudic sea for corroborative texts congenial to the spirit of the age. And because of the paucity of structured ethical theory in Judaism and because of the casual and unsystematic form of ethics in traditional literature, these constructions selected from the classics may readily be woven together to form an ethics with "major tendencies." By virtue of repetition and its understandable acceptance by the contemporary Jewish audience, these latter day transformations appeal as the authoritative version of Jewish tradition. In the insulation of the ghetto and in moments of medieval catastrophe for the people, however, quite contrary versions are acknowledged as authentic.[13]

III. *The Christian-Jewish Polemic*

Christian theologians, from Paul onward, have for the most part felt the need to loosen Christianity from its antecedent anchorage, to prove its independence and its advancement over the "old" tradition. Ancient Israel is forever portrayed as obsolescent, "concerned with rites and ceremonies, with the maintenance of obsolete, useless and even harmful customs; it has been narrowly nationalistic; it has been socially and intellectually unprogressive . . .";[14] "The principle of love. . .

and the principle of moral inwardness" are distinctive Christian contributions."[15]

The defensive reactions to this exaggerated critique not infrequently entail an emasculation of Jewish ethics which rips asunder peoplehood from religion, ritual from ethics, law from the prophetic conscience.

In this polemical spirit both extremes err profoundly in their analysis of Jewish ethics. The fundamental error common to those who would overrate and to those who would berate her, is the assumption that love of people and mankind, law and spirit, ceremony and inwardness, cultus and social consciousness are inherently incompatible. In the Jewish religious civilization, these features did and do persist to co-exist uncoercedly.

IV. *Nation and Mankind*

The early rabbinic mind experienced no contradiction in holding Israel in special relation to God and holding at the same time to a firm belief that "the pious and virtuous of *all* nations participate in eternal bliss." (Sifra on Leviticus 19:18.) The prophet who spoke lovingly of God's interest in raising the fallen tabernacle of David could still rebuke the "chosen" with: Are ye not as children of the Ethiopians unto Me, O children of Israel?" (Amos 9:7). The prophet who conceived of Israel as the Suffering Servant persecuted by the nations

---

[13] Gershom G. Scholem's *Major Trends in Jewish Mysticism* illustrates the wide influence of these moods in critical times; p. 244 ff.

[14] Albert C. Knudson *The Principles of Christian Ethics* (New York, 1943). p. 285.

[15] *Ibid.*, p. 39: see the New Testament critique of Pharisaic morality in such sections as John 7:22–24; Matthew 23:23–26; Acts 15:24–29; Romans 3:28–29.

could speak of God's blessing "Egypt My people and Assyria, the work of My hands." (Isaiah 19:25.) Nor does the particularism in Judaic literature stifle Israel's High Holy Day prayer for God to impose His awe upon all mankind that *"all* Thy works may revere Thee . . . that they may form a single band to do Thy will with a perfect heart."

So too rabbinic law, with its alleged parochialism, could demand that giving charity to the poor, burying the dead, attending funerals, eulogizing the deceased, consoling the bereaved be extended to non-Jew as well as Jew.[16] The rabbinic imagination could also spin a legend in ethics in which God chastizes the ministering angels singing a hymn of praise over the destruction of the Egyptians in the Red Sea: "My children lie drowned in the sea and you would sing hymns of triumph?" (Megillah 10b). To be sure, there looms always the danger that love of peoplehood may take the ascendency and degenerate into zealous ethnocentrism; but the risk is at least as real that universalism may be perverted to imperialism.

V. *Ritual and Ethics*

In regard to the relationship between ritual and ethics, something of the polemicist's assumptions often seeps into the defense walls of the apologists without due consideration. Many of the latter are found interpreting Jewish religion as "essentially . . . the emergence of ethical ideals out of a background of purely ritual and ceremonial observances . . ."[17] The apology thereby accepts the strange logic which sets up ethics in opposition to ritual by placing each in a separate stage, one primitive (ritualistic), the other emergent (ethical). In truth, however, these hard disjunctives between the status of rite and righteousness, cult and conscience, are virtually unknown in Biblical and Talmudic literature. Within breath of the same Biblical chapter, for instance, divinely commanded ritual law prohibiting the wearing of wool and linen together, is coupled with the sensitive injunction against removing young ones or eggs from the nest in the presence of the mother bird.[18]

The prophets condemn the hypocrisy and mechanism of ritual, but their vision aspires to sacrifice *with* mercy, adoration *with* charity, rite *with* justice, form *with* inwardness. Statute and ordinance of both ethical and ritual significance lay equal claim to Divine sanction, and the Rabbis thus admonish man to be "heedful of a light precept as of a grave one." (Pirke Aboth 2:1.)

The ritual itself was often invested with so great a degree of ethical purpose that the two elements are in fact, inseparable. "For indeed, what difference does it make to God how we slaughter an animal or of what kind of food we partake, except that He desires by such laws and regulations to benefit His creatures, to purify their hearts

---

[16] Mishna Gittin 5:8; Tosefta 5:4–5.

[17] *"Ethics"* Universal Jewish Encyclopedia. Vol. IV (1941), p. 175.
[18] Deuteronomy 22:11, 22:6.

and to ennoble their characters."[19] Ritual observance is at times taken as a pedagogic means to instruct man in self-control, in obedience to Divine Law, to dramatize hygienic principles, repudiate idolatry, etc.[20]

Ritual serves an indispensable function as an active mnemonic intensifying ethical resolutions. It is however regarded as dispensable when its observance would violate ethical principle. "Even the entire body of Biblical precepts and rituals are not equal to one ethical principle."[21] Respect for the personal dignity of a human being supercedes a negative Biblical injunction.[22]

The obduracy with which ritual observance is often maintained makes it clear that there is more here than legalism for its own sake. Observance or abandonment of ritual is not solely an issue of religious ideology. Many a ritual came to be associated with the supreme virtue of loyalty, and often a history of martyrdom added emotive value to the ritual far beyond the initial expectation. The rabbis wisely observed that "every commandment for which the Israelites gave their lives in times of persecution they now observe

openly; the others have grown effete among them."[23] The struggle in the Chanukah story was initiated by a ritual struggle whose symbolic meaning was augmented by the question of disloyalty to a people and surrender to tyranny. "Even to change one's shoe strap"[24] in moments of religious persecution may cause a minor precept to be elevated to demand martyrdom.

In much the same way did Pauline anti-nomianism and anti-ceremonialism give additional impetus to the conservation of rituals. Retention of many ceremonial laws, following the destruction of the Temple, was invested with survival value. The early Christian opposition to dietary laws and circumcision was considered a double pronged attack upon the efforts to preserve the peoplehood of Judaism and the relevance of the tradition and rabbinic law. Ceremonial laws, more than the more abstract universal laws of ethics, were focused upon for they retained their indigenous national symbolism. Their importance reached unparalleled heights as a unifying and stabilizing factor especially where political independence was lost or as in the Diaspora where both territorial and political integrity were absent.

Questions as to the value of specific ritual could no longer be regarded as a matter of intellectual dialectic, but as incidents in the *ethics of loyalty*. The license of doubt and debate was held expendable. It became important for the rabbis to insist that Abraham, though living ages before the Sinaitic

---

19 Genesis. Rabba 44.1: Tanchuma, Shemini 15b; Buber's edition.

20 See Moses Maimonides' *Guide to the Perplexed*, Part III, Chapters 43–49 for such ethical interpretations of Sabbath, Festivals, dietary laws, among others.

21 Jerusalem Talmud, Peah 16a. as cited by J. Z. Lauterbach in his essay on the *"Ethics of Halakah."* He quotes similar Talmudic passages: Sukkoth 30a; Nazir 23b. in his notes on page 271.

22 Sabbath 81b.

23 Sifre Deuteronomy Ra'eh 90b.

24 Sanhedrin 74b.

revelation, had observed all the precepts and regulations of the Law[25] though earlier tradition assured his justification by faith alone.[26] For the Pauline principle setting up the justification of faith over that of works sought its sanction from the merit of the pre-Sinaitic religious heroes of the Bible. "Therefore it is of faith, that it might be by grace . . . not to that only which is of the law but to that also which is of the faith of Abraham, who is the father of us all."[27] So it is that the cleavage between ritual and ethical law is introduced in the practical polemics over the justification by faith or works. And so it is too that ritual works are catapulted to a level of importance, nearly eclipsing the sphere of ethics.[28]

VI. *Law and Theology*

Partly because of this historical pitting of Christian creed and faith against Jewish deed and act and partly because of Judaism's inherent distrust of abstract theory, it is Law which identifies the dominant trait in the Jewish ethic. The Christian antithesis of faith and works finds its Jewish analogue in the debate over which is more important in the pursuit of the religious life: the study of the law or the practice of good deeds.[29] Neither

study nor ethical practice, however, is tied to beliefs, creeds, faith or dogmas. Even the study was not academic. In the Talmudic controversy over which is more important, study or doing, Rabbi Tarphon emphasizes study while Rabbi Akiba insists upon doing. But then "they all agreed that study was greater, for it led to doing."[30]

It seems more accurate then to speak of Jewish ethics as rooted in religious nomianism than of its frequent modern formulation as essentially "theologic."[31] Judaism's religious ethics is not theological in the sense that Aquinas' systematization of Christian ethics is theologic. The problems of evil, atonement, sin, free will in Judaism developed less as metaphysical or theologic issues than as practical morality or law. So it was that the medieval endeavors to theologize Judaism, to extrapolate a system of belief, were mainly abortive.

All of this is not to deny an implicit theocentric source of Jewish ethics. But while the legitimization of Halacha or Law was dependent upon conception of a Divine Ruler who revealed His will, the theologic implications were taken for granted, not subjected to reflective analysis. The Law and its study was applied theology. The aspirations of the Bible and ideals of the prophets were there; no question as to its enduring legitimacy. The

25 Yoma 28b.
26 Mechilta Beshallach 6; edit. Weiss, 40b.
27 Romans 4:16.
28 For additional illustrations see Lauterbach's and Kohler's articles on *"Nomism"* in *The Jewish Encyclopedia.*
29 See Pirke Aboth for consistent emphasis giving primary value to works over wisdom and erudition. 1:17, 3:12, 3:22; 4:6.

30 Kiddushin 40b.
31 M. Lazarus, *The Ethics of Judaism,* Vol. I, p. 109f.
Emil Hirsch, *"Ethics" Jewish Encyclopedia, passim.*
K. Kohler, *Jewish Theology,* p. 477.

ethical utterances of the prophets remain to be rescued from the empty fate of eschatology, from the mistiness of generalized good-will and from the facile resolution of problems through apothegm, parable and epigram. The excitement and drama of prophetic denunciation and vision must be translated into prescribed, detailed, concrete, daily activity. Goodness and virtue require more than good will and intention with which the road to moral laxity is liberally paved. Fences must be erected to guide the wayward, and transgressors must feel the reality of this-worldly punishment, if ideals are not to go up in the smoke of pious verbiage. "The task of prophecy," declares a Talmudic passage, "was taken from the prophets and given to the wise men,"[32] to promulgate and enforce regulatory law.

Such guiding principles of ethics as the conservation of health, life and property and their use for the ennoblement of man and society are consequently concretized into legal precepts. The issue of philanthropy, for example, is not left solely to the whim and caprice of the individual. There are laws of tithing and restrictions even as to the generosity of the charity given. Man should not "squander more than one-fifth of his wealth, lest he himself becomes indebted to society."[33]

The Levitical formula "to love one's neighbor as oneself" is likewise not allowed to waste away into pious declaration. The rights of adjoining neighbors are spelled out pragmatically in the Talmud. A property owner has a prior claim to purchase adjoining property over any other person. If the owner, lacking neighborly feeling, ignores his neighbor's rights by selling the property to a third person, the latter may be compelled to turn over the bought property to the adjacent neighbor for the purchasing price.[34] Theological ethics find the breadth of reality through the implementation of law in the daily activities between man and man.

The dangers of such a law-abiding ethic turning into monuments of inflexible injunctions and prohibitions are patent. As the Spirit may turn into the empty Word, so too the Law may freeze into the impersonal Letter. Spontaneity and inwardness in ethical decision could shrivel into deadening conformity to the book of statutes. Law as instrument can, with imposing power, turn into the end itself, the noble search to seek out God's will may deteriorate to a prosaic casuistry. The Talmud cautions knowingly, "For those who make a right use of the Law, it is a medicine for life; for those who make a wrong use, it is a drug for death."[35]

Many of these dangers have indeed engulfed the consecrated end of Jewish law. It appears that the further removed from independence and political normality, the further distanced from the respected age of practiced legislation, the more stringent grew the conservative urge, the more timid

---

[32] Baba Bathra 12a.
[33] Ketuboth 50a.
[34] See Lauterbach, *The Ethics of the Halakah*, p. 283.
[35] Sabbath 88b.

the changes and amendments which rabbinic predecessors once courageously introduced. Dependence upon the past for authentic rendition of the Law and reliance upon the Talmudic rabbis "greater in number and wisdom than we" increased. In its ascendancy, rabbinic law was different.

VII. *Revelation and Interpretation*

The Pharisaic revolt against Sadducean Biblical literalism encouraged a popularization of study which cut afoot the adoration of charismatic personalities. The democratization of learning weakened the influence of miracle-men and their personal magnetism. The text, not the prophet, could be called Holy, Perfect, Divine. And the text was open to all. Neither voices from Heaven moving carob trees nor falling walls could detract from the law based on verse and chapter, and applied contextually by human intelligence.[36] Interpreters of the text, often locked in contradictory judgments were equally regarded: "These and these are both the words of the living God."[37]

The Law in the hands of the rabbinic scholars humanized Revelation, allowed it growth, continuity and change. God's wisdom was not exhausted with the Sinai theophany. "Things not revealed to Moses were revealed to Akiba."[38] This, the rabbis explained, was due to the omniscience of His word. Divine truth, if given at once, would overwhelm a generation

and congeal the hearts of a nation with fear.[39]

With such a concept of progressive revelation, the rabbis could free the people from priestly and patrician bibliolatry.[40] They could transform the Pentateuchal lex talionis into a complex code entailing monetary compensation in consideration of pain, unemployment, medical expenditures, humiliation, etc. They could, through the subtleties of hermeneutics, so qualify the conditions under which the Biblical "stubborn and rebellious son," the "idolatrous city" and "the leprous house" were to be condemned as to render each case practically impossible.[41] These are made to serve as jurisprudential theory, whose instances "never were nor will be." Their function is for "you to study and receive thereby reward."[42] So too was Halachah able to circumvent the Deuteronomic law (15:1–2) which cancelled all debts on the Sabbatical year by the imaginative institution of Hillel's Prosbul. A magnificent mistranslation of a text in Psalms (119:126) "It is

---

36 Baba Mezia 59b.

37 Erubin 13b.

38 Numbers Rabbah 19:6.

39 Tanchuma, Debarim 1a.

40 For illustration of the democratic "plebeian" character of the Pharisaic reforms through Law, read Louis Finkelstein's suggestive chapter: "The Oral Law" in his two-volume The Pharisees (Jewish Publication Society, Philadelphia, 1946).

41 Deuteronomy, 21:18; Deuteronomy, 13: 17; Leviticus, 14:34 ff.

42 Sanhedrin 71a. The Rabbis' humanitarian employment of law and exegesis allows them to boast that the Sanhedrin (religious Supreme Court) which executes a person once in 7 years is called destructive. Rabbi Eliezer Ben Azzariah corrected, "once in 70 years."

time for the Lord to work; They have made void Thy Law." allows it as rationale for the rabbinic abolition of laws in the interest of the preservation of its spirit.[43]

VIII. *Ethical Absolutes*

Jewish ethics allows itself few immutable absolutes. The notable exceptions are the absolutes which prohibit murder, incest and idolatry. Whereas, ritual ordinances of the highest importance may be transgressed in the interest of the conservation of health and life, the three aforementioned cardinal sins are excluded. "We may cure ourselves with all (forbidden) things except idolatry, incest and murder."[44]

Yet, in the face of brutal Hadrianic persecutions, the Rabbinic sense of realism attenuated even these absolutes. Consideration of the public or private character of the transgression, distinctions as to who decreed the transgression, the motivation of the transgressor, the number and nature of the public witnessing the prohibited act were introduced.[45] The rabbinic role in legalizing morality carried with it a liberating force which encouraged reason and experience to free men from indiscriminate obedience to unyielding categorical imperatives.

IX. *Religious And Autonomous Ethics*

Jewish ethics falls under the category of religious or theistic ethics. Traditionally this category is contrasted with philosophic, natural or secular ethics. The differentiating characteristics of each involves the considered origin and authority of the ethical principle and performance. The genesis of and sanction for secular ethics is said to lie in experience, intuition, human reason, appeal to natural consequences, individual and social, physical and psychical.[46] Secular ethics prides itself in the autonomous and therefore uncoerced manner of arriving at the ethical decision. Existing for its own sake, morality does not cringe before the voice thundering from above, is free of the external restraint of the Other's Will. Theistic ethics legitimizes its moral philosophy through reference to its purportedly Divine Source, through revelatory experiences or by virtue of the logic which derives ethical principles from those of theology. Secular ethics dismisses theistic ethics as either arguing in circular fashion, or as "pseudo-heteronomous morality" (Von Hartmann), unreflected obedience to Divine Imperative. Theistic ethics considers the secular effort in ethics to result in anthropocentrism with its accompanying arrogance and unbridled subjectivism.

The hard and fast distinctions of heteronomy and autonomy are unknown in Jewish ethics despite the efforts of Lazarus and others who were

43 Mishnah: Berachoth 9:5, end.
44 Pesachim 25a.
45 Sanhedrin 74 a, b.

46 Mordecai M. Kaplan in his introduction to *Messilat Yesharim* discusses the basic traits and divergent methods of approach to the problem of human conduct. pp. XIV–XXX.

anxious to anticipate Kantian moral a priori in the rabbinic tradition.[47] Autonomous ethical discoveries are traced back to divine source; heteronomous ethical revelation is laden with autonomous discovery. Since man's intellect is a divine gift and his conscience a manifestation of his divine image, discoveries are one side of the coin of Revelation. Since God's will must be accepted and distinguished from that of the masked Satan, Revelation is autonomy in disguise.

How, for example, do the Rabbis understand the Noahide laws which primitive men discovered? The prohibition against shedding blood, robbery, idolatry, adultery, blasphemy, eating flesh from live animals, and the injunction to set up courts of justice are pre-Sinaitic, no special revelation of these principles being recorded in the Bible. Autonomous or not, that origin is tagged on to an innocuous verse in Genesis 2:16 and becomes somehow divinely ordained.[48] Moritz Lazarus, determined to show that "Reason (as opposed to Revelation) was the source of his (Abraham's) ethical instruction"[49] thereby gaining for Judaism the character of autonomous ethics quotes an oft cited Mishnaic passage: "Abraham observed the whole

Torah before it was given . . ." But the Mishnah[50] bases its claim of this knowledge upon the quoted verse from Scripture: "because that Abraham obeyed My voice, and kept My charge, My commandments, My statutes and My laws." (Genesis 26:5.) The illustration seems more compatible to a theory of special revelation than that of autonomy.

The Rabbis were oblivious to the bifurcated realms of nature and the supernatural in the sense that theologians employ it. Natural law is congenial to Divinity because the thesis that "the earth is the Lord's" was taken seriously. Chastity could be learned from the dove, modesty from the cat, not to rob from the ant, propriety from the cock, and "if they had not been written (in Scripture) they should have been written."[51] Man's discoveries in nature are no blasphemy to God but His glory.

X. *In Summation*

We have made much of Jewish ethics' resistance to academic classification. The people whose spirit it reflects, the opinion leaders, judges and scholars whose attitudes it records, were not consciously concerned with formulating a uniform and unambiguous code of ethics. No reduced principles or articles of belief may be drawn up from whose logic may be extracted the essence of its ethical character. But the difficulty is more than codifying a subject matter without

---

[47] For a discussion of this issue in Jewish philosophy, see Felix Perles Königsberg's "Die Autonomie der Sittlichkeit in Jüdischen Schriften" in the Judaica Festschrift in honor of Hermann Cohen (Berlin, Verlag Bruno Cassirer, 1912).

[48] Sanhedrin 56a end.

[49] Lazarus *The Ethics of Judaism* I, p. 118.

[50] Kiddushin 4.14.

[51] Yoma 67b.

system. The difficulty lies in appreciating the civilizational character of Jewish ethics; an ethical outlook which cannot be comprehended discretely, as an isolable phenomenon. Rather, if it is to be understood at all, it must be apprehended as an indispensable part of an organic totality which weaves jurisprudence and theology, legend and philosophy into a religious civilizational fabric. Within this schema the generalized aim of Jewish ethical life may be considered that of "KIDDUSH HA SHEM," the sanctification of God's name: binding heaven with earth, countenancing no rupture in God's universe, transforming the secular into the holy, knitting together the torn fragments of what was originally whole, praying towards the day when His name shall be One. Sanctification uses every means at its command: prayer and charity, piety and social action, body and soul, heart and mind.

The ethics of Judaism clings therefore to both prophet and priest; holds to love of Israel with that of mankind; eyes the world to come with faith while laboring in this world with expectancy; extols human freedom yet recalls its frustrating limitations; is God-centered without losing its passionate interest in man's lot and striving for his daily salvation. These achievements are not taken as glittering paradoxes throwing man into despair or helplessness. Within the complex organism of religious civilization these varied moods and divergent approaches are the healthy signs of a normal ethics seen whole without the grinding of a special lens.

Bibliography

Moritz Lazarus, *The Ethics of Judaism,* translated by Henrietta Szold, Jewish Publication Society (Philadelphia, 1900).
Israel Mattuck, *Jewish Ethics (Hutchinson's* University Library, London, 1953).
Leo Baeck, *The Essence of Judaism* (New York, 1936).
Mordecai M. Kaplan, "The Contribution of Judaism to World Ethics" in *The Jews,* edited by Louis Finkelstein, Vol. I (New York, 1949).
C. G. Montefiore and H. Loewe, *A Rabbinic Anthology.*
Emil Hirsch, "Ethics" in *The Jewish Encyclopedia.*
J. Z. Lauterbach, "The Ethics of Halakah" in *Rabbinical Essays* (Hebrew Union College Press, Cincinnati, 1951).
M. Mielziner, "Ethics of the Talmud" in *Judaism at the World's Parliament of Religion,* pp. 107–113.

Source Material

Ibn Gabirol, *The Improvement of Moral Qualities,* translation and introduction by Stephen S. Wise (New York, 1901).
Bachya Ibn Paquda, *Duties of the Heart,* translated by Moses Hyamson (New York, 1925).
Moses Hayyim Luzzatto, *Messilat Yesharim,* translation and introduction by Mordecai M. Kaplan (Jewish Publication Society, Philadelphia, 1936).
Moses Maimonides, *The Eight Chapters on Ethics,* translated with introduction by Joseph I. Gorfinkle (New York, 1912).
Pirke Aboth, Rabbi. *Ethics of the Fathers.*

Harold M. Schulweis
Temple Beth Abraham
Oakland, California

K

Kabbalah: *see* Jewish Ethics and Its Civilization.

Kames: *see* Moral Philosophy in America.

Kant, Immanuel

Immanuel Kant was born on April 22, 1724, in the provincial city of Koenigsburg, East Prussia. He died on February 12, 1804, never having been more than fifty miles away from the place of his birth. He was not, however, a provincial man; the range of his intellectual concerns was universal, he was deeply interested in the revolutionary political movements of the eighteenth century, and as a philosopher he must be placed beside Plato and Aristotle as one of the chief architects of Western thought. His life was outwardly uneventful; his personal background and history are important only as they illuminate his intellectual achievements. The significant biography of Immanuel Kant concerns the development of his philosophy.

Kant's father was a saddler, and both his parents were simple and sincere Pietists. Recognizing the intellectual promise of their son, they sent him, at the age of ten, to the Collegium Fredericanum, a Pietist school, where he remained for seven years, engaged in the conventional classical studies.

He then entered the University where he studied mathematics and philosophy, and partly supported himself by tutoring some of his fellow-students. When his father died in 1746, Kant left the University to become a resident tutor in several families. After nine years he returned to the University as a lecturer on a variety of subjects, including mathematics, physics, philosophy, natural theology, physical geography and anthropology. Kant's personality as well as his quality as a teacher are revealed in Herder's description of him:

> I have had the good fortune to know a philosopher who was my teacher; he had the happy sprightliness of youth . . . His open, thoughtful brow was the seat of unruffled calmness and joy; discourse full of thought flowed from his lips; jest and wit and humor were at his command, and his lecture was the most entertaining conversation . . . Nothing worth knowing was indifferent to him . . . He encouraged and urged independent thought.

Not until 1770 did Kant obtain a professorship, when he was made Professor of Logic and Metaphysics, a position he held until advancing years forced him to retire. Never married, Kant led the simple life of an academic bachelor, observing a daily routine of lecturing and writing in the forenoon, dining at noon (always in the company of friends), walking in the afternoon, and general reading in the evening before an early retirement. He adhered to routine so strictly that people were said to set their watches when he began his daily walk. Always of frail health, he relied upon a strict regimen for keeping well; the volume of his works testifies that he made effective use of his limited physical strength. Not only in the discipline of his own life but in generous provision for the needs of members of his own family and in his philanthropic activities toward others, Kant's life exemplified in large measure his own teaching that the inclinations should be subordinated to the demands of duty.

Two factors in Kant's historical background are important for understanding his philosophy, especially his ethics. One of these is the Christian faith, particularly the Pietistic form of Protestantism in which Kant was reared. The other is the ideas of the Enlightenment which characterized the thought of his country.

German Pietism emphasized the personal relationship of the individual to God, purity of heart, saintliness of character, and devotion to human welfare. It re-emphasized the priesthood of all believers, and thus had democratizing implications. Although Kant rebelled against the rigor of the religious practices at the Pietist Collegium Fredericanum, and in later life dissociated himself from organized religion, he did not hesitate to affirm that sincere Pietists like his parents

"had the root of the matter in them." It may be argued that the whole of Kant's moral philosophy was an attempt to provide a rational purification of what he regarded as the root principles of Christian ethics. Thus his Formula of the End in Itself and the Formula of the Kingdom Ends have obvious parallels in the Christian principle of the worth and dignity of the individual and the idea of the Kingdom of God. Indeed, Kant spoke of his own work as "that of a poor bungler who is trying as best he can to interpret Christ's teaching."

The ideas of the Enlightenment too are reflected in Kant's moral philosophy. That the ideals of the American and French Revolutions, with their emphasis upon freedom as the basis of progress and political justice were congenial to him appears in his essays, "What is Enlightenment?" and "Perpetual Peace." Kant was also profoundly influenced by the rationalism of his era. Although he was to bring the prevailing extravagant beliefs in the capacities of pure reason under decisive criticism in the *Critique of Pure Reason,* and to reject the empty and formal perfectionism of rationalist ethics, he did not become a skeptic. A critic of unwarranted pretensions of reasons, he yet remains a great champion of the role of reason, within its proper limits, in both theory and practice.

Kant's first great critical work was the *Critique of Pure Reason* (1781). Although this is primarily concerned with the theory of knowledge, it lays the basis in method and general conception not only for Kant's philosophy of nature but also for his philosophy of morals. While Kant's first definitive treatment of ethics, the *Foundations of the Metaphysics of Morals* (1785), popularly known as the *Grundlegung*, can be and often is read without previous acquaintance with the critical point of view developed in the *Critique of Pure Reason*, the argument of the *Grundlegung* presupposes the doctrine of the first Critique, particularly in the discussion of moral freedom. The *Critique of Practical Reason*, (1788), in turn, presupposes the two previous works. Indeed, both Kant's philosophy of nature and his philosophy of morals are part of one well-knit structure, and an understanding in depth of his ethics requires a knowledge of the whole system. For the present exposition of Kantian ethics it will, however, be feasible to follow the structure of the *Grundlegung*, making, however, references to the first two Critiques as well as to Kant's later ethical writings, including *Religion Within the Limits of Reason Alone* (1793) and the *Metaphysics of Morals* (1797).

The Nature of Morality

The starting point of Kant's discussion of ethics is the moral experience of ordinary men. "Concerning the ruling ideas in the practical part of Kant's system," said Schiller, "only philosophers disagree, but men have always been unanimous." The essential feature of that unanimous agreement is that there is a distinction between what is expedient and what is morally required, between inclination

and duty, between what, in some instances, we should like to do and what we ought to do. "Nothing in the world —indeed nothing beyond the world— can possibly be conceived which could be called good without qualification except a *good will*." Thus Kant begins the First Section of the *Grundlegung*. "The good will is not good because of what it affects or accomplishes or because of its adequacy to achieve some proposed end; it is good only because of its willing, i.e., it is good in itself." Kant is often mistakenly interpreted as saying that morality is not concerned with consequences; his point, however, is merely that intended consequences, "some proposed end," being relative cannot be the *criterion* of an absolutely good will. The criterion of a will that is to be esteemed as good in itself is that the actions to which it leads are done *from* duty. Actions of this sort alone have moral worth. This is "the first proposition of morality." To make his meaning clear Kant draws the distinction between actions which are merely in accordance with duty when the subject has some direct interest in the result, and actions done for the sake of duty. Even acts of kindness cannot derive their moral worth from altruistic feelings or inclinations; only when such acts are done from duty do they have genuine moral worth. He seems to say that so long as we have *any* inclination for an action it can have no moral worth. This would lead to the absurd teaching that the *presence* of a natural inclination to do good actions, or a feeling of satisfaction in doing them, would detract from their moral worth. Kant's language in the *Grundlegung* certainly lends some support to Schiller's satire of Kant's doctrine:

Gladly I serve my friends, but, alas, from inclination, .
And often I'm troubled because I am not good.

Nothing else will do: You must try to despise them,
And with revulsion do what Duty orders you.

However, it should be remembered that Kant is contrasting the motives of inclination and duty taken in isolation, in order to make clear which of them is the source of moral worth. Whether these two kinds of motive can be present in the same moral action at the same time is a question that interpreters still debate, but Kant's teaching as a whole supports the view that the presence of the motive of inclination does not rob an action of its moral worth *provided* the motive of duty is determinative.

"The second proposition (of morality) is: An action done from duty does not have its moral worth in the purpose which is to be achieved through it, but in the maxim by which it is determined." Thus Kant not only reiterates his rejection of intended consequences as the test of moral action, but states his doctrine in terms of 'maxims.' A maxim is any principle on which we act, be it good or bad. Insofar as our action is at all reflective, it will be action upon some general principle, (such as "Honesty is the best policy" or "An eye for an eye, a tooth

for a tooth"). If the maxim of our action generalizes a particular action with its particular motive and its intended result, it will be a *material* maxim. Since the moral goodness of an action cannot, according to Kant, be derived from its intended results, it follows that it cannot be derived from a material maxim. The only maxim which can give moral growth to an action is the principle of doing one's duty. Since this maxim is empty of any particular matter, it is a *formal* maxim. The man of good will tests, and adopts or rejects, his material maxims by the test of conformity to the "formal principle of volition as such."

In his analysis of duty Kant adds a third principle: "Duty is the necessity of an action done from respect for the law." The law here referred to is, of course, the moral law. As such it must be embodied in the formal maxim. Since this cannot be a maxim of satisfying our desires, it must be a maxim of acting rationally, i.e., acting on law valid for all rational beings regardless of their particular desires. "We stand under a discipline of reason . . ." Since this law often checks our desires, it appears as a command. Or, failing to check our desires, we none the less acknowledge it as a law of duty. We respect it, or hold it in reverence.

Thus the common rational knowledge of morals leads to the supreme principle of morality: "That is, I should never act in such a way that I could not will that my maxim should be universal law." Conformity to law as such serves as the principle of the morally good will, and, Kant holds, it must serve as such a principle if duty is not to be a vain delusion. Kant illustrates the principle by the example, among others, of making a deceitful promise to extricate oneself from difficulty. One might, of course, reject this maxim as being, on the whole, imprudent. "To be truthful from duty, however, is an entirely different matter from being truthful out of fear of disadvantageous consequences . . ." The test is, could I will that my maxim should become universal law. Kant's answer is that the maxim of telling a lie to extricate oneself from distress would destroy itself as soon as it was made a universal law.

Although the moral knowledge of common human reason contains the principle of the law of duty, it does not formulate the principle in abstraction. The claims of man's needs and inclinations, i.e., man's quest for happiness, tempt him to neglect the claims of duty and to provide plausible arguments for what he does. Since a false moral philosophy may be disastrous for morality in practice, the solution can be found only in a critical philosophy of morality which will formulate and justify the supreme principle of morality.

The Categorical Imperative

Although Kant argues that an analysis of ordinary moral judgments discloses the principle of morality, he denies that this was or could be done by generalizing from examples of morally good actions. We can, in the first place, never be certain that any given action is in fact motivated by duty. We cannot read the motives of others, and even in ourselves the chances of self-deception are great. Moreover, what we are looking for is not a generalization about actual human behavior but a moral law valid for all rational beings as such. Finally, we cannot even identify an example of a morally good action unless we already possess the criterion of moral worth. Moral principles, to be universal and necessary, must stem from the requirements of reason alone, i.e., they must be a priori. Although all genuinely moral actions must conform to the a priori, no example is adequate to its universality. Hence, before we attempt to apply moral principles we must try to formulate them precisely, independently of all empirical considerations. This requires a critique of practical reason.

Practical reason is the capacity of rational agents to subject their inclinations to principles. Insofar as we are determined by causal influences acting upon us, no question of morality can arise. The moral question concerns what principles shall guide our action. Rational agents have a subjective principle or maxim of action, but since men are imperfectly rational these subjective principles must be distinguished from objective principles, i.e., principles on which a rational being would necessarily act if reason were in full control. When the will and objective principles are in disharmony, the objective principle seems to constrain or "necessitate" the will. "The conception of an objective principle, so far as it constrains a will, is a command (of reason), and the formula of this command is called an imperative." All imperatives, whether moral or not, are expressed by an "ought," and express the relation of *necessitation* which holds between a principle recognized as objective and an imperfectly rational will. A perfectly rational or wholly good agent would necessarily act on objective principles and hence would not be "necessitated." Such an agent would be under no imperatives; he would have a 'holy' will.

Practical reason has non-moral and well as moral functions and these various functions involve different kinds of imperatives. When objective principles are *conditioned* by a will for some end which we *wish* to achieve, the imperatives that follow are *hypothetical*. They have the form, "If I will this end, then I ought to do so and so." Kant divides hypothetical imperatives into two kinds, problematic or technical and assertoric or pragmatic. When the end (like success at tennis) is one that we might will, then we ought to cultivate the necessary skill to achieve it. When the end is one that every rational agent naturally wills (his happiness), then he ought to order his life so as to achieve his goal. But some objective principles are *unconditioned*: they are not based on the previous willing of some further end but would necessarily be followed by a fully rational agent. These principles give rise to *categorical* imperatives. The hypothetical imperatives have an 'if' before the 'ought;' they are rules of skill and counsels of prudence. The categorical imperative has no conditions; it is a command or law of morality.

There is but one Categorical Imperative, but Kant gives the following five formulations of it, each of which brings out some different emphasis.

I. *The Formula of Universal Law*

"Act only according to that maxim by which you can at the same time will that it should become universal law." This formula is *the* Categorical Imperative. It commands us to test the maxims of our action by their fitness to become universal law, i.e., to act on a principle valid for all rational beings as such, and not merely on a principle that is valid if we wish to realize some further end. It has often been objected that the categorical imperative is empty, since no specific guidance for action can be derived from it. Although Kant appears, in the *Grundlegung*, to believe that particular moral rules like "Thou shalt not kill" can be 'derived' from the categorical imperative as their principle, elsewhere he firmly asserts that the supreme principles of morals "do not determine any specific purpose, but merely the moral form of every purpose." Like other formulas, the formula of ethics does not supply the variables; it merely provides a procedure for making a moral decision. It is a necessary but not a sufficient condition for moral action. The *content* of morality must be derived from elsewhere, and in the *Critique of Practical Reason* Kant held that for this purpose we must make use of Formula Ia.

Ia. *The Formula of the Law of Nature*

"Act as though the maxim of your action were by your will to become a universal law of nature." This formula is subordinate to Formula I because it does not state the essence of morality but rather formulates a principle to aid us in making moral judgments. The principle is the analogy of the moral law to the law of nature. Of course the moral law is not a law of nature. If it were there would be no moral obligation; we would naturally do what we ought. There is an analogy between the universal law of nature and the universal law of morality, but it is only an analogy. The laws of nature are causal but when Kant asks us to treat our maxims *as if* they were universal laws of nature he treats them as purposive. The test provided by Formula Ia is whether our maxims, if adopted, would further a systematic harmony of purposes. This formula anticipates the Formula of the Kingdom of Ends.

II. *The Formula of the End in Itself*

"Act so as to treat humanity, whether in your own person or in that of another, always as an end and never as a means only." This formula calls attention to the fact that all rational action besides having a principle must also set before itself an end. Because subjective and relative ends have only relative and conditional value, they can produce only hypothetical imperatives. Only if there are ends in themselves can they be the ground of a categorical imperative. Every person as a rational agent, potentially capable of having a good will, is such an end. As Kant says, "it is just the fitness of his maxims to a universal legislation that indicates that he is an end in himself." Since persons are of unconditioned value it is wrong to treat them simply as a means to an end that is only relative. They are to be treated as befits the dignity of autonomous moral agents.

III. *The Formula of Autonomy*

"Act only so that the will through its maxims could regard itself at the same time as universally lawgiving." This formula is not merely a repetition of Formula I; its emphasis adds something new. Although the moral law is objective and universal, it is not *imposed* on man. The law which we are bound to obey is the product of our own will as rational agents. Thus Kant makes clear his divergence from any authoritarian ethics. The moral law is not the will of God or any other external authority; it is the necessary expression of our nature as rational beings. Since the principle of autonomy leads directly to the idea of freedom, its importance for Kant's moral philosophy is central.

IIIa. *The Formula of the Kingdom of Ends*

"Act according to the maxims of a universally legislative member of a merely potential realm of ends." This formula springs directly from the preceding two formulas. Insofar as rational agents are subject to universal laws which they themselves legislate, they constitute a moral commonwealth or kingdom. Since these laws command that all members be treated as ends, the kingdom is a kingdom of ends. These ends include not only persons as ends in themselves, but also the personal ends which each of these may set before himself in accordance with the moral law. As legislative members of such a kingdom, rational agents have 'dignity,' an unconditional worth that has no price. This conception of a kingdom of ends in which each agent is at once the giver and the subject of laws is a picture, in moral terms, of the essence of pure democracy in which freedom and law are reconciled.

The analysis of the Categorical Imperative and its presuppositions constitutes what Kant called the "Metaphysics of morals." It sets forth the characteristics and conditions of a moral action. Since one of the essential characteristics of moral action is the autonomy of the agent, it follows that unless the will of man is free, i.e., capable of being determined by respect for the law, morality is impossible. The justification of morality, therefore, requires a justification of moral freedom.

Moral Freedom

Negatively, freedom means the power of the will to act causally without being determined by external causes. Positively, freedom is the capacity of the will to act under laws that the will itself imposes. Thus conceived freedom is identical with autonomy. Now, as we have seen, morality and autonomy are correlative concepts; the one implies the other and can be derived from it by analysis. The propositions of morality are, however, synthetic, and cannot be established analytically. We cannot use the *concept* of morality to establish the *reality* of autonomy, or vice versa. The argument that "we must be free because we are morally obligated" is fatally circular. In the *Grundlegung* Kant explores the possibility of deducing freedom from the concept of pure practical reason, but in the *Critique of Practical Reason* he abandons this thesis and rests his case for freedom on the recognition of the categorical imperative, arguing that rational agents must presuppose freedom *practically* even if it cannot be demonstrated theoretically. But freedom is not only *practically necessary,* it is also *theoretically possible.* In defense of the latter he reviews the conclusions of the *Critique of Pure Reason* to the effect that man can and must be regarded from two standpoints. In the Kantian theory, nature is a system of appearances or phenomena connected by causal laws. Regarded from the standpoint of natural science, e.g., psychology, man is a part of nature and under its causal determination. But behind nature as a system of phenomena is a real world of things-in-themselves that we do not and cannot know, and behind man as appearance there is "something else as its basis, namely, his ego as it is in itself." This ego must be presupposed as the unifying principle in knowledge (the transcendental unity of apperception), and generally in the pure activity of reason, both theoretical and practical. In the exercise of this "pure activity," the transcendental ego can be and must be conceived as a "kind of causality" which effectively frees a rational agent from causal determination in nature. Hence, viewed as a rational agent man may be presumed to be free, although viewed as a part of nature he is under the mechanism of nature. This double standpoint is an essential feature of Kant's moral philosophy.

The conclusion of the argument, quite apart from moral considerations, is that man can transcend nature and thus be free from its laws while he is at the same time, but regarded from a different standpoint, also a part of nature and determined. As a rational agent he gives laws to himself as a sensuous being. The constraint of these laws over man's natural inclinations is expressed in the categorical imperative. Kant never claims that we can have any theoretical knowledge of the supersensible world in which we are citizens and lawgivers. The proper role of philosophy is to point out that freedom is possible and to expose as merely dogmatic the arguments of determinists and materialists which would undermine the foundations of morality. In the words of the *Critique of Pure Reason,* he "found it necessary to deny knowledge, in order to make room for faith. The dogmatism of metaphysics . . . is the source of all that unbelief, always dogmatic, which wars against morality." Although we cannot demonstrate the reality of freedom and thus 'justify' the categorical imperative theoretically, we can show that freedom is practically necessary and theoretically possible. This, he holds, is all that can "be fairly demanded" of moral philosophy.

Bibliography

English translations of Kant's chief ethical writings:

Kant's Critique of Practical Reason and Other Works on the Theory of Ethics, translated by Thomas Kingsmill Abbott (London, Sixth Edition, 1909).

Immanuel Kant: Critique of Practical Reason and Other Writings in Moral Philosophy, translated by Lewis White Beck (Chicago, 1949).

The Moral Law or Kant's Groundwork of the Metaphysics of Morals, translated by H. J. Paton (New York, 1950).

Discussions:

Lewis White Beck, "Introduction" to *Immanuel Kant: Critique of Practical Reason and Other Writings in Moral Philosophy,* listed above.

H. J. Paton, *The Categorical Imperative* (Chicago, 1949).

Sir David Ross, *Kant's Ethical Theory* (Oxford, 1954).

Paul Arthur Schlipp, *Kant's Pre-Critical Ethics* (Chicago, 1938).

H. H. Schroeder, "Some Common Misinterpretations of Kantian Ethics," *Philosophical Review,* XLIX (1940), 424–46.

J. W. Scott, *Kant on the Moral Life* (London, 1924).

A. E. Teale, *Kantian Ethics* (Oxford, 1951).

Herman A. Brautigam
Colgate University

ard, H. A.; Reid, Thomas; Scheler, Max; Schopenhauer, Arthur; Soviet Morality, Current; Stoics, the.

"Kantian" Marxists: *see* Soviet Morality, Current.

Kaplan, M. M.: *see* Jewish Ethics and Its Civilization.

Karaja Indians: *see* Tapirapé Morals, Some Aspects of.

karma, law of: *see* Zoroastrian Morals.

Karmayoga, doctrine of: *see* China, Moral Philosophies of.

Katcina cult: *see* Rio Grande Pueblo Indians.

Katha Upanishad: *see* Hindu Ethics.

Kautsky, K.: *see* Soviet Morality, Current.

Keith, A.: *see* Primitive Morals.

Kenya: *see* Pakot, the Moral System of.

Keres, the: *see* Rio Grande Pueblo Indians.

Khomiakov, Alexey

The second half of the 19th century was marked in Russia by an important intellectual and religious movement called Slavophilism, of which Alexey Khomiakov, was one of the initiators and most profound spokesmen. This movement, as indicated by its name, sought to restore in Russia the Slav, i.e., the Eastern cultural and spiritual tradition as opposed to Western civilization. This did not mean that the Slavophils rejected Western culture *in toto;* but they felt that this culture had been "imported" and even forced upon Russia, without proper judgment and discrimination. They believed that Peter the Great, who in the early 18th century had transformed Russia into a European, scientifically and technically equipped empire, had done this at the expense of her authentic social, ethical and religious structure. In other words, Peter had *secularized* Russia, and his hastily introduced and drastically applied reforms, had, the Slavophils believed, a disastrous effect on the true Russian way of life. The Slavophils not only criticized Russian "secularization" in the past, but also, and even more, Russian pro-Western tendencies of their own time. Their opponents, who took up the challenge, called themselves "Westerners." Both camps presented an imposing array of intellectual forces: writers, political and social leaders, scientists and philosophers. But the Westerners lacked something which the Slavophils considered the most important element of the true Russian spirit; *religious tradition.*

Well armed in science, and sincerely devoted to humanism the Westerners had embraced the social doctrines of France and Germany. They were West-European radicals, and as such, atheists and agnostics. They believed that Russian- Orthodoxy was the religion of a superstitious, "backward people," unable to improve themselves and others. The most advanced Westerners were adamant against the Church. The more moderate ones (to which belonged the famous novelist I. Turgenev) observed the rites prescribed by Russian ecclesiastical authorities, without considering them essential. Against this background of hostile, sceptic or "blasé" intellectualism, the Slavophilism acquired the colorful, romantic, almost heroic traits of 19th century crusaders. Khomiakov became the fervent disciple of Kireievsky's Slavophil teaching.

Ivan Kireievsky, a talented and original writer, was the senior Slavophil leader. Together with his brother Peter, and a few other gifted authors, such as Konstantin Aksakov, Yury Samarin, joined by Khomiakov, Kireievsky formed the nucleus of Russian national and religious revival *versus* the West. This revival was later developed by Dostoyevsky (see Dostoyevsky) and Soloviev (see Soloviev), who took over the defense of Russian-Orthodoxy against Western rationalism. But neither Dostoyevsky nor Soloviev strictly adhered to original Slavophilism. The movement as such finally deteriorated, after the death of Kireievsky and Khomiakov. In the 80's, Slavophilism became narrowly ritualistic, nationalistic and monarchist. It actually produced a new brand of reactionary Church and State policy, criticized by Soloviev. This later school of Slavophilism had no influence whatever on creative Russian religious and ethical thought: whereas the Slavophil initial group, and especially Alexey Khomiakov, are recognized today as Russia's spiritual authorities, not only by Russian-Orthodox writers, but also by Catholics and Protestants.

Born in 1804, Alexey Khomiakov was the son of a land-owner, and spent most of his childhood in the country. He later studied at Moscow University. After graduation he served in the army, and was noted for excellent horsemanship and endurance. But at heart, Khomiakov was a scholar, and also tried his hand at poetry and drama. Re-

tiring after two years of service, he went abroad, visiting France, Italy, Austria, and other countries. In 1828 he re-enlisted to fight in Russia's war against the Turks. He was known for his courage and at the same time avoiding useless manslaughter. When peace returned, Khomiakov resigned and settled in his family homestead. He married, had several children, and his family life was peaceful and happy. He was very fond of the country, but spent many winters in Moscow, and often went abroad. Most of his time was devoted to study, writing, and philosophical discussions which during those years almost continually went on in Russian intellectual circles. Khomiakov expressed the Slavophil idea in round-table talks, as well as in his essays, poems (which became very popular) and letters to friends sharing his immediate interests.

Compared to the works of other Russian authors and religious thinkers, his writings are by far the least numerous. These writings however, had a tremendous influence on Russian religious philosophy of the late 19th and early 20th century, and up to the 1950's.

Khomiakov's extraordinary prestige is due in part to his excellent academic training and philosophical formation. Though opposed to infatuation with Western culture, he was thoroughly steeped in it. He had personally met abroad prominent Western scholars, among them Schelling. Beside philosophy, he was interested in history, linguistics, mathematics and mechanics. He was the inventor of a steam engine, a rifle, and various gadgets. A brilliant

277

intellectual in Moscow, he was at home an experienced farmer, continually working at the improvement of agricultural methods. He died in 1860.

More important of course, was Khomiakov's religious formation. The first seeds of a deep and fervent faith had been sown by his mother. A woman of exceptional character, she brought up her young son in the best traditions of Russian-Orthodoxy, at the same time inspiring him with a heroic conception of the Christian. At the age of eleven, Khomiakov wanted to be a martyr, and tried, at seventeen, to run away from home, to fight for the liberation of the Greeks. When serving in the army, he insisted on wearing the heaviest equipment, even when relieved of it; this and many other hardships he suffered not merely as a "Spartan," but as an ascetic. He was also known to fast most strictly, far beyond the usual mortifications imposed on Russian-Orthodox laymen.

This profoundly religious attitude in everyday life, was based on his consciousness of Russian-Orthodoxy: a) as a total faith taking hold of the whole man; b) as the true faith of the Russian people which the secularization effected by Peter the Great had weakened and adulterated. This is why he spontaneously adhered to the Slavophil movement, and drew from it extreme implications. He even wanted to give the example of the Russian way of life in his daily routine, wearing Russian national dress instead of European clothes. In spite of these outward preoccupations with Russian popular traditions, Khomiakov was not a nationalist of the fanatical type, as were unfortunately his successors. Neither was he a religious fanatic, blind to the errors and failings of his church. On the contrary, he bitterly criticized it in his writings. Though a champion of Russian-Orthodoxy, and an initiator of its revival, he was *not* favored nor encouraged by the Russian ecclesiastical authorities of his time.

Khomiakov's essay, entitled *The Church is One,* considered his major contribution to Russian religious thought, was written in the 40's, but was published *after* his death, in 1864, when the Church in Russia manifested more leniency than during his life. Very important too, for the understanding of his teaching are his articles concerned with Catholicism and Protestanism, which he refuted in the name of what he considered as the One True Church, i.e., Russian-Orthodoxy. One might conclude, therefore, that Khomiakov's main theological preoccupation was with the Church. But, as we shall see, the Church was in his mind so closely knit with man, both spiritually and morally, that his *ecclesiology* is at the same time an *ethical* system, which informed Russian Christian moralists who followed in his steps. This ethical system is part of a wider range of Russian religious thought, known as *Sobornost:* a word difficult, almost impossible to translate into English, and, for that matter, into other European languages. *Sobornost* hast been best rendered by the term: commonalty (used by Prof. N. Lossky).

Sobornost is an idea founded on two basic principles: the *freedom* of the human person, taken as a separate entity, and the organic whole, formed by the *free* associations of these human entities, an association founded on *Christian love*. This, then, is the *communal body*, i.e., commonalty, expressed by the Russian term "*sobornost*"; (derived from the verb *sobiraty;* to gather together). The communal body *is* the Church, in Khomiakov's mind, and is entirely free, just as each human person is free, and knows no other bond except love, no other authority, than Christ, Who is love incarnate.

The idea of Sobornost was actually first developed by I. Kireievsky, Khomiakov's senior and teacher, who, together with the latter, led the Slavophil movement. Against abstract speculation and scientism, essentially considered as the *sins* of Western civilization, the Slavophils advanced an *organic* idea. This idea was based on the cognition of The Holy Trinity. As Prof. Lossky describes it, this teaching connected the idea of consubstantiality, expressed in the dogma of the Trinity, with the idea that the structure of the created spiritual world also has the character of immediate inner unity. The direct consequences of such a structure are obviously as follows a) moral and religious solidarity and interdependence of all men linked by an 'inner unity;" b) freedom of each of its members, since the link is not natural but supernatural; c) recognition of an order (moral, social, political), determined by absolute values.

Such is Sobornost which Khomiakov took over from Kireievsky and which

under his creative pen, acquired a new, amplified, dynamic content. Khomiakov's concept of inner unity, achieved through love and therefore essentially *free,* is guided by direct and immediate *faith*. In his mind, faith is "an inward consciousness and forms the personality of every man." Lossky defines Khomiakov's concept of faith as "intuition,"[1] while Berdyaev describes it as "religious experience."[2] Khomiakov's philosophy, (Berdyaev tells us) depends upon religious experience to such an extent, that he even speaks of the dependence of philosophical apprehension upon belief in the Holy Trinity.[3] The human will, according to Khomiakov partakes in and is guided by this religious experience *only*. This is why he essentially advocates the will, which is the free will, and therefore "belongs to the sphere of the pre-objective." In other words, as Berdyaev puts it, "the will perceives the existent before rational thought. With Khomiakov, the will is not blind and not irrational, this is not irrationalism but super-rationalism."[4]

From immediate "super-rational" knowledge and will, Khomiakov built his own *ecclesiology,* and at the same time the *ethical* system applicable to every member of Sobornost. The Church, in his mind, i.e., the Russian Orthodox Church, is the ultimate manifestation of Love, binding all its members into the Body of Christ. Therefore, the Church does not mean rules

---

1 Lossky, *History of Russian Philosophy*.
2 Berdyaev, *The Russian Idea*.
3 *Ibid.*
4 *Ibid.*

and regulations. Neither does it mean authority represented by the hierarchy. The Church is the *sum* of all those who through faith and free will are its members. There is no other authority above these members, except Christ.

Catholic and Protestant writers have carefully analyzed Khomiakov's writings, pointing out divergencies and possible convergencies of his doctrine with other established Churches. Fr. Y. Congar suggests that unity through love is also expressed in the Catholic idea of love through the Holy Ghost informing the Church.[5] As to the Protestants, they have Khomiakov's correspondence with the Anglican scholar, Palmer, with whom Khomiakov was in sympathy, at the same time stressing that the Protestant approach to the Bible lacked the mystery of revelation, as described by St. Gregory.[6] Among Western scholars, concentrating on Khomiakov's teaching, the Catholic writer, A. Gratieux, is the most clear and outstanding one, as acknowledged by the Russian-Orthodox themselves.[7]

In Khomiakov's concept, the Church, constituted by *all* its members, is the supreme authority on earth; however, it has no authority *per se*. No hierarchy is the *magister,* Christ alone is the head of the Church, and all the faithful are members of His mystical body.

Because every member is part of its body, and is at the same time entirely free, each member acquires in Sobornost his own, full moral value, i.e., the dignity and freedom of the human person *per se*.

"We are free," writes Khomiakov, "because God wanted this to be so, and because Christ conquered this freedom, through his own free sacrifice in the name of freedom. We would be unworthy of the understanding of Truth, if we did not obtain it freely, if we did not attain to it through heroic effort and the tension of all our moral forces."[8]

To conclude our exposition of Khomiakov's influence on contemporary Russian religious thought, let us recall Berdyaev's "summing up": "Khomiakov had an extraordinary love of freedom and he connected the organic with it. . . . This conception of the organic existed only in the ideal of the future, not in the actual historical past."[8] However, in Khomiakov's mind, this "future" should be striven for *hic et nunc,* (and by each member of the *Ecclesia*). "The unity of the Church is nothing else than the agreement of individual freedom . . . unity and freedom are the two powers to which the mystery of human freedom in Christ is worthily committed."

No Russian religious thinker to date, has more fully expressed the absolute moral value of the individual in connection with the Church. *Sobornost* concerns all men, united in the *Ecclesia* through faith, and *Sobornost* concerns each separate man, as member of Christ's mystical body.

---

[5] Y. Congar. O.D, *Chretiens Desunis.*
[6] Khomiakov, *Essays.*
[7] A. Gratieux, *A. S. Khomiakov et le Mouvement Slavophile.*

---

[8] *Ibid.*

Bibliography

A. Khomiakov, *Complete Works*. In Russian (Moscow 1900–1907).

——, *Izbrannye Sochinenya*. Selected Works. In Russian (Chekhov Publ. New York, 1955).

N. Berdyaev, *Alexey Khomiakov*. In Russian (Moscow, 1912).

——, *Alex. Khomiakov*. In English (Publ. unknown).

N. Zernov, *Three Russian Prophets*. In English (New York, 1937).

A. Gratieux, *A. S. Khomiakov et le Mouvement Slavophile*. In French (Paris, 1939).

Y. Congar, O. P., *Chretiens Desunis*. In French (Paris, 1937). English transl. (New York).

N. O. Lossky, *History of Russian Philosophy* (International University Press, New York, 1951).

Helen Iswolsky
Fordham Institute of Contemporary Russian Studies

Khomiakov, A.: *see* Berdyaev, Nicolas.

Khurshed: *see* Zoroastrian Morals.

Kierkegaard, Soren

About one hundred years ago, in the city of Copenhagen, there died at at the age of forty-two the man who is called "the father of existentialism," Soren Kierkegaard. Except for a few trips to Berlin to hear Schelling's lectures against Hegelian philosophy, he spent his entire life in his native city. He studied philosophy and theology at its university and received his degree from there in 1840. His father had left him a considerable fortune which allowed him to continue his literary and philosophical activity for the rest of his life. As a youth he was an enthusiastic believer in Hegel's philosophy but as he read and reread Hegel's *Logic* his own thought began to formulate itself and broke the spell which Hegel's genius had cast over him. Kierkegaard began to see in Hegel a philosopher who had confused himself with "speculative philosophy in the abstract" and who had forgotten that he was an existing human being. Hegel, according to him, had tried to "walk out of existence into the system" thereby dissipating the only reality an individual has: his own. In the *Concluding Unscientific Postscript* Kierkegaard tells us how he became an author. One Sunday afternoon he was sitting out of doors in a cafe in Copenhagen's Frederiksberg Garden smoking a cigar and lapsing into a reverie. He thought that although he had never been lazy he had never really done anything, either. On the other hand, there were all the prominent figures of his time—much admired and talked about —who tried to make life easier for mankind. Some did so by inventions, others by writing summaries of everything worth knowing and still others by making "spiritual existence systematically easier and easier." And what was he doing? Since the best brains were already busy with simplifying everything, maybe he could with equal energy and enthusiasm make something harder. This notion, he says, pleased him immensely; it was, he felt, the only task left to him and it was one that speculative philosophers and theologians had overlooked because they were too busy with theories concerning nature and the world, and logical proofs for the existence of God. And so his one and ultimate problem he found to consist in this: how to become a man. The question is "What am I to do?" not "What am I to know?" And this simple but overwhelming question is the core of Kierkegaard's work. Everything he wrote serves to illuminate it, everything centers around it. It is as if his works were milestones marking different stages of his own development, by-products of his creative energy which he concentrated on becoming an individual, or as he expresses it on "becoming subjective."

For Kierkegaard this task constitutes the ethical. While in traditional thought different solutions of problems of ethics have been proposed, such as the super-natural solution with its eternal and absolute norms and commands to regulate man's actions, or the rationalistic and naturalistic solutions with their relative standards and values to guide men's activities, Kierkegaard's ethics rejects ready made solutions, it has no dogmas or norms, no generally accepted principles or rules, no objectively valid standards by which to act. Ethical contemplation for Kierkegaard is self contemplation, it is concerned not with mankind like traditional ethics, but with the particular human being, with "each and every one by himself." The first lesson in Kierkegaard's ethics is to learn that the individual stands alone since the only reality with which the ethical deals is the individual's own reality. The ethical question for him is "What it means that you and I and he are human be-

ings, each one for himself." In his Journals he writes: "There are many people who reach their conclusions about life like schoolboys: they cheat their master by copying the answer out of a book without having worked the sum out for themselves." In fact, in Kierkegaard's eyes, the great ethical doctrines of the past, just because they are doctrines or guides for human behavior would not belong to the sphere of the ethical at all and the individual who acts in accordance with them would forever remain on the "aesthetic" level. His choice is not the fruit of his labor since it is based on outward and objective criteria. Of such a man Kierkegaard says in the *Concluding Unscientific Postscript* that even if he should "contrive to reform an entire generation through his zeal and teaching . . . in relation to the ethical he is a deceitful lover; he too is one for whom Judas became the guide; he too sells his God-relationship, if not for money." For Kierkegaard, each individual is confronted with an "Either/Or." *Either* he may lose himself in the concerns of the world, in its pleasures, its achievements, its theories, its sciences and its philosophies, *or* he may be infinitely absorbed with his own self, i.e., with the study of the ethical. The first alternative leads him away from himself into the distant, to abstractions and theories. It may bring him success and money and the admiration of his contemporaries but "exist" he would not since all his endeavors lie in the sphere of objectivity and represent a kind of "dying away from the self." Such a man lives in "immediacy" i.e., as that which he already and accidentally is. His concerns are finite and relative and many. Like "Johannes the Seducer" in Kierkegaard's *Either /Or,* he may be endowed with acute intelligence and encompass the whole world in his reflections. But his very reflections keep him from the concreteness of his existence, he loses himself in them, he does not commit himself to anything in life. He is one of those whose "passions are sleepy," he remains forever a possibility. The second alternative calls him away from the marketplace, back to himself. It will reduce him to nothing in the eyes of the world. He will give up everything for nothing in order to become a particular individual, which, from the objective point of view is absolutely nothing but from the subjective point of view is everything, for "only in the ethical is your eternal consciousness . . . it is the only true and highest significance of a human being, so much higher as to make every other significance illusory; not in and for itself but always illusory if supposed to be the highest." In the strict Kierkegaardian sense only the subjective individual "exists" because only he realizes that his own self is given to him as a possibility, a task and the decision to grasp the possibility, to transform the "posse" into an "esse" is the one and absolute concern of the ethical individual. Such an individual does not look for results, he demands nothing else but the ethical itself. "A truly great ethical personality" Kierkegaard tells us in the *Concluding Unscientific Postscript* would "seek to realize his

life in the following manner: He would strive to develop himself with the utmost exertion of his powers; in so doing he would perhaps produce great effects in the external world. But this would not seriously engage his attention, for he would know that the external result is not in his power, and hence that it has no significance for him, either pro or contra. He would therefore choose to remain in ignorance of what he had accomplished, in order that his striving might not be retarded by a preoccupation with the external, and lest he fall into the temptation which proceeds from it. . . . He would therefore keep himself in ignorance of his accomplishment by a resolution of the will; and even in the hour of death he would will not to know that his life had any other significance than that he had ethically striven to further the development of his own self. If then the power that rules the world should so shape the circumstances that he became a world-historic figure: aye, that would be a question he would first ask jestingly in eternity, for there only is there time for carefree and frivolous questions."

Since the ethical individual transforms the "posse" into an "esse" action is one of the characteristics of the ethical. It is action not as external act but inward activity, the individual identifying himself with the content of his thought in order to exist in it. The ethical individual lives in the strain of becoming, his striving is a passionate tension which is acute suffering. While the aesthetic individual is forever dependent on external facts and accidents, on prosperity and success, the ethical man, since he does not postulate external conditions, is in full control of his existence since he himself creates it. The aesthetic man belongs to the public; he knows the latest theories in science or literary criticism; he may even speak contemptuously of the public and yet belong to it since he is not an individual in the existential sense but loses his self in outward concerns. He has ceased to be an individual and has become an abstraction. It is not by choice that man finds himself in the realm of the aesthetic, he is always already there, precisely because he never made the choice, namely to choose. Despair within him may lead the aesthetic individual to his self choice and the leap into the ethical, he leaves his aesthetic stasis or what he is accidentally, for the "dynamics" of the ethical to become what he is essentially. The ethical individual realizes the possibilities given to him, he gives all his energy to build his self through his actions, i.e., to transform potentiality into actuality. This constitutes his ethical enthusiasm. While "aesthetic pathos" finds its expression in scientific hypotheses or philosophical systems, "ethical pathos" is expressed in the transformation of one's existence, in turning from the outer to the inner world. While aesthetic enthusiasms vary in intensity and depth with the gifts of the individual, ethical enthusiasm is open to all men since all have the same task. "There is no waste of human lives; for even if the individuals were as numberless as the sand of the sea, the task of becoming subjective is given to each."

The realization of his true self constitutes man's contact with the divine. The religious realm therefore hovers on the horizon of the ethical. Man, for Kierkegaard becomes man through his relation to transcendence. The intensity of this relation determines the intensity of existence, the self is constituted in this tension. The ethical individual fights the aesthetic indirectly through his inwardness but he also fights the religious in which he could realize his most authentic possibility, by doing his utmost to defend himself against the decisive form of a higher standpoint, and in the *Concluding Unscientific Postscript* Kierkegaard says of him: "That he should thus defend himself is quite in order, since he is not a standpoint but an existing individual." The self expression of the ethical personality may turn into self-assertion, i.e., the ethical itself may become a temptation. The ethical task is absolute but the individual has aesthetic passions as well and finds himself committed to relative ends. To resolve this conflict a change must come over him, the first step in its direction being the realization of his own inadequacy. He cannot by himself overcome it but needs the help of the divine. The immediate expression for this is suffering which is the mark of the religious sphere as pleasure and enjoyment characterize the aesthetic realm. Suffering has its root in the incommensurability between the finite individual and his infinite task. God is the absolute other and in the face of God the personality is completely invalidated and thus also released from the fulfillment of universal demands, from having to be right or wrong, since he is unable to comply with any. Man, according to Kierkegaard, is man completely and fully when in total isolation he stands in the realization of his own nothingness in the face of God. This is something incomprehensible, paradoxical for the intellect and pure suffering for the spirit. But only then is man reborn and reintegrated. The reintegration is the gift of God and the consequence of the individual's new passion: faith. It is on this level that the suspension of the ethical takes place. The absolute requirement of the ethical is still ever present but the individual is no longer able to fulfill it, not because his striving is imperfect but because there has been a break between him and the divine. His relation to it is no longer one between potentiality and actuality but between possibility and impossibility. "Thus the individual is suspended from the requirements of the ethical in the most terrible manner, being in the suspension heterogeneous with the ethical, which nevertheless has an infinite claim upon him: each moment it requires itself of the individual, and each moment it thereby only more definitely determines the heterogeneity as heterogeneity." This is the Christian "sense of sin." In *Fear and Trembling* Kierkegaard illustrates the ethical and religious spheres with the example of Abraham and Agamemnon respectively. The relationship between Aga-

memnon and his daughter Iphigenia remains within the ethical, the sphere of morality, while the relationship between Abraham and Isaac represents the suspension of it. By no ethical code could Abraham's action be justified. He did not sacrifice his son for the sake of a whole nation as was the case with Agamemnon, but simply for the sake of his personal relationship to God. "He did it for God's sake because God required this proof of his faith; for his own sake he did it in order that he might furnish the proof. The unity of these two points of view is perfectly expressed by the word which has always been used to characterize this situation: it is a trial, a temptation . . . what ordinarily tempts a man is that which would keep him from doing his duty, but in this case the temptation is itself the ethical—which would keep him from doing God's will." Abraham as the individual is lifted above the universal. Agamemnon remains within the sphere of the universal. He gives up what he has for something more certain still and "the whole nation will know of his exploit." But he who gives up the universal for something that is still higher, what if he is mistaken? He renounces everything "he suffers all the pain of the tragic hero, he brings to naught his joy in the world . . . and perhaps at the same time debars himself from the sublime joy which to him was so precious that he would purchase it at any price. Him the beholder cannot understand nor let his eye rest confidently upon him . . ."

Ethical existence is an open kind of existence. It holds no secrets. The ethical individual's relation to God is common to all men in terms of their duty. The religious sphere has its mysteries and its privacies. The God relationship is a personal one. Reason is subjected to faith, self assertiveness to the consciousness of sin.

The how of an individual's existence is a result of his relation to the eternal. When subjectivity is truth then the mode of the relationship determines its truth and not the question of the objective "what" of the relation. This is why the aesthetic individual has forgotten how to exist. He is not himself dialectical but has his dialectic outside himself. He may bring about outward changes but inwardly he remains the same. The ethical individual is inwardly dialectical in self-assertion. If the individual can be defined by self-annihilation before God, if all connection between the individual and the eternal is broken, then we have paradoxical religiousness in which the individual is brought "to the utmost verge of existence." Since the religious individual comprehends the contradiction through suffering and in self-annihilation, he is prevented from becoming abstract as he might if he were a speculative philosopher of Hegel's school who dissolves existence into pure being. The ethical individual too posits the contradiction but only within self-assertion and the aestheticist sees the contradiction not in existence but outside of it and so existence is dissipated. The degree of intensity of existence corresponds to the degree of inwardness the individual has reached and which is brought to the highest pitch on the religious level. Kierkegaard's three stages are perspectives from which to view the transformation of the "knight of despair" into the "knight of faith" who is reconciled to life in its entirety and who pronounces the ultimate "Yes" to existence.

Ria Stavrides
Vassar College

Kierkegaard, S.: *see* French Existentialism and Moral Philosophy. Hegel, G. W. F.

kindness: *see* Aboriginals of Yirkalla; Hindu Ethics; Kant, I.; Muslim Morals; Riffian Morals; Tapirapé Morals, Some Aspects of; Utilitarianism.

King, J.: *see* Primitive Morals.

King, William: *see* Utilitarianism.

kingdom of ends: *see* Kant, I.

Kingdom of God: *see* Berdyaev, Nicolas; Quakerism, Classical, The Morality of; Spinoza.

kingdom of heaven: *see* Christian Moral Philosophy; Dostoyevsky, Fyodor.

Kireievsky, Ivan: *see* Khomiakov, Alexey.

Kluckhohn, Clyde: *see* Mundurucu Indians, A Dual System of Ethics.

knowledge: *see* Aquinas, Thomas, Moral Views of; Cudworth, Ralph; epistemology; Freud, Sigmund; Hindu Ethics; Kant, I.; Liguori, St. Alphonsus and Catholic Moral Philosophy; Major Ethical Viewpoints; Moore, George Edward; Muslim Morals; Prichard, H. A.; Ross Sir (William) David; Stoics, The.

knowledge, three kinds of: *see* Spinoza.

Kollontai, A. M.: *see* Soviet Morality, Current.

Koran: *see* Qurān.

Krylenko: *see* Soviet Morality, Current.

kshattriya: *see* Hindu Ethics.

Kydd, R. M.: *see* Wollaston, William.

L

Labadists, the: *see* Puritan Morals.

labor, manual: *see* Augustine and Morals; Hindu Ethics; Marxist Theory of Morals; Puritan Morals; toil; work.

laissez faire: *see* Green, T. H.; Marxist Theory of Morals.

language: *see* Dewey, John; Major Ethical Viewpoints; Meta-ethics and Normative Ethics; Moore, George Edward; Reid, Thomas; Rio Grande Pueblo Indians; Schlick, Moritz.

Language and Ethics

Those areas of human research which seem, at any moment, to be making the most significant progress become intensely interesting to the philosopher, especially if these successes are the result of the introduction of something new; for the philosopher sees in every useful intellectual device a possible solution of his own perennial problems, and he is quite understandably impressed and intrigued by success, tasting so little of it himself, so regularly the butt of jokes. Sciences may grow by slow and steady accretions, but they more often seem to be driven violently forward by the force of one or a few tightly clustered and signal discoveries. It is these forward leaps which capture the imagination. The philosopher will appropriate from the most active science what seems to him responsible for the advance: the application of another method or a different set of explanatory categories, the construction of a new point of view, or a revised conception of what constitutes a "true" solution to the problems of that science. Consequently, we can quite properly speak of biological and psychological ethics, and more particularly, of evolutionary and behaviorist ethics, for example, and of mathematical, physical, and linguistic ones. The philosopher who borrows in this way has a great advantage, for the devices he is adopting come to his hand already clothed with achievement and surrounded by excitement. They *are* informative. They *cannot* fail. And the theory which is yielded by their use is at once "scientific," up-to-date, and couched in the symbols of success.

Recent developments in mathematics, logic, and the physical sciences, particularly physics itself, have vigorously revived an early Greek belief that philosophical disagreements are basically or even entirely linguistic in character, and that the function of philosophy is, negatively, to eliminate those philosophical problems which draw their life from verbal confusion and vagueness, through the introduction of clarity, rigorous standards of reasoning, and the specification of what can be meaningfully said; and, positively, to serve the various scientific disciplines by standing guard over the character and function of their concepts.

While many of these philosophers are empiricists in the sense that they demand empirical confirmation for the sentences of science, they do not regard philosophy as an empirical discipline, but as an analytic one. Ethics can no longer be defined, as it normally used to be, as the normative science, but takes as its subject matter ethical judgments and their terms; with the result that the recent hold of psychology and the social sciences upon the subject has been temporarily broken.

The degree to which this analytic approach has been accepted by moral philosophers varies considerably, as do the results of their analyses of ethical language, but there is no doubt that some form of "semantic" or "linguistic" method is dominant in ethics today. The most influential theories, beyond the ones dealt with elsewhere in this encyclopedia,[1] are those of Rudolf Carnap, representative of the Vienna Circle positivists, who interprets ethical judgments as imperatives, Stephen Toulmin, who applies the methods of Ludwig Wittgenstein to ethics, and the attitude theory of Charles L. Stevenson.

Carnap regards physics as providing the methodological paradigm for science, and he holds that all knowledge

which pretends to be synthetic is empirical and scientific. There is a criterion for verification such that every sentence, to be verifiable, either asserts something about a "here and now" experience (thereby verified by it), or is deducible from such protocols, or permits them to be derived from it, together with other already verified propositions.

This criterion determines the theoretical sense of any sentence. Value judgments purport to express propositions and contain theoretical sense. The expression, "Killing is evil," for example, is a value judgment expression. From this expression we can derive the following expressions: 1) "Do not kill!" 2) "I wish that there were no killing." 3) "Killing is not a suitable way to further a harmonious community." 4) "Killing is intrinsically evil." Expression (1) is a command and has no theoretical sense. Expression (2) is a statement about a desire or wish. It is a sentence of psychology, not philosophy. Expression (3) is a statement about instrumentality. It has theoretical sense but is primarily a sentence of sociology. Expression (4) is a normative value judgment. It is the kind of expression which belongs to ethics.

But expression (4), like (1), is not a statement. It looks like a statement, as (1) does not, but it is actually equivalent to (1); for "Killing is intrinsically evil" does not assert anything about a "here and now" experience; neither is it deducible from any other proposition making a "here and now" assertion; nor from it can either protocols

---

[1] Consult A. J. Ayer, G. E. Moore, B. Russell and M. Schlick.

or other already verified propositions be determined. Value judgments, therefore, contain no theoretical sense. They are commands in misleading grammatical form.

Statements about values, unless they are descriptions of the values people actually have, are expressions of feeling, and they have the effect of stimulating similar feelings and corresponding volitions in others. They cannot be regarded as making any truth claim (although, of course, they appear to do so), and while they can be obeyed or disobeyed, they cannot be rendered true or false.

Charles L. Stevenson believes that value judgments do have some theoretical, or as he prefers to say, descriptive sense, although they also possess an imperative element. The descriptive meaning of a statement form like "X is good" resides in the assertion it makes about the speaker's attitudes. Whatever a person designates as good, is approved by that person. A statement like "Pacifism is good, but I don't approve of it" is self-contradictory. A value judgment is more than the description of the speaker's or writer's attitudes. It commands his auditors or readers to approve of the same things he does. This is the imperative factor —the emotive, non-cognitive meaning of value judgments. The proper translation of a statement form like "X is good" is "I approve of X; do so as well!" The translation serves as a characterizing formula. It does not pretend to catch the subtle meanings of actual speech. It indicates the kind of meaning present in ethical speech.

In so far as ethical disputes are the result of disagreements of belief, they may be resolved by rational methods. If I hold that slippery elm is bad for the teeth because it contains a powerful acid, explaining to me that no such acid is present may change my belief about slippery elm and so my judgment of it. *Reasons* have been given which help to change my mind, reasons whose relation to my judgment are at least indirectly factual.

It is clear that it is possible to change my mind by an appeal "to the facts," not only because my opinions rest upon them, but because I regard the care of one's teeth to be important—to be good. My disapproval of slippery elm rested upon my approval of "sound" teeth, and my misunderstanding of the facts.

It is doubtful whether all ethical disputes are really instrumental. There appear to be cases in which an appeal to facts would be fruitless, because the attitude expressed by the judgment in such cases is not the result of any rational belief, and perhaps is of a nature incapable of being the subject of rational belief, as one's approval of God in the expression "God is good," for instance. These cases, moreover, seem the really important ones.

The primary purpose of ethical language is to influence feelings, and the attitudes based upon these feelings. Language has this power because its action is causal. The descriptive meaning of a sign is its disposition to produce cognitive mental processes, while the emotive meaning of a sign is its disposition to produce a range of emotions. Since *the* problem of ethics is the resolution of ethical disagreements, and since these disputes are due to opposing feelings, except in those cases where disagreement is grounded in competing beliefs, only the skillful use of emotively charged language, or other non-cognitive measures, can expect success.

Stephen Toulmin directs his attention to the nature of ethical reasoning. We must try to discover what criteria we use in deciding that a reason, offered in an ethical argument to support some conclusion, is a good reason and does support the conclusion, and how such reasons go about lending their support. It is impossible to find criteria for recognizing good reasoning in general, for it is not all alike. We can only discover how scientific reasoning proceeds by examining actual instances. We must do the same for ethics. In so doing, we must be satisfied to give an account of how we recognize valid ethical arguments in individual cases. We cannot generalize for all of ethics.

Our examples are likely to fall into two basic types: those cases in which we try to justify specific acts by appealing to rules which are socially recognized (such as what side of the road one drives on); and those cases in which we seek to justify social practices (practices we accept if we accept the above rules) by an appeal to the social welfare, or what is necessary to the very existence of a community (such as whether to keep promises or not). The criteria appropriate to the criticism of individual acts must not be confused with those appropriate to the criticism of social practices.

As an American citizen, my decision to fight, if called, can be justified by appealing to principles I am accepting in accepting citizenship. The only other relevant reasons, pro or con, must be expressions of other such principles. It may not be entirely correct that one ought, when in Rome, to do as the Romans do, but one ought, *if a Roman*. Any request for a justification for one's going to war, beyond giving reasons expressing accepted principles, is actually a request for a justification of the entire social practice of national defense. The argument now falls outside the context of commitment to special principles, and the appeal can only be to the wider consequence of the community welfare. To persist in requesting a justification is to demand a reason where none can be given, and if this is done from the belief that in science there is no limit to justification, it is mistaken. Nor can this limitation be regarded as a weakness, for there is no need for a "further" justification. The limitation is limiting only in the way a man is limited by his manhood from all true tigerishness, and not in the way he may be limited by the size of his purse in his purchase of a home. The request has no meaning.

The application of linguistic analysis to the problems of philosophy has not produced any specifically "new" conclusions. G. E. Moore reflects the intuitionist tradition; Carnap and Ayer speak anew for Gorgias; Stevenson is indebted, as is Russell, to the ethical writing of Hume; Toulmin accepts a form of utilitarianism. There is no novelty, either, in the general nature of the linguistic method. All its originality resides in the form the method takes in the hands of its most acute practitioners.

Bibliography

R. Carnap, *Philosophy and Logical Syntax* (1935).
A. C. Ewing, *The Definition of Good* (1947).
R. M. Hare, *The Language of Morals* (1952).
C. K. Ogden and I. A. Richards, *The Meaning of Meaning* (1923).
C. L. Stevenson, *Ethics and Language*. (1944).
S. Toulmin, *Reason in Ethics* (1950).

William H. Gass
Purdue University

Lao Tzu: *see* China, Moral Philosophies of.

Latsis: *see* Soviet Morality, Current.

laughter: *see* Jewish Ethics and Its Civilization.

Lauterbach, J. Z.: *see* Jewish Ethics and Its Civilization.

Law, Edmund: *see* Utilitarianism.

law: *see* Clarke, Samuel; Jesuits, the, Moral Theology of; Jewish Ethics and Its Civilization; More, Henry; Roman law; Sophists, the; Soviet Morality, Current; universal laws.

law, eternal: *see* Augustine and Morals; Spinoza.

law, moral: *see* Aquinas, Thomas, Moral Views of; Hammurapi, Code of; Jewish Ethics and Its Civilization; Kant, I.; Muslim Morals.

law, the: *see* Christian Moral Philos-

ophy; Liguori, St. Alphonsus and Catholic Moral Philosophy; Utilitarianism; Zoroastrian Morals.

law and morality: *see* Clarke, Samuel; Hindu Ethics; Marxist Theory of Morals; Puritan Morals; Soviet Morals, Current.

law and order: *see* Dewey, John.

law of inverse variation of strength and height: *see* Hartmann, Nicolai.

law of Israel: *see* Christian Moral Philosophy.

law of Manŭ: *see* Nietzsche, Friedrich.

law of Moses: *see* Hammurapi, Code of; Moses.

law of motivation: *see* Schlick, Moritz.

laws of nature: *see* Kant, I.; Moral Philosophy in America; Soviet Morality, Current; Spinoza; Stoics, the.

Lazarus, Moritz: *see* Jewish Ethics and Its Civilization.

laziness: *see* Aboriginals of Yirkalla; Navaho Morals; Rio Grande Pueblo Indians.

LeClerc: *see* Cooper, Anthony Ashley.

legal codes: *see* Hammurapi, Code of; Soviet Morality, Current.

legal nihilism: *see* Soviet Morality, Current.

legal systems: *see* Muslim Morals.

legalism: *see* Berdyaev, Nicolas; Jewish Ethics and Its Civilization; Quakerism, Classical, The Morality of.

legalization of morality: *see* Soviet Morality, Current.

Legalist School: *see* China, Moral Philosophies of.

legislation: *see* Green, T. H.; Hammurapi, Code of; Jewish Ethics and Its Civilization; Soviet Morality, Current.

Lehm Kuhl, A.: *see* Jesuits, the, Moral Theology of.

Leibniz, G. W.: *see* Clarke, Samuel; Cooper, Anthony Ashley; Cudworth, Ralph; Goethe, Johann Wolfgang von.

Lenin, V. I.: *see* Marxist Theory of Morals; Soviet Morality, Current.

Leonardo: *see* Goethe, Johann Wolfgang von.

Lessing: *see* Cooper, Anthony Ashley.

Lessuis, L.: *see* Jesuits, the, Moral Theology of.

lewdness: *see* Hindu Ethics.

lex talionis: *see* Hammurapi, Code of; Jewish Ethics and Its Civilization; Zuni Indians, Morals of.

Li Ssu: *see* China, Moral Philosophies of.

liberality: *see* Aristotle.

liberation: *see* Hindu Ethics.

libertarianism: *see* Soviet Morality, Current.

liberty: *see* Aquinas, Thomas, Moral Views of; Jesuits, the, Moral Theology of; Liguori, St. Alphonsus and Catholic Moral Philosophy.

liberty, religious: *see* Quakerism, Classical, The Morality of.

liberty, spiritual: *see* Zoroastrian Morals.

Lien Tzu: *see* China, Moral Philosophies of.

lies: *see* lying; Soviet Morality, Current.

life insurance: *see* Price, Richard.

Liguori, St. Alphonsus and Catholic Moral Theology

The most noted and authoritative moral theologian in the Roman Catholic Church is Alphonsus de' Liguori.

In unique ways the Church has sealed with approval his life and work. On July 5, 1831, the Sacred Penitentiary in Rome issued a decree stating that all the moral opinions set forth by Alphonsus could safely be followed in the confessional. This tribute was singular, accorded to no other moral theologian in the history of the Church. However, it was not intended to include any opinions which subsequently might be rejected by the Church. On May 26, 1839 Alphonsus de' Liguori was declared a saint. Such a distinction constitutes the Church's authoritative and infallible statement that the soul of the canonized person has been admitted to the happiness of heaven. Pope Pius IX on July 7, 1871, numbered St. Alphonsus among the Doctors of the Church and declared the saint particularly renowned for his wisdom in moral theology. On April 26, 1950 Pope Pius XII declared St. Alphonsus the patron saint of confessors and moral theologians. This last honor places the vast labor of guiding souls in the Church through the Sacrament of Penance under the special protection and intercession of this renowned doctor and saint of the eighteenth century.

Alphonsus Maria de' Liguori was born at Marianella near Naples on the 27th of September 1696. His family was of the Naples nobility, his father being a captain of the Royal Galleys. Don Joseph dreamed great dreams of worldly success and prestige for his son. With this view in mind he guided Alphonsus into the legal profession. Here were seen the shadows of the great mind that had come to shed light in the confusion of the eighteenth century. At the early age of sixteen—four years below the required twenty—Alphonsus brilliantly acquired a doctorate in both laws, civil and canon, at the University of Naples.

Eight years of legal practice followed. Things boded well for Don Joseph's dream. But at this time the young lawyer struck a crisis which was to change the entire course of his life. He had prepared a case for a prominent client in a litigation over property rights. With the certain confidence of a man who has labored long and astutely over his brief, Alphonsus argued his case point by point through the maze of technical law. All were in awe of his ability. All but his opponent. Alphonsus had missed one technicality which should have been obvious. This changed the complexion of the entire case. He lost.

The first reaction of confusion, chagrin and despondency gave way to a new and deeper realization. He began to question his motives. Was he too greatly attached to his career, to his personal success and glory? Were these the things for which a man should be striving? Was this the road to his soul's salvation, to God's honor and not his own?

After much pondering, prayer and wise counsel, Alphonsus changed the direction of his entire life. He renounced the legal profession, despite his father's protests. God was his greater father. In 1726 he was ordained to the priesthood.

To evaluate the work of Alphonsus de' Liguori as a priest, one must appreciate the blending of so much outstanding talent in one personality, a personality passionately devoted to God and the things of God. Alphonsus possessed the great culture of his lineage, the religious conviction of a great people. He combined learning, artistic abilities, native Italian shrewdness, a warm sympathetic understanding, the ability to think and carry out great plans for God and the Church. He was never at rest. It is known that he took a vow never to waste a moment of time. Not content to be a dynamic force for good himself, he founded a congregation of priests that would keep his great spirit alive down through the centuries. This group has grown into the world-wide Redemptorist Congregation, a society which profits by the wisdom and holiness of its founder and is pledged to imitate his zeal in laboring for the spiritual welfare of mankind.

Alphonsus wrote unceasingly—theological, ascetical, devotional works. In his moral writings we have the man at his best. He wrote principally to guide young priests along a safe way in moral theology at a time when moral error was rampant. Both Jansenism with its rigorist religious teaching and the materialistic ideas of the French atheists were flooding Italy. The works of Alphonsus rose like a beacon light guiding troubled priests in their direction of souls. Here was a man moored to the eternal verities with the saintly and legal genius to hold essentials sacred while wisely adapting accidentals to his turbulent times.

His principal work in the field of morality was *Theologia Moralis,* the first edition of which appeared in 1748, and which he revised several times in the course of his lifetime. The most critical edition of this work, richly annotated, is published in four large tomes (See Bibliography).

Of course he had his critics. He was roundly taken to task for being too lax in an age of irrational rigorism, for over-stressing purity and chastity while the world gave vent to license, for being a casuist in the wrong sense of the word—this because the concrete problems of his age were so much a part of his concern. No one man who has read his scientific moral treatises could countenance this latter criticism.

The saint lived a long full life. He died on August 1, 1787, a bishop of the Catholic Church and Superior General of the Congregation of the Most Holy Redeemer.

The greatest tribute to the moral theology of St. Alphonsus is the acclaim of the ages. His work has lived and flourished. In the shifting of the years his wisdom and norms were usable practical tools, modern tools. So much so, that the Church has lauded him continually, theologians consult him in all difficulty, confessors lean on his opinions with gratitude and confidence.

Before discussing the particular moral system of St. Alphonsus, it is well to have the basic tenets of Catholic moral theology in perspective. Only in the light of these can a moral system be understood and evaluated.

Morality is not a wholly relative science, as many think today. It is rooted in absolute values, which are as immutable as God himself. And to deny the immutability of God, is to deny the very idea of God and to leave the world to the chaos of atheism.

Catholic moral theology presupposes three basic principles, demonstrated in fundamental theology:

1. There is an immutable, all-perfect God.
2. God has freely created man, an intellectual and free being with an immortal soul.
3. Man is ordained to God as his ultimate end in life.

The basic norm for judging human activity—which is activity of man as man, that is, action proceeding from knowledge and free will—is the ultimate end or purpose which God had for man in creating him. This purpose specifies the nature of man, and through this specification, the moral activity of man. To change the ultimate purpose of man, as intended by God, would entail changing man's nature, so that man would no longer be man. It becomes important to determine why God has made man.

Reason can infer that man has been created to know, to love and to serve his Creator, in the present life and to be happy with Him forever in the life beyond the grave. This is made clearer by God's own message to man. The burden of the New Testament is to tell man what the ultimate purpose of his life and activity are. "Beloved, now we are the children of God and it has not yet appeared what we shall be. We know that when he appears, we shall be like to him, for we shall see him just as he is." (*I John*, 3:2, 3), "Even as he (God) chose us in him (Christ) before the foundation of the world, that we should be holy and without blemish in his sight. In love he predestined us to be adopted through Jesus Christ as his sons, according to the purpose of his will unto the praise of the glory of his grace with which he has favored us in his beloved Son." (*Ephesians*, 1:6). "Blessed is the man who endures temptation; for when he has been tried, he will receive the crown of life which God has promised to those who love him." (*James*, 1:12).

Elevated by supernatural grace, man is destined through knowledge and love of God to be intimately united with God in an eternal union of knowledge and love. This destiny or purpose, decreed by God, is what ultimately determines the morality of man's human activity. All man's actions consonant with that goal are morally good and bring him closer to it; all man's actions not in harmony with that goal are morally bad and turn him from it, thus endangering his eternal salvation. Here we have the basic demarcation between good and evil, virtue and vice.

But what are the norms man has whereby he can know what path will lead him to his ultimate destiny and what deter him? In general there are two such norms: law, which is the external objective rule, conscience, the internal subjective rule.

Law is an ordination of reason for the common good, made by him who has the care of the community, according to the definition of St. Thomas Aquinas (*Summa Theologiae*, I–II, Q. 90, art. 4). The source of all law, for He has care of the entire human race, is God. The law as an ordination of intellect in God is called the Eternal Law. Such law has its fount and roots in the divine essence or immutable nature of God. It is an aspect of divine wisdom, insofar as such law is the directive of all created activity to its ultimate end. As far as man is concerned, this Eternal Law is applied in three ways, through natural law, divine positive law and finally human positive law.

The natural law is man's participation in the Eternal Law as it is found in man's essential makeup or in his human nature. Human nature, as the Creator has intended it for temporary existence in this life and eternal existence in the life to come, determines the acts to be performed as morally good or to be omitted as morally bad by the person possessing such a nature. (We qualify this statement in favor of the supernatural laws which will be additionally necessary for man to achieve his supernatural destiny. This will be treated later). Through the humble and honest use of his rational powers, by studying human nature adequately taken, man can come to some knowledge of his rights and obligations rising from his relationship to his Creator, his fellow man and to himself. Thus it is through human nature as constituted by God that natural law is determined and manifested to men.

However, even this purely natural law is not in the present state of man easily knowable in all its details by human reason. This is because of original sin. The punishment of all mankind, with two exceptions, Jesus Christ and Mary his Mother, incurred as a result of original sin, included a wounding and weakening of the human principles of operation. The intellect no longer knows even natural truths with its full potential, nor does the will elect what is truly good with its pristine vigor. As a result man does not come to a full knowledge of the natural law by his unaided human reason. The primary principles of the natural law are indeed sufficiently evident, as are proximate conclusions; but more remote conclusions and logical deductions are often not clearly perceived by man's wounded intellect. A man can clearly know he must do good and avoid evil; he can know, if he has average intelligence, that only in matrimony is it lawful to procreate children; but his knowledge may be vague as to the morality of divorce, or of the legality of euthanasia. Revelation and divinely authorized interpretation of the law are necessary for man to know in its entirety even this purely natural phase of God's law for men.

By his natural power of intelligence man can only know God as the author of creation. But divine revelation tells us man is ultimately destined to attain God in his most intimate being and to love him in this supernatural order. Human nature alone is not adequate for such knowledge and love. There must be an additional source of knowledge, of power and activity, and finally a new law arising from these. This additional knowledge is found in revelation, containing the divine positive law as found in Sacred Scripture and in the Sacred Tradition as handed down from Christ through his apostles and authentically interpreted by the Roman Catholic Church. This divine positive law builds on the natural law, thus regulating the whole edifice of man seeking his supernatural purpose in life.

There is one further refinement of the objective norm of morality. That is the human positive law, which is the particular clarifications of the natural law and the divine positive law as adapted to time and place. Its purpose is to protect the common good by facilitating the understanding and observance of the more basic laws through particularization and safeguards. This law leads man more surely to his final destiny. The ruling bodies of Church and State are commissioned by God to make such positive laws and those subject to these laws must obey them in conscience.

These laws, then, are the objective exterior norms of morality. However, the difficulty of reading the law into particular situations still confronts every individual, even though the general terms of law may be known. Is there a law for this situation? If there is, can it be said to bind under these concrete circumstances? Will fear or force mitigate its binding force? Does this person have sufficient knowledge of the law to render it obligatory for him? These and untold questions arise from the law and its relation to the human act. This is the field of the moral theologian.

Thus far the law. But it is external and objective. It is a norm or rule by which man can measure the conformity or non-conformity of his actions with his final destiny. But what of the process by which the individual holds this rule up to his own actions, performed or intended, and judges whether he is free or bound by the law? This process is found in the functioning of man's own intellect through the act of conscience.

The intellect of man, as regards morality, first knows most general principles of morality—one must do good and avoid evil; God is to be honored. Such a basic knowledge of law is called synderesis. Through a further process of reason man attains more definite principles of moral knowledge, conclusions from general principles. For example, it is evil to dishonor God by blasphemy. This further refining of moral knowledge is called moral science. The intellect then applies the knowledge derived through synderesis and moral science to a particular given situation confronting the individual himself and forms a practical judgment that this action is in conformity with the ultimate end or is not. In other words, the individual decides that if he follows a certain course, he will do good or evil. This judgment is conscience. On the way in which he follows his conscience or departs from it, man will be judged by God. It has the final word in the moral activity and responsibility of man.

Conscience may be correct, that is, in conformity with the objective external norm of law; or it may be er-roneous, not in conformity with the objective norm. An erroneous conscience may be invincibly erroneous, in that suitable effort in seeking the truth has been attempted, but has failed to bring one to the objective truth. On the contrary, it mistakenly judges good for evil, or vice versa. If so, then a man must follow such a conscience. He must follow what to him seems true. Thus, subjectively, he acts in good conscience and will not be held accountable for his mistake by God. But an erroneous conscience may be vincibly so. Here proper diligence would dispel error and bring the judgment into line with the objective norm of law, but the individual has failed to give this diligence. To act with a vincibly erroneous conscience is wrong and not in keeping with right reason, since the possibility of error has not been reasonably excluded.

In any problem of conscience there are two propositions from which a choice is to be made. One is for law, one for liberty. If there are sufficient reasons for the mind to adhere to one proposition, say the one for liberty, without reasonable fear that the other proposition, for law, might be true, then the conscience is said to be certain. If the mind cannot decide which proposition is true, so that it is in suspended judgment, then such a conscience is said to be doubtful. Ordinarily a man would not be acting reasonably, or in conformity with his ultimate purpose in life were he to act in favor of liberty with a doubtful conscience without first making further inquiry. Such a man would be exposing himself to unreasonable danger of violating the law. For instance, a man has a real and positive doubt whether or not divorce is permitted by God's law. For him to seek a divorce in such a state of doubt would be most unreasonable because of the probable danger of violating God's law and of endangering his salvation. He must endeavor to solve the problem by seeking objective truth.

At times, however, the doubt persists even after a thorough inquiry, and the question arises whether a person, in such a situation, can form sufficient certitude in favor of liberty if he has a good (though not fully convincing) argument for the permissibility of such a course. Certainly, in matters so abstruse as concrete problems of morality we could not expect the Almighty to require so great a degree of certainty for the permissibility of an act as, for example, the certainty one has that two and two make four or that Washington was our first President. Ordinarily, only practical moral certainty, which can be based on solid probability, is required to justify a person in choosing to act in favor of liberty.

The question of certain and doubtful conscience bring us to the question of moral systems. How much certitude does one need in favor of liberty in order to act honestly and reasonably with the conviction that he is morally free to act thus? What set of rules can be devised for forming a certain conscience? These are the questions a moral system seeks to answer. The natural law, the divine positive law, the human positive law all open up many questions upon which innumerable cases of conscience may be based. In all these cases there are reasons to believe a law binds, and yet there are reasons to believe that one is not bound by the law. It behooves the moral theologian to study these cases and to determine, if possible, which side has sufficient weight to win intellectual acceptance. And even more basically, the theologian must determine just what degree of certitude is necessary for a licit judgment of conscience in favor of liberty. In other words, when a person is confronted by the problem: "Am I allowed to perform this act or is there a law against it?" how much certainty must he have that he may be allowed to perform the act with a safe conscience?

There are several moral systems in Catholic theology. Their differences hinge on what constitutes sufficient certitude for licit action and what degree of probability is necessary to override probable reasons for the opposite proposition. We shall treat only that of St. Alphonsus, which is called equiprobabilism.

There are important distinctions to be made with regard to certitude. Certitude, first of all, can be had on a speculative or on a practical level. Speculative certitude is concerned with the truth arising from the nature of an action in itself. Practical certitude is concerned with the lawfulness of performing a particular action here and now. A speculative doubt can and often does exist together with practical certitude. For example, a man may not be able to determine speculatively whether or not he is paying just wages to his employees, yet he must determine some reasonable wage on a practical norm of action. Because of the nature of moral activity, with its daily demands for relatively immediate action, theologians have reasonably concluded that God demands only practical certitude for moral action.

Practical certitude is based on probabilities. It does not exclude a speculative prudent fear that the opposite opinion may be true, but it does exclude a practical prudent fear that the opposite opinion may be true. For example, in the case of the just wage, cited above, an employer simply may not be able to make the sociological studies to determine with complete certitude an objectively just wage, nor if he had such studies at hand already, would he necessarily be speculatively certain that they were accurate. Yet the problem of paying wages is immediate and demanding. So he must pay a wage which appears just, at least with good probability. He would fail against justice if he gave a wage so low, that there was only a slight probability of its justice.

Practical certitude is reached in one of two ways. First, from intrinsic arguments arising from the very case of conscience in doubt. For example, a man may doubt whether he can claim certain exemption in his income tax. The arguments arising from the wording of the law and the nature of the particular expenditure in question incline him to regard it as practically certain that such an expenditure comes under the heading of charity. Acting on those arguments as a norm for practical action, he deducts that amount from his tax. Such a man acts licitly on the practical certitude reached through intrinsic argumentation. It must be clearly understood that this is the top level of certitude that can be reasonably reached in the particular circumstances. But practical certitude may also be attained through extrinsic arguments or from reflex principles. After examining all the intrinsic arguments, pro and con, a man may still have a doubt of conscience, in that the intrinsic arguments just about balance one another. Such a man may yet resolve his conscience by calling on general principles of morality extrinsic to the particular case. For example, a man several years ago may have filed his income tax. He has no record of it now, nor can he reasonably get one. Yet at this present time he has a doubt whether or not he accounted certain receipts in his income of that year. He is unable to resolve the doubt on an intrinsic level. But by citing an extrinsic moral norm or reflex principle, he can come to extrinsic practical certitude. In this case the norm would be: if the major fact is rightly done (the filing of the income report in good conscience at the time), then all subordinate factors (the particular phase of his income he is now in doubt about) are presumed rightly done. Such a man has practical certitude that he has paid his full tax. Extrinsic principles must be based on an objective study of the ways of divine and human law, and the cases that come under the law.

However, there are certain areas

where no Catholic theologian will permit the use of the moral systems of probabilities. Probable certitude may not be used when there is danger of the nullity of a sacrament, grave spiritual or temporal harm to oneself or one's neighbor. For example, a druggist may not sell medicine to a customer if there is even a slight probability that it contains poison, even though it is much more probable that it is good medicine.

What reflex principles have validity in resolving a doubt on the basis of extrinsic practical certitude? Here will be found divergence of opinion among the various moral systems. The equi-probabilism of St. Alphonsus holds basically the following:

1. If there is a strict doubt (that is, a doubt in which the arguments for both sides are about equal), then freedom is in possession, when the doubt concerns the existence of the law, at least for the individual in doubt. One need not obey.

2. If there is a strict doubt about the cessation of a law (a doubt whether or not a law that surely bound one still binds), then the law is in possession, and must be fulfilled.

3. It is not licit to follow an opinion for liberty, when the opinion for law is certainly more probable. On this point many Catholic theologians disagree with St. Alphonsus, contending that a probable opinion for liberty may be followed even though the opinion for law is certainly more probable.*

This in basic principles is the system of equi-probabilism as advocated by St. Alphonsus. A further treatment of the system and of basic Catholic teaching on morality may be found in the works given below.

Bibliography

Theologia Moralis Sancti Alphonsi, editor, P. Leonard Gaudé, C.Ss.R. (Romae, 1912).
Aertnys-Damen, C.Ss.R., *Theologia Moralis* (Marietti, Turin, 1950).
Austin Berthe, C.Ss.R., *Life of Saint Alphonsus de' Liguori* (Dublin, 1905).
Henri Renard, S. J., *The Philosophy of Morality* (Milwaukee, 1953).
Kannengieser, "Alphonse de Liguori," *Dictionnaire de Theologie Catholique* (Paris, 1930), I, col. 906–19.
Ryan, *The Norm of Morality* (Washington, D.C., 1946).

Francis J. Connell

The Catholic University of America
limitation: *see* Goethe, Johann Wolfgang von.
Lippmann, W.: *see* Primitive Morals.
literalism: *see* Jewish Ethics and Its Civilization; Puritan Morals.
Livingstone, D.: *see* Primitive Morals.
Locke, John: *see* Clarke, Samuel; Cooper, Anthony Ashley; Cudworth, Ralph; Hume, David; Hutcheson, Francis; Moral Philosophy in America; Price, Richard; Reid, Thomas.
logic: *see* Balguy, John; Meta-ethics and Normative Ethics; Spinoza.

* The argument for this principle of St. Alphonsus is that the human mind is bound to seek truth, and when it cannot discover what is certainly true it should choose the opinion more likely to be true.

logic, Stoic and Aristotelian: *see* Stoics the.

logical empiricism: *see* Ayer, Alfred J.

logical positivism: *see* Ayer, Alfred J.; Major Ethical Viewpoints; Moral Philosophy in America.

Logicians, The (Chinese): *see* China, Moral Philosophies of.

logos: *see* Hegel, G. W. F.; Stoics, the.

longevity: *see* Rio Grande Pueblo Indians.

love: *see* Aquinas, Thomas, Moral Views of; Aztec Morals; Berdyaev, Nicolas; Butler, Joseph; China, Moral Philosophies of; Christian Moral Philosophy; Clarke, Samuel; Cooper, Anthony Ashley; Cudworth, Ralph; Dante, Alighieri; divine love; Dostoyevsky, Fyodor; Eucken, Rudolf; French Existentialism and Moral Philosophy; Freud, Sigmund; Hindu Ethics; Jewish Ethics and Its Civilization; Khomiakov, Alexey; Liguori, St. Alphonsus and Catholic Moral Philosophy; Major Ethical Viewpoints; Moral Philosophy in America; More, Henry; Muslim Morals; Plato; Puritan Morals; Quakerism, Classical, The Morality of; Ross, Sir (William) David; Schopenhauer, Arthur; Spinoza; Stoics, the; Tapirapé Morals, Some Aspects of; Tolstoy, Leo; universal love; Zoroastrian Morals.

love, perfect: *see* Augustine and Morals.

love of enemies: *see* Hammurapi, Code of.

love of God: *see* Augustine and Morals.

Lowies, R. H.: *see* Primitive Morals.

loyalty: *see* allegiance; China, Moral Philosophies of; Jewish Ethics and Its Civilization; Marxist Theory of Morals; Moral Philosophy in America; Navaho Morals.

Loyola, Ignatius: *see* Jesuits, the, Moral Theology of.

luck: *see* Aztec Morals.

Lunacharski: *see* Soviet Morality, Current.

lust: *see* Cudworth, Ralph; Dante, Alighieri; Dostoyevsky, Fyodor; Hindu Ethics; Tolstoy, Leo.

lusts: *see* Augustine and Morals.

Lutheranism: *see* Puritan Morals.

luxury: *see* Jewish Ethics and Its Civilization.

Luzzatto, Moses: *see* Jewish Ethics and Its Civilization.

Lycophron: *see* Sophists, the.

lying: *see* Augustine and Morals; Aztec Morals; deceit; falsity; Hindu Ethics; Kant, I.; lies; Navaho Morals; Pakot, The Moral System of; Puritan Morals; Riffian Morals; Rio Grande Pueblo Indians; Stoics, the; Tapirapé Morals, Some Aspects of.

M

Macaulay: *see* Utilitarianism.
Mach: *see* Soviet Morality, Current.
Machiavelli, Niccolo

Culturally pre-eminent, the Italy Machiavelli knew was politically divided, militarily impotent, and morally corrupt. The institutions which had served Italy and its people throughout the Middle Ages now functioned poorly or not at all, and a rapidly changing political, economic, and intellectual climate was draining the ideals these institutions represented of all relevance. The Middle Ages had placed in a dominating position the idea of a religiously dedicated and morally informed life—a life, for all its narrowness, intolerance, and contradiction, which could be righteous, rich, and orderly; for if one's being was not secure from priest or bandit, princeling or plague, one's reason for being was; if there was promise only of a short life here, there was also promise of a life everlasting; and if men were in no discernible way better than they had been before, when they were without the Father and his Son, the way of salvation now was open, the prospect of glory was clear, and it stretched radiantly forever; while rite and ideal, the hero, the beloved, the God, symbol and meaning, were carved in stone and limmed in tile and glass, for worship, along its path.

The church, the fiefs, the guilds and communes had absorbed the individual, finding him a station, a manner of life, a set of values and beliefs. With remarkable swiftness, and for innumerable reasons, in Italy, these beliefs became untenable. The values grew obsolete. The accustomed life proved impossible; and the accepted station was found to be profitless, senseless, and full of new dangers. From all the restrictions, safeguards, and guarantees which made medievalism, the individual was suddenly released. No path was marked. The strong might hew his own. No man's place was sacred. Any might steal or buy it, and a Borgia became Pope.

Machiavelli, as diplomat and historian for the city of Florence, watched with both his contemporary and his historical eyes the bloody struggles of audacious and ambitious men whose only object was the acquisition of power in every form in which power was possible: wealth, dominion, learning, art. These men came from everywhere. The Medici were bankers, the first Borgia a bishop. Piccinini was a butcher, Carmagnola a herdsman, the first Sforza a field-laborer and stable-boy. Machiavelli was to be famed for the hard, clear, completeness of his perception, but even he was blinded by the spectacle of bloodshed and terror these men mounted, until Italy was one great academy of murder, manslaughter and deceit, of which Machiavelli's own history of Florence is one of the coldest and most appalling records. The city-states of Italy were continually at one another's throats. Milan and Venice had wars innumerable. The Papacy was bought and sold, as were the Papal favors. Thrones were overturned by ignorant barbarians and stolen by cultured thieves. Naples had five kings in three years. Captains, princes, bankers, with fine indiscrimination, were thrown from windows, assassinated in cathedrals, garroted in dungeons, poisoned at table. No one was immune to the dagger, and the man who played longest at this deadly game was one who calculated the profit to his power of every breath; who never took offense but weighed the cost, and never gave it but counted up the gain; who, with Egyptian persistence, and a thoroughly complete and pagan knowledge of the ways of man, kept ever to his single aim: the securing, maintenance, and exercise of power.

It is not surprising, in the face of the ruin that was Italy, that Machiavelli failed to see how most men's hearts were still medieval, including, in so many ways, his own. Because he observed it daily, in the captains, cardinals, and kings he dealt with, Machiavelli concluded that men were governed by their passions and their inclinations. They desire everything, he thought, but cannot attain it; therefore they find themselves in continual discontent. Anger and envy and eager greed twist their judgment and destroy their peace. They are driven from one ambition to another; unsafe in their power, always fearful of loss and desirous of gain, either augmenting their wealth or preserving it, they secure themselves against attack in order to attack others; and they must rewin their fortunes daily and safeguard their kingdoms by perpetual reconquest.

The common men are better than their princes, but they are readily corrupted. They are prompt to blame and slow to praise. They see no further than the goods or evils of the present, and so are entirely taken with appearances and results. They are simply flattered, and easily duped. They ask only that they do not feel oppressed. Nor do religion and morality influence the motives of men. Machiavelli could not help but observe that the interests of the Papacy were purely secular, and like the interests of the other Italian principalities. Moreover, Rome, with Venice, stood to profit most from a weak, divided peninsula. So Machiavelli sensed no reformation.

Everywhere, then, personal ambition, with an assist from chance, directed the course of events, and there was a measure of order, peace, and security only where one strong man united a city or a nation. The French and Spanish people got no credit from Machiavelli for their relatively peaceful countries, for they too were corrupt, and would go the way of Italy if they did not have a king who kept them united.

Thus Machiavelli could only conclude that traditional morality and religion, if practiced faithfully by a prince (and Machiavelli gravely doubted whether a prince could continue long before being overcome by his humanity), would in these times deliver himself and his people into the brutal hands of their enemies, and run their lands, wealth, and culture to destruction.

Of an old Tuscan family, Machiavelli was born in 1469 near Florence, although history saw him first at the age of 29, when he entered the service of the Republic as the secretary of the Florentine war office. He was a witness, as a youth, to the tyrannies of the Medici and of Savonarola, who went to the scaffold a few months after Machiavelli took up his secretarial duties. Soon he was being sent on diplomatic missions, and these steadily increased in importance until he had the most confident trust of the heads of the Florentine state. His dispatches were regarded as models of what such dispassionate reports should be. Among those Machiavelli was set to watch was the Duke of Urbino, Caesar Borgia. This man Machiavelli came to admire to a degree dangerous for a diplomat. Imagination, indeed dream, mingled with fact, even in such a factual man as Machiavelli was, and the perceived Borgia became a creature of theory, an archetype, the prince of *The Prince*.

In 1512 the Medici returned to Florence, upsetting the Republic Machiavelli had served and loved, imprison-ing him for a time—a time he chose for the composition of sonnets. Forcibly retired to private life, he devoted himself to study, completing *The Prince* in 1513, and the first three books of his commentary on the history of Titus Livy (known as the *Discourses on the First Ten Books of Titus Livy*), a work he never concluded. He finished *The Art of War* in 1520, and in that year was commissioned to write a history of Florence, of which he completed eight books before his death. In 1525, Machiavelli returned to public life for a short but bitter time, and died on the 22nd of June, 1527.

Machiavelli has no moral *system*. Despite his reputation as a teacher of evil, he accepts, on the whole quite uncritically, the standard virtues. He does not attempt, as Nietzsche did, a transvaluation of values. He thinks charity, integrity, humanity, uprightness, and piety to be fine things. He has greater reservations about humility and the medieval emphasis upon the contemplative life, but these reservations are characteristic, and actually applicable to all the virtues he admires—they make men easy prey.

There are three principal reasons for Machiavelli's black reputation. The first is that he became known to Elizabethan poets and playwrights through a misrepresenting French attack on him by a man named Gentillet which appeared in English in 1577. Ironically, Machiavelli was associated in English minds with Popery, and through the figure of Catherine de'-Medici with the St. Bartholomew Massacre. With Marlowe's Barabas, the cruel, scheming Italinate villain obtained an overwhelming popularity with English audiences, the type culminating in the figure of Shakespeare's Iago. These characters were generally so overdrawn, however, that Ben Jonson was soon parodying them successfully. The second reason is that Machiavelli's work itself is often chilling. He sustains a matter of fact, unperturbed, reportorial tone in the face of the most harrowing narrative circumstances. It is not so much what Machiavelli praises or blames that shocks people. It is the absence, throughout, even when praise or blame are levied, of any *feeling* of moral approval or condemnation. The impression is sometimes conveyed, for all Machiavelli's magnificence of style, and greatness of mind, that the author of what you read is inhuman; that he appreciates too indifferently well the relative skills of peaceful mediation and bloody execution; so that in the final chapter of *The Prince,* where Machiavelli exhorts his imaginary savior to deliver Italy from the foreigner, the emotion seems incongruous and displeasing. Finally, Machievelli does appear, at times, to be recommending immoral practices. This is felt the worse because Machiavelli does not claim to be redefining the good, or even lifting his Prince beyond the touch of good and evil; for he always declares directly this or that act's evil character, even when he regards it as necessary. It may be *unfortunately* necessary, but it *is* evil.

What Machiavelli clearly saw was that morality and religion, and all the values which were their consequences, could not be practiced, nor the consequences gained, in an environment which supported no settled beliefs, no long term plans for ordinary men, no real hope for a peaceful and relatively happy life, no guarantee of those essential safeties which permit the multitude to rise above the condition of beasts. Power, in Italy, was in movement. No one could be certain where it might next collect. Unless power is brought to rest, and placed in the hands of a few (or as Machiavelli preferred, a single king), it will, like an unruly sea, wreck all petty states and drown all decency.

No moral scruples should be permitted to interfere with any measures necessary to the safety of the state; for morality cannot extend itself beyond the borders of the moral environment. In this sense, Machiavelli judges political acts by their utility. Will they strengthen and preserve the state or not? But the reason for preserving the state is not so that the Prince can despoil it or flatter himself with rank or station or preen himself before the multitude. It is because the values of the other-worldly, contemplative, medieval scheme of things can *now* only be regained by the careful practice of thoroughly pagan virtues and knowledge. It is good for a prince to have all the virtues (although Machiavelli doubts that anyone can have all of them all the time), but because of the present circumstances of men and the world, he must be ready to change from his virtues to the opposite, and so his possession of the virtues cannot be inflexibly fixed within him, but must to a great degree be feigned, and valued not for themselves, but for their utility.

The prince has his own utility. He is to establish order, corral power, and make for domestic tranquility. When this has been accomplished, however, a government of people and law, a Republic, should replace his absolute authority, for the reason again, that absolute monarchs are seldom so powerful or so consistently and *expediently* virtuous in its exercise, that they do not soon prove tyrants, and as Machiavelli had ample occasion to observe, power quickly runs out of their hands and is caught by a quarreling multitude, whereupon the peace necessary to the practice of ordinary human virtue and a modest pursuit of a good life is impossible.

Bibliography

Niccolo Machiavelli, *Il Principe*. Edited by L. A. Burd. Introduction by Lord Acton (1891).

——, *Discorsi*. Translated by L. J. Walker (1950).

——, *The Historical, Political, and Diplomatic Writings of Niccolo Machiavelli*, 4 vols. Translated by C. E. Detmold (1891).

J. W. Allen, *A History of Political Thought in the Sixteenth Century* (1928). Pt. IV, ch. 2.

Louis Dyer, *Machiavelli and the Modern State* (1904).

M. B. Foster, *Masters of Political Thought*, Vol. I (1942).

John Morley, *Machiavelli* (1897).

G. H. Sabine, *A History of Political Theory*, ch. 17 (1937).

P. Villari, *The Life and Times of Niccolo Machiavelli*. Translated by Linda Villari (1892).

J. H. Whitfield, *Machiavelli* (1947).

William H. Gass
Purdue University

Machiavelli, Niccolo: *see* China, Moral Philosophies of; Marxist Theory of Morals.

Machiavellianism: *see* Soviet Morality, Current.

Mackintosh, James: *see* Utilitarianism.

madness: *see* Minor Socratics.

magic: *see* Aboriginals of Yirkalla; Pakot, The Moral System of; religion and magic; Rio Grande Pueblo Indians; Schopenhauer, Arthur; Zuni Indians, Morals of.

magic, black: *see* Mundurucu Indians, A Dual System of Ethics.

magnanimity: *see* China, Moral Philosophies of.

magnificence: *see* Aristotle.

Mahan, Asa: *see* Moral Philosophy in America.

maieutic method: *see* Freud, Sigmund.

Maimonides, Moses: *see* Jewish Ethics and Its Civilization; Spinoza.

Mainlaender, P.: *see* Schopenhauer, Arthur.

Major Ethical Viewpoints

An ethical viewpoint may be understood as a more or less systematic attempt to provide an account of the meaning of moral terms, such as "right" and "wrong." As such it may be distinguished from a *moral* viewpoint, which consists in the application of the term "right" or "wrong" to a given instance of human conduct. If someone were to say that "right" means "conducing to human happiness," he would be expressing an ethical viewpoint. If he were to say that telling the truth is right, he would be expressing a moral viewpoint.

Perhaps the broadest distinction that can be made among ethical viewpoints is between a) those which interpret moral judgments as statements asserting something which is claimed to be true and b) those which interpret moral judgments as being simply the expression of attitudes or emotions. Theories of type a) have been called "cognitivist" theories. Those of type b) have been called "non-cognitivist" theories. Cognitivist theories may in turn be distinguished as intuitionistic, naturalistic, and metaphysical. An ethical viewpoint is intuitionistic to the extent that it explains moral knowledge as resting on or consisting in an "intuition" (some form of direct awareness) of the moral value of actions or situations. An ethical viewpoint is naturalistic so far as it defines moral terms by reference to "natural" (for instance, psychological, biological, social, etc.) processes. (An example: " 'Right' means 'approved by the upper classes.' ") An ethical viewpoint is metaphysical, in the broad sense, when it derives the notions of rightness and wrongness from or identifies them with some metaphysical conception such as a transcendental absolute or the will of a god. (An example: " 'Right' means 'in accordance with the will of Allah.' ")

Ethical viewpoints may also be distinguished as absolutistic or objective, on the one hand, and as relativistic or subjective, on the other. For the most part, intuitionistic and metaphysical views tend to be absolutistic and objective in that they regard moral truths as holding universally and apart from their relation to the experiences of any particular individuals or groups. Many naturalistic views, on the other hand, are subjective and relativistic in that they tend to regard moral truths as depending upon the desires, interests, and valuings of individuals and societies and hence as capable of varying from one place or time to another.

The ethical viewpoints to be discussed in this article are not always easy to classify unambiguously. A theory such as hedonism, for instance, may be asserted as a special form of intuitionism or as a form of naturalistic ethics—or it may even in different respects share in both forms at the same time. Clearly this makes the task of the classifier something less than simple, and requires the reader to prepare himself for various overlappings and cross-classifications which an ideal system of classification would shun. But our task is to report the facts about ethical viewpoints and their interrelations as we find them and not as we might like to have them.

Intuitionism. Intuitionists in ethics have ordinarily emphasized the *directness* and sometimes the *uniquenss* of the faculty by which we are held to become aware of (intuit) moral truths Often also they have affirmed the uniqueness and indefinability of the ethical characteristics intuited, such a rightness, goodness, duty, etc. Many intuitionists have conceived the aware ness of moral truths as being of the same order as that by which we perceive the validity of a mathematical or logical truth. The moral truth perceived is grasped immediately and by the same sort of rational self-evidence through which we may be held to perceive the validity of a syllogism or of a theorem in geometry. Other intuitionists, such as Shaftesbury and Hutcheson (English writers of the late seventeenth and early eighteenth centuries), have referred to the faculty by which moral deliverances are obtained as a "moral sense," a unique and special faculty more akin in nature to feeling than to reason.

The truths held to be revealed by intuition may be very specific or very general. Thus a given instance of cruelty may be directly intuited as evil. Or the *principle* that wanton cruelty is evil may be intuited as true and then applied by ordinary processes of inductive and deductive reasoning to a given action. Or an even more general principle such as the right of all persons to an equal share of available good experience may be invoked as a self-evidently true moral intuition and then applied as ruling out the practice of cruelty.

So far as intuitionism asserts the possibility of knowing directly that individual acts are right or wrong, it is opposed to *teleological* standpoints in ethics, that is, to those views which evaluate individual acts *indirectly* by reference to the value of their consequences. But it is quite possible to combine intuitionism, construed in a more general sense, with an ethics of consequences. One might, for instance, assert the possibility of intuiting the value of a certain sort of experience or situation and then define as right whatever actions tend to produce experiences or situations of this kind. On such a view the main ethical burden, so to speak, is placed on the intuition of value perceived to belong to the experience or situation. And the definition of "right" becomes purely derivative from this intuited value. Alternatively, intuitions might enter into a teleological ethics which conceived "right" in terms of consequences whose value was defined without reference to any intuition. This would be the case, for example, if such an ethics included the claim that one's *obligation* to do the right was intuitively recognizable. Thus one might define the right act as the act which produces the most happiness and then intuit the truth of the proposition that he *ought* to perform this act. Such a proposition would be held by many intuitionists to be synthetic, asserting a necessary connection between "ought" and "right" without reducing either notion to the other—just as other intuitionists might assert a necessary synthetic connection between the occurrence of happiness and the occurrence of value. Indeed it has been a conspicuous feature of intuitionist views to insist upon the unique and unanalyzable nature of intuited moral and value predicates and therefore upon the primitive and underivable status of propositions containing these predicates. An outstanding instance of this position is found in the writings of the Cambridge moralist,

Prof. G. E. Moore (1873–). Moore, in a passage in his *Principia Ethica,* labels as the "naturalistic fallacy" any attempt to derive moral notions such as "good" from non-moral notions such as "being an object of desire." "Good," he contends, is a simple quality like "yellow" and therefore not analyzable in terms of other concepts. Because, intuitionists claim, predicates like goodness or rightness or oughtness cannot ultimately be analyzed into purely descriptive or natural characteristics such as happiness, desire, preference, etc., it follows that ethics cannot be reduced to or derived from a natural science such as psychology or sociology.

Naturalism. It is, on the other hand, the distinctive assertion of naturalistic ethical viewpoints that ethics is not an autonomous science and that moral propositions may be analyzed into or derived from those of the empirical sciences. Questions of right and wrong would be settled, on this view, not by reference to unanalyzable intuitions, but by reference to the findings of one or another of the sciences. Definitions of moral terms are expected to conform to the same requirements as those demanded for any scientific concept, viz., they must be testable in terms of empirically specifiable criteria. Naturalists, for example, might define "good" as "preferred by most people" or as "containing no conflicting elements." They might define "right" as "contributing to human happiness" or as "approved by Society X." "Obligatoriness" or "duty" might be defined naturalistically as "tending to produce a feeling of tension in a situation involving choice."

Three ethical viewpoints which, as usually propounded, are naturalistic in the sense just described will be discussed: evolutionism, hedonism, and pragmatism.

Evolutionism. Under the heading of evolutionary ethics may be classified those several theories of human good which, largely inspired by the Darwinian doctrine of biological evolution, describe moral value in terms of the conformity of conduct with developing natural or social processes. The classical prototype of this sort of view is to be found in the evolutionism of Herbert Spencer (1820–1903). Spencer, who prided himself on being a precursor of Darwin and on his application of the law of evolution to many areas besides that of biology, described conduct as good to the extent that it represented a successful adaptation to the environment. His dictum that "the conduct to which we apply the name good is the relatively more evolved conduct; and that bad is the name we apply to conduct which is relatively less evolved" has served as a basic thesis which has been variously modified by his followers. At times Spencer's dictum has been interpreted quite literally as a doctrine of "Might makes right." Any trait which makes for the survival of its owner, including such animal adaptations as ruthlessness and cunning, has been considered morally justified, at least at the particular evolutionary level at which it is effective. An example of such an interpretation of naturalism is the ethics of Friedrich

Nietzsche (1844–1900), German philologist and philosophical psychologist. The fundamental concept in Nietzsche's system, that of a "will to power," is an evolutionary force which in human beings represents their active will to exist, to achieve, and to dominate both physically and spiritually. The development of this will, dangerously effete Nietzsche thought in his own culture, is synonymous with moral progress and provides justification for whatever violence, suffering, and disdain of the traditional virtues are necessary to its accomplishment.

It will be noticed that this theory is naturalistic in two senses. It defines good in terms of a natural concept (the direction of evolution, adaptation, a will to power) and at the same time it makes conformity to nature or to natural tendencies the criterion of moral progress. Other theories of ethics which have related morals to the evolutionary process have rejected or greatly modified the doctrine that right means simply being in line with the direction of evolution. For example, the English scientist, Julian Huxley, has used the concept of evolution, particularly in relation to the biological and social development of the individual, to explain the origin of the moral consciousness. The sense of guilt and the feeling of oughtness he contends derive from a "proto-ethical mechanism" in the infant which arises out of the ambivalent relation (of love and hate) in which the child stands to his mother and later to society. The concepts of psychoanalysis have, indeed, led a considerable number of recent writers in ethics to explain various aspects of man's evolving moral experience as emergent products of deeper life forces.

Hedonism. The designation "hedonistic" has been conferred on those ethical viewpoints which equate the end of action with pleasure or happiness and accordingly describe acts as right or virtuous to the extent that they promote a happy life. Hedonism may take either of two forms: egoistic or universalistic. It is egoistic if the "happy life" whose promotion determines right conduct is taken as one's own. It is universalistic if the happiness by which the value of conduct is judged is taken as that of all persons whom the conduct in question affects. Egoistic hedonism was given an explicit formulation as an ethical philosophy as far back as the ancient Greek period by such persons as Aristippus (435?–356? B.C.) and Epicurus (342?–270 B.C.) and has won various more or less notable adherents through the history of ethical speculation up to the present time. *Ethical egoism,* or the view that a person *ought* to act to further his own well-being or pleasure, must be distinguished from *psychological egoism,* which is a theory (about human motivation, rather than human good) to the effect that people *do,* in all of their actions, seek their own well-being.

Universalistic hedonism is better known as Utilitarianism, a title given currency chiefly through the writings of the English philosophers, Jeremy Bentham (1748–1832) and John Stuart Mill (1806–1873). Another English-

313

man, Henry Sidgwick (1838–1900), gave the position a more systematic formulation. The essence of Utilitarianism is its so-called Principle of Utility, which defines rightness as belonging to any act which, of all the acts open to the agent, will actually or probably produce the greatest amount of pleasure or happiness among those persons to whom the acts in question would make a difference. Moral value, then, is an instrumental property of acts. It belongs to acts only so far as they result in something that has intrinsic value, i.e., which is good in itself and apart from its accompaniments or effects. It is the hedonists' thesis that nothing possesses positive intrinsic value except pleasurable or happy consciousness (and correspondingly that nothing possesses negative intrinsic value except unpleasant consciousness). The view is naturalistic so far as the property of goodness is *identified* with happiness. It may, however, assume a non-naturalistic or intuitionist form (as with Sidgwick) if goodness, taken as an intuitively perceived unique quality, is held to attach to pleasant consciousness and to nothing else.

Sometimes Utilitarianism is given a meaning which differentiates it from universalistic hedonism. Such would be the case when the intrinsic goodness, in terms of which rightness is defined, is taken generically. Universalistic hedonism would be a *species* of Utilitarianism on this broader definition. Another species would be the view advocated by G. E. Moore and others under the title *Ideal Utilitarianism.*

This view holds that, besides happiness, such other qualities as beauty, love, knowledge, and friendship possess intrinsic goodness.

It may be noticed that any ethical point of view which defines rightness or moral value in terms of consequences which are themselves valuable in a non-moral sense, requires for its complete formulation a general theory of value. One such general theory of value closely identified with the naturalist tradition in the ethics is the so-called *Interest Theory.* On this theory, especially as propounded by its chief contemporary advocate, Professor R. B. Perry of Harvard University, value belongs to "any object of any interest." Interest may be favorable or unfavorable, thereby determining positive or negative value. In his *General Theory of Value* (1926) Perry defines interest as an "all-pervasive characteristic of the motor-affective life," . . . a state, act, attitude or disposition of favor or disfavor." The highest good, he holds, would come about with a maximum fulfilment of interests—"an all inclusive harmonious system of interests"— whether within the individual or among the members of a society.

Pragmatism. No viewpoint in ethics has been more proud of or more insistent upon its naturalistic affiliation than the pragmatic. Associated with a theory of knowledge which conceives the truth of an idea in terms of its usefulness in a human or social context, pragmatism describes the good as the resolution of conflicts which impede social advance. John Dewey (1859–1951) has been the most prominent exponent of this position, which first gained popularity at the hands of William James (1842–1910). A moral valuation, according to Dewey, never occurs except in a concrete situation characterized by a felt tension or disorder. Such a state of affairs, he points out, demands the application of intelligence in the exploration of means for producing a more satisfactory situation. However, this does not mean, Dewey insists, that the moral end of action can be defined merely in terms of satisfaction or the production of pleasure. Though Pragmatism has much in common with hedonistic utilitarianism and its psychological theory of value, traditional hedonism and the conventional interest theory of value are held by the pragmatist to be inadequate for several reasons. For one thing, it is an oversimplification to speak of pleasure or interest-satisfaction as being good or the final end of action in any unqualified sense. Satisfactions are always particular and can therefore never be identified with any general concept of the good. What may constitute the resolution of a problem in one social or cultural context may be totally inappropriate under different historical or cultural conditions. Hence no absolute moral ideal or principle can be specified. Ideals are simply hypotheses, projections of the moral imagination, or better, tools in the analysis and solution of particular social problems. Moral standards must change—and along with them, of course, rights and duties—with changing social conditions. The moral ideal that might have been appropriate, say,

in Czarist Russia would become wholly obsolete following the proletarian revolution.

Another reason why pragmatists like Dewey tend to object to a theory which takes pleasure—or any other single thing—as a final end is that such a theory seems to them to separate ends too sharply from means, and accordingly to encourage a disregard of the values and disvalues which attach to the means. In an adequate theory of valuation, they contend, means and ends will be seen as part of a continuing life process and it will be recognized that there is no end which is not also a means to other ends.

An analogous criticism is applied by pragmatists against those psychological theories which define value in terms of desire or interest. The good, as Dewey puts it, is more than what we want on a given occasion, more than what simply *feels* good. What is good must be good in the long run. It must not only be *desired,* but be *desirable* in the sense of being able to maintain itself as the object of desire under critical examination and under the stresses and strains of changing experience. Knowledge that something is good, then, involves more than reference to one's feeling about it or one's desire for it. It involves the use of intelligence, of reflective analysis upon one's desires and the situations in which they occur. It is absurd, according to the pragmatist, to speak of any moral end as given to men prior to action, as an infallible guide to conduct. Moral judgment, acting reflectively in a given situation, must as it proceeds be fully

315

prepared to modify and reconstruct the concept of the good with which it began its analysis. In a philosophy of on-going process, such as pragmatism, no good is ever final. All goods must submit themselves constantly to the test of social usefulness.

Metaphysical Ethics. In sharp contrast to naturalistic theories which restrict the notions of ethics to the categories of psychology and the other sciences, metaphysical ethical theories seek a deeper foundation for morality than that which is provided by individual desire or the practical-social interests of groups. These deeper foundations are found sometimes in a religious conception of the universe which defines the duty of man in relation to the absolute will of God, sometimes in a metaphysical conception of the "true" nature of the self which defines its underlying essence in terms which go beyond the ordinary thought-forms of the psychological or social sciences. Metaphysical theories of the first type may be designated "theological." Those of the second type may be referred to as "self-realization" theories. It is possible for the two theories to be combined, as for example in certain "natural law" doctrines.

Theological ethics. Theories of this kind may place stress either on the definition of right, or on the nature of moral authority and obligation, or upon both of these. A contemporary theologian, Emil Brunner has provided a theological definition of "right" in saying, "What God does and wills is good; and all that opposes the will of God is bad. The Good has its basis and its existence solely in the will of God." Other theologians have denied that the rightness and wrongness of acts consists in the fact that God approves or disapproves them, but, while allowing that right and wrong have meanings that are independent of God's will, insist that we would be under no obligation to perform what is right and abstain from what is wrong except for the compulsion exercised by the authority of God's will over us. It should be noticed that an ethical viewpoint does not become theological in a metaphysical sense simply because it acknowledges the possibility that men may have duties to God as well as to their fellow men. That which gives an ethical system a theologico-metaphysical character is its derivation of its basic ethical notions from a metaphysically conceived divine source or principle. It is one thing to say that duty gets its meaning from such a source. It is another thing to assert that men in considering what their duty is, may wish to take into account their belief in the existence and nature of God.

Self-Realizationism. In the widest sense of the term, self-realizationism in ethics is not necessarily allied with metaphysical ethics, but may be given a naturalistic or even an intuitionist formulation. This view, which has been given the names "perfectionism" and "humanism," describes the good for man as consisting basically in the fulfilling or actualizing or perfecting of potentialities that lie within the self. When these potentialities are conceived as human capacities, the definition of the good in terms of them may be wholly naturalistic and humanistic. When the self that is to be realized is conceived as somehow identified with an Absolute or Divine Self, interpreted in metaphysical terms, then self-realizationism must be categorized as a metaphysical ethics. It is in this latter, narrower sense that the name "self-realizationism" has been applied to the characteristic ethics of the modern Idealistic school of philosophy, represented by such nineteenth and twentieth century writers as G. W. F. Hegel, T. H. Green and F. H. Bradley.

The notion that man can find his good by discovering his true nature and bringing it into perfect functioning can be found in the ethical views of Socrates, Plato and Aristotle in ancient Greek times. Each of them conceives of man's essence as lying in his capacity to exercise reason. It is debatable to what degree their views of man's essential nature are metaphysical and to what degree humanistic. At any rate, their doctrine that "virtue is knowledge," that man's chief good is to be found in the use of his rational capacities, is a prototype for many theories of "ethical rationalism," a position to which we shall refer below.

In Stoicism and in Thomas Aquinas (1225–1274), the conception of a "natural law," ordained by God and impressed on man to be followed as the law of his own nature, provided an ethical position which combined self-realizationism with a theologico-metaphysical viewpoint.

Self-realizationism as a special and avowedly metaphysical position associated with the general doctrine of Absolute Idealism, came into being in the nineteenth century. Following Immanuel Kant (1724–1804), who despite his repudiation of metaphysical knowledge had based morality on faith in a free metaphysical ego, Hegel interpreted the individual self which we find in experience as simply the partial manifestation of an Absolute Self or Rational Will which gives its laws to the whole universe. The good for any individual consists in recognizing his relation to the Absolute Self and in willing to make the good of this eternal spiritual Self his own good. The realization of one's absolute self-hood is achieved gradually by becoming aware of the unreality of the contrast between one's self and others. The self is seen to be in reality a social self, only realizing itself as it discovers its unity of purpose and interest with others in the family, the civic community and the state—and finally in art, religion and philosophy where the ultimate identification of the finite self with the infinite spirit is accomplished.

Humanism. Plainly the contention that the individual self can realize what is truly valuable in itself by recognizing its ties with society or that a man is better off when he has achieved a unified personality by means of a rational understanding of himself does not need to be tied in with a metaphysical or supernatural account of man's origin and nature. If a man's good does consist in realizing his social nature or his rational nature or his inner integration, then self-realization on these terms does become a human end, which like happiness or any other natural state may be equated with the supreme good. Many self-realizationists today conceive their position in precisely this way, defining "right" teleologically as marking whatever conduct will contribute most effectively to human self-realization. If self-realization, construed in naturalistic terms, is *identified* with the good, the view will be to that extent naturalistic. If self-realization is *intuited* to possess the quality of intrinsic value, then the position will be in so far intuitionistic.

In its widest meaning, then, humanistic ethics will be any ethics that derives its conception of the good from the nature of man, rather than from the nature of any superhuman or metaphysical entity. The more special forms that humanism may take will depend upon the interpretation put on the "nature" of man. Some humanists, like Plato and Aristotle, emphasize some one side of man's nature, one which they consider uniquely or peculiarly definitive of his humanity, as, for example, his spiritual nature, his ability to use reason, his capacity for social relationships, his loyalty or honor, etc. Other humanists conceive of humanistic self-realization as involving the development and perfection of all sides of a man's nature, involving either the maximum functioning of as many as possible of his latent capacities or the developing into a harmonious pattern of a selected set of them

chosen in terms of their contribution to an integrated personality.

Humanism has also in the present century been used as the name for a view taken by a rather loosely related group of writers who adopted as a criterion of personal and social criticism the fulfillment in men's experience of the more distinctively human responses and activities. Professors Warner Fite and Irving Babbitt exemplify this position in America, though each gives the notion of the "distinctively human" a different interpretation, Fite emphasizing the processes of consciousness in which man is immediately and critically aware of what he is doing, Babbitt finding the epitome of the human to be in the restraint and discipline which the mind of man can bring to his experience.

Rationalism. Rationalism in ethics has meant several things. The name has been applied, for example, to the moral ideal of the Stoics, who regarded the universe as a whole as a rational organism and man's duty as that of accepting as reasonable and therefore good whatever circumstances befell him. The enemy of reason or of virtue on this view is emotion, which stands in the way of understanding and needs to be brought under the control of the rational self. A similar position regarding the supremacy of reason over the other aspects of the self was, as we have seen, taken by Plato and Aristotle.

The designation "rationalistic" has also been applied to ethical theories which describe our perception of moral truths as mediated by or inherent in our reasoning powers or our rational

318

nature. René Descartes (1596–1650), for example, who believed that knowledge of moral laws is innate in the reason of man, has on this account been called an ethical rationalist. But most famous of those who have been called rationalists because of their conception of the relation of reason to moral knowledge is Immanuel Kant. As did Plato and the Stoics, Kant sets reason off against impulse, emotion, and desire. A will directed by impulse or natural inclination is not a good will. A will is good, according to Kant, only when it is rational. And it is rational when it wills consistently, that is when it doesn't become involved in contradictions. Kant calls the supreme moral law the "categorical imperative" and formulates it as follows, "Act as though the maxim of your action were by your will to become a universal law of nature." The moral law issues, says Kant, from pure reason, and is categorical because it holds for all men as rational beings, quite apart from their special circumstances or inclinations. Since we are creatures of desire as well as reasoning beings, tensions arise between our rational and irrational natures. Such tensions account for the feeling of moral obligation, for the sense of duty. Duty itself is always performed when our rational will has its way, refusing to compromise with irrational impulse or inclination.

Relativism. Several of the views which have been discussed have been characterized, either explicitly or implicitly, as relativistic. It may be worthwhile at this point to devote some brief consideration to relativism as a general point of view in ethics. Any ethical position is relativistic which defines rightness or goodness in relation to the attitudes of individuals or societies, so that what is right or good for one individual or society may be wrong or evil for another individual or society. It should be noticed that the simple *fact* of differences in moral standards or beliefs from person to person or from society to society does not in itself constitute or necessarily even support the relativist position. That polygamy is not accepted either legally or morally in the United States while it is practiced and approved by, say, the Fiji Islanders is often referred to as an example of the relativism of morals. There would be less danger of confusion if this fact of the diversity of moral norms were referred to as "sociological relativism" rather than as "ethical relativism." For it is perfectly consistent with ethical absolutism— that is with the view that there is one fixed ultimate standard by which all actions everywhere are to be judged— that there should exist different moral beliefs and practices among different people. For some of these people might simply be ethically mistaken or ignorant. It is even consistent with ethical absolutism that the same type of act should be right in one place and wrong in another. For example, if "right" meant "making for the greatest happiness of the greatest number," polygamy might very well be right in the Fiji Islands but wrong in the United States, since circumstances such as an excess of females in the one place might be such as to require for the happiness of the inhabitants quite different marital arrangements from those required in the other place for the happiness of the people there.

That which in strictness distinguishes ethical relativism from ethical absolutism is that moral terms on the former view refer to the ultimate interests, or needs, or attitudes of persons or to their conduct in relation to these interests, needs, or attitudes. To the extent that people's interests, needs and attitudes do differ, fundamentally and finally, right and wrong will accordingly also differ from people to people. Absolutism, on the other hand, defines moral terms objectively, that is, out of relation to the potentially differing desires or approvals of persons or groups. Just as absolutism in ethics is for this reason associated with objective definitions of moral terms, so relativism is associated with subjective definitions. *Subjectivism* in ethics is described by one of its proponents, Edward Westermarck, as asserting "that the qualities assigned to the subjects of moral judgments really are generalizations derived from approval or disapproval felt with regard to certain modes of conduct." Moral values, that is to say, do not on the subjectivist view belong to actions or objects independently of human reactions. They consist in these reactions—or at least they do so originally, since custom may come to determine a man's approval of something without his feeling an emotional reaction to the thing at the time he approves it. For this reason subjectivism is not to be understood simply in the unsophis-

ticated version which identifies "X is good" with "I like X." But it does require that ultimately the goodness of X go back to *someone's* liking it.

Non-cognitivism. Of the ethical points of view so far considered, each may be described as "cognitive" in the sense, referred to earlier, that they regard moral utterances as making claims to knowledge. In these views, moral utterances are statements or propositions—assertions of truth. We turn now to a position in ethics which stands in the broadest possible contrast to these views. This position has been referred to as non-cognitivism because it denies that moral utterances have any literal or descriptive meaning which could qualify them as expressions of knowledge. On this view the only kind of meaning which such utterances possess is "emotive," i.e., their function is to express and evoke emotions, and not to convey truths or falsehoods.

In origin and to a large degree in current discussions, non-cognitivism in ethics has been associated with a more general philosophical point of view, that of *logical positivism*. This latter view had its genesis only a little more than 30 years ago (the date usually given being 1922, when Ludwig Wittgenstein published his *Tractatus Logico—Philosophicus*). This modern form of positivism, while a true heir to the nineteenth century positivistic tradition represented by August Comte (1798–1857) and Émile Durkheim (1858–1917), has nevertheless added some radically different theses to the earlier statements of the position. It would agree with the positivistic repudiation of supernaturalism and metaphysics and the assertion that all knowledge is summed up in the descriptive findings of the sciences, (except, of course, for the tautologies of logic and mathematics, which, however, tell us nothing about the world). They would agree that much of what has been called the language of morality is really the language of sociology, and that it is possible to talk of ethical facts if we mean simply descriptive facts which sociologists may discover about human conduct. But such facts are not normative. They *describe*, rather than *prescribe*. They say what is, rather then what ought to be as genuinely moral utterances seem to do. The sociological positivism of Comte is therefore judged to have failed in its analysis of the nature and function of normative or value assertions. The logical positivist, on the other hand, who conceives his philosophical task as that of the logical analysis and clarification of language, recognizes that normative assertions of value, moral or otherwise, are more than descriptive. Yet he cannot consistently with his empirical criterion of meaningfulness interpret them as does the intuitionist or the metaphysician. Analysis of the use of normative assertions leads him to the conclusion that they are not really *assertions* at all, in the sense of claims to truth, but are rather pseudo-statements, symbolic expressions with an emotive function. Such expressions show what the attitude or feeling of their users may be, and by so doing serve to evoke or influence attitudes

and feelings in others than their users. To say "You ought to admit your guilt" is to exhibit your own favorable attitude toward the admission of guilt and at the same time to persuade others to adopt an identical attitude. So moral utterances are, as C. L. Stevenson has recently argued in his *Ethics and Language* (1944), both expressive and persuasive. They may be taken as imperatives ("Admit your guilt!"); or as optatives ("If only you would admit your guilt!"); or as exclamations ("How fine a thing it is to admit one's guilt!"); or as directly persuasive ("I admire anyone who admits his guilt; you should feel the same way as I do").

The significance of the non-cognitivist or emotivist view of ethics can perhaps best be seen by considering its analysis of moral disagreements. Ordinary disagreements arise from differences of opinion about facts. They are potentially resolvable by appeal to facts. If two persons differ in their judgment of the weight of an object, the use of a scale will usually settle the dispute. On the other hand, if the non-cognitivist is right, differences of opinion about the value of an object cannot be settled in this manner. (We are talking now of *intrinsic* value, and not of instrumental value. Once what is intrinsically good is agreed on, then whether something does or does not lead to that good is a question of descriptive fact and a proper subject of debate.) Where intrinsic value is in dispute, the disagreement arises from differences in the disputants' emotional attitudes. But it cannot be settled by a descriptive reference to these attitudes. The subjectivist and the naturalist are wrong, according to the emotivist, in supposing that moral utterances *describe* attitudes or *report* likings and dislikings. Two people may report different feelings about the same object without the statements in which their reports are made being contradictory. There is no logical inconsistency in A's liking what B dislikes. On the other hand, the non-cognitivist points out, if it is recognized that value expressions are simply emotive utterances, it is clear that ultimate moral (i.e., attitudinal) agreement is possible only as disputants come to entertain the same emotive attitudes towards the value-object. In this way, and in this way alone, it is held, can it be determined whether or not an argument about moral matters has been settled. At the same time, as Stevenson has been careful to point out, while moral arguments are not ultimately *about* attitudes, nor about any sort of facts, it is nevertheless true that the introduction into a dispute of new facts, including facts about attitudes, may alter these attitudes. In this sense, emotive and descriptive meanings may play mutually contributory rôles in moral discussion. So that although normative ethics is not itself a science, science can yet, in good positivist fashion, play an important part in the resolution of moral disagreements.

Bibliography

C. D. Broad, *Five Types of Ethical Theory* (New York, 1930).

T. E. Hill, *Contemporary Ethical Theories* (New York, 1950).
C. E. M. Joad, *A Guide to the Philosophy of Morals and Politics* (New York 1938).
A. I. Melden, *Ethical Theories* (New York, 2nd ed., 1950).
B. Rand, *The Classical Moralists* (Boston, 1909).
Sellars and Hospers, *Readings in Ethical Theory* (New York, 1952).
H. Sidgwick, *Outlines of the History of Ethics* (London, 1892).
R. A. Tsanoff, *The Moral Ideals of our Civilization* (New York, 1942).

Lucius Garvin
University of Maryland

malice: *see* Dante, Alighieri; Hobbes, Thomas; Schopenhauer, Arthur; Zuni Indians, Morals of.
Malinovski: *see* Soviet Morality, Current.
man, nature of: *see* human nature.
Manichaeans: *see* Augustine and Morals.
manliness: *see* Muslim Morals.
Mann, T.: *see* Schopenhauer, Arthur.
manners: *see* Aztec Morals; Muslim Morals; Navaho Morals.
Marcel, Gabriel: *see* French Existentialism and Moral Philosophy.
Marcus, Aurelius: *see* Stoics, The.
Maritain, Jacques: *see* Moral Philosophy in America.
Marnyu, the Twin: *see* Zoroastrian Morals.
marriage: *see* Aboriginals of Yirkalla; Aztec Morals; Augustine and Morals; China, Moral Philosophies of; Christian Moral Philosophy; Hindu Ethics; Marxist Theory of Morals; Muslim Morals; Navaho Morals; Primitive Morals; Puritan Morals;

Marxist Theory of Morals, The

Moral principles are best regarded (for purposes of this article, at any rate) as a set of rules, a code of human behaviour. To be moral is to obey the moral code. We may evade, in this context, the question of what makes the rules of morality unique, and different from, say, a legal code, or the rules of etiquette.

The chief functions of a theory of morals are to explain and justify the moral rules or principles. One type of ethical theory explains the origin of morals by reference to a man's social needs and justifies them by their usefulness. Marxist moral theory belongs to this general category of utilitarian theory, but with differences so substantial that it would be quite misleading to classify Marx (1818–1883) with Bentham or Mill.

Marx's social theory is well known, and may be summed up in the broad statement that economic forces determine the course of history. It is true that the determinism is of a peculiar, dialectical sort; yet it is determinism nonetheless, and without the economic determinism there would be nothing unique in Marxism. The economic foundation is also said to determine the entire superstructure of society, including the systems of laws, politics, morals, religion, philosophy and art—the whole way of life, or culture.

The Marxist theory thus puts morality among those elements in the superstructure of society which are a reflection of the economic foundation. And since all societies have been class societies—the argument runs—the morality prevailing at any one time has been a code devised to serve the interests of the ruling class. The process need not be a deliberate conspiracy on the part of the ruling class who may be quite sincere in their beliefs, and dupes of their own ideology. The Communist Manifesto is quite plain on this: the bourgeoisie have exalted their rules of class-interest into eternal laws of "nature" or reason; law, morality, religion are—to the proletariat—so many bourgeois prejudices.

If Marx's theory is true, he thus effectively dismisses the moral "ought," as it is usually understood. All other theories of morality distinguish between what is right, and what is to our economic advantage. Marxist theory defines morals in purely naturalistic terms, and always relative to the class structure, since different ruling classes may devise different rules to serve their interests. Marxist theory is not unique in its naturalism and relativity, but is unique in basing morals on a purely class basis.

If morality is class determined, in what sense can the judgment be made that one moral code is better than an-

323

other? Marx was a great believer in economic progress, and since economics determines classes, which in turn determine morals, his answer is that the morality of the advanced economic system is "better" than that of the more backward system. Slavery, feudalism, and capitalism form an ascending economic and moral series. Moreover, within feudalism, say, the morality of the rising bourgeois class is better or higher than that of the decaying feudal ruling class. It will be better just *because* it is the morality of a rising class, of the class that will inherit the future. In the same way, proletarian morality is judged to be higher than capitalist morality because the proletariat will inevitably supersede the bourgeoisie.

It is stretching the point, I think, to call this type of thinking a theory of morals at all. If morality is *defined* in this way, right and wrong cease to have any of the ordinary meanings attached to them, and become merely the expedient or successful in terms of what promotes the interest of the proletariat—as Marxists interpret these interests. It is very close to the position that might is right, or Hitler's view that right is what promotes the interests of the German folk. In Marx's case it is also a doctrine of historical necessity: what is coming is right. Hence we can see why Marxism (and Hegelianism) have been described by Popper as a kind of "moral futurism."[1] Notice, too, that Marx's argument is circular. Only by assuming that his forecast is

[1] K. R. Popper, *The Open Society and Its Enemies* (Princeton, 1950), p. 385.

true, i.e., that the proletariat *will* inherit the future, can the proletariat be called progressive, and hence its morality be called "better."

In strict logic, when Marxists label capitalism and the capitalists immoral, they ought to mean merely unprogressive, or out of date. But from Marx onwards, Marxists can hardly find language strong enough to express their moral condemnation of bourgeois society and actions; and in passing judgment they invariably judge by traditional moral standards, common throughout all the western world. Similarly, communists often fail in practice to worship success (other than communist success) with its corollary that power alone gives right; and in speaking of the future classless society they describe it in terms of high social ideals which any good liberal may accept. Ordinary moral standards emerge too in the selfless behaviour of many communists, both among the rank and file, and in leaders such as Marx and Lenin. Marxist practice is thus openly inconsistent with its own moral theory, but the inconsistency is seldom recognized and never admitted.

Marx's so-called theory of morals is perhaps the most cavalier part of his system of thought. It is fragmentary, being scattered in incidental remarks and angry footnotes throughout the vast pile of Marxist writings. Indeed, there are so many moral judgments in Marxism, uttered or unexpressed, that the Marxist system may fairly enough be regarded as a treatise on social ethics disguised in the pseudo-science of economic determinism and historical necessity.

Marx's purpose was simple and grandiose: to overthrow capitalism. He raged against the common notion of his day that there was something eternal about the capitalist economy, and hence he castigated also the ideals of moral rightness, of natural rights, and of divine law, which were often used to justify private ownership, laissez-faire, and the existing social structure and income distribution. Occasional Marxists admit this interpretation when they say that in moral principles there is both an eternal and a relative element, that Marx merely concentrated on the relative element, and that when he did this he was usually correct.[2] There is a lot to be said for such a modest appraisal, and it is certainly an advance on what Marx, Engels (1820–1895) and Lenin (1870–1924) wrote.

Although Marxism contains only suggestions for the beginning of an introduction to a theory of morals, it is worth examining these suggestions in more detail, if only because there are so many Marxists in the world today. In the *first* place, Marx's theory—if we may call it that—applies only to a part of life. To say that morality is only a matter of property interest, is to say that man is shaped wholly by economic interests and relationships, which in a sense is a doctrine that life is work, and this in turn accords closely with the spirit of earlier industrialism, and its

stern Puritan outlook. (Work, in Marx's view, is what has raised man from the animals). The importance of all that large area of life outside of working hours is left out of account. Marx's theory is thus incomplete, and the very most that could be claimed for it, even if it were true, is that it is true of only a part of the moral life.

A *second* more searching question, is this: cannot the moral code transcend class interest? The Marxist reply is somewhat contradictory: (a) the common element in morals throughout history is traceable to the fact that all ruling class morality has something in common, just because it exists to support a ruling class; (b) the oppressed classes are induced by propaganda to believe in the ruling class morality. Yet, oddly enough, the proletariat are also shrewd enough to "see through" bourgeois morality and to reject it—that is, once they have been enlightened by Marxism.

Such a reply is altogether too superficial since in fact the severest critics of the bourgeoisie come from within that class, Marx and Engels themselves being outstanding examples. A part of the moral code has always been critical of some features of capitalism, even of private property itself; while within the bourgeois class, ideas on what is right or wrong may often differ, as they do on the important subjects of drink, divorce, pacifism and euthanasia. In some fundamental respects the moral code is the same in any kind of social structure and has already survived Hebrew pastoralism, Roman slavery, and feudalism, although no doubt the de-

[2] Jack Lindsay, *Marxism and Contemporary Science* (London, 1949), pp. 209–212.

tailed application has often varied. But the commandment "thou shalt not steal" is not abrogated merely by extending the prohibition from private to public property. Neither is duty to one's neighbour superseded when the meaning of "neighbour" is broadened to include all one's fellow citizens, or even all human beings. Finally, there is the point that the moral code of the west is identical, over a large area of conduct, with that in the U.S.S.R. where, presumably, there are no exploiting and exploited classes.

For these reasons alone it is hard to deny that all classes can and often do agree on many moral principles, transcending economic interests, and that such agreement is not merely common belief in ruling class propaganda. Classes, or any other groups, may naturally have conflicting interests, as a result of which they may differ on what is right in some specific cases. It is impossible to see however, that this constitutes a *different kind of morality*. Classes or other groups may also have common interests, best promoted by co-operation, but Marxism ignores this.

A *third* question must also be raised: can morality only alter when the economic foundation, the "modes of production," are altered? This query, of course, is part of the wider problem whether any elements in the superstructure or mental life of society may alter except under the influence of changing methods of production. It thus involves nothing less than the truth or falsity of the entire Marxist interpretation of history, a question

which is much too large to be examined here. Suffice it to say that the many weighty objections which may be brought against the Marxist theory of history in general damage its essential case beyond repair, and apply *a fortiori* to the particular case that changes in morals can only come about as the result of economic changes. When the economic foundation of society alters, or any other social change occurs, there will be some changes also in the detailed application of moral principles: that is the grain of wheat in the Marxist chaff.

A *fourth* difficulty with Marx's theory is that of bridging the gap between the self-interested individual and class loyalty. Engels sometimes spoke as though a person's will is determined by his class position, but on the whole that was not Marx's view. To ensure class loyalty Marx gave the answer given by every moralist from time immemorial: exhortation and the call to duty. The Russians sometimes give the same answers, as when in the recent war they appealed not to class interest, but to the traditional values of duty and patriotism in order to stimulate the fighting spirit of the Soviet people.

Marx's theory of a class-determined morality led him to an extraordinarily hopeful view of man's potential virtue once private property is abolished. (Presumably a kind of classless morality also prevailed under primitive communism before man was corrupted by private property). Marx spoke as though all crime—or even sin, if one may use that word in connection with Marxism—would disappear in the

326

classless society. Man has been corrupted by society (an old theme in moral philosophy), and when society is changed man's natural virtue will blossom in all its beauty.

Yet granting in full the Marxist assumptions of public ownership and a high standard of living, no one, however slight his knowledge of human nature, could possibly expect this to give us an entirely new morality. The elaborate Soviet penal system shows how ingenious and frequent offences against public property may be; while in addition most of the ordinary "bourgeois" type of crime still continues in the U.S.S.R., i.e., offences against the person, and against private property in consumer goods. In short, all that one can say is that the causes of some types of crime, and the temptations to some types of sin will have been removed. We may be quite sure that no institutional reorganization is going to do more than that. Selfishness, sin and crime did not come into the world with capitalism, nor will they go out with it.

Much the same considerations apply to the "Marxist view of human nature" of which so much has been made.[3] It comes down to very little: that self-interest has dominated human behaviour through history, but that once capitalism is abolished, man will transcend self-interest and be "naturally" good. Marx, like every other radical reformer, was thoroughly indignant at man's present and past

[3] For instance, in V. Venable, *Human Nature: The Marxian View* (New York, 1945).

lot, with invincible faith in man's future potentialities.

Few theories are wholly wrong, and even in Marx's partial moral theory there is a residue of truth behind the extremism. Psychology has taught us that individuals do often rationalise their behaviour, and produce excellent moral reasons for doing what will benefit them. Many observers other than Marx have noted also a class element in morals. Thus Mill wrote: "Wherever there is an ascendant class, a large portion of the morality of the country emanates from its class interest, and its feelings of class superiority."[4] The content of the moral code must also usually be socially useful, although this need not always be so, and many useless remnants from an older and superseded code may be retained and practiced with great tenacity. But Marxism gives no explanation why they are retained, since on Marxist principles they should be altered with the changed methods of production.

The emphasis on the social content of morality, and on the emptiness of vague principles which give no help in dealing with specific everyday problems, the warning that when the spectacles of economic interest are worn we can so easily adapt our morals to our interest, and the strictures on the inhumanity of so much of the philosophy of competition: all these are useful hints from whatever source they come. They embody ideas which today are commonplace, but Marx has helped to make them so. Any theory of morals

[4] *On Liberty*, (Everyman's Edition), p. 70.

must take notice of these factors, but they are not enough in themselves to constitute a theory of morals.

Marx's ostensible theory is one thing, but his conduct and the bulk of his writings are another. That is why it is never wise to take Marx's theory of morals, such as it is, at face value. Most communists too rest their case against capitalism on a moral judgment common to all classes, and seldom indulge in moral cynicism, except as a matter of routine in explaining the actions of their opponents. The one kind of behaviour which Marxism cannot explain, on its own principles of economic determinism, is that of Marxists themselves.

This point is so often misunderstood that it is worth emphasizing. It is quite evident, for example, that the Communist Manifesto does not enunciate any theory of class determined morality with respect to marriage, but is full of righteous indignation at the exploitation which made it impossible for the worker to enjoy a decent family life. Engels too, strongly condemned the double standard of sexual behaviour for men and women and looked forward to the day when there would be no economic exploitation of woman by man, but when love between equals would be the only tie holding the family together.

Some communists have occasionally dismissed all moral standards—especially the Bolsheviks in the first years after the Revolution. But Lenin was notorious for his strong, prudish views on sex, and today the Russians often show an almost puritanical attitude; the laws of marriage, divorce and abortion, for instance, being nowadays stricter than in many western countries. Moral discipline and training are much emphasized in school education, along of course, with indoctrination in communism. Again, the reliability of loose-living communists is regarded with deep suspicion by Party leaders everywhere, since what is demanded is self-control to the point of austerity, and dedication to the Party interests. Finally, there is abundant evidence to show that high-minded people join—and later leave—the communist party for moral reasons, such as the injustices and cruelties of society. This brings us to the essential principle on which Marxists operate, as distinct from the casual hints at theory in Marxism. It is the doctrine that the end or result justifies the means, a view usually attributed to Machiavelli and, perhaps unjustly, to the Jesuits.

The doctrine easily follows from Marx's view that the interests of the proletariat are a higher form of morality. Since by definition the communist party acts only in the interests of the proletariat, whatever the party does is thus morally justified. Admittedly there can be some confusion here, and two quite different ideas are easily mixed: (a) whatever the party or proletariat does is right, by definition; (b) some of the means adopted, though admittedly wrong in themselves if judged by ordinary canons of morality, are nevertheless to be condoned as the shortest or the only means that can promote the good end in view. It is extremely difficult to separate the two ideas in practice, but it seems to me that the latter is the one usually put forward to justify communist action. Some support is lent to this by the statement of ideals incorporated in the Stalin constitution of 1936. Many parts of the constitution are clearly ignored in practice, but within the Soviet Union they still seem to be widely regarded as ultimate goals.

It is easier to explain the communist behaviour and conscience on the means and results principle than on any other, especially when communists can, like Lenin, regard themselves as "agents of history." The suffering caused by the forced collectivization of farming ("the party appeared less disturbed by dead kulaks than by dead cows"), the immoral and ruthless behaviour of communist parties all over the world, are all justified in the name of high ideals. Men are used—despite Kant's maxim—entirely as means, and ostensibly for great good in the future. It is one of the ironies of history that this kind of working principle should actuate the followers of Marx, whose moral indignation was based on the charge that capitalism treated workers as mere instruments of production, and who himself dreamed of the classless society when such "exploitation" would cease. "Communism is the doctrine of humanitarianism driven to an extreme in the pursuit of offensive and defensive methods."[5] Despite the apparent relativity of its moral theory, Marxist movements become absolutist, and subordinate everything to their objectives.

A lack of scruple in promoting noble objectives is common enough in western history, and this fact should be enough to keep us from being self-righteous. The Machiavellian and Marxist principle of the ends justifying the means is nevertheless in profound conflict with the theory of democracy, which places such high value on means, and on the compromise of methods and conflicting ultimate ends.

Bibliography

The Marxist theory of morals can only be assembled from the many references to morality in the whole corpus of writings by Marx, Engels, Lenin and others. Convenient collections are found in:

Selected Works of Marx and Engels, 2 Vols. (London, 1942 and 1951).

Lenin, *Selected Works*, 2 Vols. (Moscow, 1947 and 1951).

Note in particular:

Engels, *Anti-Duhring*, and *Origin of the Family, Private Property and the State* (London, 1940).

Lenin, *On Communist Morality*, (in Sel. Works, Vol. II).

Other useful works are:

R. H. S. Crossman, ed., *The God That Failed* (London, 1950).

K. Kautsky, *Ethics and the Materialist Conception of History* (Chicago, 1913).

R. Schlesinger, ed., *The Family in the U.S.S.R.* (London, 1949).

L. Trotsky, *The Revolution Betrayed* (New York, 1937); and his pamphlet *Their Morals and Ours*. –

[5] I. Berlin, *Political Ideas in the Twentieth Century*, Foreign Affairs, (April, 1950), pp. 364 ff.

H. B. Mayo
University of Alberta

Masai: *see* Primitive Morals.

master morality: *see* Nietzsche, Friedrich.

masters and slaves: *see* China, Moral Philosophies of; Hammurapi, Code of.

master-slave morality: *see* China, Moral Philosophy of; Christian Moral Philosophy.

mastery: *see* Hegel, G. W. F.; Sophists, the.

materialism: *see* Berdyaev, Nicolas; Jewish Ethics and Its Civilization; Kant, I.; Stoics, the.

materialism, historical: *see* Soviet Morality, Current.

mathematics: *see* Balguy, John; Clarke, Samuel; Cudworth, Ralph; Meta-ethics and Normative Ethics; More, Henry; Prichard, H. A.; Reid, Thomas; Spinoza.

Mather, Cotton: *see* Moral Philosophy in America; Puritan Morals.

Mather, Increase: *see* Puritan Morals.

matriarchy: *see* Zuni Indians, Morals of.

matrilineal descent: *see* Aboriginals of Yirkalla.

matrilineal household: *see* Zuni Indians, Morals of.

matrimony: *see* Liguori, St. Alphonsus and Catholic Moral Philosophy.

Matthews, W.: *see* Primitive Morals.

maxims: *see* Jewish Ethics and Its Civilization; Kant, I.

maya: *see* Hindu Ethics; Schopenhauer, Arthur.

Mayhew, Jonathan: *see* Moral Philosophy in America.

Mazdā worship: *see* Zoroastrian Morals.

Mc Cosh, James: *see* Moral Philosophy in America.

mean, the (middle): *see* Dante, Alighieri.

mean, theory of: *see* Aristotle.

meaning: *see* Ayer, Alfred J.

means: *see* Major Ethical Viewpoints.

means and ends: *see* Dewey, John; Jesuits, the, Moral Theology of; justification of means; Kant, I.; Marxist Theory of Morals; Soviet Morality, Current.

measure of man: *see* Sophists, the.

mechanism: *see* China, Moral Philosophies of; Kant, I.

Medici, the: *see* Machiavelli, Nicollo.

medicine men: *see* Tapirapé Morals, Some Aspects of.

meditation: *see* contemplation; Hindu Ethics.

meekness: *see* Augustine and Morals; Dostoyevsky, Fyodor. Zoroastrian Morals.

Megaric school, the: *see* Minor Socratics.

memory: *see* Freud, Sigmund; Psychology and Morals.

Mencius: *see* China, Moral Philosophies of.

Mendelssohn: *see* Cooper, Anthony Ashley.

mendicant: *see* Minor Socratics.

Menippus: *see* Minor Socratics.

Mensheviks, Russian: *see* Soviet Morality, Current.

mercy: *see* Christian Moral Philosophy; Jewish Ethics and Its Civilization; Reid, Thomas.

merit: *see* Cooper, Anthony Ashley; Hindu Ethics; Jesuits, the Moral Theology of; More, Henry; Price, Richard; Reid, Thomas.

Merleau-Ponty, Maurice: *see* French Existentiatism and Moral Philosophy.

Meta-ethics and Normative Ethics

The distinction is intended roughly to separate statements about normative ethical judgments from statements which are themselves expressions of moral or ethical judgments. Examples of the former are such epistemological statements as, "the logic of moral arguments reveals a unique validity model," "the evidence for a moral statement is non-empirical," and "two moral judgments are never contradictory." Examples of the latter are actual moral judgments or imperatives such as "stealing is wrong" or "you ought to treat others as you expect to be treated yourself." The first kind are meta-ethical and are about statements of a moral kind, while the second kind express actual moral directives. Such a distinction is not new and, except for terminology, was made at least in principle by Plato in the Apology where Socrates is concerned to clarify terms and was later used quite self-consciously by Hume and Sidgwick.

The distinction is only vaguely analogous to the division of language into a meta-language and an object-language. An important difference is the fact that the distinction between meta-ethics and normative ethics is based essentially on context: whether in fact a statement or a theory asserts something about a moral judgment or whether it expresses a moral judgment. The distinction between a meta-language and object-language is a relative one based entirely on the question as to which language is the one being talked about and it is often the case that the object language may itself have the relation of meta-language to some other object-language. This relativity is not a character of the meta-ethical and normative distinction. It is not, therefore, to be supposed that the distinction will have the same logical consequences as the distinction between a meta-language and object-language, between meta-logic or meta-mathematics and logic or mathematics all of which are useful in solving certain problems in the foundations of mathematics.

In contemporary ethical thinking the usefulness of the distinction depends on how it is formulated, though it is an open question as to whether in any sense it has proved itself useful terminologically or has merely proved misleading. In current theorizing the distinction takes at least two different general forms, the consequences of which are distinct.

One formulation makes the distinction at the level of entire ethical theories and seeks to show that the theories of naturalism, intuitionism, and non-cognitive ethics are neutral with respect to moral commitments. If the distinction depends on the fact that these theories are devoid of normative principles, then the distinction on the level of whole theories is patently wrong; for all three theories make rather general normative pronouncements to the effect that men should solve their moral problems without supernatural aid, that reason in some sense should be followed and that the human person is the highest value in our society. On the other hand, if the meaning of "meta-ethics" is intended to be analytic rather than descriptive, then the definition appears to be circular; for the definition depends upon the fact that there be some agreement as to what is normative and non-normative, but such agreement has not been reached by members of the three schools mentioned and in fact their very differences as schools rest in part on this disagreement. The same difficulty seems to arise for those who set up an ethical theory like a logical system (a method which perhaps at this time imposes more rigor than is commensurate with the subject matter) in terms of which the distinction between meta-ethics or meta-ethical terms and normative ethics is controlled by arbitrary rules. As long as one confines oneself to making statements within the system, then one is clear about the meaning of the distinction. However, it is always possible that a comparison of systems would reveal differences as to what criteria have been used to make the distinction. Nor can the distinction be maintained at the level of entire ethical theories on the ground that holding an ethical theory or meta-ethics (the terms are used interchangeably) will not affect actual moral behavior. The ineffectualness of an ethical theory on conduct is not a necessary consequence of the theory's moral neutrality, but may be due to the fact that the theory is simply uninteresting.

Another formulation avoids reference to a whole theory of ethics and distinguishes meta-ethical factors such as logical, epistemological, and ontological statements from what are obviously moral injunctions. Accordingly, meta-ethical elements consist of answers to the questions as to what constitutes the evidence for a moral judgment, by what criteria do we determine the good, and to what kind of reality do our hypotheses commit us. In this case the distinction is indicated only roughly, if at all, and at least one way of making it is to hold that meta-ethical elements are not sufficient logically to support a substantive position in ethics. However, it is always possible that the alleged meta-ethical factors will implicitly contain recommendations of a methodological sort and that the distinction between this so-called "moralizing" about moral judgments and other normative statements is not at all clear. To make the distinction even roughly between what are obviously epistemological questions and what are moral questions is to assume that there is general agreement concerning the differences between what is normative and non-normative, between what is prescriptive and descriptive, between what is a value and what is not. At the present time, at least, there seems to be only wide disagreement about such differences if they are held to be differences at all. And the distinction between meta-ethics and normative ethics reveals epistemological (and possibly metaphysical) problems which either must be solved or given up as misleading.

332

Bibliography

A. J. Ayer, "On the Analysis of Moral Judgments," *Philosophical Essays* (London, 1954), pp. 231–249.

Abraham Edel, "The Logical Structure of Moore's Ethics," *The Philosophy of G. E. Moore*, P. A. Schilpp, ed. (New York, 1942), pp. 135–176.

William K. Frankena, "Moral Philosophy at Mid-Century" *Philosophical Review*, Vol. 60 (1951), pp. 44–45.

R. M. Hare, *The Language of Morals* (Oxford, 1952).

Mary Mothersill, "Moral Philosophy and Meta-Ethics," *Journal of Philosophy*, Vol. 49 (1952), pp. 587–594.

Frank A. Tillman
College of Wooster

metaphysics: *see* China, Moral Philosophies of; Clarke, Samuel; Cudworth, Ralph; Green, T. H.; Hindu Ethics; Kant, I.; Kierkegaard, Soren; Major Ethical Viewpoints; Meta-ethics and Normative Ethics; philosophy; Price, Richard; Psychology and Morals; Reid, Thomas; Rio Grande Pueblo Indians; Schopenhauer, Arthur; Sophists, The Spinoza; Stoics, The.

metaphysics of morals: *see* Kant, I.

metron: *see* Sophists, The.

Mexico: *see* Aztec Morals.

Meyer, Lodwijk: *see* Spinoza.

Mictlan: *see* Aztec Morals.

might: *see* power.

militarism: *see* Mundurucu Indians, A Dual System of Ethics.

military service: *see* Tolstoy, Leo.

Mill, James: *see* Utilitarianism.

Mill, J. S.: *see* Cumberland, Richard; Green, T. H.; Major Ethical Viewpoints; Marxist Theory of Morals; Moore, George Edward; Moral Philosophy in America; Prichard, H. A.; Utilitarianism.

mind and body: *see* Hindu Ethics.

Minor Socratics

Of men more or less decisively influenced by Socrates, three—Antisthenes (c. 455–360), Aristippus of Cyrene (c. 435–356), and Eucleides of Megara (c. 450–380)—became founders of schools (or sects) often referred to as "minor Socratic schools." These schools are the Cynic, the Cyrenaic,[1] and the Megaric, respectively. The names of the last two are self-explanatory. That of the first means something like "dog (*kyón*)-like." By some it is assumed to have been derived from the meeting place of Antisthenes with his followers, the gymnasium of *Kynos*arges; others believe it to be contemptuously indicative of the dog like life of the members of the sect (shamelessness, begging, barking, biting). In this sense it was proudly and defiantly accepted by the members themselves. What we know of the ethical teachings of the Megaric school amounts to hardly more than one sentence, in which the Good seems to have been identified with the One. All we can say of this formula is that it, in some way, links the Megarians to the Eleatic school but also to some aspects of Plato's *Philebus* and his *Laws*, and also to the *Epinomis*. And though we know that many Megarians were engaged in po-

---

[1] The theory that it was his namesake grandson who founded the school and that Aristippus the Elder was Socrates' companion rather than his pupil cannot be here discussed.

litical activities, we do not know in what way, if any, that highly abstract ethical doctrine was linked to practice. It is entirely different with the other two schools, in which ethical theory is immediately applied to life and theoretical aspects of philosophy are often neglected or even absent.

However, there is some doubt as to whether Antisthenes can actually be considered the fountainhead of Cynicism. He seems to have undergone the influence of Socrates late in his life, when he had already been active as a "sophist" (a very misleading term, to be sure) and perhaps he retained his sophistic interest also later. And probably he never adopted the Cynic way of life. Finally, though the seriousness of his logico-epistemological theories is in doubt, he seemed to have had a considerable interest in purely speculative problems in which Cynicism takes almost none. Many scholars assert in connection with all this, that only his student Diogenes of Sinope was the true founder of the sect. But for the present purpose this problem cannot be discussed, and Antisthenes will be classed together with his followers. The best justification of this procedure is a saying of his, most adequately expressing the spirit of Cynicism: "Better to rave with madness than to be ravished by pleasure." Whence came this enmity to and contempt for pleasure (if this is a good word to translate *hédoné;* sometimes "joy" or "enjoyment," sometimes "transport" or "ecstasy" are more appropriate)? The goal sought after by all men is happiness; but only he can

be happy who for happiness depends on himself alone, he who in this sense of the word is self-sufficient and is, by not depending for happiness on external circumstances, free—not in any legal sense of the word, but free inwardly, which is the only true freedom. But obviously there is hardly any condition in which man is more beside himself, more "possessed," than when he is in the grip of pleasure and there is nothing for which he more depends on external circumstances than pleasure. Therefore all pleasure is to be shunned; it makes man a slave. This contempt for pleasure is matched by the contempt for fear of hardship (*ponos*) and, in this sense at least, for suffering. And just as a man who wants to become happy must train himself to go without pleasure, so he also must train himself in exposing himself to hardships and privations such as voluntary poverty (or even self-inflicted suffering), hard work, verbal and practical insults, etc. A man who has become indifferent to pleasures and privations (hardships), is the truly wise man. He achieved *areté,* a word misleadingly translated "virtue" (actually sometimes the term "excellence befitting man" or even "life virtuosity" is a better translation); and *areté* alone is sufficient to assure his permanent happiness. After Antisthenes it became customary to present problems of ethics by describing the self-sufficient sage, who is the only one who knows what, when, and how to do anything (including loving, or cooking a lentil soup, or being king), because he alone knows what makes man happy, whereas the fool, no matter what he has or does, will always achieve unhappiness.

Voluntary hardship (exertion) is rewarded and followed by a pleasure of its own kind, the only one which we shall never repent. It would seem that the voluntary undergoing of hardships and the shunning of pleasure contradicts our natural inclinations, but Antisthenes undertook to prove that the true wants of man are extremely few and simple and easily satisfied (a conviction which could perhaps originate only in the mild Mediterranean climate), whereas the great variety of them, without the satisfaction of which we fancy to be unhappy, are unnatural and the product of civilization with its merely conventional and, in this sense, illusionary values. To get rid of these illusions it takes insight (knowledge) which thus, becomes an indispensable guide on the road to happiness; in this sense virtue (virtuosity) is teachable.

It was also Antisthenes who gave the Cynics their major patron saint in the person of Heracles, whose works became symbols of life devoted to voluntary privation (and he himself the model of the true king) and a minor in the person of Cyrus the Elder (characteristically, a non-Greek). Conversely, Prometheus as the founder of civilization in many Cynic writings is presented as a man, suffering because puffed up by conceit and vanity (*typhê*), symbolized by the vulture, and cured of them by Heracles (an example of the allegoric interpretation of myths, favored by Cynics).

In the followers of Antisthenes we admire mainly the courage with which they developed and sometimes applied their principles with all their most radical consequences and expressed them in their way of life. It is particularly Diogenes of Sinope (d. shortly after 325 B.C.) who became the hero of countless anecdotes, some undoubtedly invented to illustrate his doctrines (it is impossible to assume that had he lived the life of absolute poverty and beggary ascribed to him in most of the stories he would ever have had a chance to write his *Republic*, dialogues and tragedies, to have regular students, etc.), but some probably genuine and proving that occasionally he would not shrink to display utter shamelessness thus showing the seriousness of his doctrines. Hunger and thirst are natural desires, but to satisfy them with anything "better" than beans, onions, or garlic and water, to drink from a cup instead of the hollow of one's hand, is unnatural. To satisfy the natural desire for shelter by building houses is unnatural. The sexual drive is natural; to hide its satisfaction or accept limitations such as the prohibition of incest is unnatural. It is sheer fancy to prefer one woman to another; if at all, the ugly ones deserve preference, because they will be happy that they found somebody who has use for them. If no female is in reach, masturbation (no reason to practice it only in secret) is perfectly natural (Diogenes said that he wished hunger were equally easy to satisfy). Natural also is cannibalism.

Among illusions is allegiance to one's own country. Diogenes was perhaps the first to call himself a cosmo-polite—not in the sense of feeling allegiance to mankind at large, but because of his feeling of contempt for any feeling of allegiance to a particular place. Indeed, only a completely herd-like society (with community of women and children, without any private property, and with those "naturally" better as leaders) would have satisfied him.[2] The Cynics often presented the tyrant as in reality a slave (to pleasures, etc.); the ideal king they saw as a Cynic sage, truly free even if he happened to be in slavery, truly rich, even if he happened to live in poverty. More than once they were banished from imperial Rome, obviously because they were considered close to the republican opposition.

His contempt for hardship Diogenes expressed by such acts as rolling in hot sand in summer, embracing ice-cold statues in winter, thus practicing the enuring of oneself (*askêsis*); this behavior was on the verge of turning into what we later mainly mean by asceticism.

The typical Cynic is characterized by his appearance: unshaven, he wears only a cloak, and carries a staff and a knapsack. If necessary, he begs. Out of "philanthropy" he preaches in the streets, with full license of speech (*parrêsia*). Thus he reminds us of the *bikshu* (he was compared to the Hindu ascetics by Onesicritus, one of the philosophers who accompanied Alexander the Great to Asia) on one

hand, of the medieval mendicant friar and itinerant preacher on the other.

Diogenes asserted that it was his task to "recoin legal [i.e. conventional] currency" (a phrase which obviously inspired Nietzsche, who knew it very well, to call his undertaking "transvaluation of values"). In that it implied rejection of all values of civilization (including education) in favor of values "coined" by nature, it makes the Cynics forerunners of men like Rousseau or Tolstoy.

Among those close to Cynicism we find the historian Theopompos (b. c. 378 B.C.) perhaps identical with the so-called historian of Oxyrrhynchus, who might have been attracted to the Cynic ideal of "natural" leadership (aristocracy). Remarkable is the existence of a Cynic statesman in the person of Cercidas of Megalopolis (3rd cent. B.C.) who protested against social injustice and oppression.

Cynicism survived down to the 6th century A.D. Among later Cynics we find Crates (fl. c. 328–325 B.C.), whose mendicant life was shared by his "wife" Hipparchia and who presented the ideals of the Cynics in the form of a utopia describing the City of Knapsack (and who also coined the formula that lovesickness which neither hunger nor time can cure, should be cured by the rope); Menippus (3rd cent. B.C.), one of the masters of a new literary style in which prose and poetry, the earnest and the jocular mix and mingle; Demetrius, close to the anti-monarchical opposition of the 1st century A.D.; Oinomaos of Gadara (c. 120 A.D.), sharp critic of popular religion with its

---

[2] Swift's Utopia, the island of the horse men, exhibits many traces of Cynicism.

polytheism (he shared this position with all Cynics) and specifically of oracles, to which he opposed the free will theory; Dio of Prusa (c. 40–120), whom political exile converted to Cynicism and whose orations, eminently readable, are full of passages that are reports or perhaps even literal quotations from Antisthenes and Diogenes; and Peregrinus Proteus (c. 100–165) who, to prove his detachment from life, announced in advance and publicly committed suicide by throwing himself into the flames of a pyre. Bion the Borysthenite (c. 325–255), perhaps the originator of the so-called *diatribe,* i.e. the moral sermon in an extremely lively style, addressed mainly to the common man, and precursor of the Christian sermon, exhibiting the same qualities as the writings of Menippus (see above) and who seems to have been the first to have compared life to a play in which everybody should play the role assigned to him by circumstances as well as he can, but with the detachment of an actor, and Teles (fl. c. 240 B.C.) will also be mentioned later, as they sometimes are classed as hedonistic Cynics. Letters ascribed to Cynics (probably *bona fide* fiction) by unknown authors originated probably in the 1st and 2nd centuries. In the 4th century A.D. Emperor Julian expressed his admiration for the true Cynic (he himself dressed like one) and sharply criticized as pseudo-Cynics some contemporaries for reasons sometimes clear (e.g. their attacks on popular cults which Julian wanted to revive), sometimes unclear, but perhaps connected with their proximity to the Cyrenaics, to whom we now turn.

Being reproached for conduct unbecoming a philosopher in practicing sexual intercourse with the expensive courtesan Lais Aristippus answered: I possess [scil. her or the pleasure of the intercourse] but I am not possessed [by her or that pleasure]. An interpretation of this saying is at the same time the best interpretation of the philosophy of Aristippus. He was a hedonist; i.e. he maintained that the supreme good in life and what makes man happy is pleasure of the moment, whatever its source (pleasures of the body being on the whole stronger), which he proved by pointing out that all living beings from the very beginning strive after pleasure. Therefore the sage takes pleasure where he can find it, not caring whether or not his actions are socially reprehensible; but at the same time his attitude towards pleasure is different from that of the ordinary man. He knows that in the very same moment when he is engaged in the pursuit of pleasure, he stands above it: "I am not possessed" is the equivalent of: "I know that I could equally well go without it." And it is only this detached attitude (*adiaphoria*) towards pleasure, the certainty that one is not and never will be its slave, that one will always retain mastery over it and in this way remain one's own master, which makes hedonism the philosophy of the sage. He takes what he, as he knows, could with equal ease leave. What matters is not to abstain from pleasure, but to indulge in it without being mastered by it. Living this kind of life implies that it will entirely depend on circumstances which pleasures the sage will pursue, although the sage himself never depends on the circumstances; he takes them as they come, or even may pursue them with the same kind of detachment which he observes with regard to the actual enjoyment.

The pursuit of momentary pleasures (in this sense of the word) being the goal of life, the sage lives strictly for himself and does not recognize any sociopolitical bonds or duties. He also is a cosmopolitan not in the sense of adherence to an ideal society but in the sense of being able to live under any sun and derive all the pleasures according to circumstances. This is, of course, not quite what we usually mean by a hedonist; we almost feel reminded of Horatio whom Hamlet praises because he had been "as one, in suffering all, that suffers nothing, A man that fortune's buffets and rewards hath ta'en with equal thanks," not being "passion's slave."

By defining pleasure as change (or motion, *kinêsis*) Aristippus opened hedonism to the objection that as there is no definite limit to change, pleasure cannot be conceived as a goal. Furthermore, to his hedonism the objection was raised that it linked happiness to unhappiness, inasmuch as pleasure lasts only as long as we are engaged in the process of removing the corresponding pain (unhappiness). It seems that Epicurus defined pleasure as the condition of painlessness, i.e. as a definite limit of a process and a condition free from any admixture of pain, precisely to avoid these objections. On the other hand it may be that under the impact of Epicureanism the followers of Aristippus somewhat changed and consolidated their doctrines. Otherwise we are not too well informed on these followers[3]; it seems that they disagreed among themselves on the question whether there are any unselfish pleasures (e.g. in the welfare of our country, our friends, etc.). They seemed also even more than the founder to have stressed that it is the momentary pleasure which is the goal, not a pleasant life as a whole. On the contrary, in life taken as a whole pains outbalance pleasures, so that if happiness is to be taken as a condition of life as a whole, it would be unattainable. In other words, contrary to what some scholars assert, the Cyrenaics rejected the felicific calculus. This seems to have been the attitude of Annikeris (c. 283 B.C.), Theodoros "the Atheist" (b.c. 340 B.C.) who replaced the terms of pleasure and hardship by joy and grief, and Hegesias (c. 283 B.C.) who so impressively presented that unfavorable balance mentioned above that he was nicknamed "the persuader to suicide" and who also asserted that nothing is pleasant or unpleasant by nature and that only circumstances make it so.

At first glance the doctrines of the Cynics and the Cyrenaics seem quite incompatible: strict anti-hedonism there, hedonism here. But in fact there is great similarity between them in that

---

3 Among whom we find (as a unique case) his daughter Aretê and her son Aristippus (on whom see above) nicknamed "mother's pupil."

both teach the ideal of inner freedom and self-sufficiency of the sage, though the Cynic achieves it by a life which shuns pleasure and does not shun pain, the Cyrenaic by indifference to pleasure which he enjoys and indifference to any privations to which he might be exposed. Scholars who deny this similarity face the difficulty of explaining how both Antisthenes and Aristippus could have claimed Socrates for their master; of explaining the presence of Cynicism in some actions attributed to Aristippus, or in some doctrines of Theodorus (e.g. that sexual intercourse should be practiced in public); or of explaining the presence of Cyrenaic doctrines and a Cyrenaic way of life in Bion and Teles (who, e.g., asserted that they live like migratory birds, i.e., always being able to make the best of circumstances) in some way more satisfactory than by assuming that they became untrue to the original doctrines of Cynicism. The essential similarity seem to have been stated by Diogenes himself. He who with relish compared himself with various breeds of the dog and was by Crates called the heavenly dog, said of Aristippus, with obvious reference to his life of pleasure at the court of a tyrant that he was a royal (or perhaps a king's) dog. The taunt is obvious; but so is the recognition of similarity.

The two schools are apparented to the Stoics and the Epicureans respectively. In fact the Stoa could almost be described as Cynicism gone respectable and Epictetus almost admitted that Stoicism was Cynicism made easier. Both teach a strictly individualistic, a-social ethics. Both are a way of life much more than a system of thought. Both are popular rather than esoteric. For these reasons they will always attract some and repel others.

Bibliography

A. Sources. An edition of texts by O. Gigon (For the *Bibliotheca Teubneriana*) is in preparation. Some of the fundamental texts with an English translation are available in the Loeb Classical Library, notably Diogenes Laertius, *Lives of Eminent Philosophers,* Books 6 and 2, and Dio Chrysostom (of Prusa), *Discourses* 4, 6, 8, 9, 10, 13, 60, 62.

B. Secondary Literature: E. Zeller, *Socrates and the Socratic Schools* (London, 1885), chs. 12–14; *idem, A History of Eclecticism in Greek Philosophy* (London, 1883), ch. 10; T. Gomperz, *The Greek Thinkers,* vol. 2 (London, 1905), chs. 7–9; P. E. Moore, *Hellenistic Philosophies* (Princeton, 1923), chs. 1, 3, 6; A. O. Lovejoy, G. Boas, *Primitivism and Related Ideas in Antiquity* (Baltimore, 1935); D. R. Dudley, *A History of Cynicism* (London, 1937); R. Höistadt, *Cynic Hero and Cynic King* (Upsala, 1948).

Philip Merlan
Scripps College

Pakot, The Moral System of; Rio Grande Pueblo Indians; Stoics, The.

Mishnah, the: *see* Jewish Ethics and Its Civilization.

misogyny: *see* Schopenhauer, Arthur.

mistakes: *see* error; More, Henry; Reid, Thomas.

Mithra: *see* Zoroastrian Morals.

mixed life, the: *see* Plato.

Mo Ti: *see* China, Moral Philosophies of.

Mo Tzu: *see* China, Moral Philosophies of.

Mo Tzu, the: see China, Moral Philosophies of.

mockery: *see* Goethe, Wolfgang von.

moderation: *see* Muslim Morals; Navaho Morals; Plato; Puritan Morals; Zuni Indians, Morals of.

modes: *see* Spinoza.

modesty: *see* Jewish Ethics and Its Civilization; Puritan Morals.

Mohammed: *see* Muhammed.

moieties: *see* Aboriginals of Yirkalla.

Moism: *see* China, Moral Philosophies of.

Molina, L.: *see* Jesuits, the, Moral Theology of.

monastic: *see* Hindu Ethics; monks.

monism: *see* Hindu Ethics; Stoics, The.

monks: *see* Augustine and Morals; monastic life.

monogamy: *see* Aquinas, Thomas; Moral Views of; Soviet Morality, Current.

monotheism: *see* Goethe, Wolfgang von.

monpsychism: *see* Schopenhauer, Arthur.

Moore, George Edward

The "great" philosophers are those who articulate the animating concerns of contemporary and later thinkers, those who define the problems and the categories employed for their analysis, which chiefly engage philosophical reflection. So considered, G. E. Moore is the pre-eminent moral philosopher of the twentieth century. A survey of the most influential ethical theories at the middle of this century[1] formulates the central points at issue between them by use of the concepts and even the terms familiarized by Moore. His *Principia Ethica,* published in 1903, overhauled and gave new direction to ethical thought as his "Refutation of Idealism," which appeared in the same year, did in epistemology and metaphysics. And indeed *Principia* was avowedly dedicated to this end (cf., e.g., pp. 223–224). It was intended to do away with the verbalism and confusion of traditional ethics by relentless insistence on clarity in framing and distinguishing the questions to be asked and by appeal to the convictions of moral common-sense in answering them. Most traditional ethics are thereby found wanting. Moore's own view proclaims the uniqueness and irreducibility of moral experience and discourse which cannot therefore be grounded upon or analyzed in terms of any other field of inquiry. Thus he calls into question, on the one hand, theological and metaphysical ethics, such as the reigning Idealism of that day, and on the other, scientifically inspired "Naturalistic" ethics which take the meaning and confirmation of

---

[1] William K. Frankena, "Moral Philosophy at Mid-Century" in *Philosophical Review,* vol. LX, no. 1 (Jan., 1951), pp. 44–55.

moral judgments to be wholly empirical. This controversy has been at the heart of much ethical discussion since *Principia*. Further, Moore's sweeping indictment of the definitions of moral terms presented in foregoing ethical theories has directed the attention of later thinkers to the logical character of the foundational definitions and postulates of an ethical system and to determining in which senses, if any, these can be said to be validated.

Though Moore is historically a trailbreaking figure, his work reveals the influence of his great predecessors in British ethics, Mill and Sidgwick. Hedonism is among the doctrines which are ostensibly destroyed by the critical technique of *Principia* and it is again disavowed in Moore's later *Ethics*. Yet in fixing upon "good" as the central concept in ethics and in defining rightness of conduct by reference to the promotion of the good, Moore's is a teleological ethic. His argument in *Principia*, chap. V, that moral obligation can be justified as such only if it gives rise to value and that "no moral law is self-evident" (p. 148) is squarely in the tradition which has ever been an indispensable corrective to mere traditionalism and obscurantism in law and morals (cf., 1:p. 106). Later in *Principia* he gives eloquent expression to the genius of Utilitarianism in saying of the felt values of experience "that it is only for the sake of these things . . . that any one can be justified in performing any public or private duty; that they are the *raison d'être* of virtue; that it is they . . . that form the rational ulti-

mate end of human action and the sole criterion of social progress" (p. 189). However Utilitarianism is not employed by Moore, as it was by his early and mid-nineteenth century forebears, as an instrument of vigorous social concern, for it is accompanied by a detailed argument on behalf of conservative acquiescence in existing rules of conduct. And in general his predilection appears to be for the relishing of refined and non-competitive values rather than for missionary involvement in political and social issues. In this, Lord Keynes testifies,[2] Moore reflected the temper of his immediate contemporaries. Sidgwick's importance for Moore consists chiefly in his recognition that an ethical system must rest on principles which are incapable of being established inferentially. Moore's development of this insight in his treatment of "good" is decisive for his system and is, in turn, a chief historical source of the intuitionistic analyses of rightness and duty found in such later thinkers as Broad and Ross. In his own thinking Moore rivals the sobriety and clarity of Sidgwick, though it cannot be said that he displays the catholicity and warmth of concern with which the latter examined the concrete data of moral experience.

In recent years, and particularly in the last decade, there have been radical departures from Moore in three directions chiefly. Emotivism, charging Moore and others with undue emphasis on the cognitive and referential

2 John Maynard Keynes, "My Early Beliefs" in *Two Memoirs* (London 1949) pp. 82 ff.

341

aspects of language, has repudiated the view that such terms as "good" denote objective properties. Moore has said that he finds both this theory and his own cogent and confesses that "I simply do not know whether I am any more strongly inclined to take the one than to take the other" (5: p. 545). Further, Moore has been accused of failure to recognize the different senses of such terms as "good" and "right" in ordinary discourse and the nuances of meaning which they acquire in different contexts of usage. There is a kind of irony in this for few men have been more responsible for calling attention to the philosophical significance of ordinary language. It should be pointed out that Moore has taken note of this plurality of meanings (4: p. 117), though not perhaps sufficiently in his early writings (cf., however, 2: pp. 161, 250), but that in any event, his discussion has been concentrated chiefly on one single sense of "good." Related to the foregoing and most fundamental of all, is the transference of attention in recent ethics away from the meaning of the ethical predicates to the processes of reasoning characteristic of moral debate and persuasion. But though it may plausibly be argued that Moore has failed to develop an adequate theory of ethics, so construed, it is simply unjust to say that he has been oblivious to the issues of practical reasoning. At the beginning of *Principia* he asserts that the primary goal of ethics is that of establishing which reasons legitimately support a moral judgment (p. 6) and he takes this to be "my main object" (p. ix). Indeed he considers it sufficient refutation of an ethical theory that it fails to provide good reasons for moral injunctions (p. 12). He holds, however, that such questions cannot be intelligibly treated until the meanings of the ethical predicates have been ascertained (cf., pp. 142–143).

George Edward Moore was born in 1873 in a suburb of London. He entered Trinity College in 1892. In his formative years he was influenced by Sidgwick, James Ward and McTaggart but it is of Bertrand Russell that he says "I certainly have been more influenced by him than by any other single philosopher" (5: p. 16). He was a Fellow at Trinity 1898–1904, returned to Cambridge in 1911 as Lecturer in Moral Science and remained there for twenty-eight years, being appointed Professor in 1925. Following his retirement he taught and lectured at Oxford and at a number of American universities. He served as editor of *Mind* from 1921 to 1947. His bibliography is quite small relative to his significance in the movements of ethical and epistemological Realism and linguistic analysis.

There are certain respects in which Moore's writings are appropriate to a "defence of common sense," in the most eulogistic sense of that phrase. They are marked by a clarity not usually attained by philosophers, meticulous care in framing the question at issue and great tenacity in refusing to be diverted from its analysis by irrelevancy or glibness. Also, Moore has eschewed any large-scale metaphysical system-building. On the other hand, many of Moore's positive conclusions, particularly in ethics, are far removed from the area of uncritical conviction. And not only is it true that his thought has, as he says, been stimulated by the technical problems posed by philosophers (5: p. 14) but also it has become widely known almost exclusively within professional circles. The naiveté which he sometimes affects is deceptive, for it is generally a device for setting forth exceedingly sophisticated and incisive reasoning. However, probably no philosopher of comparable stature has been more candid and humble in avowing his perplexities and in repudiating his errors.

Moore's best-known work, *Principia Ethica,* is as much an essay in the theory of value as ethics. For he takes it as his central task to ascertain the meaning of "good" in the sense in which it is synonymous with "intrinsic value" or "ought to exist for its own sake." This question, he insists, must not be confused, as it has been traditionally, with that of determining which things are good, to which it is logically prior. He will not accept a definiens which is merely a verbal equivalent for he is concerned only with that kind of definition which analyzes the complex of the "object or idea" to which the term refers. But "'in this sense 'good' has no definition because it is simple and has no parts" (p. 9). We can be assured "by inspection" (p. 16) that any proposed definitional analysis will be inadequate, for "we are all aware of a certain simple quality, which (and not anything else)

is what we mainly mean by the term 'good'" (p. 38).

The generic error of all such definition consists in attempting to identify two properties which we know to be different. It is committed by those ethical theories which confuse properties which may universally accompany goodness with goodness itself, e.g., even if it be true that whatever is "more evolved" is always "better," it does not follow that the former term *means* the same as the latter. The error is, however, compounded because good is a unique sort of property, a "non-natural" property. Hence this particular definitional mistake deserves to be singled out and it is dubbed "the naturalistic fallacy" (cf., pp. 13–14, 58, 59). However the distinction between "natural" and "non-natural" properties proves difficult for Moore. In *Principia* he asserts that good, by contrast to "natural" properties, cannot exist "*by itself* in time" (p. 41, Italics in original; cf., also, pp. 38, 110–111). Confronted with the criticism that this is also true of "natural" properties e.g., roundness, Moore later conceded that his account of the distinction was untenable (5: pp. 581–582). At the same time he holds to the view suggested hesitantly in a later essay (3: p. 274) that intrinsic properties which are "natural" describe" the thing which possesses them whereas those which are "non-natural" do not (5: p. 591). This, of course, merely defers the problem, which remains unresolved because of Moore's failure to specify the relevant meaning of "describe" (idem.). Moore holds, however, that the existence of good is always "dependent upon" the intrinsic "natural" properties of the object (3: pp. 260, 274; 5: p. 603).

Moore's critics have pointed out the obscurity of the notion of "non-natural" properties and that "the naturalistic fallacy" argument is inconclusive if, as they avow, others are incapable of discerning the unique quality of goodness of which Moore speaks. Some thirty years after *Principia,* Moore himself described his argument that "good" is indefinable as "certainly fallacious" (4: p. 127) and asserted that he thought that it might be definable. Nonetheless, there is great significance for the understanding of moral reasoning in the conclusions which he drew in *Principia:* all judgments that something is good must necessarily be synthetic; they are known "intuitively" in the sense that they are incapable of being proved or disproved: "from no other truth, except themselves, can it be inferred that they are either true or false" (p. viii; cf., also, p. 143); though in a given instance we may be mistaken about their truth, when they are true, they are so universally. Because value-judgments are never merely tautologous, their truth is always an "open question." Since they cannot be established by any of the usual processes of inference, deductive or inductive, the inferences drawn in e.g., Stoic or theological ethics, to "this is good" from "reality is of this nature" are necessarily invalid. Despite the undeniable epistemological and metaphysical shortcomings of Moore's analysis, and the difficulties which it puts in the way of ad-

judicating value-disputes, it does mark off value-judgments from other areas of discourse and it points up the uniqueness of the way in which they are justified, while at the same time preserving their meaningfulness and knowability, as well as the impersonality which is indispensable to their normative authority. Moore's theory has therefore been seminal for the study of "practical reasoning" which has been so prominent in recent ethics and for the attempts to clarify more nearly than he was able to do, the relations between ethical ("non-natural") and non-ethical ("natural") characteristics, which are crucial to such reasoning.

To decide which things possess the quality of goodness, Moore uses the "isolation method" i.e., "consider what things are such that, if they existed *by themselves,* in absolute isolation, we should yet judge their existence to be good" (p. 187, italics in original). He finds an enormous diversity of good things which, moreover, do not possess any other property common and peculiar to themselves. He imputes to all those who have reflected upon it the conviction that "the most valuable things, which we know or can imagine" are "personal affection and the appreciation of what is beautiful" (p. 188). Though Moore concedes that these and similar intuitions, upon which he expatiates at great length in *Principia,* chap. VI, may appear "unduly arbitrary" (p. 222), it is worth quoting Keynes' remark that "(Moore's) way of translating his own particular emotions of the moment into the language

344

of generalised abstraction is a charming and beautiful comedy."[3] Moore does not hold in *Principia* that only states of sentient experience or things in relation to such experience are intrinsically valuable. He alters his position in later writings, though his precise statement is different in each case (cf., 4: p. 124, 5: p. 618). In *Principia* he argues that an utterly beautiful world would be good even if it were never the object of contemplation (pp. 83–85). However there is an increase in the value of the whole when it is apprehended, which need not be equivalent to the goodness of the components, on the principle of "organic unities": the *"value of . . . a whole bears no regular proportion to the sum of the values of its parts"* (p. 27, italics in original; cf., also, 2: p. 246). Hence a whole may be good though it contains an element which is evil and ugly e.g., compassion, the object of which is pain. Moore fails, however, to set forth a criterion for calculating the relative degree of values or their "summation."

Though intuitionism has generally been most widespread in the area of right conduct and obligation, *Principia* takes "right" to be definable, in terms which allow judgments of conduct to be validated differently than value-judgments. To judge that an act is right demands both a judgment of the goodness of something and a causal proposition concerning the conduciveness of the act to the achievement of this goodness. The latter can be confirmed or denied by the usual methods of empirical knowledge. The action

which it is the agent's duty to perform is defined as that "which will cause more good to exist in the Universe than any possible alternative" (p. 148). Moore draws the distinction between an obligatory act so defined and a "right" action, which will produce at least as much value as any alternative (idem.; cf., also, 2: pp. 32 ff.), thus leaving open the possibility that there may be a number of equally right acts. In the later *Ethics* he no longer takes the relation between obligation and value to be definitory (pp. 61, 66, 173), justifying this in a recent statement by contending that we can think the one without thinking the other (5: pp. 599–600). He now holds that the function "the world is intrinsically better because x chose act y than it would have been had he made another choice" is "logically equivalent" to "x did his duty in choosing y" i.e., each follows from the other (5: pp. 610–611).

Moore is prepared to accept the frequently paradoxical conclusions which follow from defining "rightness" in terms of all of the actual consequences brought about by an act. Primarily, to know that an act is our duty demands complete knowledge of whatever value it may possess together with that of its effects "throughout an infinite future," along with such knowledge of all possible alternative acts. But since our knowledge always falls short of this, "we never have any reason to suppose that an action is our duty" (p. 149). We must therefore restrict ourselves to calculating which of the viable alternatives which present themselves to the agent will most probably bring about

3 *Op. cit.:* p. 92.

345

the better results, though even so the probability will be relatively small. The implications of such skepticism are two-faced. Obviously it tells against the claim that any law or rule of conduct is binding under all circumstances; however it also seems to preclude taking exception to laws which are generally useful: "In short, though we may be sure that there are cases where the rule should be broken, we can never know which those cases are, and ought, therefore, never to break it" (pp. 162–163). There is nothing more startling about these conclusions than the equanimity with which the author accepts them. Furthermore it follows that a well-intentioned and carefully calculated act which, because of unforeseeable circumstances does not bring about the best possible consequences, is wrong (2: pp. 190–195).

In rigorous Utilitarian fashion, Moore finds little intrinsic value, if any, in the performance of certain acts, the motive to do what is right, or the "virtues," taking their value to be chiefly instrumental. The motive determines in part, though not wholly, the praiseworthiness or blameworthiness of the agent, but Moore also holds to the teleological view that blame and punishment may be inflicted on a man who performs a right act, if it is socially beneficial to do so. Moore faces up to the chronic objection to Utilitarianism that it blurs the distinction between acts which are merely expedient and those which are genuinely dutiful. He takes both to be means for the attainment of value and denies that the latter are any more obligatory than

the former. He argues skilfully that the distinction has arisen because of the contingent circumstances that duties generally arouse moral emotion, that people generally try to avoid doing them and that they usually affect other people in addition to the agent.

Moore's criticisms of the theories which imply, in opposition to his own view, that one and the same moral act can be both right and wrong or change from right to wrong (2: chaps. III–IV), have become extremely well-known. They have been very largely taken over by such thinkers as Ross and Ewing and most emotivist and subjectivist theorists have thought it incumbent upon them to meet these arguments. Moore says in *Ethics* that this view cannot be "proved" (p. 86) wrong, for he considers its opposite self-evident, but he then addresses himself to the definitions of "right" in terms of some feeling, opinion or attitude, which entail this conclusion. Thus, to hold that a moral judgment is merely an assertion about the speakers' feeling implies that, given opposite feelings had by different men, the same action can be both right and wrong. Moore rejects this view on the grounds that in such a case the judgments do not contradict each other and yet it is "plain matter of fact" (p. 102) that there can be genuine difference of opinion about the rightness of actions. Then, rightness cannot be equated with social or historical approval, for one may judge an action to be right though he believes that it is not generally approved. Further, to take "right" to mean that one believes something to be right, is open to the same criticisms and has the further shortcoming that it generates an infinite regress in which moral judgments always assert that a belief is held but can never assert *what* is believed. On these views, ethics as such is destroyed by being reduced to the collection of psychological and historical information.

One of the most perplexing discussions in Moore is that of "free will." Moore wishes to preserve the common view that an act cannot be considered moral if the agent cannot do anything other than what he actually does. He therefore defines a voluntary act as one such that the agent could have acted otherwise *if* he had chosen to do so. This sets it off from e.g., contracting disease, which cannot be avoided irrespective of choice and provides a basis for therapeutic reward or punishment. Moore is uncertain however what it means to say that the agent "could" have chosen differently (2: pp. 218–222; 5: p. 626) though he insists that unless a different action could have been chosen, the act is not properly moral (5: p. 624).

Any estimate of Moore's ethics will have to take account of the avowed incompleteness of the theory of free will, along with the inconclusiveness of the "naturalistic" fallacy," the opacity of "non-natural" and "non-descriptive" properties, and the questionable epistemology invoked to explain their relations to each other and to non-ethical characteristics. More important for ethics than the validity of these particular views, it has been suggested, are

the insights which underlie them and the direction which they give to further inquiry. But though Moore has asked pregnant and searching questions, and has pursued them with great patience and acumen, we must probably accept the judgment which, with characteristic frankness and humility, he delivers on himself—that he has been an "unsatisfactory answerer": "I did want to answer questions, to give solutions to problems, and I think it is a just charge against me that I have been able to solve so few of the problems I wished to solve" (5: p. 677).

Bibliography

G. E. Moore, *Principia Ethica* (1903).
G. E. Moore, *Ethics* (1912).
Philosophical Studies (1922) chaps. VIII, IX, X.
Symposium, "Is Goodness a Quality?" in *Phenomenology, Goodness and Beauty:* Aristotelian Society, s. v. XI (1932), pp. 116–131.
Paul Arthur Schilpp, ed., *The Philosophy of G. E. Moore* (1942).

Jerome Stolnitz
University of Rochester

Moore, G. E.: *see* Ayer, Alfred J.; Broad C. D.; Language and Ethics; Major Ethical Viewpoints; Moral Philosophy in America; Price, Richard; Ross, Sir (William) David; Russell, Bertrand; Utilitarianism.
Moore, G. F.: see Jewish Ethics and Its Civilization; Primitive Morals.
moral absolutes: *see* absolute morals.
moral codes: *see* Aboriginals of Yirkalla; Freud, Sigmund; Marxist Theory of Morals; Psychology and Morals; Puritan Morals; Rio Grande

Pueblo Indians; Sophists, the; Spinoza; Zoroastrian Morals.

moral disease: *see* Psychology and Morals.

moral freedom and responsibility: *see* Kant, I.; Soviet Morality, Current.

moral futurism: *see* Marxist Theory of Morals.

moral intuitionism: *see* intuitionism.

moral judgments: *see* Dewey, John.; judgment; Meta-ethics and Normative Ethics.

moral law: *see* Aquinas, Thomas, Moral Views of; Hindu Ethics.

moral obligation: *see* duties; obligation.

Moral Philosophy in America

The purpose of this article* is to give a sketch and an interpretation of the history of ethics or moral philosophy in the United States which will be of interest, not only to philosophers, but to scholars in other fields and to educated readers generally. An effort will therefore be made to avoid technicality, and to relate moral philosophy to other subjects like literature and politics.

The history of ethics in America has been a neglected subject, possibly because few, if any, of the moralists who play a part in it deserve to be ranked with Spinoza, Butler, Hume, Kant, or even Mill. Nevertheless it is interesting in several respects. Some of the parts of it are interesting in themselves, and the history as a whole illus-

trates certain themes with which any intellectual historian will be familiar but which he will not often, if ever, find clearly represented. The parts we shall come to in due course, but the themes portrayed by the picture as a whole should be stated here. There are four: 1) a gradual separation of ethics from theology, 2) an effort to find an adequate ethical basis for a democratic conception of society, 3) an increasing tendency toward empiricism and naturalism in ethics, and 4) a drift in the direction of this-worldliness and utilitarianism.

Being an offshoot of European culture and relatively little influenced by the Orient, American thought is, roughly speaking, the result of three influences, interacting with the native intelligence of our thinkers and with the American scene itself. These influences are: (a) Christianity, especially Protestantism, (b) the culture of Greece and Rome, (c) modern European science and philosophy. The themes to be described are largely the result of these three influences acting on intellects faced with life in America. In fact, any culture which has such ingredients is bound to have certain problems: the place of reason and revelation in ethics, the role of experience in ethics, the conflict of this-worldliness and other-worldliness, and the worth of the individual as against society.

I

With this, we may paint in the details of our picture, beginning with the Puritans. Perhaps no society has ever

---

* The substance of this article is taken from a lecture given to the American Studies Seminars at the University of Tokyo during the summer of 1954 and already published in Japanese.—Editor

been more strictly moralistic than theirs, and their influence on American morality has been very great (beneficial according to a "last Puritan" like R. B. Perry but baleful according to a Latin like Santayana). But to systematic moral philosophy they contributed very little, being hostile to philosophy, as well as too busy to indulge in it. We must remember that they settled in New England when modern philosophy was just beginning. They were contemporaries of Bacon and Descartes. Like them they had broken with medieval scholastic philosophy, and they believed even less in the authority of the Church. They had no help but the Bible, nor did they ask for more. They looked for their ethics, not to the Catholic Church nor to philosophy, but to Scriptural revelation as they themselves interpreted it. Moral philosophy was, indeed, taught at Harvard from the beginning with the aid of European textbooks, but the Puritans themselves did not write moral philosophy. In fact, they distrusted it. For moral philosophy means a reliance on the human intellect to discover moral truth apart from revelation. This distrust comes out nicely in Cotton Mather, writing as late as 1726, when the works of Locke, Wollaston, and perhaps Hutcheson were known. "There are," he says, "some very unwise Things done—One is the Employing of so much Time upon Ethicks in our Colleges." This he goes on, is "a vile Peece of Paganism."[1] In the eyes of Puritans like Mather, philosophy is powerless to save us, and even moral philosophy cannot provide us with true or saving virtue; to rely on it is therefore worse than foolish, it is tragic.

This position, with some modifications, was worked out most fully by Jonathan Edwards in the second half of our Colonial Period. He was gifted in philosophy and well-trained, having studied Locke and other English philosophers, and he did write an essay or two of moral philosophy, one on virtue and one on the freedom of the will. But here, as always, he was using philosophy only to support the Calvinistic theology which he was trying to defend. "True virtue," he writes, "most essentially consists in benevolence to Being in general."[2] In other words, true virtue is love—love of God, man, and all being. But he argues, man is naturally quite incapable of such disinterested benevolence. He is naturally ruled entirely by self-love; even his natural social feeling and moral sense are really forms of enlightened egoism. Reason as well as scripture can discover all this. But it follows that for true virtue and salvation man is utterly dependent on God; he can do nothing of himself but must rely wholly on God's regenerating grace, for without being regenerated he cannot love as he ought. Reason and moral philosophy cannot avail him here.

II

Edwards had followers (Joseph Bellamy, Samuel Hopkins, and others)

---

[1] Quoted by P. R. Anderson and M. H. Fisch in *Philosophy in America* (1939), p. 5.

[2] *The Nature of True Virtue* (1765), Ch. I.

but he was really fighting a rear-guard action against philosophy with philosophy as his weapon. Among his contemporaries of the 18th century a rather different point of view was arising—that human reason is capable of discovering religious and moral truth, and that human nature is capable of true virtue. Some of them were "Arminians," meaning to be fairly orthodox but insisting on human capacity and free will. They believed in the necessity of revelation, but also held that reason is morally competent— that, besides revealed law, there is a natural moral law which reason can discover and which man is able to follow with little if any special assistance from divine grace. Of these the chief was the American Dr. Samuel Johnson, who published the first systematic work on moral philosophy in America, *A New System of Moral Philosophy* (1746). Unfortunately it was not very new, being based on Wollaston, Hutcheson, etc., nor very clear either.

Others took a more radical point of view, following in English and French footsteps, namely the free-thinkers and deists. They held not only that there is a natural or rational morality and religion which reason by searching can find out, but also that divine revelation can add nothing important to this natural morality and religion, in fact, that there has been no such special revelation at all. This was in effect Benjamin Franklin's position in the 1720s and it became the creed of a number of our revolutionary leaders and founding fathers—Ethan Allen, Thomas Paine, and Thomas Jefferson,

for example. According to the deist, reason suffices for morality and therefore for salvation—it can prove God's existence and providence and the immortality of the soul; it can discover the moral law without the help of revelation, and this rationally discoverable moral law is the only moral law there is; it can see that God should be worshipped and that one's fellow-man ought to be benefited; and it can show that God will reward virtue and punish vice either here or hereafter. Moreover, its instruction on all these points is sufficiently clear and persuasive to lead a man to virtue and salvation, if he chooses, his choice being his own, not God's. This is the creed summarized by Franklin in his autobiography and by Jefferson in his letters, and the heart of it is a belief in the competence and efficacy of moral philosophy.

Even so, none of these free-thinkers wrote any moral philosophy of permanent value, except in a fragmentary way, either in the Colonial Period or in the Age of Revolution and Enlightenment. For their philosophy they looked to Locke, Hutcheson, Kames, the French *philosophes,* etc. Such as it was, their moral philosophy was somewhat confused, since it was partly utilitarian and partly non-utilitarian. In fact the ideology on which our country was founded was a eclectic combination of utilitarianism with the doctrine of natural rights. For example, Jefferson in a very interesting letter on ethics says that "nature has constituted *utility* to man, the standard and test of virtue,"[3] as nice a statement of utilitarianism as Bentham could have desired, but he had also written in the Declaration of Independence one of the classic statements of the doctrine of natural rights, which Bentham called "nonsense on stilts."

Something more should be said here of this doctrine of natural rights. It arose, under the influence of Locke, Puffendorf, and others in the second part of the Colonial Period and flourished, of course, in the Revolutionary Era. It was, in fact, the outstanding doctrine in our 18th century moral and political philosophy. It was adopted by both groups of thinkers who believed in the existence of rational morality or natural law, i.e. both by the deists and by the more orthodox who admitted the need of revelation to supplement natural faculties. One of the first to appeal to the doctrine was John Wise in 1717, arguing for a democratic form of church government against the Puritan aristocracy represented by Mather.[4] Wise argued his case partly from Scripture and partly from the law of nature. In the latter section he speaks of "the prime Immunities of Nature," in other words, natural rights. The doctrine was taken up by Jonathan Mayhew and James Otis who contended that the laws and rights of nature represent a "higher law" than that of kings and parliaments, and that rebellion is justified if this higher law is violated. Thus the

philosophical stage was set for the Adamses, Paine, Jefferson, and the Revolution.

Put into philosophical terms the doctrine of natural rights involves the following propositions: 1) that every man simply as a man has certain natural rights, such as "life, liberty, and the pursuit of happiness," equally with every other man, 2) that the fact that men possess these rights is intuitively known or self-evident, 3) that individual men possess these rights independently of all human legislation or custom, and of any connection with the welfare of society, 4) that, as a consequence, these rights are to be respected by others and even by the government, in fact, government exists only to protect the natural rights of each individual from violation by the others and may encroach upon an individual's natural rights only if and in so far as this is necessary for the protection and fulfillment of the rights of all, 5) that if a government does encroach unnecessarily on the natural rights of the people they have a right to revolt and to institute a new government. The only point, perhaps, which was not clear in this philosophy was the relation of these natural rights to God. It was agreed that "the laws of nature" were the laws "of Nature's God," and that God has "endowed" his creatures with certain "inalienable rights"— rights inalienable by other men or by society (though of course violable by them). But are these rights inalienable by God? Has he endowed us with them in such a sense that he can take them away again, although no human agen-

---

[3] *Letters,* to Thomas Law (1814).
[4] *A Vindication of the Government of New England Churches* (1717).

cy can do so? It is a familiar question whether an act is right because God commands it or commanded by God because it is right. The question here is a parallel one: have I a right because God says so or does God say so because I have the right? Are "natural rights" ours simply because of our nature, independently of the will of God as well as of human beings? On this question, I say, the thinking of our 18th century ancestors was not clear (Locke's own position was not clear), though it would seem that they should answer it in the affirmative. Practically, it was perhaps not an important question; they were rebelling against George III, not against God. But theoretically it was of some importance, for "the moral argument against Calvinism," as W. E. Channing later called it, used by deists and Arminians alike, depended on the assumption that our rights cannot be abrogated by God at his pleasure.

We have now moved well into the period of the Revolution and Enlightenment (1776 to 1830). Before we proceed to the next period we must take note of a few further facts. 1) Our philosophy of the 18th century was dominated by Locke and the British and French writers who followed in his train. Thus it was more or less empiricistic. 2) Toward the end of the century there was a conservative reaction, both politically and religiously, partly due to the excesses of the French Revolution. Democracy was attacked by the Federalists and deism by almost everyone. 3) The political reaction did not last, but the religious reaction did,

because the common people who asserted themselves under Jefferson and later under Jackson were more orthodox than were the upper classes on the eastern seaboard.

4) For a good share of this period the main textbook of moral philosophy in American as in British colleges was Paley's *Principles of Moral and Political Philosophy* (1785). Its use here may have been due in part to the followers of Edwards, for their position was close to utilitarianism. Indeed, one of them, Timothy Dwight (who is known in literature as one of the "Connecticut Wits"), proclaimed in a sermon that utility is the "foundation" of virtue, although we must take the Bible as our "measure" of virtue, since we are not wise enough to know what is useful for human happiness without God's aid.[5] Paley is thoroughly empiricistic in his theory of knowledge (apart from revelation) and argues against the existence of moral intuitions, natural rights, etc. For him duties and rights are all derivative from the general happiness, and the promotion of the general happiness is right because it is commanded by God, not vice versa. This view, which stems from Locke, combines voluntarism and utilitarianism and is therefore often called "theological utilitarianism." It was a favorite target of attack in the next period of our history, though it had proponents even then.

III

So far as ethical theory goes, the next period begins about 1830 and ends

[5] *System of Theology*, Sermon XCIX.

with the Civil War in 1865. For in 1830 moral philosophy began to flourish, as did literature and other elements in our culture, although it unfortunately took the form of textbooks, due to the need brought about by the founding of colleges and universities, which sprang up like mushrooms at this time.

This was the age of Jacksonian democracy, religious revivalism, social reform, and transcendentalism, and it needed a moral philosophy. For it did not look merely to the Bible for its ethics; like those of the previous age its moralists believed that reason can discover moral truth. However, unlike the deists, most of them held that on some points it is necessary to appeal to revelation, so that the typical position was that ethics depends on a harmonious cooperation of faith and reason, revelation and philosophy, although some of the transcendentalists, like Emerson, identified reason and revelation in such a way that both were resolved into intuition, and neither meant quite what it had before. In any case, the moralists of this generation believed in moral philosophy with a real enthusiasm, however dry some of their books may seem to us now. They did not, however, go to experience for their ethics; in fact, the main point about their thinking is that it began with a radical rejection of the philosophy of Locke and his empiricist followers, which had been more or less dominant since the days of Edwards. This philosophy had issued in scepticism (Hume), deism, materialism, unitarianism, and utilitarianism (especially Paley), and this offspring was objectionable to

them. They therefore denied its first premise—that all of our ideas originate in experience. Philosophically this denial of Lockian empiricism is the essence both of transcendentalism and of the textbook philosophy of this era.

One of the first to reject empiricism in this way was W. E. Channing, the forerunner of transcendentalism, and he says it was the British moralist Richard Price who saved him from Locke and opened his mind to "the transcendental depth," with a little help from Platonism.[6] But there were other sources to whom his younger friends and successors appealed: (a) the Scottish intuitionist Thomas Reid and his followers, (b) Kant and the German Idealists, and (c) Victor Cousin and other French philosophers of the first part of the 19th century who were influenced both by the Scottish and the German modes of thought. The influence of these three European schools on American philosophy was very great, and it was all anti-empiricistic.

The chief resulting moral philosophy was intuitionism. According to intuitionism our moral ideas, especially the ideas of right and wrong or of obligation, do not arise from experience as Locke said. They are ideas of reason, whether innate or not—ideas which reason can somehow form without depending merely on experience. They are, furthermore, simple or indefinable ideas which cannot be reduced to or explained in terms of anything

6 See H. W. Schneider, *A History of American Philosophy* (1946), p. 63.

else. Therefore, moral truths or principles are not objects of any sort of discursive proof, inductive or deductive; they are "intuitions of the mind," as James McCosh later called them. They are self-evident truths which the mind can intuit when it is thinking calmly and clearly.

There are intimations of this position in Emerson, who certainly believed that moral truths are objects of an intellectual perception or intuition. When a man's "heart or mind opens to the sentiment of virtue," he writes, "then he is instructed in what is above him. . . . *He ought.* He knows the sense of that grand word, though his analysis fails to render account of it. . . . The sentiment of virtue is a reverence and delight in the presence of certain divine laws. . . . These laws refuse to be adequately stated. They will not be written out on paper, or spoken by the tongue. They elude our persevering thought. . . . The intuition of the moral sentiment is an insight of the perfection of the laws of the soul."[7] Somewhat similar passages occur in Theodore Parker's statement of the Transcendentalist position in ethics.[8]

The best piece of moral philosophy by a Transcendentalist, however, is an essay by George Ripley, leader of the Brook Farm experiment. It is one of the best statements of intuitionism in ethics, and almost the first by an American (1833).[9] Besides stating the essential points of intuitionism, which have already been given, he carries on a very forceful attack against utilitarianism, marshalling argument after argument, most of which occur over and over again in the many books on ethics which began to appear a year or two later. For it was characteristic of transcendentalism or intuitionism in ethics in the 19th century that it was opposed to utilitarianism. The utilitarian holds that we have fundamentally one and only one duty, namely, to promote the greatest general happiness. As against this Ripley and his fellow intuitionists held that, while we have a duty to promote the general happiness, we also have other duties, e.g. to tell the truth, keep promises, worship God, etc., and these duties are independent of the duty to promote the general happiness and may even in some situations take precedence over it. Or in other words, they maintained that what makes an action right or wrong is not always its consequences in terms of happiness; it may be right or wrong just because it involves keeping or breaking a promise, telling or denying the truth, etc.

Well, this sort of intuitionism was the prevailing moral philosophy of the Transcendentalists as well as of most of the textbooks writers of the 19th century: Francis Wayland, Joseph Haven, Asa Mahan and many others. The most important of these was Wayland. His *Elements of Moral Science*

---

[7] Divinity School Address.

[8] See W. G. Muelder and L. Sears, *The Development of American Philosophy* (1940), p. 135.

[9] "The Connection between Virtue and Utility," *The Christian Examiner,* vol. XIII (1833), pp. 311–332.

(1835) was comparatively speaking the most used philosophy textbook in our history, possibly in the history of the world. It ran to 77 editions before 1875 and was translated into several languages. It also figured prominently in the anti-slavery agitation of its day, for Wayland like most of the intuitionists was against slavery.

Morality was, however, not entirely in the hands of the intuitionists at this time. There was Richard Hildreth, a historian and a utilitarian. There were also followers of Edwards who held that virtue is benevolence and consists in striving to promote the good or happiness of being. In fact, one of the first critics of Ripley and Wayland was N. W. Taylor, a Yale theologian of the Edwardian school. According to Taylor, the idea of moral rightness is complex and definable; to say that an action is right is simply to say that it is intelligent, voluntary, and conducive to the greatest general happiness.[10] This was the baldest utilitarianism, and so the issue was joined, with most people on the intuitionist side.

One of the debates involved in this controversy between intuitionism and utilitarianism was between Asa Mahan and C. G. Finney, both connected with newly founded Oberlin College, the latter, who was also a famous evangelist, taking the part of the Edwardians.[11] This discussion and others like it resulted in a synthesis of the two opposing views, and J. H. Fairchild, also of Oberlin, took this position:[12] that the idea of obligation is simple and indefinable and an object of intellectual intuition, as the intuitionists claimed, but that we have one and only one self-evident obligation, namely to promote the greatest good, as the Edwardians contended. This is an interesting and plausible doctrine but it had little vogue. As a result the controversy went on into the 20th century, without the happy ending which he sought with such a fine Edwardian love of being to provide.

It is worth noticing that in this debate the two political philosophies which had been confusedly combined in American thinking and often still are, were clearly distinguished and opposed to one another. For the intuitionists naturally accepted the theory of natural rights, which fits most readily into an intuitionist epistemology, and argued for democracy on this basis, contending that only in a democracy are people's self-evident rights respected as they ought to be. The Edwardians and other utilitarians, on the other hand, sought to justify the democratic conception of society by maintaining that only in a democracy can the love of mankind be fully expressed and the general happiness which is its object realized.

IV

The next epoch in moral philosophy runs from 1865 to 1910 or 1920, and includes two main movements,

10 "Wayland's *Elements of Moral Science,*" *Quarterly Christian Spectator,* vol. VII, pp. 597–629.

11 C. G. Finney, *Lectures on Systematic Theology* (1846); Asa Mahan, *Science of Moral Philosophy* (1848).

12 *Moral Philosophy* (1869), Ch. I and II.

evolutionary ethics and idealism. In-tuitionism was still on the scene, of course, but its day was drawing to a close, and pragmatism, which came in-to existence in this period, may be treated under the next period, when it became strong. With evolutionary ethics we can deal briefly. Here for the first time the main influence is science. Consequently we have again a move-ment to free ethics from religion, or at least from anything like orthodox Christianity, and to put it on what used to be called an independent basis. Perhaps we should rather say on a new dependent basis, for the evolutionists were only substituting biology for the-ology as a foundation for ethics. The intuitionist position they undermined by explaining away alleged moral in-tuitions and the sense of obligation as by-products of the process of evolu-tion; they even suggested that such ex-periences will evolve out of existence again in the future. Thus they made ethics an empirical science.

The evolutionary moralists looked to the process of evolution for light on the function and standard of morality. And, while a few of them followed Nietzsche's lead and used evolution as a base of attack on utilitarianism and democracy, as well as on Christianity and natural rights, most of them be-lieved, as Darwin did, that the general direction of evolution, in the human world at least, is toward the promo-tion of the greatest general happiness, and so ended up as utilitarians, using then the usual utilitarian line of argu-ment for democracy, but providing it with a cosmic setting.

Evolutionary ethics, therefore, nice-ly exemplifies all of the themes stated at the beginning. Its chief apostle was John Fiske, a follower of Herbert Spencer, whose works are obtainable in all our second-hand bookstores at very low prices, along with those of his mas-ter, a fact which shows how widely they were once read. According to Fiske, "In no department of enquiry is the truth and grandeur of the Doctrine of Evolution more magnificently illus-trated than in the province of Eth-ics."[13] The central fact in the genesis of man, he says, is the enormous in-crease in the duration of infancy re-quired for the development of his in-creased intelligence. This necessitated the evolution of a form of society, and of the sentiment of maternity which was the germ of the more general feel-ing of humanity or altruism which came later. For the situation required the individual to take as his concern the welfare of his family and even of the larger group of which it was a part. Thus arose the moral sense and ethics, for the essence of ethical conduct is al-truism or a concern for the general happiness. Thus also ethics finds a sanction in the cosmic process.[14]

It is more difficult to deal with the ethics of idealism in America. Here the chief influence was, not science nor Christian theology, but German phi-losophy from Kant to Schopenhauer, with help from Berkeley and the

---

[13] *Outlines of Cosmic Philosophy* (1875), vol. II, p. 356.
[14] See *Through Nature to God* (1899), Ch. VI–XII; *Outlines of Cosmic Philosophy*, Ch. XXII.

Greeks. In its opposition to empiricism and to evolutionary ethics, idealism was the successor of Transcendentalism, and W. T. Harris, the early Hegelian, quite naturally taught in the Concord School of Philosophy headed by Bronson Alcott, a Transcendentalist. Yet, although some personalistic idealists like B. P. Bowne sought to incorporate intuitionism into their ethical theories, idealism was in general opposed to intuitionism also. Its coherence theory of meaning and truth could hardly cohere with a belief in intuitions or simple qualities. And it regarded the ethics of intuitionism as formalistic, like Kant's; its own point of view was teleological—what is right is not right merely because it is right, it is right because it is conducive to good or well-being. On this point the idealists were with the Edwardians and utilitarians. But they did not identify the good with pleasure, as the utilitarians did; the good, they argued, was self-realization. And it was not the greatest general good which they held to be the goal of conduct, it was the individual's own good or self-realization which he was to strive for; they did, however, insist, as Hegel did, that the individual cannot realize himself in isolation, but only by being a full-fledged and loyal member of society and the state, which they thought of more as an organism than as an aggregate of individuals. Thus their position was at once more egoistic and less individualistic than that of either the utilitarians or the intuitionists.

The idealists consistently rejected both the doctrine of natural rights

and utilitarianism as bases for democracy, except when they took self-realization to be our one natural right, as did W. E. Hocking. But most of them were firm believers in democracy. They had therefore to offer a new line of argument—that a democratic form of society is the one which is most conducive to the realization of true selfhood, providing as it does both the necessary freedom and the necessary contact with others in a variety of institutions. But they also found it necessary to modify the metaphysical monism which is characteristic of absolute idealism, in order to find for the individual person the reality and value which the democratic faith requires. This is typical of American idealists as compared with the British idealist F. H. Bradley or even Bernard Bosanquet.

Thus American idealism illustrates some though not all of our four themes. Its position is best exemplified by Josiah Royce, although he does not talk the language of self-realization. In his *Philosophy of Loyalty,* he reasons that "my duty is simply my own will brought to . . . self-consciousness."[15] But I can have a will only if I am loyal to some cause in the way in which the Japanese samurai under the Bushido code was loyal to his feudal lord. But to what cause shall I be loyal? Royce's answer is: Be loyal to loyalty! Respect and foster loyalty in all men wherever you find it. ". . . do what you can to produce a maximum of devoted service to causes, . . . and of selves that

15 p. 25.

choose and serve fitting objects of loyalty."[16] This is the principle for determining what my rights and duties are; it includes both the justice emphasized by intuitionists and the benevolence stressed by Edwardians, so far as these have validity.

Coming to the metaphysics of the matter, Royce writes, "Loyalty is the will to manifest . . . the Eternal, that is, the conscious and superhuman unity of life, in the form of the acts of an individual Self."[17] This was in 1908. Later, apparently to guarantee more fully the reality of the individual on which American democracy, and morality itself, insists, he came to conceive of "the conscious and superhuman unity of life" more as a community of many minds organically related than as a single Absolute Mind.[18] Then he spoke of "loyalty to the Great Community," as the central principle of morality.

V

We come thus to our last period— from 1910 or 1920 to today. Intuitionism was well-nigh dead by this time in America, although it was being revived in England, and the doctrine of natural rights was generally regarded as discredited. And, although idealism was still defended by W. E. Hocking, W. M. Urban, and Brand Blanshard, it had lost its dominance in ethics as well as metaphysics, through the attacks of realists and pragmatists. Two

sorts of ethical theory became prevalent in place of intuitionism and idealism. The first is called ethical naturalism. Here "naturalism" has a special meaning, due to G. E. Moore. It means the view that ethical notions are complex, and are definable in terms of natural or empirical concepts like "being desired," "being approved by society," etc. On this view, ethical judgments are not self-evident or intuitive; they are simply empirical statements about what is desired, approved, etc. We may put both the realist R. B. Perry and the pragmatists James and Dewey under this heading. James in an essay called "The Moral Philosopher and the Moral Life" applies the pragmatic theory of meaning (which is roughly that handsome is as handsome does) to the terms "ought" and "good," concluding that both may be defined by reference to desire. The good is that which satisfies desire, and the right or obligatory is that which satisfies the most desire and frustrates the least in the world as a whole. He contends therefore that there are no such fixed principles in ethics as the intuitionists claim to find; in fact, his position is a form of utilitarianism, even though his psychology is not that of Bentham or Mill. The same is true of Perry, who is essentially elaborating James' position in his two important books on the theory of value.[19]

Dewey does not agree with James and Perry that anything is good which is desired or satisfies desire; a thing is good, he says, only if it is satisfactory

[16] p. 201.
[17] p. 357.
[18] See *The Problem of Christianity* (1913), vol. II.

[19] *The General Theory of Value* (1926); *Realms of Value* (1954).

on the whole and in the long run.[20] But this also is something which can be found out on the basis of experience, and for Dewey as much as for the others, or perhaps more so, ethical judgments are amenable to empirical testing and experimentation. For him, too, as for them, an essentially utilitarian goal is to be our criterion of the satisfactoriness of any action or institution, though he never quite admits this. Pragmatism in ethics is, in fact, merely a more up to date form of utilitarianism resulting from the theory of evolution and a new psychology.

Being metaphysical pluralists, Perry, James, and Dewey all hold to a kind of individualism in political philosophy, but Dewey's "new individualism," as he calls it, is less like that of traditional liberalism than that of James or Perry, perhaps because he was for a long time a Hegelian. Indeed, one may say that all of them are essentially philosophers of democracy in all of their writings, however abstruse the topic, and it is significant that they agree in finding the ethical basis of democracy in similar forms of naturalism and utilitarianism.

The other main type of ethical theory obtaining in the last thirty years may be called the non-cognitive theory. It is suggested by some passages in the writings of George Santayana, in which he describes ethical judgments as expressions of preference, which may be sincere or insincere, well-founded or ill-founded, but which are not true or false in the way that other judgments are.[21] But it has been most popular with the various schools of analytical philosophy which have obtained recently, from logical positivism to the ordinary language school, and its vogue is increasing. In America its outstanding representative is C. L. Stevenson, whose book, *Ethics and Language* (1944), has been widely read and discussed.[22] Its proponents agree with the intuitionists that ethical statements cannot be translated into factual or descriptive statements, as naturalists think they can. But they cannot accept intuitionism because they are empiricists in their theories of knowledge, and do not admit the existence of non-natural qualities, a priori intuitions, etc.; and because they are impressed by various familiar arguments against the objectivity of ethical judgments, based on anthropology, psychology, etc. They therefore conclude that ethical terms do not stand for properties at all, and that ethical statements, in spite of their declarative form, have no cognitive meaning and are not true or false. For them ethical statements like "Killing is wrong" are not intended to embody and convey information as are statements like "Tokyo is large." They are more like interjections, or commands, or expressions of wish, which are not true or false. If I say, "Close the Red Gate!" you do not say in reply, "How true!" or "You are mistaken," for I am not

[20] *The Quest for Certainty* (1929), Ch. X; *Theory of Valuation* (1939).

[21] See "Hypostatic Ethics," *Winds of Doctrine* (1913); *The Realm of Truth*, Ch. VIII.

[22] My account of Stevenson's view, and of non-cognitivism in general, is somewhat over-simplified.

making an assertion, I am expressing a desire of mine in such a way as to produce a certain action on your part. Similarly, the non-cognitivists believe, ethical judgments are expressions of attitude intended to produce certain responses on the part of their hearers.

It does not follow, Stevenson insists, that there is no disputing about right and wrong, as there is no disputing about tastes. It is true that if my statement, "Killing is wrong" is only an expression of my feelings, then I cannot prove that it is true. But I will still want you to share my attitude toward killing and, if you do not, I will then give you reasons why you should be against killing. I may remind you, for instance, that other people have feelings and desires and wish to go on living just as you do, that society disapproves of killing, etc.; and thus I may persuade you to give up your position, or rather attitude, and to adopt mine.

Many of the writers who take this point of view would be utilitarians, i.e. the ultimate reason they would give in support of their judgments on conduct would consist in an appeal to the general welfare. But it is interesting to notice that some of the most recent non-cognitivists are critical of utilitarianism, and appeal to a number of principles, as the intuitionists did, and that a few of them are even willing to speak of natural rights.

One more development ought to be mentioned. There has been something of a revival of Christian ethics along orthodox lines, since at least the beginning of the war. Thomistic ethics with its doctrine of natural law has gained ground under the influence of men like Jacques Maritain, and the neo-orthodox Protestantism of Reinhold Niebuhr, Paul Tillich, and Emile Brunner, which is close to existentialism and is often critical of the doctrine of natural law and of moral philosophy in general, is receiving a wide hearing. A favorite thesis of both of these schools, and of other religious groups as well, is that American philosophers have been maintaining and defending ideals like democracy, social justice, and universal benevolence, which have their roots historically and logically in Christian theology, while at the same time attacking and rejecting the theology on which they are based. This, they insist, is a vain endeavor, and if America is to continue to adhere to its democratic and humanitarian ideology, it must return to the fundamental articles of the Christian religion. Thus the theologians argue, correctly or incorrectly, against the trends we have found among philosophers.

William K. Frankena
University of Michigan

moral principles: *see* Meta-ethics and Normative Ethics.

moral worth: *see* Stoics, the.

morality accidental: *see* Cudworth, Ralph.

morality, natural: *see* Cudworth, Ralph.

morals: *see* Primitive Morals; Soviet Morality, Current.

morals and Christian theism: *see* Christian Moral Philosophy; Dostoyevsky, Fyodor.

morals and ethics: *see* Major Ethical Viewpoints.

morals and religion: *see* Christian Moral Philosophy; Dostoyevsky, Fyodor; Kant, I.; religion and morality; Tolstoy, Leo; Zoroastrian Morals.

morals and psychology: *see* Psychology and Morals.

Morals and Religion

Morals and religion have frequently been identified as one and the same or, if not the same, to be mutually indispensable. Among traditionalists one frequently hears the claim that without religion morals lack vitality. On the opposite side, one hears that morals are independent of religion (e.g., some humanists); or, that religion is something beyond the scope of morals (e.g., some mystics and even among some ecclesiastical traditionalists).

There is here much confusion. The concepts of "morals" and "religion" are often vague and if not vague frequently mistaken. Unless the terms mean the same they should be clearly marked as to their special provinces. Probably the most common cause of confusion is the failure to distinguish fact from evaluation, description from certain implicit standards, what actually is presented from judgments of what ought to be.

Descriptively speaking, morals are the tacit or explicitly accepted standards of behavior among persons by which acts or intentions to act are said to be good or bad, worthy or unworthy, mistaken or ideal. The standard is set up by group opinion in some social context. The individual may conform or depart from these standards; if he conforms he is said to behave well; if he departs, he is said to behave badly. Morals, thus, reflect the culture, age-level, tradition and customs of people and are thus identified with the "mores" of the group. This is singularly evident in close-contact groups such as tribal societies which by circumstance are in close bond of mutual sharing and undertaking.

Normatively speaking, morals, acceptable to a given group, are said to be good or bad, worthy or unworthy, provincial or ideal, in terms of some ideal norm (however arrived at, by philosophical considerations, by another accepted group opinion, by a claimed revelation) apart from the context in which they occur. Thus, what is morally good in a given context (descriptively) may become immoral in a larger framework of reference. Thus, a Jewish prophet may decry against the morals of his people in terms of some larger vision which he may possess although the behavior condemned may have valid moral consideration in terms of its practice and historic context. Polygamy may be moral in the setting where men are scarce and communal living intimate but immoral from the point of view of a complex society where promiscuity may work havoc with established family units and in the proper responsibility and care of the helpless.

In religion, similarly, there is a wide difference between what it is in practice and even theory and what it ought to be. Descriptively religion is one thing and normatively another. The norms will differ according to the context in which they occur. "Religion" may be defined as a generic term (which it is) referring to many particular religions of the greatest variety. "Particular religions" would be defined as those patterns of behaviors and meanings which have been crystalized into form by people who are (actually or potentially) to some degree religious. And people "are religious" for whom there is a serious concern over what they regard to be their ultimate destiny. Thus, people "have" or "possess" religions because they themselves are (or have been) religious. "Particular religions" take on the social context in which they appear, revealing the limitations and necessities of environment, insight and experience. Any religion may be said to be bad or unworthy and provincial in terms of reference to others which reflect experiences based on better or worthier and wider vistas. In a larger context, many particular religions may appear far from worthy although, in their own context, they may be valid and significant.

Thus, it is possible for a religion to be immoral viewed from a wider context. To say, therefore, that morals need religion for support is to fail to distinguish between values in their specific contexts. A person may act morally without commitment to any given religion. For example, he may share his possessions with others less fortunate without any concern that his action has anything to do with his own destiny. Conversely, a person may be religious, i.e., give himself utterly to something which he understands and feels to be worthy of his greatest concern in life (such as his tribal god or his Society) and behave immorally or even a-morally in terms of his own societal context or in terms of a wider social world which would condemn his behavior as immoral or regard it as a-moral. As Rudolph Otto has pointed out in his studies of primitive religions (*The Idea of the Holy* tr. by J. W. Harvey, 3rd ed., 1925) persons who are religious may have a profound reaction to life's ultimate meaning as a kind of *mysterium tremendum* (an awareness of the holy) which to them has no moral associations (according to whether their reactions are good or bad). Moreover, a person may isolate himself from society motivated by a religious impulse and have the minimum concern for those interpersonal relationships which are involved in morality.

The above distinctions are not theoretical. They are descriptive of what has obtained through the long centuries. Morals have varied greatly and so have religions. We tend to judge both from our own point of view and of our own society. Our judgments tend to confuse the normative with the descriptive, thus reading norms promiscuously where such norms do not apply. All morals and religions stand in relation to social contexts. No man is religious or moral in the circle of egocentrism. Whether any morality or any religion is a purely relative matter is a question of an entirely different sort, a question having to do with the kind of metaphysics that is accepted as criterion for judgment. One may avow the principle of the societal relationship of morality without committing oneself forthright to the principle of ultimate relativity of morals. Philosophically one may be a relativist or an absolutist and still acknowledge the fact that all moralities and all religions are in relation to contexts. A philosophical judgment must not be confused with a scientific description nor, conversely, should a description necessarily provincialize a philosophical theory. *Ideal* morals and *ideal* religion belong to the realm of philosophical judgments and, though they may well consider the facts of life involved, they need not be limited to accomplishments but may pronounce prophetically about what *ought* to be (as an end or purpose by which morals and religions should ultimately be judged).

When it is said that a religion enhances morals what should be meant is that when morals are attached to religious sentiment they are given a psychological thrust or possess a dynamic which would otherwise be lacking. A person who does what he thinks is a good motivated by the commitment that the doing of it has the favor of the gods has a zeal which may not be found in the person doing the same thing without such conviction or commitment. At the same time, such a person who does what he thinks is moral in the conviction that there is religious significance to his behavior becomes a more difficult person to be persuaded to change (if desirable) to a more valid morality. There are religious persons who continue to behave badly because of their religion which enhances the conduct. It would, therefore, seem to be a cautious statement to say that the enhancement of a morality by a religion is no sign that the morality is good or better because of such enhancement. It is only where there is a fundamentally good religion coupled with a good sense of moral values that such enhancement may be justified. It can be said that a given morality *without* religion is more hopeful of reconstruction and redirection toward the better than one committed religiously. Enthusiasm and commitment standing alone are dangerous handicaps to deliverance even among the genuinely religious.

To sum up: An ideal religion motivating an ideal morality can only come about by discrimination in terms of wider contexts. This discrimination is the task of philosophical criticism (and here is where the discipline of philosophical ethics comes into play). Such discrimination must come, it would seem, by a kind of detachment which can be attained more objectively by philosophical inquiry rather than within the framework of a religion (which represents a commitment) or of a religious sentiment (which is always subjectively motivated). Both religion and morality, thus, need to be subject to the diagnosis and prognosis of the philosophical mind which, by definition, is that mental awareness of cross-possibilities in the discernment of values apart from commitment to them. Thus, the philosophers will always remain the heretics to the religious and moral claims of people and, at the same time, their potentially true benefactors. The great prophetic reformers of traditional religions and of traditional morality were, by and large, philosophical critics analyzing and evaluating codes, customs and the general mores from a wider perspective. Their task has been to correct the disease of myopic traditionalism which, without criticism, tends to pervert morality and religion; and their mission is to keep pointing to a larger vision or context to promote the vitality and health of both.

Bibliography

Vergilius Ferm, *First Chapters in Religious Philosophy* (New York, 1937), Part I.
——, editor, *Forgotten Religions* (New York, 1950), Editor's Preface.

Vergilius Ferm
The College of Wooster

morals and theism: *see* Dostoyevsky, Fyodor.
moral science: *see* Liguori, St. Alphonsus and Catholic Moral Philosophy.
"moral sense": *see* Balguy, John; Broad, C. D.; Cooper, Anthony Ashley; Hume, David; Hutcheson, Francis; Major Ethical Viewpoints; More, Henry; Reid, Thomas; Schlick, Moritz; Utilitarianism.
More, Henry
Henry More was born at Grantham, Lincolnshire, England in 1614. He attended Eton before entering Christ's College, Cambridge. He received his bachelor's degree in 1639 and was immediately chosen a fellow. He re-

mained in this position the remainder of his life, refusing all offers of preferment. He did accept the prebendary of Gloucester, but resigned after a brief period in favor of Dr. Edward Fowler, possibly having accepted the post merely in order to make certain that Fowler would get it. It is also probable that he refused the mastership of his college, Cudworth, who accepted, being a second choice.

More was a man of mystical tendencies, inclined to animation and uncritical enthusiasms rather than to careful and precise thought. He was a voluminous writer, both in prose and verse, many of his works being written in a country retreat that became the center for mystical thaumaturgy and spiritualism. He died in 1687.

Although many of More's writings touch on topics that could be considered ethical, his main work in ethics is the *Enchiridion Ethicum,* published first in Latin in 1666 and translated into English in 1690 by Edward Southwell.

More states that his purpose is "to excite the minds of men unto virtue." To this end he discusses the nature of ethics, and goodness, the fundamental principles of morality, the nature and types of virtue and how virtues are to be acquired, the nature and uses of the passions, and free-will.

He defines ethics as the art of living well and happily. It has two parts: knowledge of happiness and acquisition of happiness. Happiness is the pleasure which the mind enjoys from a sense of virtue, and a consciousness of well-doing; and of conforming in all things to the rule of both. Happiness is a pleasure of the mind, not an operation of it. But since desires of the soul pursue their objects not as they are intelligible but as they are "good or congruous or grateful" or tending so, it follows that supreme happiness is not merely a thing of the intellect. Its proper seat must be called the "Boniform Faculty," a divine faculty that enables us to distinguish what is simply and absolutely best and to relish it. It resembles the part of the will which moves us toward what we judge to be absolutely the best. Acting in conformity to the Boniform Faculty is acting according to the best and divinest thing in us.

Virtue is an intellectual power of the soul by which it over-rules the animal impressions or bodily passions; so that in every action it easily pursues what is absolutely and simply the best. It is a power rather than a habit because it is "the internal cause of a thing that is essential to it" and a man can have this power (indeed he is not a man without it) without necessarily acquiring it from repeated acts. It is an intellectual power because it resides in the intellectual part of the soul rather than in the animal and, more importantly, it is excited only by some intellectual or rational principle. The highest virtue is to pursue constantly what seems best to Right Reason.

There are such things that seem best to right reason and they can be formulated in, or reduced to, certain axioms or intellectual principles. These may be called "noemata" because of their essential relation to the intellectual faculties. They are "immediately and irresistibly true, need no proof; such . . . as all Moral Reason may in a sort have reference unto: even as all Mathematical Demonstrations are found in some first undeniable Axioms." More lists twenty-three of these, the first twelve dealing with duties to ourselves, the last eleven with duties to others, God, man and to virtue itself. Somewhat paraphrased, they are as follows:

1. Good is that which is grateful, pleasant and congruous to any being with life and perception or that contributes in any degree to the preservation of it.
2. Evil is the converse of good.
3. Some sensible beings are more excellent than others.
4. One good may excel another in quality or duration or both.
5. What is good is to be chosen, evil avoided.
6. We must accept qualified authority where we are not qualified.
7. It is more justifiable not to enjoy or pursue a good than to endure evil of equal weight and duration.
8. What will necessarily happen ought to be regarded as present.
9. Good things which excel less, are distinguished by weight and duration from those things which excel more.
10. A present good is to be rejected or moderated to the degree that a future good of infinite value is probable.
11. A present evil is to be borne if there be a probable future evil infinitely more dangerous.
12. A mind unaffected by passions judges better than one so affected.
13. We must pursue the greater good with greater zeal, the lesser with less.

365

14. Do unto others as you would be done by.
15. Do not unto others as you would not be done by.
16. Return good for good, and not evil for good.
17. It is good for a man to have the wherewithal to live well and happily.
18. It is twice as good for two to have this wherewithal, a thousand times for a thousand, and so on.
19. It is better to prevent one man from living voluptuously than that another should live in calamity.
20. It is good to obey the magistrate in things indifferent, even where there is no penalty to disobey.
21. It is better to obey God than man, or even our own appetites.
22. It is good to give every man his due.
23. A man may so behave that what was his by acquisition or donation may of right cease to be his.

The nature, essence and truth of the absolute good that is made manifest in these noemata is to be judged by Right Reason, but the relish and delectation of it is to be enjoyed by the Boniform Faculty.

More discusses the passions much in the manner of Descartes. Like Spinoza, he reduces Descartes's primary passions to three: Admiration, Love and Hate. Generally, a passion is a corporeal impression with sufficient power to interfere with Right Reason of the Boniform Faculty. In themselves the primary passions are not evil. Their ethical significance is that they can and ought to be controlled, such control constituting a great part of virtue. They also can result in a cleansing and purifying of the spirit; overcoming them or directing them gives us pleasure, since it shows the dominance of Right Reason. They often "engrave a more lively impression on the soul" and the degree of passion a thing arouses can be used as a measure of its merit. In general the passions are good and needful for perfecting human life, but they must be aimed at those that are good and with proper correlation of degree so the best things are pursued with the chief passion, the lowest things by the least passion.

Such pursuits result in the acquisition of the virtues. Prudence, sincerity and patience are the primitive virtues, others derivative or "reductive" (since they can be reduced to the primitive virtues). There is a correlation between the three basic passions and the three basic virtues, the latter "in some sort answering and succeeding [the former] so as either to perfect or correct them." Prudence, for example, "stands in balance to" admiration, sincerity to love (concupiscence), and patience to hatred (fury). Prudence is a virtue by which the soul has such dominion over the passions that they cannot impede the mind in judging correctly what is absolutely and simply the best. Sincerity is a virtue of the soul by which the will is entirely and sincerely carried on to that which the mind judges to be absolutely and simply the best. Patience is a virtue of the soul whereby it is enabled, for the sake of what is simply and absolutely the best, to undergo all things. There are three principal derivative virtues: justice, fortitude, and temperance. More's discussion of each and their subdivisions is strongly influenced by Aristotle.

More concludes with a discussion of the means of acquiring these virtues, taking each in order. The precepts dealing with the acquisition of the virtues are either general or specific. There are three general precepts: that we ought to "labor after virtue," that we can achieve it, and that some precepts are efficacious to that end. The first is self-evident, the second requires free-will, and examples of the third are as follows: we acquire prudence by realizing that "precipitation is the root of most mistakes," therefore, suspend assent until the thing be clearly and distinctly understood. To acquire sincerity, recognize that while circumstances are the same we are mutually obliged to treat each other in the same manner. To acquire patience we must set ourselves to abstain from what is most grateful to the corporeal life.

A question remains, however, whether we *can* do these things, which calls for a theory of human freedom. Liberty of the will "seems almost to imply the having a power within ourselves to act or not." Still an honest man acts voluntarily in a given case though we would say that it was not in his power to act otherwise. Therefore, a distinction must be recognized between a "voluntary agent" and an "agent with free-will." The former is a more general category than the latter. A voluntary agent is one who can act, an agent with free will is one who can act or not as he pleases. A voluntary agent is merely one whose principle of action is in himself and who understands and takes cognizance of his own actions and the circumstances that relate to them, although in the meantime it may not be in his power to act otherwise than he does. The opposite of a voluntary act, then, is one that proceeds either from ignorance or outward force. In the case of outward force the principle of action is the external compelling force. In the case of ignorance although the principle of action is internal there is no awareness of moral circumstances that would have prevented the action. Free-will on the other hand supposes a free election or choice. Such a power is a great perfection when it operates to avoid actions that are base and dishonest, but it is a great imperfection when it leads to actions that are dishonest or vicious. That we in fact have such a power is shown by the fact that we check our passions, we repent, we blame and praise ourselves and others.

In his own day and since More has been better known as a divine than as a moral philosopher. Among others, there are two consequences of this. In the first place it is difficult to evaluate his historical influence as a moral philosopher. In general, it was less than that of his colleague and fellow Cambridge Platonist, Ralph Cudworth, but more than that of other Cambridge men, e.g., Whichcote, Wilkins, and Worthington. He was one of the earliest to write in opposition to Hobbes, although he mentions the great exponent of self-interest and civil authoritarianism only once in the *Enchiridion Ethicum*. Hobbes himself said, however, that if his own philosophy should ever be shown untenable he would embrace that of More. The influence of Descartes upon More is strong and pervasive, particularly in More's discussion of the passions, but also in the precepts he proposes for acquiring prudence. More's precepts are very similar to Descartes's *Rules for the Direction of the Mind.* There also is a suggestion of a Cartesian influence in More's frequent use of 'absolute and simple' with regard to what is good, although it is difficult to be sure as Descartes's notion of "simple" is not entirely unambiguous and More's adaption of it can only be described as obscure. Another similarity between More and Descartes is their emphasis upon the existence of laws in any subject matter dealing with natural states or events. More's attempt to formulate the axioms of morality that are known immediately (one is tempted to add "by the natural light") can be read as an attempt to carry over into the field of morality the Cartesian belief in a "universal mathematics." It is also tempting to suggest that in addition to doing his bit in contributing and furthering rationalism in ethics More contributed to the empirical or sentimental tradition. The closest parallel would be between his Boniform Faculty and the Moral Sense of Shaftesbury and Hutcheson. Granting the sympathy Shaftesbury had for doctrines of the Cambridge Platonists and his knowledge of their writings, it is possible that there was such influence. But it would take detailed scholarship that has not yet occurred to show that it is more than a possibility. Furthermore, if we take More's most definite

statement about the Boniform Faculty and the doctrine of the Moral Sense as it was developed by Hutcheson in his first essays there is a significant difference of doctrine. For More it is Reason that discerns the moral qualities and therefore Reason that recognizes moral distinctions. The Boniform Faculty is a source of delight in this recognition or a power to motivate action. For Hutcheson, in some of his most definite passages, moral distinctions derive from a Moral Sense, not from Reason and it is Moral Sense not Reason that is the organ of moral judgment. (cf. W. E. Frankena, "Hutcheson's Moral Sense Theory," *Journal of the History of Ideas,* Vol. 16). It must also be recognized, however, that there are some passages in Hutcheson's writings and some in Shaftesbury's where cognitive characteristics are not ruled out of the Moral Sense and there are also passages in More where the sharp distinction between cognition on the one hand and affection and conation on the other is not maintained.

A second consequence of the fact that More was not primarily a moral philosopher is that his theory is not carefully worked through. His distinctions are not carefully drawn, e.g., between Right Reason and the Boniform Faculty; he is frequently superficial, e.g., in his discussion of the epistemological status of the moral axioms; his discussion is sometimes banal, e.g., how to acquire the specific virtues. But no one can deny that there are frequent flashes of insight, e.g., his discussion of free-will, and throughout he manages to exude a sincerity and enthusiasm for the cause of morality that could fail to engage only the cynical and blasé.

Bibliography

Henry More, *An Antidote Against Atheism* (London, 1652).
———, *The Immortality of the Soul* (London, 1659).
———, *Enchiridion Ethicum* (London, 1666).
———, *Enchiridion Metaphysicum* (London, 1671).
———, *Letters Philosophical and moral between John Norris and Dr. H. More* (Oxford, 1688).
———, *An Account of Virtue: or, Dr. Henry More's abridgment of morals, put into English by Edward Southwell* (London, 1690).
William Whewell, *Lectures on the History of Moral Philosophy* (London, 1852).
John Tulloch, *Rational Theology and Christian Philosophy in England in the Seventeenth Century*, Vol. II (London, 1874).
G. N. Dolson, "The Ethical System of Henry More," *Philosophical Review* (1897).
A. O. Lovejoy, "Kant and the English Platonists," in *Essays Philosophical and Psychological in Honor of William James* (New York, 1908).
Marjorie Nicholson, "More's Psychozoia," *Modern Language Notes* (1922).
F. I. Mackinnon, *The Philosophical Writings of Henry More* (New York, 1925).

Bernard Peach
Duke University

More, H.: *see* Clarke, Samuel.
mores: *see* Ayer, Alfred J.; Primitive Morals; Utilitarianism.
Moroccan Berbers: *see* Riffian Morals.

mortal sin: *see* Jesuits, the, Moral Theology of.
mortification of the flesh: *see* Puritan Morals; Schopenhauer, Arthur.
Moses: *see* Hammurapi, Code of; Jewish Ethics and Its Civilization; Spinoza.
motivations: *see* Cudworth, Ralph; Jewish Ethics and Its Civilization; law of motivation; Major Ethical Viewpoints; Muslim Morals; Psychology and Morals.
motive feeling: *see* Schlick, Moritz.
motives: *see* Balguy, John; Butler, Joseph; China, Moral Philosophies of; Cumberland, Richard; Hindu Ethics; Kant, I.; Moore, George Edward; Price, Richard; Prichard, H. A.; Ross, Sir (William) David; Schlick, Moritz; Stoics, the; Utilitarianism.
Muhammed: *see* Muslim Morals.

Mundurucú Indians, A Dual System of Ethics

The Mundurucú Indians, an aboriginal people of central Brazil, share with most of mankind a propensity to apply one moral standard to relationships among themselves and quite another to their conduct towards the rest of humanity. One may say that this phenomenon is universal. This paper shall maintain the view common to many social scientists that ethical values, whether norms implicit in observed behavior or overt ideals, are parts of social systems. It is to be expected, therefore, that desired and valued behavior will be different among members of any one system than between participants in different systems.
In a sense, all members of modern,

complex societies are a part of the same social system. Therefore, the moral values of in-groups are commonly extended outward to a considerable degree. Moreover, the ethical norms reflected in everyday social interaction are complicated by class differences and other categories of sub-cultural variation. The individual is an actor in many situations, each of which prescribes rather different modes of behavior. He may be the bearer of several standards of ethics, which become manifest according to the particular status and role context in which he is acting. Our "real," as opposed to "ideal," values are heterogeneous in the extreme.

The complexity of our ethical values arises from the very complexity of the social structure of which they are an integral part. Beyond the realm of situationally desirable behavior, the general ideal value system, or thematic moral values, in Kluckhohn's terms, shows somewhat more uniformity and internal consistency.[1] But they are frequently in conflict with sentiments, which, while less lofty, are just as strongly value charged.

Since it is more simple, and because it is less ambivalent, the Mundurucú ethic should provide some insight into our own. It varies from our own in degree of intensity of ingroup harmony and outgroup hostility and is perhaps

different in kind, for the central theme makes a sharp and conscious dichotomy between desirable behavior within Mundurucú society and toward the outside world. These opposite aspects of their dual ethic did not conflict but served to reinforce each other and are essential parts of an internally self-consistent view of humanity.

The Mundurucú first came to the attention of colonial Brazil as a tribe of dauntless warriors inhabiting the forests and savannah country east of the upper Tapajós River in the state of Pará. Their reputation for unmitigated ferocity and hostility towards other Indian groups and white settlers grew until 1795, when Brazil authorities established peace with them and diverted their energies into attacks on tribes still unpacified. They achieved considerable success in their service as mercenaries, and by the end of the nineteenth century, there were no hostile Indians within hundreds of miles of Mundurucú territory. Mundurucú warfare ended with the general pacification of the region in the beginning of this century, and they now pursue a peaceful existence, hunting, tilling their gardens, and collecting crude rubber for sale to white traders.

Mundurucú warfare represents one side of a dually oriented system of ethical values. If one is to view them from this perspective, they appear, to use the descriptive terminology followed by Ruth Benedict, to be true Dionysians.[2] But the internal social order stressed harmony, cooperation, and

---

[1] Clyde Kluckhohn, "Values and Value-Orientations in the Theory of Action: an Exploration in Definition and Classification" in *Towards a General Theory of Action* (Talcott Parsons and Edward A. Shils, eds., Cambridge, 1952).

[2] Ruth Benedict, *Patterns of Culture* (New York, 1946).

non-aggression to an extent comparable to the Zuni Indians of Arizona; in this light their culture is Apollonian.

The apparent disparity between these two concepts of desirable conduct towards one's fellow man points to a weakness in the configurational approach of Benedict and others. According to their interpretation, ethics are a part of a central theme which pervades all aspects of any one culture and endows it with a total and unique pattern. If major ethical themes are analyzed, on the other hand, as being an integrated and integrative part of the social structure, moral values can be related in a functional and pluralistic way to the total culture. Such a dual system of ethics, when viewed functionally, does not have to show ideational consistency, for its rationality lies in the structure of the society and, ultimately, of the culture.

The major unifying theme of the Mundurucú view of humanity lies in the division which they make, explicitly and verbally, between those who are Mundurucú and those who are not. Only the former are called "people," while the latter are referred to categorically as "outlanders." In times past, all "outlanders" were considered to be enemies and proper objects of attack.

This is not a racial or genetic concept; the name "outlander" is frequently applied today to many fellow tribesmen who have adopted white men's ways to such an extent that they no longer operate within the closed circle of Mundurucú society. Further-

more, children were captured from other tribes and raised as Mundurucú without prejudice. To adult "outlanders" of either sex, however, the Mundurucú gave no quarter; the enemy was summarily dispatched and the head severed and taken as a trophy.

The taking of the trophy head was not an end in itself, although it did serve to bring glory to the successful warrior. The enemy head became the subject of a series of ceremonies and ritualistic observances which had as their object the furtherance of the material well-being of all the "people." Beyond this, the Mundurucú derived great pride from their collective strength, and, even today, the older men speak of their warrior days with animation and no little nostalgia.

The establishment of peaceful and symbiotic relations with the whites added a further dimension to the values connected with warfare, which the Mundurucú now pursued as paid allies of the Brazilians. Identification with the cause of the whites and attraction to the material delights of Western culture gave the Mundurucú a "civilizing" mission. They fought only against the "outlanders of the forest," the "savage" Indians, and they construed their role to be one of forceful pacification of these recalcitrants. This added goal provided a rationale for the acceptance of the white man and his culture and served to smooth relations between the two groups during the acculturative process. The means used to attain the new ends were traditional. Enemy villages were burned, men and women killed and decapitated, and children stolen.

It has been said that, although individual warriors sought glory, the primary purpose of war was social and only secondarily the gratification of individual egos. The patterns of boasting and vainglory common among North American Indians of the high plains were absent among the Mundurucú. A young man who made great claims of prowess was pushed to the fore during the actual attack as a means of suppressing ego-assertion and not to validate it.

The suppression of individual interests in favor of those of the collectivity of Mundurucú is consistent with the dual ethic and world-view of this war-oriented society. The joy and pride that they obtained from external aggression is matched only by the horror aroused by internal strife. A Mundurucú man never struck another in anger. If dissension arose, the principals temporarily avoided each other rather than show open hostility. Intra-group tensions did exist for a variety of causes, among which rivalry over women and fear of sorcery were predominant. The culture provided few internal cathartic mechanisms for latent aggression, and, in fact, it enjoined social harmony most positively.

The execution of sorcerers was the only situation in which drastic action was taken against another Mundurucú, and the decision to kill the suspected witch had to be taken by the group as a whole. Sorcery and accusations of sorcery were common in all villages, and the subject was so feared that people were loathe to even speak of it. Interestingly, the sorcerer was not thought to practice his art against particular individuals, but was believed to make and disperse evil spirits which might attack anyone with whom they came into contact. A general malevolence was said to pervade the sorcerer; he was simply "angry at everything."

Sorcery provides interesting insights into the mechanisms by which the Mundurucú ethic was maintained and the dangerous forces which they believed to be inherent in man and nature kept in check. While the practice of black magic may be considered as a covert channel for the latent aggressions of the sorcerer, only persons who had inherited shamanistic power were able to manipulate the evil forces. But the locus of sorcery and its punishment was social and not individual. Just as black magic was directed towards society, at large, so was the ultimate function of retribution of importance to the well-being of the social system. The universe of the Mundurucú was permeated with potentially harmful supernatural beings and forces, which could be appeased and controlled with proper techniques, and the killing of the sorcerer was a personalized means towards this important end. Furthermore, the generalized anti-social tendencies attributed to the sorcerer were a projection of similar suppressed emotions carried by the population. The destruction of the practitioner of black magic was effectively the destruction of centrifugal tendencies within the society.

Internal harmony within the house

hold and within the village were thought to be a necessary part of social and economic life. The men of the village as a whole hunted and cleared forest for gardens in cooperation, and the women of the large, extended family-household carried out their tasks in unity. Foods were shared among house members and by all the people of the village. The individual and the biological family of man, wife, and children had no independent existence external to their roles within the extended family and the village.

Cooperation and collectivism were recognized as positive, desirable values. A Mundurucú would be ashamed to unstintingly deny goods or services to his fellows. The actual extent and mode of mutual obligations were determined in specific situations by the roles connected with kinship status, but beyond this, the central ethical theme stressed generosity, hospitality, and aid between all Mundurucú.

The suppression of individual strivings is manifest in the total lack of patterns of competition or ego-assertion within Mundurucú culture. A Mundurucú man never strove to prove himself the better of others in any situation. An individual took pride in recognition as a proficient hunter, a valiant warrior, or a repository of lore, but he did not openly and competitively seek such honors for their own sake. It is to be noted, also, that all of these goals were of value to the society which benefited by it.

Although prestige was attainable through the above accomplishments, it was not considered good for a man to stand too far above his fellows. A Mundurucú never boasted of his achievements, nor would he compare himself to others. In fact, it is most difficult to elicit any sort of comparative evaluation of the moral worth of particular individuals from any Mundurucú.

The prevailing tone of Mundurucú values is perpetuated in the modern trade situation, for Mundurucú do not make commercial transactions among themselves. Trade with whites is expected and sought, but those Mundurucú who conduct trade with their fellows as employees of the whites and on behalf of them are recognized to operate outside the ethical system and attract considerable antagonism. Thus, the modern economic ethic of the Mundurucú is colored by the same dualism as existed in their warrior period.

The duality of Mundurucú ethics is closely associated with the institutional core or nexus of the culture. Hostility towards the outer world goes beyond mere distrust and suspicion; it is a positive assertion and celebration of the integrity and cohesiveness of the society. While acting as an escape-valve for intra-social aggressions, warfare served to produce tensions which, paradoxically, contributed towards maintaining balance in the social structure. Witchcraft may be said to have functioned in much the same way.

Manly virtues were esteemed in Mundurucú culture, and hunting ability was valued second only to strength in war. Male unity in a hostile world was expressed in the semi-military organization of the men's house, which also formed a focus for male social participation. Cooperation in the economy was elaborated far beyond the minimum necessary for effective exploitation of the environment; warfare was pursued beyond the requirements of security and its overt magico-religious purposes.

War and fraternity were ritualistic in nature. The relationship between them was causal in the sense that they were interdependent; intense militarism was made possible by male cohesiveness and male cohesiveness was fostered by warfare. Mundurucú society was welded by kinship and the ethic of harmony and cooperation. No commitments were owed to those outside the system; the humanity of others was recognized, but it entailed no duties. To have extended the intense moral obligations between Mundurucú to persons outside the system would have effectively vitiated and devitalized it.

Robert F. Murphy
University of California

murder: *see* Aborginals of Yirkalla; Augustine and Morals; Aztec Morals; Freud, Sigmund; Hammurapi, Code of; Hindu Ethics; Jewish Ethics and Its Civilization; Navaho Morals; Pakot, The Moral System of; Quakerism, Classical, The Morality of; Soviet Morality, Current; Tapirapé Morals, Some Aspects of; Zuni Indians, Morals of.

Murngin, the: *see* Aborginals of Yirkalla.

music: *see* Puritan Morals.

Muslim Morals

Muhammad and the Qur'ān

Our knowledge of religion and morals in pre-Islamic times is not extensive. There existed an animistic conception of spirits and local deities. Belief in these gods was not rigid and religion seems to have presented no serious ethical concepts. These local shrines required some ritual, the resident deity was consulted as an oracle but no formal demand was placed upon the worshipper. There were vague beliefs concerning the after-life; a shadowy existence which was neither reward nor punishment for the deeds of this world. The hedonistic nature of the morality of the time is reflected in their poetry. A famous pre-Islamic ode speaks of "Three things in which the young man takes delight . . . Red wine that bubbles when water is poured on it . . . Charging on my noble steed at the call of distress . . . To while away the rainy day—wonderful is a rainy day—with a fair maiden under a well propped woolen tent" (Tarafa ll. 58–61).

Lacking codes of conduct with express legal and religious sanction these Arabs were guided by certain traditional standards, such as were demanded by the customs and sentiment of the day. Society was organized on a loosely arranged tribal system with little or no central authority. Blood revenge was a duty. Raiding of neighboring tribes was honorable. Such adventures were to be undertaken with courage and loyalty. A single virtue "maruwwa" (manliness), expressed this view of Arab chivalry, calling for honor, bravery and generosity. Hospitality was highly praised and literature contains many tales recounting the extremes to which men went to display this virtue, even to passing strangers.

Over against this we have the preaching of Muhammad, with a religious and moral message which is clear and vigorous. In this message we should observe three basic concepts: a) an absolute monotheism, b) the reality of the judgment to come and c) Islam as a theocratic community. These views were conveyed to the people by the Prophet in eloquent and forcible terms. Their influence upon morals was inevitable. A strict monotheism provided a new and absolute authority for moral sanction. To be sure, Muhammad incorporated many of the old tribal ideas in his religious system but moral correctness no longer had its source in tribal custom but in the will of Almighty God. God's will was made manifest to mankind through the verbal revelation of the Qur'ān. Thus we have the concept of an absolute Law-Giver and a system of absolute and universal morality. God is the author of moral law. What God commands is right. What pleases God is good conduct, what displeases God is bad conduct.

Muhammad's declaration concerning the reality of the judgment to come brought a new consciousness of man's moral accountability. Over and over again, in vivid and moving rhetoric, Muhammad pictures the day when all men shall stand before God and be given the reward of Paradise or the punishment of Hell in accordance with their belief and conduct in this life. That this should give a strong otherworldly note to Muslim ethics is natural. Islam has, in many ways, been a practical and wordly religion, but its views have always been strongly flavoured by the idea of the world to come. The fear of Hell and the hope of Paradise has colored their theology and their popular practices. It has inspired men to meet death in battle. It has given them endurance in the misery of poverty and oppression. It has added to their inclination to fatalism, for to die is but to go to the Garden of Delight. It has given rise to such fantastic schemes as the famous "assassins" in the twelfth and thirteenth centuries and their modern counter-parts.

The third significant element of Muhammad's prophetic message was the belief that Islam is a theocratic community. Early in his teaching, the Prophet began to promulgate ideas which ran counter to the tribal society of that day. After his flight to Medina, we see a more evident development of Islam as a theocratic system whereby religion tends to regulate all phases of life. Essential to the understanding of Muslim morals is the realization that, in the Islamic community, both social and political life are subject to the regulations of divine law and that it is impossible to separate religious and moral codes or to distinguish secular and sacred affairs. For the Muslim, matters of the state and its laws, as well as the details of daily life, are within the realm of his religion. Indeed, such a theocratic system assumes that all elements of life are to be regulated by the authoritative will of God. Hence, the Qur'ān contains not only statements concerning the nature of God and the universe but an attempt to give specific regulations for daily conduct.

It should be understood that the Qur'ān is basically a collection of rhetorical and liturgical statements and not a book of systematic theology or a treatise on ethics. In the Medinan *suras* there is a greater amount of didactic and legalistic material but the book, as a whole, is not an organized presentation either of metaphysics or of ethics; however, it does contain many moral admonitions as well as definite regulations for the conduct of life.

Kindness, proper speech and generosity are advised. The believer is commanded to humility, patience, moderation, truthfulness, faithfulness to pledges and similar common virtues. Respect should be shown to parents and orphans should be treated with kindness. The old custom of blood revenge is recognized but settlement by mediation and conciliation is preferred. Regulations are given in regard to food; pork, blood and improperly slaughtered animals are prohibited. The drinking of wine is forbidden. Usury and games of chance are condemned. There are regulations concerning marriage and divorce. A Muslim is allowed four wives and is carefully admonished to treat them equally (used as a modern polemic to prove that polygamy was forbidden in that

no man can treat four wives equally). A man may divorce his wife, not without just cause but without being required to state that cause. The nearest attempt to give a systematic moral code is found in *sura* 17: 23–40 which may be summarized as follows: "Worship none but God. Show kindness to parents, speaking respectfully to them and never with reproach. Render what is due to kinsfolk, the poor and the wayfarer; yet not wastefully. Kill not your children for fear of want. Have nought to do with adultery. Slay not anyone whom God has forbidden you to slay, unless for a just cause. Touch not the substance of the orphan. Perform your covenant. Give full measure when you measure and weigh with just balance. Follow not that of which thou hast no knowledge. Walk not proudly on the earth."

Early Expansion and Development

Islam had its origin in the simple society of the Arabian peninsula, with its limited economy and relatively small contact with the outside world. The Qur'ān gave a minimum statement of moral principles and religious law; a statement of faith and practice which was not only adequate for the religious and social environment of Arabia but one of the great religious expressions in the history of mankind. The spread of Islam was amazingly rapid and within a century it had extended its rule from India to the Atlantic. With this expansion and the foundation of a vast Islamic empire, there was encountered a complex society and systems of thought unim-

376

agined by the desert Arab. As new situations arose, Islam was forced to develop in order to meet these changing needs and it did so with a remarkable flexibility. This development took two general directions; a) legal and practical considerations to meet an expanding society and b) theological and philosophical discussions arising out of the contact of Islam with other thought systems. On the more practical side, we see the collection of the Traditions (hadīth) and the growth of legal systems (sharī'a). On the theological side, we have the development of sects, religious movements, theology and philosophy where men gave their attention to the more theoretical aspects of religion and morals.

The Traditions

In situations where the Qur'ān failed to supply an answer to the problem in hand, appeal was made to the memory of men to recall the words or deeds of Muhammad (or his close companions) which might elucidate the issue. Thus there grew up a body of tradition which was eventually codified in canonical books, serving as secondary scripture for the Muslim. Like the Qur'ān, the traditions do not present a systematic discussion of religion and morals but in these collected sayings there is much in the nature of moral instruction; indeed, there are admonitions on the widest possible range of subjects. Obviously there are instructions concerning the usual religious duties in Islam; prayer, fasting, alms-giving and pilgrimage. There is also mention of many seemingly lesser important personal matters; food, clothing, clipping one's mustache or the dying of the beard, nursing of infants, proper salutations, sneezing and yawning, etc. All this is in keeping with the basic idea that Islam is concerned with the totality of life and that there is no clear distinction between religion and moral conduct. The general tone of the more moralistic aphorisms is similar to that in the Qur'ān. Generosity, kindness and self-restraint are commended. Hatred, envy and harsh words are condemned. There is a section on *Buying and Selling* and another on *Marriage*. The section on *Good Manners* gives many advices pertaining to politeness and good conduct. "God loves kindness in all matters." "Kindness to children and old people is a characteristic of Muslims." "He is the most perfect Muslim whose disposition is most liked by his own family." "If I were to order men to worship one another, verily, I would order wives to worship their husbands." "The search for knowledge is an incumbent duty on every Muslim, male and female." "Who are the possessors of learning? Those who practice what they know." These sayings will suffice to indicate the nature and tone of the moral teaching of the Traditions. The most systematic statements concerning morals are the attempts to list the greatest sins. These lists vary in detail but are somewhat as follows: "Avoid seven destructive things. . . . The associating of anything with God, magic, the taking of life except for a just cause, the taking of interest, the taking of property of an orphan, turn-

377

ing back in the day of battle and charging with adultery good women. . . ." (Goldsack, p. 5.)

These books of Traditions were the handbooks for the regulation of the Muslim community, but there arose the further necessity of interpretation and application. Thus, we have the development of legal systems. Without dealing with this rather large chapter in Islamic history, we should note that in the process of regulating the community early Islam provided a considerable amount of variety and flexibility. 1) The various schools of jurisprudence differ considerably in their positions, yet the tendency was for the community to consider the interpretation of any one school as acceptable. 2) Such principles as consensus (*ijma'*) allowed a local community to agree upon certain immediate matters awaiting their gradual acceptance or rejection by the broader Islamic community. 3) A system of degrees of correct action was developed which softened the absolutism of a theocratic system. Actions could be classified according to five categories.

a. Obligatory actions—omission of which is wrong.

b. Recommended actions—performance of which is good but omission is not wrong.

c. Permissible actions—neither recommended nor disapproved.

d. Disapproved actions—performance of which is not forbidden but not considered good.

e. Forbidden actions—commission of which is wrong.

Ascetico-Mystical Movement

In the more theological phase of this developing Isalm we must give careful attention to an ascetico-mystical movement which not only supplied many writings on ethical topics but gave to Muslim morality a special character. The early caliphs, especially Abū Bakr and Umar, are famous for the simple and pious lives which they lived even after their rise to political power. In contrast to these patriarchs of Islam, the Umayyid princes of Damascus (and later in Baghdad) indulged in luxury and revelry which shocked the conscience of good Muslims. In reaction to this worldliness and based upon the essential piety of the Qur'ān there arose an asceticism in Islam which deeply influenced the entire course of its moral and religious development. Truly, "there is no monasticism in Islam" but the ascetic movement, with varying degrees of extremity, drew out of the Qur'ān this thread of otherworldliness and cast a tone of ascetic pietism on much of later moral consideration.

On the more positive side there also developed, as early as the ninth century, a very fine and deeply spiritual type of ethical mysticism. A large number of excellent scholar-saints belonged to this movement and we have from their pens many admirable treatises pertaining to the deeper concerns of the moral and spiritual life. Their demand for complete sincerity in daily conduct, in the performance of religious duties and in the inner life had a significant influence upon the history of Muslim morals.

We possess only limited writings of some of these men; e.g., Hasan al-Basri (d. 728) Dhu al-Nūn Misri (d. 859) and al-Junaid (d. 910). Authors like Ibn al-Fārid (d. 1235) Ibn al-'Arabi (d. 1240) are too speculative and esoteric to give us the clearest statement of moral considerations. Al-Muhāsibi (d. 857) and al-Ghazāli (d. 1111) were the most important of this group and may be taken as representatives. Al-Muhāsibi is the first person to give a systematic account of these teachings and al-Ghazāli brought the movement to the point of its highest development. That their thought is basically similar can be readily observed. The extant works of both authors are numerous (even though some are still in manuscript form) but each has a primary work of easy availability (in Arabic) which can be recommended to the student of Muslim morals: al-Muhāsibi, *al-Ri'āya li Huqūq Allah;* al-Ghāzali, *Ihyā' 'Ulūm al-Dīn.*

These writers reduced the standard of right conduct to the simple formula, "doing what God likes and avoiding what He dislikes" (*al-Ri'āya* p. 5). Morality has two phases, outward actions and inner attitudes. The former may be directed to one's fellowmen in good or bad conduct or towards God in proper or improper observances of the regulations of religion. The latter is concerned with the genuineness and sincerity of his attitude and conduct toward men and God. These two phases of conduct are described as "actions of the bodily members" and "actions of the heart." The good man will be careful to keep guard over his bodily members (al-Ghazāli lists seven) so that the tongue will not speak unkind words, the hand commit evil deeds, etc. However, these men were more seriously concerned with the actions of the heart; the more subtle inward sins. These sins are often listed, and the lists vary in detail but they generally include hypocrisy, pride, vanity, envy, avarice, self-delusion, heedlessness, covetousness and evil thought (*al-Ri-'āya,* p. 10; *Ihyā',* IV, p. 366).

Much attention is given to pride, hypocrisy and envy as the most insidious of sins and the most difficult to eradicate. These sins are likened to diseases from which men must seek a cure. Persistent sinning is like a chronic disease and the cure must be patiently and diligently applied (*al-Ri'āya,* p. 30). These men were not ethical theorists but genuine moralists in that they were eager to eradicate these evils from men's lives. They were earnest in their search for the methods of doing this and in applying these methods to their hearts. There must be careful and systematic self-examination (*muhāsaba*). One needs daily to reflect upon his actions and thoughts to be sure that there has not crept into them something of pride or envy or self-delusion (*ghirra*). This requires practical methods of reflection and meditation; methods which are expounded in these manuals of spiritual life.

Some motivation is needed to cause a person to engage in this rigorous self-discipline of inner examination and outward moral rectitude. "The root of piety is the fear of God" (*al-Ri'āya,* p. 5; *Ihyā,* IV, 123ff.). For most of these moralists the fear of Hell and the hope of Paradise are combined as a double-edged motivation for spiritual exercises and good conduct. Such activity leads to repentance. This must be completely genuine and we are often warned that this is not easily attained. The lower self (*nafs*) and Satan are allies in trying to prevent men from true repentance (*al-Ri'āya*, p. 200; *Ihyā'*, III, p. 23). Throughout these writings great emphasis is placed upon sincerity (*al-Ri'āya*, p. 109; *Ihyā'*, IV, p. 309ff.). All conduct must be based upon inner sincerity. "True piety in the inner life is a desire to perform all the ordinances of religion with sincerity of action toward God" (*al-Ri'āya*, p. 9). We are given discussions of other inner virtues such as patience, thankfulness, reliance upon God, satisfaction, love and, since these men are mystics, coming into an intimate relationship with God.

We must observe that this mystical movement, vital as it was in the formation of moral thought in Islam, displayed some tendencies towards ethical negativism. Extreme asceticism occasionally led to excesses (e.g., Abū Sa'id (d. 1094) suspended himself head downward all night) and produced attitudes slightly antinomian in character. This same Abū Sa'id, in his desire to rise above the formalism of religious observances, taught that the *sufi* could disregard these regulations and live according to the higher law of mystical insight. An exaggerated trust in God (*tawakkul*) led to an excessive quietism which produced an indifference to the demands of this life. The emphasis upon inner purity held the danger of an interiorization with much attention given to psychological states and less to social conditions. Many of these writers were aware of these tendencies. Men like al-Muhāsabi and al-Ghāzali gave careful warning against them. We should also note that these men were not unaware of the bearing of inner purity upon right conduct among men. "Sufism is not composed of practices and sciences, but it is morals" (Hujwīri, *Kashf al-Mahjūb*, tr. Nicholson, p. 42). "Sufism is to know God in the heart and to walk with justice among men in the market-place." "The true saint goes in and out amongst the peoples, and eats and sleeps with them, and buys and sells in the market, and marries and takes part in social intercourse and never forgets God for a single moment" (Abū Sa'īd, quoted in *Legacy of Islam*, p. 219). It should also be observed that many of these books dealing with the mystical method have chapters devoted to such subjects as *Good Character, Manners, Generosity* (e.g., al-Qushairi's *Risāla), Earning a Living* and *Friendship* (al-Ghazāli's *Ihyā*).

Greek Ethics and Islam

Another phase of our subject is that of philosophical ethics, especially those ideas which had their origin in Greek thought. In that same flow of Greek ideas into the Arab world which influenced all phases of scientific and philosophic thought we find the ethical concepts of the classical Greek writers. An example of an Arabic work representing these ideas is a treatise by Ibn Maskawaihi (d. 1030) entitled *Tahdhīb al-Akhlāq* (*The Improvement of Ethics*). This is the most significant discussion of theoretical ethics which exists in Islam. Based, most probably, on a book by the same title by Yahyā Ibn 'Adi (d. 974), a Syriac Christian, it is more Greek in thought than Islamic. Frequent mention is made of Aristotle and knowledge of the *Nichomachean Ethics* is instructive in the reading of Ibn Maskawaihi. Early in the book the author deals with the three faculties of the soul and discusses the primary virtues; wisdom (*hikma*, p. 15), moderation or self-restraint (*'iffa*, p. 16), courage (*shuja'a*, p. 17) and justice ('adāla, p. 18). The student of Greek moralistic theory will readily recognize the source of these ideas. These topics are expanded and consideration is given to such items as manners, courtesy, the training of youth, love, friendship, how to choose friends, love in its various kinds, contentment, pride, anger and fear. Justice is given full treatment and happiness is discussed at some length including the Greek concept of complete felicity. This small treatise became widely known in the Muslim world and is a standard book in the Middle East today. Important translations and elaborations of it were made into Per-sian; for example, *Akhlāq-i-Nāsiri* by Nāsir al-Dīn Tūsi (d. 1274).

T. J. de Boer, "Ethics and Morality (Muslim)," in the *Encyclopaedia of Religion and Ethics*.
Edwin E. Calverley, "The Ethos of Islam," in *Religion in Life*, (Summer, 1953), pp. 420–430.
Carra de Vaux, "Akhlāq," in the *Encyclopaedia of Islam*.
Carra de Vaux, Ch. VI, "La Morale," *Gazali* (1902).
Dwight M. Donaldson, *Studies in Muslim Ethics* (1953).

Kermit Schoonover
The American University at Cairo

Muslims: *see* Dante, Alighieri.
Musonius Rufus: *see* Stoics, the.
mysterium tremendum: *see* Morals and Religion.
mysticism: *see* Jewish Ethics and Its Civilization; Khomiakov, Alexey; Morals and Religion; More, Henry; Schopenhauer, Arthur; Soloviev, Wladimir.
mysticism, ethical: *see* Muslim Morals.
mysticism, naturalistic: *see* China, Moral Philosophies of.
mythology: *see* Aboriginals of Yirkalla; Rio Grande Pueblo Indians; Zuni Indians, Morals of.

N

Nahuatl Indians: *see* Aztec Morals.
Napoleon: *see* Hammurapi, Code of; Hegel, G. W. F.
Nasir al Din Tusi: *see* Muslim Morals.
nationalism: *see* Broad, C. D.; Jewish Ethics and Its Civilization; Soloviev, Wladimir.
natura, naturans; natura, naturata: *see* Spinoza.
natural and moral law: *see* Hartmann, Nicolai.
natural good: *see* Cudworth, Ralph.
natural law: *see* Aquinas, Thomas; Cumberland, Richard; Jewish Ethics and Its Civilization; Liguori, St. Alphonsus and Catholic Moral Philosophy; Major Ethical Viewpoints.
natural man: *see* Hobbes, Thomas.
natural moral law: *see* .Aquinas, Thomas, Moral Views of; Moral Philosophy in America.
natural rights: *see* Marxist Theory of Morals; Moral Philosophy in America.
natural slave doctrine: *see* Aristotle.
naturalism: *see* China, Moral Philosophy of; ethical naturalism; Jewish Ethics and Its Civilization; Kierkegaard, Soren; Major Ethical Viewpoints; Marxist Theory of Morals; Meta-ethics and Normative Ethics; Rio Grande Pueblo Indians.
naturalism, ethical: *see* Hume, David.
naturalistic ethics: *see* French Existentialism and Moral Philosophy; Moore, George Edward; Moral Philosophy in America; Ross, Sir (William) David; Soviet Morality, Current.
naturalistic fallacy: *see* Major Ethical Viewpoints; Moore, George Edward.
naturalistic theory: *see* Russell, Bertrand.
nature: *see* Balguy, John; Kant, I.; laws of nature; Rio Grande Pueblo Indians; Soviet Morality, Current; Spinoza; Stoics, the.
nature, law of: *see* Utilitarianism.
nature, state of: *see* Cooper, Anthony Ashley.
nature of man: *see* Augustine and Morals; Goethe, Johann Wolfgang von; Green, T. H.; Hegel, G. W. F.; Hindu Ethics; human nature; value of man.

Navaho Morals*

The Navaho Indians live in western New Mexico, eastern Arizona, and southern Colorado and Utah. Numbering close to seventy thousand, they are the largest tribe in the United States. The size and inaccessibility of their reservation has isolated them from much White influence until quite re-

* This study has been facilitated by the Comparative Study of Values in Five Cultures Project, Laboratory of Social Relations, Harvard University; and by the writer's fellowship (1954–5) at the Center for Advanced Study in the Behavioral Sciences (Ford Foundation).

cently. Even today not a quarter of the population can use the English language with even reasonable adequacy, and the majority speak no English at all. In the more remote regions life goes on much as it did a hundred years ago. The Navaho and the closely related Apache tribes probably did not enter the American Southwest until about 1000 A.D. Many peoples speaking similar languages reside in western Canada and Alaska and a few in northern California and elsewhere in the Pacific Northwest. The Navaho as we know them in historic times have a quite different way of life from these northern tribes. The Navaho have been much influenced by their long contact with the Pueblo Indians. To the general public the Navaho are probably best known for their weaving and for their work in silver.

We shall be concerned almost exclusively with Navaho mode and theory as these prevailed at about the turn of the present century. The contemporary picture, due to Christianity and other Western influences, is too complicated to discuss adequately in a brief essay. Some account of the recent situation will be found in Kluckhohn and Leighton, *The Navaho* (1946). Since no adequate records on Navaho behavior of fifty or sixty years ago are available, this presentation will be limited to Navaho prescriptions and prohibitions with a sketch of the underlying Navho theory. Scattered observations in the literature published at that time do, of course, make plain the obvious fact that Navaho behavior often departed from the prescribed code.

A summary of Matthews (1899) may well serve as an introduction. Restoration must be made for theft, but the thief is not punished in any formal way. Theft and indeed fraud on the part of supernaturals is pictured approvingly and rewarded by good fortune when directed against alien peoples. Incest is severely tabooed. The terrible crimes are, in fact, incest and witchcraft. Only witches and cannibals are guilty of incest. Adultery is disapproved, and a deviant woman is sometimes punished by a slight whipping. Formerly, the husband, with the consent of his erring wife's relatives, might amputate her nose or administer other mutilations. Truthfulness is not inculcated in Navaho myths, though evasion and prevarication should cease when a question has been repeated four times. Solemn promises are of a very sacred character. And Matthews records that he has not found Navahos in practice "less truthful than the average of our own race." The legends record benevolent and philanthropic actions on the part of gods and man alike. Hospitality, courtesy, and deference to age are enjoined. Good conduct is not supported by a doctrine of rewards and punishments in a future life. But a belief in the consequences of one's acts tends to reinforce the ethical code.

Subsequent research requires only some amplification and slight modification of these statements.

Prescriptions

Examining 335 statements from 77 informants interviewed over a fifteen year period, Hobson (1954) found the following recurrent positive themes related to wealth accumulation and socio-economic values: "make a good living," "have lots of property," "take care of things," "work hard and don't be lazy," "look after your family," "help people out." Actually, these themes state or imply almost all that is central in Navaho ethics. Moreover, although Hobson considered slightly less than half of his sample as "conservative," all these injunctions are crucial in the Navaho code of the period before Western influence became maximal.

Security—Health and long-life are primary Navaho goals, accentuated the more because there is no thought of happiness in or of preparation for a future life. Industry and accumulation are means to these ends, both directly and indirectly in that the ceremonials required to ward off or cure illness demand a reserve of property. The four good things of life are often stated to be: fire, maize, sheep, and horses. An old man used to tell vividly how his father would say (making an embracing gesture), "When you get something, hold on to it like that." A man who does not want to appear lazy must get up before his wife in the morning and make the fire. It is very damning for one Navaho to say of another, "He is too lazy even to tell a story." The Protestant virtue of care of possessions (though not the often paired one of cleanliness) is shared by the Navaho. Destructiveness, waste, carelessness, even clumsiness are disapproved. Gambling is wrong "if you lose your mother's jewelry." Racing,

wrestling (for men), and other exercises are good "because they make you strong and not lazy." Games must not interfere with work. One must not even attend ceremonials too often lest this become a way of loafing. Knowledge, including ceremonial knowledge and sound judgment, are good because conducive to health and long life.

Decorum—Sobriety, self-control, and adherence to old custom are valued. Women are praised when they do not cry at desertion by their husbands or "too much" at the death of children. Display of anger, "bad talk" and quarrels should be avoided, particularly in front of those outside the immediate family. Drinking is wrong if it results in loss of super-ego control, if one "becomes wild and without sense." One should talk "pretty nice" to everyone. General courtesy and careful manners are enjoined. It is good to teach one's children to answer the questions of outsiders if the children know the answers. One should marry at the proper age and not marry again too soon after the death of a spouse. One should dress all of one's children (even those who may be defective) as well as one's means permit. One should carry out the ceremonials properly not sloppily. Respect the customary ways of life as maintaining stability and regularity. Many of the older people say today to their children something like this: "I am not going to throw away the things that have come down to my people." It is good to do old things, "things that started with the Navaho." It is shameful for a Navaho family to lack a sweathouse. "Good people think about the sweathouse all the time." A ceremonialist will say to his approving audience, "This arrowhead is about three hundred years old. My old folks used to carry it." Or, "This is the earth the oldest people picked up from the top of the Holy Mountains. It is good."

One must also mind one's own business. One should give instructions or information only when asked. One should discipline one's own children, but it is bad to whip the children of others. Some informants hold indeed that while one's own children must be taught to act responsibly and properly they need not be given formal instructions in the old ways: "just keep them yourself."

Reciprocity—One must look after one's parents in old age and otherwise repay them for what they have done for you. Reciprocal behavior among all relatives is the key ethic of interpersonal relations among the Navaho. Loyalty to one's family takes precedence over all other loyalties. The Navaho volunteered in large numbers for World War II, and both volunteers and draftees served well. But in occasional cases where a young man tried to evade service in response to the wishes of his mother the Navaho community applauded.

But the principle "one good turn deserves another" is also given a wider application. Some of the Ramah Navaho refused attractive employment as U. S. Army scouts against Geronimo on the ground that the Chiricahua and Mescalero Apache had behaved kindly to them during the time of the Fort Sumner captivity.

Benevolence—The widest ethical generalization enunciated among the Navaho is perhaps "Behave to everybody as if they were your relatives." One often hears of injunctions to give food and money to unrelated poor people even when there is no realistic hope of repayment. If one has nothing else to give to the starving, one should feed them with one's sacred corn pollen. It is good not to interfere with those in economic distress when they trespass on your range. Hospitality and other forms of generosity are widely praised.

In accord with the foregoing injunctions, such specific virtues as cooperation, personal independence and autonomy (so long as these do not transgress duty to relatives), general competence, truthfulness and trustworthiness, obedience to parents, discretion, control over one's impulse life (e.g., avoidance of theft and violence), readiness to meet contingencies are valued. Courage is good. Bravery is good if it does not lapse into foolhardiness. Pity is a worthwhile emotion—especially pity for loneliness or unusual distress. A sense of humor is a genuine virtue. Fluency in speech is prized. Fertility and having a good time are advocated.

Prohibitions

These, inevitably, will be largely the negatives of the above, but the ventative formulations will add content to and clarify the positive injunctions. Hobson (1954) lists two negative themes: "don't be too rich," and "never get poor." These can be generalized under the "avoid excess" prohibition (see below), but further comments are in order. Anyone who is too prosperous is, by Navaho thinking, strongly suspect of failing in his obligations to his relatives and in general benevolence. A very poor person is by that very fact suspect of lacking in industry and competence. Moreover, from the Navaho point of view, there are excellent practical reasons for avoiding the extremes. Riches provoke jealousy and antagonism. Both wealth and poverty are likely to arouse witchcraft gossip and the eventuality of the stringent sanctions that may be applied against those accused of witchcraft.

Father Bernard Haile (1943) lists the negative commandments of the Navaho as follows:

1. One should not commit rape.
2. One should not steal.
3. One should not stealthily touch a sleeping woman.
4. One should not sex-jealously quarrel because your (pollen) bag becomes blood.
5. One should not (say or wish) that this person and his livestock shall die.
6. One should not laugh about men (and womenfolk) because the same (defect) may be your punishment.
7. One should not commit adultery.
8. Man must not be killed.
9. Lies should not be told.

Most of these are the prohibitions necessary to orderly life in any group. There must be restrictions upon sex behavior; against crimes of violence; against theft, lying, vicious ridicule.

The Navaho phrasing of the last-named is characteristic. It recalls other Navaho ethical cliches, such as: "Don't laugh at old people because they might have a daughter or granddaughter you want to marry." Number 3 refers to a distinctive Navaho sex crime (see Dyk, 1951). Number 5 refers specifically to witchcraft. Only one general category of Navaho negative morality needs to be added.

Avoid Excess—Excess even in approved behavior is evil. Too much industry is bad because over-work leads to nocturnal emissions and other undesirable events. Food is good, but one should not eat too much. Wrestling in moderation is approved; engaging in it too often runs the risk of injury and death. Gambling is sometimes condemned altogether on the ground of waste, but, more often, it is only addiction which, like any other form of excess, will lead to such consequences as blindness, "going crazy," "getting wild," "getting dizzy in the head." Sex in general is a good thing. The female and male sexual organs were created for enjoyment. But sexual promiscuity is strongly disapproved, partly, to be sure, on the grounds of interference with the stability of subsistence activities and social relations, but at least equally on the basis of the dangers of excess. There are special ceremonies to remove the inordinate passions of men and women. Occasional adultery is condemned no more strongly than laziness, poverty, or lapses from truth.

Other Points—Again there are, expectably, certain specific vices implicit in the more general categories. Stinginess, sneakiness, and meanness are bad. It is "mean," for instance, if a mother punishes her children overmuch for small things. One should not "talk rough" to others nor should one cheat them. Stupidity and anger and irresponsibility are vices. Young men who marry rich girls only to squander their money are looked down upon. Drinking is bad when it leads to fighting, poverty, or destroying the dignity and efficacy of a ceremonial. One should avoid places and situations where fighting is likely to take place. Arrogance and "acting smart" are frowned upon. Unpleasantness, ugliness, or repulsiveness—anything contrary to the general harmony—are evil.

Perhaps a few words should be added on the negative aspects of the sex code. While Navaho sex is generally lusty, there are "Puritanical" notes too. There is generally some fear of the initial sex experience on the part of both boys and girls. Nakedness or any form of exposure is to be avoided lest "those around feel bad." Bestiality is condemned. The attitude toward adultery is complicated by the Navaho notion of property as well as by the "excess" theme and by the sense of danger and of affront to personal pride of the injured party. The Navaho code says, "Don't bother other people's property, including their women." On the other hand, sexual jealousy is a threat to other economic arrangements and to a wide circle of interpersonal relations. One hears statements of this sort: "You don't own it, and she can do what she likes with it as long as she does her work and looks after your children. You got yours." The Navaho notion could be generalized like this: "Adultery is not bad in and of itself, but it is better for all concerned if you do not commit adultery." In the myths the supernaturals indulge themselves sexually without much comment. Only in adultery does friction or a moral tone enter into the text.

Navaho Ethical Theory

Reichard (1950, p. 124) says, "In Navaho life ethics is empirical rather than theoretical or theological . . ." Father Bernard Haile (1943, pp. 83–4) notes that while Navahos may speak of the mind of a culprit as "twisted" or "pink" or "full of meanness," a crime like murder or theft is "primarily a social crime, involving no personal guilt." Reichard (1950, p. 125) correctly observes:

The code tells a Navaho what he should or should not do, what the punishment is—not for the transgression, but for the correction of error . . . The nearest Navaho approach to the concept of sin is 'being out of order, lacking control,' a definition that involves rationalization, not salving a bad conscience; confession of error, not a feeling of guilt . . .

In short, the Navaho conceives of nothing as good or bad in and of itself. Correct knowledge and following the rules emanating therefrom are good because they lead to long life and happiness. Morals are relative to situation and to consequences rather than absolute. Everything is judged in terms of its consequences. An old Navaho says, "I've obeyed my father, that's why I have gotten on so well." But the context of this interview indicates plainly that the Navaho does not attribute his success to the *virtue* of having obeyed his father but rather to the ineluctable result of this event in a chain.

The clearest paradigm appears in the ceremonial lore. One does not benefit from placating or pleasing the supernaturals in the sense that they are then motivated to intervene in one's behalf. The supernaturals themselves are bound by the rules. Transgressions (and this does not mean solely willful violations but mere mistakes as well) bring penalties. As one myth says: "If you make any mistakes you will become blind and warped and crippled; your mouth will be twisted." To be sure, the consequences may under certain conditions be averted or mitigated by resorting to correct ceremonial procedures. Yet this is also an invoking of the lawful course of things. The Navaho is certainly a determinist if not a mechanist. In the case of human beings the course of events is enormously complicated by the ceremonial order. Naive Navahos sometimes express surprise that dogs and other animals also get sick—presumably because animals are not under obligation to observe the ceremonial taboos. There is a generic Navaho term for crime or transgression (Haile, 1943, p. 86) which can best be translated "he took the chance"—i.e. acted in the face of realizing that human life is mechanically governed by rules that have supernatural origin.

To say that Navaho morality is dominantly empirical, situational, and deterministic is not to assert that there is no explicit theory. Ladd (1956) rightly emphasizes that the Navaho moralist is a rationalist par excellence. Reasons are given for everything, particularly, of course, by the more articulate Navahos. Death and sickness are rationalized on the ground that otherwise both people and animals would become so numerous that the earth couldn't accomodate them. Rationalism is evidenced in the basic Navaho premise that knowledge is power. Hence everything must be "talked over," and reasons must be found for everything that happens. Failing everything else, the Navaho will say, "That was the way the Holy People did it long ago," or, in effect, "That is just the nature of things." But acts rather than beliefs count. Behavior is judged—not verbal adherence to a theological or ethical code.

Bibliography

E. Albert, "The Classification of Values: a Method and Illustration," *American Anthropologist* 58:221–248 (1956).

W. E. Curtiss, "Education and Morals among the Navajos and Pueblos," *The American Antiquarian and Oriental Journal*, 27:259–64 (1905).

Walter Dyk, "Notes and illustrations of Navaho Sex Behavior," pp. 108–20 in *Psychoanalysis and Culture*, G. Wilbur and W. Muensterberger, eds. New York: International Universities Press, 1951).

Father Berard Haile, "Soul Concepts of the Navaho," *Annali Lateranensi*, 7:59–94 (1943).

R. Hobson, "Navaho Acquisitive Values," *Papers of the Peabody Museum of Harvard University,* vol. 42, No. 3 (1954).

C. Kluckhohn, "The Philosophy of the Navaho Indians," pp. 356–85 in *Ideological Differences and World Order,* F. S. C. Northrop, editor (New Haven, 1949).

C. Kluckhohn, and D. Leighton, *The Navaho* (Cambridge, 1946).

John Ladd, *The Structure of a Moral Code: A Philosophical or Ethical Discourse Applied to the Ethics of the Navaho Indians* (Cambridge, 1956).

R. McNair, *The Ideas of the Good in the Mythology of the Navaho Indians* (Ph.D. thesis, Harvard University, 1948).

W. Matthews, "The Study of Ethics among the Lower Races," *Journal of American Folklore,* 44:1–9 (1899).

R. Rapoport, "Changing Navaho Religious Values," *Papers of the Peabody Museum of Harvard University,* Vol. 41 No. 2 (1954).

G. Reichard, "Navaho Religion," Chapter 8, *Ethics* (New York, Pantheon Books, 1950).

E. Z. Vogt, "Navaho Veterans: A Study of Changing Values," *Papers of the Peabody Museum of Harvard University,* Vol. 41 No. 1 (1951).

Clyde Kluckhohn
Center for Advanced Study in the
Behavioral Sciences (California)
and Harvard University

Nazirites: *see* Jewish Ethics and Its Civilization.

necessity: *see* Hindu Ethics.

Nechayer: *see* Soviet Morality, Current.

needs: *see* Schlick, Moritz.

negation: *see* French Existentialism and Moral Philosophy.

negative freedom: *see* Hartmann, Nicolai.

negativism: *see* Muslim Morals.

negativity: *see* Hegel, G. W. F.

neighbors: *see* Freud, Sigmund; Hindu Ethics; Marxist Theory of Morals.

Neo-Freudianism: *see* Psychology and Morals.

Neo-Hegelianism: *see* Green, T. H.

Neo-intuitionism: *see* Ross, Sir (William) David.

nescience: *see* Hindu Ethics.

Nettleship, R. L.: *see* Green, T. H.

Neurath: *see* Schlick, Moritz.

neurotics: *see* Freud, Sigmund.

New England: *see* Puritan Morals.

New Mexico: *see* Rio Grande Pueblo Indians; Zuni Indians, Morals of.

New Testament: *see* Augustine and Morals; Hammurapi, Code of; Liguori, St. Alphonsus and Catholic Moral Philosophy; Quakerism, Classical, The Morality of; Spinoza.

New Testament and ethics: *see* Christian Moral Philosophy.

New Zealand: *see* Primitive Morals.

Newton: *see* Clarke, Samuel; Schopenhauer, Arthur.

Niebuhr, Reinhold: *see* Moral Philosophy in America.

Nietzsche, Friedrich

Nietzsche was born in Röcken (Germany) on October 15, 1844, the son of a Protestant minister. He attended the universities of Bonn and Leipzig and, in 1869, was appointed professor of classical philology at the University of Basel (Switzerland). He became a Swiss subject, but when the Franco-Prussian War broke out in 1870, he took leave from the university to serve with the

Prussian army as a medical orderly. Soon, however, he returned to Basel, his health badly shattered. He offered courses on Greek literature and philosophy and became a close friend of Richard Wagner, then in Tribschen, not far from Basel. Wagner was exactly the same age as Nietzsche's father and appreciated Nietzsche as a brilliant apostle and errand boy. Nietzsche's first book, *The Birth of Tragedy from the Spirit of Music* (1872) won Wagner's enthusiastic approval—precisely for its poorest part, the rhapsody on Wagner in the last ten sections. Wherever Nietzsche showed an independent mind, Wagner was not interested. A break was thus inevitable, and Wagner's removal to Bayreuth merely hastened it. Wagner's chauvinism and racism, which had seemed less important when he was the lonely genius of Tribschen, now became institutionalized as part of the meaning of Bayreuth. It is true that Nietzsche considered Wagner's *Parsifal* an insincere obeisance to Christianity and had no sympathy for the idealization of pure foolishness. But any attempt to explain the break of the two men this way overlooks the fact that Wagner's inscribed copy reached Nietzsche even as Nietzsche's enlightened *Menschliches, Allzumenschliches* (1878), with a motto from Voltaire, reached Wagner; and Wagner had much less interest in Nietzsche's work by that time than Nietzsche had in Wagner's.

In 1879, Nietzsche resigned from the university, pleading his ill health, and devoted the next ten years solely to writing. He lived very modestly and drove himself relentlessly. Every book represented a triumph over his half-blind eyes, migraine headaches, and sheer physical agony. All his major works belong to this period. They were written in utter loneliness in Switzerland and Italy and ignored by the public until Georg Brandes began to lecture on Nietzsche at the University of Copenhagen in 1888. In January 1889, Nietzsche suffered a mental breakdown and remained insane until he died, August 25, 1900. During the last decade of his life, his works were reprinted and translated, and a huge literature began to develop around him. By now there can be no doubt that he was one of the most influential thinkers of modern times. In the following article, only his ethics shall concern us.

Nietzsche's ideas about ethics are less well known than some of his striking coinages: immoralist, overman, master morality, slave morality, beyond good and evil, will to power, revaluation of all values, and philosophizing with a hammer. These are indeed among his key conceptions, but they can be understood correctly only in context. This is true of philosophic terms generally: Plato's ideas or forms, Spinoza's God, Berkeley's ideas, and Kant's intuition all do not mean what they would mean in a non-philosophic context; but scarcely anybody supposes that they do. In Nietzsche's case, however, this mistake is a commonplace—surely because few other philosophers, if any, have equalled the brilliance and suggestiveness of his formulations. His phrases, once heard, are never forgotten; they stand up by themselves, without requiring the support of any context; and so they have come to live independently of their sire's intentions. The following pages represent an attempt to sketch the context from which Nietzsche's central conceptions derive their meaning.

Nietzsche revolutionized ethics by asking new questions. As he saw it, his predecessors had simply taken for granted that they knew what was good and what was evil. Moral judgments had been accepted as incontrovertible facts, and the philosophers had considered it their task to find reasons for them. In other words, traditional moral philosophers made it their business to rationalize the moral idiosyncrasies of their environment. What F. H. Bradley was to say of metaphysics in his preface to *Appearance and Reality* (1891), is what Nietzsche said in effect of traditional ethics: it is "the finding of bad reasons for what we believe on instinct." But Nietzsche would not have added like Bradley that "to find these reasons is no less an instinct." Nor indeed did he consider moral idiosyncrasies instinctive in any literal sense. For from construing them as part of our biological make-up, Nietzsche was struck by the great variety of moral views in different times and places.

To cite Nietzsche's *Zarathustra* ("On Old and New Tablets" 2): "When I came to men I found them sitting on an old conceit: the conceit that they have long known what is good and evil for man. All talk of virtue seemed an old and weary matter to man; and whoever wanted to sleep well still talked of good and evil before going to sleep." With Nietzsche, our common moral valuations are suddenly considered questionable, and ethics, instead of being a matter of inconsequential rationalizations, becomes a critique of culture, a vivisection of modern man.

In *Beyond Good and Evil* (186) Nietzsche presents the other side of the coin: in a sense, his undertaking is more modest than that of his predecessors. "One should own up in all strictness what is still necessary here for a long time to come, what alone is justified so far: to collect material, to conceptualize and arrange a vast realm of subtle feelings of value and differences of value which are alive, grow, beget, and perish—and perhaps attempt to present vividly some of the more frequent and recurring forms of such living crystallizations—all to prepare a *typology* of morals. To be sure: so far one has not been so modest. With a stiff seriousness that inspires laughter, all our philosophers demanded something far more exalted, presumptuous, and solemn from themselves as soon as they approached the study of morality: they wanted to supply a *rational foundation* for morals; and every philosopher so far has believed that he has provided such a foundation. Morality itself, however, was accepted as 'given.' How remote from their coarse pride was that task which they considered insignificant and left in dust and dirt— the task of description, although the subtlest fingers and senses can scarcely be subtle enough for it. Because our moral philosophers knew the facts of morality only very approximately in arbitrary extracts or in accidental epitomes—for example, as the morality of their environment, their class, their church, their time, their climate and part of the world—because they were poorly informed and not even very curious about different peoples, ages, and the past, they never laid eyes on the real problems of morality; for these emerge only when we compare *many* moralities. In all previous studies of morality one thing was lacking, strange as that may sound: the problem of morality itself; what was lacking was the suspicion that there was anything at all problematic here. What the philosophers called 'a rational foundation for morality' and tried to supply was, properly considered, only a scholarly variation of a common *faith* in the prevalent morality; a new means of *expression* of this faith; in short, itself simply another feature of, or rather another fact within, a particular morality; indeed, in the last analysis, a kind of denial that this morality might ever be considered problematic—certainly the very opposite of an examination, analysis, questioning, and vivisection of this very bad faith."

Nietzsche is prepared to press two new questions. How does our prevalent morality compare with other moralities? And what can be said about morality in general? To begin with the first question, the morality of his society does not strike Nietzsche as divine or as supremely venerable; and he has no wish, any more than Freud

a quarter of a century later, to defend its surpassing wisdom. On the contrary, he finds it far from admirable in many respects, and in some ways quite contemptible in comparison with other moralities, developed elsewhere.

We have quoted Nietzsche's demand for "attempts to present vividly some of the more frequent and recurring forms . . . to prepare a *typology* of morals." Later in *Beyond Good and Evil* (260) he suggests two types: "Wandering through the many subtler and coarser moralities which have so far been prevalent on earth, or still are prevalent, I found that certain features recurred regularly together and were closely associated—until I finally discovered two basic types and one basic difference. There is *master morality* and *slave morality*. I add immediately that in all the higher and more mixed cultures there also appear attempts at mediation between these two moralities, and yet more often the interpenetration and mutual misunderstanding of both, and at times they occur directly alongside of each other—even in the same human being, within a single soul. The moral discrimination of values has originated either among a ruling group whose consciousness of their difference from the ruled group was accompanied by delight—or among the ruled group, the slaves and the dependent of all degrees. In the first case, when the ruling group determines what is 'good,' the exalted, proud states of the soul are experienced as conferring distinction and determining the order of rank. The noble man separates from himself those in whom

393

the opposite of such exalted, proud states finds expression: he despises them. It should be noted immediately that in this first type of morality the opposition of 'good' and '*bad*' means about the same as 'noble' and 'contemptible.' (The opposition of 'good' and '*evil*' has a different origin.) One feels contempt for the cowardly, the anxious, the petty, those who are intent on narrow utility; also for the mistrustful with their unfree glances, those who humble themselves, the doglike people who allow themselves to be maltreated, the begging flatterers, above all the liars: it is part of the fundamental faith of all aristocrats that the common people lie. 'We truthful ones'—thus the nobility in ancient Greece referred to itself. It is plain that moral designations were everywhere first applied to *human beings* and only later, derivatively, to actions. Therefore it is a gross mistake when historians of morality start out from such questions as: why was the compassionate action praised? The noble kind of man experiences *itself* as determining values. . . . Such a morality is self-glorification. In the foreground there is the feeling of fullness, of power that wants to overflow, the happiness of high tension, the consciousness of wealth which would give and bestow. The noble man too helps the unfortunate, but not, or almost not, out of pity, but more prompted by an urge which is begotten by the excess of power. The noble man honors himself as one who is powerful—also one who has power over himself, who knows how to speak and be silent, who delights in

being severe and hard with himself and respects all severity and hardness."

This contrast of the two types is elaborated in the first of the three inquiries which constitute Nietzsche's next book, *Toward a Genealogy of Morals*. The first chapter is entitled "Good and Evil versus Good and Bad." Here Nietzsche attempts a detailed portrait of slave morality which contrasts not good and bad but good and evil. Slave morality, he suggests (section 10), is created by "the *ressentiment* of those who are denied the real reaction, that of the deed, and who compensate with an imaginary revenge. Whereas all noble morality grows out of a triumphant affirmation of oneself, slave morality immediately says No to what comes from outside, to what is different, to what is not oneself: and this No is its creative deed. This reversal of the value-positing glance—this *necessary* direction outward instead of back to oneself—is of the nature of *ressentiment:* to come into being, slave morality requires an outside world, a counterworld." The noble morality begins with self-affirmation, "and its negative concept, 'base,' 'mean,' 'bad,' is only an afterborn, pale, contrasting image." Slave morality, on the other hand, begins with a negation; and its positive ideals are afterthoughts, contrasts to what is hated.

Misconceptions about Nietzsche's two types are legion, and they shall not be catalogued here. But another passage from the section just cited may dispel some of them: nobility precludes resentment. "To be unable to take one's own enemies, accidents, and misdeeds seriously for long—that is the sign of strong and rich natures. . . . Such a man simply shakes off with one shrug much vermin that would have buried itself deep in others; here alone it is also possible—assuming that it is possible at all on earth—that there be real '*love* of one's enemies.' How much respect has a noble person for his enemies! And such respect is already a bridge to love. After all, he demands his enemy for himself, as his distinction; he can stand no enemy but one in whom there is nothing to be despised and *much* to be honored. Conversely, imagine 'the enemy' as conceived by a man of *ressentiment*—and here precisely is his deed, his creation: he has conceived 'the evil enemy,' '*the evil one*'—and indeed as the fundamental concept from which he then derives, as an afterimage and counterinstance, a 'good one'—himself."

We are now ready to understand the phrase "beyond good and evil." The first chapter of the *Genealogy* ends: "*Beyond Good and Evil*—at least this does *not* mean 'Beyond Good and Bad.' " Nietzsche associates the contrast of good and *evil* with the morality of resentment; and the suggestion that we might go "beyond good and evil" invites comparison with Zarathustra's challenge in the chapter "On the Virtuous": "you are too *pure* for the filth of the words: revenge, punishment, reward, retribution." The same chapter contains a typology of different conceptions of virtue with vivisectional intent. The conception of resentment as the source of many moral judgments is one of Nietzsche's central themes. A powerful early statement will be found in *The Dawn* (202); and in *Zarathustra* the theme is developed in the chapters "On the Adder's Bite," "On the Pitying," "On the Tarantulas" ("For *that man be delivered from revenge,* that is for me the bridge to the highest hope"), and "On Redemption."

It will have been noted that Nietzsche presents master and slave morality as two types without claiming that every morality must represent either one or the other; and least of all does he claim, as is often supposed, that every man is either a master or a slave. When he speaks of these two types, he uses the words master and slave in a fairly literal manner to suggest that moral judgments will differ, depending on whether they were developed among men who ruled or men who were oppressed. And immediately after first introducing the terms he adds, as we have seen, "that in all the higher and more mixed cultures" the two types interpenetrate, and moral views derived from both strains may be encountered in the same person. Here he is of course referring to our own culture. And he devoted much effort to pointing up the inconsistencies in our moral judgments; and particularly he sought to uncover the ways in which the Christian virtues were molded by the resentment of the oppressed classes among which Christianity first made headway.

What Nietzsche opposed in Christian morality was not, as is often claimed, a humane attitude. On the contrary, what he opposed were such features as these: resentment, an antagonism against excellence, a predisposition in favor of mediocrity or even downright baseness, a leveling tendency, the conviction that sex is sinful, a devaluation of both body and intellect in favor of the soul, and the devaluation of this whole world in favor of another. In the end, he suggests that all these traits are rooted in resentment.

"How one philosophizes with a hammer" is the subtitle of one of Nietzsche's last works, *The Twilight of the Idols,* and he explains in the preface what he means: he speaks of idols "which are here touched with a hammer as with a tuning fork"; and instead of crushing the idols he speaks of hearing "as a reply that famous hollow sound which speaks of bloated entrails." The book was originally to bear the title "A Psychologist's Idleness," and Nietzsche's instrument is clearly the little hammer of the psychologist, not a sledge.

It is similar with the "revaluation of all values." Nietzsche does not arbitrarily invert our traditional valuations but tries to show, by an act of internal criticism, how the moral judgments of Christianity are born of resentment, and how Christian morality, being profoundly hateful, must be condemned by its own professed standards.

Beyond that, Nietzsche pictures Christianity as the "revaluation of all the values of antiquity" (*Beyond Good and Evil* 46). He claims that the Christians turned the embodiment of classical morality into the prototype of evil. He has in mind not only the Christian revaluation of pride, physical excellence, and sex, but also such passages as this one from the first chapter of Paul's First Epistle to the Corinthians, which Nietzsche cites in his *Antichrist* (45): "God hath chosen the foolish things of the world to ruin the wise; and God hath chosen the weak things of the world to ruin what is strong; and base things of the world, and things which are despised, hath God chosen, yea, and what is nothing, to bring to nought what is something." Far from seeing himself as a wayward iconoclast who turns upside down the whole Western tradition in morals, Nietzsche claims that Christianity stood classical morality on its head.

While the epithets master morality and slave morality are intended, first of all, to be descriptive and to refer to origins, Nietzsche's contrast is of course hortatory too. He wants to wean us from those elements in our moral heritage which are characteristic of slave morality. But two points should be noted. First, Nietzsche's analyses do not stand or fall with his preferences, any more than his preferences stand or fall with his analyses. And secondly, his typology does not by any means commit him to any unreserved acceptance, leave alone glorification, of master morality. In the chapter on "The 'Improvers' of Mankind" in *Twilight of the Idols,* Nietzsche discusses the Indian "law of Manu" as an example of master morality and leaves no doubt whatever about his own reaction to Manu's inhumane treatment of the outcasts, the chandalas: "These regulations are instructive enough: here we encounter for once *Aryan* humanity, quite pure, quite primordial— we learn that the concept of 'pure blood' is the opposite of a harmless concept."

This brief account may give some indication of Nietzsche's answer to his own question, how our prevalent morality compares with other moralities. There remains the question: what can be said about morality in general? If we do not accept morality as simply given, and if we acknowledge that there are many different moralities, what can we make of this whole phenomenon of morality? There are two sections in *Beyond Good and Evil* (188, 198) which offer interesting suggestions in answer to this question.

"Every morality is, as opposed to *laisser aller,* a bit of tyranny against 'nature'; also against 'reason'; but this in itself is no objection, as long as we do not have some other morality which permits us to decree that every kind of tyranny and unreason is impermissible. What is essential and inestimable in every morality is that it constitutes a long compulsion: to understand Stoicism or Hedonism or Puritanism, one should recall the compulsion under which every language so far has achieved strength and freedom —the metrical compulsion of rhyme and rhythm." Nietzsche goes on to point out how all "freedom, subtlety, boldness" requires discipline; and without discipline we should not have the achievements "for whose sake life on earth is worthwhile; for example, virtue, art, music, dance, reason, spir-

ituality." And Nietzsche concludes this section (188): " 'Thou shalt obey someone, and for a long time; else thou wilt perish and lose the last respect for yourself'—this appears to me to be the moral imperative of nature which, however, is neither 'categorical' as the old Kant would have it (hence the 'else') nor addressed to the individual (what do individuals matter!), but to peoples, races, ages, classes—but above all to the human animal, to *man*."

In the other section (198) it is suggested that every morality which addresses itself to the individual is really a prescription for living with one's passions. Nietzsche tries to show this in the cases of Stoicism, Spinoza, Aristotle, and Goethe, and claims that these moralities are "without exception baroque and unreasonable in form—because they are addressed to 'all' and generalize where generalizations are impermissible." Interpreted conditionally and taken with a grain of salt, they contain a good deal of wisdom, but no moral code can be unconditionally applied to all men.

The type that Nietzsche himself most admires is by no means his own invention. He resembles Socrates and the great-souled man of Aristotle's *Nichomachean Ethics* (IV. 3) as well as Shakespeare's 94th sonnet and these lines from *Measure for Measure:* "O, it is excellent / To have a giant's strength; but it is tyrannous / To use it like a giant." To cite *Zarathustra* ("On Those Who are Sublime"): "There is nobody from whom I want beauty as much as from you who are powerful: let your kindness be your final self-conquest. Of all evil I deem you capable: therefore I want the good from you. Verily, I have often laughed at the weaklings who thought themselves good because they had no claws." The highest type to Nietzsche's mind is the passionate man who is the master of his passions, able to employ them creatively without having to resort to asceticism for fear that his passions might conquer him. But not everybody is capable of this achievement, and Nietzsche does not believe in the possibility of a universal morality. He prefers self-control and sublimation to both license and asceticism, but concedes that for some asceticism may be necessary. Those who require such a radical prescription strike him as weaker, less powerful types than men like Goethe, for example.

The will to power is, according to Nietzsche, a universal drive, found in all men. It prompts the slave who dreams of a heaven from which he hopes to behold his master in hell no less than it prompts the master. Both resentment and brutality, both sadism and asceticism are expressions of it. Indeed, Nietzsche thinks that all human behavior is reducible to this single basic force. He does not endorse the will to power any more than Freud endorses sexual desire; but he thinks we shall be better off if we face the facts and understand ourselves than if we condemn others hypocritically, without understanding.

The overman, finally, is not what Nietzsche expects from the evolutionary process (he himself rejected this misinterpretation unequivocally), but the image and incarnation of the accomplishment of man's striving. Instead of placing perfection either above the clouds or in the past, nineteen centuries ago, and instead of asking man to adore a perfection of which he is constitutionally incapable, Nietzsche places it before man as an object of will and purpose: here is what man should make of himself. In the words of Zarathustra's first speech to the people: "*I teach you the overman. Man is something that shall be overcome. What have you done to overcome him?*"

Every morality is a recipe for a certain type of man, an explication of a vision of what man might be. Nietzsche suggests that we examine every morality with this in mind, and ask ourselves what we think of this vision —or that. And he offers us a vision of his own.

Bibliography

Friedrich Nietzsche, There are many editions in German, the *Musarionausgabe* (23 vols., 1920–29) being the most complete. In English there are *The Complete Works* (18 vols.) and *The Philosophy of Nietzsche* (5 works in one volume), both in unreliable translations, and *The Portable Nietzsche* (4 complete works and selections from other works, notes, and letters, all newly translated with introduction, prefaces, and notes by Walter Kaufmann).

C. Andler, *Nietzsche: Sa vie et sa pensée* (6 vols., 1920–31).

L. Klages, *Die psychologischen Errungenschaften Nietzsches* (1926).

K. Jaspers, *Nietzsche: Einführung in das Verständnis seines Philosophierens* (1936).

G. A. Morgan, *What Nietzsche Means* (1941).

W. Kaufmann, *Nietzsche: Philosopher, Psychologist, Antichrist* (1950, 2nd ed. 1956).

Walter Kaufmann
Princeton University

Nietzsche, F.: *see* Freud, Sigmund; Goethe, Johann Wolfgang von; Hegel, G. W. F.; Machiavelli, Niccolo; Major Ethical Viewpoints; Minor Socratics; Moral Philosophy in America; Scheler, Max; Schopenhauer, Arthur; Soviet Morality, Current; Utilitarianism.

"Nietzschean" Marxist: *see* Soviet Morality, Current.

Nilo-Hamitics: *see* Pakot, the Moral System of.

Nilotics: *see* Pakot, the Moral System of.

Nirwana: *see* Schopenhauer, Arthur.

Noahide laws: *see* Jewish Ethics and Its Civilization.

nobility: *see* Hammurapi, Code of; Nietzsche, Friedrich.

noble, the: *see* Hartmann, Nicolai.

noemata: *see* More, Henry.

Noldin, H.: *see* Jesuits, the, Moral Theology of.

nomads: *see* Pakot, the Moral System of.

non-cognition: *see* Ayer, Alfred J.; Language and Ethics.

non-cognitivism: *see* Major Ethical Viewpoints.

non-cognitivist theories: *see* Major

Ethical Viewpoints; Meta-ethics and Normative Ethics.

non-conformity: *see* Rio Grande Pueblo Indians.

non-cooperation: *see* Rio Grande Pueblo Indians.

non-difference: *see* Hindu Ethics.

non-doing: *see* China, Moral Philosophies of.

non-dualistic ethics: *see* Hindu Ethics.

non-dualistic metaphysics: *see* Hindu Ethics.

non-injury: *see* Hindu Ethics; injury.

non-literates: *see* Aboriginals of Yirkalla; Rio Grande Pueblo Indians.

non-maleficence: *see* Ross, Sir (William) David.

non-naturalism: *see* Broad, C. D.; Major Ethical Viewpoints.

non-normative ethics: *see* Meta-ethics and Normative Ethics.

non-resistance: *see* Berdyaev, Nicolas; Soloviev, Wladimir; Tolstoy, Leo.

non-self: *see* Hindu Ethics.

non-violence: *see* Quakerism, Classical, The Morality of.

normal and abnormal, the: *see* Freud, Sigmund.

normative ethics: *see* Ayer, Alfred J.; Major Ethical Viewpoints; Meta-ethics and Normative Ethics.

normative science: *see* Schlick, Moritz.

norms: *see* Aquinas, Thomas, Moral Views of; Kierkegaard, Soren; Morals and Religion; Psychology and Morals; Schlick, Moritz.

norms, ethical: *see* Mundurucu Indians; A Dual System of Ethics; Soviet Morality, Current.

North American Indians: *see* Mundurucu Indians, A Dual System of Ethics; Navaho Morals; Rio Grande

Pueblo Indians; Zuni Indians, Morals of.

North-east Africa: *see* Pakot, the Moral System of.

Northeastern Arnhem Land: *see* Aboriginals of Yirkalla.

nothingness: *see* French Existentialism and Moral Philosophy.

O

oaths: *see* Cudworth, Ralph; Quakerism, Classical, The Morality of.

oaths, sanctity of: *see* Zoroastrian Morals.

obedience: *see* Augustine and Morals; Cudworth, Ralph; Hindu Ethics; Jesuits, the, Moral Theology of; Jewish Ethics and Its Civilization; More, Henry; Navaho Morals; Quakerism, Classical, The Morality of; Sophists, the; Spinoza, Stoics, the.

obedience, civil: *see* Christian Moral Philosophy.

objective ethics: *see* Hindu Ethics.

objective theory: *see* Broad, C. D.

objectivity: *see* Scheler, Max; Sophists, the.

objectivity, ethical: *see* Plato; Socrates.

object-language: *see* Meta-ethics and Normative Ethics.

obligation(s): *see* Balguy, John; Broad, C. D.; Cooper, Anthony Ashley; Clarke, Samuel; Cudworth, Ralph; Cumberland, Richard; Dewey, John; duties; Hindu Ethics; Hobbes, Thomas; Jesuits, the, Moral Theology of; Kant, I.; Major Ethical Viewpoints; Moore, George Edward; Moral Philosophy in America; Muslim Morals; ought; Price; Prichard, H. A.; Primitive Morals; Quakerism, Classical, The Morality of; Reid, Thomas; Ross, Sir (William) David; Scheler, Max; Soviet Morality, Current; Utilitarianism; Wollaston, William; Zuni Indians, Morals of.

obligation, moral: *see* Soviet Morality, Current.

obscene language: *see* Aboriginals of Yirkalla.

occult, the: *see* Freud, Sigmund; Primitive Morals; Schopenhauer, Arthur.

Oedipus complex: *see* Freud, Sigmund.

offerings: *see* Aztec Morals; Rio Grande Pueblo Indians.

Oinomaos: *see* Minor Socratics.

Okomatadi: *see* Primitive Morals.

old age: *see* Hindu Ethics; Navaho Morals; Psychology of Morals; Rio Grande Pueblo Indians.

Old Testament: *see* Christian Moral Philosophy; Hammurapi, Code of; Jewish Ethics and Its Civilization; Quakerism, Classical, The Morality of.

omen: *see* Aztec Morals.

Onesicritus: *see* Minor Socratics.

ontology: *see* Hegel, G. W. F.; Meta-ethics and Normative Ethics.

ontology, moral: *see* Psychology and Morals.

opinion: *see* Jesuits, the, Moral Theology of; Quakerism, Classical, The Morality of; Reid, Thomas; Ross, Sir (William) David; Sophists, the; Spinoza; Stoics, the.

oppositions: *see* conflicts; Sophists, the.

oppression: *see* Marxist Theory of Morals; Minor Socratics.

optimism: *see* Freud, Sigmund; Jesuits, the, Moral Theology of; Jewish Ethics and Its Civilization.

order: *see* China, Moral Philosophies of; Cudworth, Ralph; Dewey, John; Machiavelli, Niccolo; Plato; Rio Grande Pueblo Indians; Spinoza; Stoics, the.

ordinances: *see* Jewish Ethics and Its Civilization.

Orestes: *see* Sophists, the.

organic unities, principle of: *see* Moore, George Edward; Ross, Sir (William) David.

organized charity: *see* Hindu Ethics.

original sin: *see* Dante, Alighieri; Jesuits, the, Moral Theology of; Liguori, St. Alphonsus and Catholic Moral Philosophy; Psychology and Morals; Schopenhauer, Arthur; Spinoza.

orphans: *see* Muslim Morals; Tapirapé Morals, Some Aspects of.

Orthodox church, Greek: *see* Soloviev, Wladimir; Soviet Morality, Current.

Orthodox church, Russian: *see* Berdyaev, Nicolas; Khomiakov, Alexey; Soloviev, Wladimir.

other-worldliness: *see* Puritan Morals; Muslim Morals.

Otis, James: *see* Moral Philosophy in America.

Otto, Rudolph: *see* Morals and Religion.

ought: *see* Aquinas, Thomas, Moral Views of; categorical imperative; French Existentialism and Moral Philosophy; Hartmann, Nicolai; Hindu Ethics; Hume, David; Kant, I.; Major Ethical Viewpoints; Marxist Theory of Morals; Meta-ethics and Normative Ethics; Moral Philosophy in America; Prichard, H. A.; Reid, Thomas; Schlick, Moritz; Sidgwick, Henry; Utilitarianism; Wollaston, William.

outcasts: *see* Freud, Sigmund.

outlanders: *see* Mundurucu Indians, A Dual System of Ethics.

overman, the: *see* Nietzsche, Friedrich.

overpopulation: *see* Riffian Morals.

ownership: *see* Riffian Morals.

P

pacifism: *see* Aboriginals of Yirkalla; Marxist Theory of Morals; Quakerism, Classical, The Morality of; Tolstoy, Leo.

pain: *see* Aquinas, Thomas, Moral Views of; China, Moral Philosophies of; Cumberland, Richard; Freud, Sigmund; Hindu Ethics; Hobbes, Thomas; Minor Socratics; Plato; Schlick, Moritz; Spinoza; Stoics, the; Utilitarianism.

Paine, Thomas: *see* Moral Philosophy in America; Price, Richard.

Pakot, the Moral System of*

Description and analysis of the Pakot moral system must be based upon abstraction from observed behavior and statements since Pakot do not attempt to systematize it and they have no writing from which it might be deduced. Contradictions and inconsistencies in their beliefs as described here may be partly attributed to imperfection in the analysis but also to the fact that they, like us, do not attempt to erase discrepancies except when beliefs obviously clash. Since the moral sys-

tem is but a facet of the total cultural system it is first necessary to sketch briefly some pertinent facts about the total culture—who the Pakot are, what they are like and what their cosmology, which is intimately related to the moral system, consists of.

I

The Pakot (or Suk) inhabit a reserve in the north of the Rift Valley Province in west central Kenya which varies in topography and climate from low lying hot plains to 10,000 foot high wet grasslands. They are a cattle, sheep and goat herding people who also practise some agriculture and are nomadic in differing degrees depending on the number of stock which they possess and the fertility of the land. Their nomadic propensities are one of the main reasons why the government, which rests largely in the hands of the older men of the various communities, is loosely organized. The Pakot are representative of a group of similar tribes in northeast Africa called Nilotics and Nilo-Hamitics who are found from northern Tanganyika to the southern Sudan.

Pakot men are naked except for a cotton cloth or goat skin which may be loosely worn over the shoulder. A distinctive feature is the fine painted

* Debt must be acknowledged to G. Wagner whose excellent analysis of the cosmological system of the Abaluyia of Kavirondo, Kenya (in *African Worlds* edited by D. Forde, Oxford Press, 1954), which resembles that of the Pakot, gave many of the insights needed to interpret facts relating to the Pakot moral system.

skullcap-like clay headdress which marks the wearer as an adult and warrior who has been circumcised at puberty and initiated into adulthood in his late teens. The women are modest and wear goat skin capes over their shoulders and skirts carefully covering them at all times. Their ears are pierced and weighed down with a multitude of metal earrings while around their necks they wear large metal rings and bead necklaces for ornamentation. In an area of something over 3000 square miles there exist about 55,000 of these people.

To Pakot the most valuable thing in the world is stock, particularly their cattle, which they believe their god, Tororut, has given to them, and the chief pursuit of Pakot is accumulation of these animals. Cattle are desired for their subsistence, ritual and prestige value; these various uses are so closely interwoven as to make estimation of their relative importance impossible. They are essential in many social and religious rites, to maintain life and in attaining high status. Songs are composed praising their beauty, each is given a name, and it is usual for a man to take as one of his own names that of his prize steer. The focal place that these animals have in life marks the Pakot as possessors of what M. J. Herskovits has called the "cattle complex" which is present in one degree or another among most East African people but especially the above mentioned Nilotics and Nilo-Hamitics. The amount of attention devoted to cattle seems to be the chief cause for lack of elaboration in other aspects of life—religious, political, aesthetic and so forth—for which there is little time or inclination.

In the Pakot cosmology Tororut is the creator of the world and men, including the sun, stars, rain and thunder which are treated as semi-independent aspects of the deity. He is a paternal god desiring his people to be happy and free of evil; he can be called upon by them for help when disasters such as drought and disease occur, although the Pakot also feel that he brings calamities of this kind as well as others if they stray from the prescribed and normal life that he has laid down. Most feel that he also interferes in interpersonal relations to punish those who do evil to others. He is considered to be ever watchful, very close to Pakot, and constantly ready to punish deviation in one way or another.

The social system that god has created for Pakot is felt to be perfect. He wishes people to conform to it and they are continually admonished by their leaders to do so. When appealing to Tororut for help the elders often direct the deity's attention to the fact that they have behaved according to tradition.

To each man, to animals, the trees, earth and grass and even to some inanimate objects god has given a soul or spirit (anyat) which is separable, at least for humans and some animals, and can roam about observing distant events and doing harm to those who have wronged it or simply because it is inclined to evil. After death this spirit is thought to live on if it belongs to a man of high social status (and perhaps some women) acting in much the same manner as that of a living person.

In addition to this powerful creator Pakot think of a sphere of magical cause and effect which, however, has two different aspects. On the one hand life is pictured as a state of balance, or ritual "cleanness" or "sweetness" (*anyin*), any trespass of which, whether accidental, premeditated or circumstantial, automatically renders the person who has been involved "unclean" (*kololion*). The suggestion is, though this was not clearly stated to me, that such unclean persons will also be magically punished by sickness or other misfortune if they are not ritually cleansed.

Distinct from this, but still in the sphere of magic, is the belief that there is an automatic supernatural mechanism that can be activated by anyone for either good or evil purposes. Thus, for example, the community may place a spell upon an evil doer or an evil person may inflict ill on an enemy (sorcery).

Magic is thoroughly mixed with religion, as the above suggests. In fact the place of god in these two types of magic is never made clear. No one would agree that he helps the sorcerer to obtain his ends, but it is sometimes suggested that the activating force in the magical processes of uncleanness and socially acceptable magic is god himself.

II

As this description shows, most of the evil that occurs in Pakot life can be avoided (Pakot believe) by conforming to the good life. God's wrath, uncleanness and its accompanying contamination of others, and even revenge by angry ancestral and other spirits are avoided by following the moral life. In addition, as will be shown below, certain evils are avoided by adherence to man-made laws which have no supernatural connotations. The only exceptions to this seem to be those cases of people, such as certain types of sorcerers and ancestral spirits, who are naturally wicked and who must be dealt with in other ways.

The moral life is one of ritual cleanness and conformity to the laws of god and society. Possession of large numbers of cattle is not a necessary criterion of a good man though to be without cattle is a great misfortune and to lack a desire to possess them would be considered odd. Possessing many cattle and other stock brings prestige to a man and is a sign of success and, therefore, to some extent, cleanness. The good man (*paghin*) is expected to give attention to building his herds, to be circumcised and initiated, to be married and have children. Beyond these basic requirements he is conceived of as one who is fair in dividing food among his wife or wives and children, who deals fairly with his kin and helps them, who shares his beer with his neighbors and is obliging in slaughtering a steer for a feast for them when they desire it. He is also a man who does not quarrel with his neighbors or wish them evil; nor is he proud or boastful. After the puberty circumcision ceremonies all young men enter the responsible life for the first time; they are considered thenceforth to be capable of distinguishing right from wrong and during the ceremonies are lectured on the requirements of the good life and the necessity of following them.

A good woman (*tangan*) is expected to bear and care for children, herd cattle and cultivate crops when such work needs to be done. Young women are informed of their obligations at puberty ceremonies and told not to steal from their husbands, to treat them well and be willing to guard their stock when they are away from home and not abuse them in words or acts. They are admonished to refrain from committing adultery and told to work hard in the fields to produce food for their families, to learn well how to grow crops, cook, make baskets and do the other things necessary in keeping a proper home. While women and children, in contrast to adult men and older boys, are generally not considered to have responsibility for their acts or power to control their fortunes, nevertheless adult women can be held accountable in certain circumstances.

Persons who have conformed to these prescriptions and who have avoided uncleanness achieve high moral and ritual status in the community. Old men are especially highly respected due in part to the fact that their attainment of long lives has demonstrated that they have preserved social equilibrium and have thus been good. (But it must be added that old men are also deferred to in part because they are close to death and it is felt that if they are angered their spirits will be perpetrators of harm to members of the community.) Thus far it seems that high status depends on the intentions and will of the individual, but as will be seen it is in part a result of chance.

III

Immorality occurs in two classes: 1) acts which are against the law and custom and are punishable or deprecated, and 2) acts which make a person ritually unclean. Sometimes these conditions are contiguous, sometimes not. There is, however, a considerable correspondence between the two.

In the first category (illegal acts) the simplest punishment seems to be a beating with a willow switch. Beyond that a stock fine is the more severe punishment. Stock fines may vary from a few head to a large number for serious crimes. Magical cursing, execution and expulsion from the community are the most severe punishments. Highest on the list of criminal behavior is the practise of magic designed to kill for private ends. This is in contrast to acceptable magic performed by the community or its representatives to achieve some socially desirable end such as punishment of a thief who is unknown. The practise of the former type of magic is considered premeditated murder of the most heinous kind and may be punished by execution or expulsion. But fining a person some of his stock is the most usual type of punishment. Actual premeditated murder is highly antisocial but is only punished by a fine (unless the defendant is killed in a retaliatory act by the deceased's relatives), in this case a very heavy one. Other crimes include theft (as of cattle, which is the worst sort) and lying, the latter being condemned because it may cause harm to an innocent person. A person whose lies have caused harm to others is liable to be severely fined. As for adultery, there is some confusion in the Pakot mind about it because so much of it occurs. It is adulterous for anyone but her husband to cohabitate with a woman who has been formally married and wears the wedding band on her wrist. A person caught in such an act, depending on the circumstances, is heavily fined. But so many people indulge in it that its moral status is in dispute. As one Pakot said, "Even the old men do this," which is to say, even those who are of high moral status as most old men are considered to be. The data show that theft and adultery in one form or another are the most usual kinds of crimes committed in Pakot society. In all these cases socially sanctioned magical cursing may be used by the community against the person or persons known or unknown as a punishment.

In the second category (ritual uncleanness) we find that some crimes render the guilty unclean, but, as noted above, there is no constant correlation between crime and uncleanness. Thus both a murderer of another Pakot and a warrior who kills an enemy in battle are unclean, but the warrior has not committed a crime. Rather he is praised for his bravery. People are unclean who have killed,

committed adultery, physically injured others so as to draw blood, practised magic for private ends or simply acquired a bad reputation through proximity over a long time to all kinds of misfortune or a succession of minor sins. Further, a woman and uncircumcised boy who have copulated, and a mother whose child has died are unclean. Even a diseased person if his illness seems due to his own evil acts (e.g., a proud and boastful person) is unclean and such persons often admit to immoral behavior as an explanation of their conditions.

In addition to the warrior mentioned above, there are others whose uncleanness is not correlated with crime although it is not always clear from Pakot statements who these are in every case. The following cases seem due merely to circumstances but it is possible that some may be viewed by Pakot as the result of premeditated acts of evil on the part of the sufferers: a woman during and after the birth of a child, a woman who has given birth to twins or abnormal offspring of other kinds, the widow of a man who has just died, a woman during menses or a boy during the period of circumcision seclusion. Certainly in the latter case the unclean persons are thought of as being so merely through circumstances. It is not a crime to be circumcised; rather it is necessary for all males (except in one Pakot area) and it is inevitable. The most obvious explanation is that persons in the situations just described are in some way, like criminals, in a 'transitional" or dangerously unusual position in reference to social stability that requires special care to avoid disaster and deviation.

To round out this analysis it should be noted that some illegal activities such as violating another man's water hole call only for a beating and a fine but do not in themselves make the violator unclean. Finally there are many moral trespasses which do not make the perpetrator unclean and which are punished only by a show of indignation.

It would seem that unclean persons are in a tenuous position in relation to the normal and good life. They are in danger of falling off the narrow edge and they can contaminate others. Steps are taken to cleanse them and bring them back to social health. Thus before a woman gives birth to a child a ceremony (parapara) is held to determine whether she has been contaminated by previous acts and if she has she is cleansed to protect the life of the unborn child as well as her own. Often unclean persons are quarantined in some way until the cleansing is finished. The methods of cleansing are many and varied. For less serious conditions such as menses, restriction of activities is enough and it passes away in time; for more serious conditions the persons may actually be excluded from the community until cleansed by washing their bodies with the stomach contents of a goat (grass has sacred qualities) or by painting their bodies with pigments, the latter remedy being applicable also to persons who are in danger of contamination.

To summarize this section, it seems that some acts which endanger the sta-bility of the society and the individual are both unclean and criminal (e.g., sorcery and murder); some behavior which endangers the equilibrium is acceptable (e.g.,) slaying a foreigner) and not criminal but is still unclean; some acts (e.g., violating another man's water hole) are subject to legal or other social sanctions but do not produce uncleanness.

IV

Pakot do not encourage moral behavior because they hope to obtain an eternal reward after death. To Pakot death is the greatest evil and they scrupulously refrain from talking about the dead or even discussing the subject in most cases. Any act associated with blood letting seems to be unclean because of its association with sickness and death. The spirits of adult men which live on after death are most often viewed as malevolent (*cheptomu*) visiting evil on their former households because they are cranky and vindictive about things done to them before death. They are usually placated with offerings of beer, milk and tobacco and told to go away. Death is an unenviable state—a limbo—which is not to be looked forward to. The best that can be done for the dead is to forget them.

Pakot are moral and support the system outlined above, we must conclude, because it is the best explanation of evil and way of combating it they know. Working in accordance with it they can ensure continuance of and success in this life which, without the evil, is considered a very good thing. By viewing any act that suggests death or any deviation from the "normal" as morally dirty they can take steps to restore equilibrium and insure the future continuance of the good. The fact that the preservation of the good life seems to the Westerner to be due at least in part to chance, that high status is partly accidental, that persons seem in some cases to be condemned for situations over which they have no control does not make the system any less useful and effective to Pakot as long as they believe, as they do, that they have correctly perceived the operation of the cosmos and that their own methods of control of the cosmos actually work.

Bibliography

Further writings on the Pakot, which however are not necessarily concerned directly with this problem, are:

J. G. Peristiany, "The Age-set System of the Pastoral Pakot," *Africa,* Vol. XXI, Nos. 3 & 4. July/October (1951), pp. 188–206, 279–302.

——, "Pakot Sanctions and Structure," *Africa,* Vol. XXIV, No. 1. January (1954), pp. 17–25.

H. K. Schneider, *The Pakot (Suk) of Kenya with Special Reference to the Role of Livestock in their Subsistence Economy,* University Microfilms (Ann Arbor, 1953).

Harold K. Schneider
Lawrence College

Paley, W.: *see* Moral Philosophy in America; Prichard, H. A.; Utilitarianism.

Panaetius of Rhodes: *see* Stoics, the.

pantheism: *see* Goethe, Johann Wolfgang von; Scheler, Max; Stoics, the.

parable: *see* Jewish Ethics and Its Civilization.

paradox: *see* Kierkegaard, Soren; Sophists, the.

parents: *see* Aquinas, Thomas, Moral Views of; Aztec Morals; China, Moral Philosophies of; Freud, Sigmund; Hindu Ethics; Puritan Morals; Tapirapé Morals, Some Aspects of.

Parker, Theodore: *see* Moral Philosophy in America.

parsimony: *see* Riffian Morals; stinginess.

Pascal, B.: *see* Jesuits, the, Moral Theology of; Scheler, Max.

Pashukanis: *see* Soviet Morality, Current.

passions: *see* Aquinas, Thomas, Moral Views of; Clarke, Samuel; Cudworth, Ralph; Hobbes, Thomas; Machiavelli, Niccolo; Reid, Thomas; Spinoza; Stoics, the.

Passmore, J. A.: *see* Cudworth, Ralph.

Patanjali: *see* Hindu Ethics.

pathology: *see* Psychology and Morals.

patience: *see* Augustine and Morals; Cudworth, Ralph; More, Henry; Muslim Morals; Tapirapé Morals, Some Aspects of.

patrilineal clans: *see* Aboriginals of Yirkalla.

patriotism: *see* Marxist Theory of Morality; Soviet Morality, Current.

Paul, Saint: *see* Augustine and Morals; Christian Moral Philosophy; Jewish Ethics and Its Civilization.

paying of wages: *see* Liguori, St. Alphonsus and Catholic Moral Philosophy.

peace: *see* Augustine and Morals; China, Moral Philosophies of; Hindu Ethics; Hobbes, Thomas; Kant, I.; Mundurucu Indians, A Dual System of Ethics; Quakerism, Classical, The Morality of; Spinoza.

peace of mind: *see* Quakerism, Classical, The Morality of; Stoics, the.

penal code: *see* Utilitarianism.

penal system: *see* Marxist Theory of Morals.

penalty: *see* Hammurapi, Code of; Primitive Morals.

penance: *see* Jesuits, the, Moral Theology of.

penitence: *see* Tolstoy, Leo.

penology: *see* Hammurapi, Code of.

Pentateuch: *see* Jewish Ethics and Its Civilization; Spinoza.

people's courts: *see* Soviet Morality, Current.

Pequots: *see* Puritan Morals.

perceptual intuitionism: *see* Ross, Sir (William) David; Sidgwick, Henry.

Peregrinus Proteus: *see* Minor Socratics.

perfection: *see* Aquinas, Thomas, Moral Views of; Cudworth, Ralph; Cumberland, Richard; Green, T. H.; Hindu Ethics; More, Henry; Nietzsche, Friedrich; Plato; Spinoza; Utilitarianism; Zoroastrian Morals.

perfectionism: *see* Kant, I.; Major Ethical Viewpoints; Quakerism, Classical, The Morality of; Tolstoy, Leo; Utilitarianism.

Pericles: *see* Sophists, the.

Peripatetic school: *see* Stoics, the.

Perkins, William: *see* Puritan Morals.

Perry, R. B.: *see* Dewey, John; Major Ethical Viewpoints; Moral Philosophy in America.

persecution: *see* Jewish Ethics and Its Civilization; Puritan Morals.

Persian Magi: *see* Sophists, the.

person, the: *see* Cudworth, Ralph; Hammurapi, Code of; Hartmann, Nicolai; Kant, I.

personality: *see* Hindu Ethics; Major Ethical Viewpoints.

persuasion: *see* Sophists, the.

pessimism: *see* Freud, Sigmund; Jesuits, the, Moral Theology of; Jewish Ethics and Its Civilization; Schopenhauer, Arthur.

Pharisaism: *see* Christian Moral Philosophy; Jewish Ethics and Its Civilization; Psychology and Morals.

phenomenology: *see* French Existentialism and Moral Philosophy; Hartmann, Nicolai; Scheler, Max.

philanthropy: *see* Hindu Ethics; Jewish Ethics and Its Civilization; Navaho Morals; Quakerism, Classical, The Morality of.

Philby, H. St. J.: *see* Primitive Morals.

philosopher king: *see* China, Moral Philosophies of.

philosophy: *see* criticism, philosophical; Hindu Ethics; Jewish Ethics and Its Civilization; Marxist Theory of Morals; Meta-ethics and Normative Ethics; metaphysics; Morals and Religion; Rio Grande Pueblo Indians; Spinoza.

physiology and morals: *see* Psychology and Morals.

Piccinini: *see* Machiavelli, Niccolo.

Piccolomini: *see* Jesuits, the, Moral Theology of.

pietism: *see* Kant, I.

piety: *see* Hindu Ethics; Jewish Ethics and Its Civilization; Muslim Morals;

Reid, Thomas; Socrates; Spinoza; Stoics, the; Zoroastrian Morals.

piety, filial: *see* China, Moral Philosophies of.

pilgrimages: *see* Muslim Morals.

Pilgrims: *see* Puritan Morals.

Pirke Aboth: *see* Jewish Ethics and Its Civilization.

pity: *see* Butler, Joseph; Dostoyevsky, Fyodor; Hammurapi, Code of; Hobbes, Thomas; Navaho Morals; Scheler, Max.

Plains Indians: *see* Rio Grande Pueblo Indians.

Plato

Plato was born to one of the most distinguished families of Athens in the Periclean age in 428–7 B.C. and lived until 348–7 B.C., a life as filled with action as it was with abstract speculation. In spite of the quantity of his own writing which remains, we have little direct evidence concerning the facts of his life, due to his almost unbroken silence about himself in his dialogues. All we can be sure of regarding Plato's earlier years is that the influence of his friendship with Socrates must have been an important force in the molding of his thought. Plato's letters reveal him as a young man interested in an active life, but he tells us that the death of Socrates put an end to his political aspirations and committed him to philosophy. The founding of the Academy is probably the most significant event in Plato's career, a step which realized his aim of providing rigorous scientific training for men of action. However, the greatest adventure in Plato's life

began after he was a man of sixty. Dionysius II of Syracuse had just succeeded his father, and Dion, Dionysius' uncle and the man of power, asked Plato to come to Syracuse to try to remedy Dionysius' lack of education, thus offering Plato the chance to test his ideal of the union of philosophy with the art of kingship. The venture seemed ill-fated from the beginning, and, after several attempts, Plato withdrew from Sicilian politics, grateful to have escaped with his life.

Little is known of Plato's later years, and nothing of significance remains of his important lectures in the Academy. This is not without good reason, since Plato tells us in the famous Epistle VII that "no intelligent man will ever be so bold as to put into language those things which his reason has contemplated, especially into a form that is unalterable—which must be the case with what is expressed in written symbol." (Epistle VII, 343) All of which should serve to remind us, whenever we become impatient with the difficulty of determining exactly what Plato's own views are in the dialogues, that we are lucky to have even this much left to us by a man who so distrusted direct and definitive statements.

When Plato's ethical theory is mentioned, it is usually the *Republic* which comes to mind first. However, an interesting result is obtained if one begins his account with the *Philebus*, admittedly one of Plato's very late dialogues. This can be used as a summary of the Platonic ethical view, and one then works backward to expand

411

the scope of the theory with material from the earlier writings. Although the announced topic for discussion in the *Philebus* is pleasure, the dialogue is heavily metaphysical in structure. This is exactly as it should be, since if Plato is to make good the Socratic claim for the objective existence of ethical norms, what he must do is to exhibit a subtle weaving together of ontological analysis with ethical questions, done in such a way that the solution to the ethical problem can be seen to be derived from a knowledge of ontological structure.

When the *Philebus* asks the question of which is better, the life of wisdom or the life of pleasure, someone familiar with the popular view of Platonic ethics as otherworldly and idealistic would expect the answer to be obvious: Wisdom. Yet Plato does not choose this simple alternative, and the reason for this is crucial to the understanding of both his ethics and his metaphysics. Plato actually chooses a third solution, something superior to either of these alternatives since it is a mixture which includes both elements. Even the ideal life, then, is not pure, but mixed; yet if it is to be mixed it must have a principle of mixture. Either a life of pure pleasure or of pure wisdom, Plato indicates, is a simpler alternative, because the mixed life requires a more subtle and detailed understanding. This increasing complexity of the ethical life parallels an increasing complexity in Plato's ontology. Plato's Forms, although still described as unchanging, incorporeal, not in space or in time, existing independently from the world, are now revealed to be a subtly interwoven and complicated affair, participating in one another as well as being participated in by the concrete objects of the sense world. The intricate interlocking of the forms of things now parallels the mixture of the ethical life. Thus, one who is able to understand how forms are woven together might use this as a guide for proportioning the mixtures which must enter into any human life.

The world, we find, is formed by the union of the limited and the unlimited, with mind or reason in charge of the union. Upon analysis pleasure is shown to be akin to the unlimited, since it is the kind of thing which by nature tends to go on until stopped by something outside of itself. Form, measure and proportion are the origin of ontological limit, and reason may follow their example in limiting pleasure, thereby producing the happy life for man after the pattern that produces beauty in nature. The mixed life is best, when it is well mixed, and reason can produce this controlled mixture when it operates according to natural principles of limitation.

Here the problem of the One and the Many enters, since understanding how unity can be united with plurality yields both an understanding of the structure of nature and an insight into how reason operates. Our aim is to produce a life of multiple elements, some of which tend by nature toward infinity, without destroying either unity or the harmony which unity brings. Just as in the *Parmenides* Plato rejects both of the extreme positions, that which tends to make unity absolute as well as that which tends to break it down completely, so here he tells us that wisdom lies in the life that seeks to stop between unrelieved purity and degeneration into endless pleasures. Between unity and sheer multiplicity there lies definite number. Reason alone, and this is the secret, can enable us to hold to the middle ground. "For if a person begins with some unity or other, he must, as I was saying, not turn immediately to infinity, but to some definite number." (*Philebus*, 18B)

Armed with this analysis of the scale which is established by the union of the One and the Many, we find that pleasures may be classified by this standard according to the degree to which they tend to slip off toward extreme multiplicity. It is reason alone which is able so to classify them; pleasures do not understand themselves. Basically it is a grasp of the ontological relation of the One and the Many which reason follows in making this classification of the kinds of pleasures, a fact which emphasizes the impossibility of a mixed life which could be successful without reason. The life of reason unbroken by pleasure would be intolerably dull, but pleasures cannot even be enjoyed unless you have reason to understand and appreciate them. Life must include a mixture, but this is not as easy to achieve as it sounds, since pleasure has by nature a tendency toward infinity, which, if allowed to go unchecked, will not only fail to produce a balance, but will de-

stroy any achieved equilibrium. Reason alone, operating according to the principle of the union between the One and the Many which it finds in nature, can guide us to and preserve the delicate balance upon which the happy life depends.

Now, if reason or mind is found to be the cause of the combined life, then it seems that it is also the cause of the good, which brings us to the famous Platonic supreme principle. Some pleasures are akin to and derived from truth, which makes them the purest of an essentially impure class, and similarly some kinds of knowledge or truth are purer than others. These are the kinds of knowledge which have to do with the principles of measure and number, so that it is here that the seeker after the happy life should concentrate his attention. The purer pleasures are the essential pleasures, those which we must get into life at all costs. That knowledge is best which has to do with pure being, that is, things which are eternally the same without mixture.

Just as some knowledge is preferable, so some pleasures are superior. "If there are any necessary pleasures, as there were kinds of knowledge, must we not mix them with the true?" (*Philebus*, 62E) If our blend, which has been mixed according to the priorities assigned by reason, is successful we will have Plato's ideal life: "An incorporeal order which shall rule nobly a living body." (*Philebus*, 64B) This ideal compound will be founded on the principle of measure and proportion, which leads Plato to remark that "the power of the good has taken refuge in the nature of the beautiful; for measure and proportion are everywhere identified with beauty and virtue." (*Philebus*, 64E) Through the presence of these principles the mixed life has itself been made good, and here Plato comes as close as he ever does to a direct statement about the Good: "Then if we cannot catch the good with the aid of one idea, let us run it down with three—beauty, proportion, and truth." (*Philebus*, 65A) What is particularly significant here is that at the same time that Plato reaches the pinnacle of his ontological hierarchy he also reaches the climax of his discussion of the ethically desirable life. Ontologically we learn that the Good can never be identified with Unity, since Good may best be described by a plurality of ideas; while ethically we learn the advantage of limited plurality and of a controlled mixture of carefully typed and graded pleasures.

Measure, moderation and fitness Plato places in the first rank, followed by proportion, beauty, perfection and sufficiency in the second order. Mind and wisdom are third, and sciences, art and true opinion, the affairs of the soul, come out fourth in the order of things. Only in the fifth rank do we find pleasures entering the scene, and then the pure pleasures of the soul are admitted first. The power of pleasure is fifth in this account of priority in the structure of things, and it is to this structure that the wise man looks for guidance in the mixing of his life. "It is not the infinite which supplies any

element of good in pleasure," (*Philebus*, 28A) so that pleasure, if it is not to destroy happiness, must be limited by mind; and it is to this order in the nature of the Good that the mind turns for its pattern of priorities. Pain and pleasure originate in the combined class and are sometimes good and sometimes bad, depending on the way in which reason controls their use.

In classifying the kinds of pleasures Plato gives a great deal of thought to false pleasures. "He who feels pleasure at all in any way or manner really feels pleasure, but it is sometimes not based upon realities, whether present or past, and often, perhaps most frequently, upon things which will never be realities in the future." (*Philebus*, 39D) The experience of pleasure itself is never bad; "pleasures also are not bad except by being false." (*Philebus*, 41A) Thus, pleasure is linked to knowledge, since in order to distinguish false pleasures you must know how to identify what is true. Next in order of avoidance to the pleasures based on falsities, pleasures which are dependent upon accompanying pain are to be shunned whenever possible. Such pleasures appear more intense alongside pain, but they are not as much to be desired as the pleasures which we can have without any attendant pain. The purer the pleasure the more to be desired. The most intense pleasures and "the greatest pains originate in some depravity of soul and body, not in virtue." (*Philebus*, 45E)

On the other hand, beauty of form is one instance of a pleasure which can come to us unmixed with less desirable elements. Intense pleasures may seem desirable at the moment, but they are by nature unlimited and tend to be disruptive. Whereas "any pleasure, however small or infrequent, if uncontaminated with pain, is pleasanter and more beautiful than a great deal of oft repeated pleasure without purity." (*Philebus*, 53C) Undoubtedly it is impossible to mix a life which would contain none of the impure pleasures, and this might not even be desirable; but we can learn to begin with the core of pure pleasures and add other kinds only in a quantity that can be contained within order and limit.

From the *Statesman* we learn that it is easier to know what the ideal life is than it is to practice it. The best life is no small matter, and "it is always easier to practice in small matters than in great." (*Statesman*, 286B) Some things have no sensible resemblances which are easily perceived, and since all ideal norms are of this type it is hard to discern them and harder yet to find something concrete as a guide. Furthermore, any real excellence will come only to the few, since "no multitude is able to acquire any art whatsoever." (*Statesman*, 300E) From the *Sophist* we learn the science of dialectic, which means knowing how to distinguish, kind by kind, in what ways the several kinds can or cannot combine. This is a skill important to ethics, since it is the basic knowledge which guides the mixer of the happy life in his choice of elements. If the best life is to be a mixture, then it is crucial to know what can be blended and what cannot. Furthermore, in this process we also learn how to distinguish the real from the imitation, and this is important if we are able to detect those pleasures which are based upon illusion.

The *Timaeus* is of interest for Plato's ethical doctrine primarily because of its description of the world-maker as 'good' and 'without envy.' (*Timaeus*, 29E) Because of the basic generosity in his nature the world-maker took the original disorder and made it to become as orderly as possible, following a rational and perfect pattern. Thus we are reassured to know that, although necessarily less than perfect due to its original basis in disorder, the world we live in is as orderly as possible and its maker himself operated from good motives. This means that the world is not completely alien to the achievement of good order, although analogously to the creation of the world, this depends upon the imposition of a rational form. What is encouraging to know is that chaos has been essentially contained in the founding of the world and that disorder can be overcome and forced to yield to rational purposes, although never without effort. Soul was the mistress of this original process, and it is through the mediation of the soul that good purposes must now be accomplished.

The *Laws* are admittedly the work of Plato's old age and are usually agreed to have only minimum systematic significance for the general structure of his ethical thought. On the whole, they are commentaries on specific problems, with revisions

415

recommended for certain political groups. However, the famous tenth book contains his reasons for a belief in the existence of a God, and this is the section of the *Laws* most nearly like his earlier writing and most often referred to. The point of immediate interest here is that Plato argues that the world came about by art and design, not by chance. This means that men can count on a world that is at least not alien to purpose and may even offer them some favorable circumstances for the accomplishment of their goals. Soul is the origin of motion and of life and thus has a status in the world second to none. In the *Phaedo* we hear the arguments for the soul's immortality, which would raise it to a still more dignified status in the world, deserving appropriate care and treatment. Even more important for knowledge, and consequently for ethics, is the fact that the soul is essentially immaterial and thus able to serve as an intermediary, enough like the sense world to guide the body and enough like the world of forms to be able to come to know them.

This dual nature of the soul, we learn in the *Symposium,* is what gives rise to the human phenomenon of love. If there were no plane of existence higher than his own, man would not be troubled with desire; if he were not enough like the higher level to be able to know it and to share in it, man would remain below in untroubled ignorance. As it is, love indicates man's desire for something above him which he does not have; love indicates both partial possession and in-

completeness. The presence of love defines man's place in the hierarchy of the world, since he is enough like the divine life to know and want it, and enough lower by nature to be cut off from such fulfillment. Thus love continues as a permanent indication both of man's lack and of his knowledge of a better life. Love points out the fact that "there is something halfway between skill and ignorance," (*Symposium*, 202A) and this is where man is to be found. He wants eternal possession of the good, but his nature only allows it to be momentary and passing, always in need of being regained. "The mortal nature ever seeks, as best it can, to be immortal." (*Symposium*, 207D)

Love does more, however, than just show man his intermediate status, for love reveals to the soul the presence of beauty. Following the guidance of love, passing from view to view of beautiful things, one comes at last "to that particular study which is concerned with the beautiful itself and that alone; so that in the end he comes to know the very essence of beauty." (*Symposium*, 211D) By such procedure man is almost able to lay hold of the final secret. How love reveals beauty and beauty in turn yields such knowledge, this is the job of the *Phaedrus* to try to describe to us.

"Most people are ignorant of the fact that they do not know the nature of things," (*Phaedrus*, 237C) and so we cannot take it for granted that everyone knows the nature of love and its power. When beauty is seen on earth the soul remembers the vision of true beauty which it has as its birthright. Wisdom is never grasped directly by man. Beauty alone has this privilege, that it brings us as close to wisdom as we are able to come. Love is aroused by beauty, which reveals to us an object of knowledge that we might not otherwise have recognized. Our soul, however, is a divided thing, and the lower half of it is constantly threatening to rebel, so that we are never sure of being able to follow what we see to be desirable even when we have found it. Man's ethical problem is to keep his soul in balance and unison, so that it will not be thrown off its course by impulsive and blind action. "If now the better elements of the mind, which lead to a well ordered life and to philosophy, prevail, they live a life of happiness and harmony here on earth, self-controlled and orderly, holding in subjection that which causes evil in the soul and giving freedom to that which makes for virtue." (*Phaedrus,* 256B)

As far as the essential part of Plato's ethical theory is concerned, much too much has been made of the early sections of the *Republic.* Certain forms of political organization are set up by Plato here—as he states quite explicitly —solely as an enlarged framework within which he may describe justice clearly. Certainly Plato might wish to have some features of this organization preserved, but the *Republic* was never intended as a blueprint for an actual state. The *Laws* represent Plato's only attempt to be specific about suggestions for political organization, so that to treat the *Republic* in the same light is to misunderstand Plato's conception of the function of philosophy. Philosophy does not dictate specific plans as an exact guide for present action. Instead, it tries to discover ideal norms which, although they cannot by nature ever be fully realized, may still serve as norms to guide one as he mixes actions in a concrete world. The *Republic,* then, should be approached as a purely hypothetical state unable to be fully real, established as a device to set forth certain ideal objectives, which an actual state may try to embody through whatever organizational means seem appropriate.

Although the *Republic* describes a social organization, justice for Plato, interestingly enough, is essentially a private matter. Justice may involve exterior ordering as a prerequisite, but the final test of justice is not a public one. The only question to be asked is "What effect it has upon its possessor when it dwells in his soul unseen of gods or men." (*Republic,* 366) We study justice in the state rather than in the individual, since the state is easier to examine due to its size; yet what really interests Plato is essentially the private condition of the soul of the individual. In the heated discussion over whether goods should be owned in common, for instance, this central fact about Plato's primary interest is often forgotten. No political device is ever suggested for its own sake, but rather as an illustration of a desired effect to be produced in some individual. This being the case, Plato should be glad to dispense with any piece of machinery which could be shown to be detrimental to individual

417

well-being. The political arrangements suggested in the *Republic* are for Plato merely an illustrative and nonessential means to the real point of the work: The description of that which will bring an individual into a state of well-being. Organization is necessary to this aim, but illustrative machinery should not be taken as the rigid aim of the theory proposed.

Justice is to be found in the relation of one part to another, either within or between individuals. Education enters the picture at this point, since Plato believes that one will control relations well if he has been trained properly. External controls are ultimately unsatisfactory, and internal control can only be produced by proper attention to training. Here one begins with the body, a seeming paradox for a Platonist, but the body can be trained in rhythm, form and grace as external examples of a quality of mind that cannot be developed as early as the body can. These qualities sink deeply into the character of the person and create a favorable ground for later education, so that "when reason comes, he will greet her as a friend with whom his education has made him long familiar." (*Republic,* 401) A noble and harmonious character created in the early years induces a passion for poetry and music, which will end "where it ought to end, in the love of beauty." (*Republic,* 403)

The definition which Plato gives for justice in civil relations has long been familiar: "In every well ordered community each man has his appointed task which he must perform." (*Repub-lic,* 406) Order is the foundation of justice in a state or in an individual, and from there on the central problem is to discover what task each man is best suited for and the relation of this to other functions within society. Here Plato is less specific than he was concerning the exact form of education, since Plato feels that once education has taken hold and developed reason, men of sound education may be trusted to work out arrangements to everyone's mutual advantage. An educational program which will develop sound and keenly disciplined reason is Plato's real answer to the question of how decisions are to be made. Reasonable men can be left to work out their own arrangements, but the basic problem is to be sure that they reach this required age of reason. "There is no need to dictate to men of good breeding. They will soon find out for themselves what regulations are needed." (*Republic,* 425)

Equally familiar are Plato's three major virtues: Wisdom, courage, and temperance. When all three are present, justice comes into being. Wisdom is the fundamental virtue, since the courageous man must have knowledge enough to know what is rightly to be feared. Temperance means a kind of orderliness, a control of certain pleasures and appetites, and it results in self-mastery, which is a kind of harmony. "Justice admittedly means that a man should possess and concern himself with what properly belongs to him." (*Republic,* 433) A man is just, in the same way that a state is just, and the three parts of his soul which must be brought into harmony are the rational, the appetitive, and the spirited. Justice in the individual is the health of the soul.

Now the aim of the crucial years of early education was said to be the training of reason to the full use of its powers, with wisdom emerging as the fundamental virtue in both state and individual. Plato has been using a blank check in the first half of the *Republic*, and this is his use of 'knowledge' without any real definition of its meaning. To back up solidly his claim for the importance of knowledge in all of these processes, Plato now turns to as complete an exposition of his theory of knowledge as he ever gives us. At first this may seem incongruous, if the aim of the *Republic* is to define justice, but at every point the outline of education and the definition of justice turned out to be dependent upon knowledge. To the extent, then, that Plato can now gain agreement about the nature of knowledge, he will tend to get agreement about its central role in the production of justice.

Plato turns to this task of analyzing knowledge by beginning a discussion of his concept of the 'philosopher-king'. Philosophers are those whose passion it is to see the truth and who are unsatisfied with mere belief. Philosophers, it is true, have often been thought to be ineffectual men, and Plato agrees that this is often the case. His point here is that, however ineffectual he may be, a true philosopher still possesses genuine knowledge, so that the real problem is to unite this rational insight with the forcefulness of a man of great skill in political leadership. Philosophers have the knowledge which the state needs, and there must be no rest until this union of natures is effected. Unless political power and philosophy meet together in one person "there can be no rest from troubles for states, nor yet, as I believe, for all mankind." (*Republic*, 473) It is often thought that Platonists are impractical men, but this unequivocal statement of Plato's should show how firm is his conviction that philosophy is useless until it is wielded by a man of great practical skill, until it becomes a power and a force in the structure of society and in the lives of men. Unfortunately, "this combination will be rare." (*Republic*, 502)

The search for a definition of knowledge is the search for a measure, and, since "what is imperfect can never serve as a measure," (*Republic*, 503) the sense world must be transcended and the Good attained. "The highest object of knowledge is the essential nature of the Good, from which everything that is good and right derives its values for us." (*Republic*, 504) Thus we return to the description of the Good with which the *Philebus* ended. In the search for the knowledge to understand the structure of being, we are taken beyond being, since "Goodness is not the same thing as being, but even beyond being, surpassing it in dignity and power." (*Republic*, 508) We cross the divided line which separates the sensible from the intelligible world, and then we transcend that too.

However, Plato's famous parable of the cave is crucial here. According to this story, after the vision of the Good is obtained, those who have acquired this knowledge are not allowed to stay at the height. 'Dialectic' for Plato is a two-way process; it leads men to see the intelligible world, but it also forces them back down to the world of men and of concrete objects to apply with skill the knowledge gained. It is true that Plato felt that to acquire knowledge is good in itself, but he did not condone its selfish use. No soul would be improved, no social order established, unless the difficult job of applying the knowledge gained is forced upon those who love wisdom. If the Good is to be found through knowledge, it is necessary to turn away from the ordinary activities of men, and "without having had a vision of this Form no one can act with wisdom either in his own life or in matters of state." (*Republic,* 517)

Yet this necessity of turning away from the concrete world is done only for the sake of future action—improved and more skillful action in the affairs of men. Some men, of course, will spend more of their time in abstract endeavor, while others will spend more of their energy in practical affairs. The health of the society depends upon maintaining an overall balance of the practical and the theoretical, and no man ought to be completely unfamiliar with either phase. The Good serves as the goal of pure knowledge but also as the guide and end to human betterment. You cannot overlook either phase of this constant cycle—either the intellectual abstraction from the world or the returning

application to it. Those who have been detached for a period will seem ineffectual for a time after their return to practical affairs, but in the long run their purer intellectual discipline will make them superior in effectiveness. Dialectic is "the same thing as the ability to see the connexion of things," (*Republic,* 537) so that training in an abstract dialectical process—if it really grasps the structure of things—will enable one to discern connexions which the layman will overlook.

Perhaps the most neglected section of the *Republic* is the concluding portion which describes the degeneration of the ideal state, and without this part neither the ideal state nor Plato's ethical theory can be understood adequately. Plato is too often pictured as the pure idealist who did not understand the facts of real existence or the impossibility of his own goals. First of all it is important to understand that he was under no illusion about his ideal state or individual ever becoming a reality. To fail to recognize this is to misunderstand Platonism, since the Platonist's basic premise is that the ideal can never in the nature of the case be realized in this world. Thought can discern these ideals and use them as a guide, but "is it not in the nature of things that action should come less close to truth than thought?" (*Republic,* 473) Plato did not set out to show that his ideals could be achieved in fact, and this is made even more clear in the account of the decay of the ideal state.

For Plato every actual state and

real man is a union of some of the ideal structures described in the first part of the *Republic* combined with certain portions of the forces which tend to corrode and destroy. Thus, in the *Republic* what we are presented with are the chemical elements in their pure state, the unbroken picture of the ideal together with a list of the destructive forces. Now, with these components clearly distinguished, we may proceed to analyze any given state or individual and discern within it the good structures and the destructive elements in their individual union and proportion. Being thus able to distinguish we will know what we might profitably cut out and what ought to be saved. The surgeon needs to be able to recognize the malignancy as well as healthy tissue in his operation upon the patient who combines both, but in his study he first learns each as a pure element, although they never in fact exist this distinctly.

"All that comes into being must decay," (*Republic,* 546) and one of the primary factors in degeneration is the man "dominated by motives of ambition." (*Republic,* 545) Plato's early educational scheme was designed to try to bring the individual to a point of reason, able to consider the factors of a situation with some rational detachment, but the ambitious man will not be able so to contain himself. No matter how careful we are, some such people will appear, "since some day the moment will slip by and they will beget children out of due season." (*Republic,* 546) By education we can hope to lessen their number, but we can never rid ourselves of ambition or of ambitious men, and once civil strife is born it has a tendency to increase itself.

Unfortunately, degenerate as well as reasonable men can control power, and once a man dominated by passion gains control, he is afraid to let strong and reasonable men into positions of authority. Thus, the reasonable forces which could best control passion are made impotent and not allowed to do what they could. Reason, which could operate to better human well being, is forced into subjection and is "now confined to calculating how money may breed more money." (*Republic,* 553) Only order could cure such a situation, but once passions have broken loose and control the man, "his life is subject to no order or restraint." (*Republic,* 561) He will resist any attempt at regulation as interference with freedom, although some control of these forces is exactly what must be achieved if justice is to be restored. A man in such a condition fights any attempt to remove the factors which feed his desires, and this is "the exact opposite of medical procedure, which removes the worst elements in the bodily condition and leaves the best." (*Republic,* 568) Any corruptive force has a tendency to carry itself to completion, and this produces the opposite of the philosopher-king, the tyrant, the man who has "a master passion enthroned in absolute dominion over every part of the soul." (*Republic,* 510)

Thus, Plato has given us a complete description of all of the elements which a man seeking the good life needs to know. The virtues have been described and brought together under the concept of justice. The parts of the soul have been analyzed and the phenomenon of love used to reveal the intermediate status of man. Most important of all, however, is the classification of the types of pleasure in their relation to a knowledge of the structure of the world. When taken together, this is the key to successful blending of pleasures under the guidance of reason for the production of the well mixed life. Finally, we have been given the picture of the destructive forces which operate upon men and within societies, so we can now separate the good from the degenerate elements as they appear in the particular mixture of any person or state. With the knowledge of the Good as the guiding—although always actually unattainable—norm, we can work to remove the harmful elements and can strengthen the forces which tend to produce harmony and balance. We have the advantage of knowing that it is at least possible for reason to neutralize the destructive forces and to achieve the mixture of pleasure and knowledge that characterizes well-being. Unfortunately, since any state of well-being achieved in time is necessarily subject to decay, this is a balance which must be reestablished with the arrival of each new day.

Bibliography

J. Burnet, *Platonism* (Berkeley, 1928).
F. M. Cornford, *The Republic of Plato* (London, 1945).
R. Demos, *The Philosophy of Plato* (New York, 1939).
R. Hackforth, *Plato's Examination of Pleasure* (Cambridge, 1945).
R. C. Lodge, *Plato's Theory of Ethics* (London, 1928).
R. L. Nettleship, *Lectures on the Republic of Plato* (New York, 1901).
C. Ritter, *The Essence of Plato's Philosophy* (New York, 1933).
P. Shorey, *The Unity of Plato's Thought* (Chicago, 1904).
——, *What Plato Said* (Chicago, 1933).
A. E. Taylor, *Plato: The Man and His Works* (London, 1948).
J. Wild, *Plato's Theory of Man* (Cambridge, 1948).

Frederick Sontag
Pomona College

Plato: *see* Aristotle; Cudworth, Ralph; Freud, Sigmund; Goethe, Johann Wolfgang von; Hegel, G. W. F.; Kant, I.; Major Ethical Viewpoints; Meta-ethics and Normative Ethics; Minor Socratics; Price, Richard; Prichard, H. A.; Puritan Morals; Schopenhauer, Arthur; Socrates; Sophists, the; Soviet Morality, Current; Spinoza; Stoics, the.

Platonism: *see* Augustine and Morals; Cudworth, Ralph; Moral Philosophy in America; More, Henry.

play: *see* Puritan Morals.

pleasantness: *see* Schlick, Moritz.

pleasing: *see* Ross, Sir (William) David.

pleasure: *see* Aquinas, Thomas, Moral Views of; Aristotle; Ayer, Alfred J.; Balguy, John; Broad, C. D.; Butler, Joseph; China, Moral Philosophies of; Cumberland, Richard; Freud,

Sigmund; Green, T. H.; happiness; hedonism; Hindu Ethics; Hobbes Thomas; Hutcheson, Francis; Jewish Ethics and Its Civilization; Major Ethical Viewpoints; Minor Socratics; More, Henry; Plato; Puritan Morals; Ross, Sir (William) David; Scheler, Max; Schlick, Moritz; Sidgwick, Henry; Sophists, the; Spinoza; Stoics, the; Utilitarianism; Wollaston, William.

pleasure principle: *see* Freud, Sigmund.

pledges: *see* Muslim Morals.

Plekhanov, G. V.: *see* Soviet Morality, Current.

Plotinus: *see* Schopenhauer, Arthur.

pluralism: *see* Ross, Sir (William) David.

polemics: *see* Jewish Ethics and Its Civilization; Soviet Morality, Current.

politeness: *see* Muslim Morals; Tapirapé Morals, Some Aspects of.

political authority: *see* Aquinas, Thomas, Moral Views of.

political philosophy: *see* Green, T. H.; Marxist Theory of Morals; Soviet Morality, Current.

political theory: *see* Machiavelli, Niccolo.

politicalization: *see* Soviet Morality, Current.

politics: *see* Marxist Theory of Morals; Sophists, the.

polygamy: *see* Major Ethical Viewpoints; Morals and Religion; Muslim Morals.

Polynesia: *see* Primitive Morals.

polytheism: *see* Aztec Morals; Goethe, Johann Wolfgang von; Zuni Indians, Morals of.

poor, the: *see* Augustine and Morals; poverty.

Pope: *see* Clarke, Samuel.

population, control of: *see* Soviet Morality, Current.

Posidonius: *see* Stoics, the.

positivism: *see* logical positivism; Major Ethical Viewpoints.

positivistic ethics: *see* Soviet Morality, Current.

possessions: *see* Hindu Ethics; Navaho Morals.

possessions, desire for: *see* Quakerism, Classical, The Morality of.

potencies: *see* Aquinas, Thomas, Moral Views of.

potentialities: *see* Hindu Ethics; Major Ethical Viewpoints.

poverty: *see* Hindu Ethics; Minor Socratics; Navaho Morals; Quakerism, Classical, The Morality of; Stoics, the.

power: *see* Butler, Joseph; Hindu Ethics; Hobbes, Thomas; Machiavelli, Niccolo; Marxist Theory of Morals; Nietzsche, Friedrich; Soviet Morality, Current; Spinoza.

practical certitude: *see* Liguori, St. Alphonsus and Catholic Moral Philosophy.

practical reason: *see* Clarke, Samuel; Kant, I.; Reid, Thomas.

pragmatism: *see* Dewey, John; Kant, I.; Major Ethical Viewpoints; Moral Philosophy in America; Navaho Morals; Quakerism, Classical, The Morality of; Russell, Bertrand; Soviet Morality, Current.

praise: *see* Cudworth, Ralph; Moore, George Edward; More, Henry; Price, Richard; Reid, Thomas.

precepts: *see* Hindu Ethics; More, Henry; Spinoza.

precepts, Chinese: *see* China, Moral Philosophies of.

predestination: *see* Puritan Morals.

predeterminism: *see* Aztec Morals.

pre-existence: *see* Hindu Ethics.

preference: *see* Major Ethical Viewpoints; Stoics, the.

prejudice: *see* Augustine and Morals; Puritan Morals.

preliterate society: *see* Zuni Indians, Morals of.

Preobrazhenski: *see* Soviet Morality, Current.

Presbyterianism: *see* Puritan Morals.

prescription: *see* Major Ethical Viewpoints.

prescriptive ethics: *see* Meta-ethics and Normative Ethics; Schopenhauer, Arthur.

prestige: *see* Aztec Morals; Mundurucú Indians, A Dual System of Ethics; Pakot, the Moral System of.

Preston, John: *see* Puritan Morals.

Price, Richard

Richard Price was born in 1723 at Tynton, Glamorganshire, and died in 1791 at Hackney, Middlesex. His life was devoted mainly to preaching; a practice which, as a Unitarian minister, he carried on in London, Stoke-Newington and Hackney for almost fifty years. His accomplishments in other fields, however, were not inconsiderable.

He is regarded as the founder of modern life insurance. His *Observations on Reversionary Payments* is a classic in the field. His tables of mortality based on Northampton registers were for a century the most important basis of calculation by sound companies in Great Britain and were adopted by the courts as a part of common law. His accomplishments in the field of finance led the younger Pitt to appeal to him for a program to meet the public debt. The French government in 1776 adopted many of his financial proposals. In 1762 the demands of preaching made it impossible for him to accept the editorship of the works of Sir Isaac Newton. He was an accomplished mathematician and in 1763 contributed to the Royal Society an important solution to a problem in the doctrine of chances which had been unsolved by his friend Thomas Bayes. He was a friend of Hume and admitted a philosophical debt to him much in the manner of Reid and Kant. Hume, in turn, valued Price's friendship and criticism highly. He admitted that Price convinced him that his arguments on a particular point were inconclusive. There is no record of what the point was, but it seems likely, from the evidence available in letters, and from Price's application of his principles of probability to the question of miracles, that it was Hume's argument for a "complete impossibility of miracles."

Price championed the cause of American colonial independence and his support of the French Revolution earned him the title in that country of "Apostle of Liberty." Price's writings, along with those of Thomas Paine, were influential in the decision of the colonists to declare independence. His support continued throughout the Revolution and in 1781 he and George

Washington were awarded honorary degrees by Yale University. At the same time he was invited to become a citizen of the United States of America and to aid in establishing its financial foundations. Although already failing in stength at the outbreak of the French Revolution he delivered two sermons supporting its principles. Burke's *Reflections on the French Revolution* appeared in direct response. When Price died in 1791, before the excesses of the revolution had developed, the National Assembly went into mourning for six days.

Price's moral philosophy is contained almost entirely in one smallish book entitled *A Review of the Principal Questions in Morals,* first published in 1758 when he was thirty-five. It reached a third edition in 1787, undergoing only relatively minor changes.

Price approaches moral philosophy from the standpoint of epistemology because he considers the fundamental question of morals to be an epistemological question. There are three possible meanings of the question 'What is the foundation of virtue?': 1) What is the true account or reason that such and such actions are right? 2) What are the primary "heads of virtue" or the general principles that render particular actions right? 3) What are the motives to virtuous conduct? Though important, and discussed in detail by Price, the second and third questions are about the subject-matter of morality, not its foundations. The first question is the one strictly about foundations and is the question of the epistemology of morals. The alternative answers that Price considers are a) that right is a species of sensation, not a real quality of actions, to be known by sense; or b) that right is a real character of actions, something true of actions, to be known by the understanding. Price's account of morality is an attempt to establish the second alternative and he therefore opposes the empiricism of Locke, Hutcheson and Hume with a theory of rationalistic intuitionism. He finds that sense and understanding are very different: the former is aware only of particulars, the latter of universals; sense "suffers" and is passive, understanding discerns and judges, and is "active." The two functions of the understanding are intuition and deduction. There are, consequently, he claims, many simple ideas ("original and uncompounded perceptions of the mind") that cannot be accounted for as derived from sense observation, e.g., impenetrability, inertia, substance, duration, space, necessity, infinity, contingency, possibility, impossibility and causation. The source of these ideas of science and epistemology, therefore, must be the understanding itself. In the area of morals there are also simple ideas, viz., right and wrong. That the idea of right is a simple idea is shown by the indefinability of 'right:'

Right and wrong when applied to actions which are commanded or forbidden by the will of God, or that produce good or harm, do not signify merely that such actions are commanded or forbidden or that they are useful or harmful, but a *sentiment* [opinion] concerning them and our consequent approbation or disapprobation of the performance of them. Were not this true, it would be palpably absurd in any case to ask, whether it is *right* to obey a command, or *wrong* to disobey it; and the propositions, *obeying a command is right,* or *producing happiness is right,* would be most trifling, as expressing no more than that obeying a command is obeying a command or producing happiness is producing happiness. (Chapter 1, Section 1).

Indefinability is shown by that fact that it is always possible to ask of any definiens of 'right' "But is that right?" without asking a tautologous question or changing the subject. Indefinability indicates simplicity and simplicity indicates that rightness must be the object of an immediate perception. Against Hutcheson, who asserted in his early writings that this immediate perception is by sense, Price claims it is by understanding. Among his arguments are the following: 1) There are many ideas derived from the intuition of truth. It is therefore possible that the ideas of right and wrong are among them. 2) Introspection and common opinion maintain that we express necessary truth when we say of some acts that they are right and of others that they are wrong. 3) If Rightness and wrongness were only ideas of sense it would be "the greatest absurdity" to attribute them to actions. Yet they are attributed to actions without absurdity. 4) Actions must be either right, wrong, or indifferent. On Hutcheson's and similar theories they cannot be either right or wrong. Therefore they must be indifferent, but they are not. Therefore, Hutcheson's

theory, and "sentimental" theories generally, must be false.

Price concludes that rightness and wrongness are real properties of action known by rational intuition. He derives as a "strict corollary" that morality is eternal and immutable. Right and wrong denote what actions are by nature and necessity. Moral judgments therefore are *a priori,* and also synthetic.

The judgment that an act is right is for Price, then, an ultimate judgment in at least two senses. If true, the judgment is the intuitive discernment of *the* basic moral property and therefore the ultimate moral justification for any act in which it is discerned. The discernment of rightness is ultimate cognitively and theoretically. It is also, however, and consequently, ultimate practically. Price maintains that there is a necessary connection between the discerning of rightness and obligation. This is indicated cognitively by the equivalence of the two ideas. It is indicated practically by the impossibility of discerning the rightness of an act without being subject to the appropriate obligation. There is also a necessary connection between rightness and "good desert." Cognitively this is indicated by the fact that good desert (merit) can be analyzed in terms of right. To say of a person that he is meritorious is the same as to say that it is morally right that his actions be rewarded by happiness. This necessary connection calls for a distinction between "abstract or absolute virtue" and "practical or relative virtue:"

426

ABSTRACT virtue is, most properly, a quality of the external action or event. It denotes what an action is, considered independently of the *sense* of the agent; or what, *in itself* and *absolutely*, it is right *such* an agent, in *such* circumstances should do; and what, if he judged truly, he would judge he ought to do.—PRACTICAL *virtue*, on the contrary, has a necessary relation to, and dependence upon, the opinion of the agent concerning his actions. It signifies what he ought to do, *upon supposition* of his having such and such sentiments. (Chapter 7).

While there is no necessary connection between abstract virtue and happiness there is further necessary connection between practical virtue and happiness. When an agent does what he believes he ought to do he necessarily deserves happiness. As Price puts it, "It is right that he be happy." (Chapter 7).

Practical virtue in turn requires that the agent be free. This means, for Price that the agent must have the ability "to act and determine" and that he must have a motive which is the occasion (though not the efficient cause) of his action. Practical virtue also requires the ability to judge that actions are right or wrong, such a judgment providing the motive to the practically virtuous act. Although in such a doctrine Price is subscribing to the view that reason can be practical he also maintains that there are certain "rational desires" (which he calls, after Butler, "affections") that necessarily accompany judgments of rightness although they are distinguishable from them. Price consequently claims that motivation due to the discernment of rightness is the "only spring of action in a reasonable being, as far as he can be deemed morally good and worthy." (Chapter 8) Degree of virtue is therefore determined by degree of regard for what is right. And although degree of virtue in a particular act varies directly with the strength of any obstacle that may stand in the way of its performance such obstacles are not necessary for the practice of virtue and their existence may in fact indicate previous lack of virtue. The highly virtuous man is therefore likely to be one who has fewer obstacles to overcome than the less virtuous; and, extrapolating the series, God is of course perfectly virtuous without having any obstacles to His virtue.

Conflicts do not, however, take place merely between motives to virtue and motives to vice. Conflicts may occur within the realm of virtue itself between the various "heads of virtue" of which Price gives a partial list. We have at least the following duties: 1) Reverence for God, 2) Prudence, 3) Benevolence, 4) Gratitude, 5) Honesty and 6) Justice. The general principles that would be formulated 'We have duties to God, to ourselves, to contribute to the welfare of others, to benefactors, to tell the truth and keep promises, and to be just' are all self-evident and necessarily true. But the general duty to tell the truth may conflict with the general duty to contribute to the welfare of others, for example, in a particular case, such as that of a doctor who has discovered that a patient has an incurable disease. In such conflicts, which arise in many cases when we must apply the general principles to particular cases, a greater degree of duty "cancels" a lesser degree. He admits that this is an extremely complicated and difficult matter, in which only a mind capable of universal and unerring knowledge can reach certainty.

The independence, immutability and eternity of morality raise a theological problem, since this seems to limit God's power. Price meets the problem by maintaining that morality is a "branch of necessary truth." Although necessary truth is independent of God's will it is not independent of His understanding. In fact it just *is* His understanding. Arguments supporting these views are part of Price's program of "tracing the obligations of virtue up to the truth and nature of things, and thus to Deity."

In evaluating Price it is advisable to distinguish three parts of his moral philosophy: The first is directly polemical of Locke, Hutcheson and Hume, the empirical theory of knowledge and the "sentimental" account of morality. Price's criticisms are important in bringing out the inadequacies of this kind of account although he falls short of refuting such an account. His own positive attempt to provide an account of morality that is not subject to as many, or the same kinds of, inadequacies has a more extreme part and a more moderate part. Certain extreme doctrines in his constructive theory are open to serious objection; for example, his extreme rationalism in which he sometimes suggests that

the understanding is the *sole* faculty involved in moral knowledge, the claim to absolute and necessary factual connections between knowledge and conduct, the eternity and immutability of morality in a metaphysical sense and his consequent suggestions of the independence of morality from human nature. The more moderate part of his constructive theory arises from his concern to establish the adequacy of his account of morality by making it "conform to the facts" or by showing that it does conform to the facts, including the facts of common opinion and to human nature as it is available to natural observation: Here he takes account of the role of the affections in motivation and recognizes the need to justify our rational faculties. In the latter process he attributes functions of motivation and "active powers" generally, to the understanding that would not be attributed to it in an account of morality that did not attempt to argue for the sufficiency of the understanding both for the recognition of moral distinctions and the performance of virtuous actions. He also recognizes that the processes involved in moral knowing are more complex than can be included under the rubric of "intuition and deduction." He implicitly admits a place for sensing and inducing, and recognizes that intuiting is not a simple act in the sense of being obvious or easy or isolated; but that it usually culminates a series of more pedestrian processes of observation and reasoning which are necessary for its occurence. This is particularly apparent in his recognition of the possible conflicts between the various "heads of duty" and the extreme difficulty of knowing which among the duties enjoined by these general principles is the real duty that properly cancels opposing duties. In his recognition of the distinction between abstract and practical virtue he emphasizes the need to be wary of oversimplification in problems of applying general moral principles to particular cases, a wariness that leads him to admit that the relation between knowledge and conduct in many cases of practical virtue must remain a matter of "practical certainty" rather than absolute certainty.

Price is often classed with the "Intellectualistic" school of moralists and his theory does incorporate epistemological elements from Plato and Descartes and the preceding British moralists Cudworth, Clarke, Wollaston and Balguy. Rationalism is to be found in them all and intuitionism in most of them, although Price was the first to use the term 'intuition' in the moral realm with the sense it carries in the twentieth century. But he rejected the intellectualism of his British rationalistic predecessors in two ways: He criticized them for attempting to define 'right' and he made a more definite and systematic place for emotion within his system than Wollaston, Clarke or Balguy. (Cudworth's overall position was not so intellectualistic as appears from *The Treatise on Eternal and Immutable Morality* but the manuscripts in which this philosophy is presented have never been published.) Thus although he rejected the sentimentalist school, he saw that an adequate moral philosophy must include a place for the "relish" of morally right conduct as well as for its stability and impersonal imperativeness. He is therefore a more moderate rationalist than many of his predecessors in the intellectualistic tradition.

He also laid down lines that were influential in the development of the Scottish school of Common Sense. Thomas Reid acknowledged an indebtedness to Price's writings, though he went far beyond Price in his appeal to Common Sense. There is no evidence, however, that Kant, whose ethical system so strongly resembles Price's on many points, knew of his writings at all. For other explicit acknowledgements of indebtedness to Price we must turn to the twentieth century. G. E. Moore, who used virtually the same argument for the indefinability of 'good' as Price used for 'right' did not derive his doctrine from Price; but W. D. Ross and E. F. Carritt both acknowledge a debt to Price. And Hastings Rashdall regarded Price's *Review* "as the best work published on Ethics till quite recent times. It contains the gist of the Kantian doctrine without Kant's confusions." (*Theory of Good and Evil,* Vol. I, p. 81). F. C. Sharp also regards Price's theory as clearer and more cogent than Kant's, in addition to being the clearest expression of rationalism in the eighteenth century. C. D. Broad considers W. D. Ross's *The Right and the Good* the first book since the *Review* comparable in merit to it as a statement and defence of a rationalistic type of ethics. Certainly Ross, Prichard, Carritt, Moore and Ewing have been concerned with problems very similar to those with which Price was concerned, particularly questions of definability, *prima facie* duties and real duties and the conflict of duties, complications arising from the distinction between abstract and practical virtue, problems of praise and blame, merit and responsibility, and the foundations of ethics.

Aside from the influences and opinions, it is instructive to read Price's *Review* because it not only indicates the inadequacies of empiricism and sentiment as the foundations of moral philosophy, but also indicates the inadequacies of rationalism and abstract truth to serve this purpose. Neither theory in any crude or extreme way is going to provide a satisfactory basis for moral philosophy. And writers in both cases, Price as well as Hutcheson and Hume (particularly Hutcheson in his later writings), move from an extreme rationalism on the one hand or an extreme empiricism on the other, toward positions within which both have a legitimate and, in fact, a necessary place.

Bibliography

Richard Price, *Four Dissertations* (London, Jones and Eaton, 1811).
——, *Observations on Reversionary Payments* (London, T. Cadell, 1783).
——, *A Review of the Principal Questions in Morals* (Oxford, Clarendon Press, 1948).
——, *Two Tracts on Civil Liberty: The War with America and The Debts and Finances of the Kingdom* (London, T. Cadell, 1778).
T. S. Jouffroy, *Introduction to Ethics,* translated by C. W. Channing (Boston, Hilliard, 1841), Lectures 21, 22, 23.
William Whewell, *Lectures on the History of Moral Philosophy in England* (London, J. W. Parker and Son, 1852).
James Martineau, *Types of Ethical Theory* (New York, Macmillan, 1886), vol. II.
W. H. F. Barnes, "Richard Price—A Neglected 18th Century Moralist," *Philosophy,* vol. 17 (1942), pp. 159–173.
C. D. Broad, "Some Reflections on Moral Sense Theories in Ethics," *Proceedings of the Aristotelian Society,* N.S., vol. 45, (1944–45).
D. Daiches Raphael, *The Moral Sense* (Oxford, The Clarendon Press, 1947).
C. B. Cone, *Torchbearer of Freedom, The Influence of Richard Price on 18th Century Thought* (Lexington, Ky., University of Kentucky Press, 1952).
Bernard Peach, "The Indefinability and Simplicity of Rightness in Richard Price's *Review of Morals,*" *Philosophy and Phenomenological Research,* vol. 14 (1954), pp. 370–385.
Henry Aiken, "Ultimacy of Rightness in Richard Price's Ethics," *Ibid,* pp. 386–392.

Bernard Peach
Duke University

Price, Richard: *see* Clarke, Samuel; Cooper, Anthony Ashley; Cudworth, Ralph; Moral Philosophy in America.

price system, one: *see* Quakerism, Classical, The Morality of.

Prichard, Harold Arthur

Born October 30, 1871, H. A. Prichard was educated at Clifton and New College, Oxford where he became a disciple of Cook Wilson. In 1898 he was elected to a fellowship at Trinity and after a quiet residency he retired for a brief period in 1924 because of ill health. In 1928 he was elected White's Professor of Moral Philosophy and held this chair until 1937. Prichard died after a short illness in 1947 at the age of seventy-six. Before death he was at work on what promised to be a fully sustained work in moral philosophy later entitled *Moral Obligation* which appears in an unfinished state in his collected writings on moral philosophy under the same title and published in 1949.

The central thesis of Prichard's moral philosophy is the belief that obligations are unique and indefinable and are accordingly apprehended directly by reflection in certain circumstances. It is a mistake in principle and in fact to try to convince another individual that he has an obligation, for there are no proofs relevant to notions which are immediate and irreducible. The only legitimate use that may be made of argument in matters of moral obligation is to direct attention to what circumstances prevail or to inquire whether the facts of the case are as we first perceived them. In an early paper "Does Moral Philosophy Rest on a Mistake?" (1912), Prichard maintains that justification of an obligation has a correlate in epistemology when according to which the theory of knowledge is understood to be the attempt to find a proof or criterion by which an individual may assure himself of the fact that he really knows what he knows, e.g., whether he really knows that $7 \times 4 = 28$. According to Prichard's strict sense of the term "knowledge," such mathematical truths are grasped immediately (as are obligations) and doubts about such experiences can never be laid to rest; there is no way to justify them other than doing the mathematical sum again. Such questions as "Why ought I to perform this moral act?", if it is interpreted to mean that the agent in question demands a proof or reason for feeling obliged, can never finally be answered by showing that it is to the agent's advantage to perform such acts. The question actually demands a proof of what in fact is already believed without proof; namely, that the agent *has* an obligation. The fatal mistake of much work that may be described as moral philosophy was to offer reasons for that for which no reasons were relevant. Prichard finds that the peculiar barrenness of recent and traditional moral philosophizing is due to this alleged mistake in principle and is the reason why the pursuit of moral philosophy has been so disappointing.

In working out his moral philosophy he was concerned to do two things. First, he strengthened his fundamental notion that moral obligation is not reducible to anything other than itself, and to this end he answered possible objections to the notion. Secondly, he set about to rid moral philosophy of the alleged mistake in principle. He examines the moral thought of Plato, Aristotle, Butler, T. H. Green, Sidgwick, and Mill with the view of ridding moral philosophy of confusion. We shall consider the latter task first.

History of moral philosophy reveals the fact that answers to the question as to why an individual ought to perform his duty have taken two general forms: one attempts to show that an individual ought to act because it is to his advantage in the long run, and the other states that an individual ought to act because it can be shown that some good will be realized in or by his action.

A theory which makes the agent's own interest the sole ground of obligation can be disposed of easily. To show that obligation to act is that which conduces to the agent's happiness does not prove that the agent is thereby obligated. Accordingly, Prichard shows that Plato, Butler, Hutcheson, Paley, and Mill each in his own way assumed that the individual ought to act in ways considered moral because it is to his advantage. His penetrating analysis of Plato's argument concerning justice in the *Republic* may stand in its own right as a critique of Plato's moralizing. But his analysis is intended to show that (providing we assume "justice" carries the connotation of obligation) regardless of Plato's deepened sense of profit and the conclusion that it is absurd even to ask whether the just man gains by just action, Plato makes a mistake which we least suspect him of making. If we suppose that Plato's argument is completely successful, i.e., the just man in doing his duty is happy, then Plato has only made us want to do our duty but has failed to convince us that we ought to.

The other alternative is the view which bases obligation to act on some good to which the action will lead or on the intrinsic goodness of the action itself. An example of the former is a generic utilitarianism according to which if an action leads to some good such as happiness then it ought to be done. But this involves the assumption that what is good ought to be. Yet it is clear that a premise which asserts that an action will lead to some good cannot support a conclusion which asserts that the action therefore ought to be done.

If it is maintained that the intrinsic goodness of an action itself is the reason it ought to be done, then this view leads on the only two interpretations possible to an unacceptable dilemma. If the intrinsic goodness of an act means that the action was done from a sense of duty, then this interpretation at the very outset makes goodness dependent on a prior obligation. If, according to the other interpretation, the intrinsic goodness of an action means that the action was done from an intrinsically good desire, then it is sufficient to point out that obligation has nothing to do with motives. It may well be the case that an individual knows his motives and that further he knows them to be good, but this is no guarantee that he shall thereby know his obligation. Thus goodness in no sense is a source of obligation. Nor do these considerations necessitate the view, attributed to Kant, that an act is morally good because it is done from a sense of obligation. Prichard assumes categorically that goodness and obligation are distinct and irreducible. Obligation has solely to do with the potential action of an agent, while goodness has solely to do with motives. Present motives, virtuous or conscientious, are always dependent on certain mental states which are not within the agent's control. The necessary condition for there to be an obligation is that its fulfillment be in fact within the agent's power. With this in mind, Prichard further qualifies the relation between obligation and action, holding that, in the interest of accuracy, it is necessary to say that an individual does not so much have an obligation to act as he has an obligation to set himself to act. To do an action is to change an existing state of affairs in the physical world and this is not always in the agent's power. Thus it is his obligation to set himself to act, but not necessarily to effect an actual change. Accordingly the agent may fulfill an obligation even though it coincides with having a bad motive, e.g., repaying a debt to some agent whose power we fear; he fulfills his obligation if he sets himself to pay the debt but is in fact prevented by circumstances from doing so. Thus Prichard refuses to leave open any possibility that obligation be reducible to good, or any other predicate.

By way of defending his intuitionist position, Prichard entertained and answered three important objections. The first objection is one which holds that if we accept his strict theory of knowledge it seems to follow that we can never know what the circumstances are and hence can never know our obligation nor whether it is fulfilled. Prichard holds that our belief as to what our obligation is depends on our belief as to what circumstances exist. We may see a man lying beside the road and believe that he has fainted and feel that we ought to help him. Later we may discover that he was asleep or dead, but we have nevertheless realized and fulfilled our obligation, though we may immediately feel a new obligation with a change in our belief. A second objection concerns the situation in which people may agree about their belief as to what circumstances prevail, but may disagree as to their beliefs concerning what ought to be done. To answer this, Prichard assumes that only a fully developed moral being is capable of feeling obligations. Disagreements occur because the moral development in all people is not equal and in some it is rudimentary. It is natural that there are some people who are morally blind, just as it is natural that some do not grasp mathematical truths as quickly as others if at all. The third objection concerns the question as to how we decide between conflicting obligations. Prichard maintains that we may resolve the question by considering which obligation is the most urgent; for he assumes that their urgency is a matter of degree. We then ought to set ourselves to act on the most urgent one even though the decision leaves a feeling of unrelieved tension regarding the other unfulfilled obligation.

The thought of H. A. Prichard has been a strong point in the philosophy of moral intuitionism. His work influenced W. D. Ross and Ross in his *Foundations of Ethics* (1939) tells how he was persuaded to Prichard's view that it is what is intended by an act that makes it right or wrong and accordingly distinguishes intention from motive. Recently Stuart Hampshire in "Fallacies in Moral Philosophy" (*Mind* 1949) sees his own approach as in direct line with the critique of moral philosophy begun by Prichard. With the publication of *Moral Obligation* (1949) some of the most perceptive thought of our century in ethical thinking appears in print for the first time.

Bibliography

H. A. Prichard, "Does Moral Philosophy Rest on a Mistake?", *Mind* (1912).
——, *Duty and Interest* (Oxford, 1928).
——, "Duty and Ignorance of Fact," *Proceedings of the British Academy* (1932).
——, *Moral Obligation*. Essays and Lectures (Oxford, 1949).
——, *Knowledge and Perception* (Oxford 1950).

Frank A. Tillman
The College of Wooster

Prichard, H. A.: *see* Price, Richard; Ross, Sir (William) David.
pride: *see* Aristotle; Augustine and Morals; Dante, Alighieri; Dostoyevsky, Fyodor; Freud, Sigmund; Muslim Morals; Riffian Morals.
Prierias, Sylvester: *see* Jesuits, the, Moral Theology of.

Priestly: *see* Utilitarianism.
priests: *see* Jewish Ethics and Its Civilization; Rio Grande Pueblo Indians; Zuni Indians, Morals of.

Primitive Morals

It is advisable to keep in mind that these two words, separately and in combination, have come to mean many things to many people and that attempts to confine them by definition have more often than not simply added to the number of definitions without substantially adding to the common enlightenment concerning them.

Morals, however, historically speaking, means *mores* (Latin: *mos,* plural mores, and *moralis*—first used in this sense by Cicero, *De Fato* I. 1) and *mores* (first made popular in this country by W. G. Sumner, *Folkways*) bespeak that which is customary, that which is customarily done. All the available evidence discovers that the customary varies not only from one group of human beings to another but also within any given group of human beings whose customs we can observe, directly or indirectly, over a period of time. It has been truly said that custom "is the great guide of human life" (D. Hume, *Inquiry concerning Human Understanding* IV. 30. 30) but it is nonetheless true that custom is in a state of "perpetual flux" (J. G. Frazer, *The Golden Bough* III. vi-vii).

Primitive, largely because of misguided fastidiousness, has lately given rise to endless discussion, much of it quodlibetical to the point where it borders, sometimes, on the silly. Suffice it, that primitive in this article implies that there were earlier ancestor of ours prior to the beginning of civilization slowly revealing itself perhaps 6,000 years ago, and that there were also many other human beings who for myriad reasons—not a few of which may be accidental—did not enter into the orbit of civilization in the several key places where civilization would seem to have started, such as the Nile and the Tigris-Euphrates Valleys, whose descendants survive, in one way or another, into modern times. We know vastly more about these surviving contemporary primitive peoples than we may ever be able to learn directly about their earlier counterparts. We must be expertly circumspect in drawing inferences by comparison, but, by and large, we can agree that "wherever man lived ten or twenty thousand years ago his condition was that of the modern 'savage'" (R. H. Lowies, *Introduction to Cultural Anthropology* 10) and that "features common to recent groups of savages in widely separated parts of the world are likely to reflect broadly those obtaining among the savages of primeval antiquity" (G. Clark, *From Savagery to Civilization* 27). In fact, the differences between us who claim some degree of civilization and the primitive are very slight and there is no evidence to warrant our assuming that they are permanently established. We are, indeed, "only precariously civilized" (W. Lippmann, *The Public Philosophy* 86).

This is not the place to discuss the very earliest forms of mankind (for which, see, for example, E. A. Hooton, *Up from the Ape*). There is, however, no evidence that convincingly does away with the possibility that man is a *special creation,* yet, year by year, the evidence grows that makes his *special creation* increasingly unlikely and makes, also, the hypothesis that he is a *special creation* more and more difficult to defend. All the available evidence discovers that "even the most savage tribes have reached their low level of culture from one still lower" (J. G. Frazer, *Belief in Immortality* I. 88–9). In other words, it would seem that mankind has evolved and, for that matter is still evolving; yet many stages of the how and the where are still unknown. Bear in mind, of course, that evolution, though apparently universal, is not the same thing as progress, which, historically, is rare (cf. J. B. Bury, *The Idea of Progress*).

Suffice it, that by the time man became reasonably fully human, so that we can begin to understand him, he had been on earth many thousands of years—the over all period "may well have occupied more than a million years" (M. C. Burkitt, *The Old Stone Age* 1). Organically, certainly, we were abundantly well endowed (cf. A. S. Romer, *Man and the Vertebrates*). By the time we are fully human beings, even the most primitive human beings, the differences between us and the sub-human primates are so great as to be, still, a stumblingblock (S. Zuckerman, *Social Life of Monkeys and Apes* 315). The significant differential factor was, and is, the brain of man, for "it is in the evolution of his brain that we find the most telling clues to his emergence from the

435

brutes" (G. Clark, op. cit. 2). It is what primitive man with his brain has done with his incomparably older biology that marks the history of man as human being—*homo sapiens*—on earth. What he did formerly unconsciously, he has slowly become conscious—or he can be made conscious—of doing. In this sense, surely, it can be said that "morals arise only in man" (G. G. Simpson, *The Meaning of Evolution* 345). Slowly becoming conscious of his actions, he has also, from time to time, become a prey to tinkering with them, sometimes for good and sometimes, perhaps more often, for bad.

Now these things that he did, first and through by far the longest period of his evolution unconsciously, and now slowly with increasing consciousness of them as he became what we refer to as *homo sapiens*, were the sum total of his *mores* at any given stage. And since certainly some of our primitive ancestors survived successfully (how many failed to survive is yet another question), then their *mores* were, in a very real sense, the sum total of their successful procedures—customary doings—directly, or, indirectly, of those procedures which did not permanently interfere with their successful survival. Of the former, namely, directly successful procedures, it is likely, for example, that the many rules against brother-sister marriages were for the common good (J. G. Frazer, *Totemism and Exogamy*). Of the latter, namely, those that did not prevent his successful survival, an example might be the mutilation of fingers among, for example, the Australian

Larakia (B. Spencer, *Wanderings in Wild Australia* II. 610—similar practices would seem to be as old as Upper Paleolithic man, as probably shown in the prehistoric cave of Gargas; see Abbé H. Breuil, *Four Hundred Centuries of Cave Art* 246-7). These customary procedures (*mores*) mark, therefore, the very "condition of existence for the individual and the species" (G. F. Moore, *Birth and Growth of Religion* 3-4). Their functional motivation is self preservation of the individual and the group. "The one key-phrase to the whole bustling scene seems 'urge-to-live'" (C. Sherington, *Man on his Nature* 170) motivated, it would seem, always to the survival of the group.

The origins and meanings of these customary procedures will now often escape us; indeed, they often escape the surviving practitioners of them, who know only that such and such custom has always been done and must, therefore, continue to be done. Often, at best, they find their origins, when severely questioned about them by modern investigators, in the far off times of mythological ancestors (B. Spencer & F. J. Gillen, *Native Tribes of Central Australia* 394 or W. Mathews, *Navaho Legends* 40).

Looked at in this light, it is not hard to see that much of primitive *mores* (morals) is basically the same as that of modern civilized man. Obviously, for example, primitive man was terribly interested in his food supply. Note, however, what modern Christians, for example, first ask for from the monotheistic deity in the Lord's

Prayer. Merely as another example, primitive man inherited from his sub-human background a more immediately moving interest in his own particular group than in that of some other group. Thus, when the Cherokees were questioned about right and wrong: "Right is to steal horses from another tribe or from a white man; wrong is to steal from my own tribe" (G. W. Foster, *Sequoyah* 32—see on this subject, A. Keith, *A New Theory of Human Evolution*). But primitive man's concern for his food, along with practically all his other concerns, were for the welfare of the group. His morality is, indeed, "the sum of the preservative instincts of a society" (L. Stephen, *Science of Ethics* 208). It is his inherited condition of survival from his pre-human stage, now increasingly consciously held to. The animal or primitive man that dares go it alone is the rogue that does not survive. For the most primitive man it is probably unthinkable for him to act independently of the group.

The vital factor, therefore, in primitive morals (the successful customary procedures) is that they have the at least tacit approval of the group. Stated in other words, the effective sanction of all conduct was the group. What we nowadays might call right is, with primitive man, what the group approves of. Contrariwise, what we nowadays might call wrong is any act or procedure that excites or provokes the disapproval of the group. In short, our primitive ancestors arrived at the human stage conditioned to conform to their group *mores*. And primitive

morals are simply and wholly this primordially conditioned conformity to the group *mores*. It is beside the point that many primitive customs now seem immoral to us—such, for example, as the cannibalism of our primitive ancestors (thus, A. Keith, *Essays on Human Evolution* 178) or the human suckling of monkeys and puppies (thus, among the Okomatadi, for which see G. Gheerbrant, *Journey to the Far Amazon* 314). It is beside the point that other customs do not now seem to have any connection with morals—such, for example, as the horrible mutilation in certain circumcision rites (thus, H. St. J. Philby, *Arabian Highlands* 449–50) or head shrinking practices (thus, B. Flornoy, *Jivaro*). And much of primitive morals will not for us nowadays make any sense at all—as, perhaps, not a few of modern man's customs will puzzle some future investigator—such, for example, as the apparently arbitrary mutilation of the king's chief cooks (thus, J. Martin, *The Tonga Islands* 76–7). To primitive man these customs are part and parcel of his *mores*. It does not matter that they seem incomprehensible to us. For, speaking of the Bedouin social codes, "Without these rules of the game, indeed, all human life in nomad Arabia would have become extinct long since" (C. S. Raswan, *Black Tents of Arabia* 89). In short, the group "would have disintegrated without strict adherence to its own savage morality" (E. W. Hopkins, *Origin and Evolution of Religion* 253). So, everywhere for primitive man.

In addition to the imposing significance of his biological past, which so severely conditioned him to conformity to the group *mores,* there were at least three other factors which militated against man's disturbing or neglecting this conformity to the group *mores.* He lived in constant danger of attack by real foes or the conjured up threat of attack by ones his brain now allows him to imagine. He also lived with an almost complete lack of privacy, wherein it is likely his every act was exposed. And he also lived in relatively small close-knit groups, not much beyond an enlarged family unit most of the time, wherein defection of any sort is immediately conspicuous and immediately pounced upon because it is more tragically significant to the survival of the smaller group.

The effective working of primitive morals is therefore dependent on the functioning identity of interest within the group and the unanimity of its approval or disapproval. We can guess that the intensity of the group's reactions was greatest when it manifested disapproval and it is likely that anyone to whom this group censure was directed felt it deeply. It is probable that the origins of conscience are to be found in this remorse based on the group reproof which gnaws at the very being of the member on whom the group censure falls. The efforts we expend even now to avoid being cut by the group point up the fact. On the other hand, it is probable that the individual's anticipation of the group's approval is the foundation of moral obligation. In such primitive groups, approval and disapproval admit of no compromise and, therefore, no confusion of standards.

Along with these customary procedures (*mores*) are the starkly negative withdrawals and refusals to do certain things. Certain things that must not be done appear to have had a sanction of mysteriously deadly force over and above that of the group itself. Certain things just must not be done, for doing them, in the vital experience of the group, brings—often immediately and, in any case, soon—disaster or even destruction, always to the individual and not seldom to his group. Certain things or actions are Taboo (tabu). The word itself is originally Polynesian, as first discovered by Captain Cook (J. Cook & J. King, *A Voyage to the Pacific Ocean* 1776–80 [London, 1784] I. 286 *et passim*) and its meaning seems to have been "absolutely marked [or] marked off." Current usage, universally applied, renders it as "prohibited" (verboten). The origins of taboo are lost in prehistoric obscurity but it is likely that it is based on experience, or, rather, on the interpretations—not always sound—of experience, that the doing of certain things brings disastrous, often fatal, consequences beyond the group's power to alter. Even innocent or inadvertent violation of a Taboo made no difference—the consequences were automatically inevitable. A classic example of the residual principle of taboo being violated is to be found in the Bible (II Sam. vi. 1–7 wherein Uzzah reached out his hand to steady the ark being shaken by the oxen pulling the cart in which it was being carried—certainly an innocentl well-meant act—and immediately dropped dead. The ark was taboo to profane hands.

It is probable that violation of these most primitive taboos was exceedingly rare. The effectiveness of its extra-social sanction soon led the leaders of primitive groups to extend arbitrarily beyond its natural basis the things covered by taboo—until ultimately in many groups it can be defined as "observances established for political purposes" (R. Taylor, *Te Ika A Maui; or New Zealand and its Inhabitants* 55). Despite this historic and arbitrary enlargement of scope, which inevitably tended to weaken it, taboo remained awesomely effective, so that, for example, when a Balonda has set his beehive in a tree, he ties a "piece of medicine" (taboo) around the trunk and this is full protection against thieves (D. Livingstone, *Missionary Travels and Researches in South Africa* 285). Inevitably, too, with such extensions of taboo in primitive societies, there was added the group sanction itself—to make doubly sure, sometimes; thus, among the Masai, where the boiling of milk is taboo, lest the cows run dry, the violator "can only atone for the sin with a fearfully heavy fine, or, failing that, the insult to the holy cattle will be wiped out in his blood" (H. H. Johnston, *The Kalima-njaro Expedition* 425).

Primitive morals are, therefore, basically the things customarily done or not done as they traditionally elicit either the approval or disapproval of the group and also the things which are taboo, which in the beginning are beyond the approval or disapproval of the group and work automatically—as though through some mysteriously occult power. The *mores,* as a whole and in their several parts, become increasingly consciously the responsibility of the group, which early must take upon itself the teaching of its myriad details. They center around, in general, such crucial phases of the individual and group life as the gathering and raising of food, self-defense and the survival of offspring starting with pregnancy, birth, puberty, menstruation, marriage, and death. In addition to what the young child would pick up in its earliest years merely by living with the group, the *mores* are often inculcated on the young at the time of their admission to full-fledged manhood. These rites of admission, of which primitive peoples make much, often take place at puberty and they are so set out—often involving impressively complicated drama and exquisite pain —to make sure that the initiate indelibly learns the *mores.* Only the strongest survived such initiation ceremonies; they often last through several years of studied initiation. Among the Torres Straits tribes, for example, "death was the penalty for infringing the rules connected with the initiation period" (A. C. Haddon, *Journ. Anthrop. Inst.* XIX. 335).

The responsibility of inculcating the *mores* upon the young and of enforcing them later on fell, naturally, upon the elders of the group. They alone had the requisite experience, for without all the modern materials and instruments of education, only experi-

439

ence could adequately be the basis for wisdom founded on ancestral usage. In all crucial ways, only the elders could know the rules for survival and they could but pass them on by oral precept and example—thus their universal authority among primitive peoples —and it fell to them to see to it that the young learned. Indeed, generally, "In each family the word of the old man is accepted law by the young people; they never dispute authority" (so, for the Fuegians, R. Fitzroy, Surveying Voyages of H.M.S. Adventure and Beagle II. 179).

In the earliest stages, the development of the mores, as a whole, is independent of religion and its developing premises. Indeed, the earliest religious practices are but a part of the general mores. Their sanction, we have seen, is wholly social, namely, that of the group. And so long as the group remained an integral unit, with a unanimity of approach to its mores, there is no reason to assume that it would have become otherwise. Yet primitive man could not long have remained in such isolated groups and very early there must have been mixing and coalescing of groups—though till the dawn of history proper such resultant groupings seem never to have been very large. If, however, as seems likely, man's chief enemy very early became other men, then inevitably he would have been drawn to the larger groupings for his best chance of survival. With the mixing of groups, there arose confusing standards, for the mores of two once distinct groups would not be identical, thus breaking the unanimity of the group sanctions of conduct and thereby invalidating them.

It is probable that those groupings survived whose religion had reached the stage wherein it could become the new sanction of the mores. Violation of taboo, which could have marked the crucial transition, became, for example, understood as the explosive disapproval now of the spirits or gods and much of the mores became peculiarly closely the province of these same spirits or gods. The customary procedures survived and developed as before but their sanctions slowly became religious and gradually the spirits, ultimately for some the gods, became responsible for certain spheres of morals. Gradually, the gods became not only the guardians and even vindicators of the mores but even the divine authors of them. In this way, primitive morals acquired the new and timely authority and sanction of religion. This acquisition marks one of the crucial advances in human history, for religion was the only available substitute for the previously unchallenged—but now increasingly being challenged through the mixing and contaminating of the mores—social sanctions of the group. Any transgression became now an offense against the spirits and the gods and, ultimately, against the divine laws of the gods, whose earthly representatives became the kings and priests. It is in this stage that some groups arrived at the dawn of civilization.

Bibliography

In a subject so vast and crucially complicated it is best to go first to the traditional classics in the field. The fundamental reference work is: Hastings, *Encyclopaedia of Religion and Ethics*. To mention other works risks the invidious but the following, each with full and trustworthy bibliographies, should be mentioned.

J. G. Frazer, *The Golden Bough*, 3rd edition.

E. Westermarck, *The Origin and Development of the Moral Ideas* (London 1917–24).

L. T. Hobhouse, *Morals in Evolution* (London, 1951).

E. B. Tylor, *Primitive Culture* (London, 1903).

G. Landtman, *The Origin of the Inequality of the Social Classes* (London, 1938).

Horace Abram Rigg, Jr.
Western Reserve University

primitive morals: *see* Aboriginals of Yirkalla; Jewish Ethics and Its Civilization; Zoroastrian Morals; Zuni Indians, Morals of.

primitive virtues: *see* More, Henry.

principles: *see* moral principles.

principles, first: *see* Aquinas, Thomas, Moral Views of; maxims.

prison reform: *see* Quakerism, Classical, The Morality of.

private property: *see* Marxist Theory of Morals; Minor Socratics; Soviet Morality, Current.

privation: *see* Minor Socratics.

probabiliorism: *see* Jesuits, the, Moral Theology of.

probabilism: *see* Jesuits, the, Moral Theology of; Liguori, St. Alphonsus and Catholic Moral Philosophy.

procreation: *see* Augustine and Morals.

Prodicus: *see* Sophists, the.

production, economic: *see* Marxist Theory of Morals.

profanity: *see* Puritan Morals.

profit: *see* Hindu Ethics.

profit, mutual: *see* China, Moral Philosophies of; gain.

progress: *see* Green, T. H.; Hegel, G. W. F.; Hindu Ethics; Jewish Ethics and Its Civilization; Kant, I.; Major Ethical Viewpoints; Marxist Theory of Morals; Primitive Morals.

progress, moral: *see* Quakerism, Classical, The Morality of; Stoics, the.

prohibitions: *see* Jewish Ethics and Its Civilization; Navaho Morals; Primitive Morals; Puritan Morals.

proletarian revolution: *see* Marxist Theory of Morals; Soviet Morality, Current.

proletariat: *see* Marxist Theory of Morals; Soviet Morality, Current.

Prometheus: *see* Minor Socratics; Sophists, the.

promiscuity: *see* Navaho Morals.

promise keeping: *see* Ross, Sir (William) David.

promises: *see* Aztec Morals; Broad, C. D.; Moral Philosophy in America; Navaho Morals; Stoics, the.

proofs: *see* Balguy, John; Prichard, H. A.

propaganda: *see* Marxist Theory of Morals.

property: *see* Cumberland, Richard; Hammurapi, Code of; Hume, David; Jewish Ethics and Its Civilization; Marxist Theory of Morals; private property; Stoics, the; Zuni Indians, Morals of the.

prophet and morals: *see* Christian Moral Philosophy; Jewish Ethics and Its Civilization; Morals and Religion; Spinoza.

propitiation: *see* Rio Grande Pueblo Indians.

proportion: *see* Clarke, Samuel; Cooper, Anthony Ashley; Cudworth, Ralph; Plato.

propriety: *see* Jewish Ethics and Its Civilization.

prosperity: *see* Aristotle; Quakerism, Classical, The Morality of.

prostitution: *see* Soviet Morality, Current.

Protagoras: *see* Stoics, the.

Protestantism: *see* Kant, I.; Puritan Morals; Rio Grande Pueblo Indians.

Proverbs, the: *see* Christian Moral Philosophy.

providence: *see* Moral Philosophy in America; Reid, Thomas; Stoics, the.

prudence: *see* Aquinas, Thomas, Moral Views of; Augustine and Morals; Butler, Joseph; Cudworth, Ralph; Dante, Alighieri; Dewey, John; Hobbes, Thomas; Hume, David; Jesuits, the, Moral Theology; Kant, I.; More, Henry; Price, Richard; Reid, Thomas; Riffian Morals; Sidgwick, Henry; Utilitarianism.

psyche: *see* Freud, Sigmund.

psychiatry: *see* Soviet Morality, Current.

psychoanalysis: *see* Freud, Sigmund; Major Ethical Viewpoints.

psychological egoism: *see* Butler, Joseph; Major Ethical Viewpoints.

psychology: *see* Ayer, Alfred J.; Cooper, Anthony Ashley; Cudworth, Ralph; Freud, Sigmund; Marxist Theory of Morals; Psychology and Morals; Utilitarianism.

Psychology and Morals

Morals are affected by many factors, such as physical well- or ill-being, environmental conditions of geography, climate and temperature, food supply, economic conditions, by the exigencies of coping with the elements,—to name but a few at random. Among these factors are the psychological, such as attitudes, habits of response, sensory stimuli and responses, memory, anticipation, reason, drives, suggestion, imitation, social pressure,—not to mention those complicated pathological conditions brought on by anatomical or physiological impediments. The recent emphasis on psychosomatics in medicine will undoubtedly bring about some special attention in this field to the understanding of moral behavior.

Psychology itself is grouped into a variety of schools. Chief among the most recent schools which particularly has considered the role of mind upon moral behavior is, of course, the so-called school of depth psychology. Depth psychology is a recent term for old observations, viz., that much of the mental processes lies below the surface of the conscious state. Stirrings in the unconscious mind go on unabated and man's behavior is far from the result merely of his decisions. Neo-Freudianism would hold up man as the victim of his forgotten past (racial and individual), a past seething with frustrations, fears and inner conflicts. Man is not healthy in mind since his psychologic substructure is itself pathologic.

There is psychologic disease and man is truly what the traditional theologians carelessly but realistically called "original sin." Morality has roots deep in the underground, and what man may call his "will" is often but a shallow covering of unconscious motivations greater and more powerful than choice. He is the victim even of forgotten experiences traceable, if they could be traced, to the non-re-called yesterdays of innocent infancy and childhood. A bleak picture, indeed. Moral codes demand the impossible since urges (sex, egocentricity, inferiority—depending upon which Freudian is speaking) like the tropical storms sweep away fragile decisions, determinations and commitments.

Before the onset of present-day depth psychology there arose in England a school of psychologists (the Dynamic School of British Psychologists) which took seriously the question of psychology and morality in terms of the unconscious drives. Chief among this group was the physician and psychologist J. A. Hadfield whose publication *Psychology and Morals* was a masterpiece of diagnosis with case studies of the maladjusted. The motivation of this school was therapeutic and the subjects, for the most part, the psychological casualties of World War I. This school, it would now appear, was more conservative in its analysis and hopeful of restoration (with a friendly disposition to a given traditional religion) than those depth psychologists who followed the more radical Freudian principles of determinism and fatalism. From this British

school much may be learned as to the relation between psychology and morals and, therefore, some account of their general approach may here be expounded.

Psychologically, the term "moral" involves a conflict between powerful impulses or drives and the will to pursue some norm or ideal course or, again, between two or more impulses which flare into the open, frustrating the will. The failure to resolve conflicts in the open arena of decision only accentuates the situation of frustration the next time a decision is called for. "Moral disease" is the term given to this psychological inability to resolve the underlying conflicts which bring about actions undesired or undesirable.

Psychologically, each age-level has its own set of moral standards. A boy may be pugnacious and approvingly get out there and fight nobly with his fists for his "honor." He may be forgiven if he refuses to be a tattle-tale to his companions. But that boy grown to manhood would be expected morally (in a given society) to behave differently in similar situations of provocation. Men are not expected to act like fist-fighting boys in the settling of their disputes; nor are they regarded without respect if integrity and duty force them to give honest testimony against some malefactor although it may embarrass a long-standing friendship. It would be bad ethics to impose norms of moral behavior suitable for disciplined and mature minds upon those who have not reached that stage even as it would be immoral to expect the handicapped to do what would reasonably be expected of the healthy. A preacher's son is not the preacher and as a son he may be permitted actions not permissible to his father. Young people acting like old people and, conversely, old people acting childish, are tragic examples of misplaced social behavior. In the moral sphere indiscriminately imposed codes may well move into the realm of immoral expectancy. The age-level of psychological experience and its possibilities may be as wide a difference in the case of individuals as the cultural difference between some aboriginal tribe and the social habits of a modern technological society.

Such psychological considerations need not imply that there is no universal standard of morality. Universality need not neglect situational contexts. It needs only to recognize as a *principle* the psychologic fact that morality is always a relationship of concrete situations proper to age and circumstance, thus recognizing the facts as they are. Psychologically, "good" is a *principle* and not a series of minute observances. The ethics of ancient Pharisaism (in the best sense of the term) and old-fashioned Puritanism were not so much at fault on details prescribed (commonly emphasized by critics) as they were on the immoral principle that all people are indiscriminately and situationally alike. The "good" will be good and the "bad" will be bad contextually. Such is the moral principle which can be said to be universally valid for humans. So far as a metaphysical standard of goodness or badness—whether the world is on the side of angels or that of devils or whether goodness is or is not at the heart of things—such a question (important as it may be) is no part of psychology but rightfully the province of metaphysics itself. Psychology has to do with human relationships and their possibilities and not with theology nor moral ontology.

The above is the account, in general, of those who in recent times pioneered the work of depth psychology. But there is more to this account. "Sin" is a term to be reserved for conscious and deliberate and responsible disobedience to whatever norm is posed (whether that norm itself is valid or not). "Moral disease" is a condition that lies beneath the surface in the conflicts of the unconscious mind and, of course, is not in the same category as "sin." ("Original sin" is a poor term, however valid psychologically, for "moral disease.") Disease, of course, suggests a qualification to "moral" in that the moral outcome is not of the same status as a purely moral action (involving responsible decision) since, in the former case, the basis lies beyond the realm of responsible choice. An alcoholic is not a sinful man; he is a sick man although he may conduct himself immorally. The responsibility lies not in the overt act of drunkenness (motivated by deep-seated and overwhelming desires) but only in his conscious desire (sincere enough to make the attempt) to align himself on the side (however feeble the result) of some attempt at cure. He is sinful only as he is unwilling to begin to take step

444

toward reconstruction. (This goes for over-eaters who too may be in the state of psychologic and even moral disease.)

In this general psychological frame of reference the terms "temptation" and "conscience" take on illuminating meaning. It is Hadfield who suggests that both temptation and conscience are types of suppressed desires. "Temptation" is the condition of conflict wherein a good is consciously dominant but harassed and impeded by a suppressed impulse to evil; "conscience" is the condition of conflict wherein an evil is consciously dominant but harassed and checked by a suppressed good. Both involve conflicts between the conscious desire or will and the unconscious impulse. When one is tempted one is tempted *within* oneself: one is consciously aware of a desired good but one is frustrated by the unconscious drive to express evil. When one is "conscience stricken" one is harassed *within* oneself: one is consciously aware of a desired bad but one is frustrated by the unconscious drive to express the good. No experience of temptation and no experience of conscience stand *outside* oneself. One is not tempted by the world, nor by the flesh, nor by the devil—only by oneself. Thus, a temptation for one person is not necessarily a temptation for another nor for the same person at some other moment or situation. What makes for the condition of conscience, similarly, is not something that happens *to* a person but something that is provoked *within* a person. Matters of conscience thus are relative to an inner history. What

hurts one does not hurt another nor for the same person at all times and all circumstances. The roots of both temptation and conscience are surface (conscious) conditioned and below-surface (unconscious) motivated. The surface side represents what may have been *taught* as good or bad and accepted and desired and remembered as such; the deep or below-surface side contains the lively registrations of memory (often forgotten as to origins) and *fundamental* desires. Temptation and conscience, thus, are conditioned by the varieties of experience, the codes of one's society, the mores in general and the memories which are unconsciously not forgotten.

It is, then, precarious to trust one's conscience since this is a psychological variable based on doubtful norms. Only where one can be reasonably certain that the norms are critically defensible (in the give and take of long social experience) can matters of conscience be taken seriously as norms for wider areas of people. Morality cannot rest securely on mere conscience for conscience may reflect a conflict which is unhealthy or abnormal.

There are more facets to this type of depth psychology than here outlined (for example, in the areas of religious sentiment, repressions, sublimation, faith, belief, regeneration, conversion, personal salvation, etc.).

In another section of this volume the reader will find under the name of Sigmund Freud the approach of the psychoanalytic school which the master of that school has developed in terms of its implications for moral theory.

445

Again, in another section, under the heading of John Dewey, the functionalistic school (particularly instrumentalism) is given exposition as to its implications for the understanding of the relationship between psychology and morals. But such a psychology moves in another frame of reference.

There still remains an unwritten chapter to the understanding of the relationship between psychology and morals in the field of body chemistry, the function of glands, etc., which may more properly be called physiology and morals. Such studies must come from sources disciplined in areas strictly beyond the purely psychological but which—more than we may surmise—affect human psychology and therefore moral behavior.

Bibliography

Wilhelm Wundt, *Elements of Folk Psychology* (Eng. tr., 1916).
J. A. Hadfield, *Psychology and Morals* (1926).
A. A. Roback, *The Psychology of Character* (1927).
George A. Coe, *The Motives of Men* (1928).
Vergilius Ferm, *A Dictionary of Pastoral Psychology* (New York, 1955).

Vergilius Ferm
The College of Wooster

psychology and morals: *see* Cudworth, Ralph.
psychology, social: *see* Hobbes, Thomas.
psychopathology: *see* Freud, Sigmund.

psychosomatics: *see* Psychology and Morals.
public opinion: *see* Soviet Morality, Current.
public ownership: *see* Marxist Theory of Morals.
Pueblo Indian tribes: *see* Rio Grande Pueblo Indians; Zuni Indians, Morals of.
Puffendorf: *see* Cumberland, Richard.
pugnacity: *see* fighting; Psychology and Morals; Riffian Morals.
punishment: *see* Aboriginals of Yirkalla; Augustine and Morals; Aztec Morals; Balguy, John; capital punishment; China, Moral Philosophies of: Clarke, Samuel; Cumberland, Richard; Dante, Alighieri; Freud, Sigmund; Hammurapi, Code of; Hindu Ethics; Hobbes, Thomas; Jewish Ethics and Its Civilization; Moral Philosophy in America; Muslim Morals; Navaho Morals; Pakot, the Moral System of; Puritan Morals; Reid, Thomas; Rio Grande Pueblo Indians; Schlick, Moritz; Tapirapé Morals, Some Aspects of; Utilitarianism; Zuni Indians, Morals of.
punishment, capital: *see* Quakerism, Classical, The Morality of; Sophists, the.
punishment, divine: *see* Pakot, the Moral System of; penal.
pure reason: *see* Kant, I.
purification: *see* Hindu Ethics; More, Henry; Tolstoy, Leo.
Puritan Morals
Moral seriousness lay basic to the power of Puritanism, and the Puritans, of course, deserve much of their reputation for moral severity. Moral

severity is one of the things that saw them through a severe time. But they only partly deserve the popular notion that imputes to them the revivalistic "puritanism" after about 1750, when the Puritan period proper came to a close. In their heyday the old Puritans revealed themselves capable of surprising cruelty and bigotry on occasion, as in slaughtering Pequots and persecuting Quakers. But the same disposition to bigotry and cruelty characterized other religious groups of the period and may reflect human fears and prejudices that had no necessary basis in religion at all. The 17th century was harsher in almost every way than the mid-18th, and the harshness that Puritanism displayed may have been in most respects no more Puritan than was any other religion, insofar as it was religious. A case could be made out that Puritanism effectively mitigated much of the harshness it had to cope with in that coarser, ruder age. The puritanical attitudes that prevailed among "Puritan" sects after 1750 may, by the same token, reflect the folk-prejudice of rural, hard, unlettered life more than a propensity of Puritanism itself. Puritan leadership had been in the hands of a cultivated, educated elite; and the decisive change toward rigidity of morals significantly coincides with the social assertion of the lower classes. The old Puritan morality, in this light, appears as the morality of the English gentry—i.e., it was aristocratic—, and the later, more negative morality that of the lesser yeomanry, social class making a bigger difference than Puritanism-as-a-philosophy. The Puritan philosophy itself, on the other hand, probably had less dependence on social and economic class than has been thought; but that is another story.

Puritans nevertheless from the first took a high hand with regard to morals, and one reason they did grew out of a doctrinal implication. That was their determination to *enforce* a morality professed by all groups of the time and as sternly, or more sternly legislated by the Anglican government of England and the Anglican House of Burgesses in Virginia. The Puritans did not differ from the Anglicans or the Roman Catholics in thinking the civil government should enforce religion; but, as John Winthrop said on the way across the Atlantic, "That which the most in theire Churches maineteine as a truthe in profession onely, wee must bring into familiar and constant practise." (*A Modell of Christian Charity,* 1630, *Winthrop Papers,* II, 293.) Furthermore, the Puritans we are talking about when we refer to colonial New England were mostly Congregationalist Puritans who conceived of themselves as directly covenanting with God to follow in all His ways. For them to compromise their morality would be worse than for others, they felt, because they would thereby be breaking a sacred contract; and such a breach could bring divine retribution upon the whole commonwealth. "Neither must wee think that the lord will beare with such faileings at our hands as hee dothe from those among whome wee haue liued," says Winthrop. "When God giues a speciall

447

Commission [to plant a holy common-wealth] he lookes to haue it stricktly obserued in every Article . . . soe that if wee shall deale falsely with our god . . . and soe cause him to withdrawe his present help from vs, wee shall be made a story and a by-word through the world." (*Ibid.*, 293–95.)

For non-members, who had not undertaken the full dedication entailed in subscribing to the church covenant, the Puritan elect showed an indulgence that is a far remove from fanaticism. They did not expect the lower orders to live up to the exacting code they freely imposed on themselves. John Cotton, speaking for orthodox Bay Puritanism, also expresses a greater leniency toward those who would subscribe to the covenant than Roger Williams, who insisted on a strictly pure church uncorrupted by communion with the unregenerate. In the trial for admission to membership, Cotton says,

wee doe not exact eminent measure, either of knowledge, or holinesse, but doe willingly stretch out our hands to receive *the weake in faith* . . . for we had rather 99. hypocrites should perish through presumption, then one humble soule belonging to Christ, should sinke under discouragement or despaire. . . . (*The Way of the Churches of Christ in New-England*, 1645, p. 58.)

But Williams, despite his Separatist strictness toward church membership, felt that the civil government had no business enforcing the religious policies of the elect upon the population at large. No matter how saintly, the elect still suffered from human fallibility and might mistakenly erect error and trample truth. Religious truth, he therefore held, would be safer if left completely alone by government. This discrepancy between the two Puritan ministers made for much of the difference in moral stringency between the Bay and Providence Plantation. Some Bay Puritans accused Rhode Islanders of profaning the Sabbath by plowing. They made this accusation to the Archbishop of Canterbury, even though, as Williams points out, all England played away the Sabbath. The difference came not in the professed morality of the various groups but in the degree of enforcement of it; and "forced worship stincks in Gods nostrils," Williams declared. (Letter to Major Mason 22 June 1670, 1 MHS *Colls.*, I, 281, 282.) In New Plymouth, in Massachusetts, and in Connecticut the "unregenerate" must keep quiet on the Sabbath, whatever they believed. William Bradford would not interfere with the consciences of those who wished not to work on Christmas, 1621, but at the same time he would not permit them to play while others worked. Thomas Shepard years later at Cambridge made a sort of official pronouncement concerning the disposition of children, servants, and strangers to profane the Sabbath:

we are therefore to improve our power over them for God, in restraining them from sinne, and in constraining them (as farre as we can) to the holy observance of the Rest of the Sabbath; lest God impute their sinnes to us who had power (as Eli in the like case) to restrain them and did not. . . . (*Theses Sabbaticae*, 1654, p. 310.)

Government in the interest of religion was possible and insured by the 1631 law which confined the franchise to church members. The morality they tried to enforce and the way they went about enforcing it can perhaps best be illustrated by the action of the General Court (the central government) of Massachusetts in its first order of business of the session opening 3 November 1675. It followed the lead of the clergy in assuming that God was punishing New England for specific sins in bringing upon them the calamities of King Philip's War, then underway.

The Court, apprehending there is too great a neglect of discipline in the churches, and especially respecting those that are their children . . . doe solemnly recommend it vnto the respective elders and brethren of the seueral churches throughout this jurisdiction to take effectual course for reformation herein.

The Court points out the "manifest pride openly appearing amongst us in that long haire, like weomens haire, is worne by some men, either their oune or others haire made into perewiggs, and by some weomen wearing borders of hajre, and theire cutting, curling, & immodest laying out theire haire, which practise doeth prevayle & increase, especially amongst the younger sort"; wherefore the Court exhorts moderation and empowers all grand juries to present offending persons to the county courts, which it authorizes to admonish, fine, or correct at their discretion. Notwithstanding "wholesome lawes" already in force, "the euill of pride in apparrell, both for costljnes

in the poorer sort, & vajne, new, strange fashions, both in poore & rich, with naked breasts and armes, or, as it were, pinioned with the addition of superstitious ribbons both on hajre & apparrell" moves the Court to order the county courts to present offenders to the grand jury and to fine the jurors if they should neglect their duty. The Court notes "so mutch profanes amongst us in persons turning their backs vpon the publick worship before it be finished and the blessing pronounced," and orders either the church officers or the selectmen to appoint persons to shut the meeting-house doors "or any other meete way to attajne the end." The Court finds "much disorder & rudeness in youth in many congregations in time of the worship of God," and instructs that "graue & sober" persons be placed as supervisors over the children and youth in church with the charge of presenting a list of delinquents to the nearest magistrate or court, where the delinquents will be admonished for the first offense and their parents fined five shillings for the second, or the delinquents whipped, and for incorrigible cases, ten lashes or three days in the house of correction. "The name of God is prophaned by common swearing and cursing in ordinary communication, which is a sin that growes amongst us," and the Court's remedy is to order that the laws already in force against this be vigorously prosecuted and that anybody failing to report swearing when hearing it shall be penalized the same as the swearers. "The shamefull and scandelous sin of excessive drinking,

tipling, & company keeping in tavernes . . . grows vpon us," wherefore
the Court asks the county courts not to
license any more public houses "then
are absolutely necessary in any towne"
and to license only persons of approved sobriety and law-abidingness.
The Court further orders that all private, unlicensed houses be diligently
searched out and that

the selectmen of euery towne shall choose
some sober and discreete persons, to be authorized from the County Court, each of
whom shall take charge of ten or twelve
familjes of his neighbourhood, and shall
diligently inspect them, and present the
names of such persons so transgressing to
the magistrate, commissioners, or selectmen of the toune . . . and the persons so
chosen . . . shall haue one third of the
fines allowed them. . . .

"There is a wofull breach of the fifth
commandment to be found amongst
us," wherefore "this Court doeth declare, that sin highly provoaking to the
Lord" but sets the penalty on conviction at mere admonition for the first
offense and a small fine and/or whipping for subsequent offenses. Despite
the laws in force against "the sin of
idlenes," it "doeth greatly increase,"
and the Court orders the constables to
"inspect particcular familjes" to compile a list to turn over to the selectmen
who are to proceed according to law.
The Court complains of overcharging
—"oppression"—not only by shopkeepers and merchants but also by mechanics (artisans) and day laborers;
and anybody who feels oppressed in
this way the Court accords liberty to

bring complaint before the grand jurors. Then

there is a loose & sinfull custome of going
or riding from toune to toune, and that
oft times men & women together, vpon
pretence of going to lecture, but it ap-
peares to be meerely to drincke & reuell
in ordinarys and tavernes, which is in itself
scandalous, and it is to be feared a notable
meanes to debauch our youth and hazard
the chastity of such as are draune forth
therevnto. . . .

Any offending in this way will be liable to be summoned before any county court if single persons. (*Records of
the Governor and Company of the
Massachusetts Bay,* V, 59–63.)

Even Roger Williams, who did not
share his fellow Puritans' belief in civil
coercion of conscience, fell in with
their custom of analyzing sins to determine which ones must have brought on
some community misfortune. While
minister of the Salem church, during a
day of humiliation, as he says.

I discovered 11 publike sins, for which I
beleeved (and doe) it pleased God to inflict, and further to threaten publike calamities. Most of which 11 (if not all) that
Church then seemed to assent unto. . . .
(*Mr. Cottons Letter Lately Printed, Examined and Ansvvered,* 1644, p. 2.)

All this moral preoccupation on an
official basis certainly had effect,
though it could not quite change human nature or reverse the trend of the
times. The Puritans had to admit that
laws, like those against costly apparel,
could hardly be enforced because
some of the highest-placed Puritans (or
their wives) disregarded them. In-

crease Mather and his friend Samuel Sewall got apoplectic about periwigs, but clergymen in general went with the vogue, including Cotton Mather and Jonathan Edwards (whose wife raised eyebrows with her expensive dress). The Puritans appear to have succeeded pretty well in minimizing drunkenness and public disorder, but one night even the venerable Judge Sewall barely made it home. Indications are that many a gentleman's agreement passed between respectable citizens and the spying selectmen, constables, and tithingmen. Two Labadist preachers visiting Boston in 1680 and 1681 thought there was no more devotion in the Puritan churches than elsewhere, "and even less than at New York"; drinking and fighting, they said, occurred there not less than elsewhere; "and as to truth and true godliness, you must not expect more of them than of others." When it came to business, the Labadists said they found the Bostonians the same as the English everywhere, "doing nothing but lying and cheating, when it serves their interest." The two Dutch divines, however, had nothing but admiration for the old Puritan preacher of Roxbury, John Eliot, who frankly "deplored the decline of the church in New England, and especially in Boston, so that he did not know what would be the final result." (Jasper Dankers and Peter Sluyter, *Journal of a Voyage, Memoirs* of the Long Island Hist. Soc., I, 380, 383, 386, 394.)

One of the most revealing passages in the account of these travelers describes the suspicion they met with in some of the townspeople of Boston, who

said we certainly were Jesuits, who had come here for no good, for we were quiet and modest, and an entirely different sort of people from themselves; that we could speak several languages, were cunning and subtle of mind and judgment, had come there without carrying on any traffic or any other business, except only to see the place and country; that this seemed fabulous as it was unusual in these parts; certainly it could be for no good purpose. . . . This suspicion seemed to have gained more strength because the fire at Boston over a year ago was caused by a Frenchman. (*Ibid.*, 387.)

When the clergy gradually lost its grip on the leadership of society—coinciding with the weakening of religious sanctions in general by modern secular forces and with the royal interference that separated church and state—the study-disciplined clergy also lost much of its power to resist folk-prejudice, like the incipient suspicion the Labadist visitors encountered. They succumbed to it in part themselves. Puritanism, generally speaking, cannot be equated with the provincialism and pre-Christian folklore that formed much of its milieu; yet a continuous interaction cannot be denied. The Puritan elite did not succeed in imposing their morals on the whole of society, at least for very long, but did impart a moral consciousness and moral cast to society that proved durable—even if least conspicuously so in Boston itself.

Puritanism from the first inclined to asceticism, which would be implied in its stress on other-worldly values. It also arose partly as a reaction to the dislocating effects of the beginning of the industrial revolution that left large numbers demoralized. The Puritans thought society heading for a universal shipwreck and, in their desire to salvage values and decency, took morality closer to heart. Winthrop records his affront at the general devaluation of human life in England:

This lande growes wearye of her Inhabitantes, so as man which is the most pretious of all Creatures, is heere more vile and base, then the earthe they treade vpon . . . especi[ally] if they be poore. . . . (*General Observations for the Plantation of New England*, 1629, *Winthrop Papers*, II, 114.)

Much of Puritan morality stems from this concern over outraged human dignity; reflects a desire to restore or conserve more than to repress. In any event, the heightened Puritan morals do not present a picture of extreme renunciation or mortification of the flesh.

Winthrop, a saintly and a moderate man, denied himself many legitimate pleasures for the sake of peaceful concentration on progress toward the divine. But he used tobacco as freely as that restrained non-Puritan Thomas Jefferson later; he dressed in lace ruff and cuffs and undoubtedly a scarlet waistcoat; he gave up card-playing at his English manor only because it encouraged the servants to waste too much of their time at it; he enjoyed bountiful venison feasts in America; and he drank wine and beer. (Even Puritan women used tobacco, including the brave minister's wife, Mary Rowlandson.) Winthrop discouraged the custom of drinking toasts, but the holiest of the Puritans drank heavier than Jefferson, who in his old age temperately confined himself to three glasses of light wine a day (unless a friend were present, when it would be four and a half) and to malt liquors and hard cider at dinner and supper. (Jefferson to Dr. Vine Utley, 21 Mar. 1818, *Writings*, Lipscomb ed., XV, 187.) The *Arbella* that Winthrop came over on carried about 10,000 gallons of beer, as against 3,500 gallons of water (mostly for cooking purposes), for beer was the common drink in England and long continued so in America. It came to cost a penny for an ale-quart, the quantity usually consumed per person per meal. Having to drink water produced one of the crises of early Pilgrim history. Elder William Brewster is the only Pilgrim recorded to have stuck with water, and Bradford marvels that he could have lived to a healthy old age despite it. Wine was the proper refreshment to serve guests. Both Governor Simon Bradstreet and the students at Harvard, for instance, formally served wine to the visiting Labadist clergymen. At church Communion, the Puritans passed real wine around in the single chalice. That it was ardent is proved by the Puritan preacher whose sermons became incoherent from his habit of a long draught both before and after the rest. When drunkenness became a worse and worse problem as the century wore on and rum came in,

Increase Mather railed constantly against the taverns and ale-houses of Boston, but said "I know that in such a great Town as this, there is need of such Houses, and no sober Minister will speak against the Licensing of them; but I wish there be not more of them then there is any need of." (*Wo to Drunkards*, 1673, p. 29.) The Puritans stood for temperance, not teetotalism. Calling total abstinence "temperance" and making it a crucial test of religiousness began with the great revival period when the great Puritan era was over.

In taking morality as something that should be enforced as well as professed, the Puritans actually did tend toward repressiveness, though not perhaps as much as has been thought. But the disjunctive repression that came from regarding sport, alcohol, etc. as innately sinful did not typify Puritanism during the Puritan period proper. Increase Mather took the text Jer. 10. 3: "The Customs of the People are Vain" and picked out carding, dicing, promiscuous dancing, health-drinking, New-Year's gifts, Christmas-keeping, stage-plays, and costly apparel among other things to castigate. He sounds at first like the revivalistic preachers of a century later. But he fundamentally differs from them in that he does not regard all these customs as *innately* sinful.

For a Christian to use Recreations is very Lawfull, and in some cases a great Duty, but to waste so much Time in any Recreation, though never so innocent and laudable, as Gamesters usually do at Cards and Dice, and Tables, is haynously sinfull.

Every mans Eternity in another world, will be according to his improvement of time here. (*A Testimony against Several Prophane and Superstitious Customs*, 1687, p. 17.)

This world is a temporary way-station to be held in contempt, the Puritans said, and the natural predisposition of man in this evil world is to evil. They found it necessary, therefore, to make a special effort to transcend human nature, the temporal, and the material, in a concentration on the supremely superseding goal of eternal union with the Godhead. Everything from fiddling to whittling would be suspect, partly because it tended to confirm man in his prior inclinations, and partly because it proved unimportant in the light of the higher quest, and so a distraction from that quest or a waste of precious time. Puritans had almost as terrible a consciousness of time as they had of sin. But the Puritans' strong sense of sin also existed in a somewhat different sense from the later period. It came from their measuring themselves against the divine perfection they held as their ideal, and feeling inadequate and worthless before their exalted task. This sin-sense was more self-directed than directed righteously against others (as John Cotton admonished the proud heretic Ann Hutchinson), and in the vital phase of Puritanism always occurred in terms of their other-worldly emphasis. Their very concentration on this ideal rendered questions of dress, drink, and demeanor relatively inconsequential. Increase Mather and Jonathan Edwards

453

talked about them (perhaps out of public responsibility more than out of religious dictation), but what is significant is that they talked about them very little compared to the extent they talked about the large themes like divine love. If the Puritan elite didn't have time to dissipate, neither did they have time to give dissipation more than a subordinate place in their sermons and treatises. When what these men subordinated became dominant and an end in itself; when what they deplored because it took time from the other-worldly goal became deplored because it was held to be bad in itself; then Puritanism underwent not only a partial stultification but a revolution (cloaked as a revival): obsession with the pettier betrayed the orientation as having become, beneath the surface, this-worldly.

The unofficial leader of the Congregational Puritans before the sailing of the *Arbella*—William Ames—said that "all morall actions" and "any Spirituall or Religious act or habit in the minde of man . . . ought evidently to be prescribed by the word of God, or els ought not to be done. . . ." (*English Pvritanisme*, 1640, p. 4) The Puritans took the Bible literally and undertook to follow it as the infallible revealed law. They differed from the post-Great Awakening literalists, however, in holding that the literal meaning was not self-evident but could only be won by the most painstaking scholarship. Even in their literal-mindedness, then, the Puritans discovered a subtlety and flexibility that saved them

from the later crassness of untutored literalism.

The Puritan clergy had long urged a revival of a people they thought had sadly declined from the peerless first generation. "The Lord rebuke that worldly, earthly, profane & loose spirit up & down in the country, & give us to be instructed before laid desolate," one minister wrote in 1687. (John Bishop to Increase Mather, 18 Oct., 4 MHS *Colls.*, VIII, 315) It was only natural that they should pay increasing attention to external deficiencies which inevitably followed a dying-down of the original internal flame. Jonathan Edwards set about to revive the inner flame—while also brightening the intellectual light—, but he could not help raising an opposition to bundling and other "immoral" practices that had grown beyond the bounds that the first generation had to contend with. The father of many daughters, he deplored "frolicking" or, for that matter, any social activity after 9 p.m. among youth. The lassitude of the times probably spurred his repressiveness as well as his efforts to revive emotional participation in religion. John Wesley reacted much the same way to a similar situation in England at the same time. Yet Edwards looked indulgently upon the "irregularities" of the early Great Awakening, as Winthrop had looked indulgently upon the minor law violations of the first years of settlement. The Puritan clergy had long called for a revival, but when this universal one came, it took a course that horrified them; and it is they who at last acted, to a man, to terminate it. This indicates again that the New Light or revivalistic puritanism was not what the Puritan leaders of old called Puritanism.

The sexual attitudes of Puritans remained patriarchal after the Great Awakening as they had been before—maybe less so; but the conviction that sex was innately bad too, like dancing, cards, and rum, may also post-date the Puritan period proper. The laws regarding sex do not tell much because they do not essentially differ from Anglican or Quaker or Roman Catholic laws of the same time. There was a Massachusetts law that forbade husbands to beat their wives or even use "hard words" with them. Does such a law suggest a relaxation of the patriarchal code or the existence of wife-beating? The Puritans certainly wanted to keep sex within the bounds of the decency and dignity they strove for in general. Beyond that, it is hard to generalize; but there seems nothing to contradict the conclusion that they held sex to be good if only kept private and decorous; whereas we have ample testimony to contradict such a blanket conclusion for later "Puritan" views. The starting from decorum and working back the other way to a negative verdict on sex itself appears to be a later procedure. Edwards and Winthrop are two good examples of Puritans who married precipitately and who remained in love with their wives and vice versa. The Puritans in general give the impression of having been more passionate rather than more cold than the norm, and more tender rather than more callous. The Puri-

tans were possibly the most civilized because most fully conscious and deeply feeling of the groups of the time. Their constant cultivation of divine love—which is what the old Puritanism basically concerned itself with —seems to have made them more susceptible to romantic love and female beauty, and both Winthrop and Edwards spoke at times in a delicate poetic way both about religion and about their wives, as did Ann Bradstreet in her poems to her husband. The disconcerting Puritan haste to remarry after the death of man or wife must have been more than merely customary or economic. An old or middle-aged Puritan widower would sometimes take a very young woman for a second or third wife, from John Endecott on. And at the weddings the guests sang psalms and got joyously high on sack-posset. The marriages of the most circumspect Puritan preachers and Puritan magistrates definitely did not turn out less fruitful than others'. And if Puritans demanded much of their children in the way of moral exactitude, it is the preachers and magistrates who remain most notable of all for tender and patient devotion to their children.

* * *

The ultimate modern model for the Massachusetts commonwealth of God was John Calvin's regime in Geneva nearly a century earlier. Both purported to reëstablish the pure Primitive Church of the Apostles, allowing only what the Bible expressly warranted—which would obviously make for a more drastic morality than Lutheranism, which allowed whatever the Bible did not expressly forbid. Many of the exiles from the persecution of England's Catholic queen Mary fled to Geneva and returned home schooled in the Calvinist system. The Pilgrims acknowledged the example of Calvin, and the Massachusetts Puritans acknowledged agreement with Calvinist tenets except for certain features of church organization. (William Bradford, *Of Plimmoth Plantation,* facsimile edition, London 1896, p. 27; *A Platform of Church-Discipline,* 1648, London 1653, pp. 1–2; Cotton Mather, *Magnalia,* V, part I, p. 3) Cotton Mather quotes John Cotton in a *Magnalia* sketch as saying that "he that has *Calvin* has them all," and "I love to sweeten my mouth with a piece of Calvin before I go to sleep." Jonathan Edwards says in the preface to his *Freedom of Will:*

I should not take it at all amiss to be called a *Calvinist* for distinction's sake; though I utterly disclaim a dependence on CALVIN, or believing the doctrines which I hold, because he believed and taught them.

Many American Puritans resembled Calvin in their academicism, their long training in both theology and law, their strict adherence to a Reformed church protected by the state, and in a gentleness of temper especially indulgent toward children. Calvin's kindliness notwithstanding, he had the tenacity to carry out what he conceived to be God's will whatever the consequences—just as he pursued the implications of Augustine's predestination to a pitiless conclusion because he would not flinch from the truth as he could find it. His city-state, in determining to bring God's will to familiar practice, fell into the same course of censoriousness and repressiveness as Massachusetts later, without wanting either of these by-products any more than the Puritans. The numerous fines and imprisonments for minor moral violations in Geneva show much the same pattern of practice and of partial-success, partial-failure as in Massachusetts. It is after all precisely the Calvinistic conception of the state as upholder of the church, summed up in the famous chapter 20, Book IV of the *Institutes of the Christian Religion,* that John Cotton enunciates (*The Keyes of the Kingdom,* 1644, p. 50) and that the Pilgrims exemplify as fully as the Puritans.

Calvin betrays what one often suspects of the American Puritans, that he deliberately bridled a stronger rather than weaker susceptibility to beauty. He said, for instance, that music had a secret and incredible power to move the human heart, and must therefore be approached with great caution. "Whatever music is composed only to please and delight the ear, is unbecoming the majesty of the Church, and cannot but be highly displeasing to God." (*Institutes,* tr. John Allen, 6th Am. edition, 1813, II, 118) Which would leave a wide latitude for musical immorality. Like the later Puritans in general, he put great store by gravity and dignity, words he used as characteristically as Cotton Mather.

Augustine, whom Calvin directly continues, had been as sensual as anyone who ever achieved sainthood. But the whole point of Augustine and Calvin had been to rise above the senses to a disembodied spiritual pleasure. Calvin says that God "enjoins the preservation of the mind chaste and pure from every libidinous desire" (*Ibid.*, 75), and in taking this direfully moralistic point of view he does not express an animus against the senses as bad but as inadequate or distracting in a Platonic quest for Absolute Beauty. He, too, gave very little of his over-all attention to petty morality; for the most part he preoccupied himself with the theologically momentous. His worst censoriousness came in defense of the holy Trinity, not of human chastity or sobriety.

Calvinism probably reflects the same kind of reaction to rapid economic changes and moral anarchy that both Lutheranism and English Puritanism reflect. Like them, Calvinism saw the situation in religious terms from a profoundly religious orientation, which amounts to much more than mechanical reaction to external stimuli. However this powerful mood or longing may be explained, it vastly transcended conventional morality both in impetus and objective. That morality remained much a matter of class can be seen in the French Calvinists, or Huguenots. They had such a large admixture of the nobility (who partly espoused Calvinism out of opposition to the king) as to be indistinguishable in morals from royal-Catholics, or in South Carolina from high-Anglicans.

English Puritanism was Calvinistic, beginning with the first English Puritan of distinction, the Cambridge scholar and professor Thomas Cartwright. But Calvinism and English Puritanism are not exactly synonymous. The first difference between them is that which would naturally be expected from differing periods and places, much as Calvin filled a need for further systematizing and definition of Protestantism than Luther felt in Germany a generation earlier. English Puritanism continued Calvin's legalistic tendency to a split hair, the colleges at Cambridge serving as the principal focus of analytical reinforcement. But the big men in Puritan theory—the professors William Perkins, Alexander Richardson, Richard Sibbs, Paul Baynes, and John Preston, et al.—are all closely identified with Covenant Congregationalism. Even Cartwright moved gradually from Presbyterian Puritanism to Congregationalism. Only Presbyterians, strictly speaking, could be called orthodox Calvinists in Great Britain. The other forms of Puritanism took their point of departure from Presbyterianism, which found itself in time surprisingly occupying a moderate middle position between high Anglicanism and Congregational Puritanism. Presbyterians remained within the episcopal Church of England though wishing to "reform" it the rest of the way. Finally they did Presbyterianize it for a while when Parliament triumphed over the king.

The Congregationalists, as their name signifies, wanted still another mode of organization wherein each congregation would be autonomous. One branch of them professed to remain within the English episcopacy like the Presbyterians, and are known as Independents or non-separating Congregationalists. Cromwell and the Massachusetts Puritans fell in this group. Another branch outrightly separated, including our Pilgrims who, however, had gravitated to a virtual non-separating Congregationalism by the time they sailed on the *Mayflower*. Which is one basic reason why the rigid Separatist Roger Williams could not maintain a permanent alliance either with the Pilgrims or the Bay Puritans.

Congregationalism, because it made for small, zealous, independent groups unresponsible to a higher restraining authority like an episcopacy or a presbytery, amounted in practice to an extremer Puritanism than orthodox Calvinism. But in its stress on the covenant doctrine as elaborately developed at Cambridge, it mitigated the awfulness of Calvin's stark predestination, turning his absolute Sovereign into a sort of constitutional Monarch. And the Cambridge Puritans took their inspiration more from Peter Ramus, the great professor at the University of Paris, and from Augustine than from Calvin. (See Champlin Burrage, *The Early English Dissenters,* 2 vols., Cambridge University 1912; Perry Miller, "The Marrow of Puritan Divinity," *Pubs.* Col. Soc. Mass., XXXII, 247–300; *The New England Mind: the Seventeenth Century,* Harvard 1939, chap. 1; *Orthodoxy in Massachusetts,*

Harvard 1933; and William Ames, *The Marrow of Sacred Divinity,* 1642.) Leonard Trinterud emphasizes a native tradition of Puritanism in England independent of and convergent with Calvinism. He also finds a more direct influence of the Rhineland than Geneva on focal figures like William Tyndale, who appears to have pioneered the covenant doctrine in England from Rhineland sources. ("The Origins of Puritanism," *Church History,* XX, 40–43, 48–55.)

The Congregational emphasis on the covenant (which also formed the constitution that brought the congregation into being as a church) helped break down the Calvinist insistence that man could do nothing about his eternal fate; and the whole American Puritan tradition, including Jonathan Edwards, turns out to be pulverized by the Arminianism it consistently assaulted.

This condition forms part of the story of a subtle switch that occurred in Congregationalism that reoriented its theology in God's love instead of God's sovereignty. (See John Robinson, *Observations Divine and Morall,* 1625, chap. 2; Jonathan Edwards, "Concerning the End for which God Created the World," *Two Dissertations,* 1765, pp. 109–12; "Treatise on Grace," in *Selections from the Unpublished Writings,* ed. A. B. Grosart, 1865, pp. 32–33, 36–37; *An Unpublished Essay on the Trinity,* ed. G. P. Fisher, 1903, pp. 79–107; etc.) The practical result of this switch for morality is that—to oversimplify—what Calvin promulgated out of duty the

Congregational Puritans promulgated out of love. We must not forget either the presence of lovingkindness in Calvin or a stout sense of duty in the New Englanders. But for all the freer wheeling of Congregationalism as against the presbyterial restraint of Calvinism, the moral coercion of the Bay had an unsuspected softening centrally within it.

Bibliography

Thomas Shepard, *Theses Sabbaticae or, The Doctrine of the Sabbath* (London, 1655).

James Savage, ed., *The History of New England from 1630 to 1649* [Winthrop's Journal], new edition, 2 vols. (Boston, 1853).

Records of the Governor and Company of the Massachusetts Bay in New England, Nathaniel B. Shurtleff, ed., 5 vols. (Boston, 1853).

Cotton Mather, *Magnalia Christi Americana: or, The Ecclesiastical History of New-England, from its First Planting in the Year 1620, unto the Year of Our Lord, 1698* (London, 1702).

——, *Manuductio ad Ministerium. Directions for a Candidate of the Ministry* (Boston, 1726).

Increase Mather, *Wo to Drunkards. Two Sermons Testifying against the Sin of Drunkenness: wherein the Wofulness of that Evil, and the Misery of All that are Addicted to it, is Discovered from the Word of God* (Cambridge, 1673).

——, *A Testimony against Several Prophane and Superstitious Customs, Now Practised by Some in New-England, the Evil Whereof is Evinced from the Holy Scriptures, and from the Writings Both of Ancient and Modern Divines* (London, 1687).

——, *Solemn Advice to Young Men, Not to Walk in the Wayes of their Heart, and in the Sight of their Eyes; but to Remember the Day of Judgment* (Boston, 1695).

Diary of Samuel Sewall, 3 vols., 5 MHS *Colls.,* V–VII.

Charles Chauncy, *Seasonable Thoughts on the State of Religion in New England, a Treatise in Five Parts* (Boston, 1743).

Jonathan Edwards, *Some Thoughts concerning the Present Revival of Religion in New-England, and the Way in which it Ought to be Acknowledged and Promoted, Humbly Offered to the Publick, in a Treatise on that Subject* (Boston, 1742).

Jasper Dankers and Peter Sluyter, *Journal of a Voyage to New York and a Tour in the Several of the American Colonies,* Henry C. Murphy, tr. and ed., *Memoirs* of the Long Island Hist. Soc., I (Brooklyn, 1867).

H. B. Parks, "Sexual Morals of the Great Awakening," *New England Quarterly,* III (Nov., 1930), pp. 133 *ff.*

Perry Miller, *The New England Mind from Colony to Province* (Harvard, 1953).

Carl Bridenbaugh, *Cities in the Wilderness: the First Century of Urban Life in America 1625–1742* (N.Y., 1938).

Alice Morse Earle, *Customs and Fashions in Old New England* (N.Y., 1893; reprint, 1914).

John Calvin, *Institutes of the Christian Religion,* tr. from the Latin and collated with the author's last edition in French by John Allen, 7th Am. ed. (Philadelphia, 1936).

Augustine, *Confessions.*

Cyclone Covey
Amherst College

Puritanism: *see* Moral Philosophy in America; Navaho Morals; Psychology and Morals; Quakerism, Classical, The Morality of.

Puritanism, English: *see* Green, T. H.

puritanism, political: *see* Marxist Theory of Morals; Soviet Morality, Current.

purity: *see* Hartmann, Nicolai; Hindu Ethics; Kant, I.; Liguori, St. Alphonsus and Catholic Moral Philosophy; Plato; Utilitarianism.

purpose: *see* Aquinas, Thomas, Moral Views of; ends; Hindu Ethics; Kant, I.

Q

Quakerism, Classical, The Morality of
  Quaker morality rests upon a double foundation: the teachings of Jesus as recorded in the New Testament and the revelations of the Inward Light, the Spirit or Word of God, present in every human soul. These two, if rightly understood, are consistent with each other since both come from God. The revelations of the Light or Inward Christ are needed in order to interpret and apply the teachings of the New Testament; and the New Testament is needed in order to provide an outward standard by which inward guidance may be checked and aided. But the inward is primary. Only through it can any outward authority be understood or accepted and only through it can new moral problems which are beyond the provisions of an accepted code of behavior be solved. The teachings of the New Testament are understood by Quakers as applying not to some future Kingdom of God to be miraculously created at the end of history, nor to life in heaven after death, nor to some monastic or special type of community shut off from an evil world, but to life as it is lived today by ordinary human beings. Needless to say this moral standard represents for members of the Society of Friends the goal which is to be striven toward, not a goal that has been reached. Nevertheless, it is believed that this goal can be reached or has been reached by many.

  The Society of Friends originated in England in the middle of the 17th century as a part of the religious revolution which accompanied and gave rise to the political revolution under Cromwell. But the Quakers believed that the English Reformation had not gone far enough and that it had taken a wrong turn. Though Puritanism meant the purification of Christianity by removal of all that had been added since the days of the primitive Church, the Puritans can not be said to have been primitive Christians. Unlike the early Christians, they depended more on a Book and less on the Divine Spirit revealing itself within the soul and through the inspired words of apostles and prophets. But even though Protestants professed to make the Book their guide they refused to be fully guided by it. For example, Christ said, "Swear not at all." The Quakers took this literally and were forced to undergo terrible consequences. The Protestant officials attempted to force the Quakers to take an oath in court and when they refused, they were imprisoned though guilty of no crime. In the same way most Christians failed to ac-

461

cept as a moral standard such teachings of Jesus as "Love your enemies," "Resist not evil," "Whosoever shall smite thee on thy right cheek turn to him the other also," "All they that take the sword shall perish with the sword," "If my kingdom were of this world then would my servants fight."

The early Quakers claimed that Protestants preferred an Old Testament morality based on the principle of legal justice, "an eye for an eye and a tooth for a tooth," but Jesus specifically went beyond this code and taught in its place another principle based on love and forgiveness.

The ethical teachings of Jesus concerned here and now the type of life and behavior appropriate to the Kingdom of Heaven, the ideal Divine-Human society. These teachings are valid whether final consummation of the Kingdom is thought of as achieved suddenly or gradually. He who follows these teachings of Jesus is already in God's Kingdom if he lives according to the spiritual and moral principles which characterize the Kingdom. Such a person is in the world but not of it, in the sense that he is not a part of corrupt, worldly human society but a member of a new holy society, which is not to be identified with any religious sect but is the Church invisible, the very body of Christ. He who so lives is "perfect" in the New Testament sense of that term. Any person can be free from a sense of guilt if he lives up to what he believes to be the Divine requirement. Such "perfectionism" was rejected by most Protestants. To them the ethical code of Christ seemed impractical in the present state of society. It could only prevail in the life to come or when Christ should reappear to set up his earthly Kingdom. Then love of enemies might not be too difficult for in reality there would be no enemies.

Quaker perfectionism not only admitted growth but required it. A child's perfection should develop into adult completion. The chief cause of moral growth is the presence of the Light Within, revealing new principles and new applications of old principles. Early Christianity, for example, did not condemn slavery, but eventually slavery was seen to be inconsistent with the teachings of Christ. In the Society of Friends slavery was tolerated for more than a century, though the Friends first set about freeing all their slaves more than a hundred years before the American Civil War. As men remain faithful to what light they have, more light will be vouch-safed them and their sensitivity to moral truth will become more keen. The result is moral progress.

Man is under obligation to follow the Light that he has, however dim that Light may be, but its dimness is due to his own shortcomings and not to the Light itself. Man's weaknesses and sins stand between him and the Light. They distort and hinder his vision. If the Light is a source of new and truer moral sensitivity it is not because the Light changes and gives new instructions, but because the Light, if not resisted, will penetrate and inform conscience which is the organ of moral insight. Conscience is partly conditioned by the influence of environment and education. Accordingly the requirements of conscience differ in individuals. The Divine Light shines into conscience and seeks to transform it but the Light does not wholly succeed because conscience is also influenced by the conventionalities and prejudices of society. Through prayer, worship, reading of religious literature and by means of other spiritual exercises conscience can become more sensitive to the revealed Will of God. For example, a young man may find that his conscience permits him to kill other men in battle but, as his religious life matures, he may discover that his conscience forbids it. Conscience affords a man's highest moral guidance. He must always obey it. As his conscience improves he will find it more closely in accord with the recorded teachings of Jesus. The Light or Inward Christ and the Outward Christ are one.

There is a third basis for Quaker morality in addition to the teachings of Jesus and the Inward Light. This can be termed philosophic or rational. Such is the belief that all men are fundamentally one. The Light is not divided in such a way that part is in one man and part in another. In classical Quakerism the word "spark" is not used to designate the Light. The entire Light, or Word or Spirit which comes out from God and creates the world and which is God Himself is present in every man. This is the vine of which we are all branches. It is the center of the circle of which all are radii. As we draw nearer to Him we approach nearer to one another. The Light is therefore the Source of Unity. In silent worship the Quaker seeks to become aware of and to commune with the one Life which is the ground of all our separate lives. In that communion certain moral truths related to the need of realizing unity and overcoming conflict among men become evident. Because this unity exists in the depths it is also possible on the surface of life. However degraded a man may appear to be, it is always possible to appeal to him to heed that within which speaks to him with the same Voice that speaks to all men. By using this peaceful method a bond of unity is discovered. Violence creates disunity. All acts of high moral value are in some sense the expression of a deep underlying human unity and all immoral acts express some form of superficial disunity. Hence the basis of morality is belief in and obedience to the one Divine Life in which we all "live and move and have our being." George Fox, the founder of the Society of Friends, wrote to Friends advising them "to walk cheerfully over the earth answering that of God in every man."

The Quaker religion was from the first directed quite as much toward social reform as toward individual salvation. Fox did not intend to be the founder of a sect. He felt himself to be the prophet of a new age. At the very beginning of his ministry, as he writes in his journal, "he was sorely exercised in going to their courts to cry for justice and speaking and writing to judges and justices to do justly." He preached often against the callous brutality of the criminal law which hung a man for a trifling theft. Letters were addressed to merchants and magistrates containing plans for improving the lot of the poor. An early appeal of Fox for commercial honesty (1661) was entitled "The Line of Righteousness and Justice stretched forth over all Merchants." This became a standard for Quaker business ethics and was read to Quaker meetings once a year. Emphasis on social responsibility as an integral part of religion has been characteristic of Friends. An early Quaker work (1660) entitled "An Appeal to the Parliament concerning the Poor that there not be a Beggar in England" contained various suggestions for social reform. Sensitivity to the needs of others extended even to the animal world. Hunting or killing for sport was severely condemned. The Quakers were kept busy relieving the poverty of their own members because of losses through fines and imprisonment. This effort was also extended far beyond the Quaker community through the devotion of many generations of Quaker philanthropists. Perhaps the most systematic attempt to deal with social problems was made by John Bellers (1654–1725), pioneer of modern Christian Socialism, who was cited by Karl Marx as a "veritable phenomenon in the history of political economy." Bellers' careful plans for providing work and security for the poor had far reaching consequences.

In the voluminous writings of the early Friends there are few references to the fate of their own souls or the souls of others in a life hereafter. The emphasis was on obedience to the Divine Will here and now and the kind of action resulting from such obedience. Disobedience, Friends believed, produced an inner sense of tension and discomfort, a division of the soul between forces from above pulling in one direction and forces from below pulling in the opposite direction. Peace of mind results from obedience to the Divine Will by which the soul becomes unified with the highest that it can realize. This inner sense of peace is an important moral test. If a Friend rose in a meeting for business to advocate a certain course of action he frequently began by saying "I would feel most comfortable if . . ." When John Woolman persuaded slave holders to give up their slaves he did not speak much about the sufferings of the slaves or the injustices of slavery. He simply asked "Does it make thee feel comfortable to keep these Negroes in bondage?" The slaveholder was forced to admit that he did not feel comfortable.

Since religion and morality have been so closely integrated, the Society of Friends has produced few writers who devoted themselves exclusively to morality. The most important Quaker moralist was Jonathan Dymond whose *Essays on the Principles of Morality* first appeared in 1829. These essays passed through many editions and were used throughout the 19th century as a text book in Quaker schools. Dymond declares that "the communicated will of God is the final standard of right and wrong." By this he means direct and immediate communication, given to all men and not to Christians only. The New Testament is accepted by Dymond as a communication of God's will, but not as a set of rules to be blindly obeyed. The Scriptures must be understood in the light of the immediate divine communication. Other ethical systems, particularly utilitarianism, are discussed at length and rejected. In Dymond's discussion of specific moral problems he takes issue with many conventional judgments of his time and presents a point of view in advance of his day. He rejected the current classical educational curriculum and advocated methods now generally accepted.

A chronological record of Quaker morality appears in the consecutive Books of Discipline issued by Yearly Meetings of the Society of Friends over the period of 300 years. A Yearly Meeting includes all Quakers resident within a limited geographical area. Under the title *Book of Extracts* the early Quaker manuals of Christian practice gathered up in manuscript form the "minutes" or decisions of a given Yearly Meeting concerning behavior. Eighteenth century *Book of Extracts* record the growth of moral insights, new provisions being added from time to time. The most informing portion is the "Queries," a series of questions which are considered once a year. They are a means of confronting the membership with the whole code of Quaker morality and of estimating the degree of adherence to it. It is significant that these are put in the form of questions rather than of moral rules. Rules,

like creeds, tend to become formal and to arrest development.

The moral principles characteristic of the Society of Friends are generally referred to today as "the social testimonies." Sometimes they have been called the "minor testimonies," the major testimonies being the doctrine of the Inward Light, and the principles that govern the public meeting for worship and the meeting for transaction of the business of the church. These two meetings are special communities in which the social testimonies are embodied through the relationships of the members with each other. The meeting itself exists as a kind of training ground for life outside the meeting. In the meeting for worship or for business there is 1) equality of opportunity to participate, 2) simplicity and sincerity in the sense that no words, rituals or actions are prescribed in advance which may not be, at a given time, genuine expressions of inward states, 3) an effort of each individual to adjust his own attitudes and opinions to those of others, without overcoming his fellow members by individual authority or by majority rule through voting, and 4) care extended equally to any who may be in need, spiritual, intellectual, or economic. These four moral principles may be summarized as Equality, Simplicity, Harmony and Community. We shall discuss a few of their applications to areas outside the meeting.

Equalitarianism appears to have been the earliest social testimony. Some Quakers were equalitarians before they became pacifists and were dismissed from Cromwell's army because they refused the customary deference to their officers. From the beginning men and women were on terms of complete equality in the vocal ministry. The long hard struggle for religious liberty in England and America which produced so many Quaker martyrs was based on the concept of equality of opportunity as well as the insistence upon religious sincerity. The Quakers refused to use words which recognized class distinctions. This made them appear ill-mannered and aroused antagonism, especially on the part of judges and officials. Since the plural pronoun was used to superiors and the singular "thou" to inferiors, the Quakers used only "thou." The inferior word was chosen as less likely to flatter. For the same reason they refused to take off their hats or bow even before the King. They used no expressions such as "Mister" or "Mistress," "Your honour," "Your humble servant," "The Reverend," not only because these titles recognized class distinctions but because they flattered the person addressed and were in many cases thought to be untrue. Equality has not meant equality of economic status. Each person was expected to follow a vocation or call, appropriate to his ability and interest. But no calling was considered inferior or superior to any other calling. Equality meant equality in respect. The master remained a master and the servant a servant but the master must treat the servant as an equal. The three centuries of Quaker educational work

for Negroes and Indians is one expression of this social testimony.

In their doctrine of *Simplicity* the Quakers agreed with the Puritans. Like the Puritans they condemned elaborate dress, luxurious living and "worldly" amusements, under which they classed such arts as music, the theatre, and literary fiction. It should, however, be noted that in many cases the basis of the Quaker condemnation was somewhat different from that of the Puritans. The Puritans desired to "mortify the flesh" in order that the soul might not become too much attached to this earthly existence. The Quakers were interested in the removal of superfluities which absorbed unnecessary time and made work. They also wanted to eliminate what could not be rated as completely sincere and genuine. Partly in consequence of fashions of the day, art of all kinds appeared frivolous, unnecessary and untrue to life. Science, on the other hand, seemed close to reality. Therefore, science became the hobby or profession of many Friends. Modern Friends have more clearly understood that art has its own peculiar form of truth. Hymns and collective readings were omitted from public worship as putting into the worshipper's mouth words not necessarily an expression of his feelings at the time. The formulation and recital of creeds was avoided for the same reason. Simplicity in speech in the sense of eliminating unnecessary or untrue words was striven for to such an extent that humorous stories about old-time Quakers are often based on extreme instances of this peculiarity. Modern

Friends neglect this testimony against verbalism. Quaker merchants were the first to adopt the one price system. They were unwilling to state a price higher than that which they would ultimately accept. Virtue in this case led to prosperity. But Quaker merchants generally would not sell goods which they could not conscientiously use themselves. This was a financial hardship. Such trades as that of tailor, silversmith, printer, book seller and funeral director were difficult for Friends, as they could not depend exclusively on a Quaker clientele.

The Quakers, along with the Puritans, are accredited with responsibility for the rise of capitalism. There is some truth in this theory. Like the Puritans, they exalted diligence in business, but did not esteem it a virtue to spend what was earned. On the other hand, the Quaker autobiographies give many examples of deliberate reduction of business for religious reasons. This was particularly necessary in the Quaker Society since the ministry and affairs of the church were carried on by nonprofessionals. It was important that the claims of business should not interfere with religious duties. Some Friends condemned superfluity of possessions on other grounds. For example, John Woolman found in the desire for possessions the seed of war.

Friends are best known for their refusal to take part in war. Perhaps this arises from the fact that the peace testimony is the one which has, as yet, been the least generally accepted. In every war some Friends have volunteered as soldiers, but no regularly constituted body of Friends has ever endorsed participation in war or the preparation for war. Friends have not objected to some use of force by parents, police or others if restraint is exercised sympathetically on behalf of the offender as well as of society. They would stop at the taking of life for any reason whatever and they consistently oppose capital punishment. The object of punishment should be reformation of the criminal, not revenge or fear. The prisons of early Pennsylvania under Quaker government were the first to operate on the principle of reformation. For this reason they became models for prisons in other countries.

Many Christians today are willing to say, as the "First Assembly of the World Council of Churches" said at Amsterdam in 1948, that "war is contrary to the will of God . . . and the teachings of Christ," but they add that man is a sinner and war must sometimes be chosen as a lesser evil than submission to tyranny. The Quakers believe there is a third choice better than either fighting or submitting which may indeed involve suffering and loss of outward freedom, but which preserves inward freedom, integrity, and loyalty to conscience. Man is never forced to sin. Recognition of the claims of government is in most cases a virtue but, when the government demands an immoral action, it should be disobeyed. This is not belief in anarchy. During American colonial days the Quakers for a period of time controlled the governments of five colonies, Pennsylvania, Rhode Island,

467

New Jersey, Delaware and North Carolina. They were able to govern in a fair degree of consistency with their principles. These principles, more than those embodied in the theocracy of New England or the aristocracy of the South, influenced the character of the Constitution of the United States of America and the ideal of the American State. The Quaker colonies were unlike the others in not having had a state-supported church.

This third still controversial testimony in favor of harmony has led to social pioneering. The use of non-violent methods in mental hospitals, prisons and schools initiated by Quakers in the eighteenth century has become generally accepted. That violent methods are also out of date in settling international disputes is becoming increasingly evident.

Under the fourth moral principle here labelled *Community,* are included efforts to view society in terms of one family in which it is natural to relieve poverty, misfortune and injustice. Here the Quakers stress the "social gospel," which every Christian body subscribes to, in some degree. That all men are children of one Divine Father is a doctrine which few Christians would deny. Whatever is unique in Quakerism in the field of social service arises from Quaker pacifism. Being unable to take part in war, members of the Society of Friends feel a special sense of obligation to heal the wounds of war and overcome hatreds generated by war. In every war in the Western world during the past three centuries the Quakers have been active in relief work both during and after the fighting. If possible, help is given to both sides of the conflict. Overcoming hatred and the misunderstandings which result from war or which may become causes of war is an educational process. The whole of Quaker life and Quaker religious organisation is in theory at least an effort to achieve harmony. There are also specific efforts carried on with a view to peace such as institutes, so-called seminars, work camps and conferences of an international character. This educational process is based on an important moral principle. It is believed that men are more inclined to good than to evil and that, if opportunities are afforded for personal acquaintance, eventual understanding and friendship will result. This belief has been justified by experience.

The Society of Friends does not offer any theory of an ideal social order which would involve revolutionary change from the present social order but many of its members seek to promote a slow change which will modify the harsh competition of the capitalistic system and introduce cooperation. The following query indicates the hoped-for direction of advance, "What are you doing as individuals and as a meeting to create a social and economic system which will so function as to sustain and enrich life for all?"

It is evident that the basis of Quaker morality is closer to what is sometimes called intuitionism than it is to utilitarianism, self-realization, reverence for life and other ethical systems. Modern Quakers sometimes speak of "reverence for personality" as a basis for morality but this expression or its equivalent cannot be found in classical Quakerism. Quakers believe that the dictates of conscience must be followed regardless of apparent consequences. Though the consequences of good actions are always good, the ultimate consequence of any action cannot be discerned by our human finite minds. Hence something more is needed than a knowledge of immediate results. The pragmatic test is useful but not sufficient. The same may be said regarding the rational test. Robert Barclay, the great Quaker Apologist, points out that many evil acts recorded in history, such as the tortures of the Inquisition, have been based on careful reasoning. Reason is useful in determining the consistency of a proposed action with actions already accepted as right but reason, to be creative and to lead man beyond conventionalities and accepted opinions, must be so inspired and transformed by the Inward Light that man may sometimes be led to do what seems unreasonable even to himself. Our ultimate dependence is upon moral insight. Man possesses a sense of judging what is good or evil just as he possesses a sense for judging what is beautiful or ugly or what is pleasant or unpleasant. But this moral sense must be continually cultivated and improved so that it becomes increasingly able to perceive what is Absolutely Right. The Quakers are not moral relativists. Cultivation of the moral sense takes place through a reverent reading of the New Testament and other inspired writings and through prayer and worship as man seeks to commune with the Divine Spirit of Truth. Religion is therefore the basis of Quaker morality.

Bibliography

George Fox, *Journal* (First Edition, 1694; Latest Edition, 1952).

Robert Barclay, *Apology for the True Christian Divinity* (1676 and later editions).

John Woolman, *Journal* (First Edition, 1775; Latest Edition, 1950).

Thomas Clarkson, *A Portraiture of Quakerism* (1806 and later editions).

Jonathan Dymond, *Essays on the Principles of Morality* (1829 and later editions).

William C. Braithwaite, *The Beginnings of Quakerism* (1912).

——, *The Second Period of Quakerism* (1919).

Rufus M. Jones, *The Quakers in the American Colonies* (1923).

——, *The Later Periods of Quakerism* (1921).

Margaret E. Hirst, *The Quakers in Peace and War* (1923).

Auguste Jorns, *The Quakers as Pioneers in Social Work* (1931).

A. Ruth Fry, *Quaker Ways* (1933).

Arnold Lloyd, *Quaker Social History* (1950).

John Kavanaugh, *The Quaker Approach* (1953).

Howard H. Brinton, *Friends for 300 Years* (1952).

Howard H. Brinton
Pendle Hill Graduate School of
Religious and Social Study

quarreling: *see* Tapirapé Morals, Some Aspects of.

quarrelsomeness: *see* Aztec Morals; Zuni Indians, Morals of.

question-answer method: *see* Freud, Sigmund.

quibbling: *see* Sophists, the.

quietism: *see* Muslim Morals.

Qur'ān: *see* Muslim Morals; Riffian Morals.

R

rabbinic law: *see* Jewish Ethics and Its Civilization.

rabbis: *see* Jewish Ethics and Its Civilization.

Radek: *see* Soviet Morality, Current.

rage: *see* Augustine and Morals; Dante, Alighieri.

Ramus, Peter: *see* Puritan Morals.

Rank, Otto: *see* Freud, Sigmund.

rape: *see* Zuni Indians, Morals of.

Rappists: *see* Schopenhauer, Arthur.

Rashdall, H.: *see* Price, Richard; Ross, Sir (William) David; Utilitarianism.

Rashnŭ: *see* Zoroastrian Morals.

rational appetite: *see* Aquinas, Thomas, Moral Views of.

rational ethics: *see* Aristotle; Major Ethical Viewpoints; Plato; rationalism; Socrates.

rationalism: *see* Balguy, John; Clarke, Samuel; Cooper, Anthony Ashley; Cudworth, Ralph; Hobbes, Thomas; Kant, I.; Major Ethical Viewpoints; More, Henry; Price, Richard; Reid, Thomas; Spinoza; Wollaston, William.

rationalistic intuitionism: *see* intuition, rational; Price, Richard.

Raymund of Penafort: *see* Jesuits, the, Moral Theology of.

realism, ethical: *see* Hartmann, Nicolai.

realists: *see* Moral Philosophy in America.

realization feeling: *see* Schlick, Moritz.

reason: *see* Aquinas, Thomas, Moral Views of; Balguy, John; Clarke, Samuel; Cudworth, Ralph; Cumberland, Richard; Hegel, G. W. F.; Hobbes, Thomas; Jesuits, the, Moral Theology of; Jewish Ethics and Its Civilization; Kant, I.; Language and Ethics; Major Ethical Viewpoints; Meta-ethics and Normative Ethics; Moral Philosophy in America; More, Henry; practical reason; Prichard, H. A.; Quakerism, Classical, The Morality of; Reid, Thomas; Sophists, the; Spinoza; Stoics, the; theoretical reason; Zoroastrian Morals.

reason and faith: *see* Kierkegaard, Soren.

reasonableness: *see* Balguy, John.

rebellion: *see* Augustine and Morals.

rebirth: *see* Zoroastrian Morals.

rebirth and renewal: *see* Dostoyevsky, Fyodor.

Rechbites: *see* Jewish Ethics and Its Civilization.

reciprocity: *see* China, Moral Philosophies of.

recognition: *see* Hindu Ethics.

reconstruction: *see* Major Ethical Viewpoints; Morals and Religion; Psychology and Morals.

recreation: *see* Puritan Morals.

redemption: *see* Hegel, G. W. F.; Hindu Ethics.

Redemptorist Congregation: *see* Liguori, St. Alphonsus and Catholic Moral Philosophy.

redirection: *see* Morals and Religion.

reflex: *see* Liguori, St. Alphonsus and Catholic Moral Philosophy.

reform: *see* Morals and Religion.

reformation (personal): *see* Hammurapi, Code of; Quakerism, Classical, The Morality of.

reformers, social: *see* Hindu Ethics.

refutation of psychological egoism: *see* Butler, Joseph.

regeneration: *see* Moral Philosophy in America; Soloviev, Wladimir.

regulations: *see* Jewish Ethics and Its Civilization; Muslim Morals.

Reid, Thomas

Thomas Reid was born April 26, 1710 at Strachan, Scotland. He attended the parish school of Kincardine before going to the University of Aberdeen. He entered Marischal College in 1722 at twelve years of age and graduated four years later. He was then appointed librarian of the university and held that post for ten years, pursuing his studies in classical literature and also making a careful study of mathematics, concentrating on Newton's *Principia*. Visits to London, Oxford and Cambridge during this period introduced important variety into his life and greater intellectual stimulation into his studies. His frequent references to the blind mathematician, Saunderson, derive from these visits. In 1737 he was presented by King's College, Aberdeen, to the ministry of New Machar, an instance of the Scottish theory of closely connecting College and Church. He was not well received at first, but his conscientiousness and kindness soon improved his relationships with the parishioners. His marriage to Elizabeth Reid, a cousin, in 1740, in turn added, by association, to his popularity because of her help to the sick and poor. In 1752 he was elected professor of philosophy in King's College. He introduced major revisions into the curriculum, and was instrumental in founding the Aberdeen Philosophical Society, where he presented many papers which were afterward developed into his books on the human mind. In 1763 he accepted the professorship of moral philosophy in the University of Glasgow. His instruction was primarily devoted to the intellectual and active powers of man, but he also worked out a system of ethics which included general views on jurisprudence and principles of politics. He continued teaching at Glasgow for the greater part of the remainder of his life, the main body of his publications coming during this period. He died October 7, 1796.

Reid's first published work in philosophy was an essay criticizing Hutcheson's attempt to introduce the mathematical mode of reasoning into moral subjects. His main stimulus to philosophical thought, however, as in the case of Kant, came as a reaction to Hume. Briefly stated, his reaction developed into an epistemological system based upon a denial of the theory of representative perception (the "theory of ideas," as Reid put it) and an acceptance of "common sense," the latter, as might be expected, taking different forms in different parts of his system. Reid in fact thought of his philosophy as an attempt to "re-establish experience" after the attacks of Hume. Although he set out to refute Hume's sceptical empiricism he did not fall into an extreme rationalism, but rejected both extremes equally. He anticipated his more famous successor, Kant, in maintaining that the pre-analytic data of experience are complex unifications of sensation and judgment. He therefore, like Kant, needed to identify components of knowledge that were not the resultants, either of experience or reason, yet were necessary for experience and reason. In Reid's assertion that there are such principles underlying experience and reason he also asserts that they are necessary for conduct:

A due attention to these two opinions which govern the belief of all men [that sensible qualities must have a subject which we call body, and that thought must have a subject we call mind], even sceptics in the practice of life, would probably have led [Locke] to perceive that sensation and consciousness are not the only sources of human knowledge, and that there are principles of belief in human nature of which we can give no other account but that they necessarily result from the constitution of our faculties; and that, if it were in our power to throw off their influence upon our practice and conduct, we would neither speak nor act like reasonable men. (*Essays on the Intellectual Powers of Man,* ed., A. D. Woozley, p. 397.)

Reid believes that there are some general characteristics of all first principles; for example: that all knowledge got by reasoning is built on first principles; that these principles yield conclusions from the lowest to the highest degree of probability; that agreement about first principles can be reached, e.g., by an appeal to the majority when local and temporary prejudices are removed, by the use of ridicule (when opinions contradict first principles), by the use of *argumentum ad hominem,* reduction *ad absurdum,* and appeal to agreement of all ages (with special attention to the significance of common speech), by noting whether the belief appears before education, and by noting its necessity in reasonable practices in living. He lists twelve "First Principles of Contingent Truth." These include:

1. Everything of which I am conscious exists.
3. Those things did really happen which I distinctly remember.
4. Our own personal identity continues as far back as we remember anything distinctly.
6. We have some degree of power over our actions.
7. The natural faculties by which we distinguish truth from error are not fallacious.
9. Certain features of the countenance, sounds of the voice and gestures of the body, indicate certain thoughts and dispositions of the mind.
10. There is a certain regard due to human testimony in matters of fact, and even to human authority, in matters of opinion.

473

12. In the phenomena of nature what is to be will probably be like unto what has been in similar circumstances.

He lists six categories of "First Principles of Necessary Truths:" grammatical, logical, mathematics, taste, morals, and metaphysics. Of these we may notice the first principles of morals which he divides into three categories, general, specific and "resolving:"

General Principles:

1. There are some things in human conduct that merit approbation and praise, others that merit blame and punishment; in different degrees.
2. What is in no degree voluntary can neither deserve moral approbation nor blame.
3. What is done from unavoidable necessity may be agreeable or disagreeable, useful or hurtful, but cannot be the object either of blame or of moral approbation.
4. Men may be highly culpable in omitting what they ought to have done, as well as in doing what they ought not.
5. We ought to use the best means we can to be well informed of our duty by serious attention to moral instruction; by observing what we approve by reflecting often in a calm and dispassionate hour, on our own past conduct; by deliberating coolly and impartially upon our future conduct as far as we can foresee the opportunities we may have of doing good or temptations of doing wrong.
6. It ought to be our most serious concern to do our duty as far as we know it, and to fortify our minds against every temptation to deviate from it.

Specific Principles:

1. We ought to prefer a greater good, though more distant, to a less; and a less evil to a greater.
2. As far as the intention of nature appears in the constitution of man we ought to comply with that intention.
3. No man is born to himself alone; therefore, every man ought to consider himself as a member of the common society of mankind and of those subordinate societies to which he belongs, such as family, friends, and neighborhood, country, and to do as much good as he can, and as little harm to the societies of which he is a part.
4. In every case we ought to act that part towards another which we would judge to be right in him to act toward us, if we were in his circumstances and he in ours. If there be any such thing as right and wrong in the conduct of moral agents it must be the same to all in the same circumstances.
5. To every man who believes the existence, the perfections, and the providence of God, the veneration and submission we owe to him is self-evident.

First Principles in Cases of Conflicts:

1. Unmerited generosity should yield to gratitude, and both to justice.
2. Unmerited beneficence to those who are at ease should yield to compassion to the miserable; and external acts of piety to works of mercy.
3. Acts of virtue which ought to yield in the case of a competition have more intrinsic worth when there is no competition; thus there is more worth in pure unmerited benevolence than in compassion, more in compassion than in gratitude, and more in gratitude than in justice.

474

Reid classifies these first principles of morals as necessary principles because "They are matters of judgment." In making the distinction between them and first principles of contingent truth he seems to have in mind, although he does not explicitly assert this, the distinction between principles that are logically necessary and principles that can be considered true on the basis of factual evidence. In view of the distinction which Reid draws between practical reason and theoretical reason, it is interesting to note that he does not provide a class of "practically necessary principles" into which the first principles of morals would fit. All the materials for this development are present in Reid, even his most characteristic doctrine, his appeal to "common sense," fitting into it.

He makes an explicit distinction between theoretical and practical reason:

To judge of what is true or false in speculative points, is the office of speculative reason; and to judge of what is good or ill for us on the whole, is the office of practical reason. (*Essays on the Active Powers of Man*, Essay III, Part III, Ch. 2.)

In his discussion of general characteristics of first principles he offers a criterion of a practical principle:

. . . when an opinion is so necessary in the conduct of life that, without the belief of it, a man must be led into a thousand absurdities in practice; such an opinion, when we can give no other reason for it, may safely be taken for a first principle. (*Essays on the Intellectual Powers of Man*, ed. Woozley, p. 372.)

If we now notice what Reid says about the function of common sense we find it similar to, in some cases identical with, practical reason. One of the chief activities attributed to common sense by Reid is the awareness of first principles. Reid holds that an "inward light" of good sense is given to every man, although in different degrees. Reid justifies the term "common sense" because such an "inward light" is common to all men who can be considered responsible for their conduct or with whom it is possible to transact business. It is the degree of understanding that makes it possible for a man to act from prudence and to distinguish truth from falsity in matters that are self-evident. It is what makes each man a competent judge of the first principles of any subject matter, so long as they are clearly conceived. This accounts, often, for the termination of an argument by appealing to common sense. 'Common sense' properly means 'common judgment.' There is no opposition between common sense and reason. The province of common sense is "to judge of things self-evident." (Reid explains a self-evident proposition as one that may, logically, be false, but which is obvious to common sense—which one could not bring himself seriously to disbelieve.) This branch or degree of reason is properly called common sense because in many men no other degree of reason is to be found. It is the minimal condition of being a rational creature. It is naturally given or not had at all, in this respect differing from the other branch or degree of reason by which deductions are drawn from first principles. Deductive reasoning can be improved by education, not common sense, although common sense is a necessary condition of deductive reasoning. Finally, common sense more frequently functions in refutation than in confirmation. For example, if a mathematician in some intricate demonstration, by taking one false step, comes to the conclusion that two things equal to a third are not equal to each other, a man of common sense is entitled to reject the conclusion, although he cannot claim to judge the processes of demonstration.

It is in terms of common sense that Reid claims to know the first principles of morals that have been enumerated: They have an intuitive evidence which he cannot resist. He can express them in other words, illustrate them by examples, and perhaps deduce one from another; but he cannot deduce them from other principles that are more self-evident.

When we turn from the metaphysical and epistemological foundations of Reid's ethical theory to the doctrines themselves we find, not surprisingly, considerable agreement with other doctrines in the western tradition.

The rational principles of action (as opposed to mechanical principles, e.g., habit, and animal principles, e.g., appetite) are prudence and duty. Prudence is regard for our own good on the whole; duty is too simple for definition. It can only be explained by synonyms. Duty cannot be resolved into self-interest. This is supported by common language as well as by other facts: When we disregard our interests we are called "foolish," when we disregard our honor we are called "vicious." Concern for honor is not merely concern for our reputation (self-interest) since it operates whether our reputation is involved or not. These principles are a result of the operation of common sense. In such a capacity Reid refers to common sense variously as conscience, moral sense, reason, moral faculty. He justifies each name by appealing to common usage, particularly emphasizing that in common usage 'moral sense' implies reasoning more than feeling. The operation of the moral sense accounts for our sense of duty, our conceptions of right and wrong, merit and demerit; also for our perception of these qualities in human conduct.

Conscience comes to maturity by degrees. It is peculiar to man, animals lacking it. It is evidently intended to direct our conduct. It is both an intellectual and an active power, that is, one that accounts both for the perception (understanding, recognition) of moral qualities and the impetus to action. He recognizes that conscience may make mistakes, but holds that it is morally right to act in accordance with such mistakes. With the exception of the fifth specific principle of morals (veneration of God if one believes in His existence) and the three principles in cases of conflict, Reid's doctrine of conscience does not provide definite guidance for conduct. And although he claims that the first principles enable the deduction of specific duties, he does not provide such deductions, even in his discussions of "The Liberty of Moral Agents," "Systems of Morals," "Systems of Natural Jurisprudence" or the "Nature and Obligation of a Contract." The fact is that Reid did not consider it necessary or important to work out a detailed system of morality since, by an easy transition, he held that we know not only the first principles of morality by the moral faculty, but also particular instances of morality. Therefore, all that is necessary to know what is right and wrong is to listen to one's conscience, moral sense, moral faculty, moral sentiments, or reason.

In relation to his predecessors Reid stands between the rationalism of such men as Samuel Clarke and William Wollaston, on the one hand, and the empiricism of such men as Hutcheson and Hume, on the other. He argues against Hume (and, implicitly, against Hutcheson) that having a pleasant feeling and approving conduct are different; and supports the denial by appealing to common linguistic usage which distinguishes between them. He further supports the distinction by pointing out that it is quite acceptable to doubt whether an act is worthy of moral approval, but insulting to doubt a man who is reporting how he feels about an act. He criticizes Hume's doctrine that reason is the slave of the passion by pointing out that Hume reaches his conclusion by defining 'passion' so it denotes every principle of action. The doctrine is therefore a mere tautology based upon a definition that violates common usage. In opposition, he asserts that morally significant feelings are dependent upon judgment or knowledge. After all the facts are gathered, not merely a feeling remains to be had in order to pronounce the act morally good or bad, a judgment remains to be made; in particular, whether the act in question ought to be done. Furthermore, fact and common language both support a distinction between two principles of action. Passions are violent and disorderly, reason is calm and orderly. Action in accordance with the first principles of morals, therefore, is rational action and such principles are rational principles of action; and the motivating factor is reason, rather than emotion. On this basis Reid also denies Hume's doctrine that our ends are determined by our passions and asserts that they are discovered by, and pursued because of, practical reason. This is simply common sense as an intellectual and active power of the human mind.

Although Reid is critical of the empiricists he is not therefore ready to embrace an extreme rationalism: Although the moral faculty is reason, this term being condoned by common usage, it is not deductive reason. We do not, for example, arrive at any knowledge of obligation deductively. Being subject to an obligation depends upon the nature of the person and the circumstances he is in. The circumstances and the relations can be known only by empirical observation. Therefore it is impossible correctly to consider morality a deductive system.

477

Furthermore, if morality depended upon accurate deductive reasoning, few men would be moral. Yet many men who are incapable of accurate deductive reasoning know perfectly well what their moral obligations are, and in most cases act in accordance with such knowledge.

Reid's position in relation to the rationalists and empiricists has been put neatly in three syllogisms (A. N. Prior, *Logic and the Basis of Ethics*): The position of the early rationalists (e.g., Samuel Clarke) can be presented as:

> All things discoverable by reason are capable of proof.
> All ethical precepts are discoverable by reason.
> Therefore: All ethical precepts are capable of proof.

The position of Hutcheson and Hume can be presented as:

> All things discoverable by reason are capable of proof.
> Not all ethical precepts are capable of proof.
> Therefore: Not all ethical precepts are discoverable by reason.

Reid's position differs from both:

> Not all ethical precepts are capable of proof.
> All ethical precepts are discoverable by reason.
> Therefore: Not all things discoverable by reason are capable of proof.

Unfortunately Reid's final position is not so clear-cut as this presentation suggests. This is due largely to the looseness and ambiguity with which he uses the terms 'reason,' 'common sense,' 'practical reason,' and 'conscience.' At one place or another in his writings the following senses of these phrases occur: the mind in its empirical aspect, in which data of the several senses are combined as a knowledge of objects; perception of self-evident principles; taking for granted immediately and unreflectively; principles accepted as true by all competent men at all times; principles that it is necessary to accept practically in order to live satisfactorily; the general opinions of mankind as expressed in ordinary language; the facts of reality as expressed in language; a body of statements generally accepted as true, although not demonstratively true; the principle of self-evidence underlying those statements; the power of the mind to recognize the truth of those statements. With such a range of meanings it is not surprising that readers complain that it is difficult to pin Reid down on a given point. In addition to the vagueness, there are cases of verbal inconsistency and possibly doctrinal inconsistency, e.g., in his saying that common sense is native and uninstructable, identifying common sense and conscience, and saying that conscience is instructable. It is difficult, however, to assert flatly that Reid is actually inconsistent because he emphasizes different facets of common sense, reason, or conscience in various places in his writings, depending upon the argument in question.

The tendency to shift between the

concepts of reason, common sense, or conscience as rational intuition and as immediate unreflective acceptance of a statement leads him to hold that we know general principles of morals in the same way we are aware of particular instances, say, of obligation. He was aware, however, even though vaguely, that this doctrine was unsatisfactory because in his attempt to explicate it he drew an analogy between sense perception and recognition of an instance of obligation. In suggesting the analogy, he emphasized that the point of similarity was the unreflective acceptance of the instance as one falling under a general principle. Also it is possible to find suggestions in his description of the nature of first principles, particularly "first practical principles," that there is an element of decision, affected by reasoning and reflection but not fully explicable in terms of reasoning and reflection. These suggestions, not fully worked out by Reid, are currently receiving detailed attention from such writers as Toulmin, Hampshire, Hare, Frankena and Aiken. When these considerations are combined with Reid's strong appeal to ordinary language as an important, though partial, arbiter of philosophical opinion, it is plain that he marks an important development in ethical theory that has had a continuing, though perhaps indirect, influence.

Bibliography

Thomas Reid, "An Essay on Quantity; occasioned by reading a treatise [Hutcheson's *Inquiry*] in which simple and compound ratios are applied to virtue and merit," *Philosophical Transactions of the Royal Society* (London), Vol. 45 (1748).

——, *An Inquiry into the Human Mind on the Principles of Common Sense* (Edinburgh, 1764).

——, *Essays on the Intellectual Powers of Man* (Edinburgh, 1785).

——, *Essays on the Active Powers of Man* (Edinburgh, 1788).

——, *Philosophical Orations* (Aberdeen, 1753).

——, "Observations on the Danger of Political Innovation," *Glasgow Courier* (December 18, 1794).

Joseph Priestley, *An Examination of Dr. Reid's Philosophy* (London, 1774).

J. F. Ferrier, "Reid and the Philosophy of Common Sense," *Blackwood's Magazine* (Edinburgh, 1847).

Sir W. Hamilton, (Ed.), *The Works of Thomas Reid* (Edinburgh, 1872).

James McCosh, *The Scottish Philosophy* (New York, 1875), Article 26.

J. Seth, "Reid's Moral Philosophy," *The Philosophical Review*, Vol. 7 (1898).

E. P. Robbins, "Reid's Theory of Judgment," *The Philosophical Review*, Vol. 7 (1898).

J. C. Gregory, "Reid's Theory of Perception," *The Philosophical Review, Vol.* 30 (1921).

E. M. Jones, *Empiricism and Intuitionism in Reid's Common Sense Philosophy* (Princeton, 1927).

A. D. Woozley, (Ed.), *Essays on the Intellectual Powers of Man,* (London, 1941).

Sydney C. Rome, "The Scottish Refutation of Berkeley's Immaterialism," *Philosophy and Phenomenological Research*, Vol. 3 (1942).

D. D. Raphael, *The Moral Sense* (Oxford, 1947), Chapter 5.

A. N. Prior, *Logic and the Basis of Ethics* (Oxford, 1949).

P. G. Winch, "The Notion of 'Suggestion' in Thomas Reid's Theory of Perception," *The Philosophical Quarterly*, Vol. 3 (1953).

Bernard Peach, "Common Sense and Practical Reason in Reid and Kant," *Sophia*, vol. 24 (1956).

Bernard Peach
Duke University

Reid, Thomas: *see* Moral Philosophy in America; Price, Richard.

Reik, Theodor: *see* Freud, Sigmund.

re-incarnation: *see* Hindu Ethics.

rejection: *see* Freud, Sigmund; Stoics, the.

relations: *see* Clarke, Samuel; Green, T. H.

relative morals: *see* Navaho Morals.

relativism: *see* Augustine and Morals; French Existentialism and Moral Philosophy; Major Ethical Viewpoints; Marxist Theory of Morals; Sophists, the.

relativistic ethics: *see* Hindu Ethics; Major Ethical Viewpoints.

relativity: *see* China, Moral Philosophies of; Meta-ethics and Normative Ethics; Morals and Religion.

relativity, moral: *see* Quakerism, Classical, The Morality of; Soviet Morality, Current.

religion: *see* Clarke, Samuel; Cudworth, Ralph; Freud, Sigmund; Morals and Religion; Soviet Morality, Current.

religion and ethics: *see* Aquinas, Thomas, Moral Views of; China, Moral Philosophies of; Hutcheson, Francis; Jesuits, the, Moral Theology of; Kant, I.; Khomiakov, Alexey; Moral Philosophy in America; morals and religion; Quakerism, Classical, The Morality of; Scheler, Max; Soloviev, Wladimir; Spinoza; Theology and ethics; Utilitarianism.

religion and magic: *see* Pakot, the Moral System of.

religion and morality: *see* Augustine and Morals; Aztec Morals; Clarke, Samuel; Cooper, Anthony Ashley; Cudworth, Ralph; Hindu Ethics; Jewish Ethics and Its Civilization; Kierkegaard, Soren; Liguori, St. Alphonsus and Catholic Moral Philosophy; Machiavelli; Niccolo; Major Ethical Viewpoints; Marxist Theory of Morals; Morals and Religion; Muslim Morals; Pakot, the Moral System of; Primitive Morals; Puritan Morals; Riffian Morals; Rio Grande Pueblo Indians; Zoroastrian Morals; Stoics, the; Zuni Indians, Morals of.

religion, natural: *see* Wollaston, William.

religious wars: *see* Aztec Morals; war.

remorse: *see* Broad, C. D.; Primitive Morals.

renunciation: *see* Hindu Ethics; Puritan Morals; Schlick, Moritz; Schopenhauer, Arthur.

reparation: *see* Ross, Sir (William) David.

repentance: *see* More, Henry.

repression: *see* Freud, Sigmund; Puritan Morals.

reputation: *see* Reid, Thomas; Stoics, the.

resentment: *see* Goethe, Johann Wolfgang von.

resentment, morality of: *see* Nietzsche, Friedrich.

resignation: *see* Cudworth, Ralph; Stoics, the.

resistance: *see* Freud, Sigmund.

resolution: *see* Hindu Ethics.

respect: *see* Aztec Morals; Muslim Morals; Riffian Morals; Sophists, the.

respect for parents: *see* Muslim Morals.

respectable, the: *see* Freud, Sigmund.

responsibility: *see* Aquinas, Thomas, Moral Views of; Dante, Alighieri; Dewey, John; Green, T. H.; Jesuits, the, Moral Theology of; moral freedom and responsibility; Price, Richard; Psychology and Morals; Quakerism, Classical, The Morality of; Reid, Thomas; Soviet Morality, Current; Stoics, the.

restitution: *see* Tapirapé Morals, Some Aspects of; Zuni Indians, Morals of.

restoration: *see* Psychology and Morals.

restraint: *see* Major Ethical Viewpoints.

results: *see* Hindu Ethics; rewards.

retaliation: *see* Butler, Joseph; Hammurapi, Code of.

retribution: *see* Puritan Morals.

revelation: *see* Aquinas, Thomas, Moral Views of; Cumberland, Richard; Hutcheson, Francis; Jewish Ethics and Its Civilization; Moral Philosophy in America; Morals and Religion; Schlick, Moritz; Spinoza; Utilitarianism.

revenge: *see* Quakerism, Classical, The Morality of.

reverence: *see* Hindu Ethics.

reverence for life: *see* Price, Richard; Quakerism, Classical, The Morality of.

reverence for personality: *see* Quakerism, Classical, The Morality of.

revivalism: *see* Puritan Morals.

revolutions: *see* Dewey, John; proletarian revolution; Soviet Morality, Current.

rewards: *see* Aztec Morals; Balguy, John; Clarke, Samuel; Cudworth, Ralph; Cumberland, Richard; Dante, Alighieri; Hindu Ethics; Jesuits, the, Moral Theology of; Minor Socratics; Moral Philosophy in America; Muslim Morals; Navaho Morals; Pakot, the Moral System of; Schlick, Moritz; Spinoza; Stoics, the; Utilitarianism.

rhetoricians: *see* Sophists, the.

Ricardo, David: *see* Utilitarianism.

Richardson, Alexander: *see* Puritan Morals.

rich in experience, the: *see* Hartmann, Nicolai.

ridicule: *see* Navaho Morals; Reid, Thomas; Rio Grande Pueblo Indians.

Riesman, David: *see* Freud, Sigmund.

Riffian Morals

The Moroccan Berbers are generally considered to be divided into three distinct linguistic and geographical units: the Shluh of the Grand Atlas and the Sus Valley, the Sinhaja Birabir of the Middle and Central Atlas, and the Riffians, whose morals are the subject of this article. The Riffians are a congeries of thirteen discrete groups recognized as tribes (*thiqba'ir,* sing. *thaqbitsh*), six of which (Ibuqquyen, Aith Wariyaghir, Aith 'Ammarth, Igzinnayen, Tamsaman and Asht Tuzin) fall geographically and culturally into the central part of the low but steep mountain chain which buttresses the northern Moroccan littoral. The rest (Aith Sa'id, Aith Urishik, Thafarsith, Ibdharsen, Aith Bu Yihyi, Iqar'ayen and Ikibdhanen) possess their tribal territory further to the east, where the mountains begin to give way to open rolling country, and finally, near Melilla, to flat plains. It is, however, the central mountain region which shows itself the purest from a cultural standpoint, and the cultural nucleus of the Central Rif as thus defined consists of three tribal groups: Aith Wariyaghir (62,000 souls), Aith 'Ammarth (14,500) and northern Igzinnayen (30,000). All the Riffian tribes are located in Spanish Morocco with the exception of Igzinnayen, and it, bordering both Aith Wariyaghir and Aith 'Ammarth on the south, is just across the frontier in the French Zone. When in this paper the word "Riffian" is employed, it is to these tribes in particular that the authors refer.

It is difficult, if not impossible, to divorce purely *Riffian* morality as such from Moroccan and, by extension, Islamic, morality as a whole, of which it forms but one small segment. Due to the Arab invasions and the introduction of Islam into North Africa, the morals and morality of all Moroccans, and, by the same token, of all Muslims the world over, are remarkably uniform. Irrespective of their ethnic origins or present-day political affinities, all Muslims are members of one religious community (*umma*), which constitutes one-seventh of the total population of the globe and which, by comparison with Christianity, shows

itself to be extremely homogeneous, not being, generally speaking, split up into divergent sects.

The keynote of Islamic doctrine is an uncompromising monotheism, as expressed in the first of the famous five "Pillars" of the Muslim faith: *La ilaha illa 'llah wa Muhammadun rasulu 'llah,* "There is no god but The God (Allah) and Muhammad is the Apostle of The God." The acceptance of this simple statement of belief as a common creed, plus the acceptance of a common ritual language (Arabic, the tongue in which the Qur'an, Book of Books, was directly revealed by God to the Prophet Muhammad) and of common ritual values, exemplified by the other four "Pillars" (prayer five times a day, compulsory almsgiving, fasting during the month of Ramadan, and the pilgrimage to Makka, enjoined upon every Muslim at least once in his lifetime), serve to unify all the faithful within their own religious community and in the face of the rest of the world, with which, theoretically, they are in a permanent state of armed truce, if not of war.

The Religion of God (*Din Illahi*) enjoins its practitioners to "obey the divine commands (e.g., that which is *halal,* or required of all believers, such as the five "Pillars") and makes them abstain from, and prevent others from doing, what God forbids" (M. Gaudefroy-Demombynes, *Muslim Institutions,* London 1950, p. 175). Acts classified as *haram,* or forbidden by God, include the eating of pork and the consumption of alcoholic beverages. Because all Muslims comply, to a greater

482

or lesser extent, with the divinely decreed precepts of the Qur'an, which in their practical application consist of a clear-cut list of "do's" and "don'ts" set down in black and white in the various *suras* of the Holy Book, their religious values are of necessity moral ones as well, and vice versa. In short, in orthodox Islam, religion and morality are one.

Thus the mere fact of their profession of the Muslim faith indicates that any special moral characteristics and any differences from a hypothetical Islamic moral norm which the Riffians exhibit or which are attributed to them by outsiders must be based largely on cultural factors which were already present when Islam entered the area and which therefore are not determined by it. These factors may be summed up in one word: environment, in the widest sense of the term.

Considered in this light, orthodox religion (Islam) and environment (the Rif) work against each other, for if the former inhibits the development of a morality which is uniquely Riffian, the latter has always fostered it, particularly because the Rif itself is a marginal refuge area and because Riffian culture developed in a state of almost complete isolation. To gain a proper understanding of the role of their environment in the moral values of the Riffian people, we must bear in mind two cardinal points made at the beginning of this article: 1) that the Riffians are not Arabs, but Berbers, and 2) that they are organized into tribes, each one of which possesses a kinship system and a social structure. Let us examine

a little more closely each of these points in turn.

At the time of the Arab conquests, the Badawin armies of the Caliphs discovered everywhere throughout the area now known as the Middle East that the various peoples with whom they came into contact and subsequently converted to Islam spoke languages and participated in cultures different from their own. These peoples had long since worked out their own sets of ritual symbols and techniques to cope with the supernatural and had devised and perfected their own methods of maintaining equilibrium within their own cultures, and of reducing interpersonal friction to a minimum. The new religion, however, was something outside their previous experience, and hence they drew the line between disturbances involving it and disturbances which they were already equipped to resolve (C. S. Coon, *Caravan, The Story of the Middle East*, New York, 1951, pp. 102–3). The Muslim peoples to whom the above remarks particularly apply are those of non-Arab origin who kept their ancient tongues: Persians, Turks, Indonesians and Berbers.

The fact that the Berbers took over Arabic as a ritual medium and grafted the five "Pillars," the concepts of *halal* and *haram,* and other fundamental Qur'anic precepts, onto their existing religious beliefs was more than anything else a necessary concession to the invaders, the majority of whom were nearly as ignorant of the Prophet's religion as they themselves were. The religious system of the early Berbers of the Neolithic has continued virtually unmodified, and in the Rif today spirits, ghosts and demons (most of which have been incorporated into and sanctioned by the Qur'an under the collective name of *jnun*) are still propitiated, divination is still practiced, dreams and omens still have set interpretations, and belief in the evil eye and in the power of charms and amulets is still universal. All these religious elements antedate Islam and seem at the very least an excellent indication of the fact that Islam in the Rif is only skin deep, although any Riffian would be horrified to hear that he might not be considered a good Muslim. Today, too, the Shari'a, or orthodox Muslim law, of the Maliki school, prevails in the Rif, and is invoked in all criminal cases, some of which fall under protectoral jurisdiction as well; but most disturbances of an interpersonal nature which are not offensive to the community at large are still resolved by the *'urf*, or customary law. Up to thirty years ago and the establishment of the Protectorate, customary law was the final arbiter in all legal questions, civil and criminal, and the Shari'a had no place in the Riffian legal system whatsoever. In the days before 'Abd al-Karim and the Riffian War, custom was king in an explicit sense; it was legislated and administered by the quorum of the *Aith Arba'-in*, the council of elders (*imgharen*, sing. *amghar*) who formed the tribal body politic and in whose collective hands lay tribal responsibility and tribal destiny. At present, custom is still king implicitly, although more from a

moral than from a legal point of view, because, hallowed and sanctified by tradition, it still represents to all Riffians an ethical ideal to which social pressure forces them to conform. As a regulator of moral conduct, it therefore functions as a most effective social control, applied by the imgharen of the Aith Arba'in.

We may now turn to the second environmental factor in the moral makeup of the Riffians, the tribal system, which will be considered in the light of its relationship to Riffian economics. Rocky and infertile, the Rif is a land too palpably poor to support its population, whose basic economy is one of subsistence level agriculture coupled with a small-scale animal husbandry. A fundamental economic problem is lack of water, for rain is erratic and infrequent, and the Riffian farmer is eternally, and justifiably, preoccupied with whether or not his meager harvest will see him through a hard winter. Bad years are common and droughts are periodic: the worst of these was in 1945, a year in which Riffians died like flies owing to crop failure, and in which as many others were rendered destitute and forced into mass migration to Algeria and Tangier, where temporary soup-kitchens were set up for them. To survive, therefore, in a physical environment as harsh as this, one must be tough, and the Riffian is nothing if not that. That he does survive, and to the extent of overpopulation, is due at least in part to the fact that he manages to produce a maximum number of crops (including barley, wheat, rye, tares, broad beans, onions, peas, tomatoes, carrots, olives, walnuts, almonds, pomegranates, figs and grapes) in a minimum amount of land. His diet, supplemented by a little meat bought in the market once a week, plus a certain amount of milk and butter, as well as tea, is thus more varied than that of the plains villager, and the mountain air which he breathes is better air. The naturally rugged physical constitution which this combination of factors produces is enhanced by an aptitude for hard work.

Overpopulation is thus another grave economic problem in the Rif, which throughout Riffian history has been met by two alternative solutions: the seasonal migration of young men to the rich plains of western Algeria to find work on the farms of French colons, or violent death at the hands of enemy families in the bloodfeud if they stayed at home. The first solution has reached the status of big business at the present day, and Riffian workers are eagerly sought out by owners of Algerian estates who always give them job preference over the local natives. The second solution, although now officially abolished by the Spanish Government, still finds overt expression when two men, oftener than not related consanguineally, get into an argument over the possession of a miserable little plot of land or over which of them has the right to use the irrigation water coming from the communal ditch on that particular day, and one stoves in the other's skull with a bill-hook in the process. In the old days arguments were terminated by rifle shots,

after which the feud, family against family, lineage against lineage, and tribe against tribe, could be said to have commenced. Women were also a frequent cause of feuds, and although they were immune from attack, they could and did contribute their share by poisoning the food of unwary men of the enemy group.

What does all this have to do with the kinship and tribal systems? Simply the following: that in the tumultuous and chaotic life of the average Riffian, his kin group and, by extension, his tribe, was the one stable institution to which he belonged. The mere fact of belonging to it and of participating in its activities gave, and gives, him a security he would not otherwise possess. The social structure of a Riffian tribe is expressed in terms of segmentation, and there is opposition between these segments. Thus, when the issue of his loyalty to any given social grouping in any given situation arises, the Riffian aligns himself with his own group as opposed to other groups of the same type in the social structure: with his own family against other families, with his own kinship group against other kin groups, and with his own tribe against other tribes. He will likewise align himself with Riffians of other tribes as opposed to Arab tribes of the Ghumara or Jibala, for instance, and, in the last analysis, against Arabs and townsmen of any sort. This group "we-feeling" was solidly maintained in the centuries of Riffian cultural isolation and political independence, and the martial spirit which it engendered was responsible for the fact that the Moroccan sultans could never conquer the Rif.

Let us look at this same problem from another angle. When, for example, a Riffian boy who shines shoes in Tangier states proudly "Nish dh-Wariyaghri" (I am from Aith Wariyaghir) in answer to the ethnographer's inevitable question asking him where his home is, his mere tone of voice implies that he is a member of a strong and powerful tribal group and, as such, a far superior being in every way to the local Arabs, for whom he has an infinite contempt. They, on their part, hate and fear him and his fellows for the tribal power which they represent, and although they try to cover it up by making jokes at his expense, there is always an undercurrent in their words of the feeling engendered by an Arab proverb: *Ar-Rifi da'iman quddamak, ma shi murak* ("Always keep a Riffian in front of you, never behind you," the implication being that he will stab you in the back).

It is thus clear that lack of sufficient arable land and of water, plus over-population, have produced in the Rif a highly competitive society in which a man's prestige is measured by his personal power and by the number of armed followers whom he can command. A strong man became an amghar of the Aith Arba'in, while a poor and weak one became his hired ploughman. Within the tribe the achievement of personal power is the goal of everyone, and if it cannot be obtained through force or violence, trickery and cunning are resorted to, and culturally sanctioned. Notions of "good" and "bad" are thus equated with strength and weakness, respectively, and members of humble and undistinguished families, who had either never chosen to take part in the scramble for power or who had been dispossessed in the process, were and are considered of no account. A Riffian who commands any degree of personal respect in his own tribe is one whose fingers are eminently more suited to squeezing a trigger than to pushing a plough. Although the ploughman himself may be a tyrant in his own home, it behooves him, for his own safety, to be subservient and docile in the presence of the village amghar.

We have also seen that the kinship system and the tribal structure give a measure of stability and security to Riffian society, as torn by internal wars as it is, while, to hark back to earlier considerations, the customary law and early Berber religious practices provided a social norm in the abstract and an incentive to the individual to conform, in fear of the consequences if nothing else. On top of all this, Islam has added the concept of One God, and thinly diluted its religious precepts into the core of existing belief, thus producing an external religious and moral similarity with other Muslim peoples. And, finally, in the last thirty years has come the Protectorate, to whose representatives the tribal councilmembers are as obedient as their own wives, sons and ploughmen are to them.

These factors, then, are the basis of Riffian morals. As they themselves are conflicting and contrasting, so are the morals which they underly. The same man who bashes in his neighbor's head with a bill-hook will give his all to a stranger who comes to his door seeking shelter and hospitality. In the same way, bravery is inextricably linked with prudence, arrogance with obsequiousness, and xenophobia with liberalism.

If it were possible to set up a Riffian moral trinomial, the three necessary qualifications could be expressed in terms of 1) desire to pillage vs. incentive to conform to custom, 2) deceit vs. nobility, and 3) love of lucre vs. generosity. The three traits admired by Western observers would not in themselves suffce, nor would the three which are looked upon with disgust. The average Riffian is a blend, morally speaking, not only of all three but of all six.

Closer scrutiny of the Riffian moral makeup, on the basis of the data given above, yields us the following results:

Delinquency: as defined by Western standards, negative. In Aith Wariyaghir, delinquency reaches a sum total of 2%, which takes the form of theft, usually committed by men between 20 and 30 years of age, almost all of whom have resided in cities at some time in their lives, notably Tangier and Casablanca. The remaining 98% is divided up as follows: lack of respect in interpersonal relations, particularly as applied to women—3%; litigations over ownership of property—5%; and brawls and fights—90%.

Sexual Morality: very high. In the total population of Aith Wariyaghir, 62,000 souls, there is not a single known homosexual, a fact which contrasts very markedly with the Arab groups of the Ghumara, Jibala and Lukus, to the west. (One important reason why Riffians hold Moroccan Arabs in contempt is because a relatively high proportion of them are prone to sodomy.) In addition, there are only three professional prostitutes whose tribal origins are Wariyaghri (two of them are from the Plain of Alhucemas and the third from Aith Bu 'Ayyash), and they ply their trade in recognized houses in Villa Sanjurjo, the regional capital of the *Territorio del Rif.*

Family Morality: very high. As the family is the basis of Riffian society, it entails maximum respect on the part of its component members. There is not, and has not been, a single known case in which a son or younger brother is lacking in respect towards his elders. In contradistinction to Moroccan Arab society, respect towards women is more highly accentuated and lack of it is therefore more heavily punished. During a famous feud in Taurirt, in the southern mountains of Aith Wariyaghir, the belligerents kept well away from the path leading to the fountain of Ihautshen for a stipulated period of three hours every afternoon, as the womenfolk of that group went down then to fill their water jugs.

Religious Morality: would tend to give a first impression of being high, but a careful examination of the facts shows that some 75% of the men who attend the mosque where the Friday sermon is delivered are 40 years old or over. The same statistical proportion would appear to apply to those individuals who join religious brotherhoods. In the performance of the daily prayers, however, the percentage in the same age group rises to 95%. The obvious conclusion to be drawn here is that religiosity increases with age, and that fear of God becomes greater every year closer to death.

Social Morality: very high. The example given earlier of the Riffian shoeshine boy in Tangier may suffice, for a Wariyaghri, no matter where he may be and no matter how menial his job, will proudly admit his tribal origins with the implication that they are superior to all others.

Public Morality: very high. In the weekly tribal market, for example, mutual respect is so integral an element in interpersonal relationships that no disturbances are produced and that, furthermore, every economic specialist and every individual who sells articles or produce maintains the same work site week after week, bothered and molested by no one. The market provides an excellent physical location for the observance of Riffian behavior patterns in public, and almost without exception the tribesmen show themselves to be respectful, proud and dignified.

On the other hand, however, the numerical composition of an average Riffian would give us the following percentage indices:

Intriguer—50%. In this case, there is no dearth of examples. There have, in Riffian history, been numerous instances in which one man, wishing to rid himself of a powerful enemy, has given money "underneath his *jillaba*" (a woollen cloak with sleeves and hood which all Riffian men wear), as the Riffians express it, to a hired killer for this purpose. It is also not uncommon for a man to denounce his own brother in front of the tribal authorities with, most often, the idea of relieving him of his portion of the land which they have jointly inherited from their father.

In Taurirt, at the present time, the Friday mosque has no *faqih* (preceptor). Each village whose members regularly attend this mosque has put forward its own candidate for the job, and the village representatives have in each case come to the tribal administrator with a largely fabricated account of why their candidate should be given preference over those of the other villages concerned.

Money-minded—30%. Man A, for example, comes to the Wednesday market at Taurirt with a basket of eggs. These he sells there, and with the proceeds buys a *mudd* (56 kilos) of barley to provide bread for his family. Man B now steps into the picture, and offers him 5 pesetas (about 13c) more for the mudd of barley than what he paid for it originally, so A sells B the barley. With the proceeds he decides to buy a headkerchief for his wife, and, after haggling a while with a piece-goods merchant, he completes the transaction. It is now getting along towards midafternoon, and our man must return to his home in Tafsast, 6 hours away on donkey-back. When finally

488

he arrives in his native village, long after dark, a friend, Man C, sees him with the headkerchief and, realizing that *he* has not bought a present for his own wife these many months, buys it from him for 3 pesetas more than its retail price in the market. The net result is that although our friend has made a total profit of 8 pesetas during the day's business, he has not brought home the barley. The next day, therefore, he must cross the border into Igzinnayen in the French Zone, and go to the Thursday Market at Iharrasen to purchase the barley he had intended to buy in Taurirt the day before.

Untruthful—20%. The average Riffian is habitually given to telling untruths, both on a small and on a large scale. A meets B on a village path, and asks him where he is going. B replies that he is going to catch the next bus for Villa Sanjurjo. An hour or so later they both run into each other again in the Monday Market of Aith Bu 'Ayyash.

Impulsive—10%. If A insults B or his family, his life is in danger, as B, if he had a gun, would shoot A without a second thought. As no one is permitted to carry a rifle nowadays, a heavy walking stick or the bill-hook mentioned earlier comes into play under these circumstances.

A condensation of the foregoing data and a submission of it to various tests would probably produce the following results:

Psychological Test: combines and blends magnificently the following ac-tions: impulsiveness with cunning, untruthfulness with mistrust, and curiosity with indifference, all of which are directed toward entirely personal ends, in the Riffian point of view.

Moral Test: kindness (to strangers), unknown; vice, unknown; scruples, none; human respect (in face-to-face relations), much; loyalty (to any institution other than the family, kin or tribe), unknown.

Social Test: honor, much; delicacy, slight; altruism, none; pulchritude and personal appearance, much; propriety, much; correctness, much; probity, slight; honesty, medium; austerity, much (in common with all middle Eastern peoples—see C. S. Coon (1951), chapter 18); parsimony, none; splendor, much.

Finally, a "fitness report" of any Riffian would reveal, independently of the above estimates, the following adjectival combination of characteristics:

Frugal: Goat-herders subsist on a piece of barley bread and ¼ kilo of figs, although this frugality is forgotten on feast days when one man is capable of eating a whole sheep.

Noble: A Riffian does not betray his friends, and if he is not attacked, he is incapable of harming anyone.

Hardworking: Riffian workmen are given priority, as much in French Morocco as in the Spanish Zone, over those of any other ethnic group.

Proud: No matter how poor he may be and how humble his living conditions, a Riffian is always proud of being Riffian.

Courageous: In Spanish Morocco, a Riffian is always given primary consideration over an Arab in enlistment into native troops;

his entrance into the military mahallas is virtually automatic, while the Arab is put on a waiting list. In French Morocco, the young men of Igzinnayen go into the goums, although there, what with all the Berbers of the Middle Atlas, who are also hardy fighters, competition is tougher.
Docile and *Obedient:* If the tribal administrator requests ten men to work in his garden, all of them will appear the next morning, at or before the appointed hour, with hoe in hand.
Pugnacious: Although a Riffian will never attack if unprovoked (see *Noble*), he likes to get into a fight. This quality is closely allied to impulsiveness, as he will strike a blow without a moment's hesitation to defend his own honor or that of his family.

Such is the paradox presented by Riffian morals, which, to be intelligible to the Western observer, must, in the last analysis, be considered in the light of the Riffian cultural ethos.

Bibliography
Valentin Beneitez Cantero, *Sociología Marroquí* (Ceuta, 1952).
Emilio Blanco Izaga, *La Ley Rifeña,* tomo II, parte 2a—*Los Cánones Rifeños Comentados* (Ceuta, 1939).
Carleton S. Coon, *Tribes of the Rif,* Harvard African Studies, vol. IX, Peabody Museum (Cambridge, Mass., 1931).
——, *Flesh of the Wild Ox, A Riffian Chronicle of High Valleys and Long Rifles* (New York, 1932).
——, *Caravan, The Story of the Middle East* (New York, 1951).
Maurice Gaudefroy-Demombynes, *Muslim Institutions,* translated from the French by John P. Macgregor (London, 1950).
H. A. R. Gibb, *Mohammedanism, An Historical Survey* (London, 1949).
David M. Hart, "An Ethnographic Survey of the Riffian Tribe of Aith Wariyaghir," *Tamuda,* Año II, Semestre I (Tetuán, 1954), pp. 51–86.
Robert Montagne, *Les Berbères et le Makhzen dans le Sud du Maroc* (Paris, 1930).
——, "Islam and Christianity," *Thought,* Fordham University Quarterly, vol. XXVII, no. 105, Summer (1952).
Raphael Patai, "The Middle East as a Culture Area," *Middle East Journal,* vol. 6, no. 1, Winter (1952), pp. 1–21.

David M. Hart
Marruecos Español

José R. Erola
Inteventor Comarcal of Aith
Wariyaghir

right: *see* Aboriginals of Yirkalla; Aquinas, Thomas, Moral Views of; Ayer, Alfred J.; Balguy, John; Broad, C. D.; Butler, Joseph; Clarke, Samuel; Cumberland, Richard; Dewey, John; Major Ethical Viewpoints; Marxist Theory of Morals; Moore, George Edward; More, Henry; Moral Philosophy in America; Price, Richard; Prichard, H. A.; Primitive Morals; Quakerism, Classical, The Morality of; Reid, Thomas; Ross, Sir (William) David; Schlick, Moritz; Sidgwick, Henry; Sophists, the; Spinoza; Stoics, the; Utilitarianism; Wollaston, William.
right opinion: *see* Ross, Sir (William) David.
right reason: *see* More, Henry.
righteousness: *see* Augustine and Morals; China, Moral Philosophies of; Christian Moral Philosophy; Hindu Ethics; Jewish Ethics and Its Civili-

zation; Quakerism, Classical, The Morality of; Zoroastrian Morals.

rightness, concept of: *see* Clarke, Samuel.

rights: *see* Cudworth, Ralph; Moral Philosophy in America; Zuni Indians, Morals of.

rights, natural: *see* Moral Philosophy in America.

rigorism: *see* China, Moral Philosophies of.

Rio Grande Pueblo Indians, The Value and Moral Concepts of*

Introduction

The investigation of the values and moral concepts of nonliterate peoples is a comparatively recent interest among anthropologists.[1] For the most part anthropologists are and have been concerned primarily with the more explicit and overt manifestations of culture. They have described in detail the material possessions of nonliterate peoples, their ceremonies, social institutions and behavioral traits, but they

have generally neglected the more elusive aspects of their culture. Only incidentally and briefly is mention made occasionally of the attitudes and philosophical concepts of nonliterate peoples. Such information, moreover, must be secured with great difficulty by combing through many pages of monographs and the rewards are meagre indeed.[2]

The neglect of this important area of research is understandable in view of the difficulties in obtaining information of this kind. Whereas, it is possible to learn how material items are made, what the institutions of a people are like, and how people act, it is difficult to get information on how they think and what things they value and why. Partly this is because values and moral concepts of a people are rarely on the conscious level and partly because adequate techniques for obtaining this kind of information have not yet been devised. Direct questioning of informants about their society's values and morals has not been found entirely satisfactory, although materials thus obtained are not to be minimized. The difficulties in the use of this traditional anthropological technique is that the validity of informant

---

* The materials contained in this paper were obtained in field studies made possible through the assistance of the Graduate School, Northwestern University. Acknowledgement of this assistance is made with appreciation. A special note of thanks is also extended to Dr. and Mrs. Fred Eggan, University of Chicago who read an initial draft of the paper and offered constructive criticism. For content and interpretation, however, the author alone is responsible.

[1] Early in the development of anthropology scholars like Westermarck, Hobhouse and Sutherland were concerned with the evolution of moral ideas, but later writers have largely ignored the subject except for renewed interest recently (see note 2 below). See bibliography for important works by Westermarck, Hobhouse and Sutherland.

[2] For exceptions see Harvard University's Values Studies (Papers of the Peabody Museum of American Archaeology and Ethnology, Harvard University, Vol. 40 ff.). In the values series, monographs and papers by Clyde Kluckhohn, Robert N. Rapaport, J. M. Roberts and E. Z. Vogt are especially pertinent to this subject. Other important works dealing with the values and moral concepts of nonliterate peoples are the following: Brandt, 1954; Kluckhohn, 1949; Radin, 1927; Redfield, 1952.

responses cannot always be relied upon. Under direct questioning, informants are likely to censor their responses and give answers that would place their group's moral and value concepts in a favorable light. Contemporary nonliterate peoples are very much aware of Christian and Western moral and value concepts and they often modify their responses to agree with those they feel the investigator holds.

An ideal study of the moral and value concepts of a people should certainly not neglect the informant approach, but other techniques must also be employed. First of all, an analysis of the outside contacts and influences to which a society has been subject must be carefully studied. A thorough examination of the mythology, social institutions, ceremonial ritual and behavior of the people for expressions of these covert aspects of culture would also be essential. Materials from projective techniques, personal histories and dreams should be utilized. Finally a good command of the language and close observation of both social and linguistic behavior would also be important. These are admittedly optimum considerations and a tall order to demand of any investigator; yet they would appear essential for the proper characterization of the values and moral concepts of any society.

The brief discussion of Rio Grande Pueblo values and moral concepts given in this paper does not pretend to have complied strictly with the optimum considerations outlined above.

Some attempt has been made to adhere to them, but for the most part the value system and moral concepts of the Rio Grande Pueblo Indians described in this paper are impressionistic and qualitative. As such, they must be thought of as preliminary and tentative statements to be confirmed, modified or rejected by further research.

Location and Historical Background of the Rio Grande Pueblos

The Rio Grande or Eastern Pueblo Indians live in some twenty independent autonomous villages bordering the Rio Grande and its tributaries.[3] The overall population is about 10,000—the largest village has about 2,000 people and the smallest about 100. Two separate linguistic stocks, the Keres and Tanoan are found in the area. The Tanoan stock is further divided into three distinct families: Tiwa, Tewa and Towa. Intervillage communication in the native language is possible among villages belonging to the same family and also among village members of the Keres stock, although dialectical differences are sometimes extreme enough to necessitate the use of Spanish or English to

[3] These pueblos are distinguished geographically and culturally from Laguna, Acoma, Zuni and Hopi—the Western Pueblos. Acoma, Laguna and Zuni are in northwestern New Mexico, while the Hopi villages are in northern Arizona. Although all of the pueblo peoples share general cultural characteristics there are important detailed differences that make a distinction into an Eastern and Western group meaningful. For an excellent report of these differences see Eggan, 1950.

facilitate easy communication. Both Spanish and English are well known in the area and used as *lingua franca* in the frequent intercourse between members of the various villages.

The Rio Grande Pueblos have occupied essentially their present locations for several centuries; at least there have not been, except for one or two cases, pronounced changes since Spanish contact. Prehistoric sites in the region immediately north and west of the present pueblo region were indisputably occupied by the ancestors of these Indians. The intensive archaeological studies now being made in the area will eventually give us a more comprehensive picture of the early locations and migrations of pueblo peoples in the more remote past.

Since the colonization of the Rio Grande Pueblo region by the Spaniards early in the 17th century, these Indians have been in close contact with a European-type culture. In spite of this experience, however, the Rio Grande Pueblos have retained their indigenous cultural elements and orientation. Indeed to such an extent is this true that it is possible to discuss the essential features of the culture with little reference to outside influences. Alien contacts are not to be minimized, however, and their effects will also be considered. Nevertheless, it is possible to describe Rio Grande Pueblo culture almost completely in the native context, for indigenous elements and organization still remain the core of the culture today.

Dominant Characteristics of Rio Grande Pueblo Culture[4]

Although the individual villages are politically autonomous and despite linguistic differences, the cultures of the Rio Grande Pueblos bear remarkable similarity. In each village ceremonial, social and political affairs are in the hands of a hierarchical group of priests. A dual division of social and ceremonial functions is apparent in the villages, although this aspect of organization is most pronounced in the Tanoan-speaking villages. Familial organization among the Keres-speaking villages is extended along the matrilineal line and predominantly bilaterally extended in the Tanoan villages. Each village has a number of esoteric cults or societies. These societies have a curative and purificatory function. They treat individuals who are ill and rid the village periodically of "evil spirits." Health and long life are assured for a person who becomes a member of one of these societies and although the services exacted of members are rigid, recruiting members appears not to be a problem. Individuals join because they desire to be cured of an illness or as the result of a vow made during illness and subsequent

[4] For detailed descriptions of specific Rio Grande Pueblo communities see Dumarest and Goldfrank for Cochiti; Parsons for the Tewa, Isleta, Laguna, Jemez, and Taos; White for Acoma, San Felipe, Santo Domingo and Santa Ana. Parsons, 1939 is the best source for pueblos generally. See also the published papers of these writers and also of Florence Hawley Ellis and Charles H. Lange in the *American Anthropoligist* and the *Southwestern Journal of Anthropology*. For comparative materials consult Eggan, 1950.

RIO GRANDE PUEBLO INDIANS

recovery. In some cases, parents may vow a child into a society either to derive benefit for themselves or to obtain health and long life for their child.

The emphasis on curing appears to stem from a basic anxiety over illness and a constant quest for well being. Ceremonial activity revolves primarily around rituals that effect cures or in other ways minimize this anxiety. Another major emphasis of Rio Grande Pueblo culture is weather control, although this feature is most pronounced in the ceremonial activities and concepts of the Western Pueblos.[5] In the arid Southwest sufficient moisture is a crucial factor between adequate health and virtual starvation. Weather control ceremonies to bring rain and snow have been institutionalized in the important Katcina cult, a men's organization whose primary function is to minimize this anxiety by the performance of colorful masked ceremonies.

Rio Grande Pueblo villages are highly authoritarian. The head priests of the societies in each village form a hierarchical class who exert strict control over the activities of village members. Unanimity is keynoted and conformance to a rigid calendric series of ceremonies is required of all those who are physically able. Those who do not participate actively in the ceremonies are required to lend their support by mental effort. The belief is that famine and disease are offset by cooperative effort and a harmonious, happy attitude, free from ill feeling towards one's neighbors or the universe in general. The priests keep constant surveillance; any action, whether physical or verbal, which is construed to be antithetical to group concerns and the unanimous will of the village as a whole is punished by traditional social control mechanisms. These include gossip, ridicule, accusations of witchcraft, physical punishment and banishment from the village. Depending on the severity of the offense, individuals may be made to suffer one, several or all of these control measures.

Values and Moral Concepts[6]

The above is a discussion primarily of the explicit features of Rio Grande Pueblo culture and society—it is important now to examine the basic values and concepts of Rio Grande Pueblo culture. The dominant integrating factor of Rio Grande Pueblo culture appears to be the view of the universe as an orderly phenomenon. Man and the universe are conceived to be in a kind of a balance. Nothing is believed to be good or bad, but "evil" is conceived as a disturbance in the equilibrium that exists between man and the universe. The activity world of man, of the natural environment of plants and animals, the inanimate world of earth, rocks and dead vegetable matter, the ethereal world of wind, clouds, rain and snow; even the "thought world" of human beings are all believed to be in a state of balance. The activity world is one of cooperative helpfulness; everyone work-

5 See footnote 3 above.

6 No sources are known to me on this subject in the anthropological literature on Rio Grande Pueblos. The nearest approach to the subject is Aitken, 1930.

494

ing for the good of the whole. Individual subordination to group effort is believed to be an essential part of maintaining balance in the universe. Logically the "thought world" is a happy one, free of ill feeling or hostile attitudes toward any aspect of the universe. Illness, prolonged drought conditions, famines and all bad misfortunes are believed to occur as the result of a disturbance in the orderly nature of the universe.

It is important here to distinguish between the concept of "sin" as generally conceived in Euro-American culture and the Pueblo Indian's concept of "wrong doing." The latter tries to avoid in thought and deed the things that would break the harmonious whole of the universe. Misfortune comes, in his belief, not as a punishment or retaliation by a supreme being or beings, but because the interrelatedness of the universe has been disturbed. It is thus a magical concept—a concept that might best be understood as a breach of tabu. It is conceptually different from "sin"—the concept that a supernatural (or supernaturals) has been offended or angered by the transgression of a code of morals or ethics established by such a supernatural or supernaturals who then retaliate or punish the transgressors specifically for this transgression.

The Rio Grande Pueblo Indians emphasize group activity, the cooperative working together with harmonious feeling toward all things in the universe. This concept is well expressed in the following statement by an old man:

If we [human beings] do our part, the universe [man's total environment] will do its part by granting our innermost desires. On the other hand, if we fail as individuals by neglect, by "bad thoughts," by noncooperativeness, to keep the harmony of the universe, we will suffer.[7]

Man alone can break the orderliness and harmonious balance of the universe. He may break it by ill feeling toward another, or toward a number of individuals; indeed, even by disliking or perceiving ugliness in some aspect of the universe. He may do so by taking more food than is necessary for sustenance, or by not being generous in sharing and giving what he has. He may break the balance by killing more game than is essential to supply himself and his relatives with food or by taking more clay or more pigment than is necessary to make needed pottery vessels.

Not only must man use sparingly of the food and material resources of the universe but he is required to reciprocate by appropriate propitiatory rites. These range all the way from offering corn meal, corn pollen, prayer feathers and prayer sticks to elaborate ceremonial dances made "as beautiful as possible" and participated in by the whole village. On the matter of offerings Benavides made the following report as early as the first part of the 17th century, an observation which would apply today:

Their religion [Rio Grande Pueblos] though it was not formal idolatry, was nearly so, since they made offering for

[7] From my field notes on Santa Clara Pueblo.

495

whatsoever action. As, in the time when they were going out to fight their enemies, they offered up flour and other things to the scalps of those they had slain of the hostile nation. If they were going to hunt they offered up flour to heads of deer, jackrabbits, cottontail rabbits, and other dead animals. If to fish they made offerings to the river . . .[8]

The importance of ceremonies as a propitiatory rite to effect well being and bring much needed moisture to parched lands is well known to students of Rio Grande Pueblo culture. The associated and essential requisites of cooperative effort and a happy state of mind, however, have generally been ignored. It is significant, therefore, that as early as 1912 an anthropologist made the following insightful observation:

The assertion is made [in Santa Clara Pueblo] "it will rain—we are happy; it will rain—we are dancing [ceremonializing]; we are dancing—it will rain." Cause and effect are hardly differentiated. Let us hope all people are happy; but let us make sure that they are dancing.[9]

The fact that all must participate and with harmonious good feeling to make any venture successful brings on force and coercion as important associated features of this concept of unanimous effort.[10] The Pueblo individual examines his thoughts and

attitudes to make sure that he is in a "happy state of mind," but he is also concerned with the actions and thoughts of his fellow man. If he is satisfied with his actions and his state of mind and still misfortunes and illness persist, then he is ready to cast blame on someone else. Constant surveillance of the behavior of one's neighbors even of close relatives, is a typical Rio Grande Pueblo pattern.

Rio Grande Pueblo culture thus makes rigorous demands on the individual and fills him with deep anxiety and suspicion toward his fellow man. Not only is his personal behavior and social interaction strictly circumscribed, but his thoughts, as well, are rigidly harnessed. He is constantly plagued by an apprehension that he or his fellowman may break the harmonious balance of the universe and bring illness, famine or some other form of dreaded disaster.

Rio Grande Pueblo "Conscious and Moral Code"

Much has been written about "guilt" and "shame" in nonliterate and literate cultures.[11] Euro-American culture, for instance, is said to be primarily "guilt" oriented, whereas nonliterate cultures are reported to be "shame" cultures. It is not the purpose of this paper to examine the validity of these premises; it must be emphasized, however, that "guilt" appears to be a dominant feature of Rio Grande Pueblo culture.

8 Ayer, 1916, p. 30.

9 Aitken, 1930, p. 382.

10 The use of physical coercion may have been borrowed from Spanish practices and employed to exact conformance to native ceremonial customs. Whether the use of force is indigenous or borrowed, however, it is today a strong social control mechanism in virtually all of the Rio Grande Pueblos.

11 See especially Mead, 1937. For an excellent criticism of these concepts see Piers and Singer, 1953.

Rio Grande Pueblo moral standards are established in the extended family in which the child is reared. They are reinforced by other village institutions and by traditional sanctions, but the strength of the moral code is due primarily to its strong roots firmly planted in the extended family. Although "external sanctions" in the form of ridicule, witchcraft accusations, fines and punishments are strong and constantly marshalled to prevent violation of the moral code, the nature of the Rio Grande Pueblo world view indicates that "internal sanctions" are equally as strong if not stronger. Thus, since any act, whether physical or of the mind, which is not cooperative and free from "ill feeling" is likely to bring about misfortune, it is clear that an individual may have extreme "guilt feelings" even though "he is not found out." An individual who has violated these basic moral principles of his culture awaits with apprehension unfortunate happenings either to himself personally, his family or to the village as a whole. He is thus not dependent solely on "external sanctions" for adhering to the moral code.

Other transgressions of the Rio Grande Pueblo moral code, such as lies, laziness, theft, uncontrolled anger and the like are considered violations of the concept of the harmonious and happy state of mind. On the other hand, positive attributes related to the cooperative, unanimity concept, such as fair play, honest dealings, generosity, hospitality, deference to the old and a mild and uninitiating demeanor receive high value in the culture.

These are qualities to which all Rio Grande Pueblo Indians aspire and which are esteemed and respected in the society. Conversely, failure to live up to these standards subjects the individual to censure and suspicion and assigns him to a marginal position in his society.

The behavior and conduct of the individual is thus strictly prescribed by the moral code. Moral standards are established by the host of relatives that comprise the extended family and are reinforced by village agencies and traditional sanctions. It is not dependent either solely or dominantly on "external sanctions," rather, the Rio Grande Pueblo culture has internalized the moral code as a "conscience" in the individual. Moreover, moral standards have become established as cultural values and ideals to which the individual must conform.

Euro-American and Rio Grande Pueblo moral codes

It is important to indicate what appear to be fundamental differences between the moral codes of Euro-American and Rio Grande Pueblo cultures. In the latter, the moral code might be characterized as group-centered. An individual who commits a transgression of the moral code jeopardizes the well-being of his whole village. He is thus burdened with a heavy responsibility and his feeling of guilt is an enormous one. Euro-American moral code, on the other hand, is personalized or individualized. An individual in this culture is alone responsible for his transgressions. He may become afflicted

497

with disease or misfortunes or suffer in the hereafter for his "sin," but his misconduct does not affect his society as a whole. His feeling of guilt, moreover, is restricted to misgivings about his own personal misbehavior and the possible consequences of such a transgression upon himself.

Another important distinction between the two moral codes is that the Rio Grande Pueblo Indian's reasons for guarding against transgressions of the moral code are essentially practical and temporal. He is concerned about protecting himself and others against the concrete realities of the temporal world, such as illness, bad crops, drought, and the like. The after life does not seriously concern the Rio Grande Pueblo Indian. The Euro-American, however, has misgivings about the violation of an abstract principle, an ideal or set of ideals to which he feels compelled to conform. With the individual who believes in Judeo-Christian concepts of heaven and hell, it may be because he has jeopardized his chances of a healthy and trouble-free life in the hereafter.

Another feature which distinguishes the Rio Grande Pueblo moral code from that of the Euro-American, is associated with the group-centered aspect discussed above. Since an individual's misbehavior brings misfortune not only to himself, but to the group as a whole, all members of the society are suspect until the guilty one is discovered. During disease epidemics, crop failures and drought conditions Rio Grande Pueblo villages are anxiety-ridden communities. Pueblo authorities watch closely the behavior of village members to determine the culprit or "witch." Gossip and accusations of witchcraft run rampant in the village as a whole. The lot of the individual who cannot account for curious or deviant behavior is extremely grave. If his behavior remains peculiar and misfortunes persist he falls prey to the community. Traditional sanctions of ridicule and witchcraft accusations make his life miserable. In extreme cases he may be subjected to physical punishment and may be banished from the village.

Outside Influences

It is remarkable that the Rio Grande Pueblo Indians have preserved their indigenous cultural patterns and values for so long a period of time. They have not been, however, completely immune to outside cultural pressures, although such influences appear to be minor in affecting the core of the culture. Nevertheless the content and certain important marginal features of Rio Grande Pueblo culture have been strongly influenced by outside contacts. Perhaps the most important of these, in terms of their deeply ingrained nature, are influences emanating from the Plains Indians. The second major category of influences are those from Euro-American cultures, first Spanish and more recently, Anglo-American. Euro-American contacts have brought important changes in Rio Grande Pueblo culture, but they seem to have affected only marginal features and particularly the area of material culture.

498

Plains Indian Influences[12]

Plains Indian influence is apparent in virtually all aspects of Rio Grande Pueblo culture. These are features which distinguish them most strikingly from the Western Pueblos. Attitudes toward war and the independent and aggressive personality traits of the Rio Grande Pueblos seem to stem from this source. These characteristics appear in a continuum—less pronounced in the Keres-speaking villages to the south and west and becoming more apparent in the eastern Tanoan-speaking villages. Thus, for instance, war emphases are particularly strong in Taos pueblo, the village most marginal, culturally and geographically, in the pueblo area.

The characteristics which may be attributed to Plains Indian influence are expressed in mythology, in ceremonial ritual and in songs and dances. They are also evident in social institutions, particularly in the presence of war cults or societies. More subtle, but a clearly distinguishing feature is the more independent and aggressive personality traits of the Rio Grande Pueblo Indians, especially is this strong among members of the Tanoan-speaking villages.

Spanish-Catholic influences[13]

Spanish influences in the area, although perhaps not as old as those emanating from Plains Indian sources

are still of considerable age. The Rio Grande Pueblos were first visited by Spaniards in 1540. Other expeditions followed and from 1600 the pattern of continuous contact started with the colonization of New Mexico. Although the Spaniards exerted strong pressures and effected important changes, the core of Rio Grande Pueblo culture seems not to have been drastically altered. Rather, the Rio Grande Pueblos adopted Spanish culture and religion as an added system distinct from their own. The indigenous system of values and moral concepts gave coherence and integration to both systems. It is important to discuss this phenomenon in some detail for it appears to be a unique type of acculturation and throws light on differences in value systems and moral concepts of the two groups.

The two cultural traditions are clearly distinct, yet they seem not to cause serious conflict to the members of these societies. Thus, for example, Pueblo Indians regard themselves as "good" Catholics and they attend mass and other services conducted by the Catholic Church. Some of the Pueblo Indian ceremonies have been adjusted to the Catholic calendar and on particular Catholic saint's days such obviously Spanish-Catholic features as vesper services, church processions, and the erection of a *santo* bower, have been incorporated as important marginal features. The Spanish-Catholic practices and rituals are, however, consciously purged of "native" or "pagan" features so that even the casual American tourist recognizes them as "non-

.12 For an excellent review of Plains Indian influences on the Rio Grande Pueblo Indians, see Lange, 1953.

13 For Spanish-Catholic influences see: Scholes, 1935, 1936–37, 1942. A brief survey may also be found in Dozier, 1954.

Indian." Conversely, the native ceremonies, are carefully freed of elements that are not strictly indigenous. The Rio Grande Pueblo Indians have been remarkably successful in these endeavors so that the kiva ceremonies and the ceremonies conducted by secret societies appear to be scrupulously free of Euro-American features. These restrictions are also applied to language. Rio Grande Pueblo Indians, particularly the older generation, know the Spanish language well. Spanish words are carefully deleted in the ritual language used in native ceremonies. Censorship of ceremonies open to the public has not generally been accorded as careful attention so that in the realm of costume and paraphernalia non-Indian elements occasionally appear, but in the esoteric rites, adherence to native usages is strictly maintained.

Early in the Spanish period Spanish authorities demanded from each pueblo a set of officers to represent the village in secular affairs conducted with Spanish officials.[14] These officers form an important group in each village, but they are appointed by the religious hierarchy and, moreover, they are restricted essentially to secular duties and are recognized as an imposed set of officers falling within the added Spanish-Catholic cultural tradition.[15]

This interesting phenomenon of the

existence of two cultural traditions appears to have resulted from the unpleasant contact situation between the Rio Grande Pueblo Indians and the Spanish colonists. Initially the pueblos were undoubtedly willing to accept Spanish culture and religion as integrated features in their own cultural system, but Spanish civil and church authorities were uncompromising. They had no tolerance for pueblo religious beliefs and ceremonial practices and used force and coercion to stamp them out. Many individuals and families fled the region, joined distant Indian groups and were eventually absorbed by these people. Those who remained met the situation by adopting the externals of Spanish culture and religion while their own religion went "underground." With the passage of time and under constant surveillance by Spanish authorities the Spanish-Catholic tradition became incorporated into the culture as an important, but separate cultural system.

Ethnographic evidence indicates that Spanish colonial values and concepts were never internalized. Pueblo world view has remained essentially indigenous and Spanish colonial practices and religion, though never fused with the native system, became interpreted according to pueblo concepts. Thus the view of the universe as orderly, the unanimous striving and the harmonious working together for the common good of the whole remained as basic cultural principles. The Spanish-Catholic tradition was accepted as an important but distinct method for

---

14 Bandelier, 1890–1892, p. 200.

15 In some of the pueblos these positions fall regularly to priests or assistant priests in the religious hierarchy so that such individuals have double roles—a sacred and a secular one.

keeping the universe functioning in its orderly fashion. Indeed, pueblo methods of coercion and social control sanctions were applied to exact observance of Spanish-Catholic practices, no less rigidly than to those of the indigenous pattern.

It must be emphasized, however, that over the years there were individuals and families who could not harmonize the practice of the two traditions. Every Rio Grande Pueblo community has accounts of members who left the village, either voluntarily or through pressure of the village, and joined neighboring Spanish communities. These were individuals who had been exposed to strong Spanish cultural influences. For the most part they were workers on the Spanish *haciendas* or in missionary work shops. Such individuals and families eventually became absorbed in the Spanish population and lost their pueblo identity.

Anglo-American Influences[16]

The Rio Grande Pueblo Indians first came in contact with Anglo-Americans just prior to the middle of the last century. After New Mexico became a part of the United States in 1846 increasing numbers of Americans entered the pueblo area. Prolonged and close contacts between these two peoples did not occur, however, until after New Mexico became a state in 1912. For various reasons, Americans did not become intimately or closely associated with Pueblo Indians. For one thing, New Mexico did not attract large numbers of people because of the general inhospitality of the land and the absence of productive natural resources. Moreover, the lands of the pueblos were already allotted and the best lands were already in the hands of non-Indians. Protestant missionaries did not work actively with these Indians for Spanish-Catholic missionaries had already accomplished the task of "converting" and the Rio Grande Pueblos were essentially closed as a missionary venture.

Generally, attitudes toward Anglo-Americans are more favorable than toward the Spaniards. The United States government was never involved in military exploits against these Indians. No disputes over land arose between the U.S. government and Pueblo Indians. Indeed, Anglo-Americans and the U.S. Government assumed the role of helpers and protectors against exploitation from Spanish neighbors. Toward the latter part of the last century reservations were set up, thus preventing further encroachment on their lands by non-Indians. Government schools and medical services were made available very early and although some individuals were taken away from their homes forcibly to be sent to boarding schools, for the most part, pueblo individuals sought schooling voluntarily. Moreover in the early 1920's a group of White friends worked actively to enforce the provisions of the Treaty of Guadalupe Hidalgo which had guaranteed the Indians lands originally assigned them by the Spanish Crown. On

16 Pueblo-Anglo-American acculturation is very sparsely treated in the literature. The best and virtually the only source is Parsons, 1939.

much of this land Spanish-Americans and other Whites had settled. The Anglo-American friends of the Indians succeeded in getting some of this land back to the Indians or in compensating them for lands thus alienated.

The favorable attitude toward Anglo-Americans and the latter's unconcern or tolerance of pueblo ceremonial practices are resulting in a movement of increasing numbers of individuals and families into the stream of American culture. This movement is indicated by an accelerating rate of White-Indian marriages and an increasing tendency to live away from pueblo communities in off-reservation locations. Increasing numbers of Pueblo Indians are also joining Protestant churches. Since these individuals usually forsake both Catholic and pueblo religious practices, it appears that the values and concepts inherent in the Anglo-Protestant tradition are also being accepted.[17]

The pattern of Spanish-Catholic-Indian acculturation established in the period of Spanish dominance appears to be repeated in Anglo-American-Pueblo Indian acculturation. That is, individuals and families become acculturated and move out of their pueblos, leaving these communities oriented essentially along indigenous lines as far as basic values and moral concepts

are concerned. There are today as many pueblo communities as there were when Anglo-Americans first appeared in the Southwest. Because of the tremendous increase in Pueblo Indian population the individual pueblo villages all reveal an increase in population even though large numbers of pueblo individuals have moved into Anglo-American cultural life. The individual pueblo communities, freed of noncomformists, still carry on native ceremonies, participate in the peculiarly pueblo Catholic tradition and hold strongly to the basic values and moral concepts described in this paper. A few of the Rio Grande Pueblo communities have in recent years placed ceremonial participation on a voluntary basis. The survival and vitality of ceremonies in these pueblos where compulsory participation is no longer demanded indicate the strength of indigenous values and concepts.

Summary

Rio Grande Pueblo values and moral concepts revolve around the view of the universe as an orderly phenomenon. All things, natural and supernatural, are logically in a state of equilibrium. Man alone can disturb this balance and when he does so, illness, famines, and all kinds of disastrous occurrences are likely to ensue. There are a number of specific ways in which man can bring about a disturbance in the universe, but they are all related to the basic concept of unanimous cooperation, both physical and of the mind. Rio Grande Pueblo social institutions and activities are anchored

---

17 Protestant converts are a vexing problem to pueblo authorities. In one pueblo a converted group was forced to leave the community, alienating houses and land. In another village attempts to expel another Protestant group have been unsuccessful, the newly converted group holding steadfast to houses and land against bitter opposition.

502

in this important principle. Although logically pueblo individuals should co-operate voluntarily and willingly, specific institutions and mechanisms exist in the culture to bring coercive pressure on the individual to compel him to conform. The life of the individual is thus rigidly circumscribed and he is filled with "guilt" and apprehension lest some act or thought of his own or of his fellow man should bring about misfortune.

So strong are the indigenous values and moral concepts of Rio Grande Pueblo culture that alien cultural influences have not succeeded in replacing them. Although individuals and families acculturate and a few pueblos have placed ceremonial participation on a voluntary basis, Rio Grande Pueblo communities remain essentially indigenous in cultural orientation.

Bibliography

Barbara Aitken, "Temperament in Native American Indian Religion," *Journal of The Royal Anthropological Institute*, No. 60 (1930).

E. A. B. Ayer, (Translator) *The Memorial of Fray Alonso de Benavides, 1630* (Chicago, 1916).

A. F. Bandelier, *Final Report of Investigations Among Indians of the Southwestern United States.* Papers of the Archaeological Institute of America: American Series, Vol. III, Pt. 1, and Vol. IV, Pt. 2. (Cambridge, Mass., 1890–92).

Richard Brandt, *Hopi Ethics* (Chicago 1954).

Edward P. Dozier, *The Hopi-Tewa of Arizona.* University of California Publications in American Archaeology and Ethnology, Vol. 44, No. 3. (1954).

N. Dumarest, *Notes on Cochiti, N. M.* Memoirs of the American Anthropological Association, No. 6, Pt. 3. Menasha, Wis., 1919).

Fred Eggan, *Social Organization of the Western Pueblos.* (Chicago, 1950).

Esther S. Goldfrank, *The Social and Ceremonial Organization of Cochiti.* Memoirs of the American Anthropological Association, No. 33. (1927).

L. J. Hobhouse, *Morals in Evolution* (London, 1906).

Clyde Kluckhohn, "The Philosophy of the Navaho Indians," In: *Ideological Differences and World Order* (Ed. F. S. C. Northrop) pp. 356–84 (New Haven, 1949).

Charles H. Lange, "A Reappraisal of Evidence of Plains Influences Among the Rio Grande Pueblos," *Southwestern Journal of Anthropology,* Vol. 9, No. 2, pp. 212–230 (1953).

Margaret Mead, *Cooperation and Competition Among Primitive Peoples* (New York, 1937).

Elsie Clews Parsons, *Notes on Ceremonialism at Laguna.* Anthropological Papers of the American Museum of Natural History, Vol. XIX, Part IV. (New York, 1920).

——, *The Pueblo of Jemez* (Andover, 1925).

——, *The Social Organization of the Tewa of New Mexico.* Memoirs of the American Anthropological Association, No. 36. (Menasha, Wis., 1929).

——, "Isleta," *47th Annual Report of the Bureau of American Ethnology* (Washington, 1932).

——, *Taos Pueblo.* General Series in Anthropology, No. 2. (Menasha, Wis., 1936).

——, *Pueblo Indian Religion.* 2 vols. (Chicago, 1939).

Gerhart Piers and Milton B. Singer, *Shame and Guilt* (Springfield, Ill., 1953).

Paul Radin, *Primitive Man as a Philosopher* (New York, 1927).

Robert Redfield, *The Primitive World View*. Proceedings, American Philosophical Society, Vol. 96, No. 1 (1952).

F. V. Scholes, "The First Decade of the Inquisition in New Mexico," *New Mexico Historical Review*, Vol. 10. (1935).

——, "Church and State in New Mexico," *New Mexico Historical Review*, Vol. 11. (1936–1937).

——, *Troublous Times in New Mexico, 1659–1670*. Historical Society of New Mexico, Publications in History, Vol. 11. Albuquerque, 1942).

A. Sutherland, *The Origin and Growth of the Moral Instinct* (London, 1898).

E. Westermarck, *The Origin and Development of Moral Ideas* (London, 1906).

L. A. White, "The Acoma Indians," *Forty-seventh Annual Report* [for 1929–1930]. Bureau of American Ethnology, pp. 17–192. Smithsonian Institution (Washington, 1932a).

——, *The Pueblo of San Felipe*. Memoirs of the American Anthropological Association, No. 38. (Menasha, Wis., 1932b).

——, *The Pueblo of Santo Domingo, New Mexico*. Memoirs of the American Anthropological Association, No. 38. (Menasha, Wis., 1935).

——, *The Pueblo of Santa Ana, New Mexico*. Memoirs of the American Anthropological Association, No. 60. (Menasha, Wis., 1942).

Edward P. Dozier
Northwestern University

Ripley, George: *see* Moral Philosophy in America.

rites: *see* ceremony; Jewish Ethics and Its Civilization; ritual.

ritual: *see* ceremony; Jewish Ethics and Its Civilization; Mundurucu Indians, A Dual System of Ethics; Pakot, the Moral System of; Riffian Morals; Rio Grande Pueblo Indians; rites; Zuni Indians, Morals of.

ritual and ethics: *see* Jewish Ethics and Its Civilization.

rivalry: *see* Zuni Indians, Morals of.

robbery: *see* Aztec Morals; Dante, Alighieri; Hammurapi, Code of; Jewish Ethics and Its Civilization.

Robinson, John: *see* Puritan Morals.

Roman Catholicism: *see* Catholicism; Liguori, St. Alphonsus and Catholic Moral Philosophy; Puritan Morals.

Roman law: *see* Hammurapi, Code of; Stoics, the.

Roman philosophy: *see* Augustine and Morals; Stoics, the.

romanticism: *see* Goethe, Johann Wolfgang von.

Romelly: *see* Utilitarianism.

Romer, A. S.: *see* Primitive Morals.

Ross, Sir (William) David

Sir (William) David Ross was born in Scotland in 1877, and was educated at the University of Edinburgh and at Balliol College, Oxford. He was a Lecturer, Fellow, and Tutor at Oriel College, Oxford, from 1900–1929, and Provost of Oriel College from 1929–1947, when he retired. In 1923–28 he was Deputy White's Professor of Moral Philosophy at Oxford, in 1935–36 Gifford Lecturer at Aberdeen University, and in 1938–9 Visiting Professor at Columbia University. From 1941–44 he was Vice-Chancellor of Oxford, and from 1944–47 Pro-Vice-Chancellor. He was knighted in 1938. In philosophy he is known chiefly for his editions and translations of, and commentaries on, the works of Aris totle, and for his systematic works in the field of ethics.

Ross's two books on ethics are among the few most important works in this field of the twentieth century. Of the two, *The Right and the Good* (1930) was historically the more important, for it contained the first relatively full statement of a system of ethics from the Oxford neo-intuitionist point of view which had grown up under the influence of H. A. Prichard (excepting E. F. Carritt's less influential *Theory of Morals*, 1928). The more recent and more complete *Foundations of Ethics* (1939) is largely a restatement of this system, with some additions, modifications, and replies to criticisms. It was the earlier book which brought to a height the attack on teleological ethics which Prichard had begun (it also renewed the attack on naturalistic ethics which G. E. Moore had opened), and which occasioned the counter-attacks which came from various quarters in the 1930s. Yet it represents in a sense a synthesis of the two opposing views. What is attacked is the utilitarianism of the Cambridge moralists, the view that the rightness of an action is determined wholly by its conduciveness to good; what is given up is the earlier extreme deontological position of Prichard, the view that conduciveness to good is not a right-making characteristic at all; what results is a more moderate deontological theory, the view that conduciveness to good is a right-making characteristic, but only one among others, and not always *prima inter pares*. Prichard's theory of

obligation and Moore's theory of value, both modified in certain respects, are thus united in a moral theory about the relation of value and obligation which one is tempted to call an "Oxbridge" point of view.

In *The Right and the Good,* Ross uses "right" in the sense of "objectively right," and as equivalent to "morally obligatory." He distinguishes various senses of "good" but is concerned with the sense in which it means "intrinsically good." Both rightness and goodness in these senses are, for him, indefinable and non-natural. They are independent of each other except for the fact that "being conducive to good" or "being optimific" synthetically entails "being *prima facie* right." Besides intuiting this entailment, we may also intuit, independently, certain other propositions about *prima facie* rightness and certain propositions about goodness. These intuitions about what is good are relevant to every ethical decision, since the promotion of the good is a *prima facie* duty in every situation, but what is actually a duty cannot ever be inferred merely from a knowledge of what is good or of what is conducive to good, unless no other more stringent *prima facie* duty is relevant to the situation. Thus Ross regards a consideration of consequences, even of the value of consequences, as being relevant to the determination of the rightness of an action, but not as settling the matter.

The main lines of Ross's views about the right come from Prichard. Ross first distinguishes rightness and moral goodness, act and action. An act

505

is a bit of conscious behavior, a conscious origination of something, taken by itself; an action is an act taken together with its motive. Actions are morally good or morally bad, depending on the quality of their motives; acts are right or wrong, depending on whether or not they actually do produce a certain state of affairs. Thus motives and their moral qualities have nothing to do with rightness (Ross, quite neglects to consider intentions, as most of his critics have pointed out). An act is right or wrong simply because it originates or does not originate a certain state of affairs. It may be right though its motive be bad, and wrong though its motive be good. And my duty is to act, to originate a certain state of affairs; it is not my duty merely to try to originate this state of affairs, and it is not my duty to originate this state of affairs from a sense of duty or from a good motive.

There is room for a misunderstanding here. When Ross says that success and failure in producing a certain state of affairs are the only tests of the performance of duty, he is admitting the relevance of consequences, and this admission may seem to be inconsistent with his deontologism, in particular with his assertion that the rightness of an act depends solely on its intrinsic nature. However, for Ross, an act is not one thing which produces a certain state of affairs which is another thing. An act *is* the producing of a certain state of affairs. Hence its "consequences" belong to its intrinsic nature, and must be known if we are to judge whether it has the greatest possible balance of *prima facie* rightness over *prima facie* wrongness. An act is right or wrong as being the production of the state of affairs of which it is the production. There is no legerdemain about this doctrine. Certainly it involves no admission on Ross's part of the "consequential" or utilitarian theory. For it does not involve saying that the rightness of an act depends entirely on the *value* of the state of affairs of which it is the production.

Next Ross distinguishes "*prima facie* rightness or obligatoriness" and "actual or absolute rightness or obligatoriness." What is meant by an actually or absolutely right or obligatory act will be clear. Ross says, to anyone who has asked, "What is right or obligatory for me to do in this case?" *Prima facie* rightness or obligatoriness is the characteristic, which certain types of action have, "of tending to be an actual duty." For instance, promise-keeping is a *prima facie* duty. That is, if a certain act has the characteristic of keeping a promise, then it is *prima facie* right, and will be actually or absolutely right, if it has no other characteristic which is "morally significant." Put otherwise, being an act of promise-keeping is a right-making characteristic; it makes any act which possesses it *prima facie* right or right so far as it goes. In still other words, the statement that an act keeps a promise synthetically entails the statement that it is *prima facie* right, which in turn is equivalent to the hypothetical statement that it is actually right, if certain conditions obtain. The notion of *prima facie* rightness is thus definable in terms of actual rightness, and is not another ultimate notion.

There are several *prima facie* duties, several right-making characteristics. Ross gives a list of them which he holds to be, "in principle," complete: duties of fidelity, among which are promise-keeping and truth-telling, duties of reparation, duties of gratitude, duties of justice, duties of beneficence, duties of self-improvement, and duties of non-maleficence. About the last four, it must be noted, Ross is a teleologist. Duties of non-maleficence depend on the *prima facie* duty not to bring evil into existence. Duties of beneficence, duties of self-improvement, and duties of justice all come "under the general principle that we should produce as much good as possible." It is especially noteworthy that Ross takes a teleological conception of duties of justice, which for other neo-intuitionists are "very artificially explained" or even "explained away" on any but a deontological view of them. They rest, Ross says, on the fact that it is a *prima facie* duty to bring about the "complex good" which consists in "the proportionment of happiness to virtue." Ross's deontologism appears only in his contention that duties of the first three kinds do not come under the general principle that we should produce as much good as possible.

A given act may have more than one right-making characteristic. Or, as in the familiar cases of "conflicts of duties," it may have one or more right-making characteristics and one or more wrong-making characteristics. In the latter case, is the act actually right or not? This depends on whether or not there is a balance of *prima facie* rightness over *prima facie* wrongness. But there will usually be other possible acts which are *prima facie* right or both *prima facie* right and *prima facie* wrong, and, where this is so, our question will also depend on whether or not the given act has, of all acts possible in the situation, the greatest balance of *prima facie* rightness over *prima facie* wrongness. For estimating these balances there is, however, according to Ross, no general principle. Even granting that we know all of the non-ethical characteristics of all of the acts in question, which never is the case, the difficulties of answering our problem are not over. Some *prima facie* duties are, indeed, more stringent than others, and this can often be seen, but there is no general rule for estimating their comparative stringency. The various *prima facie* rightnesses and wrongnesses are independent and cannot be compounded according to any general rule; they are irreducibly many, fall into no invariable hierarchy, and cannot be accurately measured or compared. What is our actual duty at any time cannot be known from any general principle. Our knowledge of actual duties is uninferred and immediate. Nor does it contain certainty. In fact, it consists of particular and "highly fallible" intuitions, and is not really *knowledge,* but only "more or less probable opinion." The only certain principle about actual duty is that we should do the act which actually has the greatest possible balance of *prima facie* rightness over

ROSS, SIR (WILLIAM) DAVID

prima facie wrongness. But, if we ever actually do this act, we are simply "fortunate." *Prima facie* duties, on the other hand, do represent intuitive knowledge. A proposition asserting one is an expression of a self-evident synthetic and necessary connection between a non-ethical characteristic and the ethical characteristic of rightness. We first see this connection in a particular instance of the non-ethical characteristic involved, and then, by what has been called "intuitive induction," we see that it necessarily obtains in all instances of this characteristic. Yet, in our moral decisions, this knowledge of *prima facie* duties cannot be taken as giving logical premises from which we may deduce our actual duties. It is not, however, otiose, for it is necessary as a "psychological preparation" for the intuition of these actual duties. By this doctrine Ross effects a synthesis of dogmatic and perceptual intuitionism in his theory of obligation.*

The notion of *prima facie* duties, claims, or responsibilities is the answer of contemporary dogmatic deontological intuitionism to some of the stock objections to earlier forms of that view, made alike by philosophical intuitionists like Sidgwick and Rashdall, by perceptual intuitionists like Carritt in *The Theory of Morals,* by idealists, and by naturalists. It is admitted, even insisted, that no general material rules about actual duties can be self-evident or without excep-

tion. But, it is argued, it does not follow that there can be no general material *noemata moralia* which have no exceptions. *Prima facie* obligations are general and self-evident, and do not admit of exceptions. One may be over-ruled by another, but even when this is the case, it is still a *prima facie* obligation; we feel, Ross says, a certain compunction at not fulfilling it. The alleged difficulty caused by "conflicting duties" is due to a misconception. Such conflict as there is here is a matter of *prima facie* duties. One never has an actual duty to do both of two incompatible acts or both to do and not to do a certain act. Even *prima facie* duties can conflict only when they are equal in force, and then neither is our actual duty. Both are actually right, but it is our duty only to do either one of them.

Ross's theory of value in *The Right and the Good* is, as I have indicated, similar to Moore's. Like rightness, goodness is a consequential property, which is dependent only on the intrinsic nature of the thing possessing it, and which is the object of an intellectual intuition. It is a quality, not a relation, relational property, or "objective," though it may be a quality of objectives or facts and not of substances. It is not a subjective quality, but it is a quality only of states of mind or of facts about them. The following mental states are good: virtue, pleasure, the apportionment of pleasure to the virtuous, knowledge, right opinion, and such compounds of these as aesthetic enjoyment and mutual love. In other words, there are, rough-

---

*See article "Henry Sidgwick" on dogmatic and perceptual intuitionism.

508

ly, three good-making characteristics: "being virtuous," "being pleasant," and "being an instance of knowledge." We intuit a self-evident one-way synthetic and necessary connection between each of them and goodness. The opposite characteristics are bad-making. A thing which is made good by being virtuous is *morally* good. Persons, actions, motives, and characters may be morally good. Experiences that are made good by being pleasant or by being instances of knowledge are not morally good. But it is the same quality of goodness which is possessed by all good things, however it is conditioned, and however it may vary in degree. It is self-evident that virtue is better than knowledge and knowledge than pleasure. Now, any concrete state of mind is complex, and the real question concerns our judgment as to its goodness as a whole. Is the judgment that it is good on the whole intuitive, or is it inferable from the goodness of its components? If it is intuitive, is it an instance of knowledge, as the above intuitions about the goodness of virtue, pleasure, and knowledge are, or is it only an instance of opinion? Moore holds it to be intuitive, owing to the Principle of Organic Unities. Ross admits the truth of this principle, although he doubts its importance in application. While he admits that in general the value of a whole cannot be deduced from the sum of the values of its parts, he thinks that in the case of a state of mind all of whose elements are good, we may infer, albeit not with certainty, that it is good on the whole, even if we cannot infer the degree of

its goodness. Thus he seems to think that the goodness of such complex states of mind as love and aesthetic experience can be inferred from the goodness of their components, though he immediately adds that, even so, our judgment that love is good is actually intuitive and not inferred. At the same time, he agrees that in the case of wholes which have both good and bad elements, our judgments are more doubtful, and are neither self-evident nor inferable from judgments on the elements, that is, they are intuitive, and they are matters, not of knowledge, but of opinion. In such cases our intuitive knowledge of the value of the elements of the whole serves only as a psychological preparation for our intuitive opinion as to its own value.

Thus Ross's theory of value is almost exactly analogous to his theory of obligation. Both are pluralistic, the one involving an irreducible plurality of good-making characteristics, the other an irreducible plurality of right-making characteristics. Both provide a synthesis of dogmatic with perceptual intuitionism. In both there is intuitive knowledge of general propositions; in both there is, nevertheless, only intuitive opinion in particular concrete cases. The conception of the relation of the intuitive knowledge of general truths to the intuitive opinion in particular cases is, in its main features, the same in both. Yet just here appear such differences as there are between them. In the theory of obligation the impossibility of determining what is actually right in concrete cases on the basis of general truths is due chiefly to the fact that right-making characteristics fall into no fixed hierarchy. In the theory of value *this* difficulty in passing from general truths to a decision on the goodness of concrete experiences does not obtain, since good-making characteristics do fall into a fixed hierarchy. What renders impossible the estimation of the goodness of concrete experiences on the basis of general truths is a principle which does not apply to rightness but which does apply to goodness—the Principle of Organic Unities or Values.

We may now state briefly the somewhat altered position put forward by Ross in *Foundations of Ethics*. Rightness Ross here regards as an indefinable, non-natural relation. He still holds that to act from a certain motive is no part of the content of duty. Emotions and desires may be right, he grants, as well as morally good, but they cannot be obligatory. In general, however, he brings rightness and moral goodness closer together than they were in *The Right and the Good*. This he can do, in part, because he has rejected the objective theory of obligation in favor of the subjective theory. My duty, on his present view, is simply to *set myself* to do what I *judge* to be morally most suitable in the circumstances as I *take* them to be; it is not my duty to do what is *actually* most suitable in the circumstances as they *are*.

In his theory of value Ross has also made some changes. He distinguishes three senses of the word "good," when used as a predicate, not counting the sense in which it means "useful." In

the first sense "good" is synonymous with "being a worthy object of admiration," in the second with "being a worthy object of interest," and in the third with "being an actual object of interest." Ross then denies the view which he previously held, along with Moore, that intrinsically good things are all good in the same sense. Virtue, knowledge, and aesthetic experience, he says, are good in the first two senses. The pleasure of others and the distribution of pleasure in proportion to virtue are good in the second sense but not in the first. My own pleasure is good only in the third sense. Now "only what is good in our first or in our second sense is a thing which for that reason we have a duty to produce." Thus we have a *prima facie* duty to produce virtue, knowledge, and aesthetic experience, and a *prima facie* duty to produce pleasure for others and a fair distribution of pleasure among others, but no duty, even *prima facie*, to produce pleasure for ourselves.

In the first sense, Ross still holds, "good" stands for a simple non-natural quality; the synonym assigned is a mere synonym, not a definition, for the emotion of admiration presupposes the thought that what is admired is good. In the other two cases, however, the synonyms assigned are definitions. Hence, in the other two senses, "good" stands for a definable relation, in the second for one which is non-natural, and in the third for one which is natural. "Worthiness" Ross explains in two different ways. In one place, he explains "being a worthy object of interest" as meaning "being the object of an interest which is *morally good.*" Here he is defining "good" in the second sense in terms of "good" in the first sense. In another place, he explains the phrase in question as meaning "being the object of an interest which is right." Here he is defining "good" in its second sense in terms of "right." In neither case does "worthiness" involve any new ethical notion.

Ross denies, then, that what we *mean* when we call an object good is always that we are taking some attitude toward it. What we mean is sometimes that we ought to take a certain attitude toward the object, and sometimes even that it has in itself a certain goodness. What we *express* is another matter. "What we *express* when we call an object good is our attitude towards it." In this way Ross finds an element of truth in the emotive theory of ethics, just as he finds, in the way indicated a moment ago, an element of truth in ethical naturalism. Here again, then, he offers a synthesis of opposing views.

Bibliography

Aristotle (1923).
Aristotle's Nicomachean Ethics. Translated with Introduction (1925).
The Right and the Good (1930).
Foundations of Ethics, Gifford Lectures (1939).
Kant's Ethical Theory (1954).

William K. Frankena
University of Michigan

Ross, W. D.: *see* Broad, C. D.; Clarke, Samuel; Cumberland, Richard; Moore, George Edward; Price, Richard; Prichard, H. A.

Rousseau: *see* Minor Socratics.
Royce, Josiah: *see* Moral Philosophy in America.
rudeness: *see* Hindu Ethics; Puritan Morals.
Rudnyov: *see* Soviet Morality, Current.
rules: *see* Aboriginals of Yirkalla; Aquinas, Thomas, Moral Views of; Cudworth, Ralph; Dewey, John; Green, T. H.; Jesuits, the, Moral Theology of; Marxist Theory of Morals; Meta-ethics and Normative Ethics; Muslim Morals; Navaho Morals; Quakerism, Classical, The Morality of; Soloviev, Wladimir.
rules, general: *see* Ross, Sir (William) David.
rules of conduct: *see* Hobbes, Thomas.
ruling class: *see* Marxist Theory of Morals.

Russell, Bertrand

In ethics, as in other areas of philosophy, Bertrand Russell has not hesitated to change his mind about the most basic questions. Nowhere is his intellectual catholicity more conspicuous, for he has traversed all of the major positions in contemporary ethics in the course of his writings. However his contributions to ethics fall far short of the caliber of the work which has distinguished him in other fields. For the most part his ethics has been derivative from other thinkers. His first extended essay on the subject is, as Russell points out, "largely based on" Moore's *Principia Ethica* (1:p. 1, n.1). His most recent statement, though radically opposed to the theory presented in the earlier work, contains, as he says, "nothing startlingly original"

511

(6:p. 7). And though he was among the first to advance an "emotive" theory in recent thought, this view is not elaborated systematically by Russell, so that it is simply asserted rather than argued and defended.

Russell (b. 1872), perhaps the best-known philosopher of this century, has not found rigorous thought in logic, epistemology and the philosophy of science to be incompatible with first-hand involvement in the vital social and political questions of his day. It seems clear that he has been less concerned with ethical *theory* than with such specific issues as education and peace and war, and with the advancement of his own well-known axiological ideal—creating, in a world alien to human values, a life for all mankind which will be directed by knowledge and informed by love and hope. His deep concern with the disputes and wars that have ravaged the modern world has, however, given direction to his ethical thought. "Ethics," he says, "is necessary because men's desires conflict."[1] As will be pointed out, all of his later writings have been addressed to the "political" questions how, if at all, value-disagreements can be adjudicated, and how the conflicting aspirations of different individuals and groups can be made harmonious with each other.

In the early essay, "The Elements of Ethics," referred to above, however, Russell denies that ethics is concerned with "practical" questions of choice

and conduct. In seeking knowledge it is numbered among the "sciences" (1:p. 2). "Good" or "intrinsic value" is the central concept in ethics, but, like Moore, Russell contends that it is indefinable. This is established by appeal to our "state of mind" when confronted with an ostensible definition of "good," which is not that of assent to a linguistic analysis of meaning (p. 9). Hence Russell can only "characterise" good as that which "on its own account ought to exist" (p. 5). Since goodness is an intrinsic property of things, Russell holds, in contrast to his later views, that it exists independently of our desires. Thus he seeks to preserve the common-sense conviction that disagreements concerning intrinsic value are meaningful. Though Russell says little about the cognition of values, he holds out the hope that "a very large measure of agreement on ethical questions may be expected to result from clearer thinking" (p. 57). He follows Moore in other particulars, e.g., the principle of "organic unities" (pp. 54–55).

He also takes over from Moore a teleological interpretation of "right" and with it the implication that judgments of right action are empirically confirmable. Russell wishes to take account, as any utilitarianism must, of the disparity between the actual consequences of the moral act and those which could reasonably have been anticipated, and to distinguish these further from the conscientiousness and praiseworthiness of the agent. Here, uniquely, his analysis is somewhat more detailed and revealing than

---

[1] Bertrand Russell, *A History of Western Philosophy* (New York, 1945) p. 779.

Principia. The act which produces the greatest amount of good is the "most fortunate" act (p. 22). The act which is "objectively right" is that which "of all that are possible, will probably have the best consequences" (p. 25; cf., p. 57), though Russell does not hold consistently to the view that this is a definition (cf., pp. 25, 26). The "subjectively right" or "virtuous" act is that which the agent would judge to be right after considering the choice "candidly and with due care" (p. 28). The distinction can then be drawn between those agents whose conception of "objective rightness" is "erroneous" and those whose decisions are thoughtless or insufficiently reflective. In "Elements of Ethics," as in later writings (cf., 6:pp. 97–98), Russell espouses determinism, using the familiar argument that it is not this theory but that of "free-will" which renders moral deliberation and praise and blame, senseless and futile.

Many years after the publication of this paper, Russell testified[2] that he had been led to abandon the doctrines of the indefinability and objectivity of good because of the criticisms advanced against him by Santayana in the essay "Hypostatic Ethics."[3] There Santayana had argued that value has no existence apart from human desire and interest, that morality is therefore based upon irrational preferences, and that Russell's theory, which is intended to make moral debate meaningful,

actually issues in obscurantism and intransigent dogmatism.

In his succeeding writings, accordingly, Russell executes a volte-face. He now says that "it is we who create value, and our desires which confer value" (2:p. 17). No reasons can be given in justification of desire and conflicting desires for mutually incompatible ends are not amenable to rational argument (cf., 4:p. 139). Whereas science can determine the effectiveness of means for the attainment of some objective, it "cannot decide questions of value . . . because they cannot be intellectually decided at all, and lie outside the realm of truth and falsehood" (3:p. 243).

We remain confronted, however, with the most grievously "practical" of human problems—that the fulfillment of the desires of some individual, institution or nation demands the frustration of those of other persons or groups. We are therefore constrained to try to overcome the conflict of desires, if we are not to have recourse to violence. Though "proof" of the "validity" of any desire is, in the nature of the case, impossible, we may try to alter and re-direct desires so that they become more nearly inclusive and cooperative. "Only passion can control passion, and only a contrary impulse or desire can check impulse."[4] Value-judgments atempt to serve just this function. Although they appear grammatically to be assertive, they are optative (cf., 5:p. 719): "this is good in itself" is equivalent to "would that

2 Sellars and Hospers, eds.: *Readings in Ethical Theory* (New York, 1952) p. 1, n.

3 George Santayana, *Winds of Doctrine* (New York, 1913) pp. 138–154.

4 Bertrand Russell, *Principles of Social Reconstruction* (London, 1916) p. 12.

everybody desired this" (3:p. 235; cf., 4:p. 247). Russell's "political" concern is made manifest by the fact that he never considers seriously any other of the possible "emotivist" analyses of the value-judgment. The judgment is always a hortatory injunction addressed by the speaker to those whose desires are parochial or divisive. Ethics, Russell says, "can have no importance" (2:p. 30) unless it directs human desire toward common goals. Hence he contends that even the foundational definitions of moral theory are persuasive in character: "When I say that the morality of conduct is to be judged by its probable consequences, I mean that I desire to see approval given to behaviour likely to realize social purposes which we desire" (2:p. 30).

Ethical judgments and ethical theory are, then, devices of social control comparable to educational institutions and legal codes. Although Russell calls his theory "subjectivistic" (3:p. 238), he has always recognized and insisted upon a salient feature of ethical discourse which other "subjectivists" have either ignored or denied viz., its impersonality. The ethical judgment, on Russell's translation, makes no reference to the speaker, but rather urges the kind of world which would permit the greatest possible satisfaction of any and all desires (4:p. 274). Russell does not, however, claim any greater validity or authoritativeness for such a judgment, other than the increase in persuasive force which is thereby gained. It is in this way that we "seem to give universal importance to our

desires" (3:p. 233). But "the desire remains mine even when what is desired has no reference to myself."[5]

Russell's most extended treatment of ethics, recently published, suffers from an inner duplicity which can be understood in the light of his earlier works. *Human Society*, characteristically, places ethics in a social context: "One may lay it down broadly that the whole subject of ethics arises from the pressure of the community on the individual" (6:p. 124; cf., also, pp. 16, 60). Russell presents definitions of the chief ethical predicates which seem to constitute the foundations of a straightforward "naturalistic" theory: "good" is defined as "satisfaction of desire" (p. 55); the sole criteria of "better" are the number and intensity of desires; " 'right' conduct is that which, on the evidence, is likely to produce the greatest balance of good over evil" (p. 50; cf., also, pp. 125, 145). It follows that all axiological and moral judgments are, in principle, empirically verifiable. And it is then meaningful to say that one moral code is superior to another (cf., pp. 45, 128).

Recurrently, however, Russell abandons this position. The difficulty is no longer, as in the days of *Principia Ethica,* that of distinguishing between a definition and a "significant proposition." When Russell mentions this problem at all, his discussion is undeveloped and inconclusive (cf., pp. 72, 88). The difficulty arises, rather, for Russell, as for many contemporary ethicists, within the "pragmatic" dimension of language—these definitions

[5] *History of Western Philosophy*: p. 116.

cannot "serve any purpose" (pp. 80–81) or they are of "no practical importance" (p. 84) unless they are efficacious in altering the motives to behavior. Merely to adduce evidence is frequently futile in the face of intractably partisan desires. Hence Russell thinks himself compelled to revert to the view that ethical judgments cannot be established factually (p. 25) and that they are significantly different from "scientific" propositions (pp. 88, 104–105). Though he seems, on the whole, more inclined here than in earlier writings, to the belief that moral judgments are meaningful and reasonable, he wavers between this view and its opposite, which he appears to believe is implied by the fact that ethical judgments are not coercive when addressed to those whose convictions are obdurate.

This inconsistency is never overcome by Russell and it is fatal to the adequacy of his theory. It is the philosophical expression of the perplexity of a man whose courageous life-long struggle on behalf of a humane and liberal way of life has been beset by the implacable fanaticism and irrationalism of his time.

Bibliography

B. Russell, *Philosophical Essays* (1910).
——, *What I Believe* (1925).
——, *Religion and Science* (1935).
——, *Power: A New Social Analysis* (1938).
——, *Human Society in Ethics and Politics* (1954).
Paul Arthur Schilpp, (ed.), *The Philosophy of Bertrand Russell* (1944).

Jerome Stolnitz
University of Rochester

Russell, Bertrand: *see* Ayer, Alfred, J.; Language and Ethics; Moore, George Edward.

Russia: *see* Berdyaev, Nicolas; Dostoyevsky, Fyodor; Khomiakov, Alexey; Marxist Theory of Morals; Soloviev, Wladimir; Soviet Morality, Current; Tolstoy, Leo.

Russian Social Democratic Party: *see* Soviet Morality, Current.

S

Sabbath observance: *see* Hammurapi, Code of; Puritan Morals.

sacred: *see* Aboriginals of Yirkalla.

sacred and secular: *see* Muslim Morals.

sacrifice: *see* Aztec Morals; Hindu Ethics; Jewish Ethics and Its Civilization.

Sadducees: *see* Christian Moral Philosophy; Jewish Ethics and Its Civilization.

Sa, Emmanuel: *see* Jesuits, the, Moral Theology of.

sage: *see* China, Moral Philosophies of; Minor Socratics.

sagehood: *see* China, Moral Philosophies of.

Sailer, Johann M.: *see* Jesuits, the, Moral Theology of.

Saint-Cyran: *see* Jesuits, the, Moral Theology of.

saintliness: *see* Jewish Ethics and Its Civilization; Muslim Morals.

saints: *see* Aztec Morals; Schopenhauer, Arthur.

salvation: *see* Augustine and Morals; Cudworth, Ralph; Hegel, G. W. F.; Moral Philosophy in America; Quakerism, Classical, The Morality of; Schopenhauer, Arthur; Spinoza.

salvation, secular: *see* Soviet Morality, Current.

Sanchez, Thomas: *see* Jesuits, the, Moral Theology of.

sanctification: *see* Jewish Ethics and Its Civilization.

sanctions: *see* Aboriginals of Yirkalla; Primitive Morals; Rio Grande Pueblo Indians; Utilitarianism.

sanctity of human life: *see* Soviet Morality, Current.

Sanhedrin: *see* Jewish Ethics and Its Civilization.

Santayana: *see* Moral Philosophy in America; Russell, Bertrand.

Sartre, Jean Paul: *see* French Existentialism and Moral Philosophy.

satisfaction: *see* Dewey, John; Major Ethical Viewpoints.

Savonarola: *see* Machiavelli, Niccolo.

scepticism: *see* Hume, David; Moral Philosophy in America; Sophists, the.

Scheler, Max, The Moral Philosophy of

Of German Protestant and Jewish parentage, Max Scheler (1874–1928) was born in Munich and received his university training at Berlin, Heidelberg, and Jena. At the latter institution he received his doctorate under the idealist philosopher of religion, Rudolf Eucken, and taught philosophy for several years. Subsequently, he held professorships at Munich, Cologne, and Frankfort-on-Main. Scheler was associated with Edmund Husserl in

517

editing the *Annual for Philosophy and Phenomenological Research,* the first two volumes of which contained his most important ethical treatise: *Formalism in Ethics and the Ethics of Intrinsic Value* (1913, 1916). In 1913, there also appeared his phenomenological study of sympathy, love, and hate, which was later issued in a considerably revised edition as *Nature and Forms of Sympathy* (1923). These two books were his major contributions to moral philosophy and immediately established his reputation as a leading philosopher, representing the typical concern of the Munich School of phenomenology for problems of value and real objectivity.

In 1916, Scheler returned to the Catholic Church, which he had entered briefly as a youth. His Catholic period lasted until about 1922, and was marked by a series of works on the philosophy of religion and the means of reconciliation between traditional religious and moral values and the modern mind. The most influential of these writings was *On the Eternal in Man* (1921), which examined the nature of philosophy, the relation between religion and metaphysics, and the cultural renewal of Europe. But Scheler moved on restlessly from Catholicism to his own religious and intellectual position. His two main lines of interest after 1922 were the sociology of knowledge and a philosophical anthropology, represented by his treatises on *The Forms of Knowledge and Society* (1926) and *Man's Place in the Cosmos* (1928). He had just settled in Frankfort-on-Main and

written the preface to the latter publication when he suffered a heart attack and died, without completing his projected metaphysics and philosophical anthropology.

Max Scheler had an engaging but somewhat unstable personality. His private life was tumultuous and undisciplined, but it was also marked by an admirable gentleness and warmhearted sympathy. Intellectually, he was bold enough to attempt a synthesis between traditional doctrines and the newest methods. In describing man as a beast avid for the latest novelties, however, he was portraying his own restlessness and inability to abide for long in any position. Nevertheless, there was an underlying continuity in his odyssey from phenomenology to Catholicism to the evolutionary pantheism of his closing years. They represented the progressive stages in which he sought to give a basis in actuality to the essential objects which were his point of departure and abiding interest.

Scheler's standpoint in ethics can be stated in three basic propositions. 1) There is an a priori structure on the side of the intrinsic content and relations of moral values. 2) There is an objective hierarchy of moral values, correlated with an order of value-responses on the part of the ethical person. 3) Love is the chief means for obtaining ethical insight, and the order of love determines the ethical status of the person.

1) Although he often criticized Kant's formalism in ethics, Scheler

518

also regarded his philosophy as sound in many respects, especially in its repudiation of earlier systems. Kant's philosophy is incomplete but not fundamentally mistaken. Thus, Scheler accepted the distinction between a priori and a posteriori truths, as well as the relation between a priori truths and experience. But he refused to be bound down by the limits which Kant set for the sphere of a priori truths which are relevant to experience and knowledge. In Husserl's phenomenological method, he saw a tool for extending the boundaries of human knowledge. The descriptive approach shows that more is given in intuition than just its sense contents. Among the given factors are the intelligible essential objects, which are grasped through a proportionate intuitive act called by Scheler an "essential insight." These objects must also be included in the scope of experience.

Our intuition of essential structures is an a priori act, in that it liberates the mind from purely psychological, contingent circumstances and opens up the essential laws governing all actual conditions. It uncovers a priori determinations on the side of the given, material content of knowledge, distinct from the formal structures of consciousness. Scheler challenged the Kantian assumption that the only a priori factors open to our mind are purely formal ones. Our essential insight manifests the a priori aspects precisely as belonging to the given materials of intuition.

This epistemological position entails some significant consequences for ethics, as Scheler is quick to point out. There is an a priori content of moral value objectively given to our essential insight, and not constructed out of the form of legality or the categorical imperative alone. Because of this intuitive presentation of the determinate modes and relations of ethical values, the ethical judgments expressive of these a priori factors are fully objective and experientially grounded. Hence there is no good reason for refusing to regard such judgments as strict instances of knowledge, in as complete a sense as the judgments in physics and mathematics. Ethical judgments have all the requisite marks of universality, necessity, intuitive content, and objective reference, and indeed possess these qualifications in a more absolute way than do the physical sciences. It is not so much the Kantian fact of freedom as the insight into essential moral structures that assures the objectivity and scientific status of ethical judgments, in Scheler's eyes. He is therefore ready to establish a sharper distinction than Kant deemed advisable between ethical knowledge and ethical action. The will is guided in its action by ethical knowledge, which is gained by our view of, and feeling for, the inherent a priori patterns of moral value.

Ethical judgments are objective only because of the objectivity and availability of moral values themselves. Distinct, intrinsic moral values and their relations are just as open to our a priori knowledge as is any general, formal principle of morality, such as the Kantian categorical imperative.

Kant had been reluctant to admit any other basis of morality than the purely formal motive of respect for self-imposed law, because he thought that any foundation in the material aspect of morality would reduce it to a pursuit of success and utility. Scheler followed Kant in rejecting any ethical standard based on a relation of the will to ends, goods, success, or utility. But he denied that the only alternative is ethical formalism, since this supposes the limitation of knowable a priori elements to the form of ethical conduct. Once granted that the inherent content and modality of ethical values are open to our intuitive gaze, the way is prepared for avoiding formalism without falling into associationism and utilitarianism. The intrinsic content of ethical knowledge is furnished not by ends or goods or results of action, but by intuited values. Thus without revoking the Kantian critique of a morality of ends and one based on psychological factors, Scheler went beyond the limits of ethical formalism.

2) A further development of this same theme concerns the precise way in which values confront us. They are not given to our essential insight as discrete, atomic units but within a context of objective relations. The hierarchy of values is not a subjective creation or a formalistic imposition, but is the way in which the world of values reveals itself to our inspection. Scheler offers a description of the several spheres of value presented to man. There is an order of rank ascending from material values (useful things and biological satisfactions) to cultural values (projects of an esthetic, scientific, speculative, or political sort), and culminating in religious values. All of these values have an ethical significance, depending on the manner in which we establish relations with them.

There is a proportionate response on the part of the evaluating person. Moral duty is not based on the purely formal principle of respect for the law, any more than it is on the empirical links of association. Beyond both Kant and Hume is a new alternative proposed by Scheler. Obligation rests on the essential law binding the human person to respond to values in accord with their objectively given hierarchy. The essential ranking of value-structures in themselves places a correlative demand upon man to conform his valuing acts with this ordered pattern. His valuational acts are just as "intentional" or regulated by the inherent content of given objects as are his more theoretical operations. Husserl's intentionality of consciousness is extended by Scheler into the sphere of the objective reference of our ethical valuation and choice, as responding to the exigencies of the hierarchy of values among real essences.

For all his stress upon moral objectivity, Scheler also injects a strong dose of personalism into his theory of conduct. Moral values are not objectifiable, in the sense of belonging primarily to things or of being capable of an utterly impersonal reduction. Ethical good and evil always involve a reference to persons, no matter how mediate and tenuous the reference may seem to be. The person or spiritual center in man is the original bearer of values, the locus of moral inspiration and response. In order to avoid a determinist and associationist explanation of personal action, however, Scheler is compelled to maintain a sharp dualism in man between the psychophysical unit and the person. The latter is neither an empirical complexus nor a metaphysical substance: it is the concrete unity of the acts of knowing, willing, and otherwise establishing intentional relations with the objective sphere of essential structures. Moral autonomy refers to this personal center of intending acts, and not to Kantian reason as such, which leaves the personal agent as a morally inscrutable factor. Ultimately, the moral life is constituted by the mode of correlation between the person and the given hierarchy of values. In addition to the individual person, however, Scheler contends that the social group can be treated as a collective person—a view conducive to totalitarianism.

Persons may be bearers of higher or lower values, depending upon the level at which they organize their intentional acts and influence others to do likewise. Kant and Scheler are at one in refusing to ground ethics on the results of moral acts, since they regard such results as being ethically indifferent as far as the original moral determination of the person is concerned. What counts is the inner disposition or attitude of the agent, but this attitude is far more than a formal mode of striving. For Scheler, the moral disposition consists chiefly in a direction of one's intended acts toward some determinate positive or negative values.

In the actual specification of one's attitude toward the world of values, Scheler recognized the paramount role of personal models. Our moral disposition is affected most strongly, when we see correctly how a living person organizes his existence according to a certain pattern of values. The personal bearer of values affects us much more intimately and permanently than a leader, to whose will we may have to submit. A moral exemplar provides a contagious and inspiring example, soliciting our free engagement at some level of value. The pioneer, the hero, the genius, the saint—all these personal models are concrete pleas that we choose a ranking of values similar to their own. Like the existentialists in more recent times, Scheler deplored the depersonalization of modern society and the suppression of the moral inspiration of personal exemplars.

3) It is vital for the purpose of his moral philosophy that Scheler establish the reality of interpersonal knowledge. He denies that it is obtained through some kind of analogical reasoning or through empathy. These theories suppose that it is our own self which is primarily given to us, and that others are first known through perception of their bodily movements. Quite to the contrary, our original experience is of a community life, of others as existing in us. Later on, a man differentiates himself from others and sets up an egoistic barrier. Sympathy and love are required to overcome the obstacles, by grasping others

521

precisely as personal wholes or concrete unities of action. The person cannot be objectified, but it can be known through performing the same acts which sympathy and love reveal to be present in the other self. Scheler criticizes Schopenhauer for regarding sympathy primarily as pity or compassion, since it expresses itself also as an act of rejoicing in the perfections of another. Furthermore, sympathy is not precisely an act of identifying oneself with another but of discerning his personal worth and value-outlook, considered precisely as another person.

Since sympathy is not the same as pitying identification with another, Nietzsche is mistaken in regarding it as a sign of weakness or hidden resentment. Sympathy does not stand alone, but wells out of the strength of a generous love for another. The basic moral act is love, and for this truth we are indebted to Christianity. What Nietzsche takes to be resentment of the Christian slave mentality is, in point of fact, the despairing and cynical attitude of the modern world, from which the Christian ideal of love has almost disappeared. Scheler advocates a renewal of the ethics of love as the necessary condition for a recovery of the moral awareness of ranked values and the dignity of the person.

For his account of the nature of love, Scheler appropriates elements from St. Augustine and Pascal, but he dissociates their doctrine from the context of the relation of will to the good and the end. Love sets up an order between the person and the levels of value. Thus, corresponding to the hierarchy of vital, cultural, and religious values are the responses of sexual love and pleasure, mental love or dedication to scientific and esthetic pursuits, and spiritual love in terms of moral purity and holiness. A man's love betrays his personal attitude and moral quality. Scheler is specially insistent on adapting to his own purpose the statement of Pascal that love has a logic of its own, a type of cognition distinct from that gained through reason. The feeling of sympathy and love is not simply a condition for discovering the personal values of another: it is the sole means of knowledge at our disposal for this type of reality. The aim of such loving penetration is not to evaluate or improve the other person, but to discern his personal core of value-relations, at least as much as is possible. Yet ethical love has a distinguishing feature about it. It illuminates not only what a person *is,* but also what he *may become:* it reveals the capacities in his spirit and recalls to him an ideal which he has not yet reached. In this sense, there is something creative about love, even though it does not depend upon what the other person actually makes of himself.

The love of oneself and the love of neighbor are modal aspects of one's love of God. He is the source of all values and their proper ordering. Scheler maintains that there is an ultimate convergence of values upon God, as well as a corresponding demand upon us to seek sanctity through repentance and reorientation of our life toward Him. The religious act is the plenary expression of the human

522

search after values in an ordered totality. Its distinguishing traits are: transcendence of the world, dissatisfaction with finite values as consummatory, and demand for personal response from the supreme center of values. Scheler bases his chief proof of God's existence on the existence of the religious act. By its very structure, this act intends an object which must give a personal response and which must therefore exist as the infinite, personal God. Just as love always provides our basic insight into persons and values, so religious love is our main assurance of God's actuality. Metaphysics can indicate and exhibit the absolute, once religion has established the reality of its object. But religion is intrinsically independent of metaphysics. Its roots are sunk into the same value-ordination of personal existence which gives rise to ethical life at all levels.

In his final phase, Scheler sought to give ethical significance to his evolutionary pantheism. Man is obliged to participate in and facilitate the process of divine becoming. This he does by making a preliminary, ascetic break with given vital conditions. This negative moment is only a means, however, for achieving the double aim of vitalizing the spirit and spiritualizing the vital urges. The dualism of person and self is projected on a cosmic scale and even read into the divine nature. God contains the original dualism between spirit and life, and man's work is to provide a point of partial reconcilation between these two principles. But the synthesis is never completed. Scheler's final counsel is to have the patience of bitter wisdom, in a world where power is never wholly tamed by spirit.

Scheler did not establish any special school of his own, but many of his views have had a seminal influence. The application of phenomenological description to problems involving value and reality was given a definite impetus by his pioneer research. He also gave a new lease to ethical trends stressing the objectivity and gradation of values, in opposition to the prevailing naturalism which he criticized. In philosophy of religion, he both vindicated Christian ideal of love, repentance, and communal responsibility, and at the same time raised fundamental questions about the relation between religion and metaphysics. Scheler's investigations in the area of the sociology of knowledge have suggested to sociologists a way of taking account of the influence of social conditions upon human outlooks, without going to the extreme of Marxist determinism. He anticipated the need of anthropologists and psychologists for a philosophical anthropology, although few have accepted his evolutionary pantheism as a groundwork.

Bibliography

J. Collins, "Scheler's Transition from Catholicism to Pantheism," *Philosophical Studies in Honor of The Very Reverend Ignatius Smith, O. P.*, edited by J. K. Ryan (1952).
J. Hessen, *Max Scheler* (1948).

523

P. Muller, *De la psychologie à l'anthropologie, à travers l'oeuvre de Max Scheler* (1946).

J. Oesterreicher, "Max Scheler and the Faith," *The Thomist* (1950).

E. Przywara, *Religionsbegründung: Max Scheler—J. H. Newman* (1923).

M. Scheler, *Gesammelte Werke* (to be in 13 vols., Bern, Francke Verlag, 1954 ff.), edited by Maria Scheler.

——, *The Nature of Sympathy,* translated by P. Heath (1954), with 50-page Introduction by W. Stark.

"Symposium on the Significance of Max Scheler for Philosophy and Social Science," *Philosophy and Phenomenological Research* (1942).

James Collins
St. Louis University

Scheler, M.: *see* Hartmann, Nicolai.

Schelling, M.: *see* Hartmann, Nicolai.

Schelling: *see* Goethe, Johann Wolfgang von; Kierkegaard, Soren; Schopenhauer, Arthur.

Schiller: *see* Freud, Sigmund; Kant, I.

schism: *see* Augustine and Morals; Dante, Alighieri.

Schlegel, F.: *see* Goethe, Johann Wolfgang von.

Schleiermacher, F.: *see* Schopenhauer, Arthur.

Schlick, Moritz

In 1922 the chair for Philosophy of the Inductive Sciences at the University of Vienna was offered to Moritz Schlick, and it was not long before a group of philosophers, scientists, and mathematicians, who shared Schlick's desire for a scientific philosophy, was gathering regularly to discuss philosophical problems from this strongly empirical and scientific point of view. In time, the group itself (especially Carnap, Neurath, Waismann, Feigl, Goedel, and of course, Schlick), and those closely associated with it, although they attended no meetings (particularly, Wittgenstein), were internationally recognized as the Vienna Circle, probably the most influential philosophical school of recent years.*

The geographic center of the circle was destroyed by the appointment of its members to widely separated university faculties. The symbolic center, too, was lost when Schlick was shot and killed as he entered his classroom at the University by a mentally unbalanced former student, June 22, 1936. Schlick was 54.

Along with his highly significant work in the philosophies of science, logic, and language, Schlick undertook the formulation of a scientific ethics. Written while on vacation along the Dalmatian coast, *Fragen der Ethik* is distinguished by a hard clear style, enormous concision, and a brilliant understanding of the whole subject.

According to Schlick, ethics is a system of knowledge which has for the object of its understanding the things, actions, and characteristics designated by the terms 'good,' 'right,' 'ought,' 'moral,' and the like, in all their connections, and under all the laws of their natures. It does not set for itself merely the task of explicating the meaning of the concepts listed above, although the clarity of them, and their easy comprehension, are essential; nor

*Consult entries under Ayer, A. J., Moore, G. E., Russell, B., and Language and Ethics in this encyclopedia.

does it ever attempt to supply these concepts with content, where content may otherwise be thought lacking or improper; but it always endeavors to treat its subject matter in a systematic, factual, and scientific way.

The subject matter of ethics is not given in sensation or through a specializing "moral sense." It has the purely formal characteristic of being demanded or required, but its material characteristics must be discovered by examining and grouping together the individual cases (where something is called morally good) until the elements which these cases have in common shows itself. The statement of these similiarities can be put in the form of a rule or norm, such as: "A mode of action must have such and such properties in order to be called 'good' (or 'evil')." There may be a hierarchy of these norms, reaching to a general rule, although there is no reason, initially, to expect the hierarchy to be topped by one rather than by a number of independent principles. An action may be justified by citing the rule to which it conforms, and the rule may be justified, in turn, by citing a yet more general norm, an so on, until a rule is reached which is subsumed under no rule. To ask for any further justification is to ask for the impossible, but this impossibility is logical and indicates no weakness in the subject.

In so far as ethics is a purely normative science its task is concluded with the discovery of the *actual* norms which are *in fact* invoked to justify the assertion that some person or act is morally good or bad. The norms are themselves given facts. They constitute the meaning of the moral good. The further task of ethics is to seek a causal explanation of these facts. The question of the theory of norms is: what serves as the standard of conduct? The question of explanatory ethics is: why does it serve as the standard of conduct?

Since the central problem concerns the causes or motives of moral behavior, the method of ethics must be psychological, and we must seek first an answer to the larger question: what are the motives of human conduct in general? before we can hope to answer the more limited, though no more modest, request for an explanation of moral and immoral behavior in particular. However, it is immediately necessary to restrict the area of behavior and treat only that human behavior which is the result of *decision* or which is an act of *will*, as opposed to that unreflective and undisturbed flow of common activity which is so great a part of life. It is only when this flow is checked, when the answers our organism attempts to give to its stimuli are forestalled (the door whose knob I turn won't open), that we have that feeling of exertion, of struggle, which we call the exercise of will. For ethics, only those cases are important in which the struggle is the result of inner opposition—where two or more motives collide, not a single aim with a contrary condition of nature.

What is it, in any conflict of aims, which enables one of them to overcome the other and become our motive and the content of our will? Schlick declares that every idea and every state of consciousness is surrounded by a certain emotional tone, and that this aura of feeling is either pleasant or unpleasant, not in any really measurable way (as Bentham believed), but in a way, all the same, permitting comparison and unambiguous preference. Schlick refuses to regard the possibility of qualitative differences between kinds of pleasantness with any concern.

The opposition of pleasure and pain in the transition from one idea to the other leads us toward the pleasant or inhibits us from the painful. That we always choose the most pleasant or the least unpleasant course, Schlick calls the Law of Motivation. He defends this Law from the objection which consists in advancing cases of self-sacrifice by maintaining that a close analysis of any such cases will disclose a profound joy in the idea of reunuciation, or in something similar, to be present in them; and he answers the charge of terminological vagueness by claiming his use of 'pleasantness' and 'unpleasantness' to be perfectly natural, and justified by its utility in formulating a fundamental law.

The more serious objections, that the Law of Motivation is tautologous, or if not that, ethically insignificant, Schlick answers by saying that the Law is tautologous only if it confuses desiring with willing. It is true that expressions like 'to consider better,' 'to find more satisfying,' 'to imagine with pleasure,' and so on, may be treated as synonyms of 'to desire,' with the result, if one further identifies will with desire, that to say something is more satisfying than something else is to say that it is more desirable, and therefore that it is willed, and such statements would be mere redundancies; but the idea of desire is not necessarily joined to the idea of action, whereas the idea of volition is. We can easily imagine a world where one always willed what one least desired. The correspondence between what we will and what we most desire is an empirical fact, not a linguistic stipulation, and it is the law-like character of this correspondence which leads us to suspect it of tautology.

The knowledge that men will act only upon what pleases them most, the other objection runs, is ethically useless knowledge, since it is the mark of a good man that he is pleased by the good and wills it, and it is the sign of an evil man that he is pleased by evil and his will is won by it. The Law is not ethically insignificant, however, because it tells us something whose contrary has often been maintained. It tells us that moral behavior is not distinguished from other kinds of behavior by its lack of hedonic motivation. Moral action can never proceed against pleasure, in the line of greatest resistance, and the merit of duty can never lie in its distastefulness, since *all* action is governed by the Law. We know that the "good" man is pleased by what is called "good," while the "bad" man is not. It remains, then, to discover the laws of feeling, so that we may understand why one idea is

526

entertained with pleasure and another with pain, displeasure, or despair.

The moral judgments we make of men and men's acts express nothing other than our emotional reactions to the joyous or sorrowful, pleasant or painful, consequences which flow from men's natures and the natures of their acts. Egoism, for instance, is universally condemned, because the egoist is inconsiderate. He acts without taking account of the feelings of others. The *idea* of such behavior causes men pain because egoistic acts cause them pain directly. The moral evaluation made of selfishness expresses the emotional reaction of the members of society to action which does not take account of them, and in consequence threatens them with pain.

Now the idea of the good, for the individual, is that which he considers with pleasure, and the idea of evil, that which he considers with pain. This is to say, as the Greeks did, that the good is what is desired. Greek ethics was an ethics of desire. Christian ethics, on the other hand, is an ethics of renunciation, an ethics of duty; of demand; for it emphasizes, not the desires of the individual, but those of society, and so its moral laws appear to the individual as demands made on him by others. He is asked, not merely to accede to these demands, but actively to renounce those of his own desires which conflict with his group, in favor of the desires of the group.

There is no unbridgeable gap between an ethics of self-realization and one of self-limitation. The theory of duty, the theory, that is, of the demands of society, will be deduced from the theory of goods and pleasures. If duties were ultimate and underived from any desires, the virtuous person would be happy only by accident, and virtue *would have to be* its own reward. A connection between duty and happiness exists, however, since moral commands arise from the needs of man, and moral norms measure the joy or sorrow society expects to receive from the acts which fall under them.

Whatever is morally approved promises to increase the joys of society. This expected effect is the only reason why it is approved.

The Utilitarian (whose position, as Schlick makes clear, is very close to this one) tends to make his principle absolute, and finds himself, therefore, advocating a demand, not describing one. He then tries to make his recommendation precise, as Bentham tried, with wholly unsatisfactory results. The greatest happiness principle is utterly inapplicable. Acts, by their consequences, stretch eternally into time. Indeed, 'the greatest happiness of the greatest number,' is a senseless combination of words. It supposes that the pleasures of different persons are comparable in magnitude, and additive, when they are not. Schlick does not desire to advocate a demand, but rather to describe what, as a matter of fact, society requires of its members, and to explain why it makes these requirements. He says, therefore, that "in human society, that is *called* good which is *believed* to bring the greatest happiness."

The meaning of the word 'good' is

527

determined by the prevailing opinion of society, and is applied only to those forms of conduct and to those kinds of character which appear advantageous to it. Society makes moral demands only because the fulfillment of these demands is deemed useful. But however useful their fulfillment may be, they are not always "justified" by their utility. The idea of moral behavior may gain its halo of pleasantness from other, even quite contrary, beliefs; for example that these demands are validated by a divine revelation or through a rational intuition; or in many other ways, entirely non-rational.

A man is moral in so far as he is pleased by the idea of what appears to society as useful to it. Sometimes there is this harmony of individual feeling and social utility, and sometimes not. What remains to be explained is why men act morally; that is, why is it that, on more than a few occasions, this harmony exists? We must not understand this question as asking how men can ever be got to act well, as if moral action were unnatural and morality due to a special gift, either of conscience, soul, or reason; but rather as asking how we go about increasing human dispositions toward the right and good—dispositions which are certainly already present and active.

We may influence human inclinations from without by suggestion, by punishment, and by reward, but the subtler modifications come from within the individual himself, and are the result of his actions.

The feeling which attaches to the end a man decides in any instance to pursue, Schlick calls the *motive feeling*. The feeling which comes when some end is achieved, he calls the *realization feeling*. Obviously, the motive feeling preceding an act, and the realization feeling which follows it, need not be the same. We may imagine with pleasure what realizes itself with pain; we may, in fact, imagine with pleasure an end whose successful realization we know in advance will be painful. On the whole, however, the discrepancy between motive feeling and realization feeling, where it exists, cannot survive. Goals we imagine with pleasure will ultimately be imagined with pain if their realization consistently involves pain. Contrarily, situations we fear as painful will be imagined pleasantly, if they prove pleasant. The discrepancy between the two kinds of feeling tends to be assimilated, and this tendency is a law of the emotional life.

We may conclude from the Law of Assimilation of Motive Feeling to Realization Feeling that any set of dispositions which possesses a disagreement between motive and realization feeling cannot endure. It is impossible to demand as permanent behavior what brings pain, for the necessary motive pleasure will finally be unattainable. Men insist on the pursuit of happiness. Schlick says, "there is only one way to create motives of conduct which will prevail against all influences; and this is by *reference to actual happy consequences.*" If moral conduct is not a source of pleasure, men will not be moral long. If it is, they will grow to it.

We are now in a position to answer the earlier question concerning the harmony of the social demand and the individual desire. Virtue leads to happiness, by and large. The social impulses (where pleasure is taken in the idea of another's pleasure), more consistently than any other impulses, tend to yield the pleasure they promise, and they do so without decreasing the individual's capacity for pleasure. Instead, they increase it. For Schlick, this is the ultimately important fact. If the good consists in pleasure (happiness), then any pleasure which paves the way for pleasures to come is doubly valuable. The social pleasures are the most fecund of all. They are the most valuable. Men are virtuous because, on the whole, the virtuous man has the better prospects for happiness.

Of course, society's opinion as to what is useful to it may be shortsighted or mistaken, and it may demand action which limits an individual's capacity for happiness. Society may be criticized when this happens, though not on the ground that it is immoral, for society sets the standards of the moral; but on the ground that it has decreased the likelihood of happiness for the virtuous man, and has, in consequence, increased the possibility of disobedience.

Bibliography

Moritz Schlick, *Fragen der Ethik* (1930), translated as *Problems of Ethics* by David Rynin (1939).

——, *Gesammelte Aufsätze* (1938).
——, "Meaning and Verification," *The Philosophical Review*, XLV (1936), pp. 339–369.

William H. Gass
Purdue University

Schlick, M.: *see* Ayer, Alfred J.
schools of psychology: *see* Psychology and Morals.

Schopenhauer, Arthur

Schopenhauer, born in 1788, spent his early years in Dantzig, Hamburg, and travelling in Europe. After another grand tour (his travel diary indicates that pessimism was natural with him) he, at sixteen, became apprenticed in a commercial house, according to the wishes of his father, a well-to-do banker. But when the latter died (by suicide), Arthur soon gave up his business career and, in 1807, started preparing himself for the university. First he moved to Gotha, then to Weimar. Here, after her husband's death, his mother had settled and established a literary salon, which was frequented by Goethe, to whom she introduced Arthur; here she also developed into a writer (as did later Arthur's younger and only sister Adele), whose collected works contain twenty-four volumes. At twenty-one Schopenhauer entered the University of Goettingen. He soon became acquainted with the writings of Plato and Kant. After two years he moved to Berlin (at that time under French occupation) where he studied with Fichte and Schleiermacher (both of whom he later ridiculed and abused).[1] In 1813 the War of Liberation broke out. Schopenhauer, intensely disliking anything having to do with German nationalism (in fact, of Germans as a nation he always spoke with great contempt) and feeling himself to be a cosmopolitan, left Berlin for Rudolstadt and there wrote and published his doctoral dissertation, *On the Fourfold Root of the Principle of Sufficient Reason* (enlarged ed. 1847). From Rudolstadt he returned to Weimar (where at this time he was introduced to Hindu thought) to find that his mother had established life-community with von Gerstenbergk—a man considerably her junior. Schopenhauer, always quarrelsome and very outspoken, intensely disliked the situation and didn't conceal it. The result was a break with his mother; he left Weimar never to see her again. He settled down in Dresden (1814–1818); here he published an essay *On Vision and Color* (siding by and large with Goethe against Newton); but above all, he here completed his magnum opus, *The World as Will and Idea* (published in 1819; second, considerably enlarged, edition in 1844; third in 1859). From now on no change, nor further development ever took place in his ideas, contrary to what some scholars undertook to prove. From Dresden Schopenhauer went to Italy for a year. When in Venice he had a letter of introduction to Byron from Goethe, but made no use of it, afraid that his mis-

tress, if given a chance, would betray him with Byron, who had impressed her strongly. He had to return, particularly to take care of financial matters (a commercial house in which he had invested money declared its bankruptcy), which he did with success. In 1820 he became Privatdozent at the University of Berlin, partly to improve his finances. But after one semester he stopped lecturing, disappointed by the exceedingly small number of registrants (caused probably also by his intentionally listing his course at an hour at which Hegel, at that time the greatest attraction in philosophy, had scheduled one of his) and in 1822, again left for Italy. On his return to the Germanies he first lived in Munich and Dresden, but in 1825 went back to Berlin.[2] Here he remained until 1831, in which year, to escape an outbreak of a cholera epidemic he moved to Frankfurt/Main, where, virtually without interruption, he spent the rest of his life. In 1836 he published *On the Will in Nature;* in 1840/41 *The Two Fundamental Problems of Ethics.* In 1848, the year of the Spring of the Peoples, also in Frankfurt a democratic (liberal) and nationalistic revolution broke out, to be put down by an Austrian army. So intense was Schopenhauer's dislike for the democratic revolutionaries that he left the bulk of his estate to a fund established to provide for the victims among the counter-

---

[1] Regardless of the fact that he learned much from Fichte, as he did from Schelling, another philosopher most violently vilified by him.

[2] Of his love affairs the one in Venice and another in Berlin seem to have been the only ones somewhat above the merely sexual level. His sexual desires seem to have been very strong and he loathed it.

revolutionary Prussian soldiers. In 1851 Schopenhauer published his *Parerga and Paralipomena*. At about this time his fame, late in coming, finally arrived. In his last years Schopenhauer found an ever-increasing circle of admirers and disciples. He died, suddenly and peacefully, while sitting at his breakfast table, in 1860.

As Schopenhauer's ethics is rooted in his metaphysics, some knowledge of the latter is indispensable. Schopenhauer, maintaining that he merely is following Kant, sums up his transcendental idealism by the formula: All reality (or as he says, the universe, including my own body) is only my idea.

Would man be a knower alone, this would be his highest insight into the nature of ultimate reality. But already Kant insisted that the full nature of reality is disclosed to man only to the extent that he is more than a knower. As a (moral) agent or a doer man gains access to (though no knowledge of) the realm of things-in-themselves, thus transcending the world of appearances to which he as a knower would remain confined. This idea of Kant reoccurs in his successors in various forms. In Schopenhauer one finds it as the assertion that the non-cognitive experience by which the nature of ultimate reality (Kant's thing-in-itself) is disclosed to man is the experience which he has of his body in every act of his *will*. In and by that experience man's body is disclosed as essentially will. It is simply will having become manifest (objectified). And in the same act of experience in which his own body is disclosed to

him as being essentially will, also the nature of all the reality surrounding him is revealed to him: each piece of this reality is not only his idea but will become manifest.

To capture Schopenhauer's vision of the will as the true thing-in-itself (or ultimate reality) it is advantageous to think of the realm of appearances in their dynamic rather than static aspects. Behind every change there seems to be something analogous to our will. Let us take a look at an agitated sea: we seem to know that all its flood and ebb is the result of merely mechanical forces, attraction and repulsion, gravitation, etc. But a slight switch of the focus—and we perceive these forces as so strictly analogous to what we call will in us that we suddenly can have a live experience identical with that of Schopenhauer: what agitates the sea is to the sea in the same relation as our will to our body and the sea is what our body is: this will having become visible. True, the will which agitates the sea is blind (unconscious) whereas will in us is illuminated by intellect (knowledge, consciousness) or is conscious will. But this is of secondary importance. There are simply different levels of being, and on each the original will produces a different kind of will. We see inorganic forces, in lifeless things; ability to react to stimuli, in organic beings; intelligence, i.e., ability to perceive motives and present them to the will, in man. Thus, far from being what it had always been assumed to be, viz., the highest of man's faculties, taking precedence over will, intelligence is only another tool of the

531

blind will, called into existence to do will's bidding and not different in this respect from forces in the inorganic realm or from instinct in animals. We thus speak of Schopenhauer's system as voluntarism (primacy of the will).

But if the essence of reality is will, reality is inexorably suffering. Will is incessant, striving, endless agitation—agitation without any permanent satisfaction. Again the sight of the sea illustrates Schopenhauer's thought. The perpetual motion of the waves—reaching the shore only to recede again—what else are they but expressions of will's impossibility of rest? Of course, as the will in the sea is unconscious, there is no true suffering resulting from this. But the higher we ascend on the scale of beings, the more conscious their will—and therefore the more intensive their suffering. In man the consciousness of the will reaches its climax and so does the suffering. Here it appears as the unbreakable, endless chain of want and desire, which are suffering; satisfaction leading only to new want, or, in the interval, to boredom, which is also suffering. To will there is no goal, no end; it is aimless drive. Therefore we speak of Schopenhauer as a metaphysical pessimist.

And there is one more aspect of this universal, restless urge. All things hurt themselves permanently against other things which are their obstacles; the satisfaction of the drive of one means the destruction of others; constant warfare is the condition of visible reality. In man this permanent warfare of all against all takes the form of egoism—often of malice and cruelty.

If everything is only manifestation of one and the same unconscious will, then there is ultimately no difference between the several manifestations and all things are ultimately one. Individuality is nothing but an illusion. Anything that destroys the other only destroys itself.

In one of his books Hemingway tells what often occurs when a bullet, without killing the hyena, happens to tear a hole into his belly. The hyena starts pulling out through the hole his own intestines and devours them with obvious relish. A terrible spectacle—and a perfect simile of Schopenhauer's vision of reality turning against itself—reality seemingly divided into individuals who are blind to the fact of their fundamental oneness.

Therefore there is in the last resort no suffering to which there is no corresponding guilt: on the whole, the balance is perfect. The same will which caused the suffering and appeared as the will of the one who inflicted the suffering is the will of the sufferer too.

Some of the most impressive pages of Schopenhauer are devoted to the illustration of the thesis that life is suffering, due to the insatiability of the will, but also to the mutual inflicting of injuries. And when finally death comes, nobody in his senses can face it without admitting that the play was not worth the candle. Deep down in his heart everybody feels very well that to have come into existence is something which ought not to have taken place; that it is an evil thing to be; and that the act of procreation, which brought us and brings others into being, is something nefarious; that we justly are ashamed of sex and its organs. Sexual intercourse was the original sin and still is whenever repeated. And yet the sexual urge in man is most powerful; in it the whole will to live is concentrated. It guarantees the conservation of the species and, with it, the continuation of suffering. This world is the worst of all possible worlds.

Is there no way to escape from suffering? Indeed there is. We know it from experience, and Schopenhauer, far from prescribing it (to him the idea of a prescriptive ethics is self-contradictory and to tell man what he ought to do, entirely futile), describes it to us. It is the denial of the will to exist. How does it come about that anybody should take this way and where does it lead? The way is marked by two stages: the esthetic and the ethical stage. To understand the former, again we must become familiar with a metaphysical theory of Schopenhauer.

Before the will becomes manifest in time and space, it manifests itself in ideas of all the realities—ideas taken in the Platonic sense of unchangeable patterns for the realm of becoming, themselves not in time and space. According to Schopenhauer it is these ideas which are the object of the esthetic experience, by which he means both the experience preceding the act of artistic creation and also the experience of the enjoyment of a work of art. In other words, the esthetic experience reveals the ideas of beings. Moreover, Schopenhauer adopts the theory of Kant, according to which the essence of an esthetic experience (or according to the more traditional terminology, the experience of beauty) is disinterested liking, i.e. a liking in which there is no desire and which therefore does not stimulate us to any action, but on the contrary, as long as it lasts permits us to live in pure contemplation, released from the leash of the will.

What the esthetic experience anticipates, for moments only and in an imperfect manner, some ethical experiences continue. These experiences have in common that in them the principle of individuation or of selfishness weakens. The decision to be just is the first awakening; then comes love—*agape*, not *eros*—and finally we fully experience compassion, i.e. the implicit assertion that there is no difference between one's own sufferings and those of any fellow man.

Compassion Schopenhauer considers the cornerstone of morality. This compassion he extends also to animals. In denouncing cruelty inflicted by man to man (e.g., slavery) and to animals (he therefore is a warm friend of organizations for the prevention of cruelty to animals), Schopenhauer is most eloquent.

But even these ethical experiences are preparation only. The climax comes when in man the will becomes completely conscious of itself and sees through the illusion of individuality. In this moment of illumination will can make a completely free choice. It can either reaffirm itself, i.e., to decide to continue doing consciously what it has so far done unconsciously and so to reassert itself as the will to exist and to act as an individual; or else, the will can turn against itself and renounce its will to exist. It is this abnegation, renunciation, or denial by which the individual can escape from suffering by escaping from existence. Chastity, mortification of the flesh, starvation resulting from lack of desire to eat—these are the natural expressions of the denial of the will to exist. Before our very eyes we see a miraculous contradiction: a saint, i.e. a person whose body (i.e. will manifest) still exists, but no longer does will's bidding. By this denial man achieves salvation. What the artist began, the saint completes. In the moment of his death, he becomes forever reabsorbed into the source of all beings. He has overcome the illusion of individuality; Nirwana opens to him. This Nirwana, from the ordinary point of view, presents itself as Nothing; but he who overcomes the will to live sees the ordinary world as a mere Nothing.

Death destroys our individuality, but it does not destroy our essence, which is the one universal will. Thus we are immortal, though it is not a personal immortality. With a strange lack of consistency Schopenhauer admits the possibility that in some way, though cognition will be gone after one's death, consciousness still might be preserved. In other words, at this point the concept of blind, i.e., unconscious, will changes to a concept of blind, but in some way conscious, will.

Indestructibility of our essence instead of personal immortality—a remarkable perspective opens here. One of the most characteristic doctrines of the middle ages was that of the unicity of the intellect (usually ascribed to Averroës), sometimes referred to as monopsychism. According to this doctrine, thinking (as different from sensation), i.e., the knowledge of universals, is an activity common to all men; there is only one (the so-called active) intellect, and what is called thinking in the individuals is a participation in the thinking of this universal intellect. Our thinking is connected with our bodily structure; and as our body dissolves at our death, our individual thinking dissappears. What survives is the universal or unique intellect. This is the only immortality which man can expect. His thoughts survive—because and to the extent that they have never been his own, individual thoughts. Schopenhauer denied the primacy of the intellect and replaced it by that of the will. In him it is will that is common to all individuals. The unicity of the intellect is replaced by the unicity of the will. And the consequences for the problem of immortality are identical: no personal immortality, but indestructibility of our essence.

Schopenhauer is unaware of the similarity of his theory of the unicity of the will with that of the unicity of the intellect. But he is aware of its similarity with the doctrine of monopsychism as it appears in Plotinus. Plotinus asked whether all souls are only one and answered in the affirmative. As a result, he had to ask: Why, then, don't we all think the same? Why can we not know immediately what somebody else thinks? Schopenhauer, by implication, faces a similar problem, but he has a ready answer. In many so-called occult phenomena (magnetism, telepathy, second sight, sympathetic cures, perceptions of apparitions, and many other phenomena, usually called magic) the essential unity of all wills is indeed revealed. Only to the extent that the activity of the will in us is linked to that of the intellect, the original unity is prevented from revealing itself; but in those occult phenomena, all of which presuppose a weakening of the activity of the intellect (intelligence) and of the principle of individuation, the unicity of the will is restored.

To the main aspects of Schopenhauer's ethics we should add two more. First, Schopenhauer adopted Kant's theory concerning the difference between our empirical character and what he calls our intelligible character, the former being the character which we have as members of the realm of appearances, whereas the other is the one which we have as members of the realm of things-in-themselves. The empirical character is determined entirely according to the principle of causality (as are all other appearances, because they can become appearances only in the form of links in the chain of cause and effect). Therefore, to the extent that we are members of the realm of appearances, our actions are determined, and any talk of the freedom of will is erroneous. But to the extent that we are things-in-themselves, our character no longer is determined by the law of causality. We must act according to what we are, but what we are is the result of our having chosen ourselves to be what we are. This act, by which we decided to be what we are, of course, does not belong to the realm of appearances; it is a transcendental act. Therefore we are not responsible for what we do; but we are (morally) responsible for what we are.

Secondly, it is obvious and was stressed by Schopenhauer himself that there is a great similarity between his and Hindu thought. That the essence of life is suffering caused by the desire to live; that the insight "tat twam asi" ("this art thou") destroys the illusion of individuality (or rends the veil of Maya); that salvation (emancipation) is the result of the overcoming of the will to live and is followed by absorption into Nirwana—all these principles Schopenhauer found in Hindu writings. New as his philosophy of the denial of the will to live was in Western civilization, it would, Schopenhauer said, be trivial in India. By his unlimited admiration of India's thought, Schopenhauer did probably more than any other writer to make the West aware of it.

Next to Hinduism Schopenhauer admired Christianity, interpreted by him as a pessimistic and ascetic religion. For Judaism (from which he accepted only the narrative of man's original sin and whose concept of a God, who can look at this world which He allegedly created and find His creation good, he detested) and modern Protestantism he feels only contempt because of their optimism. It is sects like the Shakers and the Rappists who express the true spirit of Christianity. He also is full of sympathy for mystics, whose union with God he interprets as absorption into Nirwana.

A side aspect of Schopenhauer's ethics is his misogyny. For him, women are the favorite and, on the whole, very willing tools of the will to live, which has assigned to them two functions only: to attract men and to bear children.

Schopenhauer's influence was manifold. Among philosophers we find as his most faithful disciple, P. Deussen, perhaps the first to pay full attention to Hindu speculation in the context of a general history of philosophy. Others, more independent, were E. V. Hartmann, J. Bahnsen, and P. Mainlaender (whose striking idea that the universe is nothing but the decaying body of God who had died is strangely reminiscent of Hardy's lines: . . . we are but "live remains of Godhead dying downwards, brain and eye now gone"). Also O. Weininger, too famous for a while, too much forgotten at present, deserves a mention. Among men of letters T. Mann felt particularly indebted to Schopenhauer. But most remarkable is his effect on Wagner and Nietzsche. *Tristan and Isolde* in its second part is essentially a variation of Schopenhauer's idea of the denial of the will to live, except that in Wagner it is an illumination not of the intellect, but of love (desire, sex), which, at its climax, becomes capable of renunciation and so instead of satisfaction leads to death and Nirwana as its true fulfillment. And the hero of *Parsifal*, "wise by compassion," because he remains chaste, becomes the savior of himself and Kundry (whose curse is her laughter, symbol of lack of compassion), the embodiment of sexual attraction and, by this, perdition even for herself. As to Nietzsche, he, after a period of admiration of both Schopenhauer and Wagner, in obvious competition with them, preaches the gospel of what we could call joyful pessimism. His hero longs not for Nirwana, but precisely for its opposite, the eternal return or re-occurrence of life with all its horror. The artist and the saint become replaced by the superman, who is strong enough to renounce renunciation.

Bibliography

A. Sources

The great edition by P. Deussen, *Saemtliche Werke* (1911–   ) is still incomplete.

A. Schopenhauer, *Werke,* ed. by E. Grisebach, 3rd ed. rev. by E. Bergmann, (1921–1924). First section (6 vols.): *Werke.* Second section (4 vols.): *Handschriftlicher Nachlasz.*

——, *Werke,* ed. by A. Huebscher, 2nd ed., (1946–1951), 7 vols.

——, *Gespraeche,* in: *XX. Jahrbuch der Schopenhauer-Gesellschaft* (1933) Suppl., *ibid.,* XXVI (1939).

English:

The World as Will and Idea, tr. by R. B. Haldane and J. Kemp (1883–1886), 3 vols. (repr. 1948–1950).

On the Fourfold Root of the Principle of Sufficient Reason. On the Will in Nature, tr. by Mme. Karl Hillebrand, rev. ed. (1891).

The Philosophy of Schopenhauer, ed. by I. Edman (1928).

Selections, ed. by De Witt H. Parker (1928).

536

The Living Thoughts of Schopenhauer, Presented by T. Mann (1939).
Complete Essays, tr. by T. B. Saunders (1942).

B. Secondary

V. J. McGill, *Schopenhauer* (1931).
R. Tsanoff, *The Problem of Evil* (1931), chs. 10 and 11.
H. Zimmern, *Schopenhauer*, rev. ed. (1932).
F. Copleston, *Arthur Schopenhauer* (1946).

Philip Merlan
Scripps College

Schopenhauer, A.: *see* Freud, Sigmund; Goethe, Johann Wolfgang von; Moral Philosophy in America; Scheler, Max.
Schwindt: *see* Freud, Sigmund.
scientific ethics: *see* Schlick, Moritz.
scientific method: *see* Dewey, John.
Scriptures, the: *see* Augustine and Morals; Bible, the; Clarke, Samuel; Hindu Ethics; Jewish Ethics and Its Civilization; Moral Philosophy in America; Quakerism, Classical, The Morality of; Spinoza.
Seal of Solomon: *see* Zoroastrian Morals.
secretiveness: *see* Hindu Ethics.
secular and sacred: *see* Muslim Morals.
security: *see* Hobbes, Thomas; Navaho Morals; Quakerism, Classical, The Morality of.
seduction: *see* Dante, Alighieri.
seeker: *see* Hindu Ethics.
self: *see* ego, the; Hindu Ethics.
self-abuse: *see* Clarke, Samuel.
self-annihilation: *see* Kierkegaard, Soren.

self-assertiveness: *see* Zuni Indians, Morals of.
self-contemplation: *see* Kierkegaard, Soren.
self-contradiction: *see* Wollaston, William.
self-contradiction of the ought: *see* Hindu Ethics.
self-control: *see* Augustine and Morals; Hindu Ethics; Jewish Ethics and Its Civilization; Marxist Theory of Morals; Navaho Morals.
self-culture: *see* Hindu Ethics.
self-deception: *see* Freud, Sigmund; Kant, I.
self-delusion: *see* Muslim Morals.
self-denial: *see* Hindu Ethics.
self-discipline: *see* Hindu Ethics.
self-evident, the: *see* Major Ethical Viewpoints; Ross, Sir (William) David.
self-evident principles: *see* Broad, C. D.
self-evident truths: *see* Moral Philosophy in America; Reid, Thomas.
self examination: *see* Muslim Morals.
self-improvement: *see* Hindu Ethics; Ross, Sir (William) David.
self-interest: *see* Clarke, Samuel; Hobbes, Thomas; Marxist Theory of Morals; More, Henry; Reid, Thomas; Utilitarianism.
self-interest, enlightened: *see* Butler, Joseph.
self-knowledge: *see* Freud, Sigmund; Hindu Ethics.
self-limitation: *see* Schlick, Moritz.
self love: *see* Balguy, John; Butler, Joseph; Cudworth, Ralph; egoism; Moral Philosophy in America.
self preservation: *see* Aquinas,

Sherington, C.: *see* Primitive Morals.
Sibbs, Richard: *see* Puritan Morals.
Sidgwick, Henry

Henry Sidgwick was born in 1838, and educated at Rugby and Trinity College, Cambridge. He was elected a fellow of Trinity, and tutored and lectured, first in classics, but after 1865 in moral science or philosophy. Because his religious views were not those expected, he resigned his fellowship in 1869, but continued to lecture in moral science. In 1881 he was made an honorary fellow of Trinity. In 1872 he applied, unsuccessfully, for the Knightbridge Professorship of Moral Science, to which he was appointed in 1883, holding it until 1900. He was married in 1876 to Eleanor Mildred Balfour, a sister of Arthur Balfour. In 1874 he published his famous *Methods of Ethics,* in 1877 his well-known article in the *Encyclopedia Britannica* which later appeared as the book, *Outlines of the History of Ethics.* He also lectured and wrote on political economy, was active in the affairs of Cambridge University, and was much interested in the education of women and in psychical research. He helped found the Society for Psychical Research in 1882, and served as its first president. He died in 1900.

Sidgwick's later influence and reputation depend almost entirely on his works in ethics, especially *The Methods of Ethics.* In general, his bent of mind was analytical, critical, realistic, common-sensical, unmetaphysical. He was critical alike of empiricism, evolutionism, Kantianism, and idealism, both in ethics and in general philoso- phy, and may be regarded as a precursor of the later Cambridge school of analytical or critical philosophy. In ethics he was no one's pupil; his views were formed, as he says in an autobiographical sketch included in the preface to the seventh edition of *Methods of Ethics,* through reflection on the writings of Mill, Kant, Butler, More, Clarke, and Aristotle. He began by rebelling against the dogmatic intuitionism of Whewell and adhering to the utilitarianism of Mill, its psychological as well as its ethical hedonism. He ended with a system in which are combined rationalistic intuitionism and utilitarianism, egoism and universalism (the synthesis of which was his acutest problem), and ethical hedonism (the point on which he was most attacked). Throughout, except for his brief adherence to Mill's psychological hedonism, he warred against all attempts to derive the "ought" of ethics from any "is," whether metaphysical, psychological, sociological, biological, or historical. It was largely out of this relentless campaign which he carried on, and in which he was joined by W. R. Sorley, H. Rashdall, and G. E. Moore, that the completely self-conscious intuitionism of this century developed, with its insistence on the simplicity, uniqueness, and non-naturalness of ethical characteristics. Besides this insistence, another element in his novel and unstable combination lived on after him. His hedonism and his egoism were dropped, but his utilitarianism became characteristic of Cambridge ethics.

Sidgwick recognizes a difference between the term "right" and the terms "duty," "ought," and "obligation," but he generally uses them all as equivalent. He distinguishes several meanings of "right" in its ethical use. We sometimes say with truth that a man who is performing some action in the belief that it is right is mistaken as to his duty. In this case, Sidgwick says, the man's action is subjectively right, and it may be formally right, but it is not objectively or materially right, and it is not completely right. An action is objectively or materially right if, the agent's beliefs and desires apart, it is what he really should do. An action is subjectively right if it is done in the belief that it is objectively or materially right, and formally right if it is done from a desire to do what is objectively or materially right. Finally, an action is completely right if it is objectively or materially right, and if it is subjectively right or at least not subjectively wrong.

Ethics is concerned, for Sidgwick, with the determination of what conduct is objectively or materially right. Now objective rightness, he maintains, is simple and non-natural. "What definition can we give of 'ought,' 'right,' and other terms expressing the same fundamental notion? . . . the notion is too elementary to admit of any formal definition . . . it cannot be resolved into any more simple notions." ". . . the fundamental notion represented by the word 'ought' or 'right' . . . is essentially different from all notions representing facts of physical or psychical experience." ". . . propositions for the form 'x is right' or 'good'

. . . , relating as they do to matter fundamentally different from that with which physical science or psychology deals, cannot be inconsistent with any physical or psychological conclusions." "Right" is not even definable as "conducive to the greatest good on the whole." "The Utilitarian, in my view . . . does not—or ought not to—mean by the word 'right' anything different from what an anti-utilitarian would mean by it." The notion that the words "right" and "ought" have in common is the same in all ethical systems, and it is "ultimate and unanalysable."

Thus Sidgwick rejects all definitions of "right" in terms of "good." In fact, he regards "good" and "right" as distinguishable notions, respectively emphasized by ancient and modern ethics. Apart from explicit utterances, this is shown by the fact that, having argued that "right" is indefinable, he goes on to seek a definition of "good." One of the passages quoted above implies that "good" is not definable in non-ethical terms. Sidgwick begins by denying that "x is good" means "x is pleasant" or "x is desired." But he goes on to consider a more complicated definition, which he does not clearly reject, according to which "a man's future good on the whole" means "what he would now desire and seek on the whole if all the consequences of all the different lines of conduct open to him were accurately foreseen and adequately realized in imagination at the present point of time." He finds that this definition is rather "elaborate and complex" to be "what we commonly *mean* when we talk of a man's 'good on the whole,' " but he "cannot deny that . . . [it] supplies an intelligible and admissible interpretation of the terms 'good' (substantive) and 'desirable,' as giving philosophical precision to the vaguer meaning with which they are used in ordinary discourse." Some interpreters go so far as to say that Sidgwick accepts this account of the meaning of "good." If so, then he is a naturalist about "good," holding it to be "entirely interpretable in terms of *fact,* actual or hypothetical."

But other readers are of the opinion that Sidgwick rejects this definition as inadequate, and in this they appear to be correct. For Sidgwick goes on to say, "It seems to me, however, more in accordance with common sense to recognize . . . that the calm desire for my 'good on the whole' is *authoritative;* and therefore carries with it implicitly a rational dictate to aim at this end, if in any case a conflicting desire urges the will in an opposite direction." This seems to mean that a reference to the notion of "ought" or "right" is involved in the meaning of "good." Thus Sidgwick proceeds to define, not only "the ultimate good on the whole for me," but also "the ultimate good on the whole, unqualified by any reference to a particular subject," both with an implicit reference to the notion of "ought." The former is "what I should practically desire if my desires were in harmony with reason, assuming my own existence alone to be considered," while the latter is "what as a rational being I should desire and seek to realize, assuming my-

self to have an equal concern for all existence."

If this interpretation of Sidgwick's discussion of "good" is correct, then his conclusion is that "good" can be defined in terms of "ought" and "desire," and he is not a naturalist about "good." That this is his conclusion is suggested by the fact that he often employs, as synonyms of "good" as applied to ends, such expressions as "right and proper end of human action," "rational end," "end at which all men ought to aim," and "ultimate end categorically prescribed," and it would seem to be proved by the fact that he once or twice explicitly states that "good" may be defined as "what one ought to aim at," and that the proposition "we ought to promote the good" is tautological.

But then it is hardly accurate to say, as G. E. Moore does, that Sidgwick was the first to recognize that "good" is indefinable, for it was "right" or "ought" that Sidgwick regarded as indefinable, not "good," and "right" and "ought" had been regarded as indefinable already in the eighteenth century by Richard Price and after him by many others.

Of course, judgments of value are intuitive on this view, but they will consist of intuitions of the *rightness* of promoting something, for example, happiness. Perhaps it is more accurate to say that they will consist of intuitions of the *prima facie* rightness of promoting something. For Sidgwick holds that the judgment that a certain action is right involves a definite precept to perform it, and implies that it is in our power, whereas the judgment that a certain action is good does not imply that it is in our power in the same strict sense, and does not involve a definite precept to perform it, "since it still leaves it an open question whether this particular kind of good is the greatest good that we can under the circumstances obtain."

So much for what Sidgwick has to say about "right" and "good." We must now see what propositions about "right" and "good" he regards as intuitive or self-evident. He begins by contending, in opposition to what he calls perceptual and dogmatic intuitionism and to common sense morality, that only one material proposition involving "right" or "ought" is self-evident, namely, the proposition "We ought to aim at pleasure," which he also expresses by saying "Pleasure is the good." The only other propositions about "right" and "good" that are self-evident are certain formal ones, significant and synthetic, but too abstract to determine any duties, and essentially negative in force. Mostly they are concerned with laying down the right way to distribute the good (pleasure). All other supposed intuitions "have only dependent and subordinate validity." They record the kinds of action which long experience has shown to produce the most good (pleasure) in the required distribution.

Sidgwick lists two formal principles about "right" which together embody his interpretation of the Golden Rule and of Kant's first principle.

(1) "Whatever is right for me must be right for all similar persons in similar circumstances."

(2) "Similar cases ought to be treated similarly."

Then he gives further principles about "good." We have seen that for Sidgwick the utilitarian principle that we ought to promote good is analytic or true by definition and, therefore, not intuitive. But he does list as self-evident the basic proposition of hedonism, namely,

(3) "Happiness (pleasure) is the only thing ultimately and intrinsically good." In other words, happiness and happiness alone ought to be promoted. This is the proposition which gives content to Sidgwick's system. He then goes on to offer certain formal propositions which he thinks of as qualifying or limiting this duty to promote good (pleasure).

(4) "The good of any one individual is of no more importance, from the point of view of the universe, than the like good of any other."

(5) "I am bound to aim at good generally,—so far as it is attainable by my efforts,—not merely at a particular part of it." From (4) and (5) Sidgwick deduces the maxim of benevolence, viz.,

(6) "Each one is morally bound to regard the good of any other individual as much as his own." Propositions (3), (5), and (6) together yield Sidgwick his utilitarian or universalistic hedonism, that is, the view that we ought to do what will produce the greatest amount of happiness on the whole. But some modes of distributing a

given quantum of happiness, Sidgwick holds, are to be preferred to others. To the question which mode is to be preferred the utilitarian formula provides no answer. "We have to supplement the principle of seeking the greatest happiness on the whole by some principle of just or right distribution of this happiness." This is the role of (2) and (4), both of which are referred to by Sidgwick as the principle of justice.

But the problem of distribution is complicated by the fact that Sidgwick also regards ethical egoism as self-evident. He says,

(7) "I ought to seek my own good on the whole," "my own happiness is a manifest obligation," "it is irrational for me to sacrifice my happiness to any other end." With (7) Sidgwick associates the maxim of prudence, viz.,

(8) "One ought not to prefer a present lesser good to a future greater good." (7) and (8) together yield Sidgwick his rational egoism, which he maintains side by side with his rational benevolence or universalism.

Thus, in spite of his dictum that two propositions cannot both be self-evident if they are inconsistent, Sidgwick holds both universalism and egoism to be self-evident, even though it seems clear that they might dictate different courses of action. This "dualism of the practical reason," he says, is "the profoundest problem of ethics." His solution of the difficulty is to suggest a theological postulate providing for a harmony between the principle of individual happiness and that of universal happiness. This postulate granted, we may use the principle of seeking the greatest general happiness (rational benevolence), limited by the principle of justice, as our basis for the practical determination of objectively right conduct.

It will be clear from this account that Sidgwick's position is not easy to classify. It cannot, for example, be put under any of the three "methods of ethics" which he discusses—ethical egoism, intuitionism, and utilitarianism—without serious qualification. He himself speaks of it sometimes as a form of "philosophical intuitionism," sometimes as a form of "utilitarianism." If we consider his views about the meaning or nature of ethical terms and judgments, the first label is clearly appropriate. He is an intuitionist because he holds that rightness and obligation are indefinable and non-natural, and that the basic propositions of ethics are intuitive or self-evident, and he is a "philosophical" intuitionist because he regards only a few general and abstract principles as self-evident, not a number of more concrete rules, as the "dogmatic" intuitionist does, and not any particular judgments, as does the "perceptual" intuitionist.

But if we try to classify Sidgwick according to his basic normative principles for determining what we should do (i.e. his "method of ethics"), the matter is more difficult. He does regard the principle of utility—that we ought to do what will promote the greatest general happiness—and the principle

543

of hedonism—that pleasure and pleasure alone is good as an end—as self-evident. But this hardly makes him a utilitarian. For he also regards ethical egoism as self-evident, as we have seen. It is true that he postulates a harmony between this and the principle of utility, and so does not admit that it contravenes or limits the latter. But he also holds that the principle of justice is self-evident, that it is independent of the principle of utility, and that it may on occasion require conduct which does not produce the greatest *quantity* of happiness which is possible. Here he is with the deontologist and against the strict utilitarian, even though he does not credit as self-evident the more concrete rules which the deontologist usually holds to be basic.

Even if Sidgwick did not affirm such a deontological principle of justice, and even though he is a hedonist, he would still not be a utilitarian of the sort which has traditionally been opposed to intuitionism. For he accepts the intuitionist view that "right" or "ought" is simple and indefinable, and that the basic principles about what is right or obligatory are intuitive. And he is with the deontologist as against the teleologist also in taking "right" as more basic than "good" in the sense that the latter can be defined in terms of the former.

It seems best, therefore, to regard Sidgwick as synthesizing the positions which had been opposed since early in the eighteenth century, rather than as belonging wholly or even mainly to one of them.

Bibliography

Henry Sidgwick, *The Methods of Ethics* (first edition 1874; seventh edition 1907).
——, *The Principles of Political Economy* (1883).
——, *Outlines of the History of Ethics* (first edition 1886; sixth edition 1931).
——, *The Elements of Politics* (1891).
——, *Lectures on the Ethics of Green, Spencer, and Martineau* (1902).
——, *Philosophy: Its Scope and Relations* (1902).
——, *The Development of European Polity* (1903).

William K. Frankena
University of Michigan

Sidgwick, Henry: *see* Broad, C. D.; Green, T. H.; Major Ethical Viewpoints; Meta-ethics and Normative Ethics; Moore, George Edward; Prichard, H. A.; Ross, Sir (William) David.
silence: *see* Hindu Ethics.
simony: *see* Dante, Alighieri.
simplicity: *see* Quakerism, Classical, The Morality of.
Simpson, G. G.: *see* Primitive Morals.
sin: *see* Aquinas, Thomas, Moral Views of; Augustine and Morals; Aztec Morals; Christian Moral Philosophy; Cudworth, Ralph; Dante, Alighieri; Dostoyevsky, Fyodor; Freud, Sigmund; Hindu Ethics; Jesuits, the, Moral Theology of; Jewish Ethics and Its Civilization; Kierkegaard, Soren; Marxist Theory of Morals; Muslim Morals; Navaho Morals; Psychology and Morals; Puritan Morals; Quakerism, Classical, The Morality of; Rio Grande

Pueblo Indians; Tolstoy, Leo; Zoroastrian Morals.

sin, origin of: *see* Augustine and Morals.

Sinai: *see* Jewish Ethics and Its Civilization.

sincerity: *see* More, Henry; Muslim Morals.

sinlessness: *see* Hindu Ethics.

"skins": *see* Aboriginals of Yirkalla.

slave morality: *see* Masters and slaves; Nietzsche, Friedrich.

slavery: *see* Aristotle; China, Moral Philosophies of; Christian Moral Philosophy; Green, T. H.; Hammurapi, Code of; Hegel, G. W. F.; Marxist Theory of Morals; Minor Socratics; Moral Philosophy in America; Quakerism, Classical, The Morality of; Schopenhauer, Arthur; Stoics, the; Zuni Indians, Morals of.

slavophilism: *see* Khomiakov, Alexey.

slips: *see* Freud, Sigmund.

sloth: *see* Dante, Alighieri.

smiling: *see* Tapirapé Morals, Some Aspects of.

Smith, Adam: *see* Cooper, Anthony Ashley; Cumberland, Richard; Hutcheson, Francis.

Sobornost: *see* Berdyaev, Nicolas; Khomiakov, Alexey.

sobriety: *see* Navaho Morals; Puritan Morals.

social acceptance: *see* Dewey, John.

social conventions: *see* Freud, Sigmund.

social ethics: *see* Aristotle; Christian Moral Philosophy; Hindu Ethics; Marxist Theory of Morals; Mundurucú Indians, A Dual System of Ethics; Plato; Russell, Bertrand.

social gospel: *see* Quakerism, Classical, The Morality of.

social instincts: *see* Soviet Morality, Current.

social justice: *see* Christian Moral Philosophy.

social nature of man: *see* Cooper, Anthony Ashley.

social pleasures: *see* Schlick, Moritz.

social self: *see* Green, T. H.

social service: *see* Hindu Ethics.

social testimonies: *see* Quakerism, Classical, Morality of.

social utility: *see* Hume, David.

socialism: *see* Berdyaev, Nicolas.

socialism, Christian: *see* Quakerism, Classical, The Morality of.

socialism, European: *see* Soviet Morality, Current.

socialism, Marxian: *see* Soviet Morality, Current.

society: *see* Aboriginals of Yirkalla; Aquinas, Thomas, Moral Views of; Augustine and Morals; Berdyaev, Nicolas; Green, T. H.; Hindu Ethics; Jewish Ethics and Its Civilization; Marxist Theory of Morals; Quakerism, Classical, The Morality of; Reid, Thomas; Rio Grande Pueblo Indians; Schlick, Moritz; Sophists, the; Stoics, the.

society and ethics: *see* Dewey, John.

Society of Friends: *see* Quakerism, Classical, The Morality of.

Society of Jesus: *see* Jesuits, The, Moral Theology of.

sociological relativism: *see* Major Ethical Viewpoints.

sociology: *see* Ayer, Alfred J.

sociology of knowledge: *see* Scheler, Max.

Socrates

Socrates was put to death at Athens under a charge of impiety in "the year of Laches" (399 B.C.), and we are more certain of the fact of his death than we are of the circumstances of his life. It is probable that he was born in or before 469 B.C., but the accounts of the intervening years are either incomplete or not consistent. Socrates himself left no record of his own thought or action, and we have no other record of anything done or said by him until he was close to fifty. Of the three contemporary accounts which we do have, those of Plato, Aristophanes and Zenophon, Plato's account is by all means the most familiar and the most accepted. The material preserved for us in Diogenes Laertius' *Lives* does not reflect a very high level of historical accuracy, so that it is not strange that Plato's readable, consistent and attractive account of Socrates has gained in circulation.

Despite his acknowledged importance, the account of Socrates' thought cannot be given without first trying to determine which biographical account we are to accept. Thus, the exposition of the Socratic ethical doctrine becomes side-tracked and turned instead into a quest for an historically accurate biography. Since the inadequacy of the material available precludes any final statement, in order to escape immobility the account accepted here will be that of Plato. In addition to the argument from the reliability of Plato's historical account, a factor which cannot be ignored is the fact that Socrates' major effect on the history of philosophy has been through the medium of the Platonic account. More than anywhere else, the place where philosophers since his time have encountered Socrates is on the pages of Plato's dialogues. Since it is here that his influence is to be found, it is not illogical that it is here that his doctrine should be sought for, in spite of the conflicts in historical and factual material.

The usual division of Plato's work into the early, middle and later dialogues will be of assistance in this problem, since the early works are commonly known as the 'Socratic dialogues.' In these early writings the subject under discussion is directly ethical. Usually the subject is the definition of some particular moral virtue or excellence, while the form is straightforward dialogue, with some attention given to literary style, and Socrates is the central figure. Taking the earlier dialogues as a unit, then, we get a comparatively consistent and complete view of the ethical doctrine of Socrates. Such a procedure also has the virtue of preserving a more consistent Platonic ethics found in the middle and late dialogues, now that the earlier and simpler dialogues have been removed and interpreted as defining Socrates' thought. Admittedly this is a reconstructed Socrates, rather than the exact historical figure, but, since the data available prevents us from ever recovering the actually existing man, we are almost left with Plato's Socrates or none. This is a fact which should not cause us to lament long, since Plato, as Socrates' most important successor, has made his Socrates influential for some twenty-five centuries, whereas the historical Socrates disturbed the complacency of a few Athenians for a brief seventy years.

Socrates is usually pictured as being completely uninterested in physical speculation, and this is certainly borne out in the account of his interests which Plato reflects. We always find Socrates discussing familiar, important-to-everyday-life, moral questions. The specific topic is usually some particular moral quality, for example, piety or temperance. Yet, there is no doubt that the overall aim is to discuss the nature of virtue in general and that piety or temperance are merely examples chosen in order to work in terms of a specific illustration of an admitted quality of virtue. The aim seems to be to arrive at a universal definition, to discover what is essential to moral excellence, so that we will not be confused into identifying virtue with any of its accidental associations.

Such a goal for ethics leads us away from ethics to the second, but necessarily related, purpose of the Socratic dialogues: To determine something about the nature of knowledge, the status of the objects of knowledge, and the relation of knowledge to moral excellence. It could even be argued that Socrates' major aim is really to establish the existence of universal forms as the objects of knowledge and that the whole subject of moral virtue is merely illustrative, used only as a topic which will be of popular interest, and that he could have used a morally neutral topic just as well to illustrate his views on objectivity of knowledge. This is too extreme a view and is too simple an explanation, since it misses the intimate relationship which Socrates wanted to establish between questions of knowledge and issues of practical conduct. Everyone wants to know what virtue is, and Socrates' intent is to force us all to face the fact that we cannot have an answer without first deciding about some difficult problems of knowledge. Philosophy, then, can be ignored only at the risk of discovering that you really do not know how to recognize what you want in life, since, lacking the required theoretical knowledge, you cannot distinguish the essentials of virtue from its accidental trappings. The important issues of public life are inescapably dependent upon difficult theoretical questions—this is the philosopher's message to the people of Athens.

Returning to the *Charmides,* we find Socrates discussing a typical ethical question: What is the Quality of Temperance? He rejects Charmides' appeal to authority in the argument over temperance and forces him to consider the more difficult question of how one establishes what is true. "The point is not who said the words, but whether they are true or not." (*Charmides,* 161) It is easier to talk of different opinions about ethical questions than it is to establish something about the nature of truth, but Socrates never allows an ethical discussion to ignore problems of knowledge. Temperance goes hand in hand with self-knowledge, since the wise man must know "what he knows, and what he does not know," (*Charmides,* 167) and in order to know this one must understand both himself and the nature of knowledge. Thus the familiar Socratic injunction for the beginning of virtue: 'Know thyself.' "If you discard knowledge, you will hardly find the crown of happiness in anything else," (*Charmides,* 173) and knowledge in this case means primarily the 'essence of the good.'

To 'be a philosopher' and to 'study virtue' seem to mean the same thing for Socrates, but this is because the study of virtue involves one in a study of knowledge, since one finds that he cannot deal with ethical problems successfully until he knows what knowledge is and how it may be used. In the *Euthydemus* the participants agree that every human being desires happiness, but then they learn that objects cannot be regarded as being good in themselves. We often think that the mere possession of some object or personal quality would in itself be good, but this is not so if goodness is not intrinsic to objects. "The degree of good and evil in them depends on whether they are or are not under the guidance of knowledge," (*Euthydemus,* 281) which means that to acquire certain possessions and to fail to gain knowledge is to miss the happiness we seek. 'Good' appears only when objects or personal qualities are used intelligently, and this is possible only after one has found out what knowledge is and how it can be acquired. "Is not this the result—that other things are indifferent, and that wisdom is the only good, and ignorance the only evil?" (*Euthydemus,* 281)

The *Meno* purports to consider the question of "whether virtue can be taught, or is acquired by practice." (Meno, 70) Actually, the issues are (1) what is a universal, and (2) how does a universal function in the process of acquiring knowledge. While it is important to see how Plato has Socrates interweave questions of ethics with problems of epistemology, it is even more important to see that Socrates seldom reaches a very decisive conclusion on the original ethical question, whereas the question of knowledge increasingly occupies the major part of the discussion and comes to much more definite results. It is as if Socrates wished to induce you to begin philosophy through the lure of moral problems, then led you into the technical problems involved and finally, after suggesting an answer to the more abstract questions, turned you loose to apply to the original ethical subject what philosophy had taught you.

In the *Meno* the ethical question posed at the start seems to get lost in the discussion, but the moral of this story seems to be that the best way to answer a practical problem is to leave it alone for a while and to try to reach a decision on the problems of knowledge which are involved before returning to the original issue. Before I can know whether virtue can be taught, I must know its nature; but I cannot know its nature until I know how to define what a thing is. If we try to settle this by using commonly accepted definitions, we find out, upon analysis, that these accepted definitions are more vague than we had realized, which brings us right back to the fact of our ignorance about the fundamental questions of knowledge.

Socrates characteristically begins his treatment of an ethical question by taking several accepted definitions, no one of which is adequate by itself, and then he tries to find what it is that is similar about all of them. Do you not understand that I am looking for that which is the same common element in all these?, he asks. If we can find the universal quality which is present in these ordinary definitions of a moral quality, then we can know its nature, but in order to do this we must know what a universal is and how it functions in the process of knowledge. Only when we know what a universal is and how it operates can we decide whether or not a moral characteristic can be taught, since what we want to teach is not a particular aspect of the virtue but its essential properties. "Do you suppose that anyone can know a part of virtue when he does not know virtue itself?" (*Meno*, 79C) Socrates' answer is no, but this makes a theory of knowledge central to any ethical discussion, since it forces us to decide first about the status of universals.

In the course of what began as a simple discussion, Socrates reveals the ignorance of his associates concerning these technical questions and in return brings down their anger upon him, together with the charge that all he does is benumb those who approach him and cast them into doubt. This brings to light the central Socratic teaching: You really know more than you think you do if only you had the skill to bring it to the surface. Doubt is a necessary stage through which you must pass, since only doubt can reveal the inadequacy of a partial definition. Admittedly this is a painful process, so much so that if left alone without outside questioning you might never begin the process voluntarily. It is philosophy's job to speed this discovery by uncovering the difficult and technical problems involved in a simple ethical question. The optimism of the Socratic position lies in its doctrine of universals. Even in extreme doubt the mind is aware of and has within its grasp that for which it is looking. Although any particular definition of virtue can easily be shown to be hopelessly inadequate, even such an unacceptable definition contains within it the universal quality you are looking for, and, more important, it is possible to train the mind to recognize this through the process of learning what universals are and how they operate in relation to the mind.

You cannot even look for something of which you know nothing at all. Doubt reveals, not that the mind is completely ignorant, but that it is in mid-passage and must be helped by philosophical thinking to go further and uncover that of which it basically has a grasp but is not able to bring unaided to consciousness. This is the meaning of the famous Socratic doctrine: There is no teaching but only recollection. As long as you think that your definition of virtue is adequate, you will take the easy way out and go on acting as if you know what you are saying when you talk about virtue. Somewhere beneath the surface the mind does have a grasp of reality. The function of Socrates and of philosophy is not to provide anyone with answers to the ethical questions which he asks, but to reduce the questioner to the perplexity of "realizing that he did not know" (*Meno,* 84C) and to try to induce in him a craving to know and to know what it means to possess knowledge.

The result of all this is that when we ask the normal, the usual ethical questions we are really seeking to learn what knowledge is, although we may not know it. Temperance and virtue are what we say that we desire, but we will achieve them only by accident unless we learn that knowledge is the basic factor and these ethical qualities only its manifestation. "He who has knowledge will always hit on the right way, whereas he who has right opinion will sometimes do so, but sometimes not." (*Meno,* 97C) The Socratic quest for virtue has turned into a search for knowledge, and this is something which a man can only find for himself. We cannot, of course, ignore the fact that some men seem to succeed even when they do not know what they are talking about, but such achievement is shown to be purely a matter of luck and chance and not anything a cautious man could afford to depend upon for something so vital as his well being. Life and the achievement of happiness are, it is true, never certain, but the basic search for knowledge is the only insurance policy a sane man can buy. If you can discover knowledge you can create well being. Without knowledge, even supposed goods can be turned to mistaken uses. "We ended by agreeing that one ought to pursue wisdom, did we not? And this pursuit—called philosophy—is an acquiring of knowledge." (*Euthydemus* 288D)

In the *Cratylus,* which supposedly concerns names and definitions, when Socrates asks whether you agree with him in opposition to Protagoras that "things have a permanent essence of their own" (*Cratylus,* 386) he is making what is probably the crucial point of his ethical doctrine. If things do not fluctuate according to our fancy but are independent and "maintain to their own essence the relation prescribed by nature," (*Cratylus,* 386) then we are not free to make judgments in any way that we please. This belief in the objective existence of the objects of knowledge (the doctrine of Forms) is what makes Socrates feel that ethical questions must also be settled by an appeal to criteria which we discover to exist independently from our desires. This is the central theme of the *Euthyphro,* which in many ways contains the core of Socrates' ethical position. The issue there supposedly is piety or holiness, but actually Socrates wants to settle what it is that makes us approve of any moral quality. Euthyphro tries to say that what is holy is what is dear to the Gods, which would make moral qualities dependent upon someone giving approval. If this were true, then the value would shift as the approval shifted and would vary from person to person, with the possibility of shifting full cycle from positive to negative. Approval is a changing thing such that, if virtues depend upon it, then they have no independent standard.

Socrates has stated the issue very well. Do things become good because we approve of them, or do we approve of things according to criteria which we find to exist independently from us? Socrates' own preference for the latter alternative is clear, since it alone can give ethics a stable footing. Yet nowhere in the earlier or Socratic dialogues do we have anything like a detailed description of what these norms are, how they exist, and how the mind discovers and deals with them. Granted that there are certain structures which exist independently from us, how can these function as ethical norms? This is the question which the later Platonic dialogues is left to deal with. The Socratic tendency toward objectivity in ethics is clear; the detailed analysis of these objective structures and their function in ethics is bequeathed to Plato. Socrates points out clearly that, if the value of an object is made to depend upon the desire and approval of various individuals, then you have the undesirable consequence that values shift as interests shift and may even become involved in contradictions. That is, it would be possible for an object to be called both good and bad at the same time, due to opposing desires. What remains to be established is that there really are norms existing independently which function in ethical situations without radical fluctuations and contradictions.

In the *Gorgias* we find one of the most characteristic of all Socratic comparisons, that between the skilled artisan or craftsman and the virtuous man in action. The well-trained craftsman operates with discipline, with knowledge of his material, and with attention to established patterns of excellence. The artisan makes his material yield to form, and this is also the task of the moral man. Many people are swayed by flattery and persuasion, but the craftsman pays attention to nothing other than his material, his objective and the canons of procedure. To acquire such skill is a matter of long training for which there is no short cut, and to rid ourselves of bad habits of procedure is never a pleasant business. We always seek the good, but do we know what the good is? The answer to this question will provide us with the norm according to which the virtuous man will operate, just as the craftsman operates according to the standards of his trade. However, the discovery of the standards for the good as they exist independently will require an elaborate construction. This job will appear to take Plato a long way from the central Socratic concern with ethical problems, but such digression is necessary if the Socratic belief in objectivity of ethical norms is to be given a solid foundation.

Bibliography

J. Burnet, "The Socratic Doctrine of the Soul," in *Proceedings of the British Academy* (1915–16), p. 235 ff.

——, Article "Socrates," in Hastings' *Encyclopaedia of Religion and Ethics,* vol. xi.

F. M. Cornford, *Before and After Socrates* (Cambridge, 1932).

Diogenes Laertius, *Lives of Eminent Philosophers,* Trans. R. D. Hicks (London, 1925).

G. Grote, *Plato and the Other Companions of Socrates* (London, 1888).

C. Ritter, *Socrates* (Tubingen, 1931).

A. E. Taylor, "Plato's Biography of Socrates," in *Proceedings of the British Academy* (1917–1918), p. 93 ff.

A. E. Taylor, *Socrates* (London, 1933).

Frederick Sontag
Pomona College

Socrates: *see* China, Moral Philosophies of; Freud, Sigmund; Goethe, Johann Wolfgang von; Major Ethical Viewpoints; Meta-ethics and Normative Ethics; Minor Socratics; Plato; Sophists, the; Stoics, the.

Socratic schools: *see* Minor Socratics.

sodomy: *see* Riffian Morals.

Sokolov: *see* Soviet Morality, Current.

solitude: *see* Hindu Ethics.

Soloviev, Wladimir

Among the representative men of the late 19th century in Russia, Wladimir Soloviev, is no doubt one of the most outstanding personalities. Philosopher, religious thinker, historian, poet, literary critic, sociologist, Soloviev was all this, and produced during his short span of life a tremendous amount of writings (some twelve volumes not including his correspondence, separately published). Soloviev was, moreover, a champion of the ecumenical movement; in fact, he was a pioneer of the Union of Churches. Last, but not least, Soloviev was a man of extraordinary charm, a brilliant conversationalist, an ardent polemicist. Not satisfied with teaching his system of Christian philosophy, he gave a constant example of Christian virtues; his kindness, unselfishness, generosity and devotion to his fellow-men, became proverbial, almost legendary.

Wladimir Soloviev was the son of Professor Sergey Soloviev, the distinguished historian, and the grand-son of a priest. Born in 1853 in Moscow, where his father held a chair at the University, Soloviev acquired at home the best principles of Russian culture together with a solid Russian-Orthodox religious formation. However, when he went to school, he became aware of the mounting rebellion against the established Church, which marked at that time Russia's younger generation. This was due in part to the low level to which religious education had sunk, as well as to the subservient position of Russian ecclesiastical authorities in regard to the State. On the other hand, atheistic books, though officially prohibited, were widely circulated in class and eagerly read. He was soon impregnated with them, and with nothing else. At fifteen, Soloviev was a confirmed atheist; he even tore off the ikons from the walls of his student rooms, and threw them out of the window. A few years later, he was miraculously saved in a railway accident, and after this event, he cast away for ever the mantle of agnosticism. He entered the Russian-Orthodox Divinity School besides studying at the Mos-

552

cow University. After graduating, he taught at the Women's Higher School in Moscow, and gave a series of public lectures which made him famous. These lectures, later published under the title of *Godmanhood,* are considered as one of his major works. From that time on, Soloviev was hailed as the leader of the Russian Christian revival versus materialism and empiricism. In 1882, he had to resign from his academic career because he publicly protested against the execution of the terrorists who in that year murdered Tsar Alexander II. In this protest, Soloviev was supported by Tolstoy. It must be noted, however, that Soloviev did not subscribe to Tolstoy's doctrine of non-resistance to evil, and engaged in polemics with him on that subject. During these early years, he was very friendly with another great Russian novelist, Dostoyevsky. It is believed that the young Christian philosopher had a considerable influence on the aging writer, this influence being reflected in *The Brothers Karamazov.* Soloviev was a pall-bearer at Dostoyevsky's funeral, and made three profound speeches dedicated to his late friend.[1] After the end of his academic activities Soloviev went abroad. At that time, he was deeply concerned with two major problems: the spiritual reform of modern society, according to the teaching of Christ (reflected in his work: *The Future of Theocracy*), and the reunion of the Russian-Orthodox Church with Rome. In Russia, his

---

[1] These speeches, one of which was delivered on Dostoyevsky's grave, were later published in Soloviev's collected works.

ideas on that subject would have been strictly supervised and censored by ecclesiastical authorities. Abroad, mainly in Paris and then in Zagreb (Croatia), where he visited Bishop Strossmayer (an ardent advocate of ecumenism), Soloviev was free to develop his teaching to its utmost conclusions. These conclusions he expressed in a number of important works: *The Russian Idea, Russia and the Universal Church,* etc. Soloviev stated the fundamental thesis of reunion as follows: a divided Christianity was a tragedy, due to historical mistakes, misinterpretations and misunderstandings, which brought about the schism between East and West: "But," he wrote, "if the separation of the Churches was historically necessary, it is even more necessary morally for Christianity to put an end to it." Not only did he prove that Unity was indispensable for the salvation of Russia, he further asserted, that actually Russia had never fallen away from the *One flock;* the Russian Church recognized the teachings of the Fathers of the Church, and was therefore not schismatic. Suffice it to accept these teachings fully, including the primacy of the Pope, and Russia would be *organically one* with the Universal Church. When Soloviev returned to Russia, and pursued his writing in Moscow, he followed the ecumenical trends abroad. In the 90's he made a solemn profession of faith at a private ceremony and in a private Catholic chapel where he was received into the Universal church. This event, long held secret, was later revealed, and is now admitted by the Russian-Orthodox themselves,[2] who for a long time, did not recognize its validity. However, the last years of Soloviev's life throw no further light on his exact position as to Russian-Orthodoxy and the Catholic Church. True, his last work, published shortly before his death *The Three Conversations* project his vision of the reunion of the Churches fulfilled at the *end of times,* after the defeat of Antichrist. *The Three Conversations* appeared in the late 90's, at a time, when he seems to have abandoned the hope of immediate unity.

In 1900, Soloviev was taken seriously ill in the country-home of his friend, Prince Trubetzkoy. He asked for a priest, and the rector of the near-by parish (Russian-Orthodox) administered to him the last rites. After his death (1900) the Russian-Orthodox claimed that he returned to his native Church. The Catholics contend that there being no Catholic priest at hand, Soloviev was fully entitled to receive *in extremis* absolution and holy communion from a Russian-Orthodox priest. A third opinion prevails, i.e., that Soloviev had a *prophetic* vision of the *end of times,* as depicted in *The Three Conversations.* On his deathbed, and perhaps even earlier, he was no longer aware of the divisions, but only of the ONE Body of Christ. The controversy around Soloviev's allegiance to Eastern or Western Christianity will probably go on. But the proper answer can scarcely be reached if we fail to take into consideration Soloviev's *entire* philosophical, religious and moral out-

look. This outlook is based, not on this or that aspect of truth, but on all these aspects at once; because he believed that all human manifestations, provided they are good, are potentially part of absolute truth, of that which he describes as *The Kingdom of God.* This Kingdom is ONE, it is "all-unity," and all shall be finally reunited in it through the incarnation, death and resurrection of Jesus Christ. This fundamental principle is expressed throughout Soloviev's entire work, and is the source of its extraordinary dynamism.

We must moreover hold in mind, that Soloviev attained this dynamic impulse, not merely through rational, discursive methods, but through direct religious experience. True, he did approach the problem rationally, and as a philosopher was thoroughly trained in abstract speculations. But, there is *another* Soloviev, not only philosopher, but also *mystic.* This mysticism is projected in many of his works in prose, but also in his poetry, especially in his famous poem: *Three Encounters.* In this poem, he describes his peculiar religious experience. Three times in his life, the same symbolic vision appeared to him: once in church, when he was a child, a second time in the London British Museum where he was studying ancient documents, and the third time in the Egyptian desert, where an inner voice ordered him to go. Three times Soloviev had a direct revelation of the supernatural world; it was projected in the shape of a woman, wearing a mantle of azure and gold, and looking down on him from

2 See C. Motchoulsky, *Wladimir Soloviev.*

the morning sky. He was mysteriously informed that the apparition was "The Wisdom of God," (*sophia* in Greek), who is especially venerated in the Greek and Russian-Orthodox Church. Of Sophia it is said in the book of Proverbs: "The Lord possessed me in the beginning . . . I was with him forming all things" (Pr. 8, 22–31). Soloviev interpreted Sophia as the World-Soul, and also as the Eternal Feminine. She is the link between God and man. God is the absolute good, He is All Unity; creation strives toward it, but is separated, divided, torn by sin. However, the world retains *potential* unity, and this potentiality is the world-soul, Sophia. Christ calls all created things to the supreme reality of Union; He is the Logos (the Word), and He is also God's Wisdom in its fullness. Such an interpretation would need to be further clarified. "In Soloviev's doctrine of Sophia," writes Prof. N. Lossky,[3] "there is vagueness and inconsistency: he now speaks of Sophia as of a being eternally perfect . . . and now as of a world-soul temporarily fallen away from God." However that may be, Soloviev's *Sophiology* created an important school of Russian-Orthodox theology (Fr. S. Bulgakov). Sophia also inspired a group known as the "Russian symbolist poets." Sophiology, no doubt, is an important element of Soloviev's religious system. But it has often been overestimated by his followers, on one hand; on the other hand, it was viewed with suspicion even by some of his most fervent ad-

mirers. Soloviev himself clearly emphasizes (in the preface to his collected poems) that Sophia, the world-soul, the eternal-feminine, is *not* a deity, and has "from all eternity accepted the power of Godhead." Attractive as Sophiology may seem to those who are inclined to a mysticism verging on the occult, this attraction would not suffice to explain Soloviev's persuasive force. His was a creative and active appeal: As Prof. N. Lossky writes:

It became the work of his [Soloviev's] life to build up a Christian Orthodox philosophy revealing the wealth and the living efficacy of the principal dogmas of Christianity . . . Soloviev showed what importance they have as a philosophical basis for a scientific study of nature, as a guidance for the moral life of the individual and as a starting point for working out an ideal of Christian politics. Soloviev's entire literary work reveals his activism: his theoretical search for truth always aims at the practical goal of reforming the world, conquering selfishness, achieving the Christian ideal of love.[4]

Essentially, Soloviev's teaching is founded not on Sophia, but on Christ Himself. It is Christ who draws all creation toward Him, through Sophia, the world-soul who seeks Him. He *is* that all-unity, of which Soloviev so often speaks in his prose as well as in his poems. "Christianity," he says, "has a content of its own. . . . The only thing in it that will be new, and specifically different from other religions, is Christ's teaching about Himself, his speaking of Himself as the living, incarnate truth: I am the way, the truth,

---

[3] N. Lossky, *History of Russian Philosophy.*

[4] *Ibid.*

and the life; he that believeth in me hath everlasting life" (Lect. on Godmanhood).

In Soloviev's mind, therefore, Christian morals are not merely the morals taught in other religions, which also prescribe righteousness, love, mercy. Christian morals are part of the fullness of truth, of potential all-unity. Christianity is not an abstract conception, nor a mere set of rules: "The essence of Christianity is the regeneration of mankind and the world . . . the transformation of the kingdom of this world into the kingdom of God (which is not of this world)" (Lect. on Godmanhood). This does not mean, however, that Soloviev turned away from the world and things temporal. On the contrary, the temporal, in his mind, must acquire an eternal content. He further developed his active, dynamic doctrine of regeneration in such works as *The Justification of the Good, The Future of Theocracy, The Meaning of Love, The Three Conversations,* etc. He was deeply concerned with the transformation of society. At one time he conceived a plan of a theocracy, in which man would not be forced to obey authority, but would *freely* accept the divine order. Later, he gave up theocracy as an extreme utopia. But he did retain the basic values of a Christian society: freedom, human dignity, the rejection of every kind of racial or religious exclusiveness, condemnation of nationalism (which he branded as "bestial"), the protection of minorities, and in particular of the Jews, at that time persecuted in Russia. "The spirit of God in mankind," he wrote, in other words, the Kingdom of God, "demands for its true manifestation the most perfect social organisation." Throughout his works, we find clearly indicated the spiritual values to be developed both in society and in the individual. All mankind and each separate human person are called to the fullness of life, and to all-unity in Christ. However, he goes on to say that the Kingdom can be attained *only* on certain conditions: there must be a restoration of *true* Christianity. This means the "inner" acceptance of Christ, i.e. the acceptance of "spiritual regeneration, in the birth from above or of the spirit which was spoken of in the discourses with Nicodemus" (Lect. on Godmanhood). But unfortunately, as Soloviev points out, there is also another, "merely outward" Christianity, which follows the Gospel teaching only "in the letter," and not as a living content.

This then is the *measure* with which Soloviev gauges man's advance or retreat, on the way to the kingdom. Mankind is called to this supreme test on all levels: the state, the nation, society, politics, the church and the individual. This basic difference between *true* (inner) and *false* (outward) Christianity is forcifully stressed in Soloviev's last work *The Three Conversations.* This is the record of an imaginary symposium between various representatives of Russian society: the narrow-minded, conservative, and blunt "general" (outward) Christianity; the sophisticated and blasé "politician," ready for every compromise which could smooth out matters (here obviously there is no Christianity at all); the humanistic and idealistic "prince" (Tolstoy), who accepts Christian ethics, *without* their supernatural content; the prince believes that evil does not exist, it is merely the absence of good; *nonresistance* will disperse that which is only a delusion. The fourth interlocutor of this round-table talk, is "Mr. Z." (Soloviev himself). He has no difficulty in dealing with the general and the politician, by merely demonstrating the emptiness of their minds and souls. Then, turning to the prince, "Mr. Z." puts his finger on the impotence of morals *severed* from the life-giving vine of Christ in His fullness:

Evil actually exists [says Mr. Z.] and is expressed not only in the absence of good. . . . There is individual evil—it means that the lowest element in man, his animal and bestial passions oppose the best aspirations of the soul and *overpower* them; it means that the human masses, individually enslaved by evil, oppose the salutary efforts of a few good men, and defeat them. Finally there is the physical evil in man . . . the lowest material elements of his body oppose the living force which binds them into a harmonious form . . . they disrupt this form . . . and that means the extreme evil called death. . . . Against ultimate pessimism and despair no moral verbalism will defend us.

Is there such a thing as a remedy against despair?—the members of the symposium demand. "Mr. Z" answers:

The remedy is the true resurrection. We know that the struggle between good and evil is pursued not only in man's soul, but also in society, and deeper still, in the physical world. And we know of one victory of life's good principle in the past: individual resurrection.

This is obviously the resurrection of Christ, and "Mr. Z." concludes: "So we await one thing: the future victories of the collective resurrection of all men."

The "round-table" ends with "Mr. Z" gazing into the far away future, into the "latter days." This is the tale he relates about the coming of Antichrist, represented eschatologically and realistically; Antichrist is the epitome of evil, pretending to be the good. He is a learned, subtle, proud man, exercising his fascination on the "masses enslaved to him" individually and collectively. He seeks to substitute Christianity with his own cult. The leaders of the churches: Catholic, Protestant and Russian-Orthodox, as well as the Jews, oppose him; many are persecuted and destroyed, and a false religion is set up. But Antichrist's triumph is short lived; he is defeated by Christ's surviving followers and the Jews, their allies. After the fall of evil, all the victims are resurrected. Victory also marks the reunion of the Churches, the martyred and resurrected pope, being hailed by all as "*Tu es Petrus.*"

And thus, "Mr. Z" concludes, no "counterfeit" good can defeat evil. No set of man-made rules can resurrect us. The world cannot convince us that good is stronger than evil. But good *was* raised from the tomb in the person of Christ,—Godmanhood has made good immortal. This is the "*expecto resurrectionem mortuorum*" from which Soloviev drew his ultimate conclusions. Their moral implications are immense, echoing the words of his early lectures: "If we are Christians not in name only, but in deed, it de-

557

pends upon us that Christ should rise from the dead in His Humanity."

Bibliography

W. Soloviev, *Complete Works,* 10 Vols. Poems, Letters. In Russian (St. Petersburg-Leningrad, 1901–1923).

——, *Tri Razgovora* (Three Conversations). In Russian (Chekhov Publ., New York, 1954).

——,*Three Conversations,* Translated and Introduction by Stephen Graham (London, 1915).

——, *Three Conversations,* Translated by A. Bakshy (London, 1915).

——, *The Meaning of Love,* Translated by Jane Marshall (London, 1946).

——, *The Justification of the Good,* Translated by N. A. Duddington (London, 1918).

——, *Russia and the Universal Church,* Translated by Geoffrey Bless (London, 1948).

——, *Lectures on Godmanhood,* Translated and introduction by P. P. Zouboff (London, 1948).

——, *A Soloviev Anthology* In English from various translations, Edited by S. L. Frank (New York, 1951).

Michel D'Herbigny, *Vladimir Soloviev:* A Russian Newman. Translated from the French (London, 1918).

N. O. Lossky, *History of Russian Philosophy.* In English (Int. University Press, New York, 1951).

Helene Iswolsky
Fordham Institute of Contemporary
Russian Studies

Soloviev, W.: *see* Berdyaev, Nicolas; Khomiakov, Alexey.
Songs of Zarathushtra: *see* Zoroastrian Morals.

Sophilology: *see* Soloviev, Wladimir.
Sophists, the

Liberal or higher education is distinguished by a conscious concern for self-improvement in moral and political matters. In this respect the Sophists were the first liberal educators in Western Civilization. There had of course been pedagogues in Greece who taught music (in the Greek sense of poetry, music, and dancing), and even reading and writing. There had also been a long tradition of gnomic or moralizing poetry. But the pedagogue was concerned with teaching the very young, and the poet was not critical enough to see himself as a systematic educator. The Sophist took over where the pedagogue and the poet left off. His aim was far more ambitious than theirs: to teach special intellectual skills that would give his pupils special power in society. For doing this the Sophist received a fee, often a large one. It is not, however, the receiving of fees that distinguishes the Sophist; it is rather his claim to be able to teach those special mental powers that are advantageous in a city-state, advantageous either to the individual, or to the society, or to both. The Sophists, therefore, were the first professional educators of Greece. Although their reign was short, from approximately 450 B.C. to not much after 350 B.C., from Protagoras through Isocrates, their influence endured, indirectly through the effect they had on higher or liberal education, and directly, though to a lesser extent, through their philosophy.

The Sophists do not fit into the

mainstream of Greek philosophy in a direct and simple way. They were the heirs more of the gnomic poets than of the natural philosophers. The latter, of course, were concerned primarily with explaining the natural world. Some, it is true, did reflect upon man and his nature, but it was the Sophists who made man the focal point of philosophy. The explanation for this shift of emphasis from the universe to man seems to be twofold: As Socrates discovered, the natural philosophers had nothing to say about human purposes or final causes, whereas the Sophists, like Socrates, were interested in exactly these things. In addition, the philosophy or the science of the period had reached an impasse. Eleatic philosophy had shown that all previous theorizing belonged to the realm of mere opinion and that knowledge of the natural world was impossible. This, of course, led to scepticism and the Sophists, unlike Socrates, were sceptics almost without exception. Natural science for them was discredited and they turned their interest to more practical human affairs.

There were two species of Sophists. There were, on the one hand, the humanists, of whom Protagoras was the most famous. These maintained that they could teach virtue—political virtue, that is, since to all Greeks man was a political animal. There were, on the other hand, the rhetoricans, of whom Gorgias was the most famous. The rhetoricians maintained that they could teach the art of persuasion, and, like Gorgias, disclaimed any capacity to teach virtues. The difference between the two is, however, more one of scope. In effect even the rhetoricians were humanists of a sort, the art of rhetoric being to them the only human virtue.

The Sophists did not arise out of a social vacuum; they met a need that was determined by historical and political conditions, and by the Greek character. Ancient Greece was not a 'country'; it was a conglomeration of separate city-states, most of which were very small by modern standards. But these city-states were not isolated; extensive travel, mostly commercial, brought them together in a tentative way at least. At times they combined for common defense. Further, these city-states were frequently democratic or relatively so, such that the male citizens did have some say in political affairs. Each city-state had its own constitution, customs, moral codes, and conventions, and there were both similarities and differences from one city-state to the next. The differences could not escape the attention of the intelligent traveller, with the result that he would see his own traditional ways of doing things in a new, perhaps more sceptical light, especially if, as was often the case, his attachment to his own city-state was not iron-clad. Thus there were many who, seeing their own institutions in this new light, were ready to adopt different ways of doing things. This could only result in the breakdown of a tradition-dominated society and the emergence of a society where individual skill and knowledge in political matters was given considerable free-play. This was doubly so in any society where democracy had any foothold at all, and under these circumstances advantages accrued to both the skilful individual and the state. The older education was unable to equip the individual with any special skill to advance or even meet the changes. This applied particularly in a democracy, where skill in persuasion was essential. No one could even defend himself in court, much less advance his own interests, without some skill in the art of persuasion. It is here where the Sophist steps in, the itinerant and therefore politically unattached teacher of the political art and the art of persuasion. Thus the Sophists inaugurated what later, in the hands of the philosophers, became liberal education.

The Sophists were primarily teachers, not writers. They directed their efforts towards influencing immediate, not remote, followers. Consequently their writings were to them of secondary importance—many seem to have been exercises or models rather than 'original' works. Very little of their writing has survived. Most of this is fragmentary, often only quotations in the works of not always friendly writers. Plato is the principal source of our knowledge of the Sophists. While he is generally hostile, holding that the Sophist argues with no eye for the truth, he is not always as unsympathetic as some writers take him to be—for example he has great respect for Protagoras, the most famous of the Sophists.

Protagoras came from Abdera in Thrace and lived from about 486–5

B.C. to about 411 B.C. He was apparently influenced by the Persian Magi, who "while invoking the gods in their secret rites, seek to undermine public belief in the divine power because they do not wish to be thought to derive their own power therefrom,"[1] Protagoras may have had some connection with Democritus, although probably not as a pupil. Later Protagoras visited Athens, became acquainted with Pericles, and in 444 B.C. was given the task of preparing legislation for the new colony of Thurii in Italy. He travelled extensively, returning to Athens several times. One story, whose truth is uncertain, says that his final visit was disastrous. Having been accused of impiety and apparently ordered to trial, he left Athens, either before or after the trial, and was lost in a ship-wreck. His two principal works were *The Antilogiae* and *On Truth*. The former apparently had sections on the gods, on being, on laws and political problems, and on the arts. Only the opening sentence of each work survives.

The following discussion of Protagoras will focus on his famous dictum that man is the measure of all things. There are four discernible stages in his thought. First, he developed more than any previous thinker the significance of the *dissoi logoi*, 'twofold arguments' or 'conflicting explanations.' Second, he tried to resolve the conflict of the *dissoi logoi* by his dictum. Third, he developed this dictum as a rule for *dealing with things* rather

---

[1] Philostratus as quoted by Untersteiner, M., *The Sophists* translated by K. Freeman (New York, 1953), p. 1.

than as a principle for the *cognition of things*. Finally, he set forth a theory on virtue, education, and society consistent with the first three points.

The problem of 'twofold arguments' is an old problem in Greek thought. An example of the problem is found in the plight of Orestes, who is helpless before the conflicting demands made upon him, the divine edict to revenge his father by murdering his mother, and the divine edict not to commit matricide. *Diké* conflicts with *Diké;* justice conflicts with justice. In his *Antilogiae* Protagoras apparently brought the *dissoi logoi* to bear on the philosophic problems concerning the gods, being and the physical world, the laws and the state, and the arts. The results were negative; all explanations fall into the realm of mere opinion. The opening sentence of the *Antilogiae* sets the theme: "concerning the gods, I am not in a position to experience their phenomenal existence or otherwise, nor their nature with regard to their external manifestation; for the difficulties are many, which prevent this experience; not only the impossibility of having sense-experience of the gods, but also the brevity of human life." Man is such that all conceptions of the nature and existence of the gods belong to opinion; there is no way to choose from the great variety of conflicting conceptions put forward; all are based upon appearance. There is therefore no cognition of the gods, either by sense experience or reason. The conclusion applies to cognition of reality, of being, and of the natural world. Thus, according to

Protagoras, when the pre-Socratic natural philosophers, beginning with Thales, had set themselves to this problem of explaining reality, they proposed many different answers, but all in terms of appearances. Reasons could be given both for and against any view, hence all were mere opinion.

There is a text[2] on the twofold arguments by an unknown author who seems to be repeating arguments of Protagoras, among others. It is a superficial attempt to show that there are two sides to every question. Good and bad are dealt with by showing first that they are the same because one thing is good for one person, bad for another; and second, that they are different because, if the same, to do good is to do ill. Right and wrong in the sense of honorable and dishonorable are then dealt with in the same way: the same act is both right and wrong—e.g., to treat friends well is right, to treat enemies well is wrong. Hence right and wrong or honorable and dishonorable are the same. But they must be different on the ground that one and the same act cannot be both right and wrong. Justice and injustice are dealt with similarly, also truth and falsity, ignorance and wisdom, the teachability and the non-teachability of wisdom and virtue, and several other contrasting concepts. The most extensive text on twofold arguments is the second part of Plato's *Parmenides,* which deals with metaphysical subjects.

Protagoras was not provincial in his outlook; he travelled widely and was

2 H. Diels, *Die Fragmente der Vorsokratiker,* 5th Ed. (Berlin, 1934), Chap. 90.

acquainted with the great variety of laws and constitutions in his world. Is there absolute law? Can one system be justified against all others? No, all are equally justifiable and equally unjustifiable; the arguments for and against are equally valid. All laws then belong to the realm of opinion. Untersteiner[3] cites the discussion between Protagoras and Pericles concerning the blame for the death of Epitimus of Pharsalus by a javelin thrown at the games. Who was to blame? The thrower? Yes. The supervisor? Yes. The javelin itself? Yes. These oppositions of opinions cannot be resolved. Hence the concept of absolute justice or right is abolished; there is nothing but opinion. *Diké*, or justice, covers far more than the modern term; it covers moral as well as legal rightness, and in addition moral goodness. There is then no absolute meaning to the term 'good.' Thus the opposition of opinions and the regulation of all discourse to opinion removes the possibility of absolute moral standards.

The second stage in Protagoras' thought may be interpreted as merely summing up the first, or it may be interpreted as a positive advance. Most writers have taken the first view. Protagoras' famous dictum is: "Man is the measure of all things, of the things that are in so far as they are, of the things that are not in so far as they are not." This is a difficult saying to interpret. Is it an assertion of mere relativism? If it is, then it means that there is no objective truth, no objective

right, no objective good, no objective reality; things are significant only when man is the focus; without man there is nothing. Plato interpreted Protagoras this way for the most part, and showed that the position so interpreted is absurd—it cannot be stated without contradicting itself because it asserts as an objective truth that there is no objective truth. Under this interpretation we have Protagoras observing the great variety of conflicting moral and legal codes, customs and opinions, the great variety of conflicting opinions concerning the nature of reality, all depending upon the untrustworthy senses and paradoxical reason. We then have Protagoras concluding that everything is anthropocentric. Thus 'true' means 'true for man,' 'good' means 'good for man,' 'right' means 'right for man.' Is man here the individual or the species? Is Protagoras an individualistic relativist or is he a universalistic relativist? The ancients were inclined to take him as the former; some modern writers insist that he was the latter.

There is an alternative to this simple relativist interpretation of Protagoras' dictum. This turns on the meaning of *metron*. 'Measure' is obviously a vague term. Plato, and after him Sextus Empiricus, interpret *metron* to mean criterion. But as Aristotle had pointed out and Plato himself had insisted, the conception is absurd. In another context a similar difficulty is brought out in Plato's *Republic* when Thrasymachus gives his famous definition of justice as the interest of the stronger. Socrates asks in effect if the

---

[3] *Op. cit.*, pp. 30–31.

stronger is to be the model for all persons or the beneficiary of all actions. Clearly Thrasymachus intends the latter although his definition is ambiguous. To go back to Protagoras and *metron*. If we take Protagoras as a universalistic relativist we could say that the universal nature of man is a measure or model or criterion for each individual. This seems to me to be a very doubtful view of Protagoras' meaning, since it necessitates setting up the universal 'man' as an objective standard, and Protagoras has denied the possibility of objective standards. But the individualistic relativism gives sheer nonsense if we interpret *metron* to mean measure or criterion. An individual is not a criterion unless it be for other individuals, but then not just any individual will do; we must do as Thrasymachus' definition suggested and take some particular individual because of some characteristic peculiar to him, such as strength. Protagoras' dictum suggests nothing like this.

However *metron* may not mean criterion at all. Untersteiner suggests that it means *master*.[4] We then have: 'Man is the master of all things, of the things that are in-so-far as they are, and of the things that are not in so-far-as they are not.' Man is therefore a practical focus, not merely a cognitive measure of all things. This brings us beyond cognitive subjectivism; there

are no objective things to control man's mind and deed; the reality and the worth of things are not independent somewhats to which man must submit. Reality has meaning only when man abandons the search for an impossible objectivity and seizes control of 'things' for himself, 'things' here being subjective, i.e. appearances, or experiences.

This interpretation of *metron* receives support from the Protagorean position put forward by Socrates in the *Theatetus*.[5] Here Plato suggests that he is giving us something Protagoras might have said. How much is Plato and how much is Protagoras is hard to say. Briefly the theory is this: In spite of the relativism expressed by the dictum there is a vital distinction between the wise and the ignorant. To the sick man food seems and is bitter; to the healthy man food seems and is the opposite. Since the healthy state is the desirable one a change from illness to health is needed. The doctor with his medicines brings this change about through a process of curing or healing. The same holds of virtue and vice, and the process of educating is similar to that of healing. The Sophist effects this change from vice to virtue, from the worse state to the better, with arguments. The wise teacher, the Sophist, therefore replaces worse with better experiences.[6] Protagoras puts

---

4 Untersteiner, *op. cit.*, pp. 41 fol. and pp. 79 fol. Untersteiner gives examples of *metron* used elsewhere in this sense. In addition he cites the etymology of the word from the verb 'to rule.' There are further changes he suggests in the traditional interpretation, but there is not space to go into them here.

5 106C–107D.

6 Plato shows in the *Republic*, Book I, that the art of healing and the art of justice are different in this respect: healing is specific, covering a specific subject matter, whereas the art of justice is general, covering everything, as an 'overlord' art, we might say.

563

'better' in place of 'true.' The Sophist does not give us true experience and belief; he gives us better ones. Thus the Sophist or wise man is the master of experience, of things. 'Better' may mean merely 'more pleasing' or 'more desirable'; it does not and cannot have any objective meaning. Thus the ambiguity, the contradictory character, of experience is resolved when man masters it. Knowledge, or rather argument, is therapeutic and practical, not cognitive.

From this it would seem clear that Protagoras' dictum of man the *metron* requires something more than the mere 'measure' interpretation. 'Measure' is more cognitive in meaning, less manipulative, less practical than the *Theatetus* doctrine requires. But give 'measure' a practical significance, and we do in fact get a concept like 'master,' as Untersteiner suggests, something active in meaning, not something merely reflective; the experience to be measured becomes a material to work with rather than a picture to contemplate. The Sophists in general did not see thought apart from practical life; the 'measure' interpretation fails to convey this practical turn.

This leads to the last logical stage of Protagoras' thought, his theory of virtue. For this we are dependent again on Plato. In the *Protagoras* the subject of virtue and its teachability is examined. For Protagoras all the virtues are one, and virtue can be taught. His position is stated in a myth: the gods fashioned all things out of the elements. To Prometheus and Epimetheus the gods gave the task of distri-

buting various capacities to living things. Epimetheus began this but by the time he came to man he had used up all the available powers. Man was left physically weak. Prometheus then stole from the Gods and gave to man fire and knowledge of the crafts. Thus man was able to take care of himself by his technical skills. But men lacked political virtue and could not live together harmoniously, hence their communities fell apart and the very existence of mankind was threatened. Zeus sent Hermes to give two powers or virtues to all men equally, *viz.* respect and justice. Thus men, in addition to power over nature, were given the art of politics whereby they achieve mastery over one another. Protagoras, as a Sophist, specialized in the teaching of this political art, the art of justice, and taught it to anyone for a fee. The art tended to be literary and included as its core the art of persuasion. We must understand it in the light of the dictum and the substitution of 'good' for 'truth.' We have, therefore, the basic conflicts of nature resolved by the peculiarly human art of justice. All existing legal and moral codes, as well as all customs are more or less unskilful attempts to obtain a harmonious society. The Sophist is the one who properly speaking has the required skill to improve matters—to use a modern phrase, his knowledge is not of *what* but of *how*. The Greeks of the period were very ambitious and eagerly sought the key to success that the Sophists claimed to possess. Protagoras was a very successful Sophist, and his theory, if true, would justify his practice.

The second of the two Sophists to be examined is Thrasymachus. What we know of his views is derived almost entirely from Plato's *Republic*. Of his life practically nothing is known. He was born in Chalcedon in Bithynia, a Colony of Megara, around 459 B.C., and he was active during the period 427 B.C. until near the end of the century. Unlike Protagoras, but like Gorgias, Thrasymachus seems to have been interested primarily in rhetoric, and did not concern himself with the teaching of virtue. In fact, by the very nature of the views attributed to him by Plato, virtue in the ordinary sense would be the last thing to concern him.

Thrasymachus' position is presented in *The Republic*, Book I, by a Thrasymachus who exactly fits the name and the view he presents—a brash fighter. He is presented as bursting with indignation because of the "quibbling" of Socrates, failing to see how constructive Socrates' argument really is. He will have none of this logic-chopping and will present his views in a set speech for a fee. Socrates does not want a speech and could pay only praise if praise is due. His friends offer to foot the bill and Thrasymachus agrees to the question and answer procedure. "Justice is the interest of the stronger." This is the first form of his famous definition. He is surprised when there is no applause, showing that he is not interested in either understanding or truth but in rhetorical effect. Socrates points this out by saying that he must first understand this definition and then test it for its truth. The definition is ambiguous, as was pointed out earlier. Does it mean that the stronger is the model for all? Or does it mean that the stronger is the beneficiary? Thrasymachus intends the latter. The details of the subsequent argument are too lengthy to be dealt with here. Along with the definition given above, Thrasymachus attempts to maintain that although the stronger makes mistakes, it is right to obey him. Socrates shows that this position involves inconsistency. Thrasymachus attempts to avoid contradiction by giving up the premise that the stronger makes mistakes. He does not want, of course, to give up his definition of justice. His tactics involve changing the meaning of 'stronger;' the stronger is no longer the *de facto* ruler, but a hypostatized craftsman, a possessor of the political art, hence by definition infallible. Socrates has no trouble in showing that a craftsman *qua* craftsman works, not for his own interest, but for the interests of someone else; e.g. the physician works for the interest of his patient, hence of the weaker. Next Thrasymachus gives us what Plato wants us to take as an example of Sophistic rhetoric as opposed to philosophic dialectic. Thrasymachus goes on at great length trying to show the the shepherd is not interested in the sheep except in-so-far-as they benefit him: hence his real interest is in his own benefit. In this speech Thrasymachus surreptitiously turns his position around and gives the second form of his definitions, his real view. *Injustice* is the interest of the stronger. The political art then is the art of injustice. Again we must omit the details of Socrates' refutation whereby he seeks to prove that the just, not the unjust life is the happy life. The whole *Republic* is devoted to this theme.

Thrasymachus' position is refuted in theory by the end of Book II. But his theory and its refutation are abstract. The theory is amplified by Glaucon and Adeimantus. They do not believe this amplified version but are puzzled by it. Plato seems to be telling us that it was what the leading Sophists and their numerous pupils were generally thought to believe and that it was a popular conception and had much influence on the ambitious youth of the time. The Sophist Lycophron (about 470 B.C.) appears to have held this view. I see no reason to assume that Plato's version of the theory is inaccurate; he was hostile, but this was all the more reason to present the theory at its best; his own refutation would then be all the more effective. A similar view is presented by Plato through the mouth of Callicles in the *Gorgias*.

Glaucon presents the version as follows: Everyone desires to do evil; no one desires to suffer evil. (This is another perhaps more precise way of saying that injustice is the interest of the stronger.) However most people are not always in a position to do what they want or to avoid suffering what they don't want. Furthermore and this is crucial, in any action the good to the doer is always less than the harm to the sufferer. Hence, after a certain amount of experience of both good and evil people get together and make a compact among themselves such that each agrees not to do harm to others in return for not having to suffer harm from others. Justice is anything consistent with the compact, injustice anything inconsistent with the compact. Laws, customs, morality are all derived from convention or compact. Justice is a question of man-made law, convention, or *nomos,* not of nature or *physis.* Of course if anyone can successfully get around the compact, around the law, then there is nothing, no natural moral force, to stop him. As Adeimantus goes on to show, the result of this is that the man who *is* thoroughly unjust will *appear* to be thoroughly just. He will be successful, or in Thrasymachus' terms he will be the stronger and will benefit the most. On the other hand the thoroughly just person will appear to be thoroughly unjust. Only the fool will be just; he who possesses the art of injustice will possess the art of deception such that his own interest will be served. We must conjecture here that the interest of such a person, in fact of any person, is pleasure, in part at least. The theory then is that pleasure and duty are *always* in conflict; only human weakness makes duty advantageous, and then only to the ordinary run of men. Socrates'—and Plato's—view is that duty and justice are natural and that man's interests are served only by justice. The theory presented by Glaucon is of interest primarily for its conception of justice as the result of a contract and the radical distinction between *nomos,* law or convention, and *physis* or nature. Some of the premises of the theory are obviously false, e.g. that everyone desires to do evil or harm to others, or that the good to the doer is always less than the harm to the sufferer. Furthermore the idea of a compact is extremely vague, to say the least.

Other Sophists include Gorgias, Prodicus, Hippias, and Antiphon. Brief mention of each of these is all that space permits. The first, Gorgias of Leontini, is usually classed as a Sophist, although he did not so regard himself. He was born sometime between 490 and 485 B.C. He was a disciple of Empedocles and was influenced by Zeno the Eleatic. He travelled widely and had much influence. He lived to the very old age of one hundred and nine, and allowed himself to die of starvation when the weakness of old age became a burden. Among his works, of which only fragments survive, were orations on various popular subjects, a treatise on rhetoric, and a treatise entitled "On Not-Being, or on Nature." He regarded himself primarily as a rhetorician, but his being a rhetorician was not unrelated to his sceptical ideas on natural science and epistemology. In his treatise *On Not-Being, or on Nature* he maintained that nothing is, or, if anything is it cannot be known, or if anything can be known it cannot be expressed in speech. "But," according to Untersteiner, "after the elimination of existence in the world of appearance, he [Gorgias] must . . . have brought back appearance into existence and have restored in fact what he had lost in the-

ory: in this way Gorgias became an orator, who wished to transform appearance into reality by persuading his hearers."[7] In moral matters the same principle apparently was used by Gorgias; there is no rational solution to moral questions; there are only conflicting explanations. Unlike Protagoras, who resolved these by transforming knowledge from a cognitive to a manipulative process, Gorgias apparently accepted the ultimate irrationality of each practical decision. Consequently the virtues are irrational, and according to Plato in the *Gorgias* are derived from *nomos* or convention. However, Gorgias' position may have been that the virtues were derived from nature or *physis* and share its conflicting nature, hence are irrational. He held, unlike other Sophists, that the virtues were not teachable.

Prodicus of Ceos was born sometime between 470 and 460 B.C. and taught in Athens with great success. Socrates was one of his students but said he didn't learn anything from him. Prodicus was, like Protagoras, a teacher of virtue, hence a humanist, and again like Protagoras used literature as the means to this end. His work, *Heracles at the Crossroads* survives in substance, although not in form, through Xenophon's restatement of it in the *Memorabilia*. It is the story of Heracles at the end of boyhood choosing virtue instead of vice, moving from nature or *physis* to law or *nomos,* the latter being something taught not inherited. Furthermore vir-

7 *op. cit.,* p. 92.

tue is one, not many. Like most of the humanistic Sophists, Prodicus seems to have accepted the existing moral codes, merely interpreting them in terms of *physis* and *nomos*.

Hippias is another of the humanistic Sophists and is chiefly noted as a polymath; he professed to teach all subjects. He was born in Elis around the year 443 B.C. He had considerable political influence and travelled widely. He was killed while involved in a political plot in Elis near the middle of the fourth century. He believed that true knowledge of reality, of nature, was essential to virtues. From this he derived his notion of the superiority of natural law and justice over convention or *nomos,* the latter being a tyrant over man except when it happens to be a universal convention, in which case it coincides with natural law. His agreement with Protagoras is only over the teachability of virtue, and he is classed as a Sophist more for his pretensions and acceptance of fees than anything else.

Antiphon the Sophist is an obscure figure. He appears to have been an Athenian, active during the last third of the fifth century. He was a rhetorician and interpreter of dreams. He wrote a treatise entitled *Truth* in which he distinguished reality from appearance. He is famous for the argument that matter is the real—if you plant a bed, wood, not a bed sprouts up! According to Antiphon the laws of the state are artificially imposed and are more often than not directly opposed to the laws of nature. Antiphon expressed the idea, the first part of

which is strange to Greek thought, that when alone one should obey the laws of nature, in company the laws of the state. Punishment for disobedience of nature is inevitable; punishment for disobedience of the laws of the state depends only on detection. Antiphon attacked the view that giving evidence in legal cases is right. Justice requires that no wrong be done to someone who has not wronged the witness. But to testify against someone is to wrong him. Plato, of course, insisted that a distinction be made between 'harm' in the sense of the surgeon's giving pain, and 'harm' in the sense of making a person less virtuous. 'Harming' an accused man with testimony may be harming him in the first sense, but not in the second.

A second work by Antiphon is the essay *On Concord* in which he stresses the importance of education and the fact that good education cannot be destroyed by adversity. The task of education is to teach concord, which holds together the individual and society.

Of course there were many other Sophists, some thorough-going like Lycophron, others partial, like Isocrates, the fourth century orator. The latter did not regard himself as a Sophist although his contemporaries frequently referred to him as such owing to the fact that he set up a school to teach the art of rhetoric. By the middle of the fourth century Plato's Academy was well established and flourishing, and Aristotle's Lyceum was soon to begin. Between them they attracted the more brilliant intellects of the time, leaving little room for the itin-

568

erant Sophist. Permanent educational institutions replaced the isolated and transitory individual educator.

Bibliography

H. Diels, *Die Fragmente der Vorsokratiker*, 5th Ed. (Berlin, 1934).
K. Freeman, *The Pre-Socratic Philosophers* (Cambridge, 1946).
H. Jackson, article on Sophists in 11th Edition, *Encyclopedia Britannica*.
W. Jaeger, *Paideia*, Vol. I, translated by G. Highet (New York, 1939).
M. Untersteiner, *The Sophists,* translated by K. Freeman (New York, 1954).

Nathaniel W. Roe
Wellesley College

Sophist(s): *see* Minor Socratics; Spinoza.

Sophocles: *see* Freud, Sigmund.

sorcery: *see* Mundurucu Indians, A Dual System of Ethics; Pakot, the Moral System of; Zuni Indians, Morals of.

sorrow: *see* Schlick, Moritz.

soul: *see* Aztec Morals; Freud, Sigmund; Hindu Ethics; Pakot, the Moral System of; Stoics, the.

South American Indians: *see* Tapirapé Morals, Some Aspects of.

Soviet Morality, Current

1. *Introduction. Russian Marxist Ethical Theory before 1917*

Marxism was received in Russia, as were earlier Western philosophies and scientific theories before it, not primarily as a technical or academic doctrine, but as a total world-view, a way of life, indeed, a vehicle of secular salvation. This, plus the related fact of extraordinary interest in problems of ethical theory and moral practice on the part of nineteenth-century Russian intellectuals generally, made Russian Marxists particularly sensitive to the chief systematic gaps in classical Marxism—those in ethics and theory of knowledge. Very soon after Marxism emerged as a dominant force in Russian intellectual life (in the early 1890's) Russian Marxists split into three opposed groups, in accordance with the ways in which they attempted to fill these gaps. One group, made up of P. B. Struve (1870–1944), S. N. Bulgakov (1871–1944), and N. A. Berdyaev (1874–1948), turned to Kant for both an ethical theory and a theory of knowledge to supplement historical materialism. A second group—including A. V. Lunacharski (1874–1933), A. A. Bogdanov (real name Malinovski) (1873–1928), S. A. Volski (real name Sokolov) (1880–1936?), and V. A. Bazarov (real name Rudnev) (1874–1931?)—turned to Nietzsche for ethics and to Mach and Avenarius for a theory of knowledge. (Maxim Gorky was closely associated with this group.) A third, relatively orthodox, group—including G. V. Plekhanov (1857–1918), L. I. Akselrod-Ortodoks (1868–1946), and A. M. Kollontai (1872–1952)—wrote comparatively little on ethical theory, but their ethical views represented an eclectic mixture of Marx, Engels, Spinoza, and Kautsky.

Both the "Kantian" Marxists and the "Nietzschean" Marxists rejected what they regarded as the impersonalism and anti-individualism of Marx (and Hegel), the doctrine that "the individual is only a point of intersection of socio-economic relationships." They sought a theoretical ground—in Kant or in Nietzsche—for the defense of the dignity, autonomy, and freedom of the individual person. The "Kantians," naturally enough, centered their attention on the problem of moral freedom and responsibility, and the origin and status of moral obligation and values. The "Nietzscheans" sharply rejected the categories of duty and obligation (Volski even called them "bourgeois"), stressing the free creation of values, the "artistic" shaping of ideals, aesthetic self-expression and growth. Both groups were markedly libertarian in their political philosophy.

"Kantian" and "Nietzschean" Marxism in Russia reached its summit in the first decade of the present century, and, though it produced much of theoretical promise—especially the work of the "Nietzscheans" in naturalistic ethics and value theory—the movement was short-lived. Berdyaev, Bulgakov, and Struve soon abandoned both the Russian Social Democratic Party and, to a large extent, Marxist theory, subsequently returning to the folds of the Orthodox Church. Lunacharski, Volski, Bogdanov, and Bazarov, though they remained Marxists, broke sharply with Lenin and the Bolsheviks during the decade before 1917. Only Lunacharski attained a position of power in Lenin's government, and this appears to have been at the cost of his Nietzschean, and, in general, libertar-

ian views. The other three men fell into disgrace or neglect during the 1920's and early 1930's. An unsympathetic observer might conclude that the attempt to combine Hegelian-Marxian determinism with Nietzsche's assertion of freedom and creativity, Hegelian-Marxian impersonalism with Nietzsche's stress on the individual as artist, creator and transvaluator of values; Marx's socialism and egalitarianism with Nietzsche's aristocratic cult of the *Übermensch,* was theoretically abortive. In any case, both the "*Kantian*" and "Nietzschean" "deviations" gave way completely, after 1917, to Lenin's more orthodox position.

2. *Lenin's Views on Morality*

Though close to both Plekhanov and L. I. Akselrod on many philosophic issues, Lenin, to the extent that he had an ethical theory, was neither a Spinozist nor a Kautskyan, but a pure Machiavellian, in the technical sense of the term: he systematically subordinated questions of individual and social morality to the tactical problem of the acquisition and maintenance of political power. "Our morality," he declared in 1920, "is wholly subordinated to the interests of the class struggle of the proletariat."[1] Whatever furthers the cause of Communism is "moral," whatever obstructs that cause is "immoral." "The only scientific criterion of morality," according to a current Soviet formulation, is "the defense of the interests of the victory of Com-

[1] V. I. Lenin, *Sochineniya* [Works], fourth ed., XXXI, 410.

570

munism. . ."[2] "In our time only what furthers the destruction of capitalism and the victory of Communism is moral."[3]

The instrumental role assigned to morality by Lenin, its subordination to political ends—which has become increasingly characteristic of Soviet theory and practice during the past quarter century—must not be misconstrued as a deprecation or minimizing of the role of morality. Quite the contrary, in October 1920, at the height of the civil war in Russia, Lenin declared that the whole concern of contemporary education should be the indoctrination of young people in the principles of Communist morality. He and his followers have always viewed morality as a crucially important weapon in the class struggle.

Lenin combined in his ethical views the Marxian doctrine of the class-character of all moral norms and judgments with the revolutionary asceticism and Machiavellianism of such mid-nineteenth-century Russian radicals and nihilists as Bakunin, Nechayev, and Tkachyov. This is a perfectly consistent combination. On the question of free will and determinism, however, Lenin "deviated" from the classical Hegelian-Marxian position in a less consistent way. Furthermore, his mitigation of determinism was deliberately selective. He continued to assert that

nature was causally determined, subject to universal, necessary laws. But he introduced significant elements of freedom, creativity, and choice into individual and historical action, insisting upon the function of the striving human will, especially the will of the dedicated, disciplined revolutionist. At the same time, however, like Plekhanov, he continued to pay lip service to strict and total historical determinism. This quite inconsistent combination has been interpreted by at least one recent Soviet writer (P. A. Shariya, see Bibliography) as a genuine modification of determinism and an assertion of "relative freedom of choice."

3. Ends and Means. Terrorism and Class-Struggle.

Lenin took over from P. N. Tkachyov (1844–86) and from Bakunin-Nechayev, especially the latter's notorious *Revolutionist's Catechism* (1869), the doctrine that the "good" revolutionary end justifies beforehand any means whatever, however "immoral" such means may appear from the viewpoint of a conventional or traditional (e.g., Kantian or Christian) ethics. Reminiscences recently published by an ex-Bolshevik, closely associated with Lenin in 1904, make it clear that as early as that year Lenin considered himself a "Jacobin" and as such a follower of Tkachyov. "Jacobinism" Lenin defined as resolute struggle to realize a goal, conducted without kid gloves, "not afraid to have recourse to the guillotine."[4]

2 "Nravstvennost kommunisticheskaya" ["Communist Morality"], *Bolshaya sovetskaya entsiklopediya,* second ed. (1954), XXX, 207.

3 M. Z. Selektor, "Politika i moral" ["Politics and Morals"], *Voprosy filosofi,* No. 4 (1951), p. 67.

4 N. Valentinov (real name Volski), *Vstrechi s Leninym* [Encounters with Lenin] New York, 1953), p. 185.

The problem of ends and means was posed sharply, not only at the level of theory, but even more urgently at the level of policy and practice, during the early years of the Soviet régime. During this period Lenin continued to put his Machiavellian theory into practice; but the task of theoretical defense of this position fell to Trotsky, and to a lesser extent to Radek and Bukharin. The most forthright statement of Lenin's position in the period immediately following the October Revolution was made by Latsis, a member of the ruling *collegium* of the Cheka (Secret Police): "Murder, lies, and treachery," he wrote, "are immoral and shameful if they are harmful to the cause of the proletarian revolution; these same lies, treachery, and murder are moral and laudable if they serve this revolution."[5]

Trotsky's "theoretical justification" (1920) of the use of terrorism, violence, and fraud by a revolutionary "dictatorship of the proletariat" was a polemical response to the critique of the German Marxist Karl Kautsky (see Bibliography). It may be reduced to four "theses": 1) Ends and means are separable, and a good end justifies any means; furthermore, different socio-economic classes may use the same means (e.g., terrorism) to achieve very different, even opposed, ends. 2) Socialism cannot be achieved without revolutionary violence and repression.

Whoever desires the end of socialism must accept the means of terrorism. 3) All governments use violence to stay in power, and all historical revolutions have used violence to break this power. 4) The reign of terror in Russia was started not by the Bolsheviks but by the counter-revolutionary forces.

Trotsky, of course, differed from later Soviet Marxists, especially Stalin and his followers, in the frankness with which he acknowledged that terroristic methods were being employed, as well as the openness of his repudiation of democratic processes and respect for human dignity. He had only scorn for the "Kantian-clerical, vegetarian-Quaker chatter about the 'sanctity of human life' . . .," and asserted that, wherever necessary, individuals are, and should be, treated merely as means.[6]

Two questions naturally arise. The first concerns the *effectiveness* of terrorism as a means to the end of socialism. A disagreement on this question would be a *scientific* one and could presumably be settled by appeals to evidence and logic, the ultimate argument being a pragmatic one: but terror *is* working, and it *has* worked. The second, and more important, question concerns the *moral* admissibility of such means, in cases where they are found to conflict radically with some other value or principle (e.g., respect for human life and liberty). One who

---

[5] *Mech* [The Sword], No. 1 (1918); quoted in V. S. Grechko, *Kommunisticheskoye vospitaniye v SSSR* [Communist Education in the U.S.S.R.], (Munich, 1951), p. 6.

[6] L. D. Trotsky, *Terrorizm i kommunizm* [Terrorism and Communism] (Moscow, 1920), p. 61.

finds terrorism morally unacceptable even though demonstrably effective, may either: 1) have recourse to alternative and perhaps less effective means for realizing the given end (this is what Kautsky and the European Socialists did in their appeal to constitutional, parliamentary reform), or else: 2) if it can be shown (as Trotsky tried to do) that terrorism, violence, and fraud are the *only* possible means, he must either a) accept them, recognizing their immorality, but asserting that they are justified by the good end (the Lenin-Trotsky position) or b) give up the end altogether.

Both parties to this controversy—Lenin, Trotsky, Radek, and Bukharin, on the one side, and Kautsky and John Dewey,[7] on the other—are stronger in their critical assaults upon the opposed position than in their own constructive contributions. Ultimately, both sides draw their polemical power from the alleged arbitrary absolutism of their opponents. There is more than a grain of truth in Trotsky's charge that Kautsky had taken an essentially Kantian, or quasi-Kantian, position, inconsistent with Marxian moral relativism. It is precisely the insistence that there are certain moral principles or values which set absolute limits to the choice of means for realizing given socio-political ends that distinguishes Kautsky, Dewey, and most of the Russian Mensheviks from Lenin, Trotsky, and the Bolsheviks. It is not easy to decide

which of these groups was more nearly "orthodox," since both Marx and Engels made many conflicting statements concerning ends, means, terrorism, and the dictatorship of the proletariat. But it is clear that Kautsky and Dewey are much closer to the liberal and humanistic traditions of the West than were the Bolsheviks. To be sure, neither Lenin nor Trotsky would be impressed by such a charge, since they repudiate this entire tradition, challenging their opponents to produce a rational (not merely historical) ground or justification for their libertarian and humanistic values. Candor forces one to admit that, despite the strenuous theoretical efforts of both Kautsky and Dewey in the domain of naturalistic ethics—the former with his Darwinian theory of social instincts, the latter with his attempted assimilation of value judgments to the assertions of the empirical sciences—this challenge has not been satisfactorily met. On the other hand, Trotsky's critics who demand a rational ground or justification for his own passionate and exclusive commitment to the end of Communism and the means of violent class struggle, are offered nothing but dogmatic Marxist-Leninist assertion. Trotsky's unsparing candor and incisiveness in polemical attack hardens, at just this critical point, into dogged authoritarian dogmatism. And Soviet "moralists" of the Stalinist period, though lacking both Trotsky's brilliance and his candor, have succeeded in surpassing him in dogmatism.

Generally speaking, the Soviet per-

---

[7] In his critique of Trotsky: "Means and Ends: Their Interdependence . . ." *The New International*, Vol IV (1938).

iod has been marked by a progressive elimination, or at least, ossification of ethical theory, contrasting sharply with the lively theoretical activity of the "Kantian" and "Nietzschean" Marxists before 1917. In the 1920's a few works of theoretical interest—notably, those of Dembski, Gurvich, Preobrazhenski, and Deborin—were published; but they were essentially reformulations of Kautsky's Darwinian-Marxist ethics. After 1931, when Deborin's group was officially repudiated, Kautskyan ethical theorists ceased to publish. Deborin himself was accused, among other things, of "holding erroneous Kautskyan views in ethics," and no one else ventured to raise a voice in defense of a Kautskyan, or indeed any other non-Leninist ethical position. By 1936, when the Stalinist Constitution was adopted, original work in ethical theory had virtually ceased in the Soviet Union. What remained was a repetition of the views of Marx, Engels, and Lenin, with Stalinist modifications as necessary to justify changes, some of them drastic, in Soviet policy and practice.

The two most important changes were with respect to law and the state, on the one hand, and sexual morality, marriage, and the family, on the other.

4. Law and Morality. The "Legalization" of Ethics.

Engels had held that law was inextricably bound up with the capitalist state as a system of legalized coercion, and would logically disappear with the "withering away" of the latter. During the 1920's Soviet theorists pushed this doctrine to the extreme of what was later characterized as "legal nihilism," asserting that "socialist law" was a contradiction in terms, and branding law as a "bourgeois fetish," an "opium for the people," and calling the legislature "a temple of bourgeois domination." Furthermore, the theoretical nihilism of such eminent Soviet jurists as Pashukanis and Stuchka was matched by the nihilism of Soviet legal practice. Tsarist legal codes and precedents were discarded in favor of "People's Courts" and "revolutionary legal consciousness." The test for the legality, as for the morality of an act, was its revolutionary expediency, the extent to which it was felt to further the interests of the socialist revolution. Elaborate codes, criminal and civil, were to be abolished; the only thing to remain was a kind of basic administrative law. This tendency prevailed almost unchallenged throughout the 1920's. But by 1930 it had been bluntly rejected; and this reversal of policy took a dramatic turn with the promulgation of the Constitution of 1936 and the definitive acceptance of law and the state as bulwarks of "socialist construction." In 1937 Vyshinski wrote that the "withering away" of the state would be "preceded by a vast period of time, and, probably, not by a single period, but by a whole series of periods, of epochs."[8] One has an image of centuries, if not millennia!

---

[8] A. Ya. Vyshinski, *K polozheniyu na fronte pravovoi teori* [The Situation on the Front of Legal Theory] (Moscow, 1937), p. 54.

574

In any case, Vyshinski seems to have provided a firm doctrinal basis for the existence of law and the state "in our time." Stalin himself made this doctrine fully authoritative in March 1939 (addressing the Eighteenth Party Congress) when he declared that the state would have to be preserved at maximum strength even after the achievement of full Communism, so long as non-Communist states continued to exist.

During the 1920's it was widely held that morality, as well as law, would "wither away" under socialism. This view is now explicitly repudiated: morality, it is asserted, will retain its full force even after the eventual disappearance of legal compulsion.[9] Similarly, in the early period a number of Soviet writers formulated the distinction between law and morality in essentially Kantian terms: law rests on external compulsion, state sanction; morality springs from inner conviction, conscience. One can be compelled to act lawfully but external compulsion destroys morality. By the early 1930's, however, such views were no longer expressed. Rather, both law and morality were viewed as resting on external compulsion, with the sole difference that in the one case the sanction was supplied by state power and in the other by "public opinion."[10]

The "legalization" of morality, which became apparent soon after 1936, has been especially striking in postwar writings. The Soviet Constitution is spoken of as the "moral code of Soviet society." Morality is subsumed under legality, and both, in turn, are subordinated to political ends. To be a moral man is to obey the laws of the Soviet state and to despise and denounce violators of these laws. "In the U.S.S.R. law and morality reinforce one another. A man who is condemned by a Soviet law is also morally condemned. If some one has violated a Soviet law, we can no longer respect such a person."[11] Thus, obedience to law, in a socialist society, is declared a *moral* duty, and law, in turn, is held to develop morality. This last is quite opposed to Marx's view that you cannot legislate men into being moral, since the foundations of morality are economic. It implies an un-Marxian assumption that a part of the superstructure (legal norms) can directly modify human conduct, independently of the appropriate economic forces and institutions. In recent years, Soviet writers have emphasized the "enormous creative role" of Soviet law and the Soviet state, their "great influence in transforming the economic base of Soviet society."[12]

---

9 M. Z. Selektor, "Pravo i nravstvennost" ["Law and Morality"], *Voprosy filosofi*, No. 2 (1954), p. 72.

10 Recently there has been a slight but not unequivocal shift in the direction of the Kantian position. Cf. *loc. cit.*

11 M. P. Baskin, *Moral kak forma obshchestvennovo soznaniya* [Morality as a Form of Social Consciousness] (Moscow, 1946), p. 13.

12 M. P. Kareva, *Pravo i nravstvennost v sotsialisticheskom obschestve* [Law and Morality in Socialist Society] (Moscow, 1951), pp. 21–22.

The general narrowing of the area where law and morality do not coincide is in accordance with the increasing control exercised over the lives of individual Soviet citizens. To transfer a given rule or norm from the realm of morality to that of legality is to bring it within the orbit of positive sanctions, the control of the coercive apparatus of the state. And the widening of the area of such control is a clear phenomenon of the Stalinist period of Soviet history.

This process of "legalization" and "politicalization" has also invaded areas of personal relationships traditionally considered private and intimate *par excellence*—sex, marriage, and the family.

5. *Sexual Morality. Marriage and the Family.*

The classical Marxian position with respect to sexual morality, marriage, and the family was most fully stated by Engels. The monogamous marriage structure, he held, was indissolubly bound up with the institution of private property, inheritance rights, and a "commercial" attitude toward the marriage contract. Under socialism the family as a social unit would "wither away," and monogamous marriage would give way to easily dissolvable relationships under conditions of perfectly free divorce. The care and education of children would be taken over in an increasing degree by social agencies. In a word, under socialism there would be no place for the "bourgeois" family, just as there would be no place for law, the state, religion, or the church.[13]

In the early years of the Soviet regime this view was publicly espoused by influential Bolshevik intellectuals, including Trotsky, Bukharin, Lunacharski, and Krylenko. Lenin himself did not take a clear position on the "withering away" of the family, but he was vigorous in his insistence upon absolute freedom of divorce.

The early Soviet legislation followed Engels' predictions and proposals. In 1917 divorce was made free and easily accessible. In 1918 abortion was legalized, and the divorce and abortion rates rose rapidly to (and then above) the levels then prevalent in Western Europe and the United States. Prostitution, which was viewed by most Soviet theorists as a basically economic, rather than social or psychological, problem, was energetically attacked, and the incidence of prostitution declined considerably, at least for a time. At the forefront of this whole movement stood Mme. A. M. Kollontai, People's Commissar for Social Welfare, who, in pamphlets, short stories, and novels defended a doctrine of "free love," "erotic friendship," and a cult of what she called "winged eros" as a goal of socialism. She considered the

13 Bakunin had advocated the abolition of the family and social upbringing of children in his *Narodnoye delo* program of 1868, nearly two decades before Engels' statement. Of course, the *Communist Manifesto* (1848) contained some very brief critical remarks on the bourgeois family and bourgeois marriage. And the communal upbringing of children has been urged by many political theorists, from Plato on down.

family and monogamous marriage "relics of the dead past." There is much evidence that a large majority of Soviet young people accepted (and practiced) her doctrines. For example, in 1922, over 1500 Moscow University students filled out questionnaires indicating what they regarded as the ideal form of sex relations.[14] The results are given below:

	Men	Women
1. Marriage	21.4%	14.3%
2. (Relatively) lasting liaisons	50.8	67.3
3. Brief liaisons	12.0	6.9
4. Casual sex relations	2.9	1.7
5. Free liaisons, duration unspecified	10.4	8.9
6. Prostitution	.1	0
7. Other (presumably homosexual)	2.4	.9
	100.0%	100.0%

Thus, 78.6% of men and 85.7% of women preferred sex relations other than marriage. This was in the era of "postcard divorce," when many people married two or three times a year over a period of several years. Thus, the "relatively lasting liaisons" are to be construed in terms of weeks, or at most months, the "brief liaisons" in terms of a few days or at most weeks.

This general picture is corroborated by the accounts of Soviet émigrés and Western visitors who were in the Soviet Union at this time. It is even supported by isolated statements in the current Soviet press. Thus in 1939 a Soviet writer remarked disapprovingly

that during the early 1920's "a girl who refused to give herself to a young man after their first date was declared Philistine and middle-class."[15]

However, the theory and practice of "free love" soon ran into stubborn resistance. Kollontai's views were caricatured and attacked by a number of writers, and most violently by the psychiatrist Zalkind, who advocated instead a kind of "revolutionary sublimation," and went so far as to formulate "Twelve Commandments" of sexual behavior. His "Twelfth Commandment," for example, reads as follows: "The class, in the interests of revolutionary expediency, has a right to intervene in the sex life of its members. Sexual matters should be subordinated in all respects to class considerations . . ."[16] Sex, Zalkind declares, is an "essential part of the fighting arsenal of the proletariat. . . ."[17] And he makes the extreme assertion that "sexual attraction toward . . . a member of a hostile class . . . is just as perverted as sexual attraction of a human being for a crocodile or orangutang."[18] The "politicalization" of personal relationships could hardly be carried further!

Soviet policy shifts with respect to sex, marriage, and the family cannot

---

[14] I. G. Gelman, *Polovaya zhizn sovremmenoi molodyozhi* [The Sex Life of Contemporary Young People] (Moscow, 1923), p. 95.

[15] V. N. Kolbanovski, "Voprosy kommunisticheskoi morali" ["Questions of Communist Morality"], *Bolshevik*, No. 15–16 (1939), p. 103.

[16] A. B. Zalkind, *Revolyutsiya i molodyozh* [The Revolution and the Young People] (Moscow, 1925), p. 90.

[17] *Ibid.*, p. 76.

[18] *Ibid.*, p. 80.

be considered in detail here.[19] Only the major changes can be briefly mentioned: In 1936 divorce regulations were suddenly tightened, a process continued in 1944 and 1948 (in part by rulings of the Soviet Supreme Court). Today it is extremely difficult and almost prohibitively expensive for the ordinary Soviet citizen to get a divorce. Current statements emphasize the consolidation of the Soviet family as a unit of "Communist education."

In 1936 abortion, too, was made illegal; it still is, although in 1954 anti-abortion penalties were slightly relaxed. Refugee reports indicate that abortions are still fairly frequent, but are often carried out by untrained village women. All Soviet spokesmen assume, without argument, that anyone who has sex relations either has children or resorts to abortion. The possibility of employing contraceptives is never mentioned. This silence is clearly a deliberate policy. Contraceptives were apparently never widely used in the Soviet Union, although until the early 1930's they were available (but of extremely poor quality, according to émigré reports). The evidence is strong that in recent years contraceptives have been wholly unavailable to the ordinary Soviet citizen (military personnel alone provide an exception). The refusal of the Soviet government to publicize even such a

birth-control technique as the "rhythm method" makes it clear that Soviet policy in this area is not a result of economic shortages, as some Western commentators have suggested, but constitutes a deliberate attempt to bolster the birth rate at whatever cost to the individual.

From the viewpoint of sexual morality, one of the paradoxical results of this drive for increased population is that, in contrast to the general tendency toward stabilizing and strengthening the family and monogamous marriage, it is possible for an unmarried woman to make a profitable (and perfectly legal) profession of bearing children, by one or a variety of fathers, and turning them over to the state for upbringing. The apparent contradiction between such a situation and current Soviet "puritanism" in matters of sex becomes less acute when we realize that this "puritanism" is not based, as was that of Plato and the Calvinists, upon a distrust of the "flesh" or the "senses." Rather, it is what might be called a "*political* puritanism," grounded in a mistrust of any kind of behavior which in principle eludes the control of the state.

The reversal of official policy and attitude with respect to marriage and the family has been both more thoroughgoing and more final than that with respect to law and the state. As we have seen, Soviet theorists, even after 1936, continued to admit that the "withering away" of law and the state, though postponed to an indefinite future, would eventually take place. But no Soviet writer since 1936

19 See, for example, R. Schlesinger (ed.), *The Family in the U.S.S.R.* (1949); M. Hindus, "The Family in Russia," in *The Family, its Function and Destiny*, ed. by R. N. Ashen (1949); L. A. Coser, "Some Aspects of Soviet Family Policy," *The American Journal of Sociology* Vol. LVI (March 1951).

has ventured to assert that the withering away of the family had merely been deferred. On the contrary, recent statements all stress that a new kind of family, the "firm, stable socialist family," has made its appearance on the stage of history, and is here to stay.

6. *Conclusion*

The specific moral principles and obligations emphasized by contemporary Soviet writers may be summed up very briefly. The central principle is the "correct" and "harmonious" combination of individual and social interests, i.e., the subordination of the former to the latter in all cases of conflict. Corollary to this are such obligations as "respect for social property"; Soviet patriotism—sharply distinguished (but it would appear to be a distinction without a difference) from "bourgeois chauvinism"; socialist internationalism, also sharply distinguished from "bourgeois cosmopolitanism." These are all variations on the root theme of the individual's subordination, loyalty, and devotion to the "collective."

An intriguing, but almost unanswerable, question concerns the extent to which the Soviet "politicalization" of personal and moral relationships has been successful, in other words, the degree to which current official moral exhortation influences the actual moral attitudes and choices of individual Soviet citizens. At least one perceptive and informed observer reports that this influence is relatively slight, that in practice most Soviet citizens observe traditional humanistic moral norms

and principles.[20] And this verdict is borne out, in part at least, both by refugee reports and, indirectly, by Soviet press criticisms of recurrent violations of "Communist morality." On the other hand, there is considerable evidence that the bureaucratic complexities of Soviet institutions, together with chronic economic shortages, have exerted a pervasive and almost irresistible pressure toward surface conformity, hypocrisy, and petty corruption of personal morals (e.g., the ubiquitous phenomenon of *blat*— "pull," or "influence," with a suggestion of "connivance"). Soviet writers, of course, insist that the incidence of actual crime in the Soviet Union is decreasing, in contrast to the situation in the "decadent" Western countries; but there is no way at present to check the truth of such claims.

As for ethical theory, current Soviet writings, with very few exceptions —one of them being the work of Shariya already mentioned (see Bibliography)—are principally exhortations aimed at making the Soviet citizen meet his "moral obligations," as set forth above. The most interesting contribution of contemporary Soviet writers is to be found in their polemic and criticism—some of it quite relevant and intellectually respectable— directed against pragmatic, positivistic, and existentialist ethics. But that is a subject which cannot be explored in the present article.

20 George F. Kennan, "Russia and the United States" *The New Republic* (June 26, 1950), p. 16.

Bibliography

Karl Kautsky, *Terrorismus und Kommunismus: Ein Beitrag zur Naturgeschichte der Revolution* (1919). (The English translation, *Terrorism and Communism,* is extremely inaccurate.)

Leon Trotsky, *In Defense of Terror* (1921). (Russian original: *Terrorizm i Kommunizm* [1920].)

John Hazard (ed.), *Soviet Legal Philosophy* (1951).

Rudolf Schlesinger (ed.), *The Family in the U.S.S.R.* (1949).

P. A. Shariya, *O nekotorykh voprosakh kommunisticheskoi morali* [On Certain Questions of Communist Morality] (Moscow, 1951).

George L. Kline, *Russian Ethical and Social Theory* (in press).

George L. Kline
Columbia University

Soviet morality: *see* Marxist Theory of Morals; Russia.

Spaniards: *see* Rio Grande Pueblo Indians.

speech: *see* Hindu Ethics.

speech, proper: *see* Muslim Morals.

spell: *see* Pakot, The Moral System of.

Spencer, B.: *see* Primitive Morals.

Spencer, Herbert: *see* Major Ethical Viewpoints; Moral Philosophy in America; Utilitarianism.

Spentā-Ārmaiti: *see* Zoroastrian Morals.

Spinoza

Baruch Spinoza (Benedict de Spinoza) was born on November 24, 1632, in Amsterdam, where his parents, Spanish-Portuguese Jews, had sought refuge from the Inquisition in the Iberian Peninsula. At the Jewish high school (Heder) he familiarized himself with Bible and Talmud as well as those secular subjects which the directors of the school considered not to be in contradiction with the Torah (the five books of Moses). Although the study of Latin, being the language of the Catholic Church, was frowned upon by Jewish authorities of the time, Michael de Spinoza, Baruch's father, consented to his son's wishes and secured for him a special Latin tutor, the physician Van den Ende. With Van den Ende Baruch read the New Testament and the works of the natural scientists of the early 17th century.

When it became known in the Jodenburt, the center of Amsterdam's Jewish quarters, that the young Spinoza harbored rather unorthodox views with regard to the scriptural traditions, Jewish and Christian alike, and when after the death of his father Baruch moved out of the ghetto into the home of his Latin teacher who, though Catholic, was suspected of atheism, the Amsterdam Jewish authorities, conscious of the precariousness of the Jewish position in those days, at first pleaded with the young scholar not to criticize publicly any of the established religious doctrines and to return to their communion. When he rejected their admonition and showed no sign of repentance, they pronounced the Herem, the great ban excommunicating him for the "horrible heresies which he practiced and taught." The writ of excommunication, dated July 27, 1656, written in Spanish, is still to be found in the archives of the Amsterdam synagogue Beth Yaakov.

Separated from his kindred, Spinoza substituted for his Hebrew name Baruch (the Blessed) the Latin equivalent Benedict; but he never accepted baptism; nor did he ever join any Christian congregation. In accordance with the time-honored Jewish custom that even the most learned Rabbi (teacher) should know a manual trade, he had learned the art of polishing optical glasses. Lens-grinding served him from now on as the means for earning a living. In 1661, he moved to Rhijnsburg, a small town near Leyden. The memory of his sojourn in Rhijnsburg is preserved in the name Spinoza Laan and the small house in which he had found lodging; today this house is a museum dedicated to his memory.

Having outlined some of his fundamental philosophical principles in the *Tractatus Brevis de Deo et Homine ejusque Felicitate* (A Short Treatise on God, Man and His Well-Being), he now proceeded to explain his objections to Bacon's *Novum Organum* and Descartes' *Discourse on Method* in an essay entitled *Tractatus de Intellectus Emendatione* (On the Improvement of the Understanding).

Though he conceded to Bacon the value of empirical observation, he felt that the surer way of attaining "truth" and to arrive at safe conclusions was by the establishment of "clear ideas," i.e., some fundamental hypothesis which, if borne out by logical reasoning, would lead to further postulates. Conceiving all actual and potential existence as a vast unity, an infinite universe operating in accordance with certain eternal and immutable laws, the whole direction of inductive reasoning seemed to him inappropriate. To Spinoza there are three kinds of knowledge: 1) opinion, which may be the cause of error; 2) rational knowledge consisting of "adequate ideas" of the particular properties of things; 3) intuitive knowledge, which is philosophical rather than scientific, synthesis rather than description and analysis. Significant as sound intuition may be, the question, however, is: What are the criteria of such intuitional knowledge? Spinoza tried to establish them in his *Tractatus de Intellectus Emendatione*. But he did not succeed and left the essay a fragment.

The quiet and peace which he had sought in Rhijnsburg did not last long. In the nearby University of Leyden professors and students soon discovered that there was a scholar in their immediate neighborhood who knew Hebrew better than any of them and who also was familiar with "the new philosophy" which was then in vogue in academic circles throughout Western Europe, the *cogito ergo sum* of Descartes.

All available accounts indicate that Spinoza, though but thirty years of age, was himself by now a rather well-known philosopher. When after two years of residence in Rhijnsburg he moved to Voorburg near the Hague, a brief detour via Amsterdam must have shown him that he had quite a few loyal disciples. Men and women had even formed a club to study his views and clamored for their publication.

It was on their insistence that he left with Lodwijk Meyer, a physician and Latinist and Rieuwertz, an Amsterdam publisher, his *Geometric Version of Descartes' Philosophy,* with the appendix containing the "Metaphysical Cogitations." No sooner was the book published in Latin than a Dutch translation came on the market. The intellectual leaders of the time, foremost among them Huyghens, considered it an honor to frequent his small bare room. The "Israelite of Voorburg" or "Juif Protestant" (The Reform Jew), as some of them called Spinoza, also attracted the most critical thinkers in the government of Holland. Johann Hudde, for many years mayor of Amsterdam, and Jan de Witt, the Grand Pensionary, were in his circle of friends. "Had he gone no further," writes John Colerus, minister of the Lutheran Church, at the Hague, in *The Life of Benedict de Spinosa* (published in 1706 in London), "he might have preserved to this day the deserved Reputation of a Wise and learned philosopher."

On February 16, 1673, Lewis Fabritius, in the name of the Elector Palatine, offered Spinoza the post of professor of philosophy at Heidelberg University under very liberal conditions. It was not false modesty which caused Spinoza to reject the offer; but there was a sentence in Professor Fabritius' letter of invitation which caused him to say "no." It was the reference to the publicly established religion in the Palatinate and the hope that Spinoza would say and write nothing which might upset the official applecart. This sentence and its implication were not to his taste.

Spinoza had gone farther than Pastor Colerus would have liked him to go. While he continued to grind his lenses during the day, he spent his nights writing his masterwork, *The Ethics.* At the time he had arrived in Voorburg, only a portion of the book had been written. Two years later the fourth part, entitled "Of human bondage," neared completion. Then, suddenly, he stopped.

When, in 1664, the Dutch possessions in North America were captured by the British and a costly war broke out between Holland and England, the liberals, who had come into office in 1653, lost their power in Holland. After the first defeat of the Dutch navy, in June 1665, hysteria swept over the country. Jan de Witt, who had managed to keep the clergy out of politics, was now attacked by them as one who by opening the floodgates to "freethinking" and "atheism" had brought about the political ruin of Holland. In Voorburg the task of choosing a new pastor had divided the population into two camps. Since the liberal elements were headed by a Daniel Tydemann, Spinoza's landlord, their opponents charged them with being under the influence "of a certain Spinoza, a Jew by birth, an atheist, a scoffer at religion and a tool for evil in the republic."

Bigotry was closing in; and Holland, the one country of Europe which had been relatively free of intolerance, seemed to be destined to join the vast camp of barbarism. Knowing the Bible as few of his contemporaries and realizing that this book had become the source of most of the superstitions rampant in the country, Spinoza now took to writing his *Tractatus Theologico Politicus* (A Theologico-Political Treatise) with the significant subtitle:

"Containing certain discussions wherein is set forth that freedom of thought and speech not only may, without prejudice to piety and the public peace, be granted; but also may not, without danger to piety and the public peace, be withheld."

When the book was published in 1670, a storm broke loose. The Synod of North and South Holland condemned it and urged its suppression by pastors and magistrates. The professors of theology in the leading universities of Holland and Germany joined the chorus of the less learned in denouncing it as "blasphemous," "godless" and "impudent."

Suffering since his childhood from tuberculosis of the lungs, Spinoza had aggravated this condition by his lens-grinding. He was in bad health. His friends, who also feared for his safety in Voorburg, therefore, urged him to move into the capital. He found an attic room and board in a house which was then on a back wharf called Stille Verkade, the same house in which Colerus took lodgings some twenty years later when he became pastor of the local Lutheran Church and wrote in his spare time the biographical sketch which furnished the raw material of all later biographies of Spinoza—this one included.

Having spoken out for freedom of thought in the treatise on theology and politics, Spinoza devoted himself again to *The Ethics*. When, in 1675, the book was finished, he added this note: "I have thus completed all I wished to set forth touching the mind's power over the emotions and the mind's freedom. Whence it appears, how potent is the wise man, and how much he surpasses the ignorant man, who is driven only by his lusts. For the ignorant man is not only distracted in various ways by external causes without ever gaining the true acquiescence of his spirit, but moreover lives, as it were unwitting of himself, and of God, and of things, and as soon as he ceases to suffer, ceases also to be ...

"If the way which I have pointed out as leading to this result (true acquiescence in an eternal necessity) seems exceedingly hard, it may nevertheless be discovered. Needs must it be hard, since it is so seldom found. How would it be possible, if salvation were ready to our hand, and could without great labour be found, that it should be by almost all men neglected? But all things excellent are as difficult as they are rare."

Apart from revising the *Tractatus Theologico-Politicus* he had plans for a treatise on the rainbow which was undoubtedly inspired by his craft. He also began writing a manual on Hebrew grammar which he felt was necessary for a better understanding of the Old Testament. But when he felt that the Prince of Orange was about to bring ruin to the land of his birth, he again set out to enter the political arena by publishing his *Tractatus Politicus*, "Wherein is demonstrated, how the society in which monarchical dominion finds place, as also that in which the dominion is aristocratic, should be ordered so as not to lapse into a tyranny, but to preserve inviolate the peace and freedom of the citizens."

When he came to Chapter XI, entitled "Of Democracy," he halted. He was too ill to go on. Sensing that his death was near, he authorized Rieuwertz to publish *The Ethics* after his death, but without mentioning the author's name. He knew that it was his life's work; but he saw no reason for the praise of posterity. He burnt whatever he had written of a translation of the Pentateuch and distributed his library among his friends. On February 21, 1677, at the age of 44, he passed away.

In considering Spinoza's system of philosophy as he developed it chiefly in *The Ethics,* we must not forget that the problem of the universe seemed somewhat simpler in his time than in our own. We may, therefore, no longer share his serene confidence that "truth" was something definite which could be grasped by everybody as long as he possessed a good mind, diligence and a logical method of research. It has often been stated that Spinoza adopted the geometrical method in *The Ethics* because he believed that it alone insured absolute freedom from error. But this appears to be a misconception. In the fragment *On the Improvement of Understanding,* Spinoza himself tells us why he was prompted to turn to philosophy. It was not abstract philosophical specu-lation but a thorough utilitarian impulse which guided him in all his thinking. Unlike Descartes he did not seek "to walk with certainty" but rather to find human happiness for himself and for his fellow man. Though he tried to see all natural phenomena *sub specie eternitatis,* he was essentially a moralist who searched for the "good life" or, as some may say, "the kingdom of God on earth." He adopted the geometrical method not because he had succumbed to the notion that mathematics would guarantee a flawless truth but because he wanted to reduce all arguments to their simplest terms and prevent as much as possible any semantic confusion.

In Spinoza's view, man's freedom is man's understanding of himself. The power on which we humans depend for the realization of our best potentialities, for our harmony with the universe, cannot be a capricious power. While we may not always comprehend it, there would be no "holiness" in the world if this power were chaos. All existence, actual and potential, must be part of a vast unitary system. If a thing does not exist, there must be some reason that renders it impossible. This unity he calls Substance or God; and the first part of *The Ethics* is devoted to an analysis of God's nature. Being the sum of all existence, God is necessarily infinite. He must operate in absolute freedom. For if He were controlled and limited by any external force, He would not be the creator of all existence. Yet, He must operate also in accordance with eternal laws, fulfilling the perfection of His own nature. God is, therefore, both "natura naturans" and "natura naturata."

Substance expresses itself in a number of attributes, among them "thought" and "extension" which are but different aspects—different to human observation—of the same substance. Hence all questions of the dependence of mind on body or body on mind are removed with one stroke. Every manifestation of either is at the same time a manifestation of the other, seen under a different aspect. Attributes are, in turn, sub-divided into modes. They may be compared to waves in relation to the ocean. The phenomenal world consists of an infinite number of such modes. Among them may be named the human mind and the human body. Together these two modes form "man."

"The nature and origin of the human mind" is the subject of the second part of *The Ethics*. Man is conscious. His mind takes cognizance not only of the human body but also of the entire external world in so far as it affects the human body. But the succession of ideas of bodily states cannot be arbitrarily controlled by the mind. While we may believe that we can direct our thoughts "at will," they are actually determined by laws as fixed as those which regulate the properties of the triangle or the circle. The illusion of freedom in the sense of an uncaused volition results from the fact that we are usually conscious of our actions but often unconscious of the causes which determine these actions.

The third part of *The Ethics* is devoted to "the origin and nature of the emotions." In so far as the mind has rational ideas, it can be said to be active. In so far as it has inadequate or irrational ideas, it can be said to be passive, i.e., subject to emotions. Everything desires to persist in its own being. Everything which adds to the bodily or mental powers of activity is pleasure; while everything which detracts from them is labeled as pain. From these three fundamentals—desire or appetite, pleasure and pain—Spinoza deduces the entire list of human emotions. "Love is pleasure, accompanied by the idea of an external cause . . . hate is nothing else but pain accompanied by the idea of an external cause . . . Hatred, the exact opposite of love, arises from error which is the outcome of superficial opinion. For when someone has come to the conclusion that a certain thing is good, and another happens to do something to the detriment of the same thing, then there arises in him a hatred against the one who did it, and this, . . . could never happen if the true good were known. For, in comparison with the true good, all indeed that is, or is conceived, is naught but wretchedness itself; and is not such a lover of what is wretched much more deserving of pity than of hatred? . . . Hatred, lastly comes also from mere hearsay, as we see it in the Turks against Jews and Christians, in the Christians against the Jews and Turks, &c. For, how ignorant is the one multitude of the religion and morals of the others!"

At this point we must remember the

585

definition which Spinoza gives to terms like "good" or "bad." By "good," he means "that which we certainly know to be useful to us . . . In so far as a thing is in harmony with our nature, it is necessarily good . . . If different, it can be neither good nor bad; if contrary, it will be contrary to that which is in harmony with our nature, that is contrary to what is good—in short, bad. Nothing, therefore, can be good, except in so far as it is in harmony with our nature; and hence a thing is useful, in proportion as it is in harmony with our nature, and vice versa."

Consequently, "service of God" means to Spinoza the harmonization of man's interests notwithstanding their diversity. There can be no conflicting "goods" since there is no multiplicity of Gods on whom human self-preservation relies. Since man is, however, a finite part of nature and bound to encounter situations of which he is not the sole cause, he is apt to be subject to emotions. Every man necessarily seeks his own interest. But his own interest does not lie in selfishness. For man is, as Aristotle said, a political animal, always in need of external help; and nothing is as useful to man as his fellow man. Hence, man's well-being is best promoted by cooperative social effort. A reasonable man, Spinoza concludes, will therefore desire nothing for himself which he does not desire for other men. He will love his neighbor as himself and be just and faithful to him.

This code of morals, developed in the fourth part of *The Ethics,* entitled "Of human bondage" is essentially in the Stoic and Judeo-Christian tradition. The idea, however, expressed in the famous proposition XIV that "a true knowledge of good and evil cannot check any emotion by virtue of being true, but only in so far as it is considered as an emotion," is uniquely Spinozistic. What Spinoza says in this sentence which was to become the keystone of all modern psychology is that emotion can be conquered only by an understanding and, therefore, control of one's emotions and not by pure intellectualizing.

The means through which man can learn to master his emotions are set forth in the fifth part, "Of the power of the understanding, or of human freedom." "An emotion," he writes, "which is a passion, ceases to be a passion, as soon as we form a clear and distinct idea thereof." For "the mind has greater power over the emotions and is less subject thereto, in so far as it understands all things as necessary," i.e., as determined in existence and operation by a chain of causes. "No one pities an infant, because it cannot speak, walk, or reason, or lastly, because it passes so many years, as it were in unconsciousness. Whereas, if most people were born full-grown and only one here and there as an infant, everyone would pity the infants; because infancy would not then be looked on as a state natural and necessary, but as a fault or delinquency in Nature; and we may note several other instances of the same sort." As long as we do not possess a perfect knowledge of our emotions, the best we can do "is to frame a system of right conduct, or fixed practical precepts, to commit it to memory, and to apply it forthwith to the particular circumstances which now and again meet us in life, so that our imagination may become fully imbued therewith, and that it may be always ready to our hand."

If we try to understand the universe as a necessary result of God's nature, a sense of joy will undoubtedly arise in us. This Spinoza calls the "intellectual love of God." It is the highest, most serene happiness that man can possibly experience. It seeks no special favors from the Deity (which would imply a change in God's nature and therefore chaos.) It knows no envy and jealousy and actually increases in proportion as our fellow men participate in it. In other words, virtue is its own reward. It needs no other. Few things have moved Spinoza to more scornful remarks than the popular creed that supernatural rewards and penalties are necessary as incentives to a virtuous life.

"Most people seem to believe . . . that piety, religion, and, generally, all things attributable to firmness of mind, are burdens, which, after death, they hope to lay aside, and to receive the reward for their bondage, that is, for their piety and religion; it is not only by this hope, but also, and chiefly, by the fear of being horribly punished after death, that they are induced to live according to the divine commandments . . . If man had not this hope and this fear, but believed that the mind perishes with the body, and that no hope of prolonged life remains for the wretches who are broken down with the burden of piety, they would return to their own inclinations, controlling everything in accordance with their lusts. . ."

The concluding words of *The Ethics* have caused more controversy than any other part of Spinoza's system of thought. Some interpreters have seen in them a doctrine of personal immortality and have called Spinoza a mystic. Others have called him a stubborn materialist who denies all moral values. "The human mind," Spinoza writes, "cannot be wholly destroyed with the body, but somewhat of it remains which is eternal." The mind, let it be repeated, consists of adequate and inadequate ideas. In so far as its ideas are adequate, the mind partakes of the infinite mind of God and is, therefore, necessarily eternal. Inadequate ideas will pass away with the body. For they are the result of conditions which are merely temporary and inseparably connected with the finite human body.

God then is eternity, law and order. To the extent to which we seek Him, to that extent we shall be blessed. At the end of his short career in life Spinoza landed where he had started as a student in the Heder praising God for His name's sake. When at the three hundredth anniversary of his birth, in 1932, a representative assembly at the Hebrew University in Jerusalem acknowledged Spinoza as one of the most outstanding Jewish philosophers it must have been conscious of the fact that Spinoza, while trying to substitute reason for revelation and for blind obedience to human authority, had never surrendered that moral severity

587

which characterizes all great Jewish thinkers from the prophets to our own day.

Against the contention of the Sophists that morality is just a social convention and that "might makes right," Plato and Aristotle had already established certain universal principles of justice which man, by virtue of his reason, can discover if he so desires. The Stoics who substituted for the ancient polis the cosmopolis or citizenship of the world, added, that the individual achieves serenity by comprehending the inevitability of natural causation. But it was not before Judaism taught the world the great message of its prophets that man learned to recognize history not as a meaningless and repetitious cycle but rather as the march of humanity toward the Messianic Age, the kingdom of God on earth. While this concept was obscured by Augustine's emphasis on the "original sin" of all mankind, Spinoza, in the footsteps of Maimonides and as a prelude to Sigmund Freud, promises man salvation not by unquestioning faith in any religious doctrine, not by adherence to any church, however powerful, but by a rational search for God, by a steadily progressing understanding of his natural environment and of himself.

Bibliography

John Colerus, *The Life of Benedict de Spinosa* (Out of French.) (London, 1706).

F. Pollock, *Spinoza: His Life and Philosophy* (1880).

C. Gebhardt, *Spinoza Opera,* (In German) 4 vols. (Heidelberg, 1926).

H. A. Wolfson, *The Philosophy of Spinoza* (1934).

R. H. M. Elwes, *The Chief Works of Benedict de Spinoza* (New York, 1951).

D. D. Runes, *Spinoza Dictionary,* (New York, 1951).

Joseph Dunner, *Baruch Spinoza and Western Democracy* (New York, 1955).

Joseph Dunner
Grinnell College

state and individual: *see* China, Moral
  Philosophies of.
stealing: *see* Aboriginals of Yirkalla;
  Ayer, Alfred J.; Marxist Theory of
  Morals; Meta-ethics and Normative
  Ethics; Primitive Morals.
Stephen, L.: *see* Primitive Morals.
Stevenson, C. L.: *see* Ayer, Alfred J.;
  Cumberland, Richard; Language
  and Ethics; Major Ethical View-
  points; Moral Philosophy in Amer-
  ica.
stinginess: *see* Navaho Morals; parsi-
  mony.
Stirling, John: *see* Utilitarianism.
Stoicism: *see* Augustine and Morals;
  Freud, Sigmund; Goethe, Johann
  Wolfgang von; Major Ethical View-
  points; Minor Socratics; Nietzsche,
  Friedrich; Spinoza; Stoics, the.

Stoics, the

"Once pronounce anything to be
desirable, once reckon anything as
good, other than moral worth, and you
have extinguished the very light of
virtue, moral worth itself, and overthrown virtue entirely."[1] Thus Cicero
has Cato pronounce the fundamental
idea of Stoicism, an idea that found expression in the thought or practice of
a large but diverse number of Greek
and Roman philosophers, orators,
writers, statesmen and public servants,
beginning with Zeno of Citium at the
end of the fourth century B.C. and extending through Marcus Aurelius at
the end of the second century A.D. Not
that its influence ceased with Marcus
Aurelius; the Stoic writings of Seneca,

Cicero, Epictetus and Marcus Aurelius
have been and still are widely read.
With the rise of Christianity, however,
Stoicism declined from its position as
a dominant philosophy—we might
even say religion, for the motivating
passion of Stoicism was more religious
than philosophic in spite of the absence of any belief that the basic doctrines were of supernatural origin.

The following brief account of Stoic
ethical philosophy will not attempt to
trace the intricacies of the details;
rather it will seek to elucidate the main
theoretical principles generally accepted by the leading Stoics, both
Greek and Roman. Hence, only the
briefest reference will be made to the
detailed moral precepts and practical
rules for the good life, even though
Stoicism itself asserted the supremacy
of practice over theory.

Zeno of Citium, a Greek colony in
Cyprus, was the founder of Stoicism.
This took place about 294 B.C. when
Zeno began lecturing in Athens at the
Stoa Poikilé, the Painted Porch,
whence the name "Stoic." To quote
Cicero again, this time a harsh and not
entirely true statement: ". . . Zeno
their founder was rather an inventor of
new terms than a discoverer of new
ideas."[2] As the first quotation from
Cicero clearly shows, the Stoics identified virtue, or moral worth, with the
highest good. The Cynics in their condemnation of pleasure and the passions, had already raised the virtues of
the simple or natural life to this supreme position. But the Cynics made

[1] Cicero, *De Finibus*, Book III 10. Loeb edition, translated by H. Rackham, Heinemann
(London, 1931).

[2] Cicero, *op. cit.*, 111, 5.

the doctrine almost absurd by their extremes, both in theory and practice—for example Diogenes, living in his tub and searching for his good or virtuous man could not be taken very seriously. Also Aristotle had examined quite explicitly the doctrine that virtue is the good, only to reject it on the ground that virtue, as a disposition, is a potentiality, not an actuality, whereas the highest good must of necessity be an actuality,[3] a requirement Cicero recognized. But the Stoics did not think of virtue as a disposition. As Cicero said: "The whole glory of virtue is in activity."[4] Previously Plato had set up virtue as the necessary condition of happiness; man is happy only when he functions well and he functions well only by virtue of justice, temperance, courage and wisdom. Pleasure is an added concomitant of happiness or functioning well, not an ingredient. 'Functioning well' is what the Stoics thought of as the good, i.e. 'functioning virtuously.' Finally there is Socrates, who maintained that all virtues reduce to wisdom and that nobody does well knowingly, the two principles combining to make virtue of supreme importance.

Thus Zeno's identification of the highest good with virtue was not new with him. The lack of novelty in Zeno's basic principle was obscured in part at least by the fervor with which the idea was adopted by both the Greek and Roman Stoics. This fervor reflects a deep disdain for pleasure and an enormous—although perhaps narrow—respect for the dignity of man as a creature whose worth is entirely internal, not in any way dependent upon external circumstances and the vicissitudes of life. Indeed Stoicism is one solution, an extreme one it is true, of the old Greek problem of the conflict between moral worth and external rewards. The Stoics, following the Cynics made virtue its own reward. It was, therefore, a philosophy admirably suited to inspire if not to produce efficient, conscientious public servants, which it in fact did in Rome when Rome was at its best.

The highest good, then, is virtue or moral worth. What is moral worth? The Stoics did not neglect the theoretical task of defining fundamental terms. To the query 'Why define virtue?' the Stoic doctrine of the subordination of theory to practice gives the answer: What is sought is the good life, and knowledge, both theoretical and practical, is necessary to its attainment. Thus the definition of virtue is of the utmost importance and in the details of the definition we find the distinctive Stoic doctrines.

The first part of the Stoic definition of moral worth gives a formula that goes back again to the Cynics. The chief good, virtue, is "to live in accordance with nature."[5] ('Nature' here is *physis*. Aristotles' conception of *physis* in terms of an internal principle of movement and rest, growth and decay, merely expresses in philosophic

---

[3] *Nicomachean Ethics,* I, iv.

[4] *De Officiis* I, 19. Loeb edition, translated by W. Miller, Heinemann, London, 1938.

[5] Cicero, *De Finibus,* IV, 14.

language a common idea accepted by both Cynics and Stoics). The idea peculiar to the Stoics emerges clearly in their interpretation of this formula. The Stoics were supposed to have said that the formula meant: "to live *in the light* of a knowledge of the natural sequence of causation."[6] It is in this interpretation of the general principle that we have the essentially Stoic definition of moral worth, of the rightness of all right actions in the primary sense, of absolute duties (*Katorthōma*), as opposed to another kind, of lower degree, which will be referred to as 'appropriate actions' and discussed later on.

In order to explain the significance of this definition a brief discussion of Stoic metaphysics and epistemology is necessary. In spite of the fact that the Academic and Peripetetic schools had undermined any simple materialism, Zeno was avowedly a materialist. He was more concerned with practice than theory, and consequently ignored the finer points of philosophic criticism. Later Stoics did attempt to soften the crudities of the theory with the result that it is scarcely correct to say that Stoic philosophy is materialistic. Zeno

6 Cicero, *De Finibus*, IV, 14. Italics mine. With the exception of the *Hymn to Zeus* of Cleanthes nothing substantial survives from the founders of the school; what we know of their doctrines is through secondary sources and later, not always trustworthy, Stoic writers. Chrysippus seems to have held that the highest good is consciousness of existence, and this refers to both the common nature and the particular nature of the individual; cf. Diogenes Laertius in *Source Book in Ancient Philosophy*, C. Bakewell (New York, 1907), pp. 272–277.

held that everything is matter, even God, mind, reason, the soul, and virtue. Furthermore the Stoics were or tried to be monists. For them fire is the substance or reality of everything. But fire has two principles, active and passive. The first is God or spirit (*Pneuma*), the second is matter in an undefined sense. God is active matter and permeates the whole universe as its active principle or force. The metaphor of 'seeds' is used to express this. The seeds are the 'reasons' for all things that grow, move, and decay. They derive from God or active matter, which is identified with reason or mind, and fate or providence. Hence every event in the universe is determined by rational causation—with the exception of men's evil actions, which are the result of ignorance, a disease. Finally, the whole universe is not only intelligent, it is beautiful, good, and harmonious, with the emphasis on the harmony.

One would suppose that this conclusion is inconsistent with the initial materialism of Stoicism, and in fact Cleanthes'[7] doctrine of 'tensions' is an attempt to achieve the missing consistency without giving up either matter as the real or harmony as an essential feature of the real. According to Cleanthes, the whole universe is matter interrelated by tensions; in God or spirit there is the utmost tension or heat; 'lower' things are distinguished by their lesser and different tensions. All combine to give a harmonious whole. Harmony is thus the key value term; the harmony is an active har-

7 For a brief account of the principal Stoics see end of this article.

mony of tensions. The general formula of right action is implied by this metaphysics. It is more than implied; it is transformed from the almost vacuous formula of Cynicism into a formula having definite ethical implications.

The Stoic definition of virtue follows from this metaphysics, but this is not altogether obvious until several psychological and epistemological points have been established. The first point is that although the human soul is material it is an off-spring of world-soul, or spirit, or active tension, which is God. Man is of all things in the world the most like God; only man recognizes the harmony of nature; only man has a feeling for order; only man seeks truth; only man is moved by his own reason; all other animals are moved simply by immediate causes, i.e. by stimulation of the senses. All things in nature naturally strive for their own preservation, seeking what is needed and avoiding what is harmful. In man this striving takes a form most resembling the action of God or spirit, being in fact the action of spirit in man. This is the psychological ground for man's moral worth.

The second point is epistemological and has to do with the nature of knowledge. Just as spirit is the active tension of the universe, so the soul of man is the active tension of man, and all his activities are ways in which his soul manifests itself. But soul is reason, and this is evident even in sense perception. Sensation is of course physical action; some physical quality of the object is transmitted to the sense organ, giving to the mind a representation of the object. True perceptions involve the *logos* or reason, according to Zeno's view. Chrysippus elaborated this to give the Stoic criterion of truth: a true representation is a 'comprehensive' representation commanding assent. Apparently this means that the object and the perceiver prehend each other, giving the tension of assent. This, according to Chrysippus, is obvious in true perceptions by reason of their clearness and distinctness. Such are comprehensive representations, and they resemble the real object. 'Assent' (*synkatáthesis*) is the key term, and the act of assent arises out of the processes of reason or world-soul in the particular perceiver.

We are now in a position to appreciate the moral significance of the Stoic interpretation of the general formula of right action "to live *in the light* of a knowledge of the natural sequence of causation." First of all, the Stoic metaphysics shows that nature or God or the universe or providence are different ways of referring to the same thing, which is a harmonious causal whole. Stoic philosophy is monistic and almost deterministic. Secondly, for man knowledge is what distinguishes him from everything else in the universe and is the basis for his happiness and moral worth. It is knowledge that produces, or rather is, the assent and this assent is not mere resignation to but active cooperation with the tensions of reality. Thus the wise man will regulate his will, his desires, and his actions to conform to the harmony of the real; he will see through the appearance of things, withholding assent from what is only apparently favorable, giving it to the apparently unfavorable when such is really in accord with nature and the work of God, reason and providence. The wise man is therefore independent of the vicissitudes of life, independent of appearances. He is in tune with reality. His will is, as both Cleanthes and Epictetus maintain,[8] conformable to nature. This is his moral worth, and it is entirely internal in the sense that the wise man is distinct from the ignorant by reason of his mental act, the act of assent which he has and the ignorant does not. In many cases the actual deeds done by the wise and the ignorant are the same. The question then is one of will or motive, as in Kant's theory. When Queen Hecuba laments "Assured happiness? There is no such thing!" the Stoic could reply: "There is, in every situation—for the wise man."

But where is there a wise man? The Stoics had difficulty with this query, and for two reasons. First, most Stoics interpreted the above doctrine to mean that there were no degrees of moral goodness; it was all or nothing. Being six inches under water was no better than being six hundred fathoms—one drowns in either case. With assent it is all or nothing. Nor is there any moral progress. One cannot be more or less virtuous, although one can approach nearer and nearer to virtue. And second, the wisdom required was extremely exacting, involving knowledge not just of the immediate situa-

tion but of the whole of reality, past, present and future. Few, if any, among men possess this wisdom. Socrates had the best claim—not that he himself would have dreamt of asserting it! The practical emphasis of Roman, if not of Greek, Stoicism is shown by the fact that Cato was also thought of as a likely candidate. Everyone else was ignorant, hence altogether lacking in moral worth.

Is each person responsible for his lack of virtue? Yes, say the Stoics. Here they seem to depart from their absolute determinism. Evil, i.e., ignorance, is voluntary and is a depravity or decline of the soul. Evil, unlike good, is not a positive factor in the universe. The Stoics do not accept both of the beliefs of Socrates, that virtue is knowledge and that no one does evil knowingly; they accept the first and reject the second. But both positions are paradoxical.

Before proceeding two remarks concerning the ethical theory discussed above are in order. For any ethical theory the basic problem is usually thought to be either "What makes good things good?" or "What makes right actions right?" How is 'good' to be defined? How is 'right' to be defined? The Stoic philosophy seems to identify 'good' with 'harmony or beauty of the whole.' To live virtuously is to live in accord with this harmony of the whole. But there is an obvious circularity in the theory. The terms 'rational,' 'natural,' 'right,' and 'harmonious' or 'consistent' are so used by the Stoics that when any one of them is in question it is defined by one

---

[8] Cleanthes, *Hymn to Zeus*, in Bakewell, *op. cit.* pp. 277–278; Epictetus, *Encheiridion*, translated by G. Long, (London, 1877), I. iv.

or more of the others. Thus: to be virtuous is to be natural. But to be natural is to be rational, hence to be virtuous is to be rational. But what is being rational? To be in accord with nature or the real. Again: to be virtuous is to be rational; to be rational is to be in harmony with the real. What is the harmony of the real? It is the rationality of the universe. Or, in other words, nature is the standard for reason and reason is the standard for nature, and either is the standard for harmony and virtue, which in turn are the standards for reason and nature.

The second remark concerns the concept of nature as the universe and the concept of nature as the individual human being. A right action is an action in accord with nature. 1) An action in accord with nature could mean an action in accord with the whole system of natural events, and hence with the laws of the universe. 2) An action in accord with nature could mean an action in accord with the whole system of events that make up the life history of the individual and hence with the moral laws of the individual man. Under this view the individual could be either the individual in isolation or the individual as a political being. 3) An action in accord with nature could mean an action in accord (a) with the universe as the only real substance or (b) with the individual as a real self. The Stoic position is with varying emphasis a combination of all of these. There is thus asserted by the Stoics an exact parallel between the macrocosm and microcosm. Some Stoics bring in a further ambiguity by sometimes taking

'accord with the nature of the individual or with the whole' to mean 'accord with the best part, i.e. reason.' This ambiguity is found also in Aristotle's ethical theory.

In practice it would make no difference whether one followed the individual or the whole owing to the parallel between the microcosm and the macrocosm. But if there seems to be a difference then the formula should be applied primarily to the individual. From this it follows that although there are universal laws of nature and hence universal moral laws, the application of these laws must take into consideration individual differences. There will be, therefore, exceptions or at least what appear to be exceptions, to the universal law. "But occasions often arise, when those duties which seem most becoming to the just man and to the "good man," as we call him, undergo a change and take on a contrary aspect. It may, for example, not be a duty to restore a trust or to fulfill a promise,—."[9] This leads to the discussion of imperfect duties and 'appropriate actions.'

The Stoic doctrine so far is a harsh doctrine allowing no compromises, no middle positions; moral worth is all or nothing. But the Stoics did soften their view considerably, for which they are charged with inconsistency. Inconsistent or not the Stoics did attempt to make room for the judgments of worth made by the ordinary man. They distinguished two kinds of worth, the primary or moral, already discussed, and a secondary kind, appli-

9 Cicero, *De Officiis* I, 30.

cable either to things or to actions, both of which are morally neutral. Let us take actions first.

Clearly there is some difference between truth-telling and lying. What is it? The former is in most cases an appropriate action (*kathēkon*). An appropriate action is either an action in accordance with nature or an action which produces an action in accordance with nature. Each has worth (*axia*). The first in itself, the second through the first. Appropriate actions may be connected with right actions (*kathorthōma*), but how? The latter are actions in accordance with *knowledge* of nature, i.e. rational intention is essential. The appropriate actions are merely actions in accord with nature. There are five stages between appropriate actions and right actions.[10] The basic appropriate action is to preserve one's natural constitution; and this is instinctive in all beings. The second stage is to retain what is in accord with this and to repel what is contrary. In the third stage the principle of appropriate actions becomes the condition of choice—i.e. one chooses *because* the action is seen to be in accord with nature, whereas previously the choice was instinctive. In the fourth stage the choice becomes a habit. Finally, it is when the *choice itself* is seen to be in harmony with nature that the highest good emerges. The highest good is the understanding of the harmony of the whole, including the choice. This is what is desired; all else is merely *chosen*. The harmony

now is fully rational and is the essence of right action (Kathorthōma) as previously defined.

To illustrate this Cicero gives a crude metaphor: the archer aims at the target, but the target is not his real objective; his real objective is to aim straight. The explanation might be as follows: In order to achieve moral worth some action or other must be done, and the archer must have some target or other in order to aim. The morally significant aspect of the action is not the action itself but the understanding of the conformity or harmony of the choice of the action with nature. Hence it does not matter morally whether the action is successful. The chief good is *to endeavour* to obtain what is in accord with nature, and "that this endeavour even though unsuccessful is itself the sole thing desirable and the sole good is actually maintained by the Stoics."[11] It is the endeavour that has moral worth, not the action. Nevertheless, the action does have some worth, even though secondary: it is 'appropriate.' The particular harmonious action is *chosen,* the harmony is *desired.* Parenthetically we might note that this 'endeavour' is, according to Stoic metaphysics, a tension, presumably the highest, and is therefore rational. As rational it is the understanding of the harmony of the whole, i.e. it is a comprehensive representation demanding assent.

Next let us examine the secondary worth of things. According to the Stoic doctrine of moral worth, health, free-

---

10 Cf. Cicero, *De Finibus*, III, 20–21.

11. Cicero, *De Finibus*, V. 20.

dom, wealth, and the like have no moral worth. But does that not put them on a level with disease, slavery, poverty, and the like? Or with clearly indifferent matters, such as whether the number of hairs on one's head are odd or even? No, it does not. The first belong to the class of preferred things (*proēgmena*), the second, to the class of rejected things (*apoproēgmena*), and the third to the class of indifferent things. The first has positive worth, the second negative, and the third has no worth. All are morally neutral. Preferred things are such that they give grounds for choice, i.e. reasons can be given for the choice. Rejected things are such that reasons can be given for the rejection. What are the grounds or reasons for choice or rejection? The grounds for choice are simply this: preferred things are natural, i.e., are in accord with nature. Health, for example, is natural, it accords with nature, but it still does not have moral worth. Anyone, not only a morally good person, will choose health. A morally good person will be able to give the reason for this, an ignorant person will not. The metaphor of the archer applies here: just as the archer aims at the target so one chooses health. But moral worth and happiness depend in no way upon health. The morally good choose health but may not achieve it.

There are, therefore, many preferred things, such as health, freedom, wealth, and the like, and their opposites, just as there are many appropriate actions such as paying debts, telling the truth, and so on, and their opposites. Nevertheless, only the wise man can have moral worth because only he has the knowledge of how the particular does in fact fit into the total harmony of nature. It is the harmony that the wise man seeks, not the particular things. The ignorant choose preferred things out of instinct or at best out of immediate rational grounds, as was seen in the stages of appropriate actions leading up to moral worth. The choosing of preferred things and the doing of appropriate actions are at best steps in the direction of virtue; they are not degrees of virtue. The final step is a total transformation of the individual from ignorance to wisdom, vice to virtue. Only when so transformed is man really happy. Such happiness is independent of the variations of external factors, which are only superficial. Even time is external; the temporal duration of happiness is irrelevant to its nature and worth.

We come now to the actual moral precepts of the Stoics. A brief resumé of the more basic of these must suffice. A more complete discussion of these will be found in the Stoic writings of Epictetus,[12] Cicero,[13] Seneca[14] and others. The general rule is to seek only what is in one's power. One's opinions, desires, aversions, are within one's power. Reputation, property, offices, bodily conditions are not. To attempt to avoid mortality, for example, can result only in unhappiness. The primary thing in one's power is the will or intention, and this means maintain-

---

[12] *The Encheiridion or Manual*, and *Discourses*.

[13] *De Officiis, De Finibus*, etc.

[14] Moral essays and letters.

ing one's will in a way conformable to nature. This really comes to: "Seek not that the things which happen should happen as you wish; but wish the things which happen to be as they are, and you will have a tranquil flow of life."[15] In the popular mind this is the essence of Stoicism, and rightly so, inso-far as we are concerned with practical moral precepts. The Stoic can be accused quite justly of apathy, of taking life the way it comes.

Related to the doctrine of apathy—perhaps 'active apathy' is better—is the Stoic doctrine of pleasure. In practice there is a sense in which both Stoicism and Epicureanism have the same goal, tranquility. Epicurus asserted that pleasure was the sole good, but the means required to obtain this good involve pain, hence the best state is the absence of both pleasure and pain—unless tranquility itself is taken to be a special pure pleasure. The Stoics deny that pleasure has any worth at all; it is purely a concomitant (*epigennēma*). This applies to intellectual as well as to bodily pleasures as is clear from Chrysippus' criticism of Aristotle's doctrine of the relation of pleasure and contemplation. The pleasures of contemplation are mere amusement, according to Chrysippus. There is no evidence that he really understood Aristotle's doctrine that pleasure is a property of contemplation, hence is neither accidental nor essential to it.

The precept to wish for things as they really are has many concrete applications. For example in the case of

sympathy for the misfortunes of another person: show sympathy, even lament with the other person, but do not lament internally.[16] The misfortunes are not real, and do not touch one's own reality. Again, "disease is an impediment to the body, not to the will unless the will itself chooses. Add this reflection on the occasion of everything that happens; for you will find it an impediment to something else, but not to yourself."[17]

Connected with this general precept is the rule of piety. "As to piety towards the Gods you must know that this is the chief thing, to have right opinions about them, to think that they exist, and that they administer the ALL well and justly; and you must fix yourself in this principle (duty), to obey them, and yield to them in everything which happens, and voluntarily to follow it as being accomplished by the wisest intelligence."[1] All one's duties to other persons, family, friends, fellow citizens, fellow humans, are subordinate to the above. In some cases it might be right to abandon one's family: ". . . if the captain shall call, run to the ship, and leave all those things without regard to them."[19]

On the other hand the Stoic doctrine enlarged the area of moral responsibility from the narrow confines of the Greek city-state, or even the Roman Empire, to include all men. Everyone is a citizen of one and the same state,

---

15 Epictetus, *Encheiridion* I. viii.

16 Epictetus, *op. cit.* I, xvi.
17 *Ibid.* I, ix.
18 *Ibid.* I, xxxi.
19 *Ibid.* I, vii.

Humanity. In the area of practical thought this is perhaps the chief contribution of Stoic moral philosophy. Cosmopolitanism became popular in part because of the work of the Stoics. In Rome the Stoic doctrine of natural law, i.e. certain moral laws binding on all men because of a common nature as rational beings, gave the Roman lawyers a basis for dealing with the large numbers of strangers who had business there. There were specific laws for Romans,[20] other laws for all men, including Romans. This concept of humanity was carried on by Christianity, although with a difference. The modern concept is more Christian than Stoic because of the emphasis on an emotional rather than a metaphysical or legal bond between all men, on love instead of reason. Thus the Stoics laid the ground-work for a universal morality. But they did not develop the details. Certain obvious universal duties were accepted, such as promise-keeping, abstinence from cruelty and harm to others, defense of society, and most of the duties more or less universally accepted. There was for the most part no rigid asceticism—any action that was obviously natural was at least appropriate[21] if not obligatory. Sexual relations were no exception to this; Zeno even followed Plato in extending the family to include the whole state, with the implied community of wives. The Stoics however never seriously attempted to reorganize the whole of society in accordance with a single universal code of morals; they were content to accept the local code of their respective communities, or, if they did reject these codes it was only to retreat to the life of private retirement.[22] The Stoics were not reformers.

A few words concerning the leading Stoic writers are in order. As has been stated Zeno of Citium (335–265 B.C.) is considered the founder of Stoicism. He began as a Cynic and was much influenced by Socrates. He worked out the principal doctrines of Stoicism, its materialism and its emphasis on reason or logos, not only of the individual but of the universe. From this the ethical doctrines are derived, as has been stated above. Zeno was followed by Cleanthes (300–220 B.C.), often, although perhaps incorrectly, represented as lacking in any originality of mind. Where Zeno had inclined to a dualism of active and passive matter, Cleanthes had adopted quite explicitly a pantheistic philosophy. His *Hymn to Zeus* is the only surviving writing of the Old Stoa, and shows a strong religious turn of mind. He is supposed to have originated the idea of the varying tensions throughout the universe. Then there is Chrysippus (280–208 B.C.) who is credited with putting Stoicism on a firm systematic basis. Outside of this systematizing his main contribution was to logic; in fact he is really the founder of the Stoic proposi-

20 Roman law being law binding on Roman citizens no matter where they might be, in contrast with Anglo-Saxon law, which is law binding on all, citizens or otherwise, within a defined geographical area.

21 i.e. 'right' in the usual sense.

22 cf. Cicero's *De Officiis*, I. 69, 70, 92.

tional logic.[23] These three were the leaders in Greece of the Old Stoa, which is given the dates 294–208 B.C. The Old Stoa established all the principal doctrines of Stoicism.

Later Stoics modified, altered, but did not advance Stoic doctrines. Panaetius of Rhodes (180–112 B.C.) is considered to be the philosopher who introduced Stoicism to Romans. He softened down the Stoic doctrine somewhat, perhaps owing to his admiration for Plato and to criticisms of Stoic philosophy stemming from the Academy. Posidonius (130–51 B.C.) was a pupil of Panaetius, and in turn a teacher of Cicero. Cicero (106–43 B.C.) set to himself the task of bringing Greek philosophy to Rome, and in this he was extremely successful. In ethics he himself inclined toward Stoicism. Some of his writings on the subject have been mentioned above. Seneca (3 B.C.–65 A.D.), like Cicero, wrote extensively on ethical problems. He was more concerned with practical than theoretical problems and wrote in a popular style. His ethical position was explicitly Stoic. Epictetus (60–117) a freed slave was the author of the works cited earlier. He was a Greek, born in Hierapolis in Phrygia, and studied under Musonius Rufus (1st century A.D.), the most famous Stoic teacher. Epictetus followed Rufus' stern ethical philosophy and in fact may have merely echoed the teaching of his master. The extant works of Epictetus are in Greek and were committed to writing by Arrian. Finally there is the Emperor Marcus Aurelius (121–180 A.D.). His *Meditations* are primarily concerned with how to obtain peace of mind in a world of cares. Stoic philosophy provided the answer, but the more theoretical aspects of Stoicism did not interest the Emperor and his philosophy is extremely religious in tone.

Bibliography

E. V. Arnold, *Roman Stoicism* (Cambridge, 1911).

E. Bevan, *Stoics and Sceptics* (Oxford, 1913).

R. D. Hicks, *Stoic and Epicurean* (New York, 1910).

G. Murray, *The Stoic Philosophy* (London, 1915).

St. G. Stock, *Stoicism* (London, 1908).

E. Zeller, *The Stoics, Epicureans and Sceptics* (London, 1870).

Nathaniel W. Roe
Wellesley College

strangers: *see* Hindu Ethics.

strife: *see* Augustine and Morals; Hindu Ethics.

striving: *see* Goethe, Johann Wolfgang von.

stronger, the: *see* Sophists, the.

struggle: *see* Hindu Ethics.

Struve, Peter: *see* Berdyaev, Nicolas; Soviet Morality, Current.

Stuart, John: *see* Utilitarianism.

Stuchka: *see* Soviet Morality, Current.

stupidity: *see* Navaho Morals.

---

[23] Stoic logic, especially with Chrysippus, was distinct from Aristotelian logic in that it was a logic of propositions, the Aristotelian a logic of classes. Much valuable work was done by Stoic logicians. cf. B. Mates, *Stoic Logic,* (Los Angeles, 1953).

T

Tapirapé Morals, Some Aspects of

The Tapirapé

The Tapirapé are a small Central Brazilian Indian tribe who live near to the river of the same name, a left tributary of the Araguaya. Professor Charles Wagley of Columbia University and I visited them on several occasions and described their culture in various articles published in English, Portuguese and German. When I met them for the first time in the big forest they inhabited, men and women were naked and had their bodies painted. One day a man asked me: "You white people have to die also?" Never before had I felt so strongly that I had entered another world quite different from ours. This was in 1935.

Today the Tapirapé have left that big forest and are living nearer to the white men. They have begun to use white people's clothes and they have learned that white people have to die also.

The following notes refer to the time of my first stay in their isolated jungle village *Tampiitáwa*.

Relations between Generations

On the day the child is born, the parents must not eat anything. Then, for a long time, they have to abstain from bananas and peanuts, two kinds of food which play an important role in the Tapirapé alimentation. They believe that the child would die if they disregarded this rule. I was told that parents of an ill child can eat only manioc flour and a soup of maize and manioc even when the child is older than six years. The Tapirapé affirmed this in order to show me that they are better parents than the neighbouring Karajá Indians who, they asserted, eat everything in such a case. I do not know if this is true or only a defamation of their neighbours. What I know is that the parents in both these tribes

601

show much love to their children. This love manifests itself through the comprehension with which the adults treat the child. When asked a question by his son, an Indian father would never say: "That is a thing of adult people you can't understand." He would never destroy, by speaking with an air of superiority, the confidence with which the boy comes to him as a friend who knows better. But already before the child's reaching the age of asking questions, the Tapirapé proves his spirit of patience. I shall never forget Uanomanchi's attitude when a little baby sitting on his lap urinated on his naked legs. No agitation! The grave man did not even stand up. He took from the ground a piece of straw and cleaned the fluid away. He did not clean his legs by rubbing or washing. Nor did he say a word nor did he make any movement which could trouble the child.—Nor shall I ever forget the behaviour of Maeyma, another Tapirapé man, during his little daughter's illness. Many women stood weeping around the girl's hammock. Maeyma was the only weeping man. He was covering his face with his hands and sobbing. He seemed emaciated. When on the next day the girl was recovering, Maeyma was lying with her in his hammock, holding her in his hands like a fragile thing, and when he moved his hands he did it with timidity and embarrassment.

But I also remember a touching scene of a Tapirapé mother. Under the burning rays of the mid-day sun, a young woman has to pass over the village plaza with her few months old baby. She holds it pressed against her abdomen and runs deeply bent so that the child is in the shadow produced by her nude body. Only when she arrives at the hut on the other side of the plaza, does she walk erect and carry the baby in her arms.

The Tapirapé never speak harshly to a child nor have they any punishment for children. Their indulgence is characterized by the following example: Kamairahó, the most important leader, entering his hut in order to lie down in his hammock, finds a little boy sitting in it. The great man says nothing and leaves the hut. Another aspect of the same man in his relations with children is that he doesn't hesitate to ask a child to share his food with him and really accepts the part given to him.

When a child who is not ill, weeps, Tapirapé's reaction is laughter.

It is noteworthy that the same people, willing to make any sacrifice for their children, do not show any scruple about killing the new-born who exceeds the small number of children admitted in a Tapirapé family, i.e., three, being no more than two of the same sex. This infanticidal custom would be better understandable in a society of nomadic hunters than among so sedentary agriculturists as the Tapirapé. But also among this tribe young mothers suckle puppies at their own breasts and nobody feeds an adult dog. And contrasting with the affection dedicated to their own children was the cruelty with which these Indians treated a three-year-old boy without parents. He was the plaything of the whole village, victim of everybody's good or bad humour, and always looking sad and dirty. The elder orphans, however, did not differ in behaviour and appearance from the other children of the same age. And among the Tapirapé, child and adult behaviour were not so different as among us. Among these Indians the activities of the children differ from adult work in degree, but not in kind. The Tapirapé child learns while playing the various kinds of adult work. A three-year-old boy already has a little bow and arrows of a size in proportion to the size of the owner. A three-year-old girl already possesses a small sieve of a size in proportion to her own size. Thus, the two children go to fish like an adult couple: the little man shooting the fish and the little woman gathering them in the sieve. Naturally, the size of the fish corresponds also to the size of the fishers. When they returned home, they put the little fish in the glowing fire in order to roast them. Then they eat them and so they show that the three-year-old Tapirapé already knows how to manage life. As the boy and girl grow, the bow and a sieve also become bigger until they reach the size of a man's bow and a woman's sieve when their owners enter puberty. And the same happens with everything handled by the Indians: with the clubs, baskets, mortars, spindles and other implements. But this does not mean that the boys before puberty participate so seriously in the economic life as the girls. A daughter, from her infancy, helps her mother in proportion to her strength and the

capacity of her age and forms in this way an increasingly productive factor.

Naturally the Tapirapé children do not only imitate the adults in their work. They practice the almost automatic smiling which characterizes these Indians, a certain coquettishness and that which more than anything else moves the soul of their tribe: singing and dancing. I have seen four to seven-year-old boys making for themselves dance-masks, putting them on their heads and then dancing and singing according to the spirit represented by the species of mask they were using.

The same kindness and indulgence shown by the adults in relation to the children are shown by these—towards each other and in regard to elder people.

The really old people were represented by a few persons older than forty. They were treated well.

Relations between the Sexes

From infancy the difference between the sexes is emphasized in adornment, behaviour, and division of labor. A woman would never paint her body in the manner of a man. Man's mark is the lip plug. Woman's sign is the tattooing on her cheeks. Woman has to be soft and gentle, also in gesture and speech. Women do not only in certain cases use different words from the men, but they also like to put many things and the personal name in the diminutive form and to talk always in a gentle voice.

When women are sitting they cover their genitals with the hand or with the legs, while the men sit with open legs. But the men have the glans covered by the prepuce which is pulled through the funnel-shaped penis sheath. So, both sexes exert themselves to cover the more sensitive parts of the genitals. Probably this custom was originated as a defense against pernicious insects. But since then it has become a real custom, every disregard of it is cautiously avoided. That has nothing to do with the sense of shame developed in our culture by means of ideas of chastity and other non Tapirapé concepts. When standing or walking, the woman of this tribe do nothing in order to cover the vulva.

Besides these differences in the behaviour of the sexes there are others referring to food taboos. Many species of animals can be eaten exclusively by men, but there is no animal reserved only for women.

Man's work is house building, woodcutting, fetching firewood, hunting, broiling the big venison, fishing with bow and arrow, carrying burdens and the bigger children on the marches, and basketery. Woman's work is going for water, cooking boiled food, preparing food in the mortar, spinning, producing all the cotton objects, and making pottery. I met a man who liked to eat boiled food and got into serious trouble when his wife left him. He had to beg for food from other women.

Generally the couples live well together, and there are not many divorces. But sometimes a Don Juan appears and has his adventures. And there are also women who take the initiative for an escapade. Maeyma was an assiduous, hard working, ugly man married to a beautiful and lazy woman. One day he beat her with a club because she had not prepared food for him. Moreover, she had had intercourse with Kamairá during Maeyma's absence. Then, the adulteress left her husband in order to live together with the widowed Kamairá, a strong, good-natured man. For a few days Maeyma was angry at him and kept out of his way. He sat down in the men's house and composed a satirical song about the adulterous couple which he sang loudly innumerable times. Then he was reconciled to Kamairá and remained without boiled food while the woman continues living with the strong, good-natured man.

The following dialogue with Kamairahó, the most important leader, gives an idea of the difference between wished and real behaviour. K.: "Are white men's women quarrelsome?"—I (anxious to know the background of this question): "No."—K.: "All Tapirapé women quarrel" (he means: with their husbands).—I: "Do the men quarrel also?"—K.: "Men's quarrel is small, the women quarrel big."—I: "Man flees with his feather ornaments and hammock when wife is quarreling."—K. smiles and confirms it. I have observed too often that an angry woman threatens to throw in the fire these most valuable possessions of her husband.—I: "Your wife is quarrelsome also?"—K. (lying): "No. But Watanamy's wife quarrels big, and Tanupantshoa's wife quarrels." These two leaders are his political rivals. K.

continues: "When woman is angry, she moved to another house. Maeyma's wife moved to another house, Mangambi's wife moved to another house."—I: "Maeyma and Mangambi have beaten their wives."—K. (lying): "They haven't beaten them." He adds: "Many women beat their husbands." (I never observed this.)—I: "Are the men afraid of their wives?"—K.: "Man is afraid.—I: "Are the women afraid of their husbands?"—K.: "Women have no fear. All Tapirapé women quarrel big."—I: "All?"—K.: "All." —I: "Your wife also?"—K.: "My wife doesn't quarrel."—After a while he asked: "Does your wife quarrel when you will make a great journey?" (He wants to travel with me.)—I: "No. And yours?"—K.: "Mine? Oh no!"

Characteristic of these Indians is continual tenderness. As far as possible the couples sit together, frequently with arms around each other and smiling. This honeymoon atmosphere I also observed in a couple immediately after the husband had beaten his wife.

Naturally, in the behaviour between sexes as among all the Tapirapé individuals in general there is no complete uniformity. In an Indian village as Tampiitawa we find a series of the same psychological types we meet in the most different social groups of white people, i.e., types such as the expansive and the surly, the generous and the avaricious, the aggressive and the peaceful, the rebel and the obedient, the arrogant and the servile, the disinterested and the selfish, the courageous and the coward, the modest and the conceited, and many others.

Integrating Forces in Tapirapé Society

Three social groupings further solidarity among the Tapirapé: 1) the work groups are men's associations for clearing away parts of the forest in order to prepare gardens, for hunting and for various ceremonials; 2) the eating groups are bilinear associations which gather when one or more of their members get too much food for their own family and not enough to distribute usefully and equitably among all the inhabitants of the village and which also, at certain occasions, unite all the population for ceremonial meals; 3) the kinship groups are a kind of compound family which not only extend relationship until the most distant cousins, but are enlarged also by adoptions.

Opportunity for exclusive reunion of all the male members of the tribe is offered by the large ceremonial men's house situated in the center of the village. It represents a school of public spirit for the young men.

An institution of special importance for the coherence of Tapirapé society is shamanism. The shaman is the expert on supernatural problems and has to protect the people against supernatural dangers, that means, against nearly every danger. I was told that three Tapirapé villages forfeited their independence, moving their inhabitants to Tampiitawa for the unique reason that they had lost their medicine-men.

As regards certain leaders' influence for tribal integration I observed that nobody dared in Kamairahó's presence

605

to talk about the origin of those who were not born in Tampiitawa, but in one of the three abandoned villages. In the evening there were also public speeches in the plaza in which Kamairá appealed to the sense of mutual responsibility.

A unifying function like that of the crown in the British empire is exercised by the institution of the "favorite child" in which a boy or a girl is treated with special attention and tenderness by everybody and mainly by the leaders, is always more adorned than the other children and placed as the central figure in various ceremonies.

A feeling sometimes disagreeable for me, but probably always welcome to a Tapirapé is given by the fact that one is never left alone in Tampiitawa. The continuous mutual control takes the form of proprieties. When you open your eyes in the morning, you will hear from the neighbouring hammock: "You awake," and you have to answer: "I awake." Always when you withdraw, you have to say where you are going and why, and the person nearest to you has to answer: "Go!" The mental narrowness so produced can probably only be endured by discipline and tolerance. Really the Tapirapé prove their love of order not only on occasions which gather all the people to common labor, common meals and common ceremonies, but also when two men of different huts are quarreling. In such a case each one remains in his own house and, invisible to his opponent, pronounces his accusation in a monotonous voice. The

other will never interrupt his speech and only begin to answer when his adversary has finished. The spirit of tolerance is manifest, as we have seen, in cases of adultery, when the offended husband, instead of killing the culprit, composes a satirical poem. If something is stolen, nobody demands its restitution or will even speak about this directly with the thief. A person who lies or gives some false alarm will not hear any reproof. The general behaviour pattern requires a person never to be violent in public relations with the other inhabitants of the village, always to show the smile of politeness and also a good sense of humour, and to be unlimitedly generous.

Disruptive Forces in Tapirapé Society

But this general behaviour pattern is sometimes seriously disregarded. We remember the bad treatment given to a young orphan. I observed that the hatred against certain persons induced their hut companions to bring their hammocks close to the fire in order to burn them during their absence. And since the death of a person is always attributed to the magical influence of another person, many Tapirapé, mainly shamans, have already died as supposed murderers under the club of an avenger.

With regard to disruptive forces in Tapirapé society we have to consider also that growing up without authoritarian guidance may favour the spirit of tolerance, but, on the other hand, it strengthens the tendency to political disintegration and to the formation of

606

new local groups, a tendency frequently apparent among this tribe.

Behaviour in Relation to Foreigners

The Tapirapé are not a warlike people. It is not their ideal to be hard on themselves and on others. They cry "Ai" at a mosquito's sting. When they are afraid of something, they do not conceal their fear and they are not ashamed of it. They like to ridicule the neighbouring tribes by means of contemptuous comparisons. But when foreigners enter Tampiitawa, they are received with magnificent hospitality. Then, not only all their possessions, but also all the intimate parts of their body are studied with the greatest curiosity. Once a missionary took a bath in the brook near the village and all the women and girls came running, gathered around him, and commented with the serenity of experts on the dimensions and possibilities of his penis.

But Tapirapé behaviour in relation to a foreigner can become really disagreeable when they consider the community menaced by his presence. They insisted, for instance, upon the same missionary's leaving the village immediately when he fell ill with malaria. And when in the house I inhabited with several Tapirapé families, a child fell ill, all the kindness before shown to me by the Indians was transformed suddenly into hatred against the foreigner as the probable cause of the evil.

Behaviour in Relation to The Supernatural

The Tapirapé sees the supernatural world populated by many kinds of dis-

agreeable beings which inspire fear. There are the souls of the dead he has to avoid. By agitating a glowing log when he goes out of the hut during the night he defends himself against many other spirits.

The Tapirapé do not suppose that the violation of the tribal behaviour pattern could offend supernatural beings or that those beings could punish them for anything. There is no interaction between such beings and what we would call moral conduct.

"Moral" behaviour in relation to the supernatural world is singing and dancing in order to defend the community against unknown dangers and to increase fertility in the world of nature.

Good and Bad

So we can say that, for the Tapirapé, "good" is what conserves the community, and "bad" is what injures it. What we would call "moral responsibility" is not attributed to the thief, liar or adulterer, but to the person supposed to be the magical author of death in the community, i.e., of diminishing its number. "Bad" is what was presumably done by this "murderer," and "good" is to "punish" him by killing him.

Bibliography

Herbert Baldus, *Ensaios de Etnologia Brasileira* (S. Paulo, 1937).
——,"Os Tapirapé, tribo tupi no Brasil Central," *Revista do Arquivo Municipal*, vol. XCVI–CXXVII (S. Paulo, 1944–49).

607

——,"Caracterização da cultura tapirapé. Indian Tribes of Aboriginal America," *Selected Papers of the XXIXth International Congress of Americanists,* edited by Sol Tax (Chicago, 1952).

——, *Biblografia Critica Da Etnologia Brasileira* (São Paulo, 1954).

Charles Wagley, *Tapirapé Shamanism. Boletim do Museu Nacional. N.S., Antropologia* n. 3. (Rio de Janeiro, 1943).

——, *Cultural Influences on Populations: A Comparison of two Tupi Tribes.* Revista do Museu Paulista, N.S., vol. V (S. Paulo, 1951).

Charles Wagley and Eduardo Galvão, *The Tapirapé.* Handbook of South American Indians. Edited by Julian H. Steward. vol. III (Washington, 1948).

Herbert Baldus
Museu Paulista
Sao Paulo, Brazil

Tarphon, rabbi: *see* Jewish Ethics and Its Civilization.

taste: *see* Ayer, Alfred J.; Cooper, Anthony Ashley; Reid, Thomas.

tattle-tale: *see* Psychology and Morals.

Taylor, Harriet: *see* Utilitarianism.

Taylor, N. W.: *see* Moral Philosophy in America.

Taylor, R.: *see* Primitive Morals.

Tecospan Indians: *see* Aztec Morals.

teetotalism: *see* Puritan Morals.

teleological ethics: *see* Major Ethical Viewpoints; Moore, George Edward; Utilitarianism.

teleology: *see* Aquinas, Thomas, Moral Views of; Cumberland, Richard; Moore, George Edward; Ross, Sir (William) David.

teleology, ethical: *see* Hartmann, Nicolai.

teleology, metaphysical: *see* Plato.

telepathy: *see* Schopenhauer, Arthur.

Teles: *see* Minor Socratics.

telling the truth: *see* Aztec Morals; Broad, C. D.; Stoics, the; truth

temperance: *see* Aquinas, Thomas, Moral Views of; Aristotle; Augustine and Morals; Clarke, Samuel; Dante, Alighieri; Hume, David; More, Henry; Plato; Puritan Morals; Socrates; Stoics, the.

temptation: *see* Jesuits, the, Moral Theology of; Kierkegaard, Soren; Liguori, St. Alphonsus and Catholic Moral Philosophy; Psychology and Morals; Reid, Thomas; Zoroastrian Morals.

tenderness: *see* Puritan Morals; Tapirapé Morals, Some Aspects of.

tensions: *see* Cudworth, Ralph; Dostoyevsky, Fyodor; Kierkegaard, Soren, Major Ethical Viewpoints; Prichard, H. A.; Stoics, the.

terror: *see* French Existentialism and Moral Philosophy.

terrorism: *see* Soviet Morality, Current.

testimony: *see* Hammurapi, Code of.

tests: *see* Major Ethical Viewpoints.

tests and morals: *see* Dewey, John.

Tezcatlipoca: *see* Aztec Morals.

Thales: *see* Sophists, the.

thankfulness: *see* Butler, Joseph; Muslim Morals.

theater: *see* Puritan Morals.

Theatetus: see Sophists, the.

theft: *see* Augustine and Morals; Dante, Alighieri; Hammurapi, Code of; Hindu Ethics; Navaho Morals; Pakot, The Moral System of; Riffian Morals; Rio Grande Pueblo Indians; Zuni Indians, Morals of.

theism: *see* Aquinas, Thomas, Moral Views of; Butler, Joseph; God; Jewish Ethics and Its Civilization; Liguori, St. Alphonsus and Catholic Moral Philosophy; Moral Philosophy in America; Muslim Morals; Quakerism, Classical, The Morality of; Zoroastrian Morals.

theocentrism: *see* Jewish Ethics and Its Civilization.

theocracy: *see* Berdyaev, Nicolas; Jewish Ethics and Its Civilization; Muslim Morals; Quakerism, Classical, The Morality of; Soloviev, Wladimir; Zuni Indians, Morals of.

Theodoros: *see* Minor Socratics.

theological determinism: *see* Hutcheson, Francis.

theological ethics: *see* Major Ethical Viewpoints; Moore, George Edward.

theological utilitarianism: *see* Moral Philosophy in America; Utilitarianism.

theology and ethics: *see* Christianity; Cumberland, Richard; Hindu Ethics; Jewish Ethics and Its Civilization; Price, Richard; Puritan Morals; religion and ethics; religion and morality; Spinoza; Utilitarianism.

Theopompos: *see* Minor Socratics.

theoretical reason: *see* Clarke, Samuel.

therapy: *see* Freud, Sigmund; Psychology and Morals.

thirst: *see* Aztec Morals.

Thomism: *see* Aquinas; Moral Philosophy in America.

Thrasymachus: *see* Sophists, the.

Tillich, Paul: *see* Moral Philosophy in America.

time wasting: *see* waste of time.

tithing: *see* Jewish Ethics and Its Civilization; Puritan Morals.

Tkachyov, P. N.: *see* Soviet Morality, Current.

Tlalocan: *see* Aztec Morals.

Tlazolteotl: *see* Aztec Morals.

tobacco: *see* Aboriginals of Yirkalla; Puritan Morals.

toil: *see* Jewish Ethics and Its Civilization; labor, manual; work.

Toland: *see* Cooper, Anthony Ashley.

Toledo, F.: *see* Jesuits, the, Moral Theology of.

tolerance: *see* Goethe, Johann Wolfgang von; Rio Grande Pueblo Indians; Spinoza; Tapirapé Morals, Some Aspects of; Zoroastrian Morals.

Tolstoy, Leo

It is a well recognized fact in the world of contemporary literature that Leo Tolstoy was one of the greatest novelists of the 19th century decades. During that period his influence as a writer was very considerable. It must be recalled, moreover, that Tolstoy died in the first decade of our own 20th century, and must therefore be listed among great authors of our time. This appreciation, however well deserved, does not exhaust Tolstoy's contribution to world culture. Tolstoy was not only a literary genius, he was also a religious and ethical thinker. In these spiritual fields, Tolstoy's role is no less important, no doubt, than his role as a novelist. Even though often baffling and controversial, Tolstoy's moral message has an impact of its own, and is still meaningful today. His moral outlook on man and society is reflected in his novels, stories, as well as in his didactic writings. But this is not all. Tolstoy's entire life from childhood to old age is a series of experiments and probings of the moral law. From these experiments and testings, the student of Tolstoy's ethics can gather a great deal: from his fiction, from his teachings, and from his diaries and notebooks. He kept a faithful record of his life and spiritual development from his teens up to his old age; his last Diary entry was made on the eve of his death, at the age of 82.

Born in 1828, in the family's country-home of Yasnaya Polyana (Province of Tula), Tolstoy was a member of the titled family of the Tolstoys, granted the count's coronet by Peter the Great. Though not exceptionally wealthy, according to the standards of the time, the Tolstoys were well-to-do landowners. Leo's childhood and youth are masterfully described by himself.[1] The first period of his life was spent in his country home. He later studied at the University of Kazan, but did not graduate because he was disappointed in the philosophy of law, in which he had intended to major. Both in Kazan and later in Moscow, Tolstoy was confused and dissipated. He found an escape in accompanying his brother to the Caucasus, where he joined the army. After seeing some active service in the campaign against Caucasian rebel tribes, Tolstoy took part in the Crimean War. He fought on the most dangerous lines of the defense of Sevastopol and wrote a magnificent record of this, his unique war experience: *The Tales of Sevastopol.* As a well established writer he published almost simultaneously *Tales of Sevastopol, Childhood and Youth, and The Cossacks.*

Tolstoy retired to his country-home of Yasnaya Polyana. He had always been attracted by life in the country, among the peasants whom he loved and admired for their solid Christian tradition. He was therefore deeply concerned with the Russian people's welfare. In 1861, the liberation of the serfs marked a new period of Russia's social and cultural development. He devoted himself to the improvement of Russian rural life and to the spreading of education. He created his own rural schools, wrote alphabets and text-books for them. He also tried to stabilize the conditions of land-ownership and peasant land-problems which arose after the liberation of the serfs. These efforts were not immediately rewarded. Meanwhile, Tolstoy was seeking stabilization in his own personal life. He realized, that such a stabilization could only be achieved in marriage and a family. In 1862, he married Sophia Behrs, and for a number of years, the family was for him the solution of his ethical problem. Many children were born to Tolstoy, some of them died in childhood, others survived him. His youngest daughter, Alexandra Tolstoy, has written an exhaustive book about her father's life, his literary creation and ethical teaching.[2] Tolstoy's family life, *per se,* was a happy one, at least in the beginning.

During that first period of peaceful existence Tolstoy may have been satis-

---

[1] *Childhood, Boyhood and Youth,* translated by L. and A. Maude.

[2] Alexandra Tolstoy, *Tolstoy, a Life of My Father* (New York, 1953).

fied with a solution of the moral problem which had haunted him during his youth and which now seemed decisive. Moreover, it was during that period that Tolstoy wrote his two great novels: *War and Peace,* published in the 60's and *Anna Karenina,* which appeared in the 70's. Tolstoy had not attained the summit of his literary fame. Other important writings followed: *Resurrection,* the *Kreuzer Sonata,* several plays, and a number of short stories. However, it was precisely at that time, when he was sixty years old and after, that Tolstoy became a moral teacher. In 1882 appeared his *Confession,* followed by *What I Believe* and other didactic writings, in which he described his own dramatic religious and moral crisis.

The aftermath of this crisis is well-known: Tolstoy now based his entire life on the teaching of the Gospels, and most particularly so on the Sermon on the Mount. He repudiated his own condition of a wealthy land-owner, and wanted to share the simple life and manual labor of the Russian peasant. He declared himself a champion of "non-resistance to evil," and therefore a pacifist. He rejected the state, law, and its enforcement, and all its consequences, especially capital punishment and military service. Though founding his teaching on the Gospels, Tolstoy rejected the Church, which he considered as a distortion and misinterpretation of the Evangelic message. He spoke of Christ, as "the son of man," but did not believe in His Divinity. Because of his outspoken attacks on the church and his denial of

the sacraments, Tolstoy was excommunicated by the Holy Synod, representing ecclesiastical authority of the Russian-Orthodox Church.

Tolstoy's criticism of literature was also startling and controversial. In his essay; *What is Art,* Tolstoy denounced all literature, including his own, (and with only a few exceptions) as a useless amusement offered to the rich. The people, half educated or not at all, could not enjoy literature. And so, he attempted to create a literature for the people only. Hence his folk-tales and his special people's "readers."

The epilogue of Tolstoy's life was as dramatic as his religious crisis. Actually, from 1882 and up to 1910, Tolstoy lived in a perpetual struggle with himself, in order to attain the perfection he taught others, and in order to free himself from his own family environment which opposed him. Tolstoy's wife, Sophia, did not share her husband's convictions, nor could she subscribe to the practical application of these convictions in their everyday life. Sophia's main concern was about her husband's will, in which he renounced all copyright and royalties due to his heirs; his entire writings, according to this will, were to become the people's property. Because of dissensions with his wife, and with other members of his family, Tolstoy's life at home became unbearable. On October 28, 1910, Tolstoy left his home; after a short stay with his sister, a nun of a nearby community, he went on his way, accompanied by his daughter, Alexandra. Stricken with pneumonia, he had to interrupt his voyage, and died in the station-master's house at Astapovo, November 7th, 1910.

Tolstoy's ethical views are fully presented in his didactic teachings. But these are not enough to enlighten us on his moral outlook. Beside these didactic teachings, we have Tolstoy's diaries, note-books and letters. We have, moreover, many testimonies of the members of his family and closest associates. Last and not least, we have Tolstoy's creative writings, novels and stories, *which all reflect his search for moral and religious truth.*

In Tolstoy's *Childhood and Youth,* we have a detailed and candid picture of his earlier years. We can see him as a sensitive, emotional boy devoted to his family, and religiously inclined. The description of his confession to a priest, for instance, is extremely moving; not having confessed all his sins, the young Tolstoy returned to confession and was only then satisfied with absolution. In Tolstoy's diaries, the first entry is self-accusation: "I have," wrote Tolstoy in 1846, "entered all my weaknesses under these headings: laziness, lying, greediness, indecision, desire to show off, sensuality, lack of self-respect, and so on. . . . All such minor shortcomings." Staying in Moscow at that time, he visited the shrine of "Our Lady of Iberia." He writes concerning this visit: "My remorse was terrifying. I never felt it so deeply before. . . . I grew devout and became even more so when in the country." At the same time, he wrote out a schedule of his every day work: studying, reading, rising early, every discipline which could curb him was self-prescribed. This strict schedule did not, however, work. Tolstoy sought to flee temptation in the Caucasus; then at the siege of Sevastopol, he discovered the true values of life and death, heroism, and the frailties of human nature, —all of them exposed by war and shared by himself. Each of the men Tolstoy observed during that siege could be, he tells us "the villain or the hero of this tale." And he concludes: "The hero of my tale whom I love with all my heart and soul, whom I have tried to depict in all its beauty, and who always was, is and will be beautiful, is—truth."

In the tales of Sevastopol, as well as in the early diaries, we have already the main patterns of Tolstoy's ethical teachings. War is evil, vanity is evil, lust is evil,—all of these sins draw man away from Truth. Later, Tolstoy will complete this by saying: "Truth is one, truth is in Christ."

But before Tolstoy reached this conclusion, he had still a long way to go. And every step he made is reflected in his writings. In *War and Peace,* he presents the picture of a society, to which he himself belonged. He chose the setting of an unstable peace, and of many years of war, the Napoleonic age. Some of his characters are villains, others heroes. The main characters of *War and Peace,* Pierre Bezukhov and Andrei Bolkonsky, are truly admirable young men. Each of them seeks to solve the moral problem. Bolkonsky is wounded at the battle of Austerlitz. Let us recall Tolstoy's famous lines:

"Above him there was nothing but the sky—the lofty sky, not clear, yet immeasurably lofty, with gray clouds gliding slowly across it. How quiet, peaceful, and solemn; . . . Yes! all is vanity, all falsehood, except that infinite sky."

This is Andrei Bolkonsky's first step toward purification. But he is to face many other trials. He falls in love with the young girl Natasha, then loses her, and is wounded, this time mortally, at the battle of Borodino. Now Andrei Bolkonsky learns the meaning of suffering,—the scene described in the field-hospital is a continuation of the Tales of Sevastopol, and even more horrible. And here Andrei Bolkonsky not only suffers, he also learns to forgive his enemies. For next to him, on the operation table is Anatole Kuraguine, the man who seduced Andrei's fiancée, Natasha. Anatole Kuraguine is amputated under Andrei's very eyes. And so Andrei pities his former rival; he feels "compassion, love of our brothers, for those who love us and for those who hate us, yes, that love which God preached to us on earth." Through the trials and sufferings of war, purification also comes to Pierre Bezukhov. On the battlefield of Borodino he is appalled and shocked by the massacre: " 'Now they will stop it, now they will be horrified at what they have done,' he thought, aimlessly going toward a crowd of stretcher-bearers . . ." Later, witnessing the shooting of prisoners by the French, Pierre once more experiences horror: "breathing heavily, Pierre looked around, as if asking what it (the shooting) meant. On the faces of all the Russians and of the French soldiers and officers without exception, he read the same dismay, horror and conflict that were in his own heart." " 'But who, after all is doing this? they are all suffering as I am. Who then is it? Who?' flashed for an instant in his mind." As Tolstoy himself, Pierre finds the solution of his problems in the soul of the Russian people. Captured by the victorious French, he meets Platon Karatayev, a fellow-prisoner: Karatayev is a peasant, who offers him an example of primitive faith, wisdom and kindness: "he loved and lived affectionately with everything life brought him in contact with, particularly with man— not any particular man, but those with whom he happened to be. He loved his dog, his comrades, the French, and Pierre who was his neighbor." Through Karatayev, Pierre finds peace of mind which will remain with him after his liberation and the end of the war. In one of the last chapters of his great novel, Tolstoy speaks of Pierre's "new attitude to life and his fellow men." Formerly, Tolstoy tells us, Pierre had used a "mental telescope," in order to look into "remote space." In other words, Pierre had only an abstract and distant view of the meaning of life. He had tried every kind of remedy: philosophy, philanthropy and all other sophistication of his time. Through Platon Karatayev he encountered reality: "he had learned to see the great, eternal and infinite in everything. . . ." To that terrible question: What for? a simple answer was now always ready in his soul:

"Because there is God, that God without whom will not one hair fall from a man's head."

In *Anna Karenina,* published some ten years later, Tolstoy once more raised religious and moral issues. Once again he portrayed Russian society, as he knew it, but carried his problem far beyond this limited field. In *Anna Karenina,* Tolstoy depicted the impact of conventional, artificial and false ethics on human destiny. The so-called "elegant" Petersburg and Moscow circles have no ethical foundations whatever: Karenin, the hypocritical husband, the sensual and carefree Vronsky, the depraved *"bon-vivant,"* Steva Oblonsky, follow a personal and social pattern, which breeds confusion, unhappiness, and finally destruction. Anna is the victim of this corruption, which she shares, almost unaware of what she is doing. Carried away by her passion, she yields to it step by step and there is absolutely nothing to stem it, until she commits adultery, then meets her fatal end: despair and suicide. This terrible moral defeat is opposed and so to say highlighted by the positive character of the story,— Levin, the man who seeks truth, and finds it, or more correctly speaking *is* truth as Tolstoy sees it. But Levin himself does not discover truth all at once. He moves toward it gradually: in his marriage and family life, in the mystery of his child's birth and of his brother's death. In continuous and often torturing examinations of conscience, Levin's path winds amid the rugged psychological landscape of a perfectionist's world. Actually, Levin's final

solution is reached at the end of the novel; it is described in less than a page. Levin, talking with one of his peasants, hears the man say, that while some only live to "fill their belly," others "live for their soul." They do not "forget God." At the peasant's words, "undefined but significant ideas seemed to burst out [in Levin's soul], as though they had been locked up, and all striving towards one goal, they thronged whirling through his head, blinding with their light."

The tremendous impact of Levin's enlightenment is felt in every word of the lines quoted above. Perhaps, because of the novel's intense development and dramatic intent as a whole Levin's "conversion," just as Pierre's in *War and Peace,* are often not sufficiently understood, or fully interpreted. However, no serious reader of *Anna Karenina* can possibly miss this unique message. It is clear that, while Anna dies, and Vronsky is torn by fruitless regrets—and doomed to life-long remorse—Levin is reborn. Writes R. P. Blackmore, commenting on *Anna Karenina:*[3] "With no less force in him than drove Anna, Levin turned the other way. He too had been at the point of death and for months at a time, but through the death of his brother and the delivery of his wife found himself alive instead."

Indeed, it is already quite clear, both in *War and Peace* and in *Anna Karenina,* toward what "goal," Tolstoy himself was striving. In fact, this goal is apparent in Tolstoy's earliest

3 *Kenyon Review,* July, '49.

diaries. The *Confession,* published in 1882, starts with an examination of conscience very much like the one he wrote in his student days: "I cannot think of those years" writes Tolstoy in his *Confession,* recalling his past life, without horror, loathing and heartache: I killed men in war and challenged men to duels in order to kill them. I lost at cards, consumed the labour of the peasants, sentenced them to punishment, lived loosely and deceived people. Lying, robbery, adultery of all kinds, drunkenness, violence, murder—there was no crime I did not commit, and in spite of that people praised my conduct and my contemporaries considered me to be a comparatively moral man." Such an enumeration of sins, mostly mortal, with only here and there a venial one, has been rarely, perhaps never, listed by a penitent, including Saint Augustine himself. Should we draw the conclusion that Tolstoy suffered from a guilt complex? We do not think so. It is obvious that Tolstoy *was* endowed with an over-sensitive, over-scrupulous conscience. But this was *not* a closed circle; on the contrary, this was a series of testings and checkings performed by a man who *wanted* to advance on the path leading toward Truth. Like Levin, Tolstoy was a perfectionist. Like Levin, Tolstoy was for a time "at the point of death." He tells us, how he was ready to commit suicide, if Truth was not finally revealed to him. He scanned the Christian religions: Russian-Orthodoxy, Catholicism, Protestantism; he read the Bible in Hebrew; he studied the Moslem faith

and he examined Buddhism. Then, finding no solace in any of these doctrines, he re-read the Gospels. The Sermon on the Mount offered him the key; from that one chapter he drew what he called his five commandments: 1) "Do not be angry", 2) Do not lust, 3) Do not swear oaths, 4) Do not resist evil, 5) Love your enemies.

As we have pointed out, Tolstoy's ethical doctrine *per se* had a very great influence inside and outside of Russia from the publication of the *Confession* on and up to his death. True, some of his declarations seemed extreme, almost fantastic, and actually impossible to put into practice: as, for instance, his criticism of marriage in the *Kreutzer Sonata,* or of man's creative genius in *What is Art?* But Tolstoy's very demand on himself and others was a challenge which moved the hearts of men. His teaching about non-resistance to evil seemed the most difficult, the most paradoxical and obscure. However, it stirred the young Gandhi, who became Tolstoy's follower, and performed, long after his teacher's death, an extraordinary feat: India came of age through non-resistance.

This, no doubt, is the most notorious result of Tolstoy's teaching, so that we still live in his world. However, his didactic writings are no longer read with the feverish emotion they awakened when he lived. There are few Tolstoyans in our time, and scarcely any perfectionists able to obey the "five commandments *al la lettre.* Even among Tolstoy's most fervent admirers today, there is a feeling, that his didactic writings were forced, artificial, striking the wrong key, whereas his two great novels render Tolstoy's creed in a vivid, dynamic and infinitely persuasive manner. Indeed, both *War and Peace* and *Anna Karenina,* together with the *Tales of Sevastopol* and Tolstoy's beautiful short stories and folk-tales, all convey the same message, which he later summed up in the Five Commandments. Each of Tolstoy's fictional works, besides being a literary masterpiece, can and should be considered as a *parable*. Each of them stirs the reader's conscience and makes demands, rarely formulated in the field of literary creation. These demands were not addressed to the reader, but to the author himself: "Everybody understood," writes V. Maklakov, one of Tolstoy's contemporaries, "that he had an extraordinarily acute conscience, which could neither justify nor hide from others its own errors."[4] Tolstoy himself knew the extent to which human conscience can be tried, and how far it can atempt to reach perfection. He wrote, that the moral ideal, as an absolute value, is a magnetic pole, toward which the needle can only point on the compass dial. He also liked to repeat that when a boat is about to land on a fast river current, the helmsman usually guides his craft toward a point beyond and above the actual landing place. He knows that the current will drive the boat back to its proper location. And this, of course, is another parable, so typical of Tolstoy, artist and moralist,

whose entire life and life-work were directed toward one goal: "Seek ye first the Kingdom of God and His justice."

Bibliography

The Tolstoy quotations are from *War and Peace,* translated by Louise and Aylmer Maude (New York, 1942); from *Anna Karenina,* translated by Constance Garnett (New York, 1950); from *A Confession* and *What I Believe,* translated by Aylmer Maude (The World's Classics).

Diaries quoted in Ernest Simmons' *Tolstoy* (Atlantic Monthly Press).

Other sources indicated in footnotes.

Helene Iswolsky
Fordham Institute of
Contemporary Russian Studies

---

[4] V. Maklakov, "Tolstoy," article published in Russian in the literary review *Vozrozhdenye* (Paris, 1954).

gion: Muslim Morals; Pakot, The Moral System of; Primitive Morals; Riffian Morals; Rio Grande Pueblo Indians.

tragedy: *see* French Existentialism and Moral Philosophy.

tranquility: *see* Aztec Morals; calmness; Cumberland, Richard; Hindu Ethics; serenity; Stoics, the.

transcendentalism: *see* Moral Philosophy in America.

transformation: *see* Hegel, G. W. F.; Stoics, the.

transgressions: *see* Jewish Ethics and Its Civilization; Rio Grande Pueblo Indians; sin.

transvaluation of values: *see* Machiavelli, Niccolo; Minor Socratics; Soviet Morality, Current.

treachery: *see* Aboriginals of Yirkalla; Dante, Alighieri; Soviet Morality, Current.

tribal custom: *see* custom; Muslim Morals.

tribal societies: *see* Morals and Religion.

tribal systems: *see* Riffian Morals.

tribulation: *see* Augustine and Morals.

Trotsky: *see* Soviet Morality, Current.

trust: *see* Stoics, the.

trustworthiness: *see* China, Moral Philosophies of; Navaho Morals.

truth(s): *see* a posteriori truths; a priori truths; Aquinas, Thomas; Moral Views of; Augustine and Morals; Ayer, Alfred J.; Balguy, John; Clarke, Samuel; Cudworth, Ralph; Dante, Alighieri; general truths; Hindu Ethics; Jewish Ethics and Its Civilization; Kant, I.; Language and Ethics; Liguori, St. Alphonsus and Catholic Moral Philosophy; Major Ethical Viewpoints; Moral Philosophy in America; Plato; Price, Richard; Prichard, H. A.; Puritan Morals; Quakerism, Classical, The Morality of; Reid, Thomas; Riffian Morals; Scheler, Max; Soloviev, Wladimir; Sophists, The; Spinoza; Stoics, The; Telling the truth; Tolstoy, Leo; Wollaston, William; Zoroastrian Morals.

truthfulness: *see* Freud, Sigmund; Muslim Morals; Navaho Morals.

truth-telling: *see* Ross, Sir (William) David.

tsarism: *see* Soviet Morality, Current.

Tucker, Abraham: *see* Utilitarianism.

Turgenev, I.: *see* Khomiakov, Alexey.

tutiorism: *see* Jesuits, the, Moral Theology of.

twofold arguments: *see* Sophists, the.

Tydemann, D.: *see* Spinoza.

typology of morals: *see* Nietzsche, Friedrich.

tyrannicide: *see* Jesuits, the, Moral Theology of.

tyranny: *see* Machiavelli, Niccolo; Minor Socratics; Quakerism, Classical, The Morality of; Spinoza.

U

ugliness: *see* Cooper, Anthony Ashley; Rio Grande Pueblo Indians.

Ulmar: *see* Muslim Morals.

ultimate truth: *see* Hindu Ethics.

Umayyid Princes: *see* Muslim Morals.

unanimity concept: *see* Rio Grande Pueblo Indians.

unchastity: *see* Jesuits, the, Moral Theology of.

uncleanness: *see* Pakot, the Moral System of.

unconscious, the: *see* Freud, Sigmund; Psychology and Morals.

unconscious will: *see* Schopenhauer, Arthur.

unfitness: *see* Clarke, Samuel.

unhappiness: *see* Aztec Morals; Dewey, John; Minor Socratics; Stoics, the.

unity: *see* Aquinas, Thomas, Moral Views of; Cudworth, Ralph; Hindu Ethics; Khomiakov, Alexey; Quakerism, Classical, The Morality of; Spinoza.

unity of existence: *see* Hindu Ethics.

universal: *see* Aquinas, Thomas, Moral Views of; Hindu Ethics; Schopenhauer, Arthur.

universal good: *see* Clarke, Samuel.

universal laws: *see* Kant, I.; Stoics, The.

universal love: *see* China, Moral Philosophies of; Cudworth, Ralph; Hindu Ethics.

universal misery: *see* Clarke, Samuel; misery.

universal moral code: *see* Nietzsche, Friedrich.

universal morality: *see* Nietzsche, Friedrich; Psychology and Morals; Stoics, the.

universal virtues: *see* Hindu Ethics.

universalism: *see* Berdyaev, Nicolas; Jewish Ethics and Its Civilization; Major Ethical Viewpoints.

universalistic hedonism: *see* Major Ethical Viewpoints; Sidgwick, Henry.

universality: *see* Hindu Ethics; Scheler, Max; Zoroastrian Morals.

universals and ethics: *see* Kant, I.; Socrates.

unpleasantness: *see* Schlick, Moritz.

unreason: *see* Freud, Sigmund.

unregenerate: *see* Puritan Morals.

unrighteousness: *see* Hindu Ethics.

unselfishness: *see* Hindu Ethics.

untruth: *see* French Existentialism and Moral Philosophy.

Upanishads: *see* Hindu Ethics.

Urban, W. M.: *see* Moral Philosophy in America.

urgency: *see* Prichard, H. A.

USSR: *see* Marxist Theory of Morals; Russia; Soviet Morality, Current.

usury: *see* Dante, Alighieri; Muslim Morals.

Utilitarianism

I

Utilitarianism was one of the leading schools of moral and political philosophy in England for approximately a hundred years, from the middle of the 18th century to the middle of the 19th century. There were continental representatives of the school, such as Helvetius in France and Beccaria in Italy, but Utilitarianism was essentially English and its most noted proponents were Englishmen or Scotchmen, John Gay, William Paley, Jeremy Bentham, James Mill, John Stuart Mill and, in a limited sense, David Hume.

On its political side the movement was aimed at social reform, the extension of political privilege, the realization of a higher standard of living for the less fortunate, and a correction of the injustices arising from a harsh penal code and its corrupt administration. It sought to secure for the mass of men not only greater material comforts but also opportunities for education and self-improvement that would enable them to achieve "human dignity." The Utilitarians were interested not only in theoretical speculation but also in direct action and participation in political life, and their activities constituted one of the important factors that brought about the sweeping political reforms in England of the second quarter of the 19th century. Justification for the humanitarian doctrines was found in elaborate theories of morals and in psychological interpretations of human nature. Utilitarian political philosophies were conclusions drawn from ethical premises.

On its ethical side Utilitarianism was a form of hedonism that attempted to unite individualistic hedonism with social or universalistic hedonism, to reconcile an egoistic theory of motives with a morality of sympathy and benevolence. It followed the empirical methods and commonsense practicality characteristic of British philosophy; it was frequently concerned with analysis and clarification of ethical terminology; it rejected the egoism of Hobbes, that it considered so repellent but it frankly recognized the selfishness that it found present in human nature; in all cases, it tried to reconcile the hedonistic character of human conduct with the altruistic and benevolent traits of men, to resolve the conflict between concern for the self and concern for the common good; in some cases, this reconciliation was achieved by a pious reliance upon the just and omnipotent Deity of the Christian religion, a God who wills the happiness of all men. In general, however, the central principle of Utilitarianism, the greatest happiness of the greatest number, was derived inductively from a study of man and society, not from the revelations of religion or from a priori metaphysical principle.

Classical utilitarianism was opposed to all forms of ethical intuitionism, but in the latter part of the 19th century Henry Sidgwick combined utilitarianism with a form of intuitionism. In his *Principles of Ethics,* written in installments between 1879 and 1893, Herbert Spencer restated the principle of utility in an evolutionistic form. At the close of the century and the beginning of the 20th century Hastings Rashdall and G. E. Moore, among others, developed an ideal non-hedonistic form of utilitarianism; but by granting that pleasure is not the sole good but one among other ends, such as virtue and perfection of capacities, they transformed Utilitarianism into an ethical theory that Bentham and James Mill would have found intolerable.

II

In 1731 Edmund Law, Bishop of Carlisle, published an *Essay on the Origin of Evil,* a translation of a Latin treatise, *De origione mali,* written by William King, Archbishop of Dublin, which had first appeared in 1702. There was printed with the translation a brief supplementary dissertation, *Concerning the Fundamental Principle of Virtue or Morality,* by the Rev. John Gay (1699–1745). Gay was a Fellow of Sidney Sussex College, Cambridge, and later vicar of Wilshampstead, Bedfordshire. His work, clear and concise in exposition, is probably the earliest statement of the Utilitarian doctrines, antedating Hume's *Treatise of Human Nature,* Book III (1740), by nine years. Hume, however, cannot be thought of as Gay's successor since he derived little or nothing from the *Fundamental Principle of Virtue or Morality* and can be considered a Utilitarian only in a limited sense. Gay's true followers are to be found in a later generation. It was Abraham Tucker's *The Light of*

Nature Pursued (1768–77) and William Paley's *Principles of Moral and Political Philosophy* (1785) that carried on the theories of "theological utlitarianism."

The basis of Gay's treatise is a psychological account of human nature. As a sensible creature man feels pleasure and pain; but he is also capable of foreseeing the pleasurable or painful future consequences of things and actions, and therefore his conduct is governed by a desire to avoid pain and to seek pleasure. The one end he pursues for its own sake is pleasure or happiness, "the sum total of pleasure," and that which is apt to produce pleasure he calls good. As a rational agent he recognizes that his own good is dependent upon other men and he desires to promote the happiness of other men in order to excite in them the same concern for his happiness. Approbations and affections thus arise in men's social relations from a prospect of private or individual happiness. Even in those instances of approval when men do not seem concerned about their own happiness or even when they find that their own happiness is lessened, their motives remain hedonistic. To explain this seeming contradiction Gay appeals to the doctrine of association of ideas. We do not always trace every action to its ultimate end, our own happiness, but rest content as soon as we perceive the action to be subservient to a known or presumed means of happiness. From our own observation and experience or from our imitation of others we have come to associate certain actions with pleasure.

This is fixed into a habit and these "Rest Places," as Gay calls habitual thinking, become our principles, so that without considering the occasions that gave rise to the original pleasure, we approve actions from which we may now derive no personal pleasure at all. These things we love and approve of and pleasure "are so tied together and associated in our minds, that one cannot present itself, but the other will also occur. And the association remains even after that which at first gave them the connection is quite forgot, or perhaps does not exist, but the contrary."[1] This is a very early formulation of the "genealogy of morals" of the English psychologists—utility, forgetting, habit, error— against which Nietzsche later inveighed. We need not thus appeal to the moral sense of Hutcheson, or to innate ideas, or to public affections. Intuitionism of all kinds is emphatically rejected.

Gay is essentially hedonistic, it is seen, but he is no "mere Hobbesist." His psychological account of morals is not sufficient in itself; egoistic hedonism is reconciled with humanitarian benevolence by means of God's will. Virtue is defined as "the conformity to a rule of life, directing the actions of all rational creatures with respect to each other's happiness; to which conformity every one in all cases is obliged."[2] Obligation is "the necessity of doing or omitting any action in order to be happy."[3] There are four kinds of obli-

gation: first, "natural obligation," that which arises from our perceiving the natural consequences of acts; second, "virtuous obligation," that which follows from the approval or disapproval of our fellow creatures; third, "civil obligation," that which arises from the authority of the civil magistrate; and fourth, "religious obligation," which arises from the authority of God. The last is the only full and complete obligation. It is evident from God's nature, since he is infinitely happy in himself from all eternity, that he wills only the happiness of mankind. He consequently wills that the individual's behavior should be a means to the happiness of men in general. Each man's actions must be directed towards fulfilling the divine will. Therefore the criterion of virtue is the happiness of mankind since that is God's will. Private ends are reconciled with public good through the mediation of Gay's theology. All men pursue pleasure or happiness but the guiding criterion of virtue prevents a conflict between the desires of the individual and the happiness of mankind in general.

III

Dr. William Paley (1734–1805), a rather worldly, pleasure-loving, 18th century divine, was the author of a most successful textbook on ethics, *Principles of Moral and Political Philosophy* (1785), which went through eighteen editions in twenty-five years. The book, together with his *View of the Evidences of Christianity* (1794) and *Natural Theology; or Evidences*

---

[1] *British Moralists*, ed. L. A. Selby-Bigge, (Oxford, 1897), Vol. II, p. 283
[2] *Ibid.*, p. 272.
[3] *Ibid.*, p. 273.

of the Existence and Attributes of the Deity (1802), both of which were also used as textbooks, gave Paley a reputation and importance greater than that which the originality of his thought would justify. In the preface to his *Principles of Moral and Political Philosophy* he acknowledges his debt to Abraham Tucker's *The Light of Nature Pursued* and admits that he has simply shortened and reorganized the mass of material in the long work of seven volumes. The basic thesis of Paley's book, however, had already been formulated by Gay, and the picture of man as purely selfish had already been drawn by Hobbes. Every man desires only his own happiness and approves of other men's actions only in so far as they are means to his happiness. As in Gay's treatise, God conciliates the clash of selfish passions. "God wills and wishes the happiness of his creatures,"[4] and those actions which promote that will and wish must be agreeable to him. We are all thus obliged to promote the general happiness of mankind. "Private happiness is our motive, the will of God our rule."[5] Fear plays as important a role in Paley's system as in Hobbes' but in the former it is a fear of the wrath of the almighty in the hereafter and not the fear of other men or of the sovereign as in the latter.

Paley defines moral philosophy as "that science which teaches men their duty and the reasons for it."[6] Like Gay he rejects all theories of moral sense or moral instincts or innate moral ideas and he cites all the objections to these theories. We are all motivated solely by pleasure, and the sentiment of approbation that accompanied an action beneficial to ourselves will continue to rise in our minds whenever we again consider such action, even though the private advantage (pleasure, benefit) no longer exists. By a process of association we tend to approve what originally gave rise to a feeling of pleasure. Habit, custom, and imitation, especially in childhood, all have a role in the development of our moral approbation, but their origin is always found in the fundamental human motive, a desire for happiness. And any condition may be called happy in which the amount of pleasure exceeds that of pain. "Whatever is expedient, is right. It is the utility of any moral rule alone, which constitutes the obligation of it."[7] Does this principle then justify acts of plunder or perjury or murder? No, "these actions are not useful, and for that reason, and that alone, are not right."[8] If properly understood, they they do not produce happiness. Acts of prudence and acts of duty seemingly have different motives but in both cases we consider solely what we ourselves shall gain or lose by the acts. The difference is this: "in the one case, we consider what we shall gain or lose in the present world; in the other case, we consider also what we

---

[4] *The Works of William Paley, D. D.* (London, 1837), Vol. I, p. 45.

[5] *Ibid.*, p. 39.

[6] *Ibid.*, p. 1.

[7] *Ibid.*, p. 46.

[8] *Ibid.*, p. 47.

shall gain or lose in the world to come."[9] Prudential considerations guide all action but such calculations must always keep in mind a future life. The Christian religion assures us that after this life there will be a just distribution of rewards and punishments. When God created the human species, he wished their happiness and the general happiness of mankind is obviously his will. Hence, when we inquire what our duty is, or what we are obliged to do, we are really asking what the will of God is, for we, as his creatures, must fulfill his purpose.

Virtue, then, is "the doing good to mankind, in obedience to the will of God, and for the sake of everlasting happiness."[10] Why am I obliged not to perjure myself, even when it might be to my advantage? The answer is: "I am urged by a violent motive—resulting from the command of another (namely, of God),"[11] The ultimate motive is expectation of heavenly bliss or other-worldly pleasure. Man, the egoistic hedonist, becomes moral by obeying the will of an omnipotent and benevolent God.

Men, of course, are not constantly calculating their chances of eternal misery or happiness; they are saved from the perplexing problem of judging the contribution of individual acts to the general happiness by social habits and customs. Before the expedient act may be declared right, its consequences in all respects should be determined. The past experience of men has produced general rules, codes of action, tables of natural rights, which aid the individual in determining his particular duties. Nevertheless, all laws and social structures ultimately rest upon the principle of utility.

IV

Although David Hume (1711–1776) did not invent the word "utilitarian," which John Stuart Mill claimed he brought into use, and although he never used the formula "the greatest happiness of the greatest number," he did develop the concept of "utility," which was the starting point of the moral reflections of Bentham and James Mill. Hume's exposition is not always completely clear and consistent and the relationship of "useful," "pleasant," and "good" is not precisely stated in his two works on morals, *A Treatise of Human Nature,* Book III (1740) and the *Enquiry concerning the Principles of Morals* (1751). It is clear, however, that Hume rejected Hobbesian egoism. Self-interest is an observable fact of human nature but not all benevolence is mere hypocrisy and the feelings of kindness, the humane sentiments, must also be included in a true account of man. Hume also rejected all appeals to religious or metaphysical sanctions in morals in order to keep his study of moral phenomena completely and consistently empirical. In this respect Hume's method set him apart from theological utilitarianism and from all a priori metaphysical ethical theories. Furthermore, Hume was of the opinion that morality is not a matter of

---

9 *Ibid.*, p. 40.
10 *Ibid.*, p. 27.
11 *Ibid.*, p. 39.

reason but of feeling only. Reason and judgment cannot arrive at distinctions between good and evil, since reason is confined to judging relations of resemblance, contrariety, degrees in quality and proportions in quantity and number. Vice and virtue are not relations or qualities; they are not matters of fact which can be observed. Examine as we will that which we call vice, we can never find it since it is not an object. Only when we turn our reflection inward do we find a sentiment of disapprobation toward an object or action. "Here is a matter of fact; but it is the object of feeling, not of reason. It lies in yourself, not in the object. So that when you pronounce any action or character to be vicious, you mean nothing, but that from the constitution of your nature you have a feeling or sentiment of blame from the contemplation of it."[12] Judgments concerning genuine matters of fact, propositions containing the copula "is" are not the same as propositions about moral feelings, propositions containing "ought," and the latter cannot be deduced from the former. "Morality, therefore, is more properly felt than judged of."[13] Furthermore, "we pronounce the impression arising from virtue to be agreeable, and that proceeding from vice to be uneasy."[14] A character or quality is admired because it is useful or agreeable to us. "An action, or sentiment, or character, is virtuous or vicious; why? because its

view causes a pleasure or uneasiness of a particular kind."[15] The quotations may not be interpreted to mean that pleasure, utility or happiness constitute moral value. Hume is not saying that a character is good because it is useful or pleasant. Even the statement that a virtuous action or character causes pleasure perhaps means no more than that we do admire certain characters, we have feelings of approbation about them and then these sentiments may, as a matter of fact, be observed as useful or pleasant. Such an interpretation would be in keeping with Hume's strict empiricism.

But Hume is not committed by these doctrines to egoistic hedonism. It can be observed that men do show concern and love for others, that among the humane sentiments expressed by men are feelings of sympathy and that these sentiments are also pleasing or useful. Through a careful analysis of benevolence and justice Hume shows how sympathy engenders respect for rights, feelings of obligation, regard for duties to others —in short, the whole moral character of social relationships. Private or individual sentiments, Hume thought, would, in general, be in harmony with the sentiments of most people.

V

Jeremy Bentham (1748–1832), the most typical of all the Utilitarians, was a precocious youth, who entered Oxford at the age of twelve, studied law in accordance with his father's

---

12 *A Treatise of Human Nature*, Everyman's Library (London, 1911), Vol. II, p. 177.
13 *Ibid.*, p. 177.
14 *Ibid.*, p. 178.

15 *Ibid.*, p. 179.

wishes, and took his B.A. degree at fifteen. Although he considered his years at the university wasted, it was during this early period of his life that he discovered the concept of utility in Part III of Hume's *Treatise of Human Nature,* and he declared he felt as if scales had fallen from his eyes. In the *Deontology, or the Science of Morality* he tells how on a visit to Oxford in 1768 he first came upon the phrase "the greatest happiness of the greatest number," with which all Utilitarianism, rightly or wrongly, has since become identified. He discovered the sacred formula in a pamphlet by Priestly entitled *Essay on Government,* then recently published, while he was browsing through a small circulating library in a coffee house near his old college, Queen's. It is generally agreed, however, that the formula was not coined by Priestly but by Francis Hutcheson in his *Enquiry concerning Moral Good and Evil* (1725). Beccaria in the preface to his essay *Dei delitti e delle pene* (1764) used a similar phrase, "la massima felicità divisa nel maggior numero."

In the preface to his first work, *Fragment on Government,* published anonymously in 1776, Bentham stated the conviction held throughout his life, that it is the greatest happiness of the greatest number that is the measure of right and wrong. The *Fragment* was in part an attack on Blackstone's contract theory of government but it was primarily an attempt to apply the principle of utility to the codification of law and to the development of a moral and legal theory. The book

at first attracted considerable attention and was praised and denounced until its authorship became known and then interest in its controversial subject waned. It did, however, bring Bentham to the attention of Lord Shelburne through whom he learned to know Dumont, the Geneva Protestant minister who became one of his most devoted disciples and who popularized the Utilitarian doctrines on the continent. It was also at Lord Shelburne's Bowood that Bentham met Lord Camden, Dunning, Pitt and Romelly, the last of whom became the chief supporter of Utilitarian measures in Parliament.

In 1785 Bentham left England to join his brother Samuel, who had gone to Russia to supervise an industrial establishment. While there he wrote his *Defence of Usury* (1788), which was widely approved. It was while Bentham was in Russia that Paley published his *Principles of Moral and Political Philosophy* and since the book contained ideas similar to those of the great project upon which Bentham had been working for many years and which had already been printed in 1780 but had remained unpublished, his friends urged him to return to England to publish his theories and establish a reputation. Encouraged by such advice and by the success of the *Defence of Usury,* Bentham brought out in 1789 what was perhaps his most important work, *An Introduction to the Principles of Morals and Legislation.*

The violent events in France during 1789 did not greatly disturb Bentham. He did, however, prepare three treatises intended for the use of the new French government: *Essai sur la Représentation* (1788), *Essay on Political Tactics* (1789), sent to Abbé Morrelet for the benefit of the French assembly, and *Draught for a Code for the Organisation of the Judicial Establishment in France* (1790). Need for social and legal reforms at home, not the French revolution, converted Bentham to democracy. Typical of his interest in practical reforms were the *Panopticon,* a scheme he drew up in 1792 for a model prison, which unfortunately the government would not support, and the *Chrestomathia,* published in 1816, an educational scheme for inculcating Utilitarian principles in the children of the middle and upper classes, in which a number of his disciples were interested. With the publication in Paris in 1802 of the *Traités de Législation Civile et Pénale,* compiled by his friend Dumont from his manuscript notes, Bentham's reputation was established on the continent and his writings aroused great interest in America.

In 1808 Bentham met James Mill, who became an intimate friend and devoted follower and who more than any other of his numerous disciples helped him formulate the principles of Utilitarianism. More and more Bentham depended upon his followers to spread his doctrines, frequently supplying them with materials from his own writing. He supported the *Westminster Review,* which first appeared in the spring of 1824, as the semi-official organ of the Utilitarian movement. Gradually the Utilitarians were recognized as one of the leading schools of English political thought and the reform movement they supported grew in strength by attracting allies in governmental circles. After meeting Mill Bentham's political thinking became more radical, but his was a moderate kind of radicalism, always presented in skilful arguments that won a hearing. The fear and opposition that English reformers had to face during the upheavals in France gradually disappeared after the defeat of Napoleon, and English public opinion was more disposed to listen to the Utilitarian spokesmen. It was the Utilitarians under Bentham's leadership who in part were responsible for bringing to the consciousness of the people and their government the need for correcting the many injustices and oppressions that existed in English social life. In the last years of his long life Bentham achieved honor and fame, and although he did not live to see the triumph of his doctrines, the influence of his circle was undoubtedly one of the factors that made the passage of the great Reform Bill possible. After his death in 1832 his last disciple John Bowring published from MSS left by Bentham the *Deontology, or the Science of Morality* (1834). The Mills rejected the book as spurious but it is now generally agreed that it is Bentham's work.

Had Bentham written no more than those portions of his works that deal with general ethical principles, he probably would hold only a minor position in the history of English philosophy. He was not an original thinker and acknowledged his debt to others for the greatest happiness principle. His original contribution was not a new doctrine but the application of a doctrine to specific practical problems of law and government. His *Introduction to the Principles of Morals and Legislation* is only a fragment of a projected long work on the general problems of legislation and the penal code, but his investigations led him back to the foundations of law in morals and to the general principles of ethics. The exposition of these general principles in the opening chapters of the *Introduction* is not always clear and the principles are not thoroughly consistent, but Bentham was not primarily interested in the formulation of a theory and was anxious to get on to an analysis of specific human motives, offenses, and punishments. His ethics was to furnish a foundation for social and political reconstruction.

The central thesis of Bentham's moral philosophy is the principle of hedonisms, i.e., pleasure is the only thing men desire in itself, and pleasure is but synonym for benefit, advantage, good, happiness. Furthermore, each man's pleasure or happiness is as desirable as every other man's. An act, therefore, is right if it tends to augment the happiness and to prevent or to diminish the pain of the person concerned. The famous opening sentences of the *Introduction* declare that "Nature has placed mankind under the governance of two sovereign masters, pain and pleasure. It is for them alone to point out what we ought to do, as well as to determine what we shall do.— They govern us in all we do, in all we say, in all we think."[16] It is not clear whether Bentham here at the start of his treatise is adopting a kind of Hobbesian hedonism, i.e., that all men by their nature always seek pleasure, or whether he is saying that all men ought to seek pleasure. Is he giving a psychological account or description of men's actual behavior, or is he stating what men's motives should be? Is the doctrine egoistic hedonism or is it a normative and ethical hedonism? Bentham, in spite of all his efforts to define and redefine his terms in the text and in elaborate footnotes, is not always clear in his meanings. Perhaps we can say that, as the doctrine is applied, he does hold 1) that pleasure is the only thing men desire in itself, 2) that each man's pleasure is as desirable as any other man's or that each man's pleasure counts as one, and 3) that men are in the main selfish but that they are also benevolent. Men not only seek their own happiness and avoid unhappiness but also seek other people's happiness as well. The formula he employed as his foundation, the principle of utility, became the greatest happiness of the greatest number. At first he thought he had discovered the general principle of his system in Hume's concept of utility but this proved unsatisfactory because utility was often interpreted in a non-hedonistic fashion. Hume had not identified that which we approve with that

16 *The Works of Jeremy Bentham,* ed. by John Bowring (Edinburgh and London, 1843), Vol. I, p. 1.

which is pleasant. If an act is to be approved because of its utility, i.e., if an act is to be judged by its consequences, as Bentham thought, then the goal of a right act has to be indicated. Pleasure, then, must be designated as the supreme end of action for Bentham's teleological ethics. Hume's utility concept also failed to take into consideration the number of interests affected and hence Bentham's standard of right and wrong was formulated as the greatest happiness of the greatest number.

In his later years Bentham found this formulation of his central principle subject to still another difficulty. In the *Deontology* he imagines a community of 4,001 persons, divided into a majority of 2,001 and a minority of 2,000, each possessing an equal share of happiness. Then he supposes that the happiness of the minority is taken from them and distributed among the 2,001. The result will not be the augmentation of happiness but a vast decrease. The implication seems to be that it would be a better course of action to make the 2,001 a little less happy and relieve the 2,000 of some of their misery than to make the 2,001 completely happy and the 2,000 utterly wretched. This is so because, says Bentham, "such is the nature of the receptacle, the quantity of unhappiness it is capable of containing, during any given portion of time, is greater than the quantity of happiness."[17] Apparently Bentham considered the earlier formulation of his principle of utility incorrect and chose to refer to it finally as simply "the greatest happiness principle."

Some interpreters hold that Bentham may have considered the "greatest happiness of the greatest number" an ambiguous statement and simply in need of the further clarification in the *Deontology*, but not fundamentally wrong. On this view Bentham consistently expounded a purely quantitative hedonism. Considerations of number enter into the criterion of rightness of acts because the happiness of men will be close to their numbers since their capacities for pleasure and pain do not vary widely. The distribution of happiness resulting from an act is not an independent criterion of its rightness; quantity remains the major criterion. In view of the passage from the *Deontology* and Bentham's egalitarianism, this interpretation may be open to some question.

Proof of the principle of utility Bentham admits is impossible, "as impossible as needless." The best way to convince a man of the soundness of the principle is to examine others he would have to substitute if he discards utility. Theories that are opposed to utility Bentham divides into two groups: the principle of asceticism and the principle of caprice. The first condemns all acts that produce pleasure and approves all acts that diminish happiness. The second considers an act right simply because some one approves it. Under this principle Bentham lists all traditional theories of moral sense, common sense, the law of

---

[17] *Deontology or The Science of Morality*, ed. by John Bowring (London and Edinburgh, 1834), Vol. I, p. 329.

reason, the law of nature, the will of God and others. Asceticism is really a disguised form of utility since the fear of pain in a future life recommends it to the pious. The principle of caprice is really a denial of all principle, since appeals to moral sense or moral reason are merely attempts to defend private preferences. The avowed standards of value are not capable of verification.

An act is judged by its consequences, in Bentham's view, and hence he attaches much importance to the distinction he draws between motive and intention. By motive he means the desire for pleasure, the driving power behind the will. Although in themselves neutral, motives may lead to good or bad acts. By intention he means all the consequences that are expected by the agent to follow from the act. It is the intention alone that determines the moral worth of an act. From an elaborate analysis of motives and intentions, Bentham is able to establish rules for guiding the legislator in determining punishments for violations of the law.

To Bentham the egoistic tendencies of man do not stand in contradiction to his benevolent inclinations. Certain factors in motivation, various hopes and fears, considerations of likely consequences, tend to draw private and public interests together. These sources of pleasure and pain that make selfishness and benevolence both possible Bentham calls sanctions. They are the forces that govern human conduct and tend to make a man recognize the coincidence of his own greatest happiness

and that of his fellow men. They are four in number: 1) the physical, 2) the political, 3) the moral, and 4) the religious. Later in his life Bentham added three more: 1) the retributive, 2) the sympathetic, and 3) the antipathetic. The basic source of pleasure and pain is, of course, nature, and since the other three, the law, the community, and God himself can operate only through the first, the physical sanction is primary and embraces the other three. The political or legal sanction refers to those forces which are utilized by the state through courts of law to control the actions of its citizens. The moral or popular sanction is meant to designate those compulsions from society which make a man seek approval and avoid disapproval so that he may enjoy the advantages and avoid the disadvantages of such approval or disapproval. The term "moral" for Bentham is closely connected with "mores" and is not meant to suggest that men desire to do what is right for its own sake. Finally, "a supreme invisible being" may also be the source of pleasurable or painful compulsions, and these may be said to issue from the religious sanction and may be experienced either in the present life or in a future life.

Bentham was of the opinion that our pleasures and pains, our likes and dislikes, could all be calculated quantitatively, although he was ready to admit that these calculations could not be made precisely. It is evident to all men that they do roughly quantify their evaluations, and Bentham's well-known "hedonistic calculus" was intended simply to clarify our highly imperfect knowledge of the quantities of pleasure and pain we experience and to help us to calculate more accurately. "The ablest moralist will be he who most successfully applies right calculations to conduct."[18] In order to provide greater accuracy in measuring the quantity of pleasures and pains, Bentham devised rules for estimating. The value of a pleasure or a pain varies with its intensity, duration, certainty or uncertainty, propinquity or remoteness. To these four elements or dimensions of value Bentham added three more: fecundity (the chance a pleasure or pain has of being followed by sensations of the same kind), purity (the chance it has of not being followed by sensations of the opposite kind) and extent (the number of persons who are affected by it). Critics of Bentham's felicific calculus, among them J. S. Mill, have pointed to the neglect of qualitative distinctions, the practical and theoretical impossibility of such quantitative calculations, and to the confusion of measurements of quantity with comparisons of effects. Bentham's Utilitarianism, however, does not stand or fall on his theory of quantitative standards.

VI

James Mill (1773–1836), of humble Scottish parentage, gave early promise of intellectual superiority and attracted the attention of Sir John Stuart, who became his patron. He studied at the University of Edinburgh and

after his course in theology was completed, he was licensed to preach in 1798. With his patron, who was about to take his seat in Parliament, Mill went to London in 1802. He attended debates in the House of Commons and as his interests in political economy and social philosophy developed, he gradually turned to a career in journalism, writing and editing. By 1805 he was making about five hundred pounds a year and felt he was able to marry and support a family. In spite of the fact that Mill was a man of great physical and mental vigor, he found life a struggle against debt and to the constant toil of hack writing he added the labor of preparing a great work on the history of British India. In addition to his professional responsibilities he undertook the direction of the education of his children, a stern and rigorous education of which his first child, John Stuart Mill, has left a famous account in his *Autobiography*.

The elder Mill met Bentham in 1808 and their friendship became the most important influence on Mill's life. For a number of years they lived in the closest intimacy, sharing the same house. Mill was perhaps Bentham's most devoted disciple and no one could have spread propaganda for Benthamism more faithfully; but Mill's ideas were no mere copies of his master's. In truth, Mill's own strong original mind had quite as much influence on Bentham as the theories of the older man had upon the young Scotchman. Mill dropped his interest in theology entirely and devoted all his energies to the propagation of Utilitarian prin-

---

18 *Ibid.*, Vol. II, p. 77.

ciples. More and more through his writings and political activities his career became identified with the reform movement.

In 1811 he met David Ricardo. Of their relationship Bentham said, "I was the spiritual father of Mill and Mill was the spiritual father of Ricardo." In economics Mill was actually a disciple of Ricardo but the two friends influenced each other reciprocally. Mill's *History of British India* was finally published in 1817. Although it lacked imaginative insight, primarily because of Mill's lack of first hand information, it was a solid piece of work and won him the kind of recognition he sought. In 1819 he applied for a position in the India House and was made Assistant to the Examiner of India Correspondence. Through a series of promotions he rose to the position of Examiner by 1836, the year he died. His official duties came to absorb most of his energies in his later years but the appointment did free him from the burden of hack writing and allowed him to devote his leisure time and vacations to formulating his theories, which had long been in incubation, in a systematic fashion. The numerous educational schemes of the Utilitarians had never proven successful. In 1825 agitation was begun for the founding of a university more in line with modern thought than the older universities of Oxford and Cambridge. Mill became one of the most active members of the movement, which succeeded in raising sufficient funds to open in 1828 the institution which became the University of Lon-

don. Official duties prevented Mill from taking the editorship of the *Westminster Review,* which Bentham supported, and accordingly the position was given to Bowring, Bentham's young disciple, but Mill contributed to the journal frequently. His most important work, *Analysis of the Phenomena of the Human Mind,* was published in 1829. Although it was criticized for its philosophical defects by many, it does possess the virtue of a consistent and vigorous statement of the psychology which served as the foundation for Mill's view of utilitarian ethics. Unlike the often confused and ambiguous writings of Bentham, Mill's *Analysis* presents the familiar doctrines with clarity. In 1835 he published a *Fragment on Mackintosh,* a violent attack upon Sir James Mackintosh, who in 1829 had written a treatise on *Ethical Philosophy* for the Encyclopedia Britannica that was highly critical of the Utilitarians. Mill's polemic against the moral sense theory defended by Mackintosh contains the fullest account of his ethics. Before his death he contributed several articles to the *London Review,* an organ of the "philosophical radicals," which was in part under the editorship of his son, John Stuart Mill.

Mill's theory of morals rests upon a foundation of association psychology. In the *Analysis* he explains that all the phenomena of thought can be understood in terms of sensations and ideas, which are copies of sensations. Sensations are pleasant, painful, or merely indifferent. A desire is an idea of a pleasant sensation which has the future associated with it; an aversion is the idea of a painful sensation with which anticipations of future consequences are associated. From his doctrine of association Mill could not develop a satisfactory theory of expectation or anticipation of the future. Nevertheless, he holds that an idea—as he understands the term—can have a future reference and hence a desire, i.e., the idea of a pleasant sensation, may excite to action. This is possible because we associate pleasures and pains with their causes, and when the idea of a future pleasure is associated with our own action as its cause, then a motive for action has come into being. But not all motives lead to action since we may have several motives at the same time and the action from one of them may prevent the others from functioning.

For Mill there can be no freedom of the will. The so-called act of willing is, in fact, a kind of association. All muscular contraction, Mill argues, follows as an effect from sensations or ideas. Since there can be no willing until an idea is present and since ideas cannot be called up voluntarily, mind only appears to have a power over its associations and thus over action. The mind might possibly guide or control a train of associations by preventing an idea from calling up the idea with which it is spontaneously associated. This would call for the injecting of a new idea into the chain and this is impossible because mind cannot originate ideas. Freedom is only apparent freedom.

Like Bentham Mill attaches the mo-

rality of an act not to the motive but to the intention of the act. The motive of an act is the idea of future pleasures associated with our action as its cause; an intention is all the consequences of an act expected by the person doing the act. Motives are neither good nor bad but simply neutral. They are the necessary driving power behind all human action, good or bad. A motive may lead to a good act on one occasion and to a bad act on another. An act is judged by its intention, which is moral when the agent expects a preponderance of good over evil consequences and immoral when the sum of its ascertainable consequences represents more evil than good or when the agent is not concerned whether the consequences will be for a greater good or not. Choice of consequences is always guided by the principle of utility.

Every man, left to himself, would seek his own pleasure without consideration for the pleasures of others. But man is not left to himself; he lives in society and has learned that society has classified some acts as moral and some as immoral. "Those acts, which it is important to other men that each individual should prefer, but in which the individual had not a sufficient interest to secure the performance of them"[19] are moral acts. Those which it is of importance to other men that each individual should abstain from but from which he has no interest in abstaining are immoral acts. In order to secure the performance of the first

[19] *Analysis of the Phenomena of the Human Mind* (London, 1869), Vol. II, pp. 310–311.

class of acts and the non-performance of the second, men had to create means. Rewards and punishments are the devices employed by society. In childhood we are taught to associate the idea of praise with moral acts and blame with the opposite; parents by the repetition of their precepts train their children to act morally from habit long before they can justify their acts rationally. If we inquire how men originally came to classify acts as moral and immoral, the reply is that they did so only because of considerations of utility. Like Bentham Mill rejects all appeals to moral sense, moral reason, right reason, or the beauty or fitness of the moral act. All of these theories, he argues, are disguised forms of utility.

VII

Because of the extraordinary and intensive education to which he was subjected by a rigorous and somewhat despotic father, John Stuart Mill (1806–1873) was prematurely adult. Naturally precocious, he had been taught Greek at the age of three and at eight he was reading Plato's dialogues in the original. He had been compelled as a boy to master the great works of antiquity and to read extensively in the fields of history, literature, logic, mathematics, and political economy. Somehow the youth managed to survive the severe regimen, to assimilate the prodigious learning, and to think for himself. Until his fourteenth year his only companions were his family and his father's friends, such men as

Bentham and Ricardo. He grew up in the midst of the debates and discussions generated by the reforming zeal of the Utilitarians, and it was inevitable that John Mill should become an ardent Benthamite. Through the influence of his father he was given a clerkship in the India House in 1823 and he remained with the company until its extinction in 1858. But with youthful energy he found time to edit Bentham's disorganized manuscripts and prepare for publication Bentham's *Rationale of Judicial Evidence,* to form with other young men he was meeting at the time the Utilitarian Society, and to become a leading figure in the London Debating Society, among whose members were Macaulay, Edward Lytton Bulwer, Wilberforce, and John Stirling. Mill was carried along by the political success of the older Philosophical Radicals and by the influence of their writings and Bentham's new *Westminster Review,* but he was beginning to develop his own views and these were bound to diverge from the extremely narrow and sectarian character of orthodox Utilitarianism.

In his twenty-first year Mill faced a crisis in his life. He was overwhelmed by disillusionment concerning all that he had been striving for, and the foundations of his life seemed to be swept away. The rigors of his intellectual training, the exacting work on behalf of the Bentham reforms, the consuming nature of his two ruling passions, love of knowledge and desire for social betterment, together with the narrowness of his social life, all contributed to the physical and mental depression in which he found himself. The most startling discovery he made was that the whole affective side of his nature had atrophied, due to his father's opposition to all displays of feeling. In 1828 John Mill read Wordsworth's poems, which, he reported, seemed to him to be the very culture of the feelings for which he was searching. Gradually his whole view of life was transformed by the discovery that feeling was at least as valuable as thought. Some of his friends now considered him a renegade and renouncer of the Utilitarian creed, but he reacted courageously against the school of thought in which he had been so carefully trained. Although he continued to express his gratitude and loyalty to his father and Bentham, he recognized the limitations and defects of their program, and by deepening and broadening his own moral and social outlook, he hoped to draw up a new Utilitarianism. Undoubtedly his friendship with Harriet Taylor, the wife of a London business man, the first young woman he had met outside of his own family, was a factor in the transformation that occurred in his thought and character. After the death of her husband, they were married in 1851 and she became a guiding influence on John Mill's thought. There is no reason to doubt his statement that the essay *On Liberty* (1859) was their joint work.

Mill continued his efforts on behalf of reform at the same time that he pursued his studies and writing in the fields of logic and scientific method and political economy. The famous *System of Logic* was published in 1843, *Representative Government* in 1861 and *Utilitarianism* in 1863, having originally appeared in *Fraser's Magazine* in 1861. In 1865 he was elected to Parliament, where he had the opportunity to bring together the intellectual left wing and the working classes, an alliance that was the foundation of British Socialism.

It is against the background of the events of his personal and intellectual life and of the whole reform movement that Mill's brilliant essay on *Utilitarianism* can best be understood, one of the shortest but most significant treatises in modern ethics.

At the start Mill points out that the principle of utility, the greatest happiness principle, has been much misjudged. By some, utility has been interpreted to mean "mere expediency," in the popular sense of the word, or calculating efficiency devoid of all moral significance, and by others it is thought of as the ideal of sensualism. Utility is neither practical usefuless nor "pig-morality." To equate man's pleasures with those of the animals is to fail to recognize the greater range of human pleasures. Qualitative distinctions must be considered. Bentham had said that "quantity of pleasure being equal, pushpin is as good as poetry,"[20] but Mill, while reaffirming the quantitative claims, argues it is absurd to neglect qualitative differences. "It is better to be a human being dissatisfied than a pig satisfied; better to be

---

[20] *Dissertations and Discussions* (New York, 1873), Vol. II, p. 414.

Socrates dissatisfied than a fool satisfied. And if the fool, or the pig, is of a different opinion, it is because they only know of their own side of the question. The other party to the comparison knows both."[21] Bentham had judged an act solely by its intention, not by its motive. Mill recognized that the motive of the act, the inner character and state of mind, are as important in judging human conduct as the consequences. Mere calculation of quantities of pleasure is not sufficient. On the one hand, Mill reaffirms the familiar Utilitarian doctrine that all men seek pleasure, but on the other hand, he recognized that they do seek other goals in the sense that something compels them to accept some pleasures and reject others. Mill calls this "something" a sense of human dignity. There must be an evaluation of pleasures; psychological hedonism must be supplemented by ethical hedonism. Not only was the problem of grading pleasures a difficult one for Mill but perhaps even more perplexing was the problem of accounting for men's sacrificing their pleasures for others. Why is the general happiness more desirable than private happiness? For almost a hundred years Mill has been criticized for confusing the desired and the desirable and for attempting to derive the ethical demand that each man should desire and promote the general happiness from the fact that each man does desire his own happiness. There are those who find no contradictions in the arguments; the difficulty lies in misunderstanding Mill's meaning.[22] Others have held that the principle of utility, as Mill expounded it, is not incompatible with a theory of perfectionism;[23] the greatest happiness principle implies the attainment of the highest human goals.

Bibliography

Ernest Albee, *A History of English Utilitarianism* (New York, 1902).

R. P. Anschutz, *The Philosophy of J. S. Mill* (Oxford, 1953).

Alexander Bain, *John Stuart Mill: A Criticism with Personal Recollections* (New York, 1882).

———, *James Mill, a Biography* (London, 1882).

Karl Britton, *John Stuart Mill* (London, 1953).

C. D. Broad, *Five Types of Ethical Theory* (New York, 1930).

Élie Halévy, *The Growth of Philosophic Radicalism* (London, 1928).

J. S. Mill, *Dissertations and Discussions* (New York, 1873), essay on Bentham.

John Plamenatz, *The English Utilitarians* (Oxford, 1949).

W. D. Ross, *Foundations of Ethics* (Oxford, 1939).

L. A. Selby-Bigge, *British Moralists* (Oxford, 1897).

Leslie Stephen, *The English Utilitarians* (London, 1900).

R. A. Tsanoff, *The Moral Ideals of Our Civilization* (New York, 1942).

Martin Eshleman
Carleton College

---

[21] *Ibid.*, Vol. III, pp. 312–313.

[22] *Philosophy and Psycho-analysis,* John Wisdom, p. 107.

[23] *The Impasse in Ethics–and a Way Out,* Brand Blanshard, University of California Publications in Philosophy, Vol. 28, No. 2, (Berkeley, 1955), pp. 108–111.

V

vaisya: *see* Hindu Ethics.

Valencia, G.: *see* Jesuits, the, Moral Theology of.

value: *see* Aquinas, Thomas, Moral Views of; Ayer, Alfred J.; Broad, C. D.; Clarke, Samuel; Dante, Alighieri; French Existentialism and Moral Philosophy; Green, T. H.; Hindu Ethics; intrinsic value; Kant, I.; Khomiakov, Alexey; Machiavelli, Niccolo; Major Ethical Viewpoints; Meta-ethics and Normative Ethics; Minor Socratics; Moore, George Edward; Moral Philosophy in America; Morals and Religion; Mundurucú Indians, A Dual System of Ethics; Puritan Morals; Rio Grande Pueblo Indians; Scheler, Max; Schlick, Moritz; Soviet Morality, Current; Stoics, the.

value judgments: *see* Dewey, John; Language and Ethics.

value of man: *see* China, Moral Philosophies of; nature of man.

value statements: *see* Ayer, Alfred J.

value theory: *see* Dewey, John; Ross, Sir (William) David; Russell, Bertrand; Soviet Morality, Current.

values, conflict of: *see* Hartmann, Nicolai.

values, hierarchy of: *see* Aquinas, Thomas, Moral Views of; Scheler, Max; Schlick, Moritz.

values and value experience: *see* Hartmann, Nicolai.

Van den Ende: *see* Spinoza.

vanity: *see* Minor Socratics; Muslim Morals; Tolstoy, Leo.

Vasquez, G.: *see* Jesuits, the, Moral Theology of.

Vedanta: *see* Hindu Ethics.

Vedas, The: *see* China, Moral Philosophies of; Hindu Ethics.

veneration: *see* Clarke, Samuel; worship.

vengeance: *see* Aboriginals of Yirkalla; Dante, Alighieri; Tapirapé Morals, Some Aspects of; Zuni Indians, Morals of.

verification principle: *see* Ayer, Alfred J.

Vermeersch, A.: *see* Jesuits, the, Moral Theology of.

vice: *see* Augustine and Morals; Aztec Morals; bad, the; Cudworth, Ralph; evil; Hindu Ethics; Sophists, the.

vice, vices, the: *see* Aquinas, Thomas, Moral Views of; China, Moral Philosophies of; Cooper, Anthony Ashley; Dante, Alighieri; evil; Hutcheson, Francis; Navaho Morals; Plato; Riffian Morals; Utilitarianism; wickedness; Wollaston, William.

vicissitudes: *see* Stoics, the.

Vienna Circle: *see* Ayer, Alfred J.; Language and Ethics; Schlick, Moritz.

violence: *see* Augustine and Morals; Dante, Alighieri; Major Ethical Viewpoints; Navaho Morals; Quak-

W

Waelder, Robert: *see* Freud, Sigmund.

Wagner, G.: *see* Pakot, The Moral System of.

Wagner, R.: *see* Nietzsche, Friedrich; Schopenhauer, Arthur.

Waismann: *see* Schlick, Moritz.

wants: *see* Minor Socratics.

war: *see* Aboriginals of Yirkalla; Aztec Morals; China, Moral Philosophies of; Dewey, John; Hammurapi, Code of; Hindu Ethics; Hobbes, Thomas; Marxist Theory of Morals; Mundurucu Indians, A Dual System of Ethics; Puritan Morals; Quakerism, Classical, The Morality of; Riffian Morals; Rio Grande Pueblo Indians; Schopenhauer, Arthur; Tolstoy, Leo; Zuni Indians, Morals of.

waste: *see* Navaho Morals.

wastefulness: *see* Zuni Indians, Morals of.

waste of time: *see* Puritan Morals.

Wayland, Francis: *see* Moral Philosophy in America.

weakness: *see* China, Moral Philosophies of.

wealth: *see* Hindu Ethics; Jewish Ethics and Its Civilization; Machiavelli, Niccolo; Navaho Morals; Stoics, the; Zuni Indians, Morals of.

weather control: *see* Rio Grande Pueblo Indians.

Weininger, O.: *see* Schopenhauer, Arthur.

welfare: *see* Butler, Joseph.

well being: *see* Clarke, Samuel; health; Rio Grande Pueblo Indians.

Wesley, John: *see* Butler, Joseph; Puritan Morals.

Westermarck, E.: *see* Major Ethical Viewpoints.

Whichcote: *see* Cudworth, Ralph; More, Henry.

whipping: *see* Puritan Morals.

whittling: *see* Puritan Morals.

wickedness: *see* evil; Freud, Sigmund; vice.

widowhood: *see* Augustine and Morals.

wife beating: *see* Aboriginals of Yirkalla; Puritan Morals.

Wilberforce: *see* Utilitarianism.

Wilkins: *see* More, Henry.

will, the: *see* Augustine and Morals; Cudworth, Ralph; Cumberland, Richard; Green, T. H.; Hindu Ethics; Hobbes, Thomas; Jesuits, the, Moral Theology of; Kant, I.; Marxist Theory of Morals; More, Henry; Psychology and Morals; Schlick, Moritz; Schopenhauer, Arthur; Spinoza.

will to power, the: *see* Major Ethical Viewpoints; Nietzsche, Friedrich.

Williams, Roger: *see* Puritan Morals.

Winthrop, John: *see* Puritan Morals.

wisdom: *see* Aristotle; Augustine and Morals; Dante, Alighieri; Dewey, John; Hindu Ethics; Jewish Ethics

641

and Its Civilization; Liguori, St. Alphonsus and Catholic Moral Philosophy; Muslim Morals; Plato; Socrates; Sophists, the; Stoics, the; Zoroastrian Morals.

Wisdom Literature: *see* Christian Moral Philosophy; Jewish Ethics and Its Civilization.

Wise, John: *see* Moral Philosophy in America.

wish fulfillment: *see* Freud, Sigmund.

wishful thinking: *see* Freud, Sigmund.

witchcraft: *see* Aztec Morals; Mundurucú Indians, A Dual System of Ethics; Navaho Morals; Rio Grande Pueblo Indians; Zuni Indians, Morals of.

witnesses: *see* Hammurapi, Code of.

Wittgenstein, Ludwig: *see* Ayer, Alfred J.; Language and Ethics; Major Ethical Viewpoints; Schlick, Moritz.

Wollaston, William

William Wollaston was born at Coton-Clanfor in Staffordshire in March 1659. He studied at Cambridge, graduating in 1681. He became assistant-master of the Birmingham grammar school, taking holy orders in the Church of England while in that position. In 1688 he inherited money from an uncle that enabled him to retire to London where he married and devoted the remainder of his life to domestic matters and the study of philosophy and natural religion. He had eleven children. His one book, *The Religion of Nature Delineated,* was printed privately in 1722. A corrected and revised edition appeared in 1724 and six more editions in the next ten years. Wollaston died October 1724.

Despite an immediate popularity with some philosophers as well as with the general public Wollaston's moral philosophy has been considered to be the rationalistic approach to morality carried to an extreme that made it absurd. It was so regarded not only by several contemporaries and immediate successors, e.g., Francis Hutcheson and John Clarke of Hull, but also by some twentieth century writers, e.g., R. M. Kydd. Wollaston's theory has been taken to be the doctrine that moral rightness is the same as truth and moral wrongness the same as falsity, because of his principle that no act that "interferes" with a true proposition can be right. It has been held e.g., that for Wollaston the moral vice of murder is contained in the denial that the victim is a man. (Leslie Stephen, *History of English Thought in the 18th Century,* vol. II, p. 9.)

John Clarke in *Examination of the notion of Good and Evil, Advanced in a late book entitled the Religion of Nature Delineated* (1725) ridicules the doctrine for its implication that a man performs morally right acts by spending his time "thrumming over such worthy and weighty propositions as these, 'a man's no horse, a horse no cow, a cow no bull, nor a bull an ass'." Francis Hutcheson was more gentle, asking "Is it virtue to say at Christmas that the mornings are sharp?" (*Essay on the Passions*). R. M. Kydd has more recently maintained (*Reason and Conduct in Hume's Treatise,* 1946) that Wollaston is to be interpreted as holding that when an act asserts a false proposition it is not merely the falsity but the self-contradiction that constitutes the moral wrongness of the act:

> . . . when an act asserts a false proposition . . . in asserting it I am contradicting myself. I am asserting both *a* and *not-a* at the same time; I am in fact making two contradictory assertions. (*Reason and Conduct in Hume's Treatise*, p. 32.)

A careful consideration of Wollaston's doctrines, however, indicates that these interpretations fail to do justice to him.

The Religion of Nature Delineated was written in answer to two questions:

> I. Is there really any such thing as natural religion properly so called?
>
> II. If there is, what is it? (p. 1.)

The most direct answer which Wollaston offers is found in his section on obligation. He there offers what he calls a "summary of natural religion:"

> They who are capable of discerning truth, tho not all truths, and of acting conformably to it, tho not in all cases, are nevertheless obliged to do these as far as they are able; or, it is the duty of such a being sincerely to endeavour to practice reason; not to contradict any truth, by word or deed, and in short, to treat everything as being what it is. (p. 111.)

Whatever the genesis of Wollaston's doctrine then, it is clear that he sets out to deal with the problem of obligation. His book is written to tell what natural religion is and his answer is that it is the sum of men's moral obligations. In the pages which intervene between the question and the answer, however, he has something to say about the way in which it is to be known that a thing is being treated as being what it is and why this is obligatory.

Wollaston did not simply rush into the view that acts are morally good or evil if they are true or false, or self-consistent or self-contradictory. This is apparent from the care with which he introduces his "preliminary propositions:"

1. That act which may be denominated morally good or evil must be the act of a being capable of distinguishing, choosing, and acting for himself.
2. Those propositions are true which express things as they are: or, truth is the conformity of those words or signs by which things are exprest, to the things themselves. (Definition.)
3. A true proposition may be denied, or things may be denied to be what they are, by deeds as well as by express words or another proposition.
4. No act (whether word or deed) of any being, to whom moral good and evil are imputable, that interferes with any true proposition, or denies anything to be what it is, can be right. (pp. 5–16.)

In the third axiom Wollaston attempts to clarify the vagueness of other rationalistic appeals to truth, falsity, and logical consistency in ethics. Although he sometimes states that acts *are* statements, he is careful, in instances where difficulties of interpretation arise, to point out that in the sense in which acts assert propositions they are extremely ambiguous. The first axiom is his attempt to specify the realm within which such propositions are morally significant. And in these cases he almost always speaks of the contradiction of the statements which "correspond to," are "implied by," are "equivalent to," or are "imported by" the acts or the situations. He considers the second axiom to be an axiom of translation according to which an act may be taken as a sign of a statement, the statement substituted for the act and inferences drawn in the usual way. He is not clear about the relation between the act and the statement or about how the statement is inferred from the act. But he does say that not all the statements which are "signified" by the act are relevant to the moral judgment: Take for example the theft of a horse:

If a man steals a horse, and rides away upon him, he may be said indeed by riding him to use him as a horse, but not as the horse of another man, who gave him no licence to do this. He does not therefore consider him as being what he is, unless he takes in the respect he bears to the true owner. (p. 35.)

In other words, in the situation where horse H is owned by person P there is, among a large number of truths "corresponding to" this situation, one statement *s* which asserts
H is owned by P.
Corresponding to the act of P, when he steals H, along with a large number of others, there is the statement, *not s:*
H is not owned by P.
The two statements are contradictory and in other respects are in accordance with the four axioms and additional ones laid down by Wollaston. But he does *not* say that the act of theft *is,* or

asserts a self-contradiction. Most significantly it is a violation of a right by an act.

The contradictoriness of *s* and *not s,* then, is one which, in so far as it has a peculiarly moral significance, is restricted by a great many qualifications. For instance, in estimating the degree of vice or virtue of an act he maintains that it is necessary to consider the truth or falsity of action—expressed statements about the happiness of the moral agents involved. Since happiness is pleasure and there can be either "higher" or "lower" pleasures, an act that expresses a truth about a higher pleasure is more virtuous than one expressing a truth about a lower pleasure. He also appeals to the "importance" of truths that are expressed or violated by acts and has an interesting way of dealing quantitatively with degrees of virtue and vice in terms of it. The degree of vice or virtue of an act is measured by the number of truths which it asserts or denies. Thus, for example, it is ten thousand times worse to defraud a person of an estate worth ten thousand pounds than to steal a book from him worth one pound, since the act of fraud in effect denies the statement ten thousand times which the theft denies but once.

Wollaston's emphasis upon the importance of happiness has led some commentators to regard his rationalistic analysis and framework as an irrelevant formalism arbitrarily joined to an essentially simple theory that morally right acts are those that are conducive to the happiness of moral agents. But there is an alternative in-

644

terpretation that falls somewhere between this interpretation and the other extreme interpretation that he identifies morality with formal categories. It is that his formalism is largely, although not entirely, an analogy to which he appeals in order to strengthen his attempt to deal with the concept of obligation.

The importance of human desire and sensitivity have been apparent from the beginning in Wollaston's postulates, particularly the first and fourth. The analogy between moral categories and logical ones has all along, then, been an adjunct to his view, although not an irrelevant one. This is apparent in many passages in addition to his postulates. For example,

. . . it is manifest that there is *as* certainly moral good and evil *as* there is true and false; and that there is *as* natural and immutable a difference between them *as* between these, the difference being *at bottom* the same thing. (pp. 32–33.) [my italics.]

There are many acts . . . such as constitute the character of a man's conduct in life which have in nature, and would be taken by any indifferent judge to have a signification and to imply some proposition, as plainly to be understood as if it were declared in words: and therefore if what such acts declare to be is not, they must contradict truth, *as much as* any false proposition or assertion can. (p. 7.) [my italics.]

These passages and others indicate that the formal analogy is not used as an argument but as a means of making an assertion in a vivid way. That is,

he does not use the doctrine that acts may be interpreted as assertions as a known similarity between logic and morals which adds to the credibility that logic and morals will also be found to agree in some other specified respect. The force of the analogy is to enliven the moral significance of instances of wilful violation of justified expectation, innocent pleasure, or personal convenience by showing how, under a certain interpretation of acts, their rightness or wrongness can be correlated with truth or falsity.

Wollaston's position, then, may be represented as follows: Acting as if 'p' were true when 'not p' is true, or conversely, is related to morality as believing that 'p' is true when 'not p' is true, or conversely, is related to abstract (logical or mathematical) theory. His qualification of the content of 'p' in the moral side of the analogy is so hedged with reference to pleasure, convenience, and expectations that truth, falsity, or contradictoriness are not in fact the criteria of virtue or vice. In response to the objection that his view introduces moral right and wrong into the sphere of inanimate objects, for example, he replies

. . . inanimate things cannot be considered as capable of wrong treatment, if the respect they bear to living things is separated from them. (p. 51.)

There are, to be sure, passages which support the more extreme interpretation of the identity of morality with formal categories but they usually have a theological significance. One of these passages refers to the general principle that everything is what it is. Any instance of a denial of this principle, Wollaston says, is an instance of an immoral act. It is not immoral, however, because there is a contradiction between 'Everything is what it is.' and 'Something is not what it is.' It is immoral because the first statement is a part of Divine decree whereas the second statement is a contradiction of this decree:

Things cannot be denied to be what they are, in any instance or manner whatsoever, without contradicting axioms and truths eternal. For such are these: everything is what it is; that which is done, cannot be undone; and the like, and then if those truths be considered as having always subsisted in the Divine mind, to which they have always been true, and which differs not from the Deity himself, to do this is to act not only in opposition to His government or sovereignty, but to His nature also: which, if He be perfect, and there be nothing in Him but what is most right, must also upon this account be most wrong. (p. 19.)

In spite of the removal of paradox which is accomplished by the analogical interpretation, however, the question still remains whether the analogy between truth and morality accounts for obligation. Wollaston puts the question from a hypothetical objector:

If a man can find out truth, may he not want the power of acting agreeably to it? (p. 109.)

Wollaston's explicit answer is his doctrine of obligation which was summarized at the beginning of this article. It is clear that there he offers no answer at all to the question whether the recognition of truth is sufficient to motivate the will, or as he puts it, to "supply the power of acting agreeably to it." He merely restates that there is an obligation to act agreeably to truth, in the sense in which he has explained that phrase. He has, however, in his general doctrine offered something more than this summary makes explicit. The analogy has a hortatory significance for Wollaston since he believed that the avoidance of contradiction in theory was an end on which everyone agreed. He drew the analogy between morality and abstract theory then, to indicate that there was as good a reason to accept the obligation of consistency in action as there was to accept the obligation of consistency in thought. But he recognized that mere consistency was a pale goal to hold up as an ideal. So he brought in the concept of happiness and its degrees. The consistency which he was urging finally, then, was an ideal of action which was consistent with the greatest happiness of rational, free, desiderative, sensitive beings. The logical analogy was a means of enforcing the "ought" which is implicit throughout: Because morality, as my analogy has shown, is similar to logic on the basis of certain postulates, the aims in morality which correspond to the aims in logic ought to determine action in the moral sphere as the aims of theory determine thought in the theoretical sphere. A second question still remains: "Even if it be granted that you have described what obligation is, have you shown that in the situations where you say there is an obligation there is any guarantee that the acts which you describe as obligatory will be performed?" To this Wollaston has no satisfactory answer. His final word is that everyone is obliged to act conformably to truth so far as he is able.

Bibliography

William Wollaston, *The Religion of Nature Delineated* (London, Knapton, 1724).
John Clarke, *Examination of the Religion of Nature Delineated* (London, 1725).
C. G. Thompson, *The Ethics of William Wollaston* (Boston, Gorham Press, 1922).
L. Stephen, *History of English Thought in the 18th Century* (London, Murray, 1876), Chapters 2, 3, 9.
R. M. Kydd, *Reason and Conduct in Hume's Treatise* (Oxford, Clarendon, 1946) Chapter I.

Bernard Peach
Duke University

Wollaston, William: *see* Balguy, John; Clarke, Samuel; Moral Philosophy in America; Price, Richard; Reid, Thomas.

women: *see* Aboriginals of Yirkalla; Riffian Morals.
wonder: *see* Hindu Ethics.
Woolman, John: *see* Quakerism, Classical, The Morality of.
Word of God: *see* Puritan Morals.
Wordsworth: *see* Utilitarianism.
work: *see* Hindu Ethics; labor, manual; Marxist Theory of Morals; toil.
worry: *see* China, Moral Philosophies of.
worship: *see* Aztec Morals; Clarke, Samuel; Hindu Ethics; Puritan Morals.
worth: *see* Stoics, the; value.
worthiness: *see* Ross, Sir (William) David.
Worthington: *see* More, Henry.
wrong: *see* Aboriginals of Yirkalla; Ayer, Alfred J.; Balguy, John; Broad, C. D.; Clarke, Samuel; Major Ethical Viewpoints; Marxist Theory of Morals; Moral Philosophy in America; Price, Richard; Prichard, H. A.; Primitive Morals; Reid, Thomas; Rio Grande Pueblo Indians; Sophists, the; Utilitarianism; Wollaston, William.
Wulamba, the: *see* Aboriginals of Yirkalla.
wu-wei: *see* China, Moral Philosophies of.

X

Xenophon: *see* Sophists, the.

Y

Yahya Ibn 'Adi: *see* Muslim Morals.

Yang Chu: *see* China, Moral Philosophies of.

Yasna, Book of: *see* Zoroastrian Morals.

yi: *see* China, Moral Philosophies of.

Yin and Yang: *see* China, Moral Philosophies of.

Yirkalla: *see* Aboriginals of Yirkalla.

young, the: *see* children; Psychology and Morals; Puritan Morals.

Z

Zalkind: *see* Soviet Morality, Current.
Zarathushtra: *see* Zoroastrian Morals.
zeal: *see* More, Henry.
Zeno of Citium: *see* Stoics, the.
Zeni, The Eleatic: *see* Sophists, the.

Zoroastrian Morals

From the very first appearance of man upon earth there has been "religion" in some shape or other. Man is distinguished from other animals by his possession of the faculty of thought. So from the very first man began to think of the relations between himself and everything else that surrounded him. It must have been obvious to him that he was extremely helpless and small amidst the stupendous forces of Nature that surrounded him. So in course of time his human reason led him to postulate some powers outside himself which were far greater and which he could hardly control. He also perceived clearly the regularity with which these forces of Nature operated, as in the ordered succession of day and night and of the seasons. And thus he soon deduced that everything happened in obedience to some definite "law." When this idea of "law" arose the next inevitable step was the notion of a "Law-giver," a "Ruler" and a "Creator." The idea of a Creator and the consideration of the relations which should subsist between man and

his Creator led ultimately to what we term "religion." The Creator was, of course, invisible to man's physical eyes, but He could be grasped somehow by the mind, and obviously He was endowed with qualities and faculties which were the highest and noblest which man could conceive.

Besides Nature man was surrounded also by his fellow men. His relations with them were determined by what we may call the "Moral Code." Even among the most primitive people there must have been degrees of goodness and virtue. There must have been individuals who possessed courage, or affection, or the spirit of helpfulness, or that of self-sacrifice in greater measure than the majority of their fellows. Such would be accepted as Rulers or Teachers. These would soon perceive that there were also "laws" governing the relations of human beings among themselves. And they proceeded to formulate these laws and laid down the moral code for the guidance of man's conduct to his fellowmen.

Very early also it was clearly perceived that religion and morality could not exist separately. "As above, so below"—and so morality should follow the loftiest precepts of religion and should draw its inspiration from religion. The laws of morality are ulti-

653

mately a special application of the Laws of God and of Nature.

Each nation developed its special set of moral laws. Still, because the fundamental laws of Nature (or God) are unchanging, the fundamental laws of morality are very similar in all lands and among all nations.

The Message of Zarathushtra was given to the people of Iran several thousand years ago.[1] This Message has brought solace to millions of human hearts during many centuries, and even today thousands of human beings find comfort in His Words.[2] Not only that but the Message of Zarathushtra was a message for the whole of humanity, because He was a World-Teacher and Zarathushtra's religion has been one of the great world-religions. It has a universal appeal and it contains Truths which can be accepted by all mankind.

Zarathushtra was among the earliest of the great teachers of humanity and He has left His mark very deep upon the religion He taught. Three special features distinguished His teaching. (i). His teaching is never opposed to human reason, and therefore it can be accepted universally. (ii). His teaching about sin and evil appeals primarily to

[1] The date of the Prophet has been given variously by different people. Pliny, Xanthus, Plato and Plutarch place him in eras varying from 6000 B.C. to 1000 B.C. Some of the modern authors give dates varying from 1200 B.C. to 800 B.C. (See Masani, *The Religion of Good Life*, p. 31.) It is not the *date* of the Prophet but His *message* that is of greater importance.

[2] The Zoroastrians of Ancient Iran numbered many millions. Their number today has dwindled down to about 125,000 in the whole world.

our reason. And (iii). His teaching about the nature of God, our Creator and Ruler, and about the methods of realizing the Supreme during our life in the world are also such as could be easily understood by ordinary human beings. The whole is an entirely *practical* way of life and from the very first we have in Zarathushtra's teachings a very efficient Moral Code. In fact we would be fully justified in calling Zoroastrianism "the Religion of the Good Life."

(i). In the very beginning of His teaching Zarathushtra gives us what might be called "The Charter of Spiritual Liberty." He says:

Hear with your ears the Highest Truths I preach,
And with your clear minds weigh them with care,
Before you choose which of two Paths to tread,
Deciding man by man, each one for each.[3]

This sounds refreshingly modern, leaving each human being free to choose his path for himself. This in itself constitutes the universal appeal of Zarathushtra's Teaching.

The "Highest Truths" He teaches are the great Laws of Nature—not understood *physically* as in modern science, but *spiritually* as all Prophets have done. They tried to understand Nature and Nature's forces, and through Nature they reached up to Nature's God.

A short time after the passing of Zarathushtra a detailed declaration of His Creed was compiled. It is known

[3] Yasna 30.2.

as Section 12 (*Hā*) of the Book of Yasna. There we find this universal Faith described in some detail.

The Faith which is of the waters and of the trees and of the bountiful Mother-Earth, the Faith which is of the Lord of Life Himself (who created the Earth and the Holy Ones), the Faith which is of Zarathushtra . . . and of everyone of the Saviours who act truly and righteously, of that Faith and a follower of that Law am I, a worshipper of the Creator of All.

I am a Mazdā-worshipper, a follower of Zarathushtra, a devoted and ardent believer in that Faith. I solemnly dedicate myself to the true-conceived thought, I solemnly dedicate myself to the true-spoken word, I solemnly dedicate myself to the true-performed action.

I dedicate myself solemnly to the excellent Faith of Mazdā-worship, which is quarrel-removing, weapon-lowering, which teaches self-reliance and holiness. This Faith is, among all that are and among all that shall be, the greatest, the holiest and the best—this Faith of Ahura and revealed by Zarathushtra.

I attribute all Good unto Ahura-Mazdā.[4]

The universality and the fundamental morality of the Creed of Zarathushtra are set forth here in very clear words. The three Commandments of the Zoroastrian Faith are also given here—true-conceived Thought (*Hu-mata*), true-spoken Word (*Hu-ukhta*), and

true-performed Action (*Hu-varshta*). These three Commandments embody everything that can be included in any moral code.

(ii). Zarathushtra's conception of sin and evil is the special feature of His Message. And it is a point which has been misunderstood by most students of Zoroastrianism. It is His so-called teaching of Dualism, of the Twin Mainyu.[5]

These two Mainyu are *two mental states or attitudes of the human mind* according as the person is attracted by things of the Earth or things of the Spirit. The words of the Prophet Himself are quite clear on this point.

Now unto eager listeners will I speak
Of the Two Mainyu Mazdā did create;

. . . .

That ye, grown perfect, may attain His Light. (1)

. . . .

The first created were these Mainyu Twain,
As Twin Co-workers they reveal themselves;
Yet in each thought and word and deed these Two
Are ne'er agreed;—one's Good, the other's Bad;
And of these Two the Wise do choose aright,
The Universe choose not thus,—and go astray. (3)

---

[4] Yasna 12.7–9.

[5] The word Mainyu is usually translated by "Spirit." But this rendering does not bring out fully the underlying idea, because "Spirit" would imply some factor or power *outside* the human being. Whereas Mainyu (from root *man—*, to think) definitely implies the mental attitude of the human being himself, and residing *within* him.

And when together did these Mainyu Twain
Foregather at Creation's early dawn,
LIFE did One make, the Other made NOT-LIFE;
And thus Creation's purpose is achieved;
Dark is the Mind that clings unto the False,
But brightly shines the Mind that holds to Truth. (4)
Of these Twain Mainyu he that is the False
Doth ever choose performing evil deeds,
But Righteousness doth choose the Holy One;
He who would clothe himself in Light of Heav'n
He who would satisfy Lord Ahura,
Let him through deeds of Truth choose Mazdā's Way. (5)
The False One did not ever choose aright
Because the Arch-Deluder close to them
Approached, as they disputing stood in doubt;
Thus did they choose the Mainyu of Worst Thought,
Misled by him they rushed away to wrath,
And thus did they pollute our mortal life. (6)[6]

The first point to note in this long quotation is that the Two Mainyu are creatures of Mazdā, the Creator of the Universe. God creates *both* Light and Darkness, Good and Evil.[7] These Two are the 'Twin Co-workers.' They both have equal power over the human being, but the man is absolutely free to choose either of the two. The wise, however, choose rightly; the unwise do not and go astray. So what we call "sin," or "going astray," is only a result of spiritual ignorance. These Two

Mainyu create between themselves LIFE and NOT-LIFE. The essential negative aspect of evil is thus made clear.[8] It has been repeatedly asserted in Zoroastrianism that evil shall be ultimately defeated and only Truth shall triumph in the end. But we need not therefore conclude that all evil in life is a mere negation. The Prophet's Teaching clearly brings out the fact that *as far as human life upon earth is concerned,* evil is something very real and has to be resisted "with the Inner Spirit's sword,"[9] and all falsehood has to be given over into the hands of Truth.[10] Zarathushtra wants His people to be ever alert against evil and to work as soldiers of Truth battling against falsehood. Those who go astray do so because they are deluded by the Arch-Deluder (the Evil Mainyu, *Aka-Mainyu*) and they are lured away by his false promises of happiness upon earth. The duty of a good soldier of Zarathusthra is also to point out the Path of Truth to those gone astray. In this he is "guided by Law Divine or by his human heart."[11] The fight is essentially the fight against temptations and ignorance. The ultimate victory of

---

6 Yasna 30.1, 3, 4, 5, 6.
7 Yasna 44.5. Cf. also Isaiah, 45.7.

---

8 The true significance of the negative aspect of evil has been very clearly brought out in Goethe's *Faust,* Part I. There Mephistopheles introduces himself as "part of that power which still produceth good while ever scheming ill." Asked to explain this "riddle" Mephistopheles goes on to say that he is "the Spirit that evermore denies! Thus all the elements which ye Destruction, Sin or briefly Evil name as my particular element I claim."
9 Yasna 31.18.
10 Yasna 30.8.
11 Yasna 46.5.

Truth is certain. The final goal of every human being is becoming perfect and being in constant union with the Supreme. A "sinner" may for the time being seem to succeed, but a time shall surely come when all his success turns to dust and ashes and then he begins to understand the Law of Truth—the Eternal Law of God—and "his mind shall thenceforth retrace its steps";[12] and he shall walk straight to his goal and attain Perfection and Immortality.

Understood thus in its true spirit Zarathushtra's teaching about the two Mainyu appears to emphasize the essential dualism in Nature, between Life and Not-Life, between Eternal and Transitory, between Spirit and Matter. As man overcomes his spiritual ignorance and gains Wisdom he advances along the Path to God.

(iii). The ancient Aryas, the ancestors of the Hindus of India and of the Zoroastrians of Iran, were worshippers of the Powers of Nature. Each of these Powers had a special circle of worshippers. Yet above and beyond them all, the ancient singers recognized the one Reality, their Creator, from whom all these Powers had emanated.[13] Thus some idea of a Supreme Being had already emerged at a very early period. Zarathushtra brought this idea to the forefront and made it the foundation of his Message. The Supreme Being has no form and is invisible and intangible to any of our senses. He can be perceived only with "the inner eye of the

Soul." All that we know as "good" and "true" and "beautiful" are but varied aspects of the Supreme Being. He is the Creator and Sustainer both of our body and our soul. He is Lord of both Life and Matter. Indeed, Zarathushtra gave Him a *double* name—*Ahura-Mazdā*—which means 'Lord of Life (and) Creator of Matter.'[14] Being formless and intangible He can only be understood through His varied "Aspects" or "Rays" (as I prefer to call them). These latter are named by Zarathushtra *Amesha-Spenta* (the Holy Immortals). These in later Zoroastrian theology correspond roughly to the Arch-angels of Judaism and Christianity. And they are placed at the head of the heavenly host. These "Rays" form the essential basis of the Message of the Prophet of Iran. They are six in number—1) Truth, 2) Love, 3) Service of Humanity, 4) Faith (or Piety), 5) Perfection, and 6) Immortality.[15] These six together with Ahura-Mazda Himself constitute the "Supreme Heptad"—the *Seven* who act with one accord.[16] In order to understand the Godhead

12 Yasna 30.10.

13 Rig-Veda, i.164.46 says quite clearly, "the Reality is one, the wise by many names call it."

14 *Ahura,* from *ahu,* life, means "Lord of Life." *Mazda* is derived from *maz,* great or vast and *da—,* to create. And so the name means "Creator of the vast (material) universe."

15 Other scholars have taken these names somewhat differently. My special point of view has been explained clearly and in some detail in the Introductory essay on "The Holy Word of the Religion of Zarathushtra and the Holy Immortals" in my book on *The Divine Songs of Zarathushtra* (Bombay, 1951), pp. 1–16. See also *Religion in the Twentieth Century* (New York, 1948), edited by Vergilius Ferm, pp. 22–27.

16 Yasht 13.82–84.

657

the human being has to realize within himself, fully and harmoniously, each of these. With their full realization comes salvation and perfect eternal life. It is also noteworthy that the first three Holy Immortals represent the Father-Aspect of Ahura-Mazda, while the other three represent the Mother-Aspect and are feminine in gender.[17]

The first among the Holy Immortals is *Asha*. The name is hard to translate accurately. It implies essentially the Eternal Law in accordance with which the Plan of God works out. This necessarily connotes Truth and Righteousness.[18] Asha is the very foundation of the Message of Zarathushtra. In the Divine Songs of Zarathushtra (the *Gathas*) the great adversary of Asha is *Druj* (Untruth). We are also told that the man who clings to Truth shall attain the lofty abode of the righteous "radiant and all-glorious." In one passage in the later hymns the wish is expressed that "through the best Asha, through the highest Asha may we get a vision of Thee, may we come near unto Thee, may we abide in full companionship with Thee."[19] And at the very end of the Book of Yasna we have the statement: "There is but one Path, the Path of Truth (Asha); all other paths are no-paths."[20] In later theology Asha is the "guardian Angel" of humanity. And the Sacred Fire, the

outward symbol of the Faith, is also named *Asha-Vahishta* (the best Asha).

Vohu Mano, the second Holy Immortal, is usually translated "Good Mind." But the name implies something far deeper; it should be translated, "Loving Mind." The name reminds us of what is taught by all Teachers that "God is Love." In the very beginning of his songs Zarathustra says:

Fain would I, Mazdā-Ahura, to You
Reach up through Vohu-Man', devoted Love.[21]

And in later theology Vohu-Mano is the Guardian of all animal creation.

Vohu-Kshathra (or *Kshathra-Vairya*) connotes the strength (the Loving Strength) of the Lord. This represents the true creative power of God. When a man performs his daily tasks in the name of "the Lord of Life" without any thought of the self he gets the blessing of Vohu-Kshathra. In other words the third Holy Immortal implies service done to humanity out of love. In later theology Kshathra is the Lord of the Mineral Kingdom.

The first Holy Immortal of the Mother-Aspect is *Spentā-Ārmaiti.* She represents firm unshaken faith or piety. In later theology she is the Genius of Mother-Earth. She seems also to correspond to the idea of the World-Mother.[22] She is close-knit with Asha. She is implanted in the hearts of all human beings by Ahura-Mazdā Himself and it is her "still, small voice" that guides every human being when

[17] All through the history of Zoroastrianism man and woman have been treated socially and spiritually as absolutely equal.
[18] Righteousness as Jesus meant it in the New Testament.
[19] Yasna 60.12.
[20] Yasna 72.11.
[21] Yasna 28.2.
[22] Cf. *Jagae-amba* in Hindu theology.

spiritual difficulties arise. She guides the man along the path of Truth "whenever doubts our reason over-whelm."[23]

The other two Mother-Aspects are *Haurvatat* (Wholeness or Perfection) and *Ameretat* (Immortality). They are regarded as Twin-Powers, because the one always implies the other. They have been described in the Gathas as "the Twin Gifts of Love." In later theology they rule over the waters and the vegetable kingdom.

The Holy Immortals are Aspects or Rays of the Supreme. They all think, speak and act as one and are in perfect accord with the Supreme Ruler of all.[24] These Seven of the Supreme Heptad might be arranged diagrammatically as two interlacing triangles making the mystic six-pointed star, well-known as the Seal of Solomon.

This wonderful and poetic teaching of the Holy Immortals may be summed up thus: Every human being must understand the Eternal Law of Truth and Righteousness. He must realize also the Power of Love. And then he must translate both these into Acts of Loving Service. All through his striving he must hold fast to Faith and thus attain the Goal of Perfection and Immortality.

This teaching of the Holy Immortals may be taken as the basis of the Teaching of Zarathushtra. Upon this Teaching as foundation has been raised the whole structure of Zoroastrian Ethics and Zoroastrian Moral Code.

Two other Divine Powers are also mentioned by Zarathushtra in His Gathas. These are *Ātar* (Fire) and *Sraosha*. Ātar is mentioned by Zarathushtra as belonging to Ahura-Mazdā and as worthy of reverence. But it is not the physical element, Fire, which is meant. The Ātar of Zarathushtra is clearly the Inner Divine Spark dwelling within and enlivening each human being. Ātar is just one Spark from the Universal Flame.[25] This original idea of the Fire has never been forgotten even in later theological writings. Because Fire-Temples were erected everywhere by Zoroastrians and because the Sacred Fire was held in great reverence by them they have been called "Fire-Worshippers" by non-Zoroastrians. What is actually worshipped in these temples is not the physical Fire, but the Inner Divine Spark. Nowhere in any of the sacred Texts is the idea of the Divine Spark entirely absent. Fire is always invoked as the "*Son* of Ahura-Mazdā." In the beautiful hymn to Atar we find this verse:

Of all passing by
The hands doth fire observe;
thus doth He ask:
'What doth the friend that fareth forth
Bring to the Friend that sits within?'

The "friend that fareth forth" is the man who goes out and engages in the every-day activities of life and "the Friend that sits within" is the Inner Spark, the Son of Ahura-Mazdā. The idea underlying this is that all outer

23 Yasna 30.9.
24 Yasht 13.92. In this passage the name *Hvare* (Sun) is used instead of Ahura-Mazda; and in Yasna 36.6. the Sun is mentioned as the radiant body of Ahura-Mazda.
25 Cf. *Mundaka-Upanishad*, 2.i.1.

activities of man should be dedicated to the Inner Spiritual Fire within.

The last verse of this hymn to Ātar says:

Thine Inner Fire, Ahura, to see
We yearn,—He blazes mightily through Truth,
He has Thy strength; our Goal and Hope is He.
He lights the Faithful clearly through life;
But, Mazdā, in the hearts of Infidels
He sees the hidden Evil at a glance.[26]

Sraosha is the most important Divine Power after the Supreme Heptad. In the list of the thirty-three Divine Powers (*Yazatas* or "Adorable Ones") the name of Sraosha stands exactly in the middle. The name is derived from the root *sru* to hear, to listen. The name therefore means listening, and implies the faculty in man of listening to the "still, small voice within," the voice of Ārmaiti. Usually the noise and turmoil of our worldly life renders us deaf to this inner voice. It is Sraosha who gives us the power to use this inner faculty. In the Gathas he is termed the greatest servant of Ahura-Mazdā. He is regarded as a Messenger of God because He inspires all true seekers after God. Sraosha is the guiding star of all meek, holy people. And the special function of Sraosha is protecting the souls of the departed. Hence all funeral ceremonies up to the morning of the fourth day after passing are performed in the name of Sraosha.

These are the Divine Powers mentioned in the Songs of Zarathushtra Himself. After His passing many of the older Aryan Divinities were re-instated in popular worship. Of these *Mithra* is the most important. A remarkable fact about Mithra is that from the very beginning he was worshipped more as a great Spiritual Idea than as a physical power. Mithra represents the Sun. But the physical Sun that lights the earth and gives to all creatures life and energy is *Khurshed* who is in one place described as the "most radiant and glorious body of Ahura-Mazdā."[27] Mithra, however, is the spiritual counterpart of this great Light of God. Mithra represents Truth, Righteousness and Justice. He is far-seeing and notes every act of man, and hears every word that is uttered. He is the embodiment of Truth and as such is the opponent of *Druj* (Untruth). More specifically Mithra demands fidelity to the plighted word and he guards the sanctity of oaths. In Avesta the word *mithra* also means "contract" or "pledged word," and being false to one's pledge (*mithro-druj*) is looked upon as one of the mortal sins. Being the Lord of Justice, Mithra judges the souls of the departed together with Sraosha and Rashnu.

Rashnu means Justice. His Justice is strict and mathematically precise. All the good and evil thoughts, words and deeds are weighed in the balance and the destination of the departed soul is determined from this. A very slight excess on either side determines the final award. In some rare cases, when the balance is exact between good and evil, the soul is left hovering midway between Heaven and Hell. This last

---

26 This verse is a quotation from Yasna 34.4.

27 Yasna 36.6.

idea however, was developed in later days.

The justice meted out is governed by the universal Law of Action and Reaction, what the Hindus call the Law of Karma. In the Faiths of India the doctrine of Rebirth is also put forward as a sort of corollary to the Law of Karma. But in Zoroastrianism although the Law of Karma is clearly laid down, the idea of rebirth is not mentioned explicitly, except in one place (Yasna 49.11) which speaks of souls coming back to "the Abode of Untruth," namely to this world of human life. There are several other passages where rebirth might be understood by implication. The belief in rebirth certainly seems logical and eminently reasonable. But it often happens that those who believe in it become slack in their efforts, because they can always depend on getting another life to make improvements. Zarathushtra, on the other hand, teaches all human beings to be *continually* active and alert in opposing evil.

As with all faiths, the Message of Zarathushtra in the purest form is found in its earliest presentation, that is, in the Gathas, which are the very words of the Founder. This pristine purity continues during the days of His immediate disciples. But in later ages, even though the Messenger was venerated, the purity of the Message was forgotten. Later followers had other, more selfish and more worldly motives and they clung to the *word* of the Message as suited their purpose. There were also influences from outside Iran which moulded the popular beliefs and customs. Thus Zoroastrian Faith in later ages was clearly different from the earlier Faith of the Gathas.

Still the lofty and spiritual personality of the Prophet has left His impress quite clearly through all these later transformations. The ultimate bases of all ethical and moral concepts of Zoroastrianism are found in the fundamental aspects of Zarathushtra's Message, namely (i) its absolute reasonableness and tolerance of belief, (ii) its conception of sin and evil and (iii) its presentation of the nature of the Godhead.

Bibliography

(In this list some of the books of general interest and in the English language are mentioned.)

Evard S. D. Bharucha, *A Brief Sketch of Zoroastrian Religion and Customs* (3rd ed., Bombay, 1928).

M. A. Buch, *Zoroastrian Ethics* (Baroda, 1919).

S. J. Bulsara, *The Religion of Zarathushtra* (Bombay, 1938).

F. C. Davar, *Iran and Its Culture* (Bombay, 1953).

M. M. Dawson, *The Ethical Religion of Zoroaster* (New York, 1931).

Dastur Dr. M. N. Dhalla, *Our Perfecting World* (New York, 1908).

——, *Zoroastrian Civilisation* (New York, 1922).

——, *History of Zoroastrianism* (New York, 1938).

L. H. Gray, *Foundations of Iranian Religions* (Bombay, 1929).

Duncan Greenlees, *The Gospel of Zarathushtra* (Madras, 1951).

Clement Huart, *Ancient Persia and Iranian Civilisation* (London, 1927).

D. J. Irani, *Gems from the Divine Songs of Zarathushtra* (Bombay, 1922).
——, *The Path to Happiness or the Teachings of Zoroaster* (Bombay, 1922).
A. V. W. Jackson, *Zoroaster, the Prophet of Ancient Iran* (New York, 1899).
——, *Zoroastrian Studies* (New York, 1928).
R. P. Masani, *The Religion of Good Life* (London, 1938).
Sir J. J. Modi, *The Religious Customs and Ceremonies of the Parsis* (2nd ed. Bombay, 1937).
J. H. Moulton, *Early Zoroastrianism* (London, 1913).
I. J. S. Taraporewala, *The Religion of Zarathushtra* (Madras, 1928).
——, "Some Aspects of the History of Zoroastrianism" (*Journal* of the K. R. Cama Oriental Institute, Bombay, 1928).
——, "The Circle of Perfection" (D. J. Irani Memorial Volume, Bombay, 1940).
——, *The Divine Songs of Zarathushtra* (Bombay, 1951).
——, "Mithraism," "Manichaeism," "Mazdakism," Three Chapters in *Forgotten Religions* (New York, 1950), edited by Vergilius Ferm.
——, "Zoroastrianism," A Chapter in *Religion in the Twentieth Century* (New York, 1948), edited by Vergilius Ferm.
——, "Zoroastrian Philosophy" A chapter in *History of Philosophical Systems* (New York, 1950), edited by Vergilius Ferm.

Irach J. S. Taraporewala
Vedic Research Institution
India

Zuckerman, S.: *see* Primitive Morals.

Zuni Indians, Morals of

The Zuni are among the largest, most traditional-minded and surely the most widely known of the Pueblo Indian tribes. Their early history is not known with certainty past the early sixteenth century when the Spaniards came upon them. The Zuni Indians then inhabited seven villages in the same locality where they now live. The southwest has been continuously inhabited by American Indians for at least 10,000 years, while Pueblo Indian culture took shape a few centuries before the beginning of the Christian era. The sole remaining Zuni village in the high, arid country of New Mexico now has a population of about 2500—an increase over past decades. Industrious farmers and herdsmen, the Zuni cultivate as they did in the past, gardens of beans, squash, melons and chilis. They also grow alfalfa and care for sizable herds of sheep and for many head of cattle and horses. On the other hand, they have yielded up their old pottery and weaving crafts for more efficient store-bought goods. The characteristic many-storied pueblo dwellings are being replaced by more modern one-story houses. Finally, the automobile, the pickup truck and many other modern appliances have been brought in to change decidedly the physical aspects of Zuni life. Changes in material culture inevitably ramify into the social sphere. Yet all observers agree upon the vitality of the traditional Zuni way of life. Recently the village elders allied with public opinion succeeded in insulating the community against the new ideas and outlooks brought back to Zuni by more than 200 of its young men who had served in the armed forces of the United States.

In their conservatism the Zuni Indians contrast strikingly with other North American Indian tribes who have seen their old standards and values shattered beyond recognition. We do not yet understand all the bulwarks that the Zuni have erected against change. Without doubt, the inflexible physical environment and the continued efficiency of the ancient modes of farming and the tribal system of land tenure have had their sheltering effects. But in the final analysis the citadel of Zuni conservatism must be sought in the values of the people.

These values have been vividly described by Ruth Benedict who characterized the Zuni as "Apollonian," followers of the middle way. The Zuni idealize moderation and deplore excess. They prefer meticulous observance of ritual to mystic ecstasy; they set compromise above competitiveness, and the welfare of the community above the private aspirations of the individual. The quiet man has the edge in popular esteem over the conspicuous individualist.

Ruth Bunzel, another close student of the Zuni, has written of them:

All the sterner virtues—initiative, ambition, an uncompromising sense of honor and justice, intense personal loyalties—not only are not admired but are heartily deplored. The woman who cleaves to her husband through misfortune and family quarrels, the man who speaks his mind where flattery would be much more comfortable, the man, above all, who thirsts for power or knowledge, who wishes to be, as they scornfully phrase it, 'a leader of his people' receives nothing but censure and will very likely be persecuted for sorcery.

Needless to say, everyday life cannot quite measure up to these ideals. And one who follows closely the lines of change in Zuni society cannot fail to notice the signs of growing individualism, contentiousness and immoderateness. In the end, the more aggressive values of the outside world are bound to prevail. For the time being, the pattern of Zuni culture as described by Benedict has been able to shield the Indians against change for more than 400 years. The pattern has been not only stable but remarkably consistent as well, encompassing under the twin ideals of moderation and collectivity almost all the areas of Zuni life. Consistency, of course, is a relative state, and even Zuni society, as we shall see, shows strains and conflicts.

The study of Zuni morals begins with religion because the religious life is the center of their interests. To this day, Zuni is strongly theocratic, while in the past the priests were the sole authorities. Responsible for rain, fertility, good health and defense against disaster, the priests commanded—as to a great extent they still do—the highest prestige and respect. However, by contrast with the ethical religions of the higher civilizations, Zuni religion seems conspicuously lacking in moral content. The Zuni regard the universe and the supernatural order as neutral forces, neither malevolent nor beneficent. They do not contemplate the universe as a battleground between forces of good and evil. The gods, it is true, punish neglect and misconduct by withholding their blessings or by bringing disaster; and in this way they maintain a moral order. However, the Zuni do not define their relationship with the gods as a moral one in terms comparable, for example, to the Judaeo-Christian concepts. In the Zuni view, man and the gods are part of a harmonious universe in which each must live up to his respective obligations. These reciprocal obligations are rather definite and limited, leaving to the individual a large private sphere of life in which he is responsible to his neighbors, but not to his gods.

The Zuni universe is essentially non-hierarchical. All phenomena and all beings including man and the gods have a place, a role and particular attributes, but nowhere in Zuni thought is there a clear statement of a higher and lower order of beings. In one version of the Zuni creation myth, the purpose of man's (Zuni, that is) appearance on earth is to relieve the loneliness of the sun:

In this world there was no one at all. Always the sun came up; always he went in. No one in the morning gave him sacred meal; no one gave him prayer sticks; it was very lonely. He said to his two children: You will go into the fourth womb. Your fathers, your mothers . . . all the Society priests, Society pekwins, Society bow priests. You will bring out yonder into the light of your sun father.

What follows is a tale of emergence from the wombs of darkness, discomfort, and human filth into the world of light, comfort and cleanliness. The emphasis is aesthetic rather than moral. The unattractive is made pleasing, the badly formed is made right and the incomplete is brought to its full development. Even the first sorcerers have their place in the emergence because they are the bearers of corn and beans.

Zuni mythology, however, is not lacking in moral lessons. Clan incest, for example, is punished by a terrifying but not all-destructive earthquake and flood. A village that wastes corn is punished with a severe crop failure. Forgetfulness in religious obligations, disrespect to the gods or to the parents inevitably bring punishment that restores the people to their senses and re-establishes the proper harmony. Misconducts that are so punished are not regarded by the Zuni as sinful in the Judaeo-Christian sense. Punishment is in the material sphere. The soul is untouched and all Zuni share the same hereafter.

The moral issues are underplayed in religious practices as well. The Zuni worship a collectivity of deities that include the tribal ancestors, the *A'thlashinawe* and the *Áwona wil'ona*, a class of supernaturals including sun father, moon mother, corn mother, salt father and salt mother, earth mother and others. In seeking the blessings of these deities the Zuni rely upon techniques that are closer to magic than to religion. Magic is basically mechanical, compelling and non-moral. Its effectiveness depends more upon proper observances than upon spiritual feeling. The Zuni rely upon fetishes and amulets and make heavy use of sympathetic magic. To bring rain they roll stones to simulate thunder, whip up suds to simulate clouds; they fill bundles of hollow reeds with water and small frogs; they plant prayer sticks, sprinkle corn meal, perform rote-perfect dances and recite letter-perfect prayers. All of these observances, they believe, will bring results.

However understated the moral features of religious observances may appear to be, they are not negligible. Religion is actually the center of Zuni morality because it embodies as well as conserves their basic moral doctrines of moderation and of collectivity. The priests, in particular, and all religious participants to a lesser degree, must purge themselves of anger and of harshness in order to deal with the supernatural. The ceremonial mood must be joyous because the gods do not appreciate gloom. The calm, dignified and rancorless behavior of the priests sets an impressive example for the community. Magic may be strong in Zuni religion, but it is not the mechanical craft of the Melanesians.

Zuni religion also enforces the morality of collectivity. All ceremonies are complexly interlocked and involve, in one way or another, the participation of all adult males and those women who are interested. Religious blessings, moreover, are asked for collectively and are granted, not to individuals, but to the community as a whole. By the same token, individual religious dereliction threatens the whole community. From the side of religion, therefore, the pressure for conformity to the Zuni creed of moderateness and of collectivity is exceptionally strong.

In the light of these religious principles, one can readily understand why the Zuni look upon witchcraft as the most serious breach of civic orthodoxy. The witch is everywhere the non-conformist, the individualist, the dweller outside the temple. In Zuni thought, the witch invokes the double dread of religious unorthodoxy and of moral delinquency in that he (or she) not only works outside of regular channels, but also bears strong animosities and perpetrates dreadful vengeances. Not too long ago the Zuni hanged and often cruelly tortured suspected witches. This vehemence of hostile feeling against witches does seem inconsistent with Zuni temperate ideals. The inconsistency seems all the greater because there is a very real doubt that any Zuni actually did practice witchcraft. Perhaps the war against witches may be explained as the use of violence to protect the community against violence. On the other hand, it may be a pathological symptom of an overly conformist society— a reaction against an immoderate pressure for moderation.

As in any society, the household is the primary source of morality. Among the Zuni, the traditional household consists of an extended family that includes a group of sisters, their husbands and their children. It unites at least three generations under one roof. Being matrilineal and matrilocal the household gives an unusually important place to women. From the point of view of the household economy—ownership of gardens, control over the food supply and general influence—Zuni society resembles a matriarchy. The men, however, as the religious leaders, are not lacking in influence. It would be correct to say that the Zuni do not define sex role in terms of inferiority or superiority.

The household is managed in a collective spirit. Authority is diffuse, a condition none is better aware of than the children. Food and goods are shared and members of a family share responsibility for one another's acts as well. Quarrelsomeness is not tolerated, and when husband and wife do not agree, the man, as the outsider, returns to his mother's household. Divorce, therefore, is as simple and unceremonious as was marriage. Divorce needs no stated reason, but the most prominent causes for it are adultery and drunkenness, in Zuni eyes both serious offenses. Most societies are intolerant of adultery, but few seem to have as intolerant a view of drunkards as does Zuni. Drinking leads to immoderate behavior, which they regard as threatening.

The household is by no means the only socializing agency in Zuni life. An individual is a member of an involved network of social relationships that covers household, family line, clans, as well as a variety of religious bodies. There are few occasions for private action.

Sex life, however, is private. Like most other preliterate societies, the Zuni do not regard sex as immoral. The infidelity of a wife, for example, is unacceptable from the viewpoint of efficient household management, but not as a moral delinquency. Adultery on the part of the male, on the other hand, is supposed to go unnoticed, although not even the Zuni have been able to deal altogether successfully with wifely jealousy. Before marriage sexual relationships are free. Even the very young are knowledgeable about sex and bodily functions. As in other things, it is immoderateness in sex that disturbs the Zuni, not the sexual activity itself. In view of their preference for a quiet and emotionally uncomplicated sex life, it is all the more interesting to learn that Zuni folktales portray the tragic consequences of a woman's jealousy. In one tale, the outraged wife commits suicide by inviting the enemy in to kill all in the pueblo.

The legal code of a society ordinarily portrays with great fidelity the details of its moral standards. Zuni law is not codified, but the record of litigation before secular authorities reveals the moral pattern.

Since Spanish days, Zuni secular authority has been vested in a governor, subordinate officials and a tribal council, all of whom were subordinate in prestige and hence in real authority to the priesthood. Secular authority is more significant today, although by no means very powerful and, certainly, with only limited prestige. Corruption, unthinkable on the part of the priests, is cynically taken for granted in the case of secular officials. The Zuni do not recognize such corruption as immoral, but reason that higher wages would strengthen resistance to graft and other forms of official venality.

Impartiality is not the main moral injunction in Zuni law. Judges tend to favor the rich and prominent over the poor and despised. Generally speaking, primitive law is a law of torts. It mediates conflicting claims, taking cognizance of the relative strength of the contestants, and does not proclaim a doctrine of Justice. Kinsmen ordinarily look after their own, and compensation for a wrong is as common a legal concept as the familiar *lex talionis*. This is essentially the legal situation at Zuni, except that under American influence some acts which once were private wrongs have now become crimes. Murder, for example, has become a crime since 1880, along with some cases of theft and such crimes of violence as rape and bodily injury. Crimes of violence, however, have always been rare. In the past they were settled through compensation payments. While malefactors clearly do not endear themselves either with their kin or with the general public, neither do they bear a permanent moral stigma for their offenses. The implication, after all, of a legal theory of compensation is that restitution is the point of emphasis, and not the moral judgment.

Moderateness and lack of contentiousness define ideal legal procedure among the Zuni. Even when the accusation concerns the dread crime of witchcraft, the witch is asked first to cooperate by confessing and making amends. Punishment is for his recalci-

trance. In any dispute the Zuni expect a quick settlement through compromise. The zealous defender of his rights is more apt to be regarded as a public nuisance than as a fighting idealist. No legal dispute is judged upon abstract merits, but personal circumstances are invariably taken into account. In one case of rape, for example, the unmarried offender offered the justification that he was "hard up." The court reminded him that he should have asked the woman's consent and advised him to take a wife, before passing judgment that he should pay damages in property to the woman and her husband.

Theft is more common than crimes of violence. It, too, is regarded as a private delict calling for compensatory damages. If sheep are stolen, the Zuni follow the harsh code of the West in dealing with rustlers—to the extent of claiming damages in the ratio of 10 to 1. A thief falls in public esteem as does any violator of the proprieties, but he is not regarded as a moral leper. If anything, the judge tries to reconcile plaintiff and defendant in order to minimize "hard feelings." Earlier observers of Zuni reported that theft was virtually unknown. Under traditional property conditions, motives for thieving were indeed scant. Not only did the family system take care of the economic needs of its members by providing all with land and other means of livelihood, but the importance of wealth itself was never overvalued. Differences in wealth always existed, but they arose from individual effort and good luck and not from the ex-

667

ploitation of others. The wealthy were expected, as they still are, to finance public religious ceremonies and to redistribute their riches. The Zuni are not indifferent to wealth. They enjoy comforts and attractive objects for their own sake as well as for the prestige of being well-to-do. At the same time, they despise miserliness and covetousness and have refused to encourage competition and rivalry for material possessions. Property attitudes, however, are changing in accordance with the standards of the white man. This is reflected in increasing frequency of litigation over property rights, particularly over inheritance. Yet even in this newer legal area, traditional Zuni values still prevail. Litigants may press their claims and receive a hearing, but their zeal costs them public favor. Judgments of the court in such cases take into account personal need and good family behavior. In effect, on questions of property, the needy have the advantage over the well-to-do.

In summary, the foundation of Zuni morality is the preservation of harmony within the community and, in a broader sense, the preservation of harmonious relationships within the Zuni cosmic order. In the Zuni moral code personal ambition, self-assertiveness, violence and individualism are wrong. Conflicts are played down rather than drawn out to their ultimate and categorical resolution—a doctrine that is not followed consistently. Zuni morality does not rest upon absolutes. It accords with what the Indians believe

human nature and the laws of nature to be rather than with what they think they should be. Because their morality does not rest upon categorical imperatives it applies mainly to their own community, to the in-group. In the past, the Zuni thought it proper to cheat the Navaho, to wage war against them and to seize their women and children as slaves.

Yet even within their own community the Zuni would be less than human if they lived up fully to their moral ideals. The case record of disputes testifies to the frictions within the community. One must add the observation that even when the Zuni do live according to their ideal of harmony they do so not necessarily through love of fellow Zuni. Observers have been impressed as much by the hot sparks of malice, envy and strong rancor generated by the Zuni in their social relations as by the benignity and moderateness of their expressed ideals. The Zuni are quick to spread uncomplimentary tales about one another. In folklore, the medium in which all peoples express some of their innermost longings and anxieties, the Zuni give prominence to tales that dwell upon themes of vengeance, secret enmities, and burning envy of the rich and the successful. The unhappy enjoy the daydream of tearing down the happiness of all. The strain for consistency with the main pattern is, however, always present because the point of vengeance is sometimes stated as teaching people to love you.

In part the evident conflict among the Zuni is the inevitable wear and tear of any small community accentuated, in the case of the Zuni, by the real clash in values between their own society and the surrounding culture of the white man. Zuni culture shows the strains of cultural change. The suspicion remains, however, that a society in which all are constrained to watch out that no one stands out above and apart from the rest is bound to reap some harvest of suspicion and ill will.

Bibliography

John Adair and Evon Z. Vogt, "Navaho and Zuni Veterans: A Study of Contrasting Modes of Culture Change." *American Anthropologist,* Vol. 51, pp. 547–61 (1949).

Ruth Fulton Benedict, *Patterns of Culture* (New York, 1934).

——, *Zuni Mythology,* 2 Vols., Columbia University Contributions to Anthropology, Vol. 21 (1935).

Ruth Bunzel, "Introduction to Zuni Ceremonialism," *Bureau of American Ethnology, 47th Annual Report* (1929–1930).

Fred Eggan, *Social Organization of the Western Pueblos,* The University of Chicago Publications in Anthropology (1950).

Irving Goldman, "The Zuni Indians of New Mexico," in *Cooperation and Competition Among Primitive Peoples,* ed., Margaret Mead (New York, 1937).

Watson Smith and John M. Roberts, *Zuni Law: A Field of Values,* Papers of the Peabody Museum of American Archaeology and Ethnology, Harvard University, Vol. 43, No. 1 (1954).

Irving Goldman
Sarah Lawrence College

Zuni Indians: *see* Mundurucu Indians, A Dual System of Ethics.

Zweig, Stefan: *see* Freud, Sigmund.

Name Index

671

Spinka, Matthew, 58
Spinoza, Baruch, 11, 31, 32, 38, 47, 58, 59, 71,
72, 98, 104, 105, 114, 117, 126, 133, 134, 157–
161, 163, 174, 178, 179, 181, 182, 184, 188, 199,
200, 207, 213, 224, 228, 229, 231, 241, 243–
245, 247, 266, 286, 293, 302, 303, 309, 330,
333, 340, 348, 366, 369, 383, 390, 391, 397,
401, 402, 403, 409, 410, 411, 422, 423, 424,
442, 480, 481, 490, 517, 537, 538, 569, 580–
584, 586, 588, 589, 600, 601, 609, 616, 617,
619, 639, 640, 641
Spinoza, Michael De, 580
Stalin, 575, 588
Stark, W., 524
Stephen, Leslie, 437, 589, 636, 647
Stevenson, Charles L., 41, 125, 290–293, 321,
322, 359, 360, 589
Steward, J. D., 31
Steward, Julian H., 608
Stirling, John, 589, 634
Stock, St. G., 599
Stolnitz, Jerome, 515
Stoughton, Dr., 114
Strahan, 230
Strauss, L., 228
Stuart, John, 599, 631
Strune, Peter, 599
Struve, Peter B., 55, 569, 570
Suarez, F., 248, 249, 600
Sumner, W. G., 600
Suslova, Appolinarya, 152
Sutherland, A., 491, 504
Swift, 336
Szold, Henrietta, 265

Tanchuma, Schemini, 259, 262
Taraporewala, Irach, J. S., 662
Tax, Sol, 608
Taylor, A. E., 31, 228, 422, 552
Taylor, Harriet, 608, 635
Taylor, N. W., 355, 608
Taylor, R., 439, 608
Teale, A. E., 275
Teles, 337, 339, 608
Theodoros "The Atheist," 338
Theopompos, 336, 609
Thompson, C. G., 647
Thrasymachus, 565, 566, 609
Tillich, Paul, 360, 609
Tillmann, F., 253
Tkachyov, P. N., 571, 609

Toland, 108, 609
Toledo, F., 248, 609
Tolstoy, Leo, 53, 54, 55, 71, 105–107, 148, 159,
181, 188, 193, 253, 303, 323, 333, 336, 361, 399,
403, 410, 446, 515, 538, 545, 553, 557, 600,
609–613, 615, 616, 617, 639, 641
Toulmin, Stephen, 290, 292, 293, 616
Toynbee, A. J., 199
Trinterud, Leonard, 458
Troeltsch, Ernest, 96, 98
Trotsky, Leon D., 136, 329, 572, 573, 576, 580,
617
Trubetzkoy, Prince, 554
Tsanoff, R. A., 322, 537, 636
Tucker, Abraham, 617, 621, 623
Tufts, James H., 136, 147
Tulloch, John, 369
Turgenev, I., 617
Turgot, 230
Tydemann, Daniel, 582, 617
Tylor, E. B., 441
Tyndale, William, 458
Tyrell, John, 125

Ulmar, 619
Ungnad, A., 199
Untersteiner, M., 562, 563, 564, 569
Urban, W. M., 358, 619
Utley, Vine, 452

Vaillant, George, 45
Valencia, G., 248, 639
Valentinov, N., 571
Van den Ende, 580
Vasquez, G., 248, 639
Venable, V., 327
Verkhovensky, 154
Vermeersch, A., 250, 639
Virgil, 128, 130, 131
Vitelleschi, 640
Vogt, Evon Z., 390, 491, 669
Volski, S. A., 569, 570, 640
Voltaire, 112, 391, 640
Vyshinski, 575, 640

Waelder, Robert, 177, 178, 641
Wagley, Charles, 601
Wagley, Sol, 608
Wagner, G., 403, 536, 641
Wagner, Richard, 391, 641
Waismann, 641
Waley, Arthur, 85

INDEX

SOCIAL MOBILITY
IN
CONTEMPORARY CHINA

**Research Group for Social Structure in Contemporary
China**

Institute of Sociology
Chinese Academy of Social Sciences

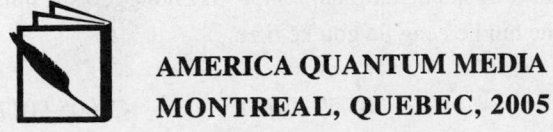

AMERICA QUANTUM MEDIA
MONTREAL, QUEBEC, 2005

Translator: *Xiaowen Bao*
Editor: *Harold W. Bashor*
Marketing Manager: *Lily Liying Zhao*
Production Administrator: *Frank Owen, Xiao Zhao*

Printed in the People's Republic of China

Library and Archives Canada Cataloguing in Publication

Social mobility in contemporary China / Research Group for Social Structure in Contemporary China, Chinese Academy of Social Sciences.

Translation of Dang dai Zhongguo she hui liu dong.
Includes bibliographical references and index.
ISBN 0-9736759-0-X

1. Social mobility--China. 2. Social stratification--China. 3. Social classes--China. 4. China--Social conditions--1949- I. Zhongguo she hui ke xue yuan. Dang dai zhongguo she hui jie ceng jie gou ke ti zu.

HN740.Z9S65 2005   305.5'13'0951   C2005-901771-6

Table of Contents

List of Tables

List of Figures

Preface and Acknowledgements

After the publication of *Social Stratification in Contemporary China* in early 2002, the tasks of the Research Group for Social Structure in Contemporary China with the Chinese Academy of Social Sciences (CASS) were twofold. First, we began to computerize and conduct statistical analysis on data drawn from a nationwide questionnaire survey among 6,000 respondents conducted by this research group in 2001; this survey covered 73 counties and cities in 12 provinces, autonomous regions, and national municipalities. Second, after discussion of this topic in several symposia, we decided to set social mobility in contemporary China as the research objective in the second phase of the project and compile our research outcomes into a monograph: *Social Mobility in Contemporary China.*

Based on proposals of collective discussions in the research group and opinions from scholars in the academic community of sociology, we developed the basic framework of this book and divided the work of study and composition among the group's members. The introduction and the first five chapters compose the general theory, while the remaining seven chapters provide detailed descriptions of particular strata as well as explanations of the adopted theory and research design of the study.

The introduction discusses the significance and goals of the study on social mobility in contemporary China which has distinct and unique characteristics. Social mobility in China over the past half century has occurred in the background of frequent transformations in social and political systems. Its driving forces, mechanisms, paths, and consequences not only have some common characteristics with industrial societies, but also depict the particularity of Chinese social structure, especially social structure transformation. Therefore, we adjusted the research methodology of the study according to China national conditions with some differences from popular textbooks. The introduction also summarizes several major findings and some important points of view in the study. Xueyi Lu, Chunguang Wang, and Chunling Li co-authored this section of the book.

Chapter 1 discusses the formation and classification of ten major social strata in China. It provides further explanation for the criteria of classification and operational methods that were proposed in Social Stratification in Contemporary China. In addition, according to the data of the nationwide survey (2001), we made some slight adjustments on the proportion of each social stratum in this chapter. The third section of this chapter explains the overall analytical framework of this book. In fact, Chapter 1 is a link between this book and Social Stratification in Contemporary China. Chunling Li and Jinguang Chen co-authored this chapter.

Chapter 2 analyzes five tides of social mobility in contemporary China. Since the establishment of the People's Republic of China in 1949, Chinese society has experienced several political-social movements. The drastic political and economic institutional transformations strongly affected the up and down of each social member's social status. Social mobility in such a historical background is different from that which has occurred in industrialized countries with basically stable socio-economic systems. Based on such historical background, this chapter divides the timeframe since 1949 into five periods and describes the process and characteristics of each period respectively. Guangjin Chen authored this chapter.

Chapter 3 proposes a pro-high-level trend in occupational structure in China and analyzes its causes. Occupation is an important criterion for classifying social members into different strata. The social mobility of stratum in modern society occurs on the basis of occupational changes. In this chapter, according to analyses on domestic and foreign data, we propose that the pace of Chinese society transforming from a traditional agricultural society into a modern industrialized society has been sped up driven by the industrialization, urbanization, and marketization since 1978. Like most industrialized countries, there has a pro-high-level trend in occupational structure in China as well. With the continuous and rapid development of Chinese economy, the growth of the secondary and tertiary industry provided numerous employment opportunities. A large amount of agricultural labor force has transferred to the secondary and tertiary industry. After the middle of the 1990s, the tertiary industry such as the modern services sector developed rapidly and provided many middle-high level job positions; as a result, a considerable number of social members became white-collar workers. However, compared with industrialized countries, the number of such occupations is still small. Therefore, we conclude that there is just a trend of pro-high-level shift in occupation structure in China. Xiuyin Shi and Wei Li co-authored this chapter.

Chapter 4 reveals origins and mobility paths of the ten major social strata in China. Based on data collected in the survey, this chapter describes and analyzes the intergenerational and intragenerational mobility in the ten social strata and uncovers the process of formation and future tendency of each stratum. Finally, we calculate the overall level of social mobility in contemporary China. Our study indicates that the rate of total social mobility has increased significantly since the reform and opening-up in China and that China has been transforming into a more open society as well. Chunling Li authored this chapter.

Chapter 5 discusses channels of social status attainment in Chinese society. Through overall analysis of relevant data, this chapter describes the influences and effects of various social mobility mechanisms on individuals' attainment of social status in different strata and groups in different historical periods. Yi Zhang authored this chapter.

From Chapter 6 to Chapter 11, we discuss and analyze social mobility of state and social administrators, private entrepreneurs, the new middle stratum, industrial workers, peasant-workers, and agricultural laborers respectively. Weibin Gong, Guangjin Chen, Wanli Zhang, Xiuyin Shi, Chunguang Wang, and Ping Fan co-authored these chapters respectively.

Chapter 12 explains the theory and methodology that we adopted in this study on social stratification and mobility and gives a detailed description about the survey procedure, data sources, and methods of statistical analysis. Wei Li and Chunling Li co-authored this chapter.

Ge Gao, a member of this research group, was in charge of matters related to collecting and organizing the literature and materials and coordinating activities of the group.

This book is the result of collective contributions. For the past three years, all members of this research group have cooperated closely and worked diligently. After the proposal was approved, this research group did a comprehensive literature review on relevant theories and studies concerning social structure and social mobility, we also conducted in-depth analyses on data from the nationwide survey and other sources. In the fall of 2002, after dividing the composition work of each chapter, group members dedicated themselves to writing this book. By August 2003, the first drafts of most chapters had been finished. After that, the research group focused on compiling and revising the text. Each section and each chapter was discussed in group meetings. Some chapters and sections were discussed repeatedly; some were completely rewritten. In this process, each member's knowledge and understanding about social mobility in China over the past fifty years were improved greatly and eventually came to an agreement on the theory, methodology, and analytical framework in research of the unique social mobility in Chinese society. All revised drafts were collected in April 2004. A special team then was formed (including Xueyi Lu, Chunguang Wang, Wei Li, Chunling Li, Guangjin Chen) in order to prepare the final version of this manuscript. In this process, some research group members, such as Wanli Zhang, Ping Fan, Linjiang Zhang, Weibin Gong, Ge Gao, and Jianzhong Dai, frequently participated in and contributed to the special team's discussions. For two months, the special team met three times to revise each chapter and section. Some chapters were condensed and rewritten. Some were supplemented and corrected. For example, Wei Li and Chunguang Wang revised and rewrote Chapter 5, Chapter 8, and Chapter 11. On June 15, 2004, the final manuscript was submitted to the editor-in-chief.

As an outcome of collective contributions, this book is important for another reason. The study of social stratification and social mobility is one of the core areas in sociology science. However, there are still not common understandings with respect to the theories and practical significance of research in this field. Fortunately, the academia in China paid great attention to our group's research project. In the process of study and composition, we held three symposia on the social mobility issue. Professors Hangsheng Zhen and Lulu Li of the Renmin University of China, Professors Sibin Wang, Shanhua Yang, Shiding Liu, and associate Professor Wen Fang of the Peking University, Professors Qiang Li and Liping Sun of the Tsinghua University, Professors Guanglei Zhu, Chuhui Wang, and Junsheng Hou of the Nankai University, Professors Zhongmin Wu of the Party School of the Central Committee of the Communist Party of China, Professors Jianzhong Dai and Yu Wang of the Beijing

Academy of Social Sciences, Professors Tiankui Jin, Peilin Lin and Ping Huang of the Chinese Academy of Social Sciences participated in our discussions and contributed valuable suggestions and insights.

In addition, Professors Jianzhong Dai, Peilin Li, and Ping Huang contributed in the design the questionnaire used in the nationwide sampling survey—the essential component of this study. Professors Shiyong Feng and Jialing Gao and Professor Huixin Ke helped us formulate the overall design of the nationwide sampling. The following colleagues in the society of sociology, departments of sociology, and institutes of sociology in provinces, autonomous regions, and national municipalities covered by the survey assisted in organizing and conducting this nationwide questionnaire survey: Professor Jianzhong Dai and associate Professor Yurong Tian in Beijing, Professor Hanlong Lu in Shanghai, Professor Nongjian Zou in Jiangsu Province, Professor Mingmei Wang and associate Professor Da Yang in Jiangxi Province, Professor Jinling Wang in Zhejiang Province, Professor Guanghai Ma in Shandong Province, Professors Zhaole Shi in Guizhou Province, Qian Liu in Henan Province, Weiwen Zhou in Hebei Province, Zhaowen Sun in Inner Mongolia, Xishun Zhao in Sichuan Province, Ruizheng Zhao in Heilongjiang Province, and so on. For six months from June 2001 to January 2002, according to the schedule set up by this research group, they trained and organized local interviewers to conduct surveys in urban and rural areas and collected the questionnaires. Without their help, it is unlikely that these difficult tasks could have been accomplished.

The publication date of this book (Chinese edition) fell on the opening date of the Thirty-sixth World Sociologist Conference. We hereby dedicate this book to colleagues from all over the world to express our sincere welcome and earnest desire for academic exchanges.

Grateful acknowledge is made to above-mentioned colleagues and friends for their generous help and valuable suggestions. We also wish to thank the leadership of the Chinese Academy of Social Sciences and the Institute of Sociology for their support and encouragement. We are indebted to colleagues in the Scientific Research Division, the main office, and the library of the Institute of Sociology for their support and assistance. Special thanks are due to the proprieter of the Social Sciences Documentation Publishing House Mr. Shouguang Xie, the Assistant of the Editor-in-Chief Mr. Guangwei Fan, and the Director of the Department of Editors Mr. Dawei Zhang. They were actively involved in our study and participated in eight meetings about manuscript composition. Their hard work has ensured the timely publication of this book.

It is a difficult task to study a country's social mobility. Especially, doing research on the social mobility in contemporary China is an extremely formidable challenge; China has a population of 1.3 billion and unbalanced development between rural and urban areas and among regions; it has experienced several drastic political, economic, and social transformations over the past fifty years as well. The difficulty is due to three aspects. First, no existing research paradigm could be applied in this study.

We did not find any works that systematically studied the social mobility at the macro level in a complicate and ever-changing background like that of China. Only a few domestic and foreign scholars have done any preliminary studies on some aspects of social mobility in contemporary China since the 1990s. Second, it is difficult to acquire materials and data about social mobility in Chinese society. Furthermore, there are few reliable longitudinal data available to be used in comparison and analysis. Third, the research group lacked adequate funding. However, by relying on cooperation, team spirit, and collective intelligence of members in the group, by relying on the supports, assistance, and instructions of a large number of colleagues, and on the data, materials, and with three years' accumulation of data, materials, and experience, we managed to accomplish this project in another three years. Today, *Social Mobility in Contemporary China* is eventually published. It is the second research report succeeding *Social Stratification in Contemporary China*. Just like the first report, it is an exploratory research. The points of view and judgments that are proposed in this book are findings with many limitations. We will cheerfully accept any suggestions and insight. However, we believe that study of social mobility and social stratification in contemporary China is very helpful both for the development of sociology science in China and for the need of balanced and sustainable development of the economy and society in China. Studies and discussions in this field will benefit the understanding of Chinese national conditions and formulation of correct social development strategy and socio-economic policy.

Research Group for Social Structure in Contemporary China
Institute of Sociology, Chinese Academy of Social Sciences
Beijing, China
June 15, 2004

Introduction

This book is the second research report published by the Research Group for Social Structure in Contemporary China with the Chinese Academy of Social Sciences (CASS); it is a continuation of the first report, *Social Stratification in Contemporary China* (2002). The research results of the first report are based on data that were collected in a questionnaire survey among 11,000 people covering ten provinces, autonomous regions, and municipalities in China as well as in the interviews with nearly one thousand people from different social strata. The findings in this book, *Social Mobility in Contemporary China*, are based on data that were collected in another nationwide questionnaire survey among 6,000 respondents conducted by the research group from 2001 to 2002. Therefore, just like the first report, this book is also an exploratory and empirical research document.

In the following sections, we will give full explanations of research themes, significance, methodology, major findings, and development tendency of the research.

SIGNIFICANCE OF THE RESEARCH

In the previous research report, *Social Stratification in Contemporary China*, the major argument is that contemporary Chinese society has been divided into ten major social strata. In this book, *Social Mobility in Contemporary China*, we focus on the following research themes:

- *How did the ten social strata evolve from the former 'two classes and one stratum' social structure?*
- *What changes have occurred in mechanisms of social mobility?*
- *How will the ten social strata continue to evolve respectively henceforth?*
- *What are the reasonable and unreasonable elements respectively in current mechanisms of social mobility?*
- *How should current mechanisms be reformed and adjusted?*

Social stratification and social mobility are analyses and descriptions of a certain social phenomenon in a country or area from two perspectives. Social stratification is a way to analyze and describe the stratification content, form, composition, and shape of the social stratum structure in a static perspective. It focuses on the process of qualitative changes in social stratum differentiation. Social mobility aims to analyze and describe the interactions between different social strata and dynamics, time-space scopes, moving directions, and rates of such movements. It emphasizes the process of quantitative changes in social stratum differentiation. The studies on social stratification and social mobility are interdependent and inseparable, and supplement each other.

Social mobility refers to the phenomenon in which social members shift from one social status to another. In a given social stratum structure, if one moves to a higher status from a lower one, it is called *upward social mobility*; and, contrariwise, it is *downward social mobility*. Both *upward mobility* and *downward mobility* are categorized as *vertical social mobility*. Sometimes, a social member shifts from one occupation to another, and meanwhile his or her income, prestige, and social status remain at the same level (for example, a lecturer at a university transfer to another research institute as an assistant researcher). This type of social movement shifting from one position to another situated at the same level is called *horizontal social mobility*.

In general, in the history of human society development, there is a tendency of constantly expanding social mobility. In the Middle Ages, in feudal society, and in ancient times, individual social status has been determined by *ascription factor*. If one were born in a certain class or stratum, usually he or she would be a lifetime member of that class or stratum. For example, in ancient China, there was a saying that "an official's son will be an official, a farmer's son will be a farmer, a worker's son will be a worker, and a businessman's son will be a businessman."[1] Boundaries between different classes or strata were strict, clear, and nearly impassable. It was a *closed society* without any social mobility. With the development of productivity and the emergence of modern socialized mass production, the mode of production and industrial structure changed constantly. Some new sectors constantly appeared, and some old ones were eliminated in competition. In this case, only the free flow of workforce could meet the requirement of socialized mass production. Karl Marx explained:

> Through the instrumentality of machinery, chemical processes, and other methods, modern industry, changing the technical basis of production, changes therewith the functions of the workers and the social combinations of the labor process. At the same time, no less continuously, it transforms the division of labor within society, incessantly shifting masses of capital and masses of labor from one branch of production to another. From its very nature, therefore, large-scale industry gives rise to changes in work, to a flux of functions, to a many-sided mobility of the worker.[2]

---

[1] Guan, Zhong. 1954. "Guan Zi · Xiao Kuang". In *Collection of Distinguished Philosophical Works*, Volume 5. Beijing: Zhonghua Book Company: 121.

[2] Marx, Karl and Frederick Engels. 1972. *Complete Works of Marx and Engels*, Chinese edition, Volume 23. Beijing: People's Publishing House: 534.

Development of science and technology, constant expansion of mass production, and the upgrade of industrial structures create new job positions and at the same time create the needs of social mobility. Only through social mobility can new job positions be filled and the reasonable allocation of the labor force and human resources be achieved. The freer the social mobility and the higher the rate of social mobility, the more active the members of each social stratum especially in middle and lower strata. Motivated by hopes, they may move upward to a higher social status through the *rule of achievement*, i.e., achieving success trough individual efforts. Objectively, social mobility can push the development of social production and realize the positive mutual-stimulative interaction between the evolutions of economic structure and social structure. Such society is an *open society*. In short, in a closed society, the *rule of ascription* is the principal social mobility rule, whereas in an open society, the rule of achievement is the leading rule of social mobility.

Since the establishment of the People's Republic of China in 1949, the country has experienced two great institutional reforms. The first one occurred just after 1949 when new China used the Soviet model for reference to build a new political and economic system. Through a series of political and economic campaigns such as land reform, socialist transformation and collectivization in agriculture, individual handicraft industry, private enterprises, state-driven industrialization, the Great Leap Forward, and People's Commune Campaign on one hand, China accomplished extraordinary achievements in economic development and industrialization. On the other hand, from the institutional reform perspective, the public ownership replaced the private ownership, and the centrally planned economy systems substituted the market economy system, which was based on individual economy. Accordingly, the overall structure of social class and stratum changed drastically. Through nationalization, socialization, and land reform, bureaucratic compradors capitalists, private entrepreneurs, and the landed class were eliminated and hundreds of millions of peasants and rural handicraft workers became members of the people's communes, otherwise known as the rural collective economy, whereas urban handicraft workers became employees of state-owned or collective enterprises. The overall structure of social strata transited to a "two classes and one stratum" society which consisted of workers, peasants and intellectuals (*cadres*).

In the following several decades, political campaigns followed one after one in China and its economic situations and social policies became extremely volatile. These changes in institutions, policies, and social structures had direct influence on social mobility. The attainment and change of social status were determined by institutions and policies of those times. Individuals, families, and even a certain stratum could not control their own destinies. From a historical perspective, before 1978, especially at the late stage of the Cultural Revolution, the overall development of Chinese society tended to a closed system, and the rule of ascription dominated the social mobility.

In 1978, the Third Plenum of the Eleventh Central Committee decided to implementation the reform and opening-up policy; it was the very beginning of the second great institutional reform in China. The reform started from economic systems, and then expanded to political and social systems. The goal of this reform was to transform the planned economy system into the socialist free-market system. This goal was achieved roughly by the year of 2000. The national economy has grown at a continuously high speed driven by the reform. Chinese society has been transiting from an agricultural- rural society to an industrial-urban society. The institutional reform, development, and structural changes in economy have accelerated the stratification of social structure. Some new strata, such as private entrepreneurs and peasant-workers, have emerged. The whole society has been divided into ten major strata. As a whole, in this period, especially in the early stage of the reform and opening-up, arrangements of national institutions and policies still have important impact on attainments and changes of people's social status. Nevertheless, the whole society becomes increasingly open, and the rule of achievement has been the leading social mobility rule.

In the gazette of the Sixteenth National Congress of the Communist Party of China, it pointed out that "the first two decades of the twentieth century, for our country, is a time full of important strategic opportunities that should not be missed, and China should make full use of it to develop itself". At present, China is at a critical moment in its history when more profound changes will happen in Chinese socio-economic structure.

> The experience of development in many countries has demonstrated that, in this stage, there are two possible results of development. One is positive, with sustained socio-economic advances and successful achievements of industrialization and modernization. Another is negative, usually with the great gaps in wealth, between urban and rural areas, and among different regions, with an increasing rate of unemployment, with violent social conflicts and polluted environments, and so on. All these issues will eventually lead to long-term socio-economic stagnations, or even social turbulences and regressions.[1]

Judging from practice since the reform and opening-up, the prospect of economic development in China is bright, and the goal of quadrupling the GDP in 20 years is attainable, because China has been running on the right track of the socialist free-market system and its government has accumulated skills and experience on regulating and controlling national economy. Whether China is able to grasp opportunities in this critical period and advance further depends on whether it can unceasingly push the development of the entire society. As for the situation of current

---

[1] Wen, Jiabao. 2004. "Speech at the Commencement of Seminar on Understanding and Application of Scientific Development Views Attended by Provincial and Ministerial Level Officials". Beijing: *People's Daily*. March 1.

China, social development lags far behind economic development. There are many conflicts between the two types of development resulting in various social issues. The six major social issues mentioned in the above quotation have pervasively emerged in China. In addition, worsening social security situation, a sharp increase of crime rate, uncontrollable corruptions, serious extravagance and waste, rushes of peasant-workers, complicated socio-economic problems related in agriculture, rural areas and peasants, and expanding pornography, gambling, drugs, and organized crimes have been endangering Chinese society. It may be a little late to talk about social development, social systems reform, and social regulation at this moment. After twenty years' reforms and opening-up, China has achieved extraordinary accomplishments in economic development, and the conditions and standard of living of ordinary people have improved greatly. However, many problems that are not approved of by many people still exist in the filed of social development. In the mid-1980s, there was a phenomenon of "scolding the government when eating good meals"; and nowadays, it turns to "criticizing the government when accepting subsistence allowances" or "cursing the society when driving a new car". These phenomena demonstrate the inharmoniousness in socio-economic development, which is worth our deepest concerns. Therefore, in the Third Plenum of the Sixteenth Central Committee holding in October 2003, the Communist Party of China proposed a new national strategy of development, i.e., "making people in the center of development, and promoting the all-round development of economy, society, and human beings with a comprehensive, balanced, and sustainable notion of development," and as well as the "five balances in development" (balancing urban-rural development, balancing development among regions, balancing economic and social development, balancing development of man and nature, and balancing domestic development and opening up wider to the outside world). These new strategic proposals are very pertinent and timely.

It is an enormous challenge to promote socio-economic development coordinately. For example, it requires adjustment of social structure, development of social undertakings, improvement of social administrations, reform of the regulatory systems of social undertakings, cultivation of harmonious social environments, and realization of basic social justice, etc. All of these are extremely difficult tasks. However, if China plans to get though this critical period, it has to accomplish all these tasks successfully. In other words, China has to make up a missed lesson of social development.

This research group was dedicated to the study of social stratum structure in contemporary China for six years with a focus on social stratification and social mobility. We believe that the structure of social strata is the skeleton of a nation's social structure. When economy in a society has developed and economic structure has changed, the social structure, especially the structure of social strata, have to adjust and change consequently in order to provide a suitable skeleton for the development of economy and changes of economic structure. Moreover, as long as there are reasonable institutional arrangements and policies, the structure of social

10

strata will certainly make corresponding adjustments and changes with the development of economic, industrial, and occupational structures.

In the first three years of this six-year research project, this research group laid an emphasis on social stratification in contemporary China.

The results of this study reveal that China has been divided into ten major social strata since its reforms and opening-up. All fundamental elements that consist of modern social stratum structure have been emerging; the order of modernized social strata hierarchy has been established; a modern social stratum structure has been forming in China.

However, this study also shows that China is just in the embryonic stage of the modern social stratum structure. In this structure, the should-be reduced stratum has not deflated because agricultural laborers still make up 44 percent of its population; whereas the should-be expanded stratum has not been enlarged because the middle social stratum only accounts for 15 percent. Therefore, it is still not a modern social stratum structure featuring justness, openness, and reasonableness and contains some structural factors that may lead to social crisis.[1] Obviously, with such social structure, the process of modernization of Chinese economy will encounter serious difficulties; even though it developed in a certain degree, it would be unstable even with the danger of depression.

In the past three years, this research group has focused on social mobility in contemporary China. We find that

China has preliminarily formed a pattern of modern social mobility mechanism in its twenty-year reform and opening-up.

This is the consequence of economic development and changes of economic and industrial structures. Diversified social mobility mechanisms and widened mobility channels are important causes as well. Before the reform and opening-up, there was a multidimensional dual status hierarchy in China. In that system, the ascription factors determined individual's social status. The rate of social mobility was extremely low. After the reform and opening-up, the dual status hierarchy has been given up gradually and more social mobility channels are available. For example, peasants can go to towns and cities to find jobs or do business; most social members can choose their occupations freely or establish their own enterprises; colleges and universities adopt the national college entrance examination system once again, etc. All these changes have made the rule of achievement instead of institutional arrangements and policies dominant in the social mobility mechanisms. A new pattern of social mobility has been emerging with a higher mobility rate and the social vigor has been

---

[1] Lu, Xueyi (ed.). 2002. *Social Stratification in Contemporary China*. Beijing: Social Sciences Documentation Publishing House.

strengthened dramatically. However, why is the middle social stratum still so small? Why is the population of agricultural laborers so large? The main cause of such phenomena is due to some existing institutional barriers in social mobility channels retained from the former planned economy (e.g., traditional residence registration system, employment system, personnel administration system, and social security system) and have blocked the upward social mobility towards higher social status. Therefore, the old mechanism and the new one co-exist in the pattern of social mobility in contemporary China. In other words, the modern social mobility mechanism featuring justness, reasonableness and openness has not yet been formed.

In conclusion, the study of social mobility in contemporary China is extreme significant both in theory and in practice. Theoretically, the study of social mobility and its mechanisms of Chinese society in which more than 1.3 billion people live will make some academic contributions to the field of sociology. More practically speaking, through the study on forms, mechanisms, paths, directions, and characteristics of social mobility in China, both active and passive factors in the process of social mobility pattern transition can be revealed. Based on these findings, we can recommend some possible strategies about further reform and adjustment of institutional arrangements and policies in order to promote the modernization of the Chinese social mobility pattern and the emergence of a just, reasonable, and open structure of social strata that coordinates with economic development.

RESEARCH FRAMEWORK AND METHODOLOGY

Social mobility is one of the most important areas in the research of social stratification. Numerous sociologists in different countries have conducted systematical studies in their own countries and large-scale cross-national comparative research. Fruitful findings and theories derived from those studies provide us indispensable references. However, social mobility over the past fifty years in China has extraordinary particularities. It occurred in the background of several significant social and political transitions and national policies strongly influenced it. These particularities resulted in some differences both in research methods and in research themes from the general social mobility study.

Generally, there are two major analytical approaches in the study of social mobility. The first one is *mobility table analysis*. By adopting this approach, sociologists investigate intergenerational and intragenerational changes of occupational status or social strata position through conjoint analysis of occupational status between parent and child, or between one's initial and current occupational status. Based on these analyses, log-linear models (such as quasi-independence model, quasi-symmetry model, or level model, etc.) are applied to analyses of opportunities, rules, and patterns of social mobility. Another method is the *Blau & Duncan's Status Attainment Model*. It is mainly used to investigate and compare influences that are made by ascription factors (for example, family background) and achievement factors (such as personal capability, ambition, and educational level, etc.) on attainment of individual occupational status. Initially, most models of status attainment adopted path analysis, but in recent studies, multiple regression analysis, event history analysis, and structural equation are also frequently used. The above two approaches have been mainstreaming research models in social mobility study. However, there are some limitations existing when applying these two methods to investigation of modern Chinese society. Usually, the mobility table analysis and the status attainment model are suitable for analysis of social mobility that occurs in stable structures of society and social stratification. However, in the past fifty years, Chinese society has experienced several significant social structure transformations. The structures of social stratification, social status hierarchy, and rules of social selection have fundamentally changed. In one significant institutional reform, some individuals or groups initially in a lower social status rose to a higher status due to the changes of social systems or national policies, while in another great institutional transitions, the social status of individuals or groups changed in opposite directions. Therefore, when applying mobility table analysis or the status attainment model to investigation of social mobility in such an environment, it is very likely that some phenomena and rules of mobility will be covered due to counteractive forces moving in opposite directions. In order to resolve this problem, in addition to mobility table analysis and status attainment model based on survey data, we also made use of historical documentation and national statistical data to conduct a systematical analysis on social-political transitions and national policy adjustments and their impact on social mobility. Thus, we could observe and describe the social mobility in contemporary China through wider perspectives.

With respect to research theme and theory orientation, this study differs somewhat from general social mobility study. Generally, studies in this field focus on the proposition of industrialization with emphasis on the relationship between industrialization and social mobility, such as whether industrialization increased opportunities of mobility (especially upward mobility), and whether there is a tendency that ascription factors (such as family background) has gradually been replaced by achievement factors (such as individual efforts) in determining opportunity of individual mobility. Usually, these studies conclude that industrialization leads to a more open social structure, or that social structure has been turning from closure into openness. On the other hand, foreign researchers who study social mobility in China often follow a theoretical framework of Neo-structuralism (theory of industry or market segmentation) and Neo-institutionalism (theory of institutional evolution and market transition). Most scholars in China also adopt these two theoretical frameworks. These studies mainly discuss changes of social mobility patterns and mechanisms in the background of institutional transitions and the complexity of social mobility mechanisms in China in the context of coexistence of state-owned planned sector and market-oriented sector (or the planned redistribution system and the market system).

However, our study did not follow the above tracks. The foremost goal of the study has been to provide a comprehensive and systematic description about the overall trend of social mobility in China over the past fifty years. Through this description, we hope that readers can see how destinies of individuals and groups are influenced by social evolution and national policy adjustment, that researchers can get some new ideas when they try to explore social transformation in contemporary China, and that decision-makers of the government can find how changes of policies may lead to significant, far-reaching socio-political consequences.

With the above-mentioned research goal, this study focuses on three aspects. First, it will give a comprehensive investigation of major socio-political changes and relevant policy adjustments since 1949 and their influences on social mobility. The reason to do so is that if we do not understand these changes, it is impossible for us to uncover the clues of changes in social mobility mechanisms and patterns, and the causes that drove these changes. Second, we will try to explain the developmental process, intrinsic property, and future trend of current social stratification in order to answer these questions:

- *Does social stratification exist in contemporary China?*
- *Where is the boundary of each stratum?*
- *What are the differences between different social strata?*
- *Is there a tendency of structuralization in social stratification?*

In other words, we plan to analyze characteristics of social stratification in contemporary China and estimate its future tendency from the viewpoint of social mobility. Third, we will conduct a comparative study on paths, mechanisms, rates, barriers, and opportunities of social mobility in different periods—especially the time around the economic reform—in an effort to judge the overall direction of social structure transitions in China over the past fifty years, that is, in what aspects of Chinese social structure the openness has been increased, and in what aspects the closure has been retained or even strengthened. Meanwhile, we will analyze how these openness and closure affect individual and socio-economic development and we will provide corresponding suggestions.

SUMMARY OF MAJOR FINDINGS

This research group adopted a study strategy combining macro-level analysis with micro-level analysis according to the particular conditions in China in order to investigate social mobility in China since 1949 qualitatively and quantitatively. Fifty years is just a short flash in the river of history. However, in the case of China, there have been five great structural social transitions. Before 1978, the social status of strata, groups, families and individuals mainly depended on the impact from the changes of the national political systems, economic systems and social policies. Sometimes it went up and sometimes it went down; it was quite unstable. Not until the reform and opening-up, the social mobility in China has taken on the similar mobile tracks usually existing in the industrialized countries. Over the past fifty years, there were five significant changes of social mobility. This study revealed the following characteristics of social mobility during this period.

> *Firstly, the pattern of social mobility in China is different from the patterns in industrialized countries. Accordingly, the theme, strategy, and methodology of research on social mobility in China should be different as well.*

The social mobility in China over the past fifty years has occurred in the background of frequent transformations in social, political, and economic systems. In contrast, scholars in industrialized countries generally study social mobility in a relatively stable context. Therefore, social mobility in China is different from industrialized countries in opportunities, rules, directions, rates, and scales of mobility. Industrialized countries usually are open societies with the principal rule of achievement in social mobility; while in China, especially before the reform and opening-up, both achievement factors and ascription factors have to take effect through intermediate institutional and structural factors, which were very significant before the reforms and still functions importantly afterwards. Merely applying mainstreaming research methods to study of social mobility in China will bring many limitations. Therefore, the research group has designed an "analytical framework for social mobility in China" after extensive exploratory studies. This book is the primary outcome of study on social mobility in China over the past fifty years based on this analytical framework.

> *Secondly, before and after the reforms in 1978, dramatic changes have occurred in patterns and mechanisms of social mobility in China.*

Before the reform and opening-up, political movements occupied the Chinese social arena one after another. The planned economy system put everything, including political, economic, and cultural resources under its control. The arrangements of national institutions and policies affected social positions and mobility opportunities of every social member or even a whole stratum directly. The vicissitudes of individual social status, the rise and decline of social strata, all depended on changes in states, governments, institutions, and social policies. In short, a politically driven pattern of social mobility dominated this period.

Since the reform and opening-up from 1978, China has turned most of its attention to economic development. A series of market-oriented reforms have been carried out, which have gradually transformed the planned economy system into the socialist free-market system and the agricultural society into industrial society. Forces of industrialization, urbanization, and marketnization have pushed economic development and the transformation of economic structure, accelerated divisions in social structure, and diversified channels of social mobility. The influence of achievement factors on social mobility mechanisms has won more weight. Impact of capability-oriented rules of social selections on attainment of socio-economic status has been prominent. However, we must point out that arrangements of national institutions and policies still have relatively important influence on social status attainment. Nevertheless, the modern social mobility mechanisms and patterns have been taking shape.

Thirdly, there is a trend of pro-high-level shift in occupational structure in China.

According to previous studies, pro-high-level shift in occupational structure is a pervasive phenomenon in industrialized countries. High-level occupations increase and account for a bigger proportion of occupation structure, whereas the proportion of low-level occupations has gradually declined, forming a trend of upward mobility.

Our study demonstrates that, since 1978, occupational structure in China has also shown a trend of pro-high-level shift. Based on data collected from the third, forth, and fifth population census in China, analysis shows that in the overall occupational structure the proportion of primary-level occupations (industrial workers and agricultural laborers) had decreased by 8.17 percent in 2000 over the 1982 figure; in contrast, the proportion of middle-level occupations had increased by 7.2 percent. Obviously, there is a pro-high-level trend in the overall occupational structure during the eighteen years from 1982 to 2000. However, compared with industrialized countries, the increase of occupations at middle and high levels was relatively small. Therefore, this trend of pro-high-level shift is still in its early stage.

The pro-high-level shift in occupational structure in industrialized countries indicates the transformation from industrialized society to post-industrialized society (or information society) after the 1950s with a trend of an increase in white-collar occupations and a decrease in blue-collar occupations. Nonetheless, the pro-high-level trend in occupational structure in China reflects a transformation from agricultural society to industrialized society after 1978 with a trend of an increase in non-agricultural employment and a decrease in farm employment. There are two driving forces in the trend of pro-high-level shift in occupational structure in China. The first one is the vast development of the tertiary industry, especially emerging tertiary sectors, impelled by industrialization and urbanization, which has provided an enlarged space of employment. The second one is the fast expansion of the private sector outside the planned economy system that has provided numerous opportunities for non-agricultural employment. Millions of peasants are employed by the private sector, and thousands of self-employed persons and private entrepreneurs emerge. In general, the overall trend of pro-high-level shift in occupational structure in China is a rapid growth both in numbers and in proportion of high-level occupations providing more opportunities of upward mobility. In such progress, occupational status will increasingly be improved and incomes will increase as well.

The trend of pro-high-level shift in occupational structure in China driven by continuous high-speed growth in economy not only causes a large number of people achieve upward mobility but also produces more significant social benefits. First of all, more people will find hopes in this progress and have more confidence about the future. They will find that upward mobility is possible as long as they can try their best to fight for it. Accordingly, such hope and confidence will reduce social conflicts through generating a more positive social identification. This may explain the following seemingly confusing phenomenon in today's China: widening gaps between urban and rural areas and among regions, in the large numbers of unemployment, and serious polarization of rich and poor, all these issues, from certain point of view, could not be tolerated any more. Yet, at the same time, Chinese society still functions in a stable condition. For example, nowadays about one hundred millions peasants are working in cities across the nation. They often cannot get reasonable remunerations and face discrimination and unfair treatment. It is puzzling that such a huge group, which is still expanding, can live in peace with urban residents. An explanation may be due to the fact that social status and economic income of peasant-workers are still higher than that of agricultural laborers who remain in rural areas.

Fourthly, in the next ten years, both the degree of pro-high-level shift in occupational structure and the size of middle social stratum in China will increase in jumps.

The research group has studied the relationship between per capita GDP in China and occupational categories and found that the growth of economy has a direct effect on the growth of non-agricultural occupational positions and middle-higher level occupational positions. The higher the level of economic development in a province or region, the greater the proportions of managerial personnel, professionals, clericals, and commercial and service personnel will be in the occupation structure.

We also find that, in the process of per capita annual GDP in a certain province increasing from 5,000 Yuan RMB to 7,500 Yuan RMB, and from 7,501 Yuan RMB to 10,000 Yuan RMB, and from 10,001 Yuan RMB to 12,500 Yuan RMB, the numbers of state and social administrators, managerial personnel, professional and technical personnel, clerical personnel, commercial and service personnel, and industrial workers increased year after year as well. At the same time, the number of agricultural laborers deceased. When per capita annual GDP was over 12,500 Yuan RMB, the number and proportion of managerial personnel, professional and technical personnel, clerical personnel, commercial and service personnel, and industrial workers increased in jumps, while agricultural laborers declined sharply. Just as Table 3-3 in

Chapter 3 shows, when per capita annual GDP was over 12,500 Yuan RMB, the proportion of managerial personnel rose from 1.6 percent to 2.7 percent; professional personnel increased from 6.7 percent to 10.9 percent; clerical personnel grew from 3.5 percent to 7.7 percent; commercial and service personnel increased from 12.3 percent to 18.6 percent; industrial worker increased from 24.1 percent to 34.1 percent. In contrast, the proportion of agricultural laborers fell abruptly from 50.9 percent to 25.2 percent. According to the data from the National Bureau of Statistics of China, in 2001 per capita annual GDP in the following provinces, autonomous regions, and municipalities were beyond 12,500 Yuan RMB: Shanghai (30,674 yuan), Beijing (20,576 yuan), Tianjin (18,327 yuan), Zhejiang (14,628 yuan), Guangdong (13,680 yuan), Jiangsu (12,932 yuan) and Fujian (12,510 yuan).[1] Occupational structures in all these regions have experienced similar changes to those mentioned-above.

How should we account for such phenomenon? This requires further exploration of the socio-economic meaning of the 12,500-yuan per capita GDP. Calculated by the official rate of exchange, 12,500 Yuan RMB is equal to 1,512 US dollar. However, if calculated by Purchasing Power Parity (PPP), 12,500 Yuan RMB is equal to 6,148 US dollar. Some researchers believe that, if calculated by the official rate of exchange, the level of economic development in China will be underestimated, whereas calculated by Purchasing Power Parity, an overestimation results. From our point of view, judging from the overall level of socio-economic development in China, the per capita annual GDP in the above seven regions at least is over 3,000 US dollar. That is to say, industrialization has been accomplished in these seven regions, i.e., these regions have entered the industrialized society. The jumps in growth that occurred in their occupational structure and stratification structure are the result of such development. Moreover, these jumps in growth provide the foundation for further social development. In the above seven regions, not only the per capita annual GDP is higher than that of the rest of China, but also the level of development in urbanization, science and technology, culture and sports, social employment, living conditions, social orders, and social development are very high or relative high. In addition to these seven regions, the per capita annual GDP of Liaoning Province reached 13,000 yuan in 2002, and Shandong Province reached 13,654 yuan in 2003. Very likely, in the next five to ten years, other provinces such as Heilongjiang, Hebei, Jilin, Hubei, Chongqing, Hainan, Hunan, Henan, Anhui, Jiangxi, Sichuan, Shannxi, Xinjiang, and Neimenggu (Inner Mongolia) will join the list. Therefore, we can anticipate that in the next five years, there will be a jump in both the occupational structure and social stratum structure of China. Accordingly, the size of middle social strata will grow in jumps. For example, when the per capita annual GDP of Beijing reached 20,576 yuan in 2001, its total number of professional and technical personnel accounted for 16.4 percent of its total employment, and the proportion of the middle stratum was around 36 percent.

---

[1] National Bureau of Statistics of China. 2003. *Statistical Abstract of China (2003)*. Beijing: China National Statistic Press: 23, 40.

Fifthly, Chinese society has been tending toward an open society.

Based on the nationwide survey data, the research group has investigated changes of social mobility patterns, shaping process and developmental tendency of ten major social strata over the past fifty years in China. The results show that there are great differences between the periods before and after the reform and opening-up.

In the perspective of intergenerational mobility, the intergenerational total mobility rate was merely 41.4 percent before 1980. More specifically, the rate of upward mobility was 32.4 percent, and the intergenerational immobility rate was 58.6 percent. In other words, it appears that nearly 60 percent of children would be expected to end up in the same occupations as their fathers, and only 30 percent or more could accomplish upward social mobility. After 1980, the intergenerational total mobility rate reached 54 percent, of which the rate of upward mobility was 40.9 percent; that is, about 40 percent of children could rise to a higher social status.

As far as the intragenerational mobility is concerned, the rate of total mobility from previous occupation to current occupation was 13.3 percent before 1979; the rate was 30.3 percent from 1980 to 1989, and 54.2 percent from 1990 to 2001. That means that 86.7 percent of social members worked in permanent positions before the reform and opening-up. From 1949 to 1979, the rate of upward mobility was 7.4 percent; from 1980 to 1989, the rate rose to 18.2 percent, and from 1990 to 2001 it reached 30.5 percent.[1]

Based on the above analyses of intergenerational and intragenerational mobility and the rate of total mobility, social mobility in China has significantly increased since 1978. It indicates that Chinese society has been tending toward an open society since the reform and opening-up.

Observations in social practice show that, with the deepening of reforms, social mobility mechanisms that affect people's social status has become more fair and reasonable and social mobility channels have been more unblocked. A series of institutions and policies that once hampered people's reasonable mobility, such as social class origins, the ownership system, the work unit system, and the dual urban-rural system, have quitted the stage or dwindled out. In contrast, achievement factors, such as personal capability and performance, are principal factors that affect status attainment. Meanwhile, rapid development in economy provides large numbers of positions in higher levels, with more opportunities for social members to gain deserved social status through ones' individual efforts. It indicates that Chinese society has been tending toward an open society since the reform and opening-up as well.

Sixthly, the modern social mobility pattern featuring justness, openness, and

---

[1] See Table 4-11 in Chapter 4.

reasonableness is still in its infancy.

Two great transformations in contemporary China, i.e., transformation from traditional agricultural society to modern industrial society and transformation from the planned economy system to the socialist free-market system, are still in process and far from accomplishment. Social mobility in an environment of such dual transformation has shown similar complexity and transition. On one hand, some important achievement factors such as education have had an increasingly significant influence on individual status attainment. Political status is being replaced by occupational status. Performance or competence has become more and more important for socio-economic status attainment as well. All these changes show that a modern social mobility pattern has been in the process of formation. On the other hand, the influence of institution and policy on social mobility is still visible, sometimes even crucial. In the process of dual transformation, such influence of institution and policy sometimes may be positive, whereas sometimes may be negative. Some institutional barriers to social mobility left by the planned economy system, such as the residence registration system (or the *Hukou* system), the personnel administration system, and the employment systems, etc., still work and are out of the agenda of reform.

Notably, some ill tendencies coexist with the open trend in contemporary Chinese society. Based on our analyses of intragenerational and intergenerational mobility in various occupational groups and social strata, since 1980 in some social strata with advantaged positions such as state and social administrators and professional and technical personnel, etc., intergenerational inheritance has risen remarkably with a significant decline in intragenerational mobility and a tendency of more in and less out. Contrastingly, children with origins in lower socio-economic positions have encountered more difficulties when they made an effort to rise to higher strata. The barriers between low-level and high-level strata are consolidated. Such tendency may indicate that boundaries between different social strata have become clear. Yet, economic, organizational, and cultural resources have shown a tendency of upward concentration since the middle of the 1990s. A large numbers of people who initially possessed only one or two of the above resources have come into possession of three forms of resource simultaneously. All these tendencies may go against the formation of the social mobility mechanism and social stratum structure featuring justness, reasonableness, and openness.

As a whole, social mobility in contemporary China shows similar characteristics to the dual transformation of social transition and institutional reform. Therefore, there is a long way to go in the shaping process of the modern social mobility pattern in China.

TENDENCIES OF SOCIAL MOBILITY IN CHINA

In the report *Social Stratification in Contemporary China*, we pointed out that there is a rudimentary form of modern social stratum structure in China and discussed evidences that support the above statement. Meanwhile, we also demonstrated that this rudimentary form of modern social stratum structure does not assort with the process of socialist modernization in China.

Judging from current international and domestic situations, we present several possible tendencies about the future of the rudiment of modern social stratum structure in China in the following three scenarios.

In the first scenario, this rudiment of modern social stratum structure is similar to a newborn infant. It would get sufficient nutrition and favorable environments in the process of future socio-economic growth and then could develop into the modern social stratum structure featuring justness, reasonableness, and openness successfully and healthfully. In the shape of its structure, it would evolve from current onion-like structure to an olive-like structure.

In the second scenario, this newborn infant would face malnutrition and could not get timely care and treatment due to stagnancy in reforms of institutions and policies and the lag of social development behind economic development. As a result, it might develop into a freak, i.e., an abnormal social stratum structure. In the shape of its structure, it might keep the current onion shape with a huge lower stratum and an undeveloped middle stratum.

In the third scenario, this newborn infant would face abominable international and domestic environments without any nutrition and care and treatment due to interruption or even disastrous mistakes in reforms of institutions and policies and serious unbalance between social development and economic development. It would be ill and weak for a time and might degenerate to a candlestick-like structure from its current onion shape. In the modern world, this is a kind of abnormal social structure with a weak skeleton, which could not support future socio-economic development at all.

Of course, we hope that we can see the first scenario coming true while leaving the second and the third one to the imagination. We believe that a modern social stratum structure featuring justness, reasonableness, and openness (in an olive shape) should be the proper social structure of a medium developed modern socialist country. In fact, Deng Xiaoping proposed the same mission in his famous "three-step strategy of development" twenty years ago. Up to now, the strategic mission in the first two steps has been accomplished and we are on the way to the third step.

Undoubtedly, the modern social stratum structure featuring justness, reasonableness, and openness is not only an essential characteristic of a modern society, but also a fundamental precondition for the formation of a modern society. Therefore, this structure should develop simultaneously in the process of formation of a modern society. In this process, the formation of the social mobility mechanisms with justness, reasonableness, and openness is not only the fundamental precondition of the development of modern social stratum structure, but also its prime driving force. The more straightway the social mobility channels, the more diverse the social mobility mechanisms, the higher the rate of social mobility, the larger the scale of social mobility, the easier the actions of people's social mobility, and the more just, reasonable, open, and vigorous a social stratum structure formed by these drives will be. In such social structure, each member in different social strata will be in his or her proper place and exert his or her own specialty. Eventually, such a social stratum structure can coordinate with the development of economy and support and promote further socio-economic development.

In this study, we find that the pattern of Chinese social mobility is shifting to a modern social mobility pattern and this new pattern is playing an increasingly important role. However, some unjust, unreasonable, and out-of-date institutions and policies are still blocking the channels of social mobility. In some important fields, there is a sign that these social mobility channels might be closed again. Therefore, this is a crucial moment in the transition of social mobility pattern in China. If China can follow the right track in constructing a socialist modern society, arrange reasonable institutions, propose right policies, deepen reforms, and remove all institutional and policy barriers left by the planned economy system, a social mobility pattern featuring justness, reasonableness, and openness will eventually be established. In contrast, if the institutional reform slows down, various institutional barriers remain, negative social mobility mechanisms thrive while positive mechanisms keep weak, or even once opened channels are blocked again, then the whole society will stagnate and the above-mentioned second and third scenarios will come true.

In our opinion, in order to promote the realization of the first scenario and avoid the second and the third one in social mobility perspective, the key is to establish a modern social mobility pattern with justness, reasonableness, and openness. We suggest that the following aspects should be considered:

First, China needs to deepen the institutional reform, remove institutional barriers that exist in the residence registration system, the personnel administration system, and the employment system, and speed up the rate of social mobility so that every social member can find his or her proper place. In particular, we should help millions of surplus rural laborers transfer to the secondary and tertiary industry in order to reduce the lower social strata as quickly as possible. The direction of reform should aim to impair the influence of ascription factors. The current ascription factors such as the residence registration and employment systems, which prevent thousands of millions of peasants from obtaining equal employment opportunities in urban areas and cause many of them become "peasant-workers" with lower social status and incomes and few upward mobility opportunities, should be abolished or redesigned as soon as possible. All these barriers have not only wasted huge numbers of human resources, but also produced enormous social tensions and led to many serious social issues.

Second, China needs to propose a series of new social policies in order to help various social mobility mechanisms featuring justness, reasonableness, and openness (especially various achievement rules that emphasize personal competence and encourage individual efforts) become stable and leading mechanisms. In doing so, the middle social stratum will be enlarged so that the shape of social stratification can become olive-like. Mechanisms of equal employment, fair competition and relevant supervisory mechanisms should be established. In modern social competition, the foremost criterion should be competence or performance. Only if people play fair in competition, if everybody can obtain the opportunity of upward mobility, and if the rule of achievement becomes common understanding, can Chinese society be an open society with a just, reasonable, and vigorous modern social stratum structure.

In particular, institutional innovations in some fields deserve greatest attention because policies in these fields will affect thousands of millions of people, if not the whole population, in China. The first one is the innovation in labor and employment policy. In some areas, especially in the private sector, there are no effective legal mechanisms and policy pressures that can ensure enterprise to provide equal employment opportunity, raise salary and wages, and offer professional training for their employees. In some enterprises, frequently firing employees before the expiration of their probation period is a most efficient strategy for cost cutting. Obviously, it will harm employees' economic accumulation and skill acquirement and reduce their opportunities of upward mobility. From employees' viewpoint, they will permanently stay in the primary blue-collar level without any opportunities of rising to middle-higher level blue-collar or white-collar positions because they lack governmental and legal supports and negotiation skills to protect their own rights and interests. The second field is the innovation in redistribution policy such as taxation. The current income redistribution policy has an effect of adverse adjustment in many areas and needs to be changed. For example, many agricultural laborers whose average monthly income is not more than two or three hundred yuan have to pay 8.4 percent tax out of it, whereas the minima taxable income for urban residents is 1,000 yuan. That is obviously unfair. The third field is the removal of limitations that are imposed on business establishment in order to encourage people to start their own business. It is very likely that the minimal capital requirement is one of the major institutional barriers that holdback people's initiatives of going into business. Such requirements cannot hold in those who have illegal funding sources, yet only restricts common people who lack money and are unable to obtain loans from banks. Removing or dropping the barrier as low as possible will allow more people to start their own business and enter the stratum of individual-operated business proprietor s or private entrepreneurs.

Third, China needs to adjust and reform the public resources allocation mechanisms in order to achieve fair and reasonable utilizations of these resources. The rationality of public resources allocation certainly should be judged from the perspective of efficiency. However, equality is an even more important criterion.

Whether the mechanisms of public resources allocation are fair or not, to a great extent, will determine the possibility that people can enjoy advantages brought by public resources allocations and that people can obtain equal opportunity in competitions at best. In this field, government should make overall plans and consider all factors in order to enable people in any stratum and any region to receive advantages of reasonable public resources allocation universally. In particular, government should assist groups that are in unfavorable situations with indigent ascription resources (e.g., families with poor economic conditions and undeveloped regions) to strengthen competitive competence. China is a country with a huge population and unbalanced development in urban and rural areas and different regions. Since the 1990s, the urban-rural and regional gaps have become wider and wider because of government's prior consideration in allocating public resources to richer regions and to richer people (economists approvingly call this "unbalanced development strategy").

From the social mobility perspective, public education is the most important field in which public resources allocation is influential. In this field, current distribution mechanisms are particularly unreasonable and unfair. The population in urban areas account for 40 percent in China. Urban residents have a higher average income than those in rural areas. The total investment in education (including various sources) was 580 billion Yuan RMB in 2002, and about 77 percent of it was invested in urban areas. By contrast, residents in rural areas who account for more than 60 percent of Chinese population only obtained 23 percent of the total educational inputs.[1] According to a survey conducted by the Ministry of Education of China, in sources of the total investment in compulsory education in inquired rural regions, the central government investment accounts for one percent, the provincial government investment makes up 11 percent, the county-level government invests 9.8 percent, and the rest 78.2 percent is raised by the town and village-level government.[2] At present, on one hand, senior high school education has been added to the compulsory education system in many cities and rich rural areas. On the other hand, in depressed villages in spacious western areas, a considerable number of teachers are often given back salary; the statutory nine-year compulsory education is far from universal and the dropout rate is relatively high. Young people in these areas are unable to obtain deserved education. To them, the inequality begins from the starting line. In this field, the allocation of public resources is obviously unreasonable. Nowadays, the annual total government revenue is over 2,000 billion Yuan RMB in China. Compared with it, the total rural compulsory education budget is relatively small. The issue of unreasonable allocation of public educational resources has been pointed out for a decade, but the situation changed little. The major reason is that the government excessively or maybe mistakenly take the so-called "efficiency first, with due consideration to equality" principle to conduct the allocation of public educational

[1] Chen, Xiwen. 2004. "Rural Economy and Rural Policy in China." Chongqing: *Reform*. Vol. 3.
[2] Lian, Yuming (ed.). 2004. *China Digital Report*. Beijing: China Times Economic Press: 385.

resources. However, education is one of the most critical factors that consist of modern achievement-led social mobility mechanisms. The government has a responsibility to adjust current mechanisms of public educational resources allocation and achieve equality and rationality in this field.

Fourth, China needs to form a proper urbanization strategy in order to speed up the process of urbanization. Urbanization has an important effect on widening social mobility channels and expediting social mobility. The intensified tendency of industrial economy pushes population to concentrate in the city, and the knowledge-based economy and information society have an even stronger concentration effect. Urbanization is an inevitable tendency, but we are hindered by traditional thinking that leads us to take detours. China will enter into a fast-developing period in the next 10 to 20 years. Chinese government should find a proper urbanization strategy in order to lead this giant tend in the right direction.

An important function of urbanization is to absorb large numbers of rural surplus laborers and help them transfer to the secondary and tertiary industry and live in cities. The expedient conception of "peasant-workers" should leave the stage. Cities, especially modernized cities, are carriers of the tertiary industry and modern service industry. In history of industrialized countries, the first occupation that agricultural laborers found after they entered cities was that of industrial workers. After the 1950s or 1960s, they started to transfer to the tertiary industry in large numbers. In current China, the situation is a little different. Over the past twenty years, industrialization has rapidly developed in both urban and rural areas. The number of employment in the secondary industry is already very large. Therefore, in the future, a part of agricultural laborers will inevitably work in the secondary industry, but most of them will transfer to the tertiary industry. Some of them with higher capability and skills will find jobs in the modern service sector. Cities are also carriers of civilization. Another important function of cities is improving the overall quality of the population through the edifying effect of the modern civilization and hence turning a traditional human into a modern human. In short, speeding up the process of urbanization, expanding the employment in non-agricultural sectors, especially in the tertiary industry, producing more high-level jobs and positions and more upward mobility opportunities, will undoubtedly expedite social mobility and impel further development of the pro-high-level trend in occupational structure.

Nonetheless, some problems in the process of urbanization deserve attention. First, the once popular makeshifts of urbanization should be superseded by the above-mentioned 'indeed' urbanization. Many empirical observations show that small towns could not become effective carriers of the tertiary industry. Second, urbanization is not equal to the beautification of cities or anything comparable. The essence of urbanization is population concentration. It means that agricultural laborers should be permitted to live and work in any cities in China. At present, in the name of urban beautification or just for the 'face' of the city, in some cities, street jobs are strictly banned and all peddlers are compulsorily driven to designated marketplaces in which high stand fees are levied. Abolishing the street jobs prevents ordinary people from starting their own business. In recent years, the number of self-employed persons in China decreased abnormally in the millions and the main cause is such an inclination of "aristocratism" in urbanization.

In conclusion, in order to establish a social mobility pattern and social stratum structure featuring justness, reasonableness, and openness, there are many things need to be accomplished in institutional innovations and many barriers should be removed. Only if these issues are resolved and barriers are removed, can the rudiment of modern social stratum structure in China have the opportunity and the conditions to become a real modern social structure.

Chapter 1   Classification of Ten Social Strata

The Research Group for Social Structure in Contemporary China of the Chinese Academy of Social Sciences (CASS) published its preliminary research results, *Social Stratification in Contemporary China* in early 2002.[1] In that report, we presented our fundamental points of view about the transition of social stratum structure in China since the reform and opening-up, and classified contemporary Chinese society into ten major strata. The classification and analyses of the ten social strata have attracted attention around the world and resulted in some controversy in academia. Since then, this research group has continued the study in more depth and in a more comprehensive manner. At this stage, we will present a more systematical theoretical explanation of the classification of the ten social strata and establish an analytical framework for social mobility in contemporary China based on the classification. First, in this chapter we will discuss theoretical analyses and operational explanations about the classification of the ten social strata. Second, we will propose a more precise estimation of the proportion of each social stratum as well as further subdivisions in order to describe the structure and characteristics of current social stratification more accurately.

CRITERIA FOR CLASSIFICATION OF TEN SOCIAL STRATA

Since 1978, the structure of Chinese social stratification has changed fundamentally. With continuous development in industrialization, urbanization, and marketnizaion, the political, institutional, and administrative criteria (such as political status, registered permanent residence status, and administrative personnel dossier identity) in the planned economy period that once determined people's socio-economic status have been replaced gradually by some new factors. The division of occupations, the widening gap in incomes, and privatization of property have made boundaries between different social strata clearer than ever. Although the evolution of the social stratum structure is still ongoing, its rudimentary shape has emerged. In the first report, *Social Stratification in Contemporary China*, we proposed the classification of ten social strata that has been widely accepted; however, a detailed explanation about the criteria for such a classification was not presented. In this section, we will offer both theoretical and operational definitions about each stratum.

---

[1] Lu (2002).

27

Classification of Occupations and Three Types of Resources

In *Social Stratification in Contemporary China*, we proposed a theoretical framework to classify social stratification by possession of organizational, economic, and cultural resources on the basis of classification of occupations.[1] The reason we classified social strata based on occupational category is not only out of consideration for convenience of conducting the research, but also for using the results of previous theoretical studies. In modern society, the classification of occupational status is one of the most basic social differentiations. People in different occupations usually reflect differences in income, prestige, education background, and authority, etc. Therefore, the classification of occupations is closely related to social stratification. In addition, from the perspectives of data collection and analysis, information about personal occupations is relatively easy to acquire and to be classified. For these reasons, many studies of social stratification have been conducted on the basis of occupation classification, the same holds true for the social stratum classification proposed by the research group.

Based on the classification of occupations, we classify basic characteristics of each stratum according to the possession of organizational, economic, and cultural resources. *Organizational resource*, or authority resource, is the capability to make use of social resources (including human resources and material resources) endowed by organizations such as governments and political parties. *Economic resource* refers to the right to own, use, and operate the means of production. *Cultural resource* means possession of knowledge and skills, which are accredited by certificates or qualifications resulting in diplomas or degrees. We believe that, in contemporary China, possession of the above three types of resources is an indicator of social positions of various social groups and each social member. It also indicates the overall socio-economic status of individuals. In the study, therefore, the classification of occupations provides the basis for classification of Chinese social strata, whereas the state of resource possession acts as the indicator for such a classification. We drew this conclusion based several years' investigations conducted by the research group. From analysis of data collected by large numbers of case interviews, we found that when people were asked to classify social groups depending on their personal experience and subjective judgment, they usually proposed three criteria: money (level of income or value of possessions), authority (level of position in public or commercial organizations), and education (level of degree or diploma).[2] Summarized

---

[1] Lu (2002).

[2] A monograph on this topic will be published soon. Some examples are offered as follows in order to show how people classify groups by the three criteria. For instance, groups are frequently mentioned as: "powerful people" (or "officials" and "cadres"), "rich people" (or "big bosses", "*Dakuan*", "factory owners", and "businessmen'), "literate people" (or "cultured people", "intellectuals", and "teachers'), "common people" (or "ordinary people", "working class", "people without power and influence", "workers", and "peasants"), and "poor people" (or "people scraping a living", "people without jobs", and "laid-off workers").

in academic languages, we may put it in this way: Generally, people tend to evaluate the social status of individuals or groups according to their possession of economic, organizational (authority), and cultural resources. In fact, sociologists often employ the three indicators to study the classification of social stratum in modern society as well. Based on analysis of existing theories and findings of empirical studies, we drew the same conclusion; in contemporary China, possession of economic, organizational, and cultural resources determines people's overall socio-economic status and their social appraisals of others and themselves. We believe that analysis of socio-economic differentiations between social strata according to possession of three types of resources will conduce an in-depth understanding of socio-economic divisions and basic characteristics of resources allocation in contemporary China.

The disparity of possession of the three types of resources among people is the result of socio-economic divisions. Nonetheless, what theorists of class (stratum) issues pay their greatest attention is not the superficial phenomenon of resource allocation, but the causes that result in such disparity, and possible socio-political consequences that may be produced by such disparity. Similarly, the objective of social stratum classification in the study is not just show whose income is higher or lower, whose power is greater or less, or who is controlling the cultural resources or not. What we really want to know is which factors in social structure enable people to possess different types or quantities of resources. In our opinion, it is people's different positions in the social structure that determine what type of resources they could possess or how much of such resources they could have, hence leading to disparity in socio-economic states. Such disparity may affect people's socio-political attitudes and behavior orientations, which is referred to as social stratification. In this study, we try to explore the foremost cause of social stratification (i.e., mechanisms of stratification) in the structure of social relationships. Only if these stratification mechanisms are found, can we explain the disparity in resources allocation and its possible socio-political consequences. Therefore, the objective of the classification of ten social strata in our study is to display the distribution of the three types of resources (which should be consistent with people's subjective feelings). The criteria for classification of social stratification that we used in the study differentiate people's positions in social structure; these different positions determine the type and quantity of resources that people possess.

Theory of Social Stratum Classification

Figure 1-1 shows the theoretical framework that we apply to analyze the process of social stratification in contemporary China. The criteria of social stratum classification are derived from this framework. There are three layers in this framework: drives of social stratification, mechanisms of social stratification, and outcomes of social stratification (i.e., the situation of resources allocation). This framework summarizes the fundamental process of social stratification in contemporary China.

Figure 1-1 Dynamics of Social Stratification in Contemporary China

First of all, social stratification in contemporary China does not occur in a relatively stable or static environment. It has been evolving with drastic socio-economic changes over the past twenty years. Twenty years ago, the shape and mechanisms of social stratification in China were different from that of the present situations. The socio-economic gaps among people were smaller. Socio-economic groups with significant differences were relatively simple (such as workers, peasants, cadres, and intellectuals, etc.). The degree of homogeneity was extremely high inside social groups. The main factors that determined people's socio-economic differences were political status (such as family background and personal political participation performance) and institutional status (such as the registered residence status—urban resident or rural resident, and the administrative personnel dossier status—cadre or worker). In contrast, in current Chinese society, socio-economic gaps keep widening, and mechanisms of social stratification are totally different from those of twenty years ago. What are the causes of these changes? What drives the evolution of social stratum structure in current China? We have to answer these questions first in the process of analyzing social stratification. In our opinion, the causes or driving forces of changes in social stratification are industrialization, marketnization, and the "dual transitions" (or "dual transformations"), i.e., transformation from traditional agricultural society to modern industrialized society and transformation from the planned economy system to the socialist free-market system.

The continuous advance of industrialization has brought about two significant consequences. The first one is subdivision and specialization in division of labor. The second one is expansion of hierarchical organizations both in number and in size. Changes in the two aspects have had crucial impact on socio-economic stratifications.

Enduring subdivision and specialization in the division of labor have produced a system of division of occupations based on the level of skills or degree of specialization. This system has become the common foundation of social stratification in nearly all industrialized societies. Abundant empirical studies have demonstrated that, in industrialized society and post-industrialized society, a person's occupation is highly related to his or her economic status (income level) and social status (social prestige). Hence, many sociologists classify classes or strata according to occupational classification or occupational prestige. People's occupations had little relationship with their socio-economic status in China before 1978. However, in the past ten years, with the hastened development of industrialization, occupational division has increasingly influenced socio-economic differences. The higher the degree of specialization an occupation has, the higher the level of its income and social prestige. Meanwhile, income and social status of manual workers relatively declined. Occupational division has been increasingly noticeable, which is a significant tendency of social stratification over the past decade in China.

At the same time, various economic and social hierarchies have developed rapidly with the expanding size of organization and the increasing levels of management. Especially remarkable is the separation of ownership right and management authority (or managerial right). All these changes have significant influenced the structure of social strata in contemporary China. In modern industrialized society, a person's control and influence on material resources or human resources are not dependent on hierarchy of status (such as aristocrat and plebeian, and landlord and tenant) as in feudal society, nor dependent on possession of the means of production (capitalist and worker) just like in the early stages of capitalism, but determined to a great extent by the level of position in organizational systems. In modern industrialized society, the foremost and largest resources (including material and human resources) are usually controlled by organizations, not individuals. Therefore, management in an organization actually possesses the right to allocate and control resources that belong to the organization. This is responsible for the differentiation of socio-economic status between management and non-management. In the past ten years in China, with the development of industrialization and integration into the global economy, the authority of the top management and their direct control on resources in large-scale commercial organizations and government agencies have been increasingly strengthened. Inside an organization, gaps of income and prestige between management and non-management have gradually widened. This is one of significant tendencies of social stratification in China over the past decade.

Two consequences of marketization have had a crucial impact on social stratification as well. The first consequence is the emergence of private property rights. The other is the emergence of the non-state-owned sector of economy. Emergence of private property rights has presented China with a new type of social relationship, that is, a relationship between owners of the means of production and their employees. With the advance of marketnizaion, the accumulation of private capital, and the expansion of the scale of the means of the means of production that gaps of socio-economic status between owners of the means of production and their employees have increasingly widened. For this reason, the ownership of the means of production has become an important factor in social stratification in contemporary China. In the process of marketnizaion, the coexistence of state-owned and non-state-owned sectors is a notable characteristic of current Chinese social structure, because this situation has created *institutional segmentation*. A series of institutional arrangements have important influences on resource allocation_and institutional barriers segment different socio-economic fields. In these different fields segmented by institutional arrangements, the rules and opportunities to acquire resources are different. In state-owned sectors (inside the system), administrative authority is the most important mechanism of social differentiation. In non-state-owned sectors (outside the system), possession of the means of production plays the role. In the current socialist market economy system in China, the government controls the most critical and largest quantity of resources. The closer a person is to the core of the state's organizations, the more likely he or she will acquire the advantaged positions in resource allocation. In short, an individual's position in institutional segmentation—inside the system or outside the system or in the core or periphery of the system—determines the types and the quantities of resources he or she may possess.

Criteria for Classification of Social Strata

Based on the above analyses, we believe that the foremost mechanisms of social stratification in contemporary China are the division of labor, hierarchy of authority, relations of production, and segmentation of institutions. *Division of labor* refers to the division of occupational skill levels, such as the division between manual and non-manual workers. Manual workers can be further divided into skilled, semi-skilled, and non-skilled workers; the level of skills of non-manual workers can be classified into senior, middle, and junior level. *Hierarchy of authority* refers to the division of management levels in hierarchical organizations, such as supervisor and supervisee, senior management and middle-lower level management. *Relation of production* refers to the division between owners of the means of production (employers and the self-employed) and employees (workers and staff members). *Institutional segmentation* refers to the division between people inside and outside the system (i.e., the state-owned and collective sectors of economy), and between people in the core sector and in the peripheral sector of the system. The above four mechanisms of stratification produce several major types of social relationships in current Chinese society. People's positions in such a structure of social relationships determine their basic socio-economic status, i.e., the types and quantities of social resources (organizational, economic, and cultural resources) that they may possess. In the above-mentioned interviews, we found that most of the interviewees approved that the three types of resources are the most important resources in modern China and are pursued by almost every social member.

In this study, we locate people's positions in the four types of social relationships through measuring a series of operational variables and hence present the classification of ten social strata. Detailed operational procedure is shown in Figure 1-2.

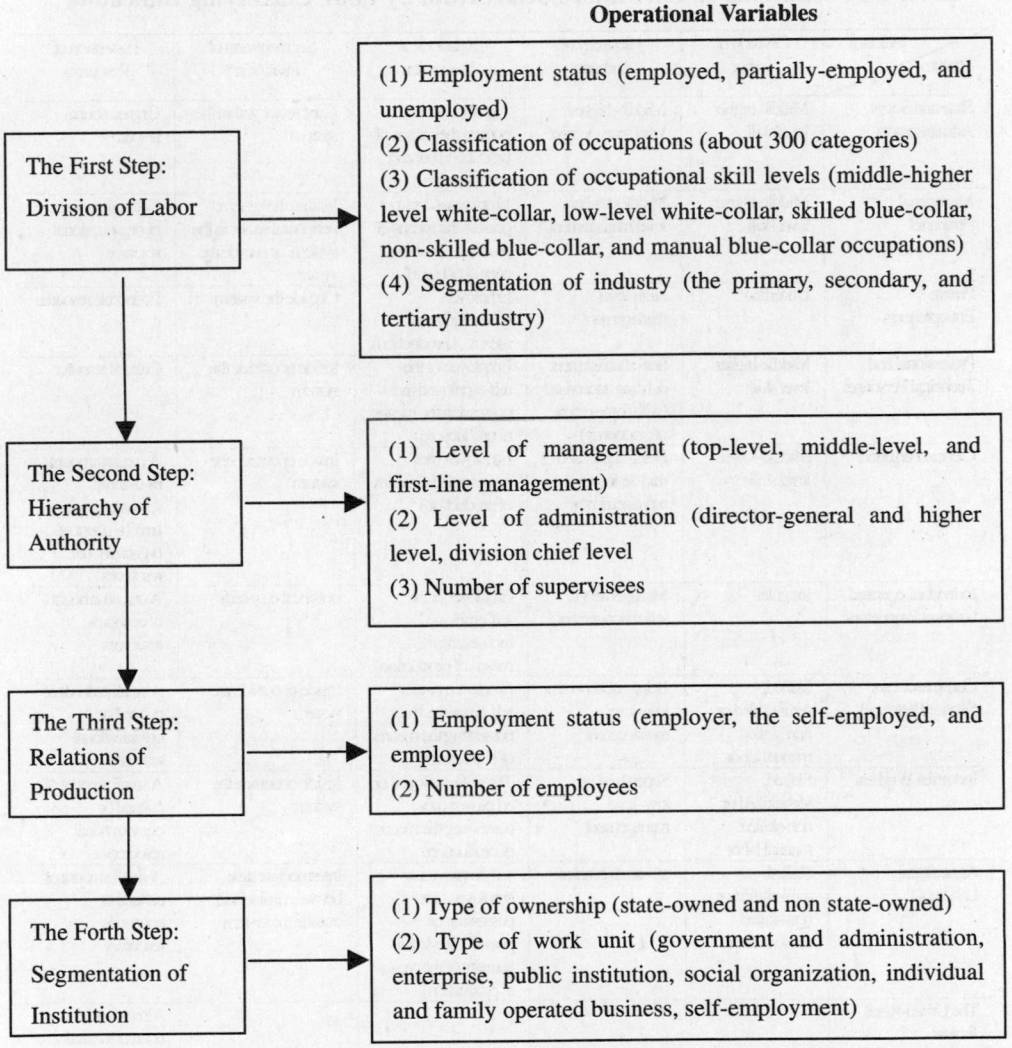

Operational Variables

The First Step: Division of Labor
- (1) Employment status (employed, partially-employed, and unemployed)
- (2) Classification of occupations (about 300 categories)
- (3) Classification of occupational skill levels (middle-higher level white-collar, low-level white-collar, skilled blue-collar, non-skilled blue-collar, and manual blue-collar occupations)
- (4) Segmentation of industry (the primary, secondary, and tertiary industry)

The Second Step: Hierarchy of Authority
- (1) Level of management (top-level, middle-level, and first-line management)
- (2) Level of administration (director-general and higher level, division chief level
- (3) Number of supervisees

The Third Step: Relations of Production
- (1) Employment status (employer, the self-employed, and employee)
- (2) Number of employees

The Forth Step: Segmentation of Institution
- (1) Type of ownership (state-owned and non state-owned)
- (2) Type of work unit (government and administration, enterprise, public institution, social organization, individual and family operated business, self-employment)

Figure 1-2   Classifying Procedure of Ten Social Strata

Based on the above classifying variables, we divide current Chinese society into ten major social strata. Because of different positions of each stratum locating in the division of labor, hierarchy of authority, relations of production, and segmentation of institution, the possession of resources by each stratum is different (see Table 1-1).

Table 1-1   Positions of Ten Major Social Strata by Four Classifying Indicators

Indicator / Stratum	Division of Labor	Hierarchy of Authority	Relations of Production	Segmentation of Institution *	Possession of Resources
State and Social Administrators	Middle-higher level skill	Middle-higher level management	Agent (do not possess the means of production but can control or use it)	Core sector within the system	Organizational resource
Managerial Personnel	Middle-higher level skill	Middle-higher level management	Employee (does not possess the means of production but can control or use it)	Within the system, peripheral sector in the system, or outside the system	Cultural resource or organizational resource
Private Entrepreneurs	Uncertain	High-level management	Employer (possessing the means of production)	Outside the system	Economic resource
Professional and Technical Personnel	Middle-higher level skill	Self-management or being supervised (with some extent of autonomy)	Employee or the self-employed (not possessing the means of production)	Inside or outside the system	Cultural resource
Clerical Personnel	Middle-lower level skill	Being supervised or middle-lower management	Employee (not possessing the means of production)	Inside or outside the system	A certain amount of cultural resources and a small amount of organizational resources
Individual-operated business Proprietors	Irregular	Management or self-management	Employer or the self-employed (possessing the means of production)	outside the system	A certain amount of economic resources
Commercial and Service Personnel	Skilled, semi-skilled or non-skilled manual labor	Being supervised or low-level management	Employee or the self-employed (not possessing the means of production)	Inside or outside the system	A small amount of cultural or organizational resources
Industrial Workers	Skilled, semiskilled or non-skilled manual labor	Supervised or low-level management	The self-employed or employee (not possessing the means of production)	Inside or outside the system	A small amount of cultural or organizational resources
Agricultural Laborers	Skilled, semi-skilled or non-skilled manual labor	self-management	self-employed or employee (not possessing or possessing a small quantity of the means of production)	Intermediate state between inside and outside the system	A small amount of cultural or economic resources
The Urban-Rural Jobless, Unemployed, and Partially Unemployed	—	—	—	—	Almost possessing none of the three types of resources

Note: "Core sector within the system" refers to government agencies and a part of public institutions and social organizations. Resource allocation in these organizations is mainly affected by governmental plans and is dependent on governmental budgets. "Peripheral sector within the system" refers to state-owned enterprises and a part of public institutions and social organizations operating like enterprises. The influence of governmental plans on resource allocation in these organizations is relatively weak.

The ten major social strata respectively are (1) the stratum of state and social administrators (possessing organizational resources), (2) the stratum of managerial personnel (possessing organizational and cultural resources), (3) the stratum of private entrepreneurs (possessing economic resources), (4) the stratum of professional and technical personnel (possessing cultural resources), (5) the stratum of clerical personnel (possessing a small amount of cultural or organizational resources), (6) the stratum of individual-operated business proprietors (possessing a small amount of economic resources), (7) the stratum of commercial and service personnel (possessing a very small amount of three types of resources), (8) the stratum of industrial workers (possessing a very small amount of three types of resources), (9) the stratum of agricultural laborers (possessing a very small amount of three types of resources), and (10) the stratum of the urban-rural jobless, unemployed, and partially unemployed (practically possessing none of the three types of resources).[1]

COMPOSITION OF TEN SOCIAL STRATA

Based on the aforementioned classifying variables and procedure, we formulated the classification of social strata from a nationwide survey. This questionnaire survey was conducted by the research group in 73 counties and cities in 12 provinces, autonomous regions and national municipalities (including Beijing, Shanghai, Zhejiang, Jiangsu, Shandong, Heilongjiang, Hebei, Henan, Jiangxi, Sichuan, Guizhou, and Inner Mongolia) from July to December in 2001. A multi-stage stratified random sampling method was employed in the survey. Subjects of the survey consisted of people at the age from 16 years to 70 years, and the effective sample size is 6,193. After being processed by weighting[2], the sample distribution in basic demographic

---

[1] Lu (2002: 9).

[2] In the initial sample distribution, in consideration of the more complicated composition of urban society and higher degree of homogeneity in rural society, we increased the proportion of the urban sample (urban and rural sample account for 66.3 percent and 33.7 percent respectively). Therefore, after such adjustment, an ex post weighting was needed to process the urban sample. This is also a prevailing method in similar surveys conducted by researchers worldwide. In addition, because of the limitation of the budget, we were unable to employ the method that some foreign scholars have used in similar investigations, i.e., only giving up after the failure of several serial visits to a chosen subject in a week. In general, we would change to another candidate if we failed to reach a subject after several serial visits in at most two days. In some areas, there were higher proportions of turning to candidates, hence this led to small errors in sample distribution of gender and age. That is because men are more likely not to stay at home than women and the younger than the older. Therefore, we needed to conduct a stratified weighting both in gender and in age. Finally, in the sample of the survey, the proportion of floating population was apparently on the low side, which is a prevailing problem in current sampling surveys conducted in China. The reason is that current sampling frame

information and major individual socio-economic background information is very close to that of the distribution of data obtained from the fifth national population census (see Table 1-2). That means the sample's representativeness in our survey is relatively good.

Table 1-2   Sample Distribution of the Survey and Proportion Distribution of 0.1% Sampling in the Fifth National Population Census

Unit: %

Category		Sample distribution before weighting	Sample distribution after weighting	Proportion distribution of data in the population census (the population aged 16~70)
Gender	Male	52.4	50.4	50.9
	Female	47.6	49.6	49.1
Age	16-20	5.4	11.2	11.1
	21-30	14.1	22.7	21.9
	31-40	25.1	26.3	26.3
	41-50	23.8	18.7	19.0
	51-60	17.6	12.5	12.8
	61-70	14.0	8.7	8.9
Registered Residence	Non-agricultural	61.5	27.1	27.1
	Agricultural	38.5	72.9	72.9
Floating Population	Non-floating population	94.5	86.9	86.9
	Floating within local areas	2.5	6.0	6.0
	Migrating from other areas	3.0	7.1	7.1
Number of Family Members*	1	2.8	3.4	2.7
	2	20.5	16.7	12.3
	3	34.7	31.5	28.9
	4	24.0	27.0	25.6
	5	11.0	13.1	17.8
	6	4.6	5.7	7.6
	7 and more	2.4	2.6	5.1
Marital Status	Single (never married)	10.9	17.6	21.3
	Married	84.2	78.8	74.8
	Divorced	1.3	0.8	0.9
	Widowed	3.6	2.8	3.0
Education Received	No education received	8.0	8.6	8.7
	Elementary school	24.3	28.8	30.3
	Junior middle school	34.2	39.6	41.1
	(Vocational)senior middle school	16.7	13.6	10.5
	Technical secondary school	7.0	4.3	4.4
	Junior college	6.7	3.5	3.3
	University	3.0	1.5	1.6
	Postgraduate	0.2	0.1	0.1
Employment Status**	Employed (in work)	66.0	76.4	75.0
	Unemployed (jobless)	34.0	23.6	25.0

generally is unable to cover all floating population. Hereby, we also needed to weight the proportion of the floating population. The weighting equation is listed as follows:

W_{total} (total weight) = W_1 (household weight) × W_2 (gender weight) × W_3 (age weight) × W_4 (floating population weight)

Notes: * In data collected by this survey, the proportion of family with less than 4 people in the distribution of number of family members is a little higher than data collected in the population census, whereas the proportion of family with more than 4 people is a little lower than in the population census data. The possible reason is that in this survey we expressed an emphasis on the permanent population (people who dwells in a residence for more than 3 months with at least 4 days in a week) when inquired respondents about the number of family members.

** In this survey, the definitions of "employed" and "unemployed" are different from those in the population census. In this survey, "employed" refers to working activity that lasts continuously more than one month (including one more month in the future), from which remunerations (including wages, salaries, and profits, etc.) can be earned. Whereas in the population census, "employed" refers to undertaking more than one hour's paid work during the one-week population census period (from October 25 to 31 in 2001). Therefore, some unstably employed and temporarily working people were defined as "employed" in the population census, whereas in this survey they were defined as "unemployed".

The subjects in the nationwide survey are the population aged 10 to 70. Therefore, stratum classification in the study is conducted in population at the age from 10 to 70. Based on the above-mentioned classifying indicators, each respondent in the sample was classified into a certain stratum. Because the framework of social stratification is based on classification of occupations, the first thing we need to explain is how to fit unemployed people into this framework. The first step of classification is to distinguish the employed from the semi-employed and the unemployed (employment status). The classification of the employed population is based on classification of occupations and relevant indicators listed in Figure 1-2.

The method of classifying the unemployed is described as follows: all unemployed people are classified in the stratum of the urban- rural jobless, unemployed, and partially unemployed except for the following four categories of unemployed people: (1) never-employed housewives (married women). which will be classified according to their husbands' stratum positions; (2) never-employed enrolled students and single young people below the age of 22 which will be classified according to their fathers' (or mothers' if father deceased) stratum positions; (3) retirees which will be classified according to their former occupations before retirement; and (4) once employed enrolled students which will be classified according to their last occupations.

In addition, the army was not included in the sampling frame of the survey; hence, compulsory servicemen were not investigated. Because in terms of the occupational and socio-economic status of compulsory servicemen are in an interim state to some extent, as a whole they were not included in social stratum classification in the study. However, families of servicemen that reside out of cantonments might be included in the sampling frame. In fact, the survey sample contains some lifers (civilians and officers). The stratum classification of these servicemen is described as

Figure 1-3 Proportion Distribution of Ten Social Strata

follows: platoon and higher-rank officers are classified as state and social administrators, whereas servicemen below platoon-rank are classified as clerical personnel.

In addition to the classification of the ten social strata, we further subdivided each stratum according to its members' specific positions in division of labor, authority hierarchy, production relations or institutional segmentation (i.e., subcategory). We believe that group disparity within each stratum is due to specific differences in one or more indicators. In such a drastically changing period of current social stratum structure, each social stratum is in the process of floating, restructuring, acclimatizing, and structuralizing; hence, the group disparity within strata is relatively conspicuous.

Figure 1-3 shows respective proportions of ten social strata and their inner compositions.[1]

---

[1] In the preliminary research report *Social Stratification in Contemporary China* (p.44), we estimated the proportion distribution of ten social strata in 1999 based on survey data obtained from eight counties and cities and official statistical data. In this book, the estimated proportions of ten social strata on the basis of the nationwide survey conducted in 2001 are approximate to the former estimations. However, there are significant differences exist in estimations of some proportions. Explanation about these differences and corresponding causes are given as follows: (1) we calculated proportions of ten social strata according to statistical data provided by governmental statistics agencies in the preliminary research report. The population covered in that social stratum classification was only the employed population (employed laborers), whereas in this study the classification based on the nationwide survey data covers all population from the age of 16 to 70. Meanwhile, because statistical measures used by governmental statistics agencies were different, calculations in the preliminary report were relatively rough. By contrast, the calculated proportion distribution based on the nationwide survey is comparatively precise. Therefore, such a situation leads to differences between the two estimations. (2) In this study, the proportion of individual-operated business proprietors (7.1 percent) is far higher than the estimated proportion in the preliminary report (4.2 percent). Before the study, the same situation happened in a sampling survey we conducted in eight counties and cities. The number of individual-operated business proprietors provided by local governments was far smaller than the calculated number based on the survey data. Some foreign economists believe that statistical data are apparently lower than the actual number because a large amount of small service businesses in China were not counted by governmental statistics agencies (Wilde, Georgina and Ken Davies. 2000. *Report on Trends in China: China to 2010 and Hong Kong after 1997*. Beijing: Xinhua Publishing House: 11, 15, and 22). The governmental statistical data apparently underestimated the number of self-employed persons. This problem is especially conspicuous in small cities, small towns, and rural areas. In the survey data, some people who are classified as individual-operated business proprietors (small storekeepers, small workshop owners, and small labor contractors, etc.) did not register at the local Administration for Industry and Commerce. Therefore, we believe that the preliminary report underestimated the proportion of self-employed entrepreneurs. (3) In this study, the estimated proportion of industrial workers (17.5 percent) is far lower than the proportion proposed in the preliminary report (22.6 percent). We believe that the number of industrial workers in the secondary industry has changed to some extent in recent years due to a large number of workers in state-owned and collective enterprises shifting to commercial, trading and service sectors or being laid off. The governmental statistical data failed to reflect such a situation completely and overestimated the number of industrial workers. Moreover, 0.95‰ sampling data of the fifth population census in China shows that the proportion of industrial workers in the secondary industry is 12.5 percent in population aged 16 to 70, and the proportion of the secondary industry workers is 16.3 percent in all of the employed population. The population census data are closer to our calculation results in the study. However, both our survey data and data of the fifth population census might underestimate the proportion of

Figure 1-4 shows the shapes of distribution of the ten social strata in the whole country, urban areas, and rural areas respectively.

State and Social Administrators

The *stratum of state and social administrators* refers to leaders who exercise actual administrative authority in party and government agencies, public institutions, and social organizations. Specifically, it includes chiefs of divisions and higher-level administrators who possess actual administrative authority in ministries and commissions of the central government and national municipalities. It also contains chiefs of sections (or townships) and higher-rank cadres and those below the chief of division (or section) level who have actual administrative authority, and chiefs of division (or section) and higher-rank cadres without actual administrative authority at the level of provincial, city, prefecture, county, and township governments.

---

industrial workers to some extent. Though the number of workers in traditional state-owned and collective enterprises has declined, at the same time a large number of peasant-workers have joined the ranks of industrial workers. Both our survey data and data of the fifth population census did not reflect the floating population completely. Therefore, the 17.5 percent proportion of industrial workers is possibly underestimated. (4) In the study, the estimated proportion of clerical personnel (7.2 percent) is apparently higher than the figure proposed in the preliminary report (4.8 percent), and is also higher than estimated proportion based on 0.95‰ sampling data of the fifth population census (accounting for 2.4 percent in the population aged 16 to 70, and 3.2 percent in the employed population). The cause of such differences is because we proposed stricter definitions of "state and social administrator" (in statistical agency and population census the corresponding category used is "principal of government agency, parties and masses organization, enterprise or institution") and "professional and technical personnel". For example, some people with nominal cadre status but without actual administrative authority are classified as "clerical personnel" in the study, whereas the governmental statistical agency classified them as "principal of government agency, parties and masses organization, enterprise or institution". In addition, heads of grass-roots level organizations (chairperson of the resident committee or the villager committee, and the secretary of the village Communist Party committee) are classified as "clerical personnel" in the study, while the statistical agency classified them as "principal of government agency, parties and masses organization, enterprise or institution". Clerks without professional and technical qualifications and personnel dealing with non-professional affairs in various institutions and enterprises are classified as "clerical personnel" in the study, while the statistical agency classified some of them as "professional and technical personnel". Therefore, the estimated proportion of "clerical personnel" in the study is higher than the figures provided by the statistical agency and the population census, whereas the estimated proportions of "professional and technical personnel" and "state and social administrators" are lower than those provided by the statistical agency and the population census. Classification in the study is relatively closer to the rule of classification of occupations which is commonly applied in international practices. In term of distribution of occupations, generally the proportion of "clerical personnel" usually should be far higher than that of "professional and technical personnel". In addition, the proportion of "clerical personnel" should be higher than the sum of proportions of "professional and technical personnel", "administrative personnel" (cadres in institutions and enterprises), and "owners of enterprise". The proportions of "clerical personnel" calculated based on the governmental statistics and the population census are apparently lower than that of "professional and technical personnel". It indicates that these data may have some errors in classification of occupations and hence seriously underestimated the proportion of "clerical personnel".

Figure 1-4   The Shapes of Distribution of Ten Social Strata, 2001

Note: 1= state and social administrators, 2= managerial personnel, 3= private entrepreneurs, 4= professional and technical personnel, 5= clerical personnel, 6= individual-operated business proprietors, 7= commercial and service personnel, 8= industrial workers, 9= agricultural laborers, 10= the urban-rural jobless, unemployed, and partially unemployed.

The above-mentioned four classifying indicators define the advantaged status of state and social administrators in the social structure. They are management with middle-high level skills in core sectors inside the system who control the most crucial resource in contemporary China—the organizational resources. Because the government agencies are in control of the most important and largest amounts of such resources, state and social administrators possessing organizational resources distinctly receive an advantaged position in resource allocation. Although they are not owners of the means of production, state and social administrators can control a part of the means of production. Therefore, they actually share a part of the economic resources as well as a large amount of cultural resources.

At present, the proportion of this stratum is about 2.1 percent in the overall social stratum structure, 2.6 percent in the urban social stratum structure, and 0.2 percent in the rural social stratum structure. The number of state and social administrators is relatively small in the whole population. Differentiation also exists within the stratum to some degree. According to the quantity of organizational resources owned by individuals and approaches of exerting such resources, this stratum can be subdivided into four groups: (1) the group of high-level administrators which consists of county (or division) and higher-level administrators who possess actual administrative authority in party and government organizations, the legal system, the People's Congress, and the Political Consultative Conference;[1] they account for 9.4 percent in the stratum; (2) the group of middle-level administrators which includes township (or section)-level cadres, who possess actual administrative authority (division principals supervising more than 3 subordinates) in party and government organizations, the legal system, the People's Congress, and the Political Consultative Conference; they account for 17.0 percent in the stratum; (3) the group of low-level administrators which refers to township (or section) -level cadres who possess actual administrative authority (section principals supervising more than 3 subordinates) in party and government organizations, the legal system, the People's Congress, and the Political Consultative Conference, etc., cadres below the section-level possessing actual administrative authority (principal of division supervising more than 3 subordinates), and section and higher-level cadres without actual administrative authority (without subordinates). They account for 57.9 percent in the stratum; (4) the group of middle-higher level administrators in public institutions[2] which refers to major principals of various public institutions, such as the president and party secretary of hospitals, the principal and party secretary of schools, the controller and party secretary of television station or radio station, the proprietor and party secretary of the newspaper press or publishing house, the director and party secretary of research institute, the president and party secretary of academy, etc. They make up 15.7 percent in the stratum.

Managerial Personnel

The *stratum of managerial personnel* refers to middle-higher level management in enterprises (not including the owners) and a part of low-level management functioning as department chiefs.[3]

---

[1] Including some mass organizations that are subject to party and government systems, such as labor unions, the Communist Youth League, and Women's Federations, etc.

[2] Low-level or first-line management in institutions are not included in the stratum of state and social administrators. In stead, they are classified as professional and technical personnel or clerical personnel.

[3] In this classification, "high-level management" refers to the top-level leadership have subordinate

42

Judging from the above-mentioned classifying indicators, the positions of members of this stratum are located within the system, in the peripheral sectors inside the system, or outside the system. They are management with middle-higher level of skills. Managerial personnel do not possess the means of production, but they actually control and manage such resources. Therefore, they are in possession of economic resources. In addition, most of them have relatively high level of education or diplomas and relatively high level of professional knowledge, so they are also in possession of cultural resources.

The stratum of managerial personnel accounts for approximately 1.6 percent in the overall social stratum structure, 3.4 percent in the urban social stratum structure, and 0.4 percent in the rural social stratum structure. The distribution of its members among regions is extremely unbalanced. Most of its members are concentrated in large and medium-sized cities, especially in developed regions. This stratum has been emerging in recent years and is still in the process of developing. The boundary between this stratum and the stratum of state and social administrators is still not very clear.

Members of this stratum mainly have three types of origins. The first origin is cadres in initial state-owned and collective enterprises. These cadres gradually moved away from the public administrative system and become professional managers. The second origin is management in large-size private enterprises or private enterprises in high-tech sectors. There has been a trend of separation of ownership rights and management authority in these enterprises since the late nineties of the twentieth century. Some owners of private enterprises employed professional managers to operate and manage business for them. Other owners shifted from start-up entrepreneurs to professional managers through demutualization. The third origin is high-level management in three forms of foreign-invested ventures in China (i.e., Sino-foreign joint ventures, Sino-foreign cooperative businesses, and exclusively foreign-owned enterprises).

At present, 37.5 percent managerial personnel in this stratum are employed in state-owned enterprises, 31.3 percent in collective enterprises, and 31.2 percent in enterprises with other forms of ownership. In other words, managerial personnel in enterprises with the public ownership make up the major part of this stratum. Two thirds of managerial personnel are employed in state-owned and collective enterprises, whereas one third of them come from private enterprises, three forms of foreign-invested ventures, and enterprises with mixed ownership. With deepening of the economic reforms and development of non-public-owned sector of economy, the distribution of the above proportions is undergoing change.

Because of different origins of members of this stratum, there are some

---

managerial personnel but without higher supervisors above them in a given enterprise. The "middle-level management" refers to managers who have higher supervisors above them in a given enterprise; meanwhile they also have subordinate managerial personnel. The "low-level management" refers to first-line managers who supervise ordinary employees directly and have no subordinate managerial personnel.

differentiations existing in the stratum. In other words, there are significant differences in socio-economic status existing among managerial personnel in enterprises with different types of ownership. Nevertheless, with growing adoption of the modern corporate system, increasing professionalization of managerial personnel, and expanding cross-ownership mobility, differences among managerial personnel in enterprises with different ownerships will gradually decrease. According to levels of management and quantities of controlled economic resources, managerial personnel can be subdivided into three groups: (1) high-level management, which refers to major principals of large-size enterprises,[1] such as general manager, Party secretary, and factory manager, etc. They account for 12.6 percent of the stratum. (2) Middle-level management, which refers to middle-level managerial personnel in large-size enterprises (such as department managers, section chiefs, workshop managers, etc.) and principals (such as factory managers, party secretaries, managers, etc.) in small-medium business.[2] They make up 41.4 percent of the stratum. (3) Low-level management which refers to low-level white-collar managerial personnel (supervising more than three subordinates) and partially blue-collar first-line managerial personnel (supervising more than 20 subordinates) in large-size enterprises, and major principals (factory managers, party secretaries, managers) in small business.[3] They account for 46.0 percent of the stratum of managerial personnel.

Private Entrepreneurs

The *stratum of private entrepreneur* refers to people who possess a certain amount of private capital or fixed assets and invest them to obtain profits with employment of other people's labors.[4] According to the four classifying indicators, the social position

---

[1] "Large-size enterprise" in this study refers to business with more than 100 employees in the secondary industry or more than 50 employees in the tertiary industry.

[2] "Small-medium business" refers to enterprise with more than 20 employees in the secondary industry or more than 10 employees in the tertiary industry.

[3] "Small business" refers to enterprise with less than 20 employees in the secondary industry or less than 10 employees in the tertiary industry.

[4] The definition of "stratum of private entrepreneurs" in the classification is a little different from the definition of "private entrepreneur" in statistics of the China Administration for Industry and Commerce. According to present regulations, a private entrepreneur is the owner of a private business employing more than eight employees. However, we found that, with the development of commerce, trade and service sectors and high-tech sectors, many small businesses have emerged in China in recent years. Although these small businesses often employ less than eight employees, they are very different from common individual-operated businesses in amount of investment, mode of operation, and level of revenue. Therefore, we classify owners of these small enterprises as small business owners in the stratum of private entrepreneurs, instead of individual-operated business proprietors. More specifically, private entrepreneurs refer to business owners who employ more than eight employees in the secondary industry or more than four employees in the tertiary industry and are not engaged in manual or partially-manual works directly. Therefore, the estimated proportion of the stratum of private entrepreneurs in the overall social stratum structure is 1.0 percent, slightly higher than the estimated proportion (0.6 percent) proposed in *Social Stratification in Contemporary*

of this stratum is defined as management who possesses the means of production and employs other people outside of the system. The most important characteristic of the stratum is the possession of the means of production, i.e., economic resources.

The stratum of private entrepreneur accounts for about one percent in the overall social stratum structure, 1.5 percent in the urban social stratum structure, and 0.7 percent in the rural social stratum structure. The amount of capital possessed by members of the stratum is very different; their socio-economic statuses differ as well. Accurate information about capital amount of every private entrepreneur is difficult to collect; hence, we could only subdivide enterprise owners into three groups (large-size business owners, medium-size business owners, and small business owners) according to the number of employees. *Large-size business owners* refer to private entrepreneurs who employ more than 100 employees in the primary and secondary industry, or more than 50 employees in the tertiary industry. They account for a very small proportion in the stratum of private entrepreneurs (0.5 percent). *Medium-size business owners* refer to private entrepreneurs who employ 30 to 99 employees in the primary and secondary industry, or 10 to 49 employees in the tertiary industry. They account for a proportion of 27.6 percent in the stratum. *Small business owners* are private entrepreneurs who employ 8 to 29 employees in the primary and secondary industry, or 4 to 9 employees in the tertiary industry. They make up the major part of the stratum with a relatively high proportion of 71.9 percent.

Professional and Technical Personnel

The *stratum of professional and technical personnel* refers to people who specialize in various professional, scientific, and technical works in organizations with various types of ownership (including government agencies, party and mass organizations, state-owned enterprises and public institutions, and non-public ownership enterprises). Most of them have received middle-higher level of vocational training of professional knowledge and specialized technology, possess professional knowledge, and specialized techniques that meet the requirements of modern socialized mass production. Classifying indicators in our classification system define the stratum of professional and technical personnel as follows: non-manual laborers who possess middle-higher level professional knowledge and techniques inside or outside the system. They are not in possession of the means of production but have certain extent of independence.

The stratum of professional and technical personnel accounts for about 4.6 percent in the overall social stratum structure, 8.6 percent in the urban social stratum structure, and 1.9 percent in the rural social stratum structure. Members of this stratum mainly concentrate in urban areas and state-owned organizations. At present, about 75.8 percent of professional and technical personnel work in urban areas, and 24.2 percent in rural areas; 65.7 percent in state-owned organizations, 15.2 percent in

China.

collectively-owned organizations, and 19.1 percent in organizations with other types of ownership. This distribution shows that the overwhelming majority of professional and technical personnel are employed in core sectors inside the system and they make up a major part of the stratum.

The factor of the type of ownership of organization leads to some differences inside the stratum. Nonetheless, with development of the market economy, expanding cross-ownership mobility of professional and technical personnel, and increasing emphasis on educational level and diploma in state-owned organizations, these differences produced by the ownership factor have been gradually declining. Furthermore, because of differences in professional level (such as senior, middle, and junior professional title), each member of the stratum may exhibit some differences in the quantity of possessed cultural resources and socio-economic status. However, because the degree of specialization is not very high in most fields, differences in economic income and social status, which are caused by the professional level, are not particularly significant. The factor that results in even more significant differences inside the stratum is the interaction between institutional segmentation (ownership) and sector segmentation (industry). Generally speaking, the traditional type of intellectuals, such as professional and technical personnel in fields of education, science, culture, and health, are mainly employed in state-owned sectors (inside the system), whereas professionals who are deeply involved in economic activities usually are employed in non-state-owned sectors (outside the system) or state-owned sectors with market-oriented operation modes (peripheral sectors within the system, such as state-owned and collectively enterprises, or enterprise-oriented public institutions). Therefore, according to the professional field and the degree of involvement in economic activity, we subdivide members of the stratum into three groups: (1) professionals in educational, scientific, cultural, and health service sectors who make up a major part of the stratum with a relatively high proportion of 69.3 percent and are mainly concentrated in state-owned organizations. Most of them are teachers. (2) Engineers and technicians who are mainly concentrated in the secondary industry. With increasing specialization and technology-intensive in the manufacturing sector in recent years, the number of engineers and technicians has grown as well. They account for 22.4 percent in the stratum. (3) Professionals in commercial, trading and service sectors who are mainly personnel engaging in economic activities, such economists, accountants, auditors, bond traders, lawyers, and designers, etc. The number of this type of professionals is increasing rapidly and accounts for 8.3 percent in the stratum.

Clerical Personnel

The stratum of clerical personnel refers to office personnel who assist principals of their organizations or divisions in dealing with administrative routines. This stratum mainly consists of middle-lower level civilians in political parties and governmental organizations, and low-level management and non-professional clerks in enterprises and public institutions with various types of ownership, etc. Clerical personnel are lower-level non-manual laborers without the means of production inside and outside the system. The stratum of clerical personnel is an important component of the middle stratum in modern society. It accounts for 7.2 percent in the overall social stratum structure. Proportion distributions of the stratum in urban and rural areas differ greatly, with a proportion of 14.2 percent in the urban stratum structure and 3.9 percent in the rural stratum structure. Members of the stratum can be subdivided into two major groups: (1) clerical personnel in political party and governmental organizations, mainly composed of officials in government agencies and ordinary clerks in public institutions. They make up 62.4 percent of the stratum; (2) clerical personnel in enterprises, referring to executive assistants and ordinary white-collar personnel in various enterprises. They account for 37.6 percent. Judging from the proportions of the above two groups, the major part of the stratum consists of officials and quasi officials employed by the government.

Individual-Operated Business Proprietors

The *stratum of individual-operated business proprietors* (or "individual industrial and commercial householder") refers to people who are in possession of a certain amount of private capital (including real estate) and invest them in business activities in manufacturing, trading, and service sectors or bonds markets and make a living on it. For example, it includes small proprietors or small employers (people who have sufficient capital to employ a small number of employees but have to participate in the activities of labor, production, and management directly) and self-employed proprietors (people who have sufficient capital to start one's own business but do not employ any other laborers), and small investors, small shareholders, and small landlords, etc.

The social position of this stratum defined by the classifying indicators is that of management or self-employed practitioners outside the system. Currently, the stratum of individual-operated business proprietors accounts for 7.1 percent in the overall social stratum structure. More specifically, in this stratum, 22.0 percent of its members are small employers with one to seven employees, and 78.0 percent are the self-employed. This stratum accounts for 12.3 percent in the urban social stratum structure, and 5.2 percent in the rural social stratum structure.

Commercial and Service Personnel

The *stratum of commercial and service personnel* refers to personnel who are engaged in non-professional, non-manual or manual activities in commercial and service sectors. Social position of this stratum defined by classifying indicators consists of employees or self-employed people in the tertiary industry inside or outside the system.

Presently, the proportion of this stratum in the overall social stratum structure is about 11.2 percent. Proportional distributions of the stratum in urban and rural areas are greatly different, with a proportion of 20.1 percent in the urban stratum structure and 5.2 percent in the rural stratum structure. Among members of the stratum, 16.5 percent of them are employed in state-owned enterprises, 7.8 percent in collective enterprises, and 75.7 percent in non-public-owned enterprises. Moreover, about 65.2 percent of members are employed in the private and individual sectors. In addition, 72.2 percent of its members work in urban areas and 27.8 percent in rural areas. Therefore, members of this stratum are mainly concentrated in the urban private and individual sectors of economy. According to levels of management and skills, this stratum can be subdivided into three major groups: First-line supervisors, quasi white-collar personnel, and blue-collar personnel in commercial and services sectors. (1) First-line supervisors in commercial and services sectors refer to people who supervise first-line personnel directly, such as foreman, team leader, etc. They make up 4.4 percent of the stratum. (2) Quasi white-collar personnel in commercial and services sectors refer to people engaging in activities requiring special skills (such as chefs, taxi drivers, barbers, beauticians, etc.), or people working in quasi white-collar environments (such as counters, salespersons, tourist guides, interpreters, and flight attendants, etc.). They account for 17 percent of the stratum. (3) Blue-collar personnel in commercial and services sectors refer to people engaging in manual or partially-manual work that does not require expertise (such as shop assistant, waiter or waitress, security, cleaner, etc.). They make up 78.6 percent of the stratum.

Industrial Workers

The *stratum of industrial workers* includes workers, builders, and relevant people engaging in manual or partially manual labor in the secondary industry. The social position of this stratum is defined by the classifying indictors as employees or self-employed people in the secondary industry inside or outside the system.

In the past ten years, the stratum of industrial workers has experienced some significant changes in the following aspects. First, member composition of this stratum has fundamentally changed. Workers in urban state-owned enterprises once made up the primary part of the stratum, while nowadays workers with peasant origin made up more than half of it and have become a major component of this stratum. More specifically, industrial workers with registered rural residence account for 54.9 percent of the stratum, whereas workers with registered non-rural residence make up 45.1 percent. Second, industrial workers once worked mainly in urban state-owned enterprises while over one third of the workers now work in rural areas, i.e., 63.6 percent of the industrial workers work in urban areas while 36.4 percent are working in rural areas. Third, industrial workers have been moving from public-owned enterprises (inside the system) to non-public-owned enterprises (outside the system) in large scale. Workers in state-owned and collective enterprises once made up the majority of industrial workers; however, currently the majority of industrial workers are employed in non-public-owned sector. More specifically, 21.5 percent of industrial workers are employed in state-owned enterprises, 16.4 percent in collective enterprise, and 62.1 percent in non-public-owned enterprises. Industrial workers still account for the highest proportion in the urban social stratum structure, which is 21.2 percent, and its proportion in the rural social stratum structure is 8.2 percent.

Before and at the early stage of the economic reform, the ownership of work unit was the major factor that led to disparities inside this stratum. Workers employed in different enterprises with different types of ownership have significant distinctions in the levels of wages and fringe benefits. Since the 1980s, the influence of the ownership factor has been gradually declining, and the registered permanent residence status has taken its place. Urban workers have significant distinctions from peasant-workers in the levels of income, fringe benefits, and social security. In recent years, with the increasing number of peasant-workers, differentiation caused by the registered permanent residence status has been diminishing. Meanwhile, differentiations produced by the level of authority and the level of skills have been increasing gradually. According to the level of authority and skills, we subdivided the stratum of industrial workers into three groups: First-line supervisors, skilled workers, and non-skilled workers in the secondary industry. (1) First-line supervisors in the secondary industry include team leaders and section chiefs who supervise first-line workers directly. They account for 3.3 percent of the stratum. (2) Skilled workers in the secondary industry refer to workers engaging in labors that require special skill training or accreditation of qualification accreditation (such as electricians, ironsmiths, and mechanics, etc.). They account for a proportion of 33.5 percent in the stratum. (3) Non-skilled workers in the secondary industry refer to manual and partially-manual workers to whom special training or qualification accreditation is not required (such as haulers, builders, and platelayers, etc.). They make up 63.2 percent of the stratum.

Agricultural Laborers

The *stratum of agricultural laborers* refers to peasants who contract in collectively owned farmland and farm with family members. Revenues gained from farming (or forestry, animal husbandry, and fishing) are their only or major source of income.[1] The social position of this stratum is self-employed people or employees who are in possession of a small quantity of means of production or do not possess any means of production in the primary industry and are intermediate between inside and outside the system.

The stratum of agricultural laborers is currently the largest stratum in China, accounting for a proportion of 42.9 percent in the overall national social stratum structure. Agricultural laborers not only work in every corner of rural areas, but also exist in suburban areas of cities in a small number. The emergence of the latter group of agricultural laborers is due to the rapidly expansion of urban areas in recent years.

---

[1] In this classification, part-time farmers whose non-agricultural income exceeds agricultural income are classified according to their non-agricultural occupations.

In this process, initially suburban villages were plotted as districts under urban administrators' jurisdiction in order to make economic development or set up economic development areas, but the occupational status of some agricultural laborers in these villages did not change. Thus, they become peasants without farmland or only with a very small amount of farmland. In the urban social stratum structure, about 2.7 percent of its members belong to the stratum of agricultural laborers, whereas in the rural social stratum structure, this proportion is 70.0 percent.

Although the number of agricultural laborers is huge, the degree of homogeneity inside the stratum is relatively high, and differentiation in socio-economic status is comparatively small. Therefore, there are no significant differentiated groups existing inside this stratum. However, three factors that have led to differences in income level and quality of life among its members. The first factor is regional disparity. The income level and quality of life of agricultural laborers are relatively high in developed regions, whereas lower in undeveloped areas. The second factor is the degree of diversification in family operated programs or the variety of cultivated crops or raised animal husbandries (including non-farm part-time jobs). The more diverse the family-operated programs or the variety of produces is, the higher the income level and standard of living of agricultural laborers will be; or vice versa. The third factor is the scale of operation. Agricultural laborers operating, cultivating, or raising livestock on a larger scale have a relatively higher level of income and standard of living; or vice versa. Therefore, according to the degree of diversification and the scale of operation, we subdivide agricultural laborers into three groups: Full-time farmers, part-time farmers, and ordinary farmers. (1) Full-time farmers (agricultural laborers) refer to agricultural laborers who operate a single agricultural program (or a single variety of produce), or run more than 10 Mu (Chinese unit of area, one Mu is equal to 1/15 of a hectare) farmland, or have an annual income of more than 3,000 Yuan RMB. They account for 12.6 percent of the stratum. (2) Part-time farmers (agricultural laborers) refer to agricultural laborers who are engaged in at least one part-time jobs or sidelines, which yields them more 1,000 Yuan RMB a year, in addition to farming major varieties of cultivated products such as grain, vegetables, or cotton, etc. They account for 25 percent of this stratum. (3) Ordinary farmers (agricultural laborers) refer to agricultural laborers who do not meet the above conditions. Their proportion in this stratum is 62.4 percent.[1]

---

[1] It should be noted that many diversified operations and part-time jobs are undertaken by different family members. For example, wives farm at home and husbands work in town, or the aged farm at home and their children work in town. Such diversification of operating or working activities among family members has an influence on farmers' household income and standard of living as well. Because questionnaires used in this study did not collect information about working activities of all family members, we have to subdivide this stratum according to respondents' individual working activity.

The Urban-Rural Jobless, Unemployed, and Partially Unemployed

The *stratum of the urban-rural jobless, unemployed, and partially unemployed* refers to people of labor age but without regular jobs.[1] The formation of this stratum is driven by the following factors. First, institutional transition and adjustment of industrial structure in China have pushed a group of workers and employees from commercial and services sectors into the unemployed or partially unemployed conditions. Second, a considerable number of young people have been unemployed for a long time since entering the labor market because of insufficient employment opportunities. Third, expropriating cropland for public and commercial use by urban governments has led to a large numbers of peasants losing their farmland; and they were usually unable to find jobs immediately in cities. In addition, many urban and rural residents are unable to work because of disability or serious illness. Most of them live in destitute conditions. Presently, the number of members in this stratum is still increasing.

There is always a certain number of unemployment in any society. However, a social stratum composed of the jobless, unemployed, and partially unemployed is the result of a special period of historical transitions in contemporary China. The number of members of this stratum is huge in China. In addition, most of them have similar socio-economic background, such as workers who were laid off from state-owned or collective enterprises and their children, and some middle-aged and young peasants who could not make a living relying on farming. A matter worthy of note is that the unemployed or partially unemployed status of a relatively large number of people in the stratum often lasts several years. This situation greatly threats to their survival.

The above characteristics of the unemployed and partially unemployed group have made them a special interim stratum. Currently, this stratum accounts for 4.8 percent in the overall social stratum structure, 10.2 percent in the urban social stratum structure, and 1.2 percent in the rural social stratum structure. More specifically, 22.8 percent of the stratum are unemployed youth, and 35.3 percent are laid-off workers of state-owned or collective enterprises, 38.3 percent belong to other types of unemployment, and 3.6 percent of its members are partially employed.

THE ANALYTICAL FRAMEWORK OF SOCIAL MOBILITY IN CONTEMPORARY CHINA

The classification of ten major social strata and the description of compositions of each stratum presented above provide a perspective to observe and analyze modern Chinese social structure. It may help people comprehensively understand basic facts

---

[1] It does not include enrolled students and never-employed housewives.

of social stratification in current China, grasp the overall structure of socio-economic resource allocation, and evaluate positions of individuals and groups in the entire social structure as well as their interrelations. However, we still need to explain the following questions: How have the ten major strata developed? What are the origins of members of each stratum? What are their future directions of social mobility? Why did some people enter into social strata with advantaged status, while some others fell into relatively junior social strata with fewer opportunities to change their social status? Which factors have an impact on the distribution of opportunity that may bring about changes of position in social strata? Efforts to answer these questions have led us into the field of social mobility study.

The themes of study on social mobility include investigations on influential factors that affect people's opportunities to obtain certain social status or move from one social status to another, the significance of such influences, channels through which these factors work and take effect, and major characteristics and general tendencies of social mobility in a society. Based on our preliminary research results on social stratification and stratum structure in contemporary China, we have conducted a pilot study on the process, mechanisms, and tendencies of social mobility in contemporary China over the past fifty years. In order to help readers to understand this study, we believe it is necessary to explain our perspectives on how to investigate social mobility in contemporary China, including our understandings about the general rules of social mobility summarized from previous studies, reflections on particular mechanisms of social mobility in China over the past fifty years, and primary findings about the relationship between these general rules and particular mechanisms.

General Rules of Social Mobility

The term *mechanism of social mobility* refers to the combined effects of backgrounds, conditions, drives, and paths through which people obtain certain social status and achieve social mobility. The term *general rules of social mobility* refers to theoretical summarizations of social mechanisms that affected people's activities of status attainment and social mobility to different extents over a long period.

In sociology, there are two basic types of social mobility rules, i.e., the *rule of ascription* and the *rule of achievement*. Sociologists generally agree that the two types of rules always relate to different social, economic, and political structures respectively. Moreover, one of them is always compatible with a certain social, economic, and political structure in a certain period and hence become the uppermost mechanism of social mobility that dominates the social mobility, including intragenerational and intergenerational mobility.

According to the logic of modernization, the rule of ascription usually dominates in traditional agriculture-based social, economic, and political structures. Under this rule, individual's opportunity of status attainment and social mobility is determined by his or her inherited social ascription. In such a society, the social stratum structure and social mobility opportunity structure are characterized as apparent closure. This means that a specific social status can only be attained or possessed by members of a particular social stratum, leaving few opportunities to members of other social strata even if they have corresponding capability.[1] In contrast, the rule of achievement mainly relies on market-oriented, industrialized, and urbanized modern social, economic, and political structures. Under this rule, individual's opportunity of status attainment and social mobility is primarily determined by one's capability and efforts. Therefore, the social stratum structure and social mobility opportunity structure in such a society are significantly open. This means that, in an open society, any social status does not belong to any particular social class (stratum), and anyone with the capability can obtain it through personal efforts. Moreover, if one does not possess the required capability or intermit one's efforts, he or she will probably be knocked down to a lower social status.[2] Therefore, the rule of ascription is regarded as the primary rule of social mobility in traditional society, while the rule of achievement is thought to be the leading rule of social mobility in modern society.

From the historical perspective, both the above-mentioned rules have existed in Chinese society, and they are general rules that we cannot neglect in any analysis of social mobility in contemporary China. However, we believe that when these rules are applied to studies and explanations of social mobility in any society, the following aspects deserve attention.

First, it is not true that above two rules must take effect in completely different periods and places. In fact, much empirical evidence show that the rules are not exclusive the in history nor in reality. Quite often, the two rules jointly determine the social mobility in a society. For example, in traditional Chinese society, the heritance of class (stratum) ascription usually determined people's social status and mobility opportunity. Nevertheless, at the same time the imperial examination system that selected talented people through national examinations also provided people with humble origins the opportunity to achieve upward mobility through individual efforts. Similarly, classic research has demonstrated that, in modern western society, both ascription factors (father's education background and occupational status etc.) and achievement factors (individual education background and early years' experience, etc.) significantly affect a person's occupational status.[3] Of course, it is also not true that the two rules always equally co-exist in a certain period and place. In fact, one type of rules always dominates in a given period and place. Therefore, we can judge the nature of the major or fundamental social mobility mechanism in a society according to the type of its dominant social mobility rule.

---

[1] The traditional Indian society that was dominated by the caste system is a typical example of such society.

[2] Xu, Jiayou. 1986. *Social Stratification and Social Mobility*. Taibei: San Min Book Company: 238-240.

[3] Blau, Peter M. and Oliver D. Duncan.1967. *The American Occupational Structure*. New York, N.Y.: Wiley.

Second, generally speaking, changes of social structure in a society closely relate to changes of its economic structure. If the national institutions and policies are relatively stable, a given economic structure is always translated into a certain amount of employment opportunities and a certain structure of occupations. Because social status attainment and mobility always happen in such space and structure, changes of economic structure usually lead to changes of employment structure and occupational structure, sequentially changing the scale, speed, opportunity, and path of social mobility, and affect the relative scope and degree of influences produced by ascription factors and achievement factors. For example, compared with the structure of traditional natural economy, the structure of modern economy, which is based on marketization, industrialization, and urbanization, is far more complicated. Moreover, it constantly evolves, expands, and upgrades following its own regularities or tendencies, thereby pushing the expansion of employment and promoting increased diversification of occupational structure and the emergence of new occupations with higher socio-economic status. In such a situation, there will be more and more upward social mobility that could be obtained by individual efforts. Therefore, changes of economic structure at the macro level are also an important perspective that is relatively independent of the ascription-achievement perspective when we observe social mobility in modern market economy.

Third, influences of the above-mentioned general rules will be comparatively significant and the observations and explanations that we achieved by applying these general rules to studies of social mobility will be relatively valid only when the institution and policy at the macro level (i.e., arrangements of political institution and policy) are stable. These macro-level factors merely provide a given space for social mobility and do not change the structure of social mobility opportunity from now and then at the macro level, nor directly intervene in social mobility at the micro level. Thus, social mobility mainly occurs at the micro level (i.e., intergenerational and intragenerational mobility at individual level) and meanwhile micro-level conditions, driving forces, and paths are relatively stable.[1] In contrast, these general rules will be insufficient to explain social mobility if not all above conditions are met.

Particular Mechanisms of Social Mobility in China

In discussion about the ascription-achievement rule that is extensively used as an analytical tool in sociology, we found that some basic limitations have to be added to the rule, that is, assumptions about the stability of macro-level institution-policy arrangements and low intervention (or indirect intervention) from such arrangements in social stratification and mobility. However, investigations on the particular process

---

[1] In such conditions, the impact of ascription factors does not disappear. However, the meaning of ascription factors changes from individual macro-social-class ascription to individual family background.

of social stratification and social mobility in China over the past fifty years show that such assumptions are not true in contemporary China.

First, the fundamental political-institutional settings and policy arrangements in China, including the socialist public ownership, the centralized system of the planned economy, and the resource allocation model stressing the development of heavy industry, etc., intervened deeply in changes of economic structure. As a result, changes of economic structure did not play a role in pushing the expansion of employment and the transition of occupational structure over a long period. For example, the economic structure in China changed fundamentally in the mid-late 1950s. By 1956, in the gross output value of industry and agriculture, the output value of industry accounted for more than 50 percent, exceeding the proportion of the output value of agriculture. However, the overall employment and occupational structure did not change accordingly. Only after the reform and opening-up starting from 1978, has the situation begun to change, albeit gradually.

Second, the arrangements of political-economic institution and policy in China have affected social position and social mobility opportunity of an individual or even a whole class profoundly. The influence of institution and policy arrangements is so enormous that sometimes it is able to eliminate one or more social classes (strata) directly, or expedite the emergence of one or more classes. Of course, the impact of institution-policy arrangements on social mobility does not always adopt the form of direct intervention. Sometimes, it may also take effect in the form of indirect and unintentional influences. For example, some people or groups may take advantage of defects and limitations in a given arrangement of institution and policy for their maximal interests.

In such situations, merely adopting the ascription-achievement rule to observe and analyze social mobility in contemporary China is inadequate. Furthermore, we could not even recognize the particular mechanisms of large-scale social stratification and mobility in China from such perspectives. However, it does not mean that these perspectives should be abandoned. We believe that the macro-level institution-policy arrangement and the micro-level ascription-achievement rule should be combined in order to study social mobility in China.

According to possible types of relationships between institution-policy arrangement and ascription-achievement rule, we theoretically classify the patterns that they affect social mobility into the following four major situations.

(1) The social mobility caused by institution-policy arrangement is irrelevant to ascription-achievement rule in some aspects. Opportunities of social mobility are directly affected by institution-policy arrangement. For example, in the movement of collectivization in the 1950s, three classes (individual handicraftsmen, individual-operated business proprietors, and capitalists) were almost eliminated, as well as the class of workers employed in private enterprises. In contrast, the reform and opening-up policy and relevant institutional arrangements since the late 1970s have reshaped the groups of individual-operated business proprietors, private

entrepreneurs, and workers employed in private enterprises.

(2) The way that institution-policy arrangement affects social mobility is to mix the ascription rule with the achievement rule to some extent, because it is indeed not so easy to find other factors as criteria for social structure arrangement. Even in modern countries with free-market economies, such mixing is inevitable. However, in China this mixing is institution-oriented rather than a spontaneous process. For example, before the reform and opening-up, if one wanted to enter the stratum of cadres that had the highest social status, generally he or she must have had a "politically reliable" family background or class origin, and should have shown loyalty through active political participation. Meanwhile, during that time, peasants hardly moved away from rural areas to work in cities. That is not because the cost of such mobility exceeded its benefit, but because the dual urban-rural system prevented peasants from moving into cities.

(3) Institution-policy arrangement may inhibit the influence of the ascription rule (or the achievement rule) while supporting the rule of achievement (or the rule of ascription), and consequently produce correcting or contorting effects on directions of social mobility. For example, the dual urban-rural system and relevant institution-policy arrangements that was created by the planned economy systems actually established the crucial impact of ascription factors on social mobility between urban and rural areas and on the shift from agricultural employment to non-agricultural employment, and blocked the channels in which achievement factors may exert their influences. People originating from families of farmers were destined to stay on farmland in their villages and could not enter cities and non-agricultural industries. Contrastingly, people born in urban families were destined to go into non-agricultural industries and enjoy various advantages that were brought by industrialization. Another example is education. If the national educational system and policy emphasize the equality-oriented universal basic education, it restrains the influence of ascription factors while having a pushing effect on the influence of achievement factors. Contrarily, if the national educational system and policy seek "education for elite" and invest limited resources into educational institutions that only serve the minority, it will favor achievement factors (such as family economic conditions or parent's occupations) rather than go against the influence of ascription factors such as individual efforts and capability.

(4) Flaws or inclinations in institution-policy arrangements that are formed intentionally or unintentionally may be utilized by some social members as a ladder to move upward, while impairing or depriving other social members' opportunities for mobility. Whether people can take advantage of such institution-policy arrangements or not depends on their possession of necessary resources (such as social networks). Generally, the latter situation is regarded as a result of non-institutional factors in social mobility. However, in our opinion, it still closely relates to the factor of institution-policy arrangement. After investigating some non-institutional factors, we find that the flaws of formal institution afford non-institutional factors the opportunity

to survive and produce significant influences. The existence of such flaws is not only due to the limitation of influence of the formal institution in social life, but also because of opportunities given by the system itself (such as so-called "opportunity for rent seeking"). Generally, only a portion of social members (mainly framers of institution or policy and people having relevant interests with them) can take advantage of these opportunities because only such people possess necessary resources, such as the authority endowed by institutions or relations with people possessing such authority.

In addition, in social mobility over the past fifty years in China, not only the above institutional factors have had significant influences, but also various non-institutional factors have played an important role as well. A large body of literature has mentioned or studied such an impact of non-institutional factors.[1] Nonetheless, as to social mobility in current China, various non-institutional factors, including so-called political capital, social networks or relation capital, etc. (for convenience, all non-institutional factors fall under the general term "social capital" in the study), are combining results of above-mentioned variables (may not include the economic structure) in essence. In other words, both ascription-achievement factors and institution-policy factors have an impact on the emergence of non-institutional factors. Ascription factors provide useful clues and initial conditions for building "social capital", while achievement factors like individual efforts are catalyzers that accelerate these clues and conditions to take effect. In some cases, the formation of "social capital" does not even have ascription factors as clues or initial conditions. For example, social connections (*guanxi*) are usually established by people who need such connections.[2] The effect of institution-policy factors is to provide "social capital" with potential or visible space to take effect. If such space does not exist, or even if institution-policy arrangement prevents "social capital" from affecting status attainment in effective ways, efforts to build "social capital" will be greatly impaired. Therefore, consider the "social capital" as an independent variable in the study. Instead, we treat it as a combining variable in the study.

---

[1] Li, Lulu. 1996. "Social Structure of Private Entrepreneurs: Developmental Mechanisms of Private Enterprises." In *China Private Sector of Economy Yearbook*. Beijing: China Industry & Commerce Associated Press; Zhang, Wanli. 1996. "Non-institutional factors and Status Attainment: Social Stratification in Current China". *Sociology Research* Vol.1; Wang, Chunguang. 1995. *Social Mobility and Social Reconstruction: Research on Zhejiang Village in Beijing City*. Hangzhou, Zhejiang: Zhejiang People's Press; Liu, Linping. 2002. *Connections, Social Capital, and Social Transformation: Study on Pinjiang Village in Shenzhen*. Beijing: China Social Sciences Press; Li, Peilin (ed.). 2003. *Peasant-Workers: Socioeconomic Analysis of Rural Workers Migrated into Cities*. Beijing: Social Sciences Documentation Publishing House.

[2] Chen, Guangjin. 1998. "Secrets of Rising and Growing of Elite in Chinese Rural Community ". In *Forum for Ten Doctors*. Beijing: China City Press.

The Analytical Framework of the Study

Based on the above discussion, the applicable analytical framework for the study of social mobility in China consists of four sets of fundamental independent variables and one set of combining variables: (1) ascription variables, (2) achievement variables, (3) socio-economic structure variables, (4) institution-policy arrangement variables, and (5) social capital (or connection networks). Generally speaking, the first and the second set of variables are micro-level variables, the third and the fourth set of variables are macro-level variables, and the fifth set of variables is a combination of micro-level and macro-level factors. It is these five sets of variables that make up the opportunity structure of social mobility in China.

On the other hand, when we try to understand and apply this explanatory framework, the following two aspects should be paid particular attention. First, each set of the above-mentioned variables includes several factors. To be more precise, we are talking about five sets of variables. Based on prior studies and actual situations in China, we can further unfold these five sets of variables as follows. (1) The set of ascription variables includes place of birth, gender, family economic condition, parents' educational background and occupations, social status (such as registered permanent residence status), and political status (such as class origin), etc. (2) The set of achievement variables includes personal educational background, capability and efforts, performance in work and labor, and performance in political participation, etc. (3) The set of socio-economic structure variable includes industrial structure (composition of output values of the primary, secondary, and tertiary industry), employment space, and occupational structure, etc. (4) The set of institution-policy variables includes institutional arrangement of ownership structure (such as the unitary public ownership system, the unitary private ownership system, or the mixed ownership system. Such an arrangement will affect the allocation of material resources and human resources), arrangement of political status of each stratum or class (such as political definitions about the leading class, the allied class, and the antagonistic class), institutional arrangements of authority allocation (such as centralization or decentralization), political party membership, and other socio-economic institutions (such as the residence registration system and the work unit system). (5) The composition of the set of social capital variables is relatively complicated; it usually includes the results that are produced by a combination of some factors of the first, second, and fourth variable sets.

Second, various influential factors in these above variable sets have different patterns and structures of combinations at different stages of social transition and social mobility in contemporary China. In other words, the combinations of factors that have a leading impact on social mobility in different periods are different. For example, before the reform and opening-up, family economic condition in the set of ascription variables might have relatively small influence on changes of individual social status, because the equalitarian orientation of institution in that period held back the tendency of expanding gap in family economic conditions. In the Cultural

Revolution period, the influence of individual educational background in the set of achievement variables on upward mobility declined significantly, because the political ideology at that time believed that "the more knowledge one has, the more likely that he or she will be reactionary in political attitude". Economic structure in the set of structure variables had no influence on changes of employment structure because of the strict restrictions of institutional arrangements (such as the pattern of industrialization and the planned economy system). Meanwhile, although the influence of social capital could be found, it was limited by many factors. In contrast, after the reform and opening-up, the influence of political status in the set of ascription variables was nearly eliminated, and the impact of social status (such as the registered permanent residence status) has been declining, whereas the effect of family economic condition has been increasing under the tendency of widening gap in income levels. In the set of achievement variables, political loyalty and performance of political participation that once played crucial roles have been dwindling, while the role of educational background has been strengthening. In the set of structure variables, transitions of economic structure have led to great changes in the structure of employment, thereby resulting in changes of occupational structure, expansion of employment, and the emergence of new occupational categories. In the set of institution variables, the influence of arrangement of class (stratum) political status has been waning rapidly, opportunities of social mobility released by institutional innovations have been increasing greatly, and the role of social capital has been rising sharply.

In conclusion, we believe that the foremost influential factors of social mobility in China over the past half century are fundamental political-economic institutions and socio-economic structures. Ascription-achievement factors that dominate in developed countries often have to attach themselves to institutional and structural factors to take effect. The channels through which various social capital affect social mobility are limited by institutional and structural factors largely. Figure 1-5 is a summary of the previous discussion, and it is taken as a preliminary analytical framework of social mobility in contemporary China in the study (the direction of arrow in this figure indicates the direction of influence).

The analytical framework of social mobility indicates our major concerns about the study, that is, combining analyses at the macro level with research at the micro level. From the macro-level perspective, the process of social mobility has experienced two major periods and five major stages in China since 1949 due to changes of institutions, policies, and socio-economic structure. In these two periods and five stages, the scale of social mobility was very large; however, the macro-level dynamic mechanisms that led to such mobility were quite different in some important aspects. Meanwhile, in the two major periods, the influences of state's institutions and policies on socio-economic structure have different characteristics. Before the reform and opening-up, the impact of changes in economic structure on changes in social structure (in the first place are employment and occupational structure) was largely blocked by some institution-policy arrangements and, hence, restricted social stratification and social mobility at that time. Contrarily, after the reform and opening –up, new institutions and policies have replaced the ole ones gradually. Changes in economic structure have directly promoted expansion of employment, diversification of occupational structure, and emergence of new occupations with higher socio-economic status and hence expedited social stratification and increased social mobility opportunities. From the micro-level perspective, ascription-achievement factors affected social mobility both before and after the reform and opening-up. However, the channels, paths, and extent of their influences were not the same in different arrangements of institution and policy. Therefore, in this study, we will follow the sequence of time over the past fifty years and move from the macro level (institution-structure) to the micro level (individual) to investigate the mechanisms of social mobility in contemporary China.

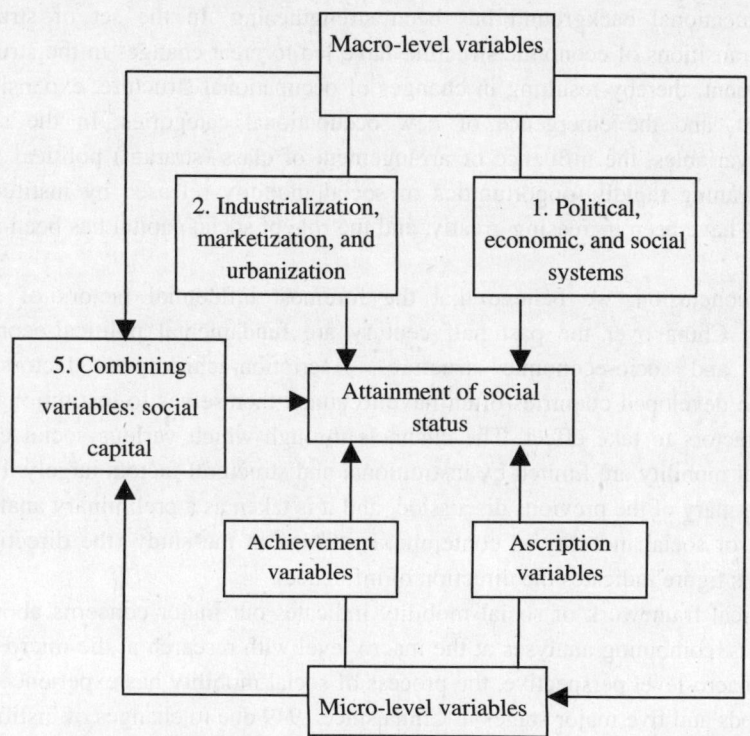

Figure 1-5   Analytical Framework of Social Mobility in China

Chapter 2 Five Tides of Social Mobility in Contemporary China

Chinese society has experienced two significant institutional transformations since 1949. In the process of these reforms, Chinese political-social status and economic conditions have greatly changed as well. Such large-scale institutional reforms and social mobility process have crucially influenced the evolution of class (stratum) structure in China over the past fifty years. In this chapter, we will describe and analyze this process of social mobility based on the before-mentioned analytical framework, and reveal the particularities of social mobility in China and, hence, providing readers with a historical and macro-level perspective to understand changes of social structure in contemporary China.

In essence, the first significant institutional transformation was an institutional revolution. In 1949, the Chinese Communist Party seized the regime and started to use the Soviet model for reference in order to establish a set of new political and economic systems, guided by Marxism and Leninism. From then on, the relationship between the government and society in China has entered a new stage. The basic characteristic of this stage is that the party-government system has comprehensively controlled Chinese society gradually. In other words, in this revolution, public ownership replaced private ownership, the highly centralized planned economy systems replaced the free-market system, and the government-led heavy-industry-first industrialization strategy became the leading strategy of economic development, and comprehensive politicalization in social life. In such situations, new institutional arrangements, policies, and economic systems regulated by them particularly influenced people's social status attainment, and the overall structure of social class (stratum) was simplified to "two classes and one stratum", which mainly consisted of the working class, the peasantry, and the cadre (intelligentsia). Of course, in addition to these major classes and stratum, some other social strata (such as landlords, rich peasants, and capitalists) still existed in the social structure at that time. People's socio-economic status was largely determined by their positions in the government-controlled redistribution system; hence, their economic interests depended on their authority status in this system and the paths and opportunities through which they could access highly centralized resources. In this sense, people's social status was decided by their positions in the highly centralized planned economy system and politicalized social structure rather than their economic income and wealth.

The second significant institutional transformation happened after the Third Plenum of the Eleventh Central Committee of the Communist Party of China. The fundamental driving force of this transformation has been economic reforms and opening to the outside world, and its goal is to establish a socialist free-market system. Usually, people called these reforms as system transition. The essential characteristic of such system transition is to transform the planned and centralized system into a market-oriented and decentralized system. The transformation of society refers to shifting from traditional agricultural society to modern industrialized society, and from a closed society to an open society. The second institutional transformation has had far-reaching influence on social stratification and mobility process. The mechanisms of resources allocation have been changed gradually, and more and more resources have been transferred from government's control to society or the market. The impact of the highly centralized redistribution system has been impaired and social freedom has been increasing. The strategy of development and structure of economy has been adjusted and, hence, expanded employment and changed occupational structure. The socio-economic differentiations have been widened, and hence promoted social stratification, brought on some new social strata, changed the socio-economic status and interrelationship of each social stratum, and shaped an incipient form of modern social stratum structure.

We also noticed that, in each significant institutional reconstruction, relevant institutional arrangements, policies, and regulations changed accordingly. Therefore, after the fundamental political-economic institutions had been established, the constantly changing relevant institutional arrangements, policies, and regulations (sometimes even the will of leaders) also affected social mobility, and hence formed various patterns of social mobility. According to changes of these social mobility patterns, we classify the process of social stratification and mobility over the past fifty years into two major periods and five major stages. The first period ranges from 1949 to 1977. It was composed of three different stages, that is, from 1949 to 1956, from 1957 to 1965, and from 1966-1977. In each stage, some landmark institution-policy changes or political events comprehensively and profoundly affected attainment of social status. In the 1949~1956 stage, the landmark events were the democratic reform and the Socialist Transformation Campaign; in the 1957~1965 stage, the landmark events were the Great Leap Forward, the People's Commune Movement, and large-scale economic adjustments; in the 1966~1977 stage the Cultural Revolution took place. The second period ranges from 1978 to the present, consisting of two stages. The first stage is from 1978 to 1991. In this stage, the planned economy system still dominated economic life, but the market mechanism also started to take effect to some extent. The second stage is from 1992 to the present. In this stage, although the influence of the planned economy system still exists in some important fields, the free-market system has arisen up to be the fundamental economic system.

In conclusion, from the history of social stratification and mobility in China over the past fifty years, we can find that there has been a profound influence of arrangement of institution and policy at the macro level on social mobility. Sometimes such an influence was indirect, potential, and unintentional, whereas sometimes they were direct, visible, and even intentional. Attainment of social status and movement from one social position to another had to be conducted under the limitations of arrangements of institution and policy. Of course, that does not mean that an individual had to accept the social status as given by the arrangements of institution and policy completely and passively. On the contrary, one still could and must seek one's anticipated position in the social status system stipulated by the institution and policy arrangements through personal efforts to take advantage of various opportunities. This is because the influences of arrangements of institution and policy on status attainment were not the same in different periods and in different fields of politics, economy, and social life. Such differences hence provided some spaces and opportunities to a certain extent for individual status attainment.

RECONSTRUCTION OF SOCIAL CLASS STRUCTURE IN

CHINA (1949~1956)

Backgrounds and Major Characteristics

At this stage, the macro-level conditions of social mobility consisted of several important political and economic events or campaigns.

The first one was the establishment of a new regime. From October 1, 1949, the old state apparatus was broken up and a new one was established. The power or authority hierarchy of this new regime extended to every town and village in China. After the accomplishment of collectivization of agriculture, about seven hundred and sixty thousand cooperative communities formed the foundation of the new regime in rural areas as grass-roots level governmental organizations. Such a new hierarchy of authority became one important ladder for later social mobility.

The second event was a series of democratic reforms and the Socialist Transformation Campaign organized and pushed by the new government, such as the rural land reform, confiscation of bureaucratic capital, and utilization, restriction, and reconstruction of agriculture, individual handicraft industry, and national capitalist industry and commerce, etc. These campaigns changed initial social class structure thoroughly. People had to seek their own positions and mobility opportunities in this new framework.

The third thing was the preliminary formation of the highly centralized planned economy system. The new regime had begun its efforts to set up the planned economy system since 1949. By the 1952, the centralized planned economy system, including the national economy planning and administration system, public finance system, finance administration system, products circulation system, foreign trade management system, material supplement system, and labor and wage system, had taken shape. However, during the period of national economy rehabilitation from 1949 to 1952, a new-democratic economic policy was carried out, the planned economy systems did not cover all fields in economic life, and market factors still wielded significant influence; hence, economic planning and the free market coexisted at the same time. China started its first Five-Year-Plan in 1953. In September 1954, the First Meeting of the National People's Congress approved the *Constitution of the People's Republic of China* and formally established the socialist state institutions, the governmental systems, and the planning and economic management systems. With the implementation of state's monopoly over purchasing and selling and the accomplishment of socialist transformations by the end of 1956, the factor of market nearly vanished, and the product market was under the control of government as well. A planned economy system with the principle of a mandatory plan first and a guidance plan second had developed. The government controlled most kinds of social resources.

Based on the above macro-level structure and institutions of society, economy, and politics, social stratification in China at this stage exhibits the following five important characteristics.

First, the hierarchy of social class (stratum) was restructured dramatically. Under the influence of institution-policy arrangements that combined the ascription rule and the achievement rule, some classes (or strata) moved downward significantly, whereas some other classes (or strata) rose up drastically. The initial social class hierarchy was nearly reserved in institutional reforms. The classes (or strata) that initially lay at the bottom of social life stood up to be masters of the society, while the classes (or strata) that initially were at the middle-high level, especially the top level, lost their economic support and fell down, in terms of political status, to the bottom of society. However, we found that these changes did not affect the intergenerational mobility significantly yet at this stage, not at least in the field of education. Meanwhile, we also found that, from then on, Chinese social class structure had been politicalized; it was dominated by the state and the space of society was squeezed.

Second, the drastic changes of politics and society in China formed a unique and complicated structure of social classes. The Communist Party of China had expected to develop a relatively simple class (stratum) structure through the socialist transformation. It would be like what Stalin had mentioned in his *Draft Constitution of the Soviet Russian* in 1936, after all classes of exploitation were eliminated. Only the working class, the peasantry, and the intelligentsia would be left. However, the actual class (stratum) structure in China at this stage was more complicated. At least two systems were included in this class structure. The first one was a multi-class system in the sense of ideology, including the working class, capitalists, petty bourgeoisie, intellectuals, and cadres in urban areas, and the landed class, rich peasants, middle peasants, poor peasants and farm laborers, and rural public administrators in rural areas. The second was the work unit-occupation hierarchy, including several strata classified by the occupational category, the hierarchy of peasant-townspeople status under the situation of urban-rural segregation (of course, the second hierarchy had still not completely come into being by the end of this stage), and so on. In addition, the class structure had a tendency of solidification. Almost every class (or stratum) had its own political boundary and socio-economic boundary. It was not an easy thing to cross these boundaries.

Third, social stratification or social mobility at this stage showed a tendency of institutionalization. A formal mechanism of social stratification and mobility with a politics-occupation axis had come into play.[1] The government monopolized the allocation of almost all critical political, economic, and culture resources. The market-oriented mobility mechanisms had been declining and replaced by the highly centralized redistribution system. Attainment of social status increasingly depended on arrangements of institution and policy.

Fourth, social mobility of social members was increasingly determined by four basic factors: (1) the macro-level arrangement of institution and policy, (2) changes of economic structure, (3) personal family origin—a typical ascription factor, and (4) individual efforts. At this stage, the combining variable—social capital—had little impact. Among all these factors, the personal family origin restricted many social members' efforts of social mobility to a great extent, especially the upward mobility in political stratification system; individual efforts usually took the form of political loyalty and working performance.

Fifth, political-administrative elite dominated the overall political, economic, and social life. The previous diverse social mobility ladders (embodied in political, economic, and cultural systems) had been simplified to the administrative-technical system. Under the control of a uniform cadre personnel system and the labor and wage system, managerial personnel in economic sectors and professional and technical personnel in scientific and technical services fields had been given certain administrative levels. Meanwhile, workers were classified according to a national skill level system, and the peasantry followed the workpoint appraisal system based on age and labor. Therefore, mobility channels in the entire society were simplified. Opportunities of upward mobility could only be obtained when one entered into politics, joined the army, was recruited into factories, was admitted into a higher school, or worked in cultural, arts, and sports fields.

The Urban and Rural Class Structure before and after 1949

The class structure at the time of establishment of the People's Republic of China was the base of latter changes of class (stratum) structure. In terms of urban and rural distribution of the national total population, in 1949, there was a total population of 542,000 thousand in China. The rural population was 484,000 thousand, accounting for 89.39 percent; and urban population was 580,000 thousand, accounting for 10.61

---

[1] Chen, Guangjin. 2004. "Segmentation of the Status Systems: The Formation of Social Stratification and Mobility Mechanisms before the Reform and Opening-up and the Issue of Justice". *Jiangsu Social Science*. Vol. 1.

percent.[1] The formation of such a structure of rural and urban population was closely related to the low-level industrialization in China at that time. The gross output value of industry and agriculture of China was 46.6 billion Yuan RMB. Of that, the gross output value of agriculture was 32.6 billion yuan, accounting for 70 percent, whereas the gross output value of industry was 14 billion, accounting for 30 percent.

There are no available commonly agreed upon estimations about the rural class (stratum) structure at that time. In this study, we adopted the results that were drawn from a survey conducted in 1954 covering 14,334 farmer families in 22 provinces. According to the results of the survey, at the time of the land reform, the rural class (stratum) structure consisted of landlords (2.6 percent), rich peasants (3.6 percent), middle peasants (35.8 percent), poor peasants and farm laborers (57.1 percent), and others (0.9 percent).[2]

As to the urban class structure before the establishment of the People's Republic of China, relevant documentation is even more difficult to find, so we can only give a very general picture here based on fragmentary data.

First, after the establishment of the People's Republic of China, the new regime temporarily retained all former officials and civilians in local governments of the old regime in consideration of political stability. According to estimations made at that time, the annual expenditure that the government had to pay every former official was equal to about 2,000 kilogram of rice, totaling about 6 billion kilogram of rice one year. Therefore, there were about three million former officials were taken over by the new regime.[3] Most of them belonged to clerical personnel. Suppose the leadership accounted for one quarter, then among them about 750 thousand belonged to the stratum of state and social administrators. However, this number does not include all former governmental officials and civilians, because a large number of them fled to Taiwan, Hong Kong, and overseas. In addition, there were also a large number of cadres functioning at various levels of governments in the areas controlled by the Communist Party of China. Therefore, summing up all of the state and social administrators in the two opposed governments in China at that time, the number was not less than 1,500 thousand.

Second, there was a class of capitalists existing in urban areas, including the so-called compradors, bureaucratic capitalists, national capitalists, and owners of various industry and commerce enterprises. According to the quantity of the means of production possessed by them, the class of capitalists could be subdivided into bourgeoisie and petty bourgeoisie. The class of bureaucratic capitalists usually belonged to the leadership in the former government, but we do not consider this

---

[1] National Bureau of Statistics of China. 1958. *National Economic Constructions and People's Living*. Beijing: China National Statistic Press: 5.

[2] Mo, Rida. 1957. *Development of Agricultural Cooperativization in China*. Beijing: China National Statistic Press: 38.

[3] Qiang, Xianzhi and Chongji Jin (eds.). 2003. *Biography of Mao Zedong*. Beijing: Central Documentation Publishing House: 67; Fairbank, John King. 2000. *The Great Chinese Revolution, 1800-1985*. Beijing: World Affairs Press: 330.

factor in the study. As to the number of other people belonging to the capitalist class, there are no reliable data available. However, according to statistical data of the number of private shareholders paid by fixed dividend after the implementation of state-private jointly operations in all industries, we estimated that the total number of members in this stratum is about 1,140 thousand.[1] As far as their agents (equal to today's managerial personnel), there are also no reliable statistical data available. We estimated that their number should be roughly equal to the number of private shareholders, because the scales of most enterprises were relatively small at that time (in fact, enterprises with more than ten employees in industrial sectors were called "large-size companies"), and business owners did not need too many managers.

Third, the stratum of clerical personnel and the stratum of professional and technical personnel mainly were composed of government employees and school staff. Some documents claimed that there were totally nine million civilians and teaching staff in China at that time.[2] Of course, a portion of them should be classified as state and social administrators. Therefore, the total number of people in the stratum of clerical personnel and the stratum of professional and technical personnel was about 7,500 thousand. In addition, some professionals were also employed in governments, enterprises, and various research institutions. In a conservative estimation, the total number of members in the two strata was less than eight million.

Fourth, the stratum of individual-operated business proprietors, including individual handicraftsmen with less than 10 employees, merchants and traders with one employee or without employee, small restaurateurs with two or less employees, boatmen and ship-owners individually operating junks, individual laborers in transportation business with automobiles or cars driven by manpower or cattle. According to calculations based on various sources, the total number of individual-operated business proprietors was 10,000 thousand to 13,000 thousand in 1949 in China,[3] of which about 7,240 thousand were in urban areas.[4]

Fifth, the laborer class (stratum) consisted of industrial workers, employees in commercial enterprises, and apprentices and helpers in individual handicraft industry. The estimated total number of members in this stratum was 8,900 thousand in 1949. Of that, 5,700 thousand were employed in individual handicraft industry, 1,600 thousand in small factories, and 1,400 thousand in medium-large size industrial enterprises.[5] The total number of employees in individual and private commercial

[1] Xue, Muqiao, Xin Su, and Zili Lin, et al. 1978. *The Socialist Transformation of the National Economy in China*, 3rd edition. Beijing: People's Publishing House: 134.

[2] Bo, Yibo. 1997. *Retrospect of Some Momentous Decision-Makings and Events*, Revised Version, Volume 1. Beijing: People's Publishing House: 22.

[3] Dong, Funreng (ed.). 1999. *Economic History of the People's Republic of China*, Volume 1. Beijing: Economic Science Press: 208-224.

[4] National Bureau of Statistics of China (1986: 124).

[5] Walder, Anderw G. 1996. *Communist Neo-traditionalism: Work and Authority in Chinese Industry*. Hong Kong: Oxford University Press: 39.

entities was 967 thousand in 1950.[1] Referring to other sources, we calculated that the total number of employees in individual and private commercial entities was 880 thousand in 1949.[2] As to the number of employees in foodservice and social services sectors, no documents about the year of 1949 are available. Nonetheless, statistical data in 1952 could be used as reference. In 1952, the number of individually owned restaurants was 849 thousand, with a working population of 1,450 thousand. The number of individual and private service entities was 440 thousand, with a working population of 910 thousand.[3] The total number of entities was 1,289 thousand, with a working population of 2,360 thousand. The ratio of the number of working population to the number of restaurants and services entities was 1.83:1 in 1952. According to the growth of individual and private commercial entities and corresponding working population between 1950 and 1952 and the above ratio, we calculated that the number of individual restaurants and services entities was not more than one million and the number of working population was not more than 1,800 thousand in 1949. If estimated by using the ratio of the number of employees to the number of the working population, the number of employees in individual and private foodservice and social service entities would be only 260 thousand. If estimated under the supposition that every entity on the average had one owner, the number of employees would be not more than 800 thousand. Therefore, the total number of employees in individual and private commercial entities, restaurants, and services entities was about 1,140 thousand to 1,680 thousand in 1949.

In addition, there were about four million unemployed people in urban areas all over China.[4] Therefore, the number of urban employment was about 29,300 thousand, plus the unemployment, and then the total work force in urban areas was 33,300 thousand, accounting for 57.4 percent of the total urban population.[5] Considering the birth control policy had not yet been implemented at that time, the family size was roughly similar both in urban and rural areas, as was the proportion of the labor force to the population both in urban and rural areas. Thus, we estimated the total population of rural labor force was about 278,000 thousand. In Table 2-1, we

---

[1] Qianhua, et al. (eds.). 1957. *Changes of Private Industry and Commerce in China over the Past Seven Years (1949~1956)*. Beijing: China Financial and Economic Publishing: 9.

[2] Some sources showed that there were 3,630 thousand individual and private commercial entities in China in 1949 (see Bao, Yujun. 2002. *Appeal for Understanding: Controversies around the Private Sector of Economy in China*. Beijing: China Industry & Commerce Associated Press: 22). In 1950 and 1951, the ratio of the number of people working in individual and private sectors to the number of entities was 1.65:1. See also Qianhua, et al. (1957: 9). Based on these data, the estimated number of working population in individual and private commercial entities was about six million. Furthermore, according to the proportion of employees in the total number of working population (14.6 percent), the estimated number of employees in individual and private commercial entities was about 876 thousand.

[3] National Bureau of Statistics of China (1988: 656).

[4] National Bureau of Statistics of China (1984: 148).

[5] This proportion approximates to the result of the first national population census. The proportion of people aged 15 to 63 to the total population was 59.31 percent in 1953 (see *China Statistical Yearbook (2003)*: Table 4-4).

summarized the estimated proportions of the population of each class (or stratum) to the total population of the labor force.

Table 2-1   Composition of Chinese Social Class (Stratum), 1949

Units: Thousand Persons, %

Class/Stratum	Number	Proportion	Class/Stratum	Number	Proportion
State and social administrators	150	0.48	People working in commercial, restaurant, and service sectors	114~168	0.45
Capitalists	114	0.37	Industrial workers	890	2.86
Managerial personnel	114	0.37	Rural labor force[3]	27,400[4]	88.10
Clerks & professionals[1]	800	2.57	The unemployed	400	1.29
Individual-operated business proprietors	1000~3,000[2]	3.70			

Source: See above paragraphs and relevant footnotes.

Notes: ① No relevant documents available to calculate numbers of the two strata respectively, thus we estimated them together.

② We used the median to calculate the proportion.

③ We did not adopt the notion of agricultural laborer here, because many landlords who did not or seldom participated in agricultural production labor were included in this stratum.

④ In the aforementioned estimation, the total number of rural labor force was about 278,000 thousand. However, because about 4,000 thousand people in this population have been classified as individual-operated business proprietors, this part should be deduced from the total number.

In conclusion, the social structure before the establishment of the People's Republic of China was still a typical non-modern social structure, although it had already contained some elements of a modern society. As a whole, the shape of such structure was like a candlestick with huge bottom and thin middle-higher level parts. The polarization of rich and poor was serious, and the entire society extremely lacked equality, which caused trouble.

Rearrangements of Class Relationships

After the establishment of the People's Republic of China, the Communist Party of China launched the democratic reforms all over the country in order to annihilate various feudal production relations, including the landlord economy and the bureaucratic comprador economy. At the same time, through utilizing, restricting, and adjusting the national capitalist economy, the new regime managed to set up a transitional new-democratic society with five types of co-existing economic elements (the state-owned economy, the cooperative economy, the state capitalist economy, the private capitalist economy, and the individual economy), and accordingly prepared the way for the transformation to socialist economy systems. The Party carried out and accomplished the land reform in a short time in newly liberated rural areas, and confiscated bureaucratic capital in urban areas in order to create a favorable environment for the development of national capitalist industry and commerce. All

69

these radical campaigns drastically reconstructed class relations in Chinese society and preliminarily established a new class structure both in urban and rural areas; in this new structure, political status was more important than economic status, and thus laid the groundwork for the new structure of social mobility.

(1)The Land Reform in Rural Areas and the Rise of Poor Peasants and Farm Laborers

The land reform in China was accomplished by the spring of 1953 except for some minor areas with a population of 7,000 thousand, and dramatically changed the relations of the socio-economic hierarchy. According to a survey conducted at that time covering 15,432 farm households in 23 provinces, after the land reform the per household cultivated area of each major rural class in newly liberated regions respectively was: poor peasant and farm laborers 12.16 Mu, middle peasants 19.01 Mu, rich peasants 25.9 Mu, and landlords 12.16 Mu.

Apparently, rich peasants became the strongest class in economic strength, but it did not mean that their socio-political status was at the same level. In fact, to the new regime, they were a politically neutral class. By contrast, though farmland and cattle possessed by poor peasants and farm laborers were only slightly more than that of landlords, their socio-political status had already risen up to the highest level and became the upholding foundation for the new regime because they had gained so much from the land reform. The economic status of middle peasants was higher than poor peasants and farm laborers, and their socio-political status was higher than rich peasants and landlords but lower than poor peasants and farm laborers as an ally of the new regime. The social status of landlords fell down to the bottom of the rural society. They possessed the least farmland, their family property was confiscated, and they were to-be-eliminated objects as a feudal exploiting class. Therefore, the basic class hierarchy was reversed, from the original order (from top to down) of landlord, rich peasant, middle peasant, and poor peasant and farm laborer to the order of poor peasant and farm laborer, middle peasant, rich peasant, and landlord. Each rural class (stratum) was endowed with its own political attribute and meaning, which gradually became their labels of political status and hence had a far-reaching impact on socio-economic life of the members of each class. Once one's class origin was established in the land reform, it would determine whether he or she could participate in the redistribution of farmland, and affect his or her opportunity and probability of social mobility in future politicalized social structure. For example, according to the policy at that time, the peasant association was the major organization in charge of the land reform, and its qualified leaders had to meet two requirements: First, having a class origin of poor peasant and farm laborer; second, actively participating in the land reform and politically loyal and reliable. Therefore, it was impossible for people with other class origins, except the middle peasant, to have the opportunity to be rural social administrators. Even activists with the middle-peasant origin could not occupy important positions in peasant associations.

(2) Economic Rehabilitation and Changes in the Urban Labor-Capital Relationship

From 1949 to 1952 was a period of rehabilitation for the national economy in China. On one hand, the new regime confiscated the bureaucratic capital and expropriated, regulated, entrusted, and requisitioned the foreign-invested capital. On the other hand, it supported the development of national capitalist industry and commerce through the policy of utilization, adjustment, and restriction. Within four years, the rehabilitation and development of industry and commerce obtained remarkable achievement. The gross output value of industry increased from 14 billion yuan to 34.3 billion yuan, annually growing by 34.8 percent.[1]

The above policies and measures had different influences on the evolution of urban social strata. First, the policy of confiscating bureaucratic capital economically eliminated the class of comprador and bureaucratic capitalists. The treatment of foreign-invested capital destroyed the living space of compradors who usually served in foreign-invested enterprises.

Second, although national capitalists developed to some extent at the time, they also began to encounter strict restrictions imposed by governmental policies. From 1949 to 1952, the number of private industrial enterprises increased from 123 thousand to 150 thousand and the number of individual and private commercial enterprises increased from 3,630 thousand to 4,300 thousand.[2] However, the new regime believed that the effects of the development of national capitalist industry and commerce were two-edged. On one hand, such development contributed to the rehabilitation of the national economy and industrialization. On the other hand, the capitalist production relation frequently conflicted with the goal of Communist Party of China, i.e., constructing the socialist systems. In the process of manufacturing, ordering, marketing, and selling, the purpose of capitalists was only profit. In addition, some capitalists bribed government officials resulting in a series of consequences. In order to solve these issues, the government carried out the Five-Antis Campaign (campaign against bribery, tax evasion, cheating, stealing, and private speculation) in urban areas from 1951 to 1952. In this campaign, capitalists were stuck by a heavy blow:

> The capitalist class was completely discredited in most enterprises. Although in a small part of small-medium enterprises they may have remaining prestige, it cannot compare with before. Thereby, workers have been taking over the authority of supervision in many enterprises, whereas many capitalists actually lost or almost lost the right of control.[3]

---

[1] National Bureau of Statistics of China (1984: 8).

[2] Bao (2002: 22); Qianhua, et al. (1957: 8-9).

[3] Political Bureau of the C.P.C. Central Committee. 1956. *Resolution on the Issue of Transforming the Capitalist Industry and Commerce*. February 24.

Third, the stratum of individual-operated business proprietors developed with the rehabilitation and development of the national economy. According to statistics in 1949, the total number of urban individual laborers was 7,240 thousand. This number increased to 8,830 thousand in 1952, an average rise of 22 percent per year.[1] They were politically defined as laborers. Even though sometimes they employed one or two employees, they did not belong to the class of exploitation. However, they did not belong to the working class neither, thus their political status was intermediate between the working class and the class of capitalists. Sometimes, individual-operated business proprietors were regarded as petty bourgeoisie; therefore, they also belonged to groups that needed to be reconstructed in later socialist transformation.

Finally, the number of working class increased significantly, and their social status rose to a great height. In the period of rehabilitation of the national economy, the development of Chinese industry drove expansion of the working class. In addition, because of the development of capitalist industry and commerce in this period, the number of employees in the private sector of economy increased as well. From 1950 to 1953, employees in private industrial enterprises increased from 1,611 thousand to 2,231 thousand, an average increase of 11.9 percent per year.[2] In the public-owned sector of economy, the expansion was even much greater. From 1949 to 1952, the total number of workers and staff members in China increased from 8,090 thousand to 16,030 thousand,[3] growing by almost 100 percent. However, the notion of "workers and staff members" included almost all people working in the public-owned sector of economy, not merely referring to industrial workers in public-owned industrial sectors. In public-owned industrial enterprises, industrial workers had become masters both politically and economically. In national capitalist industrial and commercial enterprises, although capitalists and shareholders still were owners and management, worker and staff members were employees, the socio-political status of the latter moved up significantly. In the new regime, they were politically endowed with the status of masters of the state, and their democratic rights and fundamental interests in private enterprises were confirmed and secured.

(3) Regime Construction and Formation of the New State and Social Administrator Stratum

After the establishment of the People's Republic of China, the Communist Party of China began to set up governments at the town and higher level in this country and, hence, formed a new state and social administrator stratum. The central government was founded in October 1949. The total number of top-level officials was five hundred, including officials from committee members and higher leadership in each ministry, council, national committee, and general office, to the chairperson of the

---

[1] National Bureau of Statistics of China (1986: 124).
[2] Bao (2002: 22).
[3] National Bureau of Statistics of China (1984: 107).

central government. By the end of December 1949, the regional government in Northeastern China and Political-Military Steering Committees in Eastern, Central-South, Southwestern, and Northwestern China had been established and had 262 committee members and higher officials. By the end of the fall of 1952, there were 31 provinces, one provincial-level administrative office, 160 cities, 2,174 counties and county-level administrative regions, and 280 thousand townships setting up their governments,[1] and hence formed a stratum of state and social administrators with more than 1,000 thousand members.[2]

People who entered this stratum were mainly demobilized army cadres and local cadres without military background. In addition, there were also a large number of former governmental civilians working in newly founded governmental and public administrative agencies. However, usually they did not occupy important positions with authority in these agencies. Moreover, most of them received a blow and the new regime expelled them from governmental agencies in the Three-Antis Campaign (campaign against corruption, waste and bureaucratism) from 1951 to 1952 and the Campaign of Suppressing Counterrevolutionary from 1955 to 1957. According to incomplete statistics, about 290 thousand people were purged, accounting for 7 percent of people involved in this campaign.[3]

Therefore, in the urban society, the new class structure consisted of cadres (they were politically classified into the working class), the working class (including industrial workers, and staff members or employees in commercial and service sectors), intellectuals, individual laborers, and the class of capitalists, etc. From the perspective of political status, the working class was the highest, whereas the capitalist class was the lowest. Taking the above-mentioned new rural class structure into account, the overall social class structure in China after the democratic revolution was composed of the working class (including cadres, industrial workers, employees in commercial and service sectors), poor peasants and farmer laborers (belonging to the semi-proletariat), petty bourgeoisie (including middle peasants, intellectuals, individual laborers, etc.), bourgeoisie (including national capitalists and rich peasants); the landed class, and the bureaucratic comprador capitalists, etc. Political status of the working class was the highest, poor peasants and farmer laborers were regarded as the allied force of the working class, whereas the landed class and the bureaucratic comprador capitalists were at the bottom.

---

[1] Wei, Hongyun. 2003. "The Rehabilitation of the National Economy". In *Guo Shi Ji Shi Ben Mo (1949-1999)*, Volume 1. Shenyang, Liaoning: Liaoning People's Publishing House: 8, 11, 16.

[2] For example, in Shangzhou Prefecture in Shannxi Province at that time, usually officials in a township government included one Party secretary, one township head, and one secretary (see Ding, Weizhi (ed.). 1993. *Series of China National Conditions: Socioeconomic Surveys in One Hundred Counties and Cities: Shangzhou*. Beijing: Encyclopedia of China Publishing House: 461.) In some places, there were one or several vice-heads of township. Therefore, there were more than 1,000 thousand cadres with important functions and authority in 280 thousand township governments in China.

[3] Bo (1997: 150).

The Socialist Transformation

After Chinese social class (stratum) structure was rebuilt by the top-down arrangements of new national institutions and policies, the redistribution mechanism through which the state controlled resources and opportunities began to take effect, whereas the influence of the free-market mechanism faded away. The fundamental turning point was the Socialist Transformation Movement in agriculture, the handicraft industry, and the capitalist industry and commerce carried out from 1953 according to the General Line of Socialist Transformation formulated by the Communist Party of China. After the accomplishment of this reconstruction movement, the redistribution mechanism became almost the only mechanism of social stratification and mobility in China.

Private ownership of farmland characterized the relations of production in rural society after the land reform. Under such ownership, there were differences in the composition of the labor force, operation and management skills, and quantity and quality of the means of production existing among farmer households. Such differences inevitably influenced their economic performances. As a result, social differentiation reoccurred in rural society. Many peasants began to move upward, while some moved downward for lack of sufficient labor force, the means of production, or even individual efforts. According to a survey conducted in 1954 covering 14,334 farmer households in 21 provinces, form the end of the land reform to 1954, the proportion of poor peasant and farm laborer was down from 57.1 percent to 29.0 percent, down by 49.2 percent. The proportion of middle peasants increased from 35.8 percent to 62.2 percent, up by 73.7 percent. Both the proportion of rich peasants and landlords dropped to some extent.[1] Therefore, the general tend of social mobility in rural society at that time was the move to the class of middle peasants. Such mobility was based on individual efforts. However, the mainstream viewpoint of that time believed that such changes in rural areas were unreasonable polarization. The cause of polarization was the private ownership of farmland. Only if the private ownership was abolished through the socialist transformation and only if collective ownership was establish in the form of agricultural cooperatives, could such polarization be removed. Therefore, the socialist transformation in agriculture was put on the agenda in 1953. The government managed to promote changes in rural production relations through mass movement and class struggle. By 1956, 760 thousand agricultural cooperatives had been established in China. About 111,710 thousand of farm households joined as members, accounting for 96.3 percent of the total number of rural households. After the accomplishment of the socialist transformation in agriculture, in the perspective of production relations, the rural class relations became simple: almost all peasants were members of cooperatives and entered the workpoint appraisal system based on labor capability (and labor attitude). Of course, former class relations did not disappear in the sense of political ideology

---

[1] Mo (1957: 38).

and continued to affect peasants' political status and political life, and further their social life and social mobility.[1]

In urban areas, with the Three-Antis and the Five-Antis campaigns, the government carried out the socialist transformation in urban capitalist industry and commerce through state-private joint operations from 1953. Such reconstruction consisted of two stages. Before 1955, state-private joint operations were mainly implemented by large-size enterprises. After joint operations, capitalists had the right to participate in profit distribution. They could usually gain dividends plus remunerations paid to directors of the board and managers, accounting for one fourth of the profit. After 1955, the socialist transformation was implemented at the entire industry level, and monopolistic companies were founded. After joint operations of the entire industry, fixed interests instead of dividends were paid to capitalists. The socialist transformation in capitalist industry and commerce was accomplished by the end of 1956. The basic form of socialist transformation in the individual handicraft industry was to organize individual handicraftsmen to create handicraft cooperatives. By the end of 1956, there were 104,430 cooperative organizations in the handicraft industry. Members of these cooperatives accounted for 91.7 percent of the total employment in this industry. In addition, more than 90 percent of small merchants and peddlers were organized to establish entities.

On one hand, the accomplishments of the above socialist transformations solidified the political status and interrelations of each class (stratum) in the political ideology system of the Communist Party of China, and hence became a kind of socialized cognitive paradigm on class relations. On the other hand, such socialist transformations greatly weakened the influence of the market mechanism on social mobility and replaced it with the state redistribution mechanism. For example, after the socialist transformations, the urban working class (including workers and staff members in public-owned enterprises and former employees in individual and private industrial and commercial entities) obtained relatively high economic status and political status. All wage earners got rid of their status as employed laborers. The authority of recruitment and dismissal was in control of the government. As a result, origins of urban workers changed. According to statistics, among workers and staff members who started working before 1949, 63.1 percent of them were born in peasants' families, whereas only 17.4 percent with a family background of workers. In contrast, among 6,842 thousand staff members and worker who entered the work place from 1950 to 1956, about 58.1 percent of them were veterans or came from urban workers' families, 24.4 percent had peasant origins, and 17.5 percent came from other origins (such as urban individual handicraftsmen, small merchants, and peddlers).[2]

---

[1] Zhang, Letian. 1998. *Farewell to Utopia: Research on the People's Commune System.* Beijing: Oriental Press.
[2] Gao, Guang, Zhen Li, Min Ma, and Changyuan Wang (eds.). 1990. *Social Class Structure and Class Struggles in Socialist China.* Beijing: People's Publishing House: 52-53.

After the state-private joint operation, capitalists almost lost all economic resources. Their economic conditions and mobility directions were determined by governmental policy arrangements and distributions. Although they were nominal shareholders of enterprises and possessed about 2.4 billion Yuan shares, they could only get 5 percent annual fixed interests, which ranged from several hundred Yuan to ten or more cents. Many capitalists had financial trouble.[1] In the process of state-private joint operations, the government retained all in-service capitalists and relocated them according to the principle of "assigning positions based on capability and considering due care". As a result, most of them lost former authorities and positions and became ordinary staff members in enterprises. For example, by May 1956, after the state-private joint operations accomplished at the industry level, there were 5,735 in-service capitalists in Guangzhou City of Guangdong Province. Of them, about 30 were presidents or vice presidents, 149 were on the board of directors, 4 were senior consultants, 47 were consultants, 53 were managers, 839 were section chiefs, and 725 were office heads, accounting for 32.2 percent; 3,888 were ordinary staff members, accounting for 67.8 percent.[2] In the entire country, about 710 thousand capitalists and 100 thousand agents of capitalists were emplaced to certain positions. However, only 35 percent to 40 percent of them were appointed as managerial personnel,[3] even if those who occupied managerial positions had to comply with the instructions of government representatives in enterprises. The rest of the capitalists had to retire or find their own means of livelihood.

Meanwhile, a stratum of enterprise managerial personnel with the status of government cadres was also formed under such institutional arrangements. This stratum consisted of two parts of people: managerial personnel in public-owned enterprises and cadres in state-private jointly operated enterprises (as government representatives). According to the policy at that time, every 63 workers should be assigned one cadre in state-private jointly operated enterprises in 1955, and every 160 workers should have one government representative in state-private jointly operated enterprises in 1956.[4] As a whole, government representatives in state-private jointly operated enterprises were not less than 200 thousand.[5] In addition, organizations such as committees of the Communist Party, the Communist Youth League, labor unions, and some administrative departments and offices were universally established in these

---

[1] According to statistics, there were 1,140 thousand shareholders paid by fixed interests in 1956 in China, the equity capital value was 2,105.3 yuan per capita. The government annually paid 120,000 thousand yuan fixed interests, 105.3 yuan per capita. See Dong (1999: 198-199).

[2] Qianhua, et al. (1957: 179).

[3] Dong (1999: 199). Of course, many high-level people among them were appointed as principals of government agencies as well. For example, several hundred of capitalists were appointed as deputy governor, deputy mayor, and director-general all over the country at that time.

[4] Dong (1999: 193).

[5] According to statistics, the total employment in the secondary and tertiary industry was 44,620 thousand in 1957. If we suppose that the total employment in 1956 was 30,000 thousand and every 160 workers were assigned a cadre, then there were at least 187.5 thousand of government representatives.

enterprises.[1] Cadres in these organizations were enterprise managerial personnel as well; they mainly were activists, members of the Party or the Youth League in enterprises, and veterans.

In conclusion, the socialist transformation was a process in which the market system was replaced by the state distribution system. After accomplishment of the transformation, the private ownership of the means of production was eliminated on the whole, and almost all independent market actors were cleaned out as well. The planned redistribution system based on public ownership was eventually established.

In addition to the socialist transformation, another important aspect of the General Line of Socialist Transformation was industrialization. This was a kind of state-led industrialization stressing the development of heavy industry. In the process of boosting such a pattern of industrialization, a highly centralized planned system was gradually set up to allocate resources. In order to achieve the goal of socialist industrialization, the government formulated the first Five-Year Plan and allocated almost all investment into modern industries, especially large-scale heavy industry. Under the strong impetus of government, the industrial sector of economy developed rapidly and the gross output value of industry increased by 5.5 times.[2] The industrial structure changed in a short time. In 1952, the gross output value of industry accounted for 43.1 percent and agriculture 56.9 percent, whereas in 1957, the proportion of industry was 56.7 percent and agriculture was 43.3 percent. However, industrialization with prior consideration of heavy industry was a type of capital-intensive and technology-intensive industrialization; hence, it squeezed out the labor force. In the process of industrialization, the proportion of industrial laborers to the total number of laborers decreased from 6.0 percent to 5.9 percent. Fortunately, the gates of cities were still open to peasants in that period. In order to meet of the needs of infrastructure construction, the government recruited 15,000~ 20,000 thousand rural laborers to participate in urban constructions in the cities.[3] As a result, the level of urbanization rose from 10.6 percent in 1949 to 15.4 percent in 1957. Laborers who transferred from rural areas through recruitment mainly entered into the construction and transportation industry, and a portion of them were allocated to industrial enterprises. The proportion of employment in the construction industry increased from 1.4 percent to 3.1 percent, and the transportation industry grew from 1.1 percent to 1.9 percent. The industrialization with the prior consideration of heavy industry also affected the development of commercial, foodservice and traditional services sectors. The proportion of employment in these sectors decreased from 4.7

---

[1] In a meeting called by the United Front Work Department of the Central Committee of the C.P.C. and All-China Federation of Industry and Commerce in May 1957, someone said that each factory usually had eight departments, and each workshop had eight cadres in charge of corresponding affairs (*People's Daily*. May 16, 1957).

[2] National Bureau of Statistics of China (1959: 177).

[3] Wang, Haiguang. 2003. "Macro-level Analysis of Formation and History of the Permanent Residence Registration System in Contemporary China". *Study of C.P.C. History*. Vol. 3.

percent to 3.6 percent.[1]

The New Educational System and Increasing Opportunities

Education is an important factor that affects social mobility. The influence of government is usually positive in this field. As soon as the establishment of the People's Republic of China, the government began to reform the old educational systems, contents, and methods step by step in a planned way. The First National Education Conference held in December 1949 proposed that, since the People's Republic of China was a people's democratic dictatorship regime that founded on the basis of worker-peasant alliance, the educational system should mainly benefit workers and peasants and bring up a large number of new intellectuals with origins of workers, peasants, and cadres in order to construct the new China. This meant that workers, peasants, and their families, who were once unable to go to school for poverty before the establishment of the People's Republic of China, could obtain more educational opportunities based on their family backgrounds and individual efforts, and hence gain more upward mobility opportunities. Among enrolled elementary school students in 1952, more than 80 percent of them came from workers' or peasants' families. Among secondary school students, those with worker or peasant origin accounted for 60 percent.[2] As far as the worker and peasant origins in college and university students, according to Mao Zedong's estimation, the proportion was less than 30 percent.[3] Another calculation claimed that the proportion was 36.3 percent.[4] The tendency of increasing educational opportunities for families of workers and peasants extended to the next stage of social mobility in China. According to estimations, the proportion of college and university students with worker or peasant origins increased from 36.3 percent in 1957 to 49 percent in 1960.[5]

As a whole, education in this stage achieved remarkable development, and hereby provided more opportunities of upward social mobility for more people, especially the families of workers and peasants. During two decades between 1928 and 1947, there were only 185 thousand graduates of colleges and universities in China, an average of 9,000 graduates per year.[6] By contrast, in eight years between 1949 and 1956, there were 302,514 graduates of colleges and universities in China. Of them, 89,674 students graduated in the first four years with an average of 22 thousand graduates per year; and 212,840 students graduated in the second four years, an average of 53 thousand graduates per year. In the same period, there were 968,040 graduates of technical secondary schools. Of them, 203,500 students graduated in the

---

[1] Dong (1999: 284).

[2] Wei (2003: 270-271).

[3] Mao, Zedong. 1990. *Mao Zedong Texte*, Volume 7. Beijing: People's Publishing House: 177-178.

[4] Xu, Meide. 2000. *Chinese Universities 1895~1995: A Century of Cultural Conflicts*. Beijing: Education & Science Publishing House: 129.

[5] Xu (2000: 129).

[6] National Bureau of Statistics of China (1983: 520).

78

first three years, with less than 68 thousand graduates per year; and 764,540 thousand students graduated in the second five years, nearly 153 thousand graduates per year.[1] The total number of graduates from technical secondary schools, colleges, and universities was more than 1,270 thousand. If calculated by the above-mentioned proportions of students with worker and peasant origins, i.e., 36 percent in colleges and universities and 60 percent in technical secondary schools, there were about 540 thousand graduates with worker and peasant origins.[2] Along with graduates with other origins, they were emplaced to the procession of governmental cadres according to the government's institutional arrangements.

In addition, graduates from senior middle schools were also regarded as knowledgeable persons or even intellectuals at that time, according to the opinion of Mao Zedong. He estimated that there were at least 5,000 thousand intellectuals in 1956. Of them, 4,000 thousand were senior middle school graduates and at least 2,400 thousand among them came from worker or peasant families. Usually, they were treated as intellectuals by the government.

The structure of social class (stratum) in China was changed by the year of 1956 due to the above transformations. However, because relevant data were incomplete, we have to make a very rough estimation based on data in Table 2-1 and occupational category. (1) According to statistics, the proportion of managerial personnel to the total number of the labor force was about 1.8 percent.[3] Leading cadres in the stratum of state and social administrators were included in the above estimation of managerial personnel. If calculated by a proportion of one fourth, the proportion of state and social administrators to the total number of the labor force was 0.45 percent. (2) The class of capitalists was eliminated and its members entered other strata, such as the stratum of state and social administrators, enterprises managerial personnel, and manual laborers, etc. (3) The stratum of managerial personnel consisted of management in public-owned enterprises, government representatives in state-private jointly operated enterprises, in-service capitalists, and middle-higher level management in enterprises with various types of ownership. In the process of jointly operations, the number of managerial departments in public-owned and state-private jointly operated enterprises was more than that of former private enterprises, and the number of managerial personnel inside enterprises increased. However, many enterprises were merged in this process. The proportion of merged industrial enterprises to the total number of initial private industrial enterprises was one third to two thirds, and the proportion of merged commercial enterprises was 20 percent to 40 percent, in some sectors the proportion even as high as 87 percent.[4]

---

[1] National Bureau of Statistics of China (1984a: 493, 495).

[2] College and university graduates in the first four years and technical secondary school graduates in the first three years are deducted from this estimation. According to the general educational system, those graduates usually entered schools before 1949, thus the proportion of students with worker or peasant origins must be very low.

[3] Dong (1999: 284)

[4] Qianhua, et al. (1957: 170-175).

Therefore, the total number of managerial personnel after the jointly operation in commercial and industrial enterprises only slightly increased compared with the number in 1949. Considering the growth of the total number of the labor force,[1] then the proportion of managerial personnel to the total number of the labor force would not be higher than the proportion of 0.37 percent in 1949. (4) According to statistics, from 1952 to 1957, the proportion of people who were engaged in educational, scientific, cultural, and healthcare sectors to the total number of the labor force increased from 1.8 percent to 2.1 percent,[2] with an increase of 0.06 percent per year. Thus, the proportion of the stratum of professional and technical personnel was about 2.04 percent in 1956. (5) The stratum of clerical personnel consisted of clerks in social administrative agencies and clerks in industrial and commercial enterprises. According to statistics, the proportion of clerks and office laborers in social administrative agencies to the total number of the labor force was 1.35 percent. In practice, the number of office laborers usually was much fewer than that of clerical personnel and if we suppose the proportion is one tenth, thus the proportion of clerical personnel in administrative agencies to the total number of the labor force would be 1.22 percent. The number of clerical personnel in industrial and commercial enterprises was hard to estimate. Even supposing this number was roughly equal to the number of managerial personnel (say, one section chief needed one clerk), and then its proportion to the total number of the labor force was only 0.37 percent. Thus, the total proportion of the two groups of clerical personnel was about 1.6 percent. (6) The proportion of people working in commercial, foodservice, and traditional services sectors was 4.7 percent in 1952, and then dropped to 3.6 percent in 1957,[3] with an average decrease of 0.22 percent per year. Thus, the proportion of people working in commercial and service sectors was about 3.82 percent in 1956. If we put aside managerial and clerical personnel among them, then the proportion of ordinary employees in commercial and service sectors was about 3.62 percent. (7) The stratum of industrial workers included workers in industrial enterprises, construction workers, and transportation workers. From 1952 to 1957, the total proportion of workers in industrial, construction and transportation sectors increased from 8.5 percent to 10.9 percent, up by 0.48 percent per year. Thus, the proportion of people working in these three sectors was about 10.42 percent in 1956. If we deduct managerial and clerical personnel among them, then the proportion of industrial workers was about 9.88 percent.[4] (8) According to the national statistic yearbooks, the proportion of peasants

---

[1] According to *China Statistical Yearbook (1984)*, the total number of labor force in China increased by 2.56 percent per year from 1952 to1956.

[2] Dong (1999: 284).

[3] Dong (1999: 284).

[4] The deduction of managerial and clerical personnel followed three steps: (1) summed up the proportions of people working in industries mentioned in the sixth and the seventh categories, and then calculated the proportions of people in the two categories to the summed proportion respectively; (2) summed up the proportions of managerial and clerical personnel, and assumed that they equally distributed in the above two categories; (3) calculated the proportions of managerial and clerical

declined from 88.1 percent to 80.6 percent. (9) The number of individual laborers decreased from 10,000 thousand to 160 thousand,[1] and its proportion accordingly dropped from 4.59 percent to 0.06 percent. (10) The total proportion of all the above strata to the total number of the labor force was 98.62 percent. Therefore, other persons (including jobless people) accounted for the remaining 1.38 percent.

ESTABLISHMENT OF THE MULTIDIMENSIONAL DUAL STATUS SYSTEMS (1957~1965)

Chinese society had entered into a new stage of changes since 1957. In the political arena, three large-scale political movements, i.e., the Anti-Rightist, Anti-right Opportunism, and Four Cleanups Campaigns, demonstrated that enormous tensions existed in the entire society. In fact, the source of these movements was the increasingly expanding "left-leaning" ideology. In the economic field, the planned economy system was eventually established after the accomplishment of the socialist transformation in 1956 and the People's Commune Movement in 1958. The government completely controlled the authority of allocation of economic resources in the entire society; hence, the development of the national economy was completely under control of political ideology and experienced tremendous fluctuations consisting of the Great Leap Forward, great calamity, and great adjustments. In social life, social relationships among people were increasingly politicized and ideologized. The structure, ranks, and political meanings of social classes were solidified. Meanwhile, the "left-leaning" ideology stressing class struggle gradually spread among the people, thus people still had some opportunities of cross-class mobility.

More specifically, social mobility at this stage showed the following tendencies: (1) after synchronous development in the first two or three years, industrialization and urbanization in China went back to following uncoordinated paths. The level of urbanization declined significantly. As a result, changes of economic structure caused by industrialization did not bring out synchronous changes in occupational structure. The social class (stratum) structure classified from an occupational perspective still kept the traditional shape of pyramid or candlestick. (2) The multidimensional status system was established and solidified. The government defined the identities of all social members from several different dimensions in

---

personnel in the two categories respectively, and then deducted these proportions from the proportions of the two categories to the total number of the labor force.

[1] National Bureau of Statistics of China (1984a: 107). There were 6,400 thousand individual laborers in 1955. The Socialist Transformation Movement brought a great decrease of 6,240 thousand on the former number, dwon by 39 times. The decrease of individual laborers resulted in great inconveniences to urban people's life. Thus, the government had to allow the development of individual laborers again in 1957. In that year, the number rapidly increased to 1,040 thousand.

political, economic, labor and personnel, and distribution systems. At the same time, there were two major ranks with significant political, economic, and social differences existing in each dimension of status, forming a type of dual hierarchical structure. Therefore, we believe that the multidimensional dual status hierarchy took shape at this stage. It determined people's basic social position, social role, and the boundary and opportunity of social mobility. (3) Class struggles in the political ideology field and political struggles inside the Party were spreading, and political-social status of quite a number of social members experienced significant vicissitudes.

Economic Fluctuations and Institutional Needs to Establish the Systems

The Great Leap Forward Campaign and the People's Commune Movement started immediately after the accomplishment of the socialist transformation movement from 1958. The People's Commune Movement founded a type of regime that incorporated township governments and local units of the Party organizations into cooperatives. It not only provided an institutional foundation to strictly administer peasants, but also set up an organizational foundation to mobilize peasant to participate in large-scale water conservancy projects and urban industrial constructions. The People's Commune Movement was also carried out in urban areas and thousands of people's communes were founded; however, all of these urban communes were disorganized in a short time because they conflicted with urban social life. History has demonstrated that both the Great Leap Forward Campaign and the People's Commune Movement were total failures and caused serious damages to the national economy and social development of China. Without economic development, social productions were unable to meet material needs of the people and could not ensure the advance of industrialization with emphasis on the priority of heavy industry. Therefore, how to allocate limited resources differentially under the low-level supply conditions became a critical issue that the government had to solve. As a result, establishing a type of multidimensional dual status systems that could ensure that people would accept the differentiated resources allocation system became a sort of institutionalized need.

(1) The First Tide of Large-Scale Population Movement between Urban and Rural Areas

The Great Leap Forward launched in 1958 was a rushed trial of the government-led industrialization stressing prior development of heavy industry. At that time, the iron and steel industry was regarded as the core sector of heavy industry. Therefore, the government launched the Steel-making Campaign in the industrial field. According to statistics, at the climax of this campaign, about 60,000 thousand laborers were on stream; most of them were rural laborers. Therefore, the campaign was also a trial of occupational shift in a loose sense. However, such a shift was not stable. With the bankruptcy of the Steel-making campaign, rural laborers who once were involved in industrial production had to return to the farmlands all over again. Meanwhile, the blindly expanded infrastructure constructions created unreal growth in the demand for an industrial labor force. In order to meet the increasing demand, the government decided to loosen limitations once imposed on requirements of worker recruitment, the total number of workers and staff members, and the budget of the total expenditure of wages in 1958. As a result, the number of urban workers and staff members increased rapidly. In 1958, only about 20,930 thousand people entered the procession of industrial workers and most of them came from rural areas.[1] From 1957 to 1960, the urban population in China increased from 99,490 thousand to 130,730 thousand, of which about 22,180 thousand migrated from rural areas.[2]

However, with the failure of the Great Leap Forward both in agriculture and in industry, such a huge urban population brought unbearable pressure on the government. Therefore, the government started a large-scale dismissal in urban areas from 1960 by demobilizing new workers recruited from rural areas and rural population, which were blindly flowing into cities in the period of the Great Leap Forward to return to their original locations. Moreover, the government also encouraged urban residents to migrate to rural areas. The urban population decreased by about 26,000 thousand people from 1961 to the end of 1963.[3] Therefore, such a population migration between urban and rural areas was an unsuccessful trial of rural urbanization. The consequences of its failure were serious. Not only did some 20,000 thousand peasants who had just entered the cities need to go back to their homes, but also nearly 4,000 thousand urban residents were forced to migrate to rural areas. Furthermore, the urban and rural residence registration system had been formally established since then, and the dual social structure that prevented the rural population from entering cities was eventually institutionalized in this failure.

(2) Unbalanced Economic Structure Hampered Changes of Employment Structure

Although the Great Leap Forward failed, the government-led industrialization still went on. At this stage, in the Gross Domestic Product (GDP) structure of the national economy, the proportion of the primary industry kept dropping. The proportion of the tertiary industry also showed a descending tendency after the growth at the previous stage. Only the proportion of the secondary industry was still rising (see Table 2-2). This tendency kept widening the deviation in employment structure instead of reducing it. This was a kind of unbalanced economic structure, entirely different from the general trend of global industrialization.

---

[1] National Bureau of Statistics of China (1984a: 103).

[2] Li, Ruojian. 2001. "Influences of Economic System Factors on the Great Leap Forward and Three Years of Catastrophe". *Opening Times*. August.

[3] National Bureau of Statistics of China (1984a: 103, 123).

Table 2-2   Industrialization and Employment Structure in China, 1952~1965

Units: %, Times

Year	GDP Structure			Employment Structure			Employment Structure Deviation*		
	The primary industry	The secondary industry	The tertiary industry	The primary industry	The secondary industry	The tertiary industry	The primary industry	The secondary industry	The tertiary industry
1952	50.5	20.9	28.6	83.5	7.4	9.1	-0.40	1.82	2.14
1957	40.3	29.7	30.1	81.2	9.0	9.8	-0.50	2.30	2.07
1962	39.4	31.3	29.3	82.1	7.9	9.9	-0.52	2.96	1.96
1965	37.9	35.1	27.0	81.6	8.4	10.0	-0.54	3.18	1.70

Source: Data about the GDP structure and the employment structure are from China Social Statistical Materials (2000) and China Statistical Yearbook (1984).

Note: *The calculation equation of the deviation of employment structure is: Employment structure deviation = (GDP proportion of each industry / employment proportion of each industry)–1. The result of this equation indicates that the times that the GDP proportion is more than (positive value) or less than (negative value) the employment proportion of a certain industry. The smaller the absolute value of the deviation, the more reasonable and balanced the relationship between the GDP structure and the employment structure.

In the final analysis, the heavy-industry-first industrialization strategy and the resource allocation model of the highly centralized planned system were ultimate the causes resulting in such unbalance and deviation. The unbalanced economic structure seriously hampered changes of employment structure (occupational structure), i.e., limiting the increase in employment of non-agricultural occupations and hence limiting the growth of non-agricultural employment opportunities. The deviation of employment structure was the result of such limitations with two aspects of social meaning. The first was that changes of peasant's registered residence status and occupational status were strictly restricted, supporting by the institutionalized residence registration system. The second was that the process of urbanization was hampered. According to statistics, the level of urbanization was 19.7 percent in 1960, whereas it dropped drastically to 16.8 percent in 1963. In 1964, it went up to 18.4 percent and fell to 18.0 percent in 1965.[1]

(3) Reform of Employment-Placement Systems and Institutionalized Space for Occupational Mobility

A. The Reform of Employment Systems

The urban employment mainly followed the planned job placement system after accomplishment of the socialist transformation. The main purpose of the planned job placement system was to realize full employment. The core mechanism of the system was high centralization in the administration of labor and employment and state-owned orientation in ownership. In this system, the authority of labor and

---

[1] Liu, Zhongli (ed.). 1999. *Laying Foundations: The Economy in New China over the Past Fifty Years*. Beijing: China Financial and Economic Publishing.

84

personnel administration of every work unit was taken back and concentrated into hands of its administering authority and the government labor department, thereby forming a simplified employment structure. By 1958, in the urban population, workers and staff members of state-owned work units accounted for 85.6 percent, and workers and staff members of collectively-owned work units accounted for 12.5 percent, and individual laborers 2 percent.[1]

The above institutional arrangements led to an urban employment system characterized by job-for-life (the "iron rice-bowl"), communal pot, and work unit. The top-level decision-makers found that such highly centralized employment system restrained initiatives of local governments and enterprises and, hence, decided to reform it. In order to solve the "once-in-and-never-out" malady of permanent workers and staff members, two types of employment systems were implemented at the same time from the end of 1957, i.e., the permanent position system and the contract position system. The existing workers and cadres were still eligible for the permanent position employment system, whereas newly recruited workers would follow the contract position track. Specifically, workers recruited from rural areas were required to go back to rural areas when their contracts expired. It was a so-called "semi-worker and semi-farmer" contract system. Enterprises located in the county and lower levels usually implemented the "semi-worker and semi-farmer" contract position system. Under such employment systems, there were two basic types of urban workers, i.e., permanent workers (or formal workers) and contract workers (or temporary workers). Generally, the socio-economic status of formal workers was higher than that of temporary workers. The classification of permanent workers and contract workers undoubtedly added one more ranks in the stratum of industrial workers in state-owned and collective enterprises. Thus, to many temporary workers, shifting to a formal status became a major direction to strive for in order to realize upward mobility.

B. The Reform of Distribution System

At the macro level, the urban distribution system reform aimed to transfer the budgetary and taxation authority to local governments, and thus strengthen enterprises' decision-making power in conducting independent economic activities. At the micro level, the reform focused on reforming the wage systems. In June 1956, the State Council released two relevant regulations, i.e., *Decisions on the Wage Reform* and *Provisions on Several Issues Concerning the Wage Reform*. The two regulations mainly consisted of: (1) nullifying the existing wage distribution system and dearness allowance system, and defining wage standards directly by currency; (2) unifying and revising the wage system for workers and proposing an eight-level wage system for industrial workers; (3) amending the wage level system for staff members in

---

[1] Chen, Yonghong. 2002. "Evolution and Evaluation of the Employment System in China (1949-2001) ". Pp. 46 in Hu, Angang, et al. (eds.), *Expansion of Employment and Challenge of Unemployment: Evaluation of Employment Policies in China (1949-2001)*. Beijing: China Labor and Social Security Publishing House.

enterprises, government agencies, and public institutions. Staff members in enterprises followed a thirteen-category wage system based on position levels, with several levels in each category. Personnel in government agencies and public institutions also followed a position-level wage system, in which the wage standards were divided into thirty levels and the wage standard of the highest level was 28 times higher than that of the lowest level. In addition, the whole country was divided into eleven categories of wage regions. The difference of wage standard between each category was 3 percent; and (4) adjusting the wage relations by greatly increasing wage levels in enterprises in heavy industry and some regions with priority of development, and properly increasing wage levels in all areas, especially coastal areas.

The eight-level wage system and the position-level wage system can be seen as the institutionalized mobility space inside the two status groups of workers and cadres. In addition, due to the influence of the egalitarian distribution doctrine, the length of service of urban workers and their attributions in the status system of labor and personnel dossier and the status system of work unit ownership were major factors that determined their wage levels. As far as the promotions of cadres, in addition to capability and performance, various social connections (social capital) and political needs at that time were also important influential factors. Moreover, besides individual performance and economic situations of their work units, differences in ownerships, industries, and regions also had important influences on practical income levels of cadres and workers. The same wage level was often significantly different in different industries and regions. The level of wage income (especially fringe benefits) in state-owned work units was much higher than that in collective work units. Usually, people with strong capability or social connections could find more opportunities to transfer from low-income industries or work units to high-income industries or work units. The cross-regional mobility usually occurred among senior cadres through governmental appointments or transfer. It was very difficult for ordinary workers and staff members to move between regions. The major way to overcome this situation was an exchange of position, that is, two persons working in different areas exchanged their work units for the sake of reuniting with spouses or taking care of aging parents.

Another particular distribution relationship gradually developed in rural areas as well. At the early stage of the People's Commune Movement, the rural distribution system showed the following characteristics: (1) denying the principle of distribution according to one's performance because it was a kind of "bourgeois rights"; (2) widely adopting the egalitarian supply system, i.e., people could eat free at the communal canteens without paying a cent; (3) equalizing wealth through transferring property initially owned by agricultural cooperatives to the people's communes; (4) transferring farmland, labor force, and other means of production between people's communes based on the principle of non-reimbursable allocation and transfer; and (5) the government requisitioning of a major portion of rural products by purchasing them and leaving only a small portion to peasants. Undoubtedly, such a distribution system led to serious damage in rural productions and social life, and thus only existed for a short time. At the end of 1958, the government started to rectify the development of people's communes in rural areas. Through a series of twisted and painful manoeuvres, it finally denied the improper pursuit of the "large in size and public in nature" policy and reaffirmed the collective-owned nature of it. The Central Committee of the Communist Party of China released *Directive about Changing the Basic Accounting Unit in Rural People's Communes* in February 1962. In September of the same year, the Eighth Plenum of the Tenth Central Committee of the Communist Party of China approved *Draft Amendments to the Regulation of Rural People's Communes*. These regulations formally established a system of "three-level ownership based on production teams" (i.e., the means of production were owned by communes, production brigades, and production teams; the production team was the basic accounting unit) by unifying the unit of production and the unit of distribution in order to correct the egalitarianism trends among production teams inside rural people's communes. Afterwards, at the macro level, the rural distribution relations still insisted on the principle of egalitarian distribution, however, there were two actual differences existing at the micro level in this system.[1] The first difference existed among production teams due to different amounts of possessed resources and different economic performances of agriculture production. Another difference came from different "basic workpoints" based on different individual labor capabilities and the different number of the labor force in families. In the same production brigade, families with many strong laborers would earn more workpoints and could obtain more returns in the yearend distribution, and thus had a higher standard of living. In contrast, families with more members but fewer in the labor force might be harassed with debts and live in poverty. The opportunity of migrating from poorer production brigades to richer brigades was a privilege belonging to women. They could achieve such mobility through marriage. In addition, a very small number of women could even move into cities through the same manner.

Formation of the Multidimensional Dual Status Hierarchy

After a series of political-economic movements and adjustments of national economy management systems, the centralized planned economy system and the rural-urban divided social system were eventually established at this stage. In these systems, urban and rural residents in China not only had class status, but also were attached with labels such as the registered residence status, the labor and personnel dossier status, and the work unit ownership status.

---

[1] As far as discussions about the coexistence of egalitarianism and differentiations, see Li, Shi, et al. 2000. *Empirical Analysis of Household Income Distribution in China*. Beijing: Social Sciences Documentation Publishing House: 3-4. Although this study only focused on the situation in the 1970s, we believed that its conclusions were applicable to the early 1960s as well.

(1) Formation of the Politics-Ideology-Dominated Dual Status System

The term *politics-ideology-dominated dual status system* refers to the political arrangements of class structure based on the political theory of "continuing revolution under the proletarian dictatorship". First, according to the opinions of the Party's decision-makers, especially Mao Zedong, some antagonistic classes would still exist in Chinese society even though the socialist transformation was accomplished. Second, it was their thinking and consciousness including attitudes toward the socialist system, not their economic status or positions in social production relations, which characterized these antagonistic classes. Third, thinking and consciousness of each class were determined by their initial class origins as well as changes in thinking and political viewpoints under influences of practical social life. Fourth, class struggles in the field of political ideology would continue and become the leading form of struggles when class struggles in the economic field ended. All political struggles should be explained from the perspective of class struggle. Fifthly, social members with exploiting class origins were supposed to be against the socialist system and its ideology. Furthermore, all thoughts and viewpoints different from the mainstream ideology were regarded as anti-socialist thought, and people who agreed with these opinions should be treated as anti-socialist spokespersons of the exploiting classes no matter what positions they had occupied in the new political system.

According to the above political theory, at this stage, each social member would obtain a certain fixed class (stratum) status (such as worker, impoverished and lower-middle peasant, landlord, rich peasant, or bourgeoisie) based on ascription factors, or be given some new status (such as counterrevolutionary or rightist) due to changes in political situations. These political labels were attached to people all the time and often their inheritance was intergenerational. Political boundaries between these classes or strata were definite, as were their ranks in the political appraisal system. The working class was the leading class, and members of the Communist Party of China and revolutionary cadres were vanguards of the working class. Impoverished and lower-middle peasants were allied forces of the working class, and the alliance of workers and peasants was the political basis of the socialist regime. Middle peasants and petty bourgeoisie were objects to be united, educated, and reconstructed. Other classes and strata were at the bottom of this political appraisal system and were regarded as threats to the socialist system; hence, they were objects to be governed and suppressed. Generally, people in these bottom classes had no chances of upward mobility. Even if some of them entered higher classes in some particular situations (such as to become cadres after graduation from colleges and universities), very likely they would be discriminated, beaten down, and purged in political movements.

With the expansion of the "left-leaning" ideology and class struggles, the political class structure in China was described in political ideology as a system consisting of two exploiting classes and two labor classes. The nature of political relations between these classes was accordingly defined as antagonistic and conflictive. Therefore, the political ideology dual status system was eventually established. After the accomplishment of socialist transformation, Mao Zedong and the Central Committee of the C.P.C. initially believed that, except for hostile forces that tried to undermine the socialist system, most conflicts in urban and rural China were disputes among the people, i.e., disputes on the basis of common interests.[1] However, in the movement of Rectification of Party and Working Style and the Anti-Rightist Movement, the leadership of the Party changed their attitudes. They believed that struggles between bourgeoisie and proletarians, and capitalism and socialism had become major conflicts both in political and in ideological field. The Second Meeting of the Eighth National Congress of the Communist Party of China held in May 1958 asserted that, "the conflicts between proletarians and bourgeoisie and the struggle between the socialist road and the capitalist road would be major contradictions inside Chinese society all the time before the establishment of the socialist society". It also claimed that there were "two exploiting classes and two labor classes" existing in Chinese society. The so-called two labor classes referred to the working class and impoverished and lower-middle peasants. The two exploiting classes consisted of two subgroups of people. The first subgroup was bourgeois rightists, including rightists, former landlords and compradors, and other reactionaries. Bourgeois rightists were regarded as agents of imperialists, residual feudal compradors, and the Nationalist Party in Taiwan. Another subgroup was national capitalists and intellectuals who were experiencing the socialist transformation. Most of them were regarded as in the interim of the socialist road and the capitalist road.

Therefore, all social members were classified politically into two big groups. We could call them respectively "the people" and "the non-people" group (including a part of political enemies and a part of persons belonging to neither the enemy nor the people). The two groups had two widely different types of political status, possessing different political stands and rights. Generally speaking, differences in political status and rights mean differences in economic status and interests. More than that, such political class status was not only inbred but also could be intergenerationally inherited.

The working class (including revolutionary cadres and revolutionary intellectuals), impoverished and lower-middle peasants, middle peasants, and rich middle peasants mainly possessed the political status of "the people". The status of worker and the status of impoverished and lower-middle peasant were inbred and could be intergenerational inherited. The political status of them and their families usually would not fall to a lower level, although they had also had few opportunities of upward mobility (to be revolutionary cadres and revolutionary intellectuals, for example). The status of the revolutionary cadres and revolutionary intellectuals generally could not be intergenerationally inherited. Such status neither was born with them nor could be transferred to their children. However, once people attained such status, usually they would not lose it unless they failed in political movements or

---

[1] Mao (1990: 205-206).

political struggles.

Landlords, rich peasants, and capitalists belonged to "the non-people" and their status was given in the land reform and the socialist transformation in private industry and commerce. Therefore, such status was obtained based on ascription factors. These people were political heretics and subjects of the proletarian dictatorship. Basically, "the non-people" were not entitled to various political rights prescribed by the Constitution and the law, including the rights to vote and to stand for election, and hence did not possess any upward mobility opportunities in the political status hierarchical system. Political status like "bourgeois intellectual", "anti-revolutionist", "bad element", and "rightist" were usually not given according to ascription factors but based on people's attitudes towards the socialist system and the Communist Party manifested in their words and behaviors. Some of these statuses (such as rightists) could be changed when the government and the Party decided to get rid of these political labels according to political needs. However, even then, they still could not completely enjoy their rights in political and social life. At this stage, families of "the non-people" were not given their parents' political labels; usually they were regarded as "could-be-transformed elements" instead of "the revolutionary people". Therefore, changes of their political status, especially the upward mobility opportunities, were determined by the "degree of transformation". In the early period of this stage, it was still possible for them to achieve upward mobility by entering schools. However, this road was blocked in the middle-late period of this stage. In addition, they also lost upward mobility opportunities such as joining the army and entering state-owned enterprises, etc.

(2) The Urban-Rural Registered Residence Dual Status System

At the beginning of the establishment of the People's Republic of China, the government did not strictly prevent the rural population from migrating into urban areas. In fact, the government even recruited laborers from rural areas in a planned way due to the rapid expansion of urban industry. However, in order to promote the capital-intensive industrialization, which stressed the priority of heavy industry at a relatively low social cost, it was necessary to limit the migration of rural population to urban areas.

Therefore, the government gradually institutionalized the urban-rural segregation system by following arrangements of institution and policy. The first one was the labor and employment system that prohibited urban entities from recruiting rural laborers independently. This system institutionalized the social division of labor in which rural and urban residents were destined to be peasants and townspeople respectively. The second one was the provisionment system based on the government's monopoly over purchasing and selling of agricultural products. The government was only responsible for provisioning urban residents and rural residents were left alone. The third institutional arrangement was the social welfare system that only covered urban residents. The forth was the registered residence system that strictly prevented peasants from entering into cities without permission. All these institutional arrangements eventually established the urban-rural registered residence dual status system and brought out two basic status groups: the peasantry and the townspeople. Moreover, the rural people's communes offered the strongest effective support to the operation of this dual status system.

Mobility between the two status groups was extremely difficult under the strict restriction of the registered residence dual status system. The peasantry had few opportunities to enter into cities from the 1960s, except for extremely limited opportunities such as entering schools, joining the army, and being recruited into urban entities, etc. In contrast, the townspeople were born with the right to live and work in urban areas. Only in some particular political and economic situations, some of them could be forced to move to rural areas, but they retained the eligibility to return to cities. The gaps between the two groups in economic interests and opportunities that were endowed by institutions were huge. What the townspeople enjoyed greatly surpassed that which the peasants possessed. In fact, the peasantry possessed hardly any of the rights and interests of the townspeople, but they possessed the obligations.

(3) The Cadre and Non-Cadre Dossier Dual Status System

The labor and personnel system formed at this stage divided the work force into two basic types of dossier status: cadre and non-cadre. Managerial personnel working in government and party agencies, enterprises, public institutions, and social organizations, and professional and technical personnel possessed the status of cadre, whereas the others did not. Once a person was given a certain type of status in the dossier system, usually such status would remain with him or her for a lifetime even after retirement. Dossiers about the two types of status were administrated by two different governmental agencies. The cadre dossiers were maintained by the Personnel Department (and the Organization Department of the Party), while non-cadre dossiers were preserved by the Labor Department. Agricultural laborers were excluded from this governmental dossier system. Though heads in rural production teams were nominal cadres possessing certain authority in agriculture productions, they did not possess the formal status of cadre and were still considered peasants. If they wanted to enter into the governmental cadre system, they had to climb up to higher levels through individual efforts; in addition, they had to change their registered residence status before they became formal governmental officials.

The above two types of status were entitled to different rights, powers, and interests and had significant distinctions in the distribution of economic interests, including wage level, fringe benefits, allowances, house allocation, health insurance, retirement pension, and social security, etc. Generally, cadres were supervisors, while non-cadres were supervisees. Therefore, cadres were at the middle-higher level of the society, and almost everyone hoped to obtain such status.

There were usually three channels for those pursuing the cadre status. The first channel was education. According to governmental regulations, all graduates who possessed diplomas higher than technical secondary school and accepted governmental planned placement would automatically obtain the status of cadre. Therefore, Chinese intellectuals were identical with cadres in dossier status. The second way pursue cadre status was promotion. The government would regularly assign certain authorized quota of cadres and promotion quotas to government and party agencies, enterprises, public institutions, and social organizations. People who could obtain such promoting opportunities usually were those who actively participated in politics, showed loyalty to the Party, and achieved outstanding work performance ratings. If there were no cadre quotas when an institution or organization wanted to promote someone without the cadre status, then they could adopt an expediential policy that allowed a worker to act as a temporary cadre. However, people who acquired authority through such makeshift arrangements were merely temporary cadres without the status of cadre. In addition, the process of transferring from temporary cadres to formal cadres generally was very slow. The third channel was the emplacement of demobilized army cadres. All officers with the company and higher rank would obtain the status of cadre automatically when they were demobilized and emplaced in local institutions and organizations.

In addition, the status of cadre was a lifelong privilege. The majority of cadres after the establishment of the People's Republic of China were those who were promoted in time of war. Generally, they would keep the status for life unless they were deprived of power politically. "Those who fought for it enjoy it" was their common belief.[1] Because of the limited authorized quota of cadres in a government body and the limited number of managerial positions, the stratum of cadre was a closed group lacking mobility. It was unable to accommodate too many people without cadre status. Therefore, among the above three channels of entering the cadre stratum, opportunities of promotion were limited, whereas education and emplacement of demobilized army cadres were the major ladders to climb up.

(4) The Work Unit Ownership Dual Status System

In the highly centralized planned systems, the government was in charge of socio-economic resource allocation, while various work units or entities were responsible for producing, operating, and utilizing these resources. The government allocated resources among these work units according to their levels in the ownership hierarchy and their importance in the national industrialization strategy. Units with lower-level ownership and in peripheral sectors of the national industrialization strategy generally obtained relatively fewer resources. By contrast, units with higher-level ownership and in core sectors of the national industrialization strategy generally obtained relatively more resources.

---

[1] Mao Zedong expressed his worry about this issue in the late 1950s or the early 1960s and proposed that the Party needed to pay attention to promoting young cadres and training next-generation successors. See Bo (1997a: 1201-1203).

Accordingly, people working in units with different ownerships or different importance reflected differences in resource and opportunity acquisition. The ownership hierarchy consisted of two levels: the state-owned entities and the urban collective-owned entities. Accordingly, urban workers and staff members were divided into two groups of status: urban collective unit workers and state-owned unit workers. The transfer from the former to the latter was a type of upward social mobility. However, opportunities for such upward mobility were extremely difficult to obtain. Agricultural laborers worked in rural collective units at that time, but they were not included in the work unit ownership dual status system. In relevant institutional arrangements, the notion of peasant was different from the notion of collective unit worker.

In conclusion, the work force in China at this stage was divided into different status groups based on the above-mentioned four dimensions of status. People with different types of status belonged to different social categories and hence belonged to different social strata because of socio-economic differences between these social categories. In other words, the overall characteristic of Chinese society at that time was stratification of status. From the perspective of social mobility, the political class status was relatively stable. Generally, once one's class status was determined, he or she could not change it. Only if one were attacked in political movements, would he or she move from the superior level (the labor class) down to the inferior level (the exploiting class). However, there was still some space left for social mobility in other dimensions of status hierarchy. In addition, some mobility opportunities existed inside each level of the registered residence system and the occupational status system as well. For example, both collective unit workers and state-owned unit workers had opportunities to move from the low-level workers up to the high-level workers (within the eight-level wage system of industrial workers). Inside the cadre stratum, it was possible for one to be promoted from the low level to the middle and higher level. However, in order to obtain such mobility opportunities, one had to be a member of the labor class, or at least came from the "could-be-transformed family" of the exploiting class.

Vicissitudes in Political Movements

There were three major political movements from 1957 to 1965: the Anti-Rightist Campaign in 1957, the Anti-Right Opportunism Campaign in 1959, and the Four Cleanups (or Socialist Education) Campaign in 1964. The Four Cleanups Campaign extended to the first half of 1966 and then it was replaced by the Cultural Revolution. Millions of people were under attack in the three political movements and were given various political labels.

The Anti-Rightist Campaign in 1957 was a violent and cruel movement of class struggle. Anyone could be found guilty for speaking freely. By the end of this movement, more than 550 thousand of people were given the political label of "rightist". According to archives that reported the Anti-Rightist Campaign in

Guangzhou city of Guangdong Province, rightists mainly came from cadres, members of other political parties, entrepreneurs, and intellectuals. People from the stratum of cadre were 223 persons, making up the majority of rightists. Rightists from other strata were 134 persons. This is different from the common point of view that intellectuals were hit the most heavily. Taking no account of cadres and students, people working in journalism accounted for 20 percent, personages of political parties 16.3 percent, former private entrepreneurs 14.5 percent, and intellectuals 6 percent. The average percentage of rightists in different groups of people (not including cadres and students) in Guangzhou city was 7.7 percent, exceeding the standard of 5 percent prescribed by the Central Committee of the C.P.C.. The proportions of rightists in cadres and students were not available.[1]

After the accomplishment of the socialist transformation campaign, directed under the hotheaded guideline that China should catch up with western developed countries as soon as possible and establish the socialist system and even the communist system in a short time, the Great Leap Forward and the People's Commune movement were launched. The political struggles between rash advance, equalitarianism, and "left-leaning" ideology and the opinions of anti-rash advance and efficiency first never ceased throughout that period. The direct conflict between Mao Zedong and Peng Dehuai breaking out at the Lushan Meeting of the Central Committee of the C.P.C. in 1959 abruptly turned the theme of the meeting from "correcting left-leaning" to "against right-leaning". In this tremendous movement, more than 3,000 thousand members of the C.P.C. were labeled as "right opportunist".[2] Many of them were rehabilitated in 1962. However, some others, especially senior cadres (such as Peng Dehuai, etc.), were not restored to their former positions until 1978 and most of them had passed away by that time.

Experiencing the three years of catastrophe immediately after the Great Leap Forward and the People's Commune Movement, the government had to adjust, rectify, and improve the national economy and the socio-economic life gradually went back to the right path. However, a new issue emerged, namely the capitalization of power (i.e., corruption and bribery). Decision-makers of the C.P.C. believed that the appearance of such phenomenon meant that the Communist Party was tending towards revisionism, the government was losing its revolutionary attribute, and the danger of a nationwide counter-revolutionary restoration was impending. Even Mao Zedong estimated that about one third of rural local governments were in the hands of landlords and rich peasants; in addition, they also had agents in some other governmental agencies. Based on such judgment, the Central Committee of the C.P.C. decided to launch a Socialist Education Campaign in rural areas in the form of class struggle from 1963. The main objective of this campaign was to screen out about 5 percent of rural cadres. Initially, the campaign focused on auditing accounts, financial records, inventories,

---

[1] Yiting. 2001. "Review of the Anti-Rightist Movement in Guangdong Province in 1957". *Gu Xiang Wang*. July 8th.
[2] Dong (1999: 441).

and workpoint records (usually called "small four-cleanups"). Gradually, it extended to cleaning up political attitudes, economic incomes, organizational members, and personal thoughts (usually called "big four-cleanups") and took "preventing and against revisionism" and "preventing peaceful evolution" as its theme. This movement lased four years. The total number of cadres who were purged in the movement was not available yet. Nevertheless, it seems that the proportion was far beyond the official 5 percent limitation in some places. For example, in a certain people's commune in Qinghai Province, the proportion of deposed cadres to the total number of cadres was about 47 percent. Of that, landlords and rich peasants accounted for 21 percent, and so-call "degenerates" 26 percent.[1]

As a whole, the three large-scale class struggle movements occurred at this stage brought tribulations to millions of social members in the form of downward mobility. Such mobility was not a normal social phenomenon. It was just a result of top decision-makers' political illusion about social conflicts in Chinese society and utopianism of radical equalitarianism. Such mobility severely destroyed Chinese society. It not only hurt those who were directly involved in these movements, but also affected those who were not involved. These movements disturbed and hampered the normal development of national economy and society, thereby deprived common people of opportunities of personal development. According to statistics, the total number of direct victims (including Party members, cadres, intellectuals, and common people who were animadverted, purged, and punished) in movements from 1957 to 1962 was about 8,070 thousand persons, among them 4,330 thousand were Party members and cadres, 3,740 thousand were common people. Many of them were mistreated to death or driven to suicide.[2] In addition, we are still not clear how many cadres were purged in the Four Cleanups Campaign from 1963 to 1966.

DISORDER OF SOCIAL MOBILITY (1966~1977)

Chinese society entered into a decade of turmoil with frenetic politics and fluctuant economy from 1966. The social life was highly politicalized. Ideological struggles and power struggles in the top leadership evolved into political struggles covering the entire society. Economic life was extremely unstable. Although the government-led industrialization still carried on, it did not bring any positive effects to the modernization of social stratum structure. The unilateral mobility in the closed rural-urban structure became even more severe. The peasantry had fewer opportunities to enter into cities; meanwhile urban residents migrated to rural areas on a larger scale. In short, social mobility at this stage was huge in a certain sense, but was more abnormal.

---

[1] Bo (1997a: 1160-1162).
[2] Bo (1997a: 1034-1044).

Social stratification and mobility in Chinese society at this stage had the following characteristics. First, the Cultural Revelation brought out upward and downward mobility at the same time. Some people were deprived of power in the movement, while some took power. Second, the stagnancy of economic development and high pressure of unemployment resulted in the second large-scale reverse migration of the urban-rural population. Third, the industrialization continued to advance in the form of "Simian Construction" (constructing large-size industrial enterprises in Western China) and rural industrialization. It did not promote urbanization but led to some changes in the employment structure, hence providing peasants with opportunities to change occupations without any shift of social status. Fourth, the distribution system and the labor and employment system changed once again. The distribution system became more equalitarian, but some major social inequalities still existed. The labor and employment system was simplified again and provided temporary low-paid workers with upward mobility opportunities. Fifth, the educational system constantly changed. In the early stage of the Cultural Revolution, the normal educational system was abolished and hence it blocked a normal channel for social mobility. In its late stage, the worker-peasant-soldier college system based on recommendations produced an abnormal mobility channel. Characteristics of social mobility at this stage were similar to those of the previous stage except for two distinct aspects. The first aspect was the greater distortion of normal social mobility mechanisms. For example, the higher one's level of knowledge and capability, the more possible he or she would be attacked in political struggles. The second aspect was the greater influence of power capital and social capital on school admissions, army enlistment, worker recruitment, and cadre promotion.

The Cultural Revolution: A Political Movement without Winners

The Cultural Revolution from 1966 to 1976, according to its initiator Mao Zedong's opinion, was a political and cultural revolution directed by the theory of "continuing revolution under the dictatorship of the proletariat", which was invented by Mao himself. It was also a life-and-death struggle between two classes in political, economic, and cultural fields. Therefore, it was a "great revolution" in which "one class overthrew another".

In this prolonged political movement, people suffered from strikes and persecutions were composed of the following groups. (1) "People in authority taking the capitalist road", or so-called "capitalist followers", which referred to people in authority in central and local governments. Most of them were beaten down or "stood aside", unless they surrendered to the revolt cliques. According to statistics from the Central Organization Department of the C.P.C., the total number of full-time cadres was about 17,000 thousand at that time. About 17.5 percent of them (nearly 3,000 thousand persons) were filed and investigated.[1] A large number of them were accused

---

[1] Wei, Hongyun. 2003. "The Cultural Revolution". *Guo Shi Ji Shi Ben Mo (1949-1999)*, Volume 1.

of betrayer, agent provocateur, spy, capitalist follower, or antirevolutionary.[1] Many of them died as results of mistreatment or were driven to commit suicide. The others were deprived of power and titles (according to statistics, there were more than 6,000 cadres in the central government who "stood aside"). (2) People in the cultural and educational fields whom were accused of implementing capitalist cultural or educational policy. Most of them were outstanding scholars, experts, litterateurs, artists, and publishers. Generally, they were labeled as "reactionary authorities". (3)All those people who had relations with the former two groups of people or who had voiced grievances from them. For example, in the case of Liu Shaoqi, "the greatest miscarriage of justice in the People's Republic of China", more than 28 thousand people were involved and persecuted. (4) Former landlords, rich peasants, counterrevolutionaries, bad elements, and rightists (so-called "five-category elements"). They were regarded as hidden bosses of capitalist followers and inevitably under attack again. Their families were widely discriminated against, mistreated, and persecuted in the movement as well. In urban areas, many of them were deprived of the status of urban residents and expelled from cities. For example, from the second half of August to the end of September in 1966, more than 850 thousand of five-category elements and their families were evicted out of Beijing.[2] (5) People who joined various mass organizations that supported local governments. They were labeled as "royalist", "counterrevolutionary", and "mobster", etc. Many of them were injured, disabled, sickened, and killed as results of persecutions. (6) Individuals who resisted and opposed the Cultural Revolution and Lin Biao's and Jiang Qing's cliques, such Yu Luoke, Zhang Zhixin, etc.

In short, all through the Cultural Revolution, millions of cadres, intellectuals, workers, and their families were persecuted. Undoubtedly, such persecutions drove victims' political status and social status to a lower level. Therefore, a large number of people underwent downward social mobility in this period. Meanwhile, there were many people obtaining opportunities for upward mobility through "revolting" and fixing people. The "most outstanding" among them even seized top positions in the Party and government. Therefore, the scale and span of social mobility occurring between and inside various status systems in the Cultural Revolution were unprecedented.

However, the Cultural Revolution was a movement without winners. The unique characteristic of class struggles in the Cultural Revolution was the constantly changing definition of "the enemy". This smashed the once absolute line between the "winner" and the "loser". From 1949 to the eve of the Cultural Revolution, the hereditary class origin defined the "winner" and the "loser". Nonetheless, the Cultural

---

Shenyang, Liaoning: Liaoning People's Publishing House: 695.

[1] According the report delivered by Jiang Hua at the Third Meeting of the Fifth National People's Congress, there were more than 175 thousand of misjudged counterrevolutionary cases dealt with by the legal system in the Cultural Revolution, involving more than 184 thousand of people. Of course, not all people who were labeled as "counterrevolutionary" were Party members or cadres.

[2] Wei (2003: 66).

Revolution, especially the "cleansing the class ranks" campaign in 1968, redefined the revolutionary class and the counterrevolutionary class and sequentially resulted in disorder of class structure in the whole society. Many winners suddenly became losers. After the process repeated several times, almost all "winners" in the Cultural Revolution had experienced losing something. All persecuted people fell down to the bottom. Various groups of insurrectionists replaced each other. For example, The Red Guards were dissolved and expelled to countryside because they went against the army abetted by Li Biao's group and Jiang Qing's group. Even Li Biao's group and Jiang Qing's group, who were expecting their ultimate victory, found themselves completely collapsed in one day.

The Rustication Movement: The Second Anti-Urbanization

The year of 1968 was a turning point of the Cultural Revolution. This tremendous movement led to unparalleled damages in the national economy. The shutdown of enterprises and universities made young people unable to go to school or find a job, and hence produced a large number of unemployed youth in cities. The accumulated number of graduates from senior and junior middle schools from 1966 to 1968 was more than 10,000 thousand. They made up the majority of the Red Guards at the beginning of the Cultural Revolution. Facing such a serious employment issue, Mao Zedong believed that the solution was to send middle school graduates down to the countryside, frontier, factories and mines, and grass-level units (in fact, only rural and border areas could accommodate such a huge population).

The Rustication Movement (or the "Up to the Mountains and Down to the Villages" movement) started from 1968. By 1978, the total number of rusticated educated youth was about 16,230 thousand. In addition, nearly 800 thousand were sent down to the countryside from 1979 to 1980. Therefore, the total number should be more than 17,000 thousand,[1] equal to 13 percent of the employment in urban areas at that time which involved more than one third of urban households.

In addition to urban youth who were sent to rural areas, a large number of urban workers and cadres volunteered or were mobilized to migrate to the countryside. For example, among 688 households in Huining County of Gansu Province, 191 households with 995 people were mobilized to settle in 13 people's communes in the second half of 1967.[2] The migration of these urban residents to the countryside with their entire families was called "sending down". According to some documents, about 13,000 thousand people were sent down to rural areas from 1966 to 1976.[3] Therefore, in this decade, the total number of urban population reversely flowing to rural areas was more than 30,000 thousand. Of course, some of them returned to cities again

---

[1] Wei (2003: 274).

[2] Wei (2003: 274).

[3] Chan, Kam Wing and Xueqiang Xu. 1985. "Urban Population Growth and Urbanization in China since 1949: Reconstructing a Baseline". *The China Quarterly*. No. 104.

through various channels in this period.

The migration of educated youth and urban residents to rural areas undoubtedly deviated from the worldwide trend of urbanization starting from the 1950s. As a result, the level of urbanization in China dropped from 18 percent in 1965 to 17.3 percent in 1975.

Distortion of the Educational Mobility Mechanism

Universally, education is an important channel of upward social mobility. In modern society, the universal education enables most people to obtain opportunities to move up to higher social status. However, the access of education, especially the access of high-quality education, is not necessarily determined by individual efforts. In fact, various basic institutional arrangements and individual family backgrounds have significant influences, sometimes even a crucial impact, on the attainment of educational opportunities. The majority of people in lower classes, especially the poor, usually obtained relatively fewer or even no educational opportunities at all. The Communist Party of China and its leaders like Mao Zedong had two basic educational ideals. The first ideal was that education should be open to all people, especially laborers. The second ideal was that education should serve the proletarian politics and cultivate new type of laborers with a high level of education, moral integrity, and lofty ideals. In order to achieve such goals, the government launched a series of educational institution reforms in the early 1960s. The major content of these reforms was to establish the normal full-time school education program and the non-normal work-study school education program so that workers and peasants could obtain more educational opportunities.

However, things were not always in keeping with the people's wish. The differences between the normal full-time school education program and the non-normal work-study school education program were hardly eliminated. First, various normal education opportunities were mainly shared between families of the old intelligentsia and the new political elite, even children from the families of the exploiting class.[1] In contrast, children of workers and peasants could only obtain a small portion of educational opportunities, especially in high-quality education. Most of them had to enter into the work-study schools. The educational quality of these schools was apparently worse than that of normal full-time schools. In a sense, such differences resulted in a gap in the values of human capital acquired by students in the two types of schools. Second, the institutional arrangements concerning the two types of schools further widened such inequality. For example, graduates of normal full-time technical secondary schools and higher education possessed the status of cadre and they were emplaced by the government based on employment plans, whereas graduates from non-normal technical schools and vocational schools did not possess the status of cadre. They were excluded from the governmental employment

---

[1] Fairbank (2000: 369-370).

plan and had to find jobs on their own.[1] Although such differentiated treatment was necessary because of the limitation of educational resources, it lowered the social prestige of non-normal education. Consequently, it lessened worker and peasant families' enthusiasm to let their children accept non-normal education, which made the majority of the youth feel disappointed and discontent. Some researcher even drew a conclusion from this phenomenon that it was "impossible to change the class structure in China through education".[2]

Mao Zedong realized this issue. He believed that the only solution was to carry out a thorough revolution in the Chinese educational system. On May 7, 1966, Mao Zedong released the famous *May 7th Directive*, in which he proposed that:

> Students should mainly focus on study. They should study everything in different ways, not only from teachers and schools, but also from workers, peasants, and soldiers. They should participate in political movements like animadverting capitalists. The length of schooling should be shortened. Education needs revolution. The current situation that our schools are governed by the bourgeois intelligentsia should never go on.

With the release of the *May 7th Directive*, an educational revolution started. On June 13, 1966, the Central Committee of the C.P.C. approved *Report for Instructions Concerning Reforming the Enrollment System in Higher Education* submitted by the Ministry of Education. This report believed that "the existing college entrance examination system is a bourgeois way of enrollment. It ignores the proletarian politics, merely stressing professional knowledge and grades". In order to solve this "issue", the report proposed to replace the existing enrollment system with a new system combining recommendation and selection. On the same day, the Central Committee of the C.P.C. released *Circular concerning Reforming the Enrollment and Examination Procedure in Higher Education*. The circular proposed that existing enrollment system in higher education "is basically a bourgeois framework of an examination system. It goes against the education guideline proposed by the Central Committee and Chairman Mao, and is unable to admit more revolutionary youth from the ranks of workers, peasants, and soldiers to colleges and universities. This examination system must be changed thoroughly". It meanwhile decided to "postpone the admission of new students of 1966 to colleges and universities for half a year". In fact, this postponement did not end until 1970. Colleges and universities did not admit new students for four years from 1966 to 1970 and, hence, blocked the channel through which four classes of middle school graduates could have entered into higher schools. On June 27, 1966, the Ministry of Education decided to suspend the enrollment of postgraduates in 1966 and in 1967. Thereafter, Chinese universities had stopped admitting postgraduates for twelve years.

On June 27, 1970, the Central Committee of the C.P.C. approved *Report*

---

[1] Xu (2000: 131).

[2] Fairbank (2000: 370).

submitted by Peking University and Tsinghua University Requesting Instructions on Pilot Enrollment Programs. The report suggested that, after three years of the Cultural Revolution, Peking University and Tsinghua University was ready to recruit new students and planned to start admission from the second half of 1970. It proposed a new enrollment system combining masses' recommendations, principal approval, and university selection. The eligible applicants were workers, impoverished and lower-middle peasants, soldiers, and young cadres at the age of twenty with high political loyalty, good healthy condition, more than three years' practical experience, and with junior middle school and higher diplomas. Special attention should be paid to the rusticated youth. In addition, veteran workers and impoverished and lower-middle peasants did not necessarily have to meet the requirements of age and schooling years. On October 15, 1966, the State Council gave notice to all colleges and universities in China that the enrollment in 1970 should adhere to the report submitted by Peking University and Tsinghua University. The total number of admitted worker-peasant-soldier students in 1970 was 42 thousand. This number increased year after year. The total number of enrolled students in all technical secondary schools, colleges, universities in China in 1976 reached more than 560 thousand.

Obviously, higher education is a major mechanism to achieve upward social mobility directly in modern society. However, this mechanism was largely cut off in the Cultural Revolution. According to some researchers' estimation, the secondary and higher education in China would have at least 1,000 thousand of university graduates and 2,000 thousand of technical secondary school graduates from 1966 to 1976.[1] Another estimation believed that only 4 percent of middle school graduates were recommended to enter colleges and universities by the end of the 1970s.[2]

Moreover, the new enrollment system implemented from 1970 largely distorted the mobility mechanism. In this enrollment system, an individual's class origin was taken as a prerequisite, and performance in political participation and practical experiences were adopted as criteria. Students were selected by a procedure that consisted of masses' recommendations, principal approval, and university background checks. An individual's educational background was not considered. Accordingly, this enrollment system brought about two consequences. The first was that young people with "bad" class origins were excluded from entering the gates of universities and thus lost opportunities of upward mobility obtained with higher education. The second was that this enrollment system treated the examination on knowledge and skills as an insignificant factor and hence lacked objective and fair evaluation criteria.

Another passive consequence caused by such unfair and arbitrary enrollment system was that it led to the prevalence of "getting in through the back door", In other

---

[1] Dong (1999: 584).

[2] MacFarquhar, Roderick and John King Fairbank (eds.). 1990. *The Cambridge History of China, The People's Republic: 1949-1982*. Shanghai: Shanghai People's Publishing House: 775.

words, many people managed to enter colleges through influences of power or various social networks. A scholar pointed out that:

> The composition of students reflected a more obvious tendency of education for elite compared with the situation before 1966. It was a universal fact at that time that most college students came from cadres' families, because these cadres could take advantage of their authority to manipulate the political admission criteria, which replaced the criteria of academic achievements.[1]

In such a situation, it was doubtable that whether education could affect people's social mobility as a type of ascription factor.

Rural Industrialization and Changes of Employment Structure

One prevailing viewpoint is that Chinese national economy was seriously damaged and on the verge of collapse in the decade of the Cultural Revolution. However, according to statistics, the industrialization in China still went on in this decade (see Table 2-3). The structure of employment started to change as well. In the perspective of industrial structure, both the proportions of output value and employment of the primary and secondary industry declined to some extent; furthermore, the primary industry dropped more significantly. In contrast, the proportion of output value and employment of the tertiary industry went up by 13 percent and 9 percent respectively. The proportion of employment of agriculture fell to 70 percent by the year of 1978. It indicated that a preliminary change was occurring in the employment structure.

      Table 2-3 shows that, although deviation of employment structure of the secondary industry was decreasing, the absolute value of the deviation was still as high as 2.39 in 1975. The deviation of employment structure of the tertiary industry shrank as well; its absolute value was far smaller than that of the secondary industry. However, the proportion of the output value of the tertiary industry dropped, as well as its proportion of employment. Both the proportion of the output value and the proportion of employment of the primary industry declined. In particular, its proportion of employment had fallen below 80 percent. Meanwhile, the deviation of employment structure of the primary industry increased. The above changes mean that, although the employment structure in China had started to change, the decrease rate of the proportion of employment of the primary industry was too slow. The industrialization strategy stressing the development of heavy industry still seriously excluded non-agricultural employment and held back the transformation of occupational structure.

---

[1] Xu (2000: 137).

Table 2-3　Deviations of Employment Structure, 1965~1975

Units: %, Times

Year	GDP Structure			Employment Distribution			Employment Structure Deviation		
	The primary industry	The secondary industry	The tertiary industry	The primary industry	The secondary industry	The tertiary industry	The primary industry	The secondary industry	The tertiary industry
1965	37.9	35.1	27.0	81.6	8.4	10.0	-0.54	3.18	1.70
1970	35.2	40.5	24.3	80.8	10.2	9.0	-0.56	2.97	1.70
1975	32.4	45.7	21.9	77.2	13.5	9.3	-0.58	2.39	1.35
1978	28.1	48.2	23.7	70.5	17.3	12.2	-0.60	1.79	0.94

Source: Past years' *China Statistical Yearbook*. Beijing: China National Statistic Press.

Meanwhile, we also found that there was a significant gap emerging between the change of employment structure and the progress of urbanization. The non-agricultural employment rate was 18.4 percent and the level of urbanization was 18.0 percent in 1965. The relationship between them was roughly balanced at that time. In contrast, the non-agricultural employment rate and urbanization level was 22.8 percent and 17.3 percent respectively in 1975. The cause of such a contrast was the revival of rural industrialization based on the development of rural collective enterprises. The Great Leap Forward period was the first climax of the development of rural collective enterprises. However, in the adjustment period after the three years of catastrophe, a large number of rural collective enterprises were shutdown. In the *May 7th Directive* published in 1966, Mao Zedong proposed that rural people's communes should open some small factories in appropriate conditions and hence promoted the development of rural collective enterprises again. At the North China Agriculture Meeting held in 1970, the State Council proposed a plan to accomplish the mechanization of farming in ten years. From then on, rural industrialization in China entered the second period of climax. By the year of 1978, there were 22,182 thousand of people working in rural collective enterprises (among them about 17,344 thousand were working in industrial enterprises), accounting for 7.2 percent of the rural work force. These people changed their occupational status without shifting the status of registered residence from rural to urban. Therefore, it was a kind of rural industrialization without urbanization. Although the proportion of employment of the primary industry decreased significantly in this period, the level of urbanization did not improve accordingly. Of course, the transfer of 20,000 thousand rural work force to rural collective enterprises achieved social mobility in occupations after all, and laid a preparatory foundation for future development of rural enterprises.[1]

For the most part, China in the Cultural Revolution was still a society with pan-class overviews in political life and the multidimensional dual status hierarchy in

---

[1] Besides non-agricultural employment in rural collective enterprises, there were some other non-agricultural occupations in the countryside, such as teachers in public-owned rural schools. According to statistics, there were 31,500 thousand of non-agricultural employment in rural areas in 1978. Taking away workers and staff members in rural collective enterprises, the number was about 9,312 thousand.

economic life. The differences in social status consisting of political classes and economic levels were still remarkable. Equalitarianism inside a class or rank and the disparity between each rank coexisted in this society. In addition, from the perspective of occupation, Chinese society formed the following stratum structure by the end of this stage: state and social administrators accounted for 0.98 percent, managerial personnel accounted for 0.23 percent, professional and technical personnel 3.48 percent, clerical personnel 1.29 percent, individual-operated business proprietors 0.03 percent, commercial and service personnel (including peasant-workers) 2.15 percent, industrial worker (including peasant-workers) 19.83 percent, agricultural laborer 67.41 percent, the urban-rural jobless, unemployed, and partially unemployed 4.6 percent.[1] Therefore, from the perspective of occupational structure, the class structure of Chinese society at this stage still kept the shape of a candlestick. Furthermore, its bottom was even larger that that of the previous stage.

TRANSITION OF PATTERNS OF SOCIAL STRATIFICATION AND MOBILITY (1978~1991)

Chinese society entered the second period of institutional innovations in 1978. In the political arena, class struggle was given up and past wrong policies were reclaimed. In the economic arena, a series of important institutional reforms were carried out, including introducing the market mechanism step by step, and adjusting the strategy of national industrialization. These institutional innovations brought out significant influences on social stratification and social mobility. Significant stratification occurred in original social classes (strata) and some new strata took shape gradually. The criterion that defines the relationship between each stratum is the practical difference of socio-economic interests instead of political ideology. Social mobility between different types of social status increasingly depends on possessed resources and individual efforts in changes of arrangements of institution and policy. Obvious, a transition of patterns had occurred in social stratification and mobility in China.

There are several trends emerging in the process of pattern transition. First, the reform casts its first stone to the political class status system through a series of political measures such as redressing mishandled cases and rehabilitating political prisoners (so-called "hat tipping"). The pan-political era that judged people's class positions based on political criteria eventually ended. A large number of social members returned to the normal track of political, economic, and social life. Second, the reform of the rural economic system, implementation of the household contract and responsibility system, and adjustment of prices of agricultural produces, formed a type of social stratification and mobility mechanism based on the rule of achievement

---

[1] Lu (2002: 44).

in rural areas. Some new social strata were appearing. Third, the industrialization strategy stressing the priority of heavy industry was gradually replaced by the strategy stressing comparative advantages. Labor-intensive industries developed rapidly and rural enterprises suddenly rose as a new force. The progress of urbanization accelerated, employment expanded greatly, and occupational structure became more diverse. Fourth, the educational system changed fundamentally. Resumption of the college entrance examination system and development of various educational programs provided numerous educational opportunities to the entire society. In short, institutional reforms and changes of policies still had an enormous influence on social stratification and mobility but in a different way from the previous stage. At this stage, influences of institutional arrangements promoted social stratification and mobility rather than holding them back.

The End of the Political Class Dual Status System

The Cultural Revolution nearly ended in October 1976. After then, through two years of political struggles, the influence of Mao's thoughts in his late years, including the judgment about social class relations and class struggle situations in China and the theory of "continuing revolution under the proletarian dictatorship", disappeared. These changes in ideology were accordingly transformed into a series of policies and measures. The first measure was to redress cases in which people were unjustly, falsely or wrongly charged or sentenced in and before the Cultural Revolution, i.e., the rehabilitation campaign. The second measure was to remove political labels that had been attached to various politically discriminated social classes and strata, i.e., the "hat-tipping" campaign. The Central Committee of the C.P.C. started the rehabilitation campaign and the "hat-tipping" campaign in China from 1978.

The rehabilitation campaign ended around 1981. Mishandled cases in all previous political movements were rechecked and redressed. About 3,000 thousand cadres washed sins away and regained the status of cadre. Many were restored to their original posts. In addition, millions and millions of people who were persecuted in the Cultural Revolution were rehabilitated.

The "hat-tipping" campaign was carried out at the same time. The first thing was to "tip hats" for rightists who had been given this label since 1957. In 1978, The Central Committee of the C.P.C. decided to remove the label of rightist from all these people and offer them fair treatment and consideration in promoting ranks, increasing wages, and granting professional titles, etc. Meantime, according to the regulations of the Central Committee of the C.P.C., all people who were wrongly given the label of rightist were restored to their former posts with former wage levels. Until the first half of 1981, about 540 thousand of rightists were rehabilitated, accounting for 98 percent of the total number of rightists.[1] The second measure was to "tip hats" for former

---

[1] Wei, Hongyun. 2003. "The Period of the Reform and Opening-up". *Guo Shi Ji Shi Ben Mo (1949-1999)*, Volume 2. Shenyang, Liaoning: Liaoning People's Publishing House: 120.

landlords and rich peasants. In January 1979, in *Decision on Issues Concerning "Hat-tipping" of Landlords and Rich Peasants and the Status of Their Families*, the Central Committee of the C.P.C. proposed that, to people who were labeled as landlords, rich peasants, counterrevolutionaries, and bad elements, if they had abided by the law and without crime records over the past decades, all these political labels attached to them would be removed and they would be treated as members of rural people's communes. Moreover, their families would enjoy equal treatment in education, employment, and enlistment, etc. They would be entitled to the right to vote and to stand for election. According to statistics, there were more than 20,000 thousand former "landlords, rich peasants, counterrevolutionaries, and bad elements" getting rid of these political labels and their families thus walked out of their parents' shadows.[1] The third measure was to "tip hats" for former private entrepreneurs and capitalists and their agents. By November 1981, 700 thousand of former merchants, peddlers, individual handicraftsmen regained the status of socialist laborers, and about 160 thousand former private entrepreneurs striped away of political labels.[2]

The government's intellectual policy also changed greatly in this period. In 1977, Deng Xiaoping proposed to withdraw the "two estimations" that were put forward in the Cultural Revolution (two statements proposed in the National Education Conference in 1971; that is, "in the seventeen years before the Cultural Revolution, the bourgeois seized the power in education", and "the majority of intellectuals hold a bourgeois world view and hence are bourgeois intelligentsia"). In his speech at the National Science Conference in 1978, Deng Xiaoping believed that the intelligentsia was already a part of the working class. In 1979, the Central Committee of the C.P.C. decided to recall the *Summary of the National Education Conference in 1971* and the *Briefing Concerning Ma Zhenfu Event* (a typically wrongly-charged case occurred in a middle school of the Ma Zhenfu People's Commune in Henan Province in 1973), and hence politically liberated millions of intellectuals from the imputation of "bourgeois intelligentsia". Meanwhile, the socio-economic status of intellectuals improved gradually. Besides increasing the level of salary and fringe benefits, the government set up the normal skill evaluation system and hence established a normal mobility structure and opportunity space inside this stratum. In this period, among 23,000 thousand professionals, about 950 thousand obtained various senior technical titles (or positions), and 5,420 thousand were given middle-level technical titles (or positions).[3]

---

[1] Dong (1999a: 37).

[2] Ma, Licheng and Zhijun Ling. 1998. *Cross Swords: Memoir of the Three Thought Liberation in Contemporary China*. Beijing: China Today Publishing House. In addition, from 1983 to 1987, the C.P.C. carried out another Rectifying the Party Campaign. About 500 thousand Party members were given various political punishments and lost their initial higher-level socio-political status. See also Wei (2003a: 319).

[3] Jia, Chunzeng (ed.). 1996. *The Intelligentsia and Chinese Social Reforms*. Beijing: Huawen Press: 267. After the reform and opening-up, the meaning of the term "intellectual" changed little by little. Its political and ideological meanings were fading out. Its dependence to other social classes also has become weak. Gradually, intellectuals become a new occupational group which has independent

In this way, the once paramount ideology-oriented class status system was eliminated. Accordingly, people's political class status or origin became meaningless. More than 24,000 thousand people who once were at the bottom of the political hierarchy were then equal to other social members in political status. These changes mean that, from then on, social stratification in China would no longer be the results of institutional arrangements but a spontaneously historical progress of socio-economic development.

Institutional Reforms and New Social Stratification-Mobility Mechanisms

The Third Plenum of the Eleventh Central Committee of the C.P.C. in 1978 has initiated the institutional reforms in China. This plenum oriented the central task of the C.P.C. towards in the economic field and proposed a draft to rehabilitate and develop the socialist commodity economy. Meanwhile, the government launched a preliminary reform in the political administrative system. From the perspective of social mobility, institutional reforms led to the emergence of several new social stratification-mobility mechanisms.

(1) The Reform of Rural Economic System and the Formation of Independent Achievement-Oriented Mobility Mechanism in Rural Society

The first breakthrough of economic system reforms was the implementation of the household contract and responsibility system in rural areas. This system distributed farmland to every peasant household. Accordingly, households rather than the production teams organized the agricultural activities. Meanwhile, distribution of produce followed the principle that "one portion goes to the state (governmental requisition by purchase), one portion to the collective (miscellaneous fees levied by villages and townships), and the rest to self". The household contract and responsibility system transferred hundreds of millions of peasants from collective laborers to independent household proprietors. They controlled the most important means of production in agriculture. In other words, they possessed rights to benefit from and to use farmland and the right of collective ownership of farmland entitled by the Constitution. Thus, they were similar to past peasant proprietors to some extent. In addition, other rural economic system reforms supporting the household contract and responsibility system included: reducing the scope of monopoly purchasing of farm produce by the state according to fixed prices and the quota of requisition by purchase, giving a freer rein to prices of farm produce and letting the market mechanisms work, establishing farm produce markets in rural and urban areas, adjusting rural economic

interests and attains economic interests and social status through their own professional knowledge and skills. Based on these changes, we called this group "the stratum of professional and technical personnel" in this study instead of "the stratum of intellectual".

structure and promoting diversified sectors of economy, encouraging people to get rich as soon as possible, and then help others to achieve common prosperity.

The rural economic system reforms led to several interrelated consequences and hence formed new mechanisms of social stratification and mobility in rural society. Firstly, farm households and individuals obtained rights to use and manage agricultural production resources like farmland. Accordingly, they obtained the right to dispose of surplus produce after paying tax and fees. Therefore, what determined peasants' living conditions was neither collective production capability and situations, nor farmers' competence in earning workpoints in production teams, but their individual production capability and situations. Whatever political class status once labeled them, they were now roughly equal before the scratch line and the opportunity of development. Secondly, because performance of household production was directly related to the level of income, farmers' enthusiasm for production was initiated and thereby brought about high-speed development of the rural economy and a rapid increase of peasants' incomes. More and more peasants possessed surplus produce and accumulated a certain amount of wealth. Gradually, differentiations in income and wealth accumulations emerged in the rural society. A number of peasants became rich families producing special products (so-called "household with ten thousand Yuan annual income"). Such stratification brought new mobility opportunities in the rural society. Thirdly, economic sectors that peasants were allowed to, or capable to, enter kept extending and hence provided farmers with new choices and developmental opportunities. In the progress of the reform and opening-up, the scope of farmers' sideline businesses expanded from animal husbandry, planting, and simple handicraft to manufacturing, transportation, and commerce. They could shift occupations independently among traditional channels such as working in rural and urban enterprises, entering schools, and joining the army. According to statistics, the number of the rural work force engaging in non-agricultural industries increased from 31,500 thousand in 1979 to 81,300 thousand in 1987, up by 158.1 percent and an average rise of 11.5 percent per year.[1]

In conclusion, the mechanism of rural stratification and mobility was almost completely independent and free from governmental planned arrangements in this period. Meanwhile, it also displayed significant characteristics of ascription. Farmer's production capability and performance became primary influential factors and the planned redistribution mechanism was superseded by the market mechanism in rural areas.

(2) The Reform of State-Owned Enterprise Management System and Changes of Authority Allocation in Enterprises

The adventure of urban system reforms advanced as well in this period. The most important two fields were to strengthen enterprises' independent decision-making

---

[1] National Bureau of Statistics of China (1988: 172).

power in economic activities and to restructure the enterprise distribution system. Reform in the first field formally started from 1979. A series of regulations, including the *Provisions on Independent Decision-making Power Concerning Operation and Management in State-owned Enterprises* released by the State Council, entitled enterprises several types of authority that were crucial to enterprise management, including the right to allocate a part of resources and to dispose profits and capital assets, the right to recruit, reward, and punish staff members and workers within government's planned quotas, and the right to establish functional divisions and to appoint and dismiss middle-lower level cadres within the government's authorized quota of staff.[1] After being given to enterprises, these authorities were actually in the hands of managerial personnel (especially factory managers).

The reform to strengthen enterprises' independent decision-making power affected social stratification and mobility in three aspects. First, state-owned enterprises began to shape their own interests that were independent of the government and were increasingly market-oriented. Accordingly, managerial personnel in state-owned enterprises were shifting from governmental cadres in the planned economy system to professional managers in a free-market economy. Second, changes of urban-rural employment channels led to changes in traditional relationships, especially authority-status relationship, between managerial personnel and ordinary staff members and workers. The organizational (authority) resources that were under government's control in the past were transferred to the hands of enterprises' management. Employment, rewards, and punishments were determined by managerial personnel. Therefore, ordinary staff members and workers had to follow the instructions of managers rather than the government. Such relocation of organizational resources consequently resulted in significant differences between managerial personnel and supervisees. Third, the mobility mechanism within enterprises changed as well. Enterprises could now independently establish functional divisions based on practical needs and hence increased positions of middle-level management and upward mobility within enterprises. In addition, principals of enterprises could promote and depose middle-level cadres with the power of patronage based on their own criteria. Because enterprises had been turning into independent economic interests entities, the previous criteria of political loyalty and political participation performance were replaced by economic performance and loyalty to enterprises' managers. According to Max Weber's proposition of rationalization, capable managerial personnel, and professional and technical personnel will obtain more upward mobility opportunities than ordinary staff members and workers because they possess competence that may bring more contributions to enterprises.

Thereafter state-owned enterprises reforms evolved along the above-mentioned paths, as well as changes of mechanism of social stratification and mobility within enterprises. These reforms strengthened managerial personnel's

---

[1] Dong (1999a: 66-67).

authority and at the same time inevitably raised them to a status higher than ordinary staff members and workers. Although according to the law, state-owned enterprises should practice democratic management through congresses of workers and staff members, it gradually became a mere formality.[1] In short, managerial personnel and ordinary staff members and workers in state-owned enterprises had been dividing into two strata with a completely different status of authority.

(3)The Reform of Educational System and Renovation of College Enrollment Mechanism

After the Cultural Revolution, Chinese education began to return on the right path and take effect as the major social mobility mechanism in modern society. The landmark event was the reactivation of the college entrance examination in 1977. On October 12, 1977, the State Council approved the report submitted by the Ministry of Education concerning college enrollment in 1977. According to this report, all eligible applicants, including workers, peasants, sent-down educated youth, veterans, cadres, and middle school graduates, no matter what family backgrounds and class origins they had, could attend the entrance examination. However, all applicants should have a middle school diploma or an equal level of education. The principle of enrollment was to admit the best candidates who were well developed morally, intellectually, and physically. Taking the influences of the Cultural Revolution into account, the report proposed that only 20 percent to 30 percent of the students would be recruited from that year's middle school graduates, whereas the remaining 70 percent to 80 percent would be selected from past years' middle school graduates or young people with an equal level of education. Colleges and universities in China did not completely admit graduating middle school students until 1980.

Compared with the system in the Cultural Revolution, the college enrollment system in this period was characterized itself by its single admission criterion: the grade of examination. Family background was not taken into consideration and a work unit's recommendation was not necessary. In addition, a family's economic condition, which is a very important influential factor in today's education, was not a factor that could affect an applicant's admission evaluation, because every college student was offered a sufficient stipend. In this sense, the higher education in this period became a most fair factor that influenced social mobility.

(4) The Reform of the Personnel System and Innovations of Cadre Mobility Mechanism

Cadres are always a group with higher political, economic, and social status in China. Before the reform and opening-up, if one wanted to become a cadre, he or she had to join the "revolution" before the establishment of the People's Republic of China, or

---

[1] You, Zhenglin. 2000. *Inner Stratification and Mobility: A Twenty Years' Case Study of a State-owned Enterprise*. Beijing: Social Sciences Documentation Publishing House.

had to show loyalty, enthusiasm, and hard work in production activities and political movements after the establishment of New China. The traditional cadre system produced several consequences. The first consequence was a large number of cadres being relatively old in ages, lacking modern knowledge and an innovation spirit. The second one was that the managerial authority was excessively centralized so that personnel management and operation management were out of joint. The third consequence was that out-of-date and simple management approaches held back the emergence of talented people. Finally, the unsound human resource management system led to corruption in recruitment and promotions. Therefore, the reform of the personnel system was imperative under such conditions.

Deng Xiaoping proposed some basic principles for the personnel system reform, such as "break a new path" and "training, discovering, promoting, and appointing young talents who adhere to the Four Cardinal Principles (adherence to the socialist road, the people's democratic dictatorship, the leadership of the Communist Party of China, and Marxism-Leninism and Mao Zedong Thought) and master professional knowledge".[1] The government started the personnel system reform from 1982 and achieved great success. First, a new guideline of the cadre personnel system was established, that is, making the ranks of cadres more revolutionary, younger in average age, higher in educational level and professional competence. Second, the retirement system for old cadres was set up and roughly formalized the procedure of handing over and taking over authority between old cadres and their successors. Third, the cadre personnel system was restructured. Cadres were administered according to their occupational categories and the authority of patronage was transferred to lower levels. Fourthly, various new cadre appointment procedures were adopted. In addition to the form of appointment, new approaches, such as election, examination, and engagement, were also introduced into the procedure of filling an office. Fifth, the principle that the cadre should be selected through open and fair competition was extensively accepted. The personnel system was rebuild based on laws and scientific principles.[2]

Although the cadre and non-cadre dual personnel dossier system still existed, in which the cadre was a status instead of an occupation, the above-mentioned reforms formed some new mobility mechanisms within this system after all. Firstly, the principle of appointing cadres younger in average age and the open examination system provided many people without the status of cadre with opportunities to cross the hierarchical boundary of cadre and non-cadre. Secondly, the lifelong cadre system was abolished by introducing a retirement program and hence provided more promotion opportunities for younger low-rank cadres. Thirdly, requirements about educational background and professional knowledge in cadre selection provided

---

[1] Deng, Xiaoping. 1993. *Collected Works of Deng Xiaoping*, Volume 2. Beijing: People's Publishing House: 322.
[2] Lu, Xueyi, et al. 2001. *Deng Xiaoping Theory and Transition of Social Stratum Structure in Contemporary China*. Beijing: Economic Management Press.

professional and technical personnel, who had the status of cadre but did not possess corresponding power, with opportunities to enter the core sector of the authority hierarchy. Therefore, a large number of professional and technical personnel coming from colleges and research institutes entered into authority sections and then they were appointed as leadership in this period. Since then, educational background has been an important prerequisite in cadre appointment and promotion. Fourthly, the "more revolutionary" requirement actually was a kind of capability-performance criteria. In an era focusing on the central task of economic development, cadres' performance means development of economy and progress of society instead of class struggles.

(5)The Reform of Ownership Structure and the Emergence of New Social Strata

The Socialist Transformation Movement in the middle-late 1950s transferred the ownership structure of Chinese economy into a single public ownership situation, although it did not thoroughly eliminate the non-public-owned economy. There were still 150 thousand of people working in the individual economy until 1978. However, both in ideology and in practice, the non-public-owned economy was treated as the opposite of the socialist public-owned economy. Promoting development of the non-public-owned economy meant developing capitalist economy and opposing the socialist system. After the Third Plenum of the 11th Central Committee, the Communist Party of China realized that developing the non-public-owned economy was necessary and helpful to Chinese economy when it was still at the primary stage of socialism. Therefore, the government changed its ideology-oriented preference and institutional arrangements concerning ownership and permitted the development of non-public-owned sector of economy.

The reform in institutional arrangements concerning ownership had far-reaching influences on Chinese society because it brought out two new social strata: individual-operated business proprietors and private entrepreneurs. There were 1,830 thousand of individual-operated businesses in 1978 (most of them were in rural areas) with an employment of 2,270 thousand. By the year of 1991, the number of individual-operated businesses had increased to 14,170 thousand and the employment was 22,580 thousand. The development of private enterprises was more difficult and complicated. However, development of individual-operated businesses gradually changed the arrangements of institutions and policies and hence provided opportunities for private enterprises. From 1983, private enterprises, which were beyond the legal limitation of maximal eight employees, grew up rapidly in various hidden forms. According to some studies, many township-village enterprises that suddenly rose as a new force since 1984 were actually private-owned businesses. Even rural collective enterprises had some characteristics of mixed economy and were different from traditional collective enterprises, because individuals held a relatively large proportion of shares in these enterprises.[1] According to a survey conducted by the Rural Policy Research Office of the Secretariat of the Central Committee of the C.P.C. covering 37,422 households in 272 villages in 28 provinces, among people who joined new economic combos in 1984, farmers accounted for 3.2 percent, specialized households 3.5 percent, and individual-operated business proprietors 4.4 percent. About 51 percent of these combos hired employees, with an average of 7.9 employees.[2] Judging by economic characteristics, these new economic combos in essence were private enterprises. Another survey showed that there were 225 thousand private enterprises in China by the end of 1987, employing about 3,607 thousand people, although most of them were hidden in the form of individual-operated businesses or collective enterprises. In 1988, the *Amendment to the Constitution* admitted the legal status of the private sector. According to official statistics, there were 91 thousand of formally registered private enterprises in China in 1989. This number increased to 101 thousand in 1991.[3] The number of private entrepreneurs possessing legal status was about 200 thousand.

From the perspective of social mobility, the above-mentioned reforms in arrangements of institutions and policies concerning ownership mean three things. First, it means that the so-called extra-system stratification and mobility path came into being, which is completely market-oriented. People could attain higher economic-social status through this channel rather than the traditional redistribution system. Of course, the extra-system development was still closely related to various intra-system resources.[4] Second, private possession of economic resources obtained legitimacy and became the third type of resources that could be utilized to achieve social mobility in addition to organizational resources and cultural resources. Third, such reforms created the third type of social elite, i.e., economic elite, in contras to political and cultural elite. The rise of economic elite will change the power distribution structure in Chinese society and accordingly affect the entire structure of social relationships, that is, forming an employer-employee (or labor and capital) relationship besides traditional cadre-masses (or supervisor-supervisee) relationship.

Transition of Industrialization Pattern and Expansion of Social Mobility Space

At the early stage of the reform and opening-up, there were serious problems existing in the Chinese economic structure. The proportions between agriculture, light industry,

---

[1] Zhu, Mingfang, et al. 1998. *Private Sector of Economy in China*. Beijing: China City Press: 239.

[2] The Rural Policy Research Office of the Secretariat of the Central Committee of the C.P.C. 1987. *A Cross-sectional Survey on Chinese Rural Society and Economy*. Beijing: China Social Sciences Press: 20.

[3] Zhang, Houyi and Lizhi Ming. 1999. *Report on Development of Private Enterprises in China (1978-1998)*. Beijing: Social Sciences Documentation Publishing House: 60.

[4] Li, Lulu (1996a).

and heavy industry were highly unbalanced and the development of commercial and service industries were lagging. Such unbalance and lagging, in turn, retarded the development of industry, especially heavy industry, and the improvement of people's standards of living. Therefore, adjustment of the economic structure became an imperative task. The major direction of this adjustment was to supersede the traditional heavy-industry-first industrialization strategy with the comparative advantage strategy based on the reality that capital and technology were scarce whereas human resources were plentiful in China and to accelerate the development of light industry (especially labor-intensive light industry) and commercial and service industries. All these adjustments indicated the transition of Chinese industrialization pattern. Because the employment elasticity of light industry and commercial and service industries was higher than that of heavy industry, such transition of industrialization pattern provided more non-agricultural employment opportunities and hence led to large-scale expansion of occupational mobility space and rapidly changed the employment structure, which significantly corrected the deviation between employment structure and industrial structure (see Table 2-4).

Another important factor that contributed to industrialization and expansion of non-agricultural employment was the high-speed development of rural industrialization after 1984. Such development provided a great deal of non-agricultural employment opportunities for peasants and led to great changes in the employment structure of the rural labor force (see Table 2-5). The year of 1988 was the peak of rural industrialization in this period. The proportion of non-agricultural employment in the rural labor force rose to 22.3 percent. Between 1989 and 1991, this proportion dropped to 20.7 percent for economic regression, causing improvement of deviation of employment structure stagnation in the three years as shown in Table 2-4. As an alternative, a rush of peasant-workers appeared in China in 1989, in which a large number of rural surplus labor force entered into cities to work. Hundreds of millions of the rural labor force migrated between the rural and urban areas and became a new social stratum.[1]

With the transition of the industrialization pattern, the progress of urbanization in China restarted again. According to statistics, from 1979 to 1991, the level of urbanization in China increased from 17.9 percent to 26.9 percent, growing by 0.7 percent per year.[2] Three factors contributed to the growth of urban population in this period. The first factor was the return of rusticated educated youth and cadres, and reunions of some rural-urban separated families. The second factor was the growth of the urban population itself. The third one was the migration of rural population into cities. All these three factors drove the growth of the urban population from 1978 to

---

[1] Of course, many peasants already worked in cities before this period. According to statistics, about 8,500 thousand of rural laborers transferred from agriculture per year and 16 percent of them entered into cities. See Zhang, Zhongfa and Chuanyi Cui. "Transfer of the Labor Force: History, Characteristics, and Experience of Chinese Rural Labor Force Transfer". Retrieved from http://www.ccain.com.

[2] National Bureau of Statistics of China (2003a: Table 4-1).

114

1981. However, after 1981 the main driving force was due to the natural growth of the urban population and migration of the rural labor force into cities by working in urban enterprises and studying in urban schools. According to statistics, among 98,026 thousand of entrants to the urban employment from 1978 to 1991, about 17,172 thousand came from the rural labor force (1,227 thousand per year), accounting for 17.5 percent of the total number.[1] Most of the rural labor force entered cities by being recruited by urban enterprises and then they changed their status from rural residents to urban residents in addition to the shift of occupations. Thus, they were different from "peasant-workers" that emerged later.[2]

Table 2-4   Industrial Structure and Employment Structure in China, 1978~1991

Units: %, Times

Year	GDP Structure			Employment Structure			Employment Structure Deviation		
	The primary industry	The secondary industry	The tertiary industry	The primary industry	The secondary industry	The tertiary industry	The primary industry	The secondary industry	The tertiary industry
1978	28.1	48.2	23.7	70.5	17.3	12.2	-0.60	1.79	0.94
1980	30.1	48.5	21.4	68.7	18.2	13.1	-0.56	1.66	0.63
1985	28.4	43.1	28.5	62.4	20.8	16.8	-0.54	1.07	0.70
1986	27.1	44.0	28.9	60.9	21.9	17.2	-0.56	1.01	0.68
1987	26.8	43.9	29.3	60.0	22.2	17.8	-0.55	0.98	0.65
1988	25.7	44.1	30.2	59.3	22.4	18.3	-0.57	0.97	0.65
1989	25.0	43.0	32.0	60.1	21.6	18.3	-0.58	0.99	0.75
1990	27.1	41.6	31.3	60.1	21.4	18.5	-0.55	0.94	0.69
1991	24.5	42.1	33.4	59.7	21.4	18.9	-0.59	0.97	0.77

Sources: National Bureau of Statistics of China (2003a: 36-37); National Bureau of Statistics of China (2002a: 55); Department of Population, Society, Science and Technology of the National Bureau of Statistics of China (2000: 25); Department Population, Society, Science and Technology of the National Bureau of Statistics of China, and Department of Planning and Finance, Ministry of Labor and Social Security of China (2001: 8).

Table 2-5   Distribution of The Rural Labor Force in Three Industries, 1978~1991

Unit: %

Year	1978	1980	1982	1984	1986	1988	1989	1990	1991
The primary industry	89.72	89.00	88.76	83.63	80.25	77.73	79.24	79.35	79.33
The secondary industry	6.41	6.99	7.29	9.34	11.71	12.21	11.62	11.31	11.14
The tertiary industry	3.87	4.01	3.95	7.03	8.04	10.06	9.14	9.34	9.53

Sources: *China Statistical Yearbook* (1993): 115; *China Statistical Yearbook* (1994): 328.

---

[1]   Calculated based on data drawn from page 136 in *China Statistical Yearbook (1986)* and page 118 in *China Statistical Yearbook (1992)*.

[2]   In addition, the development of small towns that started from 1984 contributed to improvement of urbanization level in this period. According to statistics, there were more than 4,540 thousand rural residents transferred as urban residents by settling down in small towns. However their grain rations were provided by themselves rather than local governments.

The development of the market economy, transition of the industrialization pattern, and restart of urbanization brought along the emergence and development of a series emerging industries and changes of administrative manners of the state, economy, and society. These changes correspondingly expanded occupational space and mobility opportunities in the entire society. Many emerging industries, such as insurance, securities, lawyer, notarization, information consulting services, and information technology industry, etc., sprang up at the end of the 1970s or in the early 1980s. These new industries provided spaces and opportunities for the emergence of the middle social stratum. These changes will be discussed in more detail in Chapter 3.

A higher level of industrialization demands modern technology and a high-caliber labor force. It was such demands that effectively promoted the development of the educational undertaking in China. In order to train more high-quality talented people, the government expanded the scale of higher education in this period by establishing more colleges and universities and increasing the number of admitted students. According to statistics, from 1978 to 1988, the number of colleges and universities increased from 598 to 1,075, up by 79.8 percent. In the following years, the number did not change much. Meanwhile, technical secondary schools increased from 2,760 to 4,022, growing by 45.7 percent. In addition, based on former non-normal education, many new forms of adult higher education grew up rapidly like bamboo shoots after a spring rain, such as radio and television broadcasting universities, staff members and workers universities, part-time colleges, night colleges, and correspondence colleges. A relatively complete higher education system that included universities, colleges, technical secondary schools and certificate programs gradually took shape. In the progress of industrialization and market-oriented transition, diplomas and degrees of higher education became a certificate of high-caliber human resources and the cultural capital to achieve upward mobility.

After a comprehensive review of the development of education at various levels in this period, we find that progress of higher education and secondary specialized education provided more upward social mobility opportunities. In our estimation, between 1980 and 1991, the number of university graduates was nearly 5,000 thousand, and graduates of technical secondary schools were more than 10,000 thousand. The two categories of graduates were still emplaced by the government based on employment plans and they possessed the status of cadre. Besides the normal education, there were more than 1,000 thousand people accepting adult higher education per year.[1]

In order to analyze the possibility of upward social mobility that was achieved through normal education in this period, we calculated the rate of entrants into higher schools at various educational levels and the relevant probability of social mobility based on statistical data (see Table 2-6). The results showed that the probability of achieving upward mobility through education for a primary school graduate changed

---

[1] Wei (2003a: 8).

in the following tendency: the probability kept rising from 1978 to 1985; after 1986, it dropped first and then rose again in a fluctuating way. As a whole, the normal higher education still only opened to a small number of people. The probability that a primary school student would enter a university was as low as 4.6 percent until 1991. It was no wonder that some scholars regarded the higher education after the reform and opening-up as a kind of elite education rather than universal education.[1] In any case, the probability almost doubled in a decade.

Table 2-6   Rates of Entrants into Higher Schools at Various Levels, 1978~1991

Unit: %

Year		1978	1980	1985	1986	1987	1988	1989	1990	1991
Rate of Entrants	Junior middle school	87.7	75.5	67.5	68.8	68.2	69.4	70.5	73.5	74.4
	Senior middle school	40.9	39.7	25.8	24.3	22.8	21.1	21.3	22.5	22.5
	Technical secondary school	2.6	4.9	6.7	6.4	6.4	6.7	6.5	6.6	7.2
	College and university	5.9	4.6	31.5	25.5	25.0	26.7	24.5	26.1	27.8
Probability of Mobility 1		2.1	1.3	5.5	4.3	3.9	3.9	3.7	4.3	4.6
Probability of Mobility 2		4.4	5.0	10.0	8.7	8.3	8.6	8.4	8.9	9.4

Source: *China Statistical Yearbook* (2003).

Notes: (1) In this table, the *rate of entrants of junior middle school* refers to the proportion of that year's primary school graduates entering junior middle schools; the *rate of entrants of senior middle school* refers to the proportion of that year's junior middle school graduates entering senior middle schools; the *rate of entrants technical secondary school* refers to the proportion of that year's junior middle school graduates entering technical secondary schools; and the *rate of entrants of college and university* refers to the proportion of that year's senior middle school graduates entering college and university.

(2) *Probability of mobility 1* refers to the probability that primary school graduates could enter colleges or universities. It is equal to the product of the rate of entrants of junior middle school, the rate of entrants of senior middle school, and the rate of entrants of college and university. *Probability of mobility 2* refers to the probability that primary school graduates could enter technical secondary schools and universities. It is the sum of the probability of mobility 1 plus product of the rate of entrants of junior middle school and the rate of entrants of technical secondary school. These probabilities were roughly calculated, taking no account of differences in enrollment dates of new students in schools at various levels.

---

[1]   Xu (2000: 292).

PRELIMINARY FORMATION OF THE NEW SOCIAL
STRATUM STRUCTURE (SINCE 1992)

Pushed by Deng Xiaoping's speeches in his official visit in South China, the theme of Chinese reform and opening-up has been formally pitched as establishing the socialist market economy since 1992. The Third Plenum of the Fourteenth Central Committee of the C.P.C. approved *Decision of the Central Committee on Several Issues Concerning Establishing the Socialist Market Economy*. Since then, the market-oriented reforms have been progressing rapidly and the pattern in which the public-owned sector remaining dominates and other sectors in diverse forms of ownership develop side by side has been taking shape. Reforms concerning establishing modern corporate system and exploring alternative ways to realize the public ownership have made significant progress in restructuring enterprises by enforcing the joint-stock and shareholding cooperative systems in state-owned and collective enterprises. The influence of market mechanisms on resource allocation and economic activities has become dominant. The level of marketization of the national economy has been increasing. By the time the Fifteenth National Congress of the Communist Party of China was held in 1997, the Chinese economic system had preliminarily accomplished the transition from the planned economy to a free-market economy at the macro level.

With the eventual establishment of a market economy, social stratification has been deepening in this period. Under influences of various factors, occupational status (authority, income, and prestige) of each social stratum has changed to a different extent. Relationships between each stratum have also experienced significant adjustments. As a result, a new social stratum structure consisting of ten major strata has come into being. Hierarchic ranks of different strata have been preliminarily established within this structure. Because such structure is similar to the class structure in a modern market economy to some extent, we call it a rudiment of modern social structure.

In this period, political institutions and relevant policies do not directly define people's class (stratum) status and social status. The socialist market system becomes the fundamental economy system in China, in which the independence of market entities is stressed. In such instances, a new social mobility pattern has been taking shape. The integration of structural mobility at the macro level (see Chapter 3) and individual mobility at the micro level (see Chapter 4) has been the major content of this new social mobility pattern. Institution-oriented and policy-oriented mobility that once dominated in past periods have been greatly weakened.

Therefore, in the perspective of social stratification and social mobility, three tendencies in this period are worthy of particular attention. The first is changes in social mobility space. Such changes provide structural mobility with indispensable conditions. The second is development of education. Since China has entered the middle phase of industrialization, worldwide experience indicates that education is crucial to individual mobility at the micro level in this phase. The third one is the future evolutionary tendencies of Chinese social structure in the process of social stratification and mobility, i.e., the formation of the new social stratum structure.

New Trends in Changes of Social Mobility Space

As mentioned earlier, industrial structure is a basic measurement of the level of a country's industrialization. Chinese industrial structure has been upgrading and the level of industrialization has been rising since 1992 (see Table 2-7), and non-agricultural employment has increased significantly. According to statistics, employment in the secondary industry kept rising from 1992 to 1998, with an increase of 25,850 thousand persons over seven years. From 1999 to 2002, the figure decreased continuously by 8,200 thousand persons in four year. It has grown again since 2003, with 2,970 thousand persons more than the previous year. With the increase and decrease balanced, employment in the secondary industry actually increased 20,620 thousand over twelve years. The tertiary industry kept expanding in this period, 94,310 thousand persons in 2003 more than in 1991. There are two notable tendencies in changes of industrial structure in this period. Firstly, balance between employment in the secondary and tertiary industry and the primary industry has been achieved since 1999, which indicates the second significant transition of Chinese employment structure. Such a balanced situation continued until 2003 and might indicate another breakthrough of industrial structure, if industrialization and urbanization could make more progress. Secondly, the proportion of employment of the tertiary industry has exceeded that of the secondary industry since 1994. This means that the main part of non-agricultural employment structure has been moving to high-end industries. Such change will undoubtedly lead to a similar change of the main part in Chinese new social stratum structure formed on the basis of occupations.

Meanwhile, employment structure deviation changed in a complicated way in this period. Deviations of employment structure increased both in the primary and secondary industry. The employment structure deviation of the primary industry increased from 1992 to 1993, then decreased from 1994 to 1996, and rose again after 1997. The employment structure deviation of the secondary industry kept growing with some small fluctuations. Only the deviation of the tertiary industry has been declining. It dropped to such a low level that it could be left out of consideration in 2003. How do we explain these changes? In the perspective of GDP structure, the proportion of the primary industry has been continuously dropping. It decreased by 9 percent in 2002 over the 1991 figure. In contrast, the proportion of the secondary industry rose by 9 percent, while the proportion of the tertiary industry changed little. From the perspective of the employment structure, the proportion of employment in the primary industry fell by 9.7 percent in 1996 over the 1991 figure. However, it has remained at the same level since 1997. The proportion of the tertiary industry has continuously increased. In 2002, it grew by 10 percent over the figure in 1991. After an increase from 1991 to 1997, the proportion of the secondary industry moved downward from 1998. In 2002, it returned to the level in 1991. Historically, we believed that such changes in the employment structure deviation might reflect influences of reforms of changing the manner of growth in industrial enterprises, downsizing for efficiency, and invigorating large-size enterprises while relaxing control over small ones. On one hand, these reforms improved the level of technology in enterprises and substituted technology for labor, and consequently limited the growth of employment in the secondary industry. On the other hand, these reforms transferred many urban laid-off workers and peasant-workers into the tertiary industry and hence increased the employment of the tertiary industry.

Table 2-7   Industrial Structure, Employment Structure, and Level of Urbanization, 1991~2002

Unit: %, Times

Year	GDP Structure			Employment Structure			Employment Structure Deviation			Level of Urbanization
	The primary industry	The secondary industry	The tertiary industry	The primary industry	The secondary industry	The tertiary industry	The primary industry	The secondary industry	The tertiary industry	
1991	24.5	42.1	33.4	59.7	21.4	18.9	-0.59	0.97	0.77	26.94
1992	21.8	43.9	34.3	58.5	21.7	19.8	-0.63	1.02	0.73	27.46
1993	19.9	47.4	32.7	56.4	22.4	21.2	-0.65	1.12	0.54	27.99
1994	20.2	47.9	31.9	54.3	22.7	23.0	-0.63	1.11	0.39	28.51
1995	20.5	48.8	30.7	52.2	23.0	24.8	-0.61	1.12	0.24	29.04
1996	20.4	49.5	30.1	50.5	23.5	26.0	-0.60	1.11	0.16	30.48
1997	19.1	50.0	30.9	49.9	23.7	26.4	-0.62	1.11	0.17	31.91
1998	18.6	49.3	32.1	49.8	23.5	26.7	-0.63	1.10	0.20	33.35
1999	17.6	49.4	33.0	50.1	23.0	26.9	-0.65	1.15	0.23	34.78
2000	16.4	50.2	33.4	50.0	22.5	27.5	-0.67	1.23	0.21	36.22
2001	15.8	50.1	34.1	50.0	22.3	27.7	-0.68	1.25	0.23	37.66
2002	15.4	51.1	33.5	50.0	21.4	28.6	-0.69	1.39	0.17	39.09
2003	14.6	52.3	33.1	49.1	21.6	29.3	-0.70	1.42	0.13	40.50

Sources: *China Statistical Yearbook* (2003): Table 3-2, Table 4-1, Table 5-2; *Statistical Abstract of China* (2004).

As a whole, industrialization is still at its middle phase in current China. Accordingly, it improved the GDP proportion of the secondary industry. The tertiary industry did not develop very well in the lower urbanization level and hence did not provide enough employment opportunities. Only if industrialization and urbanization reach a higher level, will there be a new giant change in the economic structure. Such change will correspondingly expand the space of occupations and mobility once again.

Allocation of Educational Resources and Opportunities

Through investigation on allocation of educational resources and opportunities (especially allocation of public educational resources and opportunities) in this period, we find that two opposite tendencies co-exist in Chinese education. On one hand, the educational undertaking has been developing and providing people with more opportunities to access education, especially higher education. On the other hand, there is also an unequal tendency existing in attainment of educational resources and opportunities. Therefore, the situation of educational resources and opportunities allocation is complicated, so are its results.

In this period, the educational undertaking as a whole has been developing rapidly on a large scale (see Table 2-8). Except for one year, admission to universities and colleges grew by an average annual rate of 17 percent. The growth rate sped up after 1999 because of adjustments of the national educational policy; that is, the government decided to expand university and college enrollment from 1999. The number of admitted students in technical secondary schools increased in the whole, but it also experienced a significant fluctuation. The enrollment in technical secondary schools kept growing from 1991 to 1998 by an average annual rate of 11.8 percent, faster than the growth rate of college and university enrollment in the same period (8.7 percent). The growth rate dropped from 1999 to 2001 and did not return until 2002. The tendency of changes in technical secondary school enrollment not only indicated the influence of increasing university enrollment in the same period, but also reflected the change of social perception of secondary technical education in this period. In the middle-late 1990s, the secondary technical education encountered neglect to some extent. However, with the transformation of the manner of economic growth from extensive economy, which is based on increased input of essential elements of production such as resources, capital and labor, to intensive economy, which is based on technical progress, economy of scale, and rational operation and scientific management, higher requirements of production techniques and product quality demand more technicians, especially senior technicians. Lack of technicians consequently promoted the development of secondary technical education.

Table 2-8   Growth of Enrollment in Schools at Various Levels, 1992~2002

Units: Ten thousand Persons, %

Year	College and University		Technical Secondary School		Senior Middle School		Junior Middle School		Primary School	
	Admitted Students	Growth Rate	Admitted Students	Growth Rate	Admitted Students	Growth Rate	Admitted Students	Growth Rate	Admitted Students	Growth Rate
1992	75.4	21.6	87.9	12.7	234.7	-3.7	1465.0	3.8	2183.2	5.3
1993	92.4	22.5	114.9	30.7	228.3	-2.7	1479.0	1.0	2353.5	7.8
1994	90.0	-2.6	122.5	6.6	243.4	6.6	1616.4	9.3	2537.0	7.8
1995	92.6	2.9	138.1	12.7	273.6	12.4	1752.3	8.4	2531.8	-0.2
1996	96.6	4.3	152.3	10.3	282.2	3.1	1760.7	0.5	2524.7	-0.3
1997	100.0	3.5	162.1	6.4	322.6	14.3	1805.6	2.6	2462.0	-2.5
1998	108.4	8.4	166.8	2.9	359.6	11.5	1961.4	8.6	2201.4	-10.6
1999	159.7	47.3	163.4	-2.0	396.3	10.2	2149.7	9.6	2029.5	-7.8
2000	220.6	38.1	132.6	-18.8	472.7	19.3	2263.3	5.3	1946.5	-4.1
2001	268.3	21.6	127.7	-3.7	558.0	18.0	2257.9	-0.2	1944.2	-0.1
2002	320.5	19.5	155.3	21.6	676.7	21.3	2252.3	-0.2	1952.8	0.4
Annual Average	147.7	17.0	138.5	7.2	368.0	10.0	1887.6	4.4	2242.4	-0.4

Source: *China Statistical Yearbook* (2003): Table 20-6.

As a whole, the total number of educational opportunities that people acquired in this period increased significantly, more than that in the previous period, especially in higher education. Data in Table 2-9 further confirms this conclusion. Compared with the situation in 1991, the probability that a primary school graduate would move up to the university or the probability that he or she may enter technical secondary school and university rose significantly in this period.

Table 2-9   Rates of Entrants into Higher Schools at Various Levels, 1978~1991

Unit: %

Year		1992	1993	1994	1995	1996	1997	1998	1999	2000	2001	2002
Rate of Entrants	Junior middle school	78.2	80.3	85.1	89.3	91.0	92.1	92.6	92.9	93.6	94.2	95.8
	Senior middle school	21.3	20.1	21.1	22.3	22.1	22.4	22.8	24.9	29.4	32.7	36.0
	Technical secondary school	8.0	10.1	10.6	11.3	11.9	11.2	10.6	10.3	8.3	7.5	8.3
	College and university	33.3	39.9	43.0	45.9	47.1	45.1	43.1	60.7	73.2	78.8	83.5
Probability of Mobility 1		5.6	6.4	7.7	9.1	9.5	9.3	9.1	14.1	20.1	24.3	28.8
Probability of Mobility 2		11.8	14.5	16.7	19.2	20.3	19.7	18.9	23.6	27.8	31.3	36.7

Source: *China Statistical Yearbook* (2003).

Note: In this table, the meanings of the probability of mobility 1 and 2 are the same as in Table 2-6.

When we investigated the tendency of changes of educational opportunity, the distribution of educational opportunity was also analyzed. It is well known that allocation of educational resources is closely related to the distribution of educational opportunity. What we most wanted to know concerning this issue was not the family educational inputs but the allocation of national public resources. The insufficiency of public educational inputs in China is always a serious issue that holds back the development of education and the supply of educational opportunities.[1] Furthermore, unequal allocation of educational resources was another more serious issue in this period. First of all, there is an inequality between rural and urban educational inputs. For example, rural students took up 57.2 percent of 57,215.7 thousand enrolled junior middle school students in China. In contrast, educational inputs in rural junior middle schools only took up 47.8 percent of the total educational investment in junior middle schools in China. In the fiscal budget, the average expenditure on every junior middle school student was 485.82 Yuan RMB in rural areas, while 811.69 Yuan RMB in urban areas, with an urban-rural ratio of 1.67:1.[2] Similar difference existed in the average expenditure on every primary school student between urban and rural areas. These differences in resource allocation consequently resulted in differences of

[1] Research Group of China National Institute for Educational Research. 2001. "Study on Criteria for Modernization Level of Basic Education in Chinese Developed Regions". *Education Research*. Vol. 10.

[2] Wu, Gang. 2002. "Relationship between Education and Society in the Period of Transformation". In Ding, Gang (ed.), *China Education: Studies and Reviews*, Volume 2. Beijing: Education and Science Publishing House.

educational opportunities and conditions between rural and urban areas. For example, difference in the dropout rates between rural and urban was one major consequence of difference in resource allocation. In 1998, the dropout rate of enrolled junior middle school students in China was 3.23 percent, while in rural areas the rate was 4 percent.[1]

Inequality in the structure of educational opportunity not only affects allocation of public educational resources, but also directly influences attainment of educational opportunity. For example, over the years, the admission requirements on grades in college entrance examination are different between rural and urban areas, and between different regions. Such differences leave more opportunities to students in urban areas and developed regions. Compared with Gansu Province, which lies in western China, the admission requirements on grades in college entrance examination in Beijing are 24 to 72 points lower.[2] Urban areas and developed regions acquire more public educational resource, and at the same time, students from these areas are admitted by colleges and universities based on lower requirements which means a sort of double inequality and, hence, seriously deprives students in rural and underdeveloped areas of educational opportunities.

Obviously, such inequality is institutionalized by government's institutional arrangements. In addition, because of the high tuition policy and so-called "market-oriented educational industrialization", such institutionalized inequality has been aggravated. In the late twentieth century, the governmental planned enrollment system was annulled and consequently tuition fees soared extensively in most colleges and universities, i.e., the so-called "industrialization of education" or "marketization of education". For example, the rate of tuition fees for undergraduate students was about 3,000 Yuan RMB in 1999. However, it rocketed to 4,500 Yuan RMB in 2000, up by 50 percent. In some developed cities and famous universities, the rate was even more than 6,000 Yuan RMB.[3] According to official statistics, the rural per capita net income was only 2,210 Yuan RMB in 2000. That means that an ordinary farmer could not afford even one academic year's tuition for his or her child. As a result of such institutional reform, undoubtedly it is easier for children with good family economic support to enter schools than children in low-income families. Consequently, children's upward social mobility through education is significantly influenced by ascription factors like family economic condition.

In conclusion, rural residents undoubtedly suffer more consequences brought about by unequal educational opportunities for generally worse rural economic conditions and the urban-first policy in public educational resource allocation. According to an estimation published in *China Education Daily*, until 2001 the probability of a rural primary school student entering college or university was only

---

[1] Yang, Dongping. 2001. "Report on Development of Education in China 2000". In *2001: Analysis and Forecast on Chinese Society Situations*. Beijing: Social Sciences Documentation Publishing House.

[2] Wu (2002).

[3] Wu (2002).

15 percent.[1] According to our calculation, the average level of this probability in China was 24.3 percent. That means that the probability of a rural primary school student entering college or university was 62 percent lower than the average level in China. Furthermore, because the proportion of rural population to the total population in China was 62.34 percent, the probability of urban children entering colleges reached about 40 percent, 65 percent higher than the average level in China and 1.67 times higher than the level in rural areas.

Solidification of Structure and Ranks of Social Strata

The stratum structure based on occupations in China has preliminarily taken shape through social stratification and mobility over the past twenty years since the reform and opening-up. At the same time, the rank of each stratum in this structure tends to be solidified. We discussed this phenomenon in *Social Stratification in Contemporary China* and gave a further analysis in Chapter 1 in this book. In a certain sense, this also means that a stable ladder of social mobility in Chinese society has come into being.

In the process of preliminary formation of new stratum structure and rank, determinations of socio-economic status of several major social strata like agricultural laborers, industrial workers, individual-operated business proprietors, and private entrepreneurs have produced far-reaching influences. The stratum of state and social administrators, managerial personnel, and professional and technical personnel are certainly important social strata in this new structure, but their socio-economic status have not changed much over the past twenty years because they already attained higher status in the planned economy era or at the beginning of the reform and opening-up.

(1)Disadvantaged Position of the Stratum of Agricultural Laborers

Before the reform and opening-up, the peasantry enjoyed a higher political status as the allied force of the working class. After the reform and opening-up, peasants benefited much from reforms of the rural economy system and rapid development of rural industrialization, and their economic status was improved greatly. However, the socio-economic status of peasants, especially agricultural laborers (full-time farmers and a part of part-time farmers), has begun to decline since 1997.

Firstly, the agricultural economy has entered into depression since 1997. Statistics shows that both yields and prices of farm produce have fallen at the same time. Before 1998, the growth of staple crops like corn and grain was steady. However, there was a continuous reduction of yields of corn and grain from 1999 to 2001, with an average decrease of 4.1 percent per year.[2] Before 1997, prices of farm products

---

[1] China Education Daily. 2001 "Pay Attention to the Rise of the Rural Dr)opout Rate". *China Education Daily*. June 6.

[2] National Bureau of Statistics of China (2003a: Table 12-6, Table 12-17.

124

kept rising and then started to drop after that year. In 2001 and 2002, prices of many farm products fell down to the levels of a decade ago. The drop in prices of corn and grain was especially remarkable, down by 40 percent in 1997 over the figure of the previous year. The trend of falling prices extended to the year of 2002. Prices of meat and eggs fell from 1998 and did not stop until 2001. In fact, the actual prices of meat and eggs in 2001 were 17 percent lower than those in 1997.[1] Accordingly, the gross output value of agriculture (including farming, forestry, animal husbandry, and fishing) dropped from 1997 and reached the lowest level over the past eleven years in 2000. The figure rose slightly in 2001 and 2002. In short, the growth tendency of agricultural economy in China has significantly slowed down since 1997. According to official statistics, income of peasants was increasing in this period at a lower rate. However, we hardly believe that income of full-time farmers and a portion of part-time farmers (or agricultural laborers) would keep rising rather than dropping in such instances. In fact, many experts of agriculture issues estimated that peasants' income actually fell down after 1997.

Secondly, the peasantry is facing many other issues as well. The first issue is heavy tax burdens. Since 1993, the proportion of taxes and fees imposed on the peasantry to their total income had been beyond 10 percent, in some regions even more than 25 percent. Even after the reform of rural taxes and administrative charges, the proportion was still as high as 8.4 percent. In urban areas, the minimal taxable personal income is 800 Yuan RMB per month. However, the rural per capita annual income was no more than 2,475 Yuan in 2002, i.e., about 206 Yuan per month. Therefore, the tax burdens of peasants are extremely heavy compared with urban residents. The second issue is descending governmental investment on rural public products and services and decreasing public resources enjoyed by the peasantry. For example, the proportion of expenditure on agriculture in total expenditure of public finance decreased from 10.26 percent in 1991 to 7.71 percent in 2001. In addition, the social security system in rural areas is extremely deficient. Most peasants are not covered by medical insurance and other social securities. In such situations, they have to pay considerable expenditures on education and medial healthcare. Many of them are driven to poverty for children's education or family members' illness. The third issue is increasingly serious exploitation of rural resources by cities and urban industries, such as farmland expropriation, the scissors gap between the prices of agricultural products and industrial products, reverse capital flow from rural areas to urban areas, etc. Especially, farmland expropriation is perhaps the most serious issue. There were 130,039 thousand hectare of farmland in China in 1996, while the figure dropped to 127,082 thousand hectare in 2001, a decrease of 2,957 thousand hectare over five years. All these farmlands were transferred to non-farm land. Though peasants who lost their farmland received certain compensations, some investigations showed these compensations only accounted for 10 percent to 15 percent of the actual value of appropriated land, whereas villages obtained 25 percent to 30 percent, and

[1] National Bureau of Statistics of China (2003a: Table 9-7).

local governments acquired 60 percent to 70 percent.[1] What made the situation much worse was that most lost-land peasants did not get any social security and reemployment emplacement and became sort of "vagabonds" without farmland, jobs, and social security.

In conclusion, socio-economic status of the stratum of agricultural laborers has obviously declined since 1997. The peasantry has lost its advantages obtained at the beginning of the reform and opening-up and tends to be a lower level social stratum with a disadvantaged position.

(2) Descending Status of Industrial Workers

In July 1992, the State Council released the Statute on Transformation of Management Mechanisms in Public-owned Enterprises as implementing regulations of the Law of the People's Republic of China on Enterprises. Accordingly, the independent managerial authority in public-owned enterprises was strengthened to a greater extent than in the previous period and produced significant influence on society and politics.[2] For enterprises' managerial personnel, it meant that their power of management would be strengthened. For workers in these enterprises, it meant they would lose rights to participate in enterprise management and wage negotiation.[3] However, the real problem was that strengthening independent managerial authority did not save state-owned enterprises from predicaments. The expansion of managerial authority did not significantly improve business performance but increased the risk of losing public assets. Management in enterprises could abuse such authority to gain advantages for themselves. Some enterprises even were driven to bankruptcy due to management's appropriation and embezzlement. According to statistics, "hollowed" enterprises took up 20.2 percent of 302 thousand of state-owned enterprises in China in 1995, and assets that ran up accounts in these enterprises accounted for 29.3 percent of owner's equity.[4] That means probably more than one trillion Yuan of state-owned assets were lost.[5] Obviously, a large amount of these lost assets was transferred to the hands of managerial personnel who controlled enterprises and relevant government officials.

Studies in the middle of the 1990s showed that, in large-size state-owned enterprises, deficits were the highest, but the number of enterprises running in the red was relatively smaller. Contrarily, in small-medium businesses, deficits were lower,

---

[1] "Distribution of Three Trillion Yuan Lost by Peasants for Low-price Land Expropriation". Retrieved September 11, 2003, from http://www.ccrs.org.cn.

[2] Xiao, Gen. 1997. *Property Right and Economic Reforms in China*. Beijing: China Social Sciences Press: 239.

[3] You, Zhenglin (2000); Feng, Tongqin. 2001. *Destiny of the Working Class in China*. Beijing: Social Sciences Documentation Publishing House.

[4] Wu, Jinglian, et al. 1998. *Strategic Restructuring of State-owned Economy*. Beijing: China Development Press: 26-27.

[5] According to statistics, the total amount of corporation assets in 291 thousand state-owned commercial and industrial enterprises was more than 9.6 trillion yuan RMB by the end of 1996.

but the number of money-losing enterprises was bigger. Of two evils, choose the less. Therefore, it seems that the government had no other choices except to focus on the restructuring of large enterprises and leaving small ones to fend for themselves. In September 1995, the Fifth Plenum of the Fourteenth Central Committee of the C.P.C. approved the *Ninth Five-Year Plan for Development of National Economy and Society and Long-term Goals up to 2010* and proposed the strategy of "seizing the big and freeing the small" and the policy of "downsizing for efficiency". "Seizing the big" refers to invigorating large-size enterprises through downsizing and enhancing efficiency. "Freeing the small" means loosing control over small state-owned enterprises through restructuring, coalition, merger, joint partnership, leasing, contract operation, and sell-off.

The consequence of downsizing for efficiency was large-scale layoffs rather than changes of the relationship of authority between management and ordinary staff members and workers inside enterprises. According to estimations, up to now there are more than 30,000 thousand laid-off workers because of downsizing in urban areas. Although these laid-off workers usually will find other jobs in private sectors of economy, they lost many political and economic advantages gained at the beginning of the reform and opening-up. In addition, the core of the reform of "seizing the big and freeing the small" was the transfer of public property right. This reform started at the beginning of the 1990s and reached its peak around 1996. Its basic idea was to restructure small state-owned and collective enterprises into non-public-owned enterprises. Staff members and workers in restructured enterprises either were taken over by buyers and became employees of private businesses, or were laid off and became members of the stratum of unemployment. Therefore, whether "downsizing for efficiency" or "seizing the big and freeing the small", to workers in state-owned enterprises, such reforms only meant one thing: decline of socio-economic status.

At the same time, restructuring of rural collective enterprises (township enterprises) also was launched from 1996 and accomplished around 1998. The major methods of restructuring township enterprises were auctions, joint stock systems, and shareholding cooperative systems. In the case of auction, township enterprises were thoroughly transformed into private businesses. As for joint stock systems or shareholding cooperative systems, most enterprises actually became private businesses as well because local governments usually encouraged former management to hold the majority of shares while reduce the proportion of collectively-held shares as low as possible. As a result, a large number of former staff members and workers of rural collective enterprises became employees of private businesses. Accordingly, they lost almost all the benefits that they originally enjoyed in collective enterprises. For example, after restructuring of a township business in Jiangsu Province, about 85 percent of its staff members and workers shifted to employees of privatized enterprises, without any shareholding and losing all original fringe benefits and welfare. Therefore, their socio-economic status undoubtedly moved downward.[1]

---

[1] Qin, Hui. 1998. *Case Studies on Restructuring of Township Enterprises in Jiangsu and Zhejiang*

(3) High-Speed Development of the Non-Public Sector of Economy and Rapid Rise of New Social Strata and Groups

The policy and institutional environment of non-public sector of economy development changed significantly after 1992. The pattern in which the public-owned sectors remain dominant and other sectors in diverse types of ownership develop side by side has come into being. In addition, governments at various levels released a series of policies to promote the development of the non-public sector of economy. In such a situation, the development of the non-public economy in China (including individual-operated businesses, private enterprises, foreign-invested ventures, and other private sectors) has sped up since 1992.

The influence of the development of the non-public sector of economy on social stratification and mobility is mainly shown in four aspects. First, development of individual-operated businesses formed a voluminous stratum of individual-operated business proprietors. There were 25,710 thousand individual-operated businesses in 2001. Providing one individual-operated business has one owner, members of this stratum were over 25,710 thousand. Second, development of private businesses shaped a stratum of private entrepreneurs. In 2002, the number of registered private business investors increased to 6,230 thousand persons and per capita registered authorized capital was 398 thousand Yuan. According to our previous investigations, the amount of capital actually possessed by private entrepreneurs was at least two times larger than that of registered capital. Third, development of foreign-invested enterprises brought out a group of Chinese managerial personnel and professional and technical personnel in these enterprises. They are high-income white-collar employees and a new component of the middle stratum. According to statistics, there were 208 thousand of enterprises invested by foreign entrepreneurs and entrepreneurs from Hong Kong, Macao, and Taiwan.[1] Providing every business had 10 middle-higher level Chinese managerial personnel and professional, and then more than 2,000 thousand persons belonged to this group. Some studies showed that annual per capita income of white-collar employees in Euramerican-invested enterprises was 61,000 Yuan.[2] Fourth, development of all these non-public-owned enterprises brought up a huge group of employees. According to statistics, about 34,093 thousand persons were working in private enterprises in 2002. Deducting investors among them (6,230 thousand persons), there were 27,860 thousand employees. People working in individual-operated businesses were 47,430 thousand; minus business owners among them (providing each business had one owner), there were 23,650 thousand employees. People working in foreign-invested enterprises were 6,710 thousand.[3]

Provinces. Hong Kong: Hong Kong Institute of Asia-Pacific Studies: 37.

[1] National Bureau of Statistics of China (2003: 22-23).

[2] 51job. 2003. "Secrets of White Collars' Salary: Six Factors like Hidden Income Widen the Gap". Retrieved March 27, 2003, from http://it.21cn.com. 51job is a human resources management services company in China.

[3] Zhang, Houyi, et al (eds.). 2003. *Report on Development of Private Enterprises in China (2003)*.

128

The total number of employees in the three types of non-public-owned enterprises was more than 58,220 thousand. Most employees in non-public-owned enterprises were peasant-workers. Although they were wage earners, comparing with their former occupation, i.e., agricultural laborer, their income level increased significantly. Especially, in the perspective of socio-economic status, employees in the secondary industry could be classified as members of the stratum of urban industrial workers.

Changes of the above social stratification and stratum status preliminarily defined socio-economic status and corresponding ranks of agricultural laborers, industrial workers, individual-operated business proprietors, and private entrepreneurs in the new social stratum structure. These strata, along with other social strata, consist of ten major social strata in contemporary China. According to our study, the proportion of each stratum in 2001 respectively was: 2.1 percent for the stratum of state and social administrators, 1.6 percent for the stratum of managerial personnel, 1.0 percent for the stratum of private entrepreneurs,[1] 4.6 percent for the stratum of professional and technical personnel, 7.2 percent for the stratum of clerical personnel, 7.1 percent for the stratum of individual-operated business proprietors, 11.2 percent for stratum of commercial and service sectors employees, 17.5 percent for the stratum of industrial workers, 42.9 percent for the stratum of agricultural laborers, and 4.8 percent for the stratum of the jobless, unemployed, and partially unemployed.[2] In the future, people will flow between these social strata based on their own possessed resources, individual efforts, and opportunities or constraints provided by various structural factors and institution-policy factors.

Beijing: Social Sciences Documentation Publishing House: 7, 21, 48.

[1] Calculated according to the statistical calibration used by China Administration for Industry and Commerce, the proportion of private entrepreneurs was 0.6 percent; correspondingly, the proportion of individual-operated business proprietors was 7.5 percent.

[2] Lu (2002: 44).

Chapter 3 The Pro-High-Level Trend in Occupational Structure

Occupation is an important criterion for social stratum classification; social mobility happens on the basis of occupations as well. In fact, occupational structure provides a fundamental framework for social mobility in which people's individual actions of seeking occupational status supported by personal motivations and possessed resources converge as a river of social mobility.

The social system at the macro level in China has been experiencing significant change since the reform started at the end of the 1970s. The reform has brought out profound influences on activities at the micro level, such as mechanisms of organizing and assigning works, and the transition of occupational structure. Consequently, these changes have led to significant changes of direction and opportunity in social stratum mobility. In order to understand the social mobility that occurred and has been emerging in China, it is first necessary to describe the transition of the occupational structure and then explore macro-level institutional factors that have caused such changes.

CHARACTERISTICS OF THE PRO-HIGH-LEVEL TREND IN OCCUPATIONAL STRUCTURE SINCE 1978

The Worldwide Trend of Occupational Structure Transition

It is well recognized that modern society is an open society. An important characteristic of an open society is the higher frequency of social mobility, which is continuously speeding up. Occupational structure in an open society is not a static but a dynamic process of upgrading. The basic characteristic of this process is that the number of higher-level occupations keeps increasing and so does its proportion in occupational structure, while the proportion of low-level occupations decreasing. The increase of higher-level occupations provides the majority of people with the opportunity of upward social mobility.

In one study on social mobility in the United States in the 1960s, Blau and Ducan found that the overall trend of occupational mobility in the United States was a type of vertical upward mobility. The cause of this phenomenon was the continuous increase of whit-collar and professional occupations provided more opportunities for

130

families of blue-collar workers. They accordingly drew the conclusion that upward social mobility was a general characteristic of the industrialized society and could allow for social stability and intermingling.[1]

A British scholar's study has also demonstrated this pro-high-level trend in occupational structure. The blue-collar occupations in the British manufacturing industry took up a dominant proportion of the labor force market at the beginning of the twentieth century. As time went by, more white-collar positions in the service industry emerged. More than three fourths of the labor force in Britain was manual laborers (blue-collar positions) in 1900. However, by the middle of the twentieth century, the proportion of manual laborers had decreased to less than two thirds of paid jobs, while non-manual jobs grew rapidly. Between two population censuses respectively conducted in 1971 and 1981, the proportion of male workers in blue-collar occupations dropped from 62 percent to 56 percent, and female workers declined from 43 percent to 36 percent. Meanwhile, the number of men engaging in professional and managerial occupations increased by about one million persons, and women in the same occupations grew even more.[2] Similarly, Goldthorpe and his colleagues conducted the *Oxford Social Mobility Inquiry* in 1972 and results showed that the overall social mobility of British men increased more than before. The cause of this phenomenon was the high-speed growth of white-collar occupations.[3]

The same situation occurred in Germany. From 1960 to 1995, with respect to the employment in the former West Germany, the proportions of the self-employed and family member helpers decreased from 12.6 percent and 9.9 percent to 9.7 percent and 1.6 percent respectively. The proportion of workers dropped from 50.2 percent to 34.6 percent. In contrast, proportions of officials and clerical personnel increased from 4.7 percent and 22.6 percent to 7.7 percent to 46.4 percent respectively. There were similar changes taking place in the former East Germany.[4]

After analyzing data of Britain, France, West Germany, Switzerland, Italy, Sweden, Denmark, Japan, and the United States, Lipset and Bendix drew the conclusion that the expansion of white-collar occupations occurred in all industrialized countries and there were a worldwide "trend of upward mobility".[5] Anthony Giddens asserted in his works that this trend of change in occupational structure has continued in today's world, although it has turned stabilized to some extent.[6]

The pro-high-level trend in occupational structure exists in Chinese society as well. With the development of economy and society, especially since the reform and

[1] Blau and Duncan (1967).

[2] Giddens, Anthony. 2003. *Sociology*, 4th edition. Beijing: Peking University Press: 476.

[3] Goldthorpe, John H. 1987. *Social Mobility and Class Structure in Modern Britain* (2nd edition). Oxford: Clarendon Press.

[4] Li, Peilin. *Changes of Social Structure in Contemporary Germany*. Article on the Internet.

[5] Lipset, Seymour Martin and Bendix Reinhard. 1959. *Social Mobility in Industrial Society*. Berkeley, C.A.: University of California Press.

[6] Giddens (2003: 477).

opening-up from the end of the 1970s, the occupational structure in China has experienced a pro-high-level shift that is similar to the trend in industrialized countries, but it is unique with Chinese characteristics.

The Incremental Pro-High-Level Trend in Occupational Structure

In the following section, we will investigate the process of the pro-high-level shift of Chinese occupational structure with the perspectives of change in the gross number of occupational positions, the increment of occupational categories, and the transition of occupational structure.

(1) Changes in the Total Number of Occupational Positions

From 1978 to 2001, the average annual growth rate of population in China was 1.36 percent, and the annual growth rate of occupational positions was 3.41 percent. The total number of occupational positions increased from 0.4 billion to 0.73 billion (see Figure 3-1). The absolute increase of the gross number of occupational positions means not only more employment opportunities but also an expanding space for flows between occupations.

Figure 3-1   Numbers of Occupational Positions in China, 1978~2001

Source: Past years' *China Population Statistical Yearbook*. Beijing: China National Statistic Press.

With respect to occupational category, we can find that increases of occupational positions in different occupational categories were not equal (see Table 3-1). From 1982 to 2000, the first three occupations with the highest growth in the absolute number of occupational positions was agricultural laborers (a net increase of 55,150 thousand), people working in the commercial industry (a net increase of 29,590 thousand), and production workers (a net increase of 22,900 thousand) respectively.

The increase of state and social administrators was the least, with a net increase of only 780 thousand.

Growth rates of various occupations were very different as well. The growth rates of commercial personnel and clerical personnel were the highest where these occupational positions in 2000 increased by 3.1 times and 2 times than in 1982, respectively. The second highest growth rate was that of service personnel, up by 90 percent. The third one was managerial personnel in enterprises and professional and technical personnel, with a growth rate of 43 percent. The fourth was the growth rate of state and social administrators, up by 30 percent. The growth rate of production workers was 27.5, slightly lower than the average growth rate of all occupational positions (29.4 percent). The growth rate of agricultural laborers was the lowest, merely 14.7 percent.

Table 3-1   Positions in Different Occupations, 1982~2000

Units: Ten Thousand, %

Occupation	The Year of 1982	The Year of 2000	Increased Number	Increased Proportion
Agricultural laborers	37538	43053	5515	14.7
Commercial personnel	942	3901	2959	314.1
Production workers	8337	10627	2290	27.5
Clerical personnel	679	2057	1378	202.9
Professional and technical personnel	2646	3795	1149	43.4
Service personnel	1151	2184	1033	89.7
Managerial personnel	555	798	243	43.8
State and social administrators	257	335	78	30.4

Sources: The 1982 figures are from China Population Statistical Yearbook (1985); the 1990 figures are from the Tabulation on the 1990 Population Census of the People's Republic of China; the 2000 figures are from the 2000 population census in China.

Among the above eight categories of occupations, six of them climbed steadily, and the other two grew between 1982 and 1990, and then declined after 1990. More specifically, agricultural laborers decreased by 26,290 thousand between 1990 and 2000, a negative growth rate of minus 5.8 percent. State and social administrators decreased by 660 thousand in the same period, a negative growth rate of minus 16.5 percent (see Figure 3-2).

Figure 3-2   Growth Rates of Occupations, 1982~2000

Source: Same as Table 3-1

Note: The number of occupations in 1982 =1

After comprehensively analyzing the amount and rates of growth of different occupations from 1982 to 2000 and comparing them with the growth rate of the population in the same period, we found that: (1) each occupation increased in the absolute number of positions, (2) the average growth rate of occupational positions was higher than the growth rate of the population, (3) except for agricultural laborers, growth rates of other occupations were higher than the growth rate of the population, (4) growth rates of agricultural laborers and production workers were lower than the average rate of all occupations (see Figure 3-3).

Figure 3-3   Numbers and Growth Rates of Different Occupations, 1982~2000

Source: Same as Table 3-1.

The drastic growth in both absolute numbers and proportions of occupations in China is obviously different from the changing tendency of occupation in developed countries. In Britain, for example, high-level occupations, such as legislators, senior government officials and managers, professionals and associate personnel, technicians and associate personnel, increased between 1991 and 1999. However, there was another tendency that both absolute numbers and growth rates of low-level occupations decreased simultaneously, including plant and machine operators and assemblers, craft and related trades workers, and skilled agricultural and fishing workers, etc. Figure 3-4 shows that there is a linear relationship existing among the increased numbers and growth rates of occupations in Britain. Therefore, it is a sort of "constant pro-high-level shift", while the situation in China is an "incremental pro-high-level shift" (see Figure 3-3).

(2) The Expansion of Occupational Categories

The growth of occupations in China since the reform and opening-up also means the emergence of new occupational categories. There are three major newly emerged occupations or economic groups in China since the end of the 1970s, namely, individual-operated business proprietors, private entrepreneurs, and professional managers.[1]

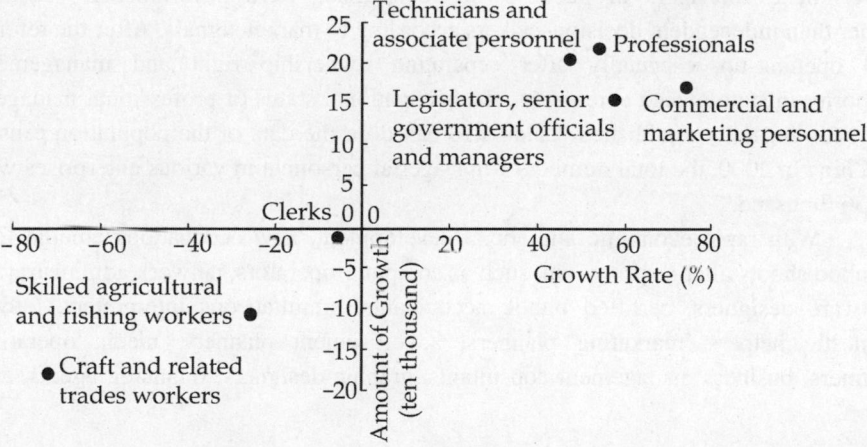

Figure 3-4   Occupational Positions and Proportions in Britain, 1991~1999

Sources: The 1991 figures are from *International Statistical Yearbook* (1999); the 1999 figures are from *International Statistical Yearbook* (2001).

---

[1] In a more rigid sense, both individual-operated business proprietors and private entrepreneurs do not belong to the occupational category, so we use the term "economic group" instead.

Individual-operated business proprietors and private entrepreneurs have experienced dramatic vicissitudes in growth over the past fifty years. There were 8,830 thousand of individual-operated business proprietors in China in 1952. After the Socialist Transformation Movement and the People's Commune Movement in the 1950s, the number fell to 2,310 thousand in 1963. Shortly thereafter, the "Cutting off the Tail of Capitalism" campaign in the Cultural Revolution almost eliminated this group completely; only 150 thousand of individual-operated business proprietors survived in 1978. However, this group resuscitated and developed rapidly after 1979. The number of its members increased to 30,098.47 thousand in 2000, with a growth of 200 times over the 1978 figure.[1]

Private entrepreneurs belonged to the exploiting classes in past political-economic stratification. They were deprived of managerial authority after 1956 and were eliminated as a stratum in an economic sense. After the reform and opening-up, starting from the *People's Daily*'s report in September 1981 about a farmer in Guangdong Province who contracted for a fishpond and hired employees to manage it, the group of private entrepreneurs has expanded rapidly. By the end of 2002, there were 2,430 thousand of private enterprises in China, involving 6,220 thousand of investors.[2]

Professional managers refer to non-investor middle-high level management in enterprises (they may possess a part of the shareholdings). Various enterprises fell into the planned economy system after 1956 and were managed and operated by the government. Managers in public-owned enterprises were governmental "cadres" rather than independent decision-makers according to market signals. After the reform and opening-up, especially after separating ownership right and management authority in state-owned enterprises, the occupational status of professional managers has been formally established. Calculated based on the data of the population census of China in 2000, the total number of managerial personnel in various enterprises was 6,756 thousand.

With rapid economic and social development, new occupations emerge like bamboo shoots after a spring rain, such as computer operators, network administrators, software designers, certified public accountants, simultaneous interpreters, tutors, domestic helpers, marketing planners, advertisement planners, media operating planners, business management consultants, graphic designers, financing agents, and so on.

(3) Changes of Occupational Structure

From 1982 to 2000, China conducted three national population censuses, i.e., the third population census in 1982, the forth population census in 1990, and the fifth population census in 2000. Data obtained from the three population censuses indicate

---

[1] National Bureau of Statistics of China (2002).

[2] Lu (2002: 17).

that there is a pro-high-level trend in occupational structure.[1] Proportions of higher-level occupations in occupational structure were increasing, while proportions of lower-level occupations were declining (see Figure 3-5).[2]

More specifically, in the years of the three censuses, proportions of five types of occupations increased: enterprise managerial personnel (1.1 percent in 1982, 1.1 percent in 1990, and 1.2 percent in 2000), professional and technical personnel (proportions in the three years respectively were 5.1 percent, 5.3 percent, and 5.6 percent), clerical personnel (1.3 percent, 1.7 percent, and 3 percent), commercial personnel (1.8 percent, 3 percent, and 5.8 percent), and service personnel (2.2 percent, 2.4 percent, and 3.2 percent).

Figure 3-5   Occupational Structure in Three Population Censuses

Sources: The 1982 figures are from the *China Population Statistical Yearbook (1985)*; the

---

[1] In this study, we adopted figures in the 1982, 1990, and 2000 population census. All figures concerning occupational structure in this chapter are from the three censuses. Because different classification criteria were adopted in the three censuses and all these criteria are different from the stratum classification of the study, we employed four different types of occupation classifications in this chapter, including the new edition of the National Standard Occupation Classifications adopted in 2000 population census, the old edition of the National Standard Occupation Classifications adopted in 1982 and 1990 population censuses, the stratum-based classification of occupations adopted in the study, and the International Standard Classification of Occupations. Different classification criteria in the three censuses led to difficulty in historical comparisons. Because data in 1982 and 1990 census were saved on paper and hard to be processed, we transformed data of the 2000 census based on the old edition of the National Standard Occupation Classifications. Domestic longitudinal comparisons discussed in this chapter are based on the old edition of the National Standard Occupation Classifications, while cross-national comparisons are based on the International Standard Classification of Occupations. Analyses about occupational structure in 2000 are based on the new edition of the National Standard Occupation Classifications and our own stratum classification. If readers find any inconsistent descriptions on occupation classifications, they were caused by these different classification criteria.

[2] The hierarchy of occupational level is consistent with the ten strata classification in the study. Because relevant data are from past years' *China Statistical Yearbook*, results of analysis are partially different from the results based on the survey conducted by the research group. However, the overall tendency revealed by these analyses is consistent.

1990 figures are from the *Tabulation on the 1990 Population Census of the People's Republic of China*; the 2002 figures are from the 2000 population census in China.

The proportion of state and social administrators rose from 1982 to 1990, and dropped from 1990 to 2000 (0.5 percent, 0.6 percent, and 0.5 percent). The proportion of workers descended from 1982 to 1990, and then ascended from 1990 to 2000, but it still did not reach the level of 1982 (16 percent, 15.2 percent, and 15.8 percent). The proportion of agricultural laborers continuously dropped from 1982 to 2000 (72 percent, 70.6 percent, and 63.8 percent).

As a result of changes in occupational proportions, employment in low-level occupations (including production workers and agricultural laborers) decreased by 8.1 percent, while employment in middle-high level occupations increased by 7.2 percent. Accordingly, the rank of overall occupations upgraded.

The trend of pro-high-level shift in occupational structure provides a possible explanation for a paradoxical phenomenon in China: the society maintains a relatively stable state while polarization of rich and poor is increasing. The rapid growth in both numbers and proportions of higher-level occupations provides the majority of people in China with upward mobility opportunities. The occupational status of most was improved and incomes increased in the process of progressive upward social mobility. The upward mobility and concomitant benefits may allow people psychologically to accept or tolerate such a social structure rather than reject it. A simple fact is that about one hundred million peasants entered cities to work or start their own businesses and hence moved from the lower-level stratum of agricultural laborers to higher-level strata, such as workers, commercial and service personnel, or individual-operated business proprietors. Although the social status of peasant-workers is very low in the city, it is higher than that of traditional peasants.

Nonetheless, the current pro-high-level shift in occupational structure in China can only be called "a trend of pro-high-level shift", i.e., it is just tending to pro-high-level shift and still at the beginning stage. Two relevant causes are listed as follows.

Firstly, middle-low level occupations rather than middle-high level or high-level occupations lead to rapid expansion of occupational structure. Figure 3-6 shows that commercial personnel, clerical personnel, and service personnel had the highest growth rates of job positions; increases in both periods were above 60 percent. Growth rates of professional and technical personnel and managerial personnel were relatively lower, in a range of 10 percent to 30 percent. The growth rate of state and social administrators, a type of high-level occupation, once was as high as 56 percent from 1982 to 1990, but then turned to negative (minus 16.5 percent) from 1990 to 2000.

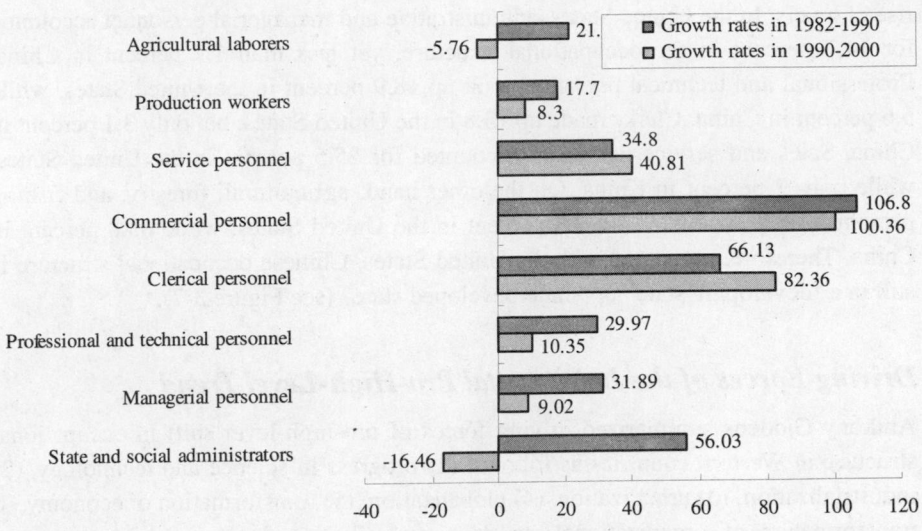

Figure 3-6   Growth Rates of Occupations, 1982~2000

Source: Same as Table 3-5.

Figure 3-7   Occupational Structure in China and the United States

Sources: Data about China are from the 2000 population census in China; data about the United States are from *World Statistical Yearbook* (2001).

Secondly, compared with developed countries, the pro-high-level shift in occupational structure in China is still at a lower level. For example, the shape of occupational structure was olive-like in the United States in 2000, in which not only proportions of middle-level occupations were very high, but also the proportion of higher-level occupations was relatively high. In contrast, the shape of occupational structure in China in the same period was pyramid-like, which had a huge base and a steepled top, and proportions of occupations between the base and the top were descending with the rise of levels. In the United States, administrative and managerial personnel accounted for 14.7 percent in the occupational structure, yet less than 1.7 percent in China. Professional and technical personnel took up 18.9 percent in the United States, while 5.6 percent in China. Clerks made up 13.8 in the United States, but only 3.1 percent in China. Sales and service personnel accounted for 25.5 percent in the United States, while only 9 percent in China. On the other hand, agricultural, forestry, and fishing personnel only accounted for 2.6 percent in the United States, while 63.8 percent in China. Therefore, compared with the United States, Chinese occupational structure is still in a "developing state" or "underdeveloped state" (see Figure 3-7).

Driving Forces of the Incremental Pro-High-Level Trend

Anthony Giddens summarized driving forces of pro-high-level shift in occupational structure in Western countries as follows: (1) progress in science and technology, (2) industrialization, (3) urbanization, (4) globalization, (5) transformation of economy, (6) transformation of organizational structure, and (7) transformation of government functions.[1] All these factors are driving forces of social transformation that focuses on development of economy, innovation of technology, and the upgrade of industrial structure in a free-market economy. However, in China, driving forces of the pro-high-level trend in occupational structure are not limited to these factors. Besides social transformation, institutional transition is a more important cause that affects changes of occupational structure.[2] In the process of restructuring the economic systems, the original allocation system in which the government monopolized almost all resources was replaced by the new system in which diverse entities possess resources. An "unintentional" consequence of the reform is the emergence of some new middle-level occupations in the occupational structure based on extra-system resources.[3] Another outcome of the economic system reform was changes of the ownership structure. Such changes resulted in emergence and development of individual-operated business proprietors and private entrepreneurs.[4]

We call the progress in science and technology, industrialization, and urbanization in current China as "modernization". The institutional reforms in China include shifting the ownership structure from the unitary public ownership to the pattern with leading public ownership and other concomitant types of ownership, restructuring the corporate structure from the unification pattern to the separation

---

[1] Giddens (2003: 67, 77-78, 366, 370-371, 477, 478, 482).

[2] Li, Lulu. 1996. "Institutional Structure of Social Stratification in Contemporary China". *Teaching and Research*. Vol.3.

[3] Social Structure Transformation Research Group of the China Society for Strategy and Management Research.1998. "Middle-short term Tendency and Hidden Troubles of Chinese Social Structure Transformation". *Strategy and Management*. Vol. 5.

[4] Li, Qiang. 1996. "Modernization and Transition of Social Stratification Structure". *Teaching and Research*. Vol. 3; Zhang, Wanli. 2000. "Review on Studies on Social Class and Stratum in China over the Past Twenty Years". *Sociology Research*. Vol. 1.

pattern of exercising ownership right and managerial authority, converting the resource allocation mechanism from the planned system to the free-market system, and altering the economic systems from the closed state to opening up to the outside world. All these reforms can be regarded as "marketization". "Modernization" is the substantive driving force of the pro-high-level trend in Chinese occupational structure, because if there is no industrialization, then the emergence of the occupation of assemblers is impossible. "Marketization" is the determinant of the process of modernization in China and the driving force of changes in occupational structure. China advanced its industrialization in the form of planned economy and public ownership from the 1950s to the 1970s. After the 1980s, industrialization has been pushed in the form of free-market economy and mixed ownership. The latter form not only brings a higher speed to industrialization, but also boosts development of the services industry and adjustment of occupations related to agriculture more rapidly.

To sum up, it is the combined force of modernization and marketization that have driven the incremental pro-high-level trend in occupational structure in China. Consequently, these changes have provided more and more opportunities of upward mobility for social members, which not only have improved individuals' benefits and promoted social development, but also have enabled Chinese society to maintain a basic stable state in the entire period of transformation.

THE PRO-HIGH-LEVEL TREND DRIVEN BY MODERNIZATION FACTORS

Economic Development

(1) Positive Relationship between Increment of Economic Growth and Increment of Occupational Positions

Changes in the total number of occupational positions in China are largely the results of economic growth. According to statistics, occupational positions have been increasing sharply in China since the 1950s. The total number of job positions was 207,290 thousand in 1952, and increased to 711,500 thousand in 2000, up by 2.4 times. Analyzing from the perspective of time sequence, the tendency of the growth rate of urban occupational positions was consistent with the tendency of the GDP growth rate, except that the change of the former was about two years behind the latter. According to the temporal order principle to determine causality, the "time-delay" relation between the two curves may indicate that the growth of GDP is an important driving force of the increase in urban occupational positions (see Figure 3-8). We named this phenomenon the "incremental effect of GDP on occupational position".

The ratio of the growth rate of occupational positions to the growth rate of GDP is called *elasticity of employment*. It reflects the capability that economic growth can lead to an increase in occupational positions. The bigger the elasticity, the stronger is the capability of a socio-economic system producing occupational positions. The elasticity of employment that was calculated according to the two-years-lag relationship (see Table 3-2) shows that the average coefficient since 1981 is 0.419. This means that, over the past years, every one percent of growth in GDP led to an average increase of 0.419 percent in occupational positions.

Figure 3-8   Annual Growth Rates of GDP and Urban-Rural Employment

Source: Calculated according to data in *China Statistical Yearbook (2001)*. For convenience of observation, we deleted several extreme figures.

Table 3-2   Elasticity of Employment Calculated According to the Time-Lag Relationship

Year	Growth Rate of Urban Employment	Year	Growth Rate of Urban Employment
1981	0.459	1991	0.163
1982	0.224	1992	0.127
1983	0.207	1993	0.190
1984	0.465	1994	0.490
1985	0.405	1995	0.420
1986	0.337	1996	0.488
1987	0.901	1997	0.282
1988	0.917	1998	0.287
1989	0.098	Average	0.419
1990	1.087		

Source: Past years' *China Statistical Yearbook*.

(2) Incremental Effect of Economic Development on Middle-High Level Occupations

The development of the economy not only directly impels the increase of occupational positions, but also promotes the upgrade of middle-high level occupations. Measuring the level of economic development and labor productivity by per capita GDP, we find that some relationships exist between the level of economic development, labor productivity, and occupational structure. The higher the per capita GDP of a province, the higher proportions of its managerial personnel, professional and technical personnel, clerks, commercial and service personnel, and workers will be. Conversely, the lower the per capita GDP of a province, the higher the proportion of agricultural laborers, and the lower proportions of the previously mentioned occupations will be (see Table 3-3).

Table 3-3   Per Capita GDP of Provinces and Proportions of Occupations

Units: Yuan RMB, %

Per capita GDP	State and social administrators	Managerial personnel	Professional & technical personnel	Clerical personnel	Commercial and service personnel	Workers	Agricultural laborers	Others
< 5,000	0.6	0.6	4.9	2.3	6.9	9.2	75.5	0.1
5,000~7,500	0.8	0.8	6.2	3.2	9.2	12.1	67.7	0.1
7,500~10,000	0.8	1.1	5.9	3.2	8.4	14.6	66.0	0.1
10,000~12,500	0.9	1.6	6.7	3.5	12.3	24.1	50.9	0.0
> 12,500	0.8	2.7	10.9	7.7	18.6	34.1	25.2	0.1

Sources: *China Statistical Yearbook* (2001), *Population Census of China* (2000).

Figure 3-9 shows that, when per capita GDP of a province increases, proportions of managerial personnel, professional and technical personnel, and clerical personnel in the occupational structure tend to rise. Furthermore, there are no intersections between the three curves. This means that, at various levels of per capita GDP, the proportion of professional and technical personnel is always higher than that of clerical personnel, and the proportion of clerical personnel is always higher than that of managerial personnel. It is a reflection of reality to some extent; that is, the number of top management in various organizations will never be more than the number of ordinary clerks.

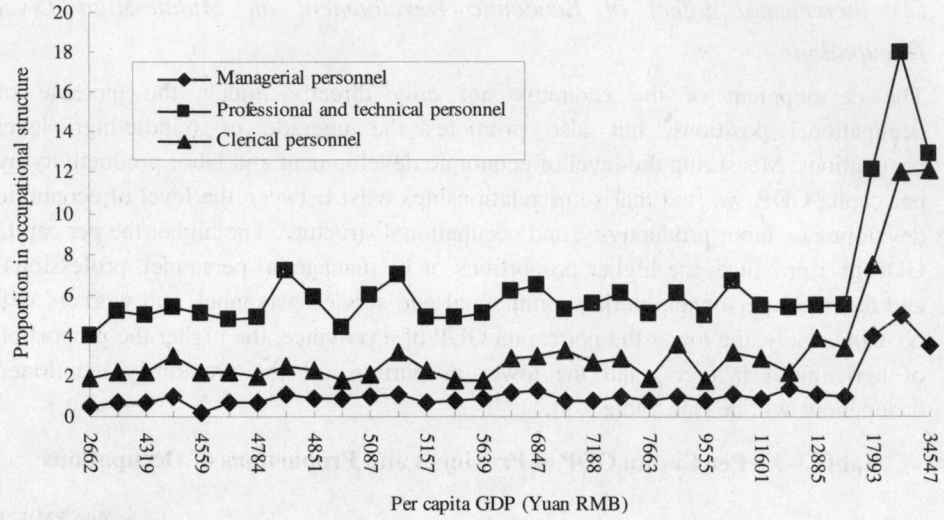

Figure 3-9 Per Capita GDP by Province and Proportions of Three Categories of Occupations

Sources: *China Statistical Yearbook* (2001), *Population Census of China* (2000).

Growth of Household Consumption

Consumption of households, which are ultimate recipients of various occupational activities, is a fundamental condition for creation and pro-high-level shift of occupations. When incomes increase, the *Engle Coefficient* descends, and the amount and proportion of non-basic consumption grow, commodities bought by people will become more and more "advanced". The "pro-high-level" tendency of the consumption of consumer goods results in growth of high-level occupations that produce "advanced" products. In addition, growth of income also indicates an increase of opportunity cost. People choose to enter into professional occupations to earn higher incomes, and these choices consequently provide job positions for people engaged in domestic service occupations such as housekeepers, babysitters, hourly workers, day workers, nurses for the aged, and infants' nurses, etc. Higher income will also elicit more demands on services and bring about the emergence of relevant occupations such as photographers, clinical psychologists, fitness coaches, ikebana and bonsai tutors, and pet feeder to name a few.

After analyzing the relationship between past years' *Engle coefficients* of rural households and that of urban households in China and proportions of various sectors, we find that, with the decline of *Engle Coefficient*, the proportion of the wholesale and retail trade industry and foodservice industry increased gradually, so did the proportion of the social services industry (see Figure 3-10). This indicates the positive

144

influence of the *Engle Coefficient* on specific industries and occupations.

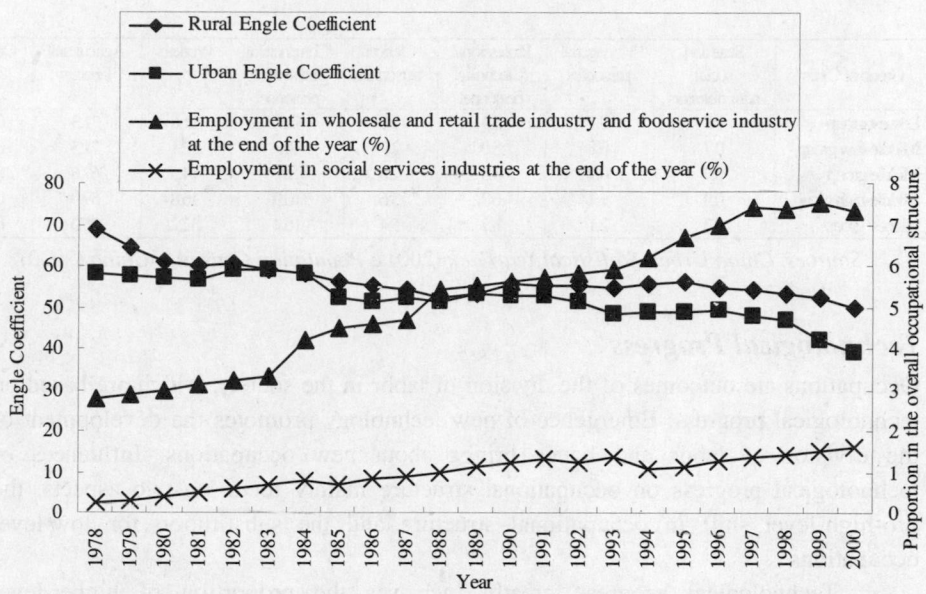

Figure 3-10   Engle Coefficients and Proportions of Two Industries, 1978~2000

Source: Past years' *China Statistical Yearbook*.

Results of lateral comparison show that there is a significant relationship between the level of household income and characteristics of occupational structure. In cities with the highest average wage, proportions of managerial personnel, commercial and service personnel, and workers are the highest. When the level of average wage declines, proportions of these occupations decrease as well. Proportions of other occupations, such as professional and technical personnel and clerical personnel, also show an increasing tendency with the rise of average wage level, but the difference between proportions of occupations, which are affected by differences of wage levels, is relatively smaller (see Table 3-4). That is to say, creation of occupations such as professional and technical personnel requires a higher increment of income. The growth of household income based on the current relatively lower level will favor the increase of proportions of managerial personnel, commercial and service personnel, and workers. Only when household income reaches a higher level can consumption on knowledge-intensive and technology-intensive products be activated, and hence result in an increase of the professional and technical personnel's proportion.

145

Table 3-4   Cities by the Level of Average Wage and Characteristics of Occupational Structure

Unit: %

Group of Cities	State and social administrators	Managerial personnel	Professional & technical personnel	Clerical personnel	Commercial and service personnel	Workers	Agricultural laborers	Others
Lowest group	0.8	0.7	5.4	2.6	7.5	11.6	71.3	0.2
Middle-low group	0.7	0.8	5.0	2.7	7.1	12.1	71.5	0.1
Middle group	0.7	0.9	5.3	2.6	8.5	14.3	67.6	0.1
Middle-high group	0.9	1.1	6.7	3.6	10.9	16.8	59.9	0.2
Highest group	0.7	2.1	8.2	5.4	16.4	32.2	35.0	0.1

Sources: *China Urban Statistical Yearbook* (2001); *Population Census of China* (2000).

Technological Progress

Occupations are outcomes of the division of labor in the society, which are based on technological progress. Emergence of new technology promotes the development of the division of labor and hence brings about new occupations. Influences of technological progress on occupational structure mainly focus on two aspects: the pro-high-level shift in occupational structure and the substitution for low-level occupations.

Technological progress greatly increases the proportion of higher-level occupations while eliminating many low-level occupations. For example, the development of robot technology brought many professional and technical occupations into existence, such as robot technology developing, designing, producing, operating, maintaining, and managing, etc. Robot technology superseded many lower-level occupations while produced many middle-high level occupations. This is the foremost mechanism of the pro-high-level shift in occupational structure.

In addition, technological progress promotes the emergence of new occupations within a sector. Development of these emerging occupations has a sort of chain effect. First, for example, the development of computer technology has created professionals taking up computer research and development and personnel engaging in computer production and sales. Then, it has driven the emergence of professionals who were related to technical support and maintenance and system administration in various industries.

Technological progress not only brings about engineering and technical occupations in specific technological fields, but also fosters other types of occupations through the process of "concomitancy" or "matching". First, technological progress leads to the growth of occupations in relevant fields. For example, robot manufacturing requires professionals in electricity, optics, mechanics, material, software, automation, bionics, and linguistics, etc. Second, it leads to the growth of technical support personnel such as laboratory assistants, cartographers, librarians, information retrieval assistants, laboratory animal feeders, and so on. Third, it results in an increase of professionals like budgeters, accountants, and counselors, etc. Fourth, it requires more clerical personnel because of a large amount of coordinating and collaborative activities such as secretaries, executive assistants, personnel assistants, etc. Fifth, because the size of technology-intensive organizations is usually small and their organizational structure tends to be flat, the process of growth in a number of such organizations requires more managerial personnel.

A report released by European Union shows that, from 1994 to 1996, positions of managers and professionals and technicians with certain special skills increased significantly with an average growth rate of 3 percent per year. In contrast, occupations that require fewer skills such as ordinary clerks, salespersons, and unskilled operators, decreased gradually.[1] For example, Shanghai Bao Steel Group Corporation introduced a technological system of production from a foreign country in the 1990s. Although the capacity of this new system was similar to that of Anshan Iron & Steel Group Corporation, which had a production technological system developed in the 1950s, the number of job positions in the latter was 20 times more than that of the former. The reason of this phenomenon is that newly increased middle-high positions in Bao Steel Group Corporation substituted a large amount of low-level positions.[2]

Technological progress is a strong driving force behind the pro-high-level trend in occupational structure in China. The number of professional and technical personnel in China increased by 43 percent from 1982 to 2000, a net growth of 11,490 thousand. In particular, the increments of teachers, business and financial personnel, and engineering, agricultural, and forestry technicians were the highest, which were 3,650 thousand, 3,580 thousand, and 2,500 thousand respectively. The growth rates of aircraft and ship technicians, lawyers, and engineering, agricultural and forestry technicians were the highest, respectively were 166.7 percent, 166.7 percent, and 85.9 percent. In contrast, the increments and growth rates of people working in entertainment, sports, and cultural industries were relatively lower.

Industrialization and Upgrade of Industrial Structure

(1) Relationship of Level Correspondence between Industrial Structure and Occupational Structure

Characteristics and evolution of occupational structure are determined by characteristics and the evolution of industrial structure. Different industries employ different methods to produce different products with different technologies and operation modes, and accordingly develop different requirements for occupations. A basic characteristic of the two structures is the corresponding relationship between the

[1] Yuan, Zhigang. 2000. "Knowledge-Based Economy and Changes in Employment: Reviews on Studies in Developed Market Economy Countries". *World Economic Forum*. Vol. 4.
[2] Qi, Jianguo. 2000. "Year of 2000: The Biggest Threat against China Economy is the Rapidly Declining Employment Elasticity". *The Journal of World Economy*. Vol. 3.

level of industry and the level of occupation. Higher-level industries have a higher proportion of middle-high level occupations. In contrast, a higher proportion of lower-level occupations exist in lower-level industries. According to the 2000 population census of China, the primary industry had the highest proportion of agricultural laborers, the secondary industry had the highest proportion of workers, and the tertiary industry had the highest proportion of commercial and service personnel, professional and technical personnel, and clerical personnel. The proportions of managerial personnel and workers in the tertiary industry were lower than that in the secondary industry, while higher than that in the primary industry. In addition, state and social administrators were concentrated in the tertiary industry (see Table 3-5).

Table 3-5   Occupational Structure in Three Industries

Unit: %

Category	State and social administrators	Managerial personnel	Professional & technical personnel	Clerical personnel	Commercial and service personnel	Workers	Agricultural laborers	Others
The primary industry	0.0	0.0	0.1	0.0	0.1	0.1	99.7	0.0
The secondary industry	0.2	3.0	6.2	4.8	7.8	76.7	1.2	0.2
The tertiary industry	3.3	2.5	24.1	11.6	41.6	15.3	1.6	0.1

Source: Population Census of China (2000).

There are four subcategories within the tertiary industry. The first subcategory is the circulation sector including transportation, storage, wholesale and retail trade, and restaurants, etc. The second subcategory is the sector of production and consumption service which provides services for production and consumer consumption including finance, insurance, geological survey, water conservancy management, real estates, service for residents, service for agriculture, forestry, animal husbandry, fishing, subsidiary services for transportation and communications, and comprehensive technical services, etc. The third subcategory is the educational and cultural service sector which provides services for improving science, culture, and qualities of nationals, including education culture and arts, radio, film, and television, health, sports, and social welfare, and scientific research, etc. The fourth subcategory is the public service sector, which provides services for public needs including government agencies, political parties, social organizations, and military and police service. A relationship of level correspondence exists between the four industries and occupational structure as well. The public service sector has the highest proportion of state and social administrators and a relatively high proportion of professional and technical personnel. The educational and cultural service sector has the highest proportion of professional and technical personnel and a certain proportion of clerical personnel, commercial and service personnel, and state and social administrators. The proportions of commercial and service personnel and workers are the highest in the production and consumer service sector (see Table 3-6).

148

Table 3-6   Occupational and Sub-Sector Structure in the Tertiary Industry

Unit: %

Sub-Sectors within the tertiary industry	State and social administrators	Managerial personnel	Professional & technical personnel	Clerical personnel	Commercial and service personnel	Workers	Agricultural laborers	Others
Circulation sector	0.3	3.3	3.9	4.9	65.9	20.7	0.9	0.1
Production and consumer service sector	1.1	3.7	22.8	10.4	39.9	18.6	3.3	0.2
Educational and cultural services sector	3.1	0.4	81.7	5.1	5.4	3.9	0.2	0.1
Public service sector	19.2	0.8	15.9	49.7	3.9	6.7	3.7	0.1

Source: *Population Census of China* (2000).

(2) Relationship of Time Correspondence between Upgrade of Industrial Structure and Pro-High-Level Trend in Occupational Structure

In the free-market economy, the levels of the primary, secondary, and tertiary industry reflect the structural evolution of industries driven by market demands. Just like the above-mentioned mechanism through which technological progress affects the occupational structure, the transition of industrial structure has the same influence on occupational structure. First, the transition of industrial structure creates new occupations. For example, the secondary industry brings out occupations like workers and engineering technicians, and the tertiary industry creates occupations like flight attendants and teachers. Second, upgrade of industrial structure creates more middle-high level occupations in high-level sectors. Third, products of high-level sectors substitute labor in low-level sectors. For example, reaping machines substitute a large number of manual-labor farmers. In addition, the squeeze-out effect and the creation effect of technological progress exist in the upgrade of industrial structure simultaneously. For example, on one hand, the automation technology in the secondary industry not only supplants workers directly, but also squeezes out clerical personnel, professional and technical personnel, and managerial personnel because of the surplus of products caused by increasing productivity. One the other hand, it also creates job positions related to the development and training of automation technology.

After the Second World War, especially since the middle of the 1970s, a trend of "servicization" in economy has emerged in almost all developed countries, i.e., both the absolute number and proportion of occupations in the tertiary industry has been increasing. Scholars like Machlup, Bell, and Alvin Toffler extended the *Clarke Law* and proposed the theory of "*post-industrialization*"; that is, developed countries have been beyond the industrial society and the future direction of economic development is "servicization".[1] Although "post-industrialization" or "servicization" in China has not developed into a "post-industrialized society" yet, this trend is significant. It is the "pro-middle-high level" transition of three industries in China that

---

[1] Machlup, Fritz. 1962. *The Production and Distribution of Knowledge in the United States.* Princeton, N.J.: Princeton University Press.

has resulted in the pro-high-level shift to middle-high level occupations in the occupational structure.

From the beginning of the 1950s to 2000, the proportion of employment in the primary industry to the total employment in three industries dropped in a wave-like manner. From 1952 to 1957, the proportion remained more than 80 percent. It fell dramatically to 58 percent in 1958 and then rose above 80 percent again in 1962. In 1979, it descended again, down to 70 percent, 60 percent in 1989, and 50 percent in 1996, and has leveled off around 50 percent since 1997.

By contrast, the time curve of the proportion of occupations in the secondary industry rose wave upon wave. After a period of steady development at the beginning of the 1950s, it reached its first peak at 26.6 percent in 1958. After then, the proportion dropped sharply and reached a trough in 1963 at 7.65 percent. It rose to 10 percent in 1970 after several years' smooth development. In 1984, it climbed above 20 percent and reached the highest point of 23.7 percent in 1997. The ascending tendency has stopped since then and turned to decline. The proportion decreased to 22.5 percent in 2000.

The time curve of the proportion of occupations in the tertiary industry ascended in a fluctuant way as well. Its level and moving trend in the 1950s were similar to the secondary industry. In 1960, it exceeded the secondary industry and dropped behind the latter in 1970 again. After several years' smooth straight climb, it rose above 10 percent in 1977 and over 20 percent in 1993. In 2000, it reached 27.5 percent. The proportion of the tertiary industry surpassed the secondary industry in 1994 once again (see Figure 3-11).

Usually, expansion of industry size always goes with upgrade of industrial structure. This means that, without any exception, the absolute size of each industry will increase in a linear way with time. First, the upgrade of industrial structure, which is represented by the progressive growth of the proportion of high-level industry, promotes the pro-high-level trend in occupational structure. Second, the expansion of industry boosts the incremental development of occupational structure (see Figure 3-12).

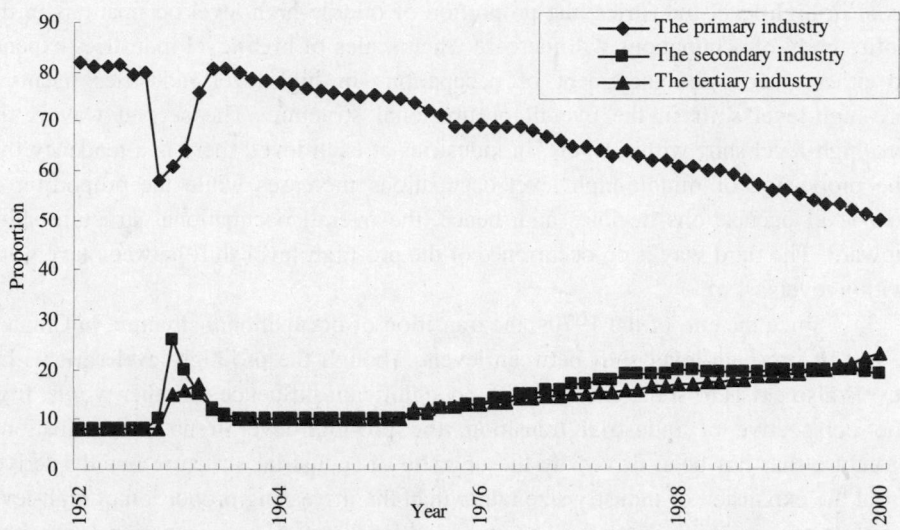

Figure 3-11   Proportions of Three Industries to the Total Employment, 1952~2000

Source: *China Statistical Yearbook* in relevant years.

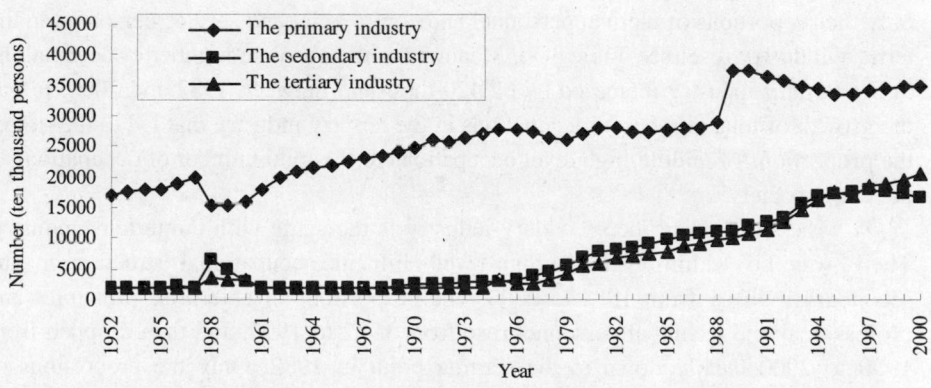

Figure 3-12   Changes of Employment in Three Industries over Time

Source: *China Statistical Yearbook* in relevant years.

(3) Impact of Upgrade of Industrial Structure on Occupational Structure

Upgrade of industrial structure affects the pro-high-level shift in occupational structure in three ways. The first is the pro-high-level shift between levels of industries. Because a relatively higher proportion of middle-high level occupations exist in high-level industries, the proportion of middle-high level occupations in the entire body of occupations will increase when scales of high-level industries expend. In other words, the increment of occupations in high-level industries means a pro-high-level shift in the overall occupational structure. The second way is the pro-high-level shift within levels. In industries at each level, there is a tendency that the proportion of middle-high level occupations increases while the proportion of low-level occupations declines and, hence, the overall occupational structure shifts upward. The third way is co-occurrence of the pro-high-level shift between levels and within levels.

Since the end of the 1970s, the transition of occupational structure in China is a sort of pro-high-level shift between levels. Though the pro-high-level shift within levels also exists to some extent, it has no significant influence. In other words, from the perspective of industrial transition, the pro-high-level trend in occupational structure that has been driven by the upgrade of industrial structure mainly derives from the expansion of industry size rather than the increasing proportion of high-level occupations inside industries. The pro-high-level trend in occupational structure discussed in the first section of this chapter is mainly achieved through the upgrade of industrial structure, whereas the occupational structure inside each industry shows much less trend of pro-high-level shift. One of the supporting proofs of this statement is that almost no pro-high-level shift caused by the increase of high-level occupations' proportion exists in the tertiary industry. From 1982 to 2000, the proportions of high-level occupations in the tertiary industry (such as professional and technical personnel, managerial personnel, and state and social administrators) declined. In fact, only the proportions of clerical personnel and commercial and service personnel in the tertiary industry rose (see Table 3-7). Meanwhile, the absolute number of occupations in the tertiary industry increased by 67,420 thousand between 1982 and 2000. It was the growth of total number of occupations in the tertiary industry that led to the rise of the proportions of middle-high level occupations to the total number of occupations in the entire society.

The situation in the secondary industry is the same with the tertiary industry. There was no within-level pro-high-level shift in occupational structure in the secondary industry from 1982 to 2000. The proportions of enterprise principles and professional and technical personnel rose from 1982 to 1990, and then dropped from 1990 to 2000, nearly down to the starting point in 1982. Only the proportions of middle-level occupations like clerical personnel and commercial personnel increased. In addition, the proportions of workers and service personnel declined. In terms of the number of occupations, enterprise principles, professional and technical personnel, and clerical personnel, all increased to a different extent (970 thousand, 1,620 thousand, and 3,560 thousand respectively). The growth amplitude of the number of worker was the largest (20,960 thousand). Increased numbers of these occupations were sources of the pro-high-level trend in occupational structure.

Table 3-7   Occupational Structure in Three Industries, 1982~2000

Unit: %

Industry	Year	State and social administrators	Enterprise principles	Professional & technical personnel	Clerical personnel	Commercial personnel	Workers	Service personnel	Agricultural laborers	Others
The primary industry	1982	0.0	0.1	0.7	0.1	0.1	0.2	1.5	97.3	0.0
	1990	0.1	0.1	0.3	0.1	0.1	0.1	1.7	95.5	0.0
	2000	0.0	0.0	0.1	0.0	0.1	0.0	0.1	99.7	0.0
The secondary industry	1982	0.7	3.0	6.5	2.2	1.8	5.4	79.1	1.0	0.3
	1990	0.7	3.4	7.9	3.2	3.2	5.1	75.9	0.5	0.2
	2000	0.2	3.0	6.2	4.8	5.1	2.6	76.7	1.2	0.2
The tertiary industry	1982	3.3	5.2	33.5	8.6	14.2	11.6	22.0	1.2	0.3
	1990	3.4	4.5	31.0	9.5	19.5	10.6	19.5	0.4	0.1
	2000	2.3	3.5	24.1	11.6	26.2	15.4	15.3	1.6	0.1

Sources: The 1982 figures are from *China Population Statistical Yearbook (1985)*; the 1990 figures are from *Tabulation on the 1990 Population Census of the People's Republic of China*; the 2000 figures are from the 2000 population census in China.

In contrast, there was a trend of "downward shift' in occupational structure within the primary industry. Proportions of higher-level occupations, such as professional personnel and service personnel decreased except for the increase of the proportion of agricultural laborers. From 1982 to 2000, the total employment in the primary industry increased by 45,690 thousand; however, 53,790 thousand were agricultural laborers and 1,160 thousand were commercial personnel (mainly individual-operated business proprietors). All other occupations declined. Therefore, the net growth of employment (i.e., 45,690 thousand) in the primary industry was the result of counteraction between this increase and decrease. In Western developed countries, the shift of national economy from the primary-industry dominated pattern to the secondary-industry dominated pattern was based on enhanced productivity in the primary industry. However, it was the pull effect caused by widening gap between the primary industry and the secondary and tertiary industry, rather than the squeeze-out effect of enhanced productivity in the primary industry that pushed rural residents in China to move to higher-level industries. In fact, the "downward shift' in occupational structure in the primary industry indicated the pro-high-level trend in the secondary and tertiary industry from another perspective.

Besides the finding that the expansion of size of high-level industries is an important source of pro-high-level trend in occupational structure, we further find that, compared with other countries, in China, the growth rate of high-end industries, which are defined according to the international standard of classification, is relatively slower, and the size of high-end industries is very small. The proportions of occupations in high-end industries in China such as social services and personal services sectors, finance and insurance, real estate, transportation, storage, postal service and communications, commerce, hotels, and tourism, etc., are not only lower than that in developed countries like the United States, Japan, and Germany, but also less than that in some developing countries like Brazil, Burma, and Pakistan. Similarly,

153

the proportions of employment in manufacturing, water, electricity, gas supply, and construction in China are not only lower than that in the United States and Japan, but also lower than that in Thailand, Malaysia, and India, and close to that in Pakistan, Burma, and Brazil. The highest proportions of employment in China are agriculture, forestry, animal husbandry, fishing, and mining and quarrying industries. In particular, the proportion of employment in agriculture, forestry, animal husbandry, and fishing is close to that in Thailand and Pakistan. Such an industrial structure and level of development suggests that China relatively falls behind in the growth of occupations and occupational structure (see Table 3-8). Obviously, the relatively lower level of industrial development in China limits the pro-high-level shift in occupational structure.

Table 3-8   Industrial Structure in China and Other Countries

Unit: %

Country	Year	Total employment (ten thousand persons)	Agriculture, forestry, animal husbandry, & fishing	Mining & quarrying industries	Manu-facturing	Water, electricity, & gas supply	Construc-tion	Commerce, hotels, & tourism	Transpor-tation, storage, & communi-cation	Finance, insurance, & real estate	Social & personal services	Others
China	1999	70586	47.45	0.94	11.49	0.4	4.83	6.73	2.86	0.76	6.02	7.04
U.S.A.	1999	13348.8	2.56	0.42	15.04	1.1	6.73	20.66	6.06	12.03	35.41	—
Japan	1999	6462	5.18	0.09	20.81	0.59	10.17	22.95	6.28	9.27	24.02	0.63
Germany	1999	3640.2	2.82	0.44	23.44	0.85	8.64	17.57	5.37	11.07	29.8	—
India	1989	2596.2	5.5	4.1	24.1	3.5	4.7	1.7	11.7	5.2	39.7	—
Thailand	1999	3208.7	48.51	0.16	13.7	0.49	4.01	14.76	3.08	—	15.25	0.05
Singapore	1999	188.6	0.32	0.05	21	0.48	6.95	21.21	10.82	15.96	23.12	0.11
Malaysia	1999	883.8	18.38	0.43	22.53	0.57	8.18	18.79	4.75	5.27	21.1	—
Pakistan	1997	3418	44.15	0.1	11.1	0.98	6.75	14.62	5.71	0.98	15.58	0.04
Burma	1998	1835.9	62.68	0.66	9.07	0.26	2.18	9.7	2.7	3.25	9.5	—
Brazil	1998	6996.3	23.35	1.23	11.76	—	7.12	13.46	3.98	1.87	37.22	—

Note: Figures about Indian only include the state-owned sector and non-farm entities with 10 or more employees. Manufacturing in Brazil includes water, electricity, and gas supply industries. The figure of commerce, hotels, and tourism in China is actually refers to employment in commerce and foodservices. The figure of social and personal services in China includes the employment in health, sports, social welfare, education, culture and arts, radio, film, and television, scientific research, general technical services, government agencies, political party institutions, and social organizations. Commerce, hotels and tourism in Thailand include finance, insurance, real estate, and industrial services.

Sources: China Statistical Yearbook (2001); International Labor Organization. Yearbook of Labor Statistics (2000).

(4) Bi-Directional Effect of the State-Led Industrialization on Industrial and Occupational Structure

In China, there is a relatively significant deviation between the distribution of occupation in industries and the distribution of GDP in industries. Scholars often use the term "deviation" to indicate the margin between the proportion of constant price GDP and the proportion of occupations in three industries. The closer the two proportions, the smaller the deviation. The GDP proportions of the primary, secondary, and tertiary industry in China respectively were 15.2 percent, 51.1 percent, and 33.6 percent in 2001. The secondary industry accounted for more than one half and the primary industry was less than 20 percent. Compared with the general pattern of industrialization around the world, it means that China has entered the middle stage of industrialization. However, the proportion of occupations in three industries respectively was 50 percent, 22.3 percent, and 27.7 percent. Such a level of occupational structure means that the level of industrialization in China is only at the beginning stage measured by the general pattern.[1] In other words, there is a great unbalance between the industrialization measured by GDP proportion and the one measured by occupational proportion (see Figure 3-13). The change of occupational structure falls behind the change of GDP structure and hence limits the pace of pro-high-level shift in occupational structure.

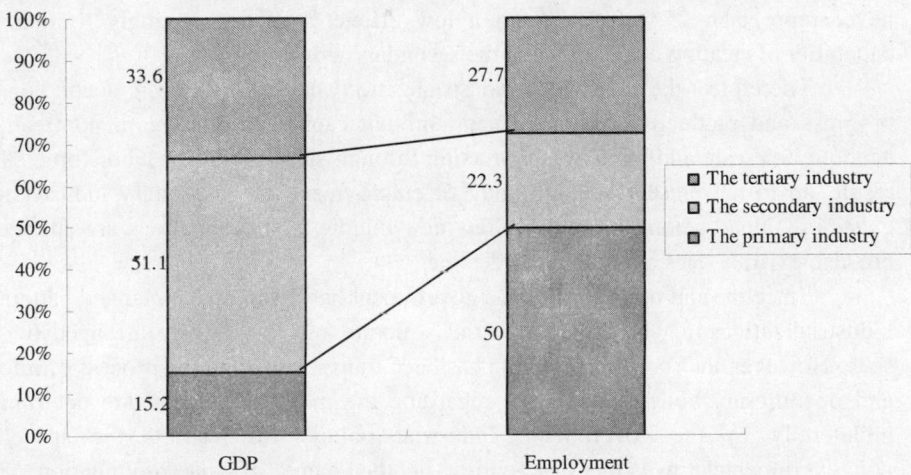

Figure 3-13   Proportions of GDP and Employment in Three Industries, 2001

Source: *China Statistical Yearbook* 2002.

---

[1] Guo, Kesha. 2000. "The Paths, Problems, and Solutions of Industrialization in China". *Social Sciences in China*. Vol. 3.

If there were no such issues, China should have had a higher proportion of middle-high level occupations and provided more opportunities of upward mobility for social members. The state-led industrialization strategy of China is responsible for the emergence of these issues.

China has carried out the state-led industrialization strategy since the 1950s. In order to achieve the "overtaking" development, the government collected capital from the primary industry through the scissors gap between the prices of agricultural products and industrial products, and by restricting the development of the tertiary industry. In order to realize high efficiency in resources allocation, the government directly operated the state-owned and collective sectors of economy. Because internal impetus from producers (enterprises) and nongovernmental investors was lacking, the state-led industrialization had two typical characteristics. First, it mainly relied on the extensive growth mode to realize the expansion of scale while overlooking technological progress and management improvement. Accordingly, the positions of workers outnumbered the middle-high level positions for professional and technical personnel and managerial personnel. Second, the economic efficiency of the industry was pretty low, as well as its capability for self-reproduction, and hence dependent upon external investment to expand the scale of industry at a very low rate. Figure 3-12 shows that, though China has been dedicated to industrialization since the 1950s, the growth rate of occupations in the secondary industry did not speed up until 1970. This growth rate lagged behind that of the tertiary industry in 1994, with a proportion never more than 25 percent. Such a low efficiency correspondingly limited the capability of creating occupations in the secondary industry.

Therefore, the state-led industrialization neither achieved technological progress and productivity enhancement through capital accumulation, nor realized economy of scale and intensive production through substitution for labor force. As a result, up to the present, a huge body of employment in the primary industry still exists in China. Among it, not only few new middle-high occupations are emerging, but also existing ones are tending to decline.

Since the end of the 1970s, the government has given up the planned pattern of industrialization, in which the industrial structure was factitiously arranged by the state. However, the state-led principle has been transplanted into the process of reform and opening-up. Policies and rules regarding the market operation are determined unilaterally by the government. Industrial policy still restricts the space of nongovernmental investment activities in the name of macro-regulation. The government still shows a sort of "fatherhood" preference to intra-system entities, intentionally or unintentionally. All these inclinations bind up non-governmental producers' inherent pursuit of efficiency. As a result, nongovernmental capital prefers industries like foodservice and entertainment that have "immediate returns" rather than manufacturing. Even those who have already entered manufacturing, most of them choose labor-intensive consumer products sectors rather than heavy processing industries, especially the equipment industry which encompasses more technology and can promote the upgrade of technology in consumer goods industries, not to mention long-term investment on technology and modern management in enterprises. All these factors prevent extra-system enterprises from transferring to the technology-intensive stage. As a result, the proportion of middle-high level occupations in China is not only lower than developed countries such as Japan, but also less than developing countries like Malaysia and Philippines (see Table 3-9).

Table 3-9   Occupational Structures in China and Other Countries

Unit: %

Country	Professionals & technicians	Administrative & managerial personnel	Clerks & related workers	Sales personnel	Service personnel	Agricultural, forestry, & fishing personnel	Production workers	Others
China	5.7	1.7	3.1	5.8	3.3	64.5	15.9	0.1
Japan	13.1	3.3	19.7	14.3	10.3	5.1	33.6	0.6
Malaysia	10.6	3.9	11.2	11.2	11.9	18.5	32.7	
Philippines	6.1	2.3	4.5	15.1	10.8	38.8	22.4	0.1

Sources: Figures regarding China are from the 2000 population census in China; figures about other countries are data in 1999.

The Clustering Effect and Spillover Effect of Urbanization

(1) Clustering Effect of City Size on Occupation Creation

Generally speaking, the city is a kind of structural arrangement based on regions to lower the cost of the allocation of production factors. The greater the city's size, the lower the cost of the allocation of production factors. Clustered production factors provide an opportunity to "select the best" for customers and suppliers and to achieve optimal allocation of production factors. In addition, the city can also lower costs of information, communications, transportation, and costs of exchanging tangible and intangible resources between organizations.

Different industries and sectors have different degrees of dependence on urban cluster. Some industries rely on the expansion of urban size to greater extent than the others do. In the current economic system of China, only in cities with a population of more than 2,000 thousand, especially more than 5,000 thousand, the proportion of occupations in the tertiary industry is over 40 percent. Compared with the tertiary industry, the degree of dependence on city size of the secondary industry is relatively lower. The proportions of the secondary industry in cities of various sizes are very close (see Table 3-10). However, the degree of dependence of sectors within the secondary industry has some differences as well. Manufacturing is more likely develop well in cities with a population of more than 2,000 thousand, and its proportion of employment may account for more than 30 percent of all industries. In cities with a population of less than 1,000 thousand, it is more likely that the quarrying industry will flourish. In addition, in cities with a population of less than

2,000 thousand, the proportion of agriculture, forestry, animal husbandry, and fishing is relatively high. In cities with a population of less than 600 thousand, the size of the public service sector is relatively large. In cities with a population of more than 2,000 thousand, the proportion of education, culture and arts, radio, film, and television is the highest. In cities with a population of more than 5,000 thousand, the proportion of scientific research and general technical services sector is the highest. In other words, in the current system in China, scientific research and general technical services sector depends most on city size (see Table 3-11).

Table 3-10   Proportions of Three Industries in Cities with Different Populations

Unit: %

Population of the City	The primary industry	The secondary industry	The tertiary industry	Population of the City	The primary industry	The secondary industry	The tertiary industry
> 5,000 thousand	10.4	44.4	45.2	600~1,000 thousand	20.9	45.4	33.7
2,000~5,000 thousand	13.2	43.7	43.2	300~600 thousand	20.7	43.1	36.3
1,000~2,000 thousand	30.0	37.4	32.7	< 300 thousand	20.9	40.6	38.5

Source: *China Urban Statistical Yearbook (1998)*, the figures are drawn from urban statistics in 1997.

Table 3-11   Proportions of Major Sectors in Cities with Different Populations

Unit: %

Population of the city	Agriculture, forestry, animal husbandry, & fishing	Mining & quarrying industries	Manufacturing	Education, culture and arts, radio, film, & television	Scientific research & general technical services sector	State organs & social organizations
> 5,000 thousand	10.4	1.2	34.5	5.5	2.5	2.7
2,000~5,000 thousand	13.2	1.3	33.4	4.6	1.8	2.7
1,000~2,000 thousand	29.9	3.6	25.5	3.1	0.7	2.2
600~1,000 thousand	20.9	6.7	30.3	3.1	0.5	2.6
300~600 thousand	20.7	6.2	29.3	3.1	0.4	3.1
< 300 thousand	20.9	8.2	24.5	3.2	0.4	4.1

Source: Same as Table 3-10.

Occupations vary differently in degree of dependence on the city as well. As a whole, cities are a more favorable environment than townships and villages for emergence and growth of middle-high occupations. Table 3-12 shows that cities bring higher proportions of managerial personnel, professional and technical personnel, clerical personnel, commercial and service personnel, and industrial workers than townships do. Similarly, townships have higher proportions of above occupations than villages do, whereas villages have the highest proportion of agricultural laborers.

Table 3-12 Occupations in Cities, Townships, and Villages

Unit: %

Category	State and social administrators	Managerial personnel	Professional and technical personnel	Clerical personnel	Commercial and service personnel	Workers	Agricultural laborers	Others
Cities	1.3	3.2	14.1	9.6	23.2	33.9	14.5	0.1
Townships	1.7	1.7	11.4	6.0	19.6	27.3	32.2	0.2
Villages	0.3	0.2	2.1	0.6	3.1	8.4	85.2	0.0

Source: *Population Census of China (2000)*.

(2)Spillover effect of the city on pro-high-level shift of occupational structure in non-urban areas

Various resources congregated in the city may radiate to adjacent non-urban areas and consequently drive the upgrade of industrial structure and the transition of occupational structure in these areas. The rapid rise of township-village enterprises in southern areas of Jiangsu Province in the 1980s largely benefited from this radiation effect from adjacent Shanghai City. Resorting to the means of production and markets spilled over from the city, occupations like managerial personnel, clerical personnel, and workers, etc., emerged in the rural areas (township-village enterprises). This may be called as "spillover effect on occupation" that the city brings to circumjacent rural areas.

The radiation effect of the city depends on the scale of resources being congregated in the city. Only when the city has developed to a sufficient size, can it produce outward radiation that may bring about the spillover effect. After analyzing occupational structures in urban and non-urban areas, we found that only in a city with a population of more than 2,000 thousand would there be a relatively high proportion of the secondary industry in its circumjacent areas. Furthermore, only in a city with a population of more than 5,000 thousand will there be a relatively high proportion of the tertiary industry in its circumjacent areas. In a city with a population of 600 to 2,000 thousand, there will usually be a relatively high proportion of the primary industry (see Table 3-13). A further analysis indicates that a major result of the radiation effect from a city with a population of more than 2,000 thousand is the creation of occupations in the manufacturing sector. In addition, there 'will be a comparatively high proportion of employment in government agencies and social organizations in such a city.

A bigger city can also boost the rate of employment in its adjacent areas as well. In the circumjacent areas of a city with a population of more than 5,000 thousand, the proportion of employment to the whole population is 56.9 percent. In cities with a population of 2,000~5,000 thousand, the proportion is 52.6 percent. The proportion is 55.2 percent in cities with a population of 1,000~2,000 thousand, 51.8 percent in cities with a population of 600~1,000 thousand, 52.1 percent in cities with a

159

population of 300~600 thousand, and 50 percent in cities with a population of less than 300 thousand. As a whole, the employment rate in cities with a population of more than 1,000 thousand is higher than that in cities with a population of less than 1,000 thousand. A city in a bigger size is more likely to diffuse more occupations in its peripheral areas.

Table 3-13   Occupations in Circumjacent Areas of Cities in Different Sizes

Unit: %

Population of the City	The primary industry	The secondary industry	The tertiary industry	Population of the City	The primary industry	The secondary industry	The tertiary industry
> 5,000 thousand	46.0	29.3	24.6	600~1,000 thousand	58.1	20.6	21.3
2,000~5,000 thousand	55.7	24.0	20.3	300~600 thousand	56.1	20.2	23.7
1,000~2,000 thousand	58.4	20.7	21.0	< 300 thousand	56.7	18.2	25.0

Source: *China Statistical Yearbook* 1998.

THE PRO-HIGH-LEVEL TREND DRIVEN BY MARKETIZATION FACTORS

The Reform of the Ownership System

(1) Characteristics of Occupations Shaped by the Ownership System

Economic organizations with different types of property rights have different functions of objectives, root in different policy environments, and have different functional orientations. All these aspects lead to differences in organizational structure and occupational structure.

In public-owned enterprises, more emphasis is laid on the objective of equality. When there is a large labor force in the society and that brings the government under pressure, the government will ask for enterprises to recruit more employees. However, sometimes these new employees only have a lower-level education and are only suitable for positions of first-line production. As a result, enterprises are overloaded with employees, especially production personnel and internal service personnel. In addition, because public-owned enterprises are directly controlled by the government, in order to keep consistent with the structure of government agencies, enterprises have to setup some corresponding positions (especially middle-high level positions) in enterprises, such as cadres who are in charge of affairs concerning the Party, the Youth League, unions, and birth control. As a result, although the proportion of middle-high level positions in enterprises is relatively low, there are still too many positions that have no "necessity of efficiency".

As economic organizations that are invested and managed by private capital, the major objective of non-public-owned enterprises is maximal economic interest. As regard to positions installment (occupational structure) in private enterprises, the number of positions is determined by the marginal benefit of each position, and the structure of positions is determined by comparative benefits and costs of different positions. Because of the development of technology and the complexity of environments and organizations, the marginal benefit of technical personnel and managerial personnel is increasing, while the marginal productivity of workers, especially odd-job workers, is relatively low. Therefore, the proportion of middle-high level positions in such enterprises is comparatively high, while the proportion of workers and internal service personnel is relatively low. The development of non-public enterprises pushed by the reform of property rights is the driving force of the pro-high-level trend of occupational structure in China. It may be called the "effect of the ownership system reform on pro-high-level trend in occupational structure".

Data from relevant surveys support the above analyses. According to the *Third Census of China Industrial Establishments* in 1995, engineering and technical personnel accounted for 7.1 percent in foreign-invested enterprises, 8.3 percent in joint-stock enterprises, 6.9 percent in state-owned enterprises, and 5.5 percent in collective enterprises. With regard to the proportion of managerial personnel, it made up 11.8 percent in joint-stock industrial enterprises, 11.6 percent in foreign-invested enterprises, and 10.6 percent in collective enterprises. Although managerial personnel also made up 11.6 percent in state-owned enterprises, it contained more positions without "necessity of efficiency" than other types of enterprises. In addition, state-owned industrial enterprises had the highest proportion of internal service personnel (10.6 percent) which suggests the overstaffed situation in state-owned enterprises (see Table 3-14).

Table 3-14   Occupations in Industrial Enterprises with Different Types of Ownership

Unit: %

Category	Worker and apprentice	Engineering and technical personnel	Managerial personnel	Service personnel
State-owned industrial enterprise	70.9	6.9	11.6	10.6
Collective industrial enterprise	80.2	5.5	10.6	3.7
Private industrial enterprise	80.1	6.7	10.3	2.9
Jointly-operated industrial enterprise	77.2	6.1	11.4	5.4
Joint-stock industrial enterprise	72.6	8.3	11.8	7.3
Foreign-invested industrial enterprise	77.2	7.1	11.6	4.1
Industrial enterprise invested by entrepreneurs from Hong Kong, Macao and Taiwan	79.6	5.9	10.7	3.8
Other industrial enterprises	70.8	9.9	13.1	6.4

Source: Calculated according to the *Third Census of China Industrial Establishments in 1996* (retrieved from the web site of the National Bureau of Statistics of China)

(2) The Creation and Incremental Effect of the Ownership System Reform on Occupations

A. Creation of New Occupational Categories

The above-mentioned creation of new occupational categories, which include individual-operated business proprietors, private entrepreneurs, and professional managers, is directly related to the reform of ownership system. In addition, other emerging occupations such as start-up entrepreneurs and technical personnel in non-public high-tech enterprises, managerial and technical personnel in foreign-invested enterprises, employees in intermediaries, and the self-employed and free-lance professionals did not exist in the former public ownership system.

B. Growth in the Number of Occupations

Based on the efficiency-oriented allocation of production factors, the non-public sector creates a large number of job positions like workers, commercial and service personnel, professional and technical personnel, and managerial personnel, and consequently promotes the rapid "extra-system" growth of occupational structure. In urban areas, the growth rate of individual economy, which has the largest increment of the number of occupations, closely synchronizes with the progress of the property-right reform. The number of occupations in the individual economy increased from 150 thousand in 1978 to 9,300 thousand in 1992 and 22,590 thousand in 1997.

The development of foreign-invested and Hong Kong, Macao, and Taiwan-funded economy started at the end of the 1970s. Up to the year of 2000, its development can be divided into two periods. Before 1990, it was a period of sluggish development. The number of occupations was 660 thousand in 1990, and then increased to 1,650 thousand in 1991, up by 1.5 times in one year. Since then, it has entered a period of rapid development. The number of occupations reached 6,420 thousand in 2000.

The development of the private sector of economy started at the beginning of the 1980s. It grew slowly before the 1990s and accelerated after 1992. The number of occupations in private enterprises was 680 thousand in 1992 and increased to 1,860 thousand in 1993, up by 1.7 times. Since then, it has entered a period of rapid development. The number reached 12,680 thousand in 2000.

The joint-stock sector of economy includes corporations limited by shares, limited liability companies, and shareholding cooperative companies. Although its emergence was relatively later than other types of economic elements, the number of occupations in joint-stock sector has increased rapidly. There are no statistics available about its development before 1992. The number of occupations in joint-stock sector was 1,640 thousand in 1993 and 12,990 thousand in 2000. Figures about the joint-stock sector in the following table include both the restructured former state-owned and urban collective enterprises and newly founded shareholding entities (see Table 3-15).

162

Table 3-15 Number of Occupations in Entities with Different Types of Ownership

Unit: Ten Thousand

Year	State-owned sector of economy	Collective economy	Jointly-operated economy	Joint-stock economy	Private sector of economy	Foreign and Hong Kong, Macao, and Taiwan-invested economy	Individual economy
1985	8990	3324	38	—	—	—	450
1986	9333	3421	43	—	—	13	483
1987	9654	3488	50	—	—	21	569
1988	9984	3527	63	—	—	31	659
1989	10108	3502	82	—	—	47	648
1990	10346	3549	96	—	57	66	614
1991	10664	3628	49	—	68	165	692
1992	10889	3621	56	—	98	221	740
1993	10920	3393	66	164	186	288	930
1994	11214	3285	52	292	332	406	1225
1995	11261	3147	53	317	485	513	1560
1996	11244	3016	49	363	620	540	1709
1997	11044	2883	43	468	750	581	1919
1998	9058	1963	48	1030	973	587	2259
1999	8572	1712	46	1167	1053	612	2414
2000	8102	1499	42	1299	1268	642	2136

Source: Relevant years' *China Statistical Yearbook*.

Table 3-16 Proportions of Occupations in Entities with Different Types of Ownership

Unit: %

Year	State-owned economy	Collective economy	Jointly-operated economy	Joint-stock sector	Private sector of economy	Foreign and Hong Kong, Macao, and Taiwan-invested economy	Individual economy
1985	70.19	25.95	0.3	—	—	—	3.51
1986	70.21	25.74	0.32	—	—	0.1	3.63
1987	70.04	25.31	0.36	—	—	0.15	4.13
1988	69.98	24.72	0.44	—	—	0.22	4.62
1989	70.24	24.34	0.57	—	—	0.33	4.5
1990	62.27	21.36	0.58	—	0.34	0.4	3.7
1991	62.81	21.37	0.29	—	0.4	0.97	4.08
1992	63.16	21	0.32	—	0.57	1.28	4.29
1993	62.08	19.29	0.38	0.93	1.06	1.64	5.29
1994	60.9	17.84	0.28	1.59	1.8	2.2	6.65
1995	58.98	16.48	0.28	1.66	2.54	2.69	8.17
1996	56.74	15.22	0.25	1.83	3.13	2.73	8.62
1997	54.65	14.27	0.21	2.32	3.71	2.88	9.5
1998	43.81	9.49	0.23	4.98	4.71	2.84	10.92
1999	40.79	8.15	0.22	5.55	5.01	2.91	11.49
2000	38.08	7.05	0.2	6.11	5.96	3.02	10.04

Source: Same as Table 3-15.

C. Substitution of Occupational Positions

Because of lack of efficiency, after breaking away from the government's "fatherhood" protection and entering into market competition, state-owned enterprises become weaker than before in competence of creating new occupations and maintaining existing occupations. As a result, the total number of occupations in state-owned enterprises has been declining after reaching its peak (112,610 thousand) in 1995. The number was 81,020 thousand in 2000, a decrease of 31,590 thousand over the figure in 1995. The efficiency was even lower in urban collective enterprises; consequently, the number of occupations in these enterprises decreased faster and earlier than that in state-owned enterprises. After the property-rights reform in 1997, the number of occupations in collective enterprises fell sharply. Not only the absolute number, but also the proportion of the number of occupations in public sector of economy to the total number of occupations in China declined. Table 3-16 shows that the proportion dropped significantly in two periods. The first period was 1989~1990, down from 70 percent to 62 percent. The second period was 1997~1998, down from 55 percent to 44 percent. In 2000, the figure decreased to 38 percent. The decline of the proportion of occupations in urban collective also occurred in these two periods. It fell from 24 percent in 1989 to 21 percent in 1990 and from 14 percent in 1997 to 9 percent in 1998. In 2000, the figure was 7 percent. The major cause of the rapid decrease of employment in state-owned and urban collective enterprises is the governmental policy of "downsizing for efficiency" in state-owned and urban collective enterprises. In addition, a large number of these enterprises have been restructured into joint-stock, joint-operated, and individually-operated or private enterprises; such a change also plays an important role in the decrease of employment.

In contrast, the proportion of occupations in non-public enterprises has been rising. Such a change indicates the significant substitution effect of occupations in non-public enterprises. Table 3-16 shows that the increase of occupations in individual, private, joint-stock, and foreign-invested and Hong Kong, Macao, and Taiwan-funded sectors of the economy was the most rapid from 1992 to 1993 and from 1997 to 1998. In 2000, the proportion of occupations in the non-public sector of the economy to total urban employment respectively was 10 percent in the individual economy, 6 percent in the private sector, 6 percent in joint-stock sector, and 3 percent in foreign-invested and Hong Kong, Macao, and Taiwan-funded sectors. Such a substitution effect leads to the incremental development of occupational structure and the tide of social mobility of employment flowing from "intra system"to"extra system.

According to a nationwide survey on private enterprise conducted by All-China Federation of Industry and Commerce in 1997, 39 percent of managerial personnel, 33.1 percent of technical personnel, and 11.1 percent of workers in private enterprises came from state-owned and collective enterprises. Calculating based on these proportions, the number of managerial personnel, technical personnel, and workers who came from state-owned and collective enterprises respectively was 214 thousand, 195 thousand, and 962 thousand persons, totaling 1,371 thousand.

According to another survey on laid-off female workers conducted by the Department of Public Administration and Sociology at Sichuan University, the proportions of managerial and technical personnel in private enterprises who came from laid-off groups respectively were 9.6 percent and 3 percent. The proportion of laid-off female workers who were re-employed in private enterprises to the total reemployment was 22.6 percent.[1]

The Arising of Business Managers from the State-Owned Enterprise Reform

After the state-private joint operation reconstruction in 1956, public enterprises were actually operated by the government. Through economic plans and administrative instructions, the central government directly managed and operated some large-size enterprises, while local governments controlled local public enterprises. As a result, the whole country was equal to a huge factory and each enterprise was equal to a workshop of this "national factory". Correspondingly, factory managers were personnel and representatives of the governmental system and responsible for implementing administrative instructions from appropriate authorities. The factory managers were not independent decision-makers and were free from any liability for consequences of decision-making and profits or losses of enterprises.

The government has been carrying out the reform of transforming management mechanisms in public enterprises since 1984. The objectives of this reform are to transform public enterprises into independent economic entities which can make their own management decisions and take full responsibility for their own profits and losses and corporations which can independently enjoy civil rights and assume civil obligations in accordance with the law. A supporting institutional arrangement is the market-oriented allocation of business managers. The separation of ownership right and management authority indicates the separation of managers in public enterprises and the status of "governmental cadres" and professionalization of business managers.

With respect to foreign-invested enterprises in China, especially Euramerican and multinationally invested enterprises, the ownership right and management authority were separated at the very beginning of their establishment and hence created the occupation of professional managers. In local private enterprises, the ownership right and management authority were initially integrated. After the 1990s, with increasingly intensive competition, more and more investors employed professional managers to operate their enterprises. Furthermore, many owners of private enterprises have been begun to transfer their business to the next generation, so obviously more and more professional managers will be employed in the future.

---

[1] Wu, Jun, et al. 2000. "Analysis of the Impact of Private Enterprises on Solving the Layoff Issue". *Journal of Chengdu Institute of Public Administration*. Vol. 1.

Influenced by these factors, the number of professional managers is increasing.

According to the Second National Basic Units Census of China, by the end of 2001 there were 3,026 thousand enterprise institutional units in China, with a net increase of 398 thousand over the figure of the First National Basic Units Census, up by 15.1 percent. By the end of 2001, the total number of establishments with commercial activities in China was 7,088 thousand with a net growth of 737 thousand over the 1996 figure, up by 11.6 percent. Of that, 3,986 thousand were establishments with production-related activities with a net increase of 315 thousand, up by 8.6 percent; 3,102 thousand were establishments with non-production-related activities with a net increase of 422 thousand, up by 15.7 percent. Supposing that each enterprise institutional unit has five managers, the net growth of senior managerial personnel was 1,990 thousand between 1996 and 2001.

Correspondingly, occupations that are related to the independent corporate governance emerged as well. According to the provisions stipulated in the Company Law, all corporations have established stockholder chapter, board of directors, and supervisory committee inside enterprises and hence created positions for chairperson of the board, directors, chairperson of supervisory committee, and supervisors. The number of directors of the board in the limited liability company was about 3 to 13 persons, and 5 to 19 persons in corporations limited by shares. These positions also are results of the creation and growth of high-level occupations and make up a part of the pro-high-level trend in occupational structure.

Market-Oriented Reforms and the Opening-Up Policy

(1) Transaction Related Positions Created by the Transformation from Administration-Led Allocation to Market-Oriented Allocation

The planned economy is a sort of "government-led allocation" economy, while the free-market economy is based on market exchanges. In the planned economy, because the government is in charge of planning, there are a large number of functional departments and personnel in governmental agencies, which leave little space for people engaging in market transactions. In contrast, in a free-market economy, the function of market allocation is fulfilled by various market-oriented entities, which accordingly create a large number of personnel related to market transaction such as salespersons, procurement personnel, and advertising personnel, etc. Therefore, the transformation from the planned economy to a free-market economy leads to adjustments in occupational structure, increases in numbers and proportion of market transaction related occupations, and decreases in planning related occupations. Analyses in the first section of this chapter have shown that the growth rate of commercial personnel was the highest among various categories of occupations, up by 106.8 percent from 1982 to 1990, and 100.4 percent from 1990 to 2000. Its proportion to the total number of occupations increased from 1.8 percent to 3 percent and then 5.8 percent.

The growth of the number and proportion of commercial personnel varies across industries. The growth rate is relatively high in sectors with a high degree of dependence on the market and a high frequency of transaction. In contrast, in sectors with a low degree of dependence on the market and low frequency of transactions, the growth rate is relatively low. The former includes sectors such as trade, foodservice, storage, manufacturing, housing management and resident services, electricity, gas, water supply, transportation, postal service and telecommunication, finance, and insurance, all with a growth rate of more than 300 percent. The latter includes sectors such as geological survey, public census, scientific research, general technical services, health, sports, social work, government and party agencies, and social organizations (see Table 3-17 and Table 3-18).[1]

Adjustments in occupational structure driven by transforming from the planned economy to a free-market economy led to cutting down on positions without "necessity of efficiency". Figures in Table 3-17 and Table 3-18 show that, from 1982 to 2000, the growth rate of the number of service-related occupations was relatively high in labor service industries in which service personnel take on the tasks of production including commerce, foodservice, and storage, transportation, postal service and telecommunications, housing management and resident services, and health, sports, and social work. In contrast, the number of service personnel decreased in non-labor service industries, such as manufacturing, geological survey, public census, scientific research, general technical services, education, culture and arts, construction, government and party agencies, and social organizations.

It was the same for workers. In manufacturing, construction, electricity, gas, and water supply, property management (housing management and residents services), finance and insurance, and transportation and postal service and telecommunications, the absolute number of workers increased as well. However, the proportions of workers in ten industries declined and did not rise in six industries. There were two causes of this phenomenon. The first one is preliminary professionalization and the pro-high-level shift in business management in industries with workers as producers

---

[1] In this study, we adopted figures of the 1982, 1990, and 2000 population census. All figures concerning industrial structure in this chapter are from the three censuses except for data in historical comparisons. According to characteristics of actually available figures, we adopted three different types of industry classifications in this chapter, including the new edition of National Standard Industry Classifications adopted in 2000 population census, the old edition of National Standard Industry Classifications adopted in 1982 and 1990 population censuses, and the International Standard Industry Classification. Because data of 1982 and 1990 censuses are saved on paper media and hard to be processed, we transformed data of 2000 census based on the old edition of classifications. Domestic longitudinal comparisons in this chapter are based on the old edition of classifications, while analyses about industrial structure and occupational structure within industries in 2000 are based on the new edition of classifications and the research group's stratum classification. Cross-national comparisons are based on the International Standard Industry Classification. The old edition of classifications is adopted in historical comparison of occupational structure within industries.

resulted in the rise of the proportion of professional and clerical personnel. The second one is the trend of outsourcing business services in industries in which workers do not make up the majority of producers. The descending tendency of the proportion of workers in government agencies, social organizations, scientific research, and general technical services were driven by the above two forces simultaneously.

Except in agriculture, forestry, animal husbandry, fishing, geological survey, public census, and manufacturing, the proportion of agricultural laborers dropped in other industries. This also shows the trend of cutting down on positions without "necessity of efficiency"; the supply of farm produce to non-agricultural organizations now depends more on market and rather than internal agricultural units.

Table 3-17   Growth Rates of Occupations in Various Sectors, 1982~2000

Unit: %

Industry	State and social adminis-trator	Enterprise managerial personnel	Professional and technical personnel	Clerical personnel	Commercial personnel	Worker	Service personnel	Agricultural laborer	Other
Agriculture, forestry, animal husbandry, & fishing	-15.8	-51.1	-71.5	-2.5	58.8	-87	-91.8	14.4	-33.3
Mining & lumbering	-61.2	-12.1	-23.8	52.5	118.9	-70.3	-14.6	-41.4	100.1
Water, electricity, & gas supply	20	141.3	249.6	523.8	1047	280.3	123.6	52.1	24
Manufacturing	-70.5	35.4	20.1	216.1	293.7	-40	29.5	226.8	-38.2
Geological survey & public census	-25.8	50.2	40	93.1	141.6	-63.2	-40.8	1252	-73.6
Construction	-60.5	97.1	78.5	126.7	370.5	-29.2	66.7	-69.4	-50.6
Transportation & communications	-26.8	1.5	33.9	128	612.8	150.9	73.9	100.6	-42.6
Commerce, foodservice, & storage	-51.6	96.5	19.8	93.4	309.5	230.6	-27	43.1	10.4
Housing management & resident services	130.9	698.6	546.1	1743.8	2009.1	445.6	569.4	67.6	553.2
Health, sports, & social work	35.5	11.4	72.9	293.3	518.5	20.5	97.4	-19.1	-49.5
Education, culture & arts	-17	-23.2	47	197.5	321.5	-29.1	-21.9	-43.9	15.3
Scientific research & general technical services	19.9	46	31.5	168.8	201.4	-23.6	-9.5	-88.3	-31.7
Finance & insurance	53.5	40.5	284.3	716.4	3989.9	38.6	753.2	-100	-55
Government and party agencies & social organizations	28.5	32	42.3	200.2	125.4	-29.3	18.2	-6.7	-68.9

Sources: The figures of 1982 are from *China Population Statistical Yearbook* (1985); the figures of 2000 are from *Major Figures of Population Census of China in 2000*.

Table 3-18　Proportions of Occupations in Various Industries, 1982~2000

Unit: %

Industry	State & social adminis- trator	Enterprise managerial personnel	Professional & technical personnel	Clerical personnel	Commercial personnel	Worker	Service personnel	Agricul- tural laborer	Other
Agriculture, forestry, animal husbandry, & fishing	0	-0.06	-0.53	-0.01	0.02	-0.16	-1.43	2.17	0
Mining and lumbering	-0.44	0.19	-0.56	2.64	1.53	-4.74	2.44	-1.39	0.32
Water, electricity, & gas supply	-0.56	-0.6	2.72	5.94	3.51	2.79	-13.06	-0.51	-0.24
Manufacturing	-0.48	0.01	-0.68	2.77	4	-3.02	-3.13	0.73	-0.2
Geological survey, public census	-0.31	1.65	6.33	4.78	1.5	-5.21	-25.5	17.1	-0.35
Construction	-0.46	0.4	0.52	0.81	1.19	-2.12	0.32	-0.44	-0.22
Transportation & communications	-0.44	-1.49	-1.85	2	2.21	3.25	-3.72	0.22	-0.17
Commerce, foodservice, & storage	-0.49	-1.9	-4.95	-1.39	20.08	2.14	-13.06	-0.33	0.12
Housing management & resident services	-0.34	0.72	-0.02	6.6	3.94	-9.16	0.73	-2.46	0
Health, sports, & social work	-0.1	-1.31	0.31	2.62	1.12	-2.77	0.58	-0.27	-0.17
Education, culture & arts	-0.2	-2.71	5.36	2.7	0.66	-3.12	-2.43	-0.25	-0.02
Scientific research & general technical services	0.02	1.27	5.38	7.17	1.5	-1.72	-6.21	-7.05	-0.36
Finance & insurance	-0.49	-9.99	1.92	6.9	1.68	-1.82	2.23	-0.05	-0.38
Government and party agencies & social organizations	-5.54	-1.21	-4.83	21.06	0.45	-3.63	-4.07	-0.59	-0.4
Other	32.3	-0.55	1.31	5.36	-0.62	-9.73	-33.6	6.4	-0.87

Sources: The 1982 figures are from *China Population Statistical Yearbook* (1985); the 2000 figures are from *Major Figures of Population Census of China in 2000*.

(2) Demand-Related Positions Created by the Transformation from State-Planned Distribution to Selling on the Market

In the process of transformation from the planned economy to a free-market economy, occupations grew in industries with increasing market demands, especially in those which are indispensable components of the market but underdeveloped in the planned system. In contrast, the number of occupations decreased in industries without sufficient market demands especially those had survived in the planned system but could not adapt in a free-market economy (see Table 3-17, Figure 3-14, Figure 3-15, Figure 3-16).

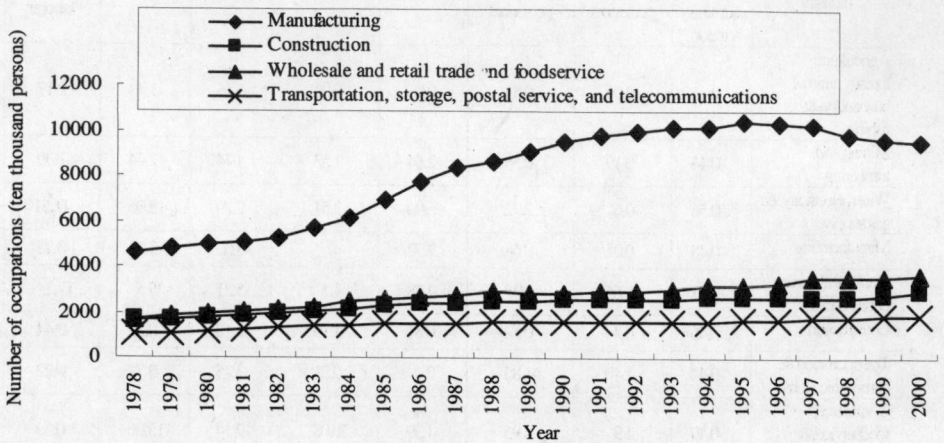

Figure 3-14   Occupations in Four Largest Non-Agricultural Sectors,
1978~2000

Source: Relevant years' *China Statistical Yearbook.*

The number of occupations in manufacturing kept increasing from 1978 to 1988 because of a strong market demand for its products. After reaching its first peak in 1988, the number declined due to the restricting policy imposed on extra-system enterprises by the government in order to protect inefficient public-owned enterprises in market competition. However, because of increasing market demand for products of the manufacturing sector, the government soon ended the restricting policy and formally introduced the free market system in 1992. The number of occupations in this sector increased again for development of extra-system enterprises. Nonetheless, it fell down again after 1995 because many state-owned enterprises were excluded from the market for inefficiency and declining market demands.

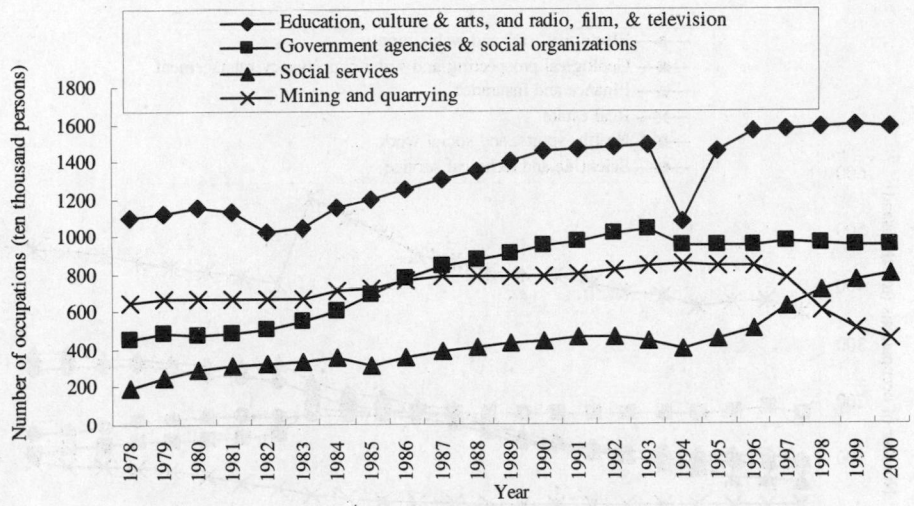

Figure 3-15   Occupations in Four Middle-Size Non-Agricultural Sectors, 1978~2000

Source: Relevant years' *China Statistical Yearbook*.

The number of occupations in the construction sector was the highest in 2000. The net increase of occupations, the increase of the occupational proportion, and the growth rate of occupations in the construction sector have been the highest since 1978. The cause of such rapid development is due to strong market demands and high efficiency. The demand for construction is composed of several different sources: investment from the government aiming to make up the insufficient housing investment of the planned system, buildings constructed in the period of the planned economy which did not meet demands of the market both in categories and numbers, emerging private-invested infrastructure construction after the property-rights reform, reconstruction of suburban and urban housings in the progress of urbanization, strong demands for housings solicited by the housing system reform and increasing household income, competition among different regions in attracting investments to construct development zones, and the increase in capital construction invested by the government in order to stimulate domestic demand. The high efficiency of the construction sector largely comes from employing cheap rural laborers on a large scale. Similarly, the number of occupations in the real estate sector has risen straight at an extremely high rate. The rapid development of real estate is driven by high profits gained in its early stage.

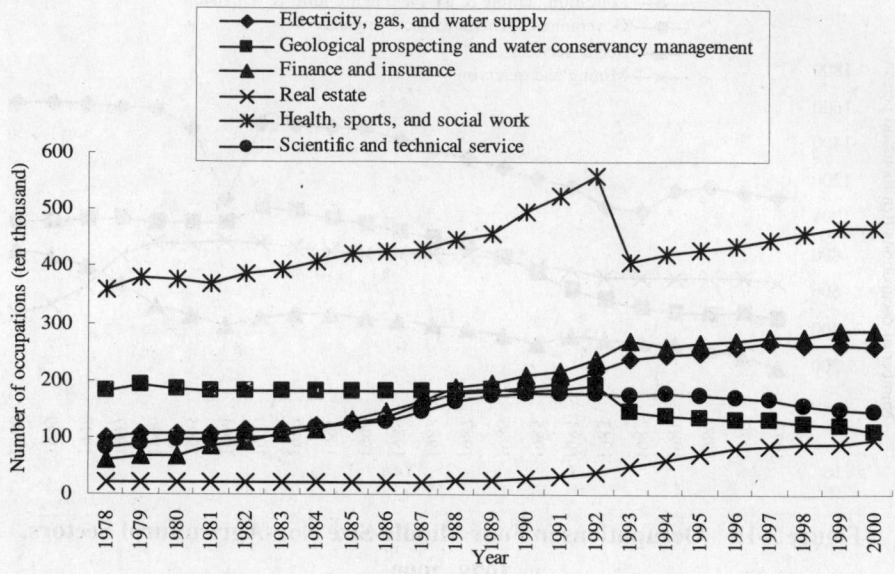

Figure 3-16   Occupations in Six Smallest Non-Agricultural Sectors, 1978~2000

Source: Relevant years' *China Statistical Yearbook*.

The wholesale and retail trade and foodservice sectors also had large numbers of occupations in 2000. These sectors have the largest net increase of numbers of occupations, the largest increase of occupational proportions, and the highest growth rate of occupations since 1978. The rapid development of occupations in these sectors is closely related to the formation of the market. The chief task of marketization is to rebuild markets and hence lead to rapidly development of trade related sectors. In addition, the reform of property rights, which first carried out in commodity circulation fields, attracted a large amount of private investment, and thus promoted the growth of occupations in these sectors.

The sectors of transportation, storage, postal service and telecommunication were also the sectors, which had the largest number of occupations in 2000 and have the highest net increase and growth rate of occupations since 1978. Such development has been driven by expanding and accelerating flows of materials, trade related personnel, labor force, and information. In addition, increasing distances of commuting traffic caused by urbanization and expansion of urban areas and growing numbers of exported and imported goods and tourists lead to greater demands in these sectors.

In sectors like education, culture and arts, radio, film, television, health, sports, social work, government and party agencies, and social organizations, the time curves of changes in the number of occupations are similar; all these curves increased straight in their early stages, but declined after reaching a certain peak, and then rose again gradually. There are two major causes of such changes. First, though market-oriented reforms in these sectors were behind other sectors and a large number of traces of the planned economy retained, they had to adjust themselves according to market demands under the pressure of competition. Second, as elements of the social system, these sectors had to adjust themselves to adapt new situations after some relevant sectors had been marketized. For example, in some culture and arts institutions operated in quasi-market-oriented modes, functional departments and personnel that were lacking the capability of producing profits were cut down or laid off. Because of financial problems in rural schools, low entrance rate caused by expensive tuition fees, and the decrease of school-age children in urban areas, many schools were cut down or merged. Former government agencies that were in charge of the economy or enterprises were removed; technical schools shrank for lack of sufficient number of students caused by marketization of the labor force. However, with the progress of marketization, demands for these sectors became increasingly strong, and accordingly the number of occupations in these sectors rose again after initial structural adjustments. For example, the number of occupations in functional departments related to market regulation in government agencies increased; social service related occupations in government agencies also grew after the reform of social security system. In addition, occupations that are related to new office technologies increased rapidly as well (for example, office automation and the "electronic-government" project lead to growing demands for computer and network engineers).

The number of occupations in the social service sector increased sharply. It was driven by an increase in productivity and household income brought by marketization and growing demands for social services, including public traffic, environmental sanitation, hairdressing, washing and dyeing, photographing, developing and printing, tourism, entertainment, advertisement, technical consulting, and data processing.

The number of occupations in finance and insurance grew straight at a highest growth rate from 1978 to 2000. The foremost condition for development of finance was expanding amount and accelerated speed of the capital flow in markets. The expansion of business scope in financial organizations and their advantage of monopoly in markets led to an increase of occupations in the finance sector. Growth of occupations in the insurance sector was related to the transformation of the social security system.

The continuous increase in the number of occupations in electricity, gas, and water supply since 1978 is largely due to their monopoly nature and the low level of marketization of this sector. In addition, the demand for energy sources brought by economic development has promoted the sale of products in this sector.

In contrast, the number of occupations in geological survey and water conservancy management declined after 1988 due to insufficient market demand.

Initially, programs of geological survey were assigned by the government, however, the governmental demands decreased significantly after the market-oriented reforms. The number of occupations related to mining and quarrying declined gradually between 1993 and 1995 due to saturation of market demands, low efficiency, and substitution of other energy sources or imported products with lower price and higher quality.

The number of occupations in agriculture, forestry, animal husbandry, and fishing has started to descend gradually since 1992. It was in that year when China formally declared to introduce the free-market economy. Agriculture in China is operated by households with outmoded technologies and equipment, and hence its productivity is relatively low. Meanwhile, slow progress of urbanization and the low level of urbanization in China have led to insufficient market demands for agricultural produce. Therefore, employment in this sector has decreased with the progress of marketization. However, such a decrease has been limited by the dual urban-rural system, especially the residence registration system, or it would have fallen to a greater extent and at a higher rate.

(3) Increment of Occupations and Substitution for External Occupations Caused by the Opening-Up

In the economic arena of China, the opening-up policy means introducing foreign investment and expanding export. Initially, the two measures did not aim to create occupations. However, they have brought about unintentional influences on the pro-high-level trend in occupational structure caused by the increment of occupations.

Foreign investment has directly created various occupations at all levels. According to calculation, every one percent of increase in foreign investment leads to an increase of 0.09 percent in the number of occupations in China.[1] In terms of the primary, secondary, and tertiary industry, every one percent of the increase in contracted foreign investment results in a decrease of 0.00537 percent in employment in the primary industry, an increase of 0.04269 percent in the secondary industry, and 0.138872 percent increase in the tertiary industry.[2]

Exporting is to sell products abroad. It can also create occupations when the domestic demands are insufficient and hence the growth of export is equal to the increase of occupations. According to calculation, every one percent of increase in export will lead to an increase of 0.1 percent in the number of occupations.[3] Another study shows that the elasticity of the total number of job positions to the export of current period is about 0.035, i.e., every one percent of increase in export will lead to

[1] Chen, Limin. 2002. "Capital Flow and Its Impact on Employment in China". Chengdu, Sichuan: *Reform of Economic System*. Vol. 5.

[2] Cao, Xiaoyan. 2003. "Quantitative Analysis of Impact of Foreign Direct Investment on Employment of the Labor Force in China". Beijing: *Statistical Education*. Vol. 5.

[3] Yu, Huixin, et al. 2002. "Influences of Trade Liberalization in China on Employment in Industry". Beijing: *The Journal of World Economy*. Vol. 10.

an increase of 0.035 percent in the number of job positions. Export from China increased by 2.5 times in the 1990s. Accordingly, the growth of export led to an increase of 8.7 percent in the number of occupations in China during that period. In other words, it directly or indirectly created more than 50,000 thousand job positions, making up about 80 percent of the newly created job positions in China in the 1990s.[1]

In sum, the reform and opening-up since 1978 have pushed the modernization-oriented and marketization-oriented "dual transformation" in China. In this process, rapid economic development and institutional innovations have led to significant adjustments in the industrial structure and corresponding great changes in occupational structure. On one hand, the absolute number of occupational positions has increased sharply. On the other hand, the growth rate of low-level occupations has slowed down, while the growth rate of middle-high level occupations has been increasing. Changes in the two aspects have resulted in a rise of occupational ranks over the past twenty-five years and hence a trend of pro-high-level shift in occupational structure. Such a structural transition has provided space of social mobility for social members.

---

[1] Gao, Weiyu. 2002. "Quantitative Analysis of Impact of Export on Employment in China". Shanghai: *Shanghai Statistics*. Vol. 2.

Chapter 4   Origins and Mobility Paths of Ten Major Social Strata

Chapters 2 and 3 have systematically described transitions of the social and political system, the adjustments of governmental policies, the progress of industrialization, and the changes of economic structure since 1949 as well as their influences on social mobility in China. It is in this background of social, political, and economic change that social mobility in China has occurred. Over the past five decades, China has experienced five significant transitions in society, politics, and economy, three of which affected social mobility profoundly. The first significant social transition is the establishment of the new regime by the Chinese Communist Part in 1949, in which the former social structure was thoroughly reconstructed, bourgeois and the landed class were eliminated and the social, political, and economic status of workers and peasants were greatly improved. The second significant social transition is the Culture Revelation between the 1960s and the 1970s, in which a large number of intellectuals and cadres were persecuted while many ordinary workers and peasants became new political nobility in revolting campaigns. The third significant transition is the economic reform starting at the end of the 1970s, in which a new-rich stratum has been fostered by the rehabilitation of private property rights and development of a free-market economy. Consequently, a large number of political and cultural elite has emerged, and the social status of workers and peasants have been descending notably. All these transitions led to enormous tides of social mobility, changes in social structure, and two very different patterns of social mobility before and after the economic reform. In this chapter, we will analyze transitions of social mobility patterns in China over the past fifty years based on intergenerational and intragenerational mobility tables in the framework of ten major social strata in China. In addition, we will describe the developing processes of ten major social strata and their prospects. We will also explore the rules and degree of structuralization of social stratification by identifying the paths and boundaries of the barriers of social mobility.

The *intergenerational mobility table* is used to investigate changes of occupational status or the position of class (stratum) between generations by conjointly analyzing the occupational status of father and children. The *intragenerational mobility table* is used to investigate changes of an individual's occupational status or position of class (stratum) by conjointly analyzing the stratum status of one's first occupation and current occupation. Based on analyses of mobility tables, researchers can calculate the intergenerational and intragenerational total mobility rate (rate of total mobility) , upward mobility rate   (it reveals how many social members move from a lower stratum up to a higher stratum), and downward mobility rate (it reveals how many social member move from a higher stratum down to a lower stratum) . In addition, mobility tables can also indicate which strata have more opportunities of upward mobility, which strata have very few upward mobility opportunities, and which strata tend to be immobile, or even move downward.

Based on data of the nationwide survey conducted by the research group, in this chapter we will calculate and compare intergenerational and intragenerational mobility tables in different periods, including tables of conjoint analysis of a respondent's occupation and his or her father's occupation (intergenerational mobility table), tables of conjoint analysis of a respondent's first occupation and his or her current occupation (intragenerational mobility table of the first occupation and the current occupation), and changes of occupational status caused by a respondent's last occupation shift (intragenerational mobility table of current occupation and the previous occupation).[1] On the basis of these tables, we will analyze the origins, mobility opportunities, and paths of each stratum respectively, and describe the developing processes and characteristics of the ten social strata and the social distance between each stratum. Moreover, through comparisons of total mobility rates and mobility patterns in different periods, we will summarize the rules of transition of social mobility patterns in China over the past five decades. Especially, we will present our judgments on the future trend of social stratification in current China based on comparisons of differences between before and after the economic reform.

MOBILITY CHARACTERISTICS OF THE STRATA WITH ADVANTAGED STATUS

The stratum of state and social administrators is the top end of the social mobility ladder in China. They are in control of a large amount of organizational resources and have strong intergenerational inheritance. The stratum of managerial personnel possesses a great deal of organizational resources but is more open than the stratum of

---

[1] The study of social mobility in international academia generally emphasizes the analysis of the intergenerational mobility table, because intergenerational mobility can reveal the long-term and steady influence of social structural factors on social mobility. However, Chinese society has changed drastically over the past fifty years, and the social structure, classifications of social stratum, and mechanisms of social mobility in different period were greatly different. Especially, social mobility mechanisms in different periods often had opposite influences, as well as governmental policies that affected social mobility had different inclinations in different periods. In such instances, intergenerational mobility is unable to completely reveal patterns and mechanisms of social mobility in a specific period because the agent of these mechanisms often had changed before it lasted for enough time to affect the next generation. Therefore, the intragenerational mobility table has an extreme significance to the study of social mobility in contemporary China. In order to show changes of social mobility in Chinese society more completely, we not only calculated mobility tables of respondents' first occupations and current occupations, but also estimated mobility tables of respondents' current occupations and previous occupations. These tables together provide more information and reveale social mobility and its changes in various periods.

state and social administrators. Most members of the stratum of private entrepreneurs build up from nothing and possess a large amount of economic resources. The three strata occupy the advantaged status in current Chinese social structure. Members of the three strata seldom move to other strata.

State and Social Administrators: More in and Less out

In this study, the *stratum of state and social administrators* refers to leaderships in government and party agencies, public institutions, and social organizations (see relevant paragraphs in Chapter 1). This stratum possesses an advantaged status in social structure and is at the top of the social stratum classification hierarchy in the study. What type of family did most members of this stratum come from? What kind of mobility path did they have to go through before attaining current stratum status? Alternatively, what type of people is most likely to become state and social administrator? Are there any barriers of mobility or distinct boundaries between this stratum and other social strata? Based on data presented in intergenerational and intragenerational mobility tables, we managed to answer the above questions and explore the demographic composition and characteristics of the stratum of state and social administrators.

Data in the intergenerational mobility table (see Table 4-1)[1] indicates the proportion distribution of family backgrounds of state and social administrators. Among current state and social administrators, about 15.4 percent of them came from the family of cadres, enterprise managerial personnel, and business owners; 9.2 percent from the family of professional and technical personnel; 9.2 percent from the family of clerical personnel; 3.1 percent from the family of the self-employed laborers and small owners; 16.9 percent from the family of workers and 46.2 percent from the family of peasants. Simply judging from the distribution of these proportions, the majority of state and social administrators came from the family of peasants and workers. However, after comparing these proportions with the proportions of various strata to the overall social structure, we found that the probabilities of people with different family backgrounds entering the stratum of state and social administrators are quite different. For example, the proportion of people with the family background of cadres, business managers, and enterprise owners in the stratum of state and social administrators is six times higher than their proportion in the overall social structure (15.4 percent / 2.6 percent). In contrast, the proportion of people from the family of

---

[1] In mobility tables, the figure in the row of "frequency" represents the frequency of each conjoint category. The figure in the row of "expectation" represents the frequency that each conjoint category should be if the mobility opportunity is exactly equal. The row of "percentage (outflow rate)" represents the percentage of people in each category in rows moving to each category in columns. The column of "percentage (inflow rate)" represents the percentage of people in each category in columns coming from each category in rows. In all mobility tables, occupations or strata are listed in the order of ranks. It means that the rank of any occupation or stratum is higher than that in rows below it (or in columns behind it). The upward mobility rate and the downward mobility rate can be conveniently calculated based on such an array.

178

peasants in the stratum of state and social administrators is only two-third of their proportion in the overall social structure (46.2 percent/ 72.9 percent). The difference in probabilities of entering the stratum of state and social administrators for people with different family backgrounds suggests that this stratum has a certain degree of intergenerational inheritance. In other words, those whose fathers are cadres, managerial personnel, or enterprise owners are most likely to become state and social administrator; seven in every one hundred of their children will be members of this stratum (6.6 percent). About three in every one hundred people from the family of professional and technical personnel and clerical personnel respectively will become state and social administrator (3.1 percent and 2.7 percent). About two in every one hundred people from the family of the self-employed laborers and individual-operated business proprietors will enter this stratum (2.2 percent). About one in every one hundred people from the family of worker will become state and social administrators. For people from the family of peasants, less than one in every one hundred persons will enter this stratum; this probability is roughly equal to their proportion in the overall social structure.

The longitudinal comparative analysis of the intergenerational mobility table (see Table 4-2 and Table 4-3) indicates that the degree of the intergenerational inheritance of the state and social administrator stratum varied in different periods. It was weaker among people who started working before 1980 (before the economic reform) than those who started working after 1980 (after the economic reform). For example, about 10.6 percent of state and social administrators who started working before 1980 came from the family of governmental cadres and enterprise managerial personnel. This proportion is five times higher than the average proportion (2.1 percent) of this category in the distribution of the overall social structure. About 25 percent of state and social administrators who started working after 1980 came from the family of governmental cadres and enterprise managerial personnel; it is seven times higher than the average proportion (3.1 percent) of this category in the overall social structure. In contrast, 53.2 percent of state and social administrators who started working before 1980 came from the family of peasants; it is about 24 percent lower than the average proportion (77.4 percent) of this category in the overall social structure. Among state and social administrators who started working after 1980, 31.3 percent came from the family of peasants and it is about 38 percent lower than the average proportion (69.2 percent) of this category in the overall social structure. That is to say, before the economic reform, the probability for children from peasant's family to be state and social administrators is higher than that after the reform. Meanwhile, after the economic reform, the probability for children from the family of

Table 4-1　The Intergenerational Mobility Table

Father's Occupation		State and social administrator	Managerial personnel	Private entrepreneur	Professional & technical personnel	Clerical personnel	Individual-operated business proprietor	Commercial and service personnel	Industrial worker	Agricultural laborer	The urban-rural jobless, unemployed, and partially unemployed	Total
							Respondent's Stratum Position					
Cadre, managerial personnel, & enterprise owner	Frequency	10	9	4	19	34	16	21	22	8	8	151
	Expectation	1.7	2.3	1.6	6.4	11.4	16.6	16.8	21.4	65.2	7.7	151.0
	Row Percentage(outflow rate)	6.6%	6.0%	2.6%	12.6%	22.5%	10.6%	13.9%	14.6%	5.3%	5.3%	100.0%
	Column Percentage(inflow rate)	15.4%	9.9%	6.3%	7.7%	7.7%	2.5%	3.2%	2.7%	0.3%	2.7%	2.6%
Professional & technical personnel	Frequency	6	8	2	49	25	18	18	24	27	16	193
	Expectation	2.1	3.0	2.1	8.2	14.6	21.2	21.4	27.3	83.3	9.8	193.0
	Row Percentage(outflow rate)	3.1%	4.1%	1.0%	25.4%	13.0%	9.3%	9.3%	12.4%	14.0%	8.3%	100.0%
	Column Percentage(inflow rate)	9.2%	8.8%	3.1%	19.8%	5.6%	2.8%	2.8%	2.9%	1.1%	5.4%	3.3%
Clerical personnel	Frequency	6	7	1	15	54	12	22	40	38	26	221
	Expectation	2.5	3.4	2.4	9.4	16.7	24.2	24.5	31.3	95.4	11.2	221.0
	Row Percentage(outflow rate)	2.7%	3.2%	0.5%	6.8%	24.7%	5.4%	10.0%	18.1%	17.2%	11.8%	100.0%
	Column Percentage(inflow rate)	9.2%	7.7%	1.6%	6.0%	12.2%	1.9%	3.4%	4.8%	1.5%	8.8%	3.8%
Small owner & self-employed laborer	Frequency	2	1	3	8	7	33	15	15	2	5	91
	Expectation	1.0	1.4	1.0	3.9	6.9	10.0	10.1	12.9	39.3	4.6	91.0
	Row Percentage(outflow rate)	2.2%	1.1%	3.3%	8.8%	7.7%	36.3%	16.5%	16.5%	2.2%	5.5%	100.0%
	Column Percentage(inflow rate)	3.1%	1.1%	4.7%	3.2%	1.6%	5.1%	2.3%	1.8%	0.1%	1.7%	1.6%

continued

Father's Occupation		State and social administrator	Managerial personnel	Private entrepreneur	Professional & technical personnel	Clerical personnel	Individual-operated business proprietor	Commercial and service personnel	Industrial worker	Agricultural laborer	The urban-rural jobless, unemployed, and partially unemployed	Total
						Respondent's Stratum Position						
Worker	Frequency	11	24	4	47	101	110	183	222	108	121	931
	Expectation	10.3	14.5	10.2	39.4	70.4	102.1	103.4	131.8	401.7	47.2	931.0
	Row Percentage(outflow rate)	1.2%	2.6%	0.4%	5.0%	10.8%	11.8%	19.7%	23.8%	11.6%	13.0%	100.0%
	Column Percentage(inflow rate)	16.9%	26.4%	6.3%	19.0%	22.8%	17.1%	28.1%	26.7%	4.3%	40.7%	15.9%
Peasant	Frequency	30	42	50	110	222	454	392	507	2346	121	4274
	Expectation	47.4	66.4	46.7	180.8	323.0	468.9	474.7	605.3	1844.2	216.6	4274.6
	Row Percentage(outflow rate)	0.7%	1.0%	1.2%	2.6%	5.2%	10.6%	9.2%	11.9%	54.9%	2.8%	100.0%
	Column Percentage(inflow rate)	46.2%	4.62%	78.1%	44.4%	50.1%	70.6%	60.2%	61.1%	92.8%	40.7%	74.9%
Total	Frequency	65	91	64	248	443	643	651	830	2529	297	5861
	Expectation	65.0	91.0	64.0	248.0	443.0	643.0	651.0	830.0	2529.0	297.0	5861.0
	Row Percentage(outflow rate)	1.1%	1.6%	1.1%	4.2%	7.6%	11.0%	11.1%	14.2%	43.1%	5.1%	100%
	Column Percentage(inflow rate)	100.0%	100%	100%	100%	100%	100%	100%	100%	100%	100%	100%

Note: This weighted sample does not include enrolled students.

Table 4-2　The Intergenerational Mobility Table of Employment before 1980

Father's Occupation		Respondent's Stratum Position										
		State and social administrator	Managerial personnel	Private entrepreneur	Professional and technical personnel	Clerical personnel	Individual-operated business proprietor	Commercial and service personnel	Industrial worker	Agricultural laborer	The urban-rural jobless, unemployed, and partially unemployed	Total
Cadre, managerial personnel, and enterprise owner	Frequency	5	2	1	8	11	3	7	9	5	2	57
	Expectation	0.9	1.0	0.3	2.1	4.6	3.9	4.1	6.4	27.5	2.2	57.0
	Row Percentage(outflow rate)	9.4%	3.8%	1.9%	15.1%	20.8%	5.7%	13.2%	17.0%	9.4%	3.8%	100.0%
	Column Percentage(inflow rate)	10.6%	3.8%	6.7%	7.5%	4.8%	1.5%	3.4%	2.8%	0.4%	1.8%	2.1%
Professional and technical personnel	Frequency	5	5	0	14	10	1	9	13	7	4	68
	Expectation	1.2	1.3	0.4	2.7	5.8	5.1	5.3	8.2	35.3	2.8	68.0
	Row Percentage(outflow rate)	7.4%	7.4%	0.0%	20.6%	14.7%	1.5%	13.2%	19.1%	10.3%	5.9%	100.0%
	Column Percentage(inflow rate)	10.6%	9.4%	0.0%	13.2%	4.3%	0.5%	4.3%	4.0%	0.5%	3.6%	2.5%
Clerical personnel	Frequency	3	5	0	7	15	4	9	16	21	5	85
	Expectation	1.5	1.7	1.5	3.4	7.3	6.3	6.6	10.3	44.1	3.5	85.0
	Row Percentage(outflow rate)	3.5%	5.9%	0.0%	8.2%	17.6%	4.7%	10.6%	18.8%	24.7%	5.9%	100.0%
	Column Percentage(inflow rate)	6.4%	9.4%	0.0%	6.6%	6.5%	2.0%	4.3%	5.0%	1.5%	4.5%	3.2%
Small owner and self-employed laborer	Frequency	2	1	0	3	4	5	5	5	0	2	27
	Expectation	0.5	0.5	0.2	1.1	2.3	2.0	2.1	3.2	14.0	1.1	27.0
	Row Percentage(outflow rate)	7.4%	3.7%	0.0%	11.1%	14.8%	18.5%	18.5%	18.5%	0.0%	7.4%	100.0%
	Column Percentage(inflow rate)	4.3%	1.9%	0.0%	2.8%	1.7%	2.5%	2.4%	1.6%	0.0%	1.8%	1.0%

continued

		Respondent's Stratum Position										
Father's Occupation		State and social administrator	Managerial personnel	Private entrepreneur	Professional and technical personnel	Clerical personnel	Individual-operated business proprietor	Commercial and service personnel	Industrial worker	Agricultural laborer	The urban-rural jobless, unemployed, and partially unemployed	Total
Worker	Frequency	7	15	1	27	56	20	58	101	45	42	372
	Expectation	6.5	7.4	2.1	14.7	31.9	27.5	28.8	44.7	192.9	15.4	372.0
	Row Percentage(outflow rate)	1.9%	1.0%	0.3%	7.3%	15.1%	1.4%	15.6%	27.2%	12.1%	11.3%	100.0%
	Column Percentage(inflow rate)	14.9%	28.3%	6.7%	25.5%	24.3%	10.1%	28.0%	31.4%	3.4%	37.8%	13.9%
Peasant	Frequency	25	25	13	47	134	165	119	178	1311	56	2073
	Expectation	36.4	41.0	11.6	82.1	170.0	150.0	160.2	249.0	1075.2	84.3	2073.0
	Row Percentage(outflow rate)	1.2%	1.2%	0.6%	2.3%	6.5%	8.0%	5.7%	8.6%	63.2%	2.7%	100.0%
	Column Percentage(inflow rate)	53.2%	47.2%	86.7%	44.3%	58.3%	83.3%	57.5%	55.3%	94.4%	50.5%	77.4%
Total	Frequency	47	53	15	106	230	198	207	322	1389	111	2678
	Expectation	47.0	53.0	15.0	106.0	230.0	198.0	207.0	322.0	1389.0	111.0	2678.0
	Row Percentage (outflow rate)	1.8%	2.0%	0.6%	4.0%	8.6%	7.4%	7.7%	12.0%	51.9%	4.1%	100%
	Column Percentage (inflow rate)	100.0%	100%	100%	100%	100%	100.0%	100.0%	100%	100%	100%	100%

Note: This weighted sample does not include enrolled students.

Table 4-3　The Intergenerational Mobility Table of Employment after 1980

Father's Occupation		State and social administrator	Managerial personnel	Private entrepreneur	Professional & technical personnel	Clerical personnel	Individual-operated business proprietor	Commercial and service personnel	Industrial worker	Agricultural laborer	The urban-rural jobless, unemployed, and partially unemployed	Total
Cadre, managerial personnel, and enterprise owner	Frequency	4	7	3	10	23	13	14	13	4	6	97
	Expectation	0.5	1.1	1.5	4.9	6.5	13.5	13.5	15.6	39.9	5.7	67.0
	Row Percentage (outflow rate)	4.1%	7.2%	3.1%	10.3%	23.7%	13.4%	14.4%	13.4%	4.1%	6.2%	100.0%
	Column Percentage (inflow rate)	25.0%	19.4%	6.1%	7.2%	10.8%	2.9%	3.2%	2.6%	0.4%	3.2%	3.1%
Professional and technical personnel	Frequency	1	2	2	34	15	16	9	12	20	12	123
	Expectation	0.6	1.4	1.9	5.4	8.3	17.2	17.2	19.7	44.2	7.2	123.0
	Row Percentage (outflow rate)	0.8%	1.6%	1.6%	27.6%	12.2%	13.0%	7.3%	9.8%	16.3%	9.8%	100.0%
	Column Percentage (inflow rate)	6.3%	5.6%	4.1%	24.5%	7.0%	3.6%	2.0%	2.4%	1.8%	6.5%	3.9%
Clerical personnel	Frequency	2	2	1	8	39	8	13	24	17	21	135
	Expectation	0.7	1.5	2.1	5.9	9.1	18.8	18.8	21.6	48.5	7.9	135.0
	Row Percentage (outflow rate)	1.5%	1.5%	0.7%	5.9%	28.9%	5.9%	9.6%	17.8%	12.6%	15.6%	100.0%
	Column Percentage (inflow rate)	12.5%	5.6%	2.0%	5.8%	18.3%	1.8%	2.9%	4.7%	1.5%	11.4%	4.3%
Small owner and self-employed laborer	Frequency	0	0	3	5	3	27	9	10	2	3	62
	Expectation	0.3	0.7	1.0	2.7	4.2	8.7	8.7	9.9	22.3	3.6	62.0
	Row Percentage (outflow rate)	0.0%	0.0%	4.8%	8.1%	4.8%	43.5%	14.5%	16.1%	3.2%	4.8%	100.0%
	Column Percentage (inflow rate)	0.0%	0.0%	6.1%	3.6%	1.4%	6.1%	2.0%	2.0%	0.2%	1.6%	2.0%

Respondent's Stratum Position

continued

Father's Occupation		State and social administrator	Managerial personnel	Private entrepreneur	Professional & technical personnel	Clerical personnel	Individual-operated business proprietor	Commercial and service personnel	Industrial worker	Agricultural laborer	The urban-rural jobless, unemployed, and partially unemployed	Total
							Respondent's Stratum Position					
Worker	Frequency	4	9	3	19	45	90	125	121	63	79	558
	Expectation	2.8	6.3	8.6	24.4	37.4	77.9	77.9	89.5	200.6	32.5	558.0
	Row Percentage(outflow rate)	0.7%	1.6%	0.5%	3.4%	8.1%	16.1%	22.4%	21.7%	11.3%	14.2%	100.0%
	Column Percentage(inflow rate)	25.0%	25.0%	6.1%	13.7%	21.1%	20.3%	28.2%	23.8%	5.5%	42.7%	17.5%
Peasant	Frequency	5	16	37	63	88	289	273	329	1035	64	2199
	Expectation	11.1	24.9	33.9	96.3	147.6	306.9	306.9	352.6	790.5	128.2	2199.0
	Row Percentage(outflow rate)	0.2%	0.7%	1.7%	2.9%	4.0%	13.1%	12.4%	15.0%	41.1%	2.9%	100.0%
	Column Percentage(inflow rate)	31.3%	44.4%	75.5%	45.3%	41.3%	65.2%	61.6%	64.6%	50.7%	34.6%	69.2%
Total	Frequency	16	36	49	139	213	443	443	509	1141	185	3174
	Expectation	16.0	36.0	49.0	139.0	213.0	443.0	443.0	509.0	1141.0	185.0	3174.0
	Row Percentage(outflow rate)	0.5%	1.1%	1.5%	4.4%	6.7%	14.0%	14.0%	16.1%	35.9%	5.8%	100.0%
	Column Percentage(inflow rate)	100.0%	100.0%	100.0%	100.0%	100.0%	100.0%	100.0%	100.0%	100.0%	100.0%	100.0%

Note: This weighted sample does not include enrolled students.

governmental cadres and enterprise managerial personnel to be state and social administrators is higher than that before the reform.[1]

Analysis of the intragenerational mobility (see Table 4-4) shows that the stratum of state and social administrators is a stratum of more in and less out to some extent. In other words, in the social mobility chain, the state and social administrator stratum usually is the final destination of social mobility. People do not want to move to other strata after entering this stratum; this also suggests the advantaged status of this stratum in the social structure. The great majority (59.1 percent) of people whose first occupation was the state and social administrator still keep the same job, while other members of the stratum moved into the managerial personnel stratum (9.1 percent) and the clerical personnel stratum (27.3 percent).[2] Since the 1990s, the proportion of state and social administrators who shifted to the stratum of managerial personnel and the stratum of private entrepreneurs has risen slightly (see Table 4-10). A large number of cadres resigned from the government and engaged in business at the beginning of the 1990s, and that may be a possible cause for such change.[3] The phenomenon that state and social administrators in control of organizational resources shifting to the stratum in possession of economic resources indicates that the importance of economic resources in the value appraisal system has been rising. However, such a movement was not very strong. After this tide of shifting to business,

---

[1] According to the difference in time of obtaining employment, respondents of the survey are divided into two groups—people who started working before and after 1980—and are analyzed by using mobility tables (Table 4-2, Table 4-3, Table 4-5, and Table 4-6) respectively; this approach contributes to understanding the different characteristics of social mobility before and after the economic reform. However, attention must to be paid to the length of service of the former group which is longer than that of the latter group; as a result, the probability of the former group to achieve social mobility, especially upward social mobility, is greater than the latter. Therefore, Table 4-8, Table 4-9, and Table 4-10 present the mobility table analysis respectively based on the time when respondent achieved his or her latest social mobility, in order to compare the social mobility of each stratum before 1980, in the 1980s and in the 1990s. Analysis of the transition of social mobility over years should consider data in the above-mentioned mobility tables comprehensively. Moreover, because of the limitation of the sample size, for some conjoint categories in Table 4-10, Table 4-11, and Table 4-12, the number of cases is too small; hence the changes of corresponding percentages are of chance to a contain extent.

[2] 27.3 percent of clerical personnel whose first occupation is state and social administrators. It seems that this proportion might be overestimated due to errors in data classification. The questionnaire used in this study focused on collecting information about the current occupation, including the number of subordinates; while similar question was not inquired as far as the first occupation was concerned. Therefore, the stratum classification of the first occupation might have some errors and some clerical personnel (cadres without administrative management authority) might be classified as state and social administrators. Usually, a state and social administrator will move downward to the stratum of clerical personnel in the following situations: (1) when a cadre loses his or her real powers, or (2) when a cadre is demoted in political movements or due to other reasons. The proportion of such situations should be very low. When taking no account of errors in data classification, the proportion of immobile state and social administrators may reach 80~90 percent.

[3] As far as the outflow channels for members of the state and social administrator stratum, besides going into business, there is another new path which has emerged in recent years; that is, some corrupt cadres are purged from this stratum. Alhough this proportion is very low, it indicates that the position of the stratum of state and social administrators is not completely immobile.

186

very few newly promoted middle-aged and young cadres (state and social administrators) followed the same path. The overwhelming majority of state and social administrators still chose to stay in this stratum and strive for promotions in administrative positions. Cadres who resigned to business usually were those without real power or any promising career in the government.

Analysis of the intragenerational mobility also shows that the inflow channel of the state and social administrator stratum is limited to a fixed path. About two-tenths of state and social administrators' first occupation is state and social administrator (21.3 percent), about six-tenths came from professional and technical personnel and clerical personnel (26.2 percent and 31.1 percent respectively), and the rest two-tenths came from industrial workers(6.6 percent), commercial and service personnel (6.6 percent), and peasants (8.2 percent) (see Table 4-4). Therefore, as a whole, the major origins of state and social administrators came from professional and technical personnel and clerical personnel, only a small portion of administrators were from workers and peasants, and hardly any managerial personnel, private entrepreneurs, and individual-operated business proprietors entered this stratum. The inflow channel of the state and social administrator stratum has changed significantly before and after the economic reform. There are certain proportions of industrial workers, commercial and service personnel, and peasants entering this stratum before the economic reform (see Table 4-5). In particular, slightly more than one-tenth of state and social administrators' first occupation was agricultural laborer (11.1 percent). After the economic reform (see Table 4-6), the probability of entering this stratum for industrial workers, commercial and service personnel, and peasants has declined sharply. Although some commercial and service personnel became state and social administrators in this period, almost no industrial workers and peasants had such opportunities. Changes in the origins of the state and social administrator stratum indicate that the selection rules of this stratum varied before and after the economic reform (for example, before the reform, the basic criteria for selecting cadres focused on the political participation performance and the political status; while after the reform, academic degrees and diplomas are emphasized in cadre promotion). Meanwhile, as a stratum with advantaged status, it has shown an increasing exclusionism towards the disadvantaged strata. Such a change inevitably affects the interest orientation of this stratum and its relationship with the stratum of workers and peasants.

Table 4-4 The Intragenerational Mobility Table

Stratum Position of the First Occupation		State and social administrator	Managerial personnel	Private entrepreneur	Professional and technical personnel	Clerical personnel	Individual-operated business proprietor	Commercial and service personnel	Industrial worker	Agricultural laborer	The jobless, unemployed, and partially unemployed	Total
State and social administrator	Frequency	13	2	0	0	6	0	0	0	1	0	22
	Expectation	0.2	0.4	0.2	0.9	1.8	2.4	2.6	2.8	9.7	0.9	22.0
	Row Percentage(outflow rate)	59.1%	9.1%	0.0%	0.0%	27.3%	0.0%	0.0%	0.0%	4.5%	0.0%	100.0%
	Column Percentage(inflow rate)	21.3%	2.2%	0.0%	0.0%	1.3%	0.0%	0.0%	0.0%	0.0%	0.0%	0.4%
Managerial personnel	Frequency	0	17	0	0	1	1	1	0	0	2	22
	Expectation	0.2	.4	0.2	0.9	1.8	2.4	2.6	2.8	9.7	0.9	22.0
	Row Percentage(outflow rate)	0.0%	77.3%	0.0%	0.0%	4.5%	4.5%	4.5%	0.0%	0.0%	9.1%	100.0%
	Column Percentage(inflow rate)	0.0%	18.9%	0.0%	0.0%	0.2%	0.2%	0.2%	0.0%	0.0%	0.8%	0.4%
Private entrepreneur	Frequency	0	0	11	0	0	0	0	0	0	0	11
	Expectation	0.1	0.2	0.1	0.5	0.9	1.2	1.3	1.4	4.9	0.5	11.0
	Row Percentage(outflow rate)	0.0%	0.0%	100.0%	0.0%	0.0%	0.0%	0.0%	0.0%	0.0%	0.0%	100.0%
	Column Percentage(inflow rate)	0.0%	0.0%	18.0%	0.0%	0.0%	0.0%	0.0%	0.0%	0.0%	0.0%	0.2%
Professional and technical personnel	Frequency	16	7	5	179	31	12	7	4	24	11	296
	Expectation	3.2	4.8	3.2	12.7	23.9	32.3	34.8	37.5	130.8	12.7	296.0
	Row Percentage(outflow rate)	5.4%	2.4%	1.7%	60.5%	10.5%	4.1%	2.4%	1.4%	8.1%	3.7%	100.0%
	Column Percentage(inflow rate)	26.2%	7.8%	8.2%	74.6%	6.9%	2.0%	1.1%	0.6%	1.0%	4.6%	5.3%
Clerical personnel	Frequency	19	20	8	13	217	21	20	26	48	27	419
	Expectation	4.6	6.8	4.6	18.0	33.8	45.7	49.2	53.1	185.2	17.9	419.0
	Row Percentage(outflow rate)	4.5%	4.8%	1.9%	3.1%	51.8%	5.0%	4.8%	6.2%	11.5%	6.4%	100.0%
	Column Percentage(inflow rate)	31.1%	22.2%	13.1%	5.4%	48.1%	3.4%	3.0%	3.7%	1.9%	11.3%	7.5%

continued

Stratum Position of the First Occupation		State and social administrator	Managerial personnel	Private entrepreneur	Professional and technical personnel	Clerical personnel	Individual-operated business proprietor	Commercial and service personnel	Industrial worker	Agricultural laborer	The jobless, unemployed, and partially unemployed	Total
							Stratum Position of the Current Occupation					
Individual-operated business proprietor	Frequency	0	1	0	0	5	185	89	18	20	3	321
	Expectation	3.5	5.2	3.5	13.8	25.9	35.0	37.7	40.7	141.9	13.7	321.0
	Row Percentage(outflow rate)	0.0%	0.3%	0.0%	0.0%	1.6%	57.6%	27.7%	5.6%	6.2%	0.9%	100.0%
	Column Percentage(inflow rate)	0.0%	1.1%	0.0%	0.0%	1.1%	30.4%	13.6%	2.5%	0.8%	1.3%	5.7%
Commercial and service personnel	Frequency	4	8	3	6	42	53	213	20	15	31	395
	Expectation	4.3	5.4	4.3	17.0	31.9	43.1	46.4	50.1	174.6	16.9	395.0
	Row Percentage(outflow rate)	1.0%	2.0%	0.8%	1.5%	10.6%	13.4%	53.9%	5.1%	3.8%	7.8%	100.0%
	Column Percentage(inflow rate)	6.6%	8.9%	4.9%	2.5%	9.3%	8.7%	32.5%	2.8%	0.6%	13.0%	7.1%
Industrial worker	Frequency	4	19	9	14	65	117	124	436	100	108	996
	Expectation	10.9	16.1	10.9	42.8	80.5	108.6	117.0	126.3	440.3	42.6	996.0
	Row Percentage(outflow rate)	0.4%	1.9%	0.9%	1.4%	6.5%	11.7%	12.4%	43.8%	10.0%	10.8%	100.0%
	Column Percentage(inflow rate)	6.6%	21.1%	14.8%	5.8%	14.4%	19.2%	18.9%	61.6%	4.1%	45.2%	17.8%
Agricultural laborer	Frequency	5	16	25	28	84	218	191	202	2259	49	3077
	Expectation	33.6	49.6	33.6	132.3	248.6	335.6	361.5	390.2	1360.2	131.7	3077.0
	Row Percentage(outflow rate)	0.2%	0.5%	0.8%	0.9%	2.7%	7.1%	6.2%	6.6%	73.4%	1.6%	100.0%
	Column Percentage(inflow rate)	8.2%	17.8%	41.0%	11.7%	18.6%	35.8%	29.1%	28.5%	91.5%	20.5%	55.1%
The jobless, unemployed, and partially unemployed	Frequency	0	0	0	0	0	2	11	2	1	8	24
	Expectation	0.3	0.4	0.3	1.0	1.9	2.6	2.8	3.0	10.6	1.0	24.0
	Row Percentage(outflow rate)	0.0%	0.0%	0.0%	0.0%	0.0%	8.3%	45.8%	8.3%	4.2%	33.3%	100.0%
	Column Percentage(inflow rate)	0.0%	0.0%	0.0%	0.0%	0.0%	0.3%	1.7%	0.3%	0.0%	3.3%	0.4%
Total	Frequency	61	90	61	240	451	609	656	708	2468	239	5583
	Expectation	61.0	90.0	61.0	240.0	451.0	609.0	656.0	708.0	2468.0	239.0	5583.0
	Row Percentage(outflow rate)	1.1%	1.6%	1.1%	4.3%	8.1%	10.9%	11.7%	12.7%	44.2%	4.3%	100.0%
	Column Percentage(inflow rate)	100.0%	100.0%	100.0%	100.0%	100.0%	100.0%	100.0%	100.0%	100.0%	100.0%	100.0%

Note: This weighted sample does not include the never-employed people.

Table 4-5　The Intragenerational Mobility Table of Employment before 1980

Stratum Position of the First Occupation		State and social administrator	Managerial personnel	Private entrepreneur	Professional and technical personnel	Clerical personnel	Individual-operated business proprietor	Commercial and service personnel	Industrial worker	Agricultural laborer	The jobless, unemployed, and partially unemployed	Total
State and social administrator	Frequency	7	2	0	0	6	0	0	0	1	0	16
	Expectation	0.3	0.3	0.1	0.6	1.4	1.2	1.3	1.7	8.5	0.5	16.0
	Row Percentage(outflow rate)	43.8%	12.5%	0.0%	0.0%	37.5%	0.0%	0.0%	0.0%	6.3%	0.0%	100.0%
	Column Percentage(inflow rate)	15.9%	3.8%	0.0%	0.0%	2.6%	0.0%	0.0%	0.0%	0.1%	0.0%	0.6%
Managerial personnel	Frequency	0	6	0	0	1	1	1	0	0	1	10
	Expectation	0.2	2	0.1	0.4	0.9	0.8	0.8	1.1	5.3	0.3	10.0
	Row Percentage(outflow rate)	0.0%	60.0%	0.0%	0.0%	10.0%	10.0%	10.0%	0.0%	0.0%	10.0%	100.0%
	Column Percentage(inflow rate)	0.0%	11.3%	0.0%	0.0%	0.4%	0.5%	0.5%	0.0%	0.0%	1.1%	0.4%
Private entrepreneur	Frequency	0	0	0	0	0	0	0	0	0	0	0
	Expectation	0.0	0.0	0.0	0.0	0.0	0.0	0.0	0.0	0.0	0.0	0.0
	Row Percentage(outflow rate)	0.0%	0.0%	0.0%	0.0%	0.0%	0.0%	0.0%	0.0%	0.0%	0.0%	0.0%
	Column Percentage(inflow rate)	0.0%	0.0%	0.0%	0.0%	0.0%	0.0%	0.0%	0.0%	0.0%	0.0%	0.0%
Professional and technical personnel	Frequency	11	2	2	74	22	4	3	3	20	3	144
	Expectation	2.4	2.9	0.8	5.8	12.8	10.8	11.7	15.7	76.2	4.9	144.0
	Row Percentage(outflow rate)	7.6%	1.4%	1.4%	51.4%	15.3%	2.8%	2.1%	2.1%	13.9%	2.1%	100.0%
	Column Percentage(inflow rate)	25.0%	3.8%	13.3%	71.2%	9.6%	2.1%	1.4%	1.1%	1.5%	3.4%	5.6%
Clerical personnel	Frequency	15	11	2	7	78	8	9	11	32	6	179
	Expectation	3.0	3.7	1.0	7.2	15.9	13.5	14.5	19.5	94.7	6.1	179.0
	Row Percentage(outflow rate)	8.4%	6.1%	1.1%	3.9%	43.6%	4.5%	5.0%	6.1%	17.9%	3.4%	100.0%
	Column Percentage(inflow rate)	34.1%	20.8%	13.3%	6.7%	33.9%	4.1%	4.3%	3.9%	2.3%	6.8%	6.9%
Individual-operated business proprietor	Frequency	0	0	0	0	1	37	21	2	4	1	66
	Expectation	1.1	1.3	0.4	2.6	5.9	5.0	5.3	7.2	34.9	2.2	66.0
	Row Percentage(outflow rate)	0.0%	0.0%	0.0%	0.0%	1.5%	56.1%	31.8%	3.0%	6.1%	1.5%	100.0%
	Column Percentage(inflow rate)	0.0%	0.0%	0.0%	0.0%	0.4%	19.0%	10.0%	0.7%	0.3%	1.1%	2.5%

Stratum Position of the Current Occupation

continued

Stratum Position of the First Occupation		Stratum Position of the Current Occupation										Total
		State and social administrator	Managerial personnel	Private entrepreneur	Professional and technical personnel	Clerical personnel	Individual-operated business proprietor	Commercial and service personnel	Industrial worker	Agricultural laborer	The jobless, unemployed, and partially unemployed	
Commercial and service personnel	Frequency	3	3	0	4	19	11	38	13	7	7	105
	Expectation	1.8	2.1	0.6	4.2	9.3	7.9	8.5	11.4	5.5	3.6	105.0
	Row Percentage(outflow rate)	2.9%	2.9%	0.0%	3.8%	18.1%	10.5%	36.2%	12.4%	6.7%	6.7%	100.0%
	Column Percentage(inflow rate)	6.8%	5.7%	0.0%	3.8%	8.3%	5.6%	18.1%	4.6%	0.5%	8.0%	4.1%
Industrial worker	Frequency	3	14	1	5	37	17	47	158	27	35	344
	Expectation	5.8	7.0	2.0	13.8	30.5	25.9	27.9	37.4	182.0	11.7	344.0
	Row Percentage(outflow rate)	0.9%	4.1%	0.3%	1.5%	10.8%	4.9%	13.7%	45.9%	7.8%	10.2%	100.0%
	Column Percentage(inflow rate)	6.8%	26.4%	6.7%	4.8%	16.1%	8.7%	22.4%	56.0%	2.0%	39.8%	13.3%
Agricultural laborer	Frequency	5	15	10	14	66	117	88	93	1279	33	1720
	Expectation	29.2	35.2	10.0	69.0	152.6	129.4	138.4	187.1	909.8	58.4	1720.0
	Row Percentage(outflow rate)	0.3%	0.9%	0.6%	0.8%	3.8%	6.8%	5.1%	5.4%	74.4%	1.9%	100.0%
	Column Percentage(inflow rate)	11.4%	28.3%	66.7%	13.5%	28.7%	60.0%	41.9%	33.0%	93.3%	37.5%	66.4%
The jobless, unemployed, and partially unemployed	Frequency	0	0	0	0	0	0	3	2	1	2	8
	Expectation	0.1	0.2	0.0	0.3	0.7	0.6	0.6	0.9	4.2	0.3	8.0
	Row Percentage(outflow rate)	0.0%	0.0%	0.0%	0.0%	0.0%	0.0%	37.5%	25.0%	12.5%	25.0%	100.0%
	Column Percentage(inflow rate)	0.0%	0.0%	0.0%	0.0%	0.0%	0.0%	1.4%	0.7%	0.1%	2.3%	0.3%
Total	Frequency	44	53	15	104	230	195	210	282	1371	88	2592
	Expectation	44.0	53.0	15.0	104.0	230.0	195.0	210.0	282.0	1371.0	88.0	2592.0
	Row Percentage(outflow rate)	1.7%	2.0%	0.6%	4.0%	8.9%	7.5%	8.1%	10.9%	52.9%	3.4%	100.0%
	Column Percentage(inflow rate)	100.0%	100.0%	100.0%	100.0%	100.0%	100.0%	100.0%	100.0%	100.0%	100.0%	100.0%

Note: This weighted sample does not include the never-employed people.

Table 4-6　The Intragenerational Mobility Table of Employment after 1980

Stratum Position of the First Occupation		State and social administrator	Managerial personnel	Private entrepreneur	Professional and technical personnel	Clerical personnel	Individual-operated business proprietor	Commercial and service personnel	Industrial worker	Agricultural laborer	The jobless, unemployed, and partially unemployed	Total
State and social administrator	Frequency	6	0	0	0	0	0	0	0	0	0	6
	Expectation	0.0	0.1	0.1	0.3	0.4	0.8	0.9	0.9	2.2	0.3	6.0
	Row Percentage(outflow rate)	100.0%	0.0%	0.0%	0.0%	0.0%	0.0%	0.0%	0.0%	0.0%	0.0%	100.0%
	Column Percentage(inflow rate)	33.3%	0.0%	0.0%	0.0%	0.0%	0.0%	0.0%	0.0%	0.0%	0.0%	0.2%
Managerial personnel	Frequency	0	11	0	0	0	0	1	0	0	1	13
	Expectation	0.1	2	0.2	0.6	1.0	1.8	1.9	1.8	4.8	0.7	13.0
	Row Percentage(outflow rate)	0.0%	84.6%	0.0%	0.0%	0.0%	0.0%	7.7%	0.0%	0.0%	7.7%	100.0%
	Column Percentage(inflow rate)	0.0%	29.7%	0.0%	0.0%	0.0%	0.0%	0.2%	0.0%	0.0%	0.7%	0.4%
Private entrepreneur	Frequency	0	0	11	0	0	0	0	0	0	0	11
	Expectation	0.1	0.1	0.2	0.5	0.8	1.5	1.6	1.6	4.0	0.6	11.0
	Row Percentage(outflow rate)	0.0%	0.0%	100.0%	0.0%	0.0%	0.0%	0.0%	0.0%	0.0%	0.0%	100.0%
	Column Percentage(inflow rate)	0.0%	0.0%	24.4%	0.0%	0.0%	0.0%	0.0%	0.0%	0.0%	0.0%	0.4%
Professional and technical personnel	Frequency	5	5	3	105	9	9	4	1	5	8	154
	Expectation	0.9	1.9	2.3	7.0	11.4	21.4	22.9	21.9	56.5	7.7	154.0
	Row Percentage(outflow rate)	3.2%	3.2%	1.9%	68.2%	5.8%	5.8%	2.6%	0.6%	3.2%	5.2%	100.0%
	Column Percentage(inflow rate)	27.8%	13.5%	6.7%	77.8%	4.1%	2.2%	0.9%	0.2%	0.5%	5.3%	5.2%
Clerical personnel	Frequency	5	9	6	6	138	14	11	15	16	21	241
	Expectation	1.5	3.0	3.6	10.9	17.8	33.5	35.9	34.3	88.4	12.1	241.0
	Row Percentage(outflow rate)	2.1%	3.7%	2.5%	2.5%	57.3%	5.8%	4.6%	6.2%	6.6%	8.7%	100.0%
	Column Percentage(inflow rate)	27.8%	24.3%	13.3%	4.4%	62.4%	3.4%	2.5%	3.5%	1.5%	14.0%	8.1%

continued

Stratum Position of the First Occupation		State and social administrator	Managerial personnel	Private entrepreneur	Professional and technical personnel	Clerical personnel	Individual-operated business proprietor	Commercial and service personnel	Industrial worker	Agricultural laborer	The jobless, unemployed, and partially unemployed	Total
Individual-operated business proprietor	F Frequency	0	1	0	0	5	145	67	16	20	2	255
	Expectation	1.5	3.2	3.8	11.5	18.9	35.5	38.0	36.3	93.6	12.8	255.0
	Row Percentage (outflow rate)	0.0%	0.4%	0.0%	0.0%	2.0%	58.0%	26.3%	6.3%	6.3%	0.8%	100.0%
	Column Percentage (inflow rate)	0.0%	2.7%	0.0%	0.0%	2.3%	35.6%	15.1%	3.8%	1.5%	1.3%	8.5%
Commercial and service personnel	Frequency	2	5	3	2	23	42	174	7	7	24	289
	Expectation	1.7	3.6	4.4	13.1	21.4	40.2	43.0	41.1	106.1	14.5	395.0
	Row Percentage (outflow rate)	0.7%	1.7%	1.0%	0.7%	8.0%	14.5%	60.2%	2.4%	2.4%	8.3%	100.0%
	Column Percentage (inflow rate)	11.1%	13.5%	6.7%	1.5%	10.4%	10.1%	39.1%	1.6%	0.6%	16.0%	7.1%
Industrial worker	Frequency	0	6	7	9	28	100	77	278	73	73	651
	Expectation	3.9	8.1	9.8	29.4	48.1	90.6	96.9	92.3	238.9	32.7	651.0
	Row Percentage (outflow rate)	0.0%	0.9%	1.1%	1.4%	4.3%	15.4%	11.8%	42.7%	11.2%	11.2%	100.0%
	Column Percentage (inflow rate)	0.0%	16.2%	15.6%	6.7%	12.7%	24.0%	17.3%	65.4%	6.7%	48.7%	21.8%
Agricultural laborer	Frequency	0	0	15	13	18	101	103	108	980	15	1353
	Expectation	8.1	16.7	20.4	61.1	100.0	188.3	201.4	192.4	496.6	67.9	1353.0
	Row Percentage (outflow rate)	0.0%	0.0%	1.1%	1.0%	1.3%	7.5%	7.6%	8.0%	72.4%	1.1%	100.0%
	Column Percentage (inflow rate)	0.0%	0.0%	33.3%	9.6%	8.1%	24.3%	23.1%	25.4%	89.3%	10.0%	45.3%
The jobless, unemployed, and partially unemployed	Frequency	0	0	0	0	0	2	8	0	0	6	16
	Expectation	0.1	0.2	0.2	0.7	1.2	2.2	2.4	2.3	5.9	0.8	16.0
	Row Percentage (outflow rate)	0.0%	0.0%	0.0%	0.0%	0.0%	12.5%	50.0%	0.0%	0.0%	37.5%	100.0%
	Column Percentage (inflow rate)	0.0%	0.0%	0.0%	0.0%	0.0%	0.5%	1.8%	0.0%	0.0%	4.0%	0.5%
Total	F Frequency	18	37	45	135	221	416	445	425	1097	150	2989
	Expectation	18.0	37.0	45.0	135.0	221.0	416.0	445.0	425.0	1097.0	150.0	2989.0
	Row Percentage (outflow rate)	0.6%	1.2%	1.5%	4.5%	7.4%	13.9%	14.9%	14.2%	36.7%	5.0%	100.0%
	Column Percentage (inflow rate)	100.0%	100.0%	100.0%	100.0%	100.0%	100.0%	100.0%	100.0%	100.0%	100.0%	100.0%

Note: This weighted sample does not include the never-employed people.

Managerial Personnel: A Growing Stratum with Free Entrances

The *stratum of managerial personnel* refers to middle-high level management in enterprises with non-owner standing and a portion of first-line management functioning as department chiefs.[1] Its rank in the social structure is only lower than that of the state and social administrator stratum. Therefore, the stratum of managerial personnel is also one of advantaged strata in current Chinese society. We pointed out in Chapter 1 that the managerial personnel stratum has just emerged in recent years and is in the process of formation. The boundaries between this stratum and the state and social administrator stratum and the private entrepreneur stratum are still not completely clear. That is also to say, the degree of structuralization of this stratum is not very high and its boundaries with other strata are not very clear. These characteristics have a great influence on the pattern of social mobility of this stratum.

Analysis of the intragenerational mobility (see Table 4-1) shows that the family backgrounds of managerial personnel and state and social administrators are similar to some extent. However, the intergenerational inheritance of the managerial personnel stratum is not as strong as the stratum of state and social administrators. People whose fathers are governmental cadres and business managers have more opportunities to be managers (6 percent), while those from the family of peasants have fewer chances (one percent). This situation is similar to that of the state and social administrator stratum. The difference between the two strata is that, for people from the family of workers, the probability of becoming managerial personnel (2.6 percent) is higher than the probability of entering the state and social administrator stratum (1.2 percent). Analysis of historical comparison (see Table 4-2 and Table 4-3) indicates that the intergenerational inheritance of the managerial personnel stratum has been strengthened since the economic reform. Among managerial personnel who started working after 1980, the proportion of people from the family of governmental cadres and enterprise managerial personnel increased significantly (the proportion was 3.8 percent before 1980, and 7.2 percent after 1980). Meanwhile, the probabilities of becoming managerial personnel for people from the family of peasants and the family of workers after 1980 (0.7 percent and 1.6 percent respectively) are lower than those before 1980 (4 percent and 1.2 percent) to some extent. This situation is also similar to the stratum of state and social administrators.

Intragenerational mobility of managerial personnel (see Table 4-4) reveals that, although this stratum has dominant status in the social structure similar to the state and social administrator stratum, it is more open and has more inflow channels than the latter. The probabilities of entering the stratum of managerial personnel for

---

[1] In this classification, "high-level management" refers to top-level leadership without higher supervisors above them in a given work unit (enterprise or institution) and meanwhile they have subordinate managers. The "middle-level management" refers to managers who have higher supervisors above them and meanwhile they have subordinate management. The "low-level management" refers to first-line managers who supervise ordinary employees directly and have no subordinate management.

industrial workers, commercial and service personnel, and peasants (respectively 21.1 percent, 8.9 percent, and 17.8 percent) is higher than those of entering the stratum of state and social administrators. The proportion of managerial personnel who came from the stratum of state and social administrators is not high (2.2 percent). This situation is surprising, because managerial personnel in former public-owned enterprises and governmental cadres belonged to the same category of occupations and had close relations. It was supposed that the mutual mobility between them should be frequent. Actually, however, few managerial personnel shifted from governmental cadres. The majority of managerial personnel were promoted from people in the same enterprise or in other enterprises in the same industry. Therefore, industrial workers, commercial and service personnel, and peasants employed in enterprises have more opportunities to move upward to the stratum of managerial personnel. Of course, clerical personnel in enterprises have the most opportunities (22.2 percent) of being managerial personnel. There are a certain proportion of professional and technical personnel entering the managerial personnel stratum (7.8 percent), but they have a much higher probability of entering the stratum of state and social administrators (26.2 percent).

The stratum of managerial personnel has a relatively low outflow rate. Among people whose first occupation is managerial personnel, about 77.3 percent of them remain in this stratum, while slightly over 20 percent of them moved to other strata. Different from the state and social administrator stratum in the rate of outflow, managerial personnel do not have complete security of employment, and they may move downward to the stratum of the urban-rural jobless, unemployed, and partially unemployed, while such a situation is impossible in the state and social administrator stratum (see Table 4-4).

The origins of managerial personnel varied before and after the economic reform (see Table 4-5 and Table 4-6). The opportunity of shifting to managerial personnel from industrial workers has dropped sharply since the reform. Among managerial personnel who started working before 1980, about 26.4 percent of them started their first occupation as an industrial worker; this proportion is almost one times higher than the proportion of industrial workers in the overall structure (13.3 percent). In contrast, among managerial personnel who started working after 1980, only 16.2 percent of people's first occupation was industrial worker; this proportion is lower than the proportion of industrial workers in the overall structure (21.8 percent). Table 4-8, Table 4-9, and Table 4-10 indicate that the probability of industrial workers moving upward to the stratum of managerial personnel has been dropping. Among managerial personnel before 1980, the proportion of managerial personnel who were directly promoted from industrial workers (26.7 percent) was nearly three times higher than the proportion of industrial workers in the overall structure (9.2 percent). In the 1980s, the proportion of managerial personnel who were directly promoted from industrial workers (13 percent) was lower than industrial workers' proportion in the overall structure (15.3 percent). In the 1990s, the proportion of managerial personnel who were directly promoted from industrial workers (14 percent) was much lower than industrial workers' proportion in the overall structure (27.4 percent). However, since the economic reform, the probability of peasants directly entering the managerial personnel stratum has been rising (see Table 4-8, Table 4-9, and Table 4-10). Most of these peasants are elders (who started working before 1980) and this may be a result of the development of township enterprises.

As a developing advantaged stratum, the exclusionism of the managerial personnel stratum towards members of lower social strata is significantly weaker than that of the state and social administrator stratum. There is a path for commercial and service personnel, industrial workers, and agricultural laborers to enter this stratum directly. Meanwhile, as an emerging stratum, its origins are relatively diverse. Members of this stratum not only include intra-system (state-owned and collective enterprises) managerial personnel, who make up the majority of this stratum, but also comprise extra-system (non-public enterprises) managerial personnel, the number of which is growing. Some managers entered this stratum through taking advantage of their cultural capital (higher level of education received); while others without higher level of education resorted to working experience. Some managers are very similar to professional managers in Western countries in lifestyle, consumer taste, and value identification, while some others are more close to the ordinary strata of workers and peasants. Therefore, the socio-economic status and value attitudes of members of this stratum vary greatly. Nonetheless, with the development of this stratum, the criteria for selecting its members will become stricter, and its exclusionism toward members of lower strata will increase.

Private Entrepreneurs: The New Rich Rising from Lower Status

In this study, *private entrepreneurs* refer to those who are possess a certain amount of private capital or fixed assets and pursue profits through investing these resources and employing a labor force. This is an advantaged stratum in control of economic resources and ranks third place in the hierarchy of social strata.

Although the stratum of private entrepreneurs is also an advantaged stratum, compared with the other two advantaged strata, the stratum of state and social administrators and the stratum of managerial personnel, it does not show any intergenerational inheritance. The intergenerational mobility (see Table 4-3) indicates that there is no significant orientation existing in the distribution of the proportions of private entrepreneurs' family backgrounds. Only the probabilities of becoming private entrepreneurs for those from the family of governmental cadres and business managerial personnel are higher than their average proportions in the overall social structure, while the probability for people from the family of workers is lower than the its average proportion in the overall structure. Probabilities of those with other family backgrounds are all similar to their average proportions in the overall structure. As a whole, the factor of family background does not have a significant influence on status attainment of the private entrepreneur. The success of private entrepreneurs relies less on parents' influences and more on individual efforts, intellectual ability, and opportunities. Most of private entrepreneurs do not possess the economic capital accumulated by the previous generation and other types of intergenerational transfer of capital (such as cultural capital or authority capital). The majority of this stratum (78.1 percent) came from the family of peasants. However, data obtained from interviews in this study show that two types of intergenerational transfer of capital affect the status attainment of owners of large-size private enterprises. First, some governmental cadres and managerial personnel in state-owned enterprises who possess the authority of allocating public resources and the privilege of business management might take advantage of their influences to help their children become owners of large-size private enterprises. Second, some large-size private enterprise owners' fathers or grandfathers once were entrepreneurs or businesspersons and they might transfer their experience and value attitudes related to business to their children and hence conduced to their children's choice of going into business and responsible for their success in a business career. However, the number of large-size private enterprise owners is very small in the overall private entrepreneur stratum.

The stratum of private entrepreneurs is an emerging stratum after the economic reform. Most of them are start-up entrepreneurs because of the lack of capital accumulated by the previous generation. Moreover, most of them have multiple experience of occupation shifting. In this stratum, only 16.9 percent of its members started their own businesses at the time they began to work, of which about half changed the scope of business. About 35.7 percent of private entrepreneurs had taken up another job before establishing a business, and the remaining 47.4 percent of owners had engaged in more than one job before starting their own businesses. About two-thirds of private entrepreneurs had taken up blue-collar jobs before starting their own businesses (see Table 4-9); among them, 9.7 percent were individual-operated business proprietors, 11.3 percent were commercial and service personnel, 11.3 percent were industrial workers, and 29 percent were agricultural laborers. Only one-tenth of private entrepreneurs' previous occupation was white-collar occupations such as state and social administrators, managerial personnel, and professional and technical personnel. That is to say, the majority of private entrepreneurs came from lower social strata, especially the stratum of agricultural laborers.

The developing process of the private entrepreneur stratum has formalized the pattern of behaviors and value orientation of its members. Because most private entrepreneurs are closely related to lower social strata in family background and personal experience, they are more close to blue-collar strata with lower social status rather than white-collar strata with higher social status in lifestyle, consumer taste, and demeanor. Compared with other advantaged white-collar strata, the literacy of the overall private entrepreneur stratum is relatively lower. All these factors hinder this stratum from shaping its identification of social status and hence the new-rich psychology and conspicuous consumption behaviors of members of this stratum are understandable. On the other hand, the laborious carve-out experience has endowed this stratum with pragmatic, shrewd, and hardworking characters.

MOBILITY CHARACTERISTICS OF THE STRATA IN
MIDDLE-LEVEL POSITIONS

The stratum of professional and technical personnel is in an advantaged position in possession of cultural resources and it is relatively steady in social mobility. The stratum of clerical personnel is a connecting link between the upper and the lower strata in the chain of social mobility and it is in control of a certain amount of organizational resources. The stratum of individual-operated business proprietors is in possession of a certain amount of economic resources and most of its members came from the lower class with few opportunities of upward mobility. These three groups compose the upper, middle, and lower tiers of the middle level in social mobility in succession.

Professional and Technical Personnel: A Bridge in Social Mobility

The *stratum of professional and technical personnel* refers to people who specialize in various professional, scientific, and technical jobs in various organizations (including government agencies, parties and mass organizations, public-owned and collective enterprises, various non-public-owned businesses). This stratum controls a large amount of cultural resources and it is a major component of the middle social strata in modern industrial society.

Analysis of intergenerational mobility (see Table 4-1) shows that the intergenerational inheritance of this stratum is relatively strong. The probability of becoming professional and technical personnel for children of professional and technical personnel is very high. Among current professional and technical personnel, the proportion of those whose fathers' occupation was professional and technical personnel (19.8 percent) is 5.6 times higher than its average proportion in the overall social structure (3.3 percent); slightly over one-fourth of children of professional and technical personnel became professional and technical personnel (25.4 percent). The probability of becoming professional and technical personnel for children of governmental cadres and enterprise managerial personnel is also high (12.6 percent), while the probability for peasants' children is low (2.6 percent). However, because of the huge population of the peasantry, the proportion of professional and technical personnel from the family of peasants to the total number of current professional and technical personnel is relatively high (44.4 percent). Analysis of historical comparison (see Table 4-2 and Table 4-3) indicates that, since the economic reform, the intergenerational inheritance of the professional and technical personnel stratum has strengthened significantly. The probability of becoming professional and technical

198

personnel for people from the family of professional and technical personnel has been increasing greatly (20.6 percent before 1980 and 27.6 percent after 1980), while the probability for people from the family of workers has been declining sharply (7.3 percent before 1980 and 3.4 percent after 1980). Among professional and technical personnel who started working before 1980, approximately 13.2 percent came from the family of professional and technical personnel; while among professional and technical personnel who started working after 1980, the proportion is 24.5 percent. Meanwhile, among professional and technical personnel who started working before 1980, about 25.5 percent came from the family of workers; while among those who started working after 1980, the proportion decreased to 13.7 percent.

The occupational characteristics of professional and technical personnel require corresponding professional knowledge or skills. In addition, people usually have to invest a certain amount of efforts and money in order to obtain professional qualifications and hence it is difficult for people to give up such professional occupations once they have engaged in these occupations. Such occupational characteristics determine the high stability of the professional and technical personnel stratum. Except for the stratum of agricultural laborers, the intragenerational mobility rate of the professional and technical personnel stratum is the lowest (see Table 4-4). Especially since the 1990s, because the intragenerational mobility rate of the agricultural laborer stratum has been rising, the stability (immobility) of the stratum of professional and technical personnel becomes the highest among the ten social strata (see Table 4-10). Among current professional and technical personnel, about three-fourths (74.6 percent) of them started their first occupation as professional and technical personnel, the remaining one-fourth mainly came from the stratum of clerical personnel, commercial and service personnel, industrial workers, and agricultural laborers. Hardly any members of the stratum of state and social administrators, managerial personnel, and private entrepreneurs moved to the stratum of professional and technical personnel; instead, a certain proportion of professional and technical personnel shifted to the above three strata. Such a direction of mobility indicates that the stratum of state and social administrators, managerial personnel, and private entrepreneurs have higher social status than the stratum of professional and technical personnel. Therefore, professional and technical personnel are willing to move to the three strata, but members of the three strata are not willing to shift to the professional and technical personnel stratum. As a whole, there are two outflow directions in the stratum of professional and technical personnel: entering into politics (moving to the stratum of state and social administrators and clerical personnel) and going into business (moving to the stratum of managerial personnel, private entrepreneurs, and individual-operated business proprietors). In addition, in rural areas, mutual mobility between professional and technical personnel and agricultural laborers happens frequently. However, the majority of professional and technical personnel (60.5 percent) remain in this stratum.

Clerical Personnel: A Buffer Zone between the Lower and Upper Strata

In this study, the *stratum of clerical personnel* refers to full-time office clerks assisting principles of organizations or departments in dealing with administrative routines, including middle-low rank officials in government and party agencies, and grassroots management and non-professional civilians in enterprises and social organizations. Most of them take up low-level white-collar jobs. This stratum is an important component of the middle social strata in modern society.

The stratum of clerical personnel is an important link in the social mobility chain. Members of this stratum are the reserve for state and social administrators, managerial personnel, and professional and technical personnel. Meanwhile, workers and peasants can achieve upward mobility through this stratum. Therefore, this stratum is an important channel for the lower class to achieve upward social mobility. Analysis of its intergenerational mobility (see Table 4-1) shows that, people from families of clerical personnel, governmental cadres, enterprise managerial personnel, and professional and technical personnel have greater chance to become clerical personnel, as well as people from the family of workers have more opportunities. In this stratum, about 22.8 percent of its members came from the family of workers, higher than its average proportion in the overall social structure (15.5 percent). In other words, the stratum of clerical personnel is an important channel for people from families of workers to achieve upward social mobility. The historical comparison (see Table 4-2 and Table 4-3) shows that, since the economic reform, the probabilities of entering the clerical personnel for people from the families of governmental cadres, enterprise managerial personnel, professional and technical personnel, and clerical personnel have been increasing, while the probabilities for people with family backgrounds of workers and peasants have declined significantly.

Judging from intragenerational mobility (see Table 4-4 and Table 4-7), about half of clerical personnel (48.1 percent and 52.4 percent) steadily remain in this stratum, about four-tenths of clerical personnel came from commercial and service personnel, industrial workers, and agricultural laborers (9.3 percent, 14.4 percent, and 18.6 percent respectively), and less than one-tenth came from professional and technical personnel (6.9 percent). Hardly any members of the three advantaged strata, i.e., the stratum of state and social administrators, managerial personnel, and private entrepreneurs, entered the stratum of clerical personnel. In addition, individual-operated business proprietors seldom moved to this stratum as well. As far as the directions of outflow from the clerical personnel stratum, about one-tenth of its members moved upward to the three advantaged strata—the stratum of state and social administrators (4.5 percent), managerial personnel (4.8 percent), and private entrepreneurs (1.9 percent), about one-tenth of its members moved into other middle social strata—the stratum of professional and technical personnel (3.1 percent) and the stratum of individual-operated business proprietors (5 percent), and nearly

200

three-tenths of clerical personnel moved downward to lower social strata—the stratum of commercial and service personnel(4.8 percent), industrial workers (6.2 percent), agricultural laborers (11.5 percent) and the urban-rural jobless, unemployed, and partially unemployed (6.4 percent). Such directions of mobility indicate that the stratum of clerical personnel is in a "buffer zone" between the upper strata and lower strata in the overall structure of social mobility. Compared with another middle-level stratum, i.e., the stratum of professional and technical personnel, the clerical personnel stratum has a greater probability of downward mobility. In other words, although both strata belong to the middle social strata, the status of the professional and technical personnel stratum is higher than that of the clerical personnel stratum in the social mobility chain.

Individual-Operated Business Proprietors: Outsiders with Few Upward Opportunities

The *stratum of individual-operated business proprietors* (i.e., individual industrial and commercial householders) refers to people who possess a small amount of private capital (including real estate), invest their capital into manufacturing, trade, and services sectors or bonds market, and live off of these businesses, including small owners or small employers (possessing sufficient capital to employ a small number of employees and directly participate in activities of labor, production, and management), the self-employed (possessing sufficient capital to start one's own business but without employees), and small investors, small shareholders, and small landlords, etc.

The distribution of individual-operated business proprietors' family backgrounds is very similar to the average distribution of various strata in the overall social structure. Except for the probability of being individual-operated business proprietors for children of small owners or the self-employed, probabilities for people with other family backgrounds are very close (see Table 4-1).

As an emerging stratum after the economic reform, origins of the individual-operated business proprietor stratum mainly consist of those who were squeezed out of the system. At the late 1970s and early 1980s, the back-to-the-city educated youth and people released from labor camps who were not admitted by the state-owned or collective enterprises and institutions became pioneers of the self-employed. In the 1980s, the unemployed youth and a portion of the surplus rural laborers entered this stratum. In the 1990s, a number of laid-off staff members and workers who were squeezed out in the restructuring reform in state-owned and collective enterprises were forced to move to this stratum; meanwhile, many peasant-workers entered into this stratum. By far the majority of individual-operated business proprietors started their individual-operated businesses in the 1990s. Among

Table 4-7 The Table of Mobility between Current and Previous Occupations

Stratum Position of the Previous Occupation		State and social administrator	Managerial personnel	Private entrepreneur	Professional and technical personnel	Clerical personnel	Individual-operated business proprietor	Commercial and service personnel	Industrial worker	Agricultural laborer	The jobless, unemployed, and partially unemployed	Total
State and social administrator	Frequency	28	6	2	3	8	1	0	0	0	1	49
	Expectation	0.5	0.8	0.5	2.1	4.0	5.8	6.2	6.2	21.7	2.1	49.0
	Row Percentage (outflow rate)	57.1%	12.2%	4.1%	6.1%	16.3%	2.0%	0.0%	0.0%	0.0%	2.0%	100.0%
	Column Percentage (inflow rate)	45.9%	6.7%	3.2%	1.2%	1.8%	.2%	0.0%	0.0%	0.0%	0.4%	0.9%
Managerial personnel	Frequency	4	28	1	1	7	1	1	2	2	1	48
	Expectation	0.5	.8	0.5	2.1	3.9	5.2	5.6	6.1	21.2	2.0	48.0
	Row Percentage (outflow rate)	8.3%	58.3%	2.1%	2.1%	14.6%	2.1%	2.1%	4.2%	4.2%	2.1%	100.0%
	Column Percentage (inflow rate)	6.6%	31.5%	1.6%	0.4%	1.5%	0.2%	0.2%	0.3%	0.1%	0.4%	0.9%
Private entrepreneur	Frequency	0	0	13	0	0	1	1	0	1	0	16
	Expectation	0.2	0.3	0.2	0.7	1.3	1.7	1.9	2.0	7.1	0.7	16.0
	Row Percentage (outflow rate)	0.0%	0.0%	81.3%	0.0%	0.0%	6.3%	6.3%	0.0%	6.3%	0.0%	100.0%
	Column Percentage (inflow rate)	0.0%	0.0%	21.0%	0.0%	0.0%	0.2%	0.2%	0.0%	0.0%	0.0%	0.3%
Professional and technical personnel	Frequency	11	6	4	183	30	11	7	3	24	9	288
	Expectation	3.1	4.6	3.2	12.4	23.3	31.4	33.8	36.6	127.3	12.3	288.0
	Row Percentage (outflow rate)	3.8%	2.1%	1.4%	63.5%	10.4%	3.8%	2.4%	1.0%	8.3%	3.1%	100.0%
	Column Percentage (inflow rate)	18.0%	6.7%	6.5%	75.9%	6.6%	1.8%	1.1%	0.4%	1.0%	3.8%	5.2%
Clerical personnel	Frequency	14	15	3	13	237	23	24	28	49	22	428
	Expectation	4.7	6.8	4.7	18.5	34.6	46.7	50.3	54.4	189.1	18.2	428.0
	Row Percentage (outflow rate)	3.3%	3.5%	0.7%	3.0%	55.4%	5.4%	5.6%	6.5%	11.4%	5.1%	100.0%
	Column Percentage (inflow rate)	23.0%	16.9%	4.8%	5.4%	52.4%	3.8%	3.7%	3.9%	2.0%	9.2%	7.7%
Individual-operated business proprietor	Frequency	0	3	6	0	7	180	95	16	24	6	337
	Expectation	3.7	5.4	3.7	14.5	27.3	36.7	39.6	42.8	148.9	14.4	337.0
	Row Percentage (outflow rate)	0.0%	0.9%	1.8%	0.0%	2.1%	53.4%	28.2%	4.7%	7.1%	1.8%	100.0%
	Column Percentage (inflow rate)	0.0%	3.4%	9.7%	0.0%	1.5%	29.6%	14.5%	2.3%	1.0%	2.5%	6.0%

continued

Stratum Position of the Previous Occupation		State and social administrator	Managerial personnel	Private entrepreneur	Professional and technical personnel	Clerical personnel	Individual-operated business proprietor	Commercial and service personnel	Industrial worker	Agricultural laborer	The jobless, unemployed, and partially unemployed	Total
							Stratum Position of the Current Occupation					
Commercial and service personnel	Frequency	2	7	7	4	41	67	230	21	36	38	453
	Expectation	4.9	7.2	5.0	19.5	36.6	49.4	53.2	57.6	200.2	19.3	453.0
	Row Percentage (outflow rate)	0.4%	1.5%	1.8%	0.9%	9.1%	14.8%	50.8%	4.6%	7.9%	8.4%	100.0%
	Column Percentage (inflow rate)	3.3%	7.9%	11.3%	1.7%	9.1%	11.0%	35.1%	3.0%	1.5%	16.0%	8.1%
Industrial worker	Frequency	1	14	7	15	69	121	144	459	130	110	1070
	Expectation	11.7	17.0	11.9	46.2	86.6	116.6	125.6	136.0	472.9	45.6	1070.0
	Row Percentage (outflow rate)	0.1%	1.3%	0.7%	1.4%	6.4%	11.3%	13.5%	42.9%	12.1%	10.3%	100.0%
	Column Percentage (inflow rate)	1.6%	15.7%	11.3%	6.2%	15.3%	19.9%	22.0%	64.6%	5.3%	46.2%	19.2%
Agricultural laborer	Frequency	1	10	18	22	52	191	146	176	2199	43	2858
	Expectation	31.2	45.5	31.7	123.3	231.2	311.5	335.6	363.2	1263.0	121.7	2858.0
	Row Percentage (outflow rate)	0.0%	0.3%	0.6%	0.8%	1.8%	6.7%	5.1%	6.2%	76.9%	1.5%	100.0%
	Column Percentage (inflow rate)	1.6%	11.2%	29.0%	9.1%	11.5%	31.4%	22.3%	24.8%	89.1%	18.1%	51.2%
The jobless, unemployed, and partially unemployed	Frequency	0	0	1	0	1	14	7	5	4	8	40
	Expectation	0.4	0.6	0.4	1.7	3.2	4.4	4.7	5.1	17.7	1.7	40.0
	Row Percentage (outflow rate)	0.0%	0.0%	2.5%	0.0%	2.5%	35.0%	17.5%	12.5%	10.0%	20.0%	100.0%
	Column Percentage (inflow rate)	0.0%	0.0%	1.6%	0.0%	0.2%	2.3%	1.1%	0.7%	0.2%	3.4%	0.7%
Total	Frequency	61	89	62	241	452	609	656	710	2469	238	5587
	Expectation	61.0	89.0	62.0	241.0	452.0	609.0	656.0	710.0	2469.0	238.0	5587.0
	Row Percentage (outflow rate)	1.1%	1.6%	1.1%	4.3%	8.1%	10.9%	11.7%	12.7%	44.2%	4.3%	100.0%
	Column Percentage (inflow rate)	100.0%	100.0%	100.0%	100.0%	100.0%	100.0%	100.0%	100.0%	100.0%	100.0%	100.0%

Note: This weighted sample does not include the never-employed people.

current individual-operated business proprietors, about 6.8 percent of them started their businesses before 1980, 19.9 percent entered this stratum between 1980 and 1989, and 73.3 percent went into business between 1990 and 2001, and among them about 38.9 percent have been in business since 1995. In other words, the overwhelming majority of individual-operated business proprietors have entered this stratum in the recent decade. Especially in the past five or six years, the growth of this stratum has been speeding up. In addition, the origins of individual-operated business proprietors are different between the 1980s and the 1990s. The major origin of this stratum was peasants in the 1980s; while in the 1990s, the proportion of people moving from the stratum industrial workers and commercial and service personnel has risen (see Table 4-9 and Table 4-10). About 15 percent of individual-operated business proprietors are laid-off staff members and workers.

Nearly one-third of individual-operated business proprietors started with individual-operated business (30.4 percent) as their first occupation; the remaining two-thirds came from three lower social strata—the stratum of commercial and service personnel (8.7 percent), industrial workers (19.2 percent), and agricultural laborers (35.8 percent). In addition, a small number of its members came from two middle social strata—the stratum of professional and technical personnel (2 percent) and the stratum of clerical personnel (3.4 percent). Very few members of the three advantaged strata—the stratum of state and social administrators, managerial personnel, and private entrepreneurs—have moved downward to the stratum of individual-operated business proprietors (see Table 4-4 and Table 4-7). Such a composition of its origins shows that the stratum of individual-operated business proprietors is a middle-level social stratum to some extent. It has admitted some from the lower social strata. However, as an intermediate link in the social mobility chain, it seems that the stratum of individual-operated business proprietors has only exerted half of its function. Although it has accommodated some members of lower social strata, usually its outflow channel is limited to but one direction: downward mobility. Compared with the other two middle social strata—the stratum of professional and technical personnel and the stratum of clerical personnel, members of the stratum of individual-operated business proprietors seldom obtained the upward mobility opportunity. It was almost impossible that they might move upward to the stratum of state and social administrators and the stratum of managerial personnel. The opportunity of entering the private entrepreneur stratum is small as well. In the second half of the 1980s and the first half of the 1990s, there were some opportunities for individual-operated business proprietors to become private entrepreneurs. However, the probability of being private entrepreneurs has declined significantly since the mid-1990s. In addition, probabilities of moving to the other two middle social strata for individual-operated business proprietors are also very low. It is not likely that individual-operated business proprietors will shift to become professional and technical personnel. A small number of individual-operated business proprietors may have entered the stratum of clerical personnel. Judging from the outflow rate of this stratum (see Table 4-7), nearly six-tenths of individual-operated business proprietors stay in this stratum and remain immobile (57.6 percent), and the remaining four-tenths moved downward to the three lower social strata, especially the stratum of commercial and service personnel (27.7 percent). In other words, in the hierarchy of social mobility, the position of the individual-operated business proprietor stratum is lower than the other two middle social strata—the stratum of professional and technical personnel and the stratum of clerical personnel. It is a middle-low social stratum. Most importantly, the mobility of members of the individual-operated business proprietor stratum is still limited by institutional barriers. It can only admit people who are squeezed out of the system and it is difficult for members of this stratum to move into the system. For many people, especially those blue-collar personnel without any special professional skills, the mobility from intra-system to extra-system is a kind of downward mobility. In the rank hierarchy of social mobility proposed in the study, moving from the stratum of commercial and service personnel and the stratum of industrial workers to the stratum of individual-operated business proprietors is a sort of upward mobility; however, in the eyes of some people who were laid off from state-owned and collective enterprises, it is a sort of downward mobility.

MOBILITY CHARACTERISTICS OF THE LOWER STRATA

Commercial and service personnel are a rapidly expanding group in the plebeian strata. Its members mainly move into the stratum of clerical personnel and individual-operated business proprietors in upward mobility. On one hand, many industrial workers move upward to be commercial and service personnel; on the other hand, the stratum of industrial workers also admits a large number of peasant-workers. Most members of the agricultural laborer stratum are fettered in rural areas by the residence registration system and become the bottom end in the social mobility chain. The three strata have disadvantaged status in possession of various social resources and have few chances to enter the advantaged strata. The frustrated people in the three strata further fall down to the stratum of the urban-rural jobless, unemployed, and partially unemployed.

Commercial and Service Personnel: Expanding with Multiple Outlets

The stratum of *commercial and service personnel* refers to people engaging in non-professional, non-manual, and manual labor in commercial and services sectors. The social position of this stratum defined by the criteria of stratum classification is blue-collar employees or the blue-collar self-employed in the intra-system or extra-system tertiary industry.

The proportion distribution of family backgrounds of members of this stratum is very close to the distribution of average proportions of various strata in the overall social structure, which means that the family background has no significant influence on the development of this stratum. Only the probability of becoming commercial and service personnel for those from families of workers is relatively high (see Table 4-1). The family backgrounds of members of the commercial and service personnel stratum changed little with time. Before and after the economic reform, probabilities of entering this stratum for people from families of governmental cadres, enterprise managerial personnel, professional and technical personnel, and clerical personnel have dropped slightly (see Table 4-2 and Table 4-3).

Analysis of intragenerational mobility (see Table 4-4 and Table 4-7) shows that about three-tenths (32.5 percent) of commercial and service personnel started their first occupation in commercial and services sectors, about five-tenths of them came from industrial workers (18.9 percent) and agricultural laborers (29.1 percent); less than two-tenths came from the middle strata, among them the majority came from the middle-low stratum, i.e., the stratum of individual-operated business proprietors (13.6 percent). Very few people came from the other two middle strata—the stratum of professional and technical personnel and the stratum of clerical personnel. Meanwhile, very few people came from the three advantaged strata—the stratum of state and social administrators, managerial personnel, and private entrepreneurs. In terms of outflow rate, more than half (53.9 percent) of commercial and service personnel steadily remained in this stratum, about one-fourth of its members moved up to higher-rank strata and the majority of them entered the middle strata, i.e., the clerical personnel stratum (10.6 percent) and the individual-operated business proprietor stratum (13.4 percent); only very few people entered the three advantaged strata—the stratum of state and social administrators, managerial personnel, and private entrepreneurs—and the professional and technical personnel stratum. In addition, less than two-tenths people flowed into the stratum of industrial workers (5.1 percent), agricultural laborers (3.8 percent), and the urban-rural jobless, unemployed, and partially unemployed (7.8 percent). The origins and outflow directions of the commercial and services stratum varied in different periods (see Table 4-5, Table 4-6, Table 4-8, Table 4-9, and Table 4-10). The proportion of commercial and service personnel was relatively low in the overall social structure before 1990. This stratum began to expand in the late 1980s and most entrants came from the stratum of agricultural laborers. The growth of this stratum has been speeding up since the 1990s and its proportion in the overall social structure has been rising rapidly. Most entrants in this period came from the stratum of industrial workers probably due to large-scale downsizing in the secondary industry. In addition, before and in the 1980s, the major destination of upward mobility for commercial and service personnel was the stratum of clerical personnel. Since the 1990s, it has turned to the stratum of individual-operated business proprietors, while people moving to the stratum of clerical personnel have decreased significantly. Meanwhile, the proportion of commercial and service personnel who moved down to the stratum of the urban-rural jobless, unemployed, and partially unemployed has been increasing since the 1990s. Before 1980, hardly anyone was ever laid off in this stratum. In the 1980s, about 3.6 percent of its members moved to the stratum of the urban-rural jobless, unemployed, and partially unemployed. This proportion has increased to 10.4 percent since the 1990s.

Industrial Workers: Changing Composition and Decreasing Size

The *stratum of industrial workers* refers to production workers, construction workers, and related personnel engaging in manual and partially manual labor in the secondary industry. The social position of this stratum defined by the criteria for stratum classification is blue-collar employees or the blue-collar self-employed in the intra-system or extra-system secondary industry.

The proportion distribution of family backgrounds of this stratum is very similar to that of the commercial and service personnel stratum. Except that the probability of being industrial workers for people from the family of workers is relatively high, proportions of people with other types of family backgrounds are very close to the proportion distribution of various strata in the overall social structure (see Table 4-1). The historical analysis of the intergenerational mobility shows that the probability of being industrial workers for people from families of workers before the economic reform is higher than that after the reform (27.2 percent before 1980 and 21.7 after 1980). In addition, the probability of becoming industrial workers for those from families of peasants after the economic reform is higher than that before the reform. Only 8.6 percent of those from families of peasants working before 1980 became industrial workers, while among those with the same family background who started working after 1980, 15 percent became industrial workers (see Table 4-2 and Table 4-2).[1]

In the perspective of intragenerational mobility (see Table 4-4 and Table 4-7), the stratum of industrial workers is similar to the stratum of commercial and service personnel to some extent. Just like the commercial and service personnel stratum, very few industrial workers came from the three advantaged strata—the stratum of state and social administrators, managerial personnel, and private entrepreneurs. In addition, only a small number of industrial workers came from the middle strata—the stratum of professional and technical personnel (1.4 percent), the stratum of clerical personnel (6.2 percent), and the stratum of individual-operated business proprietors (5.6 percent). However, the proportion of industrial workers coming from the middle

---

[1] A large number of rural migrant workers have entered the stratum of industrial workers since the 1990s. When we conducted this survey in urban areas, it was difficult to investigate them; while in rural areas them left the villages to find works in the city. Therefore, as for the proportion of workers who came from families of peasants and started working after 1980, the figure of 15 percent might be underestimated to some extent.

Table 4-8　The Table of Mobility between Current and Previous Occupations, 1949~1979

Stratum Position of the Previous Occupation		State and social administrator	Managerial personnel	Private entrepreneur	Professional and technical personnel	Clerical personnel	Individual-operated business proprietor	Commercial and service personnel	Industrial worker	Agricultural laborer	The jobless, unemployed, and partially unemployed	Total
State and social administrator	Frequency	6	2	0	0	3	0	0	0	0	0	11
	Expectation	0.1	0.1	0.0	0.5	0.5	0.3	0.4	1.0	8.0	0.1	11.0
	Row Percentage(outflow rate)	54.5%	18.2%	0.0%	0.0%	27.3%	0.0%	0.0%	0.0%	0.0%	0.0%	100.0%
	Column Percentage(inflow rate)	46.2%	13.3%	0.0%	0.0%	3.7%	0.0%	0.0%	0.0%	0.0%	0.0%	0.7%
Managerial personnel	Frequency	0	5	0	0	0	0	0	0	0	0	5
	Expectation	0.0	0.0	0.0	0.2	0.2	0.1	0.2	0.5	3.7	0.0	5.0
	Row Percentage(outflow rate)	0.0%	100.0%	0.0%	0.0%	0.0%	0.0%	0.0%	0.0%	0.0%	0.0%	100.0%
	Column Percentage(inflow rate)	0.0%	33.3%	0.0%	0.0%	0.0%	0.0%	0.0%	0.0%	0.0%	0.0%	0.3%
Private entrepreneur	Frequency	0	0	0	0	0	0	0	0	0	0	0
	Expectation	0.0	0.0	0.0	0.0	0.0	0.0	0.0	0.0	0.0	0.0	0.0
	Row Percentage(outflow rate)	0.0%	0.0%	0.0%	0.0%	0.0%	0.0%	0.0%	0.0%	0.0%	0.0%	0.0%
	Column Percentage(inflow rate)	0.0%	0.0%	0.0%	0.0%	0.0%	0.0%	0.0%	0.0%	0.0%	0.0%	0.0%
Professional and technical personnel	Frequency	1	0	0	51	6	0	0	1	7	0	66
	Expectation	0.5	0.6	0.0	2.8	3.2	1.6	2.7	6.1	48.2	0.4	66.0
	Row Percentage(outflow rate)	1.5%	0.0%	0.0%	77.3%	9.1%	0.0%	0.0%	1.5%	10.6%	0.0%	100.0%
	Column Percentage(inflow rate)	7.7%	0.0%	0.0%	71.8%	7.3%	0.0%	0.0%	0.6%	0.6%	0.0%	3.9%
Clerical personnel	Frequency	5	1	0	4	44	1	2	6	18	0	81
	Expectation	0.6	0.7	0.0	3.4	3.9	2.0	3.3	7.5	59.2	0.4	81.0
	Row Percentage(outflow rate)	6.2%	1.2%	0.0%	4.9%	54.3%	1.2%	2.5%	7.4%	22.2%	0.0%	100.0%
	Column Percentage(inflow rate)	38.5%	6.7%	0.0%	5.6%	53.7%	2.4%	2.9%	3.9%	1.5%	0.0%	4.8%

Stratum Position of the Previous Occupation		State and social administrator	Managerial personnel	Private entrepreneur	Professional and technical personnel	Clerical personnel	Individual-operated business proprietor	Commercial and service personnel	Industrial worker	Agricultural laborer	The jobless, unemployed, and partially unemployed	Total
											Stratum Position of the Current Occupation	
Individual-operated business proprietor	Frequency	0	0	0	0	0	29	19	2	4	0	54
	Expectation	0.4	0.5	0.0	2.3	2.6	1.3	2.2	5.0	39.5	0.3	54.0
	Row Percentage (outflow rate)	0.0%	0.0%	0.0%	0.0%	0.0%	53.7%	35.2%	3.7%	7.4%	0.0%	100.0%
	Column Percentage (inflow rate)	0.0%	0.0%	0.0%	0.0%	0.0%	70.7%	27.9%	1.3%	0.3%	0.0%	3.2%
Commercial and service personnel	Frequency	0	2	0	2	6	2	26	2	3	0	43
	Expectation	0.3	0.4	0.0	1.8	2.1	1.0	1.7	4.0	31.4	0.2	43.0
	Row Percentage (outflow rate)	0.0%	4.7%	0.0%	4.7%	14.0%	4.7%	60.5%	4.7%	7.0%	0.0%	100.0%
	Column Percentage (inflow rate)	0.0%	13.3%	0.0%	2.8%	7.3%	4.9%	38.2%	1.3%	0.2%	0.0%	2.6%
Industrial worker	Frequency	0	4	0	2	10	2	9	114	13	1	155
	Expectation	1.2	1.4	0.0	6.5	7.5	3.8	6.3	14.3	113.2	0.8	155.0
	Row Percentage (outflow rate)	0.0%	2.6%	0.0%	1.3%	6.5%	1.3%	5.8%	73.5%	8.4%	0.6%	100.0%
	Column Percentage (inflow rate)	0.0%	26.7%	0.0%	2.8%	12.2%	4.9%	13.2%	73.5%	1.1%	11.1%	9.2%
Agricultural laborer	Frequency	1	1	0	12	13	7	11	28	1186	8	1267
	Expectation	9.8	11.3	0.0	53.4	61.7	30.8	51.1	116.5	925.0	6.8	1267.0
	Row Percentage (outflow rate)	0.1%	0.1%	0.0%	0.9%	1.0%	0.6%	0.9%	2.2%	93.6%	0.6%	100.0%
	Column Percentage (inflow rate)	7.7%	6.7%	0.0%	16.9%	15.9%	17.1%	16.2%	18.1%	96.3%	88.9%	75.2%
The jobless, unemployed, and partially unemployed	Frequency	0	0	0	0	0	0	1	2	0	0	3
	Expectation	0.0	0.0	0.0	0.1	0.1	0.1	0.1	0.3	2.2	0.0	3.0
	Row Percentage (outflow rate)	0.0%	0.0%	0.0%	0.0%	0.0%	0.0%	33.3%	66.7%	0.0%	0.0%	100.0%
	Column Percentage (inflow rate)	0.0%	0.0%	0.0%	0.0%	0.0%	0.0%	1.5%	1.3%	0.0%	0.0%	0.2%
Total	Frequency	13	15	0	71	82	41	68	155	1231	9	1685
	Expectation	13.0	15.0	0.0	71.0	82.0	41.0	68.0	155.0	1231.0	9.0	1685.0
	Row Percentage (outflow rate)	0.8%	0.9%	.0%	4.2%	4.9%	2.4%	4.0%	9.2%	73.1%	0.5%	100.0%
	Column Percentage (inflow rate)	100.0%	100.0%	100.0%	100.0%	100.0%	100.0%	100.0%	100.0%	100.0%	100.0%	100.0%

Note: This weighted sample does not include the never-employed people.

Table 4-9　The Table of Mobility between Current and Previous Occupations, 1980–1989

Stratum Position of the Previous Occupation		Stratum Position of the Current Occupation										
		State and social administrator	Managerial personnel	Private entrepreneur	Professional and technical personnel	Clerical personnel	Individual-operated business proprietor	Commercial and service personnel	Industrial worker	Agricultural laborer	The jobless, unemployed, and partially unemployed	Total
State and social administrator	Frequency	10	1	0	0	2	0	0	0	0	0	13
	Expectation	0.2	0.2	0.1	0.5	1.0	1.2	1.3	1.5	6.8	0.2	13.0
	Row Percentage(outflow rate)	76.9%	7.7%	0.0%	0.0%	15.4%	0.0%	0.0%	0.0%	0.0%	0.0%	100.0%
	Column Percentage(inflow rate)	58.8%	4.3%	0.0%	0.0%	2.2%	0.0%	0.0%	0.0%	0.0%	0.0%	1.0%
Managerial personnel	Frequency	1	12	0	0	1	0	1	0	0	0	15
	Expectation	0.2	0.3	0.1	0.5	1.1	1.4	1.5	1.7	7.9	0.2	15.0
	Row Percentage(outflow rate)	6.7%	80.0%	0.0%	0.0%	6.7%	0.0%	6.7%	0.0%	0.0%	0.0%	100.0%
	Column Percentage(inflow rate)	5.9%	52.2%	0.0%	0.0%	1.1%	0.0%	0.8%	0.0%	0.0%	0.0%	1.2%
Private entrepreneur	Frequency	0	0	5	0	0	0	0	0	1	0	6
	Expectation	0.1	0.1	0.1	0.2	0.4	0.6	0.6	0.7	3.2	0.1	6.0
	Row Percentage(outflow rate)	0.0%	0.0%	83.3%	0.0%	0.0%	0.0%	0.0%	0.0%	16.7%	0.0%	100.0%
	Column Percentage(inflow rate)	0.0%	0.0%	41.7%	0.0%	0.0%	0.0%	0.0%	0.0%	0.1%	0.0%	0.5%
Professional and technical personnel	Frequency	3	0	0	36	8	1	3	0	6	0	57
	Expectation	0.8	1.0	0.5	2.0	4.2	5.4	5.7	6.6	30.0	0.7	57.0
	Row Percentage(outflow rate)	5.3%	0.0%	0.0%	63.2%	14.0%	1.8%	5.3%	0.0%	10.5%	0.0%	100.0%
	Column Percentage(inflow rate)	17.6%	0.0%	0.0%	80.0%	8.6%	0.8%	2.4%	0.0%	0.9%	0.0%	4.5%
Clerical personnel	Frequency	2	5	1	2	42	6	3	4	9	0	74
	Expectation	1.0	1.3	0.7	2.6	5.4	7.1	7.4	8.6	39.0	0.9	74.0
	Row Percentage(outflow rate)	2.7%	6.8%	1.4%	2.7%	56.8%	8.1%	4.1%	5.4%	12.2%	0.0%	100.0%
	Column Percentage(inflow rate)	11.8%	21.7%	8.3%	4.4%	45.2%	5.0%	2.4%	2.7%	1.3%	0.0%	5.8%

continued

Stratum Position of the Current Occupation

Stratum Position of the Previous Occupation		State and social administrator	Managerial personnel	Private entrepreneur	Professional and technical personnel	Clerical personnel	Individual-operated business proprietor	Commercial and service personnel	Industrial worker	Agricultural laborer	The jobless, unemployed, and partially unemployed	Total
Individual-operated business proprietor	Frequency	0	0	0	0	0	47	38	2	0	0	87
	Expectation	1.2	1.6	0.8	3.1	6.4	8.3	8.7	10.1	45.8	1.1	87.0
	Row Percentage(outflow rate)	0.0%	0.0%	0.0%	0.0%	0.0%	54.0%	43.7%	2.3%	0.0%	0.0%	100.0%
	Column Percentage(inflow rate)	0.0%	0.0%	0.0%	0.0%	0.0%	38.8%	29.9%	1.4%	0.0%	0.0%	6.9%
Commercial and service personnel	Frequency	0	0	1	2	9	3	25	3	10	2	55
	Expectation	0.7	1.0	0.5	1.9	4.0	5.2	5.5	6.4	29.0	0.7	55.0
	Row Percentage(outflow rate)	0.0%	0.0%	1.8%	3.6%	16.4%	5.5%	45.5%	5.5%	18.2%	3.6%	100.0%
	Column Percentage(inflow rate)	0.0%	0.0%	8.3%	4.4%	9.7%	2.5%	19.7%	2.0%	1.5%	12.5%	4.3%
Industrial worker	Frequency	1	3	2	3	19	15	22	97	25	7	194
	Expectation	2.6	3.5	1.8	6.9	14.2	18.5	19.4	22.5	102.2	2.4	194.0
	Row Percentage(outflow rate)	0.5%	1.5%	1.0%	1.5%	9.8%	7.7%	11.3%	50.0%	12.9%	3.6%	100.0%
	Column Percentage(inflow rate)	5.9%	13.0%	16.7%	6.7%	20.4%	12.4%	17.3%	66.0%	3.7%	43.8%	15.3%
Agricultural laborer	Frequency	0	2	2	2	12	48	35	40	612	6	762
	Expectation	10.2	13.8	7.2	27.0	55.8	72.6	76.2	88.2	401.4	9.6	762.0
	Row Percentage(outflow rate)	0.0%	0.3%	0.3%	0.3%	1.6%	6.3%	4.6%	5.2%	80.7%	0.8%	100.0%
	Column Percentage(inflow rate)	0.0%	8.7%	16.7%	4.4%	12.9%	39.7%	27.6%	27.2%	91.9%	37.5%	60.0%
The jobless, unemployed, and partially unemployed	Frequency	0	0	1	0	0	1	0	1	3	1	7
	Expectation	0.1	0.1	0.1	0.2	0.5	0.7	0.7	0.8	3.7	0.1	7.0
	Row Percentage(outflow rate)	0.0%	0.0%	14.3%	0.0%	0.0%	14.3%	0.0%	14.3%	42.9%	14.3%	100.0%
	Column Percentage(inflow rate)	0.0%	0.0%	8.3%	0.0%	0.0%	0.8%	0.0%	0.7%	0.4%	6.3%	0.6%
Total	Frequency	17	23	12	45	93	121	127	147	669	16	1270
	Expectation	17.0	23.0	12.0	45.0	93.0	121.0	127.0	147.0	669.0	16.0	1270.0
	Row Percentage(outflow rate)	1.3%	1.8%	0.9%	3.5%	7.3%	9.5%	10.0%	11.6%	52.7%	1.3%	100.0%
	Column Percentage(inflow rate)	100.0%	100.0%	100.0%	100.0%	100.0%	100.0%	100.0%	100.0%	100.0%	100.0%	100.0%

Note: This weighted sample does not include the never-employed people.

Table 4-10 The Table of Mobility between Current and Previous Occupations, 1990~2001

Stratum Position of the Previous Occupation		State and social administrator	Managerial personnel	Private entrepreneur	Professional and technical personnel	Clerical personnel	Individual-operated business proprietor	Commercial and service personnel	Industrial worker	Agricultural laborer	The jobless, unemployed, and partially unemployed	Total
State and social administrator	Frequency	12	3	2	2	3	0	1	0	0	1	24
	Expectation	0.3	0.5	0.5	1.1	2.5	4.1	4.2	3.7	5.2	2.0	24.0
	Row Percentage(outflow rate)	50.0%	12.5%	8.3%	8.3%	12.5%	0.0%	4.2%	0.0%	0.0%	4.2%	100.0%
	Column Percentage(inflow rate)	40.0%	6.0%	4.0%	1.6%	1.1%	0.0%	0.2%	0.0%	0.0%	0.5%	0.9%
Managerial personnel	Frequency	3	11	1	1	6	1	1	2	2	1	29
	Expectation	0.3	.6	0.6	1.4	3.0	4.9	5.1	4.5	6.3	2.4	29.0
	Row Percentage(outflow rate)	10.3%	37.9%	3.4%	3.4%	20.7%	3.4%	3.4%	6.9%	6.9%	3.4%	100.0%
	Column Percentage(inflow rate)	10.0%	22.0%	2.0%	0.8%	2.2%	0.2%	0.2%	0.5%	0.4%	0.5%	1.1%
Private entrepreneur	Frequency	0	0	8	0	0	1	1	0	0	0	10
	Expectation	0.1	0.2	0.2	0.5	1.0	1.7	1.8	1.5	2.2	0.8	10.0
	Row Percentage(outflow rate)	0.0%	0.0%	80.0%	0.0%	0.0%	10.0%	10.0%	0.0%	0.0%	0.0%	100.0%
	Column Percentage(inflow rate)	0.0%	0.0%	16.0%	0.0%	0.0%	0.2%	0.2%	0.0%	0.0%	0.0%	0.4%
Professional and technical personnel	Frequency	6	5	4	95	16	10	4	1	11	9	161
	Expectation	1.8	3.1	3.1	7.7	16.9	27.3	28.3	24.8	34.9	13.2	161.0
	Row Percentage(outflow rate)	3.7%	3.1%	2.5%	59.0%	9.9%	6.2%	2.5%	0.6%	6.8%	5.6%	100.0%
	Column Percentage(inflow rate)	20.0%	10.0%	8.0%	76.0%	5.8%	2.2%	0.9%	0.2%	1.9%	4.2%	6.1%
Clerical personnel	Frequency	7	9	2	7	150	16	18	18	21	22	270
	Expectation	3.1	5.1	5.1	12.9	28.3	45.8	47.5	41.6	58.5	22.1	270.0
	Row Percentage(outflow rate)	2.6%	3.3%	0.7%	2.6%	55.6%	5.9%	6.7%	6.7%	7.8%	8.1%	100.0%
	Column Percentage(inflow rate) (inflow rate)	23.3%	18.0%	4.0%	5.6%	54.5%	3.6%	3.9%	4.5%	3.7%	10.2%	10.3%

continued

Stratum Position of the Previous Occupation		State and social administrator	Managerial personnel	Private entrepreneur	Professional and technical personnel	Clerical personnel	Individual-operated business proprietor	Commercial and service personnel	Industrial worker	Agricultural laborer	The jobless, unemployed, and partially unemployed	Total
							Stratum Position of the Current Occupation					
Individual-operated business proprietor	Frequency	0	3	6	0	6	103	39	13	19	6	195
	Expectation	2.2	3.7	3.7	9.3	20.4	33.1	34.3	30.0	42.2	16.0	195.0
	Row Percentage(outflow rate)	0.0%	1.5%	3.1%	0.0%	3.1%	52.8%	20.0%	6.7%	9.7%	3.1%	100.0%
	Column Percentage(inflow rate)	0.0%	6.0%	12.0%	0.0%	2.2%	23.1%	8.5%	3.2%	3.3%	2.8%	7.4%
Commercial and service personnel	Frequency	2	5	6	1	26	62	179	15	23	37	356
	Expectation	4.1	6.8	6.8	17.0	37.3	60.4	62.6	54.8	77.1	29.2	356.0
	Row Percentage(outflow rate)	0.6%	1.4%	1.7%	0.3%	7.3%	17.4%	50.3%	4.2%	6.5%	10.4%	100.0%
	Column Percentage(inflow rate)	6.7%	10.0%	12.0%	0.8%	9.5%	13.9%	38.8%	3.7%	4.0%	17.2%	13.6%
Industrial worker	Frequency	0	7	5	10	40	104	113	245	92	103	719
	Expectation	8.2	13.7	13.7	34.3	75.4	122.0	126.4	110.7	155.7	58.9	719.0
	Row Percentage(outflow rate)	0.0%	1.0%	0.7%	1.4%	5.6%	14.5%	15.7%	34.1%	12.8%	14.3%	100.0%
	Column Percentage(inflow rate)	0.0%	14.0%	10.0%	8.0%	14.5%	23.4%	24.5%	60.6%	16.2%	47.9%	27.4%
Agricultural laborer	Frequency	0	7	16	9	27	136	99	108	399	29	830
	Expectation	9.5	15.8	15.8	39.6	87.0	140.8	145.9	127.8	179.7	68.0	830.0
	Row Percentage(outflow rate)	0.0%	0.8%	1.9%	1.1%	3.3%	16.4%	11.9%	13.0%	48.1%	3.5%	100.0%
	Column Percentage(inflow rate)	0.0%	14.0%	32.0%	7.2%	9.8%	30.6%	21.5%	26.7%	70.2%	13.5%	31.6%
The jobless, unemployed, and partially unemployed	Frequency	0	0	0	0	1	12	6	2	1	7	29
	Expectation	0.3	0.6	0.6	1.4	3.0	4.9	5.1	4.5	6.3	2.4	29.0
	Row Percentage(outflow rate)	0.0%	0.0%	0.0%	0.0%	3.4%	41.4%	20.7%	6.9%	3.4%	24.1%	100.0%
	Column Percentage(inflow rate)	0.0%	0.0%	0.0%	0.0%	0.4%	2.7%	1.3%	0.5%	0.2%	3.3%	1.1%
Total	Frequency	30	50	50	125	275	445	461	404	568	215	2623
	Expectation	30.0	50.0	50.0	125.0	275.0	445.0	461.0	404.0	568.0	215.0	2623.0
	Row Percentage(outflow rate)	1.1%	1.9%	1.9%	4.8%	10.5%	17.0%	17.6%	15.4%	21.7%	8.2%	100.0%
	Column Percentage(inflow rate)	100.0%	100.0%	100.0%	100.0%	100.0%	100.0%	100.0%	100.0%	100.0%	100.0%	100.0%

Note: This weighted sample does not include the never-employed people.

213

strata is far behind that of commercial and service personnel who came from the middle strata. As far as the outflow rate, the proportion of industrial workers ascending to the three advantaged strata is very low (about 3 percent), which is similar to the situation of the stratum of commercial and service personnel. In addition, about two-tenths of industrial workers moved up to the three middle strata (1.4 percent, 6.5 percent, and 11.7 percent respectively), and the proportion is slightly lower than that of the commercial and service personnel stratum. The proportion of industrial workers moving down to the stratum of the urban-rural jobless, unemployed, and partially unemployed is higher than that of the commercial and service personnel stratum. Meanwhile, in terms of the mutual mobility between the stratum of industrial workers and the stratum of commercial and service personnel, the mainstream seems to move in only one direction. In most cases, the proportion of industrial workers who moved to the stratum of commercial and service personnel is much higher than that of commercial and service personnel moving to the stratum of industrial workers. Such an occurrence suggests a tendency in changes of occupational structure and stratum structure: the number of industrial workers is decreasing while the number of commercial and service personnel is growing. After comparing the overall tendency of intragenerational mobility in industrial workers and commercial and service personnel, we found that the status of the commercial and service personnel stratum is slightly higher than that of the industrial worker stratum in the hierarchy of the social mobility chain in current China. The reason is that the chance of upward mobility for commercial and service personnel is greater than that for industrial workers and, meanwhile, the probability of downward mobility of the commercial and services stratum is lower than that of the industrial worker stratum. In addition, industrial workers tend to move to the commercial and services stratum rather than vice versa.

The historical change of intragenerational mobility in the industrial worker stratum is exactly the same with the stratum of commercial and service personnel. Before 1980 and throughout the 1980s, industrial workers mainly moved upward to the stratum of commercial and service personnel. In the 1990s, they mainly moved to the stratum of individual-operated business proprietors. In addition, few industrial workers moved downward to the stratum of the urban-rural jobless, unemployed, and partially unemployed before 1980 and in the 1980s, while in the 1990s about 14.3 percent of them moved into this stratum (see Table 4-8, Table 4-9, and Table 4-10).

Agricultural Laborers: A Highly Stable Stratum with Increasing Mobility

The *stratum of agricultural laborers* refers to farmers who contract in collective-owned farmland to run agriculture (forestry, animal husbandry, and fishery) in their households and live on it as their only (or major) occupation and income source. The position of this stratum in the social structure is the self-employed or employed laborers in possession of a small amount or none of the means of production outside the system.

The agricultural laborer stratum has the strongest intergenerational inheritance. About 92.8 percent of agricultural laborers came from peasant families and more than half (54.9 percent) of children of peasants are still agricultural laborers (see Table 4-1). The intergenerational inheritance of this stratum is a result the rural-urban divide caused by the residence registration system to some extent. Among members of the agricultural laborer stratum, about 98.4 percent of them hold the registered rural residence status and 89.8 percent reside in rural areas.

Analysis of intragenerational mobility (see Table 4-4 and Table 4-7) shows that the stratum of agricultural laborers is highly stable and only out and no in to some extent. About 91.5 percent of agricultural laborers started their first occupation as a farmer. The proportion of people coming from other strata is extremely low. In addition, among people whose first occupation was agricultural laborer, 73.4 percent nowadays are still farmers. Such an immobility rate is the highest among all social strata. About one-fourth of those whose first occupation was agricultural laborer moved to other strata. The proportion of agricultural laborers who move into the three advantaged strata—the stratum of state and social administrators, managerial personnel, and private entrepreneurs—is less than two percent. About one-tenth of agricultural laborers moved into the three middle strata—the stratum of professional and technical personnel (0.9 percent), the stratum of clerical personnel (2.7 percent), and the stratum of individual-operated business proprietors (7.1 percent). Nearly 15 percent of agricultural laborers moved into the stratum of commercial and service personnel (6.2 percent) and the stratum of industrial workers (7.6 percent). Therefore, the outflow from this stratum is very low and almost no inflow to it. Such a pattern of social mobility indicates that, on one hand, the number and size of agricultural laborers have been decreasing; one the other hand, this stratum is at the bottom of the hierarchy of social mobility chain (except for the stratum of the urban-rural jobless, unemployed, and partially unemployed). Although the opportunity of migrating between regions and finding jobs in the city for agricultural laborers has been increasing since the economic reform, in social mobility perspective the stratum of agricultural laborers has the lowest outflow rate and the fewest upward mobility opportunities.

Such a situation has changed to some extent since the 1980s. The historical comparison on intragenerational mobility shows that the social mobility of the agricultural laborer stratum varied in different periods (see Table 4-8, Table 4-9, and Table 4-10). Before 1980, this stratum was highly stable with an extremely low outflow rate (6.4 percent) and inflow rate (3.7 percent). The outflow rate of this stratum increased gradually throughout the 1980s. About two-tenths (19.3 percent) of agricultural laborers moved to other strata, mainly the stratum of individual-operated business proprietors, commercial and service personnel, and industrial workers. However, the inflow rate of this stratum was still very low (8.1 percent). In the 1990s, both the outflow rate and inflow rate of this stratum increased significantly and the immobility rate of the agricultural laborer stratum was no longer the highest. About half of farmers (51.9 percent) moved to other strata, mainly the stratum of individual-operated business proprietors (16.4 percent), commercial and service personnel (11.9 percent), and industrial workers (13 percent). At the same time, about three-tenths (29.8 percent) of its members came from other strata, mainly the stratum of industrial workers. This might be caused by a number of workers in township enterprises returning to agriculture because of downsizing of township enterprises in that period. In addition, a number of laid-off staff members and workers of state-owned enterprises moved to the countryside and farmed on contracted farmland in Northeastern China.

The Urban-Rural Jobless, Unemployed, and Partially Unemployed: An Emerging Bottom

The *stratum of the urban-rural jobless, unemployed, and partially unemployed* refers to people of working age but without regular jobs. They are a special and transient group.

Among the unemployed and partially unemployed people who ever had jobs, about half (46.2 percent) of them came from the stratum of industrial workers, 18.1 percent from the stratum of agricultural laborers, 16 percent from the commercial and services stratum, and 9.2 percent from the clerical personnel stratum. In addition, there were a few professional and technical personnel (3.8 percent) and individual-operated business proprietors (2.5 percent) moving into this stratum. It is not likely that members of the three advantaged strata will be out of work (see Table 4-7). More than nine-tenths of the unemployed and partially unemployed lost their jobs after 1990. In the 1980s, the unemployed mainly came from three lower strata—the stratum of commercial and services personnel, industrial workers, and agricultural laborers. Almost no members of middle strata and advantaged strata moved into this stratum. However, the situation has changed since 1990. There are 17.2 percent of the unemployed came from three middle strata—the stratum of professional and technical personnel, clerical personnel, and individual-operated business proprietors. Meanwhile, it is possible that members of the three advantaged strata will have lost their jobs since then.

216

SUMMARY: OPENNESS AND CLOSURE OF THE CHINESE SOCIAL STRUCTURE

Based on above analyses of the data of intergenerational and intragenerational mobility, we come to the following conclusion: As a whole, the social structure of China has been more open since the economic reform. Both the intergenerational mobility rate and intragenerational mobility rate are significantly higher than that before the reform. However, in the perspective of social mobility opportunity, closure still exists to certain degree.

Table 4-11　Historical Comparisons of Intergenerational and Intragenerational Mobility Rates *

Unit: %

Category	Intergenerational Mobility			Intragenerational Mobility (first occupation/current occupation)			Intragenerational Mobility (previous occupation/current occupation)			
	Overall	Started working before 1980	Started working after 1980	Overall	Started working before 1980	Started working after 1980	Overall	Changed jobs between 1949~1979	Changed jobs between 1980~1989	Changed jobs between 1990~2001
Immobility Rate	51.7	58.6	46.0	63.2	64.7	61.8	63.7	86.7	69.8	45.8
Total Mobility Rate	48.3	41.4	54.0	36.8	35.3	38.2	36.3	13.3	30.2	54.2
Upward Mobility Rate	37.0	32.4	40.9	23.2	23.8	22.6	20.9	7.4	18.7	30.5
Downward Mobility Rate	11.3	9.1	13.1	13.6	11.5	15.6	15.5	5.9	11.5	23.6

Note: * Mobility rates in Table 4-11 are calculated based on figures in Table 4-1, Table 4-4, and Table 4-7. The *total mobility rate* refers to the proportion of occupational or stratum status that has changed in the intergenerational or intragenerational mobility tables. The *immobility rate* refers to the proportion of occupational or stratum status that does not change. The *upward mobility rate* refers to the proportion of changes from a lower position to a higher position. The *downward mobility rate* refers to the proportion of changes from a higher position to a lower position. In Table 4-11, the sum of upward mobility rate and downward mobility rate in each column is equal to the total mobility rate. The sum of total mobility rate and immobility rate is equal to one hundred percent. The *intergenerational mobility rate* refers to changes between father's occupation and respondent's current occupation. The *intragenerational mobility (first occupation/current occupation)* refers to changes between the stratum position of respondent's first occupation and the stratum position of respondent's current occupation. *Intragenerational mobility (previous occupation/current occupation)* refers to changes between the stratum position of respondent's current occupation and the stratum position of respondent's previous occupation. In addition, the calculations of mobility rates in Table 4-11 are explained as follows: (1) the intergenerational mobility rates are calculated based on the six-category occupation classification (see the classification in Table 4-3). The intragenerational mobility rates are calculated based on the occupation classification of ten major social strata. (2) The upward and downward rate of intragenerational mobility are calculated based on the order of the ten major social strata (see Table 4-6). For example, if one's occupation is changed from the "state and social administrator" in the first place in the hierarchy to the "managerial personnel" in the second place or the "private entrepreneur" in the third place, such a move is regarded as a kind of downward mobility; conversely, it is regarded as upward mobility. However, it may be hard to say that these changes are definitely upward or downward mobility.

The intergenerational and intragenerational total mobility rate, immobility rate, upward mobility rate, and downward mobility rate are listed in Table 4-11. All figures show that the mobility rates after the economic reform are higher than those before the reform. In terms of the intergenerational mobility rate, the total mobility rate of people who started working before 1980 was 41.4 percent, while among people who started working after 1980; the rate is 54 percent, up by 13 percent. At the same time, the upward mobility rate and downward mobility rate have increased by 8 percent and 4 percent respectively.[1] The intragenerational mobility rate (first occupation/current occupation) shows the same tendency. The total mobility rate of people who started working before 1980 was 35.3 percent; while among people who started working after 1980, the rate is 38.2 percent. The rate of the latter is not much higher than that of the former. However, people who started working before 1980 have a longer working experience and hence should have a higher probability of social mobility than those who started working after 1980. Since in fact the total mobility rate of the former is lower than that of the latter, it means that the society has provided more mobility opportunities after 1980 or since the economic reform than before 1980.[2]

Figures about the intragenerational mobility between previous and current occupation show the same tendency. The total mobility rate, upward mobility rate, and downward mobility rate after the economic reform are all higher than those before the

---

[1] It should be noticed that the mobility rate of people who started working before and after 1980 may not perfectly represent the mobility rate before and after the economic reform. The reason is that a number of people who started working before 1980 were still working after 1980 and hence their social mobility might occur after 1980. This means that the mobility rate of people who started working before 1980 in Table 4-11 includes a portion of mobility occurred after 1980. In other words, the difference between mobility rates before and after the economic reform should be greater than what the figures in this table show.

[2] The intragenerational mobility rate between the first occupation and the current occupation indicates a strange phenomenon. Although the total mobility rate of those who started working after 1980 is higher than that of people who started working before 1980, the upward mobility rate of the former is slightly lower than that of the latter, while the downward mobility rate of the former is significantly higher than that of the latter. The possible reason of this phenomenon is that the working experience of people who started working before 1980 are longer than that of people who started working after 1980 and hence the former had greater chance to achieve upward mobility. In addition, the difference in downward mobility rates between the two groups may caused by the following factors: because the working experience of those who started working before 1980 were longer and their social status were more stable, or they had retired before the reform, the probability of downward mobility for them was not high. In contrast, people who started working after 1980 have greater probability of downward mobility due to influences of a series of reforms, such as administrative structure simplifying and enterprises downsizing.

reform are. In terms of changes of occupations that occurred between 1949 and 1979, only slightly over one-tenth (13.3 percent) of people achieved changes in stratum status; of which, the upward mobility rate was 7.4 percent, and the downward mobility rate was 5.9 percent. As far as changes of occupations that occurred between 1980 and 1989, less than one-third (30.2 percent) of people achieved changes in stratum status; of which, the upward mobility rate was 18.7 percent, and the downward mobility rate was 11.5 percent. As regards changes of occupations that occurred between 1990 and 2001, more than half (54.2 percent) of people achieved changes in stratum status; of which, the upward mobility rate is 30.5 percent, and the downward mobility rate is 23.6 percent. All these figures clearly show that people's upward mobility opportunity has been increased since the economic reform; meanwhile, the probability of downward mobility has grown as well.

The same conclusion can be reached from another perspective. Table 4-12 lists data about the mobility rate of different age groups in the population aged 16 to 70. People in different age groups experienced their social mobility or occupational mobility in different periods. People in different age groups have different mobility rates, which mean the social mobility in different periods is different. The working experience of people in the group of the elderly (51~60 and 61~70) mainly occurred before the economic reform and the early stages of the reform. The working experience of people in the middle-aged group (31~40 and 41~50) mainly occurred at the late stage of the Cultural Revolution and after the reform. People in the group of the youth (16~20 and 21~30) started their working experience after the reform. After comparing the intergenerational and intragenerational mobility rate in different age groups, we found that the intergenerational and intragenerational mobility rate of the middle-aged are higher than that of the old, and the upward mobility rate is especially relatively high; while although the youth have just started their career, they still show a relatively high mobility rate. In other words, people's upward mobility opportunities have been increasing significantly since the economic reform. Especially, emerging strata provide people with new channels of upward social mobility.

Table 4-12   Intergenerational and Intragenerational Mobility Rates in Different Age Groups

Unit: %

Age Group	Intergenerational Mobility			Intragenerational Mobility		
	Total mobility rate	Upward mobility rate	Downward mobility rate	Total mobility rate	Upward mobility rate	Downward mobility rate
16~20	29.1	25.1	4.0	27.5	16.0	11.5
21~30	53.0	41.4	11.6	37.0	22.4	14.6
31~40	52.4	40.1	12.0	40.9	27.7	13.2
41~50	43.0	32.6	10.4	39.8	27.9	11.9
51~60	39.2	32.8	6.4	33.4	23.2	10.2
61~70	46.0	41.4	4.6	31.7	19.3	12.4

Note: In calculation of intergenerational mobility rate in Table 4-12, the 16~20 and 21~30 age groups include a number of enrolled full-time students. According the criteria of stratum classification of the study, stratum positions of enrolled students are determined by their fathers' stratum positions. In other words, stratum positions of enrolled students are the same with their fathers' stratum positions; as a result, the mobility rate of the two age groups, especially the 16~20 group, decreased accordingly.

Judging from the tendency of the growing mobility rate, current Chinese society has been increasingly open. However, compared with the tendency of social mobility in industrialized countries, the growth of social mobility in China occurs not only in upward mobility, but also in downward mobility. This may be the consequence of the "dual transformation", i.e., the social mobility in current Chinese society occurs in the background of industrialization and institutional transition. The industrialization has brought about an upgrade in industrial structure and occupational structure and hence inevitably led to a significant increase of upward mobility opportunities. This is also a trend in all industrialized countries. The particularity of Chinese society is that the advance of industrialization goes with the institutional transition (the economic systems reform). In the progress of institutional reform, a large number of people have experienced downward mobility and hence led to an increase of downward mobility rate.

When judging the tendency of openness and closure in a social structure, besides considering changes in the mobility rate, it is necessary to investigate the relative mobility opportunity, especially the upward mobility opportunity, of each social stratum. An open society should have unobstructed channels of upward mobility. Barriers to mobility between each stratum should be relatively weak. The opportunity of entering advantaged strata should not be strongly affected by family backgrounds. In other words, the distribution of upward mobility opportunity would be relatively fair. However, according to the above-mentioned analyses on intergenerational and intragenerational mobility of each occupational groups and social strata in this chapter, we also found a series of signs that indicate the social structure of China has been tending to become more closed. For example, the intergenerational inheritance of high-level occupational groups or advantaged social strata, such as state and social administrators, managerial personnel, and professional and technical personnel, etc., has become significantly stronger since the economic reform. Meanwhile, the door for children of lower-level occupational groups to enter these high-level occupational groups has become narrower than that before the reform. The intragenerational mobility suggests the same tendency. The barriers to mobility between the upper strata (advantaged social strata) and the lower strata (disadvantaged social strata) have been strengthened to some extent. Different social strata have distinct paths and patterns of social mobility. From this perspective, boundaries between social strata have become clearer and barriers to mobility between the upper and lower strata have been increasing. In sum, the increasing openness in the overall social structure and the unfairness in mobility opportunity together make up the complicated characteristics of current social structure transition in China.

Chapter 5 Social Mobility Mechanisms in Contemporary China

As a whole, social mobility in China is currently limited by social structure at individual levels and by the institutional arrangements of the state. Adjustments in structure often change the situation, direction, and opportunity of social mobility. For example, the adjustments in industrial structure have led to a large number of workers moving to the tertiary industry. Changes in institutional arrangements and in intentions of the government not only eliminate or foster certain social strata, but also expedite the upward or downward mobility of certain social groups through opening or closing certain social channels. For example, the movement of peasant-workers to industrial workers is still fettered by the rural-urban divided dual social policy.

However, at the individual level, social mobility is a result of every social member's proactive actions to seek benefits within these structure and institutions. From the perspective of sociology, the causes that lead to every individual or group obtaining different social status, besides the influences of the structure-institution factors at the macro level, also include social resources possessed by individuals and the capability and effectiveness of exerting these resources. People normally try to make use of these crucial factors to pursue benefits in a given institutional framework and obtain corresponding social status. The possession of and exerting capability of resources varies from person to person, accordingly, so does the attainment of social status.

This chapter will try to answer the following questions: Which type of institutions, policies, and social resources do have had a significant influence on people's social mobility in different periods since 1949? What are the relationships between these factors? How do these factors have changed in the process of social transition over the past fifty years? We will also roughly evaluate the openness and fairness of Chinese social mobility through analyzing these social mobility mechanisms.

THE STRATEGY FOR ANALYSIS OF SOCIAL MOBILITY MECHANISMS

Definitions of Concepts

Analysis of social mobility mechanisms refers to the investigation of relevant factors (mechanisms) that affect people's social mobility and attainment of social status. In order to understand the process of the analysis, we first need to explain some basic concepts (such as social mobility, social status, and mechanisms that affect attainment of social status) and relevant analytical methods.

(1) Social Mobility

In sociology, *social mobility* refers to changes of an individual's social rank or stratum status. *Intragenerational mobility* and *intergenerational mobility* are two frequently adopted perspectives in analysis of social mobility. The former refers to changes of social status in one's lifetime. The latter refers to upward and downward changes between children's and their fathers' social status. By investigating people's social mobility from these two perspectives, researchers can analyze the degree of inheritance of social status attainment, which is an indicator of the degree of social openness. For example, if in a given society the social status of fathers is inherited by their children largely, we can call it a closed society, or a society of "elite reproduction".

(2) Social Status

Social status refers to people's positions in the hierarchy of social stratum rank of a society. In the study of social mobility, the social status is usually subdivided into occupational status, educational status, economic status, and authority status, etc. Generally, occupational status is analyzed by comparing the occupational status of one's first occupation (first occupational status) with that of one's current occupation (current occupational status). If one's first occupational status is the same as his or her current occupational status, it means that no social mobility has occurred in the given period. If the difference between the first occupational status and current occupational status is minor, it means that a short-distance social mobility has occurred (for example, one's occupational change in the manual labor stratum may lead to a limited increase of income, but his or her social status is not significantly improved). If the difference between the first occupational status and current occupational status is significant (i.e., spanning several social ranks), it means that a long-distance social mobility has occurred. Normally, upward changes of social status in social mobility will advance gradually. If occurrence of the long-distance mobility grows sharply, it means usually a tremendous change of social mobility rules.

(3) Ascription factors and Achievement factors

The study of mobility in sociology mainly focuses on causes and effects of social mobility. An individual's each move may enable him or her to obtain a certain social status. Therefore, the following questions are major concerns of sociologists: Whether one's acquired or inherited resources affect his or her social mobility? The former is called *achievement factors*, such as individuals' educational background and performance in political participation, etc.; the latter is called *ascription factors*, such as family background, parent's occupations, and class origin, etc. Theoretically, the greater the influence of ascription factors in a society, the more closed the society will be. In contrast, a society that is dominated by achievement factors usually provides greater space for individuals' free choices and development.

The major method that is adopted in sociology in the analysis of social mobility mechanisms is the *social status attainment model*, which is built on multiple regression analysis. This model treats an individual's social status attained in social mobility as the consequence (i.e., the dependent variable at the left end of the regression equation), and various factors that may affect the status attainment as causes (i.e., the independent variables at the right end of the regression equation). These variables are quantified into the model of multiple regression equation or path analysis and then the influence of each factor will be evaluated based on the value of standard regression coefficient of each independent variable in the regression equation.

Major Research Questions

In research on mechanisms that affect social status attainment in current Chinese society, we particularly focus on the following questions:

First, is China an open society or a closed society? In other words, does the family background (ascription factor) or individual effort (achievement factor) determine the attainment of social status and an individual's class status? Is there any constant influential factor that affects social status attainment in different institutional backgrounds and historical periods?

Second, the rapid transition of social structure since 1949 has led to significant changes of the state's institution-policy orientations. From the macro-level perspective, these factors undoubtedly affect attainment of social status as well. Comparing these macro-level factors with micro-level factors (i.e., individual ascription factors or achievement factors), which type of factors has a greater influence on status attainment? In addition, what is the relationship between factors at the two different levels? We believe that conducting a comprehensive investigation by taking account of all these factors will help us find the paths of social mobility with particular Chinese characteristics.

Third, the social transformation that has occurred over the past twenty-five

223

years since the reform and opening-up is a process of shifting from a "politics-omnipotent" society to a "market-oriented" society. Accordingly, in such a process, among various achievement factors, has any difference emerged between the influence of political capital (or authority capital) and that of educational capital on social status attainment? In other words, under the presupposition that the two types of capital shape the basis of social mobility together, when did the political capital have the greatest influence on upward social mobility? When did the proportion of the influence of the educational capital on the rise of individual social status have begun to increase? All of these questions are what scholars who study social mobility in the society pay attention.

Research Strategy and Variables

(1) Research Strategy

In the social status attainment model that we adopted in analysis of social mobility mechanisms, occupational status and educational status are treated as dependent variables; ascription, achievement, and institutional factors are treated as independent variables. Based on this model, we explored the influence of father's occupational status and educational status on children's occupational and educational status attainment, and further investigated the impact of children's first occupational status on their current occupational status. This research strategy is represented in Figure 5-1.[1]

Different institutional backgrounds have different degrees of influences on social members' status attainment; therefore, in this study we divide the past fifty years into five periods: (1) 1949 to 1956, the landmark event that ended this period is the accomplishment of the socialist transformation; (2) 1957 to 1965, the landmark event that ended this period is the start of the Cultural Revolution; (3) 1966 to 1977, the landmark event that ended this period is the end of the Cultural Revolution; (4) 1978 to 1991, the landmark event of this period is the reform and opening-up; and (5) 1991 to the present, the landmark events that started this period are Deng Xiaoping's speeches in his official visit to South China and the formally proposed policy of establishing the socialist free-market system. The purpose of our study is to investigate intergenerational and intragenerational influence in different periods and analyze the major factors that determine social status attainment.

---

[1] Figure 5-1 only represents the model of occupational status attainment. Other models like the educational status attainment are similar to this model in principle, except for some variations of variables adopted in models.

224

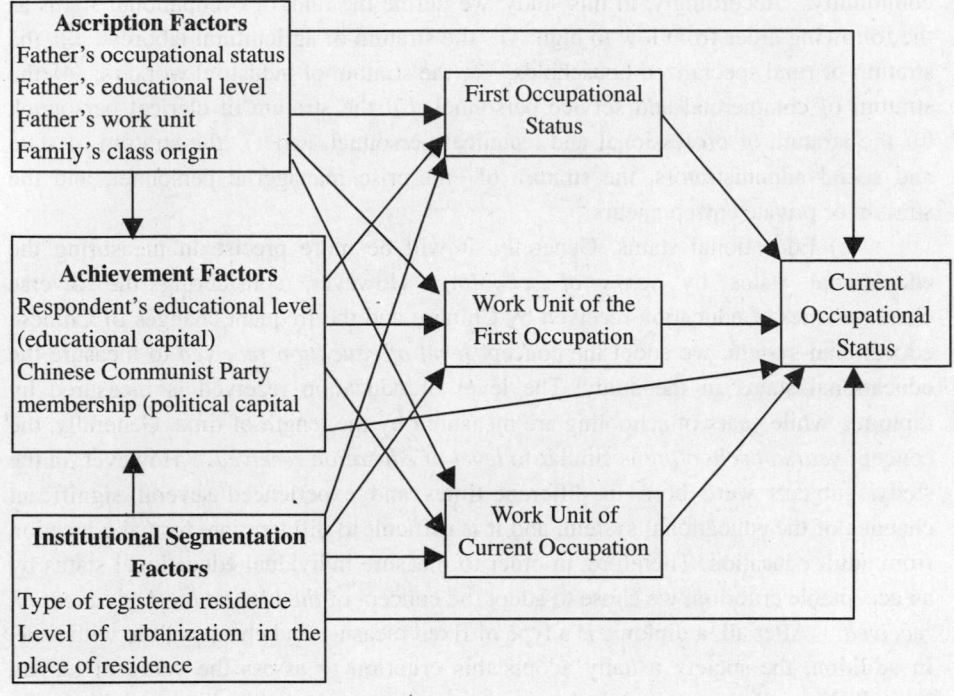

Ascription Factors
Father's occupational status
Father's educational level
Father's work unit
Family's class origin

Achievement Factors
Respondent's educational level
(educational capital)
Chinese Communist Party
membership (political capital

**Institutional Segmentation
Factors**
Type of registered residence
Level of urbanization in the
place of residence

First Occupational
Status

Work Unit of the
First Occupation

Work Unit of
Current Occupation

Current
Occupational
Status

Figure 5-1   The Analytical Model of Occupational Status Attainment

(2) Explanation of Variables

I. Dependent Variables

a) Occupational status. The first criterion for classification of occupations is the *Socioeconomic Index for All Occupations* set up by Peter M. Blau and Oliver D. Duncan. This index is determined by the regression equation between social prestige, educational backgrounds, and income levels of various occupations.[1] However, it is difficult to know the composition of educational backgrounds and income levels of various occupations in China. Moreover, there are certain differences existing between the values of social prestige in China, which were acquired in previous surveys, and the levels of income, possession of authority, and degrees of education received. Therefore, not all scholars in this field agree on the method, which replaces the *Socioeconomic Index* with occupational prestige. Recently, the *order of occupational ranks*, which is built on the basis of the occupation classification framework proposed by British sociologist John H. Goldthorpe, is frequently adopted in the academic

---

[1] Blau and Duncan (1967); Duncan, Oliver D. 1972. *Socio-economic Background and Achievement.* New York, N.Y.: Seminar Press; Duncan, Oliver D. 1975. *Introduction to Structure Equation Model.* New York, N.Y.: Academic Press.

community.[1] Accordingly, in this study, we define the rank of occupational status as the following order from low to high: ① the stratum of agricultural laborers, ② the stratum of rural specialized households, ③ the stratum of industrial workers, ④ the stratum of commercial and service personnel, ⑤ the stratum of clerical personnel, ⑥ the stratum of professional and technical personnel, and ⑦ the stratum of state and social administrators, the stratum of enterprise managerial personnel, and the stratum of private entrepreneurs.[2]

b) Educational status. Generally, it will be more precise in measuring the educational status by *years of schooling*. However, considering the diverse characteristics of education received by Chinese and the frequent changes of Chinese educational system, we adopt the concept *level of education received* to measure the educational status in the study. The level of education received is measured by diploma, while years of schooling are measured by the length of time. Generally, the concept *years of schooling* is similar to *level of education received*. However, in the study, subjects were born in different times and experienced several significant changes of the educational system, and it is difficult to differentiate formal education from adult education. Therefore, in order to measure individual educational status by an acceptable criterion, we chose to adopt the concept of *the highest level of education received*. After all, a diploma is a type of fixed measure and changes little with time. In addition, the society usually adopts this criterion to assess the value of human capital. When the level of education received was treated as an ordinal variable in the study, and we assigned its values as follows: ①without any education, ②lower primary school, ③primary school, ④junior middle school, ⑤senior middle school, ⑥ technical secondary school, ⑦ junior college, ⑧ university, ⑨ postgraduate (master's), and ⑩postgraduate (doctor's). When the level of education received was

---

[1] Although Goldthorpe believed that his system of occupational structure focused on investigating people's positions and labor relations in employment market rather than a system of hierarchic ranks, many researchers treated it as an ordinal variable when adopted his theory of stratification. Lan, Lin and Yangjie Bian employed this method as well in their article *Employment and Status Attainment Process in Chinese Urban Areas*, in which the occupational strata were defined from low to high as: ① agriculture, ② commerce, ③ manufacturing, ④ services sectors, ⑤ office works, ⑥ administration and management, and ⑦ professional and technical works. Goldthorpe (1987). See also Lin, Lan and Yanjie Bian. 2002. "Employment and Status Attainment Process in Chinese Urban Areas". Pp. 83-115 in Yanjie Bian, et al. (eds.), *Market Transformation and Social Stratification*. SJPC Book Shop.

[2] The classification of ten major social strata in this study is also a hierarchical system of occupations. However, in this chapter, because the number of people in the upper strata—the stratum of state and social administrators, business managerial personnel, and private entrepreneurs—is relatively small, we combine them into one stratum in order to meet the requirement of analysis. Contrarily, the number of agricultural laborers is too large and hence we subdivide them into two groups—agricultural laborers and specialized households—according to the degree of marketization in their agricultural operations in order to analyze the hierarchical differences between them. In addition, because the stratum of individual-operated business proprietors is not a category of occupation in a strict sense and most of them are engaged in occupations related to commerce and services sectors, in this chapter, we classify them into the stratum of commercial and service personnel. Therefore, there are seven rather than ten social strata are analyzed in this chapter.

treated as a dummy variable in this study, we divided it into the following categories: the group of primary school and lower, the group of middle school (including vocational senior middle school), and the group of technical secondary school and higher. Specific control groups were shown in tables in this chapter. What needs to be noticed is that, in analysis of educational status attainment, the level of education received is a dependent variable; while in analysis of occupational status attainment; the level of education received is one of independent variables (achievement factors).

II. Independent Variables

a) Father's occupational status. Father's occupational status is a crucial ascription factor. It is a type of social capital in the attainment of children's social status. The father can take advantage of his occupational influence or social network to help his children obtain social status. This situation is common in social mobility of Western society. In Chinese society that is dominated by the ethical philosophy of "differential order" (or hierarchical order), it is even more prevalent. In this study, this variable is operationally defined as "father's occupational status when the respondent was at the age of fourteen".

b) Father's educational level. It is a type of ascription factors as well and is measured by the same method in measuring educational status.

c) Father's and respondent's work units and sectors. The work-unit system is a unique system in contemporary Chinese society. In the planned economy system, resources were allocated through the governmental hierarchy and the system of state-owned enterprises and public institutions. The work unit was the allocator of resources. It directly reflected an individual's status, social stratum, and position to some extent. Accordingly, the work unit became a very important consideration when one chose his or her occupation. In the study, we approximately treated the work unit as an ordinal variable, and its values are listed as follows from low to high: ① private enterprise (individual-operated business), ② collective enterprise, ③ state-owned enterprise, and ④public institution and governmental agency. When the work unit was treated as a dummy variable, we divided it into three categories: public-owned unit, collective unit, and non-public and non-collective unit.[1] In this study, father's work unit was treated as a type of ascription factors, while a respondent's own work unit was regarded as a type of institutional factors.

d) Family's class origin. Undoubtedly, this is also an ascription factor. Before the reform and opening-up, it had a decisive influence on one's prospects. In this study, we treated it as a dummy variable. All people whose family backgrounds are classified as the proprietary class or exploitative class in the early 1950s are given the

---

[1] In this study, we defined peasants' work unit in the system of contracted responsibility linking remunerations to output after the reform as "non-public and non-collective unit" rather than traditional "collective ownership". The reason is that peasants take the household as the unit to arrange their activities of production and operation in this period. The "collective" only makes sense to the ownership of farmland rather than organization and arrangement of production and risk aversion.

value of "0"; while all people whose family backgrounds are classified as the exploited class or revolutionary cadres in the early 1950s are given the value of "1".

e) Membership in the Communist Party of China. The membership in the Communist Party of China is a very important indicator to distinguish one's social and political status in Chinese society. Usually, the status of Party membership is obtained through individual performance in political participation and hence it is a type of achievement factor. In addition, the status of Party membership is a type of political capital. Many studies have demonstrated that, in terms of the influence on the mobility of individual occupational status, the status of Party membership is similar to educational status to some extent.[1]

f) Type of registered residence. The residence registration system has been an important factor that affects one's social status mobility and geographical migration over the past fifty years in China. We introduce this variable into the study in order to investigate the influence of institutional factors on status attainment. The specific values of this variable are assigned as follows: the registered rural residence is given the value of "0" and the registered non-rural residence is "1".

g) Level of urbanization. The modern city is the outcome of industrialization as well as the embodiment of modern civilization. We operationally define this factor as "the residence when respondent was at the age of fourteen". The specific values of this variable are assigned as follows: the city is given the value of "1", the county is "2", the township is "3", and the village is "4".

h) Age. This is a control variable. In the study, we distinguish the cohorts of people who started working in the same period. Detailed explanation about this variable was not provided, because it is not closely related to the emphasis of the study.

i) Gender. This is a dummy variable. The male is given the value of "1" and the female is given "0".

ATTAINMENT OF OCCUPATIONAL STATUS

Attainment of the First Occupational Status

What are the major factors that determine the attainment of social status of Chinese people over the past fifty years? There is no simple answer to this question. After all, the social institutions have different channels of influence in different periods. Table 5-1[2] shows such changes with time in details.

---

[1] Lin and Bian (2002: 83-115).

[2] All data in tables and figures in this chapter are from the nationwide survey conducted by this research group in 2001.

Table 5-1 Model of First Occupational Status Attainment

(Standard Regression Coefficients)

Category \ Year	1949~1956	1957~1965	1966~1977	1978~1991	1992~2001
Father's occupational status (when respondent was 14)	0.0296	-0.0250	-0.0053	0.0729*	0.0157*
Father's educational level	0.0304	-0.0457	-0.0510	0.0436	0.0392
Family background (good class origin = 1)	-0.1646***	0.0298	-0.0106	0.0069	-0.0288
Respondent's work unit of the first occupation					
Control group=non-public & non-collective unit					
Respondent's first occupation = collective unit	0.0775	-0.0492	0.1318***	0.1629***	0.0075
Respondent's first occupation = public-owned unit	0.3571***	0.0955	0.4375***	0.2642***	0.1309 +
Type of registered residence in the first occupation	0.1147	0.1730***	0.0927*	0.1784***	0.2314***
Respondent's educational level					
Control group = Primary school and lower					
Middle school	0.2832***	0.2366***	0.0610	0.1253***	-0.0843
Technical secondary school and higher	0.3074***	0.4491***	0.2379***	0.4201***	0.2402*
Age	0.0881	0.2563***	0.0551	0.0022	-0.0104
Gender (male = 1)	-0.1289*	0.0095	-0.0735*	-0.0598*	-0.0348
R^2	0.492	0.463	0.287	0.427	0.400
N	163	360	636	779	170

Note: "***": $P<0.001$; "**": $P<0.01$; "*": $P<0.05$; "+": $P<0.10$.

First, educational level is the most important factor that determines the attainment of one's first occupational status. The influence of this factor is significant in different periods. The probability of obtaining good occupational status for those with an educational level of technical secondary school and higher is greater than that for those with lower level of education (their standard regression coefficients are greater than that of the group with an educational level of primary school and lower and that of the group with an educational level of middle school; of which, the group with an educational level of primary school and lower is the control group with the assigned value of "0"). Even in the Cultural Revolution, when the intelligentsia was treated as one of the lowest social strata, the influence of educational level on attainment of one's first occupational status was still very significant; in this period people with an educational level of technical secondary school and higher generally held relatively higher occupational status.[1]

Second, the work unit has a long-term influence on the attainment of the first occupational status. People working in public-owned work units can obtain relatively high occupational status. In the unitary planned economy, the work unit system monopolized the great majority of social resources. The rank of work unit, its capability of controlling resources, and even its degree of nationalization were

---

[1] The research conducted by Xueguang Zhou also found that, the higher the educational status people held in the period of the Cultural Revolution, the greater the probability of becoming cadres would be in attainment of the first occupation. The reason for this phenomenon is that "the majority of the Red Guards were graduates of universities, colleges, and technical secondary schools". Judging from social environments at that time, this opinion is reasonable. Zhou, Xueguang, Tuma, and Maen. 2002. "A Dynamic Analysis of Social Stratification in the State Socialism System". Pp. 379-426 in Yanjie Bian, et al. (eds.), *Market Transformation and Social Stratification*. SJPC Book Shop.

important factors that affected social status attainment.[1] If one failed to enter into a work unit with real powers after graduation with a high-level diploma, the promotion of his or her occupational status would be negatively affected. In contrast, even one held a relatively lower-level diploma, if he or she entered into a higher-rank work unit or a work unit in control of substantive resources, his or her first occupational status might be relatively high.

Third, the institutional arrangement of rural-urban divided dual social system, i.e., the residence registration system, has affected the attainment of occupational status in a long term. People who were born in the city and hence held the registered non-rural residence have a greater chance of getting good jobs and moving to the upper social strata than those born in the countryside with the registered rural residence status. Table 5-1 and Figure 5-2 show such influence in models of different periods. Between 1949 and 1956, this influence was not particular because people could migrate freely in this period. After the Municipal Standing Committee of the National People's Congress approved the *Regulations on Residence Registration of the People's Republic of China* in 1958, the impact of the registered residence status became extremely significant. Up to now, this institutional arrangement still has an unfair influence on individual employment and social development.

Fourth, compared with the above-mentioned factors, the influence of family background on attainment of the first occupational status is limited. In the early 1950s, people from families of the proprietary class could obtain relatively high first occupational status, while the first occupational status obtained by those from families of workers and peasants was slightly lower. At the early stage of the establishment of the People's Republic of China, though the former class hierarchy was overthrown in the sense of ideological appraisal, the government reconstructed the old economic system in a progressive way. In rural areas, although landlords' farmland were redistributed to farmers, the government still reserved for landlords with farmland which were equal to the area assigned to poor peasants and farm laborers. Farmlands of rich peasants were reserved for them. In urban areas, though the bureaucratic capitalists' assets were confiscated, the national capitalists and small industrial and commercial business owners still operated their enterprises. In addition, children of capitalists could still work in their own enterprises. Even after the accomplishment of the socialist transformation of the capitalist industry and commerce, these children with "bad class origins" did not receive discriminatory treatment in middle and higher education and they could work in government agencies and state-owned enterprises as professional and managerial personnel after graduation.[2] In other words, the

---

[1] This is basically the same with Lan Lin and Yanjie Ban's explanation.

[2] From the perspective of class classification, we found that, after the land reform, the family of landlords and rich peasants actually was a sort of family based on "origins of class" rather than based on "economic status of class". In contrast, capitalists and individual-operated business proprietors in the city maintained the consistency of possession of assets with their class origins in a relatively long period after the establishment of the Peoples' Republic of China. Only after the socialist transformation, especially to some individual-operated business proprietors, only in the Cultural

institutional transformation applied different policies to different social strata; providing ordinary people with mobility opportunity as well as taking account of the interests of the proprietary class. However, such a tendency ended up soon. After the accomplishment of the socialist transformation in 1956, the positive effect of "the family of the proprietary class" on the attainment of their children's first occupational status disappeared. In succeeding periods, because of the implementation of the universal employment policy, the influence of family backgrounds on employment was not greater than that of the other above-mentioned other factors.

Figure 5-2 Major Influential Factors in Attainment of First Occupational Status in Different Periods

(Standard Regression Coefficients)*

Note: *Figure 5-2 is drawn according to the standard regression coefficients in Table 5-1. In order to highlight the influences of major factors, only statistically significant regression coefficients are listed in Figure 5-2, and the rest are treated as zeros. Particularly, Figure 5-2 only compares relative influences of different factors that affected occupational status attainment in each period rather than influences of each factor in different periods. For example, based on Figure 5-2, we can say that the influence of educational status was greater than that of registered residence between 1957 and 1965, and the influence of work unit was greater than that of educational status and registered residence between 1966 and 1977. However, we cannot say that the influence of educational status between 1957 and 1965 was greater than that between 1966 and 1977. Other figures in this chapter are the same as those of Figure 5-2 at this point.

Fifth, correspondingly, between 1949 and 1977, father's occupational status, as an ascription factor, did not have a significant influence on social status attainment. With

---

Revolution, their possesions and class origins were eventually separated and hence they became the classes based on origins.

the advance of the market-oriented reform, "father's occupational status when the respondent was at the age of fourteen" has begun to affect the attainment of first occupational status since 1978.

Based on Figure 5-2, we comprehensively investigated different combinations of all the above-mentioned factors that affected the attainment of first occupational status in different periods. Between 1949 and 1956, people who worked in public-owned units with relatively high educational level and came from families of the proprietary class could obtain comparatively high occupational status. Between 1957 and 1965, the major influential factor was an individual's educational level, and the residence registration system began to show its impact. Between 1966 and 1977, the work unit system became the prime factor that affected the attainment of the first occupational status. The importance of educational level decreased. Working in public-owned units was more important than receiving a relatively higher level of education. The influence of the status of registered agricultural or non-agricultural residence was in the third place. Between 1978 and 1991, the importance of work-unit system and educational level reversed dramatically. The influence of the former declined and that of the latter began to increase. First, such a change may be due to the resumption of the college entrance examination system. A large number of students graduated from colleges, universities, and technical secondary schools successively and were assigned to relatively good work units with the status of cadres. Second, it may be due to impact of marketization. The differentiation of occupational status and corresponding benefits had been widened and started to link with the educational level. In this period, the influence of the residence registration system was still significant. In addition, father's occupational status began to affect the attainment of children's first occupation. Since 1992, the impact of work unit has been declining continuously and has become the last of the major influential factors. Meanwhile, the importance of father's occupation to children's occupational status attainment has been increasing sharply. The decline and growth of influences of the two factors indicate the tendency in which the resources used to pursue social status have been flowing from the work unit to the family. In the same period, the impact of the registered residence status on employment is extremely remarkable, next to the importance of the educational level. This phenomenon shows the barrier effect of the urban-rural divided dual system to the rural labor force moving to the city and to higher-level occupations, and reveals the sharp conflict between current market-driven social mobility and institutional barriers left by the planned economy system.

Attainment of Current Occupational Status

In this section, we will investigate the attainment of social members' current occupational status. Investigation of the attainment of the first occupational status focuses on influential factors when people started their careers, while the analysis of current occupational status attainment emphasizes causes of position changes in the course of people's careers. In other words, the former aims to understand the mechanism of employment, while the latter tries to analyze the mechanism of occupational promotion or transfer. Factors that affect the current occupational status are more complicated than those influencing the first occupational status, because one's first occupational status will undoubtedly affect changes of later occupations. The status of Party membership, which has been an important consideration in occupational promotion since 1949 in China, usually is obtained at the first-line operating positions. Therefore, the influential factors in the attainment of current occupational status have two additional independent variables: first occupational status and the Party membership. Analysis of the data in Table 5-2 indicates the following findings:

First, the Party membership, registered residence status, respondents' educational levels, and respondents' current work units are the four most important variables that significantly affect the attainment of current occupational status. Generally, the occupational status of Party members is higher than that of non-Party members. The current occupational status of people holding registered urban residence is higher than that of those holding registered rural residence. The occupational status of people with higher-level diplomas is higher than that of those with lower-level diplomas. As far as the influence of work units, it varied with time. The occupational status of people working in public/state-owned units was higher than that of those working in non-state-owned work units between 1966 and 1991. However, since 1991 this relationship has reversed. The occupational status of people working in state-owned units has declined, due to downsizing of state-owned enterprises or simplifying the administrative structure in government agencies, or being compared with high-level occupations emerging outside the system (such as entrepreneurs, managers, and high-level white-collar occupations). Influence of the five variables varied in different periods and hence indicates the transition of the institutional background.

When other variables are under control, it is worth discussing the relationship between the levels of education received and Party membership, because they represent cultural capital and political capital respectively to some extent. During the twenty years from the Great Leap Forward to the end of the Cultural Revolution, the influence of Party membership was slightly greater than that of a respondent's educational level. This phenomenon indicated the institutional orientations of emphasizing political performance, class origins, and political positions in occupational promotions. However, after 1978, though Party membership was still important, the influence of educational capital grew rapidly. For example, in the personnel system reform that aimed to make the rank of cadres younger in average age and better educated, Pparty members who had better educational background had more opportunities to be promoted. After 1992, with the deepening of marketization in China, the importance of knowledge in social distribution has been further increasing. In particular, the emerging knowledge-based economy at the end of the twentieth century provides more opportunities for knowledge workers to be promoted to higher positions. Therefore, educational status has naturally become the decisive influential factor.[1]

Second, similar to the first occupational status, "father's occupational status when the respondent was at the age of 14" has direct impact on the attainment of a respondent's current occupation after the reform in 1978, though its importance is next to the above-mentioned factors. In other words, in this period, it is more possible for a father with a good occupation to help his children get good jobs. The growing influence of father's occupational status and the declining effect of the work unit system since 1992 indicate the aforementioned substitution of family for work unit in the process of social status attainment as well.

Table 5-2   Model of Current Occupational Status Attainment

(Standard Regression Coefficients)

Category	All Cases	1957~1965	1966~1977	1978~1991	1992~2001
Father's occupational status (when respondent was 14)	0.0560*	-0.0087	0.1103+	0.0722*	0.0766*
Father's educational level	-0.0047	-0.0268	-0.0767	-0.0433.	0.0209
Family background (good class origin=1)	-0.0062	0.0163	0.1291*	-0.0506	0.0300
Type of registered residence (non-agricultural =1)	0.1574***	0.2334*	0.2574***	0.1399***	0.1478***
Respondent's educational level Control group=Primary school and lower					
Middle school	0.1121***	0.1519	0.1418*	0.0203	0.0891*
Technical secondary school and higher	0.2263***	0.1845	0.2355***	0.2265***	0.2376***
Party membership (yes=1)	0.2061***	0.2225*	0.2650***	0.1364***	0.1740***
Respondent's current work unit (public-owned=1)	0.0503*	0.0506	0.1246*	0.1126*	-0.0889*
Respondent's first occupational status	0.0970***	0.1749	0.0668	0.1444***	0.0301
Age	0.0158	0.0148	0.1681*	0.0505	0.1007**
Gender (male = 1)	0.0189	0.0501	-0.0200	0.0207	0.0077
R^2	0.199	0.375	0.418	0.233	0.197
N	2009	86	190	370	1333

Note: (1) "***": $P<0.001$; "**": $P<0.01$; "*": $P<0.05$; "+": $P<0.10$.

(2) The period of 1950~1956 is omitted because the cases of shifting occupations in that period were very few, and it is impossible to draw any statistical conclusions as a whole.

---

[1] That may indicate the transformation of political capital, i.e., Party membership is no longer a critical variable in analysis of status hierarchy. Many private entrepreneurs are former governmental cadres or Party members. They went into business after 1992 and became "extra-system officials". The social status of private entrepreneurs, individual-operated business proprietors, and white-collar workers in foreign-invested enterprises, etc., has been rising with their importance increasing in the national economy. Several surveys on occupational prestige conducted recently show that social status of all these groups are improving.

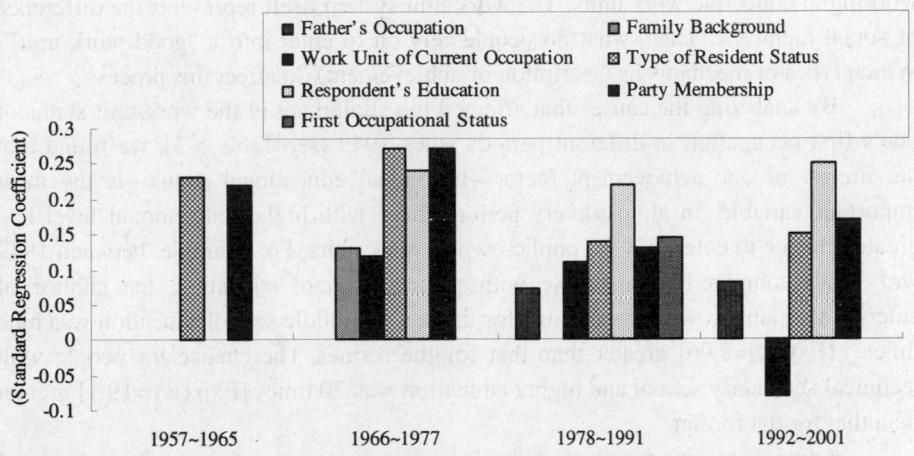

Figure 5-3   Major Influential Factors in Attainment of Current Occupational Status in Different Periods

Third, a family's class origin does not show statistical significance in the attainment of current occupational status in many periods, except in the period of the Cultural Revolution (1966~1977). In that period, people with "good" family class origins had greater chance to get good and higher-level occupations than those with "bad" family class origins. In the historical background, social class was classified by political status and the personnel arrangement of the government and work units was usually directed towards people from families of workers and peasants. For example, at the late stage of the Cultural Revolution, students with worker, peasant, and soldier origins (so-called "worker-peasant-soldier students") could enter colleges; in contrast, those with "bad" family backgrounds were tied down by their families, more or less. It was more possible for them to be "sent down" to the countryside in the rustication movement, or be assigned to a position that has few chances to obtain promotion. With the end of the Cultural Revolution, the rule of classifying social status based on class origins was ultimately abolished.

Attainment of Work-Unit Status

According to the above-mentioned analyses, we found that the work unit has been a major factor that affecting the occupational status attainment of Chinese social members in most periods since 1949. The work unit system, which still exists today, was a crucial and unique institutional arrangement in the period of the planned economy system in China. In that period, if one could work in a "core economic sector", such as the public-owned work units, he or she would obtain better fringe benefits including housing, social security, and welfare from the work unit than those working in collective work units. The work unit system itself represents the difference of social hierarchy. Then, what do people rely on to enter into a "good work unit"? Which types of mechanisms (ascription or achievement) do affect this process?

By analyzing the causes that affected the attainment of the work-unit status of one's first occupation in different periods since 1949 (see Table 5-3), we found that the impact of one achievement factor—individual educational status—is the most important variable. In almost every period, those with higher educational level had greater chance to enter into the public-owned work units. For example, between 1949 and 1956, compared with people with primary school education, the chance of entering the public-owned work units for those with middle school education was nine times [Exp(B)=8.96] greater than that for the former. The chance for people with technical secondary school and higher education was 20 times [Exp (B) =19.1] greater than that for the former.

Among ascription factors, father's work unit is one of the major influential factors as well. In the early stage after the establishment of the People's Republic of China (1949~1956), in the Cultural Revolution (1966~1977), and in the first half of the period of the reform (1978~1991), father's work-unit status had a significant influence on children's work-unit status. For example, between 1978~1991, if a father worked in a public-owned work unit, the probability of entering state/public-owned units for his children was 14 times [Exp(B)=14.07] higher than that for those whose fathers worked in non-public and non-collective units. Such a phenomenon can be explained by the work unit system. Parents in good units usually took advantage of their influences to help their children enter into the same work unit. After the reform of the personnel system in state-owned sectors in 1992, the situation in which children inherited a parent's work-unit status through intergenerational relationships has gradually faded out.

The influence of father's occupational status, educational status, and family background on children's work-unit status is not significant. However, there was an interesting phenomenon in the period between 1978 and 1991. The lower "father's occupational status when the respondent was at the age of 14", the higher the father's educational level; also, the worse the family's class origin, the higher the chance of entering state-owned work units. The reason is that children from the family of the exploitative class or "rightists" benefited from the rehabilitation policy after the Cultural Revolution. In addition, resumption of the college entrance examination system allowed parents who received relatively higher level of education to send their children to colleges and hence help them enter state-owned work units.

236

Table 5-3　Influential Factors in Attainment of Work-Unit Status in First Occupations

(Logistic Non-Standard Regression Coefficients)

Independent Variable	1949–1956		1957–1965		1966–1977		1978–1991		1992–2001	
	B	EXP(B)	B	EXP(B)	B	EXP(B)	B	EXP(B)	B	EXP(B)
Father's occupational status when respondent was 14	0.07	1.07	-0.04	0.96	-0.01	0.98	-0.08*	0.92	-0.02	0.97
Father's work unit when respondent was 14										
Control group=non-public & non-collective unit										
Father worked in collective unit when respondent was 14	-1.07*	0.34	-0.54	0.57	-0.12	0.88	0.34	1.40	0.52	1.62
Father worked in public-owned unit when respondent was 14	0.09*	1.09	0.60	1.82	1.11***	3,06	2.64*	14.07	0.58	1.78
Father's educational level	-0.12	0.87	-0.04	0.95	-0.05	0.94	0.01*	1.01	0.10	1.16
Family background (good class origin=1)	0.17	1.19	0.00	1.01	0.25	1.29	-0.24*	0.78	-0.65	0.52
Respondent's educational level										
Control group=primary school and lower										
Middle school	2.19**	8.96	1.28***	3.60	0.52***	1.68	1.20	3.34	2.02*	7.58
Technical secondary school and higher	2.95**	19.18	1.88***	6.59	1.26***	3.55	2.92	18.57	2.91**	18.52
Age	0.14*	1.16	0.22***	1.25	0.12***	1.13	0.02*	1.02	0.15***	1.17
Gender (male=1)	-0.42	0.65	0.47	1.61	0.10	1.10	0.60	1.82	0.49	1.64
Constant	-9.06*		-13.48***		-7.13		-3.7**		-7.1**	
-2LL	175.58		329.43		773.06		726.6		187.9	
N	144		329		643		766		169	

Note: "***": P<0.001; "**": P<0.01; "*": P<0.05; "+": P<0.10.

237

Analytical results of attainment of the work-unit status in current occupation are roughly similar to those of the first occupation (Table 5-4) except that influence of the work unit is more significant. In all periods, it is more possible for fathers in public-owned work units to help their children shift to a better unit. Even in the Rustication Movement between 1966~1977, many parents in public-owned units managed to help their children shift to public-owned units in various ways (in this period, the chance of entering public-owned units for children with parents in public-owned units was at least 3.06 times [Exp (B) =3.06] greater than that for children with parents in non-public-owned units and hence avoided being sent to the countryside).

In terms of the family's class origin, children from the family of workers, peasants, solders, and cadres had 1.69 times [Exp (B) =1.69] greater chance than those with bad family backgrounds to enter state-owned units between 1957~1965, and 1.38 times [Exp (B) =1.38] between 1966~1977. It was exactly twenty years later when Chinese society was dominated by the ideology of class struggle and the social hierarchy was established based on class origins. People with good class origins entered advantaged strata in occupational status attainment, while those from the family of the proprietary class received discriminatory treatment in employment and could not enter the core sectors like public/state-owned units. Although people from the family of the proprietary class in the period between 1949 and 1956 could enter non-public sectors and obtain relatively high first occupational status, these opportunities were eventually eliminated through institutional arrangements after the accomplishment of the socialist transformation. Since the reform and opening-up in 1978, the influence of such political class origins on people's social status has gradually dwindled.

Combining analyses of Table 5-3 and Table 5-4, we drew the following conclusion. In the early days of the establishment of the People's Republic of China between 1949 and 1956, the main reason that one could enter the public-owned unit was due to his or her relatively high educational level. However, after the accomplishment of the socialist transformation, "father's work unit" and "respondent's level of education received" jointly determined whether one could enter the public-owned unit. After comparing the odds ratios [Exp (B)] of the two independent variables in different periods, we found that, after the 1990s, the influence of a father's work unit has been declining; meanwhile, the impact of a respondent's level of education received has been increasing (especially on attainment of the work-unit status of the first occupation). With the changes of admission criteria of state-owned enterprises and government agencies, graduates of colleges and universities are not assigned jobs as governmental cadres any longer, but have to find jobs by themselves. Diplomas and qualification examinations have become the most important influential factors when competing in the employment market.

ATTAINMENT OF EDUCATIONAL STATUS

Our study has demonstrated that the educational level is a variable that constantly affects the attainment of social status. Although its influence has varied in different periods, the inference that the educational level determines the rank of people's social status is always tenable. This is also a common conclusion of researchers in the field of the study of social stratification around the world. As early as the model of the first status attainment built by Blau and Duncan in the 1960s, education showed the foremost positive influence on social status attainment. Therefore, a further investigation on the intergenerational inheritance of educational status will help us understand the main path of social mobility over the past fifty years in China.

Table 5-5 and Figure 5-4 indicate that father's occupation, father's educational status, and level of urbanization in residence area have jointly determined the attainment of educational status in different periods since the establishment of the People's Republic of China.

First, the influence of father's occupation is the most significant in all periods. The higher the father's occupational status, the more possible he will be able to help his children receive more school education, and the higher the value of educational capital or human capital possessed by his children will be. This phenomenon was especially well seen in the early days of the establishment of the People's Republic of China.

Second, father's educational status has a positive influence on children's level of education received since 1957. Fathers received relatively high level of education usually tends to help their children receive more education and hence increase the educational capital for the latter.

Third, only in the early days of the establishment of the People's Republic of China, family's class origin had a significant negative impact on the attainment of educational status. Families with a proprietary class origin had more opportunities to help their children obtain the advantage of receiving education. Such traditionally inherited advantage dwindled in the process of the institutional transformation after 1957.

Fourth, "residence when respondent was at the age of 14" has been an extremely significant variable. Because the educational system gives priority to cities and townships in China, children born in major cities have a greater chance to receive a better education than those born in backward countryside. The unequal distribution of educational resources between urban and rural areas has led to expanding differentiation of educational status since 1957.

In the following part, we will further investigate changes of the above factors in five periods.

Table 5-4 Influential Factors in Attainment of Work-Unit Status in Current Occupations

(Logistic Non-Standard Regression Coefficients)

Independent Variable	1949–1956 B	EXP(B)	1957–1965 B	EXP(B)	1966–1977 B	EXP(B)	1978–1991 B	EXP(B)	1992–2001 B	EXP(B)
Father's occupational status when respondent was 14	0.0790	1.08	0.13*	1.13	0.09	1.09	-0.02	0.97	-0.097	0.99
Father's work unit when respondent was 14 Control group=non-public & non-collective unit										
Father worked in collective unit when respondent was 14	-0.88**	0.41	-0.217	0.80	0.09	1.09	0.28	1.33	0.20	1.22
Father worked in public-owned unit when respondent was 14	1.22**	3.40	1.08***	2.97	1.44**	4.23	2.27***	9.71	1.20***	3.35
Father's educational level	0.0438	1.04	0.05	1.06	-0.03	0.96	0.01	1.01	0.05	1.05
Family background (good class origin=1)	-0.05	0.95	0.52*	1.69	0.32+	1.38	0.17	1.19	-0.21	0.80
Respondent's educational level Control group= primary school and lower										
Middle school	1.16**	3.19	1.35***	3.88	1.20**	3.33	1.21***	3.37	1.27	3.58
Technical secondary school and higher	1.34*	3.84	2.27**	9.03	2.83**	17.9	3.65***	38.48	3.19***	24.36
Age	0.23***	1.26	0.16***	1.8	0.11**	1.11	0.08***	1.08	0.0413	1.04
Gender (male =1)	0.3609	1.43	0.11	1.12	-0.20	0.81	0.01	1.01	0.1621	1.170
Constant	-16.01*		-11.7*		-7.8***		-6.57**		-4.9***	
-2LL	253.91	571.6	594	1054	1148.1		382.84			
N	240		594		1377		409			

Note: "****": P<0.001; "***": P<0.01; "**": P<0.05; "+": P<0.10.

Table 5-5 Model of Educational Status Attainment

(Standard Regression Coefficients)

Year of Starting to Work	1949~1956	1957~1965	1966~1977	1978~1991	1992~2001
Father's occupational status when respondent was 14	0.2778***	0.1749***	0.2350***	0.2114***	0.1964***
Father's educational level	0.0812	0.1233***	0.0667*	0.2134***	0.2211***
Family background (good class origin=1)	-0.2212***	-0.0851*	-0.0590	-0.0197	0.0034
Residence when respondent was 14	-0.1006	-0.2174***	-0.1680***	-0.1331***	-0.1149*
Age	0.0519	0.1655***	0.0174	0.0604***	0.1625***
1=Male, 0=Female	0.1526***	0.2107	0.2087***	0.1377***	0.0678
R^2	0.216	0.255	0.192	0.218	0.208
N	321	738	1249	1570	408

Notes: (1) "***": $P<0.001$; "**": $P<0.01$; "*": $P<0.05$; "+": $P<0.10$.

(2) "Residence when respondent was 14" is assigned values as follows: the city is "1", the county is "2", the township is "3", and the village is "4".

Figure 5-4 Major Influential Factors in Attainment of Educational Status in Different Periods

(1) 1949~1956. In this period, the influence of "father's occupational status when respondent was at the age of ·14" was extremely significant. Although people who started working in the time of war usually received lower level of education, most of them had relatively high occupational status in the new regime. Accordingly, their children could receive better education and obtain higher diplomas. According to many published memoirs, most cadres managed to send their children to excellent schools in this period. This was a sort of intergenerational influence in educational status attainment.

The class origin was also a momentous independent variable in this period. In the early days of the establishment of the new China, the government did not take

241

one's class origin as one of the selection criteria for college and university admission. Parents who had higher socio-economic status before 1949 could transfer their advantaged class status to their children through education. According to statistics, until September 1956, the majority of undergraduates still came from families of capitalists and landlords. Among enrolled undergraduates in colleges and universities, only 34.2 percent of them came from families of workers and peasants. Among enrolled postgraduates in universities including the system of the Chinese Academy of Science, only 23.4 percent of them had worker or peasant origins.[1] Although the Anti-Rightist Movement put a large number of intellectuals and their children in a disadvantaged position, the college entrance examination system still implemented the elite education policy. The double-tracks system of elite education and universal education produced two different consequences. The elite education expedited the differentiation of social status, while universal education improved the quality and cultural level of everyone and created better conditions to carry out the political philosophy of the government. Therefore, intellectuals who attached importance to education and children of families with lower class origins still could obtain many opportunities to enter the upper classes before the Cultural Revolution.

(2) 1957~1965. In this period, the emergence of the urban-rural dual system led to a widened gap of distribution of educational opportunities between rural and urban areas and hence became the foremost factor that affected educational status attainment. In addition, after the new regime was steadily established, the influence of father's educational status on children's educational status grew. People whose father received a relatively high level of education increased their own children's educational capital. Meanwhile, the importance of family's class origin was weakened. Such changes indicated that the inherited educational advantage of the proprietary class before 1949 disappeared in the process of institutional transition.

(3) 1966~1977. In this period, the influence of father's occupational status on children's educational status increased greatly. The difference in the level of education received caused by the urban-rural gap slightly decreased, while the influence of father's educational status declined sharply. People with better class origins could obtain more educational opportunities. In contrast, intellectuals, especially children of intellectuals who received relatively a high level of education, experienced unprecedented persecution in the Anti-Rightist Movement in previous period and the Cultural Revolution in this period. For example, the college enrollment system was changed thoroughly during the Cultural Revolution. On June 1, 1966, the Central Committee of the C.P.C. and the State Council approved and transmitted the *Report for Instructions Concerning the Reform of Enrollment System in Higher Education in 1966* submitted by the Ministry of Education. On June 13, 1966, the *Circular Concerning Reforming the Enrollment and Examination Procedure in Higher Education* was released. The government believed that "the existing college entrance

---

[1] Li, Qiang. 1999. *The Course of Life: Momentous Events and Life Courses of Chinese*. Hangzhou, Zhejiang: Zhejiang People's Press; Fairbank (2000).

examination system is a bourgeois way of enrollment" and "goes against admitting more revolutionary youth from workers, peasants, and soldiers to colleges and universities. This examination system must be changed thoroughly". On July 24, 1966, the government released the *Circular Concerning Reforming the Enrollment System in Higher Education* intending to "abolish the entrance examination and adopt a new procedure combining recommendation and examination". After Chinese universities had stopped admission for six years, on June 27[the], 1970, the Central Committee of the C.P.C. approved the *Report Submitted by Peking University and Tsinghua University Requesting Instructions on Pilot Enrollment Programs* and proposed a new enrollment system "combining recommendation of colleagues, approval of the chief of the work unit, and selection of the university". Such a change led to the prevalence of "getting in through the back door". Many people with access to educational resources managed to help their children enter colleges. On one hand, this system prevented people with lower class origins from entering colleges (such as children of intellectuals and rightists). On the other hand, it provided children whose parents' had relatively low level of education but relatively high occupational status with the opportunities of entering colleges. However, the tide of equalization in education did not reach remote rural areas—residence was still a critical variable.[1]

(4) 1978~1991. In this period, the influence of father's occupational status and educational level was stronger than that in the Cultural Revolution. The sent-down people who received a relatively high level of education returned to the city and their children had the opportunity to receive better education. People with relatively high occupational status could also help their children obtain more opportunities to enter colleges after the resumption of the college entrance examination system. From then on, the higher the father's educational level, the higher children's level of education received would be (since this period, the regression coefficient of father's educational level to children's educational level has been increasing). Furthermore, since 1978 the influence of father's educational level on children's educational level has exceeded that of "father's occupational status when respondent was at the age of 14". In other words, people with high educational level but low occupational status could create better educational opportunities for their children through inheritance of education and hence improve their children's occupational status through receiving a higher level of education.

---

[1] After the Cultural Revolution started, universities stopped admitting students and the administration of middle schools was transferred to factories, communities, or rural people's communes. Students who failed in examinations could still go up to the next grade. The elite education based on examinations was transformed to the class-based education and power-dominated education which was characterized by recommendations and exemption of the entrance examination. Although ordinary workers and peasants obtained more educational opportunities in the early days of the Cultural Revolution, they basically lost the advantage of obtaining opportunity in the succeeding institutional transformations. In contrast, social members in possession of power could help their children work in public-owned units, join the army, and enter colleges. In so-called worker-peasant-solider colleges that were established in the 1970s, the influence of power was prevalent as well.

(5) 1992~2001. The statistical tendency in this period was roughly similar to that found in the period between 1978 and 1991. With the implementation of the nine-year compulsory education, the average level of education received by Chinese ascended to some extent. However, the increase of the college tuition in the early 1990s negatively affected students from depressed families. From the perspective of regional gaps, the variable of "residence when respondent was at the age of 14" was still significant. Children in rural areas could not receive the same education with cohort children in urban areas because of the place of birth and family background. Such unfairness was the result of institutional segmentation rather than personal reasons.

In addition, statistical analysis of gender shows that the males received more education than females in all periods. In other words, there was a sort of sexual discrimination in education existing in Chinese society. In a family's educational strategy, parents tend to arrange for their sons to receive a higher level of education.

ATTAINMENT OF AUTHORITY STATUS AND ITS IMPACT ON SOCIAL MOBILITY

Among various factors that affect social mobility, educational capital that is represented by educational background, political capital that is represented by Party membership, and economic capital that is represented by income provide significant supports in the attainment of social status. We focused on influences of the above three capitals in previous sections. In this section, we will discuss the effect of authority capital.

In China, which has several thousand years' history of centralism, power has always been the center of social status. In the planned system that was established after the 1950s, administrative authority was greatly strengthened once again. Although after the reform and opening-up the control of authority on social resources has been gradually weakened by the market mechanism, its influence is still significant. Whether the power still affects social members' occupational choices or not in the field of social status attainment is a topic of concern for researchers.

After investigating the history of occupational mobility sine 1949, we found that the post of cadres or state and social administrators is always the most preferred occupational position that people are willing to choose. Obtaining such a position means that one acquires the authority that is empowered to this post by the government and hence one can exercise his or her power through managing affairs that are assigned to the post by the government. Therefore, cadres are undoubtedly the most powerful persons in current Chinese society. Before the reform and opening-up peasants thirsted for recruitment of public-owned work units, workers hoped to be promoted as cadres, military personnel awaited demobilization and emplacement as

244

cadres, and cadres pursued promotion. After the reform and opening-up, college graduates expected to be assigned to government agencies as cadres as well. Even after the 1990s, with the rapid development of extra-system economy, besides going into business, the governmental official is still the dream occupation of many college students. Therefore, authority capital has an influence on individuals' intergenerational and intragenerational mobility; fathers with power will help their children obtain the authority capital. In order to choose a relatively stable occupation to investigate the historical influence of authority capital, we focused on the stratum of state and social administrators or cadres. Table 5-6 shows influential factors in attainment of cadre status in the first occupation.

Father's cadre status has been the primary factor that affected children's attainment of cadre status over the past fifty years. Logistic regression coefficients indicate that the chance of becoming cadres in the first employment for children of cadres is 1.75 times [Exp (B) =1.75] greater than that for children of non-cadres in the entire period.

Specifically, in the period of 1949~1956, if father's status when a respondent was at the age of 14 was cadre, the probability of becoming cadre in the respondent's first employment was 2.65 times [Exp (B) =2.65] higher than those whose fathers' status were not cadres when they were at the age of 14. In contrast, in the same period the influence of father's educational level was not significant. In other words, the influence of authority capital on intergenerational mobility was obviously greater than that of educational capital in the early days of the establishment of the People's Republic of China.

However, after the accomplishment of the socialist transformation, i.e., the period of 1957~ 1965, the influence of father's educational level on intergenerational mobility began to rise. In contrast, the statistical significance of father's status of cadre declined in this period, i.e., there is only 10 percent of probability that the statistical inference is tenable. However, the impact of father's cadre status dropped as well. The probability of obtaining the cadre status for those whose fathers' status were cadres was only 1.77 times higher than that for those whose fathers' status were not cadres, smaller than the figure of 2.65 times in the early days of the establishment of the People's Republic of China.

In the Cultural Revolution (1966~1977), the statistical relationship between father's status of cadre and the attainment of cadre status in respondent's first employment dwindled. That is to say, a father's cadre status could not ensure that his children would obtain the cadre status when they got their first jobs. In this period, some cadres lost powers because of stand-asides, and hence were unable to help their children. Some cadres voluntarily sent their children "up to the mountains and down to the villages" in order to show their faith in the Cultural Revolution Movement. Such a temporary lapse of the influence of father's authority capital on the attainment of the first occupational status did not mean that people whose fathers were cadres would be more disadvantaged in social mobility than those whose fathers were not cadres. In fact, as we will soon see later, father's cadre status played an important role in the attainment of current occupational status, i.e., the process of being promoted from the ordinary position to the cadre post.

Table 5-6   Model of the Cadre Status Attainment in First Occupations

(Logistic Regression Coefficients)

Independent Variable	All Cases			1949~1956		
	Value of B	Significance	Exp (B)	Value of B	Significance	Exp (B)
Father's status when respondent was 14 (cadre=1)	0.5617	0.0034	1.7537	0.9729	0.0456	2.6455
Father's educational level	0.2016	0.0000	1.2233	0.1477	0.0976	1.1591
Respondent's age	0.0480	0.0000	1.0492	0.0241	0.6129	1.0244
Respondent's gender (male=1)	0.2107	0.0674	1.2345	-0.2962	0.2897	0.7437
Constant	-5.0684	0.0000		-2.7862	0.3727	
N	3255			281		
-2 Log Likelihood	2321.72			319.62		

	1957~1965			1966~1977		
	Value of B	Significance	Exp (B)	Value of B	Significance	Exp (B)
Father's status when respondent was 14 (cadre=1)	0.5722	0.1008	1.7721	0.4354	0.3498	1.5456
Father's educational level	0.1771	0.0065	1.1938	0.1563	0.0169	1.1692
Respondent's age	0.1280	0.0000	1.1366	0.0848	0.0011	1.0885
Respondent's gender (male=1)	0.3793	0.1072	1.4612	-0.1563	0.5615	0.8553
Constant	-9.7802	0.0000		-7.1278	0.0000	
N	397			916		
-2 Log Likelihood	494.860			437.577		

	1978~1991			1992~2001		
	Value of B	Significance	Exp (B)	Value of B	Significance	Exp (B)
Father's status when respondent was 14 (cadre=1)	0.4724	0.0908	1.6039	0.3850	0.5161	1.4696
Father's educational level	0.2342	0.0000	1.2639	0.0709	0.5201	1.0735
Respondent's age	0.0455	0.0167	1.0466	0.1165	0.0100	1.1235
Respondent's gender (male=1)	0.4008	0.0607	1.4930	1.0611	0.0186	2.8895
Constant	-4.9172	0.0000		-6.5830	0.0000	
N	1093			372		
-2 Log Likelihood	704.90135			191.703		

Dependent variable: The status obtained in respondents' first occupation was cadre.

After 1978, the probability of cadres arranging their children for entering government agencies has declined because of the increasing emphasis on educational background in the process of governmental cadre selection. In addition, the emerging stratum of enterprise owners has diversified the occupational choices of cadres' children. However, changes in attainment of the first occupational status did not eliminate the influence of authority capital. Table 5-7 shows probabilities of obtaining the status of cadre in current occupational status.

In the process of current occupational status attainment, people whose fathers had the authority capital had a greater chance to be promoted as cadres than those whose fathers lacked authority capital. The overall model shows that, if father's educational status is under control, the probability of obtaining cadre status for children of cadres is 2.1 times higher than that for those whose fathers were not cadres.

In the period of 1957~1965, the effect of father's authority capital strengthened. People whose fathers were cadres had 2.94 times greater chance to obtain cadre status in current occupation than those whose fathers were not cadres.

In the Cultural Revolution period from 1966 to 1977, people whose fathers were cadres had 4.23 times greater chance to become cadres than those whose father were not cadres. Considering the temporary lapse of the influence of father's authority capital on their children's attainment of the cadre status in the first occupation in the same period, we came to the following conclusion: although the opportunity of obtaining cadre status in the first occupation seemed equal, in succeeding position changes, a father's authority capital still could affect the process of job shift and eventually help his children enter the group of cadres and have control of authority resources.

Table 5-7 Model of the Cadre Status Attainment in Current Occupations

(Logistic Regression Coefficients)

Independent Variable	All Cases			1949~1956		
	Value of B	Significance	Exp (B)	Value of B	Significance	Exp (B)
Father's status when respondent was 14 (cadre = 1)	0.7385	0.0000	2.0927	—	—	—
Father's educational level	0.2857	0.0000	1.3307	—	—	—
Respondent's age	0.0477	0.0000	1.0488	—	—	—
Respondent's gender (male = 1)	0.5582	0.0000	1.7475	—	—	—
Constant	-5.0987	0.0000		—	—	—
N	5251			—		
-2 Log Likelihood	4052.777			—		
	1957~1965			1966~1977		
	Value of B	Significance	Exp (B)	Value of B	Significance	Exp (B)
Father's status when respondent was 14 (cadre = 1)	1.0773	0.0310	2.9366	1.4413	0.0026	4.2263
Father's educational level	0.2167	0.0352	1.2420	0.2748	0.0003	1.3162
Respondent's age	0.1283	0.0000	1.1369	0.1154	0.0000	1.1223
Respondent's gender (male = 1)	0.3676	0.2088	1.4443	0.8773	0.0003	2.4043
Constant	-10.3373	0.0000		-9.2347	0.0000	
N	490			855		
-2 Log Likelihood	372.14316			528.215		
	1978~1991			1992~2001		
	Value of B	Significance	Exp (B)	Value of B	Significance	Exp (B)
Father's status when respondent was 14 (cadre = 1)	0.4211	0.0506	1.5237	0.4587	0.0332	1.5820
Father's educational level	0.2663	0.0000	1.3051	0.2345	0.0000	1.2643
Respondent's age	0.0902	0.0000	1.0944	0.0357	0.0000	1.0363
Respondent's gender (male = 1)	0.5896	0.0000	1.8032	0.3902	0.0146	1.4772
Constant	-6.7230	0.0000		-4.0651	0.0000	
N	1794			1371		
-2 Log Likelihood	1667.102			1131.706		

Dependent variable: Respondents' current or last status was cadre.

After the Cultural Revolution, in the two periods of 1978~1991 and 1992-2001, the influence of father's authority capital on children's attainment of cadre status in current occupation was statistically significant. However, its odds ratio [Exp(B)] decreased; that is, the probability of obtaining cadre status for children of cadres was about 1.5 times higher than that for those whose fathers were not cadres, smaller than the figure of 2.94 times before the Cultural Revolution and 4.23 times in the Cultural Revolution. In other words, the positive impact of father's authority capital on children's attainment of authority capital declined to some extent. After all, the selection criteria for governmental officials have required eligible applicants to hold a certain diploma, i.e., a certain amount of educational capital. Such a requirement accordingly added an indispensable step in the process of making use of authority capital to obtain new authority capital, i.e., obtaining corresponding educational capital. If cadres' children fail to obtain necessary educational capital, the influence of father's authority capital will be limited by the institutional arrangement.

Figure 5-5   Influence of Father's Cadre Status on Children's Attainment of Cadre Status (Odds Ratios)*

Note: **Odds ratio* refers to the ratio of the chance of cadres' children becoming cadres to the chance of non-cadres' children becoming cadres. For example, in this figure, between 1949 and 1956, the odds ratio of obtaining cadre status in the first occupation is 2.65, which means that the chance of cadres' children becoming cadres was 2.65 times higher than that of non-cadres' children.

Therefore, cadres and their children realized the following fact: as long as they acquire the certificate that can testify the qualification of human capital, i.e., the diploma, cadres will easily get expected promotions and non-cadres can find ways to get into the government agencies. As a result, demands for higher education and education in Party schools have rocketed and numerous undergraduate and postgraduate education programs have emerged, which have provided more educational opportunities but also disordered the human capital market at the same time.

In addition, the decreasing odds ratio of the influence of father's cadre status on children's attainment of cadre status elicits the following two questions. First, does the occupational status of governmental officials always have great attraction? The answer is that, if the growth of officials' salary is quicker than that of other occupations, if the rigidity of currency caused by officials' actual income level and their expenditure is always larger than that of other occupations, and if the rent-seeking behaviors of the public power can continue existing and the risk of being punished is relatively small, most of current officials will to still try to affect their children's occupational choices and take advantage of their influences to help them enter the group of governmental officials. Second, if what the first point mentioned always exist, current cadres, whose children are not governmental officials and their occupational status is lower than that of the official, will continuously help their children become governmental officials by making use of their authority capital. Accordingly, the influence of father's cadre status on children's current occupational status attainment still continuously exists. Only when accurate estimation of the probability of children's last occupational status attainment is available can we precisely calculate the probability of intergenerational inheritance that whether the last occupation of cadres' children is that of cadre or not. Therefore, among groups who obtained their current occupations after the Cultural Revolution or after 1992, the odds ratio of cadres' children ultimately becoming cadres will inevitably rise in future surveys. In other words, judging from the current tendency, the influence of authority capital on social mobility is still very significant.

SOME CONCLUSIONS ON MECHANISMS OF SOCIAL

MOBILITY IN CHINA

No "Non-Stratified" Period Ever Existed in China

Evidence in countries around the world indicates that all social members in each country can be classified into different social strata. When we classify a society into a social hierarchy with the order of ranks from high to low, different persons are located in different ladders of social hierarchy. Because the society is so complicated, different sociologists may have different criteria of social class classification based on different theories in sociology. However, such differences do not mean that the no ladder disparities exist between social members.

When the class structure in a given society changes significantly, it usually indicates an epoch-making transformation of the entire society. In a certain sense, we can say that the epochal change of a society is the epochal change of its class structure. The significant changes occurring in China after 1949 are exactly the changes that happened in the process of transforming the old system into the new system. The revolution smashed the old state apparatus and a set of new institutions were established. Meanwhile, the class structure of the society changed correspondingly. The focus of the change concentrated on eliminating the private ownership system and establishing the public ownership system. Consequently, a series of social infrastructures for class structure classification related to the private ownership system left the stage gradually. The accomplishment of the socialist transformation eliminated the economic base of the proprietary classes like capitalists, individual handicraftsmen, landlord, and rich peasants, etc. At the same time, their class origins were reserved as a type of political status.

The promotion of social status of the working class and the peasantry and the decline of capitalists, landlords, and rich peasants formed two converse trends of social mobility. Classes that were located at the upper end of the social ladders before 1949 began to move down; meanwhile, classes at the lower positions before 1949 were then liberated and went up. The consequence of such tremendous social mobility seemingly resembles a kind of "non-stratification" (i.e., differentiations between classes dwindle away). However, in essence, it was a process of creating new social class structure by clearing up former class structure, that is, transforming from a society stratified by economic status into a society stratified by political status.

Accordingly, in this process, cadres emerged as a new stratum and occupied the top position in society. Although the social status of the urban working class was improved remarkably, there were great differences existing between the working class in state-owned enterprises and the workers in collective enterprises in social status and benefits. The political status of intellectuals was relatively low, but their level of income and consumption and occupational status were far higher than that of ordinary workers. In rural areas, the social status of rural cadres was relatively high. Ordinary peasants' social status was improved than that before 1949. As far as family members with lower class origins and as objects of dictatorship, although they did not need to worry about food and clothing, their social status was very low.

In short, after the accomplishment of the socialist transformation in 1956, a new hierarchy of social stratum took shape in China. In its ideology, the state aimed to eliminate economic classes and form a framework of new class structure with only two classes and one stratum (the working class, the peasantry, and the intelligentsia), and further eliminate class differentiations in the process of socialist evolution and transit to a non-class society. However, such a construct was merely a utopia. In realistic socio-economic life, the differences between the rural and the urban, and among regions, work units, and individuals inevitably exist because of underdeveloped productivity and economic level in China. Therefore, the so-call "non-stratified" period is not so in fact. In other words, in that period, the political-status-based strata were established while the economic-status-based strata were disintegrating.

Since the reform and opening-up, the diversified economy has been leading the Chinese society that was stratified by political status to transit to a society that is stratified by economic status and been shaping a unique structure in which the stratification of political status and the stratification of economic status coexist. After twenty years' development, current Chinese society is entering into a period with declining stratification of political status and strengthening stratification of economic status.

Influences of Institutional Arrangements and Intergenerational Inheritance

As we mentioned at the beginning of this chapter, ascription factors and achievement factors that affect the attainment of social status are indicators of the degree of social openness. In this study of social mobility over the past fifty years in China, we found that the ascription factors in Chinese social mobility are far more complicated than those in Western industrial society. In China, ascription factors not only contain father's occupational status and educational level (they are not very significant in data of this study), which are frequently discussed by Western researchers, but also include father's institutional resources which are entitled by specific institutional arrangements (such as father's work unit and registered residence status) and the political status given by a family's class origin.

The work unit system established after the accomplishment of the socialist transformation in 1956 was a unique institutional arrangement in the period of the planned system in China. The types of the ownership of work units determined the benefits that people obtained from work units, as well as the administrative rank of the work units that affected people's welfare level. Our study indicated that resources of the work unit showed a certain degree of intergenerational inheritance. Parents working in public-owned units would manage to arrange or transfer their children to public-owned units by all means. The replacement system (a formal institutional arrangement that enabled children to take positions in the public-owned units after their parents retired from the same unit) in work units before the reform was a typical example. Therefore, if parents benefited from a good work unit, it was very likely that their next generation would get a good work-unit status as well.

The residence registration system has negatively affected the occupational mobility of people with registered rural residence from the very beginning of its existence. People with registered non-rural residence have more opportunities for upward mobility from their birth than those born in the countryside. Social members born in rural areas were restricted within the countryside by governmental policies. Moreover, the impact of the residence registration system upon the social member is not only a lifetime influence, but also can be transferred to the next generation through family relations. Once one's registered residence status is determined, it will run for generations. Our study also found that the social segregation caused by the residence registration system not only works on people's benefits and welfare, but also seriously affects attainment of the first occupational status, accumulation of educational capital, and promotion of the current occupational status.

The classification of family's class origins was an inevitable outcome of Chinese revolution in the process of smashing the old social hierarchy and establishing the political order of a new society. However, though classes were eliminated economically, their former members still were attached with the political labels of "enemy" or "one of us". The working class and the peasantry were masters of the state all the time, while landlords, capitalists, and the petty bourgeoisie who had been deprived of the means of production were subjects to be supervised, controlled, and governed in the long term (especially in the twenty years between 1957 and 1977). Class origin was inheritable. Parent's class attributes before 1949 determined children's class origins and hence affected their attainment of individual development opportunity. This study also reveals that, between the accomplishment of the socialist transformation and the end of the Cultural Revolution, family's class origin did affect people's social mobility. Children with good family background usually had more opportunities to achieve upward mobility in promotion and transfer than those with lower family origins.

All these factors stemmed from the macro-level governmental policy, were transferred through intergenerational and family inheritance, and then jointly affected everyone's life. From the perspective of social openness, all these rules are obviously unreasonable. Therefore, the openness of Chinese society is determined by the lapse of these institutional and intergenerational factors to a great extent.

The Rise of Social Status Supported by Educational and Political Capital

After investigating important influential factors in social status attainment since 1949, we found that individual effort has been still crucial one. The importance (regression coefficient) of educational capital (such as the level of education that represents individual's capability and quality) and political capital (such as Party membership that represents individual's political loyalty) possessed by individuals is usually greater than the aforementioned ascription factors. However, by analyzing the change of its influence with time, we drew a conclusion that the influence of political capital was larger than that of educational capital before and in the Cultural Revolution, while after the reform and opening-up, the influence of educational capital on social status attainment has been increasing.

The institutional support of the importance of Party membership is the critical position of the Chinese Communist Party in Chinese society. Joining the Party usually is a kind of praise and honor to individual's political loyalty and performance. As soon as one has Party membership, it will support his or her succeeding mobility, especially in some critical promotions, for example, promoting a worker as cadre, transferring from an ordinary division to a confidential department, or raising from the deputy to the position of the chief, etc. Therefore, Party membership is a type of scarce and valuable capital. In the politics-dominated era, such political capital was much more useful than educational capital. Party membership is not equal to the power, but those who are in charge of power must come from Party members. In the redistribution system in China, the status of cadre usually means obtaining dominative power. Thus, the status of cadre is a type of political capital that is more important than Party membership, or it can be referred to as the "authority capital". The influences of authority capital and intergenerational inheritance are extremely significant, i.e., people whose fathers are cadres have far greater chance to become cadres than those from ordinary families. Even today, after the implementation of the governmental official selection system, this factor still has great influence.

The market and competition mechanisms that are introduced by the reform and opening-up stimulate people to exchange individual capability for market returns. As the embodiment of individual capability, education has displayed its growing influence; meanwhile, the importance of political performance has been decreasing. The market economy system has gradually reduced the influence of the planning authority and devaluated the authority capital. At present, educational background has paramount impact on determination of the salary standards and arrangement of occupational positions in rapidly increasing extra-system non-public-owned entities. Even though in state-owned work units, in the process of making the rank of cadres younger in average age, better educated and professionally more competent, Party members and cadres with relatively high level of education have more chance to enter high-rank posts. Therefore, improving educational level of officials, "officialization" of intellectuals, professionalization of management, and increasing authority of technical experts, are important characteristics of current Chinese society.

After the 1990s, educational capital represented by educational background has been the decisive factor in social status attainment. Nearly over night, China has become a "diploma-based society". More and more families have realized that, if there is an investment that can improve their children's social status with no risks at all, educational capital will be a good option for anybody in any social stratum.

China is Turning into an Open Society

If observing the history of status attainment of social members after the establishment of the People's Republic of China in a long-term perspective, we will find that the Cultural Revolution was like a huge maelstrom in the sea but did not change the direction of the current. In the process of social transformation with marketization of economy, industrialization and post-industrialization of sectors, urbanization of community, democratization of politics, the social mobility channels in Chinese society become opener.

The reform that has started since 1978 is a momentous landmark of advancement in Chinese society. Driven by modernization and marketization, Chinese national economy has been developing at a remarkable speed, its social stratum structure has been changing dramatically, social relationships between social members have been adjusting greatly, and mechanisms of social status attainment has become more fair and reasonable. Some important institutions and policies that indicated the social segregation such as class origins, the work unit system, and urban-rural dual system, have left the stage or have been declining. The influence of individual educational background has been growing, while that of the aforementioned ascription factors has been declining. The above growths and declines indicate that the emphasis on individual capability and corresponding performance rewards have been greatly improved in the environment of the socialist market economy. The traditional social structure that was shaped by the planned economy system has been restructured. The situation that all social members strived to enter public-owned and high-administrative-level work units has changed and new large-scale mobility channels has emerged outside the system. At present, for the majority of social members, the future of their careers is determined by individual efforts rather than governmental assignment. All these changes lead us to reach the following conclusion: the openness of Chinese society has been increasing. However, in the process of current social transformation, unreasonable and unfair institutionalized discrimination still exists in Chinese society. These institutional arrangements have resulted in unfair distribution of social mobility opportunity among social members and fettered the development of economy.

Education is a major means to promote social equity. The importance of education has been admitted by all people in China. However, some existing institutional barriers are still impeding equal distribution of educational opportunity. The unbalanced allocation of compulsory educational resources between rural and urban areas is the source of unfairness. The existing financing method in the rural compulsory educational expenditure (i.e., the expenditure is jointly paid by the central government, the local government, and students) imposes heavy burdens on families of peasants. Sometimes, in order to secure one child's education, they have to sacrifice other children's future. In addition, the so-called "industrialization of higher education" policy forces many children from families of workers and peasants to quit due to expensive tuitions. They cannot compete with children from families of cadres or private entrepreneurs by only relying on academic achievements like before the 1990s. The urban-rural segregation caused by the residence registration system still exists. Thousands of millions of peasant-workers are working in the city without enjoying corresponding urban residents' rights and interests. The employment policies implementing in some metropolises restrict the eligible employment scope of peasant-workers within the bottom of the occupational hierarchy. Wages standards and labor protection of peasant-workers are lacking protection from the law.

At present, the development of Chinese economy is in a critical period. We should be aware that the sustainable development of the economy has to rely on fair and reasonable social structure. Only if unjust institutionalized discriminations that are blocking social mobility are further cleared up can the degree of openness and equity in Chinese society be improved to a greater extent.

Chapter 6   Social Mobility of the Stratum of State and Social Administrators

The *stratum of state and social administrators* refers to the leadership who exercise actual administrative authority in Party and government agencies, public institutions, and social organizations. Specifically, it includes chiefs of divisions and higher-rank administrators who possess actual administrative authority in ministries and commissions of the central government and national municipalities. It also consists of chiefs of sections (or townships) and higher-rank cadres and a number of cadres below the chief of division (or section) level who have actual administrative authority, and chiefs of divisions (or sections) and higher-rank cadres without actual administrative authority in the government of province, city, prefecture, county, and township. In this chapter, we will mainly discuss the current situation of this stratum and its social mobility over the past fifty years, and try to understand the general rules and characteristics of the developing process of this stratum by analyzing its status in quo and the process of mobility.

THE BASIC PROFILE OF THE STRATUM OF STATE AND SOCIAL ADMINISTRATORS

State and social administrators are defined according to their positions in governmental and public administrative agencies and the administrative authority actually possessed by them. The stratum of state and social administrators has a relatively large scope and exists extensively in Party and government agencies, legislatures, judicial authorities, social organizations, and state-owned enterprises. Roughly, any managerial personnel with the status of cadre, in possession of a certain administrative authority, and holding a higher-rank position in work units financed by public revenue can be regarded as a state and social administrator.

In the Chinese personnel system, state and social administrators are classified as "cadres". The *cadre* is an ambiguous concept; initially it refers to managerial personnel and means certain positions; "cadres" is a loosely defined group in China. In a broad sense, all managerial personnel were called "cadres" after 1949, including the Chairman of the State, the Prime Minister, village heads, and even team leaders in primary schools and middle schools. In a narrow sense, the term "cadres" refers to various managerial personnel, clerks, and public office personnel who occupy certain positions, are formally listed in authorized quota of cadres, get paid by the government, and enjoy the treatment of cadres in government agencies, social organizations, state-owned or collective enterprises, army, and administrative institutions at all levels.[1] Managerial personnel and clerks enjoying the treatment of cadres in judicial courts and procuratorates at all levels are included in this concept as well. Therefore, in the narrow sense, "cadre" is first a type of legal status. Such a status needs to be ratified by the organization department of the Party and the personnel department of the government according to relevant regulations. The key criterion to judge whether one possesses the status of cadre is that whether one can enter the authorized quota of cadres assigned by the organization department and the personnel department. Usually, the treatment enjoyed by people with cadre status is better than that received by people without the cadre status. The jobs of public office personnel with cadre status are relatively stable and secured by governmental regulations and laws.

The stratum of state and social administrators and the group of cadres are similar to some extent. The common characteristic of the two groups is that they all possess the status of cadre. However, the stratum of state and social administrators usually is in control of a relatively large amount of organizational resources. They can be seen as a group with relatively high positions in cadres.

The four indicators of stratum classification define the advantaged status of state and social administrators in the social structure. They are middle-high level white-collar management in core sectors inside the system and in control of the most critical resource in current Chinese society—the organizational resource. Because the governmental organizations are in control of the most important and largest amounts of resources, state and social administrators possessing organizational resources distinctly take up an advantaged position in the allocation of resources. Although they are not owners of the means of production, state and social administrators can control a part of the means of production. Therefore, they actually share a portion of economic resources, and of course possess a large amount of cultural resources.

Currently, the proportion of this stratum is about 2.1 percent in the overall social stratum structure, 2.6 percent in the urban social stratum structure, and 0.2 percent in the rural social stratum structure. The number of state and social administrators is relatively small in the whole population.

Some differentiations also exist inside this stratum. According to the amount of organizational resources possessed by individuals and the approaches of exerting these resources, this stratum can be subdivided into four groups (see Chapter 1). As a whole, there are great differences existing among people in this stratum in social prestige and economic income because of differences in industry, sector, region, and period. People with actual administrative authority in departments in charge of projects examining and approving, administrative enforcing, and development

---

[1] Li, Qiang. 1993. *Social Stratification and Mobility in Contemporary China*. Beijing: China Economy Publishing House: 276.

planning occupy an advantaged position in the allocation of organizational resources. Therefore, their social status is usually higher than that of state and social administrators without these powers. In developed regions in China, the amount of economic resources that state and social administrators can utilize is far larger than that of those in underdeveloped regions. In recent years, because of the increasing demands for public goods like high-quality education and health care, the social status of presidents of hospitals and principals of schools is relatively high as well.

MACRO-LEVEL INSTITUTIONS RELATED TO SOCIAL
MOBILITY OF THE STRATUM

Compared with other strata, the formation and mobility of the stratum of state and social administrators receive more influence from relevant institutional arrangements, policies, and regulations of the government. Furthermore, such an influence is a leading factor, which affects this stratum at all times. In China, macro-level institutional factors that affect the development and mobility of the stratum of state and social administrators include the political and legal system, the cadre personnel system, political movements, and the reforms of these institutions. All these factors have formed different characteristics of the stratum of state and social administrators in its size, composition, and internal mobility mechanism in different periods.

Boundary, Size, and Mobility Paths

The basic institutional arrangements include the basic political and economic system and the cadre personnel system. These institutions defined the boundary, size, and major paths of outflow and inflow of the stratum of state and social administrators. The basic political system of the People's Republic of China is the people's democratic dictatorship led by the Communist Party of China and based on the alliance of workers and peasants and co-operation of major political parties. According to this system, the main body of the stratum of state and social administrators is members of the Communist Party of China, which takes the working class as its political basis and laboring people like peasants as its supportive group. At the same time, it also includes members of other political parties and personages without party affiliation. The cadre personnel system was formed on the basis of the cadre administration system set up in the time of war. This system is in charge of the entrance and exit of state and social administrators. As time goes on, the cadre personnel system has experienced continuous reforms and improvements. The influences of these reforms on formation and mobility of this stratum resulted in changes of the entrances and exits of the stratum. We will here focus on analyzing the influence of the cadre personnel system and its changes on formation and mobility of the stratum of state and social administrators.

(1) Origins of State and Social Administrators and Selection Criteria

Entering the group of cadres is the first step of entering the stratum of state and social administrators. Only if one obtains the status of cadre can he or she become a state and social administrator. Therefore, in order to explore the formation and boundary of this stratum, we must analyze the origins of and the selection criteria for state and social administrators prescribed by relevant institutions and policies.

A. Major Origins of Cadres

In the governmental personnel dossier administration system, cadre was not only a type of occupation but also a type of status. Once one obtained the status of cadre, it would be a permanent status unless he or she was dismissed from the public office. According to relevant regulations, there were three channels to obtain the status of cadre. In the first channel, demobilized army cadres were transferred to local government agencies. In the second channel, college and university students obtained the status of cadre after graduation. In the third channel, ordinary people were employed by the government agencies in open recruitments.

Therefore, there were three major origins of cadres in China since 1949. The first origin was that of demobilized army officers. The second origin was that of graduates of technical secondary schools, colleges, and universities. The third one was that of employed personnel in open recruitments. In this section, we take the employment of cadres in Jinjiang City of Fujian Province (see Table 6-1) and Haimen City of Jiangsu Province as examples in order to explain the origins of cadres in China before the implementation of the government employee system.

(a) Demobilized army cadres. The People's Republic of China was established through military struggles led by the Communist Party of China. Therefore, by the establishment of the People's Republic of China in 1949, a large amount of cadres was demobilized army cadres. In Jinjiang County of Fujian Province between 1949 and 1950, most of governmental cadres came from soldiers and officers of the Chinese People's Liberation Army (P.L.A), members of the Down-to-the-South Services Mission, underground members of the Chinese Communist Party, and guerillas. After Jinjiang city was liberated, a number of soldiers and officers of the 31st and the 28th Corps of the Chinese People's Liberation Army and members of the Down-to-the-South Services Mission were left in this city to suppress anti-revolutionary activities, carry out the land reform, and establish the new local government. The number of these cadres was 458. Most of them were assigned to leadership posts at the county and district level. A number of underground members of the Chinese Communist Party and guerillas had become cadres before the establishment of the New China, while capable people who were not cadres before 1949 were recruited as full-time cadres. According to the statistics in 1951, the number of these cadres was 55. Although these cadres had relatively long working experience, their educational levels were relatively low, so most of them were assigned to posts at the division and section level in the government. The Fujian provincial government released a mandate in 1951 to prescribe the authorized quota of cadres in Jinjiang as an A-level county: government agencies had a quota of 234 persons and public organizations had a quota of 16 persons. Before the Three-Antis Campaign in 1951, the total size of cadres in Jinjiang was 603. This number increased to 918 after reorganizing the local government.[1]

Table 6-1　Numbers and Origins of Admitted and Recruited Cadres* in Jinjiang County, Fujian Province, 1950~1988

Unit: Persons

Year	Origin	Number
1950~1951	Officers and soldiers of the P.L.A., members of the Down-to-the-South Services Mission, students of the Revaluation University and the Eastern China Military and Politics School, underground Party members, guerillas, activists in the land reform, retained former government employees	458
1953	Activists in the illiteracy elimination campaign and the land reform, etc.	178
1954	Workers, impoverished and lower-middle peasants, and unemployed youth	343
1955	Workers, impoverished and lower-middle peasants, and oddjobbers	107
1956	Shop employees, peasants, unemployed youth, and a part of capitalists and their representatives	489
1957	Peasants, unemployed youth, and others	164
1958	Workers and impoverished and lower-middle peasants	779
1959	Workers, peasants, and unemployed youth	197
1960	Workers, peasants, and unemployed youth	102
1961~1963	Cadres partially off the production jobs, workers, impoverished and lower-middle peasants, shop employees, demobilized and retired servicemen, and other oddjobbers	149
1965~1971	Demobilized servicemen	99
1972	Local-sponsored teachers were transferred to state-sponsored teachers, and probationary teachers were transferred as permanent teachers	43
1973~1980	Workers, peasants, and workers in collective units who were admitted as cadres	1120
1983	Workers as temporary cadres were transferred as formal cadres	137
1984	Workers as temporary cadres were transferred as formal cadres	534
1985	Urban unemployed youth and other idle people were recruited　by judicial court, procuratorate, police, administration for industry and commerce, and supervision agency	43
1985~1986	Personnel working in grassroots organizations such as militia departments, birth control offices, mass organizations, and township treasury stations were recruited as contract cadres	107
1987	Recruited graduates of the radio and television broadcasting universities and spare-time universities (of which 8 persons are graduates of the Liming University, a local community university)	47
1988	Personnel working in administrations for industry and commerce, tax administrations, and banks were recruited as contract cadres	52 4
Total		5150

Note: * "Admitted" refers to transferring people without the cadre status to formal cadres through a particular procedure. "Recruited" refers to recruiting eligible candidates from unemployed people as cadres, e.g., recruiting demobilized army cadres and graduates of technical secondary schools, colleges, and universities.

---

[1] Editorial committee of Jinjiang Chorography. 1989. *Jinjiang Chorography*. Xiamen, Fujian: Fujian University Press: 975.

Not only were a large number of soldiers and officers of the People's Liberation Army assigned to the government agencies in Jinjiang in the early days after the establishment of the People's Republic of China, but also many demobilized army cadres were transferred to the local institutions each year since then. According to statistics, there were total 1,167 army cadres who were transferred to Jinjiang from 1950 to 1988 (among them 250 persons were veterans). Most of them were assigned to the government agencies, judicial authorities, and grassroots organizations. In the period of the Cultural Revaluation from 1966 to 1977, the government agencies at all levels in Jinjiang County were controlled by the Revolutionary Committees that were constituted by representatives from the army, cadres, and revolt cliques.

(b) Graduates of technical secondary schools, colleges, and universities. Education is the major channel of obtaining the status of cadre. All graduates of state-sponsored formal full-time technical secondary schools, colleges, and universities who accepted the governmental planned placement could obtain the cadre status automatically. In contrast, graduates of part-time educational institutions such as staff members and workers universities, correspondence colleges, spare-time universities, radio and television broadcasting universities, cadre training seminars, and self-study examinations, etc., though they had acquired college or university diplomas, they could not obtain the cadre status directly. With the advance of the reform and opening-up and the establishment of the socialist free-market system, the types of the ownership systems have diversified and a large number of graduates of full-time technical secondary schools, colleges, and universities have been employed by newly arisen private, foreign-invested and mixed-ownership enterprises. These graduates working in non-public-owned sectors do not possess the status of cadre, though parts of them are in managerial positions. In addition, because of the development of education and the increasing level of education of the entire society, some graduates of full-time technical secondary school cannot obtain the cadre status automatically in government agencies and public institutions any more. Some work units do not treat graduates of full-time technical secondary schools as cadres, and some units admit a small number of graduates of full-time technical secondary schools into the status of cadre only after a certain procedure of ratification.

According to statistics, between 1950 and 1988, there were a total of 1,757 graduates of technical secondary school, college, and university who were assigned to Jinjiang County; among them, 611 were graduates of colleges and higher education, and 1,146 were graduates of technical secondary schools. After obtaining certain practical experience and passing through the long-term performance assessment, many of them were promoted to leadership posts at all levels in government and Party agencies, public institutions, and state-owned enterprises. In Haimen County of Jiangsu Province, most cadres came from graduates of technical secondary schools, colleges, and universities since the 1960s.[1] Table 6-2 indicates that the level of

---

[1] Editorial committee of Haimen Chorography. 1996. *Haimen Chorography*. Nanjing, Jiangsu: Jiangsu Science & Technology Press: 684.

education received by cadres in Haimen has been increasing since the 1960s. The proportion of cadres with diplomas from technical secondary school, college, and university increased from 0.44 percent in 1955 to 15.76 percent in 1971. Haimen County received a large number of graduates of technical secondary schools, colleges, and universities each year in the 1980s and they all obtained the status of cadre; the total number of them outstripped that of demobilized army cadres. For example, in 1985, graduates of technical secondary schools, colleges, and universities received by Haimen County as cadres totaled 265 persons, and demobilized army cadres totaled 259 persons. However, only after Deng Xiaoping proposed to "make the rank of cadres more revolutionary, younger in average age, better educated, and professionally more competent", did graduates of technical secondary schools, colleges, and universities with cadre status actually received attention and were promoted as leadership.

Table 6-2   Educational Background of Cadres in the Public-Owned Sector in Haimen County, Jiangsu Province, 1949~1980 *

Unit: Persons

Education \ Year	1949	1955	1957	1964	1971	1978	1980
College and higher	1	4	3	117	635	1184	1260
Technical secondary school			69			2567	1901
Senior middle school	19	86	89	464	1696		757
Junior middle school and lower	1149	814	1551	1551	1697	3047	2783

Note: * The total number of cadres before 1980 does not include the number of teachers.

(c) Open recruitments. Besides demobilized army cadres and graduates of technical secondary schools, colleges, and universities, the government agencies at all levels in China also recruited a large number of talents as cadres from various industries in each period. After the establishment of the People's Republic of China, a large number of local talents in industry, agriculture, commerce, and education sectors in Jinjiang County were recruited by government agencies, public institutions, and state-owned enterprises through examinations and performance assessment; among them, those who had passed through one year's probation period and the comprehensive assessment were formally appointed as governmental cadres. The majority of cadres have been selected by such a method especially since 1956. With the advance of the personnel system reform, the government has started to recruit contract cadres in public transportation companies, administrations for industry and commerce, tax administrations, birth control offices, and banks from urban unmarried youth with senior middle school and higher level of education since 1985. After passing the examination, interview, and background check, candidates need to sign an employment contract with the employers and then the contract will be submitted to the Personnel Bureau for approval. The first contract usually is a one-year-term contract and will be renewed according to future situations.[1] The age of recruited cadres was usually between 18 and 25, sometimes up to 35 with some exceptions. Before 1980, the government recruited many cadres from rural areas. However, this channel for rural cadres to become formal governmental cadres was abolished after 1980.

As a result of the above three origins of cadres, the composition of the cadre group consists of three major types of components: demobilized army cadres, intellectuals, and workers, peasants, ordinary personnel, and other unemployed people. The three types of components had different proportions in different periods. In the early days of the establishment of the People's Republic of China, the majority of cadres were demobilized army cadres. After the 1950s, cadres with origins from workers and peasants composed the majority of cadres. After the 1960s, the proportion of graduates of technical secondary schools, colleges, and universities increased gradually. However, the Cultural Revolution seriously damaged the normal cadre selection system and caused stagnation and even retrogression in the higher education. Intellectuals became objects of persecution and reconstruction, and a large number of old cadres stood aside. The revolt cliques and active army officers became the majority of the Revolutionary Committees. After the 1980s, higher education has resumed and developed rapidly and the social status of intellectuals has improved greatly. A large number of unemployed youth entered the stratum of cadres and many intellectuals occupied leadership posts at all levels. Before the 1990s, social members with lower stratum status could enter into the group of cadres and change their occupational and social status through joining the army, promotion, entering higher schools, and open recruitment, etc.

The implementation of the government employee system has combined the traditional open recruitment and assignment of graduates into one. Therefore, after 1993, only two channels of entering the cadre stratum still exist, i.e., the emplacement of demobilized army cadres and the examination of government employee recruitment. At first glance, it seems that the channel for social members in lower strata to enter the stratum of cadres becomes narrower. In fact, the examination system makes it possible for social members in all social strata to become government employees. Furthermore, such an expectation of upward mobility is realizable and stable and will not be changed because of leadership's personal wish. It is a type of institutionalized and regularized cadre selection mechanism. In ten years after the implementation of the government employee system, only about 5,000 peasants have entered into the group of government employees. Compared with the formal open recruitment system, the probability of being cadres for peasants seems decreases. However, such an

---

[1] On September 29, 1982, the Ministry of Personnel and Labor of China released *Several Provisions on Issues Concerning Cadres Admission and Recruitment* and proposed that in the open cadre recruitment an employment contract must be signed and an engagement letter must be sent to recruited cadres. Cadres admitted through such a method were called "employed cadres". They would posses the status of cadre in the term of contract and would lost it after the end of the contract. Therefore, employed cadres were different from former permanent cadres.

analysis has overlooked the fact that a large number of graduates of technical secondary schools, colleges, and universities who have become government employees came from families of ordinary workers, peasants, and staff members. Therefore, in this perspective, the government employee system provides more opportunities for children of families with middle-lower social status. Merely, there is a precondition, i.e., these children must have received good education, especially higher education.

B. Criteria of Cadre Selection

The family background and individual performance in political participation were important criteria for selecting cadres before 1978. People with better class origins and from impoverished families had a greater chance to enter the stratum of cadres than others did. It was difficult for the intelligentsia to become cadres from the Anti-Rightist Movement in 1957 to the end of the Cultural Revolution. They were victims of political movements.

After the Third Plenum of the 11th Central Committee of the Communist Party of China, Deng Xiaoping proposed to "make the rank of cadres more revolutionary, younger in average age, better educated and professionally more competent" and establish a normal retirement program for cadres in order to transfer leadership posts to younger cadres. These proposals promoted changes of the orientation in personnel administration from looking down on knowledge and intellectuals to emphasizing knowledge and talents. Accordingly, a large number of young intellectuals entered core positions in the public authorities and many of them held important leadership posts, becoming members of the stratum of state and social administrators.

More than 220 thousand middle-aged and younger cadres were promoted to leadership posts above the rank of division chief or chief executive of county government between 1982 and 1989 and hence entered the stratum of state and social administrators.1 By the year of 1988, the total number of cadres at the age of less than 35 was 20,048 thousand, accounting for 49.5 percent of the total number of cadres in China, up by 4.8 percent over the 1992 figure. The number of cadres at the age from 35 to 45 was 10,954 thousand, accounting for 27.1 percent of the total number of cadres in China, up by 0.12 percent over the 1992 figure. Thus, cadres with the age of less than 45 took up 76.6 percent in the total number of cadres. In terms of educational background, in 1978 cadres with primary school and lower educational background accounted for 14.62 percent, 34.85 percent of cadres had junior middle school educational background, 32.52 percent with senior middle school and technical secondary school background, and merely 18.02 percent with college and higher educational background. In contrast, in 1998 only 7.95 percent of cadres had junior middle school and lower level of education, 11.63 percent with senior middle school education, 33.9 percent with technical secondary school education, 30.99 percent with

---

1 Chinese Public Administration Society. 2002. *Brief History of the Public Administration of New China (1949~2000)*. Beijing: People's Publishing House: 413.

junior college education, 14.69 percent with university education, and 0.84 percent with postgraduate education. Therefore, in 1978 cadres with college and higher level of education only accounted for 18.02 percent in the total number of cadres in China, while in 1998, this proportion increased to 46.52 percent, up by 28.5 percent.[1]

Based on above changes in compositions of age and educational background of cadres, we inferred that, among cadres who belonged to the stratum of state and social administrators, similar changes—younger in average age and higher in level of education received—occurred as well. For example, according to a questionnaire survey among participants of the eighth, 15th, and 18th training seminars in China National School of Administration for governmental officials at the director-general level, there is an obvious trend of younger in average age and higher in level of education received among middle-higher rank governmental officials in China (see Table 6-3).

Table 6-3   Proportions of Educational Backgrounds of Participants in Training Seminars in China National School of Administration for Governmental Officials at the Director-General Level, 2002~2003

Unit: %

Category		The 8th training seminar & the seminar for Xinjiang Construction Corps	The 15th training seminar	The 18th training seminar
Educational background	Doctor's	2.0	6.5	4.1
	Master's	14.0	21.7	32.4
	Bachelor's	62.0	65.2	59.4
	College diploma	14.0	6.5	4.1
	Other	8	0	0
	Total	100.0	100.0	100.0
	Number of persons	78	72	74
Age	36~40	—	23.9	21.6
	41~45	—	28.3	74.3
	46~50	—	47.8	
	51	—	0	4.1
	Total	—	100.0	100.0

With the establishment of the government employee system, a new social mobility mechanism through which government employees can enter and leave the stratum of cadres and move up and down within this stratum has come into being since 1994. An annual performance assessment system, which links the results of assessment to the measures of encouragement and punishment, promotion, and dismissal, has been formally implemented in government agencies at all levels. Inept government employees will be demoted or dismissed.

By 1996, about 2,080 thousand of government employees in China had been graded as

---

[1] Lu, Guotai. 2002. *Public Administration in China*. Beijing: The Central Party School Publishing House: 18

264

excellent in the performance assessment. In 1996, 18,239 persons were dismissed or demoted because of low performance. Up to the present, more than 11,000 former government employees have been dismissed. The enforcement of the retirement system has been going on wheels and most government employees retired at the statutory age. Supplementing by the resignation system, the entrance of the group of government employees is unblocked. Up to the present, 11,624 persons have resigned from government employees.[1]

A number of these resigned government employees once belonged to the stratum of state and social administrators.

Major Entrance for Individuals

After one has obtained the status of cadres, if he or she wants to enter the stratum of state and social administrators, he or she has to be promoted as a leading cadre through appointment, election, and/or examination.

(1) Appointment

Appointment refers to the method of filling a non-elected office by directly designating a certain person who is supervised by the entity or person with the authority of personnel patronage according to laws, provisions, and regulations. It is a type of behavior of authorization that the superior grants the authority to the subordinate as well as a process of decentralization and redistribution of power. Appointment is a primary channel of entering the stratum of state and social administrators. It reflects the close relationship between the appointor and the appointee. First, the authority is centralized in this method and hence it is favorable for forming a high-efficient decision-making and execution system. Second, it is easy to direct the administrative system in a consistent way, which is favorable for forming the organizational cohesion. Third, it is a simple flexible and easy-to-operate method of filling offices. However, this method also has some shortcomings. First, it is difficult to know a candidate's ability and moral integrity in all instances because the person is selected from a short list of candidates by a few selectors in a unidirectional way that may lead to oversights and mistakes. Second, this method may result in nepotism or cronyism. The procedure of selection may be affected by leadership's personal favoritism. Because leading cadres are in control of the authority of selection and appointment, some are busy themselves in flattering and entertaining their superiors, resorting to deception and falsification, making use of various influences, and even bribing in order to get an office. In addition, some may feel "grateful" to their superiors for being promoted and hence turn their loyalty from the pubic to the superior. All these shortcomings may prevent many cadres with true talent and

---

[1] Chinese Public Administration Society (2002: 511).

integrity from entering the stratum of state and social administrators, impair the efficiency of state and social administration, and taint the image of the Party and the government.

(2) Election

Election refers to the mechanism of selecting leading cadres through election. It is a type of behavior that the public grants the authority to their delegates. It is also a process of centralizing the power, which means that the subjects of the rights give the authority to their representatives. This method is applied to selecting members of various congresses, councils, and committees at all levels, including administrative principals and chairpersons of committees. In China, the following offices are filled through election: (a) members of the Party Committee elected by the Congress of the Communist Party of China and members, the deputy secretary, and the secretary of its standing committee elected by the Party Committee; (b) members, chairperson, vice chairpersons, and secretary-general of the standing committee of the People's Congress, members of various special committees and director committees, members of the leader teams in governments at all levels, the president of courts, and the procurator-general; (c) members, chairman, vice chairman, and secretary-general of the standing committee of the Chinese People's Political Consultative Conference; (d) members of committees (or councils) of democratic parties and social organizations and members of the leader teams in these organizations. Some of above offices can be filled through appointment by standing committees when corresponding congresses are not in session; in addition, members of the leader team in the Party Committee can be appointed by its superior Party Committee. Elections are held regularly and have definite limitation on the term and tenure of an office; thus, it is favorable for solving the issue of lifelong official system in China to some extent.

The procedure of candidate selection is the precondition of an effective election system. In China, the procedure of producing state and social administrators through elections is under the supervision of the Communist Party of China and must reflect the intentions of the Party. Theoretically, the secretary of the Party Committee should be elected by the congress of the Party. In fact, the person holding this office is usually elected from the only candidate who is nominated by the superior Party Committee and the Organization department or is directly appointed by the superior Party Committee. In recent years, the chairpersons of the standing committees of the People's Congress in many regions of China are held by the secretaries of the local Party Committees as a concurrent post—they are elected by the People's Congress as well. Chairpersons and other leaders in various special committees of the People's Congress and a part of leaders in the Chinese People's Political Consultative Conference and its special committees are also elected from candidates who usually are retired senior cadres and nominated by the superiors.

(3) Examination

Examination refers to the mechanism of selecting the leading cadres through open examination competition, which is held by Party and government agencies based on certain standards. This method is relatively scientific and practical because it follows the principles of openness, democracy, fairness, competition, and a process of choosing the best candidate. The shortcoming of this method is that the standard examinations cannot fully investigate the actual ability of examinees. Although China has several centuries' history of selecting officials through standard examinations, they were not renovated and universally adopted until the 1980s and 1990s.

The open selection of leading cadres is a specific form of the examination system in this new period. In 1984 and 1985, in order to mitigate the shortage of talents in the process of opening-up, governments in Ningbo, Shenzhen, Guangzhou, and Xi'an, etc., started adopting the method which combined recommendations of officials with recommendations of the public, and examination with investigation to select leading cadres. In January 1996, the Central Organization Department of the Communist Party of China transmitted the *Interim Measures for Selecting Leading Cadres through Combining Open Recommendation, Examination, and Performance Assessment Together in Jilin Province* and further pushed the implementation of open selection of leading cadres in the entire China. In March 1999, the Central Organization Department released the *Circular Concerning Further Implementation of Open Selection of Leading Cadres* to give stronger impetus to the adoption of the open selection system. According to statistics, more than seven hundred cadres at the director-general level, seven thousand cadres at the division-chief level, and tens of thousands cadres at the section-chief level have been selected through open selections in all provinces, autonomous regions, and municipalities in China since 2000.[1]

Another form of the examination system is taking up middle-level offices through competition. Competition for public offices is a type of cadre selection method in which the Party and government agencies release open positions and corresponding eligible requirements and select candidates through the procedure consisting of open application, competitive examination, public comment, official investigation, and informing the public before assuming office. In the process of restructuring government agencies and implementing the government employee system, governments in some regions have proactively tried out the method of competition for offices since 1994. In July 1998, the Central Organization Department and the Ministry of Personnel released the *Instructions on Implementation of Competition for Offices in Party and Government Agencies*. In 2001, there were more than 190 thousand cadres who were promoted to leading posts through competition, equal to 68 percent of cadres selected through this method in the previous five years.[2]

---

[1] Li, Jianhua (ed.). 2002. *A Study on Strategy for Leading Talents Development in Party and Government Agencies*. Beijing: The Central Party School Publishing House: 99

[2] Wen, Shengtang. 2003. "New Development of the Anti-Corruption Struggle in 2002". Pp. 102 in Ru, Xin, et al (eds.), *Analyses and Forecasts on Social Situations in China (2003)*. Beijing: Social

The examination system with open positions, open procedure, and open examination results is supervised by the public and the government; thus, the fairness of this system is guaranteed and it gives no opportunity for those who intend to take advantage of influences to get offices. Because the implementation of this examination system is still at its beginning stage, the procedure and method of examination that vary across regions and sectors need to be further standardized. The design and coverage of examination questions and the accuracy of examination results need to be improved. In addition, it is necessary to achieve more supporting measures, a shorter selection circle, and a lower cost of the examination system.

At present, appointment and election are two major methods of forming the stratum of state and social administrators; especially, the appointment system is even more prevalent. The examination system has been tried out in selected regions and sectors in recent years as a supplementary method of forming the stratum of state and social administrators. In addition, some public institutions, such as schools, research institutes, and hospitals, have adopted the engagement system to select administrators.

The Entry and Exit Mechanisms

There are multiple institutional and policy factors which affect social members from entering and exiting the stratum of state and social administrators over the past fifty years, including the retirement and leaving post system, government agency restructuring, and political movements, etc.

(1) The Retirement and Leaving Post System

Although the government had released specific regulations on the retirement issue of the public office personnel early in the 1950s, the retirement system was not put into practice because of various reasons and accordingly it led to a lifelong official system in China. As a result, cadres could not achieve normal social mobility such as promotion and retirement, and a large number of talents, especial young people, were unable to enter the group of cadres, not to mention entering the stratum of state and social administrators.

After the reform and opening-up, because the formal cadre retirement system had not been completely established, according to Deng Xiaoping's proposal, the Central Advisory Committee of the Communist Party of China was set up as a transitional form toward the retirement system. A large number of aged senior cadres entered into this advisory committee while transferring their posts to younger cadres and hence achieved cooperation and alternation between old cadres and new ones. This system was carried out until 1992 and provided the space and opportunities of upward mobility for middle-aged and young cadres.

The Central Committee of the C.P.C. approved the *Decision on Establishing the Retirement System for Old Cadres* in 1982, which proposed that all cadres must

Sciences Documentation Publishing House.

retire at a certain age. In the same year, the State Council enacted the *Provisions on the System of Old Cadres' Leaving Posts and Resting,* which asked for all cadres who had taken part in revolutionary works before September 30, 1949 to leave their posts if they were at a certain age and met the provisions of leaving posts. Their official ranks would not be changed and remunerations and benefits would be highly compensated. Both the retirement system and the leaving post system aimed to let old cadres at a certain age retreat from public offices and transfer these positions to younger cadres. The difference between the two systems was that leaving posts was applied to senior leading cadres and the treatments of left-post cadres were slightly higher than that of retired cadres. There were 3,900 thousand old cadres who left posts or retired between 1982 and 1989.[1] Many of them were former leading cadres, i.e., members of the stratum of state and social administrators.

(2) Development of Economy and Society and Improvement of Political and Legal Systems

The development of economy and society creates conditions of social mobility for state and social administrators. With the progress of economic and social development, the social division of labor has been increasingly deepening and social administration has become complicated. Accordingly, large numbers of specialized and high-caliber administrators are in great demand. The emergence of many of the new administrative positions creates the conditions of social mobility for state and social administrators. In the process of establishing and improving the regulation system of the socialist market economy, the old administrative system is still taking effect while many new administrative institutions are established to meet the demand of economic development. The development of educational service, cultural industry, scientific and technical services, and health care has brought about vast demands for administrators. The establishment of the socialist free-market system has attracted parts of state and social administrators to leave this stratum and go into business or move into other social strata. There were two tides of officials going into business around 1993 and in 2003. This is a sort of social progress that challenged the traditional bureaucrat-centered social value system. In these days, people's value orientations and personal choices are increasingly diverse and channels of self-fulfillment are expanding. Some state and social administrators gave up the career of governmental officials for pursuing personal value by engaging in business. However, there were some negative phenomena emerged in the two tides of going into business. Some leading cadres took advantage of resources and social networks in public administration agencies to obtain undue private interests in business activities. Some took business activities as a means to legalize illegal gains obtained in public offices.

The improvement of the democratic political system in China creates chances for ordinary cadres to enter the stratum of state and social administrators as well as

---

[1] Chinese Public Administration Society (2002: 413).

provides social mobility opportunities for state and social administrators. The judicial system has been reconstructed on a large scale since 1979. Four levels of general courts and procuratorates and special courts and procuratorates were established in China. By the end of 1986, there were 29 high courts, 337 intermediate courts, 2,907 grassroots-level courts, 14,000 people's courts, and 132 special courts in China. From 1979 to 1997, the number of personnel working in courts in China increased to 292 thousand, and the number of procuratorate-related personnel grew to 215 thousand. After the Third Plenum of the 11th Central Committee of the C.P.C., the legislatures and judicial authorities have been established rapidly. By the end of 1996, there were a total of 570 thousand judicial administrative officers in China.[1]

(3) Government Agency Restructuring

Over a long period of time, government agencies at all levels in China were oversize and overstaffed with extremely low efficiency. Since the establishment of the People's Republic of China in 1949, several restructuring programs have been carried out in government agencies. Each restructuring program of government agencies inevitably affected social mobility of a considerable number of state and social administrators.

With the development of economy and society, tasks of economic and social administration have been increasing and have hence inevitably led to the expansion of government agencies and the growth of personnel. At the same time, government agencies and their personnel have a tendency of accrual, which is called *Parkinson's Law*. The former is a kind of function-driven growth, while the latter is a kind of spontaneous growth. Under the combined influences of the two types of growth, the size of government agencies and their personnel formed a series of weird circles consisting of simplifying, then expanding, simplifying again, and then expanding again. In such circles, the social status of a large number of state and social administrators went up and down. According to the five periods of social mobility in contemporary China proposed in this study, in the following section, we will investigate the influences of government agency restructuring on entering and exiting the stratum of state and social administrators in the five periods respectively.

I. 1949~1956

The tendency of government agency expanding and personnel growing came into being shortly after the establishment of the People's Republic of China. The number of government agencies increased by 20 percent in 3 years between 1949 and 1952. Except for military personnel and teaching-related personnel, the number of full-time cadres increased from 600 thousand around 1949 to 1,750 thousand in 1950, 2,710 thousand in 1951, and 3,900 thousand in 1953, up by 5.5 times in four years.[2] The government has started to increase revenue and reduce expenditure since

---

[1] Lu, et al. (2001: 184 -185).

[2] Ren, Jie and Lin Liang. 1999. *Restructuring and Transition of the Government Agency in the People's Republic of China*. Beijing: Huawen Press: 21.

November 1953. As a result, the size of administrative personnel was reduced by 160 thousand persons.

Soon after the establishment of the People's Republic of China, a large number of cadres were transferred from local governments to various departments of the central government. For example, between September and December in 1952, 5,574 cadres were shifted from local governments to Beijing in 3 batches and 80 percent of them entered economic and financial administration sectors. The major principals of each grand region took offices in both the local and the central government at the same time. They gradually shifted the focus of their work until the grand regions were abrogated. There were 163 thousand cadres shifting to industrial construction sectors from 1952 to 1954, among them 170 thousand were section-chief and higher level cadres and 103 thousand went to state-owned industrial enterprises.[1]

In 1954, on one hand, governments at all levels were simplifying administrative structure and reducing the personnel size. On the other hand, new agencies were constantly established and the size of personnel kept expanding. In addition, the proportion of operating personnel to non-operating personnel was unreasonable and people outside the authorized personnel quota and inside the quota were mixed with each other. Therefore, from the end of 1954 to the beginning of 1956, government agencies from the central, provincial, autonomous region, and municipality levels to the county and township levels carried out a large-scale program of simplification. As a result, the central government agencies reduced their personnel sizes according to the demand of operation. 36,270 persons were cut down in 51 central government agencies, accounting for 40.1 percent of the former personnel size. In addition, large numbers of cadres were shifted to lower level and grassroots production units; a considerable number of them were section-chief and higher level cadres, technical personnel, and graduates of universities who had been assigned to government agencies according to the governmental plan since 1950. According to statistics conducted by the Cadre Restructuring Committee of the Central Government Agency in 80 units, among 34,000 restructured persons, 24,400 persons were cadres of which section-chief and higher-level cadres accounted for 13 percent. Some of restructured cadres were sent to public institutions and enterprises, some of them were assigned to local governments, and some were admitted to various schools.[2] Local governments at all levels were simplified as well. In division (bureau)-level agencies in provincial, autonomous regions, and municipal governments, the hierarchy of ranks was simplified to only two levels of ranks and hence a considerable large proportion of cadres were cut down.

However, the restructure in 1955 did not trip out the simplifying-expanding circle. In less than one year, the numbers of agencies and personnel outstripped the former ones much more. By the end of 1956, in the State Council system, there were

---

[1] Ren and Liang (1999: 23-24).

[2] Composition Team. 1999. *Trans-Century Reform in China Government*. Beijing: China Economy Publishing House: 234.

48 ministries and committees, 24 departments directly under the State Council, 8 offices, and 1 secretariat, totaling 81 agencies. Personnel working in these agencies numbered 7,0649 persons, up by 93 percent in three years and with a net increase of 11 agencies within one year in 1956. The below following the behaviors of the above; local governments increased their agencies as well. For example, the number of agencies in Hunan provincial government increased from 26 in 1953 to 39 in 1956; the number of agencies in Shanghai municipal government increased from 37 in 1953 to 61 in 1956. The average number of agencies at the provincial level was about 30 in 1953, while the number increased to 45 in 1957.[1]

From 1949 to 1957, the positions and status of a considerable number of cadres changed as well; some moved down to lower positions. However, in various programs of restructuring and simplification, the increase of agencies and personnel created greater opportunities for social members of other strata to enter the group of cadres. In addition, the increase of agencies and positions inevitably provided more upward mobility opportunities for a number of cadres to become state and social administrators.

II. 1957~1966

In order to respond to the situation of simplified ownership structure after accomplishment of the socialist transformation, the central government released the *Resolution on the Reform of the Government Administrative System (Draft)* and proposed to restructure government agencies at all levels in the second half of 1956. By the end of 1959, there were 60 departments in the State Council. According to statistics, this program of personnel simplification in the central government agencies lasted to 1960; especially, the number of cut-down personnel reached its peak in 1958 and 1959. In June 1961, more than 80 thousand persons were reduced from former 240 thousand personnel in all central agencies in Beijing, down by 33 percent. Most of the cut-down personnel were sent to grassroots or production units and the countryside to participate in production activities. Government agencies at all other levels were simplified as well. About 100 thousand cadres returned to production units and 200 thousand cadres were sent down to grassroots units by 1958.[2]

China had fallen into an extremely difficult situation since 1960. Famines due to crop failures had seized the whole country. In some regions, the abnormal death rate increased sharply. The net decrease of the whole population in 1960 was more than 10,000 thousand. In order to cope with such a difficult situation and enhance the efficiency of the government, the Central Committee of the C.P.C. and the State Council released the *Decision on Further Simplifying Staff Members and Workers and Reducing Urban Population* in May 1962, which proposed that, besides simplifying the authorized quota of staff and reducing personnel on a large scale, a part of capable cadres in governments at all levels should be sent down to strengthen the grass roots.

---

[1] Ren and Liang (1999: 28).
[2] Chinese Public Administration Society (2002: 168).

272

By the end of June 1962, government agencies at the central level had reduced more than 24.7 thousand persons, accounting for 36.7 percent of the former 67.2 thousand persons, and the remaining personnel size was 42.5 thousand. However, the personnel size of the central government agencies did not reduce but increased in the second half of 1962. The actual size of personnel was 45.9 thousand by the end of February 1963, with an increase of 3,400 persons. Taking 5,000 persons in all central bureaus established in 1961 into account, the total personnel size was 50.9 thousand. The Central Committee of the C.P.C. decided to cut down 4,900 persons from 50.9 thousand personnel on March 27, 1963. As a result, the personnel size reduced to less than 46 thousand, with a decrease of 21.2 thousand over the figure at the end of June 1960, i.e., 67.2 thousand before the simplification, or down by 31.5 percent over the 1960 figure.[1] From February 1962 to 1964, a total of 810 thousand cadres were cut down in China through efforts in nearly two years. Most of the cut-down cadres were transferred to grassroots and production units.[2]

III. 1966~1977

In the Cultural Revolution, government agencies at the central and local levels experienced drastic changes and accordingly affected social mobility of the state and social administrator stratum. However, the major factor that caused social mobility of state and social administrators was not the change of agency and personnel size, but the political factor. Such social mobility was extremely disorderly without any rules. The mobility rate of the state and social administrator stratum was very high and ordinary members of this stratum were unable to take their fates in their own hands.

IV. Since 1977

After the Gang of Four collapsed in October 1977, China began to bring order out of chaos. In particular, after the Third Plenum of the Eleventh Central Committee of the C.P.C. that was held at the end of 1978, the political, economic, and social development in China have entered into a brand new era and various social undertakings have been flourishing. In this period, government agencies expanded rapidly in the consecutive five years from 1977 to 1981. For example, 48 departments were reestablished or newly set up in the State Council. The total number of functional departments in the State Council was 100 by the end of 1981, a peak since the establishment of the People's Republic of China. In the same year, Deng Xiaoping delivered his famous speech *Simplifying Administrative Structure is Another Revolution*. Accordingly, the first program of restructuring government agencies after the reform and opening-up was launched in 1982. Through agency restructuring and personnel adjustment in that year, by the end of 1982 the number of ministries and committees in the State Council dropped from 52 to 43, agencies directly under the

---

[1] Chinese Public Administration Society (2002: 204).

[2] Liu, Zhifeng. 1998. *The Seventh Revolution: Memorandum on China Government Agency Restructure in 1998*. Beijing: Economy Daily Press: 297.

State Council decreased from 43 to 15, administrative institutions were reduced from 5 to 3, and functional departments were reduced from 100 to 61. Personnel working in agencies declined from 50 thousand to 39 thousand, with a decrease of 25.4 percent. According to statistics in 38 ministries and committees, except for part-time ministers and directors, the number of ministers, vice ministers, directors, and vice-directors decreased from former 505 to 167, down by 67 percent. In newly established leader teams, the newly promoted middle-aged and young cadres accounted for 32 percent, the average age decreased from 64 to 58, and cadres with university and higher level of education increased from former 37 percent to 52 percent. Branches inside ministries and committees were simplified as well. According to statistics in 28 ministries and committees, branches at the bureau level reduced from 720 to 488, and the number of directors-general and deputy directors reduced from 2,450 to 1,398 persons, down by 43 percent. Restructuring in government agencies at the provincial, city, and county levels succeeded the reform in central government agencies. The agency restructuring program starting from 1982 lasted for three year until 1985. The focus of restructuring in local governments was readjusting and reorganizing leader teams at various levels, and meanwhile normalizing the structure of functional departments in local governments and simplifying personnel. Through this restructuring program, the personnel size of provincial governments reduced from 180 thousand to 120 thousand. Personnel working in government agencies at the city and county level decreased 20 percent, and the size of personnel in agencies at the prefecture level decreased even more.[1]

However, the expanding tendency of the government agency and personnel size was not under control even when the government agency-restructuring program from top to bottom was carried out in 1982. Old agencies were cut down while new agencies were emerging; the personnel size was reduced while the number of people working in government agencies was increasing. With the development of the free-market economy, low work efficiency and overstaffed government agencies made the functions of the government lag far behind the development of the economy and society. Therefore, the State Council started another round of government agency restructuring in 1989. Although this restructuring program was interrupted by the political event in 1989, it produced some outcomes. Functional departments in the State Council reduced from 72 to 68 and non-permanent institutions reduced from 75 to 55. The personnel size at the end of 1989 was 44,878 persons, 7,915 persons less than former 52,793 persons.

However, the growth rate of agencies and personnel was still higher than that of their decrease. The number of governmental cadres increased by one million each year. In 1990, not including the non-permanent institutions, the total number of government agencies in China increased by 55 thousand over the 1984 figure, with an average growth of 9,000 per year, or 25 per day. Section-chief and higher level cadres in provincial government agencies in China increased by more than 2,000 persons

---

[1] Ren and Liang (1999: 90).

between 1989 and 1990. By the end of 1991 personnel working in Party and government agencies and public institutions reached 33,860 thousand persons, up by 75 percent over the 1980 figure. About 740 thousand persons surpassed the authorized quota of staff in Party and government agencies at the county and higher level. At the township level, the number of supernumerary was 2,140 thousand persons.[1]

The Fourteenth National Congress of the Communist Party of China in 1992 proposed to establish the socialist market economy. According to this proposal, China government launched the third round of agency restructuring after the reform and opening-up in April 1993. This restructuring program was finished by the end of 1996. It was a comprehensive agency restructuring program. According to demands of the socialist market economy for public administration, the Party and government agencies were readjusted and personnel were cut down. In addition, the People's Congress, the Political Consultative Conference, and judicial authorities were restructured as well. After this restructuring program, ministries and committees, administrative institutions, and departments directly under the State Council reduced from 86 to 59, and non-permanent institutions decreased from 85 to 26. According to preliminary statistics, the former personnel size of these agencies was 36,716 persons. After the restructuring program, this size decreased to 29,217, down by 20.4 percent. Personnel working in local offices were reduced by 1,713 persons, with a decrease of 28 percent. Restructuring in local government agencies also achieved significant effects. According to the restructuring scheme approved by the State Council, the re-authorized quota of staff in local governments at all levels was reduced to 7,250 thousand persons from the former 9,250 thousand, down by 22 percent. Restructuring with a greater degree occurred in agencies at the city and county level, down by 650 thousand and 1,230 thousand respectively. [2]

With the establishment and improvement of the socialist free-market system, the existing administrative system and regulation methods were unable to meet the demand of socio-economic development. Government agencies at all levels in China were oversize and overstaffed with extremely low efficiency and ill-fitting functions. In 1997, the Fifteenth National Congress of the Communist Party of China proposed to start the fourth round of government agency restructuring from 1998. This restructuring program lasted for three years and achieved notable outcomes. After this round of restructuring, departments in the State Council were reduced from 40 to 29, down by 27 percent; branches inside these departments decreased by more than 200, down by 25 percent; the total personnel size reduced from 32 thousand to 16.7 thousand, down by 47.5 percent.[3]

In addition, another macro-level factor that has a significant influence on social mobility of the stratum of state and social administrators is the cadre selection system. Before 1978, the Party and governmental cadres were mainly selected through

---

[1] Ren and Liang (1999: 102).
[2] Composition Team (1999: 314, 316).
[3] Composition Team (1999: 212).

appointment. After the 1980s, major leading cadres must be elected through secret ballots. Candidates who failed in the election could not take the office. Consequently, open selecting cadres promoted reasonable mobility of the stratum of state and social administrators. In 1992, the Organization Department of the Central Committee of the C.P.C. proposed to implement the leading cadre selection method, which had been successfully tried out in Jilin Province; this method combined open recommendation with examination and assessment. Since then, more and more cadres in all regions have been selected through standardized procedures. Since 1995, more than 700 director-general level cadres, 7,000 division-chief level cadres, and tens of thousands of section-chief level cadres have been openly selected in 31 provinces, autonomous regions, and municipalities in China.[1] The cadre exchange system also has an important influence on horizontal mobility of the state and social administrator stratum.

(4) Political Movements

All previous political movements, such as the Anti-Rightist Campaign and the Cultural Revolution, significantly affected state and social administrators and hence made their social mobility go up and down.

In the Anti-Rightist Campaign launched in June 1957, 552,887 persons were labeled as rightists. Numerous people were criticized, denounced, and forced to make self-examination. More than 99 percent of rightists were undeserved and many of them were leading cadres or even senior leading cadres. Families and friends of these so-called rightists were involved and treated unjustly. Their political future was affected to some extent and was hence prevented from moving upward or even led to downward mobility. In the Anti-Rightist Campaign, the supervising authority was seriously abused; people's mistakes were intentionally aggrandized to an unreasonable degree; punishments were given in haste. As a result, a large number of Party members were wrongly punished. The number of Party members and cadres who were punished was 508,750 in 1958, more than the sum of the four years from 1954 to 1957. People who were expelled from the Party were equal to 80 percent of the sum of the seven years from 1951 to 1957.

In the Cultural Revolution starting in 1966, Party and government agencies at all levels were paralyzed. Most leading cadres were denounced and put into prison; ordinary personnel in government agencies took part in mass movements and nobody dealt with daily affairs. As a result, normal work and production order could not go on. The "Seizing Power at All Levels" campaign started in 1967 was the climax of the Cultural Revolution. Government agencies at almost all levels stopped operations; local governments were attacked universally and functions of the central government were out of order. Administrative authority was seized by the Revolutionary Committees. Leading cadres in local governments received various false accusations

---

[1] Li, Jianhua (2002: 32).

and persecutions and were deprived of personal freedom. The majority of ordinary personnel in the government were ordered to take political workshops, or were sent to the "May 7th Cadre School" to take part in compulsory labor, or were sent down to the countryside and factories, except that a few of them stayed on to work for the Revolutionary Committees. In the "Seizing Power at All Levels" campaign starting in 1967, the judicial authorities were seriously destroyed and paralyzed as well. Party and government agencies and economic administration institutions at various levels, from ministries and committees in the central government to production direction systems in enterprises and rural areas, all were serious attacked. Most of these institutions were out of action and some even were removed. The political, economic, and social life and production in the whole country was in a highly anarchic state and such anarchy made countless former state and social administrators' lives marked by vicissitudes.

In order to continue the Cultural Revolution under such a disorderly situation, Mao Zedong decided to send the army to intervene in local Cultural Revolution movement by supporting the leftists, peasants, and workers, exercising military control over some localities, departments and units, and giving military training to students. Some provinces, municipalities, and autonomous regions were under military control. The military governing committees and teams, military representatives, or preparatory panels of the Revolutionary Committees, which were mainly constituted by army cadres, were universally established in various units. The military control had extended to the whole country step by step since the beginning of 1967. A large number of servicemen were dispatched to attend this movement. More than 2,790 thousand person-time had participated in this movement by the end of 1970. At that time, more than 400 thousand persons were still taking part in the Supporting the Leftists campaign. In some regions, soldiers even served as ordinary clerks, security custodians, and typists. Before long, the military governing committees were replaced by the Revolutionary Committees.[1]

In 1967, in order to achieve so-called "turning from the great chaos to the lasting peace" that was proposed by Mao Zedong when the old state apparatus was thoroughly destroyed, Mao Zedong chose the Revolutionary Committee as a new form of regime. Revolutionary Committees were established in all regions in China to replace former Party and government agencies and exercise the administrative authority. Not only in all departments in the State Council and in local regimes at the provincial, city, county, and people's commune levels, but also in all public institutions, Revolutionary Committees were universally set up. The Revolutionary Committee was organized in the so-called approach of "combining three components", i.e., combining principals of mass organizations, principals of local garrisons, and "revolutionary leading cadres" together in the Revolutionary Committee. Of those, principals of various revolt cliques (i.e., the so-called "main body of representatives of the masses") accounted for 50 percent, representatives of the revolutionary masses of

---

[1] Ren and Liang (1999: 62).

other cliques accounted for 10 percent, and military representatives made up 20 percent. Although the Revolutionary Committee was composed of the masses, military personnel, and cadres, army cadres actually occupied the leading position and hence local Party Committees were directed by the army. The real power of the Revolutionary Committee was controlled by its standing committee, which was constituted by 20 percent of the members of the Revolutionary Committee. In September 1968, military representatives assumed 20 directors of the Revolutionary Committees at the provincial level and 5,193 directors or deputy directors of the Revolutionary Committees at the county and higher level. Military personnel occupied 78 percent of director posts in Revolutionary Committees at the county and higher level in Beijing Municipality, 81 percent in Guangdong Province, 84 percent in Liaoning Province, 95 percent in Shanxi Province, and as high as 98 percent in Hubei Province.[1]

Although the Revolutionary Committee was set up as a type of temporary authority at that time, it was actually established as the administrative agency of local governments at all levels, various departments inside the government, public institutions, and enterprises afterwards, and replaced grassroots autonomous organizations. Its existence lasted as long as twelve years.

The State Council convoked a convention to announce the establishment of core teams of Party members and the Revolutionary committees in various departments inside the State Council system on July 1, 1970. Ninety former departments were merged into 27 units (except for agencies directly under the State Council), down by 70 percent. The number of units directly supervised by the State Council was 20 and the personnel size decreased from 53 thousand to 9,000, with a decrease of 82 percent. After the September 13 Incident when Lin Biao committed treachery and fled in 1971, the State Council started to reestablish and add some functional departments to the system of the State Council.

On August 21, 1972, the Central Committee of the Communist Party of China decided to abolish the military governing committees, military propaganda teams, and leftists-supporting agencies in regions and units where the Party Committees had already been established. After certain adjustments in local Party Committees and Revolutionary Committees, more local cadres were selected to assume the principal offices. Subsequently, military representatives withdrew from most Revolutionary Committees and returned to the army one after the other; only very few military representatives continued to stay on to assume major leaders in the Revolutionary Committees at the provincial level. After 1973, the old pattern of "combining three components", i.e., combining revolutionary cadres, military representatives, and representatives of revolutionary masses together, was replaced by the new pattern of "combining three components", i.e., combining the old, middle-aged, and young cadres together.

From the very beginning of the Cultural Revolution, a large number of old

---

[1] Ren and Liang (1999: 62).

cadres were forced to withdraw from the stratum of state and social administrators and shift to other social strata and became workers and peasants, or even were persecuted to death. In the "Seizing of Power at All Levels" campaign, many leading cadres were labeled capitalist followers, betrayers, or spies and lost their power. According to statistics, by the year of 1968, more than 60 principals at the provincial, autonomous region, and municipality level were openly criticized by the Central Committee of the C.P.C. or denounced on newspapers at the national level; about 75 percent of leading cadres at the vice-minister or deputy-governors and higher level were filed and investigated. More than 184 thousand of cadres, military personnel, and ordinary people were wounded, disabled, and/or killed in the July 20 Incident in Wuhan in Hubei Province. In addition, 1,565 cadres and policemen were mistreated to death in the "Smashing the Legal System" campaign. In the "Purging the Class Troops" campaign in 1968, the entire cadre group became the subject of persecution. Cadres who were filed and investigated accounted for 17.7 percent of the total number of cadres in China. There were 29,885 cadres in the central government agencies and ministries and committees who were investigated, accounting for 16.3 percent of the total number of cadres in the central agencies, of which the proportion was over 30 percent in 11 units. The scale of persecution was unimaginable. In the "Seizing Power at All Levels" campaign, headed by Liu Shaoqi, the Chairman of the People's Republic of China, more than 34,000 persons were mistreated to death and more than one hundred million people were directly or indirectly involved in these cases.[1] In the Cultural Revolution, a large number of revolt cliques entered the stratum of state and social administrators. After the Lin Biao Incident, some old cadres were liberated in succession and held leading posts again. A number of revolt cliques who had entered administrative agencies were sent back to their former work units. However, the Jiang Qing's clique did a crash job to promote cadres and admit Party members based on the criterion of "promoting fighters against the tide of counterrevolution". For example, about 36 thousand people were admitted to the Party and 9,000 persons were promoted to be cadres in Zhejiang Province in 1974.[2] Deng Xiaoping took charge of the State Council and routines of the Central Committee from February 1975. He proposed the guideline of "general rectification" in order to reestablish the authority of the central government, strengthen the leadership of the Party Committees at all levels, and constrain the influence of Party members and cadres who rose in revolt movements, and purge Party members and cadres who were promoted in the crash job. At the end of April 1975, according to Mao Zedong's proposal and pushed by Zhou Enlai and Deng Xiaoping, the Central Committee of the C.P.C. decided to release the overwhelming majority of people who were imprisoned and investigated except for those who had relations with Lin Biao's clique. Among them, those whose cases belonged to "antagonistic conflicts between the people and the enemy" should be assigned to certain work units or given a certain amount of governmental allowance;

---

[1] Ren and Liang (1999: 63); Chinese Public Administration Society (2002: 291).
[2] Chinese Public Administration Society (2002: 273).

those whose cases belonged to "conflicts among the people" should be emplaced to certain work units and compensated for deserved salaries; those who were the Party members could take part in activities of the Party organizations again; those who were unjustly treated should be rehabilitated; those whose cases were still not closed could suspend their cases awaiting for investigation of the Central Organization Department of the Communist Party of China and the General Political Department of the People's Liberation Army. As a result of this decision, many senior cadres who had been imprisoned for a long time were released and some of them were assigned corresponding positions. However, shortly afterwards, the "Denouncing Deng Xiaoping" campaign and the "Against the Right-Opportunists' Inclination to Reverse Verdicts" campaign were launched in December 1975. Deng Xiaoping's proposal of "general rectification" came to a premature-end. In these campaigns, many old cadres were persecuted again by the Gang of Four. The Gang of Four invented a weird formula, i.e., old cadres were equal to the democratic clique, and the democratic clique was equal to capitalist followers. Old cadres who had returned to former positions and achieved many accomplishments were stigmatized by the Gang of Four as "the clique of avengers" and a political campaign of "digging out agents and the clique of avengers attempting to restore the old order" was launched in China. For example, the Minister of Education Zhou Rongxin at that time was mistreated to death in the "Against the Right-Opportunists' Inclination to Reverse Verdicts" campaign. Many other old cadres, such as Hu Yaobang and Wan Li, were denounced and persecuted. Some cadres at the local and grassroots level who insisted on correct political guidelines were denounced and deprived of authority.

MICRO-LEVEL MECHANISMS OF SOCIAL MOBILITY

Analysis on micro-level mechanisms refers to analyzing social mobility of the stratum of state and social administrators at the individual level. The major perspectives of such an analysis include the intergenerational and intragenerational mobility.

Intergenerational Mobility

From the perspective of intergenerational mobility, according to our survey in the study (see Chapter 4), the stratum of state and social administrators has a certain degree of intergenerational inheritance. People whose fathers' occupations are governmental cadres and enterprise managerial personnel have the greatest chance to be state and social administrators. People from families of professional and technical personnel and clerical personnel also have certain advantages to enter this stratum. In contrast, the probabilities of entering this stratum for people from families of peasants, the self-employed, and small owners are significantly lower than their corresponding proportions in the overall social structure. In addition, the probability for people from families of workers to be state and social administrators is roughly equal to their proportion in the overall structure.

The longitudinal comparative analysis of the intergenerational mobility indicates that the degree of intergenerational inheritance of the state and social administrator stratum varied with time. It was weaker among state and social administrators who started working before 1980s than those who started working after 1980. For example, about 10.6 percent of state and social administrators who started working before 1980 came from families of governmental cadres and enterprise managerial personnel. This proportion is five times higher than the average proportion (2.1 percent) of this category in the overall social structure. About 25 percent of state and social administrators who started working after 1980 had the same family background, and it is seven times higher than the average proportion (3.1 percent) of this category in the overall social structure. In contrast, 53.2 percent of state and social administrators who started working before 1980 came from families of peasants; it is about 24 percent lower than its average proportion (77.4 percent) in the overall social structure. Among state and social administrators who started working after 1980, 31.3 percent came from the family of peasants and it is about 38 percent lower than its average proportion (69.2 percent) in the overall social structure. That is to say, before the economic reform, the probability for children from peasant families to be state and social administrators is higher than that after the reform. Meanwhile, after the economic reform, the probability for children from the families of governmental cadres and enterprise managerial personnel to be state and social administrators is higher than that before the reform.

Intragenerational Mobility

Analysis of the intragenerational mobility   (see Chapter 4) shows that, in the social mobility chain, the stratum of state and social administrators is usually the final stop of social mobility. People do not have a strong desire to move to other strata after entering this stratum and the probability of downward mobility is relatively low. The great majority (59.1 percent) of people whose first occupation was that of state and social administrator still kept the same job, while another portion of them moved into the managerial personnel stratum (9.1 percent) and the clerical personnel stratum (27.3 percent). Since the 1990s, the proportion of state and social administrators who shifted to the stratum of managerial personnel and the stratum of private entrepreneurs, which possess economic resources, has risen slightly. A large number of cadres resigned from the government and shifted into business at the beginning of the 1990s, and that may be a possible cause of such a change. The phenomenon that state and social administrators in control of organizational resources shifting to the stratum in possession of economic resources indicates that the importance of economic resources in the value appraisal system has been rising. However, such movement was not very strong. After that tide of shifting to business, there were very few newly promoted middle-aged and young cadres (state and social administrators) following that path.

The overwhelming majority of state and social administrators still chose to stay in this stratum and strive for promotions in administrative positions. Cadres who resigned to go into business were usually those without real power or any promising career in the government, but some cadres with real power also went into business in order to take advantage of their social networks and influence to obtain undue personal interests, or to legalize illegal gains obtained in public offices through business activities.

Analysis of the intragenerational mobility also shows that the inflow channel of the state and social administrator stratum is limited to a fixed path. About two-tenths of state and social administrators' first occupations were that of state and social administrators, about six-tenths came from professional and technical personnel and clerical personnel, and the remaining two-tenths came from industrial workers, commercial and service personnel, and peasants. Therefore, as a whole, the major origins of state and social administrators are professional and technical personnel and clerical personnel, only a small portion of administrators came from workers and peasants, and almost no managerial personnel, private entrepreneurs, and individual-operated business proprietors entered this stratum. The inflow channel of the state and social administrator stratum changed significantly before and after the economic reform. There were certain proportions of industrial workers, commercial and service personnel, and peasants who entered this stratum before the economic reform. In particular, slightly more than one-tenth of state and social administrators' first occupations were that of agricultural laborers. After the economic reform (see Table 4-6), the probability of entering this stratum for industrial workers, commercial and service personnel, and peasants declined sharply. Although there are still some commercial and service personnel who have become state and social administrators in this period, almost no industrial workers and peasants have such opportunities. Changes in the origins of the state and social administrator stratum indicate that the selection rule of this stratum varied after the economic reform. For example, before the reform, the basic criteria for selecting cadres focused on their political participation performance and their political status; while after the reform, academic degrees and diplomas are emphasized in cadre promotion.

IMPACT OF INFORMAL INSTITUTIONAL FACTORS

The stratum of state and social administrators is in control of quite a number of state and social resources. Members of this stratum have relatively high social status. Being officials or cadres has been the ultimate life goal of many people in China over a long period of time. From the perspective of state and social administration, there is a demand for high-caliber talented people to take charge of such administration affairs. Therefore, people's desire to become officials and cadres is something good. People who are willing to go in for state and social administration will bring more candidates from whom competent and excellent state and social administrators will be picked out.

Supported by appropriate institutions, excellent state and social administrators will be favorable for stability and development of the society, people's wellbeing, and the solidification of the regime. Therefore, political parties and governments at all times and around the world have tried their best to find talented people to be state and social administrators. In China, as early as in the Han Dynasty (206 B.C.-200 A.C.), official selection systems such as *Cha Ju* (recommending by local administrative executives) and *Jiu Pin Zhong Zheng Zhi* (nine levels of official ranks in the imperial regime) were adopted in China. From the Sui Dynasty (581 A.C.-618 A.C.) to the Tang Dynasty (617 A.C.-907 A.C.), a set of imperial examination systems had been established gradually to select civilians and had contributed to stability and development of the feudal society in China. Various official selection systems had direct influences on social mobility of all social strata.

After the establishment of the People's Republic of China, a set of cadre personnel systems have been formed in practice and provided institutional space for the growth and development of the state and social administrator stratum. Different cadre personnel systems have different effects on the inflow of social members to this stratum and social mobility of its members. However, the institutional space created by universal institutional factors merely provides a sort of probability for members of various social strata to enter the stratum of state and social administrators. As far as who can actually enter this stratum and the direction and span of their mobility inside this stratum depend on personal factors and certain non-institutional factors to some extent. The family background, individual capability, social networks, experience, and personal hobbies of each social member will directly affect the feasibility of social mobility that is influenced by universal institutional factors. In addition, besides individual factors and formal institutional factors, informal institutional factors also have an influence on social mobility of state and social administrators; sometimes such influence has been enormous. *Informal institutional factors* refer to informal factors, which are independent of individuals and different from formal institutions. In other words, non-institutional factors are equal to a sort of "invisible rules", which reflect the characteristics of the Chinese society to some extent. "Invisible rules" are also loopholes of formal institutions or unwritten rules caused by the deviated enforcement of institutions.

Since the reform and opening-up, "making the rank of cadres more revolutionary, younger in average age, better educated and professionally more competent" has been the major criteria for selecting social members to be state and social administrators. According to these criteria, the age distribution of cadres in the twenty-first century requires that the majority of cadres at the governor and minister level should be aged 45 to 50, and a certain number of such cadres should be around 40. The majority of cadres at the city and director level should be at the age of 40 to 45, and a certain number of such cadres should be around 35; the majority of cadres at the county and division-chief level should be at the age of 35 to 40, and a certain number of such cadres should be around 30. With regard to the distribution of educational levels, it is required that cadres at the county and division-chief level and the city and director level should receive college and higher-level education, and a certain proportion of such cadres should receive university and higher-level education. Cadres at the governor and minister level should receive university and higher-level education, and a certain proportion of such cadres should receive postgraduate education and hold the master's and/or doctor's degrees. As far as the distribution of specializations, leading cadres who are familiar with modern management, ideology, Party affairs, politics, scientific and technological research, finance, economy, and trade should have a certain proportion respectively. [1] According to the above requirements, a large number of young talented social members have entered the stratum of state and social administrators and made immense contributions to the modernization of Chinese society. In practice, however, governments in some regions consider age and diploma as major criteria for cadre selection and thus there is a saying, "the age is valuable, the diploma is indispensable, and the others are nonessential". Administrative competence, experience and virtue are treated as minor references. Careers of middle-aged and older cadres have not been given appropriate considerations when large numbers of younger cadres are promoted. As a result, many extraordinarily competent middle-aged cadres lost their space of upward mobility in favor of "younger in average age" and impaired their enthusiasm. In addition, when "higher in educational level" is emphasized in cadre promotion, professional competence has been paid less attention. Many experienced cadres with lower level of education have been given a smaller chance of upward mobility when a large number of younger cadres are taking over important leading offices. Driven by the trend of "younger in average age" and "higher in educational level", some cadres practiced fraud by illegally procuring diplomas and falsifying their ages. There is another saying lashing such cadres, "the age is falsified and the diploma is bought".

Since the reform and opening-up, the social mobility mechanisms of normal entrance, promotion, and exit for state and social administrators have been established and improved. Systems concerning the election of leading cadres, informing the public before assuming office, the term of office, the probation and resignation of leading cadres, and the adjustment of incompetent incumbent cadres have been further strengthened and have consequently promoted the procedure of selection and appointment of leading cadres to be more reasonable, democratic, and institutionalized through emphasizing the criteria of virtue, competence, and performance. In practice, however, the scope of origins of cadres is still relatively narrow. The appointment system has been extensively adopted rather than a selection mechanism following the principles of openness, fairness, competition, and choosing the best. As a result, the issue that "the minority is selected from the minority by the minority" in cadre selection has not been thoroughly solved yet. The practices of giving top priority to the seniority, emphasizing sequence in promotion, and considering the balance between different groups and influences have still existed in

---

[1] Li, Jianhua (2002: 14 -15).

some regions; as a result, some competent cadres with considerable potentials have not been put in critical positions. Because of the lack of specific and reasonable criteria to define responsibility and assess the performance of leading posts, it is hard to make decisions on promotion, demotion, and dismissal of cadres on the basis of objective and accurate evaluations, which are obtained through assessing the political participation and work performance of leading cadres in a certain period. In consequence, the performance assessment is conducted in a perfunctory way, in which reports indulge in exaggeration, surveys and interviews focus on achievements while fencing with problems and shortcomings, and the conclusions of assessment are usually all in the same key, that is, too vague and too general to reflect the fact. The transparency of performance assessment and selection of leading cadres still needs to be improved. Although there is a system of informing the public before assuming offices, the published profiles usually are too simple to let the public know the personal quality, performance, achievements, and public recognition of corresponding candidates, especially those who migrate between different regions. The results of investigation and assessment are usually not released to the public and the masses do not know whether the official opinions are the same as theirs. To top it all, in some regions, the official investigation and collective decision-making on cadre selection are replaced by the principal cadres' personal opinions while ordinary cadres and the masses have little influence on promotion, demotion, and dismissal of cadres. Consequently, the phenomena of cronyism and nepotism, appointing sycophants and getting offices through making use of social networks, influences, and bribery still exist to some extent. Furthermore, there are no appropriate constraints and supervising systems, especially the responsibility investigation system, dealing with oversight and mistakes in cadre selection, to guarantee institutionally the selection of eligible and competent candidates.

There is a saying about the common practices in some local governments in China, "without influence and bribes you will stay in the same position forever; with influence but without bribes you can only get transferred at the same level; with influence and bribes you will get the important position". For example, Li Huigang, the vice general manager of the Hunan Colored Metal Industrial Controlling Company, a deputy-director level cadre, employed wizards and trickster and expensed 1.5 million Yuan RMB to procure higher offices for himself. In February 2004, Li Tiecheng, the former Party secretary of the Jingyu County in Jilin Province, Shang Dianju, the former Party secretary of the Kuandian County in Liaoning Province, Sun Kongwen, the former Party secretary of the Mengcheng County in Anhui Province, and Ma Zhaode, the former director of the Administration for Industry and Commerce of Hainan Province were arrested and accused of "selling public offices" by taking bribes. Li Tiecheng took more than 1.42 million Yuan bribes from 110 people by exploiting the opportunity of promoting and transferring cadres. Sun Kongwen took more than 350 thousand yuan bribes from 30 bribers by exploiting the opportunity of promoting cadres. All these cases indicate that the internal promotion mechanism of the state and social administrator stratum bears many problems. The existence of cadres who "sell public offices" is due to the existence of people who intend to "buy public offices"; while the existence of people who intend to "buy public offices" is due to the existence of the probability of "buying a public office". Similarly, the existence of people who try to get offices through exercising influences is due to the existence of the probability of getting public offices in such a way. Undoubtedly, the reason why the price of the public office is so high is that it is a kind of rare commodity.

Over a long period of time, the phenomena of once up and never down and lifelong posts have not been removed completely yet and are even still spreading in some regions. In consequence, members of other social strata are unable to enter this stratum and the middle-aged and younger cadres cannot get normal promotions. Some leading cadres who are mediocre, or incompetent, or even have always been making some minor mistakes still stay in the same positions or just were transferred to other leading posts unless they seriously break laws or breach regulations. In addition, some Party and governmental cadres are transferred to offices in the People's Congress and the Political Consultative Conference or in public institutions and semi-governmental associations and societies after their terms expired. All these phenomena are a type of de facto lifelong post system.

The improper social mobility mechanisms of the state and social administrator stratum have seriously affected the quality of composition, work efficiency, and overall image of this stratum and elicited discontent from members of other social strata to some extent. In order to solve this issue, it is necessary to deepen the reform of the cadre personnel system and the cadre performance assessment system and adjust the functions of the government and the role of state and social administrators. Meanwhile, greater efforts need to be exerted to improve the system and mechanism of democratic selection of cadres, especially leading cadres, and to strengthen the supervision of exercise of the public authority in order to achieve higher democracy, openness, and transparency in the promotion of cadres and rationalize the relationships between the state and social administrator stratum and other social strata. By doing so, the influence of various invisible rules may be removed to the greatest extent and accordingly it can ensure that the stratum of state and social administrators become a self-restraint, uncorrupted, and law-abiding stratum.

Chapter 7   The Formation of the Stratum of Private Entrepreneurs

The existence of the stratum of private entrepreneurs has been recognized by people in all spheres in China. This stratum has been constructed objectively and subjectively. In the objective perspective, although entrepreneurs are different greatly in possession of economic resources, as a stratum it has a tangible shape in Chinese socio-economic life. For example, the proportion of the private sector makes up one-third of the overall national economy. In regions with rapid development of the private sector such as Zhejiang Province, the proportion of the private sector accounts for two-thirds or even more than 70 percent of the local economy. In the subjective perspective, although different entrepreneurs have different points of view on their own social stratum positions, they have formed some consensus on a few issues, which involve their common interests. In this chapter, based on relevant statistics, the survey conducted by the research group, and the data of five nationwide questionnaire surveys on the private sector in China which have been conducted by the United Front Work Department of the C.P.C. Central Committee and All-China Federation of Industry and Commerce since 1993, we will investigate the process of the formation and the development of the private entrepreneur stratum in China.

The stratum of private entrepreneurs discussed in this chapter is composed of investors of various non-public-owned enterprise entities. There are two basic characteristics of the non-public-owned enterprise entity. First, it is a type of economic organization, which is officially classified as an enterprise. Such nature is confirmed by its registered category. Therefore, all organizations registered as the "individual industrial and commercial household" (i.e., individual-operated business) are not included in this investigation. Some organizations that are registered as the "individual industrial and commercial household" have relatively large economic scales and comparatively high level of household income and are operate in a mode similar to the enterprise; therefore, they are different from general individual industrial and commercial households to some extent. However, they do not think that their economic entities are enterprises and they do not regard themselves as private entrepreneurs. In recent years, the Administrations for Industry and Commerce have removed the rigid requirement on the number of employees in the economic entity registration (for example, a private enterprise must have more than eight employees). According to their own preferences and actual situations, applicants can choose to register their economic entities as "individual industrial and commercial household" or "private enterprise" (including sole proprietorship enterprise, partnership enterprise, limited liability company, and corporation limited by shares). Second, in the perspective of property rights, the non-public-owned business entity is a type of non-public-owned enterprise. The non-public ownership includes both individual ownership (such as sole proprietorship, partnership, and joint-stock system excluding public-owned shares) and mixed ownership, which mainly consists of private ownership. In general, all enterprises that are not mainly owned by the state and the collective organizations are classified as non-public-owned enterprises. Such enterprises are called "private enterprises" in short by the Administrations for Industry and Commerce in order to distinguish them from foreign-invested non-public-owned enterprises. Accordingly, the term "private entrepreneur" refers to private investors of such private enterprises.

THE DEVELOPMENT OF THE STRATUM OF PRIVATE ENTREPRENEURS

With the accomplishment of the socialist transformation in 1956, public ownership became the absolutely dominant form of ownership in the national economy. The private sector was almost eliminated and capitalists were only paid by fixed dividends. By the year of 1965, the government stopped paying fixed dividends and accordingly the bourgeoisie in China lost its economic support to survive.

The private sector resumes its development after the reform and opening-up. However, as an emerging social stratum different from the traditional bourgeoisie, the development of the stratum of private entrepreneurs has experienced a flexuous course.[1] Private enterprises initially were covered in the form of individual industrial and commercial households or collective enterprises. We cannot find any relevant statistics concerning private enterprises before 1988, because private enterprises were not legally allowed to exist in China until 1988.

The individual economy is the first form of non-public-owned economy, which emerged in China after the reform and opening-up. However, now that the individual economy was permitted to exist and develop, the emergence of private enterprises was a natural and inevitable consequence. In fact, private enterprises with more than eight employees had already emerged as early as 1980. In that year, Chen Zhixiong, a fish farmer in Guangdong Province, employed eight people to help him operate a large-size fish farm and became the first private entrepreneur in China after the reform and opening-up. However, the governmental policy at that time still strictly restricted the development of the private sector and therefore private enterprises had to develop in various hidden forms. For example, according to some studies, about 80 percent of township-village enterprises that has suddenly risen since 1984 actually

---

[1] Zhang, Houyi. 1999. "A New Force Risen Suddenly: Rebirth and Development of the Private Sector Since the Reform and Opening-Up". In Houyi Zhang and Lizhi Ming (eds.), *Report on Development of Private Enterprises in China (1978-1998)*. Beijing: Social Sciences Documentation Publishing House.

were private enterprises. Even rural collective enterprises were different from collectively owned enterprises and were somewhat characteristic of mixed ownership; individual investment made up a considerable proportion in these enterprises.[1] According to a survey conducted by the Rural Policy Research Office of the Secretariat of the Central Committee of the C.P.C. covering 37,422 households in 272 villages in 28 provinces, among people who joined a new type of economic combo in 1984, 3.2 percent were farmers, 3.5 percent were specialized households, and 4.4 percent were individual industrial and commercial households. About 51 percent of these combos had an average of 7.9 employees.[2] Judging by economic characteristics, these new economic combos in essence were private enterprises. Another survey shows that there were 225 thousand private enterprises in China by the end of 1987 with about 3,607 thousand employees.

Before officially admitting the existence and development of private enterprises in 1988, the attitude of the government had become ambiguous and neutral. In October 1984 in a speech Deng Xiaoping mentioned a famous private enterprise "Shazi Melon Seeds" in Anhui Province at that time and said,

> In my opinion, we should wait and see. Will the development of this private enterprise affect the overall situation in China? If we restrict its development, the public will worry about the consistency of our policy and feel confused. Getting rid of the Shazi Melon Seeds will cause confusion in people's thoughts. It is not good.[3]

At the beginning of 1987 in *Decision on Deepening the Rural Reform*, the Central Committee of the C.P.C. proposed, "at the primary stage of socialism and in the process of development of the commodity economy, the existence of an individual economy and a small quantity of private enterprises is inevitable in a considerably long period of time". "A guideline of allowing its existence, strengthening relevant regulations, promoting its positive effects, controlling the negative influence, and instructing its development step by step" should be adopted to deal with the issue of the private enterprise.

In November 1987, the Thirteenth National Congress of the Communist Party of China formally proposed the basic line of the primary stage of socialism and the guideline of encouraging the development of the individual and private sector of economy. The political report of the Thirteenth National Congress of C.P.C. pointed out that,

> The ownership structure of the primary state of socialism should take the public ownership as the main body. At present, the development of economic elements other

---

[1] Zhu, Mingfang, et al. (1998: 239).

[2] The Rural Policy Research Office of the Secretariat of the Central Committee of the C.P.C. (1987: 20).

[3] Deng (1993a3: 91).

289

than the public ownership is not too quick but too slow. Further development of the rural and urban cooperative economy, the individual economy, and the private sector of economy should be encouraged...In different economic sectors and regions, the proportions of various types of ownerships can be different. The practice has demonstrated that a certain extent of development of the private sector is favorable for stimulating the production, activating the market, expanding the employment, and better meeting various needs of the people. It is a kind of necessary and helpful complement to the public-owned economy.

In April 1988, the Seventh National People's Congress approved *Amendment to the Constitution of the People's Republic of China* and the following paragraph was added to Article 11,

The state permits the private sector of economy to exist and develop within the limits prescribed by law. The private sector of economy is a complement to the socialist public-owned economy. The state protects the lawful rights and interests of the private sector of economy, and exercises guidance, supervision and control over it.

On June 15, 1988, the State Council enacted *Interim Regulations on Private Enterprises* and relevant supporting tax regulations. All these legal moves preliminarily established the historical status of the private enterprise in China's economic, social, and political life. Consequently, an emerging stratum of private entrepreneurs has obtained the legal right to openly exist and develop in Chinese society. After having been fostered for nearly six years, a new social stratum eventually came on the stage from underground.

After examining the overall course of the emergence and development of this stratum, we found that, at the macro level, the process in which the stratum of private entrepreneurs differentiated from other social strata and grew up gradually is closely related to the state's institutional arrangements, policies, and regulations concerning the private sector of economy. In a certain sense, without such changes in institutions and policies, that is, if the state did not permit the development of the non-public sector of economy, the emergence and development of the private entrepreneur stratum would be impossible, or would always be in a semi-underground state just as it was in the early 1980s. In order to promote the development of the non-public-owned economy and entitle it to a legal status, the government released a series of relevant policies in this period and amended the Constitution twice in 1982 and 1988. With these measures, the government attempted to redefine the social attribute and socio-economic status of the individual and private sector of economy believing that "it is a kind of necessary and helpful complement to the public-owned economy" and hence legally established the historical status of the individual and private sector in China's economic, social, and political life. Therefore, the emergence of new strata with the development of the non-public-owned economy, i.e., individual-operated business proprietors and private entrepreneurs, was the result of changes of governmental policy.

However, just like the emergence and development of the non-public-owned economy in that period, innovation of institutions and policies had substantially realistic basis and necessity. In rural areas, implementation of the reform and opening-up, especially the household contract and responsibility system, enabled a considerable number of farmers who had a relatively strong capability of operation to become rich rapidly and accomplish preliminary capital accumulation, which prepared certain amounts of capitals for the development of the rural non-public-owned economy. Because the rural farmland is owned by collectives and not permitted to be bought or sold, people who had gotten rich first could not achieve large-scale operation through concentration of landholding and hence they had to seek opportunities and channels of development in other non-agricultural sectors. Furthermore, the general law of the socio-economic development that it is impossible to be rich without industry and commerce suggested them that engaging in industrial and commercial sectors would be a more profitable choice than engaging in agriculture; thus, it provided the driving forces for behind the development of the rural non-public-owned and non-agricultural economy. In addition, the situation of a vast population and limited farmland brought about large numbers of surplus rural laborers. Implementation of the household contract and responsibility system improved labor productivity in agriculture and reduced the demand on agricultural laborers; as a result, the problem of a vast population and limited farmland became even more serious. More and more surplus rural laborers needed to find some new outlets. However, because the rural-urban divided residence registration system did not change significantly, it was difficult for them to enter the city and work there on a large scale. Such a situation prepared a sufficient supply of laborers for the development of the rural non-public-owned and non-agricultural economy.

In urban areas, there were two major driving forces of the development of the non-public-owned economy. First, the urban economy was in a difficult situation that was caused by the *ex parte* ideological inclination of "large in size and public-owned in nature" before the reform and opening-up. The government completely neglected the characteristics of underdeveloped productivity and diversified life needs in urban areas, constantly transformed the ownership system with less attention to the collective economy, and attempted to eliminate the individual and private sector. As a result, such a policy seriously impeded the development of the urban economy, distorted the economic structure, and caused a shortfall of commodities and services directly related to people's daily lives. A large number of employment opportunities disappeared in such a transformation and thereby caused serious difficulties and problems to urban residents' lives. Facing these issues, the government was forced to change its policy by supporting the development of the urban collective and individual economy and permitting the co-existence of economic elements with diverse types of ownership in order to revitalize the urban economy and promote the development of productivity. Second, tens of millions of rusticated educated youth in the Cultural Revolution began to return to the city in the late 1970s. A considerable number of them were unable to find any jobs. At the same time, millions of urban middle school graduates could not achieve full employment each year. In 1979, there were 15,380 thousand urban laborers waiting for employment in China, accounting for 8 percent of the entire urban population; and the urban unemployment was as high as 5.9 percent.[1] Facing such vast pressure of unemployment, the state had to adjust the employment policy by loosing restrictions imposed on the development of the urban collective and individual economy and carrying out the policy, which combined finding jobs assisted by the governmental labor department with the self-organized employment and self-employment. With these measures, the government attempted to support various types of cooperative and individual economies, which were responsible for their own profits or losses and encouraged the unemployed people to find jobs for themselves or run their own businesses.

The administrations started to conduct statistics on the development of private enterprises from 1989. Table 7-1 indicates that the tendency of the development of private enterprises and the private entrepreneur stratum (i.e., investors) in China between 1989 and 2002. Taking no account of the development of private enterprises before 1988, private enterprises and the private entrepreneur stratum in China have grown at a high speed since 1989. Especially after 1992, the yearly growth rate of the number of private enterprises and investors has reached two digits. By the year of 2002, the total number of private enterprises in China was 2028.5 thousand, up by 25.9 times over the 1989 figure. The average annual growth rate between 1989 and 2002 was 28.3 percent, and 31.5 percent between 1992 and 2002. The size of the stratum of private entrepreneurs has been expanding year after year. From 1990 to 2002, this size expanded by 27.3 times, with an average growth rate of 17.7 percent annually. The proportion of this stratum to the total employment in China increased by about 24 times.

Of course, in the free-market economy, it is not very easy for people to enter this stratum because of intensive competition. Frequent inflow and outflow are normal situations. According to available statistics, between 1993 and 1999, the number of withdrawn private enterprises (including those who cancelled registrations or went out of business) increased year after year. The number of private enterprises that withdrew from business in 1999 was 17.8 times more than that in 1993; and the rate of withdrawn increased from 5.1 percent in 1993 to 8.3 percent in 1999 (see Table 7-1). There were various reasons for this withdrawal. Some private enterprises took withdrawal as a strategy of transfer (for example, canceling the registration of an enterprise while establishing another new one). However, most of withdrawn enterprises were actually closed down, meaning that owners of these enterprises withdrew from the stratum of private entrepreneurs. Some of them returned to the former strata before they had entered the stratum of private entrepreneurs (for

---

[1] Xiao, Zhuoji (ed.). 1992. *Introduction of China Economy*. Beijing: Economy Daily Press: 82-83.

example, a part of professional and technical personnel and governmental cadres who had gone into business took up their former occupations once again), some were employed by other enterprises and then became managerial personnel or even ordinary employees, and some were temporarily unemployed and seeking opportunities to stage a comeback. At present, the number of people moving into this stratum is far beyond that of people leaving the stratum. As a result, the size of this stratum keeps expanding rapidly.

Table 7-1   Development of Private Enterprises, 1989~2002

Year	Basic Profiles of Enterprises			Investors		Proportion to Total Employment in China(%)
	Number of enterprises	Growth rate of enterprise number (%)	Number of withdrawn enterprises	Number of investors (ten thousand)	Growth rate (%)	
1989	90581	—	—	—	—	—
1990	98141	8.3	—	22.0	—	0.034
1991	107843	9.9	—	24.0	9.1	0.037
1992	139633	29.5	—	30.0	25.0	0.046
1993	237919	70.4	12689	51.4	71.3	0.077
1994	432240	81.7	41089	88.9	73.0	0.132
1995	654531	51.4	56895	134.0	50.7	0.197
1996	819252	25.2	56446	170.5	27.2	0.247
1997	960726	17.3	80601	204.2	19.8	0.292
1998	1200978	25.0	74651	263.8	29.2	0.373
1999	1508857	25.6	136407	322.4	22.2	0.452
2000	1761769	16.8	—	395.3	22.6	0.538
2001	2028548	15.1	—	460.8	16.6	0.631 ①
2002	2435282	20.1	—	622.8	35.2	0.845

Sources: China Administration for Industry and Commerce Yearbook (in corresponding years), China Administration for Industry and Commerce Statistical Collection (past years), and China Statistical Yearbook (past years).

Note: ① This proportion is different from the one in Chapter 1 because of different statistical calibrations. In addition, a big problem lies in the official statistics. After the middle of the 1990s, traditional township-village enterprises were restructured on a large scale and millions of former managerial personnel in collective enterprises became private entrepreneurs holding the majority of shares in former collective enterprises. It seems that these private entrepreneurs were not included in the official statistics of private enterprise investors.

SOCIAL ORIGINS OF PRIVATE ENTREPRENEURS

The stratum of private entrepreneurs who are in possession of economic resources is in advantaged status in the social structure. Our study indicates that there is almost no intergenerational inheritance existing in this stratum. The intergenerational mobility table   (see Table 4-1 in Chapter 4) calculated by the research group shows that no significant orientation exists in the distribution of proportions of private entrepreneurs' family backgrounds. Only the probability of becoming private entrepreneurs for those from families of governmental cadres and business managerial personnel is higher than the average distribution in the overall structure, and the probability being private entrepreneurs for those from families of workers is lower than the average distribution. Probabilities of being private entrepreneurs for people with other family backgrounds are all close to the average distribution. As a whole, the success of private entrepreneurs relies less on parents' influence. However, data obtained from personal interviews in the survey show that two types of intergenerational transfer of capital affect the status attainment of owners of large-size private enterprises. First, some governmental cadres and managerial personnel in state-owned enterprises who possess the authority of public resource allocation and the privileges of business management might take advantage of their influences to help their children become owners of large-size private enterprises. Second, some large-size private enterprise owners' fathers or grandfathers were once entrepreneurs or businessmen and they might have transferred their experience and value attitudes related to business to their children and hence influence their children's choice of going into business and succeed in business career. However, the number of large-size private enterprise owners is very small in the overall private entrepreneur stratum. In addition, other studies also demonstrate that the advantaged status of fathers and spouses of entrepreneurs in the traditional system, as a type of social capital, do not bring about a contributive affect, which people generally believe that it should do so, on the size of enterprises. Only the relatively good occupations, especially leading offices, which entrepreneurs had taken up before starting their own enterprises, have such a contributive affect on the size of enterprises.[1] In other words, personal occupational experience has a relatively significant influence on the development of enterprises.

Of course, entrepreneurs' individual intelligence and competence, diligence, efforts, and ability to grasp opportunities are also important in the process of economic transition and social transformation in China. From the very beginning, people from almost all social strata went with the tide of the development of the private sector and formed an emerging private entrepreneur stratum together through exercising their individual competence and initiatives. However, results of past years' nationwide surveys on private enterprises show that the social composition of the private entrepreneur stratum varied over time. More and more newcomers of this stratum came from social strata that have relatively great advantages in the traditional system, while the proportion of entrepreneurs coming from comparatively disadvantaged strata has been decreasing and some of them have been wiped out. Such a tendency means two things. First, the requirement of establishing enterprise on entrepreneurs' personal human capital (especially the cultural resources) will become increasingly high when the free-market system develops and becomes more mature.

---

[1] Li, Lulu (1996a).

As a result, it is difficult for people with little human capital to enter this stratum; even those who have entered this stratum but with little human capital find it increasingly difficult to adapt to new market situations. Second, marketization in China has taken a progressive path and it is very easy to transfer advantages inside the traditional system to advantages outside the system. As long as people with advantaged status in the traditional system realize the vast opportunity outside the system, they will achieve success more easily than those without advantaged status in the traditional system do. We treat these two statements as hypotheses and examine them in the following study.

A Male Dominated Stratum

Table 7-2 summaries data concerning gender composition of private entrepreneurs collected in five nationwide questionnaire surveys that were conducted by the United Front Work Department of the Central Committee of the C.P.C. and All-China Federation of Industry and Commerce. According to results of these surveys, the proportion of female private entrepreneurs is relatively low at all times. Although the specific figures of the proportion may be affected by sampling errors, according to our experience, the proportion of female private entrepreneurs is actually not very high. Such a situation indicates that it is not easy for females to establish their own businesses in Chinese society. Furthermore, for this reason female entrepreneurs always receive special recognition from the society. For example, they are usually referred to as "strong women" or "women of wealth".

Table 7-2   Gender Composition of Private Entrepreneurs in Five Nationwide Surveys

Units: Persons, %

Gender	1993		1995		1997		2000		2002	
	Number	Proportion	Number	Proportion	Number	Proportion	Number	Proportion	Number	Proportion
Male	1276	90.1	1297	88.5	1782	91.8	2731	88.9	2887	88.8
Female	140	9.9	168	11.5	160	8.2	340	11.1	364	11.2
Effective samples ①	1416	100	1465	100	1942	100	3071	100	3251	100

Note: ① Effective sample refers to the sample which has answered a given question in the questionnaire. Therefore, the number of effective samples is different corresponding to different questions.

The Increasingly High Threshold of Educational Level

The comparison based on results of the past years' surveys shows that the cultural level of private entrepreneurs in China has been improving (see Table 7-3). More specifically, entrepreneurs without any education were initially few in number and decreased gradually down to zero. Entrepreneurs with primary school education and junior middle school education have decreased significantly; the proportion of the former dropped by 3.5 times and that of the latter were reduced by 1.1 times. The proportion of entrepreneurs with senior middle school and technical secondary school education grew between 1993 and 1997, decreased in 2000, and then rose again to the level of 1997 in 2002. From 1993 to 2000, the proportion of entrepreneurs with university education increased by more than 1.1 times, and decreased slightly in 2002 but still was about one times higher over the 1993 figure. The most significant rise occurred in the proportion of entrepreneurs with postgraduate education. From 1993 to 2002, this proportion increased by about 7.2 times. All these changes indicate that the cultural level of private entrepreneurs in China has been improving. A further analysis of the 2002 survey data shows that, among effective samples, the proportion of entrepreneurs with master's degree accounted for 3.2 percent and the proportion of entrepreneurs with doctor's degree made up 0.5 percent.

Table 7-3   Educational Levels of Private Entrepreneurs, 1993~2002

Units: Persons, %

Year	Without Education	Primary School	Junior Middle School	Senior Middle School and Technical Secondary School	University	Postgraduate	Total	Number of Effective Samples
1993	1.0	9.9	36.1	35.9	16.6	0.6	100.0	1419
1995	0.3	8.2	34.9	38.1	17.6	0.8	100.0	1467
1997	0.3	6.3	31.5	41.7	19.5	0.7	100.0	1937
2000	0.2	2.7	19.6	39.2	35.0	3.4	100.0	3066
2002	0	2.2	17.5	41.9	33.5	4.9	100.0	3249

In this study, we treat the level of education which is lower than junior middle school as a type of cultural resource with low value, the educational level of senior middle school and technical secondary school as a type of cultural resource with medium value, and the university and higher educational level as a type of cultural resource with high value. As a whole, from 1992 to 2002, the proportion of entrepreneurs with low-value cultural resources decreased sharply from 47 percent to 19.7 percent, down by 58.1 percent; the proportion of entrepreneurs with medium-value cultural resources increased from 35.9 percent to 41.9 percent, up by 16.7 percent; the proportion of entrepreneurs with high-value cultural resources rose from 17.2 percent to 38.4 percent, with an increase of 123.3 percent. Such changes suggest that it is increasingly difficult for people with lower levels of education to enter the stratum of private entrepreneurs.

The Rising Proportion of Party Members

As far the composition of political status of private entrepreneurs, in this study we focus on the proportion of members of the Communist Party of China in inquired private entrepreneurs. Table 7-4 shows the change of the proportion of Party members among private entrepreneurs in four surveys. Obviously, this proportion has been increasing year after year. By the year of 2002, this proportion reached as high as 30 percent. It is generally regarded that such a high proportion is unbelievable. Although such an opinion is somewhat reasonable, considering a large number of public-owned enterprises were restructured in recent years, the growth of this proportion is possible. According to statistics, among the investigated samples in 2002, there were 831 private enterprises shifting from restructured public-owned enterprises, accounting for 25.7 percent of the sample size. In this portion of private entrepreneurs, the proportion of Party members made up as high as 50.7 percent.

Table 7-4 Proportions of Party Members in Previous Nationwide Surveys on
Private Entrepreneurs

Year	1993	1997	2000	2002
Number of Party Members	189	353	609	972
Proportion of Party Members (%)	13.3	18.1	19.9	30.2
Number of Effective Samples	1421	1947	3060	3220

Compared with the proportion of Party members to the overall adult population in China (about 8 percent in 2002), the proportion of Party members in private entrepreneurs is considerably high. It indicates that the probability of Party members moving from other strata to the private entrepreneur stratum is relatively high. According to the survey in 2002, among 961 entrepreneurs with the Party membership, 157 of them joined the Party after they had started their own enterprises, accounting for 16.3 percent; 769 of them had joined the Party before starting their businesses, accounting for 80 percent and 299 of them had 15~17 years' standing of the Party membership when they went into business. For the remaining 35 entrepreneurs, the date of joining the Party and the date of establishing their enterprises was in the same year, and detailed information about which date was first is not available.

The Reproduction of Elite and Quasi-Elite

In this part, we will describe the characteristics of private entrepreneurs' occupational backgrounds in four aspects: the last occupation before starting one's enterprise, the last position, professional history, and the highest rank of cadre ever assumed. Our description and analysis demonstrate that people's perspectives about the social origins of the private entrepreneur stratum, such as the traditional viewpoint that private entrepreneurs mainly consist of people who live on the edge of society, even if it reflected the past fact, is significantly different from the current reality.

Table 7-5 indicates the distribution of the last occupation of private entrepreneurs before starting one's enterprise.[1] The designs of questionnaires adopted

---

[1] The origins of the private entrepreneur stratum in 1994 are as follows: 120,663 entrepreneurs were former individual industrial and commercial householders (individual-operated business proprietors), accounting for 13.6 percent; 109,117 entrepreneurs were former unemployed people, accounting for 12.3 percent; 27,838 entrepreneurs were dismissed or laid-off people, accounting for 3.1 percent; 61,934 entrepreneurs were people who obtained an indefinite leave of absence from original work units with their salary suspended, accounting for 7 percent; 35,830 entrepreneurs were retired and left-post people, accounting for 4 percent; 17,565 entrepreneurs were scientific and technical service

in different years are slightly different. In spite of that, certain tendencies of major changes in occupational backgrounds still can be found. (1) In the 1993 survey, the proportion of entrepreneurs who were ordinary workers before starting their businesses was the highest; while this proportion decreased by 4 times in 2002. (2) The proportion of farming peasants declined even more, down by 5.4 times. (3) The proportion of former governmental principals and professional and technical personnel dropped by 81.8 percent and 65.7 percent respectively. Such changes reflect the tendency that a large number of professional and technical personnel and governmental cadres went into business after 1992 and then returned to their former work units several years later because of overly intensive competition. However, the proportion of private entrepreneurs with such origins was still relatively high, accounting for 10 percent in 2002. (4) The proportion of former enterprise principals was the second largest one in 1993 and then increased to the first largest one in 2002, growing from one-sixth to more than the half, up by 2.6 times. (5) The proportion of individual industrial and commercial householders (individual-operated business proprietors) increased by 72.7 percent, reflecting that increasing individual-operated business proprietors are turning into private entrepreneurs. In short, as a social stratum of the elite, the origins of private entrepreneurs have been increasingly composed of elites from other social strata, especially elites in economic sectors; while the opportunities for ordinary people to start their own businesses has been decreasing sharply.

Table 7-5   Last Occupations of Private Entrepreneurs before Starting Business

Occupation	1993		2000		2002	
	Number (persons)	Percentage (%)	Number (persons)	Percentage (%)	Number (persons)	Percentage (%)
Professional and technical personnel	151	11.1	291	10.0	210	6.7
Principal of agency and institution	81	6.0	117	4.0	103	3.3
Principal of enterprise	209	15.4	1040	35.8	1738	55.4
Clerical personnel	—	—	158	5.4	126	4.0
Ordinary worker	325	24.0	256	8.8	152	4.8
Employee in commercial and service sectors	98	7.2	141	4.9	125	4.0
Farming peasant	165	12.2	165	5.7	59	1.9
Specialized household	—	—	107	3.7	—	—
Self-employed individual	120	8.8	501	17.3	478	15.2
Serviceman	14	1.0	10	0.3	15	0.5
Other	68	5.0	101	3.5	114	3.6
Handicraftsman	125	9.2	—	—	—	—
Jobless	—	—	16	0.6	15	0.5
Total	1356	100.0	2903	100.0	3135	100.0

Table 7-6 suggests that, according to the surveys in 1993 and 2002, (1) the proportion of people whose occupations before starting their businesses were governmental

personnel, accounting for 2 percent. In addition, 49,729 entrepreneurs had college and higher level of education, accounting for 5.6 percent. See *China Administration for Industry and Commerce Yearbook* (1995): 411.

cadres at the township and higher level increased from 14.6 percent in 1993 to 19.2 percent in 2002. However, the proportion of cadres at the village (or production brigade) level decreased from 10.6 percent to 2.1 percent. Such changes suggest that, with the development of the private sector and the improvement of the free-market system, governmental cadres have greater advantages than village cadres do. (2) The proportion of contractors of state-owned (or collective) enterprises increased by 1.9 times. In contrast, the proportion of private entrepreneurs from personnel in supply and marketing departments of enterprises decreased by 43.5 percent. Unfortunately, because measures adopted by the two surveys are not completely the same, we cannot compare the data more comprehensively.

Table 7-6   Last Positions of Private Entrepreneurs before Starting Business

Category of Position	1993		2002	
	Frequency (persons)	Percentage (%)	Frequency (persons)	Percentage (%)
Ordinary cadre	—	—	231	7.7
Cadre at the level of lower section	—	—	61	2.0
Cadre at the section level	68	8.8	208	7.0
Cadre at the division/county level	23	3.0	55	1.8
Cadre at the director-general level	6	0.8	6	0.2
Principal of agency or institution at the county and higher level	9	1.2	—	—
Principal of township (or people's commune)	6	0.8	15	0.5
Major cadre in village (or production brigade)	82	10.6	64	2.1
Contractor of state-owned (or collective) enterprise	41	5.3	462	15.5
Principal of enterprise	187	24.3	—	—
Manager of small-medium business	109	14.2	—	—
Manager of large-size business	139	18.1	—	—
Purchasing and marketing personnel in enterprise	94	6.6	136	4.6
Military officer	6	0.8	10	0.3
Other	—	—	1565	52.4
Without any position	—	—	174	5.8
Number of effective samples	770	100.0	2987	100.0

In fact, private entrepreneurs usually had experienced two or more changes of occupations and positions before they started their own business. Such changes are an important form of social mobility. If comprehensively considering the specific position in each change of occupation, the proportion of private entrepreneurs who were once cadres will be higher than the above figure. For example, the survey in 1997 indicated that, among 1,593 respondents, 720 people assumed the position of cadre at various levels (including village cadres), accounting for 45.2 percent. The survey in 2002 showed that, among 2,755 respondents, 1,323 people took the position of cadre at various levels, making up 48 percent. In addition, the 1997 survey revealed that 534 respondents held "other" positions before going into business, accounting for 33.5 percent of all effective samples; in the 2002 survey, 1,313 respondents held "other" positions, taking up 47.7 percent of all effective samples. Because respondents' specific explanations about the "other" positions were not statistically processed in the two surveys, we are not clear about what such type of position it refs to exactly. However, we believe that it should not mean "without any position" because an option of "without any position" was definitely offered in questionnaires used in the two surveys. The proportion of people who chose the option of "without any position" was 20.3 percent in the 1997 survey and merely 5.8 percent in the 2002 survey. Therefore, the proportion of people with experience of being cadres may be higher than the above figures. In conclusion, each survey indicates that governmental cadres and rural cadres are extremely important origins of the stratum of private entrepreneurs. The proportion of people with such experience is much higher than those with other social origins are and tends to grow.

In the formal governmental hierarchy, cadres at the section and higher levels (including principals of townships) are cadres with power and in control of certain resources. Their number is considerably large. Table 7-7 shows that the proportion of people with experience of being cadres among respondents tends to increase in the three recent surveys. The proportion of ordinary cadres is the largest but tends to decline. The proportion of rural cadres in the 2000 survey was higher than that in the 1997 survey but dropped significantly in the 2002 survey. In addition, the proportion of cadres at the section and division levels constantly rose in the three surveys. The proportion of private entrepreneurs with rural cadre experience is relatively large among all private entrepreneurs who once had the cadre status. However, because they possess less human capital (such as the ability of operation and management) and social capital (such as the relation with the government) than governmental cadres do, in increasingly intensive competition of market, it seems that this proportion will inevitably fall. Although the proportion of ordinary cadres is the largest, more and more governmental cadres at the section and higher levels who possess more human capital and social capital are entering this stratum and, hence, a decease of this proportion is predictable.

Table 7-7   The Highest Rank of Cadre that Private Entrepreneur Ever Assumed before Starting Business

Rank of Cadre	1997		2000		2002	
	Frequency (persons)	Percentage (%)	Frequency (persons)	Percentage (%)	Frequency (persons)	Percentage (%)
Ordinary cadre	349	48.5	485	42.6	582	44.0
Cadre at the level of lower section	69	9.6	97	8.5	127	9.6
Cadre at the section level	151	21.0	274	24.1	345	26.1
Cadre at the division or county level	22	3.1	57	5.0	70	5.3
Cadre at the director-general level	2	0.3	9	0.8	7	0.5
Principal of township (or people's commune)Major cadre in village (or production brigade)	112	15.6	195	17.1	164	12.4
Military officer	15	2.1	21	1.8	28	2.1
Total	720	100.0	1138	100.0	1323	100.0
The proportion of section-level cadres to the number of effective cases (%)	11.0		14.4		15.3	

The experience of being cadres is not the only way to accumulate private entrepreneurs' human capital (e.g., the ability of operation and management) and social capital (e.g., relationships with the government). For example, becoming contractors of state-owned and collective enterprises or purchasing and marketing personnel in enterprises are also very effective approaches. In the 1997 survey, 500 people had engaged in these occupations before they started their own business, accounting for 25.7 percent of all effective samples. In the 2000 survey, 796 people were contractors of state-owned and collective enterprises or purchasing and marketing personnel in enterprises before starting their own business, accounting for 25.9 percent. In the 2002 survey, people without experience of public administration and business management in Party and government agencies, public institutions, and enterprises merely made up 37.3 percent. In fact, many people held several different posts successively (see Table 7-8).

Table 7-8   Position Experience of Private Entrepreneurs before Starting Business, 2002

Combination of Position Category	Number (persons)	Percentage (%)
Cadre	995	33.3
Contractor of state-owned (or collective) enterprise	266	8.9
Purchasing and marketing personnel in enterprise	200	6.7
Cadre and contractor of state-owned (or collective) enterprise	219	7.3
Cadre and purchasing and marketing personnel in enterprise	81	2.7
Purchasing and marketing personnel and contractor	84	2.8
Cadre, Purchasing and marketing personnel, and contractor	27	0.9
Other	1116	37.3
Total	2988	100.0

As a whole, at the early stage of the development of private enterprises, people from the lower class or marginal social groups made up a relatively larger proportion. However, in the twenty-first century, this trend has changed fundamentally. Among social origins of the private entrepreneur stratum, the proportion of intra-system and extra-system elites or quasi-elites accounts for nearly two-thirds. In other words, the development of the private entrepreneur stratum is also the process of reproduction of various elites and quasi-elites in China. However, the career history of these elites and quasi-elites before they started their own enterprises is not in the scope of the study.

OBJECTIVE SOCIO-ECONOMIC STATUS OF PRIVATE ENTREPRENEURS

Objective economic status refers to the amount of economic resources controlled by private entrepreneurs. *Objective social status* refers to the contributions to socio-economic development that private entrepreneurs make by exerting economic resources controlled by them. Relevant surveys indicate that economic resources controlled by the private entrepreneur stratum and corresponding contributions to socio-economic development have been increasing year after year.

Expanding Economic Strength

Usually, the amount of registered authorized capital is used to measure the scale of private entrepreneurs' economic resources. According to statistics, the average registered authorized capital of each private enterprise was 93 thousand Yuan RMB in 1989 and increased to 97 thousand Yuan RMB in 1991, up by 4.3 percent. Since then, the amount of average registered authorized capital has been increasing at a two-digit growth rate per year. This figure rose to 1,017 thousand Yuan RMB in 2002, with an increase by 10 times over the 1989 figure (on an inflation-unadjusted basis), and on average up by 21.4 percent per year. The growth of registered authorized capital reflects the fact that the economic strength of the private entrepreneur stratum has been increasing.

However, the amount of registered authorized capital is usually far smaller than that of the actual capital size of enterprises. There are no official statistics regarding the actual capital size of private enterprises and its changes available, so we have to collect the data through relevant surveys. The five nationwide surveys on private enterprises provide relevant information. In this study, we l made use of data from the 1993, 1997, 2000, and 2002 nationwide surveys on private enterprises to analyze the possession of actual capital size of the private entrepreneur stratum. In order to make the analysis comparable, in the following statistical calculations, we deducted samples in which the composition of actual capital (or owner's equity) without liability is not definite, the total amount of paid-in capital (or the total amount of owner's equity) is not definite, and the composition of paid-in capital (or equity) contains public-owned or collectively-owned institutional capital (or equity). In addition, those cases where the total amount of paid-in capital (or the total amount of owner's equity) and/or the number of investors are/is unavailable are excluded as well. Therefore, we get the comparable data regarding the size of actual capital (equity) and the number of investors of the investigated effective samples in the four surveys. Results of this statistical analysis are list in Table 7-9.

Table 7-9 Per Capita Actual Capital (Owner's Equity) of Private Enterprise Investors

Statistical Value	1992	1996	1999	2001
Mean (ten thousand Yuan RMB)	135.4	135.7	486.0	1000.9
Median (ten thousand Yuan RMB)	35	30	75	230
Standard deviation (ten thousand Yuan RMB)	440.2	555.8	2653.0	3931.1
Number of effective samples	1184	1423	2008	2373
Number of investors	2747	3971	7343	11621

First, the size of economic capital controlled by private entrepreneurs expanded significantly in a decade. Moreover, its growth rate accelerated remarkably in the late 1990s. Such growth is indicated by the drastic increase in both the average amount of per capita actual capital of investors (the figure in 2001 was 7.4 times larger than that in 1992) and the median value of per capita actual capital (the figure in 2001 was 6.6 times larger than that in 1992). Second, the gap in economic strength among private entrepreneurs is widening, which is indicated by the drastic increase in the value of standard deviation (the figure in 2001 was 8.9 times larger than that in 1992). In a certain sense, the expansion of standard deviation year after year shows that there is a trend of concentration of resources in China since the middle of the 1990s.

The size of capital possessed by different private entrepreneurs varies and hence private entrepreneurs' socio-economic statuses are quite different. We classified private enterprises into large, medium, and small size according to the number of employees and the amount of sales. First, according to the nationwide survey in 2002, the average number of employees of 3,204 inquired private enterprises was 150 persons. If the number of employees of an enterprise is one time more than the average number, it is classified as a large-size enterprise, while an enterprise with employees less than 50 percent of the average number is regarded as a small enterprise. According to such classification, large-size private enterprises with more than 300 employees accounted for 11.5 percent, small private enterprises with less than 75 employees accounted for 55.1 percent, and medium-size enterprises with 76~299 employees accounted for 33.4 percent. Second, the average sales figures for these inquired private enterprises was 28,000 thousand Yuan RMB in 2001. Similarly, if the sales amount of an enterprise is one time more than the average amount, it is classified as large-size enterprise, while an enterprise with sales less than 50 percent of the average is regarded as a small enterprise. Of those, large-size private enterprises with more than 56,000 thousand Yuan RMB sales accounted for 10 percent, small private enterprises with less than 14,000 thousand Yuan RMB sales accounted for 70 percent, and medium-size enterprises with 14,010~55,990 thousand Yuan RMB sales accounted for 20 percent. However, although the correlation between sales and number of employees of private enterprises is statistically significant, the magnitude of the correlation is very small ($r = 0.176$, sig $= 0.01$). Considering that the sales can reflect the economic strength of private entrepreneurs more accurately, we give up the first classification while adopting the second one. As a result, in the current private entrepreneur stratum, the proportion distribution of owners of large, medium, and small enterprises was 1:2:7.

Increasing Contributions to Socio-Economic Development

We will investigate the contributions of the private entrepreneur stratum to social and economic development in three aspects: the growth of output value, the amount of paid taxes, and employment of private enterprises. Official statistics provide important reference for such investigation. However, the data in statistical yearbooks do not reflect the contributions of private enterprises completely because the statistical calibrations adopted in official statistics appear somewhat problematic. For example, from the perspective of the composition of enterprise types, among various enterprises that were classified as private enterprises by the Administration for Industry and Commerce, the proportion of limited liability companies and corporations limited by shares was 71.47 percent in 2002.[1] However, in the *China Statistical Yearbook*, limited liability company, corporation limited by shares, and private enterprise are respectively particular statistical items.[2] In addition, in the middle and late 1990s the overwhelming majority of traditional township-village enterprises were restructured to be non-public-owned enterprises in which the means of production were mainly privately owned, but no relevant statistics are available. All of these problems lead to the difficulty in analyzing the contributions of the private entrepreneur stratum to social and economic development. Because no better statistics are available, we have to make a rough analysis on such contributions according to existing sources (see Table 7-10).

Table 7-10   Contributions of Private Enterprises to Socio-economic Development, 1992~2002

Year	Output Value		Retail Sales of Consumer Goods		Paid Taxes		Employment	
	Hundred Million Yuan	Growth Rate (%)	Hundred Million Yuan	Growth Rate (%)	Hundred Million Yuan	Growth Rate (%)	Hundred Million Yuan	Growth Rate (%)
1992	205	—	91	—	4.55	—	232	—
1993	422	66.0	190	84.4	10.46	129.89	373	60.8
1994	1140	180.3	513	151.1	17.52	67.50	648	73.7
1995	2295	109.4	1006	107.9	35.59	103.14	956	47.5
1996	3227	57.0	1459	56.9	60.23	63.23	1171	22.5
1997	3923	25.5	1855	33.8	90.49	50.24	1350	15.3
1998	5853	55.1	3059	70.7	163	80.13	1710	26.7
1999	7686	29.0	4191	37.6	254.96	56.42	2022	18.3
2000	10740	32.7	5813	36.6	414.4	62.54	2406	19.0
2001	12317	19.4	6245	6.7	917.6	121.43	2714	12.8
2002	15338	25.7	7929	27.6	945.6	3.05	3409	25.6
Average annual growth rate	60.0		61.3		67.05		32.2	

Source: Past year's *China Administration for Industry and Commerce Statistical Collection*.

Table 7-10 shows that, from 1992 to 2002, the aggregate output value of private enterprises in China increased from 20.5 billion Yuan RMB to 1,533.8 billion Yuan RMB, calculated by comparable prices, up by 75.5 times over a decade with an average growth rate of 60 percent per year. The aggregate retail sales of consumer goods increased from 9.1 billion Yuan RMB to 7,92.9 billion Yuan RMB, calculated

[1] Zhang,, et al. (2003: 9).

[2] See *China Statistical Yearbook (2003)*, Table 5-1. Even in this most authoritative statistical material, the data regarding sectors with other types of ownership are not available.

by comparable prices, up by 87.3 times over a decade with an average growth rate of 61.3 percent per year. The amount of paid taxes increased from 0.455 billion Yuan RMB to 94.56 billion Yuan RMB, calculated by current prices, up by 206.8 times over a decade with an average growth rate of 67.05 percent per year. The employment in private enterprises increased from 2,320 thousand Yuan RMB to 34,090 thousand Yuan RMB, up by 13.7 times over a decade with an average growth rate of 32.2 percent per year.

It is due to the vast contributions of private enterprises to socio-economic development that the political, economic, and social status of the private entrepreneur stratum have been rising rapidly in recent years. Governments at all levels have greater and greater hope for the development of private enterprises. Many representatives of this stratum have entered the People's Congress and the Political Consultative Conference and obtained relatively high political status. The Sixteenth National Congress of the Communist Party of China formally defined this stratum as "participants of the cause of the Socialism with Chinese characteristics". Moreover, it also formally announced that elites of this stratum can be and must be admitted to the Communist Party of China in order to strengthen the supports from the masses and the society to the ruling party.

PERCEPTION OF SOCIAL STATUS AND POLITICAL PARTICIPATION

The objective formation of the private entrepreneur stratum does not necessarily mean it has been constructed subjectively at the same time. Besides all characteristics of private entrepreneurs in economic relations (such as possessing private property right of the means of production and employing other people for operation and production activities), the eventual formation of this stratum depends on the subjective development of class identification. At present, there are no sufficient proofs indicating that, as a whole, private entrepreneurs have had a type of consciousness of class identification. However, perhaps it is well founded if we said that such a subjective consciousness of class identification is still under construction. In this section, we will expatiate on this statement in two aspects. The first aspect is private entrepreneurs' perception or appraisal of their own economic status, social prestige, and situation of political participation. Their self-evaluations will indicate the perceived status of the private entrepreneur stratum in economic, political, and social life in current China. The second aspect is the actual activities of political participation of private entrepreneurs. In a certain sense, such political participation activity is an indicator of the formation of stratum consciousness in the aggregate.[1]

---

[1] In fact, many other factors may characterize the formation of private entrepreneurs' stratum

Private Entrepreneurs' Perception of Their Own Social Status

In questionnaires adopted in all previous nationwide surveys on private enterprises, many questions were designed to explore private entrepreneurs' perceptions and opinions about various social, economic, political issues. In this study, we focus on private entrepreneurs' perception of their own positions in the social hierarchy and their answers to two political and economic questions, which may characterize the property of this stratum more significantly. We will present a statistical description of the private entrepreneurs' perception of status of their social stratum, and then give a statistical analysis on it. The data adopted in this section are from the five nationwide surveys on private enterprises in China from 1993 to 2002. There were three same questions in questionnaires used in each survey asking respondents to evaluate their own income status, social prestige, and political participation status respectively. The rating scale is composed of ten ratings; the first rating is the highest and the tenth one is the lowest. Relevant statistical results are listed in Table 7-1.

Table 7-11   Perception of Private Entrepreneurs' Social Status

Unit: %

Rating		1	2	3	4	5	6	7	8	9	10	Total	N
Income Status	1993	6.5	6.9	15.8	18.6	29.1	11.4	5.8	4.3	0.9	0.6	100	1414
	1995	3.4	5.0	16.6	[9.0]	32.2	10.4	5.6	5.4	1.6	0.8	100	2859
	1997	3.4	6.2	15.4	18.3	29.6	14.2	6.8	4.4	0.9	0.8	100	1900
	2000	3.1	6.6	15.3	16.5	31.0	13.7	6.7	5.0	1.1	1.0	100	2970
	2002	2.9	6.0	18.5	17.4	29.6	11.5	6.2	5.1	1.4	1.2	100	3222
Social Prestige	1993	9.2	15.2	18.9	14.9	23.0	7.7	4.0	4.7	1.4	1.0	100	1416
	1995	6.0	12.1	20.0	15.1	26.2	8.2	4.7	3.9	2.4	1.3	100	2859
	1997	6.2	9.9	18.7	16.5	24.7	11.7	4.7	5.3	1.6	0.7	100	1896
	2000	6.5	13.0	17.5	14.6	23.9	11.8	5.6	4.4	1.5	1.1	100	2972
	2002	8.1	13.8	21.4	14.6	21.8	8.6	4.4	4.2	2.0	1.1	100	3222
Political Participation	1993	7.3	11.6	18.0	14.1	20.7	7.8	5.9	7.2	4.6	2.8	100	1413
	1995	4.6	8.4	14.5	12.0	21.8	9.6	7.3	9.6	6.0	6.3	100	2855
	1997	4.6	7.8	13.3	12.5	21.2	9.8	9.5	8.6	5.5	7.2	100	1886
	2000	4.2	10.1	15.1	12.5	19.9	10.6	9.3	8.9	5.2	4.3	100	2956
	2002	5.0	10.1	15.9	12.2	22.0	10.7	6.3	8.8	5.1	3.9	100	3216

consciousness. For example, initially some cultural elites have become the mouthpiece of the private entrepreneur stratum in governmental policy making. A few of them are independent directors of large-size enterprises and many of them are famous scholars. They give voice to the private entrepreneurs' expectations and demands on favorable policies, and propose influential and helpful strategies for the development of the private sector of economy. Second, some publications that specially target the private sector of economy (i.e., the stratum of private entrepreneurs) have emerged in China. These publications provide forums for private entrepreneurs to utter their viewpoints and opinions delivering their interests and demands in policy making. Sponsors of these publications sometimes remark arguments that are favorable or unfavorable for the development of the private sector and express appeals and counterviews (such as *Internal Reference for the Private Sector of Economy*). Third, there are more and more industrial or regional organizations of the private sector of economy in China. Along with semi-governmental organizations such as the Association of Private Entrepreneurs, these organizations have a significant influence on fostering the common consciousness of the private entrepreneur stratum.

As far as results of the 2002 survey, most respondents believed that their own economic status, social prestige, and political participation were at the middle-higher level. The differences between perceptions of the three types of status are very small. People who believed that their income status was above the fifth level accounted for 74.4 percent; people who had the similar belief about their social prestige accounted for 79.7 percent; the number of people who had the similar belief about their political participation was smaller, accounting for 65.2 percent. Therefore, as a whole, most private entrepreneurs believed that their socio-economic status was relatively high. Self-evaluation of their social prestige was the highest, economic income status was the second, and the political participation status was in third place. However, according to comparisons between the results of all previous surveys, several tendencies are more complicated.

First, in all previous surveys, it seemed that the proportion of people who believed that their own income status was at the highest level gradually declined. In contrast, the proportion of people who believed that their own income status was at a very low level rose to some extent. However, it may be not true to conclude that their income status was actually declining. Chances are that such a tendency may reflect the fact of expanding differentiation of members' economic strength within this stratum (statistical results in Table 7-9 provide evidences about differentiation within the stratum). Because of the emergence of large-size private enterprises, among samples in the 2002 survey, the largest amount of actual capital of private enterprises was 1.25 billion Yuan RMB, while the smallest amount was merely ten thousand Yuan RMB (of course, this was the net actual capital after deducting all liabilities); the standard deviation is nearly 40, 000 thousand Yuan RMB. When respondents assessed their own income status by comparing with other people, they usually took entrepreneurs who possessed business larger than theirs did as a reference point.

Second, private entrepreneurs' self-evaluation of their own social prestige was higher than that of their own income status. For example, in all previous surveys, the proportion of people who believed that their own social prestige was at the highest level was higher than that of people who believed that their income status and political participation was at the highest level. Compared with results of the 1993 survey, this proportion dropped to some extent in the four succeeding surveys. However, this proportion increased in all three surveys after 1995. Such changes also indicate the change of other social members' appraisals of this stratum, because people's self-evaluations of their own social prestige will undoubtedly be affected by social appraisals they received in real social life.

Third, as to the level of political participation, the tendency of change in private entrepreneurs' self-evaluation is roughly the same with the change in self-evaluation of their own social prestige; taking no account of the 1993 survey, the self-evaluation of the political participation level was rising in all surveys. Similarly, there was also a tendency of differentiation. After the Sixteenth National Congress of the Communist Party of China, the government endowed the private entrepreneur stratum with a significantly higher political status than before which also had an influence on private entrepreneurs' self-evaluations. The proportion of people who believed that their political participation status was at the highest or relatively high level in the 2002 survey was higher than that in the 2000 survey but lower than that in the 1993 survey, although by only several percentage points. What is the cause of such a phenomenon? Judging from the impression received in the on-site interviews, it may be due to the raise of private entrepreneurs' expectation of political participation rather than the actual decline of their political participation level.

In order to reveal private entrepreneurs' overall appraisal of their income status, social prestige, and political participation and corresponding tendencies of changes more concisely, we simplified the rating scale, that is, classifying the first to the third ratings as the higher-level appraisal, the fourth to the sixth ratings as the medium-level appraisal, and the seventh to the tenth ratings as the lower-level appraisal. Based on this simplified rating scale, we recalculated the changes of distribution of the three types of appraisals in all previous surveys and obtained the results in Table 7-12. First, in spite of whatever changes, at least one-fourth of people gave themselves a higher-level appraisal of their own status. In particular, their social prestige received an extraordinarily high level of self-evaluation. In the 1993 survey, 43.3 percent people held the higher-level appraisal to their own social prestige status; in the three surveys from 1995 to 2000, this proportion fell to some extent; it returned to the 1993 level in the 2002 survey. Second, the proportion of people who gave themselves the medium-level appraisal of the three types of status, especially the income status, was the largest. In short, in all previous surveys the proportion of private entrepreneurs who believed that their economic income status and social prestige status were at the middle-higher level in the society accounted for more than 85 percent; the proportion of private entrepreneurs who believed that their political participation was at the middle-higher level accounted for more than 65 percent.

Table 7-12 Simplified Perception of Private Entrepreneurs' Social Status

Unit: %

Rating	Year	Higher Level	Medium Level	Lower Level	Total	N
Income Status	1993	29.2	59.1	11.6	100.0	1414
	1995	25.0	61.6	13.4	100.0	2859
	1997	25.0	62.1	12.9	100.0	1900
	2000	25.0	61.2	13.8	100.0	2970
	2002	27.4	58.5	13.9	100.0	3222
Social Prestige	1993	43.3	45.6	11.1	100.0	1416
	1995	38.1	49.5	12.3	100.0	2859
	1997	34.8	52.9	12.3	100.0	1896
	2000	37.0	50.3	12.6	100.0	2972
	2002	43.3	45.0	11.7	100.0	3222
Political Participation	1993	36.9	42.6	20.5	100.0	1413
	1995	27.5	43.4	29.2	100.0	2855
	1997	25.7	43.5	30.8	100.0	1886
	2000	29.4	43.0	27.7	100.0	2956
	2002	31.0	44.9	24.1	100.0	3216

Now we have another question: Were private entrepreneurs' appraisals of their own three types of status consistent? In order to answer this question, we conducted a correlation analysis on respondents' appraisals of their own three types of status in all previous surveys. For the sake of convenience of analysis, we transformed the above rating scale into another type of scale and the results of the analysis are listed in Table 7-13.

Table 7-13   Correlation Analysis of Perception of Private Entrepreneurs' Status

Year	Category	Income Status × Social Prestige	Income Status × Political Participation	Social Prestige × Political Participation
1993	Correlation coefficient (r)	0.396	0.283	0.665
	Significance (two-sided test)	0.01	0.01	0.01
	Sample size	1415	1413	1416
1995	Correlation coefficient (r)	0.560	0.360	0.602
	Significance (two-sided test)	0.01	0.01	0.01
	Sample size	2857	2853	2855
1997	Correlation coefficient (r)	0.599	0.425	0.628
	Significance (two-sided test)	0.01	0.01	0.01
	Sample Size	1884	1885	1886
2000	Correlation Coefficient (r)	0.538	0.389	0.670
	Significance (two-sided test)	0.01	0.01	0.01
	Sample size	2953	2954	2956
2002	Correlation coefficient (r)	0.566	0.421	0.639
	Significance (two-sided test)	0.01	0.01	0.01
	Sample size	3220	3216	3216

First, the correlations between private entrepreneurs' appraisals of the three types of status are significant, but the degree of correlation between appraisals of different types of status varies. Of that, the degree of correlation between the self-evaluation of social prestige status and the self-evaluation of political participation status is the highest, reflecting the mutually driving relationship between the two types of status in real social life. In other words, the higher the social prestige is, the greater the possibility of participating in political life will be; contrarily, the higher the political participation level, the higher the social prestige status. The degree of correlation between the self-evaluated income status and political participation level is the lowest, that is, they are inconsistent to a greatest extent; considering the degree of correlation between the self-evaluated income status and social prestige is relatively high, it may well indicate that private entrepreneurs expect a higher level of political participation. Second, there is a rising trend in the degree of correlation between the self-evaluated three types of status. Of that, the degree of correlation between the self-evaluated income status and political participation level increased from 0.283 in 1993 to 0.421 in 2002, up by 48.8 percent; the degree of correlation between the self-evaluated income status and social prestige status increased from 0.396 to 0.566, up by 42.9 percent. Only the degree of correlation between the self-evaluated social prestige status and political participation status decreased slightly, but it was still the largest one among the three correlation coefficients. As a whole, private entrepreneurs feel that the consistency of the three most important types of status has been increasing over time.

In addition, the statistical analysis also indicates that private entrepreneurs' self-evaluations of the three types of status and the economic scales of their enterprises correlate to some extent. In above paragraphs, according to the amount of sales, we classified private entrepreneurs into large entrepreneurs with more than 56,000 thousand Yuan RMB sales, medium entrepreneurs with 14,010~55,990 thousand Yuan RMB sales, and small entrepreneurs with less than 14,000 thousand Yuan RMB sales. According to this classification, we analyzed the rank correlation (i.e., the Gamma correlation) between the three types of entrepreneurs and their self-evaluations of the three types of status in the 2002 survey and the results are listed in Table 7-14. Obviously, the significances of correlation passed the tests, but the degrees of correlation are not very high, of which, the degree of correlation between the size of enterprise and corresponding evaluation of income status is the highest; the degree of correlation between the size of the enterprise and the corresponding evaluation of political participation status is the highest. Judging from these data, we can only conditionally believe that the size of enterprises and corresponding self-evaluation of status positively correlate, i.e., to a certain extent, large entrepreneurs tend to believe that their own social status is relatively high. However, because the survey was conducted in different provinces in which the level of economic development is greatly different,[1] the amount of sales used to classify the size of an enterprise should be relative, that is, it should be used by referring to the overall level of development in each province. According to our estimation, if the statistical analysis could be conducted by province, the degree of correlation should have increased greatly.

Table 7-14   Correlation between Private Entrepreneur' Self-Evaluation on Social Status and Sales of Enterprise

Category	Rank Correlation Coefficient (G)	Significance	Sample Size
Sales × Income Status	0.273	0.000	2906
Sales × Social Prestige	0.134	0.000	2907
Sales × Political Participation Level	0.093	0.000	2902

Political Participation

Political participation action is an important measure of the formation of social stratum. When a stratum comes into being, i.e., its stratum consciousness begins to emerge, members of this stratum will make great efforts to participate in political affairs and governmental arrangements of institutions and policy making in order to strive for the political interests of their stratum (of course, in essence to ensure their

---

[1]   Zhang, et al. (2003: 13).

own economic interests). Therefore, the level of political participation can even be seen as the foremost indicator to measure whether a stratum has formed its stratum consciousness. Of course, in China, different social strata have different opportunities and paths, which are stipulated by governmental institutions, policies, and regulations, to participate in political affairs. As a universal convention in practice, when one enters the stratum of state and social administrators (i.e., to be a governmental official) he or her cannot continue to retain his or her status as a private entrepreneur. Therefore, private entrepreneurs' major opportunities and paths to participate in political affairs are to become deputies to the People's Congress or members of the Committee of the Political Consultative Conference; moreover, the opportunity of being members of the Committee of the Political Consultative Conference is greater than that of being deputies to the People's Congress.

Nationwide surveys conducted in 1997, 2000, and 2002 investigated the situation in which private entrepreneurs assumed the office of deputy to the People's Congress or member of the Committee of the Political Consultative Conference and the results are listed in Table 7-15. The results indicate two tendencies. First, the proportion of private entrepreneurs assuming the deputy to the People's Congress or the member of the Committee of the Political Consultative Conference tends rise. Second, the level of the People's Congress and the Political Consultative Conference in which private entrepreneurs participated tends to ascend as well. Among private entrepreneurs, the proportion of deputies to the People's Congress and members of the Committee of the Political Consultative Conference at the township level has been decreasing, while the proportion of deputies to the People's Congress and members of the Committee of the Political Consultative Conference at the city or country level has been increasing. Accordingly, political participation actions of private entrepreneurs have been increasing and their capability to affect the governmental policymaking has been strengthening as well (theoretically, the higher the level of participation, the stronger the influence of private entrepreneurs on policymaking).

Table 7-15　Political Participation of Private Entrepreneurs

Units: %, persons

Category	1997		2000		2002	
	People's Congress	Political Consultative Conference	People's Congress	Political Consultative Conference	People's Congress	Political Consultative Conference
Township level	30.5	6.5	17.6	2.1	23.8	1.0
County (city) level	35.5	57.0	44.1	63.4	33.1	61.4
Prefecture (city) level	27.4	28.1	30.0	29.1	38.5	32.7
Provincial (municipal) level	6.6	7.3	7.5	5.1	4.2	4.6
National level	0	1.1	0.8	0.3	0.4	0.2
Total	100.0	100.0	100.0	100.0	100.0	100.0
Sample size	187	458	510	1075	565	1143
Proportion to the samples	9.6	23.5	16.6	35.0	17.4	35.0

As to the growth of private entrepreneurs' political participation opportunity and the raise of political participation level, it is worthwhile to mention the following two facts. First, because of increasing economic strength of this stratum and its growing influence on socio-economic development, the government has paid more and more attention to this stratum and has constantly adjusted institutions and policies in recent years in order to provide private entrepreneurs with a larger political participation space. Second, enthusiasm and efforts of private entrepreneurs to participate in political affairs have been greatly improved and enhanced. In the process of field surveys, many private entrepreneurs expressed their intention to affect the governmental policy-making process at various levels through political participation.

Other evidence that indicates the enhancement of private entrepreneurs' intention of political participation is the active involvement of private entrepreneurs in grassroots-level political affairs. In recent years, grassroots democracy in rural China has developed rapidly. At the administrative village level, major heads of the Villagers' Committees are elected through direct elections. Therefore, in many rural areas, private entrepreneurs' enthusiasm of standing in election is growing. In this case, many local governments welcome and even proactively encourage private entrepreneurs to assume public offices at the administrative village level. For example, in 2003, Sheyang County in Jiangsu Province enacted a local regulation, which required eligible candidates for village officials must have a minimal family income of 100 thousand Yuan RMB. By report, according to this requirement, heads of the Villagers' Committees in 250 villages among 258 villages in Sheyang County were occupied by "rich people". Before then, a large number of private entrepreneurs had been elected as heads of the Villagers' Committees in provinces such as Zhejiang, Fujian, and so forth. These village officials usually are called by local governments as "cadres with double strong capabilities" (with strong leadership and strong competence to make money).[1] With the adjustment and the reform of the relationship between the Villagers' Committee and the Party Committee at the village level, it is not unusual that private entrepreneurs assume the office of major principals in the local Party Committees.

We must admit that this study has many limitations, especially lacking precise and in-depth analysis on the stratum consciousness of private entrepreneurs at the overall stratum level. In spite of this, through the above discussion and analyses, the study reveals that a relatively independent social stratum—the private entrepreneur stratum—has constructed itself objectively and subjectively. The major characteristics of this stratum have preliminarily come into being; in other words, the boundary of this stratum has been taking shape. This stratum mainly consists of the male as well as increasingly achieves its self-development through the process of the reproduction of elites or quasi elites. This stratum is in possession of three major types of resources we used to analyze the characteristics of contemporary Chinese society, that is,

---

[1] Cai, Fanghua. 2003. "Electing a Boss to be the Village Official should Follow the Legal Proceedings". On the web site of *China Rural Research of Ministry of Agriculture*. Retrieved September 11, 2003, from http://www.ccrs.org.cn.

cultural resources, economic resources, and organizational resources. Of course, possession of relatively large amount of economic resources is the marked characteristic of this stratum. Meanwhile, they also possess a relatively large amount of cultural resources, which means that, as a whole, they receive a relatively high level of education and such educational level has become increasingly high. As for the organizational resources, it not only means that they possess the organizations of enterprises and employ dozens or hundreds of employees, but also suggests that they have countless ties with government authorities. Because many of them have the occupational experience as cadres and, more importantly, they win favors and supports from the government at all levels through contributions to socio-economic development (though some problems still exist in the relationship between the two parties). It is especially worthwhile to pay attention to the tendency that more and more private entrepreneurs have taken the office of head of Villagers' Committee or Party Committee through election and hence have been directly in control of certain organizational resources (authority resources). Therefore, the social status and influence of this stratum will undoubtedly become increasingly strong; accordingly, this stratum is worth being paid more attention to by researchers who are interested in social structure of contemporary China.

Chapter 8   The Emergence of the New Middle Stratum

Has a "new middle stratum" emerged in the dual transformation of social structure—transformation from traditional agricultural society to a modern industrial society and transformation from the planned economy system to the socialist free-market system—triggered by the reform and opening-up since the 1980s as experienced in developed countries? Is there any possibility to form a "middle stratum-oriented" society? Especially since the 1990s, what is the relationship between the increasingly expanding gap in wealth in the process of rapidly evolving social transition and the formation of a mechanism of social interests coordination that will universally benefit social members on the basis of the function of "buffer layer" or "balancer" of the "new middle stratum" in modernized countries? In recent years, these questions have been the focus of controversy in academic circles and universally concerned by the public. These questions are related to how to define the "new middle stratum" and its corresponding backgrounds and how to understand the mechanisms of resource allocation in current Chinese society.

CONCEPT OF THE NEW MIDDLE STRATUM AND ITS SOCIAL ORIGIN

Definition of the New Middle Stratum

New middle stratum is a concept in opposition to the old middle stratum (class). In the study of social stratum, *old middle stratum (class)* refers to the petty bourgeois and the self-employed, such as petty farmers, shopkeepers, and independent business owners, and so forth, which usually emerged at the early stage of the Industrial Revolution. They relied on their property ownership to operate independently and make their living.[1] In contrast, the definitions of the new middle stratum are very different between various schools. Nonetheless, researchers generally agree on the following characteristics of the new middle stratum: they (1) are mainly brainworkers, (2) have relatively high level of education and received professional trainings, (3) make their living by salaries and wages, (4) possess the right of direct control in the process of labor to a varying extent and have a certain degree of right to speak and

---

[1] Gilbert, Danis and Joseph A.Carl. 1992. *Class Structure of the United States of America*. Beijing: China Social Sciences Press: 79.

314

influence on public affairs, (5) hold a moderate and conservative attitude toward politics, pursue democracy and equality, and determine the social ideology to a certain extent, (6) follow the example of the upper class in lifestyle and manner and breeding, and are particular over taste and quality, (7) emphasize self-advancement and self-fulfillment, and (8) possess sufficient private wealth, leisure time, and consumption capacity to maintain a decent lifestyle (such as possessing private automobiles and houses, making a tour or holiday with family, and so on). Of that, the key characteristic is that they do not possess the means of production and rely on organizational capital (i.e., administrative authority) and cultural capital (i.e., professional skills) to obtain their social status.

The emergence of the new middle stratum indicates the equality-oriented trend of the social status stratification in modern social structure. On one hand, the former pyramid-like structure, in which social wealth and authority were controlled by a small number of people in the upper class while the masses situated below them, has transformed into an olive-like structure, in which social wealth and authority are shared by the majority of social members. On the other hand, social members can attempt to change their initial poor life conditions and obtain upward mobility opportunities to enjoy a good living through their own efforts such as receiving modern education, etc. Therefore, the emergence of the new middle stratum will conduce to mitigate the gap between rich and poor, develop a stable, fair, and orderly structure of social interests, and hence share the achievements of socio-economic development among the majority of social members in an industrialized society.

Social Backgrounds of the Emergence of the New Middle Stratum

In 1848, when Marx and Engels wrote that the productivity created by capitalism within one hundred years was greater than the summation of productivity created by human beings in all previous periods, and that capitalism was still in its infancy. In the succeeding 150 years, the Western society experienced the second (1840~1950) and the third (since 1950) Industrial Revolution after the first Industrial Revolution (1760~1840). In the transition of modern social structure, a new social force that has influenced on the development of society has emerged in all industrial countries, that is, the new middle stratum (or new middle class), which is different from the traditional middle stratum in the early days of capitalism.[1] Although different countries have different conditions, the emergence of the new middle stratum has some similar significant social backgrounds in the process of the transition of industrialized social structure.

---

[1] Ye, Nianxian. 1990. "Chapter 2: Social Class Theories of Western Marxism Sociologists". Pp. 28-30 in Jianzhang He, et al.(eds.), *Modern Social Class Structure and Social Stratification Issues*. Beijing: China Social Sciences Press.

(1) The Emergence of Modern Industry

For the first time in 1909, man produced synthetic ammonia by synthesis technology under the direction of relevant theory. Before long, the First World War stimulated demands for chemical fertilizer and dynamite and consequently brought along the first "modern" industry—the chemical industry. Since then, science and technology have gotten rid of the characteristics of individuation, empiricism, and dispersivity in traditional "inventions" and have become the direct driving force of modern industry. Gradually, science and technology have fostered some leading industries in the "information economy" or "post-industrial society" since the 1950s,[1] such as high and new-technology industries, and pushed the traditional social status and social function of intellectuals toward the core of the social structure at a high speed and consequently brought about an emerging era in which intellectuals have become social elites.

(2) Transition of Industrial Structure from Traditional Industry to Modern Industry

Correspondingly, the industrial structure transited from traditional industry to modern industry. Large-size enterprises emerged and corporations were established universally in all capitalist countries. For example, between 1897 to 1911, 4,227 companies were merged into 257 corporations in the United States, and Ford (1903) and General Electronic (1908) automobile corporations, which had a yearly output capability of millions of automobiles, were established successively.[2]

(3) Shift from the Producer Society to the Consumer Society

Since the second Industrial Revolution, mass consumer goods have emerged; consumer durable goods, such as automobiles, radios, television sets, domestic electrical appliances, and so forth, have become the mainstream of ordinary consumables. After having entered the "post-industrial society" since the 1950s, information technology products such as videocassette recorders, mobile phones, and personal computers, etc., have led the trend of ordinary consumables.[3] The emergence of mass consumer goods shifted the human society from a producer-led society to a consumer-led society. On one hand, such a transition has improved the standard of living of lower classes (such as the working class); on the other hand, it has led to stratum differentiation in consumption.

---

[1] Bell, Daniel. 1984. *Coming of Post-Industrial Society: A Venture in Social Forecasting*, translated by Tian, Gao, et al. Beijing: The Commercial Press. McGraw, Thomas K. (ed.) 1999. *Creating Modern Capitalism: How Entrepreneurs, Companies, and Countries Triumphed in Three Industrial Revolutions*, translated by Zhao, Wenshu and Suozhang Xiao. Hangzhou, Zhejiang: Jiangsu People's Press: 15-16.

[2] McGraw (1999: 612-613).

[3] McGraw (1999: 15-16).

(4) The Proportion of the White Collars Outstripped that of the Blue Collars in Occupational Structure

The proportion of professional and technical personnel, managerial personnel, and commercial and service personnel has grown rapidly since the middle of the nineteen-century. White-collar workers, i.e., "free laborers" taking technical and management knowledge as their capital, have emerged. As a result, for the first time, the working class has encountered the challenge and differentiation of "non-proletarianization". According to employment statistics conducted in four different points of time between 1870 and 1992, occupational structures in Japan, the United States, Germany, and Britain experienced drastic changes, in which the proportion of employment in agriculture fell sharply, employment in industry gradually decreased, and employment in services sector increased rapidly. The proportion of modern services sector has been beyond 50 percent in occupational structure in all these countries since the 1990s and become the leading industry (see Table 8-1).

Table 8-1   Occupational Structure in Japan, the United States, Germany, and Britain

Unit: %

Country	1870			1913			1950			1992		
	Agriculture	Industry	Service	Agriculture	Industry	Service	Agriculture	Industry	Service	Agriculture	Industry	Service
Japan	70	30	0	60	19	21	45	25	30	10	30	60
U.S.A.	43	34	24	25	33	42	10	32	58	0.5	25	70
Germany	41	38	21	38	47	25	25	37	38	0.5	35.5	60
Britain	25	37	38	10	45	45	0.5	45	50	0.5	25.5	70

Note: Reorganized according to the table in page 610 in *Creating Modern Capitalism: How Entrepreneurs, Companies, and Countries Triumphed in Three Industrial Revolutions*, edited by Thomas K. McGraw.

With the above changes, the "new middle stratum" (or new middle class) has successively emerged in social stratification structure in industrialized countries all over the world. The new middle stratum mainly consists of the white-collar occupational groups such as professional and technical personnel, managers, clerical personnel, and commercial and service personnel. The new middle stratum accounted for 18.2 percent of the work force in United States in 1970, 19.1 percent in Britain in 1971, 16.1 percent in Federal Germany in 1970, 18.7 percent in France in 1972,[1] and 34 percent in Japan in 1975.[2]

---

[1] Ni, Liya. 1989. *Class Structure in Contemporary Capitalist Society*. Beijing: China Renmin University Press: 161.

[2] Wang, Yu and Yingying Chen. 1990. "Chapter 9: Introduction of Social Class and Stratum Structure in Modern Japan". Pp. 172 in Jianzhang He, et al.(eds.), *Modern Social Class Structure and Social Stratification Issues*. Beijing: China Social Sciences Press.

THE NEW MIDDLE STRATUM IN MODERN CHINA AND ITS

SOCIAL BACKGROUND

Definition of the New Middle Stratum in Modern China

Generally, various social structures have a middle stratum that links the upper class and the lower class. However, middle layers in different societies have different social structural functions and different significances. The new middle class in Western industrialized society is the hardcore of social structure and holds the balance because of its unique function in adjusting relationships of social interests as a "buffer" in social conflicts and a "relief valve" in social stability. In this study, based on social practice in transformation of modern Chinese social structure solicited by the reform and opening-up, referring to general rules of social development in modern society, and according to results of some preliminary empirical studies, we hypothesize that a new middle stratum will emerge in the process of social stratification in current Chinese society. This new middle stratum will have functions similar to those in developed countries but also with unique characteristics of Chinese social structure. More specifically, it has the functions of buffering polarization between rich and poor and conflicts of social interests, demonstrating examples of fair attainment of social status, exemplifying behaviors based on the socialist market economy and modern social values, and so forth.

According to empirical studies on the social stratification structure in transition of Chinese social society in recent years, referring to relevant theories in the West, we proposed a preliminary definition for the middle stratum in current China in order to investigate the process of gestation and development of the stratum.[1]

In this study, *middle stratum* refers to the group of the self-employed individuals who possess a certain amount of the means of production (such as individual-operated business proprietors) and small-medium employers (such as

---

[1] This definition was first proposed in the special report *Study on the Middle Stratum in China* released by the Research Group for Social Structure in Contemporary China taking charge by Professor Xueyi Lu in October 2001. The initial definition was as follows: "In social status hierarchy, middle stratum refers to a group of people who mainly are engaged in brainwork, rely on wages and salaries to make a living, have the capability to obtain occupations with higher income and better working conditions and corresponding family consumption capability with a certain quality of leisure living, possess a certain right of domination to control their labor activities and working objects, have civism and citizen consciousness and corresponding culture". See Zhang, Wanli. 2002. "The Fourth Special Report: Study on the Middle Stratum in China". Pp. 252-254 in Xueyi Lu (ed.), *Social Stratification in Contemporary China*. Beijing: Social Sciences Documentation Publishing House. Thereafter, with advances in relevant empirical studies, this definition was and will be constantly revised (see Zhang, Wanli. 2002. "A Pilot Study on the Middle Stratum in Current China". In *Proceeding* of the *2002 Conference of the Sociological Society of China on Globalization and Development of Chinese Society*).

owners of small-medium private enterprises). In social status hierarchy, the majority of the middle stratum consists of people who possess a certain amount of professional knowledge capital and occupational prestige capital, mainly are engaged in brainwork, rely on salaries and wages to make their living, have the capability to obtain occupations with a higher income and better working conditions, are provided with a certain right of domination to control their labor activities and working objects, hold the capability of family consumption to maintain a middle-level standard of living and corresponding quality of leisure living, and have certain social influences by employing their professional knowledge to give authoritative appraisals on public affairs. In the social status hierarchy, this group of people is called the "new middle stratum".

According to the above definition, we developed the following operational measures of the new middle stratum. (1) A certain amount of knowledge capital and occupational prestige capital. Members of this stratum received middle and higher level of national education and have professional skills training experience and qualifications such as senior middle school and higher educational backgrounds, various professional qualification certificates, various professional and technical titles, and so forth. In addition, occupations of members of this stratum have relatively high appraisal of social status. (2) The working and labor methods. Members of this stratum are engaged in occupations of brainwork, including brainwork occupations with partial manual labor such as engineers and technical workers. (3) Capability of obtaining employment: Members of the new middle stratum possess relatively high level of education and professional skills, which are in great demands and paid in higher remuneration in the labor market. (4) Occupational authority. Members of the stratum have a certain empowered right to dispatch, dominate, and control the working objects including subordinates and related office equipments, instruments, and methods, etc., and a certain degree of right to speak and make suggestions to supervisors about arrangements of business such as office secretary and engineer, etc. (5) Level of income and possessions. This refers to legal remunerations such as salaries and wages obtained from legal occupations and private possessions acquired from legal channels (including legal income and remunerations such as securities, interests, gifts, and legacies, etc.). The level of income and possessions of members of the new middle stratum should be at the middle level in the society. In current China, we take the average individual income and possessions (converted into Ren Min Bi) of 25,000~35,000 Yuan per year,[1] or the average family income of 50,000~70,000

---

[1] This figure is calculated according to the data of two relevant surveys. The first is the survey on wage levels in labor markets (i.e., the October Wage Survey) conducted by Ministry of Labor and Social Security of China in 14 medium-large size cities in 1998. The 14 cities are listed as follows: Beijing, Tianjin, Shanghai, Chongqin, Shenzhen, Foshan, Wuxi, Chengdu, Fuzhou, Qinhuangdao, Xi'an, Jinan, Harbin, and Huangshi. In each city, 40 normally operated independent accounting units were investigated; of which, 24 were state-owned units, 9 were urban collective units, 7 were other units (joint-stock, foreign-invested, and Hong Kong, Macao and Taiwan-invested enterprises), covering more than 500 thousand employees. The wage levels obtained in this survey indicated the standards of wages in October 1998. The median of per capita monthly wage, i.e., 1,479.41 yuan

Yuan per year (taking the nuclear family consisting of three members as reference, two of them are in work) as the baseline. (6) Consumption and lifestyle: Members of the stratum have the capability to afford middle-level personal and family consumption. In addition, after satisfying basic needs like food and clothing, they can provide necessary material conditions for family members to meet their various cultural and spiritual needs such as private houses, automobiles, regular tours and holidays, and corresponding cultural and social networking consumption. (7) A certain influence on public affairs: Members of the stratum possess the capability of knowledge-based and authoritative judgments on social fields related to their professional knowledge and hence have a certain degree of liberty to speak and influence public affairs.

In general, the social function of the middle stratum should aim to stabilize the social structure that is necessary to the fair, orderly, and balanced development of a modern society. Considering the particular national conditions in current transformation of Chinese social structure, the social function of the middle stratum should be defined as follows. (1) The function of buffering polarization between rich and poor and social interests conflicts. In a social stratification structure with a widening social divide and gap in wealth, the middle stratum is at the middle position in economic, political, and cultural life. Once this stratum obtains its legitimacy and social recognition, it is the time when this stratum becomes the main body in social interests structure; accordingly, it is possible for the middle stratum to make use of its buffering function to mitigate the polarization between the upper class and the lower class and among acute social conflicts. (2)The function of demonstrating examples of fair attainment of social status. The overwhelming majority of members of the middle stratum obtain a decent and comfortable life at the middle level through individual efforts, fair competition, and resorting to achievement factors such as education and market opportunities, etc. In addition, members of the stratum represent the majority of social members in social life. Therefore, the experience and accomplishments of their status attainment will certainly attract concerns from the lower class and common social members and be set as the example and hope of improving social status through upward mobility. From the perspective of social structure, it is the path and accomplishment in status attainment of the middle stratum that reveal the possibility of social fairness in equal opportunity to all social members. (3) The function of exemplifying behaviors based on the socialist market economy and

---

RMB, was taken as the baseline (see Department of Planning and Finance, Ministry of Labor and Social Security of China. 1999. *Wage Levels in Labor Markets of Medium-large Size Cities in China.* Beijing: China Labor and Social Security Publishing House.) The second one is the survey on basic family profiles conducted by the Urban Investigation Team of the National Bureau of Statistics of China among 150 thousand urban households in 1999. The data obtained in this survey indicated that the proportion of wage to the gross income was 44.5 percent, while non-wage income accounted for 55.5 percent (see *China Information.* March 8, 2000); non-wage family income was 1.5 times higher than wage income. We calculated the annual income based on the above data. With the constant growth of the household income level in China, corresponding adjustments should be made on such an indicator.

modern social values, such as the normative behaviors in market activities that follow the rules of transaction and fair competition. In social public life, members of the middle stratum pay attention to and are proactively involved in public authority and affairs such as social public security issues (e.g., environmental and resources concerns), situations of disadvantaged groups, freedom of personal choice, wealth accumulation through legal channels, construction of social trust and reciprocity, and so forth, on the basis of their peaceful psychology, conservative and moderate political attitudes, and mild manners and behaviors. As a result, they affect the formation of social custom and ethos delivering modern social values.

Seeing the above social functions and significance in social structure of the middle stratum, this chapter will focus on analysis of the emergence, composition, and characteristics of the middle stratum in modern Chinese society.

Emergence of the Middle Stratum in Contemporary China

According to general opinions, the new middle stratum usually emerges in industrial society, i.e., the developing stage of the modern society, and is closely related to some critical factors at this stage, such as industrialization, marketization, urbanization, and industrial structure, etc. Therefore, we will investigate the influences of the above-mentioned factors on the emergence of Chinese middle stratum.

First, the advance of industrialization has an important influence on subdivision and specialization of the division of labor. As a result, it has created a set of occupational differentiation hierarchy based on technical levels or degree of specialization. The socio-economic differentiations caused by the occupational differentiation become increasingly remarkable; occupations with a higher degree of specialization usually obtain growing economic income and social prestige, while income and social status of unskilled manual laborers relatively decline. Obviously, based on such occupational differentiations, the occupational structure and corresponding social status appraisal system in China provide favorable environments for the emergence of the new middle stratum. Another influence of the advance of industrialization is the expansion of hierarchical organizations both in quantity and in size. At the current stage, hierarchical organizations have developed universally in China; a large number of enterprise organizations, governmental organizations, and other organizations have emerged; the size of organizations constantly expands and the levels of management increasingly grow. Especially, the right of ownership has been separated from the authority of management; the management in organizations actually possesses the right to control and allocate corresponding resources and hence leads to differentiation of socio-economic status between the management and non-management and the emergence of the middle stratum.

From the perspective of market-oriented relationships, the progress of marketization is also a process in which the right of personal economic freedom has been gradually established, effectively implemented, and substantially guaranteed. Marketization has brought about two important consequences to the social stratification in current China. This first consequence is the emergence of the private property right; it has led to the appearance of a new type of social relationship, i.e., the relationship between owners of the means of production and employees, and consequently widened the gap in socio-economic status between owners of the means of production and employees. As a result, the ownership of the means of production has become an important aspect in social stratification in modern China. The second consequence of marketization is the emergence of the non-state-owned sector; it has led to the outgrowth of a new type of mechanism of institutional segmentation in social resource allocation, i.e., the relationship of power authorization and the relationship of market transaction. In the progress of marketization, the co-existence of the state-owned and the non-state-owned sectors has formed a unique interaction relationship between the intra-system and the extra-system sectors and accordingly made the institutional segmentation and correspondingly "price difference in status" a remarkable mechanism of status attainment in social stratification in contemporary China. Based on such a mechanism, it is possible for social stratification to provide the "free mobility space" and "free mobility resources" for the emergence of the new middle stratum.

In terms of the urban-rural structure, only when the level of urbanization in a country reaches above 50 percent is it possible for the middle stratum to become the majority of social force and exercise its functions of "buffer layer" and "balancer". In current China, although the level of urbanization is still far from 50 percent, the rapid development of urbanization from 17.9 percent in 1978 to 39.1 percent in 2002 has provided a favorable social environment for the emergence of the middle stratum.[1]

From the perspective of industrial structure, the middle stratum emerges in the transition of modern industrial structure in which the proportion of traditional industry declines while that of modern industry is increasing. Since the reform and opening-up from 1978 after the introduction of market mechanisms through economic reforms, the industrial structure in China has experienced a drastic change in which the proportion of traditional industry has declined while that of modern industry has increased. In the perspective of proportions of employment, in 1978, the primary industry accounted for 70.5 percent, the secondary industry 17.3 percent, and the tertiary industry 12.2 percent; in 2002 the proportions respectively were 50 percent (down by more than 20 percent), 21.4 percent (up by about 4 percent), and 28.6 percent (up by about 16 percent). From the perspective of proportions of GDP, in 1978 the primary industry accounted for 28.1 percent, the secondary industry 48.2 percent, and the tertiary industry 23.7 percent; in 2002, the proportions respectively were 15.4 percent (down by more than 13 percent), 51.1 percent (up by about 3

---

[1] In this study, the level of urbanization is characterized by the generally adopted proportion of the urban population to the whole population. However, because of the long history of the residence registration system and the dual urban-rural divide system in China, we believe that the level of social welfare should be included in the analysis of urbanization level in current China. The specific analysis is presented in the following text.

percent), and 33.5 percent (up by about 10 percent).[1]

The significant change of industrial structure in China is similar to the before-mentioned transition of industrial structure in the transformation of industrialized social structure in Japan, the United States, Germany, and Britain (see Table 8-1). In other words, the proportion of agriculture and its employment decreased sharply, the proportion of industry and its employment declined gradually, while the proportion of the services sector and its employment increased rapidly. As a result, the white-collar stratum, i.e., the middle stratum has grown up and gradually changed the situation of social resource allocation.

Under the influences of the above structural and institutional factors, the middle stratum of Chinese society has emerged.

First, the occupational category of the middle stratum has taken shape. When the occupational structure in a particular society transforms from the traditional occupational structure to the modern structure, i.e., the emergence of the modern occupational differentiation, new occupations related to the middle stratum will come forth in large numbers, such as certified public accountants, lawyers, financial planers, software developers, and so forth. Consequently, these emerging occupations provide economic and social space for the development of the middle stratum. In the occupational structure of China, these new occupations emerged at the late 1980s and the early 1990s. However, the paths of occupational differentiation in China are different from the typical experience in Western society. The first path is the "intra-system occupational differentiation" which occurred in former planned economy system. In this path, with the significant adjustment of industrial structure caused by the reorganization of state-owned enterprises and the reform of the personnel system in government agencies, sectors and occupations (the secondary industry) once with unfavorable status have turned to advantaged sectors and occupations such as teachers, professional and technical personnel, managerial personnel, and clerks. In addition, shifts also have occurred in characteristics of occupations, for example, shifting from former "cadres" to current "government employees". The second path is the "extra-system occupational differentiation" which has occurred in the free-market system. In this path, some new occupations have emerged, which are characterized by operating individually for the purpose of obtaining market returns by making use of private capital (including human capital), such as certified public accountants, lawyer, free lancers, business managers, marketing consultants, image consultants, and so on. In particular, the emergence of employers, i.e., private entrepreneurs, is one type of occupational differentiation that has attracted great concerns from the public.[2] The third path is the o occupational

---

[1] National Bureau of Statistics of China (2003: 34).

[2] From May 29th to September 19th in 1981, the *People's Daily* published a series articles discussing the event of contracting out a fish pound to a farmer who employed 8 people to help him in Guangdong Province. Most articles believed that "in such a way, talented people can have a chance to cut a brilliant figure and create more fortune for the society", "even if there is a certain extent of exploitation, it is unnecessarily to be startled"; contrarily, some people argued that "exploiting

differentiation caused by the emergence of high and new-technology industries (such as information industry) which are brought about by the global new technology revolution, such as scientists in life science and environmentology, senior laboratory technicians, information architects, and so forth. In particular, since the 1990s, China has carried out a strategy of human resource development by absorbing talented people from foreign countries on a large scale. As a result, a large number of Chinese students who studied abroad in the 1980s through various channels (for example, sponsored by governmental or family funding, went to foreign countries with spouses, and so on) and forms (such as pursuing academic degrees, receiving professional trainings, student and scholar exchange programs, and short-term visits, etc.) returned to China, i.e., so-called "returnees" or "turtles". Most of them have accumulated high and new-technology and cutting-edge knowledge and were edified by modern culture in foreign countries; correspondingly, they are extraordinary talents of emerging occupations which are in great demand in the domestic market and in consequence become the skeleton army of the middle stratum. According to the data of our survey, among the non-student population at the age of 16 to 70 in China, the proportion of people engaging in "middle-class occupations" reached nearly 16 percent in 2001.[1]

Second, the pattern of consumption of the middle-stratum has come into being. According to relevant experience in the West, when consumers who possess the capabilities of independent choice and effective payment to mass consumer durable goods have emerged, it is possible to identify the embryo and the actual existence of groups with the middle-class status to some extent. A consumption revolution has occurred in Chinese urban areas since the 1980s and corresponding consumer culture has been thriving.[2] There are two major characteristics of social consumption behaviors. The first characteristic is growing "autonomy in consumption" (a type of consumption behavior pattern in which the consumer is in the initiative position).[3] On one hand, such a change has become an intrinsic drive to transform the social structure and promote social progress. On the other hand, it has accelerated the social differentiation of the standard of living and quality of life between the rural and urban residents and among social members in the city and hence extended the social differentiation from the production relation to the living relation; as a result, it has

---

employees should not be permitted; it is an important issue related to the basic principle of socialism". See Zhang, Houyi. 2002. "The Third Special Report: Private Entrepreneur is an Important Component in Chinese Social Stratum Structure". In Xueyi Lu (ed.), *Social Stratification in Contemporary China*. Beijing: Social Sciences Documentation Publishing House.

[1] Li, Chunling. 2004. "Middle Stratum: A Group Worthy of Attention in Chinese Society". In Ru, Xin, et al (eds.), *Analyses and Forecasts on Social Situations in China (2003)*. Beijing: Social Sciences Documentation Publishing House.

[2] Lu, Hanlong. 2003. "Preface for the Chinese Edition: Consumption Revolution and Consumer Autonomy." In Deborahs Davis, *The Consumer Revolution in Urban China*, translated by Dai, Huisi and Hanlong Lu. Shanghai: Shanghai Academy of Social Sciences Press.

[3] The growth of consumer autonomy refers to the following phenomenon: With the development of marketization, more and more exchanges are achieved in the form of currency consumption; the expansion of categories and scope of commodities and services increases the degree of consumer choice; consumer is in the initiative position in the process of consumption. See Lu (2003).

brought about "consumption stratification". The second characteristic is the emergence of "status consumption" (a type of consumption behavior pattern in which name brands are used to show consumers' social status). Going with the growth of consumers' autonomy, personal possessions has become a feasible means to demonstrate individual achievements. The majority of consumers in "status consumption" are members of the middle stratum, who have higher income level and payment capability. The data obtained from our survey shows that at present the proportion of people in "middle-class consumption" has reached 35 percent.[1] According to the survey on white-collar consumers' behaviors in current China conducted by Jianzhong Xia and associates of the Department of Sociology at Renmin University of China, the white-collar group was 21.6 percent higher than the average level of ordinary people both in the value of individualized consumption and in the value of conspicuous consumption. In addition, the proportion of people in white-collar group who prefer to practicality accounted for 44.5 percent, while those who are in pursuit of status and conspicuous consumption made up 55.5 percent.[2]

Third, the social identification of the group with middle-stratum status has emerged as well. According to the data of the nationwide survey conducted by the research group, 46.8 percent respondents subjectively identified themselves as members of the middle stratum. Of that, less than one-tenth of respondents believed that their social status was at the high or middle-higher level. Nonetheless, nearly two-fifths of respondents believed that they were at the middle-level social status. The sum of the three proportions is 46.8 percent. That is to say, nearly half of the respondents subjectively identified themselves as members of the middle stratum.[3] According to another survey conducted by us from 2001 to 2002 in Beijing, Shanghai, and Changchun, etc., people who were engaged in occupations of the new middle stratum defined in the above text already had a strong self-identification of their middle stratum status. For example, a small entrepreneur among them frankly asked the interviewer, "Are we the middle class?" He had ever read John Naisbitt's *Metatrends* and Daniel Bell's *Coming of Post-Industrial Society: A Venture in Social Forecasting*. He believed that people like him[4] "were exactly the middle class in Western modern society", and "should be given a positive affirmation". According to respondents' answers to questions like "do you know the wording of middle class?" and "do you believe you are middle class?" we can get a glimpse of their consciousness about their status as the middle stratum.

Response of a contractor of a cultural institution (He is a middle-aged male with university educational background and around 7,000 Yuan RMB monthly incomes.

---

[1] Li, Chunling (2004).

[2] Xia, Jianzhong and Zhijie Yao. 2004. "Lifestyle of the White-collar Group: A Empirical Study". Unpublished.

[3] Li, Chunling (2004).

[4] He meant private entrepreneurs.

In the late 1980s, he obtained an indefinite leave of absence from his former work unit with his position retained and salary suspended and went into business; in the late 1990s, he formally quitted from the former work unit and deposited his personal personnel dossier in the municipal Human Resources Exchange Center):

Respondent: "Is it necessary to ask such a question? In my opinion, both of us are middle class for sure!"

Interviewer: "I am not like you. I do not have my own car and privately owned house. Don't count me in."

Respondent: "Why not? Not to mention other things, your current occupation is a standard middle-class occupation. Maybe you do not need to buy yourself a car! Moreover, our lifestyle and values can not be represented merely by money."

(Adopted from record S1 of case interview, February 17, 2002)

According to the above analyses, we believe that the middle stratum has come into being in current Chinese society and been in a budding phase. However, whether it can develop into a real force to determine the shape of modern social structure in China with its "buffer layer" and "balancer" functions still need to be tested in the future social practice.

COMPOSITION AND CHARACTERISTICS OF THE MIDDLE STRATUM

Social Origins

There are mainly four origins of the middle stratum in current China as follows:

The first type of origin is the traditional "middle class" including self-employers and individual-operated business proprietors (or individual industrial and commercial householders), such as small owners, small retailers, and so forth. They operate in a self-employed way with a small amount of capital; the size of their business usually is small with a small amount of profits. According to statistics from the National Bureau of Statistics of China, by the end of 2002 there were 23,775 thousand individual-operated businesses (individual industrial and commercial households) in China with an employment of 47,429 thousand,[1] accounting for 6.43 percent of total employment (737,400 thousand).

The second origin of the new middle stratum consists of cadres and intellectuals who came from the "middle stratum" in the planned economy system. From the 1950s to the 1980s before the reform, ordinary cadres, intellectuals, and staff

---

[1] National Bureau of Statistics of China (2003a).

members and workers in state-owned enterprises had significant advantages in economic, political, and social status in the planned economy system and were regarded as the middle stratum at that time.[1] Since the late 1980s, with the introduction of various economic elements and the institutional reforms and especially deepening restructuring of state-owned enterprises, staff members and workers in state-owned enterprises were left nothing expect for their own labor force, and their status fell sharply. In contrast, former cadres and intellectuals, relying on authority resources, high-quality social networks, and knowledge resources possessed by them respectively, retained or obtained corresponding status advantages through trading these resources in the process of readjusting their social positions in the market-oriented opportunity structure.

The third origin is emerging private entrepreneurs and township business entrepreneurs since the reform and opening-up. This group has no direct relationships with private entrepreneurs in the era of the Socialist Transformation of Capitalist Industry and Commerce in the 1950s. Completely depending on market resources and mobility opportunities released by the reform and opening-up, the emerging private entrepreneurs started their own enterprises by primitive accumulation of capital under the influence of dual mechanisms of the planned economy system and the free-market system.[2] According to statistics from the National Bureau of Statistics of China, by the end of 2002 there were 2,435 thousand private enterprises in China with 34,093 thousand entrepreneurs and employees, among them 6,228 thousand were investors,[3] accounting for 4.62 percent of total employment.

The fourth origin is the new middle stratum brought about by the introduction of foreign investment and talented people mastering high and new technology. Since the 1980s, in operation of introducing foreign investment on a large scale, some high and new-technology industries and occupations have emerged and consequently created two occupational groups. This first one is the group of modern entrepreneurs. They are experts mastering high and new technologies, or start-up entrepreneurs who once studied in foreign countries, or people who were in control of a certain authority resources in former planned systems (such as principals, purchasing and marketing personnel, and clerical personnel in state-owned enterprises and public institutions). Based on their unique advantages in technology, capital, power, and social networks, they started high and new-technology enterprises and obtained relatively high social returns. The second group consists of white-collar employees in Sino-foreign joint ventures and exclusively foreign-funded enterprises. The working and labor methods, occupational prestige, and remunerations of this group are higher than those of staff members and workers in state-owned enterprises and traditional sectors. The two

---

[1] Li, Qiang. 2001. "Some Thoughts regarding the Middle Class and the Middle Stratum". *Journal of Renmin University of China*. Vol. 2.

[2] According to analysis of this research group, the family background of capitalists in the private sector is correlated to respondents' current status attainment. See Section 1 in Chapter 4.

[3] National Bureau of Statistics of China (2003a).

occupational groups can be seen as the typical representatives of the new middle stratum in modern Chinese society. According to statistics, by the end of 2002 staff members and workers employed by foreign-invested enterprises were 3,675.6 thousand, and people working in enterprises funded by entrepreneurs from Hong Kong, Macao and Taiwan were 3,529.5 thousand,[1] the sum of the two groups were 7,205.1 thousand, accounting for 0.98 percent of total employment.

Characteristics of the Middle Stratum

In current China, the middle stratum is a status group with certain degree of heterogeneity.

The concept of *middle stratum* refers to various groups distributing in occupations with relatively strong competitive competence, comparatively high market returns and particular social influences in the system of social status allocation in industrialized social structure. In other words, it is a set of status groups with certain degree of heterogeneity; these groups are situated at roughly the same middle-level status in distribution of social resources such as occupational income, authority, prestige, and education, etc. The heterogeneity of composition of the middle stratum in current China mainly comes from two sources. The first source is the inconsistency within the allocation of three types of social status resources and the appraisal of status. The second source lies in the fact that this stratum contains a particular sub-stratum, i.e., private entrepreneurs who are in possession of a certain amount of private-owned means of production and wage labor, and having certain private property relationships.

(1) Inconsistency within Allocation of Three Types of Social Status Resources and Appraisal of Status

Inconsistency in appraisal of status refers to the (subjective and objective) inconsistent state of a certain group in evaluating their own social prestige, social authority, market returns (such as occupational income and social welfare, etc.), and so forth. For example, they may give a very high appraisal of their possession of authority whereas make a low appraisal of their possession of material wealth. The inconsistency in status appraisal of the new middle stratum is also an important characteristic of Western social structure. However, because of the dual social transformation pattern[2] and its complexity, the characteristic of inconsistency in status appraisal in modern China is different from that in Western social structure. Such a characteristic can be observed from the relationships of allocation of three types of social status resources and its impact on social members' status attainment in current China. The relationships of allocation of three types of social resources

---

[1] National Bureau of Statistics of China (2003a).

[2] It refers to the transformation from traditional agricultural society to modern industrialized society and the transformation from the planned economy to a free-market economy.

respectively are the relationship of authority delegation, the relationship of market exchange, and the networks of social relationships. Affected by the relationships of allocation of the three types of social status resources, there are three types of channels to enter the middle stratum in current China, that is, the administrative entry affected by the relationship of authority delegation, the market-oriented entry affected by the relationship of market exchange, and the social-networks-oriented entry affected by social connection capital.

A. The Relationship of Authority Delegation and the Administrative Entry

The *relationship of authority delegation* refers to the allocation of social resources by the state administrative authority and a series of corresponding institutional arrangements. Each social group and its status attainment are affected by such relationship. This type of relationship universally existed in the social structure from 1949 to 1978 and was an important relational element in that structure. In current social structure in China, this type of relationship still has an influence on the allocation of social resources and social members' status attainment to a considerable extent.[1] According to statistical analysis conducted by the research group, father's status of cadre has an important impact on social members' attainment of cadre status; especially in the two decades from 1957 to 1977, the probability of cadres' children to be cadres was 3 to 4 times higher than that of non-cadres' children. Even after the reform and opening-up, such an influence still exists although it has been weakened to a certain extent.[2]

From the perspective of origins of the middle stratum in current China, the relationship of authority delegation directly affects two major groups, that is, the group of cadres and the group of intellectuals.[3] In former planned systems, the majority of the two groups worked in administrative institutions that were financed by public revenue;[4] they possessed the cadre status, and enjoyed status privileges different from workers and peasants. This group was differentiated in the progress of the market-oriented reform and most of its members entered into the middle stratum. Compared with other social groups such as workers and peasants, they have the advantage of authority capital, educational capital, and high-quality social connection capital, which were accumulated in the former planned systems. In addition, they also accumulated and obtained plentiful experience of socio-political life and the ability of action, which are necessary for dealing with significant social reforms.

---

[1] Zhang, Wanli (1996).

[2] See Section 4 in Chapter 5.

[3] In the study, the group of cadres refers to cadres and government employees who possess political and particular authority in fields of national economy and public administration, such as the authorized right to make decision and the authority of management. The group of intellectuals refers to professional and technical personnel in science, education, culture and arts, health care, hygiene, and other social and economic domains, including researchers in natural and social sciences, teachers, actors, writers, doctors, engineers, technicians, and so forth.

[4] It means that their salaries and benefits came from funds allocated by governmental fiscal budgets.

The mobility pattern of differentiating from former systems and becoming members of the middle stratum is a type of administrative entry pattern. In other words, resorting to the institutional status in the former planned systems and intra-system social welfare security and various convenient resources, they retained their "intra-system status" for a period of time in order to adapt to the market competition and obtain returns from it. Then, under the pressure of the personnel system reform, they shifted from the "intra-system status" to the "extra-system status" and became members of the middle stratum. According to empirical observations, the administrative entry pattern has three subcategories. The first one is "having a foot in two camps". For example, one may retain his position with salary suspended and leave his former work unit to try other careers or contract in a division of his former work unit to go into business. The second one is "one family with two systems", that is, some family members stay inside the system, while others go into business outside the system. The third way is "concurrent positions in two systems", that is, when a public institution starts its own enterprise, some of its staff members are assigned from "intra-system" branches to "extra-system" divisions and hold two positions concurrently both in public institution and in the enterprise.

From the perspective of individuals, the administrative entry pattern is the outcome of their initiative choices and proactive actions. As a result, it has established the basic orientation of the middle-stratum status attainment in current China, i.e., *elite reproduction* and *professionalism*.[1] Analyzing from the perspective of social structure, the administrative entry pattern has a systematical effect on the differentiation of social structure. In other words, this pattern has led to the transformation from the former socialist redistribution system to the free-market system and established a double track system in which intra-system status and extra-system status co-exist and work. Such phenomenon indicates the complicated process of institutional transition in China, in which "the market-oriented reform in China is creating a new free-market system paralleling the planned redistribution system, rather than simply substituting the free-market system for the redistribution system".[2] Affected by the complexity of the institutional transition, the administrative

---

[1] *Elite reproduction* in this study refers to the phenomenon that the rank of cadres takes advantage of political authority and privileges in the socialist redistribution system to obtain more and more economic interests in the emerging free-market system and continue to retain their "status of elites". *Professionalism* refers to a type of public ideology which is based on professional knowledge and cultural capital transmitted through modern educational system and meanwhile with emphasis on educatees under an obligation to participate in social work. The group of professionalism refers to a new stratum consists of cultural intellectuals and technical intellectuals who differentiated from the former system or entered into this group in the new system. People with higher educational level, depending on cultural capital and professional authority possessed by them, have built up the professional authority appraisal competing with the power appraisal in the social status appraisal system which is in the progress of market-oriented transformation. See Nee, Victor. 1989. "A Theory of Market Transition: From Redistributive to Markets in State Socialism". *American Sociological Review*. Vol. 54: 663-681; Gouldner, Alvin W. 2002. *The Future of Intellectuals and the Rise of the New Class*, translated by Gu, Xiaohui and Rong Cai, Zhejiang: Jiangsu People's Press.

[2] Song, Shige.1998. "Delayed effect of Right Transition: An Explanation of Elite Reproduction and

entry and the outcomes of its market-oriented operation have led social strata with the status of "cadres" and "intellectuals" in the former system to differentiate and evolve into a part of the middle stratum—in the sense of modern social stratification structure—in current China, such as state and social administrators possessing organizational resources, managerial personnel possessing cultural or organizational resources, professional and technical personnel possessing cultural resources, and clerical personnel possessing a small amount of cultural and organizational resources.

B. The Relationship of Market Exchange and the Market-Oriented Entry

The *relationship of market exchange* refers to allocation of social resources according to commodity exchange and relevant market rules. Status attainment of members of various social groups mainly relies on the means of market exchange, which is characterized by high mobility rate of group members and the open structure. In China, since the reform and opening-up and corresponding modern society transformation from 1978, recurring to the emergence and the expansion of the free-market economy, such a distribution relationship has started its relatively independent development and operation, and consequently brought out the "extra-system" relationship of market exchange. More importantly, the impact of introduction of market mechanisms on social stratification structure in current China lies in the fact that it has broken the monopoly situation in which the rank of cadres exclusively enjoyed status advantages on the basis of authority delegation relationship in the former redistribution system. As a result, people can share socio-economic status resources and upward mobility opportunities through the market exchange relationship.

Table 8-2   The Last Positions of Private Entrepreneurs before Starting Business

Category	Party Member		Non-Party-Member	
	Number	Percentage	Number	Percentage
Ordinary cadre	36	6.8	223	11.3
Cadre at the level of lower section	21	4.0	30	1.5
Cadre at the section level	58	10.9	101	5.1
Cadre at the division or county level	17	3.2	24	1.2
Cadre at the director-general level	5	0.9	0	0.0
Principal of township (or people's commune)	3	0.6	10	0.5
Major cadre in village (or production brigade)	39	7.4	40	2.0
Contractor of public-owned enterprises	105	19.8	322	16.3
Purchasing and marketing staff in enterprises	28	5.3	119	6.0
Military officer	0	0.0	5	0.3
Other	140	26.4	590	29.9
Without position	78	14.7	509	25.8
Total	530	100.0	1973	100.0

Sources: Data are from the fourth nationwide survey on the private enterprises in China conducted by the United Front Work Department of the Central Committee of the C.P.C., All-China Federation of Industry and Commerce, and Chinese Society for Private Economy Studies in 2000. See Zhang, Houyi and Guangjin Chen. 2003. "Statistical Analysis of Survey on

Circulation in Transformation from Socialist State to Markets". *Sociology Research*. Vol. 3.

Private Entrepreneurs with the Party Membership". In Houyi Zhang (ed.), *Report on Development of Private Enterprises in China (2002)*. Beijing: Social Sciences Documentation Publishing House.

The impoverished and marginal groups in the former system, such as peasants (although they were regarded as the allied forces of the working class in ideology, because of the restriction of the rural-urban divided dual social system and the perennial scissors gap between the prices of agricultural products and industrial products, their economic status was in the poor situation), service personnel, the self-employed, and salespersons, etc., in social structure transition shifting from the planned economy system to a free-market economy and from a agricultural society to a industrial society, entered the market economy system and corresponding socio-economic arena through two major paths. As a result, they have differentiated and evolved into the stratum of private entrepreneurs, the stratum of individual-operated business proprietors, the stratum of commercial and service personnel (as a part of the middle stratum in current China), and the stratum of agricultural laborers. The first path is the social mobility from underdeveloped rural areas to relatively developed urban areas; the second path is the social mobility from the former planned system (intra-system sector) to the free-market system (extra-system sector).

As for the emerging private entrepreneurs in current China, they have three characteristics in social mobility. First, they have no direct relationships of historical inheritance with private entrepreneurs in the 1950s; this emerging social stratum has come into being completely resorting to the market-oriented transformation in economic reforms. Second, occupations of private entrepreneurs who established their enterprises in the early 1980s were usually at a relatively lower status in the former system; few of them came from state-owned enterprises and public institutions.[1] Third, many private entrepreneurs take advantage of their political status, such as Party membership and the cadre status, to help themselves develop their business.[2]

C. The Unique Effect of Social Connection Capital and Social-Networks-Oriented Entry

In this study, *social network* has a particular meaning; it refers to the effect of intimate and particular social connections among people as a type of social resources on status attainment of members of various social groups through particularism-oriented social connection mechanism. Social members in the period of drastic social transformation may feel their status unsafe and uncertain to a certain extent. When they face the institutional arrangements established by the authority

---

[1] Dai, Jianzhong (did the actual writing), China Private Enterprise Research Group. 2001. "Data and Analysis of the Fourth Nationwide Survey on Private Enterprises in 2000". In *Chinese Private Sector of Economy Yearbook (1997-1999)*. Beijing: Huawen Press.

[2] See Section 2 in Chapter 7.

relationship and the market relationship and conditioned by coerciveness of institutional arrangements, they will attempt to seek a type of non-institutional factor with affinity and certainty as a sort of compensation. As a result, as a type of social resources in status attainment, social networks are universally accepted by members of current Chinese society.

Table 8-3   Family Backgrounds of Entrepreneurs Starting Business in Different Periods

Unit: %

Family Background	Started before 1989	Started between 1989 and 1992	Started after 1992	Total
"Red" (impoverished lower-middle peasant, worker, urban pauper, revolutionary cadre, and serviceman)	78.6	84.6	79.3	71.2
"Gray" (middle peasant, small retailer, staff member, intellectual)	10.7	9.1	12.7	21.4
"Black" (landlord, rich peasant, capitalist, antirevolutionary officer and official)	10.7	6.3	8.0	7.1
Total	100.0	100.0	100.0	99.7

Sources: Four nationwide surveys on private enterprises and entrepreneurs conducted by the All-China Federation of Industry and Commerce, etc., in 1993, 1995, 1997, and 2000. Data in this table are from the 1997 survey. See Dai (2001).

Table 8-4   The Last Occupations of Entrepreneurs before Starting Business

Unit: %

Previous Occupation	Started before 1989	Started between 1989 and 1992	Started after 1992	Total
Professional and technical personnel	1.9	4.3	4.9	4.6
Cadre in enterprise and public institution	19.8	16.0	25.5	23.5
Worker, service personnel	13.2	8.6	10.8	10.7
Peasant	20.8	17.9	15.8	16.7
Individual-operated business proprietor	35.8	46.3	36.9	38.2
Other or jobless	8.5	6.8	6.1	6.5
Total	100.0	100.0	100.0	100.0

Source: Same as Table 8-3.

The impact of social networks on the emergence of the middle stratum is extraordinarily remarkable in social differentiation and the evolution of marginal groups in the former system. Because they were at a disadvantaged position in possession of economic political, and cultural resources, the only familiar and convenient social resources available to them was social networks resources. The effect of social networks is especially significant in the formation of the private entrepreneur stratum and the group of heads of labor contractors derived from peasant-workers, and status attainment of people moving from the lower class upward to the middle stratum. For a particular group in the middle stratum, social networks

333

have the effect of identity recognition and stratum identification as well. The quality of social networks (it is difficult to distinguish the quality merely according to heterogeneity or homogeneity of social networks) affects social mobility between groups at different levels and upward mobility opportunity and success ratio to a certain extent.

(2) Private Entrepreneurs: A Particular Sub-Stratum in the Middle Stratum

From the perspective of the self-employment feature of the middle stratum, the stratum of private entrepreneurs should not belong to the middle stratum, because they are in control of a certain amount of the means of production and wage labor. They have taken the right to dominate and to use the means of production as a type of capital, traded it for political and cultural resources and hence obtained certain social status in the new status opportunity structure brought by the dual-track system in which the former planned economy system and the free-market system co-exist and co-work since the reform and opening-up. However, from the perspective of social structure transition, because the social transformation in current China is a complicated process of institutional transition and is oriented to the socialist market economy, people in possession of private capital, such as private entrepreneurs, will inevitably become the majority of the middle stratum. Their success in entering the middle stratum indicates the profundity of social structure transition in current China; it has thoroughly overthrown the traditional opinion, which disdained and scorned the rationality of private wealth, and has led Chinese society to recognize and accept the reasonable value of private property in a unique way. Accordingly, the progress of modern social transformation in China has obtained a new approach of social mobilization.

Over a long period of time, the lack of consciousness of private ownership and corresponding institutions and culture in the background of Chinese social structure held back the differentiation of the middle stratum and the realization of its social functions to a certain extent. Compared with Chinese society, most developed countries belong to Western civilization (though cultural differences still exist among various ethnic groups). In the history of Western social transition, all countries experienced the enlightenment of logos to a different extent and evolved following the rules of the market economy. Therefore, in Western society the consciousness and institutions of private ownership, hierarchical management, modern social contractual relationship, and philosophy and tradition of civil society based on democracy, etc., brought about and shaped the new middle class in modern industrial society. In contrast, transition in Chinese society has a different historical background. In perspective of social stratification structure, the uniqueness in history of Chinese society is that it lacked social consciousness and institutional arrangements regarding private wealth and personal life, that is, lack of social recognition on the rationality of private wealth and personal life and corresponding legal protection and institutional arrangements. As Gerhard E. Lenski once pointed out, "private ownership of the means of production almost does not exist in most Eastern European socialist countries".[1] In March 2004, the second session of the tenth National People's Congress made an important amendment to the Constitution in order to provide private property with legal protection. From this amendment, we can see how significant the impact of this historical regret on modern Chinese society is.[2] In such a social context, classifying the emerging private entrepreneur stratum as a part of the middle stratum will be in favor of forming an advantageous social environment for the development of the middle stratum. In addition, because the authority structure in the planned system still remains in current Chinese society, the stratum of state and social administrators with public authority is in possession of the largest amount of political, organizational and authority capital and the greatest influence on society as a whole. Comparatively, private entrepreneurs, so-called "economic elites" who has arisen outside the public-owned sector, cannot stand with state and social administrators shoulder to shoulder and is merely a subgroup in the middle stratum.

---

[1] Lenski, Gerhard E. 1988. *Power and Privilege: Theory of Social Stratification*, translated by Guan, Xinping, Xianzhong Chen and Jinyu Xie. Hangzhou, Zhejiang: Zhejiang People's Press.
[2] See Xinhua Press Agency. 2004. "Synopsis of Original and Amended Provisions in the Constitution". *Guangmin Daily*. March 16.

Chapter 9   Social Mobility of Workers

In this chapter, we will use the term "workers"[1] in a broad sense and define it as follows. *Workers* refer to all personnel paid by wages and salaries that directly operate machines and instruments based on physical force and operational skills to produce material products, or are engaged in activities of transaction and exchange of tangible products and provide labor services in corresponding work units. From the perceptive of occupation classification, workers include marketing and sales personnel, service personnel, production and transportation equipment operators and related personnel, and so forth. It is worthwhile to point out that the term "workers" in this chapter is different from the commonly used concept "working class". The latter is a political concept and refers to all people who are different from "bourgeois" and obtain wage income by providing labor; while the former is an occupational concept and stratum concept in sociology. In this chapter, we will focus on the following questions: What are characteristics of workers? Who became workers? Who achieved upward social mobility among workers? Who were involved in downward social mobility? What is the intrinsic logic of such social mobility?

THE EXPLANATORY FRAMEWORK AND SOCIAL STATUS OF WORKERS

Two major sets of variables may determine whether a person will be a worker. The first set of variables includes the functional requirements and internal structure of a society; the second set of variables refers to laborer's personal resources. The particular values of the two sets of variables determine an individual's entry into the stratum of workers and his or her upward and downward occupational mobility.

The functional requirements and internal structure of a society can be simplified as the functional requirements and internal structure of an organization. An important dimension of the internal structure is the occupational structure or position structure (the terms "occupation" and "position" have the same meaning in the following text). The basic orientation of an organization is to achieve optimal structure according to its functional requirements. The optimal structure has two aspects of meaning. First, it means that the design of category and number of positions is optimal; the structure of divisions and the number of positions including

---

[1] It is necessary to point out that the meaning of the term "workers" adopted in this chapter is different from that of the term "stratum of workers" used by this research group. The latter doses not include personnel in commercial and services sectors.

principals of the organization, professional and technical personnel, clerical personnel, marketing and sales personnel, service personnel, and production and transportation personnel are optimal (according to the above definition, the last three occupations belong to workers). Second, it means that each category of position is provided with laborers in possession of the most suitable resources, that is, laborers with particular resources are allocated to positions that are most in need of such resources.

Enterprises and public institutions require three categories of resources possessed by laborers. The first category is physical and intellectual resources including physical force, skills, knowledge, and competence, etc. The second category is conformity resources including loyalty to organizations, obedience to regulations, disciplines, and superior commands, team spirit, and so on. The third category is diligence-effort resources, including the expected amount of physical and intellectual expenditure in work, efforts, and stamina, etc. The position of principal in an organization requires high-level knowledge and competence, a high degree of conformity and highly intensive diligence and efforts. Organizations always make an effort to seek laborers with as many such resources as possible to hold the position of principal. The professional and technical position requires high-level professional knowledge and corresponding capacity for work. The clerical position requires relatively high level of capacity for operation and execution and corresponding techniques. The position of worker needs a relatively high level of physical force and technique skills. Meanwhile, all these positions require corresponding conformity, diligence and efforts, while organizations always attempt to choose people with appropriate resources to match these positions.

With different functional objectives, enterprises and public institutions attach different degrees of importance to the three types of resources. In the planned economy system from the 1950s to the 1970s, consolidation of the political system and operation of the planned system were the foremost functional objectives. Organizations' conformity with the government and laborers' conformity with organizations became the principal requirements to social structure. At that time, laborers' conformity resources received high emphasis, such as loyalty to the Party, concerns for organizations, struggle with "counterrevolutionary", and so forth. Conformity resources not only can be used as a type of measure, but they can also be used to deliver values. The latter is largely affected by social status and its adjustments. Therefore, the working class who suffered bitterly in the old society before the establishment of the People's Republic of China was liberated in the new society and received extraordinary consideration. They not only had a relatively high social status with extraordinary economic benefits, but they also possessed more upward mobility opportunities. Because of their "red" family background, children of workers also had a greater chance to enter into the rank of workers who were treated as "big brothers" in the social hierarchy and further move upward from this group. In contrast, people lacking any conformity resources, such as capitalists and their children, and counterrevolutionaries and their children, could not hold critical positions in state-owned enterprises and public institutions. They were emplaced in the rank of workers as well to receive supervision and correction. Such great importance attached to the conformity resources led to the highly corresponding structure between the vertical hierarchy of occupations and the characteristics of conformity resources. People in possession of the optimal conformity resources occupied occupations at the highest level, while those with the least conformity resources had to take the lowest occupations. Comparatively, physical and intellectual resources received the cold shoulder and hence the physical difference, especial the intellectual difference, between people with occupations at different levels was relatively small.

The reform and opening-up starting from the end of 1970s have changed the economic system in China fundamentally. In the free-market system, economic efficiency and economic growth become the most important objectives of organizations. The physical and intellectual resources directly related to achievement of such objectives are attached the highest importance. Because different positions have different marginal productivity, gaps in economic and social benefits between different levels in the vertical hierarchy of occupations have been widening rapidly. The economic status and power status of workers are adjusted to a lower position. Because the physical and intellectual resources in different categories and at different levels have different marginal productivity, the vertical hierarchy of occupations is determined by possession of the physical and intellectual resources. After such a reshuffle, people with relatively large amount of physical and intellectual resources in the stratum of workers moved to higher-level occupations; while those with less physical and intellectual resources in the stratum of workers moved downward by being laid off, being forced to retire, being dismissed with compensations based on the length of service, and so on. The stratum of workers becomes a group merely in possession of physical force and basic operational skills. Unless their possession of intellectual resources is significantly improved, they will remain in the stratum of workers.

Laborers' individual resources consist of (1) human resources including the above-mentioned physical and intellectual resources, conformity resources, and diligence-effort resources, and (2) social resources.

Human resources are the most critical factor that determines the match between laborers and positions in organizations. In fact, individual's social mobility is the process in which a laborer successively matches with positions in various categories at different levels according to his particular human resources. An abundance of human resources determines an individual's social mobility space. People in possession of the highest level of physical and intellectual resources, conformity resources, and diligence-effort resources can choose among positions at almost all levels. As a rational laborer, the basic orientation of individual choice is maximization of benefits, i.e., getting the position that can bring maximal benefits (including material, social, mental, and psychological benefits, etc.) with minimal costs. In a particular social cultural context, various occupations are ranked into a vertical hierarchy in which occupations at higher levels have relatively high rates of return; therefore, people are inclined to choose high-level positions. However, because of the disparity in resources possessed by different people, those without particular resources will pay very high cost for unfitness when they take up high-level positions. Accordingly, people have to pursue the maximization of benefits within the limitation of possessed resources. For example, some workers feel that the highly intellect-based management and operation activities assumed by an entrepreneur is a kind of mental pain and psychological torture; therefore, they prefer physical labor with a regular working schedule and less apprehension to being a boss.

The match between laborers and occupational positions is a process of interaction between organizational choices and personal choices. The result of such interaction is the hierarchically corresponding relationship between discrepant human resources and vertical position structure; consequently, human resources become the most important factor for individual social mobility. As a result, in the free-market system, people occupying the positions of workers usually have relatively low level of human resources, especially with relatively sufficient physical force and skills but less professional knowledge and management capability. The upward mobility of workers is the outcome of a rise in the value of their human resources. On one hand, only in possession of the particular human resources required by higher-level positions could workers achieve upward mobility; on the other hand, pushed by the motivation to achieve maximal benefits, once a worker improve his or her personal resources significantly, it is unlikely that he or she will still stay in the position of worker. Correspondingly, workers' downward mobility is the result of devaluation of their human resources. Usually, such devaluation occurs in three situations. The first situation is degeneration of the labor force; for example, physical ability declines with age and operational skills arc hindered due to failing eyesight. The second situation is due to changes in the work itself; for example, a manually operated lathe is replaced by a digitally controlled lathe and workers' operational skills become out of date. The third situation is due to changes in work requirements; for example, workers in particular management settings of state-owned enterprises were used to being in positions of lower-level diligence and effort with poor stamina. When their enterprises were merged with foreign companies in the free-market economy and required higher-level diligence and effort, many workers maintained their original work levels. Therefore, as the result of the devaluation of human resources, some workers are laid off or dismissed. After having experienced such social selections of upward and downward mobility, people in the position of worker almost are always those who have sufficient physical force and operational skills and are deficient in other resources.

The basic condition of upward mobility for workers is the upgrade of human resources. Such upgrade is not only determined by an individual's subjective motivation, but also is restricted by his or her internal and external conditions. In other words, an individual's endowments and efforts determine the content and degree of his or her human resource upgrade. In the planned system, conformity resources such as political loyalty were attached with great importance by organizations. Some workers depended on their endowments and individual efforts to enhance such resources rapidly, such as actively participating in political activities and joining the Party, and hence achieved upward mobility. In contrast, some workers did not enhance these resources significantly; they either merely improved their skill resources based on endowments and efforts or went on as it was under the protection of "iron rice bowls" and hence permanently staying in the stratum of workers. After the reform and opening-up, the value of intellectual resources increases and the boundary between the status of workers and the status of managerial personnel is broken. Some workers enhanced their intellectual resources with advanced studies or trainings and achieved upward mobility; some workers enhanced their human resources simultaneously with the changes of assignments and tasks but failed to upgrade these resources according to the requirements of positions at higher levels, so they had to stay in the position of workers; some were still unwilling to or unable to enhance their intellectual resources and skill resources even in face of layoffs and unemployment and had to move downward. In general, due to workers' endowments and external conditions, enhancement of conformity resources (especial political loyalty) is relatively easy, while upgrade of human resources is comparatively difficult; accordingly, it is more likely for workers to achieve upward mobility in the planned system than in the free-market system. The stress of life, opportunity cost, accumulation of knowledge, and learning ability of workers limit the development of their intellectual resources or even skill resources and hence negatively affect their efforts of achieving upward mobility and holding current jobs.

Besides human resources, social resources also have an influence on the match between individuals and positions and on occupational mobility. In this study, social resources refer to social connections and corresponding actors that can facilitate the connection between individual applicants for jobs and organizational selectors and influence the latter. For example, a worker's father is the section-chief of the county labor bureau; the father is familiar with the personnel manager of a company and has a certain degree of influence on the decision making of personnel recruitment and promotion in that company. In this case, the father and his influence are that worker's social resources. The effects of social resources mainly work in four aspects. The first aspect is delivery of information. The organizational selector is in the status of incomplete information and always attempts to collect relevant information about applicants for jobs, while social networks can help applicants deliver their unique personal information to the organizational selector and attract particular attention. The second aspect is the explanation of one's resources status. The organizational selector needs to know each candidate's resource status, while social networks can help individual applicants present his or her image in an optimal way and explain how a candidate's possession of resources meet the requirements of a higher-level position to the organizational selector. The third aspect is the influence of power. According to Max Weber, social custom produces power. Over thousands of years, ethical norms in China endow the both sides in social connections with the power (or right) to put forward request and ask for help from one another and with the obligation to accept the other side's request and offer corresponding help. An individual applicant's request is delivered to decision makers in the organization through such a power-obligation relationship. The fourth aspect is social exchange. Besides the functional orientation, a decision maker in an organization also has an orientation for self-service. Social networks enable individual applicants to transfer various "personal goods" to organizational selector and help an individual with social resources obtain the desired position. Social resources are a sort of amplifier to human resources. Between two candidates with the same level of human resources, the one who possesses stronger social connections has the greater chance to obtain a position than the other does. Even though the overall quality of human resources of candidate A is better than that of candidate B, it is very likely that the latter will be the winner in the competition if candidate A has stronger social networks. Social resources are the pushing force for upward mobility but the restraining power for downward mobility.

In the planned system, personnel allocations in organizations were subjected to planning management and administrative approval; the powerful public authority limited the scope and degree of the influence of social resources. Meanwhile, because of the equalitarian orientation in distributing welfare among various strata and higher status of workers, some people with social resources (especially with backgrounds of power) entered the position of worker as well. In such situation, social resources possessed by different social strata were roughly at the same level. After the reform and opening-up, the state public authority has basically withdrawn from the field of organizational personnel allocation and the organizations obtained independent decision-making power in employment; accordingly, social resources have regained the environments to come into play. The gaps in socio-economic status between various strata have been widening rapidly. People in the stratum of workers are generally those with relatively deficient human resources and social resources. In consequence, such phenomenon leads to the negative cycle between the deficient congenital social resources, human resources, and acquired social resources. Workers now are in an even more disadvantaged situation; it is difficult for them to achieve upward social mobility, yet they have a greater possibility of being subjected to downward mobility.

In the following sections, based on the above explanatory framework, we will analyze the characteristics of workers and their upward and downward social mobility.

CHARACTERISTICS OF WORKERS: WHO ARE THEY

What are the characteristics of workers in modern China? In other words, who are in the stratum of workers? According to the above-mentioned explanatory framework, in the free-market economy employers select employees based on the principle of economic efficiency and match laborers with positions according to the mechanisms of the labor market; people in the stratum of workers are those with relatively deficient human resources and social resources.

The intellectual level of workers can be measured by multiple indicators, of which the level of education received by workers is the most important and objective one. Analysis on data of the fifth national population census in 2000 shows that the average years of schooling of workers were fewer than that of organizational principals, professional and technical personnel and clerical personnel; somewhat more than that of people engaging in agriculture, forestry, husbandry and fishing. The average years of schooling of professional and technical personnel were the highest, i.e., 12.8 years; organizational principals and clerical personnel were 11.9 years. In the stratum of workers, service personnel was 9 years, production and transportation workers 9.1 years, and commercial personnel 9.4 years. The average years of schooling of workers was more than 3 years fewer than that of professional and technical personnel.

Production and transportation workers make up a majority of the stratum of workers. Since the 1970s, because of the "reshuffle" brought about by socio-economic reforms, the average years of schooling of this group have not increased but decreased. According to the survey in two large-size state-owned enterprises conducted by this research group, the average years of schooling of production and transportation workers was 12.6 years before 1974, 12.3 years in 1975, 12.3 years in 1980, 12.1 years in 1985, 11.8 years in 1990, 12 years in 1995, and 11.8 years in 2000. In contrast, the average years of schooling of clerical personnel tend to increase; the figures in the corresponding years were respectively 13.6 years, 14 years, 13.4 years, 13.7 years, 13.9 years, 14.3 years, and 14.1 years. The general path of upward mobility for workers is to enter the group of clerical personnel at first, and then move upward to organizational principals. The expanding gap in the level of education received between production and transportation workers and clerical personnel indicates that the link between the two groups tends to be broken; as a result, many workers cannot enter the group of clerical personnel and are "frozen" in their positions.

In the stratum of workers, the average years of schooling of commercial personnel tend to increase. In two surveyed large-size enterprises, the average years of schooling of people engaging in commerce and marketing were 11.8 years before 1974, 12.6 years in 1975, 12.2 years in 1980, 12.1 years in 1985, 12.8 years in 1990, 12.9 years in 1995, and 13.3 in 2000. The educational level of these personnel was similar to that of production and transportation workers before the 1970s while significantly outstripped the latter and close to that of commercial personnel at the end of the twentieth century. Such changes mean that production and transportation workers not only have encountered intellectual barriers in the movement toward clerical personnel, but also needed greater efforts in order to enter the ranks of commercial personnel. Contrarily, commercial and marketing personnel are more eligible to move to the group of clerical personnel.

An important channel of in-service intellectual enhancement is to receive trainings, including trainings on cultural quality, professional skills, and position qualifications. In a situation in which social mobility is determined by intellectual level, the amount of training received by workers is positively correlated to the possibility of upward mobility; that is, if two people (say, A and B) have same intellectual level while A received relatively more trainings than B, A will have a greater chance to move upward. Results of the survey in two large-size state-owned enterprises indicate that, compared with organizational principals and clerical personnel, trainings received by workers are insufficient. Since the 1990s, the average length of training received by senior principals in enterprises are 548 days, middle-level principals 456 days, clerical personnel 140 days, production workers 54 days, transportation workers 49 days, and commercial and marketing personnel only 12 days. The relatively wide gaps in the length of training lead to the difference in the enhanced level of intellect between different strata and hence widen the divide, which workers have to span in the way of upward mobility.

Compared with their low intellectual level, workers' physical ability is better than that of other strata with higher status. Age, gender, and registered residence status usually are considered as objective measures of physical ability; generally, physical ability of younger people are better than that of older ones, males are more physically fit than females, and people with registered rural residence are better than those with urban registered residence (in terms of physical force paid in labor activities). Data from the national population census show that the average age of production and transportation workers is the youngest (32.8 years); service personnel (average 34 years) and commercial personnel (average 35.6 years) are also relatively young. In contrast, the average age of organizational principals is the highest (41.5 years), as is the clerical personnel (37.3 years). In terms of gender, the proportion of the males in workers is lower than that in clerical personnel and organizational principals. As to the registered residence status, the proportion of people with registered rural residence in workers is significantly higher than that in strata with higher status. The proportion of people with registered rural residence in production and transportation workers is as high as 61.8 percent; this production is 54.7 percent in clerical personnel, and 50.4 percent in commercial personnel. People with registered rural residence have become the majority of the stratum of workers (see Table 9-1).

An important indicator of workers' conformity in the planned system is the membership of the Communist Party of China. Such status indicated that one accepted the ideology of the Party and was willing to fulfill the liability endowed by the Party and follow its disciplines. In the free-market system, although the indicating effect of the Party membership has been weakening, generally the conformity of Party members is still better than that of ordinary people, such as obeying organizational commands, voluntarily providing services for organizations and others, and so forth. When this indicator is used to measure the conformity of workers, the result is significantly weaker than that of strata with higher status. According to the survey conducted in this study, the proportion of Party members in organizational principals is the highest (64.2 percent), and it is also relatively high in clerical personnel (37.5 percent); in contrast, this proportion is only 8 percent in production and transportation workers, 8.3 percent in commercial personnel, and 10.7 percent in service personnel.

Table 9-1   Average Age, Years of Education, and Proportion of Males in Various Occupations

Occupation	Age	Proportion of Males	Proportion of Registered Non-Rural Residence	Years of Education
Organizational principal	41.5	83.5	74.2	11.9
Professional and technical personnel	35.7	48.2	84.9	12.8
Clerical personnel	37.3	70.0	84.3	11.9
Commercial personnel	35.6	50.8	49.6	9.4
Service personnel	34.0	49.3	45.3	9.0
Production and transportation worker	32.8	66.5	38.1	9.1
Agricultural, forestry, husbandry and fishing Personnel	39.3	51.5	1.8	6.8

Source: The fifth national population census.

In essence, conformity means that the individual is treated as a part of the giant machine of the organization, voluntarily assume the function assigned by the organization, and closely cooperate with related co-workers. Whether a worker regards himself as a part of the organization or not depends on his perception regarding the relationship between himself or herself and the organization; that is, whether he looks upon the organization as an organic whole which integrates with him or her, or just treats it as one way to achieve his or her personal objectives. The survey in two large-size state-owned enterprises indicates that the higher one's occupational level is, the greater his or her conformity will be; he or she will consider the organization as a "collective assimilating individuals", "an enterprise to be flourish and thriving", an arena to carve out one's career, and "a completely dependable place". In contrast, the conformity of workers is significantly weaker than that of people with higher status, and they are more inclined to treat the organization as one way to "earn money and make a living", "a place to sell and buy labor", or even "a factory in which one pays much but gets very little" (see Table 9-2). The same difference is also evident in the attitudes towards the relations with colleagues. Organizational principals, professional and clerical personnel often believe that colleagues, superiors, and subordinates are "comrades with the same goals" and "staff members and workers cooperating in work"; in contrast, workers usually believe that colleagues are "rivals" and superiors are "people exploiting and oppressing us" (see Table 9-2).

Table 9-2   Perception of Respondents with Different Occupations Regarding the Meaning of Organizations

Unit: %

Occupation	A place to earn money to support family	A collective assimilating individuals	A warm and reliable family	An enterprise to be flourish and thriving	An arena to pursue a career and fulfill one's value	A factory in which one pays much but gets very little	An enterprise in which one is the master	A completely dependable place	A place to sell and buy labor
Organizational principals	53.1	24.4	4.1	12.2	64.3	27.0	17.6	10.8	—
Professional and technical personnel	66.0	18.3	5.7	6.2	55.2	15.2	11.9	19.0	7.9
Clerical personnel	60.0	20.9	8.4	2.1	52.6	19.8	14.6	21.5	8.3
Commercial & service personnel	77.3	17.4	10.1	8.6	40.6	33.4	15.4	8.3	5.6
Production and transportation workers	75.3	15.1	8.0	4.7	26.0	57.1	15.4	9.3	14.9

Source: The survey in large-size enterprises conducted by this research group.

How are workers' diligence and effort? In this aspect, they are also worse than those in strata with higher status are. As to the question "if the total energy in a working day is 100 percent, what is the proportion of energy you usually invest in your own job", the average proportion that was provided in answers of organizational principals in two surveyed large-size state-owned enterprises was 84.1 percent; clerical personnel was 82.4 percent, while production and transportation worker was merely 75.1 percent. In answers to the question "according to the situation of organization and the remunerations offered to you, what is the appropriate proportion of energy you think should be used in your own job", the expected value of organizational principals was 75.7 percent, clerical personnel was 72.7 percent, while production and transportation worker was merely 64.8 percent. Several types of behaviors that frequently occur in enterprises were listed in the questionnaire and respondents were asked to self-evaluate in which aspects their performance was outstanding. The proportion of believing oneself to "work actively without consideration of returns" was 74.1 percent in organizational principals, 62.7 percent in clerical personnel and 45.2 percent in production and transportation workers.

An important indicator of social resources is the amount of social connections and the occupational status of actors in such social connections. Seeing that usually father is the most intimate actor involved in one's social connection, who is more likely to provide help for his children proactively with all efforts, father's occupation is treated as a type of important social resources in this study. Data obtained from the nationwide survey conducted by this research group show that the intergenerational inheritance between father's occupation and children's occupation is very strong. For example, production and transportation workers' children are more likely to be production and transportation workers, commercial personnel's children have a greater chance to be commercial personnel, so do children of professional and technical personnel and organizational principals. In Table 9-3, this tendency is indicated by figures in the diagonal from the upper left to the lower right, which are higher than other figures in this table. Such a highly significant corresponding relationship between father' occupation and children' occupation shows the inheritance effect of stratum status. Workers and their fathers often situate in the same stratum.

Table 9-3   Father' Occupations of Respondents in Different Occupations

Unit: %

Father's Occupation / Respondent's Occupation	Organizational principal	Professional and technical personnel	Clerical personnel	Commercial personnel	Service personnel	Agricultural, forestry, husbandry and fishing personnel	Production and transportation worker
Organizational principal	14.2	9.0	7.1	5.6	3.7	48.5	11.9
Professional and technical personnel	8.5	23.9	8.2	4.1	4.4	35.5	15.4
Clerical personnel	12.4	8.8	17.2	5.6	6.2	31.4	18.4
Commercial personnel	5.3	3.9	7.9	9.7	4.7	47.3	21.1
Service personnel	6.3	4.9	6.3	6.3	11.1	42.4	22.9
Production & transportation worker	2.9	2.9	4.3	4.3	1.4	79.7	4.3
Agricultural, forestry, husbandry and fishing personnel	4.9	5.1	5.8	4.7	3.9	49.6	26.0

Source: The nationwide survey conducted by this research group.

ENTRIES OF THE STRATUM: WHO BECAME WORKERS

From the very beginning of one's career, the level of human resources determines those who became workers and those who became professional and technical personnel and clerical personnel. In the planned economy, the government formally stipulated that only people with technical secondary school and higher education could be cadres, while those with lower level of education could only become workers. In the free-market system, the boundary of educational background requirements between workers and cadres is removed literally, however, in recruitment activities in the labor market, a key qualification of eligible applicants for white-collar occupations, such as clerks and professional and technical personnel, is college and higher educational background, or even university and higher educational background. Very few people with education lower than the level of senior middle school are employed as clerical personnel and professional and technical personnel. Unless they start their own enterprises, people with lower level of education have little chance to be organizational principals.

Data collected from the survey of the study indicate that the first entry of occupations at various levels is positively related to the level of education received by entrants. Before 1978, the average years of schooling of people whose first occupation was service personnel was 6.7 years, people becoming production and transportation workers was 6.8 years, commercial personnel 7.6 years, clerical personnel 8.7 years, and professional and technical personnel 10.8 years. As time went on, the average years of schooling of people entering the stratum of workers has been increasing. For example, the average years of schooling of people entering the group of production and transportation workers was 6.8 years before the reform and opening-up (before 1978), 9 years in the early days of reform and opening-up (1979~1986), 9.2 years in the first stage of the labor system reform (1987~1991), and 9.6 years in the second stage of the labor system reform (since 1992). The growth of average years of schooling of people entering the group of commercial personnel is even more significant, which has increased from 7.6 years before 1978 to 11 years after 1992. However, the qualifications of educational background for people to be clerical personnel and professional and technical personnel has risen correspondingly; the qualification for clerical personnel has grown from 8.7 years to 12.3 years and professional and technical personnel from 10.8 years to 12.9 years. The growth of required years of education for organizational principals is the most significant, increasing from 8.1 years to 13 years (see Table 9-4).

Table 9-4   Years of Schooling of People Starting Their First Jobs in Different Periods

Unit: Year

Period group of the time starting the first job	Agricultural, forestry, husbandry & fishing personnel	Production & transportation worker	Service personnel	Commercial personnel	Clerical personnel	Professional and technical personnel	Organizational principal
Before 1978	6.3	6.8	6.7	7.6	8.7	10.8	8.1
1979~1986	7.1	9.0	9.8	9.7	10.1	11.1	13.8
1987~1991	6.9	9.2	8.5	8.4	12.3	12.3	10.5
After 1992	8.5	9.6	9.5	11.0	12.3	12.9	13.0

Source: Nationwide survey conducted by this research group.

Because the required level of education received is relatively low, and the time of entering the first occupation is earlier, people whose first job is that of workers are relatively young. Before 1978, the average age of people becoming production and transportation workers and commercial personnel was 19 years and people becoming professional and technical personnel and organizational principals was 20 years on average. Workers usually start to work and earn money earlier than those with higher occupational status do. Many families and people choose to end their studies early and enter into the stratum of workers. However, analysis in the following section shows that people entering occupations earlier usually will lose the key precondition of upward mobility, i.e., higher level of education received; consequently, they do not have the same upward mobility opportunity as people who enter occupations relatively later. Corresponding to the tendency that the years of schooling of workers have been increasing over time, the average age of people becoming workers has been growing as well. Before 1978, the average age of people entering the occupation of transportation workers was 19 years, which grew to 20 years after 1992. Correspondingly, the average age of people becoming professional and technical personnel and organizational principals increased from 20 years to 21 years as well.

The gender proportions of people who enter various groups in the stratum of workers are different. The majority of people whose first job is that of production and transportation workers are men. Between the 1970s and the end of the twentieth century, the proportion of males was more than 52 percent. The majority of people whose first job is service personnel is women. In the same period, the proportion of males was less than 47 percent. The proportion of females whose first job is commercial personnel is higher than that of males, which was over 55 percent. The majority of people who entered the groups of professional and technical personnel and organizational principals are men; especially, more than 60 percent of organizational principals are men.

An apparent fact is that social resources possessed by people whose first occupation was workers are relatively deficient. In other words, it is more likely that the first occupation of people with deficient social resources will be that of worker. In contrast, it is more likely that the first occupation of people with sufficient social resources will be clerical personnel or other occupations with higher status. Similar to the tendency in Table 9-3, a significant occupational inheritance is also revealed in Table 9-5; that is, the level of people's first occupation has a significantly positive correlation with the level of their fathers' occupations when they found their first jobs. For example, people whose fathers' occupation was production and transportation worker at that time were more likely to be production and transportation workers, service personnel, and commercial personnel. People whose fathers were service personnel at that time were more likely to be service personnel, and people whose fathers were commercial personnel were more likely to be commercial personnel; members of both groups had a relatively lower chance of being production and transportation workers. People whose fathers were clerical personnel at that time were more likely to be clerical personnel and professional and technical personnel and people whose fathers were professional and technical personnel were more likely to be professional and technical personnel and clerical personnel; members of both groups seldom became production and transportation workers. People whose fathers were organizational principals at that time were more likely to be organizational principals and professional and technical personnel rather than commercial personnel, service personnel, and production and transportation workers. Because workers possess deficient human resources and economic resources and have little influence on the decision making of employers, their children have to enter the stratum of workers at a lower occupational level.

Another apparent fact is that, with the advance of the reform and opening-up, the positive correlation between the level of abundance of social resources and the level of first occupation has been increasingly significant; accordingly, the phenomenon of occupational inheritance has become increasingly remarkable. In other words, as time goes on, more and more workers' children have entered the stratum of workers, while more and more children of organizational principals have assumed the positions of organizational principals in their first jobs. According to the survey of this study, before 1978 the proportion of organizational principals' children whose first occupation was organizational principal to the overall number of respondents whose first occupation was organizational principal was 6.1 percent. This proportion increased to 12.5 percent between 1979~1986; it rose to 50 percent between 1987~1991 and reached nearly 100 percent after 1992. The corresponding proportion of clerical personnel's children whose first occupation was clerical personnel was 11.8 percent before 1978, 15.3 percent between 1979~1986 and 23.8 percent after 1987. In contrast, the proportion of production and transportation workers' children whose first occupation was clerical personnel to the overall number of people whose first occupation was clerical personnel was 17.2 percent before 1978 and 31 percent between 1979~1991; it grew rapidly to 41.7 percent after 1992. On the other hand, the opportunity for children of production and transportation workers to become organizational principals and clerical personnel in their first jobs has decreased sharply. Before 1978, the proportion of production and transportation workers' children whose first occupation was organizational principal was 15.2 percent; it was reduced to 12.5 percent between 1979~1986 and fell to zero after 1987 (see Table 9-5).

Even if the status of workers in the urban occupational hierarchy is at a lower level, not everyone who wants to be a worker can achieve what one wishes. In a labor market in which the supply exceeds the demand, many job seekers are excluded from the occupation of worker. In this case, besides higher-level human resources, social resources are also important for people to enter the stratum of workers. In particular, when human resources are relatively deficient, social resources play a critical role. In other words, although workers' children have a greater possibility to be workers than children of organizational principals do, it is very likely that they even cannot enter the stratum of workers if they do not have necessary social resources. In one case, a truck driver in a state-owned enterprise quitted to be a taxi driver and then he gave up this job because the wages in this industry declined. Afterwards, he hunted for jobs in the labor market for about two years, including applying for jobs posted in employment advertisements, attending career fairs, resorting to employment agencies, etc., but he failed to find any employers who wanted to hire him. Having no choice, he had to ask for help from a distant relative who worked in local labor bureau. His relative then introduced him to a company and persuaded the company to accept him.

Table 9-5 Proportions of Respondents Whose First Occupations Were Concurrently the Same with Their Fathers' Occupations in their Own Strata

Unit: %

Respondent's First Occupation	Year	Father's Occupation						
		Organizational principal	Professional and technical personnel	Clerical personnel	Commercial personnel	Service Personnel	Agricultural, forestry, husbandry and fishing personnel	Production & transportation worker
Organizational Principal	Before 1978	6.1	—	—	6.1	9.1	63.6	15.2
	1979-1986	12.5	12.5	12.5	12.5	—	37.5	12.5
	1997-1991	50.0	—	—	—	—	50.0	—
	After 1992	100.0	—	—	—	—	—	—
Professional and Technical Personnel	Before 1978	6.4	11.8	7.5	9.1	3.7	50.3	11.2
	1979-1986	20.3	15.3	11.9	3.4	—	40.7	8.5
	1997-1991	11.9	23.8	19.0	2.4	—	33.3	9.5
	After 1992	14.3	23.8	9.5	—	4.8	33.3	14.3
Clerical Personnel	Before 1978	5.1	6.1	8.2	11.2	7.1	50.0	12.2
	1979-1986	18.8	6.3	20.8	6.3	—	25.0	22.9
	1997-1991	8.3	33.3	16.7	—	—	25.0	16.7
	After 1992	4.5	13.6	31.8	4.5	—	40.9	4.5
Commercial Personnel	Before 1978	8.5	10.6	12.8	12.8	4.3	38.3	12.8
	1979-1986	17.1	11.4	5.7	14.3	5.7	28.6	17.1
	1997-1991	5.6	—	5.6	22.2	—	27.8	38.9
	After 1992	8.7	13.0	8.7	17.4	13.0	17.4	21.7
Service Personnel	Before 1978	6.3	4.7	6.3	9.4	9.4	46.9	17.2
	1979-1986	13.2	5.3	10.5	7.9	13.2	18.4	31.6
	1997-1991	12.5	6.3	6.3	—	18.8	25.0	31.3
	After 1992	—	2.8	2.8	8.3	8.3	36.1	41.7
Production & Transportation Worker	Before 1978	5.8	4.0	5.8	9.8	5.2	37.9	31.5
	1979-1986	7.1	6.1	13.2	5.1	3.0	28.4	37.1
	1997-1991	8.2	3.5	3.5	1.2	2.4	43.5	37.6
	After 1992	7.4	2.9	5.9	2.9	2.9	50.0	27.9

Source: The nationwide survey conducted by this research group.

However, in a background check, this company found that the state-owned enterprise in which the driver formerly worked was one of its subsidiaries; according to the employment policy of the company, no one who quits from the company should be reemployed. Thus, the human resources department of the company informed the driver that he would not be hired for this reason. Fortunately, another distant relative of this driver had connections with the administering authority in charge of appointment of the general manager of the company. After the principal of the administering authority communicating with the general manager, the latter decided to make an exception to reemploy this man as a van driver. This man's experience, whose age was less than 40 years, indicates that workers with deficient social resources will be in a very disadvantaged position in the labor market with particular situations in China.

It is worthwhile to point out that, after the reform and opening-up, a large number of the rural population have started to migrate to urban areas and peasant-workers have become the main body of the stratum of workers. Chapter 10 gives a detailed analysis on this issue.

OUTLETS OF THE STRATUM: WHO MOVES UPWARD

According to the explanatory framework proposed in Section 1 and the analyses on characteristics and entries of the stratum of workers, the answer to the question "who among workers can achieve upward mobility" is palpable, that is, workers with abundant human resources and sufficient social resources have the opportunity to move upward. In contemporary Chinese society, one with lower-quality human resources but supported by sufficient social resources will still have a relatively good chance to achieve upward mobility. Similarly, even without sufficient social resources, if one's human resources are relatively abundant or rise in value rapidly, he or she can accomplish upward mobility likewise and such upward mobility has stronger potential than that of the former case. Of course, if one is in possession of abundant social resources and human resources at the same time, he or she will have a far greater chance to move upward than others do.

In this study, *upward mobility of workers* refers to social mobility in which one moves from the position of worker to the positions of clerical personnel, professional and technical personnel, and organizational principal at higher levels. In traditional state-owned enterprises, such mobility was simplified to the promotion from workers to cadres. According to the status hierarchy of various strata, the upward mobility ladder of workers usually should consist of the clerical position as the first step, the professional position as the second step, and the organizational principal position as the last step. However, in reality workers' upward mobility seldom follows such a "typical order". The "actual path of mobility" generally is as follows: moving from worker to clerical personnel and then from clerical personnel to organizational principal, or settling in the position of clerical personnel. Other possible paths (for example, moving from worker to professional and technical personnel and then from professional and technical personnel to organizational principal, or being promoting directly from the position of worker to the position of organizational principal) occur now and then but are not the main stream. The survey in two large-size state-owned enterprises shows that cadres promoted from workers are likely to take charge of the positions of office administration and department chiefs, while people who were cadres all the time are more likely to enter into development, research, design, and technical positions (see Table 9-6).

Table 9-6   Occupations of Respondents with Different Mobility Paths in Enterprises

Unit:%

Category	First-line production worker	Auxiliary production worker	Logistic Service worker	Workshop technician	Workshop/plant administrative cadre	R&D and design staff	Office administrative cadre
As a worker all the time	46.3	36.7	12.6	2.4	0.6	0.3	1.0
As a cadre all the time	0.4	0.8	6.8	15.7	8.4	11.6	56.3
Once a worker now is a cadre	0.4	0.2	4.8	7.2	21.7	2.9	62.7
Once a worker now is a temporary cadre	4.8	8.1	16.1	4.8	32.3	—	33.9

Source: The survey of large-size enterprises conducted by this research group.

Among three groups in the stratum of workers, commercial personnel have relatively more opportunities of upward mobility and can move up to higher levels; clerical personnel have the least opportunities and the shortest mobility path, and can only reach comparatively lower levels; production and transportation workers are in the middle of the first two groups. Data collected from the survey in this study show that, by the time of retirement or being surveyed, 19.2 percent of respondents whose first jobs were commercial personnel ascended to clerical personnel and 12.3 percent of them moved up to organizational principals. Among production and transportation workers, the corresponding proportions respectively were 14.4 percent and 6.6 percent; among clerical personnel, the corresponding proportions respectively were 8 percent and 4 percent. However, very few commercial personnel entered into professional and technical positions, while a lot of clerical personnel and production and transportation workers moved into these positions.

Because higher-status occupations require higher-level intellect, workers entering into higher-level positions usually have higher level of education than other ordinary workers do. According to data from the survey in two large-size state-owned enterprises, the average years of schooling of workers who were promoted to cadres are two to four years longer than that of workers in the same age group. For example, the average years of schooling of workers being promoted to cadres before 1977 were 14.5 years, while workers in the same age group were 10.5 years. For workers being promoted to cadres between 1978~1984, the figure was 14.1 years, while workers in the same age group was 9.4 years; for workers being promoted to cadres after 1992, the figure was 14 years, while workers in the same age group was 12 years.

Nonetheless, compared with respondents who had been cadres since they went into work, the average years of schooling of workers being promoted to cadres were still fewer, less than at least one year. The average years of schooling of workers being promoted to senior principals of enterprises were 14.3 years; while for those who had been cadres since they went into work and then assumed senior principal positions, this figure was 15.4 years. The average years of schooling of workers entering into professional personnel positions were 14 years; while for professional personnel who had been cadres since they went into work, this figure was 15 years. Among technical personnel, the figures were 14.5 years and 15.5 years respectively.

The higher level of education received by workers who were promoted to cadres than that of ordinary workers is due to the following two factors: First, they received longer formal schooling years before entering into the occupation of worker; second, they received more training and adult education. Among workers being promoted to be cadres, since 1990 the average length of training received by respondents who were at the age of 50 to 59 was 153 days, while workers in the same age group was only 38 days, and respondents who were cadres all the time in the same age group was 70 days. However, such difference has declined gradually as time goes on because workers have started to receive more training. For example, in the age group of 30~39, the average length of training received by respondents who were promoted from workers to cadres were 220 days, respondents who were workers all the time 135 days, and respondents who were cadres all the time 145 days.

The difference in years of schooling between cadres who came from workers and cadres who were cadres all the time means that the mobility from workers to cadres not only depends on the intellectual level determined by formal educational backgrounds, but also relies on the organizing and operating capabilities and longer practical experience based on higher-quality endowments. This statement is supported by the fact that the difference in years of schooling does not exist between managerial personnel at various levels in state-owned enterprises. Among cadres being promoted from workers, the average years of schooling of senior principals were 14.3 years, middle-level principals 14.4 years, grassroots-level principals 14.2 years, and ordinary managerial personnel 14.3 years. Workers' upward mobility to the position of cadres mainly depended on higher level of education received, while cadres' ascending in the hierarchy of cadre ranks mainly relied on general capability and special talent determined by multiple factors.

The proportion of Party members among workers who achieved upward mobility was 79.4 percent; among respondents who were workers all the time, this proportion was 27.4 percent; among respondents who were cadres all the time, it was 59.8 percent. It means that the upward mobility from workers to cadres required higher-level conformity, especially with respect to political loyalty. The difference in status and educational backgrounds between workers and people who were cadres all the time indicates that workers' upward mobility required relatively high political loyalty and loyalty to the enterprises. Besides people who were formally included in the authorized quota of cadres, a group of workers who acted as temporary cadres also existed in state-owned enterprises. These workers could not become formal cadres for some reasons, such as lower level of education received. Because the gap between this group of workers and people who were cadres all the time was even wider, correspondingly the proportion of Party member in this group was larger (82.5 percent). That is to say, entering into the position of temporary cadres required higher political loyalty and organizational loyalty than ascending from workers to formal cadres did. In addition, the earlier the time when workers were promoted to be cadres, the higher the proportion of Pparty members. For example, the proportion of Party members in workers who were promoted to be cadres was 95.7 percent in 1977, 86.4 percent in 1978~1984, 81.9 percent in 1985~1991, and 67.6 percent after 1992. One possible explanation of this phenomenon is that the earlier the time, the stricter the requirement of Party membership in promotion of cadres. Another possible reason is that people who became cadres in earlier time had more opportunities to join the Party thereafter.

In terms of conformity, compared with people who were workers all along, workers who achieved upward mobility were more inclined to regard individuals as a part of the organization, proactively assume the responsibility assigned by the organization, and closely cooperate with co-workers. Data from the survey in two large-size state-owned enterprises indicate that, in the former group, the proportion of respondents who regarded the organization as "an enterprise in which one is the master", "a collective assimilating individuals" and "a completely dependable place" was relatively larger, while in the latter group, the proportion of respondents who looked upon the organization as "a place to earn money to support family", "a place to sell and buy labor" and "a factory in which one pays much but gets very little" was relatively larger. When they were asked to answer the question "if employees have their own choice, where will their loyalty be attached", the former group inclined to stay loyal to the organization, including the Party organization in enterprises, local departments and divisions, and superiors; the latter group tended to attach their loyalty to other individuals, such as good friends in the organization. In addition, more respondents in the former group reported that they were outstanding in "obeying the leadership and commands", while more respondents in the latter group admitted that they once had conflicts with their superiors and disobedience to commands.

Not only in state-owned enterprises, but also in private enterprises and foreign-invested enterprises, the upward mobility requires higher-level conformity. Foreign-invested enterprises usually emphasize the conformity and team spirit; private enterprises give prominence to the loyalty to enterprises and employers. Many private entrepreneurs even attach more importance to loyalty than to intelligence and ability.

Higher-level diligence and effort is a critical factor for workers to achieve upward mobility. They can make up the deficiency in their educational level by diligence and effort. Moreover, their prominent achievements among colleagues are also indicated by diligence and effort. In other words, workers who achieved upward mobility successfully are usually people who take initiative and are willing, hardworking and able to endure hardships without consideration of remunerations.

Such characteristics distinguish them from people who were workers or cadres all the time. In terms of the proportion of energy invested in jobs in a working day, cadres promoted from workers and workers acting as temporary cadres were the highest (respectively 83.3 percent and 86.1 percent); while respondents who were workers all the time was the lowest (77.1 percent) as well as respondents being cadres all the time (78 percent). In terms of expected energy distribution affected by current salaries and benefits, cadres promoted from workers and workers acting as temporary cadres were the highest (respectively 76.3 percent and 76.1 percent), while respondents being workers all the time was the lowest (66 percent) as well as respondents being cadres all the time (68 percent). In addition, 71.9 percent of cadres who were promoted from workers evaluated themselves as "active with initiative and without consideration of remunerations". This proportion was 77.8 percent among workers acting as temporary cadres, while only 44.4 percent among respondents who were workers all the time, and 53.5 percent among respondents who were cadres all the time

Father's occupational background also plays an important role in workers' upward mobility. Workers whose fathers were organizational principals, professional and technical personnel and clerical personnel had a greater chance to achieve upward mobility. Workers whose fathers were commercial personnel had a greater possibility to become temporary cadres but with fewer chances of being formal cadres. Workers whose fathers were production and transportation workers had a greater chance to be workers all the time and unable to move upward. However, compared with cadres promoted from workers, it was more likely that fathers of people being cadres all the time were organizational principals or higher-rank principals, while the majority of fathers of cadres promoted from workers were grassroots principals.

Similar to the increasing impact of father's occupation on children entering different positions, its influence on the upward mobility of workers has been growing in the progress of the reform and opening-up. Before 1977, among workers who achieved upward mobility, hardly anyone had a father holding the post of organizational principal. The proportion that father's occupation was organizational principal increased to 10.4 percent between 1978~1988; it was 10.7 percent between 1985~1991 and reached 12.3 percent after 1992. Accordingly, among workers who achieved upward mobility, the proportion of fathers' occupation was agricultural, forestry, husbandry and fishing personnel has been dropping gradually, the figures in corresponding periods respectively were 32.1 percent, 14.6 percent, 16 percent, and 12.3 percent.

On the other hand, fathers' different occupational backgrounds have different influences on the level that workers can reach in upward mobility. The influence of fathers who hold the posts of organizational principals on the upward mobility of workers has some limitations as well. According to data from the survey in two large-size state-owned enterprises, among division chiefs who were promoted from workers, all their fathers did not hold the post of organizational principal but were professional and technical personnel. Among deputy division chiefs who were promoted from workers, all their fathers were not organizational principals but professional and technical personnel, clerical personnel, production and transportation workers, and commercial personnel. Only among section chiefs and deputy section chiefs who were promoted from workers, some of them had fathers who were organizational principals (see Table 9-7). To some extent, this phenomenon indicates that fathers who hold the post of organizational principal cannot assist his children to be promoted to higher-level positions in an enterprise but only to middle-level positions. The influence of power in social resources is limited, the positions of senior principals in large-size state-owned enterprises require high-level intellect and ability, and parent's authority can hardly help children break through the limitations of intellect and ability. Division chiefs in large-size enterprises are usually appointed by appropriate authorities following various formal procedures; therefore, father's authority does not have a significant influence on appointers and the appointment procedures. When children have to compete with each other, their intellectual and ability limitations will hinder them from moving upward further.

Social resources also include friendship, an achievement factor. Data from the survey in two large-size state-owned enterprises show that, friends' occupational positions and corresponding influences, i.e., whether they have relations with the appointment authority, rather than the number of friends, are important for the upward mobility of workers. Cadres who were promoted from workers usually have many friends holding the positions of principals, including leading cadres at the enterprise level, cadres in the appropriate body of the enterprise, division chiefs in functional departments of the enterprise, cadres at the plant level, principals in functional departments at the plant level, workshop managers, ordinary cadres in departments at various levels, and so on. In contrast, friends of respondents who were workers all the time were mainly first-line workers, or at most were foremen and section chiefs. Compared with respondents who were cadres all the time, people in social networks of workers who achieved upward mobility were mainly cadres in appropriate bodies, cadres at the plant level, cadres in functional departments at the plant level, workshop managers, and ordinary cadres at the plant level. In contrast, friends of respondents who were cadres all the time were mainly section-level cadres in functional departments of the enterprise, ordinary cadres in workshops, and professional and technical personnel. In other words, workers who achieved upward mobility successfully have more friends in principal positions and with authority influences.

Social resources possessed by workers in upward mobility are characterized by a positive circle. On one hand, they established close social connections with people in higher-level positions with their own human resources and other resources in order to communicate with the authority; on the other hand, after they were promoted to higher-level positions, they could further their contact with people at senior positions through formal organizational structure and possessed authority. In contrast, people who were workers all the time usually were not good at establishing relationships with superiors and did not have the capability of communication through

356

social connections that are brought about by authority. As a result, the gaps in occupations and positions between the two groups have been expanding gradually.

Table 9-7   Fathers' Occupations of Respondents Promoted from Workers to Various Managerial Positions

Unit: %

Level of Position to be Promoted from Workers	Father's Occupation					
	Organizational principal	Professional and technical personnel	Clerical personnel	Commercial personnel	Production and transportation workers	Agricultural, forestry, husbandry and fishing personnel
Division-chief level	—	50.0	—	—	—	50.0
Deputy division-chief level	—	15.0	10.0	20.0	35.0	20.0
Section-chief level	9.1	14.5	18.2	3.6	34.5	20.0
Deputy section-chief level	12.9	16.1	9.7	—	35.5	25.8
Subsection-chief level	—	—	100.0	—	—	—
Without levels	11.2	25.8	10.1	2.2	34.8	15.7

Source: The survey of large-size enterprises conducted by this research group.

OUTGOING OF WORKERS: WHO WERE LAID-OFF OR UNEMPLOYED

In the planned economy, state-owned and collective enterprises carried out the permanent worker system in which workers had complete employment security, which could guarantee that they would not be laid off once they entered the enterprise. After the 1980s, state-owned enterprises started to optimize the organization of laborers and consequently some workers were out of work and had to wait for jobs within enterprises. The labor market reform initiated since 1992 and the system of all employees signing labor contracts carried out since 1995 have led to a large number of laid-off workers. In enterprises with other types of ownership, the phenomenon of dismissal and unemployment has universally existed since the day of their establishment. Such phenomenon solicits a question: among the group of workers, who are laid off or unemployed? Who continue to stay in that position? What is the logic of social selection in this process?

There is a vast body of literature dedicating to the exploration of the layoff of workers in state-owned enterprises. Multiple factors are involved in these studies. For example, the loss incurred in an enterprise and the adjustment of industrial structure may lead to layoffs of all personnel in an enterprise, whether workers or technicians, and whether people are capable or incompetent. However, according to the explanatory framework and the analytical logic in this chapter, in social selection between being laid off and staying on the job, a basic tendency is that people with deficient human resources and social resources have a greater chance to be laid off, while those with sufficient human resources and social resources can continue to work.

The role of social resources is important in such selections, but the influence of human resources is even more critical.

The human-resources-related factors that distinguish the laid-off group from the employed group are physical ability, diligence, and effort, which are measured by age, gender and registered residence status rather than the intellectual level that is measured by years of schooling. Because the positions of workers in China mainly lie in labor-intensive sectors, such as manufacturing, commerce and foodservice sectors, which require a higher level of physical ability, basic operational skills, and diligence and efforts rather than high-level knowledge and intellect. According to the fifth national population census, the average years of schooling of workers who were laid off and dismissed from production and transportation positions were 9.9 years, while that of employed production and transportation workers were 9.1 years. The average years of schooling of workers who were laid off and dismissed from the commercial positions were 10.1 years, while that of on-the-job commercial personnel were 9.4 years. In both groups, the average years of schooling of laid-off and unemployed workers are longer than that of on-the-job workers. The reason of such phenomenon is that many enterprises cut down the number of urban workers who have higher level of education but lower-level physical ability, skills, and diligence and efforts, and replace them with peasant-workers who have higher levels of physical ability, skills, and diligence and efforts but lower levels of education. Among laid-off and unemployed workers, respondents with registered urban residences accounted for the majority (of them, 87.2 percent were production and transportation workers, 50.3 percent were service personnel, and 85.3 percent were commercial personnel). In contrast, among on-the-job workers, respondents with registered rural residences made up the majority (of them, 61.8 percent were production and transportation workers, 44.7 percent were service personnel, and 50.4 percent were commercial personnel). Meanwhile, the average age of on-the-job workers was relatively young, while that of laid-off and unemployed workers was older; the proportion of males in on-the-job workers was relatively high, while the proportion of females in laid-off and unemployed workers was higher. As a whole, the logic shown in the process of layoff and dismissal is that workers with registered urban residences, older in age with the gender of female, and having a lower level of physical ability, skills, and diligence and efforts, are laid off or dismissed. In contrast, those with registered urban residences, older in age with the gender of male, and having a higher level of physical ability, skills and diligence and efforts, can keep their jobs (see Table 9-8).

In terms of social resources, a father's occupation has a significant influence on layoff, unemployment and employment of his children. According to the nationwide survey in this study, among respondents who were laid off from the position of commercial personnel, the proportion of fathers holding the occupation of organizational principal was relatively high (18.8 percent). Among respondents who were dismissed from the position of commercial personnel, the proportion of their fathers holding the position of organizational principal was relatively low (7.1

percent). Among respondents who were still working in the position of commercial personnel, the proportion of fathers holding the position of organizational principal was even lower (5.3 percent). The logic reflected from above figures is that workers who were laid off or waiting for jobs within enterprises were relatively old (averageiy 42 years of age) and their fathers had retired from the position of organizational principal and hence lost influence in decision making of employee layoffs in enterprises; as a result, a larger proportion of their children were laid off. In contrast, the unemployed respondents were younger (averagely 36 years of age), fathers of respondents in this age group werc usually still in office, or still had an influence to some extent even if recently retired; therefore, they could successfully help their children avoid being dismissed, or help them be reemployed. The average age of on-the-job respondents was relatively young and the situation of their fathers was similar to that of the unemployed respondents; they tended to arrange their children in occupations at higher status than workers; therefore, among employed respondents, the proportion of their fathers holding the position of principal was very low. As to clerical personnel and production workers, similar differences also existed between laid-off, unemployed, and employed respondents.

Table 9-8 Comparison between the Laid-off, Unemployed, and Employed Respondents in Different Occupations

Occupation	Average Age		Proportion of Males		Proportion of Non-Rural Residence		Years of Schooling	
	The laid-off and unemployed	Employed respondents	The laid-off and unemployed	Employed respondents	The laid-off and unemployed	Employed respondents	The laid-off and unemployed	Employed respondents
Organizational principal	36.2	41.5	52.9	83.5	89.8	74.2	11.6	11.9
Professional personnel	34.8	35.7	30.9	48.2	87.6	84.9	11.7	12.8
Clerical personnel	36.8	37.3	59.6	70.0	89.9	84.3	11.0	11.9
Commercial personnel	35.7	35.6	43.9	50.8	85.3	49.6	10.1	9.4
Service personnel	36.3	34.0	58.6	49.3	50.3	45.3	8.3	9.0
Production & transportation worker	36.0	32.8	46.1	66.5	87.2	38.2	9.9	9.1
Agricultural, forestry, husbandry and fishing personnel	37.0	39.3	52.9	51.5	90.3	1.8	9.8	6.8

Source: The fifth national population census.

In contrast, among respondents whose fathers were production and transportation workers, the proportions of people being laid off and dismissed from the positions of production and transportation were very high (42.1 percent and 42.4 percent respectively); meanwhile, the proportion of respondents working in the same category of position was relatively high as well (26 percent). The logic implied in this phenomenon is that, no matter whether fathers of production and transportation workers retired or not, they cannot help their children avoid being dismissed or assist them to be reemployed. Even if their children were reemployed, most of them entered the rank of production and transportation workers rather than higher-status occupations such as clerical personnel. Although fathers who held the position of clerical personnel had a stronger social influence than those in the position of transportation worker, their influence was also limited in helping their children to avoid being dismissed; thus, the proportion of their children being laid-off and unemployed was also relatively high. To sum up, people in lower-level occupations such as workers have no influence on decision making of employment.

Chapter 10   Social Mobility of
Peasant-Workers

In the recent ten years, peasant-workers have drawn greater attention all the while. Although they do not have eminent status like politicians or screen stars, the emergence of this group has changed the original order of Chinese society and caused discomfort and tension in people's opinions, daily life, and social relationships. Such discomfort and tensions have two dimensions. The first dimension is the discomfort and tension in urban life. For example, peasant-workers have brought increasingly growing pressures on urban traffic, public order, and employment of urban residents. The second dimension refers to the concerns from people in all circles that are attracted by the unsecured rights and interests and awful living conditions of peasant-workers. Many studies on this issue have been done in academic circle and plentiful findings have been obtained. Various suggestions and proposals based on these studies have been proposed to the government and certain practical effects have been achieved. However, tension related to the issue of peasant-workers still exists and new tension has been constantly emerging.

In the 1980s and at the beginning of the 1990s, many people imputed such discomfort and tension to peasants' rush to leave home to seek jobs and go into business in the cities. At present, very few people still insist upon such a point of view. The majority of social members have realized that the shift from peasants to non-peasants is an inevitable phenomenon in the progress of the modernization in China. The Number One Document released by the Central Committee of the C.P.C. and the State Council in 2004 pointed out that:

> The shift of the rural surplus labor force to non-agricultural sectors and urban areas is an inevitable trend of industrialization and modernization. Peasants working in the city as workers can promote the increase of peasants' income, the adjustment of agricultural structure and rural economic structure, the development of urbanization, and the prosperity of urban economy and society.

Therefore, it is not necessary to discuss whether peasants should be allowed to enter cities to work and go into business. However, various difficult situations encountered by peasant-workers and related social issues are still waiting for solutions.

In such a case, one may ask questions as follows: Is being a peasant-worker the only choice in the shift from peasant to non-peasant? What is the future of peasant-workers? In the progress of modernization in other countries, none ever had such a huge group of peasant-workers as in China. Then, can we conclude that this unique group, i.e., peasant-workers, is a sort of abnormal social mobility phenomenon in the progress of modernization in China? Are many social tensions and disorders in current China caused by such abnormal phenomenon? Our answers to above questions are both yes and no. In this chapter, we will propose detailed explanations through in-depth analysis on the social mobility of peasant-workers.

DEFINITION AND SOCIAL ATRIBUTES

Definition of Peasant-Workers

Although people in China are familiar with the term "peasant-workers", a commonly accepted definition is still in the air. The two terms "floating rural population" and "peasant-workers" are often used as synonyms. However, in a stricter sense, they are different. Although the overwhelming majority of the floating rural population has become peasant-workers, some of them have come to be individual-operated business proprietors or even private entrepreneurs; in addition, many peasants do not leave their hometowns and are engaged in non-agricultural labor in local areas. In fact, they also belong to the group of peasant-workers. Thus, how should we define the concept of peasant-worker?

According to Peilin Li, the word "mobile" in the term "mobile rural laborers" has three dimensions of meanings. First, it means the movement of rural laborers between regions from rural areas to cities and from underdeveloped regions to developed regions. Second, it means the movement of rural laborers between occupations from agriculture to non-agricultural sectors such as industrial and commercial sectors. Third, it means the movement of rural laborers between social strata from the stratum of agricultural labors with lower income to other strata with higher status.[1] Although such a classification does not include all peasant-workers, it provides us with some clues to the definition of peasant-workers. For example, according to his definition, peasant-workers not only come from rural areas, but are also engaged in non-agricultural labor. Nonetheless, the concept "peasant-worker" in this study not only includes "mobile rural laborers", but also consists of workers who are engaged in non-agricultural labor in local rural areas. Based on previous studies on this issue, we believe that the concept of peasant-worker should be defined from the following four dimensions. The first dimension is occupation. Peasant-workers are engaged in non-agricultural occupations, or take non-agricultural labor as their major occupations. In other words, by far the majority of their working hours are spent on non-agricultural labor and their income mainly comes from such labor. The second dimension is institutional status. Although peasant-workers have entered into non-agricultural occupations, the status of their registered residences is still peasant. It

---

[1] Li, Peilin. 1996. "Social Networks and Social Status of Mobile Rural Laborers". *Sociology Research*. Vol. 4.

makes a great difference between them and those with registered non-rural residence status. The third dimension is labor relationships. Peasant-workers are employees hired by individual-operated business proprietors, private entrepreneurs, foreign-invested enterprises, and state-owned and collective entities. Those who have the status of registered rural residence and are engaged in non-agricultural labor but not employed by others do not belong to the group of peasant-workers; they should be classified as individual-operated business proprietors or private entrepreneurs. The fourth dimension is region. Peasant-workers come from rural areas and belong to the rural population. In short, *peasant-workers* refer to those of the rural population who have registered rural residence status and are engaged in non-agricultural labor.

According to this definition, peasant-workers make up a large group. It not only includes the great majority of the floating rural population who leaves their villages and work in cities, but also includes those of the rural population who remain in local countryside and are employed in paid non-agricultural labor. Many previous studies on peasant-workers neglected the latter but merely limited the scope of peasant-workers in the population who leave their villages and work in cities. According to our study, the population of the agricultural laborer stratum is the largest in the ten major social strata, which is more than 0.35 billion persons; the second largest stratum is the worker stratum that includes peasant-workers. The population of peasant-workers is only smaller than that of agricultural laborers. According to the nationwide survey conducted by this research group in 2001, among the rural employment, 41.88 percent of them are engaged in non-agricultural labor (see Table 10-1).

Table 10-1   Production and Operation Activities of the Rural Population in Current China

Units: Persons, %

Category	Frequency	Effective Percentage
Production & operation activities only in agriculture, forestry, husbandry and fishing	1381	58.12
Production & operation activities only in non-agricultural sectors	388	16.33
Production & operation activities both in agricultural & in non-agricultural sectors	359	15.11
Not engaged in any production & operation activities	247	10.39
No response	1	0.04
Total	2376	100

Source: The nationwide survey conducted by this research group.

According to national statistics in 1999, the total figure for the employment in China was 705,860 thousand, of which the urban employment was 210,140 thousand and the rural employment was 495,720 thousand. Meanwhile, the employment in agriculture accounted for 50.1 percent in the total employment in China, that is, 353,600 thousand. If deducting 353,600 thousand agricultural employment from the 495,720 thousand rural employment, about 142,120 thousand people remain in rural areas; most of them were engaged in non-agricultural labor. In the urban employment, 111,773 thousand of them were urban staff members and workers; nearly one hundred million people were not urban staff members and workers but peasants who came from rural areas and worked in cities, among them more than eight million people belonged to peasant-workers. As a whole, if deducting entrepreneurs or the self-employed people who came from rural areas and were engaged in non-agricultural activities, in the two hundred and twenty million rural population engaging in non-agricultural labor, at least two hundred million people belonged to peasant-workers, making up 15.9 percent of the whole population in 1999 in China, 28.3 percent of the total employment, and 40.3 percent of the total rural employment; this estimation is only about one percent smaller than the proportion (41.88 percent) acquired in the survey conducted by this research group. Among two hundred million peasant-workers, only about 36 percent of them worked and did business in the city, while the majority of peasant-workers still stayed in rural areas and were engaged in non-agricultural labor.[1]

The number of rural labor force that transferred from agriculture to non-agricultural sectors has been growing since 2001; therefore, the total number of peasant-workers in current China should be more than two hundred and ten million. In addition, according to the fifth national population census in 2000, peasant-workers made up 37 percent of the total number of workers in China, 57.5 percent of the industrial workers, and 37 percent of the employment in the tertiary industry. Therefore, peasant-workers have become a major part of the stratum of industrial workers. However, although the group of peasant-workers is very large, it does not mean that the social status of peasant-workers is very important, nor very high.

Basic Social Attributes

The composition of peasant-workers indicates the social status of this group to some extent. Who in the rural population has shifted to the status of peasant-workers? This question will be discussed from four aspects: gender, age, cultural education, and occupational characteristics. The study finds that peasant-workers display a skewed distribution in the four basic social attributes. As a whole, this group consists of the educated youth who work in non-agricultural sectors. More specifically, the group has the following characteristics.

(1) The Majority of this Group are Youth Adults

According to the nationwide survey conducted by this research group, the average age of the national overall sample is 43.35 years, and that of the rural sample is 41.86 years; the average age of agricultural laborers is 43.94 years, and that of peasant workers is 38.38 years. Among peasant-workers, respondents younger than 30 years of age account for 33.3 percent and those younger than 40 years of age account for 65 percent. In contrast, among agricultural laborers, respondents younger than 30 years

---

[1] National Bureau of Statistics of China (2000).

of age only account for 14 percent. If taking no account of peasant-workers who work in local areas, the average age of peasant-workers should be even younger, less than 30 years.[1] Data from the fifth national population census indicate that the average age of the floating rural population is 26.89 years;[2] among them, the youngest are newly born children, while the oldest are 61 years of age. People younger than 16 years old account for 10 percent of the floating rural population. The ages of 90 percent of the floating rural population are from 16 to 61 years; among them 78 percent are at the age of 16 to 40 years and 60.5 percent are f 16 to 30 years of age. The overwhelming majority of them left their hometowns and works and does business in other areas. For example, among the outgoing floating population in Anhui Province, 54 percent are people at the age of 20 to 34 years, while less than 5 percent are people older than 55 years. Similar is the situation in Zhejiang Province, and 63.6 percent of its outgoing population are people at the age of 16 to 40 year old. Therefore, the group of peasant-workers mainly consists of young people. Because they are young, they still have opportunities to change their socio-economic status and can obtain such mobility space which society provides for them. According to the *Push-Pull Theory* of urban-rural labor force mobility in Economics of Development, whatever the age is, all of the rural labor force will have equal opportunity to work and do business in the city. Under the influence of push and pull forces, all of them will choose to enter into the cities to look for jobs, no matter whether they are old or young. Obviously, such a theory is not consistent with the actual situation of peasant-workers' mobility in China.

(2) The Growing Proportion of Females is Smaller Than That of Males

In the perspective of gender composition (see Table 10-2), in rural China, 39.72 percent of the male labor force is engaged in non-agricultural labor, while only 22.63 percent of the female labor force is in non-agricultural labor. The female labor force engaged in non-agricultural labor makes up 31.85 percent of the rural labor force in non-agricultural labor. In contrast, the female labor force in agricultural labor accounts for 47.88 percent of the labor force in agricultural labor. Therefore, in rural China, the proportion of males in non-agricultural labor is far higher than that of the female labor force. The overwhelming majority of the rural population engaged in non-agricultural labor belongs to peasant workers. Judging from such a situation, the proportion of males should be higher than that of females among peasant-workers. In other words, the males are dominant in the gender distribution of peasant-workers.

---

[1] Wang, Chunguang. 2001. "The Relationship between Social Identification of the Cenozoic Floating Rural Population and Urban-rural Integration". *Sociology Research*. Vol. 3.

[2] It is hard to distinguish the peasant-workers from the data of the fifth national population census, while only the data about the floating rural population is available. In this study, we have to adopt the data of the floating rural population to describe the situation of peasant-workers, because the great majority of the floating rural population belong to peasant-workers and the difference in statistical calibrations between the two groups is not very significant.

Table 10-2 Employment Distribution of the Rural Labor Force by Gender

Units: Persons, %

Category			Employment Status				
			Agricultural Labor	Non-Agricultural Labor	Jobless	No Response	Total
Gender	Male	Number	713	520	75	1	1309
		Proportion	54.47	39.72	5.73	0.07	100
	Female	Number	655	243	176	0	1074
		Proportion	60.98	22.63	16.39	0	100
Total		Number	1368	763	251	1	2383
		Proportion	57.41	32.02	10.53	0.04	100

Source: The nationwide survey conducted by this research group.

However, according to our survey, in recent years, the number of female peasant-workers has been growing rapidly. In particular, many middle-aged and young women in rural areas have been leaving home to work and do business in other areas. In textile, foodservice, entertainment, and domestic services sectors, the proportion of the females is higher than that of the males. In construction and manufacturing sectors, etc., the proportion of male peasant-workers is higher than that of female peasant-workers. Therefore, there is a certain gender difference existing in the sector distribution of peasant-workers.

(3) The Educated People are Engaged in Industry While the Uneducated in Farming

In the Cultural Revolution, the educated urban youth went down and worked in the countryside or mountain areas; while after the reform and opening-up, the educated rural youth entered the city to work and do business. In terms of educational level, compared with other groups in the rural population, peasant-workers have a relatively higher level of education.

According to the survey in the study, the average years of schooling of those in the rural employment only were 6.31 years; of which, the average years of agricultural laborers were 5.67 years and that of non-agricultural laborers reached 7.59 years, longer than the average years of schooling of the rural employment and agricultural laborers (see Table 10-3). According to another survey:

> The average years of schooling of peasants working in other areas were 8.64 years, close to the education of junior middle school, 1.74 years longer than that of those staying in hometowns and at work in agricultural labor, while 0.01 years shorter than that of those engaged in non-agricultural labor in local areas.[1]

---

[1] Bai, Nansheng and Yupeng He. 2003. "Back Home or Enter the City". Pp. 13 in Peilin Li (ed.), *Peasant-Workers: Socio-economic Analysis on Peasant-Workers Entered into the City in China.* Beijing: Social Sciences Documentation Publishing House.

Those people who worked in other areas and those who stayed and worked in hometowns were both engaged in non-agricultural labor, most of them were peasant-workers. The fifth national population census indicated that 95.9 percent of the floating rural population were literate; among them 4.14 percent were never in school, 12.42 percent received senior middle school or a higher level of education, 52.07 percent received junior middle school education, and 30.77 percent received primary school education. In contrast, the educational level of the whole rural population was relatively low; the largest group in this population was those who received primary school education, accounting for 45.75 percent, while the illiteracy ratio was as high as more than 10 percent (see Table 10-4). Results of the nationwide survey in this study are very similar to the results of the fifth national population census: more than half of peasant-workers have a junior middle school level of education; compared with the whole rural population, the educational level of peasant-worker is relatively higher. It means that improvement of the educational level will push the rural population leave hometowns to work and do business in other areas; it is also one important channel to improve the return of rural education.

Table 10-3 Average Years of Schooling of Agricultural and Non-Agricultural Laborers

Category	Average Years	Number of Employment	Standard Deviation
Agricultural laborers	5.67	1368	3.39
Non-agricultural laborers	7.59	763	3.07
Unemployment	5.94	252	3.92
Total (rural laborers)	6.31	2383	3.47

Source: The nationwide survey conducted by this research group.

Table 10-4 Average Educational Level between Peasant-Workers and the Rural Population

Unit: %

Educational Background	The 5ᵗʰ National Population Census		The Nationwide Survey of this Study	
	Floating Rural Population	Rural Population	Educational Background	Distribution
Never in school	4.14	10.07	No educational background	0.54
Literacy class	0.59	2.19	Lower primary school	7.29
Primary school	30.77	45.76	Primary school	20
Junior middle school	52.07	36.34	Junior middle school	51.89
Senior middle school	8.28	4.62	(Vocational) senior middle school	15.94
Technical secondary school	4.14	0.81	Technical secondary school	2.97
College	0	0.14	College	0.81
University	0	0.03	University	0.27
Total	100	100	Other	0.27
			Total	100

Source: The nationwide survey conducted by this research group.

(4) In Possession of Certain Amount of "Capital for Mobility"

Compared with other parts of the rural population, most peasant-workers are more or less in possession of certain experience of occupational mobility and accumulated a certain amount of "capital for mobility", i.e., experience and know-how. According to our survey on peasant-workers who work in non-agricultural sectors in local rural areas, many of them have experience in other areas or in other occupations. Results of the nationwide survey conducted by this research group indicate that the average times of occupational shift of peasant-workers is 0.76 times more than that of rural agricultural laborers (see Table 10-5).

Table 10-5 Occupational Shifts of Peasant-Workers and Rural Agricultural Laborers

Category	Average Times of Occupational Shift	Number (Persons)
Rural agricultural laborers	1.38	1832
Peasant-workers	2.14	384
Total	1.51	2216

Source: The nationwide survey conducted by this research group.

On one hand, peasant-workers obtained the "capital for mobility" in occupational mobility, i.e., accumulating experience, knowledge, and expertise, widening their perspectives, and improving working capability. On the other hand, they could not improve their social status through occupational mobility. Most of them were in horizontal mobility between similar or relevant occupations, for example, people who once worked in blue-collar jobs usually will continue to work in blue-collar jobs after changing occupations. In China, the supply of the labor force (especially the rural labor force) is in an unlimited state; peasant-workers have limited choices in the labor market and limited opportunity and ability in wage negotiation. In addition, the legal system does not provide sufficient supports for them. Therefore, in general, peasant-workers are in a passive status in the labor market. As a result, most of them cannot obtain a permanent job in one place; naturally, job shifts occur frequently among them. Sometimes, in order to find a better job or because one is tired of having the same job for a long time, some may even leave employers without giving notice. Frequent mobility hinders them from accumulating a longer working experience; as a result, they often show up as "freshmen" and cannot obtain promotion and status improvement in organizations in which they work.

Judging from the above four basic social attributes, peasant-workers are a group with relatively better conditions in the rural population. They are young and with a relatively high level of education. Thinking the other way around, in the rural population only those who have certain conditions can become peasant-workers and are fit for corresponding jobs. The four basic social attributes are essential conditions for the upward mobility of peasant-workers.

SOCIAL MOBILITY OF PEASANT-WORKERS

Why do educated young rural people go to work as peasant-workers? Even if their jobs are unstable, why do they still choose to be peasant-workers? Will they be peasant-workers for a long time? If not, what kind of outlets will they choose for social mobility? The social mobility of such a large group of peasant-workers is not only important for their own future, but it also has a direct influence on the direction of the social structure transition and progress of modernization in China.

Social Status

Almost all rural elites have joined the group of peasant-workers. Moreover, it is difficult to find any young person to assume the position of village officials in some villages in middle and western China. When this research group conducted the survey in a western village, we found that, among seven members in the local Village Committee of the Communist Party of China, the youngest one was 67 years old, while the oldest was 83 years old. Local residents called it a committee consisting of "seven Party members with six teeth" because all people who were able to labor had left hometowns to work in other areas. It shows that the social status of peasant-workers is higher than that of agricultural laborers and hence is more attractive to the rural population. In this section, we will compare peasant-workers with agricultural laborers with respect to economical status, occupational prestige, social influence, and experience, etc., in order to explain why the social status of peasant-workers has more attraction to the rural population and why the rural population regards being peasant-workers as a kind of upward social mobility.

(1) The growth of rural income mainly comes from non-agricultural income

In recent years, the growth of rural income is very slow. In many rural regions, the agricultural income even shows a trend of negative growth. As a result, peasants have increasingly lost their interest in farming. From 1997 to 2000, the growth of per capita net income of peasants was 163 Yuan RMB. According to a study in this field:

> In the growth of net income in the past three years, the contribution of household operation was minus 28 percent, of which the contribution of crop farming was minus 98 percent, the contribution of non-agricultural labor remunerations was 115 percent, and the contribution of income from property and transfer accounted for 13 percent. If the non-agricultural labor remuneration stayed at the same level, the per capita net income in 2000 was reduced by 28.96 Yuan RMB from the figure of the previous year (down by 1.3 percent). In 2000, the negative contribution of agriculture to peasants' net income was as high as minus 112 percent, of which the negative contribution of crop farming was minus 229 percent, while the positive contribution of non-agricultural

labor remunerations was 167 percent.[1]

Therefore, agriculture has actually reduced rather than increased the net income of peasants. According to the survey conducted by the investigation team on rural society and economy of the National Bureau of Statistics of China, peasants' per capita income obtained from agricultural production fell in three successive years from 1998 to 2000, respectively down by 28 Yuan, 53 Yuan, and 48 Yuan over the figures of the previous years. The instability of agricultural income directly led to the absolute decrease of the growth rate of net income in those years. Agricultural income did not change much in 2001 and 2002, with no significant decrease or increase. However, the income of crop farming and animal husbandry dropped two Yuan RMB and one Yuan RMB from the figures of the previous years respectively; only the income of forestry increased to some extent, up by three Yuan RMB over the figure of the previous year.[2]

In some provinces, such as Sichuan and Anhui, etc., the amount of money remitted by people working in non-agricultural sectors in other areas to their hometowns was more than ten billion Yuan RMB each year. For example, The GDP of a certain city in Anhui Province was only 1.5 billion Yuan RMB in 2003, while the amount of money remitted by people working in non-agricultural sectors in other areas to their hometowns was more than 5 billion Yuan RMB. Many economic issues of a family will be solved if just one person in the family work in non-agricultural sectors. When this research group conducted the survey in the countryside of Huining County in Gansu Province, we found that most families in local villages had one or more family members working in other areas; otherwise they would not even have enough money to buy food. Thus, if just one family member works in non-agricultural sectors in other areas, the food and clothing for the whole family could be secured. Moreover, local peasants depended on their non-agricultural income to pay agricultural tax and miscellaneous fees; otherwise, they would not have enough money to pay such tax and fees. According to the survey conducted in this study, the income of non-agricultural labor is significantly higher than that of agricultural labor; the income of full-time non-agricultural labor is much higher than that of part-time non-agricultural labor; the income of part-time non-agricultural labor is higher than that of full-time agricultural labor. The income of full-time non-agricultural labor was 2.87 times higher than that of full-time agricultural labor; the income of part-time non-agricultural labor was 2.12 times than that of full-time agricultural labor (see Table 10-6). According to the survey conducted by the investigation team on rural society and economy of National Bureau of Statistics of China in 2002,

---

[1] Bai and He (2003: 22).

[2] Investigation Team on Rural Society and Economy of the National Bureau of Statistics of China. 2003. *Monitoring Report on Poverty in Rural China (2003)*. Beijing: China National Statistic Press: 5.

The growth of peasants' income almost completely came from the growth of non-agricultural income. The wage income was a major source of the growth of non-agricultural income…the growth of wage income mainly came from the income earned by peasants who worked at non-agricultural labor in other places and local areas. In the wage income, the income earned by people working in other areas, in local villages, in local township enterprises, and in non-enterprises organizations respectively were 298 Yuan RMB, 140 Yuan RMB, 240 Yuan RMB, and 162 Yuan RMB, with an increase of 33 Yuan RMB, 13 Yuan RMB, 10 Yuan RMB, and 12 Yuan RMB respectively over the figures in the same period of previous year, up by 12 percent, 10 percent, 4.5 percent, and 8.3 percent respectively.[1]

Table 10-6　Income Earned by the Rural Labor Force in Different Occupations in 2000

Unit: Yuan RMB

Employment of the Rural Population		Wage and bonus not including agricultural income	Other non-agricultural income	Income from business	Household agricultural income	Total
Production & operation activities only in agricultural sectors	Mean	706.4	872.93	235.35	4224.89	6039.57
	Standard deviation	2285.37	6563.01	1752.47	5936.66	—
Production & operation activities only in non-agricultural sectors	Mean	5500.68	1097.13	8200.89	2526.19	17324.89
	Standard deviation	6326.21	3556.92	18770.14	5061.46	—
Activities both in agricultural & non-agricultural sectors	Mean	2902.48	2206.98	4024.14	3643.13	12776.47
	Standard deviation	3325.22	3916.25	10156.58	8560.74	—
Not engaged in any production & operation activities	Mean	1201.71	443.88	484.06	2817.12	4946.77
	Standard deviation	2351.95	1696.33	1965.11	7980.98	—
No response	Mean	5124	—	—	—	5124
	Standard deviation	—	—	—	—	—
Total	Mean	2555.4	1143.19	3123.29	3836.23	10658.11
	Standard deviation	4491.42	5350.25	11218.59	6561.35	—

Source: The nationwide survey conducted by this research group.

In the field survey in rural areas, we found that the net income for grain output of one Mu farmland (one Mu is equal to 1/15 of a hectare) is around 200 yuan RMB (not deducting the labor cost). In some years, planting grain even suffered a loss; although the income will be a little more if planting cash crops, it is merely around 1,000 yuan RMB. In contrast, a peasant-worker can earn more than 400 Yuan RMB per month and 5,000 Yuan RMB per year at least, equal to farming 250 Mu of land. Therefore, rural laborers rush off to the city to be peasant-workers. For example, among around 800 laborers in a certain village in Chongqing City, more than 500 of them went out to

---

[1] Investigation Team on Rural Society and Economy of the National Bureau of Statistics of China (2003: 5).

work in other areas including those who worked in the local city (110 persons) and periodically worked in other areas and those worked in other areas for a long term (more than 300 persons). Many young people went out with their whole family, leaving their farmland to other peasants; however, they had to pay the agricultural tax by themselves, or nobody would cultivate their farmland. The income of peasant-workers ranged from 9,000 Yuan RMB to 4,000 or 5,000 Yuan RMB. If a family has no peasant-worker, the economic condition of this family will be seriously affected. Such a situation indicates that the economic status of peasant-workers is much higher than that of agricultural laborers.

(2) Being a worker rather than a farmer is promising

Being a farmer engaged in agriculture not only is toilsome but also offers lower income. This situation has a direct influence on the attitudes of the rural population toward agricultural labor. In rural areas in China, a common opinion has been accepted universally: "being a farmer is not promising." For a young man in the countryside, it is very likely that he cannot afford to get married if he only works in agriculture. A survey on occupational prestige also indicates that the occupational prestige of peasant-workers is higher than that of agricultural laborers. The prestige of farmers is the lowest; it is not as good as that of taxi drivers, babysitters, porters, mineworkers, and peasant-workers (in that survey, the term "peasant-worker" was used in a narrow sense with some difference from the definition in this study; but it still belongs to the scope of peasant-workers which are defined in the study).[1] In rural areas in middle and western China, almost all young and middle-aged men have left home to work in other areas leaving women, children, and old people at home to go into agriculture.

Of course, from the perspective of people in the countryside, the reason why being a farmer is not promising is not only due to the low return of agricultural labor, but also to the narrow perspective of a farmer who works only at home. In addition to earning money, many peasants also have another purpose when they go to work in other areas, that is, widening their perspectives, learning skills, tempering themselves, and accumulating experience. Some hope to raise funds by being peasant-workers in order to support their educational pursuits: to receive the adult education and obtain a college diploma or a bachelor's degree, or even a master's degree. Some rural youth long for urban life and wish to enjoy the modern urban lifestyle through the mobility by peasant-workers.

(3) Peasant-workers still have an embarrassing and lower social status

Although the social status of peasant-workers is higher than that of agricultural laborers, compared with other social strata, it is still at the bottom of social hierarchy.

---

[1] Wang, Chunguang. 2003. "Study on the Issue of Social Inequality in Occupational Mobility in China". *Chinese Journal of Population Science.*Vol. 2.

First, they are engaged in the most toilsome, dirtiest, and the most dangerous jobs in our society; especially in cities, they take jobs which urban residents are unwilling to do. Their working hours are the longest while remuneration is the lowest. Compared with urban permanent workers, they are given unequal pays, unequal working hours, and unequal rights and interests for equal work. In other words, although peasant-workers' jobs are more toilsome and heavier than that of urban workers, their income is much lower than that of urban workers and they are excluded from the security system for the minimum standard of living and the social security system in urban areas (such as medical insurance and endowment insurance). More often, although they work like horses, many peasant-workers cannot get their wages in time by the end of the year. In 2003, the total amount of back pay for peasant-workers in China was as high as 100 billion Yuan RMB. Second, the living condition of peasant-workers is extremely bad. They cannot enjoy the basic treatment of other citizens. Many peasant-workers live in the dirtiest bunkhouses or work sheds without clean drinking water and sanitary facilities. Many of them work as a kind of modern "indenture laborers" with limited personal freedom in their spare time. In cities, peasant-workers often encounter discriminations and exclusions. Some urban residents and administrators ascribed the chaotic public order and the dirty environment in the city to peasant-workers and treated them unequally, for example, by limiting and forbidding peasant-workers to enter into some occupations, against giving peasant-workers equal citizen treatments, and preventing their children from entering into urban public schools.

In short, the social status of peasant-workers is not only lower than other social strata (except for agricultural laborers), but also incommensurate with their social contributions. In terms of economic status, their remuneration is low and disproportionate with the value of their labor. Compared with urban workers in the same positions, their economic status is extremely lower. Table 10-7 shows that, in the same non-agricultural labor, the average wage of workers with registered non-rural residences is 1.78 times higher than that of workers with registered rural residences.[1] In terms of legal rights, peasant-workers lack self-protection, have no right to establish unions and negotiate with employers, and have no influence on decision making of the government. In terms of social prestige, peasant-workers make up a group that receives various unequal treatment and discrimination and constantly remains in a marginal state. In terms of the national treatment, peasant-workers do not have the most basic civil rights. As taxpayers, they receive very limited services from the government. Meanwhile, they often are excluded from the scope of public services provided by local governments. Even worse, such services sometimes become a kind of economic plundering in form of various fees imposed on peasant-workers.

---

[1] People with the registered rural residence status and working in non-agricultural labor are not equal to peasant-workers, but most of them belong to peasant-workers. Similarly, people with the registered non-rural residence status and working in non-agricultural labor are not equal to urban workers. In general, the wage level of urban workers is higher than that of peasant-workers. Therefore, it is just a rough comparison.

Peasant-workers have made immense contributions to the city but have to carry the burden of health care, retirement, and education of their children by themselves without any supports from the urban society. This is an extremely unfair social reality.

Despite all this, being peasant-workers is still a sort of upward mobility for the rural population. In this sense, China is different from western countries, especially European countries. In the early days of industrialization and urbanization in Europe, many workers came from handicraftsmen. Such a shift was not a type of upward mobility but downward mobility, because the social status of European workers was lower than that of handicraftsmen at that time; usually workers were bankrupt handicraftsmen. In contrast, Chinese peasant-workers are different. They come from the stratum of agricultural laborers, which is at the bottom of Chinese society; thus, they have a great improvement in social status. This fact affects the stratum identification and collective actions of peasant-workers to some degree. This is a major reason why peasant-workers can endure such heavy and toilsome works, unequal treatments, and bad living conditions.

Table 10-7   Wages and Bonus Income of Laborers with Different Registered Residences

Status of Registered Residence	Category of Occupation	Average Income (Yuan RMB)	Number (Persons)	Standard Deviation
Non-rural	Non-agricultural labor	7854.96	2758	8698.61
	Agricultural labor	330.05	424	1122.44
Rural	Non-agricultural labor	4412.47	516	5308.55
	Agricultural labor	1208.51	88	2339.26

Source: The nationwide survey conducted by this research group.

(4) Being peasant-workers is the only choice of the overwhelming majority of the rural population in search of a breakthrough in the unbalanced development in China

In current China, being peasant-workers is the only choice of the rural population in search of relative balance in the unbalanced development between urban and rural areas and among regions, because the overwhelming majority of the rural population does not have more upward mobility opportunities and channels. Therefore, the rural population has been continuously joining the group of peasant-workers. The net growth of people who left the countryside and worked in non-agricultural sectors was about 5,000 thousand in 2003. To most peasants, farming has become an unwilling choice. As long as they have a chance, peasants will try to leave agriculture and the countryside. However, the upward mobility opportunity and channels that society provides for peasants are very limited; entering higher schools and joining the army are the most desired upward mobility channels for the rural population. According to our estimation, from 1978 to 2001 there were a total of 11,638.5 thousand members of the rural population who had achieved the upward mobility of shifting from agricultural laborers to non-agricultural laborers and from villagers to urban residents through such channels. Comparing to the nearly 0.9 billion rural population in China, the proportion of those people was like a drop in the bucket, only around one percent; to the whole population in China, this proportion was even smaller, only 0.8 percent; to the 156,650 thousand mechanically increased urban population from 1978 to 1999, this proportion was only 7.4 percent. Obviously, to the overwhelming majority of the rural population, it is an unrealistic dream to achieve upward mobility by entering higher schools; those who achieved upward mobility by joining the army are even fewer than those entering higher schools.

Another channel is the social mobility achieved through the expansion of cities and towns. Many people have achieved upward mobility in such expansion. However, about 50,000 thousand peasants have become "three-no" peasants (no farmland, no jobs, and no stable sources of income) in this process; their socio-economic status has been even worse. According to other countries' experience, shifting from peasants to workers is not only the prime choice and channel for peasants to achieve upward mobility, but also meets the requirement of development of industrialization and urbanization. Nonetheless, current institutional arrangements and social structure in China prevent peasants from directly shifting to workers and hence they have to enter into an interim state of occupational status.

It is observed that Chinese peasants are a group with the most toilsome work and the lowest status. In the past, they did not have the land ownership and the right to choose occupations. After the reform and opening-up, the living condition of peasants has been improved; however, they are still the group with the least rights. Peasants have made immense contributions to the development of this country but were exploited and infringed upon. Although the national economy in China has developed rapidly, the scissors gap between the prices of industrial products and agricultural products, the rural-urban divide, and the gap among regions have not been reduced but continuously widening. For example, the gap between rural and urban income increased from 2.34:1 in 1978 to more than 3.24:1 in 2003. If we add various benefits enjoyed by urban residents, the gap should be even wider. In contrast, in addition to agricultural tax and miscellaneous fees, peasants have to afford the expenditure of rural public goods. In this case, if peasants continue to stay in the countryside, they will continue to lead a hard life. Most full-time agricultural households in rural areas are poor families. Without other choices, peasants have to leave agriculture or even the countryside to work in non-agricultural sectors or do business. It is a well-known fact that the gap among regions has expanded year after year. Over the past two decades, rural areas in western and middle China have not thrived through developing township-village enterprises as in the coastal regions; contrarily, the rural economic condition in these regions has been worsening; local peasants found that they would eventually be penniless if they continued to stay at home. As a result, they have had to leave for the developed eastern regions to find opportunity and space to improve their own economic conditions.

In sum, over the past twenty years in China, the increasingly expanding rural-urban divide and the gap among regions have forced the rural population to move into cities and the population in middle and western depressed areas to move to coastal developed regions on a large scale. With such large-scale rural-urban mobility and regional mobility, the group of peasant-workers has emerged and grown into an immense surge.

History of Peasant-Workers' Social Mobility

(1) The Past and the Present of Peasant-Workers

After all, the emergence of peasant-workers is not a new social phenomenon in China. It has forever existed in the history of China. There were various handicraftsmen in traditional rural society; from the perspective of occupations, they were very similar to modern peasant-workers who work in non-agricultural sectors in local countryside. Before 1949, it was very common that peasants sought part-time occupations in the slack season in farming. In the 1950s, a large number of the rural population was engaged in non-agricultural activities; in terms of occupations, they were very similar to modern peasant-workers as well. In fact, peasant-workers did indeed emerge in rural collective enterprises in the movement of collectivization in the late 1950s; they were non-agricultural laborers with registered rural residences.

Peasant-workers discussed in this study are both similar to and different from the above peasant-workers in the past. Both groups are non-agricultural laborers coming from agricultural laborers; the non-agricultural labor that they work in is temporary and of short term, or even part-time and unstable. The purpose for working in non-agricultural labor is to "bring home the bacon". Of course, some rural craftsmen might specialize in full-time non-agricultural labor. However, modern peasant-workers not only move on a large scale for a long geographical distance and work in more sectors, but also are restricted by the status system; with the status of registered rural residence, they cannot enjoy the same social treatments and status as people with the registered non-rural residence.

In traditional rural society in China, the number of agricultural laborers who shifted to non-agricultural sectors was not very large; in addition, most of them moved within the nearby rural and urban areas. In contrast, peasant-workers are currently seeking jobs all over the country or even the world (such as looking for jobs through exporting labor services or even illegally going into other countries). In the past, the institutionalized urban-rural divide did not exist and it was very easy for a peasant to change his or her status to be an urban resident. Even in the early 1950s, such a situation still went on. Therefore, at that time the peasant-worker was mainly an occupational concept rather than a type of institutional status.

However, since the end of the 1950s and especially from the early 1960s', the situation has changed drastically. The government implemented a strict urban-rural dual system. It was very difficult, if not impossible, for a peasant to transfer to non-agricultural sectors and migrate to the city. According to the institutional arrangements and policies, the rural areas should develop agriculture while the urban areas should focus on non-agricultural sectors. Peasants with the status of registered rural residence should stay in the countryside to live and be farmers; they were not allowed to enter the city to work and do business, or they were even not permitted to go in for non-agricultural activities in local villages. Of course, in the period of the People's Commune, in order to solve the shortage of some industrial goods, a few small-size commune-owned enterprises were established, in which the procurement of materials, production, and sale of products were all situated in local areas. A small number of rural laborers entered those enterprises and became non-agricultural laborers, i.e., peasant-workers. However, they were not paid by wages but workpoints, which were credits to participate in the distribution of their original production teams with peasants in agricultural labor. Therefore, they were not peasant-workers in a modern sense. After the late 1970s, more rural collective enterprises emerged and consequently the number of peasant-workers paid by workpoints increased to some extent.

Until the early days of the reform and opening-up, the number of peasant-workers was considerable small; most of them worked in non-agricultural labor in the local countryside, while only some of them were employed by urban entities as stillmen and cleaners, etc. Because the government had strictly restrained the rural population from entering the city and trans-regional employment and did not loose the limitation imposed on the development of rural collective enterprises and individual and private sectors of economy, the number of peasant-workers did not grow rapidly. Therefore, although peasants at that time already had the motivation to go to work in other areas, corresponding opportunities and channels were still very limited.

Three major changes that occurred in the early 1980s provided peasants with the opportunity to transfer to non-agricultural sectors. The first change was the implementation of the rural contracted responsibility system with remuneration linked to output. As a result, peasants obtained the right to handle their own affairs in agricultural production and operation and the right to dispose their labor outputs. The second change was the unprecedented development of rural collective enterprises (the name was changed to "township enterprises" in 1984); it accordingly created a large number of non-agricultural employment opportunities. The third change was the reform of the urban system starting in 1984. Limitations imposed on the development of urban individual economy were loosed and a contract system was introduced into urban commercial and services sectors. Consequentially, the extra-system employment space was developed and expanded. With these three significant changes, peasant-workers have experienced three phases of expansion of employment space: initially, peasant-workers worked at non-agricultural sector in the local countryside, and then they entered small towns and eventually worked in cities. From the perspective of time sequence of social mobility, the process of rural laborers shifting to peasant-workers consists of three steps: the first step is the change of occupations (i.e., working in non-agricultural sector in the local countryside); the second step is the change of residence (working in cities or in rural areas of other developed regions); the third step is the change of registered residence status. The last step is far more difficult than changes of occupations and residence. Because peasant-workers have not achieved the shift of registered residence status, they cannot thoroughly accomplish the mobility from the stratum of agricultural laborers to other social strata.

In terms of regions, the earliest modern peasant-workers emerged in southern regions of Jiangsu Province and in the Zhujiang delta region of Guangdong Province (at first in Shenzhen district). In the early 1980s, based on original rural collective enterprises, township enterprises in southern regions of Jiangsu Province developed rapidly. In fact, the rise of township enterprises in China mainly occurred in this area. Township enterprises employed a large number of rural laborers to work in non-agricultural labor and hence created peasant-workers who worked in non-agricultural sectors in the local countryside. Benefiting from the state's opening-up policy, foreign-invested enterprises have been established in the Zhujiang delta region since the early 1980s and many peasant-workers were employed in these enterprises. Subsequently, individual-operated businesses and private enterprises have thrived in the Wenzhou district of Zhejiang Province and in the Jinjiang district of Fujian Province and pushed a mass of peasants to shift to peasant-workers. In addition, the success of the rural reforms triggered the urban reforms and consequently provided the rural population with more non-agricultural employment opportunities. In succeeding years, township enterprises, foreign-invested ventures, individual economy, and private enterprises have spread over the whole country and hence brought about peasant-workers in every corner of China.

Since the first "peasant-workers rush" occurred in 1989, so far it has become a normal phenomenon in Chinese society. The daily life of urban residents deeply relies on the labor of peasant-workers. Meanwhile, many peasant-workers have lived in the city with their whole family for a long time and have been engaged in full-time non-agricultural occupations. The number of peasant-workers working in the city increased from thirty or forty million in the middle and late 1980s to 99 million in 2003. In the middle and late 1980s, township enterprises absorbed two million or three million peasant-workers each year; in 1997, more than 0.12 billion peasant-workers were employed in township enterprises. Although after that period most township enterprises were restructured, the number of peasant-workers did not drop. As early as the 1990s, some scholars pointed out that a very important social stratum, i.e., the stratum of peasant-workers, has taken shape in less than two decades. In modern China, peasant-workers have become a major component of the stratum of industrial workers.[1]

---

[1] Lu, Xueyi. 2003. *Socio-economic Issues on Agriculture, Rural Areas, and Peasants*. Beijing: Social Sciences Documentation Publishing House.

(2) Social Mobility of Peasant-Workers

Over the past two decades, the size of the group of peasant-workers has been growing, but it does not provide details about the change of an individual peasant-worker's life. For a society the period of two decades is just like a flash in its history; however, for individuals it is a considerably long period of life history. In this period, what kind of social mobility have peasant-workers experienced? Where are these people nowadays who became peasant-workers in the early days of the reforms? Are they still peasant-workers? Has anyone among them achieved the social mobility to enter into other strata? How is the possibility to achieve such social mobility? What kind of conditions is required for such mobility? We will try to answer these questions in the following discussion.

According to the data collected by this research group, the social mobility of peasant-workers mainly focuses on occupational mobility. The change of their social status is still difficult and slow. Therefore, we will analyze the path of peasant-workers' social mobility from the perspective of occupational mobility.

Table 10-8 is the table of occupations of peasant-workers organized on the basis of data collected in case interviews. It effectively reflects the general picture of peasant-workers' occupational mobility. Combined with previous studies, analysis of this table indicates some tracks of peasant-workers' social mobility.

First, the change of peasant-workers' occupations is relatively significant and is considerably unstable. In 39 cases in Table 10-8, the most times of occupational shift are seven, while the least are two. The duration of a certain type of non-agricultural activity is not long; the shortest is only several months, while longer ones are 3 to 5 years; very few are more than 10 years. Moreover, many peasant-workers frequently shifted between agricultural activity and non-agricultural activity. When non-agricultural jobs were hard to find, they went back to the countryside to work in agricultural labor; after a while, they went out to seek non-agricultural jobs again and thus became a kind of "pendulum peasant-workers" swinging between agriculture and non-agriculture.

The instability and inconstancy of peasant-workers' occupations are closely related to their social status; they usually do not establish a type of stable contract relationship with enterprises or employers; most peasant-workers do not sign labor contracts with employers. At the same time, the *Labor Law of the People's Republic of China* does not provide effective protection for peasant-workers' rights and interests. Therefore, many enterprises take advantage of legal loopholes and the surplus situation in rural labor force supply and adopt a strategy to save operation costs by employing peasants for a short term. For example, some enterprises intentionally pay very low wages to peasant-workers in the probation period and fire them by the end of this period with the excuse of ineligibility; then other peasant-workers are employed as probationary workers once again in their place. From the perspective of peasant-workers, because they cannot expect a stable occupation, they generally pursue maximized remunerations and attempt to find any higher-paid works; once they find such jobs, peasant-workers usually will quit their current jobs without any hesitation. Such instability has a more negative effect on peasant-workers than on enterprises. In the current labor market, the supply of peasant-workers exceeds the demand; once a peasant-worker loses his job, it is not easy for him or her to find another one. Sometimes, one may be jobless for a long time and have to go back home to be a farmer or wait for employment (In Table 10-8, case 4, 9, 10, 20, 27, 29, 33, 37, and 39 indicate such situations). Therefore, in spite of low wages and bad working conditions, many peasant-workers still work hard in order to hold their positions.

Second, the most possible upward mobility opportunity for peasant-workers is to become individual-operated business proprietors, while the possibility to be permanent urban workers and entrepreneurs is very small. In addition, it is highly possible and very easy for peasant-workers to return to positions as agricultural laborers. If we treat the peasants who went out to work in non-agricultural sectors in the 1980s as the first generation of peasant-workers, how is their current stratum status? Table 10-8 provides some clues to this question as well. The first-generation peasant-workers in the 1980s nowadays mainly situated in three occupational categories: peasant-workers, agricultural laborers, and individual-operated business proprietors.

There are a considerable number of peasant-workers returning to the stratum of agricultural laborers. This is both a kind of back flow and a type of downward mobility, because most peasant-workers initially came from agricultural laborers. Especially, in the 1980s' almost no peasant-workers directly worked in non-agricultural sectors without the experience of being a farmer. There were two peaks of back flow appearing over the past two decades, i.e., 1989~1991 and 1998~2000; the first peak was caused by the national economic depression and readjustment; the second one was brought about by the restructuring of state-owned and township enterprises. During the first peak, the government readjusted and rectified the national economy and many peasant-workers were expelled from the city. At that time, peasant-workers were treated as a kind of "blindly floating population" and hence the government had a 'reasonable' excuse. Meanwhile, in that period, due to shortage of capital, township enterprises dismissed a part of peasant-workers as well. During the second peak, the restructuring of state-owned enterprises aimed at "downsizing for efficiency" and consequently released a large number of laid-off workers. Peasant-workers were regarded as rivals of laid-off workers in the labor market (at that time, there was a saying, "peasant-workers are scrambling for rice bowls with laid-off workers"), hence many cities carried out certain discriminatory policies to restrict the employment of peasant-workers. As a result, a number of peasant-workers could not find jobs in cities and had to return to the countryside and agriculture. In addition, township enterprises had universally experienced serious problems in development since 1996 and had to restructure themselves; in consequence, many peasant-workers were dismissed and reentered agriculture.

Table 10-8　Occupational Mobility of Peasant-Workers, 2001

Case No.	Sex	Year of Birth	Occupational Experience (1)	Occupational Experience (2)	Occupational Experience (3)	Occupational Experience (4)	Occupational Experience (5)	Occupational Experience (6)	Occupational Experience (7)
1	Male	1962	Farmed at home	1977-1979, served in the army	1980-1984, farmed at home	1995-2001, worked in a brick field			
2	Male	1945	1968-1999, farmed at home	1999-2000, washed coal in a coal washery in Chongqing	2001, worked as a choreman in a company in Deyang				
3	Male	1965	1981-1985, farmed at home	1985-2001, worked as a plasterer in a construction company					
4	Female	1976	1993-1995, farmed at home	1995-1997, worked in "Hali" ice cream company	1997, worked in "Meiqile" ice cream company	1997-2000, worked as an attendant in a community service center	2000~present, farms at home		
5	Male	1948	1963-1965, farmed at home	1966-1997, worked as a plasterer	1998, farmed at home				
6	Male	1952	Farmed at home	1979, worked in a brick field	1981, farmed at home	1985-1986, worked in a brick field	1987, started a greengrocery		
7	Male	1971	1989, worked as a barber	1991, started a factory in glass processing (bankrupted later)	1995, worked as an odd jobber	1997, started a barber shop in town			
8	Male	1964	1981-1989, ran a slaughterhouse	1990, started a grocery	1990-1991, ran a jellied bean curd shop	1997-1998, worked as a cleaner in a restaurant in Beijing	1998, worked as a guard in a construction team in Zhengzhou	1998-2000, ran a car washing shop in hometown	2000~present, runs a snack bar in hometown
9	Male	1972	1988-1990, farmed at home	1990-1994, worked as a choreman in a garage	1994, worked as a choreman in another car shop	1995-1997, worked as a plasterer in a construction company	1998~present, farms at home		
10	Female	1953	1973-1993, farmed at home	1990-1997, worked in a brick field	1997~present, farms at home				
11	Female	1964	1979-1989, worked in a township enterprise	1990-1997, worked in a brick field	1998~present, works in an office of local township				

continued

Case No.	Sex	Year of Birth	Occupational Experience (1)	Occupational Experience (2)	Occupational Experience (3)	Occupational Experience (4)	Occupational Experience (5)	Occupational Experience (6)	Occupational Experience (7)
12	Female	1958	1975–1980, farmed at home	1985–1994, worked in a garment factory in Hongzhou	1995–1998, worked in another garment factory in Hongzhou	1999–present, trades small commodities as a street peddler			
13	Male	1959	1977–1979, worked as a temporary teacher	1979–1983, worked as a porter in a transportation company	1983–1984, worked as a builder in a construction company	1985–1992, jobless	1993–1994, worked as a latheman in a factory	1995–2001, worked as a plasterer in a construction company	
14	Female	1959	1978–1986, worked as attendant in a hotel in local town	1986–1989, ran a small seafood shop	1989–1997, worked as a jobber	1997–2001, ran a small flourmill			
15	Male	1976	1992–1999, worked as a operator in a large paper company	1999–2001, worked as a textile worker	2001–present, works as a independent tractor driver				
16	Female	1971	1991–1992, worked as a packer	1992–1993, worked in a small textile factory	1993–2000, worked as a kindergartener	2001, started an individual-operated business making fishing net			
17	Male	1961	1978–1980, farmed at home	1980–1985, worked in a tilery	1986–1996, worked as workshop manager in the tilery	1999–present, works as a builder in Zhoushan construction company			
18	Male	1956	1973–1976, worked as a apprentice carpenter	1978–1991, worked as a carpenter	1992–1994, farmed at home	1994–present, works as an independent forwarder			
19	Male	1970	1987–1999, worked as an electrician in a construction company	1999–2000, worked as an independent forwarder	2000–2001, worked as an electrician in a construction company	2001–present, works for another independent forwarder			
20	Female	1975	1991–1992, worked as a lathe operator in a small fittings factory	1994–1995, worked as a packer in a collective packinghouse	1995–present, stays home and jobless				

382

continued

Case No.	Sex	Year of Birth	Occupational Experience (1)	Occupational Experience (2)	Occupational Experience (3)	Occupational Experience (4)	Occupational Experience (5)	Occupational Experience (6)	Occupational Experience (7)
22	Male	1960	1977–1980, farmed at home	1980–1984, worked as a boatman in a collective enterprise	1984–1987, worked as a boatman for an employer	1987–1992, worked as a tractor driver providing farming service	1992–1994, worked as a fisher for an employer	1994–present, works as an independent forwarder	
23	Female	1959	1974–1995, farmed at home	1984–1995, worked as a jobber	1996–present, run an aquatic product shop				
24	Female	1960	1979–1985, worked as a warehouseman in a die shop	1985–1986, worked as a salesperson in another die shop	1986–present, works as a treasurer in local village office				
25	Female	1957	1974–1984, worked as a treasurer in local village office	1985–1987, ran a small restaurant	1988–2000, farmed at home	2001, worked in a die shop			
26	Female	1957	Worked as a worker in a collective silk mill	Worked as a teller in a packinghouse	As a worked in a state-owned textile company	As a worker in a textile factory	As a worker in another textile factory		
27	Female	1954	As a worker in a dyehouse	Ran a grocery	Farms at home				
28	Female	1971	Farmed at home	1986–1988, worked as a plasterer	1989, worked as a electrician	Works as a temporary electrician in local electric power station			
29	Female	1963	Worked as a brickie in building sites	Worked as a carpenter in a furniture factory in Xi'an	Worked as a storekeeper in a toy factory in Guangdong Province	Farms at home			
30	Male	1956	Farmed at home	2000, worked in a cookware factory					
31	Male	1961	1979–1991, farmed at home	1991–1992, worked in a village brick field in Shannxi Province	1992–present, is engaged in business				
32	Male	1976	1996–1999, worked as a house maintainer	2001–present, works as a choreman in building sites					
33	Male	1951	1965–1993, farmed at home	1993–1998, worked as a builder in building sites	1998–present, farms at home				

continued

Case No.	Sex	Year of Birth	Occupational Experience (1)	Occupational Experience (2)	Occupational Experience (3)	Occupational Experience (4)	Occupational Experience (5)	Occupational Experience (6)	Occupational Experience (7)
34	Male	1970	1987–1992, farmed at home	1993–1997, worked as a painter in a garage	2000–present, works as a packer in a state-owned chemical plant in Meishan				
35	Male	1981	1999–2000, worked as a security guard in Hongzhou	After 2000, unemployed					
36	Male	1966	1978–1998, farmed at home	1992–present, works in a bamboo articles factory					
37	Male	1972	1986–1991, worked as a jobber in Nongquan city	1991–2000, did business in Nongquan	After 2000, jobless and stays at home				
38	Male	1978	1992–1999, worked as an operator in a large paper company	1999–2001, worked as a textile worker	2001–present, works as an independent forwarder				
39	Female	1960	1975–1990, farmed at home	1990–1992, worked in a paper mill	1993–present, farms at home				

Source: The nationwide survey conducted by this research group.

384

In terms of peasant-workers, most first-generation peasant-workers now have become middle-aged and elderly persons. On one hand, they are unable to find jobs as easily as younger peasant-workers are, because young ages, physical strength, and low wages are the major competitive advantages of peasant-workers in the labor market. On the other hand, the employment of peasant-workers is not stable. Especially, working in other areas has more uncertainty and peasant-workers have to lead an unsecured life without institutional protections. Therefore, many older peasant-workers returned to hometowns and worked in agriculture again.

Of course, not all first-generation peasant-workers have returned to agriculture, and a certain number of peasant-workers are still engaged in non-agricultural activities; some of them are still peasant-workers; some become individual-operated business proprietors, and a few become private entrepreneurs. A tiny minority of them even accomplished postgraduate programs and entered the stratum of professional and technical personnel through individual efforts in education. However, the overwhelming majority of first-generation peasant-workers who are still working in non-agricultural sectors in other areas did not achieve upward mobility via occupational mobility. Although they frequently changed occupations, all such changes were limited in the scope of peasant-worker related occupations. For example, the respondent in case 13, from 1979 to 1983, worked as a porter in a transportation company; from 1983 to 1984 he worked as a builder in a construction company; from 1993 to 1994, as a latheman in a factory; from 1995 to 2001, as a plasterer in a construction company. Respondents in case 14, 17, and 15 were peasant-workers all along as well. Such a characteristic of peasant-workers' mobility has occurred not only in the 1980s but also in the 1990s as well.

The most possible upward mobility for peasant-workers is to be individual-operated business proprietors. After working in non-agricultural sectors for several years, many peasant-workers accumulated a small amount of money and some experience; at a certain age, they might want to find a stable occupation and being an individual-operated business proprietor becomes their first choice. In general, they will return to their hometowns and open a small business run by their family. Most peasant-workers are unable to become private entrepreneurs because of insufficient capital, technology, and management capability. Especially after the 1990s, capital, technology, and management capability have become critical factors that determine whether a person can be a private entrepreneur or not. Therefore, the most likely direction of peasant-workers' upward mobility is to be an individual-operated business proprietor. Many cases in Table 10-8 give examples for this point. In case 6 and 7, the two respondents were initially peasant-workers; later, one respondent started a greengrocery, while the other opened a barbershop. In case 8, the respondent initially was an individual-operated business proprietor and then became a peasant-worker; at present, he runs an individual-operated business again.

By report, some peasant-workers who were assiduous in studying were admitted to universities as postgraduate students, and then they entered other strata. In our survey, some peasant-workers became private entrepreneurs; one person even became a millionaire from a peasant-worker gleaning and collecting scraps. However, these are exceptional cases in the mobility of peasant-workers. Although the great efforts of some young peasant-workers who learn skills on the job and have interests in studying are worthy of praise, as a whole, the resources and conditions that are possessed by peasant-workers to achieve upward mobility are very limited. Such a situation can be observed from the social mobility mechanisms of peasant-workers.

Mechanisms of Social Mobility

Based on the above descriptions and analysis, we find some mechanisms that take effect in the social mobility of peasant-workers. Analysis on such mechanisms will be conducted from the following two perspectives: the mobility from agricultural laborers to peasant-workers and the mobility from peasant-workers to other social strata.

(1) Mechanisms of Mobility from Agricultural Laborers to Peasant-Workers

In fact, the above descriptions and analysis have significantly demonstrated the mechanisms of mobility from agricultural laborers to peasant-workers. We further summarize them into four basic mechanisms as follows.

A. The Pressure Mechanism of Employment and Income

The large number of surplus rural laborers forces a part of the rural population to seek jobs in non-agricultural sectors. At the same time, the slow growth or even negative growth of agricultural income gives a further push on rural laborers to enter non-agricultural sectors.

B. The Mechanism of Age and Gender

Many previous studies demonstrate that, in rural areas, young and middle-aged people mainly choose to work as non-agricultural laborers, while elderly people and women stay at home and are engaged in agricultural labor. Results of our survey also support this finding. Meanwhile, although young women also go out to work in other areas and their number has been increasing recently, the number of male peasant-workers is still greater than that of female peasant-workers.

C. The Mechanism of Human Resources

The human resources here mainly refer to the level of education received. According to the above-mentioned statistics, usually the level of education received by peasant-workers is higher than that of agricultural laborers. On one hand, employers have certain requirements on peasant-workers' educational backgrounds. In general, peasant-workers with junior middle school and higher education will find jobs more easily. In some coastal regions, employers currently require senior middle school and higher educational backgrounds. As a whole, the higher their educational level, the more likely peasant-workers will find jobs:

> The longer the years of schooling of peasant-workers, the higher their income level will be. Meanwhile, the income level of peasant-workers who received trainings in past five years is significantly higher than that of those without trainings.[1]

On the other hand, rural laborers with higher level of education received usually have more confidence to work as non-agricultural laborers rather than as agricultural laborers.

D. The Mechanism of Social Capital

Peasant-workers largely depend on social networks to find jobs. The basic pattern of peasant-workers in search of jobs is "relatives refer relatives, friends introduce friend, and neighbors help neighbors". Because of the effect of such social networks, the homogeneity of peasant-workers' occupations is relatively high. For example, in the same factory, peasant-workers usually come from several major regions. Similarly, in a certain sector, the places of peasant-workers' origins are highly concentrated. For example, many tailors come from Zhejiang Province, babysitters mainly come from Anhui Province and Sichuan Province, and most taxi drivers in Shenzhen City come from Hunan Province and Jiangxi Province; in Beijing, peasant-workers from particular regions usually dwell together and have formed several inhabited areas in this city, such as so-called "Zhejiang village", "Henan village", and "Xinjiang village", etc. To peasant-workers with lower educational levels, the effect of social capital is more important than that of human capital. Many previous studies have demonstrated this point.[2]

The above four major mechanisms do not take effect separately but are interconnected and combined in pushing the rural population to go in for non-agricultural labor as peasant-workers. Without sufficient social capital, even rural young men with certain level of education cannot find jobs easily. Similarly, it is difficult for peasant-workers with only social capital but no certain educational background to find jobs.

(2) Mechanisms of Mobility from Peasant-Workers to Other Strata

The knowledge of mechanisms in social mobility from agricultural laborers to peasant-workers can provides some clues to predict the future paths of social mobility of peasant-workers. In order to explain the directions of peasant-workers' social

---

[1] Wang, Fenyu and Yandong Zhao. 2003. "Economic Status Attainment of Mobile Rural Laborers and Its Determinants". Pp. 142 in Peilin Li (ed.), *Peasant-Workers: Socio-economic Analysis on Peasant-Workers Entered into the City in China*. Beijing: Social Sciences Documentation Publishing House.
[2] Li, Peilin (2003)..

mobility more clearly, it is necessary to briefly discuss the mobility mechanisms of moving from peasant-workers to other strata. These mechanisms determined the possible and impossible directions in peasant-workers' mobility. Based on our survey and study, we believe that three types of mechanisms have a significant influence on the directions of peasant-workers' mobility: the institutional mechanism, the age and gender mechanism, and the economic mechanism.

A. The Institutional Mechanism

The institutional mechanism still has an influence on shifting from peasants to peasant-workers, but not as significant as on the social mobility from peasant-workers to other strata. The occupation of peasant-worker itself is an outcome of institutional arrangements and governmental policies, in which workers who came from peasants can only be called as "peasant-workers" and do not have the same status as urban workers. According to current institutions in China, peasant-workers cannot enjoy various stipulated treatments that are endowed to urban workers through governmental policies. The mobility from peasant-workers to urban workers is blocked by institutions. On one hand, the status of peasant-workers is unstable and temporary; on the other hand, it is difficult for peasant-workers to shift to urban workers. Peasant-workers cannot participate in the recruitment examination of government employees and are ineligible to become formal employees in state-owned enterprises and public institutions. Therefore, relevant institutional arrangements restrain peasant-workers from moving into the stratum of state and social administrators, professional and technical personnel, clerical personnel, and managerial personnel; the left possible moving directions are individual-operated business proprietors, commercial and service personnel, private entrepreneurs, and agricultural laborers. Because the overwhelming majority of peasant-workers have little chance to become private entrepreneurs, only three strata are actually possible directions; of which, moving toward individual-operated business proprietors and commercial and service personnel belong to upward mobility. However, such upward mobility can only bring them very limited improvement of status, while the back flow toward agricultural laborers is not only a type of downward mobility but also the most possible direction.

B. The Age and Gender Mechanism

Age and gender always affect the occupational mobility of peasant-workers. If a peasant-worker fails to improve his or her socio-economic status when he or she is young, the possibility of upward mobility will become smaller and smaller with age. In general, if a peasant-worker cannot find a stable job at a certain age, he or she will consider returning to agriculture, or choose to start an individual-operated business according to his or her own economic condition. Compared with males, female peasant-workers tend to look to their future directions earlier. Usually, female peasant-workers at the age over 23 years will choose to return home and get married, and then they will decide whether to continue to be peasant-workers or not; some of them may choose to stay home to do housework, farm, and take care of children and elderly family members. Male peasant-workers have relatively more choices, they can continue to be workers or do business after getting married. Of course, many married women also choose to go out with their husbands to work or do business. Usually, enterprises have a certain limitation on the age of peasant-workers, and they tend to recruit younger applicants. Moreover, when employed peasant-workers have reached a certain age, some enterprises will dismiss them with various excuses and measures.

C. The Economic Mechanism

The economic condition is an extremely important factor that affects peasant-workers' choices of directions of move. After having accumulated a certain amount of money, many peasant-workers will choose to be individual-operated business proprietors. However, for many peasant-workers, it is not easy to save money because the major goal of these peasant-workers is to support their family. In fact, after many years' work, a lot of peasant-workers still do not have adequate savings.

The combination of the three mechanisms has an even more important influence on the directions of move of peasant-workers. When one is prevented from moving upward to higher strata by institutions, he or she will scrape the bottom of the barrel and choose to enter into adjacent strata with better socio-economic status. Of course, such choices still need necessary conditions. After working for a period of time, some peasant-workers with certain economic conditions will consider to start their own shops or businesses. In contrast, those without corresponding economic conditions have to continue to work as peasant-workers; after reaching a certain age, maybe they cannot find any jobs and have to reenter into agriculture as farmers. In the three mechanisms, some relevant conditions are external factors or even ascription factors and hence are out of a peasant-worker's control; some factors need to be achieved through peasant-workers' individual efforts. As a whole, conditions that can be obtained through peasant-workers' efforts are not so good, while at the same time the limitations imposed on them are so many, so unreasonable, and so rigid; as a result, the upward mobility channels of peasant-workers become extremely narrow.

According to our survey, peasant-workers can only achieve upward mobility through the following channels. First, they can excel at work and attempt to obtain certain honors (such as "outstanding peasant-workers", etc.) in their positions; hence, they may be accepted as local residents and become permanent workers. Second, they can register in colleges, universities, or even postgraduate programs while working in enterprises; after obtaining certain degrees and skills, they may find managerial positions. Third, they can save a certain amount of money and then start their own shops or businesses in their hometowns and become business owners or entrepreneurs. Fourth, they can support their children's education with all their efforts; as a result, their children may enter into universities successfully and hence achieve intergenerational upward mobility. However, the number of peasant-workers who have actually achieved upward mobility through these four channels is very limited; the overwhelming majority of peasant-workers are unable to achieve upward mobility through the above four channels.

THE PEASANT-WORKER SYSTEM AND LAG OF SOCIAL MOBILITY

Explanations of the Peasant-Worker System

Social status and mobility state are closely related to the unique peasant-worker system in China.   What on earth is this system? In fact, the above discussions have provided much relevant information. In this section, we will further propose a systematic explanation in order to help readers understand the uniqueness of the peasant-worker system from the perspective of social mobility.

The peasant-worker system is an embodiment and extension of the urban-rural dual system in non-agricultural field. According to the traditional urban-rural dual system, rural areas should develop agriculture, while urban areas should focus on industry; peasants could only work in agriculture and were not allowed to go in for non-agricultural labor and hence could not work in the city. Peasants engaged in agriculture were secured by farmland. Correspondingly, they could not enjoy urban residents' social welfare and security treatments. Now peasants can enter into non-agricultural sectors, work, and do business in the city. In this sense, it seems that the urban-rural dual system has been broken up. However, the social policy and institutional arrangements established in the planned economy era have actually taken effect; furthermore, they have extended into the city with peasants' social mobility and reproduced a type of dual system in the urban areas, i.e., the peasant-worker system.

The peasant-worker system is the outcome of reconstruction of the planned systems in the reform and opening-up with a remarkable characteristic of discrimination. In this system, peasant-workers cannot enjoy fair and reasonable treatments. Compared with urban permanent workers, they receive unequal pays and work unequal hours for the same work. Relevant unfair phenomena universally exist, such as a city with two systems, an enterprise with two systems, a union with two systems, and a school with two systems.

Compared with the planned economy era, the peasant-worker system gives peasants the opportunity to work in non-agricultural sectors; hence, it is great progress. However, such a system, which has run for two decades, is not only unfair to peasant-workers, but also unfavorable for the state. It has impaired the competence of sustainable development of this country, and the most serious disadvantage of this system is that it has neither stimulated peasant-workers to learn skills, nor promoted enterprises to pay attention to peasant-workers' skills training. Even worse, it has impaired the urban workers' enthusiasm for learning and improving skills. In many state-owned enterprises, peasant-workers are used as the first-line workers, while formal workers become "overseers", losing any ideas and motivations to learn skills. Although Chinese economy currently still grows at a high speed, it has encountered its biggest "bottleneck", that is, the lack of skilled technical workers. Compared with other major manufacturing countries, the proportion of technical workers to the overall number of workers in China is considerably low. In some major manufacturing countries, the proportion of senior workers is 30 percent, middle-level workers 50 percent, and junior workers 15~20 percent; while in China, senior workers only account for 5 percent, middle-level workers 30~35 percent, and junior workers as high as 60 percent. Such a situation largely impedes China transforming from the "world factory" to a major manufacturing country. One of key measures that can be used to remove such conditions is giving up the peasant-worker system thoroughly to help peasant-workers successfully achieve complete social mobility in which occupational mobility and a shift of social status occur at the same time and hence remove any lag in social mobility.

The Lag of Social Mobility of Peasant-Workers

The peasant-worker system is not only a discriminatory system, but also an abnormal social institution, which seriously hinders the social mobility of peasant-workers and results in the lag of social mobility. The *lag of social mobility* refers to the asynchrony and incoordination in social mobility; for peasant-workers, it is embodied as inconsistency and incoordination between occupational mobility and social status shift.

    The concept "lag" was initially proposed by an American sociologist William Ogbum. In his study on social transition, he found that the non-material cultural transition lags behind the material cultural transition and hence brings about the cultural lag. We believe that many lag phenomena also exist in the progress of socio-economic transition in China. The emergence and constant existence of the peasant-worker group is a typical phenomenon of lag. It is worthwhile to point out that the lag is not equal to stagnancy; it just means that the change in a certain aspect cannot keep up with changes in other aspects. There are certain conditions existing for rural laborers to become peasant-workers; not all rural laborers can be peasant-workers. However, merely being in possession of such conditions still cannot change the unbalanced situation in social transition and hence the lag of social mobility emerges.

    Based on the above reasons, we believe that the concept of lag can clearly reflect the characteristic of peasant-workers' social mobility. The lag of peasant-workers' social mobility mainly includes four aspects.

(1) The shift of status lags behind the shift of occupation

Peasant-worker is the outcome of occupational mobility in which agricultural laborers shift from agriculture to non-agricultural occupations in the secondary and tertiary industry; however, the social status of agricultural laborers does not change thoroughly and peasant-workers still retain their status as peasants. Of course, nowadays the status of peasant itself has changed to some extent as well, but it still cannot meet the need of occupational mobility. Peasant-workers are engaged in works that are similar to or the same as what urban permanent workers do, but they are not treated as formal workers all the time. Although recently the government has noticed that peasant-workers have become the major element of the working class, it still does not adopt effective measures to remove such lag phenomenon.

(2) The change of social status lags behind the change of economic status

The primary purpose of the rural population shifting to peasant-workers is to obtain more economic income. As a whole, the income of peasant-workers is higher than that of agricultural laborers. However, peasant-workers do not still obtain corresponding social status. Their social status is the same as that of agricultural laborers; in fact, the social status of many peasant-workers is even lower than that of farmers, because they lack basic social respect and decent lifestyles.

(3)The Shift of occupations does not integrate peasant-workers into urban society; they are still excluded from the progress of urbanization

With the development of industrialization, a large number of the rural population has transferred to non-agricultural fields and hence brought about the group of peasant-workers. However, the lag of urbanization prevents many peasant-workers from becoming urban residents with the shift of their occupations and being integrated into the urban social structure.

(4) The change of civil rights is disjointed

Although peasant-workers have obtained relative freedom in the right to employment, they do not get other civil rights such as the right of employment security, the right to migrate freely, the right to receive education and training, the right to participate in pubic administration, and so forth.

In sum, the social mobility of peasant-workers is very different from normal social mobility both in structure and in mobility mechanisms. Normal social mobility occurs under the condition that all citizens' basic civil rights are secured and hence usually such lags will not happen.

Is a New Working Class Growing Up in China?

After above analyses, the next question is whether the peasant-worker system and the lag of social mobility will be changed in the future. Alternatively, will they be solidified? In this process, will peasant-workers become a new working class? Alternatively, have peasant-workers already grown up as a new working class?

Various evidences show that peasant-workers have risen as a new social stratum in contemporary Chinese society. In this study, we treat them as a part of the stratum of workers in the ten major strata framework; in fact, peasant-workers have become a substratum in the stratum of workers, and we may call it a "new working class". Hereafter, we will discuss the possibility and feasibility of peasant-workers as a new working class from the dimensions of its social attribute, social structure, and size.

From the perspective of social attribute, there are many differences between peasant-workers and the stratum of workers in China; especially, the status of peasant-workers is still different from that of urban workers. Although the government has admitted that peasant-workers are an important element of the working class, many peasant-workers are still excluded from unions. Even if they organize their own unions, such unions will be called as "unions of peasant-workers". Furthermore, peasant-workers are excluded from the state social welfare and security systems. They cannot enjoy equal social security and welfare benefits as urban workers do. Judging from this point, peasant-workers share the same social attribute with the stratum of agricultural laborers and hence still retain the status as peasants. However, peasant-workers also are significantly different from agricultural laborers in occupation, economic status, and lifestyle.

From the perspective of social structure transition, the shift of the rural labor force from agricultural laborers to peasant-workers is consistent with the synchronous trends of urbanization and industrialization in China. Such a change is an inevitable outcome of the modernization of Chinese society; in turn, it also has promoted the modernization of Chinese society. In the progress of modernization, a large proportion of the rural population will inevitably shift to non-agricultural sectors and enter the city; without such changes, the accomplishment of modernization in China is impossible. History of developed countries provides sufficient proof; the proportions of peasants and the rural population in all these countries are very small, while the levels of urbanization are over 70 percent. At present, the rural population makes up more than 62 percent in the whole population in China. Therefore, there is a great gap between China and developed countries in social structure.

However, the efforts to remove the lag of peasant-workers' social mobility are conditioned by the rigid social structure and institutions in China, including the urban-rural interests allocation, market segmentations, interests allocation between the central government and local governments, interests allocation among local governments, and the administrative personnel system, etc. All these factors restrain peasant-workers from becoming urban formal workers and moving to other strata.

Limited by such rigid interests allocations and institutions, can peasant-workers shape a sort of new stratum identification? Will some remarkable collective actions occur? All these questions need further investigation and study. However, one thing we can confirm is that the size of peasant-workers is not negligible any longer. Meanwhile, it is observed that peasant-workers' collective actions have been growing, their consciousness to strive for rights and interests and to participate in public affairs has been strengthening, and the level of organization of peasant-workers has been increasing. If the lag of peasant-workers' social mobility lasts for a long time, a new working class will inevitably emerge.

In conclusion, peasant-workers are a unique group in Chinese society. The emergence and existence of this group reflect the unique characteristics of social transformations in China, that is, transformations from the planned system to a free-market system, from agricultural society to industrial society, and from rural society to urban society. In the process of such transformations, because changes between society, occupations, market, and institutions are not synchronous, the lag of social mobility will unavoidably occur. Compared with the past, the emergence and development of peasant-workers is a sign that indicates Chinese social structure has developed in a more rational direction; however, compared with the need for further development, such rationalization is still very limited. Therefore, in order to remove the lag of social mobility and promote peasant-workers to develop into an actually important part of the stratum of industrial workers, further institutional reforms are necessary.

Chapter 11　Social Mobility of Agricultural Laborers

In the social hierarchy and social mobility in contemporary China, agricultural laborers are both the largest occupational group and the largest disadvantaged stratum. Knowledge of the social mobility of this stratum will enhance understanding of the social structure attributes in modern China.

DEFINITION AND THE SIZE OF THE STRATUM OF AGRICULTURAL LABORERS

The drop of the proportion of agricultural laborers to the overall social labor force is a universal tendency in the process of industrialization in all countries. The key for China to achieve industrialization and urbanization is to change the employment structure by adjusting industrial structure and hence pushing the agricultural population to shift to non-agricultural population. In 1997, the proportion of the labor force in the primary industry dropped to less than 50 percent for the first time in history; since then, this proportion has still remained around 50 percent in the following years. Such a tendency indicates that, in a country with such a huge agricultural population, it is an extremely difficult task to reduce the proportion of agricultural laborers in employment in the process of economic development. At present, the proportion of agricultural population is still too high, even higher than that of Iran and North Korea (see Table 11-1), and is significantly disproportionate to the level of economic development in China.

As an internationally adopted concept, agricultural laborers refer to social members who are engaged in agricultural production labor and rely on such activities as major source of income. Because of the influence of the urban-rural residence registration system, the concept of agricultural laborers in China is different from its common meaning. In China, agricultural laborers refer to peasants who contract in collective-owned land in the form of family operations,1 are engaged in agriculture (forestry, animal husbandry, and fishery) as their only or major occupation, and live on such occupation as their only or major source of income.2 They are an

---

[1] In the stratum classification of this study, people whose income gained from non-agricultural part-time occupations is higher than agricultural income are classified according to the categories of their part-time occupations.

[2] There are two methods to define peasants. The first method is judging by the proportion of working

occupational group working in agricultural production and have the status of registered rural residence. In this definition, the status of peasants is emphasized in order to distinguish peasants from agricultural workers in state-owned farms, whom have the status of permanent workers. Agricultural laborers include self-employed laborers, employed laborers, and employers engaged in agriculture. At present, the agricultural income of Chinese agricultural laborers mainly includes income gained from self-employed labor in agriculture (such as family operations), remuneration earned from wage labor in agriculture (such as employees working for state-owned farms and agricultural entrepreneurs), and returns obtained from large-scale operations in agriculture (such as agricultural entrepreneurs who employ peasant-workers).

Table 11-1   Proportions of the Agricultural Population

Unit: %

Year	1990	1998	1999	2000	2001
World Totals	46.4	43.2	42.8	42.4	42.0
Asia	58.9	54.0	53.4	52.9	52.4
China	71.9	67.7	67.1	66.6	66.0
Bengal	65.2	57.6	56.6	55.6	54.7
India	58.2	54.6	54.1	53.7	53.2
Indonesia	50.9	45.4	44.8	44.1	43.4
Iran	32.1	27.4	26.9	26.4	25.9
Israel	4.1	2.9	2.8	2.7	2.6
Japan	7.0	4.4	4.1	3.9	3.6
Kazakhstan	—	20.6	20.2	19.8	19.3
North Korea	38.0	31.6	30.9	30.1	29.4
South Korea	16.1	10.0	9.3	8.8	8.2
Malaysia	26.0	19.2	18.4	17.7	17.0
Mongolia	32.0	25.7	25.0	24.3	23.6
Burma	73.3	70.8	70.5	70.2	69.9
Pakistan	55.5	51.8	51.4	50.9	50.4
Philippines	45.6	40.6	40.0	39.3	38.7
Singapore	0.4	0.2	0.2	0.1	0.1
Sri Lanka	49.2	46.9	46.6	46.3	46.0
Thailand	56.9	50.6	49.8	49.0	48.2
Turkey	37.3	32.0	31.4	30.7	30.1
Vietnam	71.2	68.1	67.7	67.3	66.9

Source: Statistics from the Food and Agriculture Organization, United Nations.

hours invested in agriculture; agricultural income of peasants defined by this method may make up either a major or a minor part of their total income. The other one is judging by the proportion of income gained from agriculture; agricultural working hours of peasants defined by this method may make up either a major or a minor part of their total working hours. In consideration of agricultural laborer is a type occupation based on social division of labor, we believe that the proportion of agricultural income is a more appropriate indicator of the occupational characteristic of agriculture. Furthermore, only if agricultural income becomes a persons' major source of income, will agriculture be his or her occupation rather than a hobby.

The concept of agricultural laborers is different from the concepts of "agricultural population", "rural population", and "employment in the primary industry" adopted in the governmental statistical yearbooks. Agricultural population is not the same as agricultural laborers. *Agricultural population* refers to villagers who possess the right to contract in rural land stipulated by the existing rural administration system, while agricultural laborers are just a part of agricultural population. In other words, agricultural population is equal to villagers, while agricultural laborers are a segment of the villagers. Similarly, rural population is not equal to agricultural laborers and is different from agricultural population, which is classified by the status of registered residence. *Rural population* refers to the population resides in townships which are classified by the administrative regionalism, which includes the non-agricultural population, agricultural laborers, and the agricultural population.

Agricultural laborers belong to a part of "employment in the primary industry", "employment in rural areas", and "employment in agriculture, forestry, animal husbandry, and fishery" in the governmental statistical yearbooks. Besides agricultural laborers in the rural population, *employment in the primary industry* also includes employees in state-owned farms. Comparing the figures of "employment in the primary industry" and "employment in agriculture, forestry, animal husbandry, and fishery" in the same year in the governmental statistical yearbooks, we will find that the two sets of figures are not same. *Employment in rural areas* refers to rural laborers who work in agriculture or non-agricultural sectors. *Employment in agriculture, forestry, animal husbandry, and fishery* refers to those rural laborers who are engaged in agricultural activity. The graph of changes in the rural employment structure (Figure 11-1) shows that the curve of the proportion of rural non-agricultural employment to total rural employment nearly coincides with the curve of the proportion of employment in township enterprises at the end of the year to total rural employment. In addition, the proportion of employment engaged in the primary industry in township enterprises to the total employment in township enterprises decreased sharply from 64.75 percent in 1980 to 3.62 percent in 1985, and then to 1.55 percent in 2002. This means that the non-agriculture-oriented changes in rural areas mainly are achieved through the development of township enterprises.

The general situation of the urban and rural population in the fifth national population census, the change of the population of rural agricultural laborers from 1978 to 2002, and the change of the rural employment structure from 1978 to 2002 are listed in Table 11-2, Table 11-3, and Table 11-4.

Figure 11-1   Curves of Changes in the Rural Employment Structure

Table 11-2   Urban and Rural Population in the 5th National Population Census

Unit: Ten thousand persons

Year of Census	1953	1964	1982	1990	2000
Urban population	7726	12710	21082	29971	45844
Rural population	50534	56748	79736	83397	80739

Source: Reorganized according to Table 3-4 in *China Statistical Yearbook (2003)*.

Table 11-3   Population of Rural Agricultural Laborers, 1978~2002

Unit: Ten thousand households, Ten thousand persons

Year	Rural households	Rural population	Rural employment	Rural employment in the primary industry	Rural employment in agriculture, forestry, animal husbandry & fishery
1978	17347	80320	30638	28318	28455.6
1980	17673	81096	31835.7	29122	29808.4
1985	19077	84419.7	37065.1	31130	30351.5
1989	21504	87831	40938.8	33225	32440.5
1990	22237	89590.3	42009.5	38914	33336.4
1991	22566	90525.1	43092.5	39098	34186.3
1992	22849	91154.4	43801.6	38699	34037
1993	22984	91333.5	44255.7	37680	33258.2
1994	23165	91526.2	44654.1	36628	32690.3
1995	23282	91674.6	45041.8	35530	32334.5
1996	23437.6	91941	45288	34820	32260.4
1997	23406.2	91524.7	45962.1	34840	32434.9
1998	23678	91960.1	46432.3	35177	32626.4
1999	23810.5	92216.3	46896.5	35768	32911.8
2000	24148.7	92819.7	47962.1	36043	32797.5
2001	24432.2	93382.9	48228.9	36513	32451
2002	24569.4	93502.5	48526.9	36870	31990.6

Table 11-4 Rural Employment Structure, 1978~2002

Unit: Ten thousand persons, %

Year	Employment in township enterprises at the end of the year	Employment engaged in the primary industry in township enterprises at the end of the year	Proportion of the rural non-agricultural employment to total rural employment	Proportion of the employment engaged in the primary industry in township enterprises to total employment in township enterprises	Proportion of the employment in township enterprises at the end of the year to total rural employment
1978	2826.56	1734.36	7.12	61.36	9.23
1980	2999.68	1942.3	6.37	64.75	9.42
1985	6979	252.38	18.11	3.62	18.83
1989	9366.78	239.3	20.76	2.55	22.88
1990	9264.75	236.06	20.65	2.55	22.05
1991	9613.63	243.17	20.67	2.53	22.31
1992	10624.71	261.82	22.29	2.46	24.26
1993	12345.31	285.36	24.85	2.31	27.9
1994	12017.47	260.46	26.79	2.17	26.91
1995	12862.06	313.52	28.21	2.44	28.56
1996	13508.29	336	28.77	2.49	29.83
1997	13050.42	276.96	29.43	2.12	28.39
1998	12536.55	273.91	29.73	2.18	27
1999	12704.09	247.38	29.82	1.95	27.09
2000	12819.57	222.04	31.62	1.73	26.73
2001	13085.58	200, 03	32.71	1.53	27.13
2002	13287.71	205.37	34.08	1.55	27.38

Source: Reorganized according to data about the employment in township enterprises at the end of the year in Table 12-30, *China Statistical Yearbook (2003)*.

CHARACTERISTICS OF SOCIAL MOBILITY OF THE
STRATUM BEFORE 1978

The history of social development in China from 1949 shows that the transfer of agricultural laborers from agriculture to non-agricultural sector also occurred in the planned economy. However, only after the implementation of the household contract and responsibility system with remuneration linked to output in rural areas, peasants obtained the right to choose their occupations independently and agricultural laborers could migrate freely.

The Land Reform and Cooperativization: 1949~1956

Before 1949, there were two classes in Chinese countryside, that is, landlords and peasants. In the total rural population, landlords and rich peasants accounted for 10 percent, poor peasants and farm laborers accounted for 70 percent, and middle peasants made up 20 percent. The distribution of rural land resources was extremely unbalanced. In many regions such as Sichuan Province, landlords occupied about 70 to 80 percent of rural lands. In the middle and lower areas of the Yangtze River, lands were dispersedly distributed; in general, landlords possessed about 30 percent to 50 percent of farmland and public lands, rich peasant occupied about 10 percent to 15 percent, and middle and poor peasants and farm laborers had 30 percent to 40 percent. In newly liberated areas and to-be liberated areas, as a whole, the total rented land made up about 60 percent to 70 percent of the total rural land. Although middle and poor peasants and farm laborers farmed 90 percent of rural land, they only owned a part of the land.

The system of the land in which landlords owned the majority of land fettered the development of social productivity seriously. It was one of the main causes that resulted in poverty and underdevelopment in China. Furthermore, it was a basic obstacle to industrialization in China. In order to liberate rural productivity, develop agricultural production, and create favorable conditions for industrialization, the First Plenum of the Chinese People's Political Consultative Conference approved the *Common Guiding Principles* in 1949, which encouraged farmers to realize their request of "land to the tiller" step by step in areas, in which the land reform was not yet carried out and to transfer the land ownership from the landlord-owned system to the farmer-owned system. In June 1956, the *Law of the People's Republic of China on the Land Reform* was enacted and put into practice.

From the winter of 1950 to the end of 1952, except for some minority inhabited regions such as Tibet and Xinjiang and the to-be liberated Taiwan Province, in newly liberated areas with an agricultural population of 0.27 billion, plus previously liberated areas, there were more than 0.3 billion peasants without farmland or only with a small quantity of farmland. All these peasants obtained about 0.7 billion Mu (equal to 47,000 thousand hectare) of farmland and a large number of the means of production at no cost; in addition, they were exempt from more than 30,000 thousand tons of grains which had to be paid to landlords as the rent of land each year in the past. The land reform aroused peasants' unparalleled initiative in production.

In rural areas at that time, there were two forms of organizations in agricultural production, i.e., family operations and reciprocal aids, which were universally welcomed by peasants. In February 1953, the Central Committee of the C.P.C. approved the *Draft of the Resolution on Reciprocal Aids and Cooperation in Agricultural Production* and proposed to establish agricultural producers' cooperatives, which were characterized by the pooling of land in areas with appropriate conditions. Therefore, the combination of cooperativization in agriculture and industrialization in the national economy aroused a rush of establishment of cooperatives in China. Mao Zedong pointed out that the purpose of this movement was to eliminate capitalism and small-scale production in China. The number of agricultural cooperatives reached 15 thousand in spring 1953 in China, with 2740 thousand peasant households as members, a rise of several times over the 1952 figure. In April 1953, the first National Education Conference reaffirmed that farmlands that had already been distributed to peasants were not allowed to be deprived deliberately. Peasants' ownership must be protected; engagement, debit and credit, tenancy, and trade of farmland should be conditionally permitted. However, because the government monopolized the purchase and sale of farm produce and hence had to directly contact with hundreds of millions of peasants, it was really an onerous task; in addition, the unbalanced situation in supply and demand of grain and cotton could not be mitigated by the small-scale peasant economy. Therefore, there was an increasing demand to combine dispersed individual farmers into large-scale production organizations. In February 1954, the Seventh Plenum of the Tenth Central Committee of the C.P.C. formally approved the *General Line of the Socialist Transformations* proposed by the Political Bureau. The *General Line* put forward that industrialization of the national economy was the central task and the socialist transformations of the individually operated agriculture, the handicraft industry, and the capitalist industry and commerce were supportive measures of the central task. By the end of 1956, farm households that had joined cooperatives accounted for 96.3 percent of the total number of farm households in China; farm households that had joined the advanced cooperatives made up 87.8 percent of the total number of farm households. Advanced cooperatives became the major form of production organization in rural China.

In general, the social mobility of peasants during this period has the following characteristics:

First, the rural resources were evenly distributed among peasants. The status of impoverished lower-middle peasants who made up the majority of the rural population was greatly improved and the "land to the tiller" goal was achieved. The land reform was not only a readjustment of the capital and property relations in rural areas, but also a structure-oriented social mobility that overthrew the original status order. The political status of landlords and rich peasants in rural society fell significantly. Through the land reform, most poor peasants and farm laborers obtained production conditions, which were equal to the conditions of middle peasants before the land reform, and their living conditions were improved as well. Their dream "a wife and some children in the same house, with thirty Mu of farmland and an ox" came true. A pro-middle-peasant tendency emerged in the countryside. A tiny minority of rich middle peasants grew up to new rich peasants through employing farm laborers, doing part-time business or making loans; a small number of farm households sold their farmland for various reasons and hence their standard of living dropped. As a result, the gap in wealth expanded to some extent. However, as a whole, after the land reform, agricultural production and peasants' living conditions were generally enhanced. The peasant organizations took on some governmental functions; rural education was paid great attention to and various short middle-school programs were established; the rural production environments and social environments were improved as well; the worker-peasant alliance was treated as the political foundation of the new regime. The government intensively reconstructed the infrastructure of irrigation and water conservancy in 1952; from 1950 to 1951 goods exchange fairs were held at various levels all over China to promote the sales of local and special products and handicraft wares and hence improved the purchasing power of peasants. Cooperativization transformed yeomen into collectivized peasants. As a result, some limitations started to be imposed on peasants' freedom in employment.

Second, the state-driven industrialization transformed some peasants into workers. There were 2,858 bureaucratic capitalists controlled enterprises in China before 1949, with 1290 thousand staff members and workers, among them 750 thousand were industrial workers. In the early days after the establishment of the People's Republic of China, the newly increased workers mainly consisted of two groups. One group consisted of demobilized soldiers; the other group was recruited from peasants. In fact, the majority of soldiers in the army also came from peasants. Therefore, shifting from peasants to workers became the major feature of the social mobility in that period. After the implementation of the state's monopoly over purchasing and selling, such mobility was restricted and workers in enterprises mainly came from urban residents; only in a few sectors, such as mining industry, were some workers still recruited from peasants.

The People's Commune Movement: 1957~1965

On April 8, 1958, the Central Committee of the C.P.C. released the *Proposal Concerning Merging Small Agricultural Cooperatives into Large-size Cooperatives*, and it was the beginning of the People's Commune Movement. According to Mao Zedong's opinion, the advantage of the People's Commune was that the agricultural production, industrial production, commercial, educational, and people's militia organizations were combined into one single organization and hence it was convenient for management. In August 1958, the enlarged meeting of the Political Bureau with the Central Committee of the C.P.C. approved the *Resolution on Establishment of the People's Commune in Rural Areas* and proposed to achieve the transition from collective ownership to public ownership in China within 3~6 years and explore a feasible path to evolve into a Communist society based on the practice of the People's Commune. After the release of this resolution, the People's Commune Movement reached its peak. More than 740 thousand agricultural cooperatives were restructured into 26 thousand people's communes within several months by the end of 1958. More than 0.12 billion farm households were included in these communes, accounting for 98.2 percent of the total number of farm households in China. Except for Tibet, Ningxia, Xinjiang Autonomous Regions, and Yunnan Province, all rural areas in China universally achieved collectivization.

The people's communes were characterized by "big in size and public in nature". An advanced agricultural cooperative usually had 100~200 farm households, while a people's commune generally contained 4,000~5,000 farm households. Agricultural cooperatives were mainly engaged in agricultural production, while the people's commune was a type of grassroots regime organizations that comprehensively worked in agriculture, forestry, animal husbandry, fishery, and sidelines, and put agricultural production, industrial production, commercial, educational, and people's militia organizations under a unified management. A feature of the people's commune system was that it completely fettered peasants in rural areas and farmland; peasants could not migrate freely and choose their occupations independently. The *Statute on Permanent Residence Administration and Registration* enacted in 1958 strictly restricted the free flow of population; it definitely classified urban and rural residents into agricultural population and non-agricultural population. It prescribed that "citizens who migrate from rural areas to urban areas must be in possession of an employment letter of the urban labor administration department, an admission letter of schools, or a settle-in permit of the urban permanent residence registration agency". From then on, the state-driven urban-rural dual administration system and social policy have been carried out in China. The people's commune became an administration tool of this system by which the rural population was prevented from moving into the city. After the reform and opening-up, this system has been broken down by the unpreventable rush of peasant-workers entering the city.

Meanwhile, rural collective enterprises were established in the people's communes as well, and some enterprises came from the former handicrafts industry and family sidelines. After the Socialist Transformation Movement, there were 10,000 thousand peasants in China who were engaged in part-time handicrafts production. Among 0.5 billion peasants in China, more than 0.1 billion mainly lived on sidelines income. At that time, handicrafts production and sidelines were completely subjected to agricultural production activities in agricultural cooperatives or people's communes; agricultural cooperatives or people's communes were treated as unified accounting units. Therefore, handicrafts production and sidelines were called as "collective sidelines". Such non-agricultural labor in commune-owned enterprises was merely a kind of secondary division of labor within the rural community. By the end of 1958, there were a total of 260 thousand commune-owned enterprises in China, with 6.25 billion Yuan RMB gross output value and 7,500 thousand year-round commune members; if taking account of the rural labor force invested in the Steel-Making Campaign, the total number reached 18,000 thousand.[1] However, commune-owned enterprises were established based on the principles of equalitarianism and cost-free transfer of resources, while the principles of voluntary reciprocity, equal exchange, and distribution according to work were neglected; as a result, such a system resulted in serious waste in capital, materials, and labor force. Accordingly, many commune-owned enterprises soon shut down; only a few rural collective enterprises that worked at agricultural machinery maintenance and grain and oil processing were left. In 1965, the government once encouraged people's communes to establish enterprises based on production teams. However, such enterprises mainly aimed to

---

[1] Ma, Jieshan and Yi Zhang (eds.). 1987. *China Township Enterprise Yearbook (1978~1987)*. Beijing: China Agriculture Press.

provide services for local agricultural production and the status of its staff members and workers were still peasants; rural collective enterprises did not develop on a large-scale basis during that period.

In such socio-economic and political background, the social mobility of agricultural laborers had the following characteristics: the overwhelming majority of peasants could only enter agricultural production; even if they were engaged in non-agricultural labor, they could only work in the rural areas. In addition, peasants who entered the non-agricultural labor were not paid with wages like industrial workers; in fact, they were paid by workpoints and participated in the distribution in production teams with other agricultural laborers. Therefore, they did not achieve thorough shift and mobility. Of course, a few peasants became cadres because of their outstanding performance in political participation.

The Cultural Revolution: 1966~1977

In this period, the basic situation of peasants' social mobility was similar to that in the previous period; peasants were not allowed to go out to work and do business and commune-owned enterprises did not develop much. However, political movements in this period were unprecedented both in size and in the degree of violence. The social mobility of agricultural laborers showed the following characteristics.

First, the ideological propaganda and political movements overturned the original order of the social strata; several strata were attacked and hence the political status of peasants relatively ascended. In the Cultural Revolution, the production order in urban areas was destroyed by political movements and the economic development fell into stagnation; many urban youth could not obtain employment and hence the countryside became an outlet. Between 1968~1976, there were 16,000 thousand educated youth who went down to settle in the countryside and border areas and hundreds of thousands of cadres were sent down to the "May 7th cadre schools"; most "May 7th cadre schools" were located in deserted and obscure areas with atrocious natural conditions, such as sand beaches, saline lands, swamplands, and valleys. For example, in 1968, among 1966 class university graduates who were assigned to Helongjian Province by the government, about 80 percent of them were assigned to rural areas below the county level. Intellectuals had to give up their specialties and research and learn simple labor skills from peasants; sent-down cadres must live with peasants and participate in agricultural production activities. Thus, the social status of peasants relatively rose because the status of urban youth, cadres and intellectuals were abased. In this period, peasants temporarily were not at the bottom of the social hierarchy.

Second, local small-size enterprises developed to some degree after 1970. In 1970 and 1971, local state-owned industrial enterprises directly recruited more than six million workers from the countryside and hence provided agricultural laborers with some upward mobility opportunities.[1]

---

[1] Zhang, Jingru and Songchen Li (eds.). 1999. *Illustrated History of the People's Republic of China*

Third, the development of rural collective enterprises within the peoples' communes conduced to the transfer of agricultural laborers to non-agricultural sectors. In the Cultural Revolution, the industrial production order was destroyed by political movements, while damages in the countryside were comparably small. When urban industrial enterprises stopped production, rural collective enterprises obtained the opportunity of development. Consequently, the development of rural collective enterprises promoted the occupational differentiation in the countryside. However, such occupational differentiation did not change the status of peasants in the administration system of the people's commune; workers in rural collective enterprises were rewarded by workpoints referring to agricultural laborers and participated in the distribution in production teams at the end of the year. By the end of 1978, 1,524 thousand rural collective enterprises were established in 94.7 percent of people's communes and 78.7 percent of production brigades in China, with an increase of 409 thousand over the 1976 figure of 1,115 thousand. The industrial output value of rural collective enterprises reached 38.53 billion Yuan RMB, up by 58.2 percent over the 1976 figure; rural laborers employed in these enterprises were 28,265 thousand, accounting for 9.5 percent of the total rural labor force. The gross income of rural collective enterprises was 43.14 billion Yuan RMB, up by 13.7 times over the 1965 figure, accounting for 29.7 percent of the gross income of the people's communes in the same year. The rural collective enterprises had become an important element in rural economy and fostered talented people for the transfer of the rural labor force after the reform and opening-up. Workers in rural collective enterprises were the first group that shifted from agriculture to non-agricultural sectors after the reform and opening-up.

CHARACTERISTICS OF SOCIAL MOBILITY OF THE STRATUM AFTER 1978

It was after the reform and opening-up when the large-scale social mobility of agricultural laborers emerged. With the implementation of the household contracted responsibility system with remuneration linked to output in rural areas, peasants obtained independent decision-making power in production and operation and hence they could choose their occupations independently. Agricultural laborers who once were fettered in agriculture have started to shift to non-agricultural sectors and have accordingly aroused differentiations and mobility in the rural society.

The agricultural laborers are the largest parent population of social differentiations and mobility. After the reform and opening-up, this parent population has released a large number of its members who entered other social strata. The

---

(3). Beijing: Modern China Publishing House: 1317~1318.

proportion of agricultural laborers to the total working population decreased sharply. This proportion fell from 67.41 percent to 44 percent from 1979 to 1999; at present, it roughly lingers around 50 percent. According to a survey conducted by the Rural Policy Research Office of the Secretariat of the Central Committee of the C.P.C. and the Ministry of Agriculture of China covering 312 villages in 1994, among agricultural laborers in China the proportions of peasants in various occupations respectively were: agricultural laborers 63.4 percent, peasant-workers 12.2 percent, managerial personnel in township and village collective enterprises 0.9 percent, individual laborers and owners or partners in individual-operated businesses 6.5 percent, laborers in private enterprises 0.8 percent, employed laborers 3 percent, rural cadres 0.6 percent, people working in educational, scientific and technical, health care, and cultural services 1.1 percent, household work laborers 8.1 percent, and other laborers 3.3 percent.

The social mobility of agricultural laborers is characterized by "more in and less out". According to the nationwide survey conducted by this research group in 2001, from the perspective of intragenerational outflow rate, among people whose first occupation was agricultural laborer, 73.4 percent of them were still agricultural laborers; only 26.6 percent of them entered other strata. Among them, except for 1.6 percent became jobless and unemployed people, the majority achieved upward mobility: 6.6 percent of agricultural laborers became industrial workers, 6.7 percent entered commercial and services sectors, 7.1 percent became individual-operated business proprietors, and 2.7 percent became clerical personnel. However, only very few agricultural laborers became state and social administrators, managerial personnel, private entrepreneurs, and professional and technical personnel (see Table 11-5). From the perspective of intragenerational inflow rate, among those whose current occupation is agricultural laborer, 91.5 percent of them became peasants as their first occupation, 4.1 percent of them came from workers, and the proportions of people coming from other strata were small. Almost no members from the advantaged strata moved down to the stratum of agricultural laborers (see Table 11-6).

Table 11-5　Outflow of Agricultural Laborers

Category	State and social administrator	Managerial personnel	Private entrepreneur	Professional and technical personnel	Clerical personnel	Individual-operated business proprietor
Frequency	5	16	25	28	84	218
Expectation	33.6	49.6	33.6	132.3	248.6	335.6
Outflow Rate (%)	0.20	0.50	0.80	0.90	2.70	7.10

Category	Commercial and service personnel	Industrial worker		Agricultural laborer	The jobless, unemployed, and partially unemployed	Total
Frequency	191	202		2259	49	3077
Expectation	361.5	390.2		1360.2	131.7	3077
Outflow Rate (%)	6.20	6.60		73.40	1.60	100.00

Table 11-6 Inflow of Agricultural Laborers

Category	State and social administrator	Managerial personnel	Private entrepreneur	Professional and technical personnel	Clerical personnel	Individual-operated business proprietor
Frequency	1	0	0	24	48	20
Expectation	9.7	9.7	4.9	130.8	185.2	141.9
Inflow Rate (%)	0.0	0.0	0.0	1.0	1.9	0.0

Category	Commercial and service personnel	Industrial worker	Agricultural laborer	The jobless, unemployed, and partially unemployed	Total
Frequency	15	100	2259	1	12460
Expectation	174.6	440.3	1360.2	10.6	2468
Inflow Rate (%)	0.6	4.1	91.5	0.0	100

Such a situation indicates that the social mobility of agricultural laborers in China has the following characteristics. First, the interchange between agricultural laborers and other social strata is very low. Among all social strata, the inflow rate of the stratum of agricultural laborers is the lowest (8 percent), and its outflow rate is at a lower level as well (26.6 percent). Second, the tendency in which agricultural laborers attempt to get out of their own stratum is the most significant. Although the mobility rate of the stratum of agricultural laborers is relatively low, its outflow rate is far higher than its inflow rate; the former is over 3 times higher than the latter. Third, most agricultural laborers who moved out of this stratum achieved upward mobility; only a very small proportion of them moved downward and became unemployed. Fourth, a tiny minority of agricultural laborers can achieve a long-distance upward mobility; the overwhelming majority of them moved into adjacent strata, such as the stratum of industrial workers, commercial personnel, individual-operated business proprietors, and clerical personnel.

Before 1980, the stratum of agricultural laborers was a highly stable stratum, with extremely low outflow rate (6.4 percent) and inflow rate (3.7 percent). Since the 1980s the outflow rate of this stratum has been growing, about one-fifth (19.3 percent) of agricultural laborers moved to other strata, mainly the stratum of individual-operated business proprietors, commercial and service personnel, and industrial workers. However, the inflow rate (8.1 percent) of the stratum of agricultural laborers has still remained at a lower level (see Table 4-5 and Table 4-6 in Chapter 4).

The number of the rural labor force engaged in crops and plant cultivation has dropped since 1992. Five major factors have caused such phenomenon. First, the income obtained from crops and plant cultivation is relatively low and hence it has driven a large number of young and middle-aged peasants to work in non-agricultural sectors in other areas. Second, because modern agricultural production technology has been increasingly adopted in agriculture, the labor force has been squeezed out of agricultural production and hence the number of rural laborers accommodated by agriculture has been dropping. For example, adoption of rural power-generating machines and biochemistry agriculture chemicals has enhanced labor efficiency in agriculture and the demand on the labor force has greatly decreased. Third, because the amount of rural farmland has rapidly decreased, a number of peasants could not obtain farmland. The issue of surplus of the rural labor force has been gradually transformed into the issue of serious unemployment of peasants. The expropriation of cropland for public or commercial use brought out a large number of peasants losing their farmland. Because of poor emplacement and legal services provided by the government, they encountered great difficulty in finding new jobs. Forth, in spite of the advance of agricultural production technology and the growth of investment in agriculture, abnormally high prices and poor quality of agricultural means of production have had a great negative impact on agricultural production. Fifth, the tax and miscellaneous fees imposed on peasants in some regions are extremely high; peasants who are engaged in crops and plant cultivation even are unable to maintain a minimum standard of living.

In addition, differentiation has emerged within the stratum of agricultural laborers. In rural areas, such differentiations have two major forms. The first form is the expanding scale of farmland invested in agricultural production, i.e., the transformation from household contractors to agricultural entrepreneurs in crops and plant cultivation. In the second form, with the continuous improvement of the socialized services system in agricultural production and agricultural products sale, farm households' agricultural production has become somewhat made-to-order farming, and agricultural technical services, quality management, and agricultural products sale are outsourced to social intermediaries. The first form has promoted the development of large-scale operations in agricultural production, while the second one has dispersed the market risks in supply and demand of agricultural products and hence provided relatively stable income of crops and plant cultivation and livestock breeding for farm households.

Table 11-7 Occupational Proportions of Agricultural Laborers

Occupation	Sample Size	Percentage
Grain farmer and related agricultural worker	1017	63.92
Raiser of poultry, domestic animals, bees, and silkworms	84	5.28
Farmer of fruit, tea, mulberry, sugarcane, and related agricultural worker	63	3.96
Vegetable grower and related agricultural worker	41	2.58
Cotton grower and related agricultural worker	22	1.45
Other agricultural worker	8	0.50
Horticulturist of nursery and gardens and laborer in tree planting and forestation	8	0.50
Raiser of livestock	4	0.25
Laborer in aquiculture	3	0.19
Laborer in logging	1	0.06
Fisher	1	0.06
Rural plasterer	1	0.06
Not applicable	20	1.26
No response	1	0.06
Missing value	310	19.48
Total		99.62

Source: The survey conducted by this research group in 2001.

Note: Occupations that cannot be classified are not included in Table 11-7.

Before 1990, the major channel for surplus rural laborers to transfer to non-agricultural sectors was via township enterprises, which were characterized by "working at non-agricultural labor in the local countryside and entering enterprises in stead of entering the city." From 1984 to 1988 township enterprises absorbed 10,840 thousand rural laborers each year, while laborers emigrated from the countryside were only about three million in the same period. The situation changed after the 1990s. Because the township enterprise moved toward capital-intensive and technology-intensive production, its employment capacity decreased. From 1989 to 1995 enterprises only absorbed 5,930 thousand laborers each year; meanwhile, with the rapid development of urban construction industry and services industry, the number of mobile rural laborers who left their hometowns and worked in other areas grew sharply. According to results of various large-scale surveys, we estimated that the total number of mobile rural laborers was 51,000 thousand in 1993; it increased to 71,000 thousand in 1994 and then reached around 80,000 thousand in 1995.

The frequency of agricultural laborers' mobility increased as well. Among agricultural laborers with experience of occupational shifts in the overall sample, the number of respondents with experience in just one occupation and no occupational shifts was 455, those with experience in two occupations were 153, those with experience in three occupations were 74, those with experience in four occupations were 32, those with experience in five occupations were 24, those with experience in six occupations were 6, and those with experience in seven occupations were 20. Taking account of the variable of age, we find that respondents with experience in multiple occupations were mostly born before 1970; the number of respondents with experience in just one occupation and no occupational shifts was 442, those with experience in two occupations were 150, those with experience in three occupations were 73, those with experience in four occupations were 32, those with experience in five occupations were 14, those with experience in six occupations were 6, and those with experience in seven occupations were 8.

PROSPECTS OF SOCIAL MOBILITY FOR AGRICULTURAL LABORERS

Analysis on social mobility of peasants since 1949 indicates that, in the free-market system, peasants' independent decision-making power in production and the right to use individual labor are ensured by the household contract and responsibility system, and the social openness and urban-rural social mobility are growing. In such a background, the continuous decrease of the proportion of agricultural laborers in Chinese social stratum structure is a very important indicator of the progress of Chinese society. Industrialization in 1957 absorbed a large number of the rural labor force and formed the first peak when peasants entered the stratum of workers. In 1970, six million new workers were directly recruited from rural areas. However, because of inconsistency with the rules of productivity development and the free-market economy, such mobility did not promote the development of industry and resulted in a shortage of urban provisionment because of sudden population growth; subsequently, the government had to restrict urban enterprises for recruiting workers from agricultural laborers. Therefore, the decrease of agricultural laborers can have a positive influence only in the above-mentioned three conditions. The goal of modern China is harmonious development and social progress; thus, modernization and industrialization are not simply equal to the decrease of the number of peasants, but require more concern on the improvement of a set of supportive conditions that are necessary in order to achieve a decrease in the number of agricultural laborers.

In the progress of industrialization, marketization, and urbanization in China, undoubtedly the number of agricultural laborers will continue to drop. However, the problem lies in how to achieve social justice in this process and how to enable peasants engaged in crop farming to share the fruits of social development and protect their rights and interests. Otherwise, the accumulated feeling of unfairness among agricultural laborers will eventually intensify social conflicts. Although more employment in agriculture is not the major source of relative growth of peasants' income any more, the growth of agricultural productivity is still critical to maintain the competitive competence of Chinese agriculture in the world grain market and to enhance the grain output in order to meet increasing demand. The decrease of agricultural laborers is a kind of social stratum structural adjustment; it never means that agriculture should be ignored. Agricultural laborers should obtain sufficient job remuneration that can compete with that of non-agricultural sectors. It is impossible to find a solution for the conflict of interests between the urban and rural areas in the planned economy framework that divides people into urban and rural residents. It is urgent to abolish such a dual system thoroughly and make an overall plan on urban and rural development.

(1)Paying more attention to the all-around progress in the rural society

The issue of disadvantaged people's livelihood is always a topic to which a society advocating equity and justice must pay more attention. The key to build a well-off society in an all-round way lies in the countryside and the future of agricultural laborers in the countryside is the most difficult issue to deal with. Urbanization in China should not be at the cost of destitution in rural areas and the sacrifice of peasants' legal rights and interests. Balanced development in urban and rural areas requires coordination between the interests of the urban population and peasants; especially, the legal rights and interests of agricultural laborers in the countryside should be given more considerations. In short, more attention should be paid to the all-around progress in the rural society. Favorable conditions that can facilitate the transfer of peasants from agricultural labor to non-agricultural labor should be created; meanwhile, more efforts is needed to transform rural agricultural production and rustication into a type of occupation and lifestyle that can attract a more advantaged labor force. Such purposes cannot be achieved through peasants' individual efforts. Contrarily, they require oriented arrangements of institutional innovations on supply and distribution of rural public goods.

(2) Improving reasonable mobility mechanisms of surplus rural laborers

The number of surplus rural laborers in China is very large, while the quality of these laborers is relatively low. In rural areas, production factors, such as capital and technology, etc., are relatively scarce. The surplus rural labor force does not create benefits to agriculture; contrarily, they participate in the distribution of agricultural yield. As a result, such a situation causes low labor productivity in agriculture and hampers the growth of peasants' income. According to other countries' experiences, in all countries or regions with a huge population and scarce farmland and capital, their industrial structure has evolved from a resource-intensive and labor-intensive pattern into a capital-intensive and technology-intensive pattern. For example, the major method of rural labor force transfer in Japan is to improve the productivity of agricultural labor and reduce the demand of agriculture for labor, and meanwhile absorb the surplus rural labor force via a rapidly developing industry. The government should encourage peasants to go in for sidelines in order to provide more space for labor force transfer. Relevant laws and policies should be established and revised in order to promote and guide the transfer of the rural labor force. Efforts should be intensified to develop rural education in order to foster qualified talents who meet the requirements of the non-agricultural sectors. Urbanization in rural areas should be paid more attention in order to achieve the transfer of the surplus rural labor force in local areas.

(3) Lowering educational costs and improving the quality of the rural labor force

Only if the quality of the rural labor force is improved can the surplus rural labor force achieve transfer effectively. The government should reinvestigate the actual situation in rural areas and make a greater effort to lower the cost of education and hence provide peasants with an education that is equal to that for urban residents. The content of education should be reformed and more efforts should be made in improving the educational facilities, especially in the middle and western China. If the issue of peasants' education cannot be solve, the quality of the rural labor force will not be improved and hence they will be unable to meet diverse requirements in employment; in consequence, the transfer of the surplus rural labor force will be hampered and eventually various socio-economic issues related to agriculture, rural areas, and peasants cannot be solved.

(4) Establishing and improving the rural social security system

Presently, rural social security usually is undertaken by peasants' family. Even if taking no account of sharing the benefits of social development with peasants, only from the perspective of social equality, it is a must to establish and improve the rural social security system before expropriating peasants' cropland for public use. The scale of agricultural laborer transferring to non-agricultural sectors is affected by the forces of push and pull, while the improvement of peasants' status is influenced by multiple factors in different periods, such as administration systems, policies, space of status, and personal quality, etc. The social mobility of peasants from agriculture to non-agricultural sectors and from rural areas to urban areas does not have any institutionalized stability; most agricultural laborers who entered the city are young peasants. Usually they will be replaced by younger peasants in competition in the urban labor market after several years' work in the city and have to return to the countryside. Therefore, continuous efforts should be made to establish the mechanisms that are favorable for the upward mobility of agricultural laborers.

(5) Giving consideration to both the city and the countryside in the strategy of "employment first"

In current China, the economic cluster effect and exemplary role of agricultural entrepreneurs remind us the development of *in situ* industrialization and non-agricultural sectors in local rural areas should be reconsidered. The relationship between such strategy and the industrialization in urban areas is not conflicted nor competitive but complementary. It is impossible for the city in China to create 12,000~15,000 thousand new non-agricultural employment opportunities each year.

> The alternative to the transfer of populations from the villages to new or expanded small cities and towns would be for most rural workers to remain in the villages and, for those with jobs outside the village, to commute to their jobs. If this alternative is to be a viable one and result not only in the narrowing of income differentials, but also in improving the quality of life and well-being of the villagers, the villages must be made more attractive places in which to live and work for both those who will remain employed in the villages and those who have jobs elsewhere. If this alternative is to be an attractive one, it would require that every village be on an all-weather road and that bus services be provided to permit the workers to commute on a daily basis at a reasonable cost in terms of time and money.
>
> What would be required to make villages more attractive places in which to live? Most villages in China lack several of the amenities that urban residents in China now take for granted—tap water, inside toilets, reliable and affordable electricity, and quality access to television signals…Above all else, the rural educational system must be transformed to provide the same opportunities, at the same cost, to rural students as are available in urban areas.[1]

---

[1] Johnson, D. Gale. 2002. "Can Agricultural Labor Adjustment Occur Primarily through Creation of Rural Non-Farm Jobs in China?" *Urban Studies*, Edinburgh. 39: 2163.

Chapter 12   Theories and Survey Methods

In early 2002, the Research Group for Social Structure in Contemporary China of the Chinese Academy of Social Sciences (CASS) published its preliminary research result, *Social Stratification in Contemporary China.*[1] In that report, we proposed our fundamental points of view about the transition of social stratum structure in China since the reform and opening-up and classified contemporary Chinese society into ten major strata. The classification and analysis of the ten social strata have drawn a large amount of attention across the world and brought about some controversies in academia. Meanwhile, as the largest-scale empirical study in the field of social stratification in recent years in China, it is necessary for us to illuminate the methods and channels of data collection in this study from the perspective of methodology. In this chapter, we will offer our responses to these academic arguments and explain the operational methods and corresponding techniques and instruments in detail.

THEORIES OF SOCIAL STRATIFICATION

In the preliminary research result of this research project, *Social Stratification in Contemporary China,* we provided a basic explanation for the principle of classification of the ten major social strata in China.[2] Academic controversies have been aroused after the publication of this book; some arguments even went beyond the academic sphere of sociology research and involved certain ideological issues. There are various concepts of class (stratum) and classification criteria in the field of modern social class (stratum) study; the definition of concepts and the choice of classification criteria largely depend on theoretical backgrounds and research purposes of researchers. It is hard to say which one is completely correct or totally wrong. For example, economists who are concerned about the issue of income distribution may adopt income level or wealth as the criterion to classify social class (stratum) (such as high-income stratum, middle-income stratum, and low-income stratum, etc.). Researchers in political science who are interested in political issues may classify class (stratum) based on a power relationship structure (such as the ruling class and the ruled class). In sociology, classifications of social class (stratum) adopted by different scholars are also diverse. Some scholars use the standard of income to classify class (stratum); some researchers who pay more attention to the issue of consumption employ the consumption level or consumption pattern as the criterion in

---

[1] Lu (2002).
[2] Lu (2002: 4 -10).

classification; some prefer to occupational category or occupational prestige. From the perspective of research questions that they intend to investigate, all these classifications are meaningful and conduce to an understanding of relevant questions. However, in exploration of the concept of class (stratum) and social stratification, most sociologists who have greater theoretical interest and concern over macro-level social transition pay more attention to fundamental characteristics of social structure or social relationships. These fundamental characteristics determine the basic allocation structure of social resources, people's positions in social structure, and the relationship between them; meanwhile, they also affect people's interests orientations, socio-political attitudes, behavior choices, and lifestyles to some extent. The classification of social stratum in this study is similar to the above concepts of class and stratum. Through such stratum classification, we intend to understand the most basic characteristics of social relationships in contemporary China; based on such an understanding, we plan to investigate the rules of resource allocation, describe the basic structure of socio-economic differentiations, and hence define the positions of individuals or groups in the overall social structure.

Over a long period of time, there are two schools of theory in the field of social class (stratum) study. One is Marxist class analysis; the other is Weberian social stratification study. Traditional Marxist theoreticians and Weberian sociologists stand in distinct positions in definition of class (stratum) and criteria for classification and have disputed on these issues for a long time. The distinctions of the two schools' viewpoints mainly focus on three aspects. First, Marxist theoreticians classify social class based on the ownership of the means of production, which is regarded as a classification principle of economic determinism. In contrast, Weberian sociologists attach importance to identification, which is treated as a classification principle of cultural determinism to a certain extent. Second, Marxists believe that the ownership of the means of production is the unique criterion for class classification, while Weberians adopt multiple classification criteria: status (prestige, consumption pattern, and lifestyle, etc.), economic condition (income, property, and employment relationship, etc.), and political authority. Third, Marxists believe that the class in their classification is actually existing social entity in real society, which has definite class consciousness and class interests and adopts collective actions to pursue class interests. In contrast, Weberians hold a more flexible attitude toward this issue. They generally think that the class (stratum) defined by scholars is largely a statistical classification; it is only a tool of classification (or ideal type) adopted in the study on social issues. In the real life, social entity that has a unified class-consciousness and adopts collective actions does not exist. The controversy between Marxists and Weberians has lasted for more than one century. However, in the recent three decades, there is a trend of convergence between the schools. The above-mentioned three distinctions in viewpoints between Post-Marxists and Post-Weberians have been fading to some extent. On one hand, few Post-Marxists still insist that the possession of the means of production is the unique criterion for class classification, because the polarized class structure consisting of bourgeoisie (capitalists) and proletarians (the working class) proposed by Karl Marx at that time is inconsistent with the actual situation in modern society; the emergence of the middle class is an unarguable fact which is also an important research topic of Post-Marxists. On the other hand, though more and more indicators (including race, gender, and age, etc.) have been introduced into social stratification by Post-Weberians, many of them treat the economic indicator, i.e., the possession of the means of production (the status of employer or employee), as the most important criterion in social class (stratum) classification. In fact, in the field of modern social class (stratum) research, it is difficult to tell to which school many well-known theorists belong clearly. For example, French sociologist Pierre Bourdieu had a significant influence on modern class (stratum) research because he proposed the concept of *cultural capital* and published the book *Distinction*.[1] From the perspective of the definition of class and the indicator of classification, his theory should belong to a sort of Weberian social stratification; however, because the traditional Marxist class analysis was attached to his analysis on cultural capital and his criticism on the real society, some scholars believe that he is a Marxist theorist of class analysis. Two of most famous scholars of modern Post-Weberian social stratification study, Anthony Giddens and Frank Parkin developed Max Weber's concept of *class*. However, Giddens' *theory of structuralization*[2] and Parkin's notion of *social closure*[3] were deeply affected by Marxist class theory; therefore, some scholars also call them Marxist class analysts. In contrast, the indicators adopted in the class classification by the most famous theorist of Post-Marxist class analysis, Erik O. Wright, are very similar to those used by Post-Weberians.[4] In recent years social stratification theorist David B. Grusky gained a great reputation because of the effort of "salvaging class analysis" advocated by him. He cast away the theoretical dispute between the Marxist theory and the Weberian theory and established a third school, i.e., Post-Durkheimians.[5]

The major causes that diminished the distinctions between theorists of the two schools come from two aspects. First, because of drastic social transitions, theorists of the two schools have to revise the traditional theories and reinterpreted the works of Karl Marx and Max Weber in order to adapt to the actual situation of industrialized society and post-industrialized society. Second, because empirical approach is extensively adopted in studies in sociology, many past theoretical arguments have

---

[1] Bourdieu, Pierre and Jean-Claude Passeron. 1977. *Reproduction in Education, Society and Culture*. Beverly Hills, C.A.: Sage Publications; Bourdieu, Pierre. 1984. *Distinction: A Social Critique of the Judgment of Taste*. Cambridge, M.A,: Harvard University Press.

[2] Giddens, Anthony. 1973. *The Class Structure of the Advanced Society*. New York, N.Y.: Harper & Row, Publishers.

[3] Parkin, Frank. 1974. *The Social Analysis of Class Structure*. London: Tavistock Publication.

[4] Wright, Erik O. 1979. *Class Structure and Income Determination*. New York, N.Y.: Academic Press.

[5] Grusky, David B. (ed.). 2001. *Social Stratification: Class, Race & Gender in Sociological Perspective*. Colorado: Westview Press: 18-20.

been continuously confirmed or rejected by empirical data; consequently, both Marxists' and Weberians' basic understandings about modern social class (stratum) structure or social stratification structure tend to converge. Such convergence remarkably concentrates on the classification of social class (stratum). When Post-Marxists constructed the framework of social class (stratum) classification about modern society, the largest revision they made to the traditional Marxist class theory was to weaken its polarized classification of bourgeoisie and proletarians and in turn to adopt multiple indicators in the classification. In contrast, the significant revision that Post-Weberian theorists made to traditional Weber's stratification theory was to claim that Weber's concept of class is very similar to Marx's concept of class,[1] and hence frequently adopted the indicator *possession of the means of production* in class classification. In such a situation, the criteria of class (stratum) classification adopted by Post-Marxists and Post-Weberians and corresponding results of classification (including class groups and corresponding proportions) are very similar. Nonetheless, some significant differences in research purposes and focuses still exist between theorists of the two schools. Marxist class (stratum) analysis often emphasizes the criticism of social reality with more or less revolutionary orientations or strong concerns for real socio-political issues. By contrast, the studies of Weberian theory attach more importance on objectively describing and accurately understanding social reality. All these changes indicate that, with the advance of study and improvement of research methods, scholars increasingly tend to go beyond traditional disputes of rival parties and more objectively and accurately understand the modern class (stratum) issue.

The study of class (stratum) issue conducted by scholars and theorists in China is basically divorced from the mainstream of academic development in the international sociologist community and are set in distinct socio-political environments and theoretical backgrounds. In fact, over a considerably long period of time, various theories on the class (stratum) issue proposed by Chinese scholars were always an important element of the theory of the proletarian revolution and the mainstream ideology at that time and hence were different from the academic research of class (stratum) issue in sociology both in scope and in perspective. Furthermore, the so-called Marxist class theory in China was quite different from Marx's original expatiation.[2] Many important viewpoints in Marxist class theory that were commonly

---

[1] When Post-Weberians reinterpreted Weber's works, they believed that Max Weber's notion of *class* was consistent with Karl Marx's concept, except that Weber considered one more indicator than Karl Marx did, i.e., *status group*. In contrast, traditional Weberians only focused on Weber's notion of *status group* while overlooking Weber's exploration on class issue.

[2] When we reread Marx's works today, we find that, in *Manifesto of the Communist Party* and *The Capital* (Marx's foremost discourses on class issue were included in the two books), Marx did not define what the class was and how different classes should be classified. Marx's discourses on class issue mainly focused on economic interests conflicts between capitalists and proletariats (i.e., capitalists exploited workers) and proposed that the capitalist society would eventually polarize into two major classes (bourgeoisie and proletarians) and the conflict between capitalists and proletarians would become the major contradiction of the capitalist society and hence lead the capitalist system to

accepted in China were derived from succeeding proletarian revolution theorists including Lenin and Stalin, who developed Marx's viewpoints on class issue; Mao Zedong further developed these Soviet Russian class theories in order to adapt to the need of the revolutionary struggle in Chinese society. Such a theory of revolution based on class analysis had a positive effect on the revolution in China led by the Communist Party of China, and it especially had a great impact on social mobilization (mobilizing the masses). However, the criteria of class classification in these theories were attached with strong political color, with emphasis on political attitudes or political stands. Moreover, such criteria were not consistent all the time; with the changes of political situations, these criteria and classification varied as well. More importantly, theoretical viewpoints, criteria of class classification, and the ultimate results of classification were determined by the major leaders of the Party and the government and were legitimized by the official propaganda organ, having no use for support of scholars' academic research. After the Communist Party of China seized the regime in 1949, Mao Zedong continued to develop the class theory and treated it as the major foundation in decision making on socio-political policies; he was not aware that the most needed knowledge in that period was not the theory of revolution but the theory of industrialization. In the Cultural Revolution, the class theory emphasizing class struggle developed into an extreme form and became seriously unrealistic; consequently, it resulted in enormous mistakes in decision-making of the Party and the government, intensified social conflicts, aroused social convulsions and thus caused serious damages in socio-economic development and the progress of industrialization in China. Since the reform and opening-up in 1978, the major socio-economic policies and ideological theory of the Party and the government have changed significantly. Mao Zedong' theory of class struggle and "continuing revolution under the dictatorship of the proletarians" has been criticized to some extent. At the same time, studies in sociology and political science, etc., have resumed in China and scholars have begun to conduct academic research on class (stratum) issue. However, the influence of traditional class theory still exists; it has not only caused a series of barriers in the process of economic reforms (such as whether the existence of individual-operated business is allowed, whether the legal status of private entrepreneurs is admitted, and so on), but also created some forbidden areas in the field of academic research. Due to this reason, although the class (stratum) issue has been a hot spot of research in the sociologist community in China in the past two decades, the overwhelming majority of research was empirical studies on social stratification merely involving a part of social life, while relevant theoretical issues were left untouched. As a result, the theoretical study of the class (stratum) issue in China has no significant progress yet.

Undoubtedly, most scholars and theorists in China have already realized that traditional Marxist class theory is unable to explain current social issues. It is certainly impertinent to analyze the class issue in modern Chinese society by simply borrowing

---

die out.

the class classification proposed by Karl Marx in the 19th century with the purpose to analyze social issues in the early capitalism in Europe, or the theory of class analysis developed by Mao Zedong in the context of the Chinese society in the 1920s or 1930s. However, it is also very difficult to propose a new theory which is consistent with current conditions in China and which can meanwhile be accepted by the government and the public. In current China, academic study on the class (stratum) issue is still mixed with ideological issues; academic viewpoints are still mixed with political beliefs. In this case, theoretical disputes and definitions of concepts in this area only have limited space. Obviously, it is not possible to solve such a significant theoretical issue in a short time only relying on the efforts of academic research.

Because of lack of a mature class (stratum) theory, it is difficult to propose the classification criteria according to corresponding theory. In this study, we attempt to seek the classification criteria for contemporary Chinese society based on the objective social reality; and then, we try to propose some theoretical explanations on the basis of existing theories and research findings in this area.[1] The classifying indicators we initially adopted in this study neither came from theories of Post-Marxist or Neo-Weberian schools in the field of study of class (stratum) issues, nor were derived from traditional politically-oriented class theory developed by Lenin, Stalin and Mao Zedong, etc. In fact, what we complied was ordinary people's subjective perceptions of current social differentiation. Members of this research group conducted in-depth interviews with hundreds of respondents engaged in various occupations or no occupations in urban and rural areas in China in order to understand how people classify various groups, what their classification criteria are, and how they evaluate different groups. Although respondents proposed a variety of classification criteria, some of these criteria were commonly adopted and consistent with the results of theoretical study conducted by us. In fact, the foremost indicators of class stratification adopted by respondents are similar to the class (stratum) classification criteria proposed by Post-Marxists and Post-Weberian scholars to some extent. It means that, with the development of industrialization, the rules of class (stratum)

---

[1] After the publication of *Social Stratification in Contemporary China*, aiming at the classification of ten major strata in contemporary China proposed in this book, some scholars argued that, although such a classification was very close to people's feelings for the social reality, corresponding theoretical explanation was relatively weak, lacking for a set of systematically theoretical analyses on the class (stratum) issue in contemporary Chinese society. Such critique is pertinent. Because this research project is an empirical study in sociology, its primary purpose is to collect accurate data, describe the status quo of socio-economic divisions in modern China through appropriate analyses, identify basic rules in such divisions, and explain corresponding causes. In addition, we also intend to propose an appropriate framework of class (stratum) classification as the tool to analyze the macro-level structure and discuss some theoretical findings derived from the empirical data with the purpose to challenge traditional out-of-date class (stratum) analysis theory. It is insufficient to propose a systematical class (stratum) analysis theory based on findings of the study. We merely hope that findings of this empirical study can provide some useful references for scholars engaged in theoretical study on class (stratum) theory, and more importantly, help governmental decision-makers, relevant researchers, and the public understand the actual situation of socio-economic divisions in contemporary China.

418

stratification in contemporary Chinese society are partially similar to those in other industrialized countries. Meanwhile, affected by the unique institutional characteristics of Chinese society, many respondents realized that certain institutional factors have also led to differences among various social groups in China and hence proposed some unique criteria related to institutional segmentations. In recent years, many empirical studies in sociology demonstrate that such institutional factors have an important impact on socio-economic differentiations in Chinese society. Based on the above ideas and combining the study on people's subjective perceptions of social stratification with the literature review of existing theories and findings, we defined the specific indicators of stratification and classified contemporary Chinese society into ten major strata.[1] The detailed explanation for the specific method and procedure of this classification can be found in Chapter 1.

---

[1] In this study, we adopted the term "stratum" rather than "class". Some scholars demurred at the adoption. In dispute about the class (stratum) issue in China, there is a misleading argument which believes that adoption of the term "class" means adherence to Marxist theory and the socialist principles; while adoption of the term "stratum" means to admit anti-Marxist bourgeoisie scholars' viewpoints. In response to this argument, we specially added an annotation in the book *Social Stratification in Contemporary China* (p. 6) to explain the meanings of the two terms "class" and "stratum" and people's perceptions of such terms in Chinese society. After the publication of the above book, it still aroused some questions. In this book, we present a further explanation here. It is a type of political or ideological phenomenon in China to strictly distinguish the term "class" from "stratum" and antithetic meanings are attached to them respectively. The theory of class struggle that had prevailed for several decades before 1978 has left a profound impression in people's minds. Accordingly, people usually believe that the term "class" refers to the concept of class in the traditional Marxist sense, which leads one to associate it with violent social conflicts, sharp contradictions between groups with opposite interests, and revolutionary movements and struggles among people. Since the 1980s, in discussion of the current class (stratum) issue, many scholars have tended to adopt the term "stratum" rather than "class" in order to manifest that the groups in their classifications are not "classes" with irreconcilable contradictions and conflicts used by Karl Marx or Mao Zedong and also show their deprecatory attitudes toward the out-of-date theory of class struggle. However, some others still adhere to traditional class theory and believe that the substitution of "stratum" for "class" means denial of Marxist class theory and hence is a kind of bourgeoisie point of view. Such dispute largely is a sort of ideological controversy rather than academic debate. Such strict distinction does not exist in the field of academic research. In studies on socio-economic divisions conducted by the academic circle of sociology, the difference between "class analysis" and "social stratification study" in theoretical orientations and research methods does exist. The term "class" is universally adopted by theorists of class analysis; however, the definitions of this term differ in dozens of ways and corresponding theoretical backgrounds and analytical frameworks are greatly different, including class analyses based on Marxist, Weberian, structuralist, and action theory. In most cases, researchers in social stratification also adopt the term "class" while a few scholars use "stratum" as well. However, to thoese researchers, whether the adoption of "class" or the adoption of "stratum" does not have definite theoretical meanings. It is not a significant problem to adopt "class" or "stratum"; what is more important is how these concepts are defined. As to the ten major social strata in the classification of this study, the theoretical meaning of the term "stratum" is close to that of the term "class" in English. In Chinese edition of this book, we adopt "stratum" rather than "class"; however, it is just in order to indicate that the groups in our classification are different from "classes" which were defined according to political criteria in the civil war and the Cultural Revolution.

EXPLANATIONS FOR SURVEY METHODS

The Procedure and Organization of the Survey

At the beginning of the establishment of this research group in 1999, we defined this research project as "an in-depth empirical study on transition of social structure, especially class (stratum) structure, in China since 1949". The purpose of this study is to describe the current situation and characteristics of Chinese social structure, and the process, rules, and tendencies of such transition. Therefore, a nationwide cross-sectional survey is necessary to achieve the purpose of the research. In order to ensure the validity of this nationwide survey, the research group divided the whole research procedure into three successive phases. In each phase, we revised the survey instruments (the questionnaire and the interview schedule), survey methods, and organizing approaches through trial and error in order to achieve the objectives of this phase and eventually improve the overall validity of the nationwide survey.

In the first phase of the research project before August 1999 we collected and reviewed various materials related to theories, models, methodology, and questionnaires in social stratification study presented by researchers in Europe, America, Russia, and Japan, etc. In addition, in order to follow up the frontier of study in China, we invited some scholars in this field to attend symposia held by us. In these symposia, the opinion of Professor Qiang Li of Tsinghua University about the "fragmentation of stratification" in current China and the analysis of Professor Liping Sun on the "fracture" of social structure gave us important inspiration. According to the theoretical study and the unique *status quo* of social groups in China since the reform and opening-up, we further subdivided the research questions and objectives and divided the study into four parts: (1) The cross-sectional survey and case interviews in urban areas which aim to conduct an in-depth analysis on the transition of the urban social stratum structure based on the survey data, (2) the cross-sectional survey and case interviews in rural areas which aim to conduct an in-depth analysis on the transition of the rural social stratum structure based on the survey data, (3) the special survey on particular groups (including the stratum of private entrepreneurs, cadres, individual-operated business proprietors, workers, and peasants), and (4) the nationwide survey based on above three surveys, which aims to describe the transition of social structure in current China. In June 1999, the research group finished the first draft of the questionnaire that would be used in surveys on urban, rural, and particular groups; subsequently, a pilot study with a sample size of 102 respondents was conducted in Xingrenzhuang Village in Sanhe County of Hebei Province and Yuetan community in Xicheng District of Beijing City. Based on the analysis on response methods to the questionnaire and the survey data, the theoretical framework of the study and the questionnaire were revised for the first round and consequently the cross-sectional survey in the second phase of study was launched.

From August 1998 to July 2001, the research group conducted cross-sectional surveys in 11 survey sites in China continually.[1] We defined the surveys in this phase as a pilot study, which aims to (1) systematically investigate the social structure of a relatively independent community (city/county) or organization (enterprise and college) and hence provide a classification framework for subsequent nationwide social stratum classification, (2) identify the difference between various types of social strata as extensively as possible, i.e., the patterns of social stratum hierarchy in various regions, stages of economic development, and organizational forms in order to improve the representative reliability of the nationwide social stratification indicators, and (3) explore appropriate field operational procedure and methods of administering and monitoring the nationwide survey based on these cross-sectional surveys.

In order to achieve above purpose, three roles are indispensable in organizing and conducting the survey in each survey site, including (1) local governments which are willing to support this research project, (2) local experts and scholars who are engaged in social science research and familiar with local situations and act as coordinators, and (3) a group of interviewers who have a certain level of education, a sense of responsibility, and certain knowledge about social investigation.

Any colleagues who have the experience of social investigation in China may understand the difficulty in entering the field; especially, conducting surveys in provincial areas as outsiders is really a challenge. For example, Mr. Jinqing Cao who conducted a survey single-handedly in rural areas in Henan Province frequently encountered precaution, prevarication, and resistance from local officials. In particular, because the social stratum division involved in this research project is still a sensitive topic in China and the proposed survey will cover thousands of households, even if the legitimacy of this research is guaranteed by the Chinese Academy of Social Sciences, understanding, permission, and supports from local governments are indispensable in order to accomplish the survey successfully.

On one hand, we need supports from local governments; on the other hand, we must avoid the color of "official" in order to ensure the independence and quality of the survey. Therefore, we need local scholars in the field of social science research and local scientific research institutions (such as local Academy of Social Sciences, colleges, and Party schools) to take charge of actual organization of the surveys. These scholars possess both local knowledge and professional knowledge, have channels to communicate with local governments, and are able to organize the operation of the survey; hence, they are central roles in the cross-sectional surveys.

Finally, conducting the surveys in local field sites needs a group of interviewers with good quality and a sense of responsibility. Considering interviewers should have similar backgrounds with interviewees such as dialects and the culture of community, we requested local scientific research institutions to recruit interviewers

---

[1] The 11 survey sites include Hanchuan City in Hubei Province, Haicheng City in Liaoning Province, Fuqing City in Fujian Province, Zhenning County in Guizhou Province, Hefei City in Anhui Province, Wuxi City in Jiangsu Province, Qidu Town in Wujiang City of Jiangsu Province, Shenzhen City in Guangdong Province, Yanshan Petrochemical Complex in Beijing City, the First Automobile Works in Changchun City of Jilin Province, and Nankai University in Tianjin City.

in local areas. Qualified interviewers should have certain experience of social work and hence can understand the knowledge of social stratification better, possess college and higher educational background, and work in a certain organization. In our opinion, researchers in local scientific research institutions, teachers and students in local Party schools, public administration institutes, and colleges are most eligible candidates.

Taking account of all above factors comprehensively, this research group adopted the following pattern in the phase of cross-sectional surveys: the research group, local governments, and local social science research institutions forming a survey coordination team. The research group dispatched researchers to take charge of technique instruction and supervision (including sampling, questionnaire explaining, interviewer training, and quality control); local governments took charge of providing materials and executive and logistic services; local research institutions took charge of organizing the conduct of the survey.

It is worthwhile to point out that, in order to meet the above three conditions, the choice of the aforementioned 11 survey sites did not strictly follow the requirement of nationwide representativeness in the sense of probability, but was determined by the method of subjective judgment sample. Of course, we also considered the differences in social structures between eastern, middle, and western regions in China caused by different levels of marketization and the segmentations between social strata caused by the urban-rural dual system as much as possible.

In order to accomplish such a research plan, from the summer of 1999 to the summer of 2001, the leader of the research group, Professor Xueyi Lu, and other group members frequently traveled to survey sites all over China, sought supports from local governments, engaged local research institutions and local scholars to participate in the survey, recruited and trained interviewers, and organized the conduct of surveys on the spot. Fortunately, aware of the significance of social stratification analysis for the development of local society and economy, all local governments showed great concern and interest in our research project and provided convenience for the research group as much as they could. Local research institutions and scholars invested great enthusiasm and endeavor into this project. Due to their hard work, 11,000 questionnaires and nearly one thousand interview records were efficiently collected together. All these precious empirical data subsequently became the basis of the first report of this research project, i.e., *Social Stratification in Contemporary China*.

According to the feedbacks obtained from the cross-sectional surveys, significant revisions were made on the survey instruments and operational methods. First, in order to adopt a unified framework in stratum classification, original questionnaires used in the urban and rural surveys respectively were merged into one questionnaire and the special survey on particular groups was not listed separately any more. Second, the occupational category table was expanded. Third, the sampling method in the floating population was standardized. Finally, the within-household sampling table was adjusted. On such a basis, the questionnaire and related instructions and manuals that would be used in the nationwide large-scale survey in the next phase were worked out, including the *Instruction for Survey Operation*, *Supervisor's Agenda*, *Interviewer Manual, Questionnaire Instruction*, and so forth.

In July 2001, the nationwide survey was formally started up. Instructed by two famous experts in statistical sampling, Professors Shiyong Feng of the Institute for Systems Science of the Chinese Academy of Science and Jialing Gao of the Institute of Population Studies of the Chinese Academy of Social Sciences, and adopting the *multi-stage composed sampling*, we drew 6,240 people aged 16 to 70 years old in 408 resident committees (or villager committees) of 73 cities (or counties/prefectures) from 3,300 city-level and county-level sampling units (including the urban section of the city, the county-level city, and the county). From December 2001, questionnaires were coded and verified, and then data were input into computers and reorganized in the database.

Executive Summary of the Nationwide Survey

The nationwide survey was conducted in the following steps:

Task Objectives at each stage

County /city /prefecture-level sampling	Resident /villager committee level sampling / Interviewer training	Within-household sampling / On-site interview	Data processing
(1) Draw the first level sampling units based on the national population statistical data by county/ city/prefecture	(1) Draw the second level sampling units (resident/villager committees) from each selected county/city/ prefecture (2) Organize interviewer teams and train interviewers	(1) Draw interviewee households by supervisors from the selected resident/ villager committees based on household registration re- cords (2) Draw interviewees from the selected household by interviewers based on random sampling table and conduct interview (3) Supervisors collect and examine questionnaires on the spot	(1) Code questionnaires and deal with open-ended questions (2) Data input (3) Data verification

423

(1) Sampling Design

In this study, regular residents aged 16 to 70 in China are the population for the ultimate inference of the survey.[1] Considering that the average age of people who received nine-year compulsory education and have the qualification to obtain employment is 16 years old and the social stratification in this study mainly focuses on the occupational population, we chose the age of 16 years as the base line. In addition, considering the urban-rural dual structure in China based on the permanent residence registration system, we treated the urban population and the rural population as two independent subpopulations (the domain of study) and conducted sampling respectively and used the registered urban or rural residence as the criterion to distinguish the two subpopulations. Accordingly, the domain of survey is divided into the urban domain and the rural domain; the resident/villager committee was treated as the criterion to distinguish the two domains in principle.

The major parameter that this study intends to infer through the survey is the proportion distribution of social strata. Therefore, according to the calculation formula of simple random sampling characterized by proportional parameters, at the 95 percent confidence level, if the admissible error is within 3 percent, the sample size is:

$$N_{SRS} = \frac{Z^2 \times a^2}{\Delta^2} = \frac{1.96^2 \times 0.5^2}{0.03^2} \approx 1070$$

(N_{SRS} is the sample size of the simple random sampling; Z is the coordinate value of the Z-distribution corresponding to the confidence level; σ^2 is the population variance; Δ is admissible error of sampling). According to this formula, in urban and rural areas, the sample size that can meet the requirement of the survey is 2 times 1070, i.e., 2140. However, because the multi-stage composed sampling is adopted in this study, the sample size calculated according to the simple random sampling formula needed to be revised by multiplying the Deff (design effect) of the composed sampling. Considering that the degree of occupational variance and the differentiation in urban areas is higher than in the countryside, we increased the sample size in the urban domain to 4,000 and the sample size in the rural domain to 2,000; corresponding Deff is 3.7 and 1.87 respectively.[2]

The multi-stage composed sampling is adopted in the nationwide survey, that is, drawing samples in four stages: County/city/prefecture, resident/villager committee, household, and resident. Different sampling methods are used in each stage (see Table

---

[1] A part of population with the registered collective residences and groups with their registered residences written off (such as garrison in encampment, students in on-campus residences, and persons serving sentences) are not included in the population. Because of limited survey conditions, residents in Tibet Autonomous Region, Taiwan Province, and Hong Kong and Macao Special Administration Regions are not included in the population neither.

[2] In general, the values of Deff adopted in similar studies range from 2 to 2.5. According to post hoc test of the data obtained from the survey, the Deff is round 1.25. Therefore, the designed sample size is appropriate both in the urban domain and in the rural domain.

12-1).

Table 12-1 Distribution of Sampling Units and Design of the Nationwide Multi-Stage Sampling

Stage of Sampling	Method of Sampling
Stage 1: Sample 73 counties/cities/ prefectures	Stratified proportional sampling + PPS sampling
Stage 2: Sample 404 resident/villager committees	PPS sampling (Probability Proportional to Size)
Stage 3: sample 6,000 households	Systematic sampling
Stage 4: sample 6,000 residents	Simple random sampling

In the first stage, based on the *Population Statistical Data by County and City (1998)* edited by the Ministry of Public Security of China, we treated 3,300 counties /cities / prefectures in China as the sampling frame and conducted stratified proportional sampling in it. According to the difference in economic development among regions (i.e., the eastern, middle, and western regions in China),[1] per capita GDP and the administrative level of the county/city/prefecture (see Table 12-2), we divided all sampling units in the sampling frame into 33 strata and worked out the total number of the population in each stratum and its proportion to the whole population P_s respectively; P_s multiplied by the sample sizes in the urban and rural domains is the sample size which should be drawn from each stratum. In order to avoid highly concentration of distribution of samples, we further prescribed that the sampled respondents from each resident committee (villager committee) should not be fewer than 10 persons or more than 20 persons. Resident committees drawn from each first-level and second-level prefecture and county-level city should not be less than six. The average number of villager committees in the rural domain drawn from each county/city/prefecture is 4 to 6. Accordingly, the number of resident/villager committees and the number of counties/cities/prefectures that should be drawn can be inferred from the above restrictions respectively (see Table 12-3 and Table 12-4). Finally, by using PPS (Probability Proportional to Size) sampling,[2] we drew a corresponding number of counties/cities/prefectures in each stratum.

In the second stage, from local government agencies in counties (cities/prefectures) selected in the first stage, we obtained the list of resident/villager committees (including the number of households and the number of the population of each committee) and treated it as the sampling frame. By adopting the PPS

---

[1] In this sampling, eastern regions include Beijing, Tianjin, Shanghai, Liaoning, Shandong, Jiangsu, Zhejiang, Fujian, and Guangdong Province; middle regions include Hebei, Shanxi, Jilin, Heilongjiang, Anhui, Jiangxi, Henan, Hubei, Hunan, Guangxi, and Hainan Province; western regions include inner Mongolia, Chongqing, Sichuan, Yunnan, Shannxi, Gansu, Ningxia, Qinghai, and Xinjiang.

[2] In this survey, the PPS sampling was adopted repeatedly because of its following characteristics: (1) It can conduct own-weighting within each stratum; (2) it can directly adopt the sample size formula of the simple random sampling (SRS) and the calculation is simple and convenient; (3) it can directly adopt statistical analysis software (such as SPSS, etc.) which conduct statistical inference based on the simple random sampling.

425

sampling, we drew corresponding resident/villager committees equidistantly from this sampling frame.

Table 12-2   Levels of County/City/Prefecture in China

Category of Levels	Eastern Regions	Middle Regions	Western Regions
(1) First-level prefecture	Proportion of non-rural population ≥ 80%	Proportion of non-rural population ≥ 80%	Proportion of non-rural population ≥ 70%
(2) Second-level prefecture	Proportion of non-rural population <80%	Proportion of non-rural population < 80%	Proportion of non-rural population < 70%
(3) County-level city			
(4) First-level county	Per Capita GDP ≥ 6,001 Yuan RMB	Per Capita GDP ≥ 5,001 Yuan RMB	Per Capita GDP ≥ 3,501 Yuan RMB
(5) Second-level county	Per Capita GDP 4,001~6,000 Yuan RMB	Per Capita GDP 3,001~5,000 Yuan RMB	Per Capita GDP 2,001~3,500 Yuan RMB
(6) Third-level county	Per Capita GDP ≤ 4,000 Yuan RMB	Per Capita GDP ≤ 3,000 Yuan RMB	Per Capita GDP ≤ 2,000 Yuan RMB

Table 12-3   Sampling Units and Sample Sizes of Each Stratum in the Urban Domain

Category	Eastern Regions			Middle Regions			Western Regions		
	County/city/ prefecture	Resident committee	Sample size	County/city/ prefecture	Resident committee	Sample size	County/city/ prefecture	Resident committee	Sample size
First-level prefecture	7	56	640	3	28	480	2	20	200
Second-level prefecture	4	32	320	2	16	320	1	7	140
County-level city	4	28	350	3	20	320	2	16	160
First-level county	2	4	80	1	6	120	2	6	90
Second-level county	2	4	80	3	12	240	2	6	120
Third-level county	2	4	80	3	15	200	1	4	80
Total	21	128	1550	15	97	1680	10	59	790

Table 12-4   Sampling Units and Sample Sizes of Each Stratum in the Rural Domain

Category	Eastern Regions			Middle Regions			Western Regions		
	County/city/ prefecture	Villager committee	Sample size	County/city/ prefecture	Villager committee	Sample size	County/city/ prefecture	Villager committee	Sample size
First-level prefecture	0	0	0	0	0	0	0	0	0
Second-level prefecture	2	8	80	1	4	80	1	4	40
County-level city	4	16	240	2	10	200	2	8	80
First-level county	1	4	80	2	8	120	2	8	80
Second-level county	1	4	80	3	12	240	2	8	160
Third-level county	2	6	120	3	12	240	2	8	160
Total	10	38	600	11	46	880	9	36	520

Example of Resident/Villager Committee Sampling

Design the sampling frame → Develop the list of all local resident/villager committees, including the name of resident/villager committee, the number of population, and the number of households

Arrange the list in descending sequence according to the number of households

Compute the cumulative percentage

Compute the sampling interval

Systematic sampling based on the cumulative percentage

Name of Village	Size of Population	Number of Households	Cumulative Percentage	Sample 6 villages
Zhanqian Village	33957	13481	22.44	⑥ 87.8% + 16.7% = 114.5%
Beiguan Village	31180	12388	43.06	① Random starting point: 31%
Tiexi Village	18833	7963	56.31	② 31% + 16.7% = 47.7%
Nanguan Village	18881	7760	69.22	③ 47.7% + 16.7% = 64.4%
Dongguan Village	10783	6373	79.83	
Hongguang Village	9886	3524	85.69	④ 64.6% + 16.7% = 81.1%
Sanli Village	4855	1801	88.69	
Huangling Village	4790	1657	91.45	
Dajia Village	4091	1132	93.33	
Yanjun Village	3429	1013	95.02	
Dahe Village	1597	470	95.80	
Dawang Village	1691	468	96.58	
Dongjia Village	1220	407	97.26	
Xiaowang Village	1202	339	97.82	⑤ 81.1% + 16.7% = 87.8%
Ranjia Village	832	242	98.22	
Baimiao Village	656	237	98.62	
Xiaoyao Village	783	230	99.00	
Houfang Village	865	218	99.36	
Xiaohe Village	645	196	99.69	
Erdao Village	747	190	100.00	
Total	150923	60089		Interval = 100% / 6 = 16.7%

In the third stage, the sampling of households is relatively simple. Based on the roster of resident households and the list of temporary residents obtained from local resident/villager committees, we designed the sampling frame and drew samples from it equidistantly. In order to avoid unsuccessful door-to-door interviews in the next stage, in addition to the scheduled sample size, we also drew additional 50 ~100 percent of households as alternative candidates.

In the last stage, the sampling of interviewees within households was conducted by interviewers on the spot. After entering the household, interviewers firstly collected information about all family members, filled out the *Family Member Information Form* (see Table 12-5), and then noted information about individuals who were eligible to be interviewed (at the age of 16~70 and having lived in this address for more than three months) into the *Sampling Table*. In this survey, we adopted the *Kish Sampling Table* that is commonly employed by international survey experts.[1] This table provides twelve types of random sampling methods to select interviewees respectively in case that the number of family members ranges from one to 12. Before entering the household, the interviewer randomly selected a certain type of sampling method in the twelve types of sampling provided in the *Kish Sampling Table* on the first page of the questionnaire. Then, after having filled out the *Family Member Information Form*, in the sequence of the male first and the female second and the older first and the younger second, the interviewer inserted information of eligible individuals into the "gender" and "age" columns in the *Kish Sampling Table* respectively and a sequence number was assigned to each candidate. The sequence number of the candidate who should be interviewed was determined by the number in the cross between the column of the selected type of sampling and the row corresponding to the last candidate's sequence number (see Table 12-6).

Table 12-5   The Model of Sampling (1): Family Member Information Form

S1 Family member's relationship to the person answered the door	S2 Gender	S3 Age	S4 Regular resident or not	S5 Relationship to the interviewee
The person answered the door	Female	40	Yes	
Husband	Male	41	Yes	
Daughter	Female	16	Yes	
Sister-in-law	Female	37	No	
Son	Male	12	Yes	
......				
12.				

---

[1] The *Kish Sampling Table* initially was used in the United States. Its original form had only 10 types of sampling methods and was used in the sampling in families with 1~10 members. When the number of family members is the common divisor of 10 (such as 1, 2, 5 and 10), it can ensure each member has equal probability to be selected. Because of the national birth control policy, the size of family in China usually is smaller than that of the United States. As to the family structure, the proportion of families with 3~4 members in China is higher than that of similar American family. Therefore, in this survey, we increased the types of sampling in the table from 10 types to 12 types; when the number of family members is the common divisor of 12 (such as 1, 2, 3, 4, 6 and 12), it can ensure the randomness of interviewee selection.

Table 12-6   The Model of Sampling Table (1): Kish Sampling Table

K1 No.	K2 Gender	K3 Age	1	2	3	4	5	6	7	8	9	10	11	12
1	Male	41	1	1	1	1	1	1	1	1	1	1	1	1
2	Female	40	2	1	1	2	1	2	1	2	1	2	2	1
3	Female	16	3	2	1	1	3	2	2	1	3	1	2	3
4			4	1	3	2	2	3	1	4	3	2	2	1
5			5	4	1	2	3	4	1	2	3	5	4	2
6			6	3	1	5	2	4	3	5	1	4	6	2
7			7	1	4	3	6	2	5	2	5	7	4	3
8			8	4	5	7	1	2	6	3	7	5	3	1
9			9	5	1	4	3	8	2	7	6	5	2	8
10			10	3	5	9	4	1	7	2	8	6	9	4
11			11	6	1	5	10	4	9	8	3	2	7	6
12			12	7	2	9	4	11	6	1	8	3	10	5

(2) Supervisor and Interviewer Training

From the perspective of survey execution, the probability sampling, the door-to-door interview and the face-to-face interview administrated by interviewers are critical techniques in the survey. In order to collect data by following standard procedures, referring to the interviewer training manual of the Survey Research Center at the University of Michigan and the interview norms of famous market research institutions such as AC Nielson, etc., we developed a six-session training course and gave all interviewers and supervisors involved in the survey an three-days intensive training in order to ensure that they could fulfill their roles in the survey normatively.

As to the interviewers, the purpose of the training course was to enable them to fulfill four tasks including within-household sampling, on-site interview, questionnaire examining, and questionnaire coding. We provided interviewers with a sixty-page *Interviewer Manual* and explained the use of within-household sampling instruments, possible misleading words in the questionnaire and corresponding explanations, the methods of inquiring and answering some particular questions, the standard of questionnaire coding, and so on.

The major task of supervisors was to take charge of technique instruction and quality control in the survey, including conducting household sampling, distributing questionnaires, changing inquired households and interviewees, examining questionnaires, organizing questionnaire coding, and so forth. In addition to the training that was received by interviewers, supervisors also received special trainings on household sampling, sampled households and interviewees changing, and questionnaire reexamining, etc.

Session 1: Questionnaire Trial Answer

Request interviewers to answer the questionnaire as interviewees in order to make themselves familiar with the structure of the questionnaire and the length of interview time

Session 2: Questionnaire Explanation

Make interviewers familiar with the explanations for questionnaire questions in the *Interviewer Manual*

Session 3: Within-household Sampling and On-site Interview Techniques

Make interviewers familiar with the methods of within-household sampling and the steps and procedure of interview

Section 4: Simulation Exercise

Interviewers exercise interviews in order to make themselves familiar with the role of interviewer and the whole process of the interview

Section 5: Experimental Interview

Choose a certain survey site and each interviewer conducts one or two interviews in order to identify potential problems

Section 6: Summary

Summarize the problems found in experimental interviews and making some supplementary stipulations

(3) Interview Execution

In order to control the quality of each step in the on-site survey, the nationwide survey adopted the approach of *on-site team*, that is, the survey in each resident/villager committee was conducted by 1 to 2 supervisors and 5 to 10 interviewers together. Each team finished the survey in a resident/villager committee in 1 to 3 days. On the average, each interviewer finished an interview in 1 to 1.5 hours. In order to ensure that every member in chosen households had an equal chance to be selected, in urban areas the schedule of the visit was arranged in the weekends or after working hours (6:00 P.M.~ 9:30 P.M.). In rural areas, there was no specific requirement about the time of the visit because rural residents usually did not have a time limit of work. Only if the work in one site was accomplished could the on-site team move to the next one. The purpose of such operational approach was to solve any possible problems timely on the spot. In addition, the co-work of supervisors and interviewers eliminated the nonstandard interviews to the greatest extent.[1] Specific steps of interview execution are listed as follows.

In the first step, supervisors conducted systematic sampling in the roster of residents or households provided by the local resident/villager committee and worked out the list of selected households and alternative households. In the second step, the supervisor distributed questionnaires to interviewers according to the sampling list. In order to control the quality of interview, formal questionnaires were distributed to interviewers on the spot; in addition, the supervisor should follow the rule to handing out one questionnaire first and then giving out another one only after the former one was handed in. By doing so, interview errors could be effectively controlled. In the third step, the interviewer visited the selected household and chose the interviewee with the sampling list, the sampling table and the questionnaire. If the sampling was successful, the visit would continue; if it failed, the interviewer would inform the supervisor and the latter then would make a change based on the alternative households list. The interviewer conducted the within-household sampling once

---

[1] The *on-site team* approach is different from the field operating approach commonly used by social investigation and market research institutions. In the latter approach, usually only investigators enter the field without supervisors accompanied in the whole course; in order to achieve the quality control of interviews, supervisors need to go around and inspect among several survey sites and check submitted questionnaires by telephone or conduct selective examination through second visits. Rather than such *ex post* countercheck, we prefer to on-site quality control. However, it is a kind of expensive approach to improve survey quality.

again.[1] In the fourth step, after the interviewee confirmed that the interview time was appropriate and the interview surrounding was under control, the interviewer would conduct the face-to-face interview. In the process of interviewing, the questionnaire was administrated by the interviewer, i.e., the questionnaire was in interviewer's hands all along, the interviewer would ask questions one by one and the interviewee would answer them one by one. The interviewee was not allowed to fill out the questionnaire; except for one or two questions, the interviewee was not allowed to see the questionnaire.[2] In the fifth step, after the interview was completed, the interviewer should conduct a comprehensive check on the spot in order to make sure that there were no missing or incorrectly answered questions, or no ambiguous or illogical answers. After the examination, the interviewer would appreciate the interviewee and then sign the questionnaire and submit it to the supervisor. In the sixth step, the supervisor collected the questionnaire submitted by the interviewer on the spot and then rechecked it immediately. If no problems were found, the supervisor would hand out the next household's address and another questionnaire; if there were any problems, the supervisor was to request the interviewer to go back to the inquired household immediately and conduct a supplementary interview. After double-checking by the interviewer and the supervisor, all questionnaires then entered the coding process.

(4) Ex Post Coding and Data Processing

The preliminary coding of questionnaires was conducted by interviewers on the spot. After completing that day's interviews, interviewers coded their questionnaires one by one under supervisors' instruction; and then supervisors checked the coding one by one. If any abnormal answers were found in this process, the supervisor would request the interviewer to visit corresponding interviewees once again. After all

---

[1] We stipulated that the right to change the sampled households and individuals was in hand of the supervisor. In the following four situations, samples might be altered: (1) Nobody lived in the selected address, (2) no eligible interviewees in the selected household (such as their ages did not meet the requirement of the survey), (3) the selected household refused the interview, and (4) the eventually selected interviewee refused the interview. The method of changing samples was to change the selected household, i.e., finding the corresponding alternative household in the alternative list. It was strictly forbidden to change the interviewee within a selected household.

[2] The face-to-face interview administrated by the interviewer is a time-consuming and arduous approach of interview, but it can provide the best process control for the survey. The reasons for us to choose this approach include: (1) a considerable number of interviewees are unable to read the questionnaire because of lower level of education received, (2) many concepts in the questionnaire need the interviewer to make further explanations, (3) it is necessary to remind the interviewee of the logic relationships between different questions by the interviewer in order to avoid misanswering, (4) through the approach of read and answer, the interviewer can observe interviewees' perceptions of questions and the authenticity of their answers, and (5) adopting such an approach means that the interviewer cannot leave the field at all time. Therefore, we definitely stipulated that it was not allowed to complete the questionnaires by interviewees themselves or complete the questionnaires collectively (i.e., one interviewer read the questionnaire while several interviewees completing their questionnaires respectively).

questionnaires were collected and sent to Beijing, a group of special personnel rechecked the coding of questionnaires.

EDI professional input software was used in the process of data input and all data were checked by the double-input procedure; and then, all data were transformed into a SPSS database and logic verification of data was conducted. Finally, according to results of the fifth national population census, different weights were assigned to variables such as age, gender, type of registered residence, and floating population, etc.; eventually, the formal database is established.

References

Bai, Nansheng and Yupeng He. 2003. "Back Home or Enter the City". Pp. 13 in Peilin Li (ed.), *Peasant-Workers: Socio-economic Analysis on Peasant-Workers Entered into the City in China*. Beijing: Social Sciences Documentation Publishing House.

Bao, Yujun. 2002. *Appeal for Understanding: Controversies around the Private Sector of Economy in China*. Beijing: China Industry & Commerce Associated Press.

Bell, Daniel. 1984. *Coming of Post-Industrial Society: A Venture in Social Forecasting*, translated by Tian, Gao, et al. Beijing: The Commercial Press.

Blau, Peter M. and Oliver D. Duncan.1967. *The American Occupational Structure*. New York, N.Y.: Wiley.

Bo, Yibo. 1997. *Retrospect of Some Momentous Decision-Makings and Events*, Revised Version, Volume 1. Beijing: People's Publishing House.

Bo, Yibo. 1997a. *Retrospect of Some Momentous Decision-Makings and Events*, Revised Version, Volume 2. Beijing: People's Publishing House.

Bourdieu, Pierre and Jean-Claude Passeron. 1977. *Reproduction in Education, Society and Culture*. Beverly Hills, C.A.: Sage Publications.

Bourdieu, Pierre. 1984. *Distinction: A Social Critique of the Judgment of Taste*. Cambridge, M.A.: Harvard University Press.

Cai, Fanghua. 2003. "Electing a Boss to be the Village Official should Follow the Legal Proceedings". On the web site of *China Rural Research of Ministry of Agriculture*. www.ccrs.org.cn.

Cao, Xiaoyan. 2003. "Quantitative Analysis of Impact of Foreign Direct Investment on Employment of the Labor Force in China". Beijing: *Statistical Education* 5.

Center for Population Studies of the Chinese Academy of Social Sciences.1986. *China Population Statistical Yearbook (1985)* . Beijing: China National Statistic Press.

Chan, Kam Wing and Xueqiang Xu. 1985. "Urban Population Growth and Urbanization in China since 1949: Reconstructing a Baseline". *The China Quarterly* 104.

Chen, Guangjin.1998. "Secrets of Rising and Growing of Elite in Chinese Rural Community ". In *Forum for Ten Doctors*. Beijing: China City Press.

_____. 2004. "Segmentation of the Status Systems: The Formation of Social Stratification and Mobility Mechanisms before the Reform and Opening-up and the Issue of Justice". *Jiangsu Social Science* 1.

Chen, Limin. 2002. "Capital Flow and Its Impact on Employment in China". Chengdu, Sichuan: *Reform of Economic System* 5.

Chen, Yonghong. 2002. "Evolution and Evaluation of the Employment System in China (1949-2001) ". Pp. 46 in Hu, Angang, et al. (eds.), *Expansion of Employment and Challenge of Unemployment: Evaluation of Employment*

Policies in China (1949-2001). Beijing: China Labor and Social Security Publishing House.

Chen, Xiwen. 2004. "Rural Economy and Rural Policy in China." Chongqing: *Reform* 3.

China Education Daily. 2001 "Pay Attention to the Rise of the Rural Dropout Rate". *China Education Daily*. June 6.

Chinese Public Administration Society. 2002. *Brief History of the Public Administration of New China (1949~2000)*. Beijing: People's Publishing House.

Composition Team. 1999. *Trans-Century Reform in China Government*. Beijing: China Economy Publishing House.

Dai, Jianzhong (ed.). 2001. "Data and Analysis of the Fourth Nationwide Survey on Private Enterprises in 2000". In *Chinese Private Sector of Economy Yearbook (1997-1999)*. Beijing: Huawen Press.

Deng, Xiaoping. 1993. *Collected Works of Deng Xiaoping*, Volume 2. Beijing: People's Publishing House.

_____. 1993a. *Collected Works of Deng Xiaoping*, Volume 3. Beijing: People's Publishing House.

Department of Planning and Finance of the Ministry of Labor and Social Security of China. 1999. *Wage Levels in Labor Markets of Medium-large Size Cities in China*. Beijing: China Labor and Social Security Publishing House.

Department of Population, Society, Science and Technology of the National Bureau of Statistics of China. 2000. *China Social Statistical Materials (2000)*. Beijing: China National Statistic Press.

Department Population, Society, Science and Technology of the National Bureau of Statistics of China, and Department of Planning and Finance, Ministry of Labor and Social Security of China. 2001. *China Labor Statistical Yearbook (2001)*. Beijing: China National Statistic Press.

Ding, Weizhi (ed.). 1993. *Series of China National Conditions: Socioeconomic Surveys in One Hundred Counties and Cities: Shangzhou*. Beijing: Encyclopedia of China Publishing House.

Dong, Funreng (ed.). 1999. *Economic History of the People's Republic of China*, Volume 1. Beijing: Economic Science Press.

_____. (ed.). 1999a. *Economic History of the People's Republic of China*, Volume 2. Beijing: Economic Science Press.

Duncan, Oliver D. 1972. *Socio-economic Background and Achievement*. New York, N.Y.: Seminar Press.

_____. 1975. *Introduction to Structure Equation Model*. New York, N.Y.: Academic Press.

Editorial committee of Jinjiang Chorography. 1989. *Jinjiang Chorography*. Xiamen, Fujian: Fujian University Press.

Editorial committee of Haimen Chorography. 1996. *Haimen Chorography*. Nanjing, Jiangsu: Jiangsu Science & Technology Press.

Fairbank, John King. 2000. *The Great Chinese Revolution, 1800-1985*. Beijing: World Affairs Press.

Feng, Tongqin. 2001. *Destiny of the Working Class in China*. Beijing: Social Sciences Documentation Publishing House.

Gao, Guang, Zhen Li, Min Ma, and Changyuan Wang (eds.). 1990. *Social Class Structure and Class Struggles in Socialist China*. Beijing: People's Publishing House.

Gao, Weiyu. 2002. "Quantitative Analysis of Impact of Export on Employment in China". Shanghai: *Shanghai Statistics* 2.

Giddens, Anthony. 1973. *The Class Structure of the Advanced Society*. New York, N.Y.: Harper & Row, Publishers.

_____. 2003. *Sociology*, 4th edition. Beijing: Peking University Press.

Gilbert, Danis and Joseph A.Carl. 1992. *Class Structure of the United States of America*. Beijing: China Social Sciences Press.

Goldthorpe, John H. 1987. *Social Mobility and Class Structure in Modern Britain*, 2nd edition. Oxford: Clarendon Press.

Gouldner, Alvin W. 2002. *The Future of Intellectuals and the Rise of the New Class*, translated by Gu, Xiaohui and Rong Cai, Zhejiang: Jiangsu People's Press.

Grusky, David B. (ed.). 2001. *Social Stratification: Class, Race & Gender in Sociological Perspective*. Colorado: Westview Press.

Guan, Zhong. 1954. "Guan Zi · Xiao Kuang". In *Collection of Distinguished Philosophical Works*, Volume 5. Beijing: Zhonghua Book Company.

Guo, Kesha. 2000. "The Paths, Problems, and Solutions of Industrialization in China". *Social Sciences in China* 3.

International Labor Office. 2000. *Yearbook of Labor Statistics (2000)*. Geneva: International Labor Organization.

Investigation Team on Rural Society and Economy of the National Bureau of Statistics of China. 2003. *Monitoring Report on Poverty in Rural China (2003)*. Beijing: China National Statistic Press.

Jia, Chunzeng (ed.). 1996. *The Intelligentsia and Chinese Social Reforms*. Beijing: Huawen Press.

Johnson, D. Gale. 2002. "Can Agricultural Labor Adjustment Occur Primarily through Creation of Rural Non-Farm Jobs in China?" *Urban Studies*, Edinburgh. 39: 2163.

Lenski, Gerhard E. 1988. *Power and Privilege: Theory of Social Stratification*, translated by Guan, Xinping, Xianzhong Chen and Jinyu Xie. Hangzhou, Zhejiang: Zhejiang People's Press.

Li, Chunling. 2004. "Middle Stratum: A Group Worthy of Attention in Chinese Society". In Ru, Xin, et al (eds.), *Analyses and Forecasts on Social Situations in China (2003)*. Beijing: Social Sciences Documentation Publishing House.

Li, Jianhua (ed.). 2002. *A Study on Strategy for Leading Talents Development in Party and Government Agencies*. Beijing: The Central Party School Publishing House.

Li, Lulu. 1996. "Institutional Structure of Social Stratification in Contemporary China". *Teaching and Research* 3.

_____.1996a. "Social Structure of Private Entrepreneurs: Developmental Mechanisms of Private Enterprises." In *China Private Sector of Economy Yearbook*. Beijing: China Industry & Commerce Associated Press.

Li, Peilin. 1996. "Social Networks and Social Status of Mobile Rural Laborers". *Sociology Research* 4.

_____. (ed). 2003. *Peasant-workers: Socioeconomic Analysis of Rural Workers Migrated into Cities*. Beijing: Social Sciences Documentation Publishing House.

Li, Qiang. 1993. *Social Stratification and Mobility in Contemporary China*. Beijing: China Economy Publishing House.

_____. 1996. "Modernization and Transition of Social Stratification Structure". *Teaching and Research* 3.

_____. 1999. *The Course of Life: Momentous Events and Life Courses of Chinese*. Hangzhou: Zhejiang People's Press.

_____. 2001. "Some Thoughts regarding the Middle Class and the Middle Stratum". *Journal of Renmin University of China* 2.

Li, Ruojian.2001. "Influences of Economic System Factors on the Great Leap Forward and Three Years of Catastrophe". *Opening Times*. August.

Li, Shi, et al. 2000. *Empirical Analysis of Household Income Distribution in China*. Beijing: Social Sciences Documentation Publishing House.

Lian, Yuming (ed.). 2004. *China Digital Report*. Beijing: China Times Economic Press.

Lin, Lan and Yanjie Bian. 2002. "Employment and Status Attainment Process in Chinese Urban Areas". Pp. 83-115 in Yanjie Bian, et. al. (eds.), *Market Transformation and Social Stratification*. SJPC Book Shop.

Lipset, Seymour Martin and Bendix Reinhard. 1959. *Social Mobility in Industrial Society*. Berkeley, C.A.: University of California Press.

Liu, Linping. 2002. *Connections, Social Capital, and Social Transformation: Study on Pinjiang Village in Shenzhen*. Beijing: China Social Sciences Press.

Liu, Zhifeng. 1998. *The Seventh Revolution: Memorandum on China Government Agency Restructure in 1998*. Beijing: Economy Daily Press.

Liu, Zhongli (ed.). 1999. *Laying Foundations: The Economy in New China over the Past Fifty Years*. Beijing: China Financial and Economic Publishing.

Lu, Guotai. 2002. *Public Administration in China*. Beijing: The Central Party School Publishing House.

Lu, Hanlong. 2003. "Preface for the Chinese Edition: Consumption Revolution and Consumer Autonomy." In Deborahs Davis, *The Consumer Revolution in Urban China,* translated by Dai, Huisi and Hanlong Lu. Shanghai: Shanghai Academy of Social Sciences Press.

Lu, Xueyi, et al. 2001. *Deng Xiaoping Theory and Transition of Social Stratum Structure in Contemporary China*. Beijing: Economic Management Press.

Lu, Xueyi (ed.). 2002. *Social Stratification in Contemporary China*. Beijing: Social Sciences Documentation Publishing House.

_____. 2003. *Socio-economic Issues on Agriculture, Rural Areas, and Peasants*. Beijing: Social Sciences Documentation Publishing House.

Ma, Jieshan and Yi Zhang (eds.). 1987. *China Township Enterprise Yearbook (1978~1987)*. Beijing: China Agriculture Press.

Ma, Licheng and Zhijun Ling. 1998. *Cross Swords: Memoir of the Three Thought Liberation in Contemporary China*. Beijing: China Today Publishing House.

MacFarquhar, Roderick and John King Fairbank (eds.). 1990. *The Cambridge History of China, The People's Republic: 1949-1982*. Shanghai: Shanghai People's Publishing House.

McGraw, Thomas K (ed.). 1999. *Creating Modern Capitalism: How Entrepreneurs, Companies, and Countries Triumphed in Three Industrial Revolutions*, translated by Zhao, Wenshu and Suozhang Xiao. Hangzhou, Zhejiang: Jiangsu People's Press.

Machlup, Fritz. 1962. *The Production and Distribution of Knowledge in the United States*. Princeton, N.J.: Princeton University Press.

Mao, Zedong. 1990. *Mao Zedong Texte*, Volume 7. Beijing: People's Publishing House.

Marx, Karl and Frederick Engels. 1972. *Complete Works of Marx and Engels*, Chinese edition, Volume 23. Beijing: People's Publishing House.

Mo, Rida. 1957. *Development of Agricultural Cooperativization in China*. Beijing: China National Statistic Press.

National Bureau of Statistics of China. 1958. *National Economic Constructions and People's Living*. Beijing: China National Statistic Press.

_____. 1959. *A Decade of Greatness*. Beijing: China National Statistic Press.

_____. 1983. *China Statistical Yearbook (1983)*. Beijing: China National Statistic Press.

_____. 1984. *Splendid Thirty-Five Years*. Beijing: China National Statistic Press.

_____. 1984a. *China Statistical Yearbook (1984)*. Beijing: China National Statistic Press.

_____. 1986. *China Statistical Yearbook (1986)*. Beijing: China National Statistic Press.

_____. 1988. *China Statistical Yearbook (1988)*. Beijing: China National Statistic Press.

_____. 1992. *China Statistical Yearbook (1992)*. Beijing: China National Statistic Press.

_____. 1999. *International Statistical Yearbook (1999)*. Beijing: China National Statistic Press.

_____. 2000. *China Statistical Yearbook (2000)*. Beijing: China National Statistic Press.

_____. 2001. *International Statistical Yearbook (2001)*. Beijing: China National

Statistic Press.

———. 2001a. *World Statistical Yearbook (2001)*. Beijing: China National Statistic Press.

———. 2002. *China Urban Statistical Yearbook (2001)*. Beijing: China National Statistic Press.

———. 2002a. *Statistical Abstract of China (2002)*. Beijing: China National Statistic Press.

———. 2003. *Statistical Abstract of China (2003)*. Beijing: China National Statistic Press.

———. 2003a. *China Statistical Yearbook (2003)*. Beijing: China National Statistic Press.

———. 2004. *Statistical Abstract of China (2004)*. Beijing: China National Statistic Press.

Nee, Victor. 1989. "A Theory of Market Transition: From Redistributive to Markets in State Socialism". *American Sociological Review* 54: 663-681.

Ni, Liya. 1989. *Class Structure in Contemporary Capitalist Society*. Beijing: China Renmin University Press. .

Parkin, Frank. 1974. *The Social Analysis of Class Structure*. London: Tavistock Publication.

Political Bureau of the C.P.C. Central Committee. 1956. *Resolution on the Issue of Transforming the Capitalist Industry and Commerce*. February 24.

Population Census Office of the State Council and Department of Population Census of the National Bureau of Statistics of China. 1993. *Tabulation on the 1990 Population Census of the People's Republic of China*. Beijing: China National Statistic Press.

Qi, Jianguo. 2000. "Year of 2000: The Biggest Threat against China Economy is the Rapidly Declining Employment Elasticity". *The Journal of World Economy* 3.

Qianhua, et al (eds.). 1957. *Changes of Private Industry and Commerce in China over the Past Seven Years (1949~1956)*. Beijing: China Financial and Economic Publishing.

Qiang, Xianzhi and Chongji Jin (eds.). 2003. *Biography of Mao Zedong*. Beijing: Central Documentation Publishing House.

Qin, Hui. 1998. *Case Studies on Restructuring of Township Enterprises in Jiangsu and Zhejiang Provinces*. Hong Kong: Hong Kong Institute of Asia-Pacific Studies.

Ren, Jie and Lin Liang. 1999. *Restructuring and Transition of the Government Agency in the People's Republic of China*. Beijing: Huawen Press.

Research Group of China National Institute for Educational Research. 2001. "Study on Criteria for Modernization Level of Basic Education in Chinese Developed Regions". *Education Research* 10.

Rural Policy Research Office of the Secretariat of the Central Committee of the C.P.C.. 1987. *A Cross-sectional Survey on Chinese Rural Society and Economy*. Beijing:

China Social Sciences Press.

Social Structure Transformation Research Group of the China Society for Strategy and Management Research.1998. "Middle-short term Tendency and Hidden Troubles of Chinese Social Structure Transformation". *Strategy and Management* 5.

Song, Shige.1998. "Delayed effect of Right Transition: An Explanation of Elite Reproduction and Circulation in Transformation from Socialist State to Markets". *Sociology Research* 3.

Walder, Anderw G. 1996. *Communist Neo-traditionalism: Work and Authority in Chinese Industry*. Hong Kong: Oxford University Press.

Wang, Chunguang. 1995. *Social Mobility and Social Reconstruction: Research on Zhejiang Village in Beijing City*. Hangzhou, Zhejiang: Zhejiang People's Press.

_____. 2001. "The Relationship between Social Identification of the Cenozoic Floating Rural Population and Urban-rural Integration". *Sociology Research* 3

_____. 2003. "Macro-level Analysis of Formation and History of the Permanent Residence Registration System in Contemporary China". *Study of C.P.C. History* 3.

_____. 2003a. "Study on the Issue of Social Inequality in Occupational Mobility in China". *Chinese Journal of Population Science* 2.

Wang, Fenyu and Yandong Zhao.2003. "Economic Status Attainment of Mobile Rural Laborers and Its Determinants".Pp. 142 in Peilin Li (ed.), *Peasant-Workers: Socio-economic Analysis on Peasant-Workers Entered into the City in China*. Beijing: Social Sciences Documentation Publishing House.

Wang, Yu and Yingying Chen.1990. "Chapter 9: Introduction of Social Class and Stratum Structure in Modern Japan".

Pp. 172 in Jianzhang He, et. al.(eds.), *Modern Social Class Structure and Social Stratification Issues*. Beijing: China Social Sciences Press.

Wei, Hongyun. 2003. *Guo Shi Ji Shi Ben Mo (1949-1999)*, Volume 1. Shenyang, Liaoning: Liaoning People's Publishing House.

_____. 2003a. *Guo Shi Ji Shi Ben Mo (1949-1999)*, Volume 2. Shenyang, Liaoning: Liaoning People's Publishing House.

Wen, Jiabao. 2004. "Speech at the Commencement of Seminar on Understanding and Application of Scientific Development Views Attended by Provincial and Ministerial Level Officials". Beijing: *People's Daily*. March 1st.

Wen, Shengtang. 2003. "New Development of the Anti-Corruption Struggle in 2002". Pp. 102 in Ru, Xin, et al (eds.), *Analyses and Forecasts on Social Situations in China (2003)*. Beijing: Social Sciences Documentation Publishing House.

Wilde, Georgina and Ken Davies. 2000. *Report on Trends in China: China to 2010 and Hong Kong after 1997*. Beijing: Xinhua Publishing House.

Wright, Erik O. 1979. *Class Structure and Income Determination*. New York, N.Y.: Academic Press.

Wu, Gang. 2002. "Relationship between Education and Society in the Period of

Transformation". In Ding, Gang (ed.), *China Education: Studies and Reviews*, Volume 2. Beijing: Education and Science Publishing House.

Wu, Jinglian, et al. 1998. *Strategic Restructuring of State-owned Economy*. Beijing: China Development Press.

Wu, Jun, et al. 2000. "Analysis of the Impact of Private Enterprises on Solving the Layoff Issue". *Journal of Chengdu Institute of Public Administration* 1.

Xia, Jianzhong and Zhijie Yao. 2004. "Lifestyle of the White-collar Group: A Empirical Study". Unpublished.

Xiao, Gen. 1997. *Property Right and Economic Reforms in China*. Beijing: China Social Sciences Press.

Xiao, Zhuoji (ed.). 1992. *Introduction of China Economy*. Beijing: Economy Daily Press.

Xinhua Press Agency. 2004. "Synopsis of Original and Amended Provisions in the Constitution". *Guangmin Daily*. March 16.

Xu, Jiayou. 1986. *Social Stratification and Social Mobility*. Taibei: San Min Book Company.

Xu, Meide. 2000. *Chinese Universities 1895~1995: A Century of Cultural Conflicts*. Beijing: Education & Science Publishing House.

Xue, Muqiao, Xin Su, and Zili Lin, et al. 1978. *The Socialist Transformation of the National Economy in China*. Beijing: People's Publishing House.

Yang, Dongping. 2001. "Report on Development of Education in China 2000". In *2001: Analysis and Forecast on Chinese Society Situations*. Beijing: Social Sciences Documentation Publishing House.

Ye, Nianxian. 1990. "Chapter 2: Social Class Theories of Western Marxism Sociologists". Pp. 28-30 in Jianzhang He, et. al.(eds.), *Modern Social Class Structure and Social Stratification Issues*. Beijing: China Social Sciences Press.

Yiting. 2001. "Review of the Anti-Rightist Movement in Guangdong Province in 1957". *Gu Xiang Wang*. July 8th.

You, Zhenglin. 2000. *Inner Stratification and Mobility: A Twenty Years' Case Study of a State-owned Enterprise*. Beijing: Social Sciences Documentation Publishing House.

Yu, Huixin, et al. 2002. "Influences of Trade Liberalization in China on Employment in Industry". Beijing: *The Journal of World Economy* 10.

Yuan, Zhigang. 2000. "Knowledge-Based Economy and Changes in Employment: Reviews on Studies in Developed Market Economy Countries". *World Economic Forum* 4.

Zhang, Houyi. 1999. "A New Force Risen Suddenly: Rebirth and Development of the Private Sector Since the Reform and Opening-Up". In Houyi Zhang and Lizhi Ming (eds.), *Report on Development of Private Enterprises in China (1978-1998)*. Beijing: Social Sciences Documentation Publishing House.

_____. 2002. "The Third Special Report: Private Entrepreneur is an Important Component in Chinese Social Stratum Structure". In Xueyi Lu (ed.), *Social*

Stratification in Contemporary China. Beijing: Social Sciences Documentation Publishing House.

Zhang, Houyi, et al (eds.). 2003. *Report on Development of Private Enterprises in China (2003)*. Beijing: Social Sciences Documentation Publishing House.

Zhang, Houyi and Guangjin Chen. 2003. "Statistical Analysis of Survey on Private Entrepreneurs with the Party Membership". In Houyi Zhang (ed.), *Report on Development of Private Enterprises in China (2002)*. Beijing: Social Sciences Documentation Publishing House.

Zhang, Houyi and Lizhi Ming. 1999. *Report on Development of Private Enterprises in China (1978-1998)*. Beijing: Social Sciences Documentation Publishing House.

Zhang, Jingru and Songchen Li (eds.). 1999. *Illustrated History of the People's Republic of China (3)*. Beijing: Modern China Publishing House.

Zhang, Letian. 1998. *Farewell to Utopia: Research on the People's Commune System*. Beijing: Oriental Press.

Zhang, Zhongfa and Chuanyi Cui. "Transfer of the Labor Force: History, Characteristics, and Experience of Chinese Rural Labor Force Transfer". www.ccain.com.

Zhang, Wanli. 1996. "Non-institutional factors and Status Attainment: Social Stratification in Current China". *Sociology Research* 1.

_____. 2000. "Review on Studies on Social Class and Stratum in China over the Past Twenty Years". *Sociology Research* 1.

_____. 2002. "The Fourth Special Report: Study on the Middle Stratum in China". Pp. 252-254 in Xueyi Lu (ed.), *Social Stratification in Contemporary China*. Beijing: Social Sciences Documentation Publishing House.

_____. 2002a. "A Pilot Study on the Middle Stratum in Current China". In *Proceeding of the 2002 Conference of the Sociological Society of China on Globalization and Development of Chinese Society*.

Zhou, Xueguang, Tuma, and Maen. 2002. "A Dynamic Analysis of Social Stratification in the State Socialism System". Pp. 379-426 in Yanjie Bian, et. al. (eds.), *Market Transformation and Social Stratification*. SJPC Book Shop.

Zhu, Mingfang, et al. 1998. *Private Sector of Economy in China*. Beijing: China City Press.

51job. 2003. "Secrets of White Collars' Salary: Six Factors like Hidden Income Widen the Gap". it.21cn.com.

Index